# Dewey Decimal Classification
# and Relative Index

# Dewey Decimal Classification and Relative Index

Devised by Melvil Dewey

## EDITION 23

Edited by

Joan S. Mitchell, Editor in Chief

Julianne Beall, Assistant Editor

Rebecca Green, Assistant Editor

Giles Martin, Assistant Editor

Michael Panzer, Assistant Editor

## VOLUME 4
Relative Index

OCLC
OCLC Online Computer Library Center, Inc.
Dublin, Ohio
2011

Library of Congress Cataloging-in-Publication Data
**Dewey, Melvil, 1851-1931.**
    Dewey decimal classification and relative index / devised by Melvil Dewey. — Ed. 23 / edited by Joan S. Mitchell, Editor in Chief ; Julianne Beall, Assistant Editor ; Rebecca Green, Assistant Editor ; Giles Martin, Assistant Editor ; Michael Panzer, Assistant Editor.
    v. cm.
    Includes bibliographical references and index.
    Contents: v. 1. Manual. Tables — v. 2. Schedules 000-599 — v. 3. Schedules 600-999 — v. 4. Relative index.
    ISBN-13: 978-1-910608-81-4 (set : alk. paper)
    ISBN-10: 1-910608-81-5 (set : alk. paper)
    ISBN-13: 978-1-910608-80-7 (vol. 1 : alk. paper)
    ISBN-10: 1-910608-80-7 (vol. 1 : alk. paper)
    [etc.]
    1. Classification, Dewey decimal. I. Mitchell, Joan S. II. Beall, Julianne, 1946- III. Green, Rebecca, 1952- IV. Martin, Giles. V. Panzer, Michael. VI. Title.
    Z696.D52 2011
    025.4'31—dc22                2011001112

OCLC Online Computer Library Center, Inc.
6565 Kilgour Place
Dublin, OH 43017-3395 USA
www.oclc.org/dewey

ISBN-13: (set) 978-1-910608-81-4; v. 1 978-1-910608-80-7;
v. 2 978-1-910608-76-0; v. 3 978-1-910608-79-1; v. 4 978-1-910608-78-4

ISBN-10: (set) 1-910608-81-5; v. 1 1-910608-80-7; v. 2 1-910608-76-9;
v. 3 1-910608-79-3; v. 4 1-910608-78-5

 Recycled paper

# Relative Index

# Abbreviations Used in the Index

| | | |
|---|---|---|
| T1 | Table 1 | Standard Subdivisions |
| T2 | Table 2 | Geographic Areas, Historical Periods, Biography |
| T3 | Table 3 | Subdivisions for the Arts, for Individual Literatures, for Specific Literary Forms |
| T3A | Table 3A | Subdivisions for Works by or about Individual Authors |
| T3B | Table 3B | Subdivisions for Works by or about More than One Author |
| T3C | Table 3C | Notation to Be Added Where Instructed in Table 3B, 700.4, 791.4, 808–809 |
| T4 | Table 4 | Subdivisions of Individual Languages and Language Families |
| T5 | Table 5 | Ethnic and National Groups |
| T6 | Table 6 | Languages |

| | |
|---|---|
| A.C.T. | Australian Capital Territory |
| Ala. | Alabama |
| Alta. | Alberta |
| Ariz. | Arizona |
| Ark. | Arkansas |
| B.C. | Before Christ |
| | British Columbia |
| Calif. | California |
| Colo. | Colorado |
| Conn. | Connecticut |
| D.C. | District of Columbia |
| Del. | Delaware |
| Dept. | Department |
| Fla. | Florida |
| Ga. | Georgia |
| Ill. | Illinois |
| Inc. | Incorporated |
| Ind. | Indiana |
| Kan. | Kansas |
| Ky. | Kentucky |
| La. | Louisiana |
| Man. | Manitoba |
| Mass. | Massachusetts |
| Md | Maryland |
| Me. | Maine |
| Mich. | Michigan |
| Minn. | Minnesota |
| Miss. | Mississippi |
| Mo. | Missouri |
| Mont. | Montana |
| N.B. | New Brunswick |
| N.C. | North Carolina |
| N.D. | North Dakota |
| N.H. | New Hampshire |
| N.J. | New Jersey |
| N.M. | New Mexico |
| N.S. | Nova Scotia |
| N.S.W. | New South Wales |
| N.T. | Northern Territory |
| N.W.T. | Northwest Territories |
| N.Y. | New York |
| N.Z. | New Zealand |
| Ncb. | Nebraska |
| Nev. | Nevada |
| Okla. | Oklahoma |
| Ont. | Ontario |
| Or. | Oregon |
| P.E.I. | Prince Edward Island |
| P.R. | Puerto Rico |
| Pa. | Pennsylvania |
| Qld. | Queensland |
| R.I. | Rhode Island |
| S. Aust. | South Australia |
| S.C. | South Carolina |
| S.D. | South Dakota |
| Sask. | Saskatchewan |
| Tas. | Tasmania |
| Tenn. | Tennessee |
| Tex. | Texas |
| U.S. | United States of America |
| V.I. | Virgin Islands |
| Va. | Virginia |
| Vic. | Victoria |
| Vt. | Vermont |
| W.A. | Western Australia |
| W. Va. | West Virginia |
| Wash. | Washington |
| Wis. | Wisconsin |
| Wyo. | Wyoming |
| Yukon | Yukon Territory |

35mm cameras 771.32
100 Mile House (B.C.) T2—711 75
401(k) plans 332.024 014 5

# A

A level examination 378.166 2
Aachen (Germany) T2—435 511
A'ālī al-Nīl (Sudan) T2—629 3
Aar River (Switzerland) T2—494 54
Aarau (Switzerland) T2—494 562 84
Aarau (Switzerland :
  Bezirk) T2—494 562 8
Aardvark 599.31
Aardwolf 599.743
Aargau (Switzerland) T2—494 56
Aarhus amt (Denmark) T2—489 5
Abaca
  botany 584.39
  fiber crop 633.571
Abacus 513.028 4
Abalones 641.394
  cooking 641.694
  fishing and culture 639.483 2
  food 641.394
  zoology 594.32
Abandoned children 305.230 869 45
  T1—086 945
  social group 305.230 869 45
  social services 362.73
Abattoirs 664.902 9
Abaza language 499.962
  T6—999 62
Abazin language 499.962
  T6—999 62
Abbeville County (S.C.) T2—757 35
Abbeys
  architecture 726.7
  church history 271
  religious significance of
    buildings 246.97
Abbotsford (B.C.) T2—711 37
Abbott, J. J. C. (John Joseph
  Caldwell), Sir
  Canadian history 971.055
Abbreviated longhand 653.2
Abbreviation dictionaries 413.15
  specific languages T4—315
  specific subjects T1—014 8
Abbreviations 411
  specific languages T4—11
  specific subjects T1—014 8

'Abd al-Razzāq ibn Hammām
  al-Ḥimyari
  Hadith 297.125 56
Abdias (Biblical book) 224.91
Abdomen 573.997
  biology 573.997
  human anatomy 611.95
  human physiology 612.95
  injuries 617.550 44
  regional medicine 617.55
  surgery 617.550 59
Abdominal muscles
  human anatomy 611.736
Abdominal pregnancy
  obstetrics 618.31
Abduction (Crime) 364.154
  law 345.025 4
  prevention 364.4
    self-defense 613.66
Abduction (Logic) 511.31
'Abdu'l-Bahá
  works by 297.938 24
Abdul Rahman, Tunku, Putra Al-
  Haj
  Malaysian history 959.505 1
Abdul Razak bin Dato' Hussein,
  Tun Haji
  Malaysian history 959.505 2
Abdullah bin Ahmad Haji
  Badawi
  Malaysian history 959.506 1
Abel (Biblical person)
  Bible stories 222.110 950 5
Abel Tasman National Park
  (N.Z.) T2—937 7
Abelian categories 512.62
Abelian groups 512.25
Abelian varieties 516.353
Aberconwy (Wales) T2—429 27
Aberdare (Wales) T2—429 78
Aberdeen (Scotland) T2—412 3
Aberdeen (South Africa :
  District) T2—687 54
Aberdeen Angus cattle 636.223
Aberdeenshire (Scotland) T2—412 4
Abergavenny (Wales) T2—429 98
Abergele (Wales) T2—429 27
Aberration
  astronomy 522.9
Abertillery (Wales) T2—429 95
Abhidhammapiṭaka 294.382 4
Abhidharmapiṭaka 294.382 4
Abia State (Nigeria) T2—669 45
Abidjan (Ivory Coast) T2—666 8

| | |
|---|---|
| Ability | 153.9 |
| Ability grouping in education | 371.254 |
| Ability testing | 153.93 |
|   aptitudes | 153.94 |
|   education | 371.262 |
|   intelligence | 153.93 |
|   personnel selection | 658.311 25 |
| Abitibi (Quebec : Regional County Municipality) | T2—714 134 |
| Abitibi, Lake (Ont. and Quebec) | T2—713 142 |
| Abitibi-Ouest (Quebec : Regional County Municipality) | T2—714 132 |
| Abitibi-Témiscamingue (Quebec : Administrative region) | T2—714 13 |
| Abitibi-Témiscamingue Region (Quebec) | T2—714 13 |
| Abkhaz language | 499.962 3 |
| | T6—999 623 |
| Abkhaz literature | 899.962 3 |
| Abkhazia (Georgia) | T2—475 8 |
| Abkhazo-Adyghian languages | 499.962 |
| | T6—999 62 |
| Ablation of snow | 551.578 464 |
| Ablutions | |
|   Islam | 297.38 |
| ABM (Missiles) | 358.174 82 |
|   engineering | 623.451 94 |
|   military equipment | 358.174 82 |
| Abnaki Indians | T5—973 4 |
| Abnaki language | 497.34 |
| | T6—973 4 |
| Abnormal psychology | 616.89 |
| Abnormalities | |
|   human teratology | 616.043 |
|   physical anthropology | 599.949 |
| Abodah Zarah | 296.123 4 |
|   Babylonian Talmud | 296.125 4 |
|   Mishnah | 296.123 4 |
|   Palestinian Talmud | 296.124 4 |
| Abolition of slavery | 326.8 |
|   political science | 326.8 |
|   sociology | 306.362 |
|   United States history | 973.711 4 |
| Abolitionists (Antislavery activists) | 326.809 2 |
| Abominable snowman | 001.944 |
| Aboriginal Australian languages | 499.15 |
| | T6—991 5 |
| Aboriginal Australian literatures | 899.15 |
| Aboriginal Australians | T5—991 5 |
|   religion | 299.921 5 |
| Aboriginal Malay languages | 499.28 |
| | T6—992 8 |
| Aboriginal peoples | 305.8 |
|   Australia | T5—991 5 |
|   social group | 305.8 |
|   Tasmania | T5—991 59 |
|   *see also* Indigenous peoples | |
| Aboriginal Tasmanians | T5—991 59 |
| Aborigines | 305.8 |
|   *see also* Indigenous peoples | |
| Abortifacient agents | |
|   medicine | 618.29 |
|   pharmacokinetics | 615.766 |
| Abortifacients | |
|   medicine | 618.29 |
|   pharmacokinetics | 615.766 |
| Abortion | 362.198 88 |
|   criminology | 364.185 |
|     criminal law | 345.028 5 |
|   demographic effect | 304.667 |
|   ethics | 179.76 |
|     religion | 205.697 6 |
|       Buddhism | 294.356 976 |
|       Christianity | 241.697 6 |
|       Hinduism | 294.548 697 6 |
|       Islam | 297.569 76 |
|       Judaism | 296.369 76 |
|   law | 342.084 |
|     legal right of fetuses | 342.085 |
|     legal right of women | 342.087 8 |
|     medical law | 344.041 92 |
|   medicine | 618.88 |
|   nonsurgical methods | |
|     medicine | 618.29 |
|     pharmacokinetics | 615.766 |
|   social problem | 363.46 |
|     law | 344.054 6 |
|   social services | 362.198 88 |
|   social theology | 201.763 46 |
|     Christianity | 261.836 |
|     Judaism | 296.38 |
|   surgery | 618.88 |
| Aboth | 296.123 47 |
| Abra (Philippines) | T2—599 1 |
| Abrading tools | 621.92 |
| Abraham (Patriarch) | |
|   Bible | 222.110 92 |
|   Islam | 297.246 3 |
| Abrasions | |
|   medicine | 617.13 |
| Abrasives | |
|   mineral resources | 553.65 |
| Abrogation | |
|   Hadith | 297.125 163 |

| | |
|---|---|
| Abruzzi (Italy) | T2—457 1 |
| Abruzzo (Italy) | T2—457 1 |
| ancient | T2—377 3 |
| Absaroka Range (Mont. and Wyo.) | T2—787 4 |
| Absentee ownership | |
| land economics | 333.4 |
| Absentee voting | 324.65 |
| law | 342.075 |
| Absenteeism | 331.259 88 |
| labor economics | 331.259 88 |
| personnel management | 658.314 |
| public administration | 352.66 |
| sociology | 306.361 |
| Absinthe | 641.255 |
| commercial processing | 663.55 |
| Absolute (Philosophy) | 111.6 |
| Absolute monarchy | 321.6 |
| Absolute rights | 323.01 |
| Absolute temperature | 536.5 |
| Absolution (Christian rite) | 234.166 |
| public worship | 265.64 |
| theology | 234.166 |
| Absorbency | |
| skin | 573.5 |
| human physiology | 612.791 |
| *see also* Skin | |
| Absorber oil | 665.538 4 |
| Absorption | 541.33 |
| chemical engineering | 660.284 23 |
| chemistry | 541.33 |
| gaseous-state physics | 530.435 |
| nutrition | |
| human physiology | 612.38 |
| Absorption of sound | |
| physics | 534.208 |
| Abstinence | 178 |
| ethics | 178 |
| religious practice | 204.47 |
| Buddhism | 294.344 47 |
| Christianity | 248.47 |
| Hinduism | 294.544 7 |
| Abstract algebra | 512.02 |
| Abstract data types | 005.73 |
| Abstract expressionism | 709.040 52 |
| painting | 759.065 2 |
| sculpture | 735.230 452 |
| Abstract harmonic analysis | 515.785 |
| Abstract spaces | 516.1 |
| Abstract thought | 153.24 |
| philosophy | 128.3 |
| psychology | 153.24 |
| Abstracting | |
| information science | 025.41 |
| Abstracting techniques | |
| rhetoric | 808.062 |
| Abstraction | 153.24 |
| Abstractionism | 709.040 52 |
| painting | 759.065 2 |
| sculpture | 735.230 452 |
| Abstracts | |
| collections | 080 |
| brief abstracts | 011 |
| Abstracts of title | 346.043 8 |
| Abū Dā'ūd Sulaymān ibn al-Ash'ath al-Sijistānī | |
| Hadith | 297.125 51 |
| Abu Dhabi (United Arab Emirates : Emirate) | T2—535 7 |
| Abū Ẓaby (United Arab Emirates : Emirate) | T2—535 7 |
| Abuja (Federal Capital Territory, Nigeria) | T2—669 68 |
| Abuse of power | |
| civil rights issue | 323.49 |
| law | 345.023 2 |
| government liability | 342.088 |
| public administration | 353.46 |
| Abused children | 305.230 869 45 |
| | T1—086 945 |
| pediatrics | 618.928 582 23 |
| social group | 305.230 869 45 |
| social theology | 201.762 76 |
| Christianity | 261.832 71 |
| social welfare | 362.76 |
| *see also* Child abuse | |
| Abutments | 721.3 |
| architecture | 721.3 |
| construction | 690.13 |
| structural engineering | 624.16 |
| Abydos (Egypt : Extinct city) | T2—323 |
| Abyssal zone | |
| biology | 578.779 |
| ecology | 577.79 |
| Abyssinia | T2—63 |
| Abyssinian cat | 636.826 |
| Abyssinians | T5—928 |
| Acacias | 583.748 |
| forestry | 634.973 748 |
| ornamental arboriculture | 635.977 374 8 |
| Academic costume | 378.28 |
| Academic degrees | 378.2 |
| Academic dissertations | 378.242 |
| specific places | 015 |
| Academic freedom | 371.104 |
| higher education | 378.121 3 |
| law | 344.078 |

Academic high schools 373.241
  *see also* Secondary education
Academic libraries 027.7
  administration 025.197 7
  collection development 025.218 77
  use studies 025.587 7
Academic library buildings
  architecture 727.827
Academic placement 371.264
  special education 371.904 3
  *see Manual at* 371.262 vs.
    371.264
Academic prognosis 371.264
  special education 371.904 3
  *see Manual at* 371.262 vs.
    371.264
Academic status 371.104
  higher education 378.121
Academic year 371.23
  law 344.079 2
Academies (Organizations) 060
Academy schools 371.05
Acadia 971.501 7
  T2—715
Acadia National Park (Me.) T2—741 45
Acadia Parish (La.) T2—763 56
Acadians T5—41
Acadians in Canada T5—114
  expulsion of 971.501 7
Acanthaceae 583.95
Acanthocephala 592.33
  paleozoology 562.33
Acanthodii 567.2
Acanthopterygii 597.64
  paleozoology 567.64
  *see also* Fishes
Acanthuses 635.933 95
  botany 583.95
  floriculture 635.933 95
Acari 595.42
Acarida 595.42
Acariformes 595.42
Acarina 595.42
Acarnania (Greece) T2—495 18
  ancient T2—383
Acceleration
  biophysics
    humans 612.014 414
  classical mechanics 531.112
  extraterrestrial biophysics
    humans 612.014 534
Acceleration of particles 539.73
Acceleration principle
  (Macroeconomics) 339.41

Accelerator effect
  (Macroeconomics) 339.41
Accelerometers
  aircraft 629.135 2
Accent (Linguistics) 414.6
  specific languages T4—16
Accent (Poetry) 808.1
Acceptances (Commercial paper) 332.77
  exchange medium 332.55
  law 346.096
Access control (Computers) 005.8
  management 658.478
Access points (Cataloging) 025.322
Access roads 388.13
Access to airports 387.736 2
Accessioning
  archives 025.281 4
Accessories (Clothing) 391.44
  care 646.6
  commercial technology 687.19
  customs 391.44
  home economics 646.3
  home sewing 646.48
  *see also* Clothing
Accident insurance 368.384
  government-sponsored 368.42
  industrial casualty 368.7
  law 346.086 384
Accident investigation 363.106 5
  technology 620.86
Accidents 363.1
  personal health 613.6
  psychology 155.936
  social services 363.1
    law 344.047
    public administration 353.9
  tort law 346.032 2
Accidents (Philosophy) 111.1
Accipitridae 598.94
Acclimation
  health 613.1
Acclimatization
  animals 591.42
  biology 578.42
  plants 581.42
Accomack County (Va.) T2—755 16
Accommodation (Optometry) 617.755
  *see also* Eye diseases —
    humans
Accompaniment
  musical technique 781.47
Accomplices 364.3
  *see also* Offenders

8

Accordions 788.86
  instrument 788.861 9
  music 788.86
  *see also* Woodwind instruments
Accountability
  Christian doctrines 233.4
  ethics 170
  executive management 658.402
  military administration 355.685
  public administration 352.35
  public education 379.158
  teachers 371.144
Accountancy 657
Accountants 657.092
Accounting 657
  arts 700.455 3
        T3C—355 3
  law 346.063
    corporation law 346.066 48
    public administration 343.034
  literature 808.803 553
    history and criticism 809.933 553
    specific literatures T3B—080 355 3
      history and
        criticism T3B—093 553
  malpractice 346.063 1
  management policy 658.151 1
Accounts payable 657.74
  accounting 657.74
  financial management 658.152 6
Accounts receivable 657.72
  accounting 657.72
  financial management 658.152 44
Accra (Ghana) T2—667
Accreditation 352.84
  education 379.158
  *see also* Licensing
Accreditation of prior learning 371.264
Acculturation 303.482
Accumulators
  hydraulic 621.254
Accuracy drills and tests
  keyboarding 652.307
  shorthand 653.15
Aceh (Indonesia) T2—598 11
Aceh (Indonesian people) T5—992 242
Aceh language 499.224 2
        T6—992 242
Aceh literature 899.224 2
Aceraceae 583.78
Acetabularia 579.836
Acetals 668.423
Acetates 668.423
Acetobacter 579.33

Acetylene 547.413
  chemical engineering 661.814
  gas technology 665.85
Achaea (Greece) T2—495 27
  ancient T2—387
Achaia (Greece) T2—495 27
  ancient T2—387
Acheulian culture 930.124
Achievement tests 371.262
  secondary education 373.126 2
  teacher-prepared tests 371.271
Achinese T5—992 242
Achinese language 499.224 2
        T6—992 242
Achinese literature 899.224 2
Acid-base imbalances
  medicine 616.399 2
    *see also* Digestive system
      diseases — humans
Acid mine drainage 363.738 4
  environmental protection 363.738 4
  preventive technology 622.5
  water pollution engineering 628.168 32
Acid pollution
  ecology 577.275 2
Acid precipitation 363.738 6
  *see also* Acid rain
Acid rain 363.738 6
  law 344.046 336
  meteorology 551.577 1
  pollution technology 628.532
  social welfare 363.738 6
  weather forecasting 551.647 71
  *see also* Pollution
Acid rock 781.66
Acid-soil conditioners 631.821
  chemical engineering 668.64
Acidification
  ecology 577.275 2
Acidosis
  medicine 616.399 2
    *see also* Digestive system
      diseases — humans
Acids 546.24
  aromatic chemistry 547.637
  chemical engineering 661.2
  chemistry 546.24
  human toxicology 615.921
  organic chemistry 547.037
    applied 661.86
  *see also* Chemicals
Acinonyx 599.759
Acipenseriformes 597.42
  paleozoology 567.42

| | |
|---|---|
| Acne | |
| medicine | 616.53 |
| *see also* Skin diseases — | |
| humans | |
| Acochlidacea | 594.34 |
| Acoela (Platyhelminthes) | 592.42 |
| Acoli (African people) | T5—965 |
| Acoli language | 496.5 |
| | T6—965 |
| Aconites | 583.34 |
| Acorns | |
| coffee substitute | |
| commercial processing | 663.97 |
| Acoustical communications | |
| engineering | 621.382 8 |
| Acoustical engineering | 620.2 |
| Acoustical engineers | 620.209 2 |
| Acoustical insulation | |
| buildings | 693.834 |
| Acoustical pattern recognition | 006.45 |
| engineering | 621.399 4 |
| Acoustical properties | |
| materials science | 620.112 94 |
| Acoustical prospecting | 622.159 2 |
| Acoustics | 534 |
| architectural design | 729.29 |
| engineering | 620.2 |
| *see also* Sound | |
| Acousto-optical communications | |
| engineering | 621.382 8 |
| Acquired immune deficiency | |
| syndrome | 362.196 979 2 |
| *see also* AIDS (Disease) | |
| Acquired immunity | 571.96 |
| humans | 616.079 |
| Acquisition of corporations | 338.83 |
| *see also* Mergers | |
| Acquisition of real property | 333.33 |
| economics | 333.33 |
| private ownership | 333.33 |
| public ownership | 333.13 |
| law | 346.043 62 |
| private ownership | 346.043 62 |
| public ownership | 343.025 2 |
| Acquisition of territory | 325.32 |
| law | 342.041 2 |
| law of nations | 341.42 |
| Acquisitions (Libraries) | 025.2 |
| Acquisitions (Museums) | 069.51 |
| Acrasia | 579.52 |
| Acre (Brazil) | T2—811 2 |
| Acreage allotments | 338.18 |
| law | 343.076 1 |

| | |
|---|---|
| Acrididae | |
| agricultural pests | 632.726 |
| Acrobatic gymnastics | 796.476 |
| Acrobatics | 796.476 |
| circuses | 791.34 |
| sports | 796.476 |
| Acrobats | 796.476 092 |
| circuses | 791.340 92 |
| sports | 796.476 092 |
| Acrochordidae | 597.967 |
| Acromegaly | |
| medicine | 616.47 |
| *see also* Endocrine | |
| diseases — humans | |
| Acronym dictionaries | 413.15 |
| specific languages | T4—315 |
| specific subjects | T1—014 8 |
| Acronyms | 411 |
| specific languages | T4—11 |
| specific subjects | T1—014 8 |
| Acrostics | 793.73 |
| Acrothoracica | 595.35 |
| Acrylic painting | 751.426 |
| Acrylics | 668.423 2 |
| textiles | 677.474 2 |
| *see also* Textiles | |
| Acrylonitrile rubber | 678.72 |
| Act | |
| philosophical anthropology | 128.4 |
| ACT (College testing program) | 378.166 2 |
| Act of Union, 1840 | 971.039 |
| ACTH (Hormone) | |
| pharmacology | 615.363 |
| production | |
| human physiology | 612.492 |
| Acting | 792.028 |
| motion pictures | 791.430 28 |
| radio | 791.440 28 |
| stage | 792.028 |
| television | 791.450 28 |
| Actinide series | 669.292 |
| chemistry | 546.42 |
| metallurgy | 669.292 |
| *see also* Chemicals; Metals | |
| Actinium | 669.292 1 |
| chemistry | 546.421 |
| metallurgy | 669.292 1 |
| *see also* Chemicals; Metals | |
| Actinomycetales | 579.37 |
| Actinomycetes | 579.37 |
| *see Manual at* 579.3 | |
| Actinopoda | 579.45 |
| Actinopterygii | 597 |
| *see also* Fishes | |

Actinotherapy
  medicine     615.831 5
Action
  philosophical anthropology   128.4
  psychology     150
Action games
  indoor     793.4
Action Party (Italy : 1853–1867)   324.245 026
Action Party (Italy : 1942–1947)   324.245 06
Action research     001.4
        T1—072
Action toys     790.133
  manufacturing technology   688.728
Actions (Law)     347.05
Activated carbon     662.93
  water treatment     628.166
Activated sludge process   628.354
Activewear     796
  commercial technology   687.16
  customs     391.48
  home economics     646.3
  home sewing     646.47
Activity-based costing   657.42
Activity therapy
  medicine     615.851 5
Acton (Quebec : Regional
  County Municipality)   T2—714 525
Actors     792.028 092
  motion pictures     791.430 280 92
    collected biography   791.430 280 922
      United States   791.430 280 922 73
  radio     791.440 280 92
  stage     792.028 092
  television     791.450 280 92
  *see Manual at* 780.92 and
  791.092
Actresses     792.028 092
  *see also* Actors
Acts of the Apostles   226.6
  pseudepigrapha   229.925
Actual grace     234.1
Actuarial science     368.01
Acuity (Visual perception)
  psychology     152.142 2
Acupressure
  therapeutics     615.822 2
Acupuncture
  therapeutics     615.892
Acylation
  chemical engineering   660.284 4
Ad Dakhla (Western
  Sahara)     T2—648
Ada County (Idaho)   T2—796 28
Adages     398.9

Adair County (Iowa)   T2—777 73
Adair County (Ky.)   T2—769 675
Adair County (Mo.)   T2—778 264
Adair County (Okla.)   T2—766 89
Adam
  Bible stories     222.110 950 5
  Islam     297.246
Adamawa-Eastern languages   496.361
        T6—963 61
Adamawa languages   496.361
        T6—963 61
Adamawa State (Nigeria)   T2—669 88
Adamawa-Ubangi languages   496.361
        T6—963 61
Adams, John
  United States history   973.44
Adams, John Quincy
  United States history   973.55
Adams County (Colo.)   T2—788 81
Adams County (Idaho)   T2—796 26
Adams County (Ill.)   T2—773 44
Adams County (Ind.)   T2—772 73
Adams County (Iowa)   T2—777 76
Adams County (Miss.)   T2—762 26
Adams County (N.D.)   T2—784 89
Adams County (Neb.)   T2—782 397
Adams County (Ohio)   T2—771 86
Adams County (Pa.)   T2—748 42
Adams County (Wash.)   T2—797 34
Adams County (Wis.)   T2—775 56
Adams Lake (B.C.)   T2—711 72
Adams River (B.C.)   T2—711 75
Adana İli (Turkey)   T2—564 7
  ancient     T2—393 5
Adangme (African people)   T5—963 37
Adangme language   496.337
        T6—963 37
Adaptability
  psychology     155.24
    children     155.418 24
    late adulthood   155.672
    situational influences   155.9
      children     155.418 9
Adaptation (Biology)   578.4
  animals     591.4
  plants     581.4
Adaptive control systems
  automation engineering   629.836
Addax     599.645
Added-value tax     336.271 4
Adders (Snakes)     597.963
Adder's-tongues (Ferns)   587.33

Addiction 362.29
  customs 394.14
  devotional literature 204.32
    Christianity 242.4
  medicine 616.86
  pastoral theology 206.1
    Christianity 259.429
  personal health 613.8
  religious guidance 204.42
    Christianity 248.862 9
  social theology 201.762 29
    Christianity 261.832 29
  social welfare 362.29
  *see also* Substance abuse
Addictive drugs
  pharmacokinetics 615.78
Addicts T1—087 4
Addis Ababa (Ethiopia) T2—633
Addison County (Vt.) T2—743 5
Addison's disease
  medicine 616.45
  *see also* Endocrine
    diseases — humans
Addition (Chemical reaction) 541.39
  organic chemistry 547.2
    applied 660.284 4
Addition (Mathematics) 512.92
  algebra 512.92
  arithmetic 513.2
Additive processes
  color photography 778.65
Addo Elephant National
  Park (South Africa) T2—687 53
Addresses 080
Adelaide (S. Aust.) T2—942 31
Adelaide (South Africa :
  District) T2—687 53
Aden T2—533 5
Aden, Gulf of 551.461 532
   T2—165 32
Adenauer, Konrad
  German history 943.087 5
Adenomas
  incidence 614.599 9
  medicine 616.993
Adenophorea 592.57
Adenosine triphosphate 572.475
Adenoviridae 579.244 3
Adephaga 595.762
Adhesion 541.33
  chemical engineering 660.293
Adhesiveness
  materials science 620.112 92

Adhesives 668.3
  building materials 691.99
  manufacturing technology 668.3
  materials science 620.199
  structural engineering 624.189 9
Adi Granth 294.682
Adige River (Italy) T2—453
Adipocytes
  human cytology 611.018 276
Adipose tissues 571.57
  human histology 611.018 27
Adirondack Mountains
  (N.Y.) T2—747 5
Adıyaman İli (Turkey) T2—565 2
  ancient T2—393 6
Adjectivals 415.5
  specific languages T4—55
Adjectives 415.5
  specific languages T4—55
Adjudication 347.07
  competitions T1—079
  criminal law 345.07
  law of nations 341.55
Adjustment (Insurance) 368.014
Adjustment (Psychology) 155.24
  children 155.418 24
  late adulthood 155.672
Adjustment disorders
  medicine 616.852
  *see also* Mental disorders
Adlerian psychology 150.195 3
Administration 658
   T1—068
  public administration 351
  *see Manual at* T1—068
Administration of estates 346.056
Administration of justice 347
  crimes against 364.134
  law 345.023 4
  criminal law 345.05
Administration régionale
  Kativik (Quebec) T2—714 111
Administrative agencies 351
  description and duties 351
  government publications
    bibliographies 011.534
  law 342.064
  organization and structure 352.29
    *see Manual at* 351 vs.
      352.29; *also at* 352–354
  *see Manual at* 352–354
Administrative areas
  area planning 711.551

Administrative assistants
  office management    651.3
Administrative courts    342.066 4
Administrative discretion    342.066 4
Administrative law    342.06
Administrative personnel
  office management    651.3
Administrative procedure
  law    342.066
Administrative regulations    348.025
Administrative reports    T1—06
  public administration    351.05
Administrative responsibility    658.402
  military services    355.685
  public administration    352.35
Administrative revenues
  public finance    336.16
Administrators (Public officials)    352.3
  *see also* Public administrators
Admirals    359.009 2
  role and function    359.331
Admiralty courts    347.04
Admiralty Islands (Papua
  New Guinea)    T2—958 1
Admiralty law    343.096
  *see Manual at* 341.45 vs.
    343.0962
Admissibility of evidence    347.062
  criminal law    345.062
Admission tests    371.262
  higher education    378.166 2
Admission to the bar    344.017 613 4
Admissions
  schools    371.21
    higher education    378.161
Adobe
  architectural construction    721.044 22
  building construction    693.22
Adolescence    305.235
  arts    T3C—354
  literature    808.803 54
    history and criticism    809.933 54
    specific literatures    T3B—080 354
      history and
        criticism    T3B—093 54
  psychology    155.5
  social aspects    305.235
Adolescent boys    305.235 1
    T1—083 51
  *see also* Young men — under
    twenty-one
Adolescent dentistry    617.600 835

Adolescent development    305.235 5
  psychology    155.5
  sociology    305.235 5
Adolescent girls    305.235 2
    T1—083 52
  *see also* Young women —
    under twenty-one
Adolescent gynecology    618.100 835
Adolescent literature    808.899 283
  history and criticism    809.892 83
  specific literatures    T3B—080 928 3
    history and criticism    T3B—099 283
Adolescent medicine    616.008 35
Adolescent obstetrics    618.200 835
Adolescent pharmacology    615.108 35
Adolescent psychiatry    616.890 083 5
Adolescent psychology    155.5
Adolescent surgery    617.008 35
Adolescent therapeutics    615.508 35
Adolescent toxicology    615.900 835
Adolescents    305.235
    T1—083 5
  arts    700.452 35
    T3C—352 35
  civil and human rights    323.352
  etiquette    395.123
  government programs    353.536 5
  health    613.043 3
  home care    649.125
  journalism for    070.483 3
  labor economics    331.347
    law    344.013 47
  legal status    346.013 5
    constitutional law    342.087 72
    private law    346.013 5
  libraries for    027.626
  literature    808.803 523 5
    history and criticism    809.933 523 5
    specific literatures    T3B—080 352 35
      history and
        criticism    T3B—093 523 5
  physical fitness    613.704 3
  physiology    612.661
  psychology    155.5
  publications for
    bibliographies    011.625
    reviews    028.162 5
  reading
    library science    028.535
  religion    200.835
    Christianity    270.083 5
      devotional literature    242.63
      guides to Christian life    248.83
      pastoral care    259.23

Adolescents
  religion
    Christianity (continued)
      religious education     268.433
      guides to life     204.408 35
      Judaism     296.083 5
        guides to life     296.708 35
        religious education     296.680 835
    sex hygiene     613.951
    social aspects     305.235
    social welfare     362.708 3
      law     344.032 708 3
      public administration     353.536 5
Adolf Fredrik, King of Sweden
  Swedish history     948.503 63
Adopted children     306.874
          T1—085 4
  family relationships     306.874
  home care     649.145
  psychology     155.445
  social welfare     362.829 8
Adoption     362.734
  criminology     364.18
    criminal law     345.028
  law     346.017 8
  religion     204.41
  social welfare     362.734
Adoptive parents     306.874
          T1—085
Adoration of magi     232.923
Adoration of shepherds     232.922
ADP (Computing)     004
Adrar (Algeria : Province)     T2—657
Adrenal gland diseases
  medicine     616.45
    *see also* Endocrine
      diseases — humans
  pediatrics     618.924 5
Adrenal glands     573.46
  biology     573.46
  human anatomy     611.45
  human physiology     612.45
  medicine     616.45
  surgery     617.461
  *see also* Endocrine system
Adrenal hormones     573.464
  human physiology     612.45
  pharmacology     615.364
  *see also* Endocrine system
Adrenocorticotrophic hormone
  pharmacology     615.363
  production
    human physiology     612.492

Adrianople (Turkey)     T2—496 14
Adriatic Sea     551.461 385
          T2—163 85
Adsorbent carbons     662.93
Adsorbent charcoals     662.93
Adsorption     541.335
  chemical engineering     660.284 235
  chemistry     541.335
  gaseous-state physics     530.435
  semiconductors     537.622 6
Adult baptism     234.161 3
  public worship     265.13
  theology     234.161 3
Adult child abuse victims
  medicine     616.858 223 9
  social theology     201.762 764
    Christianity     261.832 73
  social welfare     362.764
Adult child sexual abuse victims
  medicine     616.858 369
  social theology     201.762 764
    Christianity     261.832 73
  social welfare     362.764
Adult children of alcoholics
  medicine     616.861 9
  social welfare     362.292 4
Adult children of substance
  abusers
  medicine     616.869
  social welfare     362.291 4
Adult easy literature
  rhetoric     808.067
Adult education     374
          T1—071 5
  federal aid     379.121 5
  law     344.074
  public administrative support     353.84
  public support     379.114
    law     344.076 85
  special education     371.904 75
  university extension     378.175
Adultery     306.736
  criminology     364.153
    criminal law     345.025 3
  ethics     176.4
    *see also* Sexual relations —
      ethics
  social theology     201.7
    Christianity     261.835 736
  sociology     306.736
Adulthood     305.24
  psychology     155.6
  social aspects     305.24

Adults 305.24
  criminal offenders 364.3
  development
    physiology 612.66
  education 374
    *see also* Adult education
  guides to religious life 204.4
  health 613.043 4
  journalism for 070.483 4
  physical fitness 613.704 4
  psychology 155.6
  recreation 790.192
    indoor 793.019 2
    outdoor 796
  religion 200
    Christianity 230
      guides to Christian life 248.84
      religious education 268.434
  social aspects 305.24
Adur (England) T2—422 69
Advaita (Philosophy) 181.482
Advanced placement (Education) 371.264
Advent 263.912
  devotional literature 242.332
  music 781.722
  sermons 252.612
Advent Christian Church 286.73
  *see also* Adventists
Adventists 286.7
  biography 286.709 2
  church government 262.067
    parishes 254.067
  church law 262.986 7
  doctrines 230.67
    catechisms and creeds 238.67
  guides to Christian life 248.486 7
  missions 266.67
  moral theology 241.046 7
  public worship 264.067
  religious associations 267.186 7
  religious education 268.867
  seminaries 230.073 67
  theology 230.67
Adventure 904
  arts 700.458 2
    T3C—358 2
  literature 808.803 582
    history and criticism 809.933 582
    specific literatures T3B—080 358 2
      history and
        criticism T3B—093 582
  specific places 930–990

Adventure fiction 808.838 7
  history and criticism 809.387
  specific literatures T3B—308 7
    individual authors T3A—3
Adventure games 793.93
  *see Manual at* 793.932 vs.
    794.822
Adventure racing 796.5
Adverbials 415.76
  specific languages T4—576
Adverbs 415.76
  specific languages T4—576
Adversary system 347
Adverse drug reactions
  pharmacokinetics 615.704
Advertisements 381.029
    T1—029
  illustration 741.67
Advertisers 659.109 2
Advertising 659.1
  illustration 741.67
  law 343.082
  managerial organization 659.112
  medical ethics 174.26
Advertising agencies 659.112 5
Advertising campaigns 659.113
Advertising cards
  illustration 741.685
Advertising departments 659.112 2
Advertising images 659.104 5
Advertising lighting 621.322 9
Advertising media planning 659.111
Advertising themes 659.104 5
Advice to readers
  journalism 070.444
Advisory bodies
  public administration 352.743
Advocacy
  law 347.052
Advocates (Lawyers) 340.092
Adygea (Russia) T2—475 2
Adyghe language 499.962 5
    T6—999 625
Adyghe literature 899.962 5
Aegadian Islands T2—458 24
Aegean architecture 722.61
Aegean Islands (Greece :
  Periphereia) T2—495 8
Aegean Islands (Greece and 949.58
  Turkey) T2—495 8
  ancient 939.1
    T2—391
Aegean Sea 551.461 388
    T2—163 88

| | |
|---|---|
| Aeolian instruments | 786.69 |
| chamber music | 785.669 |
| construction | 786.691 923 |
| by hand | 786.691 923 |
| by machine | 681.866 9 |
| Aeolian Islands (Italy) | T2—458 11 |
| Aepyornithiformes | 568.5 |
| Aequian language | 479.7 |
| | T6—797 |
| Aeration | |
| sewage treatment | 628.35 |
| water supply treatment | 628.165 |
| Aerial cinematography | 777.6 |
| Aerial microorganisms | 579.175 |
| Aerial photography | 778.35 |
| military engineering | 623.72 |
| Aerial railways | 385.6 |
| engineering | 625.5 |
| transportation services | 385.6 |
| Aerial skiing | 796.937 |
| Aerial surveying | 526.982 |
| Aerial videography | 777.6 |
| Aerial warfare | 358.4 |
| *see also* Air warfare | |
| Aerobatics | 797.54 |
| Aerobic dancing | 613.715 |
| Aerobic exercise | 613.71 |
| sports | 796.44 |
| Aerobic gymnastics | 796.44 |
| Aerobic-microaerophilic gram- | |
| negative bacteria | 579.323 |
| Aerobic respiration | 573.2 |
| Aerodynamic load | 624.175 |
| aeronautics | 629.132 35 |
| Aerodynamics | 533.62 |
| aeronautics | 629.132 3 |
| engineering | 620.107 4 |
| space flight | 629.415 1 |
| Aeroelasticity | |
| aeronautics | 629.132 362 |
| Aeromechanics | 533.6 |
| aeronautics | 629.132 3 |
| engineering | 620.107 |
| Aeronautical charts | 629.132 54 |
| Aeronautical engineers | 629.130 092 |
| Aeronautics | 629.13 |
| law | 343.097 |
| Aerophones | 788 |
| *see also* Wind instruments | |
| Aerosols | 541.345 15 |
| chemical engineering | 660.294 515 |
| colloid chemistry | 541.345 15 |
| meteorology | 551.511 3 |

| | |
|---|---|
| Aerospace engineering | 629.1 |
| military | 623.66 |
| Aerospace engineers | 629.109 2 |
| Aerospace medicine | 616.980 21 |
| Aerospace photography | 778.35 |
| Aerospace physiology | |
| humans | 612.014 4 |
| Aerostatics | 533.61 |
| aeronautics | 629.132 2 |
| engineering | 620.107 3 |
| Aerotherapy | |
| medicine | 615.836 |
| Aesthetics | 111.85 |
| arts | 701.17 |
| literature | 801.93 |
| music | 781.17 |
| philosophy | 111.85 |
| Aestivation | 571.786 |
| Aeta (Philippine people) | T5—992 1 |
| Aetolia (Greece) | T2—383 |
| Aetolia and Acarnania | |
| (Greece) | T2—495 18 |
| ancient | T2—383 |
| Afan (Wales) | T2—429 85 |
| Afar (African people) | T5—935 |
| 'Afār kelel (Ethiopia) | T2—634 |
| Afar language | 493.5 |
| | T6—935 |
| AFDC (Social program) | 362.713 |
| Affection | |
| psychology | 152.41 |
| Affective disorders | 362.25 |
| medicine | 616.852 7 |
| social welfare | 362.25 |
| *see also* Mental disorders | |
| Affects | |
| psychology | 152.4 |
| Affenpinscher | 636.76 |
| Affine geometry | 516.4 |
| Affinity (Law) | 346.015 |
| Affirmative action | |
| education | 379.26 |
| employment | 331.133 |
| *see also* Equal employment | |
| opportunity | |
| government programs | 353.53 |
| law | 342.087 |
| constitutional law | 342.087 |
| labor law | 344.011 33 |
| Affixes (Grammar) | 415.92 |
| specific languages | T4—592 |
| Affoltern (Switzerland : | |
| Bezirk) | T2—494 572 1 |

Afforestation 333.751 52
  law 346.046 751 52
  resource economics 333.751 52
  silviculture 634.956
Afghan hound 636.753 3
Afghan language 491.593
  T6—915 93
Afghan literature 891.593
Afghan rugs
  arts 746.758 1
Afghan War, 2001– 958.104 7
Afghanistan 958.1
  T2—581
  ancient 939.6
  T2—396
Afghans T5—915 93
Afghans (Coverlets) 645.4
  arts 746.430 437
  home sewing 646.21
  household equipment 645.4
AFL (Labor) 331.883 209 73
AFL-CIO 331.880 973
Aflatoxins
  human toxicology 615.952 956 57
Africa 960
  T2—6
  geography 916
  military operations
    World War I 940.416
    World War II 940.542 3
  travel 916.04
Africa, Black T2—67
Africa, Central 967
  T2—67
Africa, East 967.6
  T2—676
Africa, North 961
  T2—61
  ancient 939.7
  T2—397
Africa, Southern 968
  T2—68
Africa, Sub-Saharan 967
  T2—67
Africa, West 966
  T2—66
Africa proconsularis T2—397 3
African American cooking 641.592 960 73
African American Methodist
  churches 287.8
  *see also* Methodist Church
African Americans 973.049 607 3
  T5—960 73
  civil rights 323.119 607 3

African Americans (continued)
  civilization 973.049 607 3
  education 371.829 960 73
  military troops
    Civil War (United States) 973.741 5
    World War II 940.540 3
  social aspects 305.896 073
  *see Manual at* T5—96073
African bush pig 599.633
African clawed frog 597.865 4
African elephant 599.674
  big game hunting 799.276 74
  conservation technology 639.979 674
  resource economics 333.959 674
African independent churches 289.93
African languages 496
  T6—96
African lilies 584.33
African literature 808.899 6
  history and criticism 809.896
  in African languages 896
African Methodist Episcopal
  Church 287.83
  *see also* Methodist Church
African Methodist Episcopal
  Zion Church 287.83
  *see also* Methodist Church
African mole rat 599.359
African National Congress (South
  African political party) 324.268 083
African religions 299.6
African sleeping sickness
  incidence 614.533
  medicine 616.936 3
  *see also* Communicable
    diseases — humans
African theater (World War II) 940.542 3
African violets 635.933 95
  botany 583.05
  horticulture 635.933 95
Africans T5—96
Afrihili (Artificial language) 499.99
  T6—999 9
Afrikaans language 439.36
  T6—393 6
Afrikaans literature 839.36
Afrikaners T5—393 6
Afro-Americans 973.049 607 3
  T5—960 73
  *see also* African Americans
Afro-Asian bloc T2—171 65

| | | | |
|---|---|---|---|
| Afro-Asiatic languages | 492 | Age-hardening metals | 671.36 |
| | T6—92 | Age of Freedom | |
| non-Semitic | 493 | Swedish history | 948.503 6 |
| | T6—93 | Age of Greatness | |
| Afro-Asiatic literatures | 892 | Swedish history | 948.503 4 |
| non-Semitic | 893 | Aged abuse | 362.682 |
| Afro-Asiatic peoples | T5—92 | criminology | 364.155 5 |
| non-Semitic | T5—93 | criminal law | 345.025 55 |
| Afro-Cuban jazz | 781.657 | social welfare | 362.682 |
| Afrohili (Artificial language) | 499.99 | Aged people | 305.26 |
| | T6—999 9 | | T1—084 6 |
| After-dinner speeches | | *see also* Older people | |
| literature | 808.851 | Agency law | 346.029 |
| history and criticism | 809.51 | Agency shop | 331.889 2 |
| specific literatures | T3B—501 | Agent Orange | |
| individual authors | T3A—5 | human toxicology | 615.951 37 |
| rhetoric | 808.512 | Aggadah | 296.19 |
| Afterimages | | Midrash | 296.142 |
| psychology | 152.148 | Talmud | 296.127 6 |
| Afternoon teas | 642 | Aggeus (Biblical book) | 224.97 |
| cooking | 641.53 | Aggregates (Materials) | 553.62 |
| light meals | 641.53 | economic geology | 553.62 |
| main meals | 641.54 | materials science | 620.191 |
| customs | 394.125 3 | mining | 622.362 |
| light meals | 394.125 3 | Aggression | 302.54 |
| main meals | 394.125 4 | law of war | 341.62 |
| Afyon İli (Turkey) | T2—562 8 | psychology | 155.232 |
| ancient | T2—392 6 | drives | 153.8 |
| Afyonkarahisar (Turkey : | | emotions | 152.47 |
| İli) | T2—562 8 | personality trait | 155.232 |
| Agadir Idda Outanane | | social psychology | 302.54 |
| (Morocco) | T2—646 6 | Agin Buriat (Russia : | |
| Agamidae | 597.955 | Okrug) | T2—575 |
| Agapes (Christian rites) | 265.9 | Agin Buriatskiĭ avtonomnyĭ | |
| Agaricaceae | 579.6 | okrug (Russia) | T2—575 |
| Agaricales | 579.6 | Aging | 571.878 |
| Agates | 553.87 | arts | T3C—354 |
| *see also* Semiprecious stones | | human physiology | 612.67 |
| Agavaceae | 584.352 | literature | 808.803 54 |
| Agaves | 584.352 | history and criticism | 809.933 54 |
| fiber crop | 633.577 | specific literatures | T3B—080 354 |
| Age characteristics | | history and | |
| animals | 591.39 | criticism | T3B—093 54 |
| physical anthropology | 599.937 | physiology | 571.878 |
| plants | 581.39 | psychology of late adulthood | 155.67 |
| Age determination | | social aspects | 305.26 |
| animals | 591.39 | Aging alcoholic beverages | 663.17 |
| physical anthropology | 599.937 | Agnatha | 597.2 |
| plants | 581.39 | paleozoology | 567.2 |
| Age discrimination in | | Agnosticism | 211.7 |
| employment | 331.398 133 | Christian polemics | 239.7 |
| law | 344.013 981 33 | philosophy | 149.72 |
| Age groups | 305.2 | philosophy of religion | 211.7 |
| | T1—083–084 | Agnostics | 211.709 2 |

Agnus Dei 264.36
  music 782.323 2
Agoraphobia
  medicine 616.852 25
  *see also* Mental disorders
Agostinho Neto, António
  Angolan history 967.304 1
Agoutis 599.359
Agrammatism
  medicine 616.855 2
  *see also* Communication
    disorders
Agranulocytosis
  medicine 616.154
  *see also* Cardiovascular
    diseases — humans
Agraphia
  medicine 616.855 3
  *see also* Communication
    disorders
Agreement (Grammar) 415
  specific languages T4—5
Ağrı İli (Turkey) T2—566 26
  ancient T2—395 5
Agricultural areas T2—173 4
  area planning 711.554
Agricultural assistance
  law 343.076
  production economics 338.18
Agricultural banks 332.31
Agricultural chemicals 631.8
  engineering 668.6
  public safety 363.179 2
  *see also* Hazardous materials
  use 631.8
Agricultural civilization 909
Agricultural commodities 338.17
  *see also* Agricultural products
Agricultural communities 307.72
Agricultural cooperative credit
  associations 334.2
Agricultural cooperatives 334.683
Agricultural credit 332.71
  law 346.073
  production economics 338.18
Agricultural ecology 577.55
Agricultural economics 338.1
Agricultural engineering 630
Agricultural enterprises 338.763
Agricultural equipment 631.3
  manufacturing technology 681.763
Agricultural experiment stations 630.724
Agricultural extension 630.715
Agricultural genetics 631.523 3

Agricultural industries 338.1
  accounting 657.863
  economics 338.1
  law 343.076
  public administration 354.5
Agricultural insurance 368.096
  crop 368.121
  livestock liability 368.56
Agricultural laborers
  social class 305.563
Agricultural lands 333.76
  biology 578.755
  ecology 577.55
  economics 333.76
  sale and rental 333.335
Agricultural libraries 026.63
Agricultural life
  civilization 909
Agricultural lower classes 305.563
Agricultural machinery 631.3
  manufacturing technology 681.763
  shortages
    economics 338.14
Agricultural marketing 381.41
  public administration 354.59
Agricultural meteorology 630.251 5
Agricultural occupations
  sociology 305.963
Agricultural pests 632.6
Agricultural pollution 363.738 498
  effect on natural ecology 577.273
Agricultural price supports
  economics 338.18
  public administration 354.528 5
Agricultural productivity 338.16
Agricultural products 338.17
  commerce 381.41
  economics 338.17
  investment economics 332.644 1
  military resources 355.245
  public administration 354.59
Agricultural runoff 363.738 498
Agricultural schools 630.71
Agricultural sociology 306.349
Agricultural structures 631.2
  architecture 725.37
  construction 690.537
  domestic architecture 728.92
    construction 690.892
  use 631.2
Agricultural systems of labor
  sociology 306.364

| | |
|---|---|
| Agricultural wastes | 363.728 8 |
| animal feed | 636.085 56 |
| animal husbandry | 636.083 8 |
| sanitary engineering | 628.746 |
| social services | 363.728 8 |
| water pollution engineering | 628.168 4 |
| *see also* Waste control | |
| Agricultural workers | 630.92 |
| economics | 331.763 |
| social class | 305.963 |
| Agricultural working class | 305.563 |
| Agriculture | 630 |
| applied science | 630 |
| art representation | 704.943 |
| arts | T3C—36 |
| economics | 338.1 |
| energy economics | 333.796 6 |
| enterprises | 338.763 |
| folklore | 398.24 |
| history and criticism | 398.36 |
| law | 344.095 7 |
| painting | 758.5 |
| public administration | 354.5 |
| Agriculture and state | 338.18 |
| Agriculturists | 630.92 |
| Agrigento (Italy) | T2—458 221 |
| ancient | T2—378 221 |
| Agrigento (Italy : Province) | T2—458 22 |
| ancient | T2—378 22 |
| Agrigentum (Italy) | T2—378 221 |
| Agroforestry | 634.99 |
| Agromyzidae | 595.774 |
| Agronomy | 630 |
| Agrosteae | 584.9 |
| Agrostis | 633.23 |
| botany | 584.9 |
| forage crop | 633.23 |
| Aguadilla (P.R. : District) | T2—729 54 |
| Aguascalientes (Mexico : State) | T2—724 2 |
| Āḥād (Hadith) | 297.125 24 |
| Aḥādīth al-Qudusīyah | 297.125 8 |
| Aharonim | 296.180 92 |
| Ahidjo, Ahmadou | |
| Cameroonian history | 967.110 41 |
| Ahilot | 296.123 6 |
| Ahimsa | 294.548 697 |
| Buddhism | 294.356 97 |
| Hinduism | 294.548 697 |
| Jainism | 294.456 97 |
| Ahmadinejad, Mahmoud | |
| Iranian history | 955.061 |
| Ahmadiyya movement | 297.86 |
| doctrines | 297.204 6 |

| | |
|---|---|
| Ahom | T5—959 19 |
| Ahuachapán (El Salvador : Dept.) | T2—728 411 |
| Ahvenanmaan lääni (Finland) | T2—489 72 |
| Aichi-ken (Japan) | T2—521 67 |
| Aid to families with dependent children | 362.713 |
| AIDS (Disease) | 362.196 979 2 |
| church work with patients | 259.419 697 92 |
| incidence | 614.599 392 |
| law | 344.043 697 92 |
| medicine | 616.979 2 |
| nursing | 616.979 202 31 |
| pediatrics | 618.929 792 |
| social services | 362.196 979 2 |
| social theology | 201.762 196 979 2 |
| Christianity | 261.832 196 979 2 |
| *see also* Communicable diseases — humans | |
| Aigaio Nēsoi (Greece : Periphereia) | T2—495 8 |
| Aigle (Switzerland : District) | T2—494 524 9 |
| Aiken County (S.C.) | T2—757 75 |
| Aikido | 796.815 4 |
| physical fitness | 613.714 8 |
| Ailanthuses | 635.977 377 |
| botany | 583.77 |
| ornamental arboriculture | 635.977 377 |
| Ailerons | 629.134 33 |
| Ailuropoda | 599.789 |
| Ain (France) | T2—445 83 |
| Aïn Chok-Hay Hassani (Morocco : Prefecture) | T2—643 8 |
| Aïn Defla (Algeria : Province) | T2—653 |
| Aïn Sebaâ-Hay Mohamed (Morocco : Prefecture) | T2—643 8 |
| Aïn Temouchent (Algeria : Province) | T2—651 |
| Ainu | T5—946 |
| Ainu language | 494.6 |
| | T6—946 |
| Ainu literature | 894.6 |
| Air | |
| gas technology | 665.82 |
| health | 613.19 |
| Air artillery | 358.43 |
| Air bags | |
| automobile | 629.276 |
| Air bases | 358.417 |
| military engineering | 623.66 |
| World War I | 940.443 |

Air bases (continued)
  World War II       940.544 3
  *see also* Air warfare
Air circulation equipment
  buildings       697.932 5
Air compression engines
  automotive       629.250 7
Air-compression-powered
  automobiles
  engineering       629.229 4
Air-compression-powered
  locomotives       385.365
  engineering       625.265
  transportation services       385.365
  *see also* Rolling stock
Air compression technology       621.51
Air compressors       621.51
Air conditioning
  aircraft       629.134 42
  automobile       629.277 2
  buildings       697.93
  health       613.5
  household management       644.5
  library buildings       697.978
    plant management       022.8
  mining       622.42
  museums       069.29
  plant management       658.25
  ships       623.853 7
  vehicles       629.040 289
Air conditioning engineers
  building trades       697.930 92
Air currents       551.517
  aeronautics       629.132 4
Air-cushion vehicles       388.35
  engineering       629.3
  land       388.35
  military engineering       623.748
  ocean       387.2
  transportation services       388.35
    inland water       386.22
Air engines       621.42
Air force personnel       358.400 92
  role and function       358.413 3
Air forces       358.4
Air freight       387.744
  airport services       387.736 4
  law       343.097 8
Air guns       683.4
  art metalwork       739.73
Air holes
  aeronautics       629.132 327
Air mail       383.144
  *see also* Postal service

Air masses       551.551 2
Air mechanics       533.6
  aeronautics       629.132 3
  engineering       620.107
Air-mileage indicators       629.135 1
Air motors       621.42
Air national guards       358.413 7
Air operations (Military science)    358.414
Air ordnance       358.418
  engineering       623.746 1
  military equipment       358.418
Air pilots       629.130 92
Air pockets
  aeronautics       629.132 327
Air pollution       363.739 2
  crop damage       632.19
  ecology       577.276
  law       344.046 342
  public administration       354.373 5
  social welfare       363.739 2
  technology       628.53
  toxicology       571.956
  *see also* Pollution
Air pollution rights       363.739 26
  law       344.046 342
Air-position indicators       629.135 1
Air pressure control
  aircraft       629.134 42
  spacecraft       629.477 5
Air propulsion       621.42
Air pumps       621.69
Air raid shelters       363.35
  civil defense       363.35
  law       344.053 5
  military engineering       623.38
  public administration       353.95
Air raid warning systems       358.414
  civil defense       363.35
  military engineering       623.737
Air raids       358.414
  civil defense       363.35
  World War I       940.442
  World War II       940.544 2
  *see also* Air warfare
Air resistance
  aeronautics       629.132 34
Air resources       333.92
  economics       333.92
  law       346.046 92
  public administration       354.37
Air rights (National airspace)       341.46
Air rights (Real estate)
  economics       333.3
  law       346.043 2

Air rights (Real estate) (continued)
  sale and rental — 333.339
  urban area planning — 711.4
  zoning — 333.771 7
    law — 346.045
Air safety — 363.124
  law — 343.097
  public administration — 353.988
  social services — 363.124
  technology — 629.130 028 9
Air-sea interactions — 551.524 6
Air seasoning
  lumber — 674.382
Air-speed indicators — 629.135 2
Air sports — 797.5
Air-supply control
  spacecraft — 629.477 5
Air-supported construction — 693.98
Air-taxi accidents — 363.124 93
  *see also* Air safety
Air temperatures
  meteorology — 551.525
Air terminals — 387.736 2
  *see also* Airports
Air-to-air guided missiles — 358.43
  engineering — 623.451 91
  military equipment — 358.43
Air-to-air missile forces — 358.43
Air-to-surface guided missiles — 358.428 2
  engineering — 623.451 92
  military equipment — 358.428 2
Air-to-surface missile forces — 358.42
Air-to-underwater guided
  missiles — 358.42
  engineering — 623.451 93
  military equipment — 358.42
Air-to-underwater missile forces — 358.42
Air traffic control — 387.740 426
  engineering — 629.136 6
  law — 343.097 6
  military engineering — 623.666
  transportation services — 387.740 426
  *see Manual at* 629.1366 vs.
    387.740426
Air traffic controllers — 629.136 609 2
Air transportation — 387.7
  engineering — 629.13
  law — 343.097
  public administration — 354.79
  safety — 363.124
    *see also* Air safety
  transportation services — 387.7

Air transportation facilities — 387.736 2
  engineering — 629.136
  *see also* Airports
Air transportation insurance — 368.093
  inland marine — 368.24
  liability — 368.576
Air transportation police — 363.287 6
Air transportation workers — 387.709 2
Air warfare — 358.4
  Algerian Revolution — 965.046 48
  Chaco War — 989.207 164 8
  Civil War (Spain) — 946.081 48
  Falkland Islands War — 997.110 244 8
  Indo-Pakistan War, 1971 — 954.920 514 8
  Indochinese War — 959.704 148
  Iraq War, 2003– — 956.704 434 8
  Iraqi-Iranian Conflict — 955.054 248
  Korean War — 951.904 248
  Persian Gulf War, 1991 — 956.704 424 8
  Vietnamese War — 959.704 348
  World War I — 940.44
  World War II — 940.544
Airborne infantry — 356.166
Airbrush drawing — 741.29
Airbrush painting — 751.494
Aircraft — 387.73
  engineering — 629.133
  law — 343.097 5
  military engineering — 623.746
  military equipment — 358.418 3
  piloting — 629.132 52
  psychological influence — 155.965
  sanitation services — 363.729 3
  sports — 797.5
  theft of — 364.162 862 913 3
    law — 345.026 286 291 33
  transportation services — 387.73
    operation — 387.740 44
  *see Manual at* 629.046 vs. 388
Aircraft accidents — 363.124
  *see also* Air safety
Aircraft carriers — 359.948 35
  design — 623.812 55
  engineering — 623.825 5
  naval equipment — 359.948 35
  naval units — 359.943 5
Aircraft detection — 358.414
  civil defense — 363.35
Aircraft engineers — 629.130 092
Aircraft failures — 363.124 16
  public safety — 363.124 16
  wreckage studies — 629.132 55
  *see also* Air safety
Aircraft gunnery — 623.555

Aircraft navigators    629.132 510 92
Aircraft noise    363.741
   engineering    629.132 3
   social welfare    363.741
   *see also* Noise
Aircraft operation
   transportation services    387.740 44
Aircraft racing    797.52
Airdrie (Scotland)    T2—414 52
Aire, River (England)    T2—428 15
Airflow
   aeronautics    629.132 32
Airfoils    629.134 32
Airframes    629.134 31
Airline cooking    641.575
Airline employees    387.709 2
Airlines    387.7
   *see also* Air transportation
Airplane accidents    363.124
   *see also* Air safety
Airplane-banner advertising    659.134 4
Airplane hijacking    364.155 2
   law    345.025 52
Airplane racing    797.52
Airplanes    387.733 4
   engineering    629.133 34
   military engineering    623.746
   piloting    629.132 52
   transportation services    387.733 4
   *see also* Aircraft
Airport facilities    387.736 2
   *see also* Airports
Airport police    363.287 6
Airports    387.736
   architecture    725.39
   area planning    711.78
   construction    690.539
   engineering    629.136
   institutional housekeeping    647.963 9
   law    343.097 7
   military engineering    623.66
   public administration    354.79
   transportation services    387.736
   *see also* Aircraft
Airships    387.732 4
   engineering    629.133 24
   military engineering    623.743
   piloting    629.132 522
   transportation services    387.732 4
   *see also* Aircraft
Airspace (Territorial right)    341.46
Airstrips    387.736
   engineering    629.136 12
   military engineering    623.661 2

Airstrips (continued)
   transportation services    387.736
   *see also* Airports
Ais-Ais/Richtersveld
   Transfrontier Park
   (South Africa)    T2—687 19
Aisén (Chile : Province)    T2—836 22
Aisén del General Carlos
   Ibáñez del Campo
   (Chile : Region)    T2—836 2
Aisne (France)    T2—442 66
Aitkin County (Minn.)    T2—776 72
Aitōlia kai Akarnania
   (Greece)    T2—495 18
Aix    598.412
Aix-la-Chapelle (Germany)    T2—435 511
Aizoaceae    583.53
Ajaria (Georgia)    T2—475 8
'Ajlūn (Jordan : Province)    T2—569 546
'Ajmān (United Arab
   Emirates : Emirate)    T2—535 7
Aka (African people)    T5—965
Aka language (Central African    496.396
   Republic)    T6—963 96
Akaishi Mountains (Japan)    T2—521 6
Akan (African people)    T5—963 385
Akan language    496.338 5
      T6—963 385
Akan literature    896.338 5
Akarnania (Greece)
   ancient    T2—383
Akbar, Emperor of Hindustan
   Indian history    954.025 4
Akershus fylke (Norway)    T2—482 2
Akhenaton, King of Egypt
   Egyptian history    932.014
Akimel O'Odham Indians    T5—974 552 9
Akimel O'Odham language    497.455 29
      T6—974 552 9
Akimel O'Odham literature    897.455 29
Akita    636.73
Akita-ken (Japan)    T2—521 13
Akkad    935.501
      T2—355
Akkadian language    492.1
      T6—921
Akkadian literature    892.1
Akkadians    T5—921
Akkala Saami language    494.576
      T6—945 76
Akkala Sámi language    494.576
      T6—945 76
Aklan (Philippines)    T2—599 5
Aklavik (N.W.T.)    T2—719 3

| | |
|---|---|
| Akoli language | 496.5 |
| | T6—965 |
| Akpes language | 496.33 |
| | T6—963 3 |
| Akron (Ohio) | T2—771 36 |
| Aksaray İli (Turkey) | T2—564 1 |
| ancient | T2—393 4 |
| Aksum (Kingdom) | 963.4 |
| | T2—634 |
| Akwa Ibom State (Nigeria) | T2—669 43 |
| Akwamu (Kingdom) | 966.701 6 |
| | T2—667 |
| Akwe-Shavante language | 498.4 |
| | T6—984 |
| Al-Jaza'ir (Algeria : Province) | T2—653 |
| Al Mafraq (Jordan : Province) | T2—569 597 |
| ancient | T2—335 97 |
| Al-Mu'talif wa-al-mukhtalif (Hadith) | 297.125 264 2 |
| Alabama | 976.1 |
| | T2—761 |
| Alabama, Battle of Kearsarge and, 1864 | 973.754 |
| Alabama River (Ala.) | T2—761 2 |
| Alabaster | 553.635 |
| economic geology | 553.635 |
| mining | 622.363 5 |
| Alacalufan languages | 498.7 |
| | T6—987 |
| Alachua County (Fla.) | T2—759 79 |
| Alagoas (Brazil) | T2—813 5 |
| Alajuela (Costa Rica : Province) | T2—728 65 |
| Alamance County (N.C.) | T2—756 58 |
| Alameda County (Calif.) | T2—794 65 |
| Alamo, Siege, 1836 | 976.403 |
| Alamosa County (Colo.) | T2—788 36 |
| Åland (Finland) | T2—489 72 |
| Åland Islands (Finland) | T2—489 72 |
| Alarm systems | |
| engineering | 621.389 28 |
| fire safety technology | 628.922 5 |
| Alaska | 979.8 |
| | T2—798 |
| Alaska, Gulf of (Alaska) | 551.461 434 |
| | T2—164 34 |
| Alaska Panhandle (Alaska) | T2—798 2 |
| Alaska Range (Alaska) | T2—798 3 |
| Alaskan Inuit languages | 497.12 |
| | T6—971 2 |
| Alaskan Inuktitut languages | 497.12 |
| | T6—971 2 |

| | |
|---|---|
| Alaskan Malamute | 636.73 |
| Alaskan Pacific seawaters | 551.461 434 |
| | T2—164 34 |
| Alastrim | |
| incidence | 614.521 |
| medicine | 616.913 |
| *see also* Communicable diseases — humans | |
| Alaudidae | 598.825 |
| Alava (Spain) | T2—466 5 |
| Alba (Romania : Judeţ) | T2—498 4 |
| Albacete (Spain : Province) | T2—464 6 |
| Albacore | 597.783 |
| Albania | 949.65 |
| | T2—496 5 |
| ancient | 939.865 |
| | T2—398 65 |
| Albania (Ancient kingdom) | 939.534 |
| | T2—395 34 |
| Albanian language | 491.991 |
| | T6—919 91 |
| Albanian literature | 891.991 |
| Albanians | T5—919 91 |
| Albany (N.Y.) | T2—747 43 |
| Albany (South Africa : District) | T2—687 53 |
| Albany (W.A.) | T2—941 2 |
| Albany County (N.Y.) | T2—747 42 |
| Albany County (Wyo.) | T2—787 95 |
| Albatrosses | 598.42 |
| Albay (Philippines) | T2—599 1 |
| Albemarle County (Va.) | T2—755 482 |
| Albemarle Sound (N.C.) | 551.461 348 |
| | T2—163 48 |
| Alberni-Clayoquot (B.C.) | T2—711 2 |
| Albert (N.B. : County) | T2—715 31 |
| Albert (South Africa : District) | T2—687 56 |
| Albert I, King of the Belgians | |
| Belgian history | 949.304 1 |
| Albert II, Holy Roman Emperor | |
| German history | 943.028 |
| Albert II, King of the Belgians | |
| Belgian history | 949.304 4 |
| Albert Falls and Nature Reserve (South Africa) | T2—684 75 |
| Alberta | 971.23 |
| | T2—712 3 |
| Albertine Statute | |
| Piedmontese history | 945.108 3 |
| Sardinian history | 945.908 3 |
| Alberton (South Africa : District) | T2—682 25 |

Albigensianism 273.6
  denomination 284.4
  persecution of 272.3
Albinism
  medicine 616.55
  *see also* Skin diseases —
    humans
Albula (Switzerland) T2—494 732 4
Albumin glue 668.32
Albumins 572.66
  *see also* Proteins
Albuminuria
  medicine 616.63
  *see also* Urologic diseases —
    humans
Albuquerque (N.M.) T2—789 61
Albury (N.S.W.) T2—944 8
Alcedinidae 598.78
Alcelaphinae 599.645
Alces 599.657
Alchemy 540.112
Alcidae 598.33
Alcohol 547.031
  *see also* Alcoholic beverages;
    Alcohols
Alcohol abuse 362.292
  *see also* Alcoholism
Alcohol-related disorders
  perinatal medicine 618.326 861
Alcohol smuggling 364.133 61
  law 345.023 361
Alcoholic beverages 641.21
  commercial processing 663.1
  cooking with 641.62
  criminology 364.133 2
    law 345.023 32
    possession and use 364.173
      law 345.027 3
  customs 394.13
  ethics 178 1
  *see also* Ethical problems
  home preparation 641.874
  product safety 363.192 9
  *see also* Food — product
    safety
  public control 363.41
    law 344.054 1
    public administration 353.37
  smuggling 364.133 61
    law 345.023 361
Alcoholics T1—087 4
Alcoholics Anonymous 362.292 86

Alcoholism 362.292
  law 344.044 61
  medicine 616.861
  pastoral theology 206.1
    Christianity 259.429 2
  personal health 613.81
  pregnancy complications
    obstetrics 618.368 6
  school problem 371.784
  social theology 201.762 292
    Christianity 261.832 292
  social welfare 362.292
  *see also* Substance abuse
Alcohols 547.031
  aromatic chemistry 547.631
  chemical engineering 661.82
  chemistry 547.031
  fuel 662.669 2
    cooking 641.585
  human toxicology 615.951 31
  pharmacokinetics 615.782 8
Alcona County (Mich.) T2—774 79
Alcorn County (Miss.) T2—762 993
Alcyonaria 593.6
Aldabra Island (Seychelles) T2—696
Aldehydes 547.036
  aromatic chemistry 547.636
  chemical engineering 661.85
Alderflies 595.747
Alderney (Channel Islands) T2—423 43
Alders 583.48
Aldosterone
  pharmacology 615.364
Ale 641.23
  commercial processing 663.42
  cooking with 641.623
  home preparation 641.873
Aleatory composition 781.32
Alekseĭ Mikhaĭlovich, Czar of
  Russia
  Russian history 947.048
Alemán, Arnoldo
  Nicaraguan history 972.850 542
Alemán, Miguel
  Mexican history 972.082 7
Alentejo (Portugal) T2—469 5
Alentejo (Portugal : Region) T2—469 5
Aleppo (Syria : Province) T2—569 13
Alessandri, Jorge
  Chilean history 983.064 4
Alessandria (Italy :
  Province) T2—451 4
  ancient T2—371 8
Alethic logic 511.314

| | |
|---|---|
| Aleut | T5—971 9 |
| Aleut language | 497.19 |
| | T6—971 9 |
| Aleut literature | 897.19 |
| Aleutian Islands (Alaska) | T2—798 4 |
| Aleutians East Borough (Alaska) | T2—798 4 |
| Alexander I, Emperor of Russia | |
|   Russian history | 947.072 |
| Alexander II, Emperor of Russia | |
|   Russian history | 947.081 |
| Alexander III, Emperor of Russia | |
|   Russian history | 947.082 |
| Alexander County (Ill.) | T2—773 999 |
| Alexander County (N.C.) | T2—756 795 |
| Alexander technique | |
|   therapeutics | 615.82 |
| Alexandria (Egypt) | |
|   ancient | T2—321 |
| Alexandria (Egypt : Province) | T2—621 |
| Alexandria (Scotland) | T2—414 32 |
| Alexandria (South Africa : District) | T2—687 53 |
| Alexandria (Va.) | T2—755 296 |
| Alexandrian philosophy | 186.4 |
| Alexis, Czar of Russia | |
|   Russian history | 947.048 |
| Alfalfa | 633.31 |
|   botany | 583.74 |
|   forage crop | 633.31 |
| Alfalfa County (Okla.) | T2—766 22 |
| Alfonsinos | 597.64 |
| Alfonso XII, King of Spain | |
|   Spanish history | 946.074 |
| Alfonso XIII, King of Spain | |
|   Spanish history | 946.074 |
| Alfred (South Africa : District) | T2—684 6 |
| Alfred, King of England | |
|   English history | 942.016 4 |
| Alfred the Great, King of England | |
|   English history | 942.016 4 |
| Algae | 579.8 |
|   paleontology | 561.93 |
|   physiology | 571.298 |
|   resource economics | 333.953 8 |
| Algarve (Portugal) | T2—469 6 |
| Algarve (Portugal : Region) | T2—469 6 |
| Algebra | 512 |
|   numerical methods | 518.42 |
|   primary education | 372.71 |
| Algebraic combinatorics | 511.6 |

| | |
|---|---|
| Algebraic curves | 516.352 |
| Algebraic function theory | 512.74 |
| Algebraic geometry | 516.35 |
| Algebraic groups | 512.2 |
| Algebraic K-theory | 512.66 |
| Algebraic logic | 511.324 |
| Algebraic number theory | 512.74 |
| Algebraic numbers | 512.784 |
| Algebraic operations | 512.92 |
| Algebraic progressions | 515.24 |
| Algebraic surfaces | 516.352 |
| Algebraic topology | 514.2 |
| Algebraic varieties | 516.353 |
| Alger County (Mich.) | T2—774 932 |
| Algeria | 965 |
| | T2—65 |
|   ancient | T2—397 14 |
| Algerians | T5—927 65 |
| Algic languages | 497.3 |
| | T6—973 |
| Algicides | 632.95 |
|   agricultural use | 632.95 |
|   chemical engineering | 668.652 |
|   pest control technology | 628.97 |
| Algiers (Algeria : Province) | T2—653 |
| Algiers, War with United States, 1815 | 973.53 |
| Algologists | 579.809 2 |
| Algology | 579.8 |
| Algoma (Ont. : District) | T2—713 132 |
| Algonkian era | 551.715 |
|   geology | 551.715 |
|   paleontology | 560.171 5 |
| Algonkian languages | 497.3 |
| Algonquian Indians | T5—973 |
| Algonquian languages | 497.3 |
| | T6—973 |
| Algonquin Indians | T5—973 3 |
| Algonquin Provincial Park (Ont.) | T2—713 147 |
| Algorithms | 518.1 |
|   computer programming | 005.1 |
| Alicante (Spain : Province) | T2—467 65 |
| Alice (South Africa : District) | T2—687 55 |
| Alice Springs (N.T.) | T2—942 91 |
| Alicyclic compounds | 547.5 |
|   chemical engineering | 661.8 |
| Alien labor | 331.62 |
|   law | 344.016 2 |
| Alien property | |
|   law | 346.040 869 1 |
|   law of war | 341.67 |

Alien species     333.952 3
   *see also* entries beginning with
     Nonnative
Alienated classes     305.568
      T1—086 94
Alienation (Law)     346.043 6
Alienation (Social psychology)     302.544
   arts     700.453
      T3C—353
   literature     808.803 53
    history and criticism     809.933 53
    specific literatures    T3B—080 353
     history and
       criticism    T3B—093 53
Aliens     305.906 91
      T1—086 91
   labor economics     331.62
   labor law     344.016 2
   law of war     341.67
   legal status     346.013
    constitutional law     342.083
    private law     346.013
   liability of states     341.26
   naturalization     323.623
   political status     323.631
   social group     305.906 91
   social welfare     362.899 1
   women
    social welfare     362.839 81
   young people
    social welfare     362.779 1
Alimony     346.016 63
Aliphatic compounds     547.4
   chemical engineering     661.8
Alismales     584.72
Alismatales     584.72
Alismidae     584.7
Aliwal North (South
    Africa : District)    T2—687 56
Alizarines     667.230
Alkali health     583.628
Alkali metals     669.725
   chemistry     546.38
   materials science     620.189 6
   metallurgy     669.725
   *see also* Chemicals; Metals
Alkaline-earth metals     669.725
   chemistry     546.39
   materials science     620.189 6
   metallurgy     669.725
   *see also* Chemicals; Metals
Alkaline-soil conditioners     631.825
   chemical engineering     668.64

Alkalis     546.32
   chemical engineering     661.3
   human toxicology     615.922
Alkaloidal plants     581.63
   agriculture     633.7
   botany     581.63
Alkaloids     572.549
   biochemistry     572.549
   chemistry     547.7
   pharmacognosy     615.321
Alkanes     547.411
   chemical engineering     661.814
Alkenes     547.412
   chemical engineering     661.814
Alkylation     547.2
   chemical engineering     660.284 4
Alkynes     547.413
   chemical engineering     661.814
All-age schools     371
All-cargo plane services     387.744
All-risk insurance coverage     368.09
All-star games (Baseball)     796.357 648
All-terrain cycling     796.63
All-terrain vehicles     388.34
   driving     629.283 042
   engineering     629.220 42
   military engineering     623.747
   repair     629.287 042
   transportation services     388.34
   *see also* Automotive vehicles
All-volunteer army     355.223 62
All-weather tactics     355.423
All-year school     371.236
Allah     297.211
Allamakee County (Iowa)    T2—777 33
Alleanza nazionale (Italian
    political party)     324.245 04
Allegan County (Mich.)    T2—774 14
Allegany County (Md.)    T2—752 94
Allegany County (N.Y.)    T2—747 84
Alleghany County (N.C.)    T2—756 832
Alleghany County (Va.)    T2—755 816
Allegheny County (Pa.)    T2—748 85
Allegheny Mountains    T2—748 7
   Pennsylvania    T2—748 7
   West Virginia    T2—754 8
Allegheny River (Pa. and
    N.Y.)    T2—748 6
Allegiance     323.6
   *see also* Citizenship
Allegory
   art representation     704.946
   arts     700.415
      T3C—15

Allegory (continued)
Biblical 220.68
Koran 297.122 68
literature 808.801 5
history and criticism 809.915
specific literatures T3B—080 15
history and
criticism T3B—091 5
paintings 753.6
Allen, Bog of (Ireland) T2—418 5
Allen County (Ind.) T2—772 74
Allen County (Kan.) T2—781 94
Allen County (Ky.) T2—769 732
Allen County (Ohio) T2—771 42
Allen Parish (La.) T2—763 58
Allendale County (S.C.) T2—757 77
Allende Gossens, Salvador
Chilean history 983.064 6
Allerdale (England) T2—427 87
Allergenic plants
botany 581.657
Allergic contact dermatitis
incidence 614.599 33
medicine 616.973
Allergies 571.972
animals 571.972
humans 362.196 97
incidence 614.599 3
medicine 616.97
pediatrics 618.929 7
social services 362.196 97
Alliaceae 584.33
edible bulbs 641.352 6
cooking 641.652 6
food 641.352 6
garden crop 635.26
Alliance for the Future of Austria
(Political party) 324.243 603
Alliances 327.116
armed forces 355.356
international relations 327.116
military science 355.031
Allied fire insurance lines 368.12
Allied forces 355.356
Allied health personnel
role and function 610.737 069
services 610.737
Allier (France : Dept.) T2—445 97
Allies (Military powers) 355.031
armed forces 355.356
Allies (World War I group) 940.332
Allies (World War II group) 940.533 2
Alligator lizards 597.959 2

Alligator pears 641.346 53
*see also* Avocados
Alligatoridae 597.984
Alligators 597.984
big game hunting 799.279 84
conservation technology 639.977 984
resource economics 333.957 984
Allocation (Rationing)
public administration 352.86
Allocation of staff 658.312 8
public administration 352.66
Allodium 333.323 2
Alloecoela 592.42
Allopathy 610
therapeutic system 615.53
Allosaurus 567.912
Allotheria 569.29
Alloy binary systems
metallurgy 669.94
Alloys 669
chemistry 546.3
materials science 620.16
metallography 669.95
metallurgy 669
ship design 623.818 2
shipbuilding 623.820 7
structural engineering 624.182
*see Manual at* 669
Allspice 641.338 3
botany 583.765
*see also* Spices
Alluvial mining 622.292 7
Alluvium 551.354
Almanacs 030
astronomy 528
Almere (Netherlands) T2—492 2
Almería (Spain : Province) T2—468 1
Almonds 641.345 5
agriculture 634.55
botany 583.73
commercial processing 664.804 55
cooking 641.645 5
food 641.345 5
Almsgiving 204.46
Christianity 248.46
ethics 177.7
*see also* Ethical problems
Islam 297.54
Almshouses 362.585
architecture 725.55
Alnwick (England : District) T2—428 87
Alodium 333.323 2
Aloe barbadensis
pharmacology 615.324 32

Aloe vera
  pharmacology 615.324 32
Aloes (Century plants) 584.352
Aloes (Hemp) 584.352
Aloes (Lilies) 584.32
  floriculture 635.934 32
Alopecia
  medicine 616.546
  *see also* Skin diseases —
    humans
Alopex 599.776 4
Alouatta 599.855
Alpaca wool textiles 677.32
  *see also* Textiles
Alpacas 636.296 6
Alpena County (Mich.) T2—774 81
Alpenhorns 788.92
  *see also* Brass instruments
Alpes de Haute-Provence
  (France) T2—449 5
Alpes-Maritimes (France) T2—449 4
Alpha cellulose 676.4
Alpha decay 539.752 2
Alpha particles 539.723 2
Alphabetic subject catalog 017
Alphabets 411
  applied linguistics 418
    specific languages T4—813
  decorative arts 745.61
  printing 686.21
  specific languages T4—11
Alphorns 788.92
  *see also* Brass instruments
Alpine biology 578.753 8
Alpine County (Calif.) T2—794 43
Alpine ecology 577.538
Alpine gardens 635.952 8
Alpine plants 581.753 8
  floriculture 635.952 8
Alpine skiing 796.935
Alpine snowboarding 796.939
Alps T2—494 7
  Austria T2—436 4
  France T2—445 8
  Italy T2—451
  Switzerland T2—494 7
Alpstein (Switzerland) T2—494 71
Alsace (France) T2—443 9
Alsatian (Dog) 636.737 6
Alsatian dialect 437.944 39
   T6—34
Alstroemeriaceae 584.353
Alta Verapaz (Guatemala) T2—728 151

Altagracia (Dominican
  Republic : Province) T2—729 385
Altai language 494.33
   T6—943 3
Altai Mountains T2—517 3
Altaic languages 494
   T6—94
Altaic literatures 894
Altaĭskiĭ kraĭ (Russia) T2—573
Altar railings 247.1
  architecture 726.529 6
Altar screens 247.1
  architecture 726.529 6
Altars 203.7
  architecture 726.529 1
  Christianity 247.1
Altay (Russia) T2—573
Altdorf (Switzerland) T2—494 774
Altenburger Land
  (Germany : Landkreis) T2—432 22
Alterations
  arts 702.874
  clothing 646.408
    commercial 687.044
    home sewing 646.408
Altered states of consciousness 154.4
Alternating current 621.31
Alternating-current machinery 621.313 3
Alternating-current transmission 621.319 13
Alternating manic-depressive
  psychoses
  medicine 616.895
  *see also* Mental disorders
Alternation of generations 571.884
Alternative education 371.04
Alternative energy resources 333.794
  economics 333.794
  engineering 621.042
Alternative higher education 378.03
Alternative histories (Fiction) 808.838 768
  history and criticism 809.387 68
  specific literatures T3B—308 768
    individual authors T3A—3
Alternative medicine 610
  health 613
  therapeutics 615.5
Alternative schools 371.04
  primary education 372.104 24
Alternative technology 338.927
Altimeters 629.135 2
Altitude sickness
  medicine 616.989 3
  *see also* Environmental
    diseases — humans

| | |
|---|---|
| Alto Adige (Italy) | T2—453 83 |
| Alto Alentejo (Portugal) | T2—469 52 |
| Alto horns | 788.974 |
| *see also* Brass instruments | |
| Alto Paraguay (Paraguay : | |
| Dept.) | T2—892 27 |
| Alto Paraná (Paraguay) | T2—892 132 |
| Alto recorders | 788.365 |
| *see also* Woodwind instruments | |
| Alto saxophones | 788.73 |
| *see also* Woodwind instruments | |
| Alto voices | |
| children's | 782.78 |
| choral and mixed voices | 782.78 |
| single voices | 783.78 |
| men's | 782.86 |
| choral and mixed voices | 782.86 |
| single voices | 783.86 |
| women's | 782.68 |
| choral and mixed voices | 782.68 |
| single voices | 783.68 |
| Altos (Guatemala : | |
| Province) | T2—728 18 |
| Altruism | |
| ethical systems | 171.8 |
| personality trait | 155.232 |
| Alumina | 553.67 |
| economic geology | 553.67 |
| technology | 666.72 |
| Aluminum | 669.722 |
| architectural construction | 721.044 772 2 |
| building construction | 693.772 2 |
| building material | 691.872 2 |
| chemical engineering | 661.067 3 |
| chemistry | 546.673 |
| decorative arts | 739.57 |
| economic geology | 553.492 6 |
| human toxicology | 615.925 673 |
| materials science | 620.186 |
| metallography | 669.957 22 |
| metallurgy | 669.722 |
| metalworking | 673.722 |
| mining | 622.349 26 |
| physical metallurgy | 669.967 22 |
| ship design | 623.818 26 |
| shipbuilding | 623.820 7 |
| structural engineering | 624.182 6 |
| *see also* Chemicals; Metals | |
| Aluminum lithography | 763.23 |
| Aluminum soaps | 668.125 |
| Alunite | |
| mineralogy | 549.755 |
| Alvarez, Luis Echeverría | |
| Mexican history | 972.083 2 |

| | |
|---|---|
| Alveolar abscesses | |
| dentistry | 617.632 |
| Älvsborgs län (Sweden) | T2—486 7 |
| Alwa (Kingdom) | 962.620 22 |
| Alyn and Deeside (Wales) | T2—429 33 |
| Alyssums | 635.933 64 |
| botany | 583.64 |
| floriculture | 635.933 64 |
| Alzheimer disease | 362.196 831 |
| geriatrics | 618.976 831 |
| medicine | 616.831 |
| social services | 362.196 831 |
| *see also* Nervous system | |
| diseases — humans | |
| AM radio stations | 384.545 3 |
| *see also* Radio stations | |
| AM radio systems | 621.384 153 |
| Amaas | |
| incidence | 614.521 |
| medicine | 616.913 |
| *see also* Communicable | |
| diseases — humans | |
| Amador County (Calif.) | T2—794 42 |
| Amalgamations of corporations | 338.83 |
| *see also* Mergers | |
| Amalgams | |
| dentistry | 617.675 |
| Amambay (Paraguay) | T2—892 137 |
| Amanzimtoti (South Africa) | T2—684 55 |
| Amapá (Brazil : State) | T2—811 6 |
| 'Amāra kelel (Ethiopia) | T2—634 |
| Amaranthaceae | 583.53 |
| Amaranths | 583.53 |
| botany | 583.53 |
| cooking | 641.631 |
| field crop | 633.1 |
| floriculture | 635.933 53 |
| food | 641.331 |
| Amaryllidaceae | 584.34 |
| Amaryllises | 635.934 34 |
| botany | 584.34 |
| floriculture | 635.934 34 |
| Amasya İli (Turkey) | T2—563 8 |
| ancient | T2—393 32 |
| Amateur cinematography | 777 |
| Amateur circuses | 791.3 |
| Amateur motion pictures | 791.433 |
| Amateur radio | 384.54 |
| communications services | 384.54 |
| engineering | 621.384 16 |
| law | 343.099 45 |
| public administration | 354.75 |

Amateur sports 796.042
  see Manual at 796.08 vs.
    796.04
Amateur theater 792.022 2
Amateur video recording 777
Amateur videography 777
Amateur workshops 684.08
Amazon Region (Colombia) T2—861 6
Amazon River T2—811
  Brazil T2—811
  Peru T2—854 4
Amazonas (Brazil) T2—811 3
Amazonas (Colombia :
  Dept.) T2—861 7
Amazonas (Peru) T2—854 6
Amazonas (Peru : Region) T2—854 4
Amazonas (Venezuela) T2—876 4
Amazónica (Ecuador) T2—866 4
Ambassadors 327.209 2
Amber 553.879
  carving 736.6
  see also Semiprecious stones
Amber Valley (England) T2—425 16
Ambient music 781.648
Ambition
  social psychology 302.54
Amblyopsidae 597.62
Amblypygi 595.453 6
Ambon (Indonesia) T2—598 52
Ambulance services 362.188
  armed forces 355.345
  World War I 940.475 3
  World War II 940.547 53
  see also Health services
Ambulances 362.188
  driving 629.283 34
  engineering 629.222 34
  health services 362.188
  military engineering 623.747 24
  military equipment 355.83
  repair 629.287 234
  sanitation services 363.729 7
Ambulatory care 362.12
  see also Health services
Ambush tactics 355.422
Ambystoma 597.858
Ambystomatidae 597.858
Amebiasis
  incidence 614.53
  medicine 616.936
  see also Communicable
    diseases — humans

Amebic dysentery
  incidence 614.516
  medicine 616.935 3
  see also Communicable
    diseases — humans
Ameiva 597.958 2
Amelia County (Va.) T2—755 634
Amenhetep IV, King of Egypt
  Egyptian history 932.014
Amenhotep, King of Egypt
  Egyptian history 932.014
Amenorrhea
  gynecology 618.172
  see also Female genital
    diseases — humans
Amens
  music 782.295
American Arctic seawaters 551.461 327
    T2—163 27
American Baptist Association 286.136
  see also Baptists
American Baptist Churches in the
  U.S.A. 286.131
  see also Baptists
American Baptist Convention 286.131
  see also Baptists
American bison 599.643
  see also Bison
American black bear 599.785
American buffalo 599.643
  see also Bison
American College Testing
  Program 378.166 2
American elk 599.654 2
  animal husbandry 636.294 42
  big game hunting 799.276 542
American English dialects (U.S.) 427.973
    T6—21
American English pronunciation
  (U.S.) 421.54
American English spelling (U.S.) 421.54
American Evangelical Lutheran
  Church 284.133 2
  see also Lutheran church
American Federation of Labor 331.883 209 73
American Federation of Labor
  and Congress of Industrial
  Organizations 331.880 973
American folk music 781.621 3
American folk songs 782.421 621 3
American football 796.332
American football players 796.332 092
American Independent Party 324.273 3

| | |
|---|---|
| American Indian languages | 497 |
| | T6—97 |
| South America | 498 |
| | T6—98 |
| American Indian literatures | 897 |
| South America | 898 |
| American Indians | T5—97 |
| South America | T5—98 |
| *see also* American native peoples | |
| American Legion | 369.186 1 |
| American literature (English) | 810 |
| American loyalists | |
| Canadian history | 971.024 |
| United States history | 973.314 |
| American Lutheran Church | 284.131 |
| *see also* Lutheran church | |
| American-Mexican Border Region | T2—721 |
| American Muslim Mission | 297.87 |
| American native languages | 497 |
| | T6—97 |
| South America | 498 |
| | T6—98 |
| American native literatures | 897 |
| South America | 898 |
| American native peoples | T5—97 |
| military troops | |
| American Revolution | 973.343 |
| War of 1812 | 973.524 2 |
| World War II | 940.540 3 |
| religion | 299.7 |
| North America | 299.7 |
| South America | 299.8 |
| social aspects | 305.897 |
| South America | T5—98 |
| tribal land | 333.2 |
| *see also* Indigenous peoples | |
| American Nazi Party | 324.273 38 |
| American opossums | 599.276 |
| American organs | 786.55 |
| instrument | 786.551 9 |
| music | 786.55 |
| *see also* Keyboard instruments | |
| American paint horse | 636.13 |
| American Party (U.S.) | 324.273 2 |
| American pocket billiards | 794.733 |
| American Reformed Church | 285.7 |
| *see also* Reformed Church (American Reformed) | |
| American Revised version Bible | 220.520 4 |
| American Revolution, 1775–1783 | 973.3 |
| societies | 369.13 |
| American saddlebred horse | 636.13 |

| | |
|---|---|
| American Samoa | 996.13 |
| | T2—961 3 |
| American Sign Language | 419.7 |
| | T6—999 87 |
| American Sign Language literature | 899.987 |
| American Standard version Bible | 220.520 4 |
| American theater (World War II) | 940.542 8 |
| American Veterans of World War II, Korea, and Vietnam | 369.186 2 |
| Americans (U.S.) | T5—13 |
| Americas | T2—7 |
| Americium | 546.441 |
| *see also* Chemicals | |
| Amerind languages | 497 |
| | T6—97 |
| South America | 498 |
| | T6—98 |
| Amerind literatures | 897 |
| South America | 898 |
| Amerindians | T5—97 |
| South America | T5—98 |
| *see also* American native peoples | |
| Amersfoort (South Africa : District) | T2—682 79 |
| Ameslan (Sign language) | 419.7 |
| | T6—999 87 |
| Amethysts | 553.87 |
| *see also* Semiprecious stones | |
| Amhara (African people) | T5—928 |
| Amharic language | 492.87 |
| | T6—928 7 |
| Amharic literature | 892.87 |
| Amherst (N.S.) | T2—716 11 |
| Amherst County (Va.) | T2—755 496 |
| Amherst of Arracan, William Pitt Amherst, Earl | |
| Indian history | 954.031 3 |
| Ami (Taiwan people) | T5—992 5 |
| Amiante (Quebec) | T2—714 712 |
| Amicicide (Military science) | 355.422 |
| Amides | 547.042 |
| chemical engineering | 661.894 |
| Amiens (France) | T2—442 625 |
| Amiiformes | 597.41 |
| Amin, Idi | |
| Ugandan history | 967.610 42 |
| Amination | 547.27 |
| chemical engineering | 660.284 4 |
| Amines | 547.042 |
| biochemistry | 572.548 |
| chemical engineering | 661.894 |
| Amino acid sequence | 572.633 |

Amino acids   572.65
   applied nutrition   613.282
   biochemistry   572.65
   humans   612.015 756
  *see also* Proteins
Aminoglycosides
   pharmacology   615.329
Amish
   biography   289.709 2
Amish churches   289.73
  *see also* Mennonite Church
Amish cooking   641.566
Amite County (Miss.)   T2—762 24
Amman (Jordan : Province)   T2—569 58
   ancient   T2—335 8
Ammeters   621.374 4
Ammonia   546.711 2
   chemical engineering   661.34
Ammonite language   492.6
  T6—926
Ammonium fertilizers   631.841
   chemical engineering   668.624 1
Ammonium hydroxide   546.711 2
   chemical engineering   661.34
Ammonium nitrate fertilizer   631.842
   chemical engineering   668.624 2
Ammonium salts   546.711 24
   chemical engineering   661.5
Ammonoidea   564.53
Ammunition   355.825
   military   355.825
    engineering   623.45
    use   355.825
   small arms engineering
    military   623.451
   small arms manufacturing
    technology   683.406
Amnesia
   medicine   616.852 32
  *see also* Mental disorders
Amnesty   364.65
   law   345.077
   penology   364.65
Amniocentesis
   obstetrics   618.320 427 5
Amniotes   596
Amniotic fluid
   human physiology   612.63
   obstetrics   618.34
Amoebas   579.432

Amoebiasis
   incidence   614.53
   medicine   616.936
  *see also* Communicable
   diseases — humans
Amoebic dysentery
   incidence   614.516
   medicine   616.935 3
  *see also* Communicable
   diseases — humans
Amoebida   579.432
Amoraim   296.120 092
Amorites   T5—921
Amorphous solids   530.413
Amos (Biblical book)   224.8
Ampere-hour meters   621.374 4
Amphetamine abuse   362.299 5
   medicine   616.864
   personal health   613.84
   social welfare   362.299 5
  *see also* Substance abuse
Amphibians   597.8
   agriculture   639.378
   art representation   704.943 278
   arts   T3C—362 78
   commercial hunting   639.13
   conservation technology   639.977 8
   drawing   743.676
   food   641.396
    cooking   641.696
   paleozoology   567.8
   resource economics   333.957 8
   zoology   597.8
Amphibious air-cushion vehicles
   engineering   629.325
   military engineering   623.748 5
Amphibious operations   355.46
   marine forces   359.904 6
Amphibious planes   387.733 48
   engineering   629.133 348
   transportation services   387.733 48
  *see also* Aircraft
Amphiboles
   mineralogy   549.66
Amphineura   594.27
Amphipoda   595.378
Amphisbaenia   597.948
Amphisbaenidae   597.948
Amphissa (Greece)   T2—383
Amphitheaters   796.068
   architecture   725.827
Amplifiers   621.381 535
   electronic circuits   621.381 535
   radio engineering   621.384 12

| | |
|---|---|
| Amplitude-modulation radio systems | 621.384 153 |
| Amplitude modulators electronic circuits | 621.381 536 2 |
| Amputation of limbs surgery | 617.580 59 |
| Amsterdam (Netherlands) | T2—492 352 |
| Amsterdam Island | 969.9 |
| | T2—699 |
| Amto-Musan languages | T6—991 2 |
| Amulets | 133.44 |
| Islamic popular practices | 297.39 |
| numismatics | 737.23 |
| religious significance | 203.7 |
| Amundsen Sea | 551.461 74 |
| | T2—167 4 |
| Amur (Russia : Oblast) | T2—577 |
| Amur River (China and Russia) | T2—577 |
| Amurskaĩa oblast′ (Russia) | T2—577 |
| Amusement parks | 791.068 |
| architecture | 725.76 |
| area planning | 711.558 |
| landscape architecture | 712.5 |
| recreation | 791.068 |
| Amusements | 790 |
| journalism | 070.444 |
| law | 344.099 |
| *see also* Recreation | |
| AMVETS (Veterans' organization) | 369.186 2 |
| Amyl nitrite abuse | 362.299 3 |
| medicine | 616.86 |
| personal health | 613.8 |
| social welfare | 362.299 3 |
| *see also* Substance abuse | |
| Amylases | 572.756 |
| *see also* Enzymes | |
| Amyloidosis medicine | 616.399 5 |
| *see also* Digestive system diseases — humans | |
| Amyotrophic lateral sclerosis medicine | 616.839 |
| *see also* Nervous system diseases — humans | |
| An Giang (Vietnam : Province) | T2—597 9 |
| Anabaptists | 284.3 |
| Anabolism | 572.45 |
| *see also* Metabolism | |

| | |
|---|---|
| Anacardiaceae | 583.77 |
| edible fruits | 641.344 4 |
| cooking | 641.644 4 |
| food | 641.344 4 |
| orchard crops | 634.44 |
| Anacondas | 597.967 |
| Anaerobic bacteria | 579.314 9 |
| Anaerobic digestion (Sewage treatment) | 628.354 |
| Anaerobic gram-negative rods | 579.325 |
| Anaerobic respiration | 572.478 |
| Anagrams | 793.734 |
| Anahim Lake (B.C.) | T2—711 75 |
| Analgesic abuse | 362.299 |
| medicine | 616.86 |
| personal health | 613.8 |
| social welfare | 362.299 |
| *see also* Substance abuse | |
| Analgesics pharmacokinetics | 615.783 |
| Analog circuits electronics | 621.381 5 |
| Analog communications | 621.382 |
| Analog computers | 004.19 |
| communications | 004.619 |
| electronic | 004.19 |
| engineering | 621.391 9 |
| interfacing | 004.619 |
| nonelectronic | 004.9 |
| programming | 005.29 |
| Analog instruments technology | 681.1 |
| Analog-to-digital converters | |
| computer engineering | 621.398 14 |
| computer science | 004.64 |
| electronic engineering | 621.381 59 |
| Analogy logic | 169 |
| Analysis (Mathematics) | 515 |
| numerical methods | 518.6 |
| Analysis of covariance | 519.538 |
| Analysis of variance | 519.538 |
| Analysis situs | 514 |
| Analytic curves | 516.362 |
| Analytic functions spaces | 515.73 |
| Analytic geometry | 516.3 |
| Analytic number theory | 512.73 |
| Analytic spaces | 515.942 |
| Analytic surfaces | 516.362 |
| Analytic topology | 514.7 |
| Analytic trigonometry | 516.34 |
| Analytical bibliography | 010.42 |

Analytical biochemistry 572.36
  humans 612.015 85
Analytical chemistry 543
  minerals 549.133
  organic chemistry 543.17
Analytical guides (Music) 780.15
Analytical mechanics 531.015 15
Analytical philosophy 146.4
Anambas Islands
  (Indonesia) T2—598 192
Anambra State (Nigeria) T2—669 48
Ananda Mahidol, King of
  Thailand
  Thai history 959.304 3
Anaphora
  linguistics 401.456
    specific languages T4—014 56
Anapsida 567.92
Anarchism 335.83
  economics 335.83
  ideal state 321.07
  political ideology 320.57
Anarchist communities 307.77
Anarchists 335.830 92
Anarcho-syndicalism 335.82
  economics 335.82
  political ideology 320.57
Anarchy 335.83
  *see also* Anarchism
Anas 598.413
Anas platyrhynchos 598.413 4
Anaspidea 594.37
Anatidae 598.41
Anatolia T2—561
Anatolian languages 491.998
   T6—919 98
Anatolikē Makedonia kai
  Thrakē (Greece) T2—495 7
Anatomic embryology
  humans 611.013
Anatomy 571.3
  domestic animals 636.089 1
  drawing
    animals 743.6
    humans 743.49
  humans 611
  *see Manual at* 599.94 vs.
    611; *also at* 612 vs. 611
  microorganisms 571.633 29
Anatosaurus 567.914
Anaxagorean philosophy 182.8
Anbār (Iraq) T2—567 4
Ancash (Peru) T2—852 1

Ancestors T1—085 3
  family relationships 306.874
  objects of worship 202.13
Ancestry 929.1
Anchor ice 551.344
Anchorages 387.1
  engineering 627.22
  *see also* Ports
Anchors 623.862
Anchovies 641.392
  cooking 641.692
  food 641.392
  zoology 597.45
Ancienne-Lorette (Quebec) T2—714 471
Ancient Arabic Order of the
  Nobles of the Mystic Shrine
  for North America 366.16
  biography 366.160 92
Ancient architecture 722
Ancient civilization 930
Ancient history 930
   T1—090 1
Ancient law 340.53
Ancient philosophy 180
Ancient remedies
  therapeutics 615.880 901
Ancient sculpture 732
Ancient world 930
   T2—3
  geography 913
  *see Manual at* T2—3; *also at*
    T2—4–9 vs. T2—3
Ancona (Italy : Province) T2—456 71
  ancient T2—374 5
Ancyclostomiasis
  incidence 614.555 4
  medicine 616.965 4
  *see also* Communicable
    diseases — humans
Andalusia (Spain) T2—468
Andalusite
  mineralogy 549.62
Andaman and Nicobar
  Islands T2—548 8
Andaman Sea 551.461 565
   T2—165 65
Andamanese T5—959
Andamanese languages 495.9
   T6—959
Andean languages 498.32
   T6—983 2
Andean Region (Colombia) T2—861 2
Andelfingen (Switzerland :
  Bezirk) T2—494 574 9

| | |
|---|---|
| Anderson County (Kan.) | T2—781 672 |
| Anderson County (Ky.) | T2—769 463 |
| Anderson County (S.C.) | T2—757 25 |
| Anderson County (Tenn.) | T2—768 73 |
| Anderson County (Tex.) | T2—764 229 |
| Andes | T2—8 |
| Andes (Chile : Province) | T2—832 42 |
| Andesite | 552.23 |
| Andhra language | 494.827 |
| | T6—948 27 |
| Andhra literature | 894.827 |
| Andhra Pradesh (India) | T2—548 4 |
| Andi languages | 499.964 |
| | T6—999 64 |
| Andorra | 946.79 |
| | T2—467 9 |
| Andreaeales | 588.2 |
| Andrés Avelino Cáceres | |
| (Peru) | T2—852 2 |
| Andrew County (Mo.) | T2—778 126 |
| Andrews County (Tex.) | T2—764 856 |
| Androgens | |
| human physiology | 612.61 |
| Androgynous behavior | |
| psychology | 155.33 |
| Androgyny | |
| psychology | 155.33 |
| Andropogoneae | 584.92 |
| Andropov, ĪU. V. (ĪUriĭ | |
| Vladimirovich) | |
| Russian history | 947.085 4 |
| Andros Island (Bahamas) | T2—729 6 |
| Andros Island (Greece) | T2—495 85 |
| Androscoggin County (Me.) | T2—741 82 |
| Androscoggin River (Me.) | T2—741 8 |
| Anecdotes | |
| literature | 808.882 |
| history and criticism | 809.982 |
| specific literatures | T3B—802 |
| individual authors | T3A—8 |
| Anelytropsidae | 597.952 |
| Anemia | |
| medicine | 616.152 |
| *see also* Cardiovascular | |
| diseases — humans | |
| Anemones | 583.34 |
| floriculture | 635.933 34 |
| Anesthesiologists | 617.960 92 |
| law | 344.041 2 |
| Anesthesiology | 617.96 |
| Anesthetics | |
| pharmacokinetics | 615.781 |
| Anesthetists | 617.960 92 |
| law | 344.041 2 |

| | |
|---|---|
| Aneuploidy | 572.877 |
| Aneurysms | |
| medicine | 616.133 |
| *see also* Cardiovascular | |
| diseases — humans | |
| Angas language | 493.7 |
| | T6—937 |
| Angaston (S. Aust.) | T2—942 32 |
| Angelfishes | 597.72 |
| Cichlidae | 597.74 |
| Pomacanthidae | 597.72 |
| Angelina County (Tex.) | T2—764 173 |
| Angels | 202.15 |
| art representation | 704.948 64 |
| arts | T3C—382 021 5 |
| Christianity | 235.3 |
| Islam | 297.215 |
| Judaism | 296.315 |
| literature | 808.803 820 215 |
| history and criticism | 809.933 820 215 |
| specific literatures | T3B—080 382 021 5 |
| history and | |
| criticism | T3B—093 820 215 |
| Anger | 152.47 |
| ethics | 179.8 |
| religion | 205.698 |
| psychology | 152.47 |
| *see also* Vices | |
| Ångermanland landskap | |
| (Sweden) | T2—488 5 |
| Angers (France) | T2—441 84 |
| Angina pectoris | |
| medicine | 616.122 |
| *see also* Cardiovascular | |
| diseases — humans | |
| Angiocardiography | |
| medicine | 616.120 757 2 |
| Angiology | 616.13 |
| Angioplasty | 617.413 |
| Angiospermae | 580 |
| *see Manual at* 583–584 | |
| Angle harps | 787.94 |
| *see also* Stringed instruments | |
| Angle trisection | 516.204 |
| Anglerfishes | 597.62 |
| Angles | 516.152 |
| Anglesey (Wales) | T2—429 21 |
| Anglican cathedrals | |
| architecture | 726.65 |
| Anglican chant | 782.322 3 |
| Anglican Communion | 283 |
| church government | 262.03 |
| parishes | 254.03 |
| church law | 262.983 |

Anglican Communion (continued)
  doctrines 230.3
    catechisms and creeds 238.3
  general councils 262.53
  guides to Christian life 248.483
  liturgy 264.03
  missions 266.3
  moral theology 241.043
  persecution by Queen Mary 272.6
  public worship 264.03
  religious associations 267.183
  religious education 268.83
  religious orders 255.83
    church history 271.83
    women 255.983
      church history 271.983
  seminaries 230.073 3
  theology 230.3
Anglican sacred music 781.713
  public worship 782.322 3
    music 782.322 3
    religion 264.030 2
Anglicans
  biography 283.092
Angling 799.12
Anglo-Boer War, 1880–1881 968.204 6
Anglo-Boer War, 1899–1902 968.048
Anglo-Dutch Wars, 1652–1653 949.204
Anglo-Egyptian Sudan 962.403
  T2—624
Anglo-Indians T5—914 11
Anglo-Irish War, 1919–1921 941.508 21
Anglo-Saxon language 429
  T6—29
Anglo-Saxon law 340.550 942
Anglo-Saxon literature 829
Anglo-Saxons T5—2
Anglo-Spanish War, 1739–1741 946.055
Angola 967.3
  T2—673
Angolans T5—967 3
Angolese T5—967 3
Angoni language 496.398
  T6—963 98
Angora cat 636.83
Angora goat 636.398 5
Angoulême, House of 944.028
Angoumois (France) T2—446 5
Anguidae 597.959 2
Anguilla 972.973
  T2—729 73
Anguilla (Eels) 597.432
Anguillidae 597.432
Anguilliformes 597.43

Anguinomorphoidea 597.959
Angular momentum (Nuclear
  physics) 539.725
Angus (Scotland) T2—412 6
Angus cattle 636.223
Anhalt (Germany) T2—431 86
Anhimidae 598.41
Anhui Sheng (China) T2—512 25
Anhwei Province (China) T2—512 25
Anhydrite
  mineralogy 549.752
Anhydrous sulfates
  mineralogy 549.752
Aniliidae 597.967
Animal babies 591.392
  domestic animals 636.07
  mammals 599.139 2
Animal behavior 591.5
  comparative psychology 156
Animal black 662.93
Animal body disposal 363.78
Animal breeding 636.082
Animal combat sports 791.8
Animal communication 591.59
  physiology 573.92
Animal communities 591.782
Animal courtship 591.562
Animal defenses 591.47
Animal-derived drugs
  pharmacology 615.36
Animal-derived poisons
  human toxicology 615.94
Animal diseases 571.91
  agricultural economics 338.14
  veterinary medicine 636.089 6
Animal ecology 591.7
Animal experimentation 590.724
  ethics 179.4
    *see also* Animals —
      treatment of — ethics
  medicine 616.027
  physiology 571.107 24
Animal fats 665.2
  food 641.36
  food technology 664.3
  home cooking 641.66
  industrial technology 665.2
Animal feeding 636.084
Animal feeds 636.085 5
  *see also* Feeds
Animal fibers 677.3
  materials science 620.197
  production economics 338.476 773

| | |
|---|---|
| Animal fibers (continued) | |
| textiles | 677.3 |
| arts | 746.043 |
| *see also* Textiles | |
| Animal flight | 573.798 |
| behavior | 591.57 |
| physiology | 573.798 |
| Animal food | 636.085 5 |
| *see also* Feeds | |
| Animal ghosts | 133.14 |
| Animal glue | 668.32 |
| Animal grooming | |
| agriculture | 636.083 3 |
| zoology | 591.563 |
| Animal heat | 571.76 |
| Animal hormones | 573.44 |
| Animal hospitals | 636.083 21 |
| Animal husbandry | 636 |
| equipment manufacturing | |
| technology | 681.763 6 |
| production economics | 338.176 |
| public administration | 354.56 |
| Animal industry | 338.176 |
| law | 343.076 6 |
| public administration | 354.56 |
| Animal intelligence | 591.513 |
| comparative psychology | 156.39 |
| Animal language | 591.59 |
| Animal locomotion | 573.79 |
| Animal magnetism | 154.72 |
| parapsychology | 133.89 |
| Animal manures | |
| waste technology | 628.746 6 |
| Animal marking | 590.723 2 |
| Animal migration | 591.568 |
| Animal models | |
| human diseases | 616.027 |
| Animal navigation | 591.568 |
| Animal oils | 665.2 |
| food | 641.36 |
| food technology | 664.3 |
| home cooking | 641.66 |
| industrial technology | 665.2 |
| Animal performances | 791.8 |
| circuses | 791.32 |
| Animal pest control | 363.78 |
| *see also* Pest control | |
| Animal pests | 591.65 |
| Animal physiology | 571.1 |
| Animal-plant relationships | 577.8 |
| Animal populations | 591.788 |
| Animal psychology | 591.5 |
| comparative psychology | 156 |
| Animal racing | 798 |

| | |
|---|---|
| Animal rescue | 636.083 2 |
| Animal resources | 333.954 |
| law | 346.046 954 |
| public administration | 354.349 |
| Animal rights | |
| ethics | 179.3 |
| *see also* Animals — | |
| treatment of — ethics | |
| Animal sacrifice | 203.4 |
| Animal shelters | 636.083 2 |
| Animal shows | 791.8 |
| animal husbandry | 636.081 1 |
| performing arts | 791.8 |
| Animal sounds | 591.594 |
| Animal swimming | 591.57 |
| Animal training | 636.083 5 |
| Animal viruses | 579.2 |
| Animal wastes | 631.86 |
| law | 344.046 22 |
| pollution | 363.738 |
| technology | 628.746 6 |
| water pollution engineering | 628.168 46 |
| Animal watching | 590.723 4 |
| Animal waxes | 665.13 |
| Animal weapons | 591.47 |
| Animal welfare | 636.083 2 |
| animal husbandry | 636.083 2 |
| law | 344.049 |
| Animals | 590 |
| agricultural pests | 632.6 |
| agriculture | 636 |
| production economics | 338.176 |
| anatomy | 571.31 |
| art representation | 704.943 2 |
| arts | 700.462 |
| | T3C—362 |
| Bible | 220.859 |
| biography | T1—092 9 |
| care and maintenance | 636.083 |
| conservation | 333.954 16 |
| *see Manual at* 333.955–.959 | |
| vs. 639.97 | |
| conservation technology | 639.9 |
| disease carriers | 571.986 |
| medicine | 614.43 |
| drawing | 743.6 |
| folklore | 398.245 |
| history and criticism | 398.369 |
| food source | 641.306 |
| agriculture | 636.088 3 |
| growth | 571.81 |
| legendary | 398.245 4 |
| *see also* Legendary animals | |

| | |
|---|---|
| Animals (continued) | |
| literature | 808.803 62 |
| history and criticism | 809.933 62 |
| specific literatures | T3B—080 362 |
| history and criticism | T3B—093 62 |
| painting | 758.3 |
| physiology | 571.1 |
| religious worship | 202.12 |
| resource economics | 333.954 |
| see Manual at 333.955–.959 vs. 639.97 | |
| smuggling | 364.133 67 |
| law | 345.023 367 |
| therapeutic use | 615.851 58 |
| treatment of | |
| ethics | 179.3 |
| religion | 205.693 |
| Buddhism | 294.356 93 |
| Christianity | 241.693 |
| Hinduism | 294.548 693 |
| Judaism | 296.369 3 |
| use in mining | 622.65 |
| use in warfare | 355.424 |
| zoology | 590 |
| see Manual at 800, T3C—362 vs. 398.245, 590, 636 | |
| Animals for specific purposes | 636.088 |
| see Manual at 636.1–.8 vs. 636.088 | |
| Animated cartoons | 791.433 4 |
| cinematography | 777.7 |
| drawing | 741.58 |
| motion pictures | 791.433 4 |
| Animated drawings | |
| drawing | 741.58 |
| Animated films | 791.433 4 |
| Animation cels | 741.58 |
| Anime | 791.433 4 |
| drawing | 741.58 |
| motion pictures | 791.433 4 |
| Animism | |
| comparative religion | 202.1 |
| philosophy | 147 |
| Anis | 598.74 |
| Anise | 641.338 2 |
| botany | 583.849 |
| see also Flavorings | |
| Aniseikonia | |
| incidence | 614.599 7 |
| optometry | 617.758 |
| see also Eye diseases — humans | |
| Anisophylleaceae | 583.76 |

| | |
|---|---|
| Anjou (France) | T2—441 8 |
| Anjou, House of | |
| Sicilian history | 945.804 |
| Southern Italian history | 945.705 |
| Ankara İli (Turkey) | T2—563 6 |
| ancient | T2—393 2 |
| Ankles | 612.98 |
| physiology | 612.98 |
| regional medicine | 617.584 |
| surgery | 617.584 |
| see also Lower extremities | |
| Anklets (Ornaments) | 391.7 |
| customs | 391.7 |
| making | 739.278 |
| costume jewelry | 688.2 |
| handicrafts | 745.594 2 |
| fine jewelry | 739.278 |
| Ankole (Kingdom) | 967.610 1 |
| | T2—676 1 |
| Ankylosauria | 567.915 |
| Ankylosing spondylitis | |
| medicine | 616.73 |
| see also Musculoskeletal diseases — humans | |
| Ann Arbor (Mich.) | T2—774 35 |
| Anna, Empress of Russia | |
| Russian history | 947.061 |
| Annaba (Algeria : Province) | T2—655 |
| Annam-Muong languages | 495.92 |
| | T6—959 2 |
| Annam-Muong literatures | 895.92 |
| Annam-Muong peoples | T5—959 2 |
| Annamese | T5—959 22 |
| Annamese language | 495.922 |
| | T6—959 22 |
| Annandale and Eskdale (Scotland) | T2—114 7 |
| Annapolis (Md.) | T2—752 56 |
| Annapolis (N.S. : County) | T2—716 33 |
| Annatto tree | 583.625 |
| Anne (Mother of the Virgin Mary), Saint | 232.933 |
| private prayers to | 242.75 |
| Anne, Queen of England | |
| British history | 941.069 |
| English history | 942.069 |
| Scottish history | 941.106 9 |
| Anne Arundel County (Md.) | T2—752 55 |
| Annealing glass | 666.129 |
| Annealing metals | 671.36 |
| Annelida | 592.6 |
| paleozoology | 562.6 |

Annexation
city government 320.859
law 342.041 3
international politics 325.32
law 342.041 2
law of nations 341.42
Anniellidae 597.959
Annihilation (Nuclear particles) 539.75
Annihilationism 236.23
Anniversaries 394.2
*see also* Celebrations
Annobón (Equatorial
Guinea) T2—671 86
Annonaceae 583.22
edible fruits 641.344 1
cooking 641.644 1
food 641.344 1
orchard crops 634.41
Annotations to cases 348.047
Annotations to laws 348.027
Announcements
etiquette 395.4
Announcing
radio performances 791.443
television performances 791.453
Annual leave 331.257 6
personnel management 658.312 2
Annual publications 050
T1—05
*see also* Annuals (Publications)
Annual wage plan 331.236
Annual wages 331.216 2
personnel management 658.322 2
Annuals (Plants) 582.12
floriculture 635.931 2
Annuals (Publications) 050
T1—05
almanacs 030
encyclopedia yearbooks 030
publishing 070.572
Annuities
insurance 368.37
personal finance 332.024 014 5
tax law 343.064
Annulment 346.016 65
Annunciation to Mary 232.912
Anodynes
pharmacokinetics 615.783
Anointing of the sick 234.167
public worship 265.7
theology 234.167
Anoka County (Minn.) T2- -776 65
Anoles 597.954 8
Anolis 597.954 8

Anomochloeae 584.9
Anomura 595.387
Anonymous works
bibliographies 014
Anoplura 595.756
Anorexia nervosa 362.25
medicine 616.852 62
social welfare 362.25
Anostraca 595.32
Anoxygenic phototrophic
bacteria 579.38
Anschluss
Austrian history 943.605 22
Anser 598.417 3
Anseriformes 598.41
paleozoology 568.4
Anserini 598.417
Anson County (N.C.) T2—756 753
Answers
books of miscellaneous facts 030
study and teaching T1—076
Ant bear 599.31
Ant lions 595.747
Antacids
pharmacokinetics 615.73
Antakya (Turkey) T2—564 8
ancient T2—394 31
Antalya İli (Turkey) T2—564 4
ancient T2—392 8
eastern T2—392 9
western T2—392 8
Antananarivo (Madagascar :
Province) T2—691
Antarctic regions T2—989
Antarctic waters 551.461 7
T2—167
Antarctica T2—989
Antártica Chilena (Chile :
Province) T2—836 48
Antbirds 598.822 6
Ante-Nicene church 270.1
Anteaters 599.314
Antelope County (Neb.) T2—782 55
Antelopes 599.64
big game hunting 799.276 4
conservation technology 639.979 64
resource economics 333.959 64
Antenatal care
obstetrics 618.24
Antennas 621.382 4
communications engineering 621.382 4
radar engineering 621.384 83
radio engineering 621.384 135

Antennas (continued)
   satellite communication   621.382 54
   television engineering   621.388 35
Antenuptial contracts   346.016 62
Anterior chambers (Eyes)
   human physiology   612.841
Anthems   782.25
   choral and mixed voices   782.526 5
   single voices   783.092 65
Anthers   575.65
Anthocerotidae   588.3
Anthologies   080
   literature   808.8
      specific literatures   T3B—08
      *see Manual at* T3B—08
         and T3B—09
      *see Manual at* 808.8
   *see Manual at* 080 vs. 800; *also*
      at 081–089
Anthozoa   593.6
   paleozoology   563.6
Anthracenes   547.616
   chemical engineering   661.816
Anthracite coal   553.25
   economic geology   553.25
   mining   622.335
   properties   662.622 5
Anthrax
   animals
      veterinary medicine   636.089 695 6
   humans
      incidence   614.561
      medicine   616.956
      *see also* Communicable
         diseases — humans
Anthribidae   595.768
Anthropogenesis   599.938
Anthropoidea   599.8
   *see also* Primates
Anthropological linguistics   306.44
Anthropologists   301.092
Anthropology   301
   arts   700.455 2
         T3C—355 2
   literature   808.803 552
      history and criticism   809.933 552
      specific literatures   T3B—080 355 2
         history and
            criticism   T3B—093 552
   philosophical anthropology   128
   physical anthropology   599.9
   theological anthropology   202.2
   *see also* Humans — religion
Anthropometric design   620.82

Anthropometry   599.94
   *see Manual at* 599.94 vs. 611
Anthropomorphism
   comparative religion   202.112
   philosophy of religion   211
Anthroposophical therapy   615.53
Anthroposophy   299.935
   biography   299.935 092
Anthuriums   635.934 64
   botany   584.64
   floriculture   635.934 64
Anti-allergic agents
   pharmacokinetics   615.796
Anti-anxiety drugs
   pharmacokinetics   615.788 2
Anti-arrhythmia agents
   pharmacokinetics   615.716
Anti-bacterial agents
   pharmacokinetics   615.792 2
Anti-federalist Party (U.S.)   324.273 26
Anti-HIV agents
   pharmacokinetics   615.792 4
Anti-infective agents
   pharmacokinetics   615.792
Anti-inflammatory agents
   pharmacokinetics   615.794
Anti-Lebanon   T2—569 14
Anti-Masonic Party (U.S.)   324.273 2
Anti-mission Baptists   286.4
   *see also* Baptists
Anti-retroviral agents
   pharmacokinetics   615.792 4
Anti-Semitism   305.892 4
   political aspects   323.119 24
   political ideology   320.569 924
   social theology   201.5
      Christianity   261.26
Anti-Trinitarianism   289.1
Antiaircraft artillery   358.138 2
Antiaircraft artillery forces   358.13
Antiaircraft defenses   355.422
   *see also* Air warfare
Antiballistic missiles   358.174 82
   engineering   623.451 94
   military equipment   358.174 82
Antibiotics   615.329
   chemistry   547.7
   pharmacokinetics   615.792 2
   pharmacology   615.329
Antibodies   571.967
   human immunology   616.079 8
Antibody-dependent immune
   mechanisms   571.968
   humans   616.079 9

| | |
|---|---|
| Antichrist | 236 |
| Anticlines | 551.86 |
| Anticoagulants | |
| pharmacokinetics | 615.718 |
| Anticommunist international | |
| leagues | 324.13 |
| Anticonvulsants | |
| pharmacokinetics | 615.784 |
| Anticosti Island (Quebec) | T2—714 178 2 |
| Anticyclones (Meteorology) | 551.551 4 |
| Antidepressants | |
| drug therapy | 616.852 706 1 |
| pharmacokinetics | 615.78 |
| Antidiuretics | |
| pharmacokinetics | 615.761 |
| Antidotes | |
| human toxicology | 615.908 |
| Antifreeze solutions | |
| automotive | 629.256 |
| Antifungal agents | |
| pharmacokinetics | 615.792 |
| Antigen-antibody reactions | 571.967 7 |
| human immunology | 616.079 87 |
| Antigen recognition | 571.964 6 |
| human immunology | 616.079 5 |
| Antigens | 571.964 5 |
| human immunology | 616.079 2 |
| Antigonish (N.S. : County) | T2—716 14 |
| Antigua | T2—729 74 |
| Antigua and Barbuda | 972.974 |
| | T2—729 74 |
| Antiguans | T5—969 729 74 |
| Antilipemic agents | |
| pharmacokinetics | 615.739 |
| Antillean Arawak Indians | T5—979 2 |
| Antilles | 972.9 |
| | T2—729 |
| Antilles, Lesser | T2—729 |
| Antilocapridae | 599.639 |
| Antilopinae | 599.646 |
| Antimacassars | 645.4 |
| arts | 746.95 |
| home sewing | 646.21 |
| household management | 645.4 |
| Antimasonic Party (U.S.) | 324.273 2 |
| Antimatter | 530 |
| Antimilitarism | 355.021 3 |
| military science | 355.021 3 |
| sociology | 303.66 |
| Antimissile defense forces | 358.174 |
| Antimissile missiles | 358.174 82 |
| engineering | 623.451 94 |
| military equipment | 358.174 82 |

| | |
|---|---|
| Antimission Baptists | 286.4 |
| *see also* Baptists | |
| Antimonides | |
| mineralogy | 549.32 |
| Antimony | 669.75 |
| chemical engineering | 661.071 6 |
| chemistry | 546.716 |
| economic geology | 553.47 |
| materials science | 620.189 5 |
| metallography | 669.957 5 |
| metallurgy | 669.75 |
| mining | 622.347 |
| physical metallurgy | 669.967 5 |
| *see also* Chemicals; Metals | |
| Antineoplastic agents | |
| pharmacokinetics | 615.798 |
| Antinomianism | 273.6 |
| Antioch (Turkey) | T2—564 8 |
| ancient | 939.431 |
| | T2—394 31 |
| Antioquia (Colombia : Dept.) | T2—861 26 |
| Antioxidants | |
| applied nutrition | 613.286 |
| Antiparasitic agents | |
| pharmacokinetics | 615.792 |
| Antiparticles | 539.72 |
| Antipersonnel devices | 623.451 4 |
| Antipodes Islands (N.Z.) | T2—939 9 |
| Antiprotons | 539.721 23 |
| Antipsychotic drugs | |
| pharmacokinetics | 615.788 2 |
| Antipyretics | |
| pharmacokinetics | 615.783 |
| Antique (Philippines) | T2—599 5 |
| Antique furniture | 749.1 |
| Antiques | 745.1 |
| *see Manual at* 745.1 | |
| Antiquities | 930.1 |
| law | 344.094 |
| Antiretroviral agents | |
| pharmacokinetics | 615.792 4 |
| Antisepsis | |
| obstetrics | 618.8 |
| public health | 614.48 |
| surgery | 617.910 1 |
| Antislavery movements | 326.8 |
| *see also* Abolition of slavery | |
| Antisocial people | 305.906 92 |
| | T1—086 92 |
| Antisocial personality disorders | |
| medicine | 616.858 2 |
| *see also* Mental disorders | |

Antispasmodics
  pharmacokinetics 615.784
Antisubmarine reconnaissance
  (Air warfare) 358.45
Antisubmarine warfare 359.93
  World War I 940.451 6
  World War II 940.545 16
Antitank artillery forces 358.12
Antitrust law 343.072 1
Antitrust policies 338.8
Antitrust violations 364.168
  law 345.026 8
  public administration 353.43
Antiviral agents
  pharmacokinetics 615.792 4
Antofagasta (Chile :
  Province) T2—831 38
Antofagasta (Chile :
  Region) T2—831 3
Antoine-Labelle (Quebec) T2—714 241
Antonines 255.18
  church history 271.18
Antonym dictionaries 413.1
  specific languages T4—312
  specific subjects T1—03
Antrim (Northern Ireland :
  Borough) T2—416 12
Antrim (Northern Ireland :
  County) T2—416 1
Antrim County (Mich.) T2—774 85
Ants 595.796
  control technology 628.965 7
  culture 638.579 6
Antsiranana (Madagascar :
  Province) T2—691
Antwerp (Belgium) T2—493 222
Antwerp (Belgium :
  Province) T2—493 22
Antwerpen (Belgium) T2—493 222
Antwerpen (Belgium :
  Province) T2—493 22
Anura 597.8
  paleozoology 567.8
Anus
  human anatomy 611.35
  human physiology 612.36
  medicine 616.35
  surgery 617.555
Anus diseases
  medicine 616.35
  *see also* Digestive system
    diseases — humans
Anvers (Belgium) T2—493 222
Anvil Island (B.C. : Island) T2—711 31

Anvils 682
  blacksmithing 682
  music 786.884 3
  *see also* Percussion
    instruments
Anxiety 152.46
Anxiety disorders
  medicine 616.852 2
  *see also* Mental disorders
Anyi (African people) T5—963 38
Anyi language 496.338
   T6—963 38
Anzoátegui (Venezuela :
  State) T2—875 2
Aomori-ken (Japan) T2—521 12
Aorta 573.185
  human anatomy 611.13
  human physiology 612.133
  medicine 616.138
  physiology 573.185
  *see also* Cardiovascular system
Aortic diseases
  medicine 616.138
  *see also* Cardiovascular
    diseases — humans
Aortic valve 573.185
  human anatomy 611.12
  human physiology 612.17
  medicine 616.125
  physiology 573.185
  *see also* Cardiovascular system
Aortic valve diseases
  medicine 616.125
  *see also* Cardiovascular
    diseases — humans
Aosta (Italy) T2—451 11
  ancient T2—372 211
Aoudad 599.649
AP ammunition 623.451 8
Apache County (Ariz.) T2—791 37
Apache Indians T5—972 5
Apachean Indians T5—972 5
Apachean languages 497.25
   T6—972 5
Apalachicola River (Fla.) T2—759 92
Apartheid 305.800 968
  political ideology 320.560 968
Apartment buildings 647.92
  architecture 728.314
  construction 690.831 4
  household management 647.92
  *see also* Dwellings

| | | | |
|---|---|---|---|
| Apartment hotels | 647.92 | Apocalypses (Biblical literature) | 220.046 |
| architecture | 728.314 | New Testament | |
| construction | 690.831 4 | pseudepigrapha | 229.94 |
| household management | 647.92 | Old Testament pseudepigrapha | 229.913 |
| see also Dwellings | | Apocrita | 595.79 |
| Apartment-house districts | | Apocrypha (Bible) | 229 |
| area planning | 711.58 | Apocryphal wisdom literature | 229.3 |
| Apartment houses | 647.92 | Apocynaceae | 583.93 |
| architecture | 728.314 | Apoda (Amphibians) | 597.82 |
| construction | 690.831 4 | Apodacea | 593.96 |
| household management | 647.92 | Apodemus | 599.358 5 |
| see also Dwellings | | Apodi | 598.762 |
| Apartments | 643.27 | Apodidae | 598.762 |
| see also Apartment houses | | Apodiformes | 598.76 |
| Apathy | | paleozoology | 568.7 |
| social psychology | 302.17 | Apoidea | 595.799 |
| Apatites | 553.64 | Apollo project | 629.454 |
| mineralogy | 549.72 | Apologetics | 202 |
| Apatosaurus | 567.913 8 | Christianity | 239 |
| Apennines (Italy) | T2—45 | Islam | 297.29 |
| Apes | 599.88 | Judaism | 296.35 |
| animal husbandry | 636.988 | Aponogetonaceae | 584.74 |
| experimental animals | | Apoplexy | |
| medicine | 616.027 38 | medicine | 616.81 |
| Aphanite | 552.2 | see also Nervous system | |
| Aphasia | | diseases — humans | |
| medicine | 616.855 2 | Apostates | |
| see also Communication | | Christian polemics | 239.7 |
| disorders | | Apostles | 225.92 |
| special education | 371.914 2 | art representation | 704.948 62 |
| Aphid flies | 595.774 | Apostles' Creed | 238.11 |
| Aphids | 595.752 | Apostleship (Spiritual gift) | 234.13 |
| agricultural pests | 632.752 | Apostolic Church | 270.1 |
| Aphorisms | 398.9 | Apostolic succession | 262.11 |
| Aphrodisiacs | | Apostolicity | 262.72 |
| pharmacokinetics | 615.766 9 | Appalaches (Quebec) | T2—714 712 |
| Aphyllophorales | 579.597 | Appalachian dulcimers | 787.75 |
| Apiaceae | 583.849 | see also Stringed instruments | |
| Apical meristem | 575.485 | Appalachian Mountains | T2—74 |
| Apiculture | 638.1 | North Carolina | T2—756 8 |
| Apidae | 595.799 | Appaloosa | 636.13 |
| APL (Educational credit) | 371.264 | Appanoose County (Iowa) | T2—777 89 |
| Aplacophora | 594.2 | Apparatus | T1—028 4 |
| Aplastic anemia | | teaching aids | 371.33 |
| medicine | 616.152 | | T1—078 |
| see also Cardiovascular | | Apparel | 391 |
| diseases — humans | | see also Clothing | |
| Apnea | | Apparitions | 133.1 |
| medicine | 616.2 | Apparitions of Mary | 232.917 |
| see also Respiratory tract | | Appeal (Law) | 347.08 |
| diseases — humans | | Appeals of labor grievances | 331.889 66 |
| Apocalypse (Biblical book) | 228 | see also Grievances (Labor) | |

| | |
|---|---|
| Appellate courts | 347.03 |
| criminal law | 345.014 4 |
| England | 347.420 3 |
| Scotland | 347.411 03 |
| United States | 347.732 4 |
| Appellate procedure | 347.08 |
| Appendages | 573.998 |
| Appendectomies | |
| surgery | 617.554 5 |
| Appendicitis | |
| medicine | 616.34 |
| *see also* Digestive system | |
| diseases — humans | |
| surgery | 617.554 5 |
| Appendix | |
| human anatomy | 611.345 |
| human physiology | 612.33 |
| medicine | 616.34 |
| surgery | 617.554 5 |
| Appennino Tosco-Emiliano | |
| (Italy) | T2—454 |
| Appenzell (Switzerland) | T2—494 714 4 |
| Appenzell (Switzerland : | |
| Canton) | T2—494 71 |
| Appenzell Ausser-Rhoden | |
| (Switzerland) | T2—494 712 |
| Appenzell Inner-Rhoden | |
| (Switzerland) | T2—494 714 |
| Apperception | |
| psychology | 153.73 |
| Appetite disorders | |
| medicine | 616.852 6 |
| *see also* Mental disorders | |
| Appetizers | 641.812 |
| Apples | 641.341 1 |
| botany | 583.73 |
| commercial processing | 664.804 11 |
| cooking | 641.641 1 |
| food | 641.341 1 |
| orchard crop | 634.11 |
| Appleton layers | 538.767 4 |
| Application frameworks | 005.1 |
| Application generators | 005.13 |
| Application programming | 005.1 |
| *see Manual at* 005.1–.2 vs. | |
| 005.42 | |
| Application software | 005.3 |
| *see Manual at* 005.3, 005.5 | |
| vs. 005.43–.45; *also at* | |
| 005.3682 vs. 005.365, | |
| 005.3684 | |
| Applications for positions | 650.142 |
| job hunting | 650.142 |
| personnel selection | 658.311 2 |
| public administration | 352.65 |
| Applied chemistry | 660 |
| law | 344.095 4 |
| Applied ethics | 170 |
| *see also* Ethical problems | |
| Applied linguistics | 418 |
| specific languages | T4—8 |
| Applied mathematics | 519 |
| Applied mechanics | 620.1 |
| Applied numerical analysis | 518 |
| Applied nutrition | 363.8 |
| *see also* Nutrition | |
| Applied optics | 621.36 |
| Applied physics | 621 |
| law | 344.095 3 |
| Applied psychology | 158 |
| Applied sciences | 600 |
| Applied sociology | 360 |
| Appling County (Ga.) | T2—758 784 |
| Appliqué | |
| textile arts | 746.445 |
| Appointment power (Legislative | |
| bodies) | 328.345 5 |
| Appomattox County (Va.) | T2—755 625 |
| Apportionment (Legislatures) | 328.334 5 |
| law | 342.053 |
| Appraisal | |
| archives | 025.281 4 |
| land economics | 333.332 |
| Appreciation | |
| arts | 701.18 |
| literature | 801 |
| music | 781.17 |
| Apprentices | |
| economics | 331.55 |
| Apprenticeship | 331.259 22 |
| | T1—071 55 |
| economics | 331.259 22 |
| union control | 331.889 6 |
| education | 371.227 |
| secondary level | 373.27 |
| personnel management | 658.312 4 |
| public administration | 354.968 |
| Approach piloting | 623.892 9 |
| Appropriate technology | 338.927 |
| Appropriation power (Legislative | |
| bodies) | 328.341 2 |

| | |
|---|---|
| Appropriations | 352.49 |
| enactment | 328.37 |
| law | 343.034 |
| *see Manual at* 300–330, 355– | |
| 390 vs. 342–347, 352–354 | |
| Approval plans | |
| library acquisitions | 025.233 |
| Approximation (Mathematics) | 511.4 |
| algebra | 512.924 |
| numerical methods | 518.5 |
| Apraxia of speech | |
| medicine | 616.855 2 |
| *see also* Communication | |
| disorders | |
| Apricots | 641.342 1 |
| botany | 583.73 |
| commercial processing | 664.804 21 |
| cooking | 641.642 1 |
| food | 641.342 1 |
| orchard crop | 634.21 |
| Aprons | 391.44 |
| commercial technology | 687.19 |
| leather | 685.22 |
| *see also* Accessories (Clothing) | |
| Apses | |
| Christian church architecture | 726.593 |
| Apterous insects | 595.756 |
| Apterygiformes | 598.54 |
| paleozoology | 568.5 |
| Apterygota | 595.72 |
| Apteryx | 598.54 |
| Aptitude tests | 153.94 |
| education | 371.262 |
| personnel selection | 658.311 25 |
| teacher-prepared tests | 371.271 |
| Aptitudes | 153.9 |
| Apulia (Italy) | T2—457 5 |
| ancient | T2—377 5 |
| Apure (Venezuela) | T2—874 2 |
| Apurímac (Peru) | T2—853 8 |
| Aqaba, Gulf of | 551.461 533 |
| | T2—165 33 |
| 'Aqabah (Jordan : Province) | T2—569 572 |
| 'Aqā'id (Islam) | 297.2 |
| Aquaculture | 639.8 |
| economics | 338.371 8 |
| Aquariums | 597.073 |
| fish culture | 639.34 |
| Aquarius (Zodiac) | 133.527 6 |
| Aquaspirillum | 579.323 |
| Aquatic animals | 591.76 |
| resource economics | 333.954 8 |
| Aquatic biological resources | 333.952 8 |
| public administration | 354.57 |

| | |
|---|---|
| Aquatic biology | 578.76 |
| *see Manual at* 578.76–.77 vs. | |
| 551.46, 551.48 | |
| Aquatic birds | 598.176 |
| resource economics | 333.958 28 |
| Aquatic ecology | 577.6 |
| marine environments | 577.7 |
| Aquatic exercises | 613.716 |
| Aquatic gardens | 635.967 4 |
| botany | 581.760 73 |
| floriculture | 635.967 4 |
| Aquatic organisms | 578.76 |
| Aquatic plants | 581.76 |
| floriculture | 635.967 4 |
| Aquatic resources | 333.91 |
| Aquatic sports | 797 |
| Aquatinting | 766.3 |
| Aqueducts | |
| water supply engineering | 628.15 |
| Aqueous humors | |
| human anatomy | 611.84 |
| human physiology | 612.844 |
| Aqueous solutions | 541.342 2 |
| chemical engineering | 660.294 22 |
| Aquiculture | 639.8 |
| Aquifers | 553.79 |
| *see also* Groundwater | |
| Aquifoliaceae | 583.85 |
| Aquila (Italy : Province) | T2—457 11 |
| ancient | T2—377 34 |
| Aquila chrysaetos | 598.942 3 |
| Aquileia (Italy) | |
| ancient | T2—373 81 |
| Aquino, Benigno S., III | |
| Philippine history | 959.905 2 |
| Aquino, Corazon Cojuangco | |
| Philippine history | 959.904 7 |
| Aquitaine (France) | T2—447 1 |
| Aquitania | T2—364 7 |
| Aqvilgjuaq (Nunavut) | T2—719 55 |
| Arab countries | T2—174 927 |
| Arab League | 341.247 7 |
| Arabesques (Music) | 784.189 4 |
| Arabia | 953 |
| | T2—53 |
| ancient | 939.49 |
| | T2—394 9 |
| Arabia, Roman | T2—394 8 |
| Arabia Deserta | 939.49 |
| | T2—394 9 |
| Lower Mesopotamia | T2—355 |
| Upper Mesopotamia | T2—354 |
| Arabia Felix | 939.49 |
| | T2—394 9 |

| | |
|---|---|
| Arabia Petraea | 939.48 |
| | T2—394 8 |
| Arabian Desert (Egypt) | T2—623 |
| Arabian Peninsula | 953 |
| | T2—53 |
| Arabian Sea | 551.461 537 |
| | T2—165 37 |
| Arabic language | 492.7 |
| | T6—927 |
| Biblical texts | 220.46 |
| Hadith texts | 297.125 04 |
| Koran texts | 297.122 4 |
| printing | 686.219 27 |
| Arabic literature | 892.7 |
| Arabic philosophy | 181.92 |
| Arabs | T5—927 |
| Sicilian history | 945.802 |
| Araceae | 584.64 |
| Arachnida | 595.4 |
| disease carriers | 571.986 |
| medicine | 614.433 |
| paleozoology | 565.4 |
| Arad (Romania : Judeţ) | T2—498 4 |
| Araeoscelidia | 567.93 |
| Arafura Sea | 551.461 475 |
| | T2—164 75 |
| Aragon (Kingdom) | 946.03 |
| Sardinian history | 945.905 |
| Sicilian history | 945.805 |
| Southern Italian history | 945.706 |
| Spanish history | 946.03 |
| Aragon (Spain) | T2—465 5 |
| Aragonite | |
| mineralogy | 549.785 |
| Aragua (Venezuela : State) | T2—873 4 |
| Arakhin | 296.123 5 |
| Babylonian Talmud | 296.125 5 |
| Mishnah | 296.123 5 |
| Aral Sea (Uzbekistan and Kazakhstan) | T2—587 |
| Arales | 584.64 |
| Araliaceae | 583.84 |
| Aramaeans | T5—922 |
| Aramaic languages | 492.2 |
| | T6—922 |
| Biblical texts | 220.42 |
| Midrashic texts | 296.140 4 |
| Talmudic texts | 296.120 4 |
| Aramaic literatures | 892.2 |
| Arameans | T5—922 |
| Aran Islands (Ireland) | T2—417 48 |
| Araneae | 595.44 |
| Araneida | 595.44 |
| Aransas County (Tex.) | T2—764 122 |
| Aranyakas | 294.592 1 |
| Arapaho Indians | T5—973 54 |
| Arapaho language | 497.354 |
| | T6—973 54 |
| Arapahoe County (Colo.) | T2—788 82 |
| Ararat (Vic.) | T2—945 7 |
| Arauan languages | 498.9 |
| | T6—989 |
| Arauca (Colombia : Dept.) | T2—861 98 |
| Araucanía (Chile) | T2—834 6 |
| Araucanian Indians | T5—987 2 |
| Araucanian languages | 498.72 |
| | T6—987 2 |
| Araucariaceae | 585.3 |
| Arauco (Chile : Province) | T2—834 2 |
| Arawak Indians | T5—983 9 |
| South America | T5—983 9 |
| West Indies | T5—979 2 |
| Arawakan languages | 498.39 |
| | T6—983 9 |
| Central America | 497.92 |
| | T6—979 2 |
| South America | 498.39 |
| | T6—983 9 |
| West Indies | 497.92 |
| | T6—979 2 |
| Arbitrage | 332.645 |
| Arbitration | |
| international relations | 327.17 |
| labor economics | 331.891 43 |
| law | 344.018 914 3 |
| public administration | 354.97 |
| law | 347.09 |
| law of nations | 341.522 |
| personnel management | 658.315 4 |
| public administration | 352.68 |
| Arbon (Switzerland : Bezirk) | T2—494 599 |
| Arborvitaes | 585.4 |
| Arboviruses | 579.256 2 |
| Arbuckle Mountains (Okla.) | T2—766 5 |
| Arc furnace practice | 669.142 4 |
| Arc length | |
| calculus | 515.43 |
| integral geometry | 516.362 |
| Arc lighting | 621.325 |
| Arc welding | 671.521 2 |
| Arcade games | 794.822 |
| *see Manual at* 793.932 vs. 794.822 | |
| Arcades | 721.41 |
| architecture | 721.41 |
| construction | 690.141 |

| | | | |
|---|---|---|---|
| Arcadia (Greece) | T2—495 22 | Architects | 720.92 |
| ancient | T2—388 | Architectural acoustics | |
| Arcellinida | 579.43 | construction | 690.2 |
| Arch bridges | | Architectural decoration | 729 |
| construction | 624.22 | *see Manual at* 729 | |
| Archaeobacteria | 579.321 | Architectural design | 729 |
| Archaeoceti | 569.5 | *see Manual at* 729 | |
| Archaeocyatha | 563.47 | Architectural drawing | 720.284 |
| Archaeogastropoda | 594.32 | Architectural drawings | 720.222 |
| Archaeological thefts | 364.162 89 | Architectural orders | 721.36 |
| law | 345.026 289 | architecture | 721.36 |
| Archaeologists | 930.109 2 | construction | 690.13 |
| Archaeology | 930.1 | Architectural schools and styles | 720.9 |
| ancient places | 931–939 | ancient | 722 |
| arts | T3C—358 301 | construction details | 721 |
| Bible | 220.93 | design and decoration | 729 |
| law | 344.094 | Architectural structure | 720 |
| literature | 808.803 583 01 | Architecture | 720 |
| history and criticism | 809.933 583 01 | art representation | 704.944 |
| modern places | 940–990 | arts | T3C—357 |
| Archaeopteris | 561.597 | landscapes | 712 |
| Archaeornithes | 568.22 | literature | 808.803 57 |
| Archaisms (Linguistics) | 417.7 | history and criticism | 809.933 57 |
| specific languages | T4—7 | specific literatures | T3B—080 357 |
| Archbishops | 270.092 | history and | |
| biography | 270.092 | criticism | T3B—093 57 |
| specific denominations | 280 | naval | 623.81 |
| *see Manual at* 230–280 | | painting | 758.7 |
| ecclesiology | 262.12 | religious significance | 203.7 |
| Archean era | 551.712 | Christianity | 246.9 |
| geology | 551.712 | *see also* Arts — religious | |
| paleontology | 560.171 2 | significance | |
| Arched harps | 787.94 | *see also* Arts | |
| *see also* Stringed instruments | | Archival materials | |
| Archeology | 930.1 | cataloging | 025.341 4 |
| *see also* Archaeology | | library acquisitions | 025.281 4 |
| Archeozoic era | 551.712 | library treatment | 025.171 4 |
| geology | 551.712 | records management | 651.56 |
| paleontology | 560.171 2 | Archival science | 020 |
| Archer County (Tex.) | T2—764 543 | Archive buildings | |
| Archers | 799.320 92 | architecture | 725.15 |
| Archery | 799.32 | Archives | 027 |
| Arches (Structural elements) | 721.41 | *see also* Libraries | |
| architecture | 721.41 | Archivists | 020.92 |
| construction | 690.141 | Archosauria | 567.9 |
| structural engineering | 624.177 5 | Archostemata | 595.762 |
| concrete | 624.183 45 | Archuleta County (Colo.) | T2—788 32 |
| Arches (Structures) | 725.96 | Arcs | 516.152 |
| Arches National Park (Utah) | T2—792 58 | Arctic animals | 591.709 113 |
| Archetype (Psychology) | | Arctic Archipelago | |
| Jungian system | 150.195 4 | (Nunavut and N.W.T.) | T2—719 52 |
| personality theory | 155.264 | Arctic Bay (Nunavut) | T2—719 52 |
| Archiannelida | 592.62 | Arctic biology | 578.091 13 |
| Architarbi | 565.4 | | |

| | |
|---|---|
| Arctic climate | |
| health | 613.111 |
| Arctic cod | 597.632 |
| Arctic cooking | 641.591 1 |
| Arctic ecology | 577.091 13 |
| Arctic fox | 599.776 4 |
| Arctic islands | T2—98 |
| Arctic Ocean | 551.461 32 |
| | T2—163 2 |
| *see Manual at* T2—163 and | |
| T2—164, T2—165 | |
| Arctic plants | 581.709 113 |
| floriculture | 635.952 |
| Arctic regions | T2—113 |
| Arctocephalinae | 599.797 3 |
| Arctocephalus | 599.797 38 |
| Ardabīl (Iran : Province) | T2—551 2 |
| Ardahan İli (Turkey) | T2—566 22 |
| ancient | T2—393 37 |
| Ardèche (France) | T2—445 89 |
| Ardeidae | 598.34 |
| Ardennes | T2—493 48 |
| Ardennes (France) | T2—443 12 |
| Ardennes, Battle of the, | |
| 1944–1945 | 940.542 193 48 |
| Ards (Northern Ireland) | T2—416 54 |
| Area planning | 307.12 |
| arts | 711 |
| community sociology | 307.12 |
| Area studies | 940–990 |
| collection development | 025.29 |
| Area treatment | T1—09 |
| Arecales | 584.5 |
| paleobotany | 561.45 |
| Arecibo (P.R. : District) | T2—729 53 |
| Arecidae | 584.5 |
| paleobotany | 561.45 |
| Arena theater | 792.022 8 |
| Arenac County (Mich.) | T2—774 73 |
| Arenaviridae | 579 256 |
| Areolar tissues | |
| human histology | 611.018 2 |
| Arequipa (Peru : Dept.) | T2—853 2 |
| Arequipa (Peru : Region) | T2—853 2 |
| Arezzo (Italy) | |
| ancient | T2—375 68 |
| Arezzo (Italy : Province) | T2—455 9 |
| ancient | T2—375 68 |
| Arfon (Wales) | T2—429 25 |
| Argenteuil (Quebec : | |
| Regional County | |
| Municipality) | T2—714 23 |
| Argentina | 982 |
| | T2—82 |
| Argentine literature | 860 |
| Argentine Republic | T2—82 |
| Argentineans | T5—688 2 |
| Argentines | T5—688 2 |
| Argeş (Romania : Judeţ) | T2—498 2 |
| Argolis (Greece) | T2—495 22 |
| ancient | T2—388 |
| Argon | |
| chemistry | 546.753 |
| gas technology | 665.822 |
| Argonne (France) | T2—443 81 |
| Argot | 417.2 |
| specific languages | T4—7 |
| Arguloida | 595.36 |
| Argument (Logic) | 168 |
| Argyll and Bute (Scotland) | T2—414 2 |
| Århus amt (Denmark) | T2—489 5 |
| Arhynchobdellida | 592.66 |
| Ari liturgy | 296.450 4 |
| Ariana | T2—396 |
| Arianism | 273.4 |
| Arias Sánchez, Óscar | |
| Costa Rican history | 972.860 521 |
| 1986–1990 | 972.860 521 |
| 2006–2010 | 972.860 526 |
| Arica (Chile : Province) | T2—831 23 |
| Arid lands | 551.415 |
| | T2—154 |
| biology | 578.754 |
| ecology | 577.54 |
| economics | 333.736 |
| geography | 910.915 4 |
| geomorphology | 551.415 |
| physical geography | 910.021 54 |
| Ariège (France) | T2—447 35 |
| Aries (Zodiac) | 133.526 2 |
| Arikara Indians | T5—979 32 |
| Arikara language | 497.932 |
| | T6—979 32 |
| Ariminum (Italy) | T2—372 686 |
| Aristocracy | 305.52 |
| | T1—086 21 |
| political system | 321.5 |
| Aristolochiales | 583.26 |
| Aristotelian philosophy | 185 |
| modern | 149.91 |
| Arithmetic | 513 |
| numerical methods | 518.45 |
| primary education | 372.72 |
| Arithmetic progressions | 515.24 |
| Arizona | 979.1 |
| | T2—791 |
| Ark of the Covenant | 296.493 |

| | |
|---|---|
| Arkadia (Greece) | T2—495 22 |
| ancient | T2—388 |
| Arkansas | 976.7 |
| | T2—767 |
| Arkansas County (Ark.) | T2—767 86 |
| Arkansas River | T2—767 3 |
| Arkansas | T2—767 3 |
| Colorado | T2—788 9 |
| Kansas | T2—781 |
| Oklahoma | T2—766 8 |
| Arkhangel'sk (Russia : | |
| Oblast) | T2—471 7 |
| Arkhangel'skaĩa oblast' | |
| (Russia) | T2—471 7 |
| Arles (France) | T2—449 18 |
| Arlesheim (Switzerland : | |
| Bezirk) | T2—494 333 |
| Arlington County (Va.) | T2—755 295 |
| Arm muscles | |
| human anatomy | 611.737 |
| Arm techniques | |
| music | 784.193 6 |
| Arm wrestling | 796.812 |
| Armada, 1588 | 942.055 |
| Armadillos | 599.312 |
| Armageddon | 236.9 |
| Armagh (Northern Ireland : | |
| County) | T2—416 6 |
| Armagh (Northern Ireland : | |
| District) | T2—416 61 |
| Armatures (Electrical equipment) | |
| generators | 621.316 |
| Armatures (Sculpture) | 731.3 |
| Armed forces | 355 |
| energy economics | 333.796 |
| *see also* Armed services | |
| Armed services | 355 |
| cooking | 641.57 |
| law | 343.01 |
| libraries | 027.5 |
| life insurance | 368.364 |
| relation to state | 322.5 |
| reserves | 355.37 |
| law | 343.012 |
| Armenia (Ancient kingdom) | T2—395 5 |
| Armenia (Region) | 956.62 |
| | T2—566 2 |
| ancient | 939.55 |
| | T2—395 5 |
| Armenia (Republic : | |
| 1920– ) | T2—475 6 |
| Turkey | 956.62 |
| | T2—566 2 |

| | |
|---|---|
| Armenia (Republic) | |
| ancient | 939.55 |
| | T2—395 5 |
| Armenia (Republic : 1918–1920) | 956.620 23 |
| | T2—566 2 |
| Armenia (Republic : 1920– ) | 947.56 |
| | T2—475 6 |
| Armenian Church | 281.62 |
| *see also* Eastern churches | |
| Armenian language | 491.992 |
| | T6—919 92 |
| Biblical texts | 220.49 |
| Armenian literature | 891.992 |
| Armenian massacres, 1894–1896 | 956.620 154 |
| Armenian massacres, 1915–1916 | 956.620 154 |
| Armenians | T5—919 92 |
| Armidale (N.S.W.) | T2—944 4 |
| Armies (Military units) | 355.31 |
| Armies (National armies) | 355.3 |
| Arminians | 284.9 |
| Armistice | 327.17 |
| law | 341.66 |
| World War I | 940.439 |
| Armor (Wearable) | 623.441 |
| art metalwork | 739.75 |
| Armor-piercing ammunition | 623.451 8 |
| Armored animals | 591.477 |
| Armored cavalry | 358.18 |
| Armored dinosaurs | 567.915 |
| Armored forces | 358.18 |
| Armored personnel carriers | 358.188 3 |
| engineering | 623.747 5 |
| military equipment | 358.188 3 |
| Armored vehicles | 358.188 3 |
| engineering | 623.747 5 |
| military equipment | 358.188 3 |
| Armored warfare | 358.18 |
| Armorial bearings | 929.6 |
| Armories | 355.75 |
| architecture | 725.18 |
| Arms (Body parts) | 612.97 |
| physiology | 612.97 |
| regional medicine | 617.574 |
| surgery | 617.574 059 |
| *see also* Upper extremities | |
| Arms (Military) | 355.8 |
| art metalwork | 739.7 |
| customs | 399 |
| engineering | 623.4 |
| military equipment | 355.8 |
| procurement | 355.621 2 |
| *see Manual at* 355–359 vs. 623 | |
| Arms (Small firearms) | 683.4 |
| *see also* Guns (Small arms) | |

Arms control 327.174
  international politics 327.174
  law 341.733
  military science 355.03
  *see also* Arms race
Arms race 327.174
  ethics 172.422
  social theology 201.727 5
    Christianity 261.873 2
  *see also* Arms control
Armstrong (B.C.) T2—711 5
Armstrong County (Pa.) T2—748 88
Armstrong County (Tex.) T2—764 833
Army artillery forces 358.12
Army engineer corps 358.22
Armyworms 595.78
  agricultural pests 633.104 978
Arnhem (Netherlands) T2—492 18
Arnhem Land (N.T.) T2—942 95
Arno River (Italy) T2—455
Arnold, Benedict
  treason 973.382
Arnsberg (Germany :
  Regierungsbezirk) T2—435 63
Aromatherapy 615.321 9
Aromatic compounds 547.6
  chemical engineering 661.8
Aromatic herbs 641.357
  *see also* Herbs
Aromatic hydrocarbons
  human toxicology 615.951 1
Aromatic teas 641.357
  home preparation 641.877
  *see also* Herb teas; Tea
Aromatization 547.27
  chemical engineering 660.284 4
Aroostook County (Me.) T2—741 1
Árpád, House of 943.902
Arpeggiones 787.6
  *see also* Stringed instruments
Arpeggios 781.252
Arraignment 345.072
Arrangement (Archives) 025.341 4
Arrangement (Music) 781.37
Arrangements (Music) 781.38
  *see Manual at* 781.38
Array processing 004.35
  *see also* Processing modes —
    computer science
Array processors 004.35
  *see also* Processing modes —
    computer science

Arrest 363.232
  law 345.052 7
  police services 363.232
Arretium (Italy) T2—375 68
Arrhythmia
  medicine 616.128
  *see also* Cardiovascular
    diseases — humans
Arrondissements 320.83
  *see also* Counties
Arrow grasses 584.74
Arrow Lakes (B.C.) T2—711 62
Arrowheads (Plants) 584.72
Arrowroot 641.336 8
  botany 584.39
  commercial processing 664.23
  cooking 641.636 8
  food 641.336 8
  starch crop 633.68
Arrows 799.202 85
Arrowworms 592.38
Arroyo, Gloria Macapagal-
  Philippine history 959.905 1
Ars antiqua 780.902
Ars nova 780.902
Arsenals 355.7
  architecture 725.18
Arsenates
  mineralogy 549.72
Arsenic 669.75
  chemical engineering 661.071 5
  chemistry 546.715
  economic geology 553.47
  human toxicology 615.925 715
  metallography 669.957 5
  metallurgy 669.75
  mining 622.341
  organic chemistry 547.057 15
    applied 661.895
  physical metallurgy 669.967 5
  *see also* Chemicals; Metals
Arsenides
  mineralogy 549.32
Arson 364.164 2
  law 345.026 42
Art 700
  investment economics 332.63
  sociology 306.47
  theft of 364.162 87
    law 345.026 287
  therapeutics 615.851 56
  *see also* Arts
Art and religion 201.67
  *see also* Arts and religion

| | |
|---|---|
| Art appreciation | 701.18 |
| Art brut | 709.040 9 |
| Art dealers | 709.2 |
| *see Manual at* 709.2 vs. | |
| 381.457092 | |
| Art deco | 709.040 12 |
| sculpture | 735.230 412 |
| Art galleries | 708 |
| architecture | 727.7 |
| law | 344.093 |
| Art libraries | 026.7 |
| Art metalwork | 739 |
| Art metalworkers | 739.092 |
| Art museums | 708 |
| architecture | 727.7 |
| institutional housekeeping | 647.997 |
| Art music | 781.68 |
| nonwestern | 781.69 |
| western | 781.68 |
| Art needlework | 746.4 |
| Art nouveau | 709.034 9 |
| architecture | 724.6 |
| decoration | 745.409 034 |
| Art paper | 676.282 5 |
| Art policy (Government policy) | 700 |
| Art posters | 769.5 |
| Art songs | 782.421 68 |
| Art therapy | |
| medicine | 615.851 56 |
| psychiatry | 616.891 656 |
| Arta (Greece) | T2—495 3 |
| Arterial diseases | |
| medicine | 616.13 |
| *see also* Cardiovascular | |
| diseases — humans | |
| Arterial embolisms | |
| medicine | 616.135 |
| *see also* Cardiovascular | |
| diseases — humans | |
| Arterial occlusive diseases | |
| medicine | 616.13 |
| *see also* Cardiovascular | |
| diseases — humans | |
| Arterial thromboses | |
| medicine | 616.135 |
| *see also* Cardiovascular | |
| diseases — humans | |
| Arteries | 573.185 |
| animals | 573.185 |
| human anatomy | 611.13 |
| human physiology | 612.133 |
| medicine | 616.13 |
| physiology | 573.185 |

| | |
|---|---|
| Arteries (continued) | |
| surgery | 617.413 |
| *see also* Cardiovascular system | |
| Arteriosclerosis | |
| medicine | 616.136 |
| *see also* Cardiovascular | |
| diseases — humans | |
| Artesian wells | |
| engineering | 628.114 |
| hydrology | 551.498 |
| Arthabaska (Quebec : | |
| Regional County | |
| Municipality) | T2—714 565 |
| Arthritis | |
| medicine | 616.722 |
| *see also* Musculoskeletal | |
| diseases — humans | |
| Arthrobacter | 579.373 |
| Arthrochirotida | 563.96 |
| Arthropoda | 595 |
| *see also* Arthropods | |
| Arthropods | 595 |
| agricultural pests | 632.65 |
| paleozoology | 565 |
| pesticides | |
| agricultural use | 632.951 7 |
| Arthur, Chester Alan | |
| United States history | 973.84 |
| Arthur, King | |
| English history | 942.014 |
| Arthur County (Neb.) | T2—782 785 |
| Arthur's Pass National Park | |
| (N.Z.) | T2—938 1 |
| Artibonite (Haiti : Dept.) | T2—729 446 |
| Artichokes | 641.353 2 |
| botany | 583.99 |
| commercial processing | 664.805 32 |
| cooking | 641.653 2 |
| food | 641.353 2 |
| garden crop | 635.32 |
| Articles (Grammar) | 415.5 |
| specific languages | T4—55 |
| Articles of Confederation, 1781 | |
| United States history | 973.318 |
| Articulata | 593.92 |
| paleozoology | 563.92 |
| Articulatae | 587.2 |
| Articulated lorries | 388.344 |
| engineering | 629.224 |
| *see also* Trucks | |
| Articulation (Education) | 371.21 |

Articulation disorders
  medicine    616.855
  *see also* Communication
    disorders
Articulations
  human anatomy    611.72
  human physiology    612.752
Artificial arms
  medicine    617.574
Artificial environments
  health    613.5
Artificial eyes
  ophthalmology    617.79
Artificial feeding
  medicine    615.854 8
Artificial flies (Fishing)
  angling    799.124
  making    688.791 24
Artificial flower arrangements    745.92
Artificial flowers
  handicrafts    745.594 3
Artificial gems    666.88
Artificial harbors    387.1
  hydraulic engineering    627.2
  military engineering    623.64
  *see also* Ports
Artificial heart
  surgery    617.412 059 2
Artificial insemination
  animal husbandry    636.082 45
  ethics    176.2
    *see also* Reproduction —
      ethics
  family law    346.017
  gynecology    618.178
  health    613.94
Artificial intelligence    006.3
        T1—028 563
  *see Manual at* 006.3 vs. 153
Artificial islands    627.98
Artificial languages    499.99
        T6—999 9
Artificial legs
  medicine    617.58
Artificial-light gardening    635.048 3
  floriculture    635.982 6
Artificial-light photography    778.72
Artificial limbs
  manufacturing technology    681.761
  medicine    617.58
Artificial minerals    666.86
Artificial modification of weather  551.68
Artificial organs
  surgery    617.956

Artificial radioactivity
  physics    539.753
Artificial recharge (Groundwater) 627.56
Artificial respiration
  medicine    615.836 2
Artificial road surfaces    625.8
Artificial satellites
  engineering    629.46
  flight    629.434
  telecommunications    384.51
    *see also* Satellite
      communication
  weather reporting    551.635 4
Artificial stone    666.89
  architectural construction    721.044 4
  building construction    693.4
  building materials    691.3
  materials science    620.139
Artificial sweeteners
  commercial processing    664.5
Artificial teeth
  dentistry    617.692
Artificial tissue
  surgery    617.956
Artigas (Uruguay : Dept.)    T2—895 36
Artillery    355.821
  art metalwork    739.742
  engineering    623.41
  military equipment    355.821
Artillery ballistics    623.51
Artillery forces    358.12
Artillery installations    355.73
Artillery projectiles    623.451 3
Artiodactyla    599.63
  paleozoology    569.63
Artisans    609.2
  labor economics    331.794
Artistic études    784.189 49
Artistic gymnastics    796.442
Artistic lettering    745.61
Artistic principles    700.1
Artistic themes
  arts    700.457
        T3C—357
  folklore    398.277
    history and criticism    398.357
  literature    808.803 57
    history and criticism    809.933 57
    specific literatures    T3B—080 357
      history and
        criticism    T3B—093 57
Artists    700.92
  labor economics    331.761 7
  *see Manual at* 700.92

| | |
|---|---|
| Artists' books | 700 |
| fine arts | 709.040 82 |
| techniques | 702.81 |
| Artists' marks | 702.78 |
| | T1—027 8 |
| Artists' sketches | |
| criminal investigation | 363.258 |
| Artois (France) | T2—442 72 |
| Arts | 700 |
| auction catalogs | 700.29 |
| awards | 700.79 |
| collections | 700.74 |
| decorative | 745 |
| exhibitions | 700.74 |
| auction catalogs | 700.74 |
| festivals | 700.74 |
| influence on crime | 364.254 |
| law | 344.097 |
| museums | 700.74 |
| primary education | 372.5 |
| public administrative support | 353.77 |
| religious significance | 203.7 |
| Buddhism | 294.343 7 |
| Christianity | 246 |
| Hinduism | 294.537 |
| Islam | 297.3 |
| Judaism | 296.46 |
| Native American religions | 299.713 7 |
| sociology | 306.47 |
| Arts and crafts | 745 |
| sociology | 306.47 |
| Arts and religion | 201.67 |
| Christianity | 261.57 |
| Islam | 297.267 |
| Judaism | 296.377 |
| Arts policy (Government policy) | 700 |
| Artvin İli (Turkey) | T2—566 22 |
| ancient | T2—393 37 |
| Aruba | T2—729 86 |
| Arums | 584.64 |
| Arun (England) | T2—422 67 |
| Arunāchal Pradesh (India) | T2—541 63 |
| Arundineae | 584.9 |
| Arundinelleae | 584.9 |
| Arusha Region (Tanzania) | T2—678 26 |
| Arutani-Sape languages | 498.9 |
| | T6—989 |
| Arvicola | 599.354 |
| Arya-Samaj | 294.556 3 |
| Aryan languages (Indo-European) | 410 |
| | T6—1 |
| Aryan languages (Indo-Iranian) | 491.1 |
| | T6—911 |
| Asante (African people) | T5—963 385 |

| | |
|---|---|
| Asante (Empire) | 966.701 8 |
| Asante (Kingdom) | T2—667 |
| Asbāb wurūd al-Ḥadīth | 297.125 162 |
| Asbestos | 553.672 |
| building material | 691.95 |
| economic geology | 553.672 |
| human toxicology | 615.925 392 24 |
| materials science | 620.195 |
| mining | 622.367 2 |
| pollution | 363.738 494 |
| law | 344.046 335 |
| *see also* Pollution | |
| public safety | 363.179 1 |
| *see also* Hazardous materials | |
| technology | 666.72 |
| textiles | 677.51 |
| *see also* Textiles | |
| Asbestos (Quebec : Regional County Municipality) | T2—714 573 |
| Asbestos paper | 676.289 |
| Asbestosis | |
| medicine | 616.244 |
| *see also* Respiratory tract diseases — humans | |
| workers' compensation law | 344.021 8 |
| Ascariasis | |
| incidence | 614.555 4 |
| medicine | 616.965 4 |
| *see also* Communicable diseases — humans | |
| Ascension Day | 263.93 |
| *see also* Ascensiontide | |
| Ascension Island (Atlantic Ocean) | T2—973 |
| Ascension of Jesus Christ | 232.97 |
| Ascension of Mary | 232.914 |
| Ascension Parish (La.) | T2—763 19 |
| Ascensiontide | 263.93 |
| devotional literature | 242.36 |
| music | 781.728 |
| sermons | 252.63 |
| Ascent to Heaven of Muḥammad | 297.633 |
| Asceticism | 204.47 |
| Buddhism | 294.344 47 |
| Christianity | 248.47 |
| Hinduism | 294.544 7 |
| Islam | 297.576 |
| Sufi | 297.446 |
| Judaism | 296.7 |
| Aschaffenburg (Germany) | T2—433 31 |
| Aschelminthes | 592.5 |
| paleozoology | 562.5 |
| Ascidiacea | 596.2 |

| | |
|---|---|
| Asclepiadaceae | 583.93 |
| Ascobolus | 579.578 |
| Ascoli Piceno (Italy : | |
| Province) | T2—456 75 |
| ancient | T2—374 8 |
| Ascomycetes | 579.56 |
| Ascomycotina | 579.56 |
| Ascophyllum | 579.888 |
| Ascothoracica | 595.35 |
| ASEAN | 341.247 3 |
| public administration | 352.115 9 |
| Asepsis | |
| obstetrics | 618.8 |
| public health | 614.48 |
| surgery | 617.910 1 |
| Asexual reproduction | 571.89 |
| microorganisms | 571.842 9 |
| plants | 575.49 |
| Asexuality | 306.76 |
| Asexuals | 306.76 |
| | T1—086 6 |
| psychology | 155.34 |
| social services | 362.896 |
| women | |
| social services | 362.839 6 |
| young people | |
| social services | 362.786 |
| Ash trays | |
| automobile | 629.277 |
| manufacturing | 688.4 |
| Ash Wednesday | 263.925 |
| devotional literature | 242.35 |
| sermons | 252.625 |
| Ashante language | 496.338 5 |
| | T6—963 385 |
| Ashanti | 966.701 8 |
| Ashanti (African people) | T5—963 385 |
| Ashanti (Kingdom) | T2—667 |
| Ashburton District (N.Z.) | T2—938 6 |
| Ashe County (N.C.) | T2—730 835 |
| Ashes (Trees) | 583.87 |
| forestry | 634.973 87 |
| Asheville (N.C.) | T2—756 88 |
| Ashfield (England) | T2—425 25 |
| Ashford (England : | |
| Borough) | T2—422 392 |
| Ashkenazic liturgy | 296.45 |
| Ashland County (Ohio) | T2—771 29 |
| Ashland County (Wis.) | T2—775 21 |
| Ashley County (Ark.) | T2—767 83 |
| Ashoka, King of Magadha | |
| Indian history | 934.045 |
| Ashtabula County (Ohio) | T2—771 34 |
| Ashuapmushuam Wildlife | |
| Reserve (Quebec) | T2—714 142 |
| Ashur (Extinct city) | T2—354 |
| 'Āshūrā' | 297.36 |
| Asia | 950 |
| | T2—5 |
| geography | 915 |
| military operations | |
| World War I | 940.415 |
| travel | 915.04 |
| Asia (Roman diocese) | 939.2 |
| | T2—392 |
| Asia (Roman province) | T2—392 3 |
| Asia, Central | 958 |
| | T2—58 |
| Asia, Southeastern | 959 |
| | T2—59 |
| Asia Minor | 956.1 |
| | T2—561 |
| ancient | 939.2 |
| | T2—392 |
| Asian Americans | T5—950 73 |
| education | 371.829 950 73 |
| Asian Arctic seawaters | 551.461 325 |
| | T2—163 25 |
| Asian flower arrangements | 745.922 5 |
| Asian intergovernmental | |
| organizations | 341.247 |
| Asiana (Roman diocese) | 939.2 |
| | T2—392 |
| Asians | T5—95 |
| Asiatic cholera | |
| incidence | 614.514 |
| medicine | 616.932 |
| *see also* Communicable | |
| diseases — humans | |
| Asiatic elephant | 599.676 |
| Asilidae | 595.773 |
| ASL (Sign language) | 419.7 |
| | T6—999 87 |
| Asmā' al-Ruwāh | 297.125 264 |
| Asmara (Eritrea) | T2—635 |
| Asocial people | 305.568 |
| | T1—086 92 |
| Aśoka, King of Magadha | |
| Indian history | 934.045 |
| Asotin County (Wash.) | T2—797 42 |
| Asp (Viper) | 597.963 6 |
| Asparagaceae | 584.355 |
| Asparagus | 641.353 1 |
| botany | 584.355 |
| commercial processing | 664.805 31 |
| cooking | 641.653 1 |

Asparagus (continued)
food     641.353 1
garden crop     635.31
Aspect (Grammar)     415.63
specific languages     T4—563
Aspect-oriented programming     005.117
Aspects (Astrology)     133.530 44
Aspens     583.65
Asperger syndrome
medicine     616.858 832
pediatrics     618.928 588 32
Aspergillus     579.565 7
Asphalt     553.27
building materials     691.96
economic geology     553.27
materials science     620.196
mining     622.337
petroleum product     665.538 8
processing     665.4
Asphalt concrete     666.893
road engineering     625.85
Asphalt pavements     625.85
Asphyxia
medicine     617.18
Asphyxiating gases
human toxicology     615.91
Aspidobothria     592.4
Aspidochirotacea     593.96
Aspidocotylea     592.4
Aspidogastrea     592.48
Aspirin     615.313 7
Assa-Zag (Morocco)     T2—646 8
Assam (India)     T2—541 62
Assamese     T5—914 51
Assamese language     491.451
    T6—914 51
Assamese literature     891.451
Assassination     364.152 4
law     345.025 24
Assateague Island (Md. and
Va.)     T2—752 21
Assault and battery     364.155 5
law     345.025 55
criminal law     345.025 55
torts     346.033
social welfare     362.885
Assaying
metallurgy     669.92
Assemblage
arts     702.814
Assemblers (Computer programs)     005.456
Assemblies (Legislative bodies)     328
Assemblies of God     289.94
Assembling machines     670.427

Assembling products     670.42
factory engineering     670.42
production management     658.533
Assembly languages     005.136
Assembly-line methods     670.42
production management     658.533
technology     670.42
Assertiveness training
applied psychology     158.2
Asses     636.18
animal husbandry     636.18
zoology     599.665
Assessment tests
education     371.262
Assimilation (Physiology)
humans     612.39
Assimilation (Sociology)     303.482
Assiniboine Indians     T5—975 24
Assiniboine language     497.524
    T6—975 24
Assiniboine River (Sask.
and Man.)     T2—712 73
Assistant teachers     371.141 24
Assisted living     362.61
Assisted suicide
criminology     364.152 3
law     345.025 23
ethics     179.7
    *see also* Right to die — ethics
medical ethics     179.7
Associate-degree nurses     610.730 92
role and function     610.730 692
Association     302.3
Association analysis     519.537
Association football     796.334
electronic games     794.863 34
Association of ideas
psychology     153.22
Association of South East Asian
Nations     341.247 3
public administration     352.115 9
Associationism
psychological system     150.194 4
Associations     060
fraternal organizations     369
Associations for religious work     206.5
Christianity     267
Judaism     296.67
Associative algebras     512.46
Associative learning
psychology     153.152 6
Associative memory     004.5

Associative processing 004.35
  *see also* Processing modes —
    computer science
Associative processors 004.35
  engineering 621.391
  *see also* Processing modes —
    computer science
Associative rings 512.46
Assomption (Quebec :
  Regional County
  Municipality) T2—714 416
Assumption of Mary 232.914
Assumption Parish (La.) T2—763 43
Assurance 368
  *see also* Insurance
Assyria 935.03
 T2—35
  Mesopotamian history 935.03
  Middle Eastern history 939.402
  Palestinian history 933.03
Assyrian Church of the East 281.8
  *see also* Eastern churches
Assyrian dialect 492.17
 T6—921
Assyrian literature 892.1
Assyrians T5—921
Assyro-Babylonian language 492.1
 T6—921
Assyro-Babylonian literature 892.1
Astatine 546.735
Asterales 583.99
Asteridae 583.9
Asterinales 579.564
Asteroidea 593.93
Asteroids 523.44
 T2—992 4
  astrology 133.539 8
Asterozoa 593.93
  paleozoology 563.93
Asters 635.933 99
  botany 583.99
  floriculture 635.933 99
Asthma
  medicine 616.238
  *see also* Respiratory tract
    diseases — humans
  pediatrics 618.922 38
Asti (Italy : Province) T2—451 5
  ancient T2—371 7
Astigmatism
  optometry 617.755
  *see also* Eye diseases —
    humans
Astrakhan (Russia : Oblast) T2—474 8

Astrakhanskaĩa oblast'
  (Russia) T2—474 8
Astral projection 133.95
Astrapotheria 569.62
Astrobiology 576.839
Astrodomes 796.068
  architecture 725.827
Astrolatry 202.12
Astrologers 133.509 2
Astrology 133.5
  natural 520
Astrology and religion 201.613 35
  Christianity 261.513
Astromechanics
  engineering 629.411
Astrometry 522
Astronautical engineering 629.47
  military 623.69
Astronautical engineers 629.409 2
Astronautics 629.4
Astronauts 629.450 092
  selection and training 629.450 7
Astronavigation 527
Astronomers 520.92
Astronomical almanacs 528
Astronomical geography 525
Astronomical instruments 522.2
Astronomical interpretation
  Bible 220.68
Astronomical observatories 522.1
  architecture 727.552
Astronomy 520
  law 344.095 2
  *see Manual at* 520 vs. 523.1,
    523.112, 523.8
Astronomy and religion 201.652
  Christianity 261.55
  philosophy of religion 215.2
Astrophotography 522.63
Astrophysics 523.01
Asturias (Spain) T2—461 9
Asua language 496.5
 T6—965
Asunción (Paraguay) T2—892 121
Aswān (Egypt : Province) T2—623
Asylum 323.631
  law 342.083
Asymptotic curves 516.362
Asynchronous machinery 621.313 6
Asynchronous transfer mode
  communications engineering 621.382 16
  computer communications 004.66
  engineering 621.398 1
Asyūṭ (Egypt : Province) T2—622

| | |
|---|---|
| Atacama (Chile : Region) | T2—831 4 |
| Atamasco lilies | 584.34 |
| Atascosa County (Tex.) | T2—764 443 |
| Atatürk, Kemal | |
| Turkish history | 956.102 4 |
| Ataxia telangiectasia | |
| medicine | 616.83 |
| *see also* Nervous system | |
| diseases — humans | |
| Atayal (Taiwan people) | T5—992 5 |
| Atchison County (Kan.) | T2—781 36 |
| Atchison County (Mo.) | T2—778 113 |
| Atelinae | 599.858 |
| Athabasca, Lake (Sask. and | |
| Alta.) | T2—712 41 |
| Athabascan languages | 497.2 |
| Athabaska River (Alta.) | T2—712 32 |
| Athanasian Creed | 238.144 |
| Athapascan-Eyak languages | 497.2 |
| Athapascan Indians | T5—972 |
| Athapascan languages | 497.2 |
| | T6—972 |
| Athapaskan languages | 497.2 |
| | T6—972 |
| Atharvaveda | 294.592 15 |
| Atheism | 211.8 |
| Christian polemics | 239.7 |
| Atheistic religions | 201.4 |
| Atheists | 211.809 2 |
| Athelstan, King of England | |
| English history | 942.017 1 |
| Athenian supremacy | 938.04 |
| Athens (Ga.) | T2—758 18 |
| Athens (Greece) | T2—495 12 |
| ancient | T2—385 |
| Athens County (Ohio) | T2—771 97 |
| Atheriniformes | 597.66 |
| paleozoology | 567.66 |
| Atherosclerosis | |
| medicine | 616.136 |
| *see also* Cardiovascular | |
| diseases — humans | |
| Atherton (Qld.) | T2—943 6 |
| Athletes | 796.092 |
| health | 613.711 |
| occupational ethics | 174.979 6 |
| physical fitness | 613.711 |
| *see Manual at* 796.092 | |
| Athlete's foot | |
| medicine | 616.579 |
| *see also* Skin diseases — | |
| humans | |
| Athletic club buildings | |
| architecture | 725.85 |

| | |
|---|---|
| Athletic fields | 796.420 68 |
| area planning | 711.558 |
| Athletic games | 796 |
| Athletic garments | 796 |
| Athletic gloves and mitts | |
| manufacturing technology | 685.43 |
| Athletic injuries | |
| incidence | 614.3 |
| medicine | 617.102 7 |
| Athletic services | |
| armed forces | 355.346 |
| Athletic sports | 796 |
| Athletics (Sports) | 796 |
| Athletics (Track and field) | 796.42 |
| Athos (Greece) | T2—495 65 |
| Atjeh (Indonesia) | T2—598 11 |
| Atkinson County (Ga.) | T2—758 822 |
| Atlanta (Ga.) | T2—758 231 |
| Atlanta Campaign, 1864 | 973.737 1 |
| Atlantic City (N.J.) | T2—749 85 |
| Atlantic Coast (Nicaragua) | T2—728 53 |
| Atlantic Coastal Plain | T2—75 |
| Maryland | T2—752 1 |
| North Carolina | T2—756 1 |
| South Carolina | T2—757 6 |
| United States | T2—75 |
| Virginia | T2—755 1 |
| Atlantic cod | 597.633 |
| Atlantic County (N.J.) | T2—749 84 |
| Atlantic intergovernmental | |
| organizations | 341.243 |
| Atlantic Islands | 997 |
| | T2—97 |
| Atlantic languages (Africa) | 496.32 |
| | T6—963 2 |
| Atlantic Ocean | 551.461 3 |
| | T2—163 |
| World War II | 940.542 93 |
| *see Manual at* T2—163 and | |
| T2—164, T2—165 | |
| Atlantic Provinces | 971.5 |
| | T2—715 |
| Atlantic region | T2—182 1 |
| Atlántico (Colombia : | |
| Dept.) | T2—861 15 |
| Atlántida (Honduras) | T2—728 312 |
| Atlantis | 001.94 |
| *see also* Legendary places | |
| Atlas Mountains | T2—64 |
| Atlases | 912 |
| | T1—022 3 |
| cataloging | 025.346 |
| geography | 912 |
| library treatment | 025.176 |

58

Atlases (continued)
  pictorial works        T1—022 2
  *see Manual at* T1—0222 vs.
    T1—0223
Atmosphere        551.5
                T2—161
  ecology        579.175
  meteorology        551.5
  public administration        354.37
Atmosphere-land interactions    551.523
Atmosphere-ocean interactions    551.524 6
Atmosphere-water interactions    551.524
Atmospheric disturbances    551.55
Atmospheric electricity    551.563
Atmospheric entry
  manned space flight    629.458 8
Atmospheric formations    551.551
Atmospheric ionization    538.767
Atmospheric nucleation    551.574 1
Atmospheric optics    551.565
Atmospheric pressure    551.54
Atmospheric radiation
  meteorology    551.527 3
Atmospheric thermodynamics
  space flight    629.415 2
Atoka County (Okla.)    T2—766 66
Atolls    551.424
                T2—142
  geography    910.914 2
  geomorphology    551.424
  physical geography    910.021 42
Atomic bomb    355.825 119
  *see also* Nuclear weapons
Atomic emission spectroscopy    543.52
Atomic energy    333.792 4
  economics    333.792 4
  law    343.092 5
  physics    539.7
Atomic mass
  chemistry    541.242
Atomic number    541.242
Atomic physics    539.7
  astronomy    523.019 7
Atomic spectroscopy    543.5
Atomic structure    539.14
  chemistry    541.24
Atomic weapons    355.825 119
  *see also* Nuclear weapons
Atomic weight    541.242
Atomism    146.5
Atoms    539.7
  theoretical chemistry    541.24
Atonality    781.267

Atonement    202.2
  Christianity    234.5
  Islam    297.22
  Judaism    296.32
Atonement Day
  Judaism    296.432
  liturgy    296.453 2
Atonement of Jesus Christ    232.3
Atopic dermatitis
  medicine    616.51
  *see also* Skin diseases —
    humans
ATP (Triphosphate)    572.475
Aṭrāf    297.125 62
Atrato River (Colombia)    T2—861 51
Atrial fibrillation
  medicine    616.128
  *see also* Cardiovascular
    diseases - - humans
Atrium buildings    720.48
  architecture    720.48
  construction    690.38
Atrocities
  World War I    940.405
  World War II    940.540 5
Atropine
  human toxicology    615.952 395 2
  pharmacology    615.323 952
Atsina Indians    T5—973 54
Atsina language    497.354
                T6—973 54
Attaché cases
  manufacturing technology    685.51
Attachment (Law)    347.077
  private law    346.077
Attack (Military science)    355.4
  tactics    355.422
Attack (Music)    781.235
Attack airplanes    358.428 3
  engineering    623.746 3
  military equipment    358.428 3
Attala County (Miss.)    T2—762 644
Attendance officers    371.295
Attention
  psychology
    learning    153.153 2
    perception    153.733
Attention deficit disorder
  medicine    616.858 9
  pediatrics    618.928 589
Attention-deficit-disordered
  children
  education    371.94

| | |
|---|---|
| Attenuators | |
| electronic circuits | 621.381 536 2 |
| Attica (Greece) | T2—495 12 |
| ancient | T2—385 |
| Attics | 643.5 |
| Attie language | 496.337 |
| | T6—963 37 |
| Attikē (Greece) | T2—495 12 |
| ancient | T2—385 |
| Attitude training | |
| personnel management | 658.312 44 |
| executives | 658.407 124 4 |
| public administration | 352.669 |
| Attitudes | 152.4 |
| psychology | 152.4 |
| sociology | 303.38 |
| Attoni, House of | |
| Tuscan history | 945.503 |
| Attorneys | 340.092 |
| *see also* Lawyers | |
| Attorneys general | |
| advisory opinions | 348.05 |
| United States | 348.735 |
| public administration | 353.422 93 |
| Attracting birds | 639.978 |
| zoology | 598.072 34 |
| Attraction (Social psychology) | 302.13 |
| Attributes of God | 212.7 |
| Christianity | 231.4 |
| comparative religion | 202.112 |
| Islam | 297.211 2 |
| Judaism | 296.311 2 |
| philosophy of religion | 212.7 |
| Attributes of the Church | 262.72 |
| Attribution (Social psychology) | 302.12 |
| Au Sable River (Mich.) | T2—774 7 |
| Aube (France) | T2—443 31 |
| Auckland (N.Z.) | T2—932 4 |
| Auckland, George Eden, Earl of | |
| Indian history | 954.031 4 |
| Auckland City (N.Z.) | T2—932 4 |
| Auckland Islands (N.Z.) | T2—939 9 |
| Auckland Province (N.Z.) | T2—931 2 |
| Auckland Region (N.Z.) | T2—932 |
| Auction bridge | 795.414 |
| Auction catalogs | T1—029 |
| bibliographic materials | |
| alphabetic subject | 017.7 |
| classed | 017.3 |
| bibliography | 017.3 |
| commerce | 381.170 29 |
| Auctions | 381.17 |
| law | 343.081 1 |
| management | 658.877 |
| *see also* Commerce | |
| Aude (France) | T2—448 7 |
| Audience participation programs | 791.443 |
| radio | 791.443 |
| television performances | 791.453 |
| Audiences | 302.33 |
| mass media | 302.23 |
| Audio books | |
| bibliographies | 011.384 |
| Audio input devices | |
| computer science | 006.45 |
| engineering | 621.399 4 |
| Audio-lingual language study | 418 |
| specific languages | T4—83 |
| Audio output devices | |
| computer science | 006.5 |
| engineering | 621.399 |
| Audio publications | 070.579 |
| Audio systems | |
| automobile | 629.277 |
| Audio systems engineering | 621.382 8 |
| recording and reproduction | 621.389 3 |
| Audiobooks | |
| bibliographies | 011.384 |
| Audiologists | 617.809 2 |
| Audiology | 617.8 |
| pediatrics | 618.920 978 9 |
| Audiotex | 384.646 |
| Audiovisual engineering | 621.389 7 |
| Audiovisual equipment | |
| libraries | |
| management | 022.9 |
| museology | 069.32 |
| Audiovisual materials | |
| art appreciation use | 701.1 |
| bibliographies | 011.37 |
| cataloging | 025.347 |
| Christian religious education | 268.635 |
| instructional use | 371.335 |
| library treatment | 025.177 |
| primary education | 372.133 5 |
| reviews | 028.137 |
| Audiovisual treatment | T1—020 8 |
| Auditing | 657.45 |
| accounting | 657.45 |
| government accounts | 657.835 045 |
| Auditoriums | |
| architecture | 725.83 |

Auditory canal diseases
  medicine 617.83
  *see also* Ear diseases —
    humans
Auditory canals
  human physiology 612.851
  medicine 617.83
Auditory memory 153.133
Auditory perception
  psychology 152.15
Auditory tube diseases
  medicine 617.86
  *see also* Ear diseases —
    humans
Auditory tubes
  human physiology 612.854
  medicine 617.86
Audits 657.45
  accounting 657.45
    government accounts 657.835 045
Audrain County (Mo.) T2—778 332
Audubon County (Iowa) T2—777 486
Auglaize County (Ohio) T2—771 43
Augmented reality 006.8
Augrabies National Park
  (South Africa) T2—687 12
Augsburg (Germany) T2—433 75
Augsburg, War of the League of,
  1688–1697 940.252 5
  North American history 973.25
Augsburg Confession 238.41
Augusan del Norte
  (Philippines) T2—599 7
Augusan del Sur
  (Philippines) T2—599 7
Augusta (Ga.) T2—758 64
Augusta (Me.) T2—741 6
Augusta County (Va.) T2—755 916
Augusta Praetoria (Italy) T2—372 211
Augusta Taurinorum (Italy) T2—372 221
Augustana Evangelical Lutheran
  Church 284.133 3
  *see also* Lutheran church
Augustinians 255.4
  church history 271.4
Auks 598.33
Aunis (France) T2—446 4
Aunts 306.87
  T1—085
Aura
  human physiology 612.014 2
  parapsychology 133.892

Aural nervous system
  human anatomy 611.85
  human physiology 612.85
  medicine 617.886
Aural nervous system diseases
  medicine 617.886
  *see also* Nervous system
    diseases — humans
Aurangzeb, Emperor of
  Hindustan
  Indian history 954.025 8
Aurich (Germany :
  Landkreis) T2—435 917
Auricle diseases (Ears)
  medicine 617.82
  *see also* Ear diseases —
    humans
Auricle diseases (Heart)
  medicine 616.12
  *see also* Cardiovascular
    diseases — humans
Auricles (Ears)
  human anatomy 611.85
  human physiology 612.851
  medicine 617.82
Auricles (Heart) 573.17
  human anatomy 611.12
  human physiology 612.17
  medicine 616.12
  physiology 573.17
  *see also* Cardiovascular system
Auriculas 635.933 675
  botany 583.675
  floriculture 635.933 675
Aurignacian culture 930.128
Aurora County (S.D.) T2—783 375
Auroras (Geomagnetism) 538.768
Auschwitz (Extermination camp) 940.531 853 858
Auscultation
  medicine 616.075 44
Ausdehnungslehre 512.5
Aust-Agder fylke (Norway) T2—483 1
Austin (Tex.) T2—764 31
Austin County (Tex.) T2—764 252
Austral Islands T2—962 2
Australasia T2—9
Australasian possums 599.23
Australia 994
  T2—94
Australian Alps (N.S.W.
  and Vic.) T2—944
Australian bass 597.73
Australian Capital Territory T2—947
Australian cattle dog 636.737

| | |
|---|---|
| Australian Country Party | 324.294 04 |
| Australian Democrats (Political party) | 324.294 095 |
| Australian football | 796.336 |
| Australian football players | 796.336 092 |
| Australian grayling | 597.55 |
| Australian Labor Party | 324.294 07 |
| Australian languages | 499.15 |
| | T6—991 5 |
| Australian Liberal Party | 324.294 05 |
| Australian literature (English) | 820 |
| Australian salmon | 597.7 |
| culture | 639.377 |
| Australian school shark | 597.34 |
| Australians | T5—24 |
| Australoid race | T5—991 5 |
| Australopithecines | 569.93 |
| Australopithecus | 569.93 |
| Austria | 943.6 |
| | T2—436 |
| ancient | 936.36 |
| Austrian Empire | 943.604 |
| | T2—436 |
| Austrian People's Party | 324.243 604 |
| Austrian school (Economics) | 330.157 |
| Austrian Succession, War of the, 1740–1748 | 940.253 2 |
| North American history | 973.26 |
| Austrian winter peas | 633.369 |
| botany | 583.74 |
| Austrians | T5—36 |
| Austro-Asiatic languages | T6—959 3 |
| Austro-Asiatic peoples | T5—959 3 |
| Austro-Hungarian Monarchy | 943.604 4 |
| | T2—436 |
| Austrian history | 943.604 4 |
| Hungarian history | 943.904 3 |
| Austro-Italian front World War I | 940.414 5 |
| Austro-Prussian War, 1866 | 943.076 |
| Austroasiatic languages | 495.93 |
| | T6—959 3 |
| Austroasiatic literatures | 895.93 |
| Austroasiatic peoples | T5—959 3 |
| Austronesian languages | 499.2 |
| | T6—992 |
| Austronesian literatures | 899.2 |
| Ausuittuq (Nunavut) | T2—719 52 |
| Autarchy (Absolute monarchy) | 321.6 |
| Autarchy (Economic self-sufficiency) | 338.9 |
| Autauga County (Ala.) | T2—761 463 |

| | |
|---|---|
| Autecology | 577.26 |
| animals | 591.7 |
| microorganisms | 579.17 |
| plants | 581.7 |
| *see Manual at* 577.3–.7 vs. 579–590 | |
| Authentic Hadith | 297.125 21 |
| Authenticating | |
| arts | 702.88 |
| Author catalogs | 025.315 |
| bibliography | 017 |
| library science | 025.315 |
| Author-title catalogs | 025.315 |
| bibliography | 017 |
| library science | 025.315 |
| Author-title indexing | 025.322 |
| Authoritarian government | 321.9 |
| Authoritarianism | 320.53 |
| Authority | 303.36 |
| ethical systems | 171.1 |
| Christianity | 241.2 |
| religion | 206.5 |
| Christianity | 262.8 |
| Judaism | 296.67 |
| social control | 303.36 |
| Authority control | |
| cataloging | 025.322 2 |
| Authority files | |
| cataloging | 025.322 2 |
| Authorized version (Bible) | 220.520 3 |
| Authors | |
| relations with publishers | 070.52 |
| Authors (Literature) | 809 |
| collected biography | 809 |
| specific literatures | T3B—09 |
| Authorship of Bible | 220.66 |
| Authorship techniques | 808.02 |
| Autism | |
| medicine | 616.858 82 |
| pediatrics | 618.928 588 2 |
| special education | 371.94 |
| Autistic disorder | |
| medicine | 616.858 82 |
| Autobiographical fiction | 808.838 2 |
| history and criticism | 809.382 |
| specific literatures | T3B—308 2 |
| individual authors | T3A—3 |
| Autobiography | 920 |
| | T1—092 |
| arts | 700.45 |
| | T3C—35 |
| literary form | 809.935 92 |
| specific literatures | T3B—094 92 |

Autobiography (continued)
  literature | 808.803 5
    history and criticism | 809.933 5
    specific literatures | T3B—080 35
      history and
        criticism | T3B—093 5
Autocorrelation | 519.537
Autocracy (Absolute monarchy) | 321.6
Autogenic training
  medicine | 615.851 22
Autogiros
  engineering | 629.133 35
Autograph scores | 780
  treatises | 780.262
Autographs | 929.88
Autoharps | 787.75
  *see also* Stringed instruments
Autoimmune diseases | 571.973
  animals | 571.973
  humans | 362.196 978
    incidence | 614.599 38
    medicine | 616.978
    social services | 362.196 978
Autoimmunity | 571.973
  incidence | 614.599 38
  medicine | 616.978
Automata | 511.35
  artificial intelligence | 006.3
Automated information systems | 025.04
  *see also* Information storage
    and retrieval systems
Automatic abstracting
  information science | 025.410 285 635
Automatic cameras | 771.32
Automatic control engineering | 629.8
Automatic data collection
  systems | 006.2
  engineering | 621.399
Automatic data processing | 004
   | T1—028 5
Automatic identification and data
  capture | 006.24
  computer science | 006.24
  engineering | 621.384 192
Automatic movements
  psychology | 152.32
Automatic piloting
  aircraft | 629.132 6
Automatic pilots
  aircraft | 629.135 2
Automatic pistols | 683.432 5
  *see also* Pistols

Automatic rifles
  military engineering | 623.442 4
  military equipment | 355.824 24
Automatic speech recognition | 006.454
Automatic sprinkler systems
  fire technology | 628.925 2
Automatic text summarization
  information science | 025.410 285 635
Automatic theorem proving | 511.360 285 63
Automatic train control
  engineering | 625.27
Automatic transmissions
  automotive engineering | 629.244 6
Automatic writing (Spiritualism) | 133.932
Automation
  agricultural economics | 338.161
  control engineering | 629.8
  economics | 338.064
  manufacturing technology | 670.427
  mineral industries | 338.26
  production management | 658.514
  secondary industries | 338.454
  social effects | 303.483 4
Automation engineers | 629.809 2
Automation training
  personnel management | 658.312 43
Automatons | 629.8
Automobile accidents | 363.125
  *see also* Highway safety
Automobile bodies | 629.26
Automobile cars (Railroad) | 385.34
  engineering | 625.24
  *see also* Rolling stock
Automobile driving | 629.283
  law | 343.094 6
  recreation | 796.7
Automobile engineers | 629.222 092
Automobile industry | 338.476 292 22
  law | 343.078 629 222
Automobile insurance | 368.092
  inland marine | 368.232
  law | 346.086 092
  liability | 368.572
Automobile noise | 363.741
  *see also* Noise
Automobile parking | 388.474
  *see also* Parking facilities
Automobile racers | 796.720 92
Automobile racing | 796.72
  electronic games | 794.867 2
Automobile rallies | 796.73
Automobile registration | 354.765 284
  law | 343.094 4
  public administration | 354.765 284

Automobile safety    363.125
   *see also* Highway safety
Automobile theft    364.162 862 922 2
   law    345.026 286 292 22
Automobile transportation    388.321
   engineering    629.222
   law    343.094
   public administration    354.765
   safety    363.125
     *see also* Highway safety
   transportation services    388.321
   urban    388.413 21
Automobiles    388.342
   engineering    629.222
   law    343.094 4
   licenses    354.765 284
     law    343.094 4
   military engineering    623.747 2
   production economics    338.476 292 22
   repair    629.287 2
   sports    796.7
   theft of    364.162 862 922 2
     law    345.026 286 292 22
   transportation services    388.342
   travel    910
   *see Manual at* 629.046 vs. 388
Automorphic functions    515.9
   calculus    515.9
   number theory    512.7
Automorphisms    511.326
   geometry    516.1
   topological algebras    512.55
Automotive electronics    629.272
Automotive engineering    629.2
Automotive industry    338.476 292
   law    343.078 629 2
Automotive vehicles    388.34
   engineering    629.2
   law    343.094 4
   military engineering    623.747
   production economics    338.476 292
   public administration    354.765
   repair    629.287
   safety    363.125
     *see also* Highway safety
   safety engineering    629.204 2
   sports    796.7
   transportation services    388.34
   *see Manual at* 629.046 vs. 388
Autonomic nervous system
   human anatomy    611.83
   human physiology    612.89
   medicine    616.856 9

Autonomic nervous system
   diseases
   medicine    616.856 9
     *see also* Nervous system
     diseases — humans
Autonomous agencies
   public administration    352.264
Autonomous Communities
   (Spain)    321.023
   *see also* States (Members of
   federations)
Autonomous Republics (Soviet
   Union)    321.023
   *see also* States (Members of
   federations)
Autonomy in education
   higher education    378.1
   public policy    379.15
Autonomy of states    320.15
Autopilots
   aircraft    629.135 2
Autopsy
   forensic medicine    614.1
   medicine    616.075 9
Autoregression    519.536
Autumn    508.2
   music    781.524 6
   *see also* Seasons
Autumn-flowering plants    581.43
   floriculture    635.953
Auvergnat dialect (Occitan
   language)    T6—491
Auvergne (France)    T2—445 9
Auxiliaries (Foreign troops)    355.359
Auxiliary party organizations    324.3
Auxiliary power systems
   spacecraft    629.474 4
Auxiliary procedures    T1—028
Auxiliary routes
   marine    387.523
Auxiliary storage
   computer science    004.56
   engineering    621.397 6
Auxiliary techniques    T1—028
Auyuittuq National Park
   (Nunavut)    T2—719 52
Available light photography    778.76
Avalanches    551.307
   snow    551.578 48
Avant-garde arts    700.411
      T3C—11
Avant-garde jazz    781.656

| | |
|---|---|
| Avant-garde literary works | 808.887 |
| history and criticism | 809.987 |
| specific literatures | T3B—807 |
| individual authors | T3A—8 |
| Avant-garde music | 780.904 |
| Avar language | 499.964 |
| | T6—999 64 |
| Avaric language | 499.964 |
| | T6—999 64 |
| Avarice | 178 |
| moral theology | 205.68 |
| *see also* Vices | |
| Avaro-Andi-Dido languages | 499.964 |
| | T6—999 64 |
| Ave Maria | 242.74 |
| Aveiro (Portugal : District) | T2—469 34 |
| Avellino (Italy : Province) | T2—457 21 |
| ancient | T2—377 31 |
| Aveneae | 584.9 |
| Average costs | 338.514 2 |
| management | 658.155 3 |
| Averaging | 519.533 |
| Aversion | |
| psychology | 152.4 |
| Avery County (N.C.) | T2—756 862 |
| Aves | 598 |
| Avesta | 295.82 |
| Avestan language | 491.52 |
| | T6—915 2 |
| Avestan literature | 891.52 |
| Aveyron (France) | T2—447 4 |
| Aviaries | 598.073 |
| animal husbandry | 636.68 |
| architecture | 728.927 |
| construction | 690.892 7 |
| Aviary birds | 636.68 |
| *see also* Birds | |
| Aviation | 387.7 |
| *see also* Air transportation | |
| Aviation fuel | 665.538 25 |
| Aviation insurance | 368.093 |
| inland marine | 368.24 |
| liability | 368.576 |
| Aviation law | 343.097 |
| Aviation medicine | 616.980 213 |
| Aviation meteorology | 629.132 4 |
| Aviation psychology | 155.965 |
| Avignon (France) | T2—449 22 |
| Avignon (Quebec) | T2—714 783 |
| Avila (Spain : Province) | T2—463 59 |
| Avila Camacho, Manuel | |
| Mexican history | 972.082 6 |
| Avionics | 629.135 |
| military aircraft | 623.746 049 |
| Avitaminosis | |
| medicine | 616.39 |
| *see also* Digestive system | |
| diseases — humans | |
| Avocados | 641.346 53 |
| agriculture | 634.653 |
| botany | 583.23 |
| commercial processing | 664.804 653 |
| cooking | 641.646 53 |
| food | 641.346 53 |
| Avodah Zarah | 296.123 4 |
| Babylonian Talmud | 296.125 4 |
| Mishnah | 296.123 4 |
| Palestinian Talmud | 296.124 4 |
| Avon (England) | T2—423 9 |
| Avon, River (Gloucestershire-Bristol, England) | T2—423 9 |
| Avon, River (Leicestershire-Gloucestershire, England) | T2—424 4 |
| Avon, River (Wiltshire-Dorset, England) | T2—423 19 |
| Avot | 296.123 47 |
| Avoyelles Parish (La.) | T2—763 71 |
| Awadhi dialect | 491.492 |
| | T6—914 92 |
| Awadhi literature | 891.492 |
| Awadhi-speaking people | T5—914 92 |
| Awards | T1—079 |
| armed forces | 355.134 |
| biography | 355.134 092 |
| *see also* Military commemorations | |
| orders and decorations | 929.81 |
| research | 001.44 |
| Awnings | 645.3 |
| household management | 645.3 |
| manufacturing technology | 684 |
| Axes | 621.93 |
| art metalwork | 739.72 |
| Axholme, Isle of (England) | T2—428 32 |
| Axiology | 121.8 |
| Axiom of choice | 511.3 |
| Axiomatic set theory | 511.322 |
| Axioms | 160 |
| mathematical logic | 511.3 |
| philosophical logic | 160 |
| Axis Powers (World War II group) | 940.533 4 |
| Axles | 621.823 |
| automotive engineering | 629.245 |
| railroad engineering | 625.21 |
| Axolotl | 597.858 |

Axons
  human cytology    612.810 46
Ayacucho (Peru : Dept.)    T2—852 9
Ayatollahs    297.092
  biography    297.092
    specific sects    297.8
  role and function    297.61
  *see Manual at* 297.092
Aydın İli (Turkey)    T2—562 6
  ancient    T2—392 3
Aye-ayes    599.83
  conservation technology    639.979 83
  resource economics    333.959 83
Ayers Rock (N.T.)    T2—942 91
Ayers Rock-Mount Olga
  National Park (N.T.)    T2—942 91
Aylesbury Vale (England)    T2—425 93
Aylwin Azócar, Patricio
  Chilean history    983.066 1
Aymara Indians    T5—983 24
Aymara language    498.324
    T6—983 24
Aymara literature    898.324
Aymaran languages    498.324
    T6—983 24
Ayrshire (Scotland)    T2—414 6
Ayrshire cattle    636.225
Aysen (Chile : Province)    T2—836 22
Aythya    598.414
Ayub Khan, Mohammad
  Pakistani history    954.904 5
Ayurvedic medicine
  therapeutic system    615.538
Ayutthaya (Kingdom)    959.302 3
Az Zarqā' (Jordan :
  Province)    T2—569 593
  ancient    T2—335 93
Azad Kashmir    T2—549 138
Azaleas    635.933 66
  botany    583.66
  floriculture    635.933 66
Āzarbāyjān-i Bākhtarī (Iran)    T2—554
Āzarbāyjān-i Khāvarī (Iran)    T2—553
Azcona H., José
  Honduran history    972.830 533
Azerbaijan    947.54
    T2—475 4
  ancient    939.534
    T2—395 34
Azerbaijan (Iran)    T2—553
Azerbaijan (Region)    T2—553
  Azerbaijan    T2—475 4
  Iran    T2—553
Azerbaijani    T5—943 61

Azerbaijani language    494.361
    T6—943 61
Azerbaijani literature    894.361
Azilal (Morocco : Province)    T2—644
Azimuth    526.63
'Azīz (Hadith)    297.125 24
Azlon
  textiles    677.472
Azo compounds    547.043
  chemical engineering    661.894
Azo-oxy dyes    667.253
Azo-tetrazo dyes    667.253
Azores    T2—469 9
Azospirillum    579.323
Azov, Sea of (Ukraine and    551.461 389
  Russia)    T2—163 89
Aztec calendar    529.329 784 52
Aztec language    497.452
    T6—974 52
Aztec literature    897.452
Aztec period    972.018
Aztecan languages    497.452
    T6—974 52
Aztecs    T5—974 52
Azua (Dominican Republic :
  Province)    T2—729 372
Azuay (Ecuador)    T2—866 24

# B

B cells    571.967
  human immunology    616.079 8
B-flat horns    788.974
  *see also* Brass instruments
B lymphocytes    571.967
  human immunology    616.079 8
Bà Rịa-Vũng Tàu (Vietnam)    T2—597 7
Baalbek (Lebanon)
  ancient    T2—394 4
'Bab el Mandeb    551.461 532
    T2—165 32
Baba Batra    296.123 4
  Babylonian Talmud    296.125 4
  Mishnah    296.123 4
  Palestinian Talmud    296.124 4
Baba Kamma    296.123 4
  Babylonian Talmud    296.125 4
  Mishnah    296.123 4
  Palestinian Talmud    296.124 4
Baba Meẓia    296.123 4
  Babylonian Talmud    296.125 4
  Mishnah    296.123 4
  Palestinian Talmud    296.124 4

Babanango (South Africa : District) T2—684 2

Babangida, Ibrahim Badamosi
  Nigerian history 966.905 3

Babblers 598.834

Babenberg, House of 943.602 3

Babergh (England) T2—426 48

Babi Yar Massacre, 1941 940.531 844 5

Babies 305.232
  T1—083 2
  health 613.043 2
  pediatrics 618.920 2
  psychology 155.422
  *see also* Infants

Bābil (Iraq : Province) T2—567 5

Babine language 497.2

Babirusa 599.633

Babism 297.92

Babists
  biography 297.920 92

Baboons 599.865

Babouvism (Socialist school) 335.2

Babur, Emperor of Hindustan
  Indian history 954.025 2

Baby animals 591.392
  domestic animals 636.07
  mammals 599.139 2

Baby blue-eyes (Plant) 635.933 94
  botany 583.94
  floriculture 635.933 94

Baby food 641.300 832
  commercial preparation 664.62
  cooking 641.562 22
  feeding 649.3
  food 641.300 832

Babylon (Extinct city) T2—355

Babylonia 935.5
  T2—355

Babylonian dialect 492.17
  T6—921

Babylonian Empire 935.502
  Mesopotamian history 935.502
  Middle Eastern history 939.402
  Palestinian history 933.03

Babylonian literature 892.1

Babylonian Talmud 296.125

Babylonians T5—921

Babysitters' handbooks 649.102 48

Bắc Giang (Vietnam : Province) T2—597 2

Bắc Kạn (Vietnam : Province) T2—597 1

Bạc Liêu (Vietnam : Province) T2—597 9

Bắc Ninh (Vietnam : Province) T2—597 2

Baca County (Colo.) T2—788 99

Bacău (Romania : Județ) T2—498 1

Baccarat 795.42

Bachelet, Michelle
  Chilean history 983.066 4

Bachelors 306.815 2
  T1—086 52

Bachelor's degree 378.2

Bacillaceae infections
  incidence 614.512
  medicine 616.931
  *see also* Communicable diseases — humans

Bacillariophyceae 579.85

Bacillary diseases
  incidence 614.512
  medicine 616.931
  *see also* Communicable diseases — humans

Bacillary dysentery
  incidence 614.516
  medicine 616.935 5
  *see also* Communicable diseases — humans

Bacillus 579.362

Back (Body part)
  human anatomy 611.9
  human physiology 612.9
  regional medicine 617.56
  surgery 617.560 59

Back muscles
  human anatomy 611.731

Back play
  American football 796.332 24
  rugby 796.333 26
  soccer 796.334 25

Backache
  medicine 617.564

Backgammon 795.15

Backhand
  tennis 796.342 23

Backpacking 796.51
  equipment technology 688.765 1

Backyards
  biology 578.755 4
  ecology 577.554
  landscape architecture 712.6

Bacon County (Ga.) T2—758 787

Bács-Kiskun Megye (Hungary) T2—439 8

| | |
|---|---|
| Bacteria | 579.3 |
|   medical microbiology | 616.920 1 |
|   paleontology | 561.91 |
|   *see Manual at* 579.3 | |
| Bacteria culture | |
|   biology | 571.638 293 |
| Bacteria-enhanced oil recovery | 622.338 27 |
| Bacterial blood diseases | |
|   incidence | 614.577 |
|   medicine | 616.94 |
|     *see also* Communicable | |
|       diseases — humans | |
| Bacterial counts | |
|   milk processing | 637.127 7 |
| Bacterial diseases | 571.993 |
|   agriculture | 632.32 |
|   animals | 571.993 11 |
|     veterinary medicine | 636.089 692 |
|   humans | 362.196 92 |
|     incidence | 614.57 |
|     medicine | 616.92 |
|     social services | 362.196 92 |
|   plants | 571.993 12 |
|     agriculture | 632.32 |
|   *see also* Communicable | |
|     diseases | |
| Bacterial food poisons | |
|   human toxicology | 615.952 93 |
| Bacterial viruses | 579.26 |
| Bactericides | 668.653 |
|   agricultural use | 632.953 |
|   chemical engineering | 668.653 |
| Bacteriological examination | |
|   medicine | 616.075 81 |
| Bacteriologists | 579.309 2 |
| Bacteriology | 579.3 |
|   medicine | 616.920 1 |
| Bacteriophages | 579.26 |
| Bacteroides | 579.325 |
| Bactria | T2—396 |
| Baculoviridae | 579.243 6 |
| Bad debts | |
|   tax law | 343.052 36 |
| Bad Doberan (Germany : | |
|   Landkreis) | T2—431 74 |
| Badajoz (Spain : Province) | T2—462 7 |
| Baden (Germany) | T2—434 64 |
| Baden (Switzerland : | |
|   Bezirk) | T2—494 566 3 |
| Baden-Baden (Germany) | T2—434 643 |
| Baden-Württemberg | |
|   (Germany) | T2—434 6 |
| Badenoch and Strathspey | |
|   (Scotland) | T2—411 58 |
| Badgers | 599.767 |
| Badges | |
|   armed forces | 355.134 2 |
| Badlands National Park | |
|   (S.D.) | T2—783 93 |
| Badminton | 796.345 |
| Badminton players | 796.345 092 |
| Badui language | 499.223 |
| | T6—992 23 |
| Baetica | T2—366 8 |
| Baffin (Nunavut) | T2—719 52 |
| Baffin Bay | 551.461 327 |
| | T2—163 27 |
| Baffin Island (Nunavut) | T2—719 52 |
| Bafia languages | 496.396 |
| | T6—963 96 |
| Bafokeng (South Africa : | |
|   District) | T2—682 41 |
| Bag lunches | 641.53 |
| Bag papers | 676.287 |
| Bagasse | |
|   fuel technology | 662.88 |
|   plastic technology | 668.411 |
| Bagasse pulp | 676.14 |
| Bagaza, Jean-Baptiste | |
|   Burundi history | 967.572 041 5 |
| Bagēmder (Ethiopia) | T2—634 |
| Baggage cars | 385.33 |
|   engineering | 625.23 |
|   *see also* Rolling stock | |
| Baggage insurance | 368.2 |
| Baggage services | 388.042 |
|   *see also* Passenger services | |
| Baghdād (Iraq : Province) | T2—567 47 |
| Bagheli dialect | 491.492 |
| | T6—914 92 |
| Bagheli literature | 891.492 |
| Bagheli-speaking people | T5—914 92 |
| Bagpipes | 788.49 |
|   instrument | 788.491 9 |
|   music | 788.49 |
|   *see also* Woodwind instruments | |
| Bags | 688.8 |
|   paper | 676.33 |
| Baguios (Hurricanes) | 551.552 |
| Bahai Faith | 297.93 |
| Bahais | |
|   biography | 297.930 92 |
| Bahama Islands | 972.96 |
| | T2—729 6 |
| Bahamas | 972.96 |
| | T2—729 6 |
| Bahamians | T5—969 729 6 |

Bahasa Indonesia 499.221
  T6—992 21
Bahasa Indonesia literature 899.221
Bahasa Kebangsaan 499.28
  T6—992 8
Bahasa Malaysia 499.28
  T6—992 8
Bahasa Malaysia literature 899.28
Bahasa Melayu 499.28
  T6—992 8
Bahá'u'lláh
  works by 297.938 22
Bahāwalpur District
  (Pakistan) T2—549 16
Bahia (Brazil : State) T2—814 2
Bahía Blanca Estuary (Argentina) 551.461 368
  T2—163 68
Bahing-Vayu languages 495.49
  T6—954 9
Bahoruco (Dominican
  Republic : Province) T2—729 326
Bahr al Ahmar (Egypt) T2—623
Baḥr al-Aḥmar (Sudan :
  Province) T2—625
Baḥr al Jabal (Sudan) T2—629 5
Bahrain 953.65
  T2—536 5
  ancient 939.49
  T2—394 9
Bahraini T5—927 536 5
Baie-D'Urfé (Quebec) T2—714 28
Baie-James (Quebec) T2—714 115
Baikal seal 599.792
Bail (Law) 345.056
Bailey County (Tex.) T2—764 844
Bailments 346.025
Bairnsdale (Vic.) T2—945 6
Bait-casting 799.126
Bait fishing 799.122
Bait worm culture 639.75
Baixo Alentejo (Portugal) T2—469 55
Baja California (Mexico) T2—722
Baja California Norte
  (Mexico) T2—722 3
Baja California Sur
  (Mexico) T2—722 4
Baja Verapaz (Guatemala) T2—728 152
Baka (West African people) T5—963 61
Baka language T6—963 61
Baked goods 641.815
  commercial processing 664.752
  home preparation 641.815
Baker County (Fla.) T2—759 13
Baker County (Ga.) T2—758 967

Baker County (Or.) T2—795 75
Baker Lake (Nunavut) T2—719 58
Bakery goods
  commercial processing 664.752
Bakhtīarī va Chahār Mahāll
  (Iran) T2—559 7
Baking
  commercial food preparation 664.02
  home cooking 641.71
Baking powder 664.68
Baking soda
  food technology 664.68
Bakongo (Kingdom) 967.320 1
  T2—673 2
Ba'labakk (Lebanon)
  ancient T2—394 4
Balaena 599.527 6
Balaenidae 599.527
Balaenoptera 599.524
Balaenopteridae 599.524
Balalaikas 787.875
  instrument 787.875 19
  music 787.875
  *see also* Stringed instruments
Balance beam (Gymnastic
  equipment) 796.442
Balance of payments 382.17
  international banking 332.152
  international commerce 382.17
Balance of power 327.112
Balance of trade 382.17
Balance sheets 657.3
  accounting 657.3
  financial management 658.151 2
  investment analysis 332.632 042
Balancing machinery 621.816
Balanopales 583.43
Balanophoraceae 583.88
Balanopsidales 583.43
Balconies 721.84
  architecture 721.84
  construction 690.184
Balcony furniture 645.8
  *see also* Outdoor furniture
Balcony gardening 635.967 1
Bald cypresses 585.5
Bald eagle 598.943
  conservation technology 639.978 943
  resource economics 333.958 943
Baldachins
  church architecture 726.529 3

| | |
|---|---|
| Baldness | |
| medicine | 616.546 |
| *see also* Skin diseases — | |
| humans | |
| Baldwin County (Ala.) | T2—761 21 |
| Baldwin County (Ga.) | T2—758 573 |
| Bâle-Ville (Switzerland) | T2—494 32 |
| Baleares | T2—467 5 |
| Balearic Islands | T2—467 5 |
| Balearic Sea | 551.461 382 |
| | T2—163 82 |
| Baleen whales | 599.5 |
| Balfour (South Africa : | |
| District) | T2—682 77 |
| Bali (Indonesia) | T2—598 62 |
| Bali language | 499.223 8 |
| | T6—992 238 |
| Bali literature | 899.223 8 |
| Bali Sea (Indonesia) | 551.461 474 |
| | T2—164 74 |
| Balıkesir İli (Turkey) | T2—562 3 |
| ancient | T2—392 1 |
| Balinese | T5—992 238 |
| Balinese language | 499.223 8 |
| | T6—992 238 |
| Balinese literature | 899.223 8 |
| Baling crops | 631.56 |
| equipment manufacturing | |
| technology | 681.763 1 |
| Balkan Mountains | |
| (Bulgaria) | T2—499 |
| Balkan Peninsula | 949.6 |
| | T2—496 |
| Balkan States | 949.6 |
| | T2—496 |
| Balkan Wars | 949.603 9 |
| Balkar language | 494.38 |
| | T6—943 8 |
| Ball bearings | 621.822 |
| Ball games | 796.3 |
| equipment technology | 688.763 |
| indoor | 794.7 |
| outdoor | 796.3 |
| Ball hockey | 796.356 4 |
| Ball lightning | 551.563 4 |
| Ballad operas | 782.14 |
| music | 782.14 |
| stage presentation | 792.6 |
| Ballades (Music) | 784.189 6 |

| | |
|---|---|
| Ballads | |
| literature | 808.814 4 |
| history and criticism | 809.144 |
| specific literatures | T3B—104 4 |
| individual authors | T3A—1 |
| music | 782.43 |
| Ballarat (Vic.) | T2—945 7 |
| Ballard County (Ky.) | T2—769 96 |
| Ballast (Railroad) | 625.141 |
| Ballet | 792.8 |
| Ballet dancers | 792.802 809 2 |
| Ballet music | 781.556 |
| Balletts | 782.43 |
| Ballina (N.S.W.) | T2—944 3 |
| Ballistic missile forces | 358.17 |
| Ballistic missiles | 358.171 82 |
| engineering | 623.451 95 |
| military equipment | 358.171 82 |
| Ballistics | 531.55 |
| criminal investigation | 363.256 2 |
| engineering | 620.105 |
| military engineering | 623.51 |
| physics | 531.55 |
| Ballistocardiography | |
| medicine | 616.120 754 |
| Balloons | |
| engineering | 629.133 22 |
| military engineering | 623.742 |
| piloting | 629.132 522 |
| sports | 797.51 |
| Ballots | 324.65 |
| Ballroom dancing | 793.33 |
| Balls (Dances) | 793.38 |
| Balls (Geometrical shapes) | 516.156 |
| Balls (Gymnastic equipment) | 796.443 |
| Balls (Recreational equipment) | 796.3 |
| manufacturing technology | 688.763 |
| Ballymena (Northern | |
| Ireland : Borough) | T2—416 13 |
| Ballymoney (Northern | |
| Ireland : District) | T2—416 14 |
| Balms | 583.77 |
| Balms (Burseraceae) | 583.77 |
| Balms (Lamiaceae) | 583.96 |
| Balneotherapy | |
| medicine | 615.853 |
| Balochi | T5—915 98 |
| Balochi language | 491.598 |
| | T6—915 98 |
| Balochi literature | 891.598 |
| Balong language | 496.396 |
| | T6—963 96 |
| Balqā' (Jordan : Province) | T2—569 55 |

Balsa
  botany                              583.68
  forestry                            634.973 68
Balsaminaceae                         583.79
Balsams (Impatiens)                   583.79
Baltic-Finnic languages               494.54
                                      T6—945 4
Baltic-Finnic literatures             894.54
Baltic languages                      491.9
                                      T6—919
Baltic literatures                    891.9
Baltic Sea                            551.461 334
                                      T2—163 34
Baltic Sea Region                     T2—485
Baltic States                         947.9
                                      T2—479
Baltimore (Md.)                       T2—752 6
Baltimore County (Md.)                T2—752 71
Balto-Slavic languages                491.8
                                      T6—918
Balto-Slavic literatures              891.8
Balts (Indo-European
  people)                             T5—919
Baluchi                               T5—915 98
Baluchi language                      491.598
                                      T6—915 98
Baluchi literature                    891.598
Baluchistan                           T2—549 15
  Iran                                T2—558 3
  Pakistan                            T2—549 15
Baluchistan (Pakistan)                T2—549 15
Balustrades                           721.8
  architecture                        721.8
  artistic ironwork                   739.48
  construction                        690.18
Bamako (Mali)                         T2—662 3
Bamana language (Mandekan)            496.345 2
                                      T6—963 452
Bamhara (African people)              T5—963 452
Bambara language                      496.345 2
                                      T6—963 452
Bambara literature                    896.345 2
Bamberg (Germany)                     T2—433 18
Bamberg County (S.C.)                 T2—757 78
Bamboo pulp                           676.14
Bamboos                               584.9
  basketwork crop                     633.58
  floriculture                        635.934 9
  handicrafts                         745.51
  textiles                            677.54
    *see also* Textiles
Bambuseae                             584.9
Bambute (African people)              T5—963 94
Bamileke (African people)             T5—963 6

Bamileke languages                    496.36
                                      T6—963 6
Bamun language                        496.36
                                      T6—963 6
Bana (African people)                 T5—963 6
Bana language                         496.36
                                      T6—963 6
Banach algebras                       512.554
Banach spaces                         515.732
Bananas                               641.347 72
  botany                              584.39
  commercial processing               664.804 772
  cooking                             641.647 72
  food                                641.347 72
  horticulture                        634.772
Banat                                 T2—498 4
  Romania                             T2—498 4
  Yugoslavia                          T2—497 1
Banbridge (Northern
  Ireland : District)                 T2—416 57
Band leaders                          784.092
Banda (African people)                T5—963 61
Banda, H. Kamuzu (Hastings
  Kamuzu)
  Malawian history                    968.970 41
Banda languages                       496.361
                                      T6—963 61
Banda Sea                             551.461 474
                                      T2—164 74
Bandages                              677.8
  manufacturing technology            677.8
  surgical use                        617.93
Bandera County (Tex.)                 T2—764 885
Bandi language                        496.348
                                      T6—963 48
Bandicoots                            599.26
Bandjoun language                     496.36
                                      T6—963 6
Bandoneons                            788.84
  *see also* Woodwind instruments
Bands                                 784
Bandundu (Congo :
  Province)                           T2—675 116
Bandy                                 796.963
Banff (Alta.)                         T2—712 332
Banff and Buchan
  (Scotland)                          T2—412 4
Banff National Park (Alta.)           T2—712 332
Bangalore torpedoes                   623.454 5
Banghāzī (Libya)                      T2—612
Bangi-Ntomba languages                496.396 8
                                      T6—963 968
Bangiophycideae                       579.89
Bangka (Indonesia)                    T2—598 196

Bangka Belitung
  (Indonesia)    T2—598 196
Bangladesh    954.92
   T2—549 2
  ancient    934.92
   T2—349 2
Bangladesh people    T5—914 126
Bangladeshis    T5—914 126
Bangor (Me.)    T2—741 3
Bang's disease    636.208 969 57
Bangui (Central African
  Republic)    T2—674 1
Banī Suwayf (Egypt :
  Province)    T2—622
Banjar    T5—992 256
Banjar language    499.225 6
   T6—992 256
Banjar literature    899.225 6
Banjar Malay language    499.225 6
   T6—992 256
Banjar Malay literature    899.225 6
Banjarese    T5—992 256
Banjarese language    499.225 6
   T6—992 256
Banjarese literature    899.225 6
Banjoists    787.880 92
Banjos    787.88
  instrument    787.881 9
  music    787.88
  *see also* Stringed instruments
Banjul (Gambia)    T2—665 1
Bank accounts    332.175 2
Bank deposit insurance    368.854
  law    346.086 854
Bank examination    657.833 304 5
Bank failures    332.1
Bank for International
  Settlements    332.155
Bank holding companies    332.16
Bank mergers    332.16
Bank notes    332.42
  central banking    332.112
  form of currency    332.404 4
Bank reserves    332.1
  macroeconomic policy    339.53
  requirements    332.113
Bankers    332.109 2
Banking    332.1
  *see also* Banks (Finance)
Banking cooperatives    334.2
Banking services    332.17
Bankruptcy    332.75
  accounting    657.47
  credit economics    332.75

Bankruptcy (continued)
  financial management    658.15
  law    346.078
    commercial law    346.078
    public finance    343.037
  public finance    336.368
Banks (Finance)    332.1
  accounting    657.833 3
  architecture    725.24
  auditing    657.833 304 5
  credit regulation
    macroeconomic policy    339.53
  government guaranty of
    deposits    368.854
  law    346.082
  public administration    354.86
Banks County (Ga.)    T2—758 143
Banks Island (N.W.T.)    T2—719 3
Banks Peninsula (N.Z.)    T2—938 4
Banks Peninsula District
  (N.Z.)    T2—938 4
Banksias    583.89
Bann River (Northern
  Ireland)    T2—416
Banned books    098.1
Banner County (Neb.)    T2—782 975
Banners    929.92
  armed forces    355.15
Bannock County (Idaho)    T2—796 47
Bannock Indians    T5—974 577
Bannock language    497.457 7
   T6—974 577
Bannockburn, Battle of, 1314    941.102
Banquets    642.4
Banská Bystrica (Slovakia :
  Province)    T2—437 34
Banskobystrický kraj
  (Slovakia)    T2—437 34
Bansuris    788.35
  *see also* Woodwind instruments
Bantams    636.587 1
Banten (Indonesia)    T2—598 23
Banteng    599.642 2
Bantoid languages    496.36
   T6—963 6
Bantu languages    496.39
   T6—963 9
  *see Manual at* T6—9639
Bantu literatures    896.39
Bantu-speaking peoples    T5—963 9
Bantustans    968.29
   T2—682 9
Banyan    583.45

Banzer Suárez, Hugo
  Bolivian history — 984.054 1
Baobabs — 583.68
Baoruco (Dominican
  Republic : Province) — T2—729 326
Baoulé (African people) — T5—963 38
Baoulé language — 496.338
  — T6—963 38

Baptism — 234.161
  customs — 392.12
  etiquette — 395.24
  music — 781.582
  public worship — 265.1
  theology — 234.161
Baptism in the Holy Spirit — 234.13
Baptism of Jesus Christ — 232.95
Baptismal fonts — 247.1
  architecture — 726.529 1
Baptismal names — 929.44
Baptismal records
  genealogy — 929.3
Baptist General Conference of
  America — 286.5
  *see also* Baptists
Baptist sacred music — 781.716
  public worship — 782.322 6
    music — 782.322 6
    religion — 264.060 2
Baptistries
  architecture — 726.4
    accessory building — 726.4
    part of church — 726.596
Baptists — 286
  biography — 286.092
  church government — 262.06
    parishes — 254.06
  church law — 262.986
  doctrines — 230.6
    catechisms and creeds — 238.6
  general councils — 262.56
  guides to Christian life — 248.486
  missions — 266.6
  moral theology — 241.046
  persecution of — 272.8
  public worship — 264.06
  religious associations — 267.186
  religious education — 268.86
  seminaries — 230.073 6
  theology — 230.6
Bar-code scanners — 006.242
  computer engineering — 621.399 4
Bar coding — 006.242
  computer science — 006.242
  materials management — 658.780 285 624 2

Bar examination — 340.076
Bar mitzvah — 296.442 4
  customs — 392.14
  etiquette — 395.24
  liturgy — 296.454 24
  music — 781.583
Baraga County (Mich.) — T2—774 973
Barahona (Dominican
  Republic : Province) — T2—729 324
Barai language — 499.12
  — T6—991 2
Baraita — 296.126 3
Baranya Megye (Hungary) — T2—439 7
Barbacoan languages — 498.2
  — T6—982
Barbadians — T5—969 729 81
Barbados — 972.981
  — T2—729 81
Barbary horse — 636.11
Barbary States — T2—61
Barbecuing — 641.76
  indoor cooking — 641.76
  outdoor cooking — 641.578 4
Barbels (Fishes) — 597.482
  sports fishing — 799.174 82
Barber County (Kan.) — T2—781 82
Barbering — 646.724
  customs — 391.5
Barberries — 583.34
  botany — 583.34
  cooking — 641.647 4
  floriculture — 635.933 34
  food — 641.347 4
  horticulture — 634.74
Barbers — 646.724 092
Barbershops
  sanitation services — 363.729 9
Barbets — 598.72
Barbeyales — 583.43
Barbiturate abuse — 362.299
  medicine — 616.86
  personal health — 613.8
  social welfare — 362.299
  *see also* Substance abuse
Barbiturates
  pharmacokinetics — 615.782 1
Barbour County (Ala.) — T2—761 32
Barbour County (W. Va.) — T2—754 59
Barbs (Fishes) — 597.482
Barbuda — T2—729 74
Barcaldine (Qld.) — T2—943 5
Barcelona (Spain :
  Province) — T2—467 2

| | | | |
|---|---|---|---|
| Barents Sea | 551.461 324 | Barking and Dagenham | |
| | T2—163 24 | (London, England) | T2—421 75 |
| Barents Sea region | T2—48 | Barkley, Lake (Ky. and | |
| Bargain theory of wages | 331.210 1 | Tenn.) | T2—769 79 |
| Barge canals | 386.48 | Barkly East (South Africa : | |
| engineering | 627.138 | District) | T2—687 57 |
| transportation services | 386.48 | Barkly West (South Africa : | |
| *see also* Canals | | District) | T2—687 11 |
| Bargello | 746.442 | Barletta-Andria-Trani | |
| Barges | 386.229 | (Italy : Province) | T2—457 59 |
| design | 623.812 9 | ancient | T2—377 56 |
| engineering | 623.829 | Barley | 641.331 6 |
| freight services | 386.244 | botany | 584.9 |
| *see also* Ships | | cooking | 641.631 6 |
| Bari (Italy) | T2—457 511 | food | 641.331 6 |
| ancient | T2—377 581 | food crop | 633.16 |
| Bari (Italy : Province) | T2—457 51 | forage crop | 633.256 |
| ancient | T2—377 58 | Barlow, George Hilaro, Sir | |
| Bari language | 496.5 | Indian history | 954.031 2 |
| | T6—965 | Barmera (S. Aust.) | T2—942 33 |
| Baric languages | 495.4 | Barn owls | 598.97 |
| | T6—954 | Barnabites | 255.52 |
| Barima-Waini Region | | church history | 271.52 |
| (Guyana) | T2—881 1 | Barnacles | 595.35 |
| Barinas (Venezuela : State) | T2—874 3 | paleozoology | 565.35 |
| Barisāl (Bangladesh : | | Barnes County (N.D.) | T2—784 32 |
| Division) | T2—549 26 | Barnet (London, England) | T2—421 87 |
| Barite | 553.662 | Barnim (Germany : | |
| mineralogy | 549.752 | Landkreis) | T2—431 53 |
| Baritone voices | 782.88 | Barnouic (Channel Islands) | T2—423 49 |
| choral and mixed voices | 782.88 | Barns | 631.22 |
| single voices | 783.88 | animal husbandry | 636.083 1 |
| Baritones (Horns) | | architecture | 725.372 |
| American | 788.975 | construction | 690.537 2 |
| instrument | 788.975 19 | domestic architecture | 728.922 |
| music | 788.975 | construction | 690.892 2 |
| *see also* Brass instruments | | use | 631.22 |
| British | 788.974 | Barnsley (England : | |
| *see also* Brass instruments | | Metropolitan Borough) | T2—428 25 |
| Barium | 669.725 | Barnstable County (Mass.) | T2—744 92 |
| chemical engineering | 661.039 5 | Barnwell County (S.C.) | T2—757 76 |
| chemistry | 546.395 | Barometric leveling | 526.37 |
| economic geology | 553.499 | Barometric pressure | 551.54 |
| metallurgy | 669.725 | Baroque architecture | 724.16 |
| physical metallurgy | 669.967 25 | Baroque art | 709.032 |
| *see also* Chemicals | | Baroque decoration | 745.409 032 |
| Barium (Italy) | T2—377 581 | Baroque music | 780.903 2 |
| Bark | 581.47 | Baroque painting | 759.046 |
| descriptive botany | 581.47 | Baroque sculpture | 735.21 |
| forest product | 634.985 | Barotse kingdoms (Zambian | |
| physiology | 575.452 | history) | 968.940 1 |
| Bark beetles | 595.768 | Barracks | 355.71 |
| Barkerville (B.C.) | T2—711 75 | architecture | 725.18 |
| | | military housing | 355.71 |

Barracudas 597.7
Barrage balloons
military engineering 623.744
Barrages
engineering 627.123
Barramunda 597.39
culture 639.373 9
fishing 639.273 9
Barrels 688.8
wooden 674.82
Barren County (Ky.) T2—769 72
Barrhead (Scotland) T2—414 39
Barrier islands 551.423
T2—142
geography 910.914 2
geomorphology 551.423
physical geography 910.021 42
Barrios de Chamorro, Violeta
Nicaraguan history 972.850 541
Barristers 340.092
Barron County (Wis.) T2—775 18
Barrow County (Ga.) T2—758 195
Barrow-in-Furness
(England : Borough) T2—427 81
Barrow Island National Park
(W.A.) T2—941 3
Barrow River (Ireland) T2—418
Barry (Wales) T2—429 89
Barry County (Mich.) T2—774 16
Barry County (Mo.) T2—778 76
Bars (Drinking places) 647.95
*see also* Drinking places
Bars (Musical instruments) 786.82
concussed 786.873
friction 786.863
set 786.863
single 786.888
percussed 786.843
set 786.843
single 786.884 3
plucked 786.85
set 786.85
single 786.887
*see also* Percussion instruments
Bars (Structural elements) 624.177 4
Bartending 641.874
Barter 332.54
Bartholomew County (Ind.) T2—772 24
Bartın İli (Turkey) T2—563 7
ancient T2—393 17
Barton, Edmund, Sir
Australian history 994.041
Barton County (Kan.) T2—781 52
Barton County (Mo.) T2—778 71

Bartow County (Ga.) T2—758 365
Baruch (Bible) 229.5
Baryons 539.721 64
Baryonyx 567.912
Barytons 787.6
*see also* Stringed instruments
Bas-Congo (Congo) T2—675 114
Bas-Rhin (France) T2—443 95
Bas-Richelieu (Quebec) T2—714 39
Bas-Saint-Laurent (Quebec) T2—714 76
Bas-Saint-Laurent-Gaspésie
Region (Quebec) T2—714 77
Basa (Cameroon people) T5—963 96
Basa (Liberian people) T5—963 3
Basaa language (Cameroon) 496.396
T6—963 96
Basal body 571.67
Basal ganglia
human physiology 612.825
medicine 616.83
Basal ganglia diseases
medicine 616.83
*see also* Nervous system
diseases — humans
Basalt 552.26
Basari (Senegal-Guinea
people) T5—963 2
Basari (Togo-Ghana people) T5—963 5
Base lines (Surveying) 526.33
Base running
baseball 796.357 27
Base sequences (Nucleotides) 572.863 3
humans 611.018 166 3
Baseball 796.357
electronic games 794.863 57
equipment manufacturing 688.763 57
Baseball cards 796.357 075
Baseball players 796.357 092
Baseband computer equipment 004.64
engineering 621.398 1
Baseband local-area networks 004.68
*see also* Computer
communications
Basel (Switzerland) T2—494 32
Basel (Switzerland :
Canton) T2—494 32
Basel-Landschaft
(Switzerland : Canton) T2—494 33
Basel-Stadt (Switzerland) T2—494 32
Baselland (Switzerland) T2—494 33
Basements
home economics 643.5
Basenji 636.753 6

| | |
|---|---|
| Bases (Chemicals) | 546.32 |
| chemical engineering | 661.3 |
| *see also* Chemicals | |
| Bases (Military installations) | 355.7 |
| law | 343.015 7 |
| Bashfulness | 155.232 |
| Bashir, Omar Hassan Ahmad al | |
| Sudanese history | 962.404 3 |
| Bashkir language | 494.38 |
| | T6—943 8 |
| Bashkirīa (Russia) | T2—474 3 |
| Bashkortostan | T2—474 3 |
| Basic Christian communities | 250 |
| ecclesiology | 262.26 |
| *see Manual at* 260 vs. 251–254, | |
| 259 | |
| Basic education | 370 |
| adults | 374.012 |
| *see also* Education | |
| Basic English | 428 |
| Basic skills education | 370 |
| *see also* Education | |
| Basic sulfates | |
| mineralogy | 549.755 |
| Basic training (Military) | 355.54 |
| living conditions | 355.129 2 |
| Basidiomycete yeasts | 579.59 |
| Basidiomycetes | 579.59 |
| Basidiomycotina | 579.59 |
| Basil | 641.357 |
| botany | 583.96 |
| *see also* Herbs | |
| Basil III, Czar of Russia | |
| Russian history | 947.042 |
| Basilan (Philippines : | |
| Province) | T2—599 7 |
| Basilan Island (Philippines) | T2—599 7 |
| Basildon (England : | |
| District) | T2—426 772 |
| Basilians | 255.17 |
| church history | 271.17 |
| Basilicata (Italy) | T2—457 7 |
| ancient | T2—377 7 |
| Basilisks (Mythical animal) | 398.245 4 |
| *see also* Legendary animals | |
| Basingstoke and Deane | |
| (England) | T2—422 71 |
| Basket stars | 593.94 |
| Basketball | 796.323 |
| electronic games | 794.863 23 |
| Basketball cards | 796.323 075 |
| Basketball players | 796.323 092 |
| Basketry | |
| handicrafts | 746.412 |

| | |
|---|---|
| Basketwork plants | |
| agriculture | 633.58 |
| Basommatophora | 594.38 |
| Basotho | T5—968 85 |
| Basotho-Qwaqwa (South | |
| Africa) | T2—685 1 |
| Basque (France) | T2—447 16 |
| Basque language | 499.92 |
| | T6—999 2 |
| Basque literature | 899.92 |
| Basque nationalism | 320.540 946 6 |
| Basque Provinces (Spain) | T2—466 |
| Basques | T5—999 2 |
| Basques (Quebec : Regional | |
| County Municipality) | T2—714 766 |
| Baṣrah (Iraq : Province) | T2—567 5 |
| Bass clarinets | 788.65 |
| *see also* Woodwind instruments | |
| Bass drums | 786.95 |
| *see also* Percussion instruments | |
| Bass flutes | 788.34 |
| *see also* Woodwind instruments | |
| Bass recorders | 788.367 |
| *see also* Woodwind instruments | |
| Bass saxophones | 788.75 |
| *see also* Woodwind instruments | |
| Bass Strait (Vic. and Tas.) | 551.461 576 |
| | T2—165 76 |
| Bass viols | 787.65 |
| *see also* Stringed instruments | |
| Bass voices | 782.89 |
| choral and mixed voices | 782.89 |
| single voices | 783.89 |
| Bassa (Cameroon people) | T5—963 96 |
| Bassa (Liberian people) | T5—963 3 |
| Bassa language (Cameroon) | 496.396 |
| | T6—963 96 |
| Bassa language (Liberia) | 496.33 |
| | T6—963 3 |
| Bassari (Senegal-Guinea | |
| people) | T5—963 2 |
| Bassari (Togo-Ghana | |
| people) | T5—963 5 |
| Basse-Côte-Nord (Quebec : | |
| Region) | T2—714 179 |
| Basse-Normandie (France) | T2—442 1 |
| Basse-taille | |
| ceramic arts | 738.4 |
| Basse Terre (Guadeloupe) | T2—729 76 |
| Basses (Fishes) | 597.73 |
| conservation technology | 639.977 73 |
| cooking | 641.692 |
| culture | 639.377 3 |
| food | 641.392 |

Basses (Fishes) (continued)
resource economics | 333.956 73
sports fishing | 799.177 3
zoology | 597.73
Basses (Stringed instruments) | 787.5
instrument | 787.519
music | 787.5
*see also* Stringed instruments
Basset horns | 788.62
Basset hound | 636.753 6
Bassetlaw (England) | T2—425 21
Basslets | 597.73
Bassoons | 788.58
instrument | 788.581 9
music | 788.58
*see also* Woodwind instruments
Basswood
botany | 583.68
forestry | 634.972 77
lumber | 674.142
Bast fibers
textiles | 677.1
*see also* Textiles
Bastille Day | 394.263 5
Bastrop County (Tex.) | T2—764 32
Basutoland | 968.850 2
| T2—688 5
Bat flies | 595.774
Bat games | 796.35
Bat mitzvah | 296.443 4
customs | 392.14
etiquette | 395.24
liturgy | 296.454 34
music | 781.583
Bataan (Philippines :
Province) | T2—599 1
Batak | T5—992 246
Batak Dairi language | 499.224 66
| T6—992 246 6
Batak Dairi literature | 899.224 66
Batak languages | 499.224 6
| T6—992 246
Batak Toba language | 499.224 62
| T6—992 246 2
Batak Toba literature | 899.224 62
Batanes (Philippines) | T2—599 1
Batangas (Philippines :
Province) | T2—599 1
Batavian Republic | 949.205
Batch processing | 004.3
*see also* Processing modes —
computer science
Batemans Bay (N.S.W.) | T2—944 7
Bates County (Mo.) | T2—778 43

Batfishes | 597.62
Bath (England) | T2—423 98
Bath and North East
Somerset (England) | T2—423 98
Bath County (Ky.) | T2—769 555
Bath County (Va.) | T2—755 87
Bathhouses
architecture | 725.73
domestic | 728.96
public | 725.73
construction | 690.573
domestic | 690.896
public | 690.573
Bathing | 613.41
child training | 649.63
customs | 391.64
health | 613.41
therapeutics | 615.853
Bathing suits
commercial technology | 687.16
customs | 391.48
home sewing | 646.47
Bathrooms | 643.52
construction | 690.42
home economics | 643.52
plumbing | 696.182
residential interior decoration | 747.78
Bathurst (N.B.) | T2—715 12
Bathurst (N.S.W.) | T2—944 5
Bathurst (South Africa :
District) | T2—687 53
Bathurst Inlet (Nunavut) | T2—719 55
Bathyal zone
biology | 578.779
ecology | 577.79
Bathyscaphes | 387.27
design | 623.812 7
engineering | 623.827
transportation services | 387.27
Bathyspheres | 387.27
design | 623.812 7
engineering | 623.827
transportation services | 387.27
Batik | 746.662
Bating leather | 675.22
Batlle Ibáñez, Jorge
Uruguayan history | 989.506 74
Batman İli (Turkey) | T2—566 78
ancient | T2—394 2
Batna (Algeria : Province) | T2—655
Batoidei | 597.35
paleozoology | 567.35
Baton Rouge (La.) | T2—763 18
Baton twirling | 791.6

| | |
|---|---|
| Batrachoidiformes | 597.62 |
| Bats (Animals) | 599.4 |
|   conservation technology | 639.979 4 |
|   paleozoology | 569.4 |
|   resource economics | 333.959 4 |
| Bats (Sports equipment) | |
|   baseball | 796.357 26 |
|     manufacturing technology | 688.763 57 |
|   cricket | 796.358 26 |
|     manufacturing technology | 688.763 58 |
| Batswana (Ethnic group) | T5—963 977 5 |
| Batswana (National group) | T5—968 83 |
| Battalions (Military units) | 355.31 |
| Batten disease | |
|   medicine | 616.83 |
| Battered wives | 362.829 2 |
|   criminology | 364.155 53 |
|     criminal law | 345.025 553 |
|   social welfare | 362.829 2 |
|   *see also* Family violence | |
| Batteries (Artillery units) | 358.123 |
| Batteries (Electric) | 621.312 42 |
|   automotive | 629.254 2 |
| Battery (Crime) | 364.155 5 |
|   law | 345.025 55 |
|     criminal law | 345.025 55 |
|     torts | 346.033 |
| Batting (Sports) | |
|   baseball | 796.357 26 |
|   cricket | 796.358 26 |
| Battle games | 793.92 |
| Battle of the Atlantic, 1939–1945 | 940.542 93 |
| Battle tactics | 355.42 |
| Battleford (Sask.) | T2—712 42 |
| Battlefords (Sask.) | T2—712 42 |
| Battles | 355.4 |
|   *see also* Land operations | |
|   *see Manual at* 930–990 | |
| Battleships | 359.835 2 |
|   design | 623.812 52 |
|   engineering | 623.825 2 |
|   naval equipment | 359.835 2 |
|   naval units | 359.325 2 |
| Bauchi State (Nigeria) | T2—669 82 |
| Baudouin I, King of the Belgians | |
|   Belgian history | 949.304 3 |
| Bauxite | 553.492 6 |
|   economic geology | 553.492 6 |
|   mineralogy | 549.53 |
|   mining | 622.349 26 |
| Bava Batra | 296.123 4 |
|   Babylonian Talmud | 296.125 4 |
|   Mishnah | 296.123 4 |
|   Palestinian Talmud | 296.124 4 |

| | |
|---|---|
| Bava Kamma | 296.123 4 |
|   Babylonian Talmud | 296.125 4 |
|   Mishnah | 296.123 4 |
|   Palestinian Talmud | 296.124 4 |
| Bava Mezia | 296.123 4 |
|   Babylonian Talmud | 296.125 4 |
|   Mishnah | 296.123 4 |
|   Palestinian Talmud | 296.124 4 |
| Bavaria (Germany) | T2—433 |
| Bavarian Alps (Germany) | T2—433 6 |
| Baxter County (Ark.) | T2—767 21 |
| Bay County (Fla.) | T2—759 95 |
| Bay County (Mich.) | T2—774 47 |
| Bay laurel | 641.357 |
|   botany | 583.23 |
| Bay of Bengal | 551.461 564 |
| | T2—165 64 |
| Bay of Biscay (France and Spain) | 551.461 338 |
| | T2—163 38 |
| Bay of Fundy | 551.461 345 |
| | T2—163 45 |
| Bay of Plenty Region (N.Z.) | T2—934 2 |
| Bay rum tree | 583.765 |
| Bayadh (Algeria : Province) | T2—657 |
| Bayamón (P.R. : District) | T2—729 52 |
| Bayberries (Myricaceae) | 583.43 |
| Bayberry wax | 665.12 |
| Bayburt İli (Turkey) | T2—565 7 |
|   ancient | T2—393 37 |
| Bayelsa State (Nigeria) | T2—669 41 |
| Bayern (Germany) | T2—433 |
| Bayesian statistical decision | |
|   theory | 519.542 |
| Bayfield County (Wis.) | T2—775 13 |
| Baylor County (Tex.) | T2—764 744 |
| Bayonet practice | 355.547 |
| Bayonets | 623.441 |
|   art metalwork | 739.723 |
| Bayono-Awbono languages | 499.1 |
| | T6—991 |
| Bayreuth (Germany) | T2—433 15 |
| Bays | |
|   law of nations | 341.448 |
|   resource economics | 333.916 4 |
| Bazaars | 381.1 |
|   architecture | 725.21 |
|   management | 658.87 |
|   *see also* Commerce | |
| Bazookamen | 356.162 |
| Bazookas | 356.162 |
|   engineering | 623.442 6 |
|     ammunition | 623.455 |
|   military equipment | 356.162 |

Beach activities
  recreation — 796.53
Beach erosion — 551.36
  engineering — 627.58
Beach flies — 595.774
Beach volleyball — 796.325 82
Beaches — 551.457
  — T2—146
  area planning — 711.558
  geography — 910.914 6
  geomorphology — 551.457
  landscape architecture — 714
  physical geography — 910.021 46
  recreational resources — 333.784
  resource economics — 333.917
  sanitation services — 363.729 2
Beacons — 387.155
  light
    navigation aids — 623.894 4
  transportation services — 387.155
Beaconsfield (Quebec) — T2—714 28
Beaconsfield (Tas.) — T2—946 5
Bead embroidery — 746.5
Beaded lizard — 597.959 5
Beadle County (S.D.) — T2—783 274
Beads — 391.7
  customs — 391.7
  handicrafts — 745.582
  home sewing — 646.19
Beagle — 636.753 7
Beak — 591.44
  descriptive zoology — 591.44
  physiology — 573.355
Beak rushes — 584.84
Beaked reptiles — 597.945
Beaked whales — 599.545
Beam bridges
  construction — 624.21
Beam warfare — 358.39
Beams (Light) — 535.5
Beams (Structural elements) — 624.177 23
  naval architecture — 623.817 723
  structural engineering — 624.177 23
  concrete — 624.183 423
Beans — 641.356 5
  botany — 583.74
  commercial processing — 664.805 65
  cooking — 641.656 5
  field crop — 633.3
  food — 641.356 5
  garden crop — 635.65
Bear Lake County (Idaho) — T2—796 44

Beard — 646.724
  care — 646.724
  customs — 391.5
Beard fishes — 597.62
Bearded pig — 599.633 2
Bearded seal — 599.796
Beardworms — 592.3
Bearing walls — 721.2
  architecture — 721.2
  construction — 690.12
  interior decoration — 747.3
Bearings — 621.822
  clockwork — 681.112
  machine engineering — 621.822
  railroad engineering — 625.21
Béarn (France) — T2—447 16
Bears — 599.78
  animal husbandry — 636.978
  big game hunting — 799.277 8
  conservation technology — 639.979 78
  predator control technology — 636.083 9
    conservation technology — 639.966
  resource economics — 333.959 78
  zoology — 599.78
Bearsden and Milngavie
  (Scotland) — T2—414 36
Beasts of burden — 636.088 2
Beatification of saints — 235.24
Beating metals
  decorative arts — 739.14
  sculpture — 731.41
Beatitudes — 226.93
  Christian moral theology — 241.53
Beatrix, Queen of the
  Netherlands
  Dutch history — 949.207 3
Beauce (Quebec) — T2—714 71
Beauce-Sartigan (Quebec) — T2—714 714
Beaufort County (N.C.) — T2—756 186
Beaufort County (S.C.) — T2—757 99
Beaufort Sea — 551.461 327
  — T2—163 27
Beaufort West (South
  Africa : District) — T2—687 39
Beauharnois-Salaberry
  (Quebec) — T2—714 32
Beauregard Parish (La.) — T2—763 59
Beauticians — 646.720 92

| | |
|---|---|
| Beauty | 111.85 |
| personal | |
| arts | 700.453 |
| | T3C—353 |
| literature | 808.803 53 |
| history and criticism | 809.933 53 |
| specific literatures | T3B—080 353 |
| history and | |
| criticism | T3B—093 53 |
| philosophy | 111.85 |
| Beauty contests | 791.66 |
| Beauty pageants | 791.66 |
| Beauty shops | 646.72 |
| arts | T3C—356 4 |
| literature | 808.803 564 |
| history and criticism | 809.933 564 |
| personal care | 646.72 |
| sanitation services | 363.729 9 |
| Beaver County (Okla.) | T2—766 14 |
| Beaver County (Pa.) | T2—748 92 |
| Beaver County (Utah) | T2—792 46 |
| Beaverhead County (Mont.) | T2—786 69 |
| Beavers | 599.37 |
| conservation technology | 639.979 37 |
| resource economics | 333.959 37 |
| trapping | 639.113 7 |
| Bebop | 781.655 |
| Bécancour (Quebec : | |
| Regional County | |
| Municipality) | T2—714 55 |
| Béchar (Algeria : Province) | T2—657 |
| Bechuanaland | 968.830 2 |
| | T2—688 3 |
| Becker County (Minn.) | T2—776 84 |
| Beckham County (Okla.) | T2—766 43 |
| Becoming | |
| philosophy | 116 |
| Bed and breakfast | |
| accommodations | 910.464 |
| *see also* Lodging (Temporary | |
| housing) | |
| Bedbugs | 595.754 |
| Bedclothes | 645.4 |
| arts | 746.97 |
| commercial technology | 684.3 |
| home sewing | 646.21 |
| household equipment | 645.4 |
| Bedding (Bedclothes) | 645.4 |
| *see also* Bedclothes | |
| Bedford (England : | |
| Borough) | T2—425 61 |
| Bedford (South Africa : | |
| District) | T2—687 53 |
| Bedford (Va.) | T2—755 676 |
| Bedford County (Pa.) | T2—748 71 |
| Bedford County (Tenn.) | T2—768 583 |
| Bedford County (Va.) | T2—755 675 |
| Bedfordshire (England) | T2—425 6 |
| Bédié, Henri Konan | |
| Ivorian history | 966.680 52 |
| Bedouins | T5—927 2 |
| Bedrooms | 643.53 |
| home economics | 643.53 |
| interior decoration | 747.77 |
| Beds (Furniture) | 645.4 |
| manufacturing technology | 684.15 |
| *see also* Furniture | |
| Bedsores | |
| medicine | 616.545 |
| *see also* Skin diseases — | |
| humans | |
| Bedspreads | 645.4 |
| arts | 746.97 |
| home sewing | 646.21 |
| household equipment | 645.4 |
| Bedwetting | |
| medicine | 616.849 |
| *see also* Nervous system | |
| diseases — humans | |
| pediatrics | 618.928 49 |
| Bee balms | 583.96 |
| Bee County (Tex.) | T2—764 117 |
| Bee eaters | 598.78 |
| Bee flies | 595.773 |
| Bee keeping | 638.1 |
| Bee lice | 595.774 |
| Bee products | 638.16 |
| Bee venom | |
| human toxicology | 615.942 |
| Beeches | |
| botany | 583.46 |
| forestry | 634.972 5 |
| lumber | 674.142 |
| Beechworth (Vic.) | T2—945 5 |
| Beef | 641.362 |
| commercial processing | |
| economics | 338.476 649 2 |
| technology | 664.92 |
| cooking | 641.662 |
| food | 641.362 |
| Beef cattle | |
| agricultural economics | 338.176 213 |
| animal husbandry | 636.213 |
| Beefwoods | 583.43 |
| Beekeepers | 638.109 2 |

Beer | 641.23
  commercial processing | 663.42
  cooking with | 641.623
  home preparation | 641.873
Bees | 595.799
  agriculture | 638.1
Beeswax
  apiculture processing | 638.17
Beet sugar | 641.336 3
  commercial processing | 664.123
  food | 641.336 3
  *see also* Sugar
Beet syrup | 641.336 3
  commercial processing | 664.123
  food | 641.336 3
  *see also* Sugar
Beetles | 595.76
  agricultural pests | 632.76
  culture | 638.576
  palcozoology | 565.76
Beetling textiles | 677.028 25
Beets | 641.351 1
  botany | 583.53
  commercial processing | 664.805 11
  cooking | 641.651 1
  food | 641.351 1
  garden crop | 635.11
  sugar crop | 633.63
Bega (N.S.W.) | T2—944 7
Beggar's lice | 583.74
Begheli literature | 891.492
Beginner cooking | 641.512
Begoniales | 583.627
Begonias | 635.933 627
  botany | 583.627
  floriculture | 635.933 627
Behavior
  animals | 591.5
  comparative psychology | 156
  educational psychology | 370.15
  evolutionary psychology | 155.7
  general psychology | 150
  plants | 575.9
  social psychology | 302
Behavior genetics
  psychology | 155.7
Behavior modification | 153.85
  educational psychology | 370.152 8
  home child care | 649.64
  teaching methods | 371.393
Behavior modification therapy
  psychiatry | 616.891 42
Behavior therapy
  psychiatry | 616.891 42

Behavioral adaptation
  animals | 591.5
Behavioral pharmacology | 615.78
Behavioral sciences | 300
  psychology | 150
  public administrative support | 352.745
Behaviorism | 150.194 3
Beijing (China) | T2—511 56
Beijing dialect | 495.1
  | T6—951 1
Being | 111
Beira (Portugal : Province) | T2—469 3
Beira (Portugal : Region) | T2—469 3
Beira Alta (Portugal) | T2—469 31
Beira Baixa (Portugal) | T2—469 33
Beira Litoral (Portugal) | T2—469 35
Beirut (Lebanon) | T2—569 25
Beja (African people) | T5—935
Beja (Portugal : District) | T2—469 55
Beja language | 493.5
  | T6—935
Bejaïa (Algeria : Province) | T2—655
Békés Megye (Hungary) | T2—439 9
Bekhorot | 296.123 5
  Babylonian Talmud | 296.125 5
  Mishnah | 296.123 5
Bekhterev, Vladimir
  Mikhailovich
  psychological system | 150.194 4
Bektashi | 297.48
Bel and the Dragon (Bible) | 229.6
Bela-Bela (South Africa :
  District) | T2—682 51
Belarus | 947.8
  | T2—478
Belarusian language | 491.799
  | T6—917 99
Belarusian literature | 891.799
Belarusians | T5—917 99
Belau | 996.6
  | T2—966
Belfast (Northern Ireland) | T2—416 7
Belfast (South Africa :
  District) | T2—682 74
Belfort (France : Territory) | T2—444 55
Belgian Congo | 967.510 24
  | T2—675 1
Belgian draft horse | 636.15
Belgian hare | 636.932 2
Belgian literature
  Flemish | 839.31
  French | 840
Belgian malinois | 636.737
Belgian tervuren | 636.737

| | |
|---|---|
| Belgians | T5—393 2 |
| Belgica | T2—369 3 |
| Belgium | 949.3 |
| | T2—493 |
| ancient | 936.93 |
| | T2—369 3 |
| Belgorod (Russia : Oblast) | T2—473 5 |
| Belgorodskaiͨa oblast' | |
| (Russia) | T2—473 5 |
| Belgrade (Serbia) | T2—497 1 |
| Belief | |
| epistemology | 121.6 |
| Belief and doubt | |
| epistemology | 121.6 |
| Belief systems | |
| social control | 303.372 |
| Belitung (Indonesia) | T2—598 196 |
| Belize | 972.82 |
| | T2—728 2 |
| Belize District (Belize) | T2—728 22 |
| Belizeans | T5—969 728 2 |
| Belknap County (N.H.) | T2—742 45 |
| Bell County (Ky.) | T2—769 123 |
| Bell County (Tex.) | T2—764 287 |
| Bell-jar gardening | |
| floriculture | 635.985 |
| Bell magpies | 598.8 |
| Bell peppers | 641.356 43 |
| *see also* Sweet peppers | |
| Bell towers | |
| architecture | 725.97 |
| Bella Coola (B.C.) | T2—711 1 |
| Bella Coola River (B.C.) | T2—711 1 |
| Belladonna | |
| botany | 583.952 |
| human toxicology | 615.952 395 2 |
| pharmacology | 615.323 952 |
| Bellechasse (Quebec : | |
| Regional County | |
| Municipality) | T2—714 733 |
| Bellenden Ker National | |
| Park (Qld.) | T2—943 6 |
| Belles-lettres | 800 |
| history and criticism | 809 |
| specific literatures | T3B—09 |
| *see Manual at* 800 | |
| Bellflowers | 635.933 98 |
| botany | 583.98 |
| floriculture | 635.933 98 |
| Belligerency | 341.62 |
| Belligerent countries | T2—171 82 |
| Bellingshausen Sea | 551.461 74 |
| | T2—167 4 |
| Bellinzona (Switzerland) | T2—494 784 4 |

| | |
|---|---|
| Bellinzona (Switzerland : | |
| Distretto) | T2—494 784 |
| Bells | 786.884 8 |
| instrument | 786.884 819 |
| music | 786.884 8 |
| *see also* Percussion instruments | |
| Belluno (Italy : Province) | T2—453 7 |
| ancient | T2—373 68 |
| Bellville (South Africa : | |
| District) | T2—687 35 |
| Belly dancing | 793.3 |
| Belmont County (Ohio) | T2—771 93 |
| Beloit (Wis.) | T2—775 87 |
| Belorussia | 947.8 |
| | T2—478 |
| Belorussian language | 491.799 |
| | T6—917 99 |
| Belorussian literature | 891.799 |
| Belorussians | T5—917 99 |
| Belt buckles | 391.7 |
| customs | 391.7 |
| making | 739.278 |
| costume jewelry | 688.2 |
| handicrafts | 745.594 2 |
| fine jewelry | 739.278 |
| Belt conveyors | 621.867 5 |
| Beltrami County (Minn.) | T2—776 82 |
| Belts (Clothing) | 391.44 |
| commercial technology | 687.19 |
| leather | 685.22 |
| *see also* Accessories (Clothing) | |
| Belts (Power transmission | |
| devices) | 621.852 |
| Beltways | 388.122 |
| *see also* Roads | |
| Beluga | 599.542 |
| Bemba (African people) | T5—963 915 |
| Bemba kingdoms (Zambian | |
| history) | 968.940 1 |
| Bemba language | 496.391 5 |
| | T6—963 915 |
| Bemba literature | 896.391 5 |
| Bembe language (Lake | 496.394 |
| Tanganyika) | T6—963 94 |
| Ben Hill County (Ga.) | T2—758 852 |
| Ben Lomond National Park | |
| (Tas.) | T2—946 4 |
| Ben M'sik-Sidi Othmane | |
| (Morocco : Prefecture) | T2—643 8 |
| Ben Slimane (Morocco : | |
| Province) | T2—643 9 |
| Bến Tre (Vietnam : | |
| Province) | T2—597 8 |

Bena-Kinga languages 496.391
    T6—963 91
Benalla (Vic.) T2—945 5
Bench marks 526.32
Bench-scale plants
  chemical engineering 660.280 71
Bendel State (Nigeria) T2—669 3
Bendel states (Nigeria) T2—669 3
Bendigo (Vic.) T2—945 4
Bending metals
  decorative arts 739.14
  sculpture 731.41
Bending tools 621.982
Bendjedid, Chadli
  Algerian history 965.053
Bends
  medicine 616.989 4
  *see also* Environmental
    diseases — humans
Benedictines 255.1
  church history 271.1
  women 255.97
    church history 271.97
Benedictions 203.8
  Christianity 264.13
  Judaism 296.45
Benedictus 264.36
  music 782.323 2
Beneficial animals 591.63
Beneficial microorganisms 579.163
Beneficial organisms 578.63
Beneficial plants 581.63
Beneficiation (Ore dressing) 622.7
Benefit cost analysis 658.155 4
  public administration 352.43
Benefit societies 334.7
  economics 334.7
  insurance 368.3
Benefits (Insurance) 368.014
Benelux countries 949.2
  T2—492
Benesh choreology 792.82
Benevento (Italy)
  ancient T2—377 32
Benevento (Italy : Province) T2—457 23
  ancient T2—377 32
Beneventum (Italy) T2—377 32
Benevolence
  ethics 177.7
  *see also* Ethical problems
Benevolent and Protective Order
  of Elks 366.5

Benevolent societies 334.7
  economics 334.7
  insurance 368.3
Benewah County (Idaho) T2—796 93
Benga language 496.396
  T6—963 96
Bengal (India) T2—541 4
Bengal, Bay of 551.461 564
  T2—165 64
Bengal cat 636.822
Bengali T5—914 4
Bengali-Assamese languages 491.44
  T6—914 4
Bengali language 491.44
  T6—914 4
Bengali literature 891.44
Benghazi (Libya) T2—612
Bengkulu (Indonesia) T2—598 17
Bengo (Angola : Province) T2—673 2
Benguela (Angola :
  Province) T2—673 4
Benguet (Philippines :
  Province) T2—599 1
Beni (Bolivia) T2—844 2
Béni Mellal (Morocco :
  Province) T2—644
Benign neoplasms
  incidence 614.599 9
  medicine 616.993
Benign tumors
  incidence 614.599 9
  medicine 616.993
Benin 966.83
  T2—668 3
Benin (Kingdom) 966.930 1
  T2—669 3
Benin (Nigeria) T2—669 3
Benin City (Nigeria) T2—669 32
Beninese T5—966 83
Benishangul-Gumuz kelel
  (Ethiopia) T2—633
Bennett, Richard Bedford
  Bennett, 1st Viscount
  Canadian history 971.062 3
Bennett County (S.D.) T2—783 65
Bennettitales 561.592
Bennington County (Vt.) T2—743 8
Benoni (South Africa :
  District) T2—682 25
Benson County (N.D.) T2—784 39
Bent County (Colo.) T2—788 97
Bent grasses 633.23
  botany 584.9
  forage crop 633.23

| | | | |
|---|---|---|---|
| Benthic biology | | Bereavement | |
| oceans | 578.777 | religion (continued) | |
| Benthic ecology | | personal religion | 204.42 |
| oceans | 577.77 | rites | 203.88 |
| Bentinck, William Henry | | Bereina (New Guinea) | T2—954 6 |
| Cavendish, Lord | | Bergama (Turkey) | T2—562 5 |
| Indian history | 954.031 4 | Bergamo (Italy) | T2—452 41 |
| Benton County (Ark.) | T2—767 13 | ancient | T2—372 268 1 |
| Benton County (Ind.) | T2—772 972 | Bergamo (Italy : Province) | T2—452 4 |
| Benton County (Iowa) | T2—777 61 | ancient | T2—372 268 |
| Benton County (Minn.) | T2—776 67 | Bergen County (N.J.) | T2—749 21 |
| Benton County (Miss.) | T2—762 89 | Berger Perdomo, Oscar | |
| Benton County (Mo.) | T2—778 493 | Guatemalan history | 972.810 533 |
| Benton County (Or.) | T2—795 34 | Bergius process | 662.662 2 |
| Benton County (Tenn.) | T2—768 33 | Bergomum (Italy) | T2—372 268 1 |
| Benton County (Wash.) | T2—797 51 | Bergsonism | 143 |
| Bentonite | 553.61 | Bergville (South Africa : | |
| economic geology | 553.61 | District) | T2—684 7 |
| mining | 622.361 | Beriberi | |
| Benue-Congo languages | 496.36 | medicine | 616.392 |
| | T6—963 6 | *see also* Digestive system | |
| Benue-Niger languages | 496.36 | diseases — humans | |
| | T6—963 6 | Bering Sea | 551.461 451 |
| Benue State (Nigeria) | T2—669 54 | | T2—164 51 |
| Benzene | 547.611 | Bering Strait | 551.461 451 |
| chemical engineering | 661.816 | | T2—164 51 |
| fuel | 662.669 | Berit milah | 296.442 2 |
| human toxicology | 615.951 1 | liturgy | 296.454 22 |
| Benzie County (Mich.) | T2—774 632 | Berkane (Morocco : | |
| Beowulf | 829.3 | Province) | T2—643 3 |
| Berakhot | 296.123 1 | Berkeley (Calif.) | T2—794 67 |
| Babylonian Talmud | 296.125 1 | Berkeley County (S.C.) | T2—757 93 |
| Mishnah | 296.123 1 | Berkeley County (W. Va.) | T2—754 97 |
| Palestinian Talmud | 296.124 1 | Berkelium | 546.444 |
| Berber languages | 493.3 | Berks County (Pa.) | T2—748 16 |
| | T6—933 | Berkshire (England) | T2—422 9 |
| Berber literatures | 893.3 | Berkshire County (Mass.) | T2—744 1 |
| Berberidaceae | 583.34 | Berkshire Hills (Mass.) | T2—744 1 |
| Berbers | T5—933 | Berlin (Germany) | T2—431 55 |
| Bereavement | | Berlin (Germany : East) | T2—431 552 |
| pastoral theology | 206.1 | Berlin (Germany : West) | T2—431 554 |
| Christianity | 259.6 | Berlin, Battle of, 1945 | 940.542 131 55 |
| Judaism | 296.61 | Berlin Wall | 943.155 208 7 |
| psychology | 155.937 | fall of Berlin Wall, 1989 | 943.108 79 |
| religion | 204.42 | Bermuda | 972.99 |
| Christianity | | | T2—729 9 |
| devotional literature | 242.4 | Bermuda Islands | 972.99 |
| personal religion | 248.866 | | T2—729 9 |
| rites | 265.85 | Bermuda Triangle | 001.94 |
| devotional literature | 204.32 | Bermudians | T5—969 729 9 |
| Judaism | | Bern (Switzerland) | T2—494 542 4 |
| personal religion | 296.76 | Bern (Switzerland : Canton) | T2—494 54 |
| rites | 296.445 | Bernalillo County (N.M.) | T2—789 61 |
| liturgy | 296.454 5 | Berne (Switzerland) | T2—494 542 4 |

Berner Alpen (Switzerland) T2—494 541
Berner Jura (Switzerland) T2—494 547
Berner-Mitteland
 (Switzerland) T2—494 542
Bernese Alps T2—494 541
Bernese mountain dog 636.73
Bernier and Dorre Islands
 National Park (W.A.) T2—941 3
Bernina (Switzerland) T2—494 732 9
Berri (S. Aust.) T2—942 33
Berrien County (Ga.) T2—758 862
Berrien County (Mich.) T2—774 11
Berries 581.464
 commercial processing 664.804 7
 cooking 641.647
 descriptive botany 581.464
 food 641.347
 horticulture 634.7
 physiology 575.67
Berry (France) T2—445 5
Berry Islands (Bahamas) T2—729 6
Berthing structures
 engineering 627.32
Bertie County (N.C.) T2—756 163
Berwick-upon-Tweed
 (England : Borough) T2—428 89
Berwickshire (Scotland) T2—413 7
Beryciformes 597.64
Beryl
 mineralogy 549.64
Beryllium 669.724
 chemical engineering 661.039 1
 chemistry 546.391
 economic geology 553.492 3
 human toxicology 615.925 391
 materials science 620.189 4
 metallography 669.957 24
 metallurgy 669.724
 metalworking 673.724
 mining 622.349 23
 physical metallurgy 669.967 24
 *see also* Chemicals; Metals
Besançon (France) T2—444 66
Bessarabia (Moldova and
 Ukraine) T2—476
Bessel function 515.53
Bessemer steel 669.142 3
Best books
 bibliographies 011.73
Beta decay 539.752 3
Beta functions 515.52
Beta Israel T5—924
Beta particles 539.721 12

Beta radiation
 biophysics 571.459
 humans 612.014 486
Betatron-synchrotrons 539.735
Betatrons 539.734
Bété language 496.33
 T6—963 3
Bethal (South Africa :
 District) T2—682 78
Bethlehem (South Africa :
 District) T2—685 1
Bethulie (South Africa :
 District) T2—685 7
Betrothal 392.4
 *see also* Engagement
 (Betrothal)
Betsimisaraka (Kingdom) 969.101
 T2—691
Betta (Fighting fish) 597.7
 culture 639.377
Better business bureaus 381.347
Betting 306.482
 *see also* Gambling
Betting systems 795.01
Betulales 583.48
Bevel gears 621.833 2
Beverage containers
 disposal 363.728 8
 *see also* Waste control
Beverage technologists 663.092
Beverage technology 663
 equipment manufacturing
 technology 681.766 4
Beverages 641.2
 commercial processing 663
 cooking with 641.62
 customs 394.12
 health 613.2
 home economics 641.2
 home preparation 641.87
 product safety 363.192 9
 *see also* Food — product
 safety
Beverley (England :
 Borough) T2—428 39
Bexar County (Tex.) T2—764 35
Bexley (London, England) T2—421 77
Bezah 296.123 2
 Babylonian Talmud 296.125 2
 Mishnah 296.123 2
 Palestinian Talmud 296.124 2
Bhagavad Gita 294.592 4
Bhakti Yoga 294.543 6
Bharals 599.649

| | |
|---|---|
| Bhedabheda (Philosophy) | 181.484 2 |
| Bhili language | 491.47 |
| | T6—914 7 |
| Bhili literature | 891.47 |
| Bhojpuri language | 491.454 7 |
| | T6—914 54 |
| Bhojpuri literature | 891.454 |
| Bhopal (India) | T2—543 |
| Bhotia | T5—954 1 |
| Bhumibol Adulyadej, King of Thailand | |
| Thai history | 959.304 4 |
| Bhutan | 954.98 |
| | T2—549 8 |
| Bhutanese | T5—914 18 |
| Biafra | T2—669 4 |
| Biafran War, 1967–1970 | 966.905 2 |
| Biała Podlaska (Poland : Voivodeship) | T2—438 43 |
| Białystok (Poland : Voivodeship) | T2—438 36 |
| Bias bindings | 677.76 |
| Biathlon | 796.932 2 |
| Bibb County (Ala.) | T2—761 82 |
| Bibb County (Ga.) | T2—758 552 |
| Bibionidae | 595.772 |
| Bible | 220 |
| biography | 220.92 |
| *see Manual at* 220.92 | |
| homiletical use | 251 |
| music | 782.295 |
| choral and mixed voices | 782.529 5 |
| single voices | 783.092 95 |
| use in public worship | 264.34 |
| Bible as literature | 809.935 22 |
| Bible Christians (Methodist denomination) | 287.53 |
| *see also* Methodist Church | |
| Bible colleges | 230.071 1 |
| Bible meditations | 242.5 |
| Bible prayers | 242.722 |
| Bible stories | 220.950 5 |
| Bible study | 220.07 |
| Biblical Aramaic language | 492.29 |
| | T6—922 9 |
| Biblical events | 220.95 |
| art representation | 704.948 4 |
| arts | 700.482 2 |
| | T3C—382 2 |
| Biblical Greek language | 487.4 |
| | T6—87 |
| Biblical moral precepts | |
| Christianity | 241.5 |
| Judaism | 296.36 |

| | |
|---|---|
| Biblical persons | |
| art representation | 704.948 4 |
| arts | 700.482 2 |
| | T3C—382 2 |
| biography | 220.92 |
| *see Manual at* 220.92 | |
| Biblical theology | |
| Christianity | 230.041 |
| Judaism | 296.3 |
| Bibliographers | 010.92 |
| Bibliographic analysis | 025.3 |
| Bibliographic centers | |
| cooperation | 021.64 |
| Bibliographic Classification (Bliss) | 025.434 |
| Bibliographic control | 025.3 |
| Bibliographic description | 025.324 |
| Bibliographic headings | 025.322 |
| Bibliographic instruction | 025.56 |
| Bibliographies | 011 |
| specific collections | 017 |
| specific forms | 011.3 |
| specific historical periods | 011.09 |
| specific languages | 011.2 |
| specific places | 015 |
| specific subjects | 016 |
| *see Manual at* 011–017 | |
| Bibliography | 010 |
| Bibliotherapy | |
| medicine | 615.851 6 |
| Bicameral legislatures | 328.39 |
| Biche, Lac la (Alta.) | T2—712 33 |
| Bichirs | 597.42 |
| Bichon Frise | 636.72 |
| Biculturalism | |
| sociolinguistics | 306.446 |
| sociology | 305.8 |
| Bicycle accidents | 363.125 9 |
| *see also* Highway safety | |
| Bicycle motocross | 796.622 |
| Bicycle paths | 388.12 |
| area planning | 711.72 |
| engineering | 625.7 |
| transportation services | 388.12 |
| urban | 388.411 |
| Bicycle racing | 796.62 |
| mountain | 796.63 |
| Bicycle theft | 364.162 862 922 72 |
| law | 345.026 286 292 272 |
| Bicycle touring | 796.64 |
| Bicycle troops (Armed forces) | 357.52 |
| Bicycles | 388.347 2 |
| engineering | 629.227 2 |
| law | 343.094 4 |

Bicycles (continued)
  repair    629.287 72
  riding    629.284 72
    sports    796.6
  theft of    364.162 862 922 72
    law    345.026 286 292 272
  transportation services    388.347 2
Bicycling    388.347 2
  sports    796.6
  transportation services    388.347 2
Bidding
  games
    contract bridge    795.415 2
Bié (Angola : Province)    T2—673 4
Biel (Switzerland :
  Verwaltungskreis)    T2—494 545 7
Bielefeld (Germany)    T2— 435 655
Biella (Italy : Province)    T2—451 76
  ancient    T2—372 236
Bielorussian language    491.799
    T6—917 99
Bielorussian literature    891.799
Bielsko (Poland :
  Voivodeship)    T2—438 58
Bienne (Switzerland :
  District)    T2—494 545 7
Biennials (Plants)    582.12
  floriculture    635.931 4
Bienville Parish (La.)    T2—763 93
Bifidobacterium    579.373
Biflagellate molds    579.54
Bifurcation theory    515.392
Big air snowboarding    796.939
Big bands    784.48
Big bang theory (Cosmogony)    523.18
Big Bend National Park
  (Tex.)    T2—764 932
Big Bend Region (Tex.)    T2—764 93
Big Black River (Miss.)    T2—762 4
Big brown bats    599.47
Big business    338.644
  economics    338.644
  management    658.023
  personnel management    658.303
Big cats    599.755
Big Cypress Swamp (Fla.)    T2—759 44
Big game animals    599.6
  conservation technology    639.979 6
  resource economics    333.959 6
Big game fishes    597.7
Big game hunting    799.26
Big Horn County (Mont.)    T2—786 38
Big Horn County (Wyo.)    T2—787 33
Big Horn Mountains (Wyo.)    T2—787 3

Big Sandy River (Ky. and
  W. Va.)    T2—754 47
  Kentucky    T2—769 2
  West Virginia    T2—754 47
Big Sioux River (S.D. and
  Iowa)    T2—783 39
  Iowa    T2—777 1
  South Dakota    T2—783 39
Big Stone County (Minn.)    T2—776 432
Bigamy    364.183
  law    345.028 3
Bigfoot    001.944
Bighead carp    597.482
Bighorn sheep    599.649 7
  big game hunting    799.276 497
  conservation technology    639.979 649 7
  resource economics    333.959 649 7
Bignoniaceae    583.95
Bihar (India)    T2—541 23
Bihari    T5—914 54
Bihari language    491.454
    T6—914 54
Bihari literature    891.454
Bihor (Romania)    T2—498 4
Bikeways    388.12
  *see also* Bicycle paths
Bikini Atoll (Marshall
  Islands)    T2—968 3
Bikkurim    296.123 1
  Mishnah    296.123 1
  Palestinian Talmud    296.124 1
Bilateral trade agreements    382.9
Bilateral treaties    341.37
  sources of law of nations    341.1
  texts    341.026 6
Bilayer lipid membranes    572.577
Bilbao (Spain)    T2—466 3
Bile    573.383 79
  biochemistry    573.383 79
  human physiology    612.35
  *see also* Digestive system
Bile acids    573.383 79
Bile duct diseases
  medicine    616.365
    *see also* Digestive system
      diseases — humans
Bile ducts    573.38
  biology    573.38
  human anatomy    611.36
  human physiology    612.35
  medicine    616.365
  surgery    617.556 7
  *see also* Digestive system

| | | | |
|---|---|---|---|
| Bilecik İli (Turkey) | T2—563 4 | Bills of exchange | 332.77 |
| ancient | T2—393 15 | exchange medium | 332.55 |
| Bilharziasis | | law | 346.096 |
| incidence | 614.553 | Bills of lading | |
| medicine | 616.963 | law | 346.025 |
| *see also* Communicable | | Biluchi | T5—915 98 |
| diseases — humans | | Biluchi language | 491.598 |
| Biliary tract | 573.38 | | T6—915 98 |
| biology | 573.38 | Biluchi literature | 891.598 |
| human anatomy | 611.36 | Bimetallism | 332.423 |
| human physiology | 612.35 | Bimini Islands (Bahamas) | T2—729 6 |
| medicine | 616.36 | Bin ʿAlī, Zayn al-ʿĀbidīn | |
| surgery | 617.556 | Tunisian history | 961.105 2 |
| *see also* Digestive system | | Binary form | 781.822 2 |
| Biliary tract diseases | | instrumental | 784.182 2 |
| medicine | 616.36 | Binary numbers | 513.52 |
| *see also* Digestive system | | Binary stars | 523.841 |
| diseases — humans | | Binary system | 513.52 |
| Bilinear forms | 512.944 | Bingham County (Idaho) | T2—796 51 |
| algebraic geometry | 516.35 | Bingo | 795.36 |
| Bilingual dictionaries | T4—32–39 | Bingöl İli (Turkey) | T2—566 73 |
| Bilingual education | 370.117 5 | ancient | T2—394 2 |
| adult level | 374.017 5 | Bình Định (Vietnam : | |
| Bilingual instruction | | Province) | T2—597 5 |
| primary education | 372.651 | Bình Dương (Vietnam : | |
| Bilingual phrase books | T4—834 | Province) | T2—597 7 |
| Bilingual programs | | Bình Phước (Vietnam : | |
| public administration | 353.7 | Province) | T2—597 7 |
| Bilingualism | 306.446 | Bình Thuận (Vietnam : | |
| linguistics | 404.2 | Province) | T2—597 5 |
| specific languages | T4—042 | Bini (African people) | T5—963 3 |
| sociology | 306.446 | Bini language | 496.33 |
| Bill (Mouth part) | 591.44 | | T6—963 3 |
| descriptive zoology | 591.44 | Binocular-vision photography | 778.4 |
| physiology | 573.355 | Binoculars | |
| Bill collection | | manufacturing technology | 681.412 5 |
| law | 346.077 | Binomial distribution | 519.24 |
| management | 658.88 | Binomial equations | 512.942 2 |
| Bill drafting | 328.373 | algebra | 512.942 2 |
| Billboards | 659.134 2 | calculus | 515.252 |
| land use law | 346.045 | Binuclear family | 306.89 |
| outdoor advertising | 659.134 2 | Bío Bío (Chile : Province) | T2—834 3 |
| Billfishes | 597.78 | Bío Bío (Chile : Region) | T2—834 1 |
| Billiard players | 794.720 92 | Bioactive proteins | 572.69 |
| Billiards | 794.72 | Bioastronautics | 571.499 |
| equipment technology | 688.747 2 | humans | 612.014 5 |
| Billings County (N.D.) | T2—784 94 | Biobibliographies | 012 |
| Bills (Legislation) | 328.37 | Biobío (Chile) | T2—834 1 |
| law | 348.01 | Biochemical engineering | 660.63 |
| United States | 348.731 | Biochemical evolution | 572.38 |
| *see Manual at* 300–330, | | Biochemical genetics | 572.8 |
| 355–390 vs. 342–347, | | humans | 611.018 16 |
| 352–354 | | *see Manual at* 576.5 vs. 572.8 | |
| | | Biochemical interactions | 572.43 |

Biochemical reactions | 572.43
Biochemicals | 572
  organic chemistry | 547
Biochemistry | 572
  ecology | 577.14
  humans | 612.015
  origin of life | 576.83
Bioclimatology | 577.22
Biodegradation
  materials science | 620.112 23
Biodiesel fuel | 665.37
  animal fats and oils | 665.2
Biodiversity | 333.95
  biology | 578.7
  conservation | 333.951 6
  ecology | 577
  resource economics | 333.95
  *see Manual at* 333.7–.9 vs.
    363.1, 363.73, 577
Biodynamics | 571.43
  humans | 612.014 41
Bioelectricity | 572.437
  electric organs | 573.97
  humans | 612.014 27
Bioelectrochemistry | 572.437
Bioenergetics | 572.43
  ecology | 577.13
  humans | 612.014 21
Bioethics | 174.2
  religion | 205.649 57
    Christianity | 241.649 57
  *see also* Ethical problems
Biofeedback | 152.188
  therapeutic use | 615.851 4
Biofeedback therapy
  medicine | 615.851 4
Biofeedback training
  therapeutic use | 615.851 4
Biogas
  technology | 665.776
Biogenesis | 576.83
Biogeochemical cycles | 577.14
Biogeochemical prospecting | 622.12
Biogeochemistry | 577.14
Biogeography | 578.09
  animals | 591.9
  plants | 581.9
Biographers | 920
Biographical dictionaries | T1—092 2
Biographical fiction | 808.838 2
  history and criticism | 809.382
  specific literatures | T3B—308 2
    individual authors | T3A—3

Biography | 920
  | T1—092
  arts | 700.45
  | T3C—35
  literary form | 809.935 92
    specific literatures | T3B—094 92
  literature | 808.803 5
    history and criticism | 809.933 5
    specific literatures | T3B—080 35
    history and
      criticism | T3B—093 5
  *see Manual at* T1—092; *also at*
    913–919; *also at* 930–990
Bioinorganic chemistry | 572.51
  humans | 612.015 24
Bioko (Equatorial Guinea) | T2—671 86
Biological agents
  law | 341.735
  military engineering | 623.459 4
Biological classification | 578.012
Biological clocks | 571.77
Biological communities | 577.82
Biological control of pests
  agriculture | 632.96
Biological control systems | 571.7
  human physiology | 612.022
  *see also* Endocrine system
Biological determinants
  psychology | 155.7
    evolutionary psychology | 155.7
    individual psychology | 155.234
Biological diversity | 333.95
Biological instruments
  manufacturing technology | 681.757
Biological invasions | 577.18
Biological oceanography | 578.77
Biological parents | 306.874
  law | 346.017
  social welfare | 362.829 8
Biological processes | 570
  internal processes | 571
  *see Manual at* 579–590 vs.
    571–575
Biological productivity | 577.15
Biological projectiles | 623.451 6
Biological resources | 333.95
  conservation technology | 639.9
  economics | 333.95
  law | 346.046 95
  public administration | 354.349
Biological rhythms | 571.77
  human physiology | 612.022
Biological sciences | 570

Biological specimens

preservation | 570.752

Biological transport | 571.64

Biological treatment

sewage | 628.35

Biological warfare | 358.38

civil defense | 363.35

ethics | 172.42

*see also* War — ethics

law | 341.735

Biological weapons | 358.388 2

disarmament | 327.174 5

engineering | 623.451 6

biological agents | 623.459 4

Biologists | 570.92

Biology | 570

ethical systems | 171.7

law | 344.095 7

social effects | 304.27

specific environments | 578.7

*see Manual at* 577.3–.7 vs.
578.73–.77

*see Manual at* 579–590 vs.
571–575

Biology and religion | 201.657

Christianity | 261.55

philosophy of religion | 215.7

Bioluminescence | 572.435 8

Bioluminescent communication | 573.95

Bioluminescent organs | 573.95

Biomagnetism | 154.72

Biomass energy | 333.953 9

animals | 333.954

fuel technology | 662.88

plants | 333.953 9

resource economics | 333.953 9

Biomechanics | 571.43

humans | 612.014 41

locomotion | 573.793 43

humans | 612.76

Biomedical engineering | 610.28

Biomedical instrumentation | 610.284

Biomes | 577

*see Manual at* 577.3–.7 vs.
579–590

Biometeorology | 577.22

Biometrics | 570.151 95

Biomineralization | 572.51

animals | 573.764 51

Bionics | 003.5

Bioparks | 578.073

Biophysics | 571.4

humans | 612.014

Biopsy

medicine | 616.075 8

Biorhythms | 571.77

human physiology | 612.022

Biosociology | 304.5

biological ecology | 577.8

sociology | 304.5

*see Manual at* 302–307 vs. 156

Biosolids | 363.728 493

sanitary engineering | 628.38

social services | 363.728 493

use as fertilizer | 631.869

Biospeleology | 578.758 4

Biosphere

resource economics | 333.95

Biostatistics | 570.151 95

Biosynthesis | 572.45

humans | 612.015 4

*see also* Metabolism

Biotechnologists | 660.609 2

Biotechnology | 660.6

food technology | 664.024

law | 343.078 660 6

Bioterrorism | 363.325 3

*see also* Terrorism

Biotic communities | 577.82

Bipolar disorder

medicine | 616.895

*see also* Mental disorders

Bipolar memory | 004.53

engineering | 621.397 32

Bipolar transistors | 621.381 528

Bira (African people) | T5—963 94

Bira-Huku languages | 496.394

| T6—963 94

Biracial people | T5—05

Birational transformations

algebraic geometry | 516.35

Birches | 583.48

forestry | 634.972 6

Bird attracting | 639.978

zoology | 598.072 34

Bird dogs | 636.752

Bird hunting | 799.24

Bird lice | 595.757

Bird watching | 598.072 34

Birdbanding | 598.072 32

Birdhouses | 636.508 31

animal husbandry | 636.508 31

architecture | 728.927

construction | 690.892 7

Birds | 598

agricultural pests | 632.68

air transportation hazard | 363.124 12

Birds (continued)
animal husbandry 636.5
arts T3C—362 8
commercial hunting 639.12
conservation technology 639.978
control technology 628.968
agriculture 632.68
disease carriers 571.986
medicine 614.434
drawing 743.68
paleozoology 568
resource economics 333.958
sports hunting 799.24
zoology 598
Bird's-eye fabrics 677.615
Bird's Head Peninsula
(Indonesia) T2—951 2
Bird's-nest fungi 579.599
Birds' nests 598.156 4
Birds of paradise 598.865
Birds of prey 598.9
conservation technology 639.978 9
resource economics 333.958 9
Biremes 387.21
design 623.812 1
engineering 623.821
handling 623.882 1
transportation services 387.21
*see also* Ships
Birmingham (Ala.) T2—761 781
Birmingham (England) T2—424 96
Birs River (Switzerland) T2—494 3
Birth 573.67
mammals 573.67
reproductive behavior 599.156
*see also* Childbirth
Birth certificates
public administration 353.59
Birth control 363.96
demographic effect 304.666
ethics 176.3
religion 205.66
Buddhism 294.356 6
Christianity 241.66
Hinduism 294.548 66
Islam 297.566
Judaism 296.366
gynecology 618.18
health 613.94
law 344.048
medicine 618.18
public administration 353.59
school programs 371.714
social services 363.96

Birth control (continued)
social theology 201.7
Christianity 261.836
Judaism 296.38
Birth defects
medicine 616.043
Birth intervals
demography 304.63
Birth of Jesus Christ 232.92
Birth order 306.87
environmental psychology 155.924
family relationships 306.87
Birth rites
religion 203.81
Birthday books
astrology 133.540 42
Birthday parties
cooking 641.568
Birthdays
customs 394.2
fortune-telling 133.335 4
Birthmarks
capillary hemangiomas
medicine 616.993 15
medicine 616.55
Births
demography 304.63
Birthwort 583.26
Bisa-Lamba languages 496.391
T6—963 91
Bisayan Islands
(Philippines) T2—599 5
Biscay (Spain) T2—466 3
Biscay, Bay of (France and 551.461 338
Spain) T2—163 38
Biscayne Bay (Fla.) 551.461 348
T2—163 48
Biscayne National Park
(Fla.) T2—163 48
Biscuit mixes 664.753
Biscuits (Breads) 641.815 7
commercial processing 664.752 3
home preparation 641.815 7
Biscuits (Cookies) 641.865 4
commercial processing 664.752 5
home preparation 641.865 4
Biscuits (Crackers) 641.815
commercial processing 664.752
home preparation 641.815
Bisexuality 306.765
ethics 176.4
*see also* Sexual relations —
ethics
psychology 155.343

| | |
|---|---|
| Bisexuals | 306.765 |
| | T1—086 63 |
| psychology | 155.343 |
| social welfare | 362.896 3 |
| Bishops (Chessmen) | 794.145 |
| Bishops (Clergy) | 270.092 |
| biography | 270.092 |
| specific denominations | 280 |
| *see Manual at* 230–280 | |
| ecclesiology | 262.12 |
| Bishops' thrones | 247.1 |
| architecture | 726.529 3 |
| Biskra (Algeria : Province) | T2—655 |
| Bislama language | 427.995 95 |
| | T6—217 |
| Bismarck (N.D.) | T2—784 77 |
| Bismarck, Otto, Fürst von | |
| German history | 943.083 |
| Bismarck Archipelago (Papua | 995.8 |
| New Guinea) | T2—958 |
| Bismarck Range (Papua | |
| New Guinea) | T2—956 |
| Bismarck Sea | 551.461 476 |
| | T2—164 76 |
| Bismuth | 669.75 |
| chemical engineering | 661.071 8 |
| chemistry | 546.718 |
| economic geology | 553.47 |
| materials science | 620.189 5 |
| metallography | 669.957 5 |
| metallurgy | 669.75 |
| mining | 622.347 |
| physical metallurgy | 669.967 5 |
| *see also* Chemicals; Metals | |
| Bison | 599.643 |
| animal husbandry | 636.292 |
| commercial hunting | 639.116 43 |
| conservation technology | 639.979 643 |
| resource economics | 333.959 643 |
| subsistence hunting | 639.116 43 |
| zoology | 599.643 |
| Bissau (Guinea-Bissau) | T2—665 7 |
| Bistriţa-Năsăud (Romania) | T2—498 4 |
| Bithynia | T2—393 13 |
| Biting lice | 595.757 |
| Bitlis İli (Turkey) | T2—566 72 |
| ancient | T2—394 2 |
| Bitterns | 598.34 |
| Bitterroot Range (Idaho and | |
| Mont.) | T2—786 8 |
| Idaho | T2—796 6 |
| Montana | T2—786 8 |
| Bittersweet (Celastraceae) | 583.85 |
| Bittersweet (Solanaceae) | 583.952 |

| | |
|---|---|
| Bitumens | 553.27 |
| *see also* Asphalt | |
| Bituminous coal | 553.24 |
| properties | 662.622 4 |
| *see also* Coal | |
| Bituminous materials | 553.2 |
| building materials | 691.96 |
| economic geology | 553.2 |
| materials science | 620.196 |
| structural engineering | 624.189 6 |
| Bituminous pavements | 625.85 |
| Bituminous sands | 553.283 |
| *see also* Tar sands | |
| Bituminous shale | 553.283 |
| *see also* Oil shale | |
| Bivalvia | 594.4 |
| fishing and culture | 639.4 |
| paleozoology | 564.4 |
| resource economics | 333.955 4 |
| Bivouac | 355.412 |
| military training | 355.544 |
| Biwas | 787.85 |
| *see also* Stringed instruments | |
| Bixaceae | 583.625 |
| Biya, Paul | |
| Cameroonian history | 967.110 42 |
| Bizana (South Africa : | |
| District) | T2—687 59 |
| Bizerte (Tunisia) | T2—611 |
| Blaby (England : District) | T2—425 41 |
| Black Africa | T2—67 |
| Black Americans | 973.049 607 3 |
| | T5—960 73 |
| *see also* African Americans | |
| Black and tan coonhound | 636.753 6 |
| Black-and-white television | 621.388 02 |
| Black art (Witchcraft) | 133.4 |
| Black authors (African origin) | |
| literature | 808.898 96 |
| history and criticism | 809.889 6 |
| specific literatures | T3B—080 896 |
| history and criticism | T3B—098 96 |
| Black basses | 597.738 8 |
| sports fishing | 799.177 388 |
| Black bear | 599.785 |
| big game hunting | 799.277 85 |
| conservation technology | 639.979 785 |
| resource economics | 333.959 785 |
| Black Belt (Ala.) | T2—761 4 |
| Black Canyon of the | |
| Gunnison National Park | |
| (Colo.) | T2—788 19 |
| Black Carib Indians | T5—979 2 |

Black Carib language 497.92
T6—979 2
Black Country (England) T2—424 9
Black Death
  European history 940.192
  incidence 614.573 2
  Italian history 945.05
  medicine 616.923 2
    *see also* Communicable
      diseases — humans
  Tuscan history 945.505
Black Down Hills (England) T2—423 87
Black duck 598.413
Black-eyed peas 641.356 592
  botany 583.74
  commercial processing 664.805 659 2
  cooking 641.656 592
  field crop 633.33
  food 641.356 592
  garden crop 635.659 2
Black-eyed Susans 583.99
Black-footed ferret 599.766 29
  conservation technology 639.979 766 29
  resource economics 333.959 766 29
Black Forest (Germany) T2—434 6
Black grouse 598.634
Black Hawk County (Iowa) T2—777 37
Black Hawk War, 1832 973.56
Black Hills (S.D. and Wyo.) T2—783 9
Black holes (Astronomy) 523.887 5
Black lead 553.26
  *see also* Graphite
Black-letter calligraphy 745.619 75
Black lung disease 362.196 244
  medicine 616.244
  social services 362.196 244
  workers' compensation law 344.021 8
    *see also* Respiratory tract
      diseases — humans
Black magic 133.4
Black mangrove 583.96
Black mass 133.422
Black Methodist churches 287.8
  *see also* Methodist Church
Black moss 584.85
Black Muslim religion 297.87
Black Muslims
  biography 297.870 92
  political science 320.558
Black nationalism 320.546
Black Panther Party 322.420 973
Black pepper 641.338 4
  botany 583.25
  *see also* Hot spices

Black powder 662.26
Black rat 599.352
Black River (S.C.) T2—757 8
Black Rock Desert (Nev.) T2—793 54
Black Sea 551.461 389
T2—163 89
Black Sea region T2—182 29
  ancient 939.5
T2—395
Black shale 553.283
  *see also* Oil shale
Black theology 202.089 96
  Christianity 230.089 96
Black vulture (New World) 598.92
Black vulture (Old World) 598.94
Blackall (Qld.) T2—943 5
Blackberries 641.347 13
  botany 583.73
  commercial processing 664.804 713
  cooking 641.647 13
  food 641.347 13
  horticulture 634.713
Blackberry lily 635.934 38
  botany 584.38
  floriculture 635.934 38
Blackbirds (New World) 598.874
Blackbirds (Old World) 598.842
Blackburn (England :
  Borough) T2—427 623
Blackburn with Darwen
  (England) T2—427 623
Blackdown Hills (England) T2—423 87
Blackflies 595.772
Blackfoot language 497.352
T6—973 52
Blackford County (Ind.) T2—772 68
Blackheads
  medicine 616.53
    *see also* Skin diseases —
      humans
Blackjack (Game) 795.423
Blacklands (Tex.) T2—764 26
Blacklisting (Labor) 331.894
  law 344.018 94
Blackmail 364.165
  law 345.026 5
Blackouts
  electrical engineering 621.319
  military engineering 623.77
Blackpool (Lancashire,
  England) T2—427 65

| | | | |
|---|---|---|---|
| Blacks (African origin) | 305.896 | Blast injuries | |
| | T5—96 | medicine | 617.19 |
| United States | 973.049 607 3 | Blast-resistant construction | 624.176 |
| | T5—960 73 | buildings | 693.854 |
| *see also* African Americans | | Blasting | 624.152 6 |
| Blacksmithing | 682 | excavation | 624.152 6 |
| Blacksmiths | 682.092 | mining | 622.23 |
| Blacktip shark | 597.34 | underwater engineering | 627.74 |
| Blackwater River (Cavan- | | Blastozoa | 563.92 |
| Meath, Ireland) | T2—419 5 | Blastulas | 571.865 |
| Blackwood River (W.A.) | T2—941 2 | Blattaria | 595.728 |
| Bladder (Urinary) | 573.49 | Blazers | 391.473 |
| biology | 573.49 | commercial technology | 687.113 |
| human anatomy | 611.62 | customs | 391.473 |
| human physiology | 612.467 3 | home sewing | 646.433 |
| medicine | 616.62 | *see also* Clothing | |
| surgery | 617.462 | Blazonry | 929.6 |
| *see also* Urinary system | | Bleaching | |
| Bladder diseases | | clothes and related materials | 667.14 |
| medicine | 616.62 | home economics | 648.1 |
| *see also* Urologic diseases — | | oils and gases | 665.028 3 |
| humans | | Bleckley County (Ga.) | T2—758 525 |
| Bladder stones | | Bledsoe County (Tenn.) | T2—768 76 |
| medicine | 616.622 | Bleeding hearts (Plants) | 635.933 35 |
| *see also* Urologic diseases — | | botany | 583.35 |
| humans | | floriculture | 635.933 35 |
| Bladdernuts | 583.78 | Blekinge län (Sweden) | T2—486 2 |
| Bladderworts | 583.95 | Blekinge landskap (Sweden) | T2—486 2 |
| Bladen County (N.C.) | T2—756 32 | Blended families | 306.874 7 |
| Blaenau Gwent (Wales : | | Blended waxes | 665.19 |
| County Borough) | T2—429 95 | Blenders | |
| Blaine County (Idaho) | T2—796 32 | use in cooking | 641.589 3 |
| Blaine County (Mont.) | T2—786 15 | Blending oils and gases | 665.028 3 |
| Blaine County (Neb.) | T2—782 772 | Blending petroleum distillates | 665.534 |
| Blaine County (Okla.) | T2—766 31 | Blenio (Switzerland : | |
| Blair County (Pa.) | T2—748 75 | Distretto) | T2—494 782 |
| Blanco County (Tex.) | T2—764 64 | Blennies | 597.77 |
| Bland County (Va.) | T2—755 765 | Blennioidei | 597.77 |
| Blanket orders | | Blessings | 203.8 |
| library acquisitions | 025.233 | Christianity | 264.13 |
| Blankets | 645.4 | Judaism | 296.45 |
| arts | 746.97 | Blida (Algeria : Province) | T2—653 |
| home sewing | 646.21 | Blighted areas | |
| household equipment | 645.4 | area planning | 711.5 |
| manufacturing technology | 677.626 | Blimps (Airships) | 387.732 7 |
| Blantyre (Malawi) | T2—689 7 | engineering | 629.133 27 |
| Blasphemy | 205.695 | military engineering | 623.743 7 |
| Christianity | 241.695 | transportation services | 387.732 7 |
| criminology | 364.188 | *see also* Aircraft | |
| ethics | 179.5 | Blind-deaf people | 305.908 1 |
| *see also* Ethical problems | | | T1—087 1 |
| law | 345.028 8 | communication | 419.4–.9 |
| Blast-furnace gas | 665.772 | | |
| Blast-furnace practice | 669.141 3 | | |

| | |
|---|---|
| Blind people | 305.908 1 |
| | T1—087 1 |
|   education | 371.911 |
|   library services | 027.663 |
|   social group | 305.908 1 |
|   social welfare | 362.41 |
| Blind play (Chess) | 794.17 |
| Blind snakes | 597.969 |
| Blind workers | 331.591 |
| Blindman's buff | 793.4 |
| Blindness | |
|   incidence | 614.599 7 |
|   ophthalmology | 617.712 |
|     *see also* Eye diseases — | |
|       humans | |
|   social welfare | 362.41 |
| Blinds | 645.3 |
|   architecture | 721.82 |
|   construction | 690.182 |
|   household management | 645.3 |
|   manufacturing technology | 684 |
| Blini | 641.815 3 |
| Bliss Bibliographic Classification | 025.434 |
| Blister beetles | 595.769 |
| Blitz tactics | 355.422 |
| Blizzards | 551.555 |
|   social services | 363.349 25 |
| Bloc québécois (Canadian | |
|   political party) | 324.271 098 4 |
| Block books | 092 |
| Block diagramming | |
|   program design | 005.120 28 |
| Block Island (R.I.) | T2—745 8 |
| Block printing | 761 |
|   textile arts | 746.62 |
| Blockades | 355.44 |
|   Civil War (United States) | 973.75 |
|   law of nations | 341.584 |
|     law of war | 341.63 |
|   military operations | 355.44 |
|   World War I | 940.452 |
|   World War II | 940.545 2 |
|   *see also* Naval operations | |
| Blockbusters (Ammunition) | 355.825 17 |
|   engineering | 623.451 7 |
|   military equipment | 355.825 17 |
| Blocking | |
|   American football | 796.332 26 |
| Blocks (Musical instruments) | 786.82 |
|   *see also* Bars (Musical | |
|     instruments) | |
| Bloemfontein (South | |
|   Africa : District) | T2—685 4 |

| | |
|---|---|
| Bloemhof (South Africa : | |
|   District) | T2—682 45 |
| Blogs | 006.752 |
| Blood | 573.15 |
|   animals | 573.15 |
|   histology | 573.153 5 |
|   human biophysics | 612.118 1 |
|   human histology | 612.11 |
|   human physiology | 612.11 |
|     biological markers | 612.118 2 |
|   medicine | 616.15 |
|   physiology | 573.15 |
|   *see also* Cardiovascular system | |
| Blood analysis | |
|   criminal investigation | 363.256 2 |
|   diagnosis | |
|     general disease | 616.075 61 |
| Blood banks | 362.178 4 |
|   law | 344.041 94 |
|   *see also* Health services | |
| Blood-brain barrier | 573.862 1 |
| Blood cells | 573.153 6 |
|   human histology | 612.11 |
|   *see also* Cardiovascular system | |
| Blood chemistry | 573.154 |
|   human physiology | 612.12 |
|   physiology | 573.154 |
| Blood cholesterol | |
|   human physiology | 612.12 |
| Blood coagulation | 573.159 |
|   human physiology | 612.115 |
|   physiology | 573.159 |
|   *see also* Cardiovascular system | |
| Blood coagulation disorders | |
|   medicine | 616.157 |
|   *see also* Cardiovascular | |
|     diseases — humans | |
| Blood diseases | 573.153 9 |
|   humans | |
|     cancer | 362.196 994 18 |
|       incidence | 614.599 941 8 |
|       medicine | 616.994 18 |
|       social services | 362.196 994 18 |
|       *see also* Cancer — humans | |
|     medicine | 616.15 |
|     pharmacokinetics | 615.718 |
|     *see also* Cardiovascular | |
|       diseases | |
| Blood-forming system | 573.155 |
|   *see also* Hematopoietic system | |
| Blood-forming system diseases | 573.155 39 |
|   *see also* Hematopoietic system | |
|     diseases | |

| | | | |
|---|---|---|---|
| Blood groups | 573.154 | Blood vessels (continued) | |
| human physiology | 612.118 25 | pregnancy complications | |
| physiology | 573.154 | obstetrics | 618.361 3 |
| see also Cardiovascular system | | surgery | 617.413 |
| Blood lipids | | see also Cardiovascular system | |
| human physiology | 612.12 | Bloodhound | 636.753 6 |
| Blood plasma | 573.156 | Bloodroot | 583.35 |
| biology | 573.156 | Bloodsucking animals | 591.53 |
| human histology | 612.116 | Bloodworts | 584.354 |
| human physiology | 612.116 | Blotting paper | 676.284 4 |
| pharmacology | 615.39 | Blount County (Ala.) | T2—761 72 |
| see also Cardiovascular system | | Blount County (Tenn.) | T2—768 885 |
| Blood plasma banks | 362.178 4 | Blouses | 391.475 |
| see also Health services | | commercial technology | 687.115 |
| Blood plasma substitutes | 615.399 | customs | 391.475 |
| Blood platelet disorders | | home economics | 646.3 |
| medicine | 616.157 | home sewing | 646.435 |
| see also Cardiovascular | | see also Clothing | |
| diseases — humans | | Blowers | 621.61 |
| Blood platelets | 573.159 | Blowflies | 595.774 |
| histology | 573.159 | Blowing glass | 666.122 |
| human histology | 612.117 | decorative arts | 748.202 82 |
| human physiology | 612.117 | Blown tableware | |
| medicine | 616.157 | decorative arts | 748.2 |
| physiology | 573.159 | Blowpipes (Chemical apparatus) | 542.4 |
| see also Cardiovascular system | | Blowpipes (Weapons) | |
| Blood pressure | 573.134 3 | sports | 799.202 82 |
| human physiology | 612.14 | Blue and white transfer ware | 738.27 |
| physiology | 573.134 3 | Blue catfish | 597.492 |
| see also Cardiovascular system | | Blue collar workers | 331.79 |
| Blood River (South Africa) | T2—684 1 | | T1—086 23 |
| Blood River, Battle of, 1838 | 968.404 2 | labor economics | 331.79 |
| Blood substitutes | 615.399 | labor force | 331.119 042 |
| Blood sugar | | labor market | 331.129 042 |
| human physiology | 612.12 | labor unions | 331.88 |
| Blood transfusion | 362.178 4 | personnel management | 658.304 4 |
| law | 344.041 94 | training | 658.312 45 |
| pharmacology | 615.39 | public administration | 354.93 |
| social services | 362.178 4 | social class | 305.562 |
| Blood types | 573.154 | see also Working class | |
| human physiology | 612.118 25 | Blue Earth County (Minn.) | T2—776 21 |
| physiology | 573.154 | Blue goose | 598.417 5 |
| see also Cardiovascular system | | Blue-green algae | 579.39 |
| Blood vessel diseases | | Blue monkeys | 599.862 |
| medicine | 616.13 | Blue Mountains (N.S.W.) | T2—944 5 |
| see also Cardiovascular | | Blue Mountains (Or. and | |
| diseases — humans | | Wash.) | T2—795 7 |
| Blood vessels | 573.18 | Oregon | T2—795 7 |
| animals | 573.18 | Washington | T2—797 46 |
| human anatomy | 611.13 | Blue Mountains National | |
| human physiology | 612.13 | Park (N.S.W.) | T2—944 5 |
| medicine | 616.13 | Blue Nile (Sudan) | T2—626 4 |
| physiology | 573.18 | Blue Nile River (Ethiopia | |
| | | and Sudan) | T2—626 4 |

| | |
|---|---|
| Blue Ridge Mountains | T2—755 |
| Georgia | T2—758 2 |
| North Carolina | T2—756 8 |
| South Carolina | T2—757 2 |
| Virginia | T2—755 |
| Blue shark | 597.34 |
| Blue whale | 599.524 8 |
| Blue-winged teal | 598.413 |
| Bluebells (Boraginaceae) | 635.933 94 |
| botany | 583.94 |
| floriculture | 635.933 94 |
| Bluebells (Campanulaceae) | 635.933 98 |
| botany | 583.98 |
| floriculture | 635.933 98 |
| Bluebells (Liliaceae) | 635.934 32 |
| botany | 584.32 |
| floriculture | 635.934 32 |
| Blueberries | 641.347 37 |
| botany | 583.66 |
| commercial processing | 664.804 737 |
| cooking | 641.647 37 |
| food | 641.347 37 |
| horticulture | 634.737 |
| Bluebirds | 598.842 |
| Bluebonnet | 583.74 |
| floriculture | 635.933 74 |
| Bluegrass music | 781.642 |
| Bluegrass region (Ky.) | T2—769 3 |
| Bluegrasses | 633.21 |
| botany | 584.9 |
| forage crop | 633.21 |
| Blueprints | 604.25 |
| building construction | 692.1 |
| printing technology | 686.42 |
| technical drawing | 604.25 |
| Blues | 781.643 |
| songs | 782.421 643 |
| Bluestone | 553.53 |
| economic geology | 553.53 |
| quarrying | 622.353 |
| Blyth Valley (England) | T2—428 84 |
| BMX (Bicycle racing) | 796.622 |
| Bo tree | |
| Buddhism | 294.343 5 |
| Boaco (Nicaragua : Dept.) | T2—728 526 |
| Boadicea, Queen | |
| English history | 936.204 |
| Boar fishes | 597.64 |
| Board games | 794 |
| equipment technology | 688.74 |
| Board of Governors of the Federal Reserve System (U.S.) | 332.110 973 |
| Board of trade buildings | |
| architecture | 725.25 |
| Board zithers | 787.74 |
| *see also* Stringed instruments | |
| Boardercross | 796.939 |
| Boarding schools | 373.222 |
| Boardinghouses | 910.464 |
| *see also* Lodging (Temporary housing) | |
| Boards of directors | |
| executive management | 658.422 |
| public administration | 352.25 |
| Boards of education | 353.822 5 |
| local public schools | 379.153 1 |
| public administration | 353.822 5 |
| Boardsailing | 797.33 |
| Boas | 597.967 |
| Boat lily | 584.86 |
| Boat racing | 797.14 |
| Boatbuilding | 623.82 |
| Boathouses | |
| architecture | 725.87 |
| Boating | 623.88 |
| seamanship | 623.88 |
| sports | 797.1 |
| Boating safety | 363.123 |
| sports | 363.14 |
| law | 344.047 6 |
| *see also* Water transportation — safety | |
| Boatmen | |
| sports | 797.109 2 |
| technologists | 623.880 92 |
| Boats | 387.2 |
| *see also* Ships | |
| Bobangi language | 496.396 8 |
| | T6—963 968 |
| Bobbin laces | 677.653 |
| arts | 746.222 |
| manufacturing technology | 677.653 |
| Bobcat | 599.753 6 |
| Bobo (African people) | T5—963 5 |
| Bobo-Dioulasso (Burkina Faso) | T2—662 5 |
| Bobo language | 496.35 |
| | T6—963 5 |
| Bobsledding | 796.952 |
| Bobwhites | 598.627 3 |
| conservation technology | 639.978 627 3 |
| resource economics | 333.958 627 3 |
| sports hunting | 799.246 273 |
| Bocas del Toro (Panama : Province) | T2—728 712 |
| Boccie | 796.31 |

| | | | |
|---|---|---|---|
| Bochum (Germany) | T2—435 632 | Body language | 302.222 |
| Bochum (South Africa : | | psychology | 153.69 |
| District) | T2—682 56 | social psychology | 302.222 |
| Bodensee | T2—434 62 | Body measurements | |
| Germany | T2—434 62 | humans | 599.94 |
| Switzerland | T2—494 597 | Body mechanics | |
| Bodish languages | 495.4 | human physiology | 612.76 |
| | T6—954 | Body piercing | |
| Bodo languages | 495.4 | customs | 391.7 |
| | T6—954 | Body shape | 613.71 |
| Bodoni type | 686.224 7 | *see also* Body contours | |
| Body (Human) | | Body size | 591.41 |
| arts | T3C—356 1 | Body temperature | 571.76 |
| literature | 808.803 561 | humans | 612.014 26 |
| history and criticism | 809.933 561 | Body weight | 591.41 |
| specific literatures | T3B—080 356 1 | Bodybuilding | 613.713 |
| history and | | physical fitness | 613.713 |
| criticism | T3B—093 561 | sports | 796.41 |
| philosophy | 128.6 | Bodyguards | 363.289 |
| religion | 202.2 | Bodywork | 629.260 288 |
| Christianity | 233.5 | Boeotia (Greece) | T2—495 15 |
| *see also* Humans — religion | | ancient | T2—384 |
| Body and mind | | Boer War, 1880–1881 | 968.204 6 |
| philosophy | 128.2 | Boer War, 1899–1902 | 968.048 |
| psychology | 150 | Bog mosses | 588.29 |
| Body and soul | 128.1 | Bog myrtle (Buckbean) | 583.93 |
| religion | 202.2 | Bog myrtle (Sweet gale) | 583.43 |
| Christianity | 233.5 | Bog of Allen (Ireland) | T2—418 5 |
| Judaism | 296.32 | Bog turtle | 597.925 7 |
| philosophy of religion | 218 | Bogotá (Colombia) | T2—861 48 |
| *see also* Humans — religion | | Bogs | |
| Body art | 709.040 752 | biology | 578.768 7 |
| Body contours | 613.71 | ecology | 577.687 |
| arts | T3C—356 1 | Bogus wrapping paper | 676.287 |
| customs | 391.62 | Bohemia (Czech Republic) | T2—437 1 |
| health | 613.71 | Bohemia (Kingdom) | 943.710 2 |
| literature | 808.803 561 | | T2—437 1 |
| history and criticism | 809.933 561 | Bohemia and Moravia | 943.703 3 |
| specific literatures | T3B—080 356 1 | (Protectorate) | T2—437 |
| history and | | Bohemian Forest | T2—437 14 |
| criticism | T3B—093 561 | Czech Republic | T2—437 14 |
| sociology | 306.461 3 | Germany | T2—433 5 |
| Body covering (Animals) | 573.5 | Böhm-Bawerk, Eugen von | |
| descriptive zoology | 591.47 | economic school | 330.157 |
| physiology | 573.5 | Bohol (Philippines) | T2—599 5 |
| Body fluid disorders | | Bohrium | |
| medicine | 616.399 2 | chemistry | 546.54 |
| *see also* Digestive system | | Bohuslän landskap | |
| diseases — humans | | (Sweden) | T2—486 7 |
| Body heat | | Boidae | 597.967 |
| humans | 612.014 26 | Boiler and machinery insurance | 368.7 |
| Body image | 306.461 3 | Boiler-house practice | 621.194 |
| | | Boiler insurance | 368.7 |
| | | Boiler operations | 621.194 |

Boilers
  heating buildings              697.07
    steam                        697.507
  ship power plants              623.873
  steam engineering              621.183
Boiling
  home cooking                   641.73
Boiling points                   536.44
Boils
  medicine                       616.523
    *see also* Skin diseases —
      humans
Boina (Kingdom)                  969.101
                                 T2—691
Boinae                           597.967
Bois-Francs Region
  (Quebec)                       T2—714 565
Boise (Idaho)                    T2—796 28
Boise County (Idaho)             T2—796 74
Bojador (Morocco :
  Province)                      T2—648
Bojutsu                          796.86
Bok choy                         641.353
  cooking                        641.653
  food                           641.353
  garden crop                    635.3
Bokhara rugs
  arts                           746.758 7
Bokkeveld Range (South
  Africa)                        T2—687 17
Bokmål language                  439.82
                                 T6—398 2
Bokmål literature                839.82
Boksburg (South Africa :
  District)                      T2—682 25
Boland (South Africa)            T2—687 34
Bolaños Geyer, Enrique
  Nicaraguan history             972.850 543
Bolas
  sports                         799.202 82
Bolctaceae                       579.6
Boletes                          579.6
Bolívar (Colombia : Dept.)       T2—861 14
Bolívar (Ecuador :
  Province)                      T2—866 16
Bolívar (Venezuela : State)      T2—876 3
Bolívar, Simón
  South American history         980.02
Bolivar County (Miss.)           T2—762 43
Bolivia                          984
                                 T2—84
Bolivia (Game)                   795.418
Bolivian literature              860
Bolivians                        T5—688 4

Boll weevil
  agricultural pest              633.519 768
Bollinger County (Mo.)           T2—778 94
Bollworm
  agricultural pest              633.519 78
Bolobedu (South Africa :
  District)                      T2—682 59
Bologna (Italy)                  T2—454 11
  ancient                        T2—372 611
Bologna (Italy : Province)       T2—454 1
  ancient                        T2—372 61
Bolshevik International          324.175
Bolshevik parties                324.217 5
Bolsover (England :
  District)                      T2—425 15
Bolton (England :
  Metropolitan Borough)          T2—427 37
Bolts                            621.882
Bolts (Locks)                    683.31
Boltzmann statistics             530.132
Bolu İli (Turkey)                T2—563 4
  ancient                        T2—393 15
Bolyai geometry                  516.9
Bolzano (Italy : Province)       T2—453 83
  ancient                        T2—373 73
Bomb disposal units
  armed forces                   358.23
Bombacaceae                      583.68
Bombala (N.S.W.)                 T2—944 7
Bombardment
  military science               355.4
  particle physics               539.73
  solid-state physics            530.416
Bombay (India)                   T2—547 92
Bombers                          358.428 3
  engineering                    623.746 3
  military equipment             358.428 3
Bombing (Terrorism)              363.325
  *see also* Terrorism
Bombing forces                   358.42
Bombs                            355.825 1
  military engineering           623.451
  military equipment             355.825 1
Bombsights                       623.46
Bombycillidae                    598.852
Bombycoidea                      595.78
Bombyliidae                      595.773
Bon (Tibetan religion)           299.54
Bon Homme County (S.D.)          T2—783 395
Bonaire                          T2—729 86
Bonaparte River (B.C.)           T2—711 72
Bonasa                           598.635

Bonaventure (Quebec :
  Regional County
  Municipality)      T2—714 785
Bond (Law)      345.056
Bond County (Ill.)      T2—773 873
Bond insurance      368.853
Bond paper      676.282 3
Bonded fabrics      677.69
  *see also* Textiles
Bonding metals      671.58
Bonding of employees
  insurance      368.83
  law      346.086 83
Bonds (Chemical forces)      541.224
  biochemistry      572.33
Bonds (Securities)      332.632 3
  accounting      657.75
  financial management      658.152 24
    capital procurement      658.152 24
    debt management      658.152 6
  income tax      336.242 6
    law      343.052 46
  investment economics      332.632 3
  law      346.092 2
    corporate law      346.066 6
  *see Manual at* 332.632044 vs.
    332.6323; *also at* 332.6322
    vs. 332.6323
Bône (Algeria : Dept.)      T2—655
Bone cancer
  incidence      614.599 947 1
  medicine      616.994 71
  *see also* Cancer — humans
Bone carving      736.6
Bone char      662.93
Bone diseases
  medicine      616.71
  *see also* Musculoskeletal
    diseases — humans
  pharmacokinetics      615.771
Bone marrow      573.155 6
  biology      573.155 6
  diseases      573.155 639
    *see also* Hematopoietic
     system diseases
  human anatomy      611.41
  human physiology      612.416
  medicine      616.41
  surgery      617.441
Bone marrow cancer
  incidence      614.599 944 1
  medicine      616.994 41
    *see also* Cancer — humans

Bone marrow diseases
  medicine      616.41
  *see also* Hematopoietic
    system diseases —
    humans
Bone meal
  use as fertilizer      631.85
Bone tissues
  human histology      612.751 045
Bones      573.76
  anthropometry      599.947
  biology      573.76
  drawing
    animals      743.6
    humans      743.46
  fractures
    medicine      617.15
  human anatomy      611.71
  human physiology      612.751
  medicine      616.71
  pharmacokinetics      615.771
  surgery      617.471
Bongo (Mammal)      599.642 3
Bongo, Omar
  Gabonese history      967.210 42
Bongo-Bagirmi languages      496.5
     T6—965
Bongos      786.95
  *see also* Percussion instruments
Bonin Islands (Japan)      T2—528
Bonito      641.392
  cooking      641.692
  food      641.392
  zoology      597.783
Bonn (Germany)      T2—435 518
Bonner County (Idaho)      T2—796 96
Bonnets      391.43
  *see also* Headwear
Bonneville County (Idaho)      T2—796 53
Bono (Kingdom)      966.701 6
     T2—667
Bononia (Italy)      T2—372 611
Bonsai      635.977 2
Bontebok National Park
  (South Africa)      T2—687 36
Bonuses      331.216 4
  labor economics      331.216 4
  personnel management      658.322 5
Bony fishes      597
  *see also* Fishes
Bony ganoids      597.41
Boobies      598.43
  resource economics      333.958 43
Booby traps      623.451 4

| | |
|---|---|
| Booidea | 597.967 |
| Book arts | |
| technology | 686 |
| Book catalogs | 025.313 |
| bibliography | 017 |
| library science | 025.313 |
| Book clubs | 070.5 |
| Book collecting | 002.075 |
| Book editors | 070.510 92 |
| Book illumination | 745.67 |
| Book illustration | 741.64 |
| Book jacket illustration | 741.64 |
| Book lice | 595.732 |
| Book numbers (Shelflisting) | 025.428 |
| Book of Common Prayer | 264.03 |
| Book of Mormon | 289.322 |
| Book paper | 676.282 4 |
| Book reports | 371.302 81 |
| Book restoration | |
| library science | 025.84 |
| Book reviews | 028.1 |
| Book scorpions | 595.47 |
| Book selection | |
| library science | 025.21 |
| Bookbinders | 686.300 92 |
| Bookbinding | 686.3 |
| library operations | 025.7 |
| notable books | 095 |
| Bookcases | |
| manufacturing technology | 684.16 |
| Booking services | |
| transportation | 388.042 |
| *see also* Passenger services | |
| Bookkeepers | 657.209 2 |
| Bookkeeping | 657.2 |
| Bookmobiles | |
| plant management | 022 |
| public library use | 027.42 |
| Bookplates | 769.52 |
| bibliography | 010.42 |
| Books | 002 |
| arts | T3C—39 |
| bibliographies | 011 |
| cataloging | 025.32 |
| folklore | 398.28 |
| history and criticism | 398.3 |
| influence on crime | 364.254 |
| literature | 808.803 9 |
| postal handling | 383.124 |
| *see also* Postal service | |
| provenance | 097 |
| publishing | 070.5 |
| sociology | 302.232 |
| technology | 686 |
| Books (continued) | |
| theft of | 364.162 800 2 |
| law | 345.026 280 02 |
| Books and reading | 028 |
| Books of Hours | 242 |
| Booksellers' catalogs | 017.4 |
| Bookselling | 381.450 02 |
| Boolean algebra | 511.324 |
| Boomerangs | |
| sports hunting | 799.202 82 |
| sports throwing | 796.435 |
| Boone County (Ark.) | T2—767 18 |
| Boone County (Ill.) | T2—773 29 |
| Boone County (Ind.) | T2—772 54 |
| Boone County (Iowa) | T2—777 544 |
| Boone County (Ky.) | T2—769 363 |
| Boone County (Mo.) | T2—778 29 |
| Boone County (Neb.) | T2—782 51 |
| Boone County (W. Va.) | T2—754 39 |
| Booster rockets | 629.475 |
| Boosters (Detonators) | 662.4 |
| Boothferry (England) | T2—428 39 |
| Boothia Peninsula | |
| (Nunavut) | T2—719 55 |
| Bootlace worms | 592.32 |
| Bootlegged editions | 364.166 2 |
| law | 345.026 62 |
| Bootlegging (Copyright | |
| infringement) | 364.166 2 |
| law | 345.026 62 |
| Bootlegging (Offense against | |
| revenue) | 364.133 2 |
| law | 345.023 32 |
| Boots | 391.413 |
| customs | 391.413 |
| manufacturing technology | 685.31 |
| *see also* Clothing | |
| Bootstrap methods | 519.54 |
| Bop | 781.655 |
| Bophuthatswana (South Africa) | 968.24 |
| | T2—682 4 |
| Boquerón (Paraguay : | |
| Dept.) | T2—892 24 |
| Borage | 583.94 |
| Boraginaceae | 583.94 |
| Borates | 553.633 |
| economic geology | 553.633 |
| mineralogy | 549.735 |
| mining | 622.363 3 |
| Borax | 553.633 |
| economic geology | 553.633 |
| mineralogy | 549.735 |
| mining | 622.363 3 |
| Bordeaux (France) | T2—447 144 |

| | |
|---|---|
| Borden, Robert Laird, Sir | |
| Canadian history | 971.061 2 |
| Borden County (Tex.) | T2—764 853 |
| Border Country (Scotland) | T2—413 7 |
| Border defense | 355.45 |
| Border disputes | |
| law of nations | 341.42 |
| Border patrols | 363.285 |
| Borderline personality disorder | |
| medicine | 616.858 52 |
| *see also* Mental disorders | |
| Borders (Floriculture) | 635.963 |
| Borders (Geography) | 320.12 |
| *see also* Boundaries | |
| Borders Region (Scotland) | T2—413 7 |
| Bordism theory | 514.72 |
| Bordj Bou Arréridj | |
| (Algeria : Province) | T2—655 |
| Boreal forests | |
| biology | 578.737 |
| ecology | 577.37 |
| Borers (Insects) | |
| agricultural pests | 634.049 7 |
| Boring | |
| mining | 622.24 |
| Boring tools | 621.952 |
| Boris Fyodorovich Godunov, | |
| Czar of Russia | |
| Russian history | 947.044 |
| Bornean languages | 499.225 |
| | T6—992 25 |
| Borneo | T2—598 3 |
| Indonesia | T2—598 3 |
| Malaysia | T2—595 3 |
| Borneo languages | 499.225 |
| | T6—992 25 |
| Bornholm (Denmark) | T2—489 2 |
| Bornholms amt (Denmark) | T2—489 2 |
| Borno State (Nigeria) | T2—669 85 |
| Bornu (Kingdom) | 966.980 1 |
| | T2—669 8 |
| Boron | 553.6 |
| chemical engineering | 661.067 1 |
| chemistry | 546.671 |
| economic geology | 553.6 |
| organic chemistry | 547.056 71 |
| applied | 661.895 |
| *see also* Chemicals | |
| Boron fuels | 662.86 |
| Borrelia infections | |
| incidence | 614.574 |
| medicine | 616.924 |
| *see also* Communicable | |
| diseases — humans | |

| | |
|---|---|
| Borrowing | 332.041 5 |
| capital management | 658.152 24 |
| public finance | 336.34 |
| *see also* Public debt | |
| Borrowing power (Legislative | |
| bodies) | 328.341 2 |
| Borsod-Abaúj-Zemplén | |
| Megye (Hungary) | T2—439 9 |
| Borstals | 365.42 |
| *see also* Penal institutions | |
| Borzoi | 636.753 5 |
| Bos | 599.642 2 |
| Boshof (South Africa : | |
| District) | T2—685 8 |
| Bosnia and Hercegovina | 949.742 |
| | T2—497 42 |
| ancient | 939.874 2 |
| | T2—398 742 |
| Bosniaks | T5—918 39 |
| Bosnian language | 491.839 |
| | T6—918 39 |
| Bosnian literature | 891.839 |
| Bosnian Muslims | T5—918 39 |
| Bosnians | T5—918 39 |
| Bosons | 539.721 |
| Bosporus (Turkey) | 551.461 389 |
| | T2—163 89 |
| Bosque County (Tex.) | T2—764 518 |
| Bossier Parish (La.) | T2—763 97 |
| Boston (England : Borough) | T2—425 37 |
| Boston (Mass.) | T2—744 61 |
| Boston ivy | 635.933 86 |
| botany | 583.86 |
| floriculture | 635.933 86 |
| Boston Massacre, 1770 | 973.311 3 |
| Boston Mountains (Ark. and | |
| Okla.) | T2—767 1 |
| Arkansas | T2—767 1 |
| Oklahoma | T2—766 8 |
| Boston Port Bill, 1774 | 973.311 6 |
| Boston Tea Party, 1773 | 973.311 5 |
| Boston terrier | 636.72 |
| Bostonnais (Quebec) | T2—714 459 |
| Bostrychoidea | 595.763 |
| Botanical drugs | |
| pharmacology | 615.321 |
| Botanical gardens | 580.73 |
| architecture | 727.658 |
| landscape architecture | 712.5 |
| Botanical medicine | |
| therapeutic system | 615.53 |
| Botanical specimens | |
| preservation | 580.752 |
| Botanists | 580.92 |

| | |
|---|---|
| Botany | 580 |
| Botetourt County (Va.) | T2—755 83 |
| Botflies | 595.774 |
| Botha, Louis | |
| South African history | 968.052 |
| Botha, P. W. (Pieter Willem) | |
| South African history | 968.063 |
| Bothaville (South Africa : | |
| District) | T2—685 2 |
| Bothnia, Gulf of | 551.461 334 |
| | T2—163 34 |
| Botoșani (Romania : Judeṭ) | T2—498 1 |
| Botshabelo (South Africa : | |
| District) | T2—685 6 |
| Botswana | 968.83 |
| | T2—688 3 |
| Botswana people | T5—968 83 |
| Bottineau County (N.D.) | T2—784 61 |
| Bottle cutting | |
| decorative arts | 748.202 86 |
| Bottle-nosed dolphins | 599.533 |
| Bottled water | |
| commercial processing | 663.61 |
| Bottles | 688.8 |
| glass | 666.192 |
| decorative arts | 748.82 |
| technology | 666.192 |
| *see also* Containers | |
| Bottling alcoholic beverages | 663.19 |
| Bottom fishing | 799.122 |
| Bottoms (Petroleum) | 665.538 8 |
| Botulism | |
| incidence | 614.512 5 |
| medicine | 616.931 5 |
| *see also* Communicable | |
| diseases — humans | |
| Bouaké (Ivory Coast) | T2—666 8 |
| Boucherville (Quebec) | T2—714 371 |
| Bouches du Rhône (France) | T2—449 1 |
| Boudicca, Queen | |
| English history | 936.204 |
| Boudry (Switzerland : | |
| District) | T2—494 386 |
| Bougainville Island (Papua | |
| New Guinea) | T2—959 2 |
| Bougainvilleas | 635.933 53 |
| botany | 583.53 |
| floriculture | 635.933 53 |
| Bougie (Algeria : Province) | T2—655 |
| Bouira (Algeria : Province) | T2—653 |
| Boujdour (Morocco : | |
| Province) | T2—648 |
| Boulaida (Algeria : | |
| Province) | T2—653 |
| Boulder County (Colo.) | T2—788 63 |
| Boulemane (Morocco : | |
| Province) | T2—643 4 |
| Boumerdes (Algeria : | |
| Province) | T2—653 |
| Boundaries | 320.12 |
| law of nations | 341.42 |
| local government | 320.8 |
| political science | 320.12 |
| Boundary County (Idaho) | T2—796 98 |
| Boundary layers | 532.051 |
| aeronautics | 629.132 37 |
| engineering | 620.106 4 |
| physics | 532.051 |
| space flight | 629.415 1 |
| Boundary surveying | 526.9 |
| Boundary-value problems | 515.35 |
| calculus of finite differences | 515.62 |
| differential equations | 515.35 |
| Bounty Islands (N.Z.) | T2—939 9 |
| Bounty Mutiny, 1789 | 996.18 |
| Bourbon | 641.252 |
| commercial processing | 663.52 |
| Bourbon, House of | 944.03 |
| French history | 944.03 |
| genealogy | 929.74 |
| Sicilian history | 945.807 |
| 1712–1799 | 945.807 |
| 1815–1860 | 945.808 3 |
| Southern Italian history | 945.707 |
| 1734–1799 | 945.707 |
| 1815–1860 | 945.708 3 |
| Spanish history | 946.054 |
| Bourbon County (Kan.) | T2—781 97 |
| Bourbon County (Ky.) | T2—769 423 |
| Bourbon Restoration, 1814–1833 | 946.072 |
| Bourbon Restoration, 1871–1873 | 946.073 |
| Bourbonnais (France) | T2—445 97 |
| Bourgeoisie | 305.55 |
| | T1—086 22 |
| Bourges (France) | T2—445 525 |
| Bourgogne (France) | T2—444 1 |
| Bourguiba, Habib | |
| Tunisian history | 961.105 1 |
| Bourke (N.S.W.) | T2—944 9 |
| Bournemouth (England) | T2—423 38 |
| Bouteflika, Abdelaziz | |
| Algerian history | 965.054 |
| Boutonneuse fever | |
| incidence | 614.526 3 |
| medicine | 616.922 3 |
| *see also* Communicable | |
| diseases — humans | |
| Boutonnieres | 745.923 |

| | |
|---|---|
| Bouvet Island | T2—971 3 |
| Bouvier des Flandres | 636.737 |
| Bovidae | 599.64 |
|   animal husbandry | 636.2 |
|   paleozoology | 569.64 |
| Bovinae | 599.642 |
| Bovine spongiform | |
|   encephalopathy | |
|   humans | |
|     medicine | 616.83 |
|     *see also* Nervous system | |
|       diseases — humans | |
| Bovines | 599.64 |
|   animal husbandry | 636.2 |
| Bow harps | 787.94 |
|   *see also* Stringed instruments | |
| Bow River (Alta.) | T2—712 33 |
| Bowed stringed instruments | 787 |
|   *see also* Stringed instruments | |
| Bowell, Mackenzie, Sir | |
|   Canadian history | 971.055 |
| Bowen (Qld.) | T2—943 6 |
| Bowen Island (B.C. : Island) | T2—711 33 |
| Bowfins | 597.41 |
| Bowhead whale | 599.527 6 |
| Bowie County (Tex.) | T2—764 197 |
| Bowing techniques | 784.193 69 |
| Bowl games (Football) | 796.332 63 |
| Bowland, Forest of | |
|   (England) | T2—427 685 |
| Bowlers | 794.609 2 |
| Bowling (Cricket) | 796.358 22 |
| Bowling (Game) | 794.6 |
|   equipment technology | 688.746 |
| Bowling alleys | 794.6 |
|   architecture | 725.84 |
| Bowman County (N.D.) | T2—784 92 |
| Bowron Lake Provincial | |
|   Park (B.C.) | T2—711 75 |
| Bows and arrows | 799.202 85 |
|   art metalwork | 739.73 |
|   manufacturing technology | 688.792 028 5 |
|   military equipment | 623.441 |
|   shooting game | 799.215 |
|   sports | 799.202 85 |
|   target shooting | 799.32 |
| Box (Plants) | 583.69 |
|   floriculture | 635.933 69 |
| Box Butte County (Neb.) | T2—782 94 |
| Box Elder County (Utah) | T2—792 42 |
| Box-girder bridges | |
|   construction | 624.215 |
| Box lily | 584.353 |
| Box lunches | 641.53 |

| | |
|---|---|
| Boxcars | 385.34 |
|   engineering | 625.24 |
|   *see also* Rolling stock | |
| Boxer (Dog) | 636.73 |
| Boxer Rebellion, 1899–1901 | 951.035 |
| Boxers (Pugilists) | 796.830 92 |
| Boxes | 688.8 |
|   paperboard | 676.32 |
|   *see also* Containers | |
| Boxfishes | 597.64 |
| Boxing | 796.83 |
|   law | 344.099 |
| Boxwoods | 583.69 |
|   floriculture | 635.933 69 |
| Boy Scout camps | 796.542 2 |
| Boy Scouts | 369.43 |
| Boyacá (Colombia) | T2—861 44 |
| Boycott | |
|   Holocaust, 1933–1945 | 940.531 813 2 |
|   international politics | 327.117 |
|   law of nations | 341.582 |
|   labor economics | 331.893 |
|     law | 344.018 93 |
|   restraint of trade | 338.604 8 |
|     law | 343.072 3 |
| Boyd County (Ky.) | T2—769 27 |
| Boyd County (Neb.) | T2—782 723 |
| Boyer Ahmadī va | |
|   Kohkīlūyeh (Iran) | T2—556 8 |
| Boyle County (Ky.) | T2—769 523 |
| Boyne River (Ireland) | T2—418 22 |
| Boys | 305.230 811 |
| | T1—083 |
|   criminal offenders | 364.36 |
|   education | 371.821 1 |
|   health | 613.042 32 |
|   home care | 649.132 |
|   journalism for | 070.483 26 |
|   psychology | 155.432 |
|   publications for | |
|     bibliographies | 011.624 1 |
|   recreation | 790.194 |
|     indoor | 793.019 4 |
|     outdoor | 796.083 |
|   sex hygiene | 613.953 |
|   social aspects | 305.230 811 |
|   *see also* Children | |
| Boys' clubs | 369.42 |
| Boys' societies | 369.42 |
| Boysenberries | 641.347 18 |
|   commercial processing | 664.804 718 |
|   cooking | 641.647 18 |
|   food | 641.347 18 |
|   horticulture | 634.718 |

Bozca Island (Turkey)    T2—562 2
Bozcaada (Turkey)    T2—562 2
Bozen (Italy : Province)    T2—453 83
Bozizé, François
   Central African history    967.410 54
Brabant (Belgium)    T2—493 3
Brabant Wallon (Belgium)    T2—493 37
Bracelets    391.7
   customs    391.7
   making    739.278
     costume jewelry    688.2
      handicrafts    745.594 2
      fine jewelry    739.278
Brachiopoda    594.68
   paleozoology    564.68
Brachycera    595.773
Brachycera-Cyclorrhapha    595.774
Brachycera-Orthorrhapha    595.773
Brachyura    595.386
Bracing equipment
   aircraft    629.134 37
Bracken (Ferns)    587.3
Bracken County (Ky.)    T2—769 325
Bracket fungi    579.597
Brackish water    553.72
      T2—169
   economic geology    553.72
   hydrology    551.48
Bracknell Forest (England)    T2—422 98
Bradford (England : City)    T2—428 17
Bradford County (Fla.)    T2—759 15
Bradford County (Pa.)    T2—748 57
Bradley County (Ark.)    T2—767 63
Bradley County (Tenn.)    T2—768 873
Bradoriida    565.3
Bradyodonti    567.3
Bradypodidae    599.313
Braga (Portugal : District)    T2—469 12
Bragança (Portugal :
   District)    T2—469 27
Braganza, House of    946.903
Brahma Samaj    294.556 2
Brahmanas    294.592 1
Brahmanism    294.5
Brahmans (Cattle)    636.291
Brahmans (People)
   biography    294.509 2
Brahmaputra River    T2—549 2
   Bangladesh    T2—549 2
   India    T2—541 6
Brahui    T5—948 3
Brahui language    494.83
      T6—948 3
Brahui literature    894.83

Braided rugs
   arts    746.73
Braiding hair    646.724 7
Braiding textiles    677.028 2
   arts    746.42
Braids (Hairstyling)    646.724 7
Braids (Mathematics)    514.224
Braids (Textile trim)    677.76
   arts    746.27
Brăila (Romania : Judeţ)    T2—498 1
Braille    411
   printing    686.282
   specific languages    T4—11
Braille publications
   bibliographies    011.63
   cataloging    025.349 2
   library treatment    025.179 2
   publishing    070.579 2
Brain    573.86
   biology    573.86
   human anatomy    611.81
   human biochemistry    612.822
   human biophysics    612.822
   human physiology    612.82
   medicine    616.8
   surgery    617.481
   *see also* Nervous system
Brain cancer
   incidence    614.599 948 1
   medicine    616.994 81
   *see also* Cancer — humans
Brain-damaged people    305.908 4
      T1—087 4
   education    371.91
   *see also* Mentally disabled
     people
Brain diseases
   humans
     cancer    362.196 994 81
      incidence    614.599 948 1
      medicine    616.994 81
      social services    362.196 994 81
     *see also* Cancer — humans
     incidence    614.598
     medicine    616.8
     surgery    617.481
Brain drain    331.127 91
Brain stem
   human anatomy    611.81
   human physiology    612.826
   medicine    616.8
Braintree (England :
   District)    T2—426 715
Brainwashing    153.853

Braising
  home cooking    641.73
Brakes (Devices)
  automotive engineering    629.246
  railroad engineering    625.25
Brakes (Ferns)    587.3
Brakpan (South Africa :
  District)    T2—682 24
Bran    641.331
  commercial processing    664.720 8
    wheat    664.722 8
  cooking    641.631
  food    641.331
Branch banking    332.16
Branch banks    332.16
Branch County (Mich.)    T2—774 21
Branch libraries
  architecture    727.84
  public librarianship    027.4
Branch stores    381.12
  *see also* Commerce
Branches of government    320.404
  law    342.044
Branching processes    519.234
Branchiopoda    595.32
  paleozoology    565.32
Branchiura    595.36
Brand name products
  sales promotion    658.827
Brand preferences
  marketing research    658.834 3
Brandenburg (Germany)    T2—431 5
Brandenburg an der Havel
  (Germany)    T2—431 54
Brandfort (South Africa :
  District)    T2—685 3
Branding animals    636.081 2
Brandon (Man.)    T2—712 73
Brands
  sales promotion    658.827
Brandt, Willy
  German history    943.087 7
Brandy    641.253
  commercial processing    663.53
Brant (Ont. : County)    T2—713 47
Branta    598.417 8
Brantley County (Ga.)    T2—758 753
Bras d'Or Lake (N.S.)    T2—716 9
Brasília (Brazil)    T2—817 4
Brașov (Romania : Județ)    T2—498 4
Brass    669.3
  decorative arts    739.52
  materials science    620.182
  metallography    669.953

Brass (continued)
  metallurgy    669.3
  metalworking    673.3
  physical metallurgy    669.963
Brass bands    784.9
Brass ensembles    785.9
Brass instruments    788.9
  bands and orchestras    784
  chamber ensembles    785
    mixed    785.2–.5
    single type    785.9
  construction    788.919 23
    by hand    788.919 23
    by machine    681.889
  solo music    788.9
Brassicaceae    583.64
Bratislava (Slovakia)    T2—437 31
Brauer groups    512.46
Braulidae    595.774
Braunschweig (Germany)    T2—435 976
Braunschweig (Germany :
  Regierungsbezirk)    T2—435 97
Braxton County (W. Va.)    T2—754 66
Brayer painting    751.49
Braziers
  ceramic arts    738.8
  heating buildings    697.1
Brazil    981
    T2—81
Brazil nut    641.345 75
  agriculture    634.575
  botany    583.76
  cooking    641.645 75
  food    641.345 75
Brazilian literature    869
Brazilian Portuguese
  dialects    T6—69
Brazilian spiderflowers    583.76
Brazilians    T5—698
Brazing    671.56
  decorative arts    739.14
  sculpture    731.41
Brazoria County (Tex.)    T2—764 137
Brazos County (Tex.)    T2—764 242
Brazos River (Tex.)    T2—764
Brazzaville (Congo)    T2—672 4
Breach of contract    346.022
Bread    641.815
  commercial baking    664.752 3
  home baking    641.815
Bread-dough handicrafts    745.5
Bread molds (Fungi)    579.53

| | |
|---|---|
| Breadfruits | 641.343 9 |
| botany | 583.45 |
| cooking | 641.643 9 |
| food | 641.343 9 |
| orchard crop | 634.39 |
| Break dancing | 793.3 |
| Break-even analysis | 658.155 4 |
| Breakfast foods | |
| commercial processing | 664.756 |
| Breakfasts | 642 |
| cooking | 641.52 |
| customs | 394.125 2 |
| Breaking | |
| materials science | 620.112 6 |
| Breaks (Rest periods) | |
| labor economics | 331.257 6 |
| personnel management | 658.312 2 |
| Breakwaters | |
| engineering | 627.24 |
| Bream (Abramis) | 597.482 |
| sports fishing | 799.174 82 |
| Breast | |
| human anatomy | 611.49 |
| medicine | 618.19 |
| men | 616.49 |
| women | 618.19 |
| surgery | 618.190 59 |
| women's physiology | 612.664 |
| Breast cancer | |
| incidence | 614.599 944 9 |
| medicine | 616.994 49 |
| *see also* Cancer — humans | |
| Breast diseases | |
| medicine | 618.19 |
| men | 616.49 |
| *see also* Endocrine | |
| diseases — humans | |
| Breast feeding | 649.33 |
| child rearing | 649.33 |
| health | 613.269 |
| human physiology | 612.664 |
| Breast implants | 618.190 592 |
| Breathing | 573.2 |
| biology | 573.2 |
| health | 613.192 |
| human physiology | 612.2 |
| musical technique | 781.48 |
| instrumental | 784.193 2 |
| *see also* Respiratory system | |
| Breathing exercises | |
| health | 613.192 |
| therapy | 615.836 |
| Breathitt County (Ky.) | T2—769 19 |
| Breckinridge County (Ky.) | T2—769 854 |

| | |
|---|---|
| Breckland (England) | T2—426 14 |
| Brecknock (Wales : District) | T2—429 56 |
| Brecon (Wales) | T2—429 56 |
| Brecqhou (Channel Islands) | T2—423 47 |
| Bredasdorp (South Africa : District) | T2—687 36 |
| Breeder reactors | 621.483 4 |
| Breeding | |
| animal husbandry | 636.082 |
| plant cultivation | 631.52 |
| Breeding stock | |
| plants | 631.52 |
| Breisgau-Hochschwarzwald (Germany : Landkreis) | T2—434 626 |
| Bremen (Germany) | T2—435 2 |
| Bremer County (Iowa) | T2—777 34 |
| Bremerhaven (Germany) | T2—435 21 |
| Bremgarten (Switzerland : Bezirk) | T2—494 566 5 |
| Bremsstrahlung | 539.722 2 |
| Brent (London, England) | T2—421 85 |
| Brentwood (England : Borough) | T2—426 76 |
| Brescia (Italy) | T2—452 61 |
| ancient | T2—373 121 |
| Brescia (Italy : Province) | T2—452 6 |
| ancient | T2—373 12 |
| Brèst (Belarus : Voblasts) | T2—478 9 |
| Brest (France) | T2—441 12 |
| Brèstskaĩa voblasts' (Belarus) | T2—478 9 |
| Bretagne (France) | T2—441 |
| Breton language | 491.68 |
| | T6—916 8 |
| Breton literature | 891.68 |
| Bretons | T5—916 8 |
| Brevard County (Fla.) | T2—759 27 |
| Breviaries | 264.15 |
| Roman Catholic | 264.020 15 |
| texts | 264.024 |
| Brewed alcoholic beverages | 641.23 |
| commercial processing | 663.3 |
| cooking with | 641.62 |
| home preparation | 641.873 |
| Brewed nonalcoholic beverages | 641.877 |
| commercial processing | 663.9 |
| home preparation | 641.877 |
| Brewster County (Tex.) | T2—764 932 |
| Brexias | 583.72 |
| Brezhnev, Leonid Il'ich | |
| Russian history | 947.085 3 |
| Brĩanskaĩa oblast' (Russia) | T2—472 5 |
| Briard (Dog) | 636.737 |

| | |
|---|---|
| Bribery of officials | 364.132 3 |
| law | 345.023 23 |
| public administration | 353.46 |
| Bribery of voters | 364.132 4 |
| law | 345.023 24 |
| Brick pavements | 625.82 |
| Bricklayers | 693.210 92 |
| Bricks | 666.737 |
| architectural construction | 721.044 21 |
| building construction | 693.21 |
| building materials | 691.4 |
| ceramic arts | 738.6 |
| materials science | 620.142 |
| structural engineering | 624.183 6 |
| Bride purchase | 392.4 |
| Bridge (Game) | 795.415 |
| Bridge circuits | 621.374 2 |
| electronics | 621.381 548 |
| Bridge engineers | 624.209 2 |
| Bridge harps | 787.98 |
| *see also* Stringed instruments | |
| Bridge River (B.C.) | T2—711 31 |
| Bridge whist | 795.413 |
| Bridgend (Wales : County Borough) | T2—429 71 |
| Bridges | 388.132 |
| architecture | 725.98 |
| construction | 624.2 |
| military engineering | 623.67 |
| public administration | 354.76 |
| transportation services | 388.132 |
| railroads | 385.312 |
| roads | 388.132 |
| Bridges (Dentistry) | 617.692 |
| Bridges (Electrical circuits) | 621.374 2 |
| Bridgnorth (England : District) | T2—424 59 |
| Brie (Cheese) | 641.373 53 |
| cooking | 641.673 53 |
| food | 641.373 53 |
| processing | 637.353 |
| Brief psychotherapy | 616.891 47 |
| Briefcases | |
| manufacturing technology | 685.51 |
| Brig (Switzerland : Bezirk) | T2—494 794 3 |
| Brigades (Military units) | 355.31 |
| Bright disease | |
| medicine | 616.612 |
| *see also* Urologic diseases — humans | |
| Brightness perception | |
| psychology | 152.143 |
| Brighton (England) | T2—422 56 |
| Brighton and Hove (England) | T2—422 56 |
| Brill's disease | |
| incidence | 614.526 2 |
| medicine | 616.922 2 |
| *see also* Communicable diseases — humans | |
| Brindisi (Italy) | T2—457 541 |
| ancient | T2—377 631 |
| Brindisi (Italy : Province) | T2—457 54 |
| ancient | T2—377 63 |
| Brine | 553.72 |
| Brine shrimps | 595.32 |
| Brining foods | 664.028 6 |
| commercial preservation | 664.028 6 |
| home preservation | 641.46 |
| Briquettes | 662.6 |
| Brisbane (Qld.) | T2—943 1 |
| Brisbane River (Qld.) | T2—943 2 |
| Brisbane Water National Park (N.S.W.) | T2—944 2 |
| Briscoe County (Tex.) | T2—764 839 |
| Bristles | |
| animal husbandry | 636.088 45 |
| manufacturing technology | 679.6 |
| Bristletails | 595.723 |
| Bristling (Fish) | 641.392 |
| cooking | 641.692 |
| food | 641.392 |
| zoology | 597.452 |
| Bristol (England) | T2—423 93 |
| Bristol (Va.) | T2—755 726 |
| Bristol Avon River (England) | T2—423 9 |
| Bristol Bay (Alaska) | 551.461 434 |
| | T2—164 34 |
| Bristol Bay Borough (Alaska) | T2—798 4 |
| Bristol board | 676.288 |
| Bristol County (Mass.) | T2—744 85 |
| Bristol County (R.I.) | T2—745 5 |
| Britain | 941 |
| | T2—41 |
| ancient | 936.1 |
| | T2—361 |
| *see Manual at* 941 | |
| Britain, Battle of, 1940 | 940.542 11 |
| Britain, Northern | 941.1 |
| | T2—411 |
| ancient | 936.11 |
| | T2—361 1 |

Britain, Southern                         942
                                          T2—42
  ancient                        936.2
                                          T2—362
British Americans            T5—13
  *see Manual at* T5—13 vs.
    T5—2073, T5—21073
British ancestry             T5—2
  *see Manual at* T5—201–209 vs.
    T5—2101–2109
British Antarctic Territory   T2—989
British Canadians            T5—112
  *see Manual at* T5—112,
    T5—114 vs. T5—2,
    T5—41
British Columbia                          971.1
                                          T2—711
British Commonwealth of
  Nations                         T2—171 241
British Empire               T2—171 241
British Guiana               T2—881
British Honduras             T2—728 2
British Isles                             941
                                          T2—41
  ancient                         936.1
                                          T2—361
  *see Manual at* 941
British Kaffraria            T2—687 5
British New Guinea                        995.402 1
British North America Act, 1867   971.049
British Open (Golf)                       796.352 66
British pronunciation                     421.55
British Sign Language                     419.41
                                          T6—999 841
British Solomon Islands      T2—959 3
British Somaliland           T2—677 3
British spelling                          421.55
British system (Measurement)              530.813
  social aspects                  389.15
British Togoland                          966.703
                                          T2—667
British Virgin Islands       T2—729 725
British western seawaters                 551.461 337
                                          T2—163 37
Britons                      T5—21
  *see Manual at* T5—201–209 vs.
    T5—2101–2109
Brits (South Africa :
  District)          T2—682 41
Britstown (South Africa :
  District)          T2—687 13
Brittania (Roman province)   T2—362
Brittany (Dog)                            636.752
Brittany (France)            T2—441

Brittle stars                             593.94
Brittleness
  materials science              620.112 6
Brixia (Italy)               T2—373 121
Brněnský kraj (Czech
  Republic)          T2—437 24
Broaching tools                           621.954
Broad beans                               641.356 51
  botany                          583.74
  cooking                         641.656 51
  field crop                      633.37
  food                            641.356 51
  garden crop                     635.651
Broad-gage railroads                      385
Broad jump                                796.432
Broad River (S.C.)           T2—757 4
Broadband computer equipment   004.64
  engineering                     621.398 1
Broadband local-area networks   004.68
  *see also* Computer
    communications
Broadbills                                598.822
Broadcast advertising                     659.14
Broadcast communications                  004.693
Broadcast media
  journalism                      070.19
Broadcast public speaking                 808.51
Broadcast videotex                        004.69
  *see also* Computer
    communications
Broadcasters                              384.540 92
Broadcasting                              384.54
  law                             343.099 4
  public administration           354.75
  *see Manual at* 384.54, 384.55,
    384.8 vs. 791.4
Broadcasting channels                     384.545 2
  radio                           384.545 2
  television                      384.552 1
Broadcasting networks                     384.540 65
  *see also* Networks
    (Communications)
Broadcasting stations                     384.545 3
  radio                           384.545 3
    *see also* Radio stations
  television                      384.552 2
    *see also* Television stations
Broadland (England)          T2—426 17
Broads, The (England)        T2—426 17
Broadsides
  cataloging                      025.342
  direct advertising              659.133
  library treatment               025.172
Broadwater County (Mont.)    T2—786 664

| | |
|---|---|
| Broca aphasia | |
| medicine | 616.855 2 |
| *see also* Communication | |
| disorders | |
| Brocade | 677.616 |
| Brocatelle | 677.616 |
| Broccoli | 641.353 5 |
| commercial processing | 664.805 35 |
| cooking | 641.653 5 |
| food | 641.353 5 |
| garden crop | 635.35 |
| Broiling | 641.76 |
| Broken Hill (N.S.W.) | T2—944 9 |
| Broken homes | 362.829 4 |
| social services | 362.829 4 |
| sociology | 306.89 |
| *see also* Families — social | |
| welfare | |
| Brokers (Securities) | 332.62 |
| law | 346.092 6 |
| public administration | 354.88 |
| Brokopondo (Suriname : | |
| District) | T2—883 92 |
| Brome-Missisquoi (Quebec) | T2—714 62 |
| Bromegrasses | 584.9 |
| Bromeliads | 584.85 |
| floriculture | 635.934 85 |
| Bromeliales | 584.85 |
| Bromes (Grasses) | 584.9 |
| Bromine | |
| chemical engineering | 661.073 3 |
| chemistry | 546.733 |
| economic geology | 553.6 |
| organic chemistry | 547.02 |
| applied | 661.891 |
| Bromley (London, England) | T2—421 78 |
| Bromoil process | 773.8 |
| Bromsgrove (England : | |
| District) | T2—424 42 |
| Bromyard (England) | T2—424 2 |
| Bronchi | |
| human anatomy | 611.23 |
| human physiology | 612.234 |
| medicine | 616.23 |
| surgery | 617.544 |
| Bronchial asthma | |
| medicine | 616.238 |
| *see also* Respiratory tract | |
| diseases — humans | |
| Bronchial diseases | |
| medicine | 616.23 |
| *see also* Respiratory tract | |
| diseases — humans | |

| | |
|---|---|
| Bronchiectasis | |
| medicine | 616.23 |
| *see also* Respiratory tract | |
| diseases — humans | |
| Bronchitis | |
| medicine | 616.234 |
| *see also* Respiratory tract | |
| diseases — humans | |
| Bronchodilator agents | |
| pharmacokinetics | 615.72 |
| Bronchopneumonia | |
| medicine | 616.241 |
| *see also* Respiratory tract | |
| diseases — humans | |
| Bronkhorstspruit (South | |
| Africa : District) | T2—682 29 |
| Brontosaurus | 567.913 8 |
| Bronx (New York, N.Y.) | T2—747 275 |
| Bronze | 669.3 |
| decorative arts | 739.512 |
| materials science | 620.182 |
| metallography | 669.953 |
| metallurgy | 669.3 |
| metalworking | 673.3 |
| physical metallurgy | 669.963 |
| Bronze Age | 930.156 |
| | T1—090 13 |
| Bronze sculpture | |
| casting | 731.456 |
| Brooches | 391.7 |
| customs | 391.7 |
| making | 739.278 |
| costume jewelry | 688.2 |
| handicrafts | 745.594 2 |
| fine jewelry | 739.278 |
| Brook trout | 597.554 |
| sports fishing | 799.175 54 |
| Brooke County (W. Va.) | T2—754 13 |
| Brookings County (S.D.) | T2—783 272 |
| Brooklyn (New York, N.Y.) | T2—747 23 |
| Brooks County (Ga.) | T2—758 874 |
| Brooks County (Tex.) | T2—764 475 |
| Brooks Range (Alaska) | T2—798 7 |
| Broom, Loch (Scotland) | T2—163 37 |
| Broomball | 796.965 |
| Broome (W.A.) | T2—941 4 |
| Broome County (N.Y.) | T2—747 75 |
| Broomfield County (Colo.) | T2—788 64 |
| Broomrapes | 583.95 |
| Brooms | 679.6 |
| Brossard (Quebec) | T2—714 37 |
| Brother-brother relationship | 306.875 2 |
| Brother-sister relationship | 306.875 3 |

Brothers   306.875
   T1—085 5
  *see also* Siblings
Brothers (Christian religious
   orders)   255.092
  biography   271.092 02
  church history   271.092
Brothers and sisters   306.875 3
  psychological influence   155.924
  psychology   155.443
   adulthood   155.646
Brothers Hospitallers of St. John
   of God   255.49
  church history   271.49
Brotulas   597.63
Broward County (Fla.)   T2—759 35
Brown algae   579.88
Brown-bag lunches   641.53
Brown bats (Eptesicus)   599.47
Brown bats (Myotis)   599.472
Brown bear   599.784
  conservation technology   639.979 784
  resource economics   333.959 784
Brown coal   553.22
  economic geology   553.22
  mining   622.332
  properties   662.622 2
Brown County (Ill.)   T2—773 473
Brown County (Ind.)   T2—772 253
Brown County (Kan.)   T2—781 34
Brown County (Minn.)   T2—776 31
Brown County (Neb.)   T2—782 736
Brown County (Ohio)   T2—771 796
Brown County (S.D.)   T2—783 144
Brown County (Tex.)   T2—764 548
Brown County (Wis.)   T2—775 61
Brown lung disease
  medicine   616.244
  *see also* Respiratory tract
   diseases — humans
Brown rat   599.352
Brown Swiss cattle   636.234
Brownian motion   530.475
  liquid-state physics   530.425
  *see Manual at* 530.475 vs.
   530.12, 531.16
Brownouts   333.793 217
  electrical engineering   621.319
Browsing   591.54
  animal husbandry   636.084 5
  descriptive zoology   591.54
Broxbourne (England)   T2—425 87
Broxtowe (England)   T2—425 26
Broye (Switzerland)   T2—494 537

Broye-Vully (Switzerland)   T2—494 524 3
Bruce (Ont. : County)   T2—713 21
Bruce, Stanley Melbourne Bruce,
  Viscount
  Australian history   994.042
Brucella   579.33
Brucellosis
  animals
   veterinary medicine   636.208 969 57
  humans
   incidence   614.565
   medicine   616.957
    *see also* Communicable
     diseases — humans
Bruges (Belgium)   T2—493 122
Brugg (Switzerland :
  Bezirk)   T2—494 562 6
Brugge (Belgium)   T2—493 122
Bruises
  medicine   617.13
Brule County (S.D.)   T2—783 381
Brunches   642
  cooking   641.52
  customs   394.125 2
Brundusium (Italy)   T2—377 631
Brunei   959.55
   T2—595 5
Brunelliaceae   583.72
Bruniaceae   583.72
Brunswick County (N.C.)   T2—756 29
Brunswick County (Va.)   T2—755 575
Bruny Island (Tas.)   T2—946 2
Brush disposal
  forestry   634.955
Brush drawing   741.26
Brush-tailed possum   599.232
Brush turkeys   598.64
Brushes   679.6
Brushes (Generator parts)   621.316
Brussels (Belgium)   T2—493 32
Brussels-Capital Region
  (Belgium)   T2—493 32
Brussels griffon   636.76
Brussels sprouts   641.353 6
  commercial processing   664.805 36
  cooking   641.653 6
  food   641.353 6
  garden crop   635.36
Bruttium   T2—377 8
Bryales   588.2
Bryan County (Ga.)   T2—758 732
Bryan County (Okla.)   T2—766 62
Bryansk (Russia : Oblast)   T2—472 5

Bryce Canyon National Park
  (Utah)     T2—792 52
Bryde's whale     599.524
Bryophyta     588
  paleobotany     561.8
  pharmacology     615.322
Bryopodales     579.835
Bryopsida     588.2
Bryozoa     594.67
  paleozoology     564.67
Brythonic languages     491.6
    T6—916
Brythonic literatures     891.6
Bubble memory     004.563
Bubbles     530.427 5
  chemical engineering     660.293
  chemistry     541.33
  physics     530.427 5
Bube-Benga languages     496.396
    T6—963 96
Bubonic plague
  incidence     614.573 2
  medicine     616.923 2
  *see also* Communicable
    diseases — humans
Bucconidae     598.72
Bucerotidae     598.78
Buchanan, James
  United States history     973.68
Buchanan County (Iowa)     T2—777 382
Buchanan County (Mo.)     T2—778 132
Buchanan County (Va.)     T2—755 752
Bucharest (Romania)     T2—498 2
Bucheggberg (Switzerland)     T2—494 359 5
Bücher, Karl
  economic school     330.154 2
Buckbeans     583.93
Buckeyes     583.78
Buckingham County (Va.)     T2—755 623
Buckinghamshire (England)     T2—425 9
Buckles     391.7
  customs     391.7
  making     739.278
    costume jewelry     688.2
      handicrafts     745.594 2
    fine jewelry     739.278
Bucks County (Pa.)     T2—748 21
Buckthorns     583.86
Buckwheat     641.331 2
  botany     583.57
  commercial processing     664.72
  cooking     641.631 2
  food     641.331 2
  food crop     633.12

Bucureşti (Romania)     T2—498 2
Budapest (Hungary)     T2—439 12
Buddha     294.363
  art representation     704.948 943 63
  arts     700.482 943 63
    T3C—382 943 63
Buddhism     294.3
  art representation     704.948 943
  arts     700.482 943
    T3C—382 943
  Islamic polemics     297.294
Buddhism and Islam     294.335
  Buddhist view     294.335
  Islamic view     297.284 3
Buddhist architecture     720.95
Buddhist calendar     529.324 3
  religion     294.343 6
Buddhist education     294.375
Buddhist ethics     294.35
Buddhist holidays     294.343 6
  customs     394.265 43
  *see also* Holidays
Buddhist monasteries     294.365 7
  architecture     726.784 3
Buddhist philosophy     181.043
Buddhist sculpture     730.95
Buddhist temples and shrines     294.343 5
  architecture     726.143
Buddhists     T1—088 294 3
  biography     294.309 2
  social group     305.694 3
Buddlejaceae     583.95
Budějovický kraj (Czech
  Republic)     T2—437 13
Budgerigars     636.686 4
  animal husbandry     636.686 4
  zoology     598.71
Budget deficits     352.48
  macroeconomic policy     339.523
  *see also* Budgets (Public)
Budget in business     658.154
Budget messages     352.48
  specific jurisdictions     352.493–.499
Budget surpluses
  macroeconomic policy     339.523
Budgeting     658.154
  armed forces     355.622 8
  public administration     352.48
  *see also* Budgets (Public)
Budgets (Business)
  management     658.154
Budgets (Public)     352.48
  armed forces     355.622 8
  specific jurisdictions     355.622 9

| | |
|---|---|
| Budgets (Public) (continued) | |
| law | 343.034 |
| legislative enactment | 328.378 |
| specific international organizations | 352.491 |
| specific jurisdictions | 352.493–.499 |
| Buds | 581.46 |
| descriptive botany | 581.46 |
| physiology | 575.486 |
| plant propagation | 631.533 |
| Budworms | 595.78 |
| agricultural pests | 632.78 |
| Buena Vista (Va.) | T2—755 851 |
| Buena Vista County (Iowa) | T2—777 18 |
| Buenos Aires (Argentina) | T2—821 1 |
| Buenos Aires (Argentina : Province) | T2—821 2 |
| Buffalo | 599.642 |
| animal husbandry | 636.293 |
| Buffalo (Bison) | 599.643 |
| *see also* Bison | |
| Buffalo (N.Y.) | T2—747 97 |
| Buffalo County (Neb.) | T2—782 45 |
| Buffalo County (S.D.) | T2—783 31 |
| Buffalo County (Wis.) | T2—775 48 |
| Buffalo gnats | 595.772 |
| Buffers | |
| railroad engineering | 625.25 |
| Buffing metals | 671.72 |
| Buffing tools | 621.922 |
| Bufo | 597.872 |
| Bufonidae | 597.87 |
| Bufonoidea | 597.87 |
| Buganda | T2—676 1 |
| Buganda (Kingdom) | 967.610 1 |
| Buginese | T5—992 262 |
| Buginese language | 499.226 2 |
| | T6—992 262 |
| Buginese literature | 899.226 2 |
| Bugis | T5—992 262 |
| Bugis language | 499.226 2 |
| | T6—992 262 |
| Bugis literature | 899.226 2 |
| Bugles | 788.95 |
| instrument | 788.951 9 |
| music | 788.95 |
| *see also* Brass instruments | |
| Bugs (Heteroptera) | 595.754 |
| Buḥayrah (Egypt) | T2—621 |
| Buḥayrāt (Sudan) | T2—629 4 |
| Buhid | T5—992 1 |
| Builders | 690.092 |
| Building | |
| enterprises | 338.769 |
| restrictive practices | 338.826 9 |
| government control | 354.642 8 |
| production economics | 338.476 9 |
| technology | 690 |
| Building and loan associations | 332.32 |
| law | 346.082 32 |
| public administration | 354.86 |
| Building codes | 343.078 69 |
| criminology | 364.142 |
| criminal law | 345.024 2 |
| enforcement | 363.233 |
| Building construction services (Armed forces) | 358.22 |
| Building cooperatives | 334.1 |
| Building engineering services | 696 |
| Building industries | 338.476 9 |
| public administration | 354.64 |
| Building management | 658.2 |
| public administration | 352.56 |
| Building materials | 691 |
| architectural construction | 721.04 |
| construction | 691 |
| synthetic | 666.89 |
| Building paper | 676.289 |
| Building remodeling | 690.24 |
| home economics | 643.7 |
| *see Manual at* 690 vs. 643.7 | |
| Building societies | 332.32 |
| Buildings | 720 |
| architecture | 720 |
| area planning | 711.6 |
| art representation | 704.944 |
| capital procurement | 658.152 42 |
| construction | 690 |
| *see Manual at* 624 vs. 690 | |
| economics | 333.338 |
| energy economics | 333.790 2 |
| investment economics | 332.632 43 |
| landscape architecture | 717 |
| management | 658.2 |
| public administration | 352.56 |
| planning | |
| museums | 069.22 |
| Built-in furniture | 645.4 |
| decorative arts | 749.4 |
| manufacturing technology | 684.16 |
| *see also* Furniture | |
| Builth Wells (Wales) | T2—429 56 |
| Bujumbura (Burundi) | T2—675 72 |
| Buka Island (Papua New Guinea) | T2—959 2 |

| | |
|---|---|
| Bukhara rugs | |
| arts | 746.758 7 |
| Bukhārī, Muḥammad ibn Ismāʻīl | |
| Hadith | 297.125 41 |
| Bukidnon (Philippines) | T2—599 7 |
| Bukovina | T2—498 4 |
| Romania | T2—498 4 |
| Ukraine | T2—477 9 |
| Bulacan (Philippines) | T2—599 1 |
| Bülach (Switzerland : | |
| Bezirk) | T2—494 572 4 |
| Bulawayo (Zimbabwe) | T2—689 1 |
| Bulbs (Plants) | 584.146 |
| descriptive botany | 584.146 |
| nursery production | 631.526 |
| ornamental plants | 635.915 26 |
| physiology | 575.495 |
| planting | 631.532 |
| ornamental plants | 635.915 32 |
| Bulganin, Nikolay | |
| Aleksandrovich | |
| Russian history | 947.085 2 |
| Bulgaria | 949.9 |
| | T2—499 |
| ancient | 939.89 |
| | T2—398 9 |
| Bulgarian Empire, 680–1014 | 949.901 3 |
| Bulgarian Empire, 1185–1396 | 949.901 4 |
| Bulgarian language | 491.81 |
| | T6—918 11 |
| Bulgarian literature | 891.81 |
| Bulgarian Macedonia | T2—499 8 |
| Bulgarian Thrace | T2—499 5 |
| Bulgarians | T5—918 11 |
| Bulimia | |
| medicine | 616.852 63 |
| *see also* Mental disorders | |
| Bulk carriers (Ships) | 387.245 |
| engineering | 623.824 5 |
| *see also* Ships | |
| Bulk mailings | 383.124 |
| *see also* Postal service | |
| Bulkley-Nechako (B.C.) | T2—711 82 |
| Bulkley River (B.C.) | T2—711 82 |
| Bull-roarers | 788.29 |
| *see also* Wind instruments | |
| Bull shark | 597.34 |
| Bull Shoals Lake (Ark. and | |
| Mo.) | T2—767 193 |
| Bull terriers | 636.755 9 |
| Bulldog | 636.72 |
| Bulldozers | 624.152 |
| engineering | 629.225 |
| repair | 629.287 5 |
| Buller District (N.Z.) | T2—937 3 |
| Bulletin boards | |
| instructional use | 371.335 6 |
| management use | 658.455 |
| Bullets | |
| military engineering | 623.455 |
| Bullfighting | 791.82 |
| Bullfinches | 598.885 |
| Bullfrogs | 597.892 |
| Bullheads (Catfishes) | 597.492 |
| Bullitt County (Ky.) | T2—769 453 |
| Bullmastiff | 636.73 |
| Bulloch County (Ga.) | T2—758 766 |
| Bullock County (Ala.) | T2—761 483 |
| Bullroarers | 788.29 |
| *see also* Wind instruments | |
| Bulls (Papal documents) | 262.91 |
| Bullying | 302.343 |
| education | 371.58 |
| social interaction | 302.343 |
| Bulrushes | 584.84 |
| Bulrushes (Cattails) | 584.68 |
| Bulrushes (Sedges) | 584.84 |
| Bultfontein (South Africa : | |
| District) | T2—685 3 |
| Bulu language | 496.396 |
| | T6—963 96 |
| Bumpers | |
| automobile | 629.276 |
| Bunbury (W.A.) | T2—941 2 |
| Buncombe County (N.C.) | T2—756 88 |
| Bundaberg (Qld.) | T2—943 2 |
| Bundling (Customs) | 392.4 |
| Bündnis Zukunft Österreich | |
| (Political party) | 324.243 603 |
| Bungalows | |
| architecture | 728.373 |
| construction | 690.837 3 |
| Bungee jumping | 797.5 |
| Bunker Hill, Battle of, 1775 | 973.331 2 |
| Bunker oils | 665.538 8 |
| Bunsen burners | 542.4 |
| Bunt (Fungi) | 579.593 |
| disease of wheat | 633.119 493 |
| Buntings | 598.883 |
| Bunun (Taiwan people) | T5—992 5 |
| Bunya Mountains National | |
| Park (Qld.) | T2—943 2 |
| Bunyoro (Kingdom) | 967.610 1 |
| | T2—676 1 |
| Buoyancy | 532.02 |
| air mechanics | 533.61 |
| gas mechanics | 533.12 |
| liquid mechanics | 532.25 |

Buoys 387.155
  navigation aids 623.894 4
  transportation services 387.155
Buprestoidea 595.763
Bur reeds 584.68
Būr Saʿīd (Egypt : Province) T2—621 5
Burbots 597.632
Burdekin River (Qld.) T2—943 6
Burdur İli (Turkey) T2—562 7
  ancient T2—392 4
Bureau County (Ill.) T2—773 372
Bureaucracy 302.35
  public administration 352.63
  sociology 302.35
Burgas (Bulgaria : Oblast) T2—499 5
Burgaska oblast (Bulgaria) T2—499 5
Burgenland (Austria) T2—436 15
Burglarproofing
  household security 643.16
Burglary 364.162 2
  law 345.026 22
  *see also* Theft
Burglary insurance 368.82
Burgos (Spain : Province) T2—463 53
Burgundian language 439.9
   T6—399
Burgundy (France) T2—444 1
Burhou (Channel Islands) T2—423 47
Burial insurance 368.366
Burial of dead 363.75
  customs 393.1
  *see also* Undertaking
    (Mortuary)
Burial of Jesus Christ 232.964
Burial of waste 363.728 5
  technology 628.445 64
  *see also* Waste control
Buriat T5—942
Buriat language 494.2
   T6—942
Buriatiia (Russia) T2—575
Burke County (Ga.) T2—758 65
Burke County (N.C.) T2—756 85
Burke County (N.D.) T2—784 72
Burkina Faso 966.25
   T2—662 5
Burkinabe T5—966 25
Burkinans T5—966 25
Burkitt lymphoma
  incidence 614.599 944 6
  medicine 616.994 46
  *see also* Cancer — humans
Burleigh County (N.D.) T2—784 77
Burleson County (Tex.) T2—764 241

Burlesque shows 792.7
Burlington (Vt.) T2—743 17
Burlington County (N.J.) T2—749 61
Burma 959.1
   T2—591
Burmanniaceae 584.38
Burmese T5—958
Burmese cat 636.824
Burmese language 495.8
   T6—958
Burmese literature 895.8
Burnaby (B.C.) T2—711 33
Burnet County (Tex.) T2—764 63
Burnet-Llano region (Tex.) T2—764 6
Burnett County (Wis.) T2—775 14
Burnie (Tas.) T2—946 5
Burnley (England :
  Borough) T2—427 642
Burnout (Psychology) 158.723
Burns
  crop damage 632.18
  medicine 617.11
Burramyidae 599.23
Burreeds 584.68
Burritos 641.84
Burros 636.182
  animal husbandry 636.182
  conservation technology 639.979 665
  resource economics 333.959 665
  zoology 599.665
Burrowing animals 591.564 8
Burrowing toad 597.865
Burrows 591.564 8
Bursa İli (Turkey) T2—563 1
  ancient T2—393 13
Bursae
  human anatomy 611.75
  human physiology 612.75
  medicine 616.76
  surgery 617.475
Bursae diseases
  medicine 616.76
    *see also* Musculoskeletal
    diseases — humans
Bursaries T1—079
Burseraceae 583.77
Burt County (Neb.) T2—782 243
Burundi 967.572
   T2—675 72
Burundi people T5—967 572
Burundians T5—967 572
Burushaski language 494.892
   T6—948 92
Burushaski literature 894.892

| | |
|---|---|
| Burusho | T5—948 92 |
| Bury (England : Metropolitan Borough) | T2—427 38 |
| Buryat | T5—942 |
| Buryat language | 494.2 |
| | T6—942 |
| Buryatia (Russia) | T2—575 |
| Burying beetles | 595.764 2 |
| Bus cooking | 641.575 |
| Bus drivers | 388.322 092 |
| Bus stops | 388.33 |
| urban | 388.473 |
| *see also* Bus transportation | |
| Bus terminals | 388.33 |
| architecture | 725.38 |
| urban | 388.473 |
| Bus transportation | 388.322 |
| law | 343.094 82 |
| public administration | 354.765 3 |
| transportation services | 388.322 |
| urban | 388.413 22 |
| law | 343.098 2 |
| public administration | 354.769 |
| Buses | 388.342 33 |
| driving | 629.283 33 |
| engineering | 629.222 33 |
| military engineering | 623.747 23 |
| operation | 388.322 044 |
| repair | 629.287 233 |
| sanitation services | 363.729 3 |
| transportation services | 388.342 33 |
| *see also* Automotive vehicles | |
| Bush, George | |
| United States history | 973.928 |
| Bush, George W. (George Walker) | |
| United States history | 973.931 |
| Bush babies | 599.83 |
| Bush clovers | 633.364 |
| botany | 583.74 |
| forage crop | 633.364 |
| Bushbuck | 599.642 3 |
| Būshehr (Iran : Province) | T2—557 4 |
| Bushman languages | 496.1 |
| | T6—961 |
| Bushmen (African people) | T5—961 |
| Bushong languages | 496.396 |
| | T6—963 96 |

| | |
|---|---|
| Business | 650 |
| arts | T3C—355 3 |
| social theology | 201.73 |
| Christianity | 261.85 |
| Judaism | 296.383 |
| *see also* Commerce | |
| *see Manual at* 330 vs. 650, 658 | |
| Business administration | 658 |
| Business arithmetic | 650.015 13 |
| Business cards | |
| illustration | 741.685 |
| Business crime | 364.168 |
| law | 345.026 8 |
| Business cycles | 338.542 |
| Business directories | 338.702 5 |
| *see Manual at* T1—025 vs. T1—029 | |
| Business districts | 307.333 |
| area planning | 711.552 2 |
| land economics | 333.77 |
| Business enterprises | 338.7 |
| dissolution | 338.71 |
| management | 658.166 |
| economics | 338.7 |
| finance | 338.604 1 |
| management | 658.15 |
| income tax | 336.241 7 |
| law | 343.052 68 |
| initiation | 338.71 |
| economics | 338.71 |
| management | 658.11 |
| | T1—068 1 |
| law | 346.065 |
| location | 338.09 |
| economic rationale | 338.604 2 |
| economics | 338.09 |
| law | 346.07 |
| management | 658.11 |
| | T1—068 1 |
| plant location | 658.21 |
| management | 658 |
| relations with government | 322.3 |
| social welfare | 361.765 |
| tax | 336.207 |
| law | 343.068 |
| valuation | 658.15 |
| *see Manual at* 338.091–.099 vs. 332.67309, 338.6042; *also at* 380; *also at* 658.04 vs. 658.114, 658.402 | |

Business ethics 174.4
  religion 205.644
    Christianity 241.644
    Islam 297.564 4
    Judaism 296.364 4
  *see also* Ethical problems
Business etiquette 395.52
Business failure
  dissolution
    management 658.166
  reorganization
    management 658.16
Business finance
  management 658.15
  production economics 338.604 1
Business forecasting 338.544
Business forecasts 338.544 3
Business forms 651.29
Business insurance 368.094
  liability 368.81
Business intelligence
  management use 658.472
Business interruption insurance 368.815
Business law 346.07
Business liability insurance 368.81
Business libraries 027.69
Business logistics
  management 658.5
Business losses
  tax economics 336.241 7
  tax law 343.052 36
Business machines 651.26
  manufacturing technology 681.14
  office services 651.26
Business management 658
    T1—068
  *see Manual at* T1—068
Business meetings
  management use 658.456
Business names 929.97
  law 346.048
  sales promotion 658.827
Business organizations 338.7
Business presentation software 005.58
Business presentations
  management use 658.452
Business records
  law 346.065
  records management 651.5
Business relationships (Personal) 650.13
Business security
  management 658.47
Business success 650.1

Business tax 336.207
  income tax 336.241 7
    law 343.052 68
    public administration 352.44
    public finance 336.241 7
  law 343.068
  public administration 352.44
  public finance 336.207
Business-to-business advertising 659.131 5
Business white pages 338.702 5
  *see Manual at* T1—025 vs.
    T1—029
Business writing 808.066 65
  *see Manual at* 658.45 vs. 651.7,
    808.06665
Businesses 338.7
Businessmen 338.092
  *see Manual at* 338.092
Businessowners insurance 368.094
Businesspeople 338.092
  *see Manual at* 338.092
Businesswomen 338.092
  *see Manual at* 338.092
Busing (School desegregation) 379.263
  law 344.079 8
Buskerud fylke (Norway) T2—482 6
Busoga (Kingdom) 967.610 1
    T2—676 1
Bustards 598.32
Busts (Sculpture) 731.74
Butadiene-styrene rubber 678.72
Butane 665.773
Butcher paper 676.287
Butene 665.773
Butler County (Ala.) T2—761 37
Butler County (Iowa) T2—777 29
Butler County (Kan.) T2—781 88
Butler County (Ky.) T2—769 755
Butler County (Mo.) T2—778 93
Butler County (Neb.) T2—782 322
Butler County (Ohio) T2—771 75
Butler County (Pa.) T2—748 91
Butomaceae 584.72
Butte (Mont.) T2—786 68
Butte County (Calif.) T2—794 32
Butte County (Idaho) T2—796 59
Butte County (S.D.) T2—783 43
Butter 641.372
  cooking 641.672
  food 641.372
  processing 637.2
Butter prints and molds
  wood carving 736.4
Buttercups 583.34

| | |
|---|---|
| Butterfat tests | |
| milk processing | 637.127 6 |
| Butterflies | 595.789 |
| conservation technology | 639.975 789 |
| culture | 638.578 9 |
| resource economics | 333.955 7 |
| Butterfly bushes | 583.95 |
| Butterfly farming | 638.578 9 |
| Butterfly fishes (Freshwater) | 597.47 |
| Butterfly fishes (Marine) | 597.72 |
| Butterfly flowers | 635.933 952 |
| botany | 583.952 |
| floriculture | 635.933 952 |
| Butterfly gardening | 638.578 9 |
| Buttermilk | 641.372 4 |
| cooking | 641.672 4 |
| food | 641.372 4 |
| processing | 637.24 |
| Butternuts | 583.49 |
| Butterworth (South Africa : | |
| District) | T2—687 58 |
| Buttock muscles | |
| human anatomy | 611.738 |
| Button accordions | 788.863 |
| instrument | 788.863 19 |
| music | 788.863 |
| *see also* Woodwind instruments | |
| Button mangrove | 583.763 |
| Button quails | 598.32 |
| Buttonbushes | 635.933 93 |
| botany | 583.93 |
| floriculture | 635.933 93 |
| Buttons | 391.45 |
| commercial technology | 687.8 |
| customs | 391.45 |
| home sewing | 646.19 |
| numismatics | 737.24 |
| Butts County (Ga.) | T2—758 585 |
| Butyrates | 668.423 |
| Buxaceae | 583.69 |
| Buyers' guides | 381.33 |
| | T1—029 |
| *see Manual at* T1—025 vs. | |
| T1—029 | |
| Buzău (Romania : Judeţ) | T2—498 2 |
| Buzzards | 598.94 |
| Buzzards (Turkey vulture) | 598.92 |
| Buzzards Bay (Mass. : Bay) | 551.461 346 |
| | T2—163 46 |
| Bwile language | 496.393 |
| | T6—963 93 |
| By-products | |
| commercial food processing | 664.08 |
| pulp | 676.5 |

| | |
|---|---|
| Byblidaceae | 583.72 |
| Byblos (Lebanon) | T2—569 2 |
| ancient | T2—394 4 |
| Bydgoszcz (Poland : | |
| Voivodeship) | T2—438 26 |
| Byelarus | 947.8 |
| | T2—478 |
| Byelorussian language | 491.799 |
| | T6—917 99 |
| Byelorussian literature | 891.799 |
| Byelorussians | T5—917 99 |
| Bylot Island (Nunavut) | T2—719 52 |
| Bypass surgery (Coronary) | 617.412 |
| Byrrhoidea | 595.763 |
| Byssinosis | |
| medicine | 616.244 |
| *see also* Respiratory tract | |
| diseases — humans | |
| Byzacium | T2—397 3 |
| Byzantine architecture | 723.2 |
| Byzantine art | 709.021 4 |
| religious significance | 246.1 |
| Byzantine decoration | 745.409 021 |
| Byzantine Empire | 949.502 |
| | T2—495 |
| Egyptian history | 932.023 |
| Libyan history | 939.740 5 |
| Moroccan history | 939.712 06 |
| North African history | 939.705 |
| Sardinian history | 945.902 |
| Sicilian history | 945.801 |
| Southern Italian history | 945.701 |
| Tunisian history | 939.730 5 |
| Byzantine Greek language | 487.3 |
| | T6—87 |
| Byzantine Greek literature | 880 |
| Byzantine law | 340.54 |
| Byzantine painting | 759.021 4 |
| Byzantine rite churches | 281.5 |
| *see also* Eastern churches | |
| Byzantine sculpture | 734.224 |
| Byzantium (City) | T2—398 618 |
| BZÖ (Austrian political party) | 324.243 603 |

# C

| | |
|---|---|
| C*-algebras | 512.556 |
| Cà Mau (Vietnam) | T2—597 9 |
| Caaguazú (Paraguay : | |
| Dept.) | T2—892 134 |
| Caazapá (Paraguay : Dept.) | T2—892 127 |

Cabala 296.16
  Jewish mysticism
    experience 296.712
    movement 296.833
  Jewish religious sources 296.16
  occultism 135.47
Cabañas (El Salvador) T2—728 426
Cabaret shows 792.7
Cabarrus County (N.C.) T2—756 72
Cabbages 641.353 4
  botany 583.64
  commercial processing 664.805 34
  cooking 641.653 4
  food 641.353 4
  garden crop 635.34
Cabell County (W. Va.) T2—754 42
Cabin pressurization
  aircraft 629.134 42
Cabinda (Angola : Province) T2—673 1
Cabinet government 321.804 3
Cabinet-level committees 352.24
Cabinet members 352.293
Cabinet organs 786.55
  instrument 786.551 9
  music 786.55
  *see also* Keyboard instruments
Cabinet secretariats 352.243
Cabinet secretaries 352.243 229 3
Cabinetmakers 684.104 092
Cabinetmaking 684.104
Cabinets (Furniture)
  decorative arts 749.3
  manufacturing technology 684.16
Cabinets (Government councils) 321.804 3
  public administration 352.24
Cabins 643.1
  architecture 728.73
  home economics 643.1
  *see also* Dwellings
Cabins (Aircraft) 629.134 45
Cable communication systems 384.6
  *see also* Telephone
Cable railways 385.6
  engineering 625.5
  transportation services 385.6
  *see also* Railroads
Cable-stayed bridges
  construction 624.238
Cable television 384.555
  engineering 621.388 57
  law 343.099 46
  *see also* Television

Cables (Electrical conductors) 621.319 34
  computer science 004.64
  engineering 621.398 1
Cables (Ropes)
  knotting and splicing 623.888 2
  metal 671.84
  structural engineering 624.177 4
Cabo Delgado
  (Mozambique) T2—679 8
Cabooses 385.32
  engineering 625.22
  transportation services 385.32
  *see also* Rolling stock
Cabs 388.342 32
  *see also* Taxicabs
Cacao 583.68
  agriculture 633.74
  *see also* Cocoa
Cacao butter 665.354
  *see also* Cocoa butter
Cáceres (Spain : Province) T2—462 8
Cachapoal (Chile :
  Province) T2—833 2
Cache County (Utah) T2—792 12
Cache Creek (B.C.) T2—711 72
Cachets (Philately) 769.567
Cactales 583.56
Cacti 583.56
  edible fruits 641.347 75
    cooking 641.647 75
    horticulture 634.775
  floriculture 635.933 56
Cactuses 583.56
  *see also* Cacti
CAD (Computer-aided design) 620.004 202 85
CAD/CAM (Manufacturing) 670.285
Caddisflies 595.745
Caddo County (Okla.) T2—766 41
Caddo Indians T5—979 3
Caddo Lake (La. and Tex.) T2—763 99
Caddo language 497.93
   T6—979 3
Caddo Parish (La.) T2—763 99
Caddoan Indians T5—979 3
Caddoan languages 497.93
   T6—979 3
Cadence (Music) 781.254
Cadenzas 784.186
Cádiz (Spain : Province) T2—468 8
Cadmium 669.56
  chemical engineering 661.066 2
  chemistry 546.662
  human toxicology 615.925 662
  materials science 620.184 6

Cadmium (continued)
  metallography      669.955 6
  metallurgy      669.56
  metalworking      673.56
  physical metallurgy      669.965 6
  *see also* Chemicals
Caecilians      597.82
Caedmon      829.2
Caen (France)      T2—442 24
Caenagnathiformes      568.5
Caenolestidae      599.27
Caere (Italy)      T2—375 9
Caerphilly (Wales : County
  Borough)      T2—429 76
Caesalpiniaceae      583.749
Caesium      669.725
  *see also* Cesium
Café Filho, João
  Brazilian history      981.062
Cafeteria meal service      642.5
Cafeterias      647.95
  *see also* Eating places
Caffeine abuse      362.299
  medicine      616.864
  personal health      613.84
  social welfare      362.299
  *see also* Substance abuse
Cagayan (Philippines)      T2—599 1
Cage birds      636.68
  *see also* Birds
Cages (Animal housing)      636.083 1
Cages (Mine elevators)      622.68
Cagliari (Italy)      T2—459 11
  ancient      T2—379 11
Cagliari (Italy : Province)      T2—459 1
  ancient      T2—379 1
Cahuapanan languages      498.9
     T6—989
Cahuilla Indians      T5—974 5
Cahuilla language      497.45
     T6—974 5
CAI (Computer-assisted      371.334
  instruction)      T1—078 5
  adult level      374.26
Caimans      597.984
Cain (Biblical person)
  Bible stories      222.110 950 5
Cairngorm Mountains
  (Scotland)      T2—412 4
Cairngorms (Scotland)      T2—412 4
Cairns (Qld.)      T2—943 6
Cairo (Egypt : Province)      T2—621 6

Caisson disease
  medicine      616.989 4
  *see also* Environmental
    diseases — humans
Caissons      624.157
Caithness (Scotland)      T2—411 52
Cajamarca (Peru : Dept.)      T2—851 5
Cajun cooking      641.597 63
Cajun French dialect      447.976 3
     T6—41
Cajuns      T5—410 763
  *see Manual at* T5—112,
    T5—114 vs. T5—2,
    T5—41
Cakchikel Indians      T5—974 22
Cakchikel language      497.422
     T6—974 22
Cakchikel literature      897.422
Cake decorating      641.865 39
Cake icing      641.865 39
Cake mixes      664.753
Cakes (Pastry)      641.865 3
  commercial processing      664.752 5
  home preparation      641.865 3
Cakewalks      791.12
  music      784.188 7
Cala (South Africa :
  District)      T2—687 58
Calabar (Nigeria)      T2—669 44
Calabash tree      635.977 395
  botany      583.95
  ornamental arboriculture      635.977 395
Calabria (Italy)      T2—457 8
  ancient      T2—377 8
Calabria (Roman region)      T2—377 6
Caladiums      635.934 64
  botany      584.64
  floriculture      635.934 64
Calamitales      561.72
Calamopityaceae      561.595
Calanoida      595.34
Călăraşi (Romania : Judeţ)      T2—498 2
Calaveras County (Calif.)      T2—794 44
Calcarea      593.42
  paleozoology      563.4
Calcaronea      593.42
Calcasieu Lake (La.)      T2—763 52
Calcasieu Parish (La.)      T2—763 54
Calcification      572.516
Calcimining      698.2
Calcinea      593.42
Calcispongiae      593.42
  paleozoology      563.4

Calcite
  mineralogy 549.782
Calcium 669.725
  applied nutrition 613.285 16
  biochemistry 572.516
    humans 612.015 24
  chemical engineering 661.039 3
  chemistry 546.393
  metabolism
    human physiology 612.392 4
  metallurgy 669.725
  organic chemistry 547.053 93
    applied 661.895
  physical metallurgy 669.967 25
  *see also* Chemicals
Calcium soaps 668.125
Calculators 681.145
  manufacturing technology 681.145
  mathematics 510.284
Calculus 515
  numerical methods 518.6
Calculus of finite differences 515.62
Calculus of variations 515.64
Calcutta (India) T2—541 47
Caldas (Colombia : Dept.) T2—861 35
Calderdale (England) T2—428 12
Calderón Fournier, Rafael Angel
  Costa Rican history 972.860 522
Calderón Hinojosa, Felipe
  Mexican history 972.084 2
Calderón Sol, Armando
  Salvadoran history 972.840 541
Caldwell County (Ky.) T2—769 815
Caldwell County (Mo.) T2—778 185
Caldwell County (N.C.) T2—756 845
Caldwell County (Tex.) T2—764 33
Caldwell Parish (La.) T2—763 76
Caledon (South Africa :
  District) T2—687 36
Caledon River (Lesotho and
  South Africa) T2—685 6
Caledonia County (Vt.) T2—743 34
Calendar reform 529.5
Calendars 529.3
  chronology 529.3
  illustration 741.682
  liturgy 264
    Anglican 264.031
    Roman Catholic 264.021
  religion 203.6
    Christianity 263.9
    Islam 297.36
    Judaism 296.43
Calendering paper 676.234

Calendering rubber 678.27
Calendering textiles 677.028 25
Calgary (Alta.) T2—712 338
Calhoun County (Ala.) T2—761 63
Calhoun County (Ark.) T2—767 64
Calhoun County (Fla.) T2—759 943
Calhoun County (Ga.) T2—758 956
Calhoun County (Ill.) T2—773 853
Calhoun County (Iowa) T2—777 43
Calhoun County (Mich.) T2—774 22
Calhoun County (Miss.) T2—762 81
Calhoun County (S.C.) T2—757 72
Calhoun County (Tex.) T2—764 121
Calhoun County (W. Va.) T2—754 29
Calibration 530.8
  electrical instruments 621.372
Calico bass 597.738
California 979.4
  T2—794
California, Gulf of (Mexico) 551.461 41
  T2—164 1
California, Southern T2—794 9
California halibut 597.69
California laurel 583.23
California legless lizards 597.959
Californium 546.448
Caligoida 595.34
Caliphate 297.61
Caliphs
  companions of Muḥammad 297.648
  religious biography 297.092
  role and function 297.61
Calisthenics 613.714
  child care 649.57
Calitzdorp (South Africa :
  District) T2—687 38
Call to Islam 297.74
Calla lilies 635.934 64
  botany 584.64
  floriculture 635.934 64
Callahan County (Tex.) T2—764 726
Callao (Peru : Province) T2—852 6
Callaway County (Mo.) T2—778 335
Callejas Romero, Rafael
  Leonardo
  Honduran history 972.830 534
Caller ID telephone service 384.64
Calles, Plutarco Elías
  Mexican history 972.082 3
Calligraphy 745.61
Calliphoridae 595.774
Callipteris 561.597
Callithricidae 599.84

| | |
|---|---|
| Callitrichidae | 599.84 |
| paleozoology | 569.84 |
| Callorhinus | 599.797 3 |
| Callosities | |
| medicine | 616.544 |
| *see also* Skin diseases — | |
| humans | |
| Calloway County (Ky.) | T2—769 92 |
| Calls (Finance) | 332.645 3 |
| multiple forms of investment | 332.645 3 |
| stocks | 332.632 283 |
| Caloosahatchee River (Fla.) | T2—759 48 |
| Caloric restriction | |
| health | 613.25 |
| Calorie counters | 613.23 |
| Calories | |
| applied nutrition | 613.23 |
| Calorimeters | |
| manufacturing technology | 681.2 |
| Calorimetry | 536.6 |
| Caltanissetta (Italy : | |
| Province) | T2—458 21 |
| ancient | T2—378 21 |
| Calumet County (Wis.) | T2—775 66 |
| Calvados (France) | T2—442 2 |
| Calvert County (Md.) | T2—752 44 |
| Calvinia (South Africa : | |
| District) | T2—687 17 |
| Calvinistic Baptists | 286.1 |
| *see also* Baptists | |
| Calvinistic churches | 284.2 |
| *see also* Reformed Church | |
| Calvinists | |
| biography | 284.209 2 |
| Calycerales | 583.9 |
| CAM (Manufacturing) | 670.427 |
| Camagüey (Cuba : | |
| Province) | T2—729 156 |
| Camarines Norte | |
| (Philippines) | T2—599 1 |
| Camarines Sur (Philippines) | T2—599 1 |
| Camas County (Idaho) | T2—796 31 |
| Cambistry | 332.45 |
| Cambium | 575.488 |
| Cambodia | 959.6 |
| | T2—596 |
| Cambodian language | 495.932 |
| | T6—959 32 |
| Cambodian literature | 895.932 |
| Cambodians | T5—959 32 |
| Cambria County (Pa.) | T2—748 77 |
| Cambrian Mountains | |
| (Wales) | T2—429 |
| Cambrian period | 551.723 |
| geology | 551.723 |
| paleontology | 560.172 3 |
| Cambridge (England) | T2—426 59 |
| Cambridge (Mass.) | T2—744 4 |
| Cambridge Bay (Nunavut) | T2—719 55 |
| Cambridgeshire (England) | T2—426 5 |
| Cambuslang (Scotland) | T2—414 57 |
| Camcorders | |
| videography | 777.34 |
| Camden (London, England) | T2—421 42 |
| Camden (N.S.W.) | T2—944 6 |
| Camden County (Ga.) | T2—758 746 |
| Camden County (Mo.) | T2—778 54 |
| Camden County (N.C.) | T2—756 135 |
| Camden County (N.J.) | T2—749 87 |
| Camelidae | 599.636 |
| Camellias | 583.624 |
| floriculture | 635.933 624 |
| Camels | 636.295 |
| animal husbandry | 636.295 |
| zoology | 599.636 2 |
| Camel's hair textiles | 677.34 |
| *see also* Textiles | |
| Camelus | 636.295 |
| zoology | 599.636 2 |
| Camembert cheese | 641.373 53 |
| cooking | 641.673 53 |
| food | 641.373 53 |
| processing | 637.353 |
| Cameos | 736.222 |
| Cameras | 771.3 |
| cinematography | 777.34 |
| manufacturing technology | 681.418 |
| television engineering | 621.388 34 |
| videography | 777.34 |
| Camerata | 563.92 |
| Cameron County (Pa.) | T2—748 66 |
| Cameron County (Tex.) | T2—764 495 |
| Cameron Parish (La.) | T2—763 52 |
| Cameroon | 967.11 |
| | T2—671 1 |
| Cameroon people | T5—967 11 |
| Cameroonians | T5—967 11 |
| Cameroun | T2—671 1 |
| Camiguin (Philippines) | T2—599 7 |
| Camillians | 255.55 |
| church history | 271.55 |
| Camouflage (Biology) | 591.472 |
| Camouflage (Military science) | 355.41 |
| engineering | 623.77 |
| Camp cooking | 641.578 2 |
| Camp County (Tex.) | T2—764 219 |
| Camp Fire, inc. | 369.47 |

Camp Fire Girls 369.47
Camp meetings
  Christian religious practices 269.24
Camp programs 796.5
  church work 253.7
  Jewish religious work 296.67
Campa Indians T5—983 9
Campa language 498.39
  T6—983 9
Campaign buttons
  numismatics 737.242
Campaign finance 324.78
  law 342.078
Campaign finance offenses 364.132 4
  law 345.023 24
Campaign literature 324.23
Campaign pins
  numismatics 737.242
Campaign strategy (Elections) 324.72
Campaigns (Military science) 355.4
  *see also* Land operations
Campaigns (Politics) 324.9
  elections 324.9
  law 342.078
  nominations 324.5
    specific countries 324.24–.29
  techniques 324.7
  *see Manual at* 909, 930–990 vs.
    320
Campania (Italy) T2—457 2
  ancient T2—377 2
Campanula 583.98
  floriculture 635.933 98
Campanulales 583.98
Campbell, Kim
  Canadian history 971.064 7
Campbell County (Ky.) T2—769 34
Campbell County (S.D.) T2—783 17
Campbell County (Tenn.) T2 768 72
Campbell County (Va.) T2—755 672
Campbell County (Wyo.) T2—787 12
Campbell Island (N.Z.) T2—939 9
Campbellites 286.6
  *see also* Restoration movement
    (Christian movement)
Campbelltown (N.S.W.) T2—944 6
Campbeltown (Scotland) T2—414 2
Campeche (Mexico : State) T2—726 4
Camperdown (South
  Africa : District) T2—684 7
Campers (Vehicles) 388.346
  cooking 641.575
  engineering 629.226
  *see also* Motor homes

Campfires 796.545
Camphors
  chemistry 547.71
Camping 796.54
  meal service 642.3
  military operations 355.412
  military training 355.544
Camping equipment 796.540 284
  armed forces 355.81
  manufacturing technology 685.53
Campo Formio, Treaty of, 1797 945.307
Campobasso (Italy :
  Province) T2—457 192
  ancient T2—377 38
Campsites 910.468
  household management 647.942
  *see also* Lodging (Temporary
    housing)
Campus Crusade for Christ 267.61
Campus ministry 259.24
Campus police 363.289
Campus unrest 371.81
Campus-wide information
  systems
  information science T2—436 6
Cams 621.838
Cần Thơ (Vietnam) T2—597 9
Canaanite language 492.6
  T6—926
Canaanite literature 892.6
Canaanites T5—926
Canaanitic languages 492.6
  T6—926
Canaanitic literatures 892.6
Canada 971
  T2—71
  English explorations 971.011 4
  French explorations 971.011 3
  Norse explorations 971.011 2
  *see Manual at* T2—73 vs.
    T2—71
Canada, Eastern T2—713
Canada, Western T2—712
Canada goose 598.417 8
Canadian Alliance (Political
  party) 324.271 04
Canadian Arctic T2—719
Canadian Arctic
  Archipelago (Nunavut
  and N.W.T.) T2—719 52
Canadian Cordillera T2—711
Canadian County (Okla.) T2—766 39
Canadian football 796.335
Canadian football players 796.335 092

| | |
|---|---|
| Canadian language | |
| English | 420.971 |
| | T6—21 |
| French | 440.971 |
| | T6—41 |
| Inuit | 497.12 |
| | T6—971 2 |
| Canadian literature | |
| English | 810 |
| French | 840 |
| Inuit | 897.12 |
| Canadian Pacific seawaters | 551.461 433 |
| | T2—164 33 |
| Canadian pronunciation | |
| English | 421.52 |
| French | 441.52 |
| Canadian Reform Conservative | |
| Alliance (Political party) | 324.271 04 |
| Canadian River (Okla.) | T2—766 |
| Canadian River, North | |
| (Okla.) | T2—766 1 |
| Canadian Rockies (B.C. and | |
| Alta.) | T2—711 |
| Canadian Shield | T2—714 |
| Canada | T2—714 |
| Manitoba | T2—712 72 |
| Ontario | T2—713 1 |
| Canadian spelling | |
| English | 421.52 |
| French | 441.52 |
| Canadians | T5—11 |
| *see Manual at* T5—112, | |
| T5—114 vs. T5—2, | |
| T5—41 | |
| Canaigre | 633.87 |
| agriculture | 633.87 |
| botany | 583.57 |
| Çanakkale İli (Turkey) | T2—562 2 |
| ancient | T2—392 1 |
| Asia | T2—562 2 |
| Europe | T2—496 12 |
| Canal Area (Panama) | T2—728 75 |
| Canal transportation | 386.4 |
| *see also* Inland water | |
| transportation | |
| Canalboats | |
| freight services | 386.244 |
| power-driven | 386.224 36 |
| design | 623.812 436 |
| engineering | 623.824 36 |
| transportation services | 386.224 36 |

| | |
|---|---|
| Canalboats (continued) | |
| towed | 386.229 |
| design | 623.812 9 |
| engineering | 623.829 |
| transportation services | 386.229 |
| Canalized rivers | 386.4 |
| engineering | 627.13 |
| *see also* Canals | |
| Canals | 386.4 |
| engineering | 627.13 |
| law | 343.096 4 |
| law of nations | 341.446 |
| transportation services | 386.4 |
| Canapés | 641.812 |
| Cañar (Ecuador : Province) | T2—866 23 |
| Canarese | T5—948 14 |
| Canaries | 636.686 25 |
| animal husbandry | 636.686 25 |
| zoology | 598.885 |
| Canary grasses | 584.9 |
| Canary Islands | 964.9 |
| | T2—649 |
| Canasta | 795.418 |
| Canberra (A.C.T.) | T2—947 1 |
| Cancellations (Philately) | 769.567 |
| Cancer | 571.978 |
| animals | 571.978 1 |
| veterinary medicine | 636.089 699 4 |
| humans | 362.196 994 |
| geriatrics | 618.976 994 |
| incidence | 614.599 9 |
| medicine | 616.994 |
| nursing | 616.994 023 1 |
| pediatrics | 618.929 94 |
| social services | 362.196 994 |
| surgery | 616.994 059 |
| Cancer (Zodiac) | 133.526 5 |
| Candelilla wax | 665.12 |
| Candidiasis | |
| incidence | 614.559 3 |
| medicine | 616.969 3 |
| *see also* Communicable | |
| diseases — humans | |
| Candleberry | 583.43 |
| Candleberry wax | 665.12 |
| Candler County (Ga.) | T2—758 773 |
| Candles | 621.323 |
| handicrafts | 745.593 32 |
| *see also* Lighting | |
| Candlesticks | 621.323 |
| ceramic arts | 738.8 |
| handicrafts | 745.593 3 |
| *see also* Lighting | |
| Candlewood | 583.628 |

| | |
|---|---|
| Candomblé | 299.673 |
| Candy | 641.853 |
|   commercial processing | 664.153 |
|   home preparation | 641.853 |
| Candytufts (Plants) | 583.64 |
| Cane fruits | 641.347 1 |
|   botany | 583.73 |
|   cooking | 641.647 1 |
|   food | 641.347 1 |
|   horticulture | 634.71 |
| Cane rat | 599.359 |
| Cane sugar | 641.336 1 |
|   commercial processing | 664.122 |
|   food | 641.336 1 |
|   *see also* Sugar | |
| Cane syrup | 641.336 1 |
|   commercial processing | 664.122 |
|   food | 641.336 1 |
|   *see also* Sugar | |
| Cane textiles | 677.54 |
|   *see also* Textiles | |
| Canea (Greece : Nome) | T2—495 9 |
| Canella language | 498.4 |
| | T6—984 |
| Canelones (Uruguay : Dept.) | T2—895 14 |
| Canes (Sticks) | 391.44 |
| Caniapiscau (Quebec : Regional County Municipality) | T2—714 117 |
| Canidae | 599.77 |
|   paleozoology | 569.77 |
| Canindeyú (Paraguay) | T2—892 133 |
| Canine police services | 363.232 |
| Canines | 636.7 |
|   *see also* Dogs | |
| Canis | 599.772 |
| Çankırı İli (Turkey) | T2—563 7 |
|   ancient | T2—393 17 |
| Canna (Scotland) | T2—411 54 |
| Cannabaceae | 583.45 |
| Cannabis | |
|   pharmacokinetics | 615.782 7 |
| Cannabis abuse | 362.295 |
|   medicine | 616.863 5 |
|   personal health | 613.835 |
|   social welfare | 362.295 |
|   *see also* Substance abuse | |
| Cannaceae | 584.39 |
| Cannas | 635.934 39 |
|   botany | 584.39 |
|   floriculture | 635.934 39 |

| | |
|---|---|
| Canned foods | |
|   cooking | 641.612 |
|   product safety | 363.192 9 |
|     *see also* Food — product safety | |
| Cannel coal | 553.23 |
|   economic geology | 553.23 |
|   properties | 662.622 3 |
| Cannibalism | |
|   customs | 394.9 |
| Cannibalism in animals | 591.53 |
| Canning, John Charles, Earl | |
|   Indian history | 954.031 7 |
| Canning foods | 664.028 2 |
|   commercial preservation | 664.028 2 |
|   home preservation | 641.42 |
| Cannock Chase (England) | T2—424 67 |
| Cannon County (Tenn.) | T2—768 535 |
| Cannons | 355.822 |
|   art metalwork | 739.742 |
|   engineering | 623.42 |
|   military equipment | 355.822 |
| Canoe racing | 797.14 |
| Canoeing | |
|   sports | 797.122 |
| Canoes | 386.229 |
|   design | 623.812 9 |
|   engineering | 623.829 |
|   transportation services | 386.229 |
| Canoidea | 599.76 |
|   paleozoology | 569.76 |
| Canon law | 262.9 |
| Canon of Bible | 220.12 |
| Canonization of saints | 235.24 |
| Canons (Music) | 784.187 8 |
| Canons regular | 255.08 |
|   church history | 271.08 |
|   women | 255.908 |
|     church history | 271.908 |
| Canopies | |
|   church architecture | 726.529 3 |
| Cant | 417.2 |
|   specific languages | T4—7 |
| Cantabria (Spain) | T2—463 51 |
| Cantabrian Mountains (Spain) | T2—462 |
| Cantal (France) | T2—445 92 |
| Cantaloupes | 641.356 117 |
|   cooking | 641.656 117 |
|   food | 641.356 117 |
|   garden crop | 635.611 7 |
| Cantatas | 782.24 |
|   choral and mixed voices | 782.524 |
|   single voices | 783.092 4 |

| | |
|---|---|
| Canteen cooking | 641.577 |
| Canteen meal service | 642.5 |
| Canteens | |
| armed forces | 355.341 |
| Canterbury (England : City) | T2—422 34 |
| Canterbury Region (N.Z.) | T2—938 |
| Cantharidae | 595.764 4 |
| Cantharoidea | 595.764 4 |
| Canticle of Canticles | 223.9 |
| Canticles | 782.295 |
| Cantilever bridges | |
| construction | 624.219 |
| Cantilever foundations | 624.156 |
| Canton (China) | T2—512 75 |
| Cantonese dialects | 495.172 7 |
| | T6—951 7 |
| Cantons | 320.83 |
| *see also* Counties | |
| Cantons-de-l'Est (Quebec) | T2—714 6 |
| Cantors (Judaism) | |
| biography | 296.462 092 |
| Cantus firmus | 781.828 |
| Canunda National Park (S. Aust.) | T2—942 34 |
| Canute I, King of England | |
| English history | 942.018 1 |
| Canvas embroidery | 746.442 |
| Canvasback | 598.414 |
| Canyon County (Idaho) | T2—796 23 |
| Canyoneering | 796.524 |
| Canyoning | 796.524 |
| Canyonlands National Park (Utah) | T2—792 59 |
| Canyons | 551.442 |
| | T2—144 |
| geography | 910.914 4 |
| geomorphology | 551.442 |
| physical geography | 910.021 44 |
| Canzonas | 784.187 5 |
| Cao Bằng (Vietnam : Province) | T2—597 1 |
| Cap-de-la-Madeleine (Trois-Rivières, Quebec) | T2—714 451 |
| Capacitance meters | 621.374 2 |
| Capacitors | |
| electrical engineering | 621.315 |
| radio engineering | 621.384 133 |
| Capacity (Law) | 346.013 |
| Cape (South Africa : District) | T2—687 355 |
| Cape Baring (N.W.T.) | T2—719 3 |
| Cape Breton (N.S. : Regional municipality) | T2—716 95 |
| Cape Breton Highlands National Park (N.S.) | T2—716 91 |
| Cape Breton Island (N.S.) | T2—716 9 |
| Cape Cod (Mass.) | T2—744 92 |
| Cape Cod Bay (Mass.) | 551.461 345 |
| | T2—163 45 |
| Cape Dorset (Nunavut) | T2—719 52 |
| Cape Fear River (N.C.) | T2—756 2 |
| Cape Girardeau County (Mo.) | T2—778 96 |
| Cape Hatteras (N.C.) | T2—756 175 |
| Cape Le Grand National Park (W.A.) | T2—941 7 |
| Cape May County (N.J.) | T2—749 98 |
| Cape Metropolitan Area (South Africa) | T2—687 35 |
| Cape of Good Hope (South Africa) | 968.705 |
| | T2—687 |
| Cape of Good Hope (South Africa : Cape) | T2—687 35 |
| Cape Peninsula (South Africa : Cape) | T2—687 35 |
| Cape Range National Park (W.A.) | T2—941 3 |
| Cape Town (South Africa) | T2—687 355 |
| Cape Verde | 966.58 |
| | T2—665 8 |
| Cape Verde Islands | T2—665 8 |
| Cape Verdeans | T5—966 58 |
| Cape Wollaston (N.W.T.) | T2—719 3 |
| Cape York Peninsula (Qld.) | T2—943 8 |
| Capercaillies | 598.634 |
| Capers | 641.338 2 |
| botany | 583.64 |
| *see also* Flavorings | |
| Capes (Clothing) | 391.46 |
| *see also* Outerwear | |
| Capetian dynasty | 944.021 |
| genealogy | 929.74 |
| Capillaries | 573.187 |
| animals | 573.187 |
| human anatomy | 611.15 |
| human physiology | 612.135 |
| medicine | 616.148 |
| physiology | 573.187 |
| surgery | 617.415 |
| *see also* Cardiovascular system | |
| Capillarity | 530.427 |
| chemical engineering | 660.293 |
| Capillary circulation | 573.187 |
| human physiology | 612.135 |
| *see also* Capillaries | |

Capillary diseases
  medicine        616.148
  *see also* Cardiovascular
    diseases — humans
Capillary hemangiomas
  medicine        616.993 15
Capital        332.041
  financial economics        332.041
  income distribution        339.21
  management        658.152
  production economics        338.604 1
Capital (B.C.)        T2—711 28
Capital accounting        657.76
Capital budgets        658.154
Capital budgets (Public)        352.48
  *see also* Budgets (Public)
Capital cities
  area planning        711.45
Capital Federal (Argentina)    T2—821 1
Capital flight        332.042 4
Capital flows        332.042 4
Capital formation        332.041 5
  agricultural industries        338.13
  economics        332.041 5
  financial management        658.152 2
  macroeconomics        339.43
  mineral industries        338.23
  production economics        338.604 1
  secondary industries        338.43
Capital gains tax        336.242 4
  law        343.052 45
  public administration        352.44
  public finance        336.242 4
    corporate income        336.243
    individual income        336.242 4
Capital levy        336.22
  law        343.054
Capital loss
  personal income tax deduction   336.242 4
Capital management        658.152
Capital markcts        332.041 5
Capital movements        332.042 4
Capital punishment        364.66
  ethics        179.7
    religion        205.697
      Buddhism        294.356 97
      Christianity        241.697
      Hinduism        294.548 697
      Islam        297.569 7
      Judaism        296.369 7
  law        345.077 3
  penology        364.66
  social theology        201.764
    Christianity        261.833 66

Capital sources        332.041 5
  financial management        658.152 2
Capital transactions (Balance of
  payments)
  international banking        332.152
  international finance        332.042 4
Capitale-Nationale (Quebec) T2—714 47
Capitalism        330.122
  economics        330.122
  social theology        201.73
    Christianity        261.85
    Judaism        296.383
  sociology        306.342
Capitalization (Finance)        658.152
Capitalization (Writing)        411
  specific languages        T4—11
Capitals (Architecture)        721.3
Capitán Prat (Chile :
  Province)        T2—836 28
Capitol Reef National Park
  (Utah)        T2—792 54
Capitols
  architecture        725.11
Capitonidae        598.72
Capiz (Philippines :
  Province)        T2—599 5
Cappadocia (Kingdom)        T2—393 4
Cappadocia (Turkey)        T2—564 1
Capparales        583.64
Capparidales        583.64
Capra        599.648
Capreolus        599.659
Capri Island (Italy)        T2—457 3
Capricorn (Zodiac)        133.527 5
Caprifoliaceae        583.92
Caprimulgiformes        598.99
  paleozoology        568.9
Caprinae        599.647
Caps (Headwear)        391.43
  *see also* Headwear
Capsicums        641.338 4
  botany        583.952
  *see also* Hot spices; Sweet
    peppers
Capstans        621.864
Capsule cockpits        629.134 386
Capsules (Pharmaceuticals)
  pharmaceutical chemistry        615.19
Captive balloons
  engineering        629.133 22
  military engineering        623.744
Captives (Military)        355.113
  war customs        399
  *see also* Prisoners of war

| | |
|---|---|
| Capture (Nuclear particles) | 539.75 |
| Capuchins | 255.36 |
| church history | 271.36 |
| Capybaras | 599.359 |
| Caquetá (Colombia) | T2—861 64 |
| Car boot sales | 381.195 |
| Car cards (Advertising) | 659.134 4 |
| Car parks | 388.474 |
| *see also* Parking facilities | |
| Car pools | 388.413 212 |
| law | 343.098 2 |
| Car sickness | |
| medicine | 616.989 2 |
| *see also* Environmental | |
| diseases — humans | |
| Carabidae | 595.762 |
| Carabobo (Venezuela : | |
| State) | T2—873 2 |
| Caracaras | 598.96 |
| Caracas (Venezuela) | T2—877 |
| Caracciolini | 255.56 |
| church history | 271.56 |
| Caradon (England) | T2—423 7 |
| Caralis (Italy) | T2—379 11 |
| Carapidae | 597.63 |
| Carapodidae | 597.63 |
| Caraş-Severin (Romania) | T2—498 4 |
| Carassius (Goldfish) | 639.374 84 |
| culture | 639.374 84 |
| zoology | 597.484 |
| Caravans (Vehicles) | 388.346 |
| engineering | 629.226 |
| *see also* Motor homes | |
| Caravels | 387.21 |
| design | 623.812 1 |
| engineering | 623.821 |
| handling | 623.882 1 |
| transportation services | 387.21 |
| *see also* Ships | |
| Caraway | 641.338 3 |
| botany | 583.849 |
| *see also* Spices | |
| Carazo (Nicaragua) | T2—728 516 |
| Carbines | 683.422 |
| *see also* Rifles | |
| Carbohydrases | 572.756 |
| *see also* Enzymes | |
| Carbohydrate-restricted diet | |
| health | 613.283 3 |
| Carbohydrates | 572.56 |
| applied nutrition | 613.283 |
| biochemistry | 572.56 |
| humans | 612.015 78 |
| chemistry | 547.78 |
| Carbohydrates (continued) | |
| metabolic disorders | 571.945 6 |
| medicine | 616.399 8 |
| *see also* Digestive system | |
| diseases — humans | |
| metabolism | 572.564 |
| human physiology | 612.396 |
| Carbon | 547 |
| biochemistry | 572 |
| chemical engineering | 661.068 1 |
| inorganic chemistry | 546.681 |
| materials science | 620.193 |
| mineralogy | 549.27 |
| organic chemistry | 547 |
| applied | 661.8 |
| *see also* Chemicals | |
| Carbon black | 662.93 |
| Carbon County (Mont.) | T2—786 652 |
| Carbon County (Pa.) | T2—748 26 |
| Carbon County (Utah) | T2—792 566 |
| Carbon County (Wyo.) | T2—787 86 |
| Carbon cycle (Biogeochemistry) | 577.144 |
| Carbon dioxide | 546.681 2 |
| gas technology | 665.89 |
| therapeutics | 615.836 |
| Carbon dioxide removal | |
| human physiology | 612.22 |
| Carbon dioxide sinks | 577.144 |
| Carbon processes | |
| photographic printing | 773.1 |
| Carbonaceous materials | 553.2 |
| economic geology | 553.2 |
| mining | 622.33 |
| Carbonate rocks | 552.58 |
| Carbonated beverages | 641.26 |
| commercial processing | 663.62 |
| home preparation | 641.875 |
| Carbonated water | |
| commercial processing | 663.61 |
| Carbonates | |
| mineralogy | 549.78 |
| Carbonia-Inglesia (Italy : | |
| Province) | T2—459 8 |
| ancient | T2—379 8 |
| Carboniferous period | 551.75 |
| geology | 551.75 |
| paleontology | 560.175 |
| Carboxylic acids | 547.037 |
| chemical engineering | 661.86 |
| Carbro process | 773.1 |
| Carbuncles | |
| medicine | 616.523 |
| *see also* Skin diseases — | |
| humans | |

| | |
|---|---|
| Carbureted-blue gas | 665.772 |
| Carburetors | 621.437 |
|   automotive | 629.253 3 |
| Carcharhinidae | 597.34 |
| Carcharhiniformes | 597.3 |
| Carcharodon carcharias | 597.33 |
| Carchi (Ecuador) | T2—866 11 |
| Carcinogenesis | |
|   biology | 571.978 |
|   medicine | 616.994 071 |
| Carcinoma | 571.978 |
|   incidence | 614.599 9 |
|   medicine | 616.994 |
|   *see also* Cancer | |
| Card catalogs | 025.313 |
| Card games | 795.4 |
| Card players | 795.409 2 |
| Card readers (Computers) | 004.76 |
|   engineering | 621.398 6 |
| Card tricks | 793.85 |
| Card weaving | |
|   arts | 746.14 |
| Cardamom | 641.338 3 |
|   botany | 584.39 |
|   *see also* Spices | |
| Cardboard | 676.288 |
| Cárdenas, Lázaro | |
|   Mexican history | 972.082 5 |
| Cardiac arrest | |
|   medicine | 616.123 025 |
|   *see also* Cardiovascular | |
|     diseases — humans | |
| Cardiac asthma | |
|   medicine | 616.12 |
|   *see also* Cardiovascular | |
|     diseases — humans | |
| Cardiac muscle tissues | |
|   human histology | 612.740 45 |
| Cardiff (Wales) | T2—429 87 |
| Cardigans | 391.46 |
|   commercial technology | 687.14 |
|   home sewing | 646.45 |
|   *see also* Outerwear | |
| Cardinal fishes | 597.7 |
| Cardinal numbers | 511.322 |
| Cardinal sins | 241.3 |
| Cardinals (Birds) | 598.883 |
| Cardinals (Clergy) | 282.092 |
|   biography | 282.092 |
|   ecclesiology | 262.135 |
| Carding textiles | 677.028 21 |
|   arts | 746.11 |
|   manufacturing technology | 677.028 21 |

| | |
|---|---|
| Cardiology | 616.12 |
|   pediatrics | 618.921 2 |
| Cardiopulmonary diseases | |
|   medicine | 616.1 |
|   *see also* Cardiovascular | |
|     diseases — humans | |
| Cardiopulmonary resuscitation | |
|   medicine | 616.102 5 |
| Cardiotonic agents | |
|   pharmacokinetics | 615.711 |
| Cardiovascular agents | |
|   pharmacokinetics | 615.71 |
| Cardiovascular diseases | 573.139 |
|   animals | 573.139 |
|     veterinary medicine | 636.089 61 |
|   humans | 362.196 1 |
|     anesthesiology | 617.967 41 |
|     cancer | 362.196 994 1 |
|       incidence | 614.599 941 |
|       medicine | 616.994 1 |
|       social services | 362.196 994 1 |
|       *see also* Cancer — humans | |
|     geriatrics | 618.976 1 |
|     incidence | 614.591 |
|     medicine | 616.1 |
|     nursing | 616.102 31 |
|     pediatrics | 618.921 |
|     perinatal medicine | 618.326 1 |
|     pharmacokinetics | 615.71 |
|     pregnancy complications | |
|       obstetrics | 618.361 |
|     social services | 362.196 1 |
|     surgery | 617.41 |
| Cardiovascular organs | 573.1 |
|   *see also* Cardiovascular system | |
| Cardiovascular system | 573.1 |
|   anesthesiology | 617.967 41 |
|   biology | 573.1 |
|   diseases | 573.139 |
|     *see also* Cardiovascular | |
|       diseases | |
|   human anatomy | 611.1 |
|   human histology | 612.104 5 |
|   human physiology | 612.1 |
|   medicine | 616.1 |
|   physiology | 573.1 |
|   surgery | 617.41 |
| Cardoso, Fernando Henrique | |
|   Brazilian history | 981.064 |
| Cards | |
|   divination | 133.324 2 |
|   games | 795.4 |
|     manufacturing technology | 688.754 |
| Carduelidae | 598.885 |

CARE (Firm) — 361.763
Career changes — 331.702
  business — 650.14
  economics — 331.702
  executive management — 658.409
Career development — 370.113
  business — 650.1
  economics — 331.702
  industrial psychology — 158.7
  *see also* Vocational education;
    Vocational guidance
Career education — 370.113
      T1—071
  *see also* Vocational education
Career guidance — 331.702
      T1—023
  *see also* Vocational guidance
Career opportunities — 331.702
      T1—023
  *see also* Vocational guidance
Caregivers — 362.042 5
Carettochelyidae — 597.926
Cargados Carajos Shoals
  (Mauritius) — T2—698 2
Cargo airplanes
  military engineering — 623.746 5
Cargo handling — 388.044
  *see also* Freight services
Cargo-handling equipment — 623.867
  port engineering — 627.34
  ships — 623.867
Cargo insurance — 368.2
Cargo ships — 387.245
  petroleum technology — 665.543
  power-driven — 387.245
    design — 623.812 45
    engineering — 623.824 5
  wind-driven — 387.224
    design — 623.812 24
    engineering — 623.822 4
  *see also* Merchant ships; Ships
Caria — T2—392 4
Carib Indians — T5—984 2
Carib Indians (Galibi) — T5—984 22
Carib language — 498.422
      T6—984 22
Carib languages — 498.42
      T6—984 2
Caribbean Area — 972.9
      T2—729
Caribbean Blacks — T5—969 729
Caribbean Islands — T2—729
Caribbean peoples — T5—969 729

Caribbean Region
  (Colombia) — T2—861 1
Caribbean Sea — 551.461 365
      T2—163 65
Caribbees — T2—729
Cariboo (B.C. : Regional
  District) — T2—711 75
Cariboo Mountains (B.C.) — T2—711 7
Caribou — 599.658
  animal husbandry — 636.294 8
  conservation technology — 639.979 658
  resource economics — 333.959 658
Caribou County (Idaho) — T2—796 45
Caricaceae — 583.626
Caricatures — 741.56
  drawing — 741.51
  genres
    history, criticism, techniques — 741.53
  geographic treatment — 741.569 3–.569 9
    *see Manual at* 741.593–.599
      and 741.5693–.5699
  *see Manual at* 741.5; *also at*
    741.56
Caridea — 595.388
Caries
  dentistry — 617.67
  incidence — 614.599 6
Carillons — 786.64
  *see also* Mechanical musical
    instruments
Caring
  ethics — 177.7
    religion — 205.677
    *see also* Love — ethics
Carjacking — 364.162 862 922 2
  law — 345.026 286 292 22
Carl XVI Gustaf, King of
  Sweden
  Swedish history — 948.505 4
Carleton (N.B. : County) — T2—715 52
Carleton (Ont.) — T2—713 84
Carlisle (England : City) — T2—427 89
Carlisle County (Ky.) — T2—769 97
Carlow (Ireland : County) — T2—418 82
Carlsbad Caverns National
  Park (N.M.) — T2—789 42
Carlton County (Minn.) — T2—776 73
Carmarthen (Wales :
  District) — T2—429 65
Carmarthenshire (Wales) — T2—429 65
Carmelite Nuns — 255.971
  church history — 271.971

| | |
|---|---|
| Carmelites | 255.73 |
| church history | 271.73 |
| women | 255.971 |
| church history | 271.971 |
| Carnallite | 553.636 |
| mineralogy | 549.4 |
| Carnarvon (South Africa : District) | T2—687 17 |
| Carnarvon National Park (Qld.) | T2—943 5 |
| Carnations | 635.933 53 |
| botany | 583.53 |
| floriculture | 635.933 53 |
| Carnauba wax | 665.12 |
| Carnival | 394.25 |
| Carnivals | 791.1 |
| Carnivora | 599.7 |
| conservation technology | 639.979 7 |
| paleozoology | 569.7 |
| resource economics | 333.959 7 |
| Carnivorous animals | 591.53 |
| Carnivorous dinosaurs | 567.912 |
| Carnivorous plants | 583.75 |
| Byblidaceae | 583.72 |
| Cephalotaceae | 583.72 |
| floriculture | 635.933 75 |
| Lentibulariaceae | 583.95 |
| Nepenthales | 583.75 |
| physiology | 575.99 |
| Sarraceniaceae | 583.36 |
| Carnot cycle | 536.71 |
| Caro, Joseph | |
| Jewish legal codes | 296.182 |
| Carob | 641.344 6 |
| botany | 583.74 |
| cooking | 641.644 6 |
| food | 641.344 6 |
| orchard crop | 634.46 |
| Carolina (South Africa : District) | T2—682 78 |
| Caroline County (Md.) | T2—752 31 |
| Caroline County (Va.) | T2—755 362 |
| Caroline Islands | T2—966 |
| Carolingian calligraphy | 745.619 74 |
| Carolingian dynasty | 944.014 |
| French history | 944.014 |
| German history | 943.014 |
| Italian history | 945.02 |
| Lombardian history | 945.202 |
| Piedmontese history | 945.102 |
| Tuscan history | 945.502 |
| Venetian history | 945.302 |
| Carols | 782.28 |
| choral and mixed voices | 782.528 |
| single voices | 783.092 8 |
| Carom billiards | 794.72 |
| Carotid body | |
| human anatomy | 611.47 |
| human physiology | 612.49 |
| medicine | 616.4 |
| Carp | 641.392 |
| cooking | 641.692 |
| culture | 639.374 83 |
| food | 641.392 |
| sports fishing | 799.174 83 |
| zoology | 597.483 |
| Carp family | 597.482 |
| Carpal tunnel syndrome | |
| medicine | 616.856 |
| *see also* Nervous system diseases — humans | |
| Carpals | |
| human anatomy | 611.717 |
| human physiology | 612.751 |
| Carpathian Mountains | T2—477 9 |
| Slovakia | T2—437 3 |
| Ukraine | T2—477 9 |
| Carpathos Island (Greece) | T2—495 87 |
| ancient | T2—391 7 |
| Carpels | 575.665 |
| Carpenter Lake (B.C.) | T2—711 31 |
| Carpenters | 694.092 |
| Carpentry | 694 |
| ship hulls | 623.844 |
| Carpeting | |
| building construction | 698.9 |
| Carpetmakers | 746.792 |
| Carpets | 645.12 |
| *see also* Rugs | |
| Carpetweeds | 583.53 |
| Carpoids | 563.92 |
| Carranza, Venustiano | |
| Mexican history | 972.082 1 |
| Carrera, Rafael | |
| Guatemalan history | 972.810 44 |
| Carriacou Island | 972.984 5 |
| | T2—729 845 |
| Carriage horses | 636.14 |
| Carriages | 388.341 |
| manufacturing technology | 688.6 |
| Carrick (England) | T2—423 7 |
| Carrickfergus (Northern Ireland) | T2—416 17 |
| Carrier language | 497.2 |
| Carrier proteins | 572.696 |
| Carrier RNA | 572.886 |

| | | | |
|---|---|---|---|
| Carriers (Common carriers) | 388.041 | Carterton District (N.Z.) | T2—936 7 |
| see also Common carriers | | Cartesian coordinate system | 516.16 |
| Carriers (Pneumatic) | 621.54 | Carthage (Extinct city) | T2—397 3 |
| Carrion beetles | 595.764 2 | Carthaginian architecture | 722.32 |
| Carrion flowers (Asclepiadaceae) | 583.93 | Carthaginian period | 939.730 2 |
| Carrion flowers (Smilacaceae) | 584.356 | Libyan history | 939.740 2 |
| Carroll County (Ark.) | T2—767 17 | Moroccan history | 939.712 02 |
| Carroll County (Ga.) | T2—758 39 | North African history | 939.702 |
| Carroll County (Ill.) | T2—773 345 | Portuguese history | 936.690 2 |
| Carroll County (Ind.) | T2—772 94 | Spanish history | 936.602 |
| Carroll County (Iowa) | T2—777 465 | Tunisian history | 939.730 2 |
| Carroll County (Ky.) | T2—769 373 | Carthusians | 255.71 |
| Carroll County (Md.) | T2—752 77 | church history | 271.71 |
| Carroll County (Miss.) | T2—762 633 | women | 255.97 |
| Carroll County (Mo.) | T2—778 225 | church history | 271.97 |
| Carroll County (N.H.) | T2—742 42 | Cartier, Jacques | |
| Carroll County (Ohio) | T2—771 67 | Quebec history | 971.401 2 |
| Carroll County (Tenn.) | T2—768 25 | Cartilage | 573.763 56 |
| Carroll County (Va.) | T2—755 714 | human histology | 612.751 7 |
| Carron, River (Scotland) | T2—411 52 | human physiology | 612.751 7 |
| Carrots | 641.351 3 | medicine | 616.77 |
| botany | 583.849 | see also Musculoskeletal | |
| commercial processing | 664.805 13 | system | |
| cooking | 641.651 3 | Cartilage cells | |
| food | 641.351 3 | human cytology | 612.751 76 |
| garden crop | 635.13 | Cartilage diseases | |
| Carrying cases | | medicine | 616.77 |
| cameras | 771.38 | see also Musculoskeletal | |
| Cars (Automobiles) | 388.342 | diseases — humans | |
| driving | 629.283 | Cartilaginous fishes | 597.3 |
| engineering | 629.222 | Cartilaginous ganoids | 597.42 |
| repair | 629.287 2 | Cartographers | 526.092 |
| transportation services | 388.342 | Cartographic materials | |
| see also Automobiles | | cataloging | 025.346 |
| Carson City (Nev.) | T2—793 57 | library treatment | 025.176 |
| Carson County (Tex.) | T2—764 826 | Cartography | 526 |
| Cartagena (Spain) | T2—467 7 | military engineering | 623.71 |
| Cartago (Costa Rica : | | military intelligence service | 355.343 2 |
| Province) | T2—728 62 | Cartomancy | 133.324 2 |
| Cartan geometry | 516.376 | Cartons | 688.8 |
| Cartels | 338.87 | paperboard | 676.32 |
| international | 338.88 | Cartoon animation | 741.58 |
| see also International | | Cartoon fiction | 741.5 |
| enterprises | | Cartoon films | 791.433 4 |
| Carter, James Earl | | cinematography | 777.7 |
| United States history | 973.926 | drawing | 741.58 |
| Carter, Jimmy | | motion pictures | 791.433 4 |
| United States history | 973.926 | Cartooning | |
| Carter County (Ky.) | T2—769 28 | techniques | 741.51 |
| Carter County (Mo.) | T2—778 892 | Cartoonists | |
| Carter County (Mont.) | T2—786 36 | biography | 741.569 3–.569 9 |
| Carter County (Okla.) | T2—766 58 | see Manual at 741.593–.599 | |
| Carter County (Tenn.) | T2—768 984 | and 741.5693–.5699 | |
| Carteret County (N.C.) | T2—756 197 | | |

| | |
|---|---|
| Cartoons | 741.56 |
| | T1—022 2 |
| drawing | 741.51 |
| genres | |
| history, criticism, techniques | 741.53 |
| geographic treatment | 741.569 3–.569 9 |
| *see Manual at* 741.593–.599 | |
| and 741.5693–.5699 | |
| humor | 741.56 |
| | T1—020 7 |
| journalism | |
| comic strips | 070.444 |
| editorial | 070.442 |
| *see Manual at* 741.5; *also at* | |
| 741.56 | |
| Cartridge tapes (Computers) | 004.563 |
| engineering | 621.397 63 |
| Cartridges (Ammunition) | 683.406 |
| manufacturing technology | 683.406 |
| military engineering | 623.455 |
| Carts | 388.341 |
| manufacturing technology | 688.6 |
| Cārvāka | 181.46 |
| Carver County (Minn.) | T2—776 53 |
| Carving | |
| artistic technique | 730.28 |
| architectural decoration | 729.5 |
| decorative arts | 736 |
| sculpture | 731.46 |
| table service | 642.6 |
| Caryophyllales | 583.53 |
| Caryophyllidae | 583.5 |
| Casaba melon | 641.356 117 |
| cooking | 641.656 117 |
| food | 641.356 117 |
| garden crop | 635.611 7 |
| Casablanca (Morocco) | T2—643 8 |
| Casablanca-Anfa | |
| (Morocco ; Prefecture) | T2—643 8 |
| Casanare (Colombia : Dept.) | T2—861 96 |
| Cascade County (Mont.) | T2—786 611 |
| Cascade Mountains (B.C.) | T2—711 5 |
| Cascade Range | T2—795 |
| British Columbia | T2—711 5 |
| California | T2—794 2 |
| Oregon | T2—795 |
| Washington | T2—797 5 |
| Cascades | |
| landscape architecture | 714 |
| Cascading style sheets | 006.74 |
| Case (Grammar) | 415.5 |
| specific languages | T4—55 |
| Case grammar (Theory) | 415.018 |
| specific languages | T4—501 8 |
| Case histories | |
| medicine | 616.09 |
| Case studies | |
| descriptive research | 001.433 |
| | T1—072 3 |
| Casein-derived plastics | 668.43 |
| Casein glue | 668.32 |
| Casein painting | 751.422 |
| Caserta (Italy : Province) | T2—457 25 |
| ancient | T2—377 23 |
| Cases (Law) | 348.04 |
| law of nations | 341.026 8 |
| Casework | 361.32 |
| Casey County (Ky.) | T2—769 66 |
| Cash | 332.041 2 |
| accounting | 657.72 |
| financial management | 658.152 44 |
| Cash balance theory | 332.401 |
| Cash flow | |
| financial management | 658.152 44 |
| Cash management | |
| financial management | 658.152 44 |
| Cash-on-delivery mail | 383.184 |
| Cash registers | |
| manufacturing technology | 681.14 |
| Cash renting | |
| land economics | 333.562 |
| Cashews | 641.345 73 |
| agriculture | 634.573 |
| botany | 583.77 |
| cooking | 641.645 73 |
| food | 641.345 73 |
| Casino (N.S.W.) | T2—944 3 |
| Casinos | |
| architecture | 725.76 |
| Casks | |
| wooden | 674.82 |
| Caspian Sea | T2—475 |
| Commonwealth of | |
| Independent States | T2—475 |
| Iran | T2—551 4 |
| Caspian seal | 599.792 |
| Casquets (Channel Islands) | T2—423 48 |
| Cass County (Ill.) | T2—773 465 |
| Cass County (Ind.) | T2—772 86 |
| Cass County (Iowa) | T2—777 72 |
| Cass County (Mich.) | T2—774 12 |
| Cass County (Minn.) | T2—776 86 |
| Cass County (Mo.) | T2—778 42 |
| Cass County (N.D.) | T2—784 13 |
| Cass County (Neb.) | T2—782 272 |
| Cass County (Tex.) | T2—764 195 |
| Cassations | 784.185 |

| | |
|---|---|
| Cassava | 641.336 82 |
| botany | 583.69 |
| commercial processing | 664.23 |
| cooking | 641.636 82 |
| food | 641.336 82 |
| starch crop | 633.682 |
| Casserole dishes | 641.821 |
| Cassettes (Computers) | 004.563 |
| Cassettes (Sound) | 384 |
| bibliographies | 011.38 |
| sound reproduction | 621.389 324 |
| *see also* Sound recordings | |
| Cassettes (Video) | 384.558 |
| *see also* Video recordings | |
| Cassia County (Idaho) | T2—796 39 |
| Cassiar Mountains (B.C. and Yukon) | T2—711 85 |
| Cassiterite | |
| mineralogy | 549.524 |
| Cassowaries | 598.53 |
| Cast iron | 669.141 3 |
| decorative arts | 739.4 |
| Cast latex | 678.533 |
| Cast tableware | |
| decorative arts | 748.2 |
| Castaneoideae | 583.46 |
| Castanets | 786.873 |
| *see also* Percussion instruments | |
| Caste systems | 305.512 2 |
| Castellón (Spain : Province) | T2—467 61 |
| Castelo Branco (Portugal : District) | T2—469 33 |
| Castelo Branco, Humberto de Alencar | |
| Brazilian history | 981.063 |
| Castile (Kingdom) | 946.03 |
| Castile (Spain) | T2—463 |
| Castilla-La Mancha (Spain) | T2—464 |
| Castilla-León (Spain) | T2—462 |
| Castilla y León (Spain) | T2—462 |
| Casting | |
| arts | 730.28 |
| ceramic arts | 738.142 |
| sculpture | 731.45 |
| Casting (Fishing) | 799.124 |
| Casting glass | 666.125 |
| Casting latex | 678.527 |
| Casting metals | 671.2 |
| arts | 730.28 |
| decorative arts | 739.14 |
| sculpture | 731.456 |
| technology | 671.2 |
| Casting plastics | 668.412 |

| | |
|---|---|
| Casting pottery | 666.442 |
| arts | 738.142 |
| technology | 666.442 |
| Castle Morpeth (England) | T2—428 83 |
| Castle Point (England) | T2—426 792 |
| Castlegar (B.C.) | T2—711 62 |
| Castlemaine (Vic.) | T2—945 3 |
| Castlereagh (Northern Ireland : District) | T2—416 51 |
| Castles | |
| architecture | 728.81 |
| domestic | 728.81 |
| military | 725.18 |
| Castles (Chessmen) | 794.143 |
| Castor oil | 665.353 |
| Castor-oil plant | 583.69 |
| Castoridae | 599.37 |
| paleozoology | 569.37 |
| Castrato voices | 782.86 |
| choral and mixed voices | 782.86 |
| single voices | 783.86 |
| Castro, Cipriano | |
| Venezuelan history | 987.063 12 |
| Castro, Fidel | |
| Cuban history | 972.910 64 |
| Castro County (Tex.) | T2—764 837 |
| Castroism | 335.434 7 |
| economics | 335.434 7 |
| political ideology | 320.532 309 729 1 |
| Casual clothes | 391 |
| *see also* Casual wear | |
| Casual wear | 391 |
| commercial technology | 687 |
| customs | 391 |
| home economics | 646.3 |
| home sewing | 646.4 |
| *see also* Clothing | |
| Casual workers | 331.544 |
| Casualty insurance | 368.5 |
| law | 346.086 5 |
| Casuariiformes | 598.53 |
| paleozoology | 568.5 |
| Casuarinales | 583.43 |
| Casuistry | |
| ethical systems | 171.6 |
| Caswell County (N.C.) | T2—756 575 |
| CAT (Air transportation hazard) | 363.124 12 |
| Cat breeds | 636.8 |
| *see Manual at* 636.82–.83 | |
| Cat briers | 584.356 |
| Cat family (Felidae) | 599.75 |
| CAT scan | |
| medicine | 616.075 722 |

Catabolism 572.48
  *see also* Metabolism
Catahoula Parish (La.) T2—763 74
Catalan language 449.9
  T6—499
Catalan literature 849.9
Catalans T5—49
Catalases 572.791
  *see also* Enzymes
Catalog marketing 381.142
  management 658.872
Catalog shopping 381.142
  law 343.081 142 8
Cataloging
  library science 025.3
  museology 069.52
Cataloging in publication 025.3
Catalogs T1—021 6
  postal handling 383.124
   *see also* Postal service
  *see also* Auction catalogs
Catalogs (Bibliographic catalogs) 025.31
  general catalogs 011
  library science 025.31
  specific collections 017
  specific forms 011.3
  specific historical periods 011.09
  specific languages 011.2
  specific places 015
  specific subjects 016
  *see Manual at* 011–017
Catalogs of exhibits 069.52
  T1—074
  museology 069.52
  *see Manual at* T1—074 vs.
   T1—029
Catalonia (Spain) T2—467
Catalpas 635.977 395
  botany 583.95
  ornamental arboriculture 635.977 395
Cataluña (Spain) T2—467
Catalysis 541.395
  chemical engineering 660.299 5
  organic chemistry 547.215
Catalytic cracking 665.533
Catamarca (Argentina :
  Province) T2—824 5
Catamblyrhynchidae 598.88
Catana (Italy) T2—378 131
Catanduanes Island
  (Philippines) T2—599 1
Catanduanes Province
  (Philippines) T2—599 1

Catania (Italy) T2—458 131
  ancient T2—378 131
Catania (Italy : Province) T2—458 13
  ancient T2—378 13
Catanzaro (Italy : Province) T2—457 81
  ancient T2—377 81
Catapults 623.441
Cataracts
  ophthalmology 617.742
   *see also* Eye diseases —
    humans
Catarrhini 599.86
  paleozoology 569.86
Catastrophes 904
  *see also* Disasters
Catastrophes (Biological
  evolution) 576.84
Catastrophes (Mathematics) 514.744
Catastrophic health insurance 368.382 8
  government-sponsored 368.42
  law 344.022
  law 346.086 382 8
Catawba County (N.C.) T2—756 785
Catawba Indians T5—975 2
Catawba language 497.52
  T6—975 2
Catawba River (N.C. and
  S.C.) T2—757 45
Catbirds 598.844
Catch-as-catch-can wrestling 796.812 3
Catch basins
  sewers 628.25
Catchers' mitts
  manufacturing technology 688.763 57
Catching
  baseball 796.357 23
Catchword indexing 025.486
Catechetics 268
Catechisms 202
  Christianity 238
Catechists 268.092
  biography 268.092
   *see Manual at* 230–280
  role and function 268.3
Catechols 547.633
Catechumenate 265.13
Categorial grammar 415.018
  specific languages T4—501 8
Categories (Mathematics) 512.62
Category theory 512.62
Catered meals 642.4
Caterers 642.409 2
Catering 642.4

| | |
|---|---|
| Catering establishments | 647.95 |
| *see also* Eating places | |
| Caterpillars | 595.781 392 |
|   culture | 638.578 139 2 |
| Catfishes | 597.49 |
| Catfishes (Channel catfish) | 641.392 |
|   conservation technology | 639.977 492 |
|   cooking | 641.692 |
|   culture | 639.374 92 |
|   food | 641.392 |
|   resource economics | 333.956 492 |
|   sports fishing | 799.174 92 |
|   zoology | 597.492 |
| Catharine, the Great | |
|   Russian history | 947.063 |
| Catharism | 273.6 |
|   denomination | 284.4 |
|   persecution of | 272.3 |
| Cathartics | |
|   pharmacokinetics | 615.732 |
| Cathartidae | 598.92 |
| Cathcart (South Africa : District) | T2—687 55 |
| Cathedral systems | |
|   Christian ecclesiology | 262.3 |
| Cathedrals | |
|   architecture | 726.6 |
|   religious significance | 246.96 |
| Catherine I, Empress of Russia | |
|   Russian history | 947.061 |
| Catherine II, Empress of Russia | |
|   Russian history | 947.063 |
| Catheterization | |
|   surgery | 617.05 |
| Cathode-ray tubes | 621.381 542 2 |
|   television engineering | 621.388 32 |
| Catholic Church | 282 |
| Catholic epistles | 227.9 |
| Catholic regions | T2—176 12 |
| Catholic schools | 371.071 2 |
| Catholicity | 262.72 |
| Catholics | 282.092 |
| Catnip | 583.96 |
| Catnip tea | 641.357 |
| *see also* Herb teas | |
| Catoosa County (Ga.) | T2—758 326 |
| Catron County (N.M.) | T2—789 93 |
| Cats | 636.8 |
|   animal husbandry | 636.8 |
|   arts | T3C—362 975 2 |
|   predator control technology | 636.083 9 |
|   zoology | 599.752 |
| Cat's cradles | 793.96 |
| Catskill Mountains (N.Y.) | T2—747 38 |
| Catsup | 641.814 |
|   commercial processing | 664.58 |
|   home preparation | 641.814 |
| Cattails (Plants) | 584.68 |
| Cattaraugus County (N.Y.) | T2—747 94 |
| Cattle | 636.2 |
|   agricultural economics | 338.176 2 |
|   animal husbandry | 636.2 |
|   theft of | 364.162 863 62 |
|     law | 345.026 286 362 |
|   zoology | 599.642 2 |
| Cattle cars | 385.34 |
|   engineering | 625.24 |
|   *see also* Rolling stock | |
| Cattle stealing | 364.162 863 62 |
|   law | 345.026 286 362 |
| Cattlemen | 636.213 092 |
| CATV systems | 384.554 6 |
|   *see also* Television | |
| Cauca (Colombia : Dept.) | T2—861 53 |
| Caucasian Albania | T2—395 34 |
| Caucasian languages | 499.96 |
| | T6—999 6 |
| Caucasian literatures | 899.96 |
| Caucasian race | 305.809 |
| | T5—09 |
| Caucasians (Peoples of the Caucasus) | T5—999 6 |
| Caucasic languages | 499.96 |
| | T6—999 6 |
| Caucasic literatures | 899.96 |
| Caucasoid race | T5—09 |
| Caucasus | 947.5 |
| | T2—475 |
|   ancient | 939.53 |
| | T2—395 3 |
|   Russia | T2—475 2 |
| Caucasus rugs | |
|   arts | 746.759 |
| Cauchy integral | 515.43 |
| Cauchy problem | 515.35 |
| Caucus nomination | 324.52 |
| Caucuses (Legislative) | 328.36 |
| Caudal anesthesia | |
|   surgery | 617.964 |
| Caudata | 597.85 |
| Caudofoveata | 594.2 |
| Caulerpales | 579.835 |
| Cauliflower | 641.353 5 |
|   commercial processing | 664.805 35 |
|   cooking | 641.653 5 |
|   food | 641.353 5 |
|   garden crop | 635.35 |

Causation
  philosophy    122
Causative (Linguistics)    415.6
  specific languages    T4—56
Cause
  philosophy    122
Causes of Holocaust    940.531 811
Causes of war    355.027
  American Revolution    973.311
  Civil War (United States)    973.711
  Mexican War    973.621
  South African War    968.048 1
  Vietnamese War    959.704 31
  World War I    940.311
  World War II    940.531 1
Caustic potash    546.383 22
  chemical engineering    661.332
Caustic soda    546.382 22
  chemical engineering    661.322
Cautín (Chile)    T2—834 6
Cavalier County (N.D.)    T2—784 37
Cavalry (Horse mounted)    357.1
Cavalry (Mechanized)    357.5
Cavalry forces    357
Cavan (Ireland : County)    T2—416 98
Cave animals    591.758 4
Cave dwellers    569.9
Cave fishes    597.175 84
Cavefishes (Amblyopsidae)    597.62
Caves    551.447
   T2—144
  biology    578.758 4
  ecology    577.584
  exploring    796.525
  geography    910.914 4
  geomorphology    551.447
  physical geography    910.021 44
  psychological influence    155.964
Cavia    599.359 2
Cavies    599.359 2
Caviidae    599.359 2
Caviomorpha    599.359
Cavitation    532.597
  engineering    620.106 4
Cavite Province
  (Philippines)    T2—599 1
Cavities (Teeth)
  dentistry    617.67
  incidence    614.599 6
Cavity resonators    621.381 332
Cayenne (French Guiana)    T2—882
Cayenne pepper    641.338 4
  botany    583.952
  *see also* Hot spices

Cayley algebra    512.5
Cayman Islands    972.921
   T2—729 21
Cayo District (Belize)    T2—728 25
Cayuga County (N.Y.)    T2—747 68
Cayuga Indians    T5—975 54
Cayuga Lake (N.Y.)    T2—747 68
Cayuga language    497.554
   T6—975 54
CB radio    384.53
  communications services    384.53
  engineering    621.384 54
CBR warfare    358.3
  law    341.735
CD-ROMs    004.565
  *see also* CDs (Compact
    discs) — computer storage
CDs (Compact discs)
  computer storage    004.565
    bibliographies    011.39
    cataloging    025.344
    engineering    621.397 67
    library treatment    025.174
    publishing    070.579 7
  music    780
  recordings    384
    bibliographies    011.38
    cataloging    025.348 2
    engineering    621.389 32
    library treatment    025.178 2
    publishing    070.579
  *see also* Sound recordings
CDU (German political party)    324.243 04
Ceará (Brazil : State)    T2—813 1
Ceasefires    327.17
  law    341.66
Cebidae    599.85
  paleozoology    569.85
Cebu (Philippines)    T2—599 5
Cebu Island (Philippines)    T2—599 5
Cebuano language    499.21
   T6—992 1
Cecal diseases
  medicine    616.34
  *see also* Digestive system
    diseases — humans
Cecidomyiidae    595.772
Cecil County (Md.)    T2—752 38
Cecum
  human anatomy    611.345
  human physiology    612.33
  medicine    616.34
  surgery    617.554 5
Cedar County (Iowa)    T2—777 66

| | |
|---|---|
| Cedar County (Mo.) | T2—778 743 |
| Cedar County (Neb.) | T2—782 58 |
| Cedar Mountains (South Africa) | T2—687 31 |
| Cedarberg (South Africa) | T2—687 31 |
| Cedars | 585.2 |
| forestry | 634.975 6 |
| lumber | 674.144 |
| Cefalonia (Greece) | T2—495 5 |
| CEGEPs | 378.154 3 |
| Ceiling coverings | |
| household management | 645.2 |
| Ceilings | 721.7 |
| architecture | 721.7 |
| construction | 690.17 |
| interior decoration | 747.3 |
| Celandines | 635.933 35 |
| botany | 583.35 |
| floriculture | 635.933 35 |
| Celastrales | 583.85 |
| Celebes (Indonesia) | T2—598 4 |
| Celebes Sea | 551.461 473 |
| | T2—164 73 |
| Celebrations | 394.2 |
| armed forces | 355.16 |
| *see also* Military commemorations | |
| cooking | 641.568 |
| customs | 394.2 |
| public administrative support | 353.77 |
| Celeriac | 641.351 28 |
| cooking | 641.651 28 |
| food | 641.351 28 |
| garden crop | 635.128 |
| Celery | 641.355 3 |
| botany | 583.849 |
| commercial processing | 664.805 53 |
| cooking | 641.655 3 |
| food | 641.355 3 |
| garden crop | 635.53 |
| Celery root | 641.351 28 |
| *see also* Celeriac | |
| Celestas | 786.83 |
| instrument | 786.831 9 |
| music | 786.83 |
| *see also* Percussion instruments | |
| Celestial bodies | 520 |
| folklore | 398.26 |
| history and criticism | 398.362 |
| Celestial Church of Christ | 289.93 |
| *see also* Christian denominations | |
| Celestial mechanics | 521 |
| engineering | 629.411 |

| | |
|---|---|
| Celestial navigation | 527 |
| nautical | 623.89 |
| Celestial reference systems | 522.7 |
| Celestines | 255.16 |
| church history | 271.16 |
| Celestite | |
| mineralogy | 549.752 |
| Celiac disease | |
| medicine | 616.399 |
| *see also* Digestive system diseases — humans | |
| Celibacy | 306.732 |
| customs | 392.6 |
| ethics | 176.4 |
| religion | 205.66 |
| Buddhism | 294.356 6 |
| Christianity | 241.66 |
| Hinduism | 294.548 66 |
| psychology | 155.3 |
| religious practice | 204.47 |
| Buddhism | 294.344 47 |
| Christianity | 248.47 |
| clergy | 253.25 |
| Hinduism | 294.544 7 |
| sociology | 306.732 |
| Cell biology | 571.6 |
| humans | 611.018 1 |
| Cell chemistry | 572 |
| Cell culture | 571.638 |
| experimental research | |
| medicine | 616.027 7 |
| Cell death | 571.936 |
| Cell determination | 571.863 6 |
| Cell differentiation | 571.835 |
| Cell digestion | 572.4 |
| Cell division | 571.844 |
| Cell lines | |
| experimental research | |
| medicine | 616.027 7 |
| Cell-mediated immunity | 571.966 |
| humans | 616.079 7 |
| Cell membrane receptors | 572.696 |
| Cell membranes | 571.64 |
| Cell metabolism | 572.4 |
| Cell movement | 571.67 |
| Cell physiology | 571.6 |
| humans | 611.018 1 |
| Cell receptors | 572.696 |
| Cell respiration | 572.47 |
| Cell walls | 571.68 |
| Cellists | 787.409 2 |
| Cello concertos | 784.274 |

| | | | |
|---|---|---|---|
| Cellos | 787.4 | Celtic regions | 944 |
| instrument | 787.419 | | T2—44 |
| music | 787.4 | ancient | 936.4 |
| *see also* Stringed instruments | | | T2—364 |
| Cells (Biology) | 571.6 | Netherlands | |
| anatomy | 571.633 | ancient | 936.92 |
| growth | 571.84 | | T2—369 2 |
| humans | 611.018 1 | Switzerland | T2—494 |
| pathology | 571.936 | ancient | 936.94 |
| reproduction | 571.84 | | T2—369 4 |
| Cells (Rooms) | | Celtic religion | 299.16 |
| architecture | 726.79 | Celts | T5—916 |
| Cellular automata | 511.35 | Cement | 666.94 |
| Cellular immunity | 571.966 | economic geology | 553.68 |
| humans | 616.079 7 | materials science | 620.135 |
| Cellular pathology | 571.936 | structural engineering | 624.183 3 |
| humans | 611.018 15 | Cement casting | |
| Cellular radio | 384.535 | sculpture | 731.452 |
| engineering | 621.384 56 | Cementum | |
| Cellular slime molds | 579.52 | dentistry | 617.634 |
| Cellular telephones | 384.535 | Cemeteries | 363.75 |
| engineering | 621.384 56 | landscape architecture | 718 |
| Cellulases | 572.756 | public administration | 353.6 |
| *see also* Enzymes | | World War I | 940.465 |
| Celluloid | 668.44 | World War II | 940.546 5 |
| Cellulose | 572.566 82 | *see also* Military | |
| biochemistry | 572.566 82 | commemorations | |
| *see also* Carbohydrates | | Cemetery records | |
| Cellulose acetate | | genealogy | 929.5 |
| textiles | 677.464 | Cenozoic era | 551.78 |
| *see also* Textiles | | geology | 551.78 |
| Cellulose derivatives | | paleontology | 560.178 |
| chemical engineering | 661.802 | Censored books | 098.1 |
| Cellulosics | 668.44 | Censored observations | 519.546 |
| textiles | 677.46 | Censorship | 363.31 |
| *see also* Textiles | | law | 344.053 1 |
| Celtic harps | 787.95 | libraries | 025.213 |
| *see also* Stringed instruments | | social control | 303.376 |
| Celtic languages | 491.6 | *see Manual at* 363.31 vs. | |
| | T6—916 | 303.376, 791.4 | |
| Celtic literatures | 891.6 | Census | |
| Celtic period | 936.401 | law | 342.08 |
| Austrian history | 936.360 2 | public administration | 352.75 |
| Belgian history | 936.930 1 | statistical reports | 310 |
| Dutch history | 936.920 1 | Census bureaus | 352.75 |
| English history | 936.202 | Census records | |
| French history | 936.401 | genealogy | 929.3 |
| Irish history | 936.150 2 | Census taking | 001.433 |
| Ireland | 936.170 2 | | T1—072 3 |
| Northern Ireland | 936.160 2 | animals | 590.723 2 |
| Liechtenstein history | 936.364 802 | birds | 598.072 32 |
| Luxembourgian history | 936.935 01 | Centaurs | 398.21 |
| Scottish history | 936.110 2 | *see also* Legendary beings | |
| Swiss history | 936.940 1 | Center Hill Lake (Tenn.) | T2—768 532 |

Center Party (Germany)　324.243 025
Centipedes　595.62
Central (Paraguay)　T2—892 122
Central (Scotland)　T2—413 1
Central Africa　967
　T2—67
Central African Empire　T2—674 1
Central African Federation　968.903
Central African Republic　967.41
　T2—674 1
Central African Republic
　people　T5—967 41
Central Africans (National
　group)　T5—967 41
Central Algonquian languages　497.31
　T6—973 1
Central America　972.8
　T2—728
Central America (Federal　972.804
　Republic : 1823–1840)　T2—728
　Costa Rican history　972.860 42
　Guatemalan history　972.810 42
　Honduran history　972.830 4
　Nicaraguan history　972.850 42
　Salvadoran history　972.840 42
Central American native　497
　languages　T6—97
Central American native
　literatures　897
Central American native
　peoples　T5—970 728
Central Americans　T5—687 28
Central Asia　958
　T2—58
　ancient　939.6
　T2—396
Central Australia　T2—942
Central banks　332.11
Central Black Earth Region
　(Russia)　T2—473 5
Central business district
　community redevelopment　307.342
Central Chernozem Region
　(Russia)　T2—473 5
Central Coast (B.C.)　T2—711 1
Central Dravidian languages　494.82
　T6—948 2
Central Dravidian literatures　894.82
Central Dravidians　T5—948 2
Central eastern Europe　943.7
　T2—437
Central Europe　943
　T2—43
Central Fraser Valley (B.C.)　T2—711 37

Central Greece (Greece)　T2—495 15
Central Hawke's Bay
　District (N.Z.)　T2—934 69
Central heating　697.03
　resource economics　333.793
Central Intelligence Agency
　(U.S.)　327.127 3
Central Italy　945.6
　T2—456
Central Java (Indonesia)　T2—598 26
Central Kalimantan
　(Indonesia)　T2—598 34
Central Kootenay (B.C.)　T2 711 62
Central Lowlands
　(Scotland)　T2—413
Central Macedonia (Greece)　T2—495 65
Central Malayo-Polynesian　499.22
　languages　T6—992 2
Central nervous system　573.86
　biology　573.86
　human anatomy　611.81
　human biochemistry　612.822
　human biophysics　612.822
　human physiology　612.82
　medicine　616.8
　*see also* Nervous system
Central nervous system diseases　573.863 9
　animals　573.863 9
　humans
　　medicine　616.8
　*see also* Nervous system
　　diseases
Central Okanagan (B.C.)　T2—711 5
Central Otago District
　(N.Z.)　T2—939 4
Central Pacific Basin　551.461 49
　T2—164 9
Central Pacific islands　T2—96
Central Powers (World War I)　940.334
Central processing units　004
　engineering　621.39
Central Province (Kenya)　T2—676 26
Central Province (Papua
　New Guinea)　T2—954 6
Central Province (Solomon
　Islands)　T2—959 35
Central Province (Zambia)　T2—689 4
Central Region (Scotland)　T2—413 1
Central Saanich (B.C.)　T2—711 28
Central-Southern Region
　(China)　T2—512
Central stations
　steam engineering　621.19

Central Sulawesi
  (Indonesia)          T2—598 44
Central Turkic languages       494.34
                              T6—943 4
Central Valley (Calif. :
  Valley)            T2—794 5
Central Vietnam          T2—597 4
Centralization
  executive management      658.402
  libraries                021.6
  public administration       352.283
  schools               379.153 5
Centralized databases
  computer science         005.75
Centralized processing        004.3
  *see also* Processing modes —
     computer science
Centrarchidae             597.738
Centre (France)           T2—445 1
Centre (Haiti)            T2—729 442
Centre County (Pa.)        T2—748 53
Centre-de-la-Mauricie
  (Quebec)           T2—714 453
Centre-du-Québec (Quebec) T2—714 5
Centrifugal blowers         621.63
Centrifugal casting
  metals                671.254
Centrifugal fans          621.63
Centrifugal force          531.113
  fluid mechanics         532.059 5
  solid mechanics         531.35
Centrifugal pumps         621.67
  hydraulic             621.252
Centrifuging latex         678.522
Centripetal force          531.113
  fluid mechanics         532.059 5
  solid mechanics         531.35
Centrist parties          324.215
  international organizations   324.15
Centro cristiano democratico
  (Italian political party)     324.245 082
Centrocercus             598.636
Centrolenidae            597.87
Centromeres             571.844
Centropomidae           597.72
Century plants           584.352
Cephalaspidea           594.34
Cephalocarida           595.36
Cephalochordata         596.4
  paleozoology          566
Cephalophinae           599.64
Cephalopoda            594.5
  paleozoology          564.5
Cephalotaceae           583.72

Cephalotaxaceae         585.3
Cepheids               523.844 25
Ceram Sea (Indonesia)      551.461 473
                            T2—164 73
Cerambycidae           595.764 8
Ceramic artists          738.092
Ceramic arts            738
Ceramic engineers        666.092
Ceramic fillings
  dentistry             617.675
Ceramic inlays
  dentistry             617.675
Ceramic materials         553.61
  building materials        691.4
  chemical engineering      666
  economic geology        553.61
  materials science         620.14
  mining               622.361
  pottery              666.42
    arts                738.12
  sculpture material        731.2
  ship hulls             623.845
  shipbuilding           623.820 7
  structural engineering      624.183
Ceramic-to-metal bonding    666.042
Ceramics
  materials science         620.14
Ceramics industry         338.476 66
  equipment manufacturing
    technology            681.766 6
Ceratophyllaceae         583.29
Ceratopsia              567.915
Cercidiphyllales          583.43
Cercopithecidae          599.86
  paleozoology          569.86
Cercopithecus           599.862
Cereal grains
  commercial processing      664.7
Cereal grasses           584.9
  forage crops           633.25
  *see Manual at* 633–635
Cereals                 641.331
  agriculture            633.1
  animal feed           636.086
  botany               584.9
  commercial processing      664.7
    ready-to-eat cereals      664.756
  cooking              641.631
  food                641.331
  forage crops           633.25
  *see Manual at* 633–635

Cerebellum
  human anatomy 611.81
  human physiology 612.827
  medicine 616.8
Cerebral commissures
  human physiology 612.826
Cerebral hemispheres
  human anatomy 611.81
  human physiology 612.825
  medicine 616.8
Cerebral infarction
  medicine 616.81
    *see also* Nervous system
      diseases — humans
Cerebral ischemia
  medicine 616.81
    *see also* Nervous system
      diseases — humans
Cerebral palsy
  medicine 616.836
    *see also* Nervous system
      diseases — humans
Cerebral peduncles
  human physiology 612.826
Cerebral sphingolipidosis
  medicine 616.858 845
Cerebrospinal fluid
  human physiology 612.804 2
Cerebrovascular circulation
  human physiology 612.824
Cerebrovascular diseases
  medicine 616.81
    *see also* Nervous system
      diseases — humans
Cerebrum
  human anatomy 611.81
  human physiology 612.825
  medicine 616.8
Ceredigion (Wales) T2—429 61
Ceremonial robes 391.48
  commercial technology 687.15
  customs 391.48
  *see also* Clothing
Ceremonials 264.022
Ceremonies 390
  armed forces 355.17
  customs 390
  religion 203.8
    *see also* Rites — religion
Ceres (Dwarf planet) 523.44
Ceres (South Africa :
  District) T2—687 33
Cerigo Island (Greece) T2—495 2

Cerium
  chemistry 546.412
Cerium-group metals
  economic geology 553.494 3
Cerro Gordo County (Iowa) T2—777 25
Cerro Largo (Uruguay) T2—895 23
Certainty
  epistemology 121.63
Certhiidae 598.82
Certificates (Awards) T1—079
  research 001.44
Certificates of deposit 332.175 2
Certification 352.84
  *see also* Licensing
Certitude
  epistemology 121.63
Cerveteri (Italy) T2—456 3
  ancient T2—375 9
Cervical caps
  health 613.943 5
  medicine 618.185
    *see also* Birth control
Cervical vertebrae
  medicine 616.73
Cervicitis
  gynecology 618.142
    *see also* Female genital
      diseases — humans
Cervidae 599.65
  animal husbandry 636.294
  paleozoology 569.65
Cervix (Uterine)
  gynecology 618.14
  human anatomy 611.66
  human physiology 612.627
  surgery 618.145
Cervix diseases
  gynecology 618.14
    *see also* Female genital
      diseases — humans
Cervus 599.654
  animal husbandry 636.294 4
Cervus elaphus
  animal husbandry 636.294 42
César (Colombia) T2—861 18
Cesarean section
  obstetrical surgery 618.86
Cesium 669.725
  chemical engineering 661.038 5
  chemistry 546.385
  metallurgy 669.725
  *see also* Chemicals
Český Les T2—437 14
Cessnock (N.S.W.) T2—944 2

Cestoda 592.46
Cestode infections
  incidence 614.554
  medicine 616.964
    *see also* Communicable
      diseases — humans
Cetacea 599.5
  conservation technology 639.979 5
  paleozoology 569.5
  resource economics 333.959 5
Cetewayo, King of Zululand
  KwaZulu-Natal history 968.404 5
Ceuta (Spain) T2—641
  ancient T2—397 12
Cévennes, Parc national des
  (France) T2—448 1
Cévennes Mountains
  (France) T2—448 1
Ceylon T2—549 3
Ceylonese T5—914 13
Chabad Lubavitch Hasidism 296.833 22
Chachalacas 598.64
Chaco (Argentina) T2—823 4
Chaco Boreal (Paraguay and
  Bolivia) T2—892 2
Chaco War, 1933–1935 989.207 16
Chaconnes 781.827
  instrumental 784.182 7
Chad 967.43
  T2—674 3
Chadians T5—967 43
Chadic languages 493.7
  T6—937
Chadic literatures 893.7
Chaetodontidae 597.72
Chaetognatha 592.38
  paleozoology 562.38
Chaetomiales 579.567
Chaetophorales 579.83
Chafers 595.764 9
  agricultural pests 632.764 9
Chaffee County (Colo.) T2—788 47
Chafing dish cooking 641.585
Chaga language 496.395
  T6—963 95
Chagas disease
  incidence 614.533
  medicine 616.936 3
    *see also* Communicable
      diseases — humans
Chagatai language 494.364
  T6—943 64
Chagga language 496.395
  T6—963 95

Chagos Islands 969.7
  T2—697
Chahār Mahāll va Bakhtīārī
  (Iran) T2—559 7
Chain banking 332.16
Chain banks 332.16
Chain drives 621.859
Chain gangs 365.65
Chain hoists 621.863
Chain indexing 025.47
Chain reactions
  nuclear engineering 621.483 1
Chain saws 621.934
Chain-stitch fabrics 677.66
  *see also* Textiles
Chain stores 381.12
  management 658.870 2
  *see also* Commerce
Chaine Annamitique
  (Vietnam) T2—597 4
Chains
  power transmission 621.859
Chair cars 385.33
  engineering 625.23
  *see also* Rolling stock
Chair lifts 621.868
Chairs 645.4
  decorative arts 749.32
  manufacturing technology 684.132
  outdoor furniture 645.8
    *see also* Outdoor furniture
  *see also* Furniture
Chaka, Zulu Chief
  KwaZulu-Natal history 968.403 9
Chalatenango (El Salvador :
  Dept.) T2—728 421
Chalcidice (Greece) T2—495 65
Chalcidoidea 595.79
Chalcids 595.79
Chalcis (Extinct city) T2—384
Chalcocite
  mineralogy 549.32
Chalcogens 546.72
Chalcolithic Age 930.153
Chaldean Empire 935.04
  T2—35
Chaldeans (Religious order) 255.18
  church history 271.18
Chaldee (Aramaic) language 492.29
  T6—922 9
Chalk 553.68
  economic geology 553.68
  petrology 552.58
Chalk drawing 741.23

Chalkidikē (Greece)   T2—495 65
Challoner Bible   220.520 2
Chamaeidae   598.834
Chamaeleontidae   597.956
Chamaemyiidae   595.774
Chamber music   785
Chamber orchestras   784.3
Chambers County (Ala.)   T2—761 56
Chambers County (Tex.)   T2—764 143
Chambers of commerce   381.06
   architecture   725.25
Chambly (Quebec : County)   T2—714 365
Chameleons   597.956
Chameleons (Anoles)   597.954 8
Chamic languages   499.22
  T6—992 2
Chamois   599.647
Chamomiles   583.99
Chamorro   T5—995 2
Chamorro language   499.52
  T6—995 2
Champagne   641.222 4
   commercial processing   663.224
Champagne (France :
   Province)   T2—443 1
Champagne-Ardenne
   (France)   T2—443 1
Champaign County (Ill.)   T2—773 66
Champaign County (Ohio)   T2—771 465
Champlain (Quebec :
   County)   T2—714 455
Champlain (Quebec :
   Regional County
   Municipality)   T2—714 37
Champlain, Lake   T2—747 54
   New York   T2—747 54
   Vermont   T2—743 1
Champlevé
   ceramic arts   738.4
Ch'an Buddhism   294.392 7
Chañaral (Chile : Province)   T2—831 42
Chance
   philosophy   123.3
   probabilities   519.2
Chance composition   781.32
Chancel railings   247.1
   architecture   726.529 6
Chancellors (Prime ministers)   352.53
   cabinet governments   321.804 3
   public administration   352.23
Chancels
   architecture   726.593

Chancroid
   incidence   614.547
   medicine   616.951 8
   *see also* Communicable
     diseases — humans
Chandeliers
   furniture arts   749.63
Chandīgarh (India)   T2—545 52
Chandra Shekhar
   Indian history   954.052
Changamire (Kingdom)   968.910 1
  T2—689 1
Change   116
   executive management   658.406
   philosophy   116
   political science   320.011
   sociology   303.4
Changing voices   782.79
   choral and mixed voices   782.79
   single voices   783.79
Chania (Greece : Nome)   T2—495 9
Channel bass   597.725
Channel catfish   641.392
   *see also* Catfishes (Channel
     catfish)
Channel Islands   T2—423 4
Channel Islands (Calif.)   T2—794 91
Channel Islands National
   Park (Calif.)   T2—794 91
Channeling (Spiritualism)   133.91
Channels (Navigation)
   engineering   627.23
Channiformes   597.64
Chansons   782.43
Chants (Music)   782.292
   choral and mixed voices   782.529 2
   single voices   783.092 92
Chanukah   296.435
   liturgy   296.453 5
Chaos
   mathematics   515.39
   philosophy   117
Chaotic behavior in systems   003.857
Chaotic systems   003.857
   mathematics   515.39
Chaouen (Morocco :
   Province)   T2—642
Chaouia-Ouardigha
   (Morocco)   T2—643 9
Chapacura-Wanham languages   498.9
  T6—989
Chaparral biology   578.738
Chaparral ecology   577.38
Chapbooks   002

Chapels
  architecture 726.4
    Christianity 726.5
Chaperonage
  customs 392.6
Chaplain services (Military) 355.347
  Algerian Revolution 965.046 7
  American Revolution 973.37
  Chaco War 989.207 167
  Civil War (Spain) 946.081 7
  Civil War (United States) 973.778
  Falkland Islands War 997.110 247
  Indochinese War 959.704 17
  Iraq War, 2003– 956.704 437
  Korean War 951.904 27
  Napoleonic Wars 940.277
  Persian Gulf War, 1991 956.704 427
  South African War 968.048 7
  Vietnamese War 959.704 37
  War of the Pacific 983.061 67
  World War I 940.478
  World War II 940.547 8
Chaplaincy 206.1
  Christianity 253
  Judaism 296.61
Chapping
  medicine 616.58
  *see also* Skin diseases —
    humans
Chapter houses
  architecture 726.69
Characidae 597.48
Characiformes 597.48
Characins 597.48
Character 155.2
  child psychology 155.418 2
  influence on crime 364.24
  psychology 155.2
Character development
  psychology 155.25
Character disorders
  medicine 616.858
Character education 370.114
  primary education 372.011 4
Character recognition 006.4
  computer engineering 621.399 4
Character sets 005.722
Character training
  home child care 649.7
Characters (Fictitious persons) 808.802 7
  history and criticism 809.927
  specific literatures T3B—080 27
    history and criticism T3B—092 7

Characters (Symbols)
  printing 686.21
Charades 793.24
Charadrii 598.33
Charadriiformes 598.33
  paleozoology 568.3
Charales 579.839
Charcoal
  chemical engineering 662.74
Charcoal cooking 641.58
Charcoal drawing 741.22
Chard 641.354 2
  cooking 641.654 2
  food 641.354 2
  garden crop 635.42
Charente (France) T2—446 5
Charente-Maritime (France) T2—446 4
Charente River (France) T2—446 5
Charge of particles (Nuclear
  physics) 539.725
Chari-Nile languages 496.5
      T6—965
Charismatic gifts 234.13
Charismatic movement 270.82
  Protestantism 280.4
Charismatic spiritual renewal 269
Charitable donations
  financial management 658.153
  tax law 343.052 32
Charitable trusts 361.763 2
  law 346.064
    income tax law 343.052 668
    tax law 343.066 8
  social welfare 361.763 2
Charities 361.7
  *see also* Welfare services
Chariton County (Mo.) T2—778 25
Chariton River (Iowa and
  Mo.) T2—778 2
Charity
  ethics 177.7
    religion 205.677
      Christianity 241.4
  *see also* Love — ethics
Charlemagne, Emperor
  French history 944.014 2
  German history 943.014
Charles I, King of England
  British history 941.062
  English history 942.062
  Scottish history 941.106 2
Charles I, King of Spain
  Spanish history 946.042

| | |
|---|---|
| Charles II, King of England | |
| British history | 941.066 |
| English history | 942.066 |
| Scottish history | 941.106 6 |
| Charles II, King of Spain | |
| Spanish history | 946.053 |
| Charles III, Duke of Savoy | |
| Piedmontese history | 945.106 |
| Charles III, King of Spain | |
| Spanish history | 946.057 |
| Charles IV, Holy Roman | |
| Emperor | |
| German history | 943.027 |
| Charles IV, King of France | |
| French history | 944.024 |
| Charles IV, King of Spain | |
| Spanish history | 946.058 |
| Charles V, Holy Roman Emperor | |
| German history | 943.031 |
| Spanish history | 946.042 |
| Charles V, King of France | |
| French history | 944.025 |
| Charles VI, Holy Roman | |
| Emperor | |
| German history | 943.052 |
| Charles VI, King of France | |
| French history | 944.026 |
| Charles VII, Holy Roman | |
| Emperor | |
| German history | 943.054 |
| Charles VII, King of France | |
| French history | 944.026 |
| Charles VIII, King of France | |
| French history | 944.027 |
| Italian history | 945.06 |
| Tuscan history | 945.506 |
| Venetian history | 945.306 |
| Charles IX, King of France | |
| French history | 944.029 |
| Charles IX, King of Sweden | |
| Swedish history | 948.503 25 |
| Charles X, King of France | |
| French history | 944.062 |
| Charles X Gustav, King of | |
| Sweden | |
| Swedish history | 948.503 43 |
| Charles XI, King of Sweden | |
| Swedish history | 948.503 44 |
| Charles XII, King of Sweden | |
| Swedish history | 948.503 45 |
| Charles XIII, King of Sweden | |
| and Norway | |
| Swedish history | 948.504 1 |

| | |
|---|---|
| Charles XIV John, King of | |
| Sweden and Norway | |
| Swedish history | 948.504 1 |
| Charles XV, King of Sweden and | |
| Norway | |
| Swedish history | 948.504 1 |
| Charles City County (Va.) | T2—755 44 |
| Charles County (Md.) | T2—752 47 |
| Charles Mix County (S.D.) | T2—783 382 |
| Charles River (Mass.) | T2—744 4 |
| Charleston (S.C.) | T2—757 915 |
| Charleston (W. Va.) | T2—754 37 |
| Charleston County (S.C.) | T2—757 91 |
| Charleville (Qld.) | T2—943 4 |
| Charlevoix (Quebec : | |
| Regional County | |
| Municipality) | T2—714 492 |
| Charlevoix County (Mich.) | T2—774 86 |
| Charlevoix-Est (Quebec : | |
| Regional County | |
| Municipality) | T2—714 494 |
| Charlotte (N.B.) | T2—715 33 |
| Charlotte (N.C.) | T2—756 76 |
| Charlotte County (Fla.) | T2—759 49 |
| Charlotte County (Va.) | T2—755 65 |
| Charlottesville (Va.) | T2—755 481 |
| Charlottetown (P.E.I.) | T2—717 5 |
| Charlottetown Conference, 1864 | 971.049 |
| Charlton County (Ga.) | T2—758 752 |
| Charm | |
| life skills | 646.76 |
| Charms (Occultism) | 133.44 |
| Charnwood (England) | T2—425 47 |
| Charophyceae | 579.839 |
| Chars | 597.554 |
| Charter schools | 371.05 |
| Charter services | 388.042 |
| air | 387.742 8 |
| bus | 388.322 2 |
| *see also* Passenger services | |
| Chartered banks | 332.122 |
| Chartered surveyors (United | |
| Kingdom) | |
| economics | 333.08 |
| Chartering | 352.84 |
| *see also* Licensing | |
| Charters | 352.84 |
| administrative law | 342.066 |
| constitutional law | 342.02 |
| private law | 346.06 |
| public administration | 352.84 |
| *see also* Licensing | |
| Charters Towers (Qld.) | T2—943 6 |
| Chartreaux cat | 636.82 |

Chartres (France) T2—445 124
Charts 912
  aeronautics 629.132 54
  diagrammatic works T1—022 3
  geography 912
  pictorial works T1—022 2
  *see Manual at* T1—0222 vs.
    T1—0223
Chārvāka 181.46
Chase (B.C.) T2—711 72
Chase County (Kan.) T2—781 59
Chase County (Neb.) T2—782 87
Chasing metals
  decorative arts 739.15
Chasms 551.442
  T2—144
  geography 910.914 4
  geomorphology 551.442
  physical geography 910.021 44
Chassis 629.24
Chastity
  ethics 176.4
    religion 205.66
      Buddhism 294.356 6
      Christianity 241.66
      Hinduism 294.548 66
  religious practice 204.47
    Buddhism 294.344 47
    Christianity 248.47
    Hinduism 294.544 7
Chat groups 004.693
Chateau Clique 971.038
Châteauguay (Quebec :
  County) T2—714 34
Chateaux
  architecture 728.8
Chatham County (Ga.) T2—758 724
Chatham County (N.C.) T2—756 59
Chatham Islands (N.Z.) T2—939 9
Chatham-Kent (Ont.) T2—713 33
Chatsworth (South Africa :
  District) T2—684 5
Chattahoochee County (Ga.) T2—758 476
Chattahoochee River T2—758
Chattanooga (Tenn.) T2—768 82
Chattanooga campaign, 1863 973.735 9
Chattel mortgages
  law 346.074
Chattisgarhi dialect 491.492
  T6—914 92
Chattisgarhi literature 891.492
Chattooga County (Ga.) T2—758 344
Chaudière-Appalaches
  (Quebec) T2—714 71

Chaudière River (Quebec) T2—714 71
Chaunceys Line Reserve
  National Park (S. Aust.) T2—942 32
Chausey Islands (France) T2—423 48
Chautauqua County (Kan.) T2—781 918
Chautauqua County (N.Y.) T2—747 95
Chaves County (N.M.) T2—789 43
Châvez Frias, Hugo
  Venezuelan history 987.064 2
Chavín (Peru : Region) T2—852 1
Cheat River (W. Va. and
  Pa.) T2—754 8
Cheatham County (Tenn.) T2—768 462
Cheating 179.8
  *see also* Vices
Cheboygan County (Mich.) T2—774 87
Chebyshev polynomials 515.55
Chechen T5—999 641
Chechen language 499.964 1
  T6—999 641
Checheno-Ingushetia
  (Russia) T2—475 2
Chechnia (Russia) T2—475 2
Chechnya (Russia) T2—475 2
Checkered beetles 595.763
Checkers 794.2
Checking accounts 332.175 22
Checklists T1—021 6
Checkoff (Union dues) 331.889 6
Checks 332.76
  law 346.096
Checks and balances 320.404
  public administration 352.88
Cheddar cheese 641.373 54
  cooking 641.673 54
  food 641.373 54
  processing 637.354
Cheeks 591.44
  descriptive zoology 591.44
  human anatomy 611.318
  human physiology 612.31
  medicine 616.31
  physiology 573.355
  *see also* Digestive system
Cheerfulness 179.9
  *see also* Virtues
Cheerleading 791.64
Cheese 641.373
  cooking 641.673
  food 641.373
  processing 637.3

| | |
|---|---|
| Cheese foods | 641.373 58 |
| cooking | 641.673 58 |
| food | 641.373 58 |
| processing | 637.358 |
| Cheese pies | 641.824 |
| commercial processing | 664.65 |
| cooking | 641.824 |
| home preparation | 641.824 |
| Cheese varieties | 637.35 |
| Cheesemaking | 637.3 |
| Cheetah | 599.759 |
| animal husbandry | 636.89 |
| Chefchaouen (Morocco : | |
| Province) | T2—642 |
| Cheilostomata | 594.676 |
| Chekiang Province (China) | T2—512 42 |
| Chelan County (Wash.) | T2—797 59 |
| Chelates | 547.590 442 42 |
| Cheliabinskaia oblast' | |
| (Russia) | T2—474 3 |
| Chelicerata | 595.4 |
| paleozoology | 565.4 |
| Cheliff (Algeria : Province) | T2—653 |
| Chełm (Poland : | |
| Voivodeship) | T2—438 43 |
| Chelmsford (England : | |
| Borough) | T2—426 752 |
| Chelmsford, Frederic John | |
| Napier Thesiger, Viscount | |
| Indian history | 954.035 7 |
| Chelonia (Genus) | 597.928 |
| Chelonia (Order) | 597.92 |
| paleozoology | 567.92 |
| Cheloniidae | 597.928 |
| Chelonioidea | 597.928 |
| Cheltenham (England) | T2—424 16 |
| Chelyabinsk (Russia : | |
| Oblast) | T2—474 3 |
| Chelydridae | 597.922 |
| Chelyidae | 597.929 |
| Chemehuevi Indians | T5—974 576 |
| Chemehuevi language | 497.457 6 |
| | T6—974 576 |
| Chemical analysis | 543 |
| minerals | 549.133 |
| organic chemistry | 543.17 |
| Chemical arms control | |
| law | 341.735 |
| Chemical bonds | 541.224 |
| Chemical communication | 573.929 |
| Chemical compounds | 546 |
| engineering | 660 |

| | |
|---|---|
| Chemical contraceptives | |
| health | 613.943 2 |
| medicine | 618.182 |
| *see also* Birth control | |
| pharmacokinetics | 615.766 |
| Chemical crystallography | 548.3 |
| Chemical diagnosis | |
| medicine | 616.075 6 |
| Chemical engineering | 660 |
| law | 344.095 4 |
| Chemical engineers | 660.092 |
| Chemical equilibrium | 541.392 |
| organic chemistry | 547.212 |
| Chemical fire extinction | 628.925 4 |
| Chemical forces (Armed | |
| services) | 358.34 |
| Chemical industries | 338.476 6 |
| technology | 660 |
| Chemical instruments | 542 |
| manufacturing technology | 681.754 |
| Chemical laboratories | 542.1 |
| Chemical lasers | 621.366 4 |
| Chemical metallurgy | 669.9 |
| Chemical mineralogy | 549.13 |
| Chemical mutagens | 576.542 |
| Chemical oceanography | 551.466 |
| Chemical pollution | 363.738 |
| Chemical preservation | |
| food | 664.028 6 |
| home economics | 641.46 |
| lumber | 674.386 |
| Chemical projectiles | 623.451 6 |
| Chemical propulsion | 621.435 |
| aircraft | 629.134 353 |
| spacecraft | 629.475 2 |
| Chemical reactions | 541.39 |
| biochemistry | 572.43 |
| Chemical reactors | 660.283 2 |
| Chemical senses | 573.877 |
| human physiology | 612.86 |
| Chemical sensory perception | |
| psychology | 152.16 |
| Chemical technologists | 660.092 |
| Chemical technology | 660 |
| Chemical terrorism | 363.325 3 |
| *see also* Terrorism | |
| Chemical treatment | |
| water supply engineering | 628.166 |
| Chemical warfare | 358.34 |
| civil defense | 363.35 |
| law | 341.735 |
| Chemical waste disposal | 363.728 8 |
| *see also* Waste control | |

Chemical wastes
  water pollution engineering 628.168 36
Chemical weapons 358.348 2
  disarmament 327.174 5
  engineering 623.445
  law 341.735
  military equipment 358.348 2
Chemicals 540
  hazardous materials 363.179
    *see also* Hazardous materials
  photography 771.5
  product safety 363.19
    law 344.042 4
Chemiculture 631.585
Chemiluminescence 541.35
  chemical engineering 660.295
Chemisorption 541.335
  chemical engineering 660.293
Chemistry 540
  applied 660
  electrical equipment 542.84
  electronic equipment 542.84
  information systems 025.065 4
  law 344.095 4
Chemists 540.92
Chemnitz (Germany) T2—432 162
Chemnitz (Germany :
  Direktionsbezirk) T2—432 16
Chemnitz (Germany :
  Regierungsbezirk) T2—432 16
Chemokines
  human immunology 616.079
Chemolithotrophic bacteria 579.32
Chemotaxonomy 578.012
Chemotherapy
  medicine 615.58
Chemung County (N.Y.) T2—747 78
Chen 598.417 5
Chenango County (N.Y.) T2—747 73
Chenaux (Quebec) T2—714 455
Chenille 677.617
Chenopodiaceae 583.53
Chepang (Nepalese people) T5—954 9
Chepang language 495.49
  T6—954 9
Chepstow (Wales) T2—429 98
Cheques 332.76
  law 346.096
Cher (France) T2—445 52
Cheremis T5—945 6
Cheremis language 494.56
  T6—945 6
Cherimoya 583.22
Cherkasy (Ukraine : Oblast) T2—477 6

Cherkas'ka oblast'
  (Ukraine) T2—477 6
Chernenko, K. U. (Konstantin
  Ustinovich)
  Russian history 947.085 4
Chernihiv (Ukraine : Oblast) T2—477 6
Chernihivs'ka oblast'
  (Ukraine) T2—477 6
Chernivets'ka oblast'
  (Ukraine) T2—477 9
Chernivtsy (Ukraine :
  Oblast) T2—477 9
Cherokee County (Ala.) T2—761 65
Cherokee County (Ga.) T2—758 253
Cherokee County (Iowa) T2—777 17
Cherokee County (Kan.) T2—781 99
Cherokee County (N.C.) T2—756 99
Cherokee County (Okla.) T2—766 88
Cherokee County (S.C.) T2—757 42
Cherokee County (Tex.) T2—764 183
Cherokee Indians T5—975 57
Cherokee language 497.557
  T6—975 57
Cherokee literature 897.557
Cherries 641.342 3
  botany 583.73
  commercial processing 664.804 23
  cooking 641.642 3
  food 641.342 3
  orchard crop 634.23
  ornamental arboriculture 635.977 373
Cherry County (Neb.) T2—782 732
Cherry pickers (Machines) 621.873
Cherubim and Seraphim Church 289.93
  *see also* Christian
    denominations
Cherwell (England) T2—425 73
Chesapeake (Va.) T2—755 523
Chesapeake Bay (Md. and Va.) 551.461 347
  T2—163 47
Chesapeake Bay Region
  (Md. and Va.) T2—755 18
Cheshire (England) T2—427 1
Cheshire County (N.H.) T2—742 9
Cheshire swine 636.484
Chess 794.1
  equipment technology 688.741
Chess players 794.109 2
Chessmen 794.1
  manufacturing technology 688.741
Chest
  human anatomy 611.94
  human physiology 612.94

| | |
|---|---|
| Chest (continued) | |
| regional medicine | 617.54 |
| surgery | 617.540 59 |
| Chest bones | |
| human anatomy | 611.712 |
| human physiology | 612.751 |
| Chest muscles | |
| human anatomy | 611.735 |
| Chester (England : City) | T2—427 14 |
| Chester County (Pa.) | T2—748 13 |
| Chester County (S.C.) | T2—757 47 |
| Chester County (Tenn.) | T2—768 265 |
| Chester-le-Street (England : District) | T2—428 69 |
| Chester River (Md.) | T2—752 34 |
| Chester White swine | 636.484 |
| Chesterfield (England : Borough) | T2—425 12 |
| Chesterfield County (S.C.) | T2—757 63 |
| Chesterfield County (Va.) | T2—755 594 |
| Chesterfield Inlet (Nunavut) | T2—719 58 |
| Chestnut bean | 641.356 57 |
| see also Chick-peas | |
| Chestnuts | 583.46 |
| cooking | 641.645 3 |
| food | 641.345 3 |
| forestry | 634.972 4 |
| lumber | 674.142 |
| nut crop | 634.53 |
| Chests (Furniture) | 645.4 |
| manufacturing technology | 684.16 |
| see also Furniture | |
| Cheviot Hills (England) | T2—428 8 |
| Chevrotains | 599.63 |
| Chewa (African people) | T5—963 918 |
| Chewa language | 496.391 8 |
| | T6—963 918 |
| Chewa literature | 896.391 8 |
| Chewing | |
| animal physiology | 573.35 |
| descriptive zoology | 591.53 |
| human physiology | 612.311 |
| Chewing gum | 641.338 |
| commercial processing | 664.6 |
| food | 641.338 |
| Chewing lice | 595.757 |
| Cheyenne (Wyo.) | T2—787 19 |
| Cheyenne County (Colo.) | T2—788 92 |
| Cheyenne County (Kan.) | T2—781 112 |
| Cheyenne County (Neb.) | T2—782 96 |
| Cheyenne Indians | T5—973 53 |
| Cheyenne language | 497.353 |
| | T6—973 53 |
| Chhattīsgarh (India) | T2—541 37 |

| | |
|---|---|
| Chhattisgarhi dialect | 491.492 |
| | T6—914 92 |
| Chhattisgarhi literature | 891.492 |
| Chi-square test | 519.56 |
| Chiapas (Mexico) | T2—727 5 |
| Chiaroscuro | 701.8 |
| Chiasmodontidae | 597.7 |
| Chiba-ken (Japan) | T2—521 37 |
| Chibcha Indians | T5—982 |
| Chibchan languages | 498.2 |
| | T6—982 |
| Central America | 497.8 |
| | T6—978 |
| Chibougamau (Quebec) | T2—714 115 |
| Chibougamau Wildlife Reserve (Quebec) | T2—714 142 |
| Chicago (Ill.) | T2—773 11 |
| Chicago breakdown | 781.653 |
| Chicago school of economics | 330.155 3 |
| Chicanos | T5—687 207 3 |
| Chich | 641.356 57 |
| see also Chick-peas | |
| Chichaoua (Morocco : Province) | T2—646 4 |
| Chichester (England : District) | T2—422 62 |
| Chichewa language | 496.391 8 |
| | T6—963 918 |
| Chichewa literature | 896.391 8 |
| Chick-peas | 641.356 57 |
| botany | 583.74 |
| commercial processing | 664.805 657 |
| cooking | 641.656 57 |
| field crop | 633.37 |
| food | 641.356 57 |
| garden crop | 635.657 |
| Chickadees | 598.824 |
| Chickamauga Lake (Tenn.) | T2—768 82 |
| Chickarees | 599.363 |
| Chickasaw County (Iowa) | T2—777 315 |
| Chickasaw County (Miss.) | T2—762 942 |
| Chickasaw Indians | T5—973 86 |
| Chickasaw language | 497.386 |
| | T6—973 86 |
| Chicken (Meat) | 641.365 |
| agricultural economics | 338.176 513 |
| commercial processing | |
| economics | 338.476 649 3 |
| technology | 664.93 |
| cooking | 641.665 |
| food | 641.365 |
| home preservation | 641.493 |
| Chicken turtle | 597.925 9 |

Chickenpox
  incidence 614.525
  medicine 616.914
    *see also* Communicable
      diseases — humans
  pediatrics 618.929 14
Chickens 636.5
  zoology 598.625
Chicory (Beverage) 641.337 8
  agriculture 633.78
  botany 583.99
  commercial processing 663.97
  cooking with 641.637 8
  food 641.337 8
  home preparation 641.877
Chicory (Salad green) 641.355 4
  agriculture 635.54
  botany 583.99
  commercial processing 664.805 54
  cooking 641.655 4
  food 641.355 4
Chicot County (Ark.) T2—767 84
Chicoutimi (Saguenay,
  Quebec) T2—714 162
Chicozapotes 583.674
  *see also* Sapotaceae
Chief executives
  executive management 658.42
  law 342.062
  public administration 352.23
Chiefs of staff
  executive management 658.42
  public administration 352.237 229 3
Chieti (Italy : Province) T2—457 13
  ancient T2—377 37
Chifley, J. B. (Joseph Benedict)
  Australian history 994.05
Chiga (African people) T5—963 956
Chiga language 496.395 6
    T6—963 956
Chiggers 595.42
Chihuahua (Dog) 636.76
Chihuahua (Mexico : State) T2—721 6
Chilako River (B.C.) T2—711 82
Chilblains
  medicine 616.58
    *see also* Skin diseases —
      humans
Chilcotin River (B.C.) T2—711 75
Child abuse 362.76
  criminology 364.155 54
    criminal law 345.025 554
  family relationships 306.874
  medicine 616.858 223

Child abuse (continued)
  social theology 201.762 76
    Christianity 261.832 71
  social welfare 362.76
  law 344.032 76
Child care 649.1
Child care services 362.7
Child cooks 641.512 3
Child custody 346.017 3
Child development 305.231
  physiology 612.65
  psychology 155.4
  sociology 305.231
Child labor 331.31
  law 344.013 1
Child molesting 364.153 6
  law 345.025 36
  medicine 616.858 36
Child neglect 362.76
  *see also* Child abuse
Child-parent relations 306.874
  *see also* Parent-child relations
Child prostitution 306.745
  *see also* Prostitution
Child protection 362.76
  *see also* Child abuse
Child psychology 155.4
Child rearing 649.1
  customs 392.13
  personal religion 204.41
    Christianity 248.845
    Islam 297.577
    Judaism 296.74
Child study 305.23
  physiology 612.65
  psychology 155.4
  sociology 305.23
Child support 346.017 2
Child training 649.6
Childbed fever
  obstetrics 618.74
Childbirth 618.4
  arts T3C—354
  customs 392.12
    etiquette 395.24
  folklore 398.274
    history and criticism 398.354
  human physiology 612.63
  literature 808.803 54
    history and criticism 809.933 54
    specific literatures T3B—080 354
      history and
        criticism T3B—093 54
  music 781.582

| | |
|---|---|
| Childbirth (continued) | |
| obstetrics | 618.4 |
| preparation | |
| obstetrics | 618.24 |
| psychology | 155.646 3 |
| social services | 362.198 4 |
| Childhood | 305.23 |
| psychology | 155.4 |
| sociology | 305.23 |
| Childhood disintegrative disorder | |
| medicine | 616.858 83 |
| pediatrics | 618.928 588 3 |
| Childhood of Jesus Christ | 232.927 |
| Childlessness | 306.87 |
| Children | 305.23 |
| | T1—083 |
| art representation | 704.942 5 |
| arts | 700.452 3 |
| | T3C—352 3 |
| civil and human rights | 323.352 |
| law | 342.087 72 |
| law of nations | 341.485 72 |
| cooking for | 641.562 2 |
| development | |
| human physiology | 612.65 |
| drawing | 743.45 |
| etiquette | 395.122 |
| government programs | 353.536 |
| grooming | 646.704 6 |
| health | 613.043 2 |
| home care | 649.4 |
| institutional buildings | |
| architecture | 725.57 |
| journalism for | 070.483 2 |
| labor economics | 331.31 |
| law | 344.013 1 |
| legal status | 346.013 5 |
| constitutional law | 342.087 72 |
| private law | 346.013 5 |
| literature | 808.803 523 |
| history and criticism | 809.933 523 |
| specific literatures | T3B—080 352 3 |
| history and | |
| criticism | T3B—093 523 |
| painting | 757.5 |
| physical fitness | 613.704 2 |
| psychology | 155.4 |
| publications for | |
| bibliographies | 011.62 |
| reviews | 028.162 |
| reading | |
| library science | 028.53 |

| | |
|---|---|
| Children (continued) | |
| recreation | 790.192 2 |
| indoor | 793.019 22 |
| outdoor | 796.083 |
| relations with government | 323.352 |
| religion | 200.83 |
| Christianity | 270.083 |
| devotional literature | 242.62 |
| guides to Christian life | 248.82 |
| pastoral care | 259.22 |
| prayer books | 242.82 |
| religious education | 268.432 |
| guides to life | 204.408 3 |
| Judaism | 296.083 |
| guides to life | 296.708 3 |
| religious education | 296.680 83 |
| sex hygiene | 613.951 |
| social aspects | 305.23 |
| social welfare | 362.7 |
| public administration | 353.536 |
| socialization | 303.32 |
| treatment of | |
| ethics | 179.2 |
| *see also* Ethical problems | |
| World War I | 940.316 1 |
| World War II | 940.531 61 |
| Children (Progeny) | 306.874 |
| | T1—085 4 |
| Children of alcoholics | |
| pediatrics | 618.928 619 |
| social welfare | 362.292 3 |
| Children of minorities | |
| home care | 649.157 |
| psychology | 155.457 |
| Children of prisoners | 362.829 5 |
| Children of substance abusers | |
| pediatrics | 618.928 69 |
| social welfare | 362.291 3 |
| Children of unmarried parents | 306.874 |
| | T1—086 945 |
| legal status | 346.017 |
| social welfare | 362.787 4 |
| Children's books | |
| bibliographies | 011.62 |
| illustration | 741.642 |
| literature | 808.899 282 |
| *see also* Children's literature | |
| publishing | 070.508 3 |
| Children's church | 264.008 3 |
| Children's clothing | 391.3 |
| commercial technology | 687.083 |
| customs | 391.3 |
| home economics | 646.36 |

Children's clothing (continued)
home sewing   646.406
*see also* Clothing
Children's cooking   641.512 3
Children's Crusade, 1212   944.023
Children's diseases   362.198 92
  medicine   618.92
  social welfare   362.198 92
Children's homes   362.732
Children's hospitals   362.198 92
*see also* Health care facilities
Children's libraries   027.625
  administration   025.197 625
  collection development   025.218 762 5
Children's literature   808.899 282
  history and criticism   809.892 82
  rhetoric   808.068
  specific literatures   T3B—080 928 2
   history and criticism   T3B—099 282
Children's parties   793.21
Children's rights   323.352
  law   342.087 72
  law of nations   341.485 72
Children's sermons
  Christianity   252.53
Children's songs   782.420 83
Children's theater   792.022 6
Children's voices   782.7
  choral and mixed voices   782.7
  single voices   783.7
Childress County (Tex.)   T2—764 754
Chile   983
  T2—83
Chile saltpeter   553.64
  economic geology   553.64
  mineralogy   549.732
Chilean cedar   585.4
Chilean literature   860
Chileans   T5—688 3
Chili   641.823 6
  commercial processing   664.65
  home preparation   641.823 6
Chili peppers   641.338 4
*see also* Hot spices
Chilko River (B.C.)   T2—711 75
Chilled dishes
  cooking   641.79
Chilliwack (B.C.)   T2—711 37
Chiloé (Chile)   T2—835 6
Chilopoda   595.62
Chiltern (England)   T2—425 97
Chiltern Hills (England)   T2—425
Chilterns (England)   T2—425
Chilton County (Ala.)   T2—761 81

Chiluba, Frederick
  Zambian history   968.940 42
Chimaerae   597.38
Chimaeriformes   597.38
Chimakuan languages   497.9
  T6—979
Chimaltenango
  (Guatemala : Dept.)   T2—728 161
Chimborazo (Ecuador)   T2—866 17
Chimbu Province (Papua
  New Guinea)   T2—956 7
Chimeras (Fishes)   597.38
Chimes   786.848
*see also* Percussion instruments
Chimneys   721.5
  architecture   721.5
  buildings   697.8
  steam furnaces   621.183
Chimpanzees   599.885
Ch'in dynasty   931.04
Chin dynasty   931.04
China   951
  T2—51
  ancient   931
  T2—31
China (Porcelain)   666.5
  arts   738.2
China (Republic : 1949– )   951.249 05
  T2—512 49
China cabinets   645.4
  manufacturing technology   684.16
*see also* Furniture
China fir   585.5
China grass plant   583.45
Chinaberry tree   635.977 377
  botany   583.77
  ornamental arboriculture   635.977 377
Chinandega (Nicaragua :
  Dept.)   T2—728 511
Chinch bugs
  agricultural pests   633.104 975 4
  zoology   595.754
Chinchilla, Laura
  Costa Rican history   972.860 527
Chinchillas   636.935 93
  animal husbandry   636.935 93
  zoology   599.359 3
Chinchillidae   599.359 3
Chincoteague pony   636.16
Chinese   T5—951
Chinese artichoke   641.352
  agriculture   635.2
  botany   583.96

Chinese artichoke (continued)
  cooking       641.652
  food       641.352
Chinese calendar       529.329 51
  religion       299.511 36
Chinese calligraphy       745.619 951
Chinese chess       794.18
Chinese communism       335.434 5
  economics       335.434 5
  political ideology       320.532 309 51
Chinese Communist Party       324.251 075
Chinese crested (Dog)       636.76
Chinese evergreen       635.934 64
  botany       584.64
  floriculture       635.934 64
Chinese flower arrangements       745.922 51
Chinese gooseberry       641.344
  *see also* Kiwi (Fruit)
Chinese ink painting       751.425 1
Chinese language       495.1
      T6—951
Chinese literature       895.1
Chinese opera       782.109 51
Chinese religions       299.51
Chinese rugs
  arts       746.751
Chinese Shar-Pei       636.72
Chinese water chestnut       584.84
Chinese wood oil       665.333
Ch'ing dynasty       951.03
Chinook Indians       T5—974 1
Chinook language       497.41
      T6—974 1
Chinooks (Winds)       551.518 5
Chinquapins       583.46
Ch'ins       787.75
  *see also* Stringed instruments
Chinyanja (African people)       T5—963 918
Chinyanja language       496.391 8
      T6—963 918
Chios (Greece)       T2—495 82
Chios Island (Greece)       T2—495 82
  ancient       T2—391 3
Chip boards       676.183
Chipaya language       498.9
      T6—989
Chipewyan Indians       T5—972
Chipewyan language       497.2
      T6—972
Chipmunks       599.364
  animal husbandry       636.936 4
Chipped soaps       668.124
Chippewa County (Mich.)       T2—774 91
Chippewa County (Minn.)       T2—776 39

Chippewa County (Wis.)       T2—775 44
Chippewa Indians       T5—973 33
Chippewa language       497.333
      T6—973 33
Chippewa literature       897.333
Chippewa River (Wis.)       T2—775 4
Chipping
  golf       796.352 34
Chiquimula (Guatemala :
  Dept.)       T2—728 141
Chiricahua Indians       T5—972 56
Chiricahua language       497.256
      T6—972 56
Chiriquí (Panama :
  Province)       T2—728 711
Chirognomy       133.6
Chiromancy       133.6
Chironomidae       595.772
Chiropody       617.585
Chiropractic
  therapeutic system       615.534
Chiropractors       610.92
  limited practice       615.534 092
  *see Manual at* 610.92 vs.
    615.534092
Chiroptera       599.4
  paleozoology       569.4
Chisago County (Minn.)       T2—776 61
Chiseling       730.28
  decorative arts       736
  sculpture       731.46
Chissano, Joaquim Alberto
  Mozambican history       967.905 2
Chita (Russia : Oblast)       T2—575
Chital       599.65
Chitarrones       787.82
  *see also* Stringed instruments
Chitin       573.774
  *see also* Carbohydrates
Chitinskaĩa oblast' (Russia)       T2—575
Chitons       594.27
Chitrāl District (Pakistan)       T2—549 122
Chittagong (Bangladesh :
  Division)       T2—549 23
Chittagong Hill Tracts
  (Bangladesh : Region)       T2—549 29
Chittenden County (Vt.)       T2—743 17
Chiusi (Italy)
  ancient       T2—375 68
Chivalry       394.7
  arts       T3C—353
  folklore       398.273
    history and criticism       398.353

Chivalry (continued)
  literature     808.803 53
    history and criticism   809.933 53
    specific literatures   T3B—080 353
      history and
        criticism   T3B—093 53
Chives     641.352 6
  botany     584.33
  cooking     641.652 6
  food     641.352 6
  garden crop     635.26
Chkalov (Russia : Oblast)   T2—474 3
Chlamydia infections
  incidence     614.573 5
  medicine     616.923 5
  *see also* Communicable
    diseases — humans
Chlamydias     579.327
Chlamydomonadaceae     579.832
Chlef (Algeria : Province)   T2—653
Chloranthaceae     583.23
Chlordane
  human toxicology     615.951 2
Chlorideae     584.9
Chlorination
  water supply treatment     628.166 2
Chlorine     553.95
  chemical engineering     661.073 2
  chemistry     546.732
  economic geology     553.95
  human toxicology     615.91
  organic chemistry     547.02
    applied     661.891
  *see also* Chemicals
Chlorite
  mineralogy     549.67
Chlorococcales     579.833
Chloromonadophyta     579.82
Chlorophyceae     579.83
Chlorophylls     572.46
  chemical engineering     661.894
  organic chemistry     547.593
Chlorophyta     579.83
Chloroplastic DNA     572.869
Chloroplasts     571.659 2
Chloroprene rubber     678.72
Chlorpromazine
  pharmacokinetics     615.788 2
Choapa (Chile : Province)   T2—832 38
Chocó (Colombia)   T2—861 51
Choco languages     498.9
    T6—989
  Central America     497.9
    T6—979

Chocolate     641.337 4
  beverage     641.337 4
    commercial processing     663.92
    home preparation     641.877
  commercial processing     664.5
  cooking with     641.637 4
  food     641.337 4
Choctaw County (Ala.)   T2—761 395
Choctaw County (Miss.)   T2—762 694
Choctaw County (Okla.)   T2—766 63
Choctaw Indians   T5—973 87
Choctaw language     497.387
    T6—973 87
Choice
  mathematics     511.65
  psychology     153.83
Choice axiom     511.3
Choice of entry (Cataloging)     025.322
Choice of vocation     331.702
    T1—023
  *see also* Vocational guidance
Choir lofts
  architecture     726.593
Choir stalls     247.1
  architecture     726.529 3
Choirs     782.5
Choirs (Structural parts)
  architecture     726.593
Chokeberries     583.73
Chokwe (African people)   T5—963 99
Chokwe-Luchazi languages     496.399
    T6—963 99
Chol language     497.428
    T6—974 28
Cholan-Tzeltalan languages     497.428
    T6—974 28
Cholera
  incidence     614.514
  medicine     616.932
  *see also* Communicable
    diseases — humans
Cholesterol     572.579 5
  applied nutrition     613.284
  biochemistry     572.579 5
Choluteca (Honduras :
  Dept.)   T2—728 351
Chon languages     498.7
    T6—987
Chondrichthyes     597.3
  paleozoology     567.3
Chondrocytes
  human cytology     612.751 76
Chondrophora     593.55

| | | | |
|---|---|---|---|
| Chondrostei | 597.42 | Chow chow | 636.72 |
| paleozoology | 567.42 | Chowan County (N.C.) | T2—756 147 |
| Chongqing (China) | T2—513 8 | Chowan River (N.C.) | T2—756 15 |
| Chontales (Nicaragua) | T2—728 527 | Chrétien, Jean | |
| Chopi (African people) | T5—963 97 | Canadian history | 971.064 8 |
| Chopi languages | 496.397 | Chrismation | |
| | T6—963 97 | Christianity | 234.162 |
| Choptank River (Del. and | | public worship | 265.2 |
| Md.) | T2—752 31 | theology | 234.162 |
| Choral music | 782.5 | Christchurch (England : | |
| Choral recitations | | Borough) | T2—423 39 |
| literature | 808.855 | Christchurch (N.Z.) | T2—938 3 |
| history and criticism | 809.55 | Christchurch City (N.Z.) | T2—938 3 |
| specific literatures | T3B—505 | Christening | 265.1 |
| individual authors | T3A—5 | customs | 392.12 |
| Choral speaking | 808.55 | etiquette | 395.24 |
| literature | 808.855 | music | 781.582 |
| history and criticism | 809.55 | Christian and Missionary | |
| music | 782.96 | Alliance | 289.9 |
| primary education | 372.676 | *see also* Christian | |
| rhetoric | 808.55 | denominations | |
| Chorale preludes | 784.189 92 | Christian art | 704.948 2 |
| Chorales | 782.27 | religious significance | 246 |
| instrumental form | 784.189 925 | Christian Brothers | 255.78 |
| Chordata | 596 | church history | 271.78 |
| Chordophones | 787 | Christian calendars | 529.4 |
| *see also* Stringed instruments | | religion | 263.9 |
| Chords (Music) | 781.252 | Christian church | 260 |
| Chorea | | history | 270 |
| medicine | 616.83 | local | 250 |
| *see also* Nervous system | | specific denominations | 280 |
| diseases — humans | | *see Manual at* 260 vs. 251–254, | |
| Choreatic disorders | | 259 | |
| medicine | 616.83 | Christian Church (Disciples of | |
| *see also* Nervous system | | Christ) | 286.63 |
| diseases — humans | | *see also* Restoration movement | |
| Choreographers | 792.820 92 | (Christian movement) | |
| Choreography | 792.82 | Christian Churches and Churches | |
| musical plays | 792.62 | of Christ | 286.63 |
| Choreology | 792.82 | *see also* Restoration movement | |
| Chorionic villi sampling | | (Christian movement) | |
| obstetrics | 618.320 427 5 | Christian County (Ill.) | T2—773 81 |
| Chorley (England : | | Christian County (Ky.) | T2—769 78 |
| Borough) | T2—427 615 | Christian County (Mo.) | T2—778 792 |
| Choroid diseases | | Christian Democracy (Italian | |
| ophthalmology | 617.72 | political party) | 324.245 082 2 |
| *see also* Eye diseases — | | Christian Democratic Center | |
| humans | | (Italian political party) | 324.245 082 |
| Choroids | | Christian democratic parties | 324.218 2 |
| human physiology | 612.842 | international organizations | 324.182 |
| ophthalmology | 617.72 | Christian Democratic People's | |
| Chosen people (Judaism) | 296.311 72 | Party of Switzerland | 324.249 404 |
| Chou dynasty | 931.03 | Christian Democratic Union of | |
| Chouteau County (Mont.) | T2—786 293 | Germany (Political party) | 324.243 04 |

| | |
|---|---|
| Christian denominations | 280 |
| | T1—088 28 |
| church government | 262.01–.09 |
| parishes | 254.01–.09 |
| church law | 262.98 |
| doctrines | 230.1–.9 |
| catechisms and creeds | 238.1–.9 |
| general councils | 262.51–.59 |
| guides to Christian life | 248.48 |
| missions | 266.1–.9 |
| moral theology | 241.04 |
| public worship | 264.01–.09 |
| religious associations | 267.18 |
| religious education | 268.8 |
| religious orders | 255 |
| church history | 271 |
| women's | 255.9 |
| seminaries | 230.073 |
| theology | 230.1–.9 |
| *see Manual at* T1—0882 *and* | |
| 200; *also at* 283–289 | |
| Christian doctrine | 230 |
| Christian education | 268 |
| *see Manual at* 207.5, 268 vs. | |
| 200.71, 230.071, 292–299 | |
| Christian ethics | 241 |
| *see Manual at* 241 vs. 261.8 | |
| Christian holidays | 263.9 |
| customs | 394.266 |
| devotional literature | 242.3 |
| sermons | 252.6 |
| *see also* Holidays | |
| Christian initiation | 265.1 |
| Christian leadership | 262.1 |
| local church | 253 |
| Christian life | 248.4 |
| Christian-Marxist dialogue | |
| Christian theology | 261.21 |
| Christian Methodist Episcopal | |
| Church | 287.83 |
| *see also* Methodist Church | |
| Christian names | 929.44 |
| Christian philosophy | 190 |
| Christian Reformed Church | 285.731 |
| *see also* Reformed Church | |
| (American Reformed) | |
| Christian regions | T2—176 1 |
| Christian sacred music | 781.71 |
| public worship | 782.32 |
| music | 782.32 |
| choral and mixed voices | 782.532 |
| single voices | 783.093 2 |
| religion | 264.2 |
| religious symbolism | 246.75 |

| | |
|---|---|
| Christian schools (General | |
| education) | 371.071 |
| Christian Science | 289.5 |
| Christian Scientists | |
| biography | 289.509 2 |
| Christian Social Party (Austria) | 324.243 602 4 |
| Christian Social Party | |
| (Switzerland) | 324.249 407 |
| Christian Social Union (German | |
| political party) | 324.243 04 |
| Christian socialism | 335.7 |
| economics | 335.7 |
| political ideology | 320.531 2 |
| Christiana (South Africa : | |
| District) | T2—682 45 |
| Christianity | 230 |
| art representation | 704.948 2 |
| religious significance | 246 |
| arts | 700.482 3 |
| | T3C—382 3 |
| religious significance | 246 |
| Islamic polemics | 297.293 |
| literature | 808.803 823 |
| history and criticism | 809.933 823 |
| specific literatures | T3B—080 382 3 |
| history and | |
| criticism | T3B—093 823 |
| Christianity and anti-Semitism | 261.26 |
| Christianity and atheism | 261.21 |
| Christianity and culture | 261 |
| Christianity and Islam | 261.27 |
| Christian view | 261.27 |
| Islamic view | 297.283 |
| Christianity and Judaism | 261.26 |
| Christian view | 261.26 |
| Jewish view | 296.396 |
| Christianity and occultism | 261.513 |
| Christianity and other religions | 261.2 |
| Christianity and politics | 261.7 |
| Christianity and secular | |
| disciplines | 261.5 |
| *see Manual at* 261.5 | |
| Christianity in public schools | 379.28 |
| Christians | 270.092 |
| | T1—088 27 |
| specific denominations | 280 |
| *see Manual at* 230–280 | |
| Christina, Queen of Sweden | |
| Swedish history | 948.503 42 |
| Christlich-Demokratische Union | |
| Deutschlands (Political party) | 324.243 04 |
| Christlich-soziale Partei (Austria) | 324.243 602 4 |
| Christlich-soziale Partei | |
| (Switzerland) | 324.249 407 |

Christlich-Soziale Union
  (German political party) — 324.243 04
Christlichdemokratische
  Volkspartei der Schweiz — 324.249 404
Christmas — 263.915
  arts — 700.434
    T3C—334
  cooking — 641.568 6
  customs — 394.266 3
  devotional literature — 242.335
  handicrafts — 745.594 12
  literature — 808.803 34
    history and criticism — 809.933 34
    specific literatures — T3B—080 334
      history and
        criticism — T3B—093 34
  sermons — 252.615
Christmas cards — 394.266 3
  customs — 394.266 3
  handicrafts — 745.594 12
Christmas carols — 782.281 723
Christmas cooking — 641.568 6
Christmas decorations — 394.266 3
  customs — 394.266 3
  handicrafts — 745.594 12
Christmas Island (Indian
  Ocean) — T2—948
Christmas Island (Kiribati) — T2—964
Christmas music — 781.723
Christmas ornaments — 394.266 3
  customs — 394.266 3
  making — 688.726
    handicrafts — 745.594 12
    technology — 688.726
Christmas roses — 635.933 34
  botany — 583.34
  floriculture — 635.933 34
Christmas seals (Prints) — 769.57
Christmas songs — 782.421 723
Christmas story — 232.92
Christmas trees
  ornamental arboriculture — 635.977 5
Christology — 232
Chromates
  mineralogy — 549.752
Chromatids — 571.844
Chromatin — 572.87
Chromatographic analysis — 543.8
Chromatography — 543.8
Chrome brick — 666.72
Chromite
  mineralogy — 549.526

Chromium — 669.734
  chemical engineering — 661.053 2
  chemistry — 546.532
  decorative arts — 739.58
  economic geology — 553.464 3
  materials science — 620.189 34
  metallography — 669.957 34
  metallurgy — 669.734
  metalworking — 673.734
  mining — 622.346 43
  organic chemistry — 547.055 32
    applied — 661.895
  physical metallurgy — 669.967 34
  *see also* Chemicals; Metals
Chromium group
  chemical engineering — 661.053
  chemistry — 546.53
Chromolithography — 764.2
Chromoproteins — 572.68
  *see also* Proteins
Chromosomal DNA — 572.86
  humans — 611.018 166
Chromosome mapping — 572.863 3
  humans — 611.018 166 3
Chromosome numbers — 572.87
Chromosomes — 572.87
  humans — 611.018 167
Chromosphere of sun — 523.75
Chronic diseases
  medicine — 616.044
Chronic fatigue syndrome
  medicine — 616.047 8
Chronic obstructive pulmonary
  disease
  medicine — 616.24
    *see also* Respiratory tract
      diseases — humans
Chronic renal failure
  medicine — 616.614
    *see also* Urologic diseases —
      humans
Chronicles — 900
  *see also* History
Chronicles (Biblical books) — 222.6
Chronobiology — 571.77
Chronographs
  astronomy — 522.5
  technology — 681.118
Chronologies — 902.02
    T1—020 2
Chronologists — 529.092
Chronology — 529

Chronometers
  astronomy 522.5
  technology 681.118
Chronoscopes
  technology 681.118
Chroococcales 579.39
Chrysanthemums 635.933 99
  botany 583.99
  floriculture 635.933 99
Chrysemys 597.925 92
Chrysobalanaceae 583.73
Chrysocloridae 599.335
Chrysocolla
  mineralogy 549.64
Chrysomelidae 595.764 8
Chrysomeloidea 595.764 8
Chrysophyceae 579.86
Chrysophyta 579.86
Chtouka-Aït Baha
  (Morocco) T2—646 6
Chubs 597.482
  sports fishing 799.174 82
Chūbu Region (Japan) T2—521 6
Chubut (Argentina) T2—827 4
Chuckchee Sea 551.461 325
    T2—163 25
Chucks 621.992
Chūgoku Region (Japan) T2—521 9
Chukchi (Russia : Okrug) T2—577
Chukchi-Kamchatkan languages 494.6
    T6—946
Chukchi Sea 551.461 325
    T2—163 25
Chukotko-Kamchatkan
  languages T6—946
Chukotskiĭ avtonomnyĭ
  okrug (Russia) T2—577
Chulalongkorn, King of Siam
  Thai history 959.303 5
Chulupí language 498.7
    T6—987
Chumash Indians T5—975 8
Chumash language 497.58
    T6—975 8
Chumash languages 497.58
    T6—975 8
Ch'ung-ch'ing shih (China) T2—513 8
Chungking (China) T2—513 8
Chuquisaca (Bolivia) T2—842 4
Chur (Switzerland) T2—494 732 24

Church 260
  ecclesiology 262
  history 270
    specific denominations 280
  local 250
Church and state 322.1
  social theology 201.72
    Christianity 261.7
  *see also* Politics and religion
  *see Manual at* 322.1 vs. 201.72,
    261.7, 292–299
Church authority 262.8
Church buildings
  architecture 726.5
  institutional housekeeping 647.985
  landscape architecture 712.7
  management 254.7
  religious significance 246.9
Church calendar 263.9
  chronology 529.44
Church camps 796.542 2
Church controversies 262.8
  local church 250
  specific denominations 280
Church etiquette 395.53
Church fathers 270
  biography 270.092
Church finance 262.006 81
  local church 254.8
Church furniture 247.1
Church government 262
  local church 254
Church group work 253.7
Church growth
  local church 254.5
  missionary work 266
Church history 270
  specific denominations 280
Church holidays 263.9
  customs 394.266
  devotional literature 242.3
  sermons 252.6
  *see also* Holidays
Church in public education 379.28
Church law 262.9
Church libraries 027.67
Church membership
  local church 254.5
Church modes 781.263
Church music 781.71
Church of Christ, Scientist 289.5
  *see also* Christian
    denominations
Church of Constantinople 281.949 61

| | |
|---|---|
| Church of England | 283.42 |
| church government | 262.034 2 |
| parishes | 254.034 2 |
| church law | 262.983 42 |
| doctrines | 230.3 |
| catechisms and creeds | 238.3 |
| guides to Christian life | 248.483 |
| liturgy | 264.03 |
| missions | 266.3 |
| moral theology | 241.043 |
| persecution by Queen Mary | 272.6 |
| religious associations | 267.183 42 |
| religious education | 268.834 2 |
| religious orders | 255.83 |
| church history | 271.83 |
| women | 255.983 |
| church history | 271.983 |
| seminaries | 230.073 342 |
| theology | 230.3 |
| Church of God General Conference | 286.73 |
| *see also* Adventists | |
| Church of God in Christ, Mennonites | 289.73 |
| *see also* Mennonite Church | |
| Church of Jesus Christ of Latter-Day Saints | 289.332 |
| *see also* Mormon Church | |
| Church of North India | 287.95 |
| *see also* Christian denominations | |
| Church of Scotland | 285.233 |
| Church of South India | 287.94 |
| *see also* Christian denominations | |
| Church of the Brethren | 286.5 |
| *see also* Baptists | |
| Church of the East | 281.8 |
| *see also* Eastern churches | |
| Church of the Nazarene | 287.99 |
| *see also* Christian denominations | |
| Church of the New Jerusalem | 289.4 |
| Church organization | 262 |
| Church polity | 262 |
| Church presses publishing | 070.594 |
| Church-related colleges and universities | 378.071 |
| *see also* Higher education | |
| Church renewal | 262.001 7 |
| Church schools (General education) | 371.071 |
| libraries | 027.83 |

| | |
|---|---|
| Church services | 264 |
| flower arrangements | 745.926 |
| music | 782.32 |
| Church Slavic language | 491.817 01 |
| | T6—918 17 |
| Church Slavic literature | 891.81 |
| Church Slavonic language | 491.817 01 |
| | T6—918 17 |
| Church Slavonic literature | 891.81 |
| Church suppers | 642.4 |
| Church welfare work | 361.75 |
| Church work (Pastoral care) | 253 |
| Church work with children | 259.22 |
| Church work with disabled people | 259.44 |
| Church work with families | 259.1 |
| Church work with juvenile delinquents | 259.5 |
| Church work with older people | 259.3 |
| Church work with the sick | 259.4 |
| Church work with young adults | 259.25 |
| Church work with youth | 259.23 |
| Church year | 263.9 |
| chronology | 529.44 |
| devotional literature | 242.3 |
| music | 781.72 |
| sermon preparation | 251.6 |
| sermons | 252.6 |
| Church youth groups | 259.23 |
| Churches of Christ | 286.63 |
| *see also* Restoration movement (Christian movement) | |
| Churches of Christ in Christian Union | 289.9 |
| *see also* Christian denominations | |
| Churches of God | 289.9 |
| *see also* Christian denominations | |
| Churchill (Man.) | T2—712 71 |
| Churchill County (Nev.) | T2—793 52 |
| Churchill River (Sask. and Man.) | T2—712 71 |
| Chūsei period | 952.02 |
| Chutes-de-la-Chaudière (Quebec) | T2—714 59 |
| Chutney | 641.814 |
| commercial processing | 664.58 |
| home preparation | 641.814 |
| Chuukese language | 499.52 |
| | T6—995 2 |
| Chuvash language | 494.315 |
| | T6—943 15 |
| Chuvash literature | 894.315 |

| | |
|---|---|
| Chuvashes | T5—945 6 |
| Chuvashia (Russia) | T2—474 6 |
| Chuvashiĩa (Russia) | T2—474 6 |
| Chyromyiidae | 595.774 |
| Chytridiomycetes | 579.53 |
| CIA (Intelligence agency) | 327.127 3 |
| Cibola County (N.M.) | T2—789 91 |
| Cicadas | 595.752 |
| Ciceŵa language | 496.391 8 |
| | T6—963 918 |
| Ciceŵa literature | 896.391 8 |
| Cichlidae | 597.74 |
| culture | 639.377 4 |
| Cicindelidae | 595.762 |
| Ciconiidae | 598.34 |
| Ciconiiformes | 598.34 |
| paleozoology | 568.3 |
| Cider | 641.341 1 |
| commercial processing | 663.63 |
| cooking with | 641.641 1 |
| fermented | 641.229 |
| commercial processing | 663.29 |
| food | 641.341 1 |
| Ciechanów (Poland : | |
| Voivodeship) | T2—438 41 |
| Ciego de Ávila (Cuba : | |
| Province) | T2—729 153 |
| Cienfuegos (Cuba : | |
| Province) | T2—729 143 |
| Cigar flower | 583.76 |
| Cigarette holders | 688.4 |
| Cigarettes | 679.73 |
| smuggling | 364.133 6 |
| law | 345.023 36 |
| Cigars | 679.72 |
| Cilia | 571.67 |
| Ciliary bodies | |
| human physiology | 612.842 |
| ophthalmology | 617.72 |
| Ciliatea | 579.49 |
| Ciliates | 579.49 |
| Cilicia | T2—393 5 |
| Ciliophora | 579.49 |
| CIM (Manufacturing) | 670.285 |
| Cimarron County (Okla.) | T2—766 132 |
| Cimbaloms | 787.74 |
| *see also* Stringed instruments | |
| Cinchonas | 583.93 |
| medicinal crops | 633.883 93 |
| Cincinnati (Ohio) | T2—771 78 |
| Cinclidae | 598.832 |
| Cinder blocks | 666.894 |
| building construction | 693.4 |
| building materials | 691.3 |

| | |
|---|---|
| Cinder blocks (continued) | |
| manufacturing technology | 666.894 |
| materials science | 620.139 |
| structural engineering | 624.183 2 |
| Cinema | 791.43 |
| Cinemas | |
| architecture | 725.823 |
| Cinematography | 777 |
| *see Manual at* 791.43, 791.45 | |
| vs. 777 | |
| Cinnabar | |
| mineralogy | 549.32 |
| Cinnamon | 641.338 3 |
| botany | 583.23 |
| *see also* Spices | |
| Cinque Ports (England) | T2—422 352 |
| Cinquefoils | 583.73 |
| CIO (Labor) | 331.883 309 73 |
| CIP (Cataloging) | 025.3 |
| Ciphers (Cryptography) | 652.8 |
| computer science | 005.82 |
| Circadian rhythms | 571.77 |
| human physiology | 612.022 |
| Circassian languages | 499.962 4 |
| | T6—999 624 |
| Circassians | T5—999 624 |
| Circle geometry | 516.18 |
| Circle-squaring | 516.204 |
| Circles | 516.152 |
| Circuit breakers | 621.317 |
| Circuit courts | 347.02 |
| Circuit switching | 621.381 537 |
| communications engineering | 621.382 16 |
| computer communications | 004.66 |
| engineering | 621.398 1 |
| Circuits | 621.319 2 |
| computer engineering | 621.395 |
| electronics | 621.381 5 |
| microwave electronics | 621.381 32 |
| radio engineering | 621.384 12 |
| Circular buildings | 720.48 |
| architecture | 720.48 |
| construction | 690.38 |
| Circular dichroism | 541.7 |
| Circular manic-depressive | |
| psychoses | |
| medicine | 616.895 |
| *see also* Mental disorders | |
| Circulars | |
| direct advertising | 659.133 |
| postal handling | 383.124 |
| *see also* Postal service | |

| | |
|---|---|
| Circulation (Biology) | 573.1 |
| biology | 573.1 |
| brain | 573.862 1 |
| human physiology | 612.824 |
| *see also* Nervous system | |
| human physiology | 612.1 |
| plants | 575.7 |
| *see also* Cardiovascular system | |
| Circulation (Meteorology) | 551.517 |
| Circulation services | |
| library science | 025.6 |
| museology | 069.13 |
| Circulation theory (Economics) | 332.401 |
| Circulatory fluids | 573.15 |
| biology | 573.15 |
| plants | 575.75 |
| *see also* Cardiovascular system | |
| Circulatory organs | 573.1 |
| *see also* Cardiovascular system | |
| Circulatory system | 573.1 |
| biology | 573.1 |
| plants | 575.7 |
| *see also* Cardiovascular system | |
| Circumcision | 392.1 |
| customs | 392.1 |
| female | |
| surgery | 618.160 59 |
| Jewish rites | 296.442 2 |
| liturgy | 296.454 22 |
| male | |
| surgery | 617.463 |
| music | 781.582 |
| Circumcision of Jesus Christ | 232.92 |
| Circumstantial evidence | 347.064 |
| criminal investigation | 363.25 |
| criminal law | 345.064 |
| law | 347.064 |
| Circumterrestrial flights | |
| manned | 629.454 |
| unmanned | 629.435 2 |
| Circus animals | 791.32 |
| animal husbandry | 636.088 8 |
| Circus performers | 791.309 2 |
| Circuses | 791.3 |
| Cire perdue casting | |
| metals | 671.255 |
| Cirques (Geologic landforms) | 551.315 |
| Cirrhosis | |
| medicine | 616.362 4 |
| *see also* Digestive system | |
| diseases — humans | |
| Cirripedia | 595.35 |
| paleozoology | 565.35 |
| Cisalpine Gaul | T2—372 |

| | |
|---|---|
| Cisalpine Republic | 945.208 2 |
| CISC (Computer science) | 004.3 |
| *see also* Processing modes — | |
| computer science | |
| Ciskei (South Africa) | T2—687 55 |
| Cispadane Gaul | T2—372 6 |
| Cistaceae | 583.625 |
| Cistercians | 255.12 |
| church history | 271.12 |
| women | 255.97 |
| church history | 271.97 |
| Citation indexing | 025.47 |
| Citations | |
| armed forces | 355.134 |
| *see also* Military | |
| commemorations | |
| Citators to cases | 348.047 |
| United States | 348.734 7 |
| Citators to laws | 348.027 |
| United States | 348.732 7 |
| Citharinidae | 597.48 |
| Cities | 307.76 |
| | T2—173 2 |
| arts | T3C—358 209 732 |
| government | 320.85 |
| influence on precipitation | 551.577 5 |
| literature | 808.803 582 097 32 |
| history and criticism | 809.933 582 097 32 |
| specific literatures | T3B—080 358 209 732 |
| history and | |
| criticism | T3B—093 582 097 32 |
| psychological influence | 155.942 |
| public administration | 352.16 |
| control by higher | |
| jurisdictions | 353.336 |
| *see Manual at* 351.3–.9 vs. | |
| 352.13–.19 | |
| public administrative support | 352.793 |
| social services to residents | 361.917 32 |
| public administration | 353.533 3 |
| sociology | 307.76 |
| *see Manual at* T2—4–9; *also at* | |
| T2—41 and T2—42; *also at* | |
| T2—713 and T2—714; *also* | |
| *at* T2—93 | |
| Citizen participation | 323.042 |
| crime prevention | 364.43 |
| election campaigns | 324.72 |
| social welfare | 361.25 |
| Citizens advice bureaus | 361.06 |
| Citizens and state | 323 |
| Citizens band radio | 384.53 |
| communications services | 384.53 |
| engineering | 621.384 54 |

| | |
|---|---|
| Citizenship | 323.6 |
|   ethics | 172.1 |
|     *see also* Political ethics | |
|   law | 342.083 |
|   political science | 323.6 |
|   primary education | 372.83 |
|   public administration | 353.48 |
|   social theology | 201.723 |
|     Christianity | 261.7 |
|     Judaism | 296.382 |
| Citric acid cycle | 572.475 |
| Citronella | 584.92 |
| Citrons | 641.343 31 |
|   cooking | 641.643 31 |
|   food | 641.343 31 |
|   orchard crop | 634.331 |
| Citrus County (Fla.) | T2—759 72 |
| Citrus fruits | 641.343 04 |
|   botany | 583.77 |
|   commercial processing | 664.804 304 |
|   cooking | 641.643 04 |
|   food | 641.343 04 |
|   orchard crop | 634.304 |
| Citterns | 787.85 |
|   *see also* Stringed instruments | |
| City churches | 250.917 32 |
|   administration | 254.22 |
|   pastoral theology | 253.091 732 |
| City colleges | 378.052 |
|   *see also* Higher education | |
| City core | |
|   community redevelopment | 307.342 |
| City directories | 910.25 |
|   *see Manual at* T1—025 vs. | |
|     T1—029 | |
| City gas | 665.772 |
| City government | 320.85 |
| City government buildings | |
|   architecture | 725.13 |
| City halls | |
|   architecture | 725.13 |
| City manager government | 320.854 |
| City managers | |
|   public administration | 352.232 16 |
| City noise | 363.741 |
|   technology | 620.23 |
|   *see also* Noise | |
| City planners | 711.409 2 |
| City planning | 307.121 6 |
|   civic art | 711.4 |
|   law | 346.045 |
|   public administration | 354.353 |
| City schools | 371.009 173 2 |
| City-states | 321.06 |
| City traffic | 388.41 |
|   law | 343.098 2 |
| City warfare | 355.426 |
| Cityscapes | |
|   drawing | 743.84 |
|   fine arts | 704.944 |
|   painting | 758.7 |
| Ciudad da La Habana | |
|   (Cuba) | T2—729 123 |
| Ciudad Real (Spain : | |
|   Province) | T2—464 5 |
| Civets | 599.742 |
| Civic action of armed forces | 355.34 |
| Civic art | 711 |
| Civic centers | 307.33 |
|   architecture | 725.1 |
|   area planning | 711.551 |
|   community sociology | 307.33 |
| Civics | 320.4 |
|   primary education | 372.83 |
| Civil actions | 347.053 |
| Civil commotion insurance | 368.125 |
| Civil defense | 363.35 |
|   law | 344.053 5 |
|   public administration | 353.95 |
| Civil disobedience | 303.61 |
|   ethics | 172.1 |
|     religion | 205.621 |
|       Buddhism | 294.356 21 |
|       Christianity | 241.621 |
|       Hinduism | 294.548 621 |
|       Judaism | 296.362 1 |
|   law | 342.085 4 |
|   political action | 322.4 |
|   public safety | 363.32 |
|   social conflict | 303.61 |
|   social theology | 201.72 |
|     Christianity | 261.7 |
|     Judaism | 296.382 |
| Civil disorder | 303.62 |
|   public safety | 363.32 |
|   social conflict | 303.62 |
|   social services | 363.32 |
| Civil engineering | 624 |
|   *see Manual at* 624.1; *also at* | |
|     624 vs. 690 | |
| Civil engineers | 624.092 |
| Civil law (Legal system) | 340.56 |
|   *see Manual at* 340, 342–347 vs. | |
|     340.56 | |
| Civil-law notaries | 346.002 3 |
| Civil liberties | 323 |
|   *see also* Civil rights | |
| Civil-military relations | 322.5 |

| | |
|---|---|
| Civil procedure | 347.05 |
|   public administration | 353.44 |
| Civil rights | 323 |
|   government programs | 353.48 |
|   law | 342.085 |
|     *see Manual at* 342.085 vs. | |
|       341.48 | |
|   legal theory | 340.112 |
|   political science | 323 |
|   social theology | 201.723 |
|     Buddhism | 294.337 23 |
|     Christianity | 261.7 |
|     Hinduism | 294.517 23 |
|     Islam | 297.272 |
|     Judaism | 296.382 |
|   social welfare | 361.614 |
| Civil rights leaders | 323.092 |
| Civil rights violations | 364.132 2 |
|   law | 345.023 22 |
|   public administration | 353.46 |
| Civil rights workers | 323.092 |
| Civil service (Merit system) | 352.63 |
|   law | 342.068 |
| Civil service (Nonmilitary | |
|   government agencies) | 351 |
| Civil service examinations | 351.076 |
| | T1—076 |
| Civil service pensions | 331.252 913 51 |
|   public administration | 353.549 |
| Civil service workers | 352.63 |
|   *see also* Government workers | |
| Civil supremacy over the military | 322.5 |
| Civil unions | 306.841 |
| | T1—086 56 |
|   law | 346.016 |
| Civil war | 355.021 8 |
|   ethics | 172.1 |
|   law of nations | 341.68 |
|   social conflict | 303.64 |
|   social theology | 201.72 |
|     Buddhism | 294.337 2 |
|     Christianity | 261.7 |
|     Hinduism | 294.517 2 |
|     Judaism | 296.382 7 |
| Civil War (Angola), 1975–2000 | 967.304 2 |
| Civil War (England), 1642–1649 | 942.062 |
| Civil War (Guatemala), | |
|   1960–1996 | 972.810 52 |
| Civil War (Lebanon), 1975–1990 | 956.920 44 |
| Civil War (Nigeria), 1967–1970 | 966.905 2 |
| Civil War (Rwanda), 1994 | 967.571 043 1 |
| Civil War (Serbia), 1998–1999 | 949.710 315 |
| Civil War (Sierra Leone), | |
|   1991–2002 | 966.404 4 |

| | |
|---|---|
| Civil War (Somalia), 1991– | 967.730 53 |
| Civil War (Spain), 1936–1939 | 946.081 |
| Civil War (Sudan), 1955–1972 | 962.404 1 |
| Civil War (United States), | |
|   1861–1865 | 973.7 |
|   societies | 369.15 |
| Civilian workers | 331.79 |
|   armed forces | 355.23 |
|     management | 355.619 |
|   labor economics | 331.79 |
|     labor force | 331.119 042 |
|     labor market | 331.129 042 |
| Civilization | 909 |
|   arts | 700.458 |
| | T3C—358 |
|   Bible | 220.95 |
|   history | 909 |
|     ancient | 930 |
|     specific places | 930–990 |
|     *see also* History | |
|   literature | 808.803 58 |
|     history and criticism | 809.933 58 |
|     specific literatures | T3B—080 358 |
|     history and | |
|       criticism | T3B—093 58 |
|   painting | 758.99 |
|   primary education | 372.89 |
|   sociology | 306 |
|   *see Manual at* 306 vs. 305, | |
|     909, 930–990; *also at* 909, | |
|     930–990 vs. 910 | |
| CJD (Disease) | |
|   medicine | 616.83 |
|     *see also* Nervous system | |
|       diseases — humans | |
| Clackamas County (Or.) | T2—795 41 |
| Clackmannan (Scotland : | |
|   District) | T2—413 15 |
| Clackmannanshire | |
|   (Scotland) | T2—413 15 |
| Cladding | |
|   buildings | 698 |
|   nuclear engineering | 621.483 35 |
| Cladding metals | 671.73 |
| Cladistic analysis | 578.012 |
| Cladocera | 595.32 |
| Cladocopa | 595.33 |
|   paleozoology | 565.33 |
| Cladoselachii | 567.3 |
| Claiborne County (Miss.) | T2—762 285 |
| Claiborne County (Tenn.) | T2—768 944 |
| Claiborne Parish (La.) | T2—763 94 |
| Claiming | |
|   library acquisitions | 025.236 |

Claims (Customer relations)
  marketing management 658.812
Claims (Insurance) 368.014
Claims adjustment
  insurance 368.014
Claims against government
  public administration 352.885
Claims courts 347.04
Clairaudience 133.85
Clairvoyance 133.84
Clairvoyants 133.840 92
Clallam County (Wash.) T2—797 99
Clam shrimps 595.32
Clamming 639.44
  sports 799.254 4
Clamps 621.992
Clams 594.4
  conservation technology 639.974 4
  cooking 641.694
  fishing 639.44
  food 641.394
    commercial processing 664.94
  paleozoology 564.4
  resource economics 333.955 44
  sports clamming 799.254 4
  zoology 594.4
Clandestine publications
  bibliographies 011.56
Clanwilliam (South Africa :
  District) T2—687 31
Clare (Ireland) T2—419 3
Clare (S. Aust.) T2—942 32
Clare County (Mich.) T2—774 71
Clarendon County (S.C.) T2—757 81
Clarinet concertos 784.286 2
Clarinetists 788.620 92
Clarinets 788.62
  instrument 788.621 9
  music 788.62
  *see also* Woodwind instruments
Clarion County (Pa.) T2—748 69
Clark, Charles Joseph
  Canadian history 971.064 5
Clark, Joe
  Canadian history 971.064 5
Clark County (Ark.) T2—767 49
Clark County (Idaho) T2—796 57
Clark County (Ill.) T2—773 71
Clark County (Ind.) T2—772 185
Clark County (Kan.) T2—781 77
Clark County (Ky.) T2—769 54
Clark County (Mo.) T2—778 343
Clark County (Nev.) T2—793 13
Clark County (Ohio) T2—771 49

Clark County (S.D.) T2—783 22
Clark County (Wash.) T2—797 86
Clark County (Wis.) T2—775 28
Clarke County (Ala.) T2—761 245
Clarke County (Ga.) T2—758 18
Clarke County (Iowa) T2—777 856
Clarke County (Miss.) T2—762 673
Clarke County (Va.) T2—755 98
Clarkias 635.933 76
  botany 583.76
  floriculture 635.933 76
Class actions 347.053
Class groups (Mathematics) 512.74
Class numbers 512.74
Class reunions 371.8
Class schedules 371.242
Class size (Education) 371.251
Class struggle 305.5
  influence on crime 364.256
  Marxian theory 335.411
  theory of union role 331.880 1
Classed catalogs
  bibliography 017
  library science 025.315
Classes (Education) 371.25
  museum services 069.15
Classical Arabic language 492.7
    T6—927
Classical Arabic literature 892.7
Classical architecture 722.8
Classical conditioning 153.152 6
Classical economics 330.153
Classical education
  secondary level 373.241
Classical geometry 516.02
Classical Greek language 480
    T6—81
Classical Greek literature 880
Classical high schools 373.241
  *see also* Secondary education
Classical languages (Greek and 480
  Latin) T6—8
Classical literatures (Greek and
  Latin) 880
Classical mechanics 531
Classical music 781.68
Classical physics 530
  theory 530.14
Classical religion 292
  temples and shrines
    architecture 726.12
Classical revival 709.034 1
Classical revival architecture 724.2
Classical revival decoration 745.409 034

| | | | |
|---|---|---|---|
| Classical revival painting | 759.051 | Clay (continued) | |
| Classical revival sculpture | 735.22 | pottery | 666.42 |
| Classical statistical mechanics | 530.132 | arts | 738.12 |
| Classical typology (Psychology) | 155.262 | technology | 666.42 |
| Classicism | | sculpture material | 731.2 |
| arts | 700.414 2 | Clay County (Ala.) | T2—761 58 |
| | T3C—142 | Clay County (Ark.) | T2—767 995 |
| literature | 808.801 42 | Clay County (Fla.) | T2—759 16 |
| history and criticism | 809.914 2 | Clay County (Ga.) | T2—758 927 |
| specific literatures | T3B—080 142 | Clay County (Ill.) | T2—773 795 |
| history and | | Clay County (Ind.) | T2—772 44 |
| criticism | T3B—091 42 | Clay County (Iowa) | T2—777 153 |
| music | 780.903 3 | Clay County (Kan.) | T2—781 275 |
| Classification | 001.012 | Clay County (Ky.) | T2—769 145 |
| | T1—012 | Clay County (Minn.) | T2—776 92 |
| information science | 025.42 | Clay County (Miss.) | T2—762 945 |
| knowledge | 001.012 | Clay County (Mo.) | T2—778 16 |
| Classified advertising | 659.131 | Clay County (N.C.) | T2—756 985 |
| print media | 659.132 | Clay County (Neb.) | T2—782 357 |
| Classified catalogs | | Clay County (S.D.) | T2—783 393 |
| bibliography | 017 | Clay County (Tenn.) | T2—768 49 |
| library science | 025.315 | Clay County (Tex.) | T2—764 542 |
| Classroom discipline | 371.102 4 | Clay County (W. Va.) | T2—754 67 |
| Classroom management | 371.102 4 | Clay pigeons | 799.313 2 |
| Classroom reading programs | | Clay pots | |
| primary education | 372.427 | use in cooking | 641.589 |
| Classroom techniques | 371.3 | Clayton County (Ga.) | T2—758 432 |
| Classrooms | 371.621 | Clayton County (Iowa) | T2—777 36 |
| Clatsop County (Or.) | T2—795 46 | Clean rooms | |
| Clauses (Grammar) | 415 | safety engineering | 620.86 |
| specific languages | T4—5 | Cleaning | |
| Claves | 786.872 | pneumatic engineering | 621.54 |
| *see also* Percussion instruments | | technology | 667.1 |
| Clavichords | 786.3 | Cleaning crops | 631.56 |
| instrument | 786.319 | Cleaning house | 648.5 |
| music | 786.3 | Cleaning metals | 671.7 |
| *see also* Keyboard instruments | | Cleanliness | 613.4 |
| Clavicipitales | 579.567 | personal customs | 391.64 |
| Clavicles | | personal health | 613.4 |
| human anatomy | 611.717 | Cleansing tissues | 676.284 2 |
| Clawless otters | 599.769 | Clear-air turbulence | |
| Claws | 591.47 | transportation hazard | 363.124 12 |
| descriptive zoology | 591.47 | Clear Creek County (Colo.) | T2—788 61 |
| physiology | 573.59 | Clearance (Banking) | 332.178 |
| Clay | 553.61 | central banking | 332.113 |
| building materials | 691.4 | commercial banking service | 332.178 |
| economic geology | 553.61 | Clearfield County (Pa.) | T2—748 61 |
| materials science | 620.191 | Clearing banks | 332.12 |
| mineralogy | 549.6 | Clearing houses (Banking) | 332.12 |
| mining | 622.361 | Clearing of land | 631.61 |
| petrology | 552.5 | Clearwater County (Idaho) | T2—796 88 |
| | | Clearwater County (Minn.) | T2—776 83 |
| | | Clearwater River (B.C.) | T2—711 72 |
| | | Clearwater River (Idaho) | T2—796 85 |

| | | | |
|---|---|---|---|
| Cleavage | | Clerks regular | 255.5 |
| geology | 551.84 | church history | 271.5 |
| mineralogy | 549.121 | Clerks Regular of Somaschi | 255.54 |
| Cleburne County (Ala.) | T2—761 64 | church history | 271.54 |
| Cleburne County (Ark.) | T2—767 285 | Clerks Regular of the Mother of | |
| Cleethorpes (England : | | God | 255.57 |
| Borough) | T2—428 34 | church history | 271.57 |
| Cleft lip | | Clermont (Qld.) | T2—943 5 |
| surgery | 617.522 | Clermont County (Ohio) | T2—771 794 |
| Cleft palate | | Clermont-Ferrand (France) | T2—445 914 |
| surgery | 617.522 5 | Cleroidea | 595.763 |
| Clematises | 635.933 34 | Clethraceae | 583.66 |
| botany | 583.34 | Cleveland (England) | T2—428 5 |
| floriculture | 635.933 34 | Cleveland (Ohio) | T2—771 32 |
| Clemency | 364.65 | Cleveland, Grover | |
| law | 345.077 | United States history | 973.85 |
| penology | 364.65 | 1885–1889 | 973.85 |
| Clemmys | 597.925 7 | 1893–1897 | 973.87 |
| Cleopatra, Queen of Egypt | | Cleveland bay horse | 636.14 |
| Egyptian history | 932.021 | Cleveland County (Ark.) | T2—767 69 |
| Clerestories | | Cleveland County (N.C.) | T2—756 775 |
| Christian church architecture | 726.594 | Cleveland County (Okla.) | T2—766 37 |
| Clergy | 200.92 | Cleveland Hills (England) | T2—428 49 |
| biography | 200.92 | Clichés | 418 |
| Christian | 270.092 | dictionaries | 413.1 |
| biography | 270.092 | specific languages | T4—31 |
| specific denominations | 280 | rhetoric | 808 |
| *see Manual at* 230–280 | | specific languages | T4—8 |
| ecclesiology | 262.1 | Click beetles | 595.765 |
| occupational ethics | 241.641 | Client-server computing | 004.36 |
| pastoral theology | 253 | Client-server processing | 004.36 |
| personal religion | 248.892 | *see also* Processing modes — | |
| training | 230.071 1 | computer science | |
| occupational ethics | 174.1 | Client-server programming | 005.276 |
| religion | 205.641 | Client-server programs | 005.376 |
| role and function | 206.1 | Cliff ecology | 577.58 |
| *see also* Rabbis; Religious | | Clifford algebras | 512.57 |
| leaders | | Clifton Forge (Va.) | T2—755 816 |
| *see Manual at* 200.92 and | | Climacteric | |
| 201–209, 292–299 | | human physiology | 612.665 |
| Clergymen's wives | | Climacteric disorders | |
| Christianity | 253.22 | gynecology | 618.175 |
| *see also* Spouses of clergy — | | *see also* Female genital | |
| Christianity | | diseases — humans | |
| Clerical celibacy | | male | |
| Christianity | 253.25 | medicine | 616.693 |
| Clerical services | 651.37 | *see also* Male genital | |
| Clerihews | 808.817 | diseases — humans | |
| history and criticism | 809.17 | medicine | 618.175 |
| specific literatures | T3B—107 | Climate | 551.6 |
| individual authors | T3A—1 | biophysics | 571.49 |
| Clerks | 651.370 92 | ecology | 577.22 |
| office services | 651.37 | health | 613.11 |
| social class | 305.965 137 | influence on crime | 364.22 |

| | |
|---|---|
| Climate (continued) | |
| psychological influence | 155.915 |
| social effects | 304.25 |
| *see Manual at* 551.5 vs. 551.6 | |
| Climate control | 551.68 |
| Climate-induced illnesses | |
| medicine | 616.988 |
| *see also* Environmental | |
| diseases — humans | |
| Climate types | 551.62 |
| Climatic changes | |
| crop damage | 632.1 |
| effect on natural ecology | 577.22 |
| Climatological diseases | |
| medicine | 616.988 |
| *see also* Environmental | |
| diseases — humans | |
| Climatologists | 551.609 2 |
| Climatology | 551.6 |
| Climatotherapy | |
| medicine | 615.834 |
| Climbing plants | 582.18 |
| floriculture | 635.974 |
| Clinch County (Ga.) | T2—758 812 |
| Clinch River (Va. and | |
| Tenn.) | T2—768 73 |
| Clingfishes | 597.62 |
| Clinical chemistry | 616.075 6 |
| Clinical drug trials | 615.580 724 |
| Clinical enzymology | 616.075 6 |
| Clinical immunology | 616.079 |
| Clinical medicine | 616 |
| diagnosis | 616.075 |
| *see Manual at* 616.075 | |
| Clinical neuropsychology | 616.8 |
| Clinical psychology | 616.89 |
| Clinical trials | 615.507 24 |
| Clinics | 362.12 |
| *see also* Health care facilities | |
| Clinton (B.C.) | T2—711 72 |
| Clinton, Bill | |
| United States history | 973.929 |
| Clinton County (Ill.) | T2—773 875 |
| Clinton County (Ind.) | T2—772 553 |
| Clinton County (Iowa) | T2—777 67 |
| Clinton County (Ky.) | T2—769 653 |
| Clinton County (Mich.) | T2—774 24 |
| Clinton County (Mo.) | T2—778 155 |
| Clinton County (N.Y.) | T2—747 54 |
| Clinton County (Ohio) | T2—771 765 |
| Clinton County (Pa.) | T2—748 54 |
| Clip spot embroidery | 677.77 |

| | |
|---|---|
| Clipper ships | 387.224 |
| design | 623.812 24 |
| engineering | 623.822 4 |
| handling | 623.882 24 |
| transportation services | 387.224 |
| *see also* Ships | |
| Clippings | |
| cataloging | 025.342 |
| library treatment | 025.172 |
| Clitics | 415.92 |
| specific languages | T4—592 |
| Clive, Robert Clive, Baron | |
| Indian history | 954.029 6 |
| Cloaks | 391.46 |
| commercial technology | 687.14 |
| home sewing | 646.45 |
| *see also* Outerwear | |
| Clock towers | |
| architecture | 725.97 |
| Clockcases | |
| art | 739.3 |
| decorative arts | 749.3 |
| Clockmakers | 681.113 092 |
| Clocks | 681.113 |
| art metalwork | 739.3 |
| technology | 681.113 |
| Clockworks | 681.112 |
| Clocolan (South Africa : | |
| District) | T2—685 5 |
| Clog dancing | 793.32 |
| Clogs | 391.413 |
| commercial technology | 685.32 |
| customs | 391.413 |
| *see also* Clothing | |
| Cloisonné | |
| ceramic arts | 738.42 |
| Cloisters | |
| cathedral | |
| architecture | 726.69 |
| monastic | |
| architecture | 726.79 |
| Clonal selection | 571.964 6 |
| human immunology | 616.079 5 |
| Cloning | 571.89 |
| biotechnology | 660.65 |
| human immunology | 616.079 5 |
| human reproduction | |
| ethics | 176.22 |
| *see also* Reproduction — | |
| ethics | |
| immunology | 571.964 6 |
| plants | 575.49 |
| Clonmel (Ireland) | T2—419 25 |
| Clontarf, Battle of, 1014 | 941.501 |

Close air support (Tactics)    358.414 2
Close corporations    338.74
   law    346.066 8
   management    658.045
   *see also* Corporations
Close support aircraft    358.428 3
   engineering    623.746 3
   military equipment    358.428 3
Close-up cinematography    777.6
Close-up photography    778.324
Close-up videography    777.6
Closed-circuit television    384.556
   *see also* Television
Closed-end mutual funds    332.632 7
Closed-loop systems
   automation engineering    629.83
Closed shop    331.889 2
Closed stacks    025.81
Closet drama    808.82
   history and criticism    809.2
   specific literatures    T3B—2
   individual authors    T3A—2
Closets    643.5
Closing (Real estate)    346.043 73
Clostridium    579.364
Clostridium infections
   incidence    614.512
   medicine    616.931
   *see also* Communicable
     diseases — humans
Cloth
   ship design    623.818 97
   shipbuilding    623.820 7
Cloth covers
   bookbinding    686.343
Clothes dryers
   home economics    648.1
   manufacturing technology    683.88
Clothing    391
   armed forces    355.81
     costume    355.14
   arts    746.92
   commercial manufacturing    687
     fur    685.24
     instruments    681.767 7
     leather    685.22
   customs    391
   health    613.482
   home economics    646.3
   home sewing    646.4
   product safety    363.19
     law    344.042 35
   psychological influence    155.95

Clothing (continued)
   social welfare    361.05
   *see Manual at* 391 vs. 646.3,
     746.92
Clothing care
   home economics    646.6
Clothing construction    646.4
   commercial technology    687
   home sewing    646.4
Clothing industry    338.476 87
Clothing workers    687.092
Clotting
   blood    573.159
     human physiology    612.115
     physiology    573.159
   *see also* Cardiovascular
     system
Cloud colors    551.567
Cloud computing    004.678 2
Cloud County (Kan.)    T2—781 25
Cloud forests
   biology    578.734
   ecology    577.34
Cloud seeding    551.687 6
Clouded leopard    599.75
Clouds    551.576
   aeronautics    629.132 4
   weather modification    551.687 6
Clove (Spice)    641.338 3
   botany    583.765
   *see also* Spices
Clovers    633.32
   botany    583.74
   forage crop    633.32
Clowns    791.33
Cloze procedure
   primary education
     reading    372.472
Club cars    385.33
   engineering    625.23
   *see also* Rolling stock
Club fungi    579.597
Club games    796.35
Club mosses    587.9
   paleobotany    561.79
Clubhouse buildings
   architecture    728.4
Clubmen    367.92
Clubs    367
         T1—06
Clubs (Gymnastic equipment)    796.443
Clubwomen    367.92
Cluj (Romania : Județ)    T2—498 4

| | |
|---|---|
| Cluniacs | 255.14 |
| church history | 271.14 |
| Clupea | 597.452 |
| Clupeidae | 597.45 |
| Clupeomorpha | 597.45 |
| paleozoology | 567.45 |
| Clusiaceae | 583.624 |
| Clusium (Italy) | T2—375 68 |
| Cluster analysis | 519.53 |
| Cluster computing | 004.35 |
| Cluster headache | |
| medicine | 616.849 13 |
| *see also* Nervous system | |
| diseases — humans | |
| Clusters of stars | 523.85 |
| Clutches (Machine parts) | 621.825 |
| Clutha District (N.Z.) | T2—939 3 |
| Clwyd (Wales) | T2—429 3 |
| Clydach (Wales) | T2—429 98 |
| Clyde, Firth of (Scotland) | 551.461 337 |
| | T2—163 37 |
| Clyde, River (Scotland) | T2—414 |
| Clydebank (Scotland) | T2—414 32 |
| Clydebank (Scotland : | |
| District) | T2—414 32 |
| Clydesdale (Scotland : | |
| District) | T2—414 57 |
| Clydesdale horse | 636.15 |
| Cnemidophorus | 597.958 25 |
| Cnidaria | 593.5 |
| paleozoology | 563.5 |
| Cnidospora | 579.48 |
| Co-dependency | 362.291 3 |
| *see also* Codependency | |
| Coach horses | 636.14 |
| Coaches (Buses) | 388.342 33 |
| *see also* Buses | |
| Coaches (Railroad cars) | 385.33 |
| engineering | 625.23 |
| *see also* Rolling stock | |
| Coaches (Sports) | 796.092 |
| Coaching (Driving) | |
| recreation | 798.6 |
| Coaching (Sports) | 796.077 |
| Coaching horses | |
| recreation | 798.6 |
| Coagulants | |
| pharmacokinetics | 615.718 |

| | |
|---|---|
| Coagulation | |
| blood | 573.159 |
| human physiology | 612.115 |
| physiology | 573.159 |
| *see also* Cardiovascular | |
| system | |
| water supply treatment | 628.162 2 |
| Coahoma County (Miss.) | T2—762 44 |
| Coahuila (Mexico : State) | T2—721 4 |
| Coahuiltecan Indians | T5  979 |
| Coahuiltecan languages | 497.9 |
| | T6—979 |
| Coal | 553.24 |
| chemical engineering | 662.62 |
| economic geology | 553.24 |
| heating buildings | 697.042 |
| mining | 622.334 |
| law | 343.077 52 |
| pipeline transportation | 388.57 |
| law | 343.093 97 |
| production economics | 338.272 4 |
| prospecting | 622.182 4 |
| public administration | 354.44 |
| public utilities | 363.6 |
| law | 343.092 7 |
| resource economics | 333.822 |
| law | 346.046 822 |
| Coal County (Okla.) | T2—766 67 |
| Coal gasification | 665.772 |
| Coal mining | 622.334 |
| law | 343.077 52 |
| production economics | 338.272 4 |
| Coal oil | 665.538 3 |
| Coal slurry | 662.623 |
| pipeline transportation | 388.57 |
| law | 343.093 97 |
| technology | 662.624 |
| technology | 662.623 |
| Coal tar | 547.82 |
| Coal tar chemicals | 661.803 |
| Coalition military forces | 355.356 |
| Coalition War, 1690–1697 | 949.204 |
| Coarse fishing (Sports) | 799.11 |
| Coast artillery | 358.168 2 |
| engineering | 623.417 |
| military equipment | 358.168 2 |
| Coast artillery forces | 358.16 |
| Coast guard | 363.286 |
| military service | 359.97 |
| police services | 363.286 |

| | |
|---|---|
| Coast guard ships | 363.286 |
| design | 623.812 63 |
| engineering | 623.826 3 |
| military service | 359.978 3 |
| police services | 363.286 |
| Coast Mountains (B.C.) | T2—711 1 |
| Coast Province (Kenya) | T2—676 23 |
| Coast Ranges | T2—795 1 |
| California | T2—794 1 |
| Oregon | T2—795 1 |
| Washington | T2—797 9 |
| Coast Region (Tanzania) | T2—678 23 |
| Coastal defense | 355.45 |
| Coastal engineering | 627.58 |
| Coastal lands | 551.457 |
| | T2—146 |
| Coastal pools | 551.461 8 |
| | T2—168 |
| Coastal regions | 551.457 |
| | T2—146 |
| Coastal wetlands | |
| biology | 578.769 |
| ecology | 577.69 |
| Coastal zones | 551.457 |
| | T2—146 |
| Coasting | |
| snow sports | 796.95 |
| Coasts | 551.457 |
| | T2—146 |
| biology | 578.751 |
| ecology | 577.51 |
| geography | 910.914 6 |
| geomorphology | 551.457 |
| law | 346.046 917 |
| physical geography | 910.021 46 |
| recreational resources | 333.784 |
| resource economics | 333.917 |
| Coastwise routes | 387.524 |
| Coatbridge (Scotland) | T2—414 52 |
| Coated paper | 676.283 |
| Coaticook (Quebec : Regional County Municipality) | T2—714 67 |
| Coating | 667.9 |
| latex | 678.527 |
| metals | 671.73 |
| paper | 676.235 |
| Coatings | 667.9 |
| Coatis | 599.763 |
| Coats | 391.46 |
| commercial technology | 687.14 |
| indoor garments | 687.113 |
| outdoor garments | 687.14 |
| Coats (continued) | |
| customs | 391.46 |
| indoor garments | 391.473 |
| outdoor garments | 391.46 |
| home economics | 646.3 |
| home sewing | 646.45 |
| indoor garments | 646.433 |
| outdoor garments | 646.45 |
| *see also* Clothing | |
| Coats Island (Nunavut) | T2—719 58 |
| Coats of arms | 929.6 |
| Cob (Building material) | 693.22 |
| Cobalt | 669.733 |
| chemical engineering | 661.062 3 |
| chemistry | 546.623 |
| economic geology | 553.483 |
| materials science | 620.189 33 |
| metallography | 669.957 33 |
| metallurgy | 669.733 |
| metalworking | 673.733 |
| mining | 622.348 3 |
| organic chemistry | 547.056 23 |
| applied | 661.895 |
| physical metallurgy | 669.967 33 |
| *see also* Chemicals; Metals | |
| Cobalt soaps | 668.125 |
| Cobar (N.S.W.) | T2—944 9 |
| Cobb County (Ga.) | T2—758 245 |
| Cobbling | 685.31 |
| Cobordism theory | 514.72 |
| Cobourg Peninsula National Park (N.T.) | T2—942 95 |
| Cobras | 597.964 2 |
| Coburg (Germany) | T2—433 11 |
| Cocaine abuse | 362.298 |
| medicine | 616.864 7 |
| personal health | 613.84 |
| social welfare | 362.298 |
| *see also* Substance abuse | |
| Cocas (Plants) | 583.79 |
| Coccidiosis | |
| incidence | 614.53 |
| medicine | 616.936 |
| *see also* Communicable diseases — humans | |
| Coccinellidae | 595.769 |
| Cochabamba (Bolivia : Dept.) | T2—842 3 |
| Cochineal dyes | 667.26 |
| Cochise County (Ariz.) | T2—791 53 |
| Cochlear diseases | |
| medicine | 617.882 2 |
| *see also* Ear diseases — humans | |

| | |
|---|---|
| Cochleas | |
| human anatomy | 611.85 |
| human physiology | 612.858 |
| medicine | 617.882 2 |
| Cochran County (Tex.) | T2—764 845 |
| Cochrane (Ont. : District) | T2—713 142 |
| Cockatiels | 636.686 56 |
| animal husbandry | 636.686 56 |
| zoology | 598.71 |
| Cockatoos | 598.71 |
| animal husbandry | 636.686 5 |
| Cocke County (Tenn.) | T2—768 895 |
| Cockfighting | 791.8 |
| Cockney dialect | 427.942 1 |
| | T6—21 |
| Cockroaches | 595.728 |
| control technology | 628.965 7 |
| Cocks (Mechanisms) | 621.84 |
| Cocksfoot (Grass) | 633.22 |
| botany | 584.9 |
| Cocktails | 641.874 |
| commercial processing | 663.1 |
| Coclé (Panama : Province) | T2—728 721 |
| Cocoa | 641.337 4 |
| beverage | 641.337 4 |
| commercial processing | 663.92 |
| home preparation | 641.877 |
| cooking with | 641.637 4 |
| food | 641.337 4 |
| Cocoa butter | 665.354 |
| chemical technology | 665.354 |
| cooking with | 641.637 4 |
| food | 641.337 4 |
| food technology | 664.3 |
| Coconino County (Ariz.) | T2—791 33 |
| Coconucos Range | |
| (Colombia) | T2—861 53 |
| Coconut milk | |
| commercial processing | 663.64 |
| Coconut oil | 665.355 |
| Coconuts | 641.346 1 |
| botany | 584.5 |
| commercial processing | 664.804 61 |
| cooking | 641.646 1 |
| food | 641.346 1 |
| food crop | 634.61 |
| textiles | 677.18 |
| *see also* Textiles | |
| Cocoons | 595.714 6 |
| Cocoparra National Park | |
| (N.S.W.) | T2—944 8 |
| Cocos (Keeling) Islands | 969.9 |
| | T2—699 |
| Cocuy National Park | |
| (Colombia) | T2—861 44 |
| Cocuy Range (Colombia) | T2—861 44 |
| Cod-liver oil | |
| pharmacology | 615.34 |
| COD mail | 383.184 |
| *see also* Postal service | |
| CODASYL databases | |
| computer science | 005.754 |
| Code generators | |
| computer science | 005.45 |
| Code of Manu | 294.592 6 |
| Code telegraphy | 384.14 |
| wireless | 384.524 |
| *see also* Telegraphy | |
| Codependency | 362.291 3 |
| alcoholism | 362.292 3 |
| medicine | 616.861 9 |
| social welfare | 362.292 3 |
| devotional literature | 204.32 |
| Christianity | 242.4 |
| medicine | 616.869 |
| pastoral theology | 206.1 |
| Christianity | 259.429 |
| religious guidance | 204.42 |
| Christianity | 248.862 9 |
| social theology | 201.762 29 |
| Christianity | 261.832 29 |
| social welfare | 362.291 3 |
| Codes (Law) | 348.023 |
| United States | 348.732 3 |
| Codes of conduct | |
| moral theology | 205 |
| Christianity | 241.5 |
| Judaism | 296.36 |
| Codex iuris canonici (1917) | 262.93 |
| Codex iuris canonici (1983) | 262.94 |
| Codiaeum | 583.69 |
| Codiales | 579.835 |
| Codification | 348.004 |
| law of nations | 341.026 7 |
| United States | 348.730 4 |
| Coding data | 005.72 |
| Coding of programs | 005.13 |
| Coding theory | 003.54 |
| | T1—011 54 |
| Codington County (S.D.) | T2—783 23 |
| Codling moth | |
| agricultural pests | 634.049 78 |
| Codons | 572.86 |
| Cods | 641.392 |
| conservation technology | 639.977 633 |
| cooking | 641.692 |
| food | 641.392 |

Cods (continued)
   resource economics — 333.956 633
   zoology — 597.633
Coeducation — 371.822
Coefficient of expansion — 536.41
Coefficient of restitution — 531.382
Coelacanths — 597.39
Coelenterata — 593.5
   paleozoology — 563.5
Coelesyria (Lebanon) — T2—394 4
Coelomycetes — 579.55
Coelophysis — 567.912
Coenopteridales — 561.73
Coenzymes — 572.7
   *see also* Enzymes
Coercion
   social control — 303.36
Coeur d'Alene language — 497.943
   — T6—979 43
Coeur d'Alene Mountains
   (Idaho and Mont.) — T2—796 91
Coevolution — 576.87
Cofactors — 572.7
Coffee — 641.337 3
   agricultural economics — 338.173 73
   agriculture — 633.73
   botany — 583.93
   commercial processing
      economics — 338.476 639 3
      technology — 663.93
   cooking with — 641.637 3
   food — 641.337 3
   home preparation — 641.877
Coffee cakes — 641.865 9
   commercial processing — 664.752 5
   home preparation — 641.865 9
Coffee County (Ala.) — T2—761 34
Coffee County (Ga.) — T2—758 823
Coffee County (Tenn.) — T2—768 64
Coffee grounds
   divination — 133.324 4
Coffee substitutes — 641.877
   commercial processing — 663.97
   home preparation — 641.877
Coffeehouses — 647.95
   *see also* Eating places
Cofferdams — 624.157
Coffey County (Kan.) — T2—781 645
Coffin flies — 595.774
Coffs Harbour (N.S.W.) — T2—944 3
Cofimvaba (South Africa :
   District) — T2—687 58

Cog railroads — 385.6
   engineering — 625.33
   transportation services — 385.6
Cogeneration — 333.793
   law — 343.092 9
   resource economics — 333.793
   steam — 621.199
Cognac — 641.253
   commercial processing — 663.53
Cognition — 153
   epistemology — 121
   psychology — 153
Cognition disorders
   medicine — 616.8
      *see also* Nervous system
         diseases — humans
Cognitive neuroscience — 612.823 3
Cognitive psychology — 153
   adolescents — 155.513
   children — 155.413
   education — 370.152
   late adulthood — 155.671 3
   men — 155.332 3
   women — 155.333 3
   *see Manual at* 153.4
Cognitive reading methods
   primary education — 372.474
Cognitive science — 153
   human physiology — 612.823 3
   *see Manual at* 006.3 vs. 153
Cognitive therapy
   pediatrics — 618.928 914 25
   psychiatry — 616.891 425
Cohabitation — 306.841
   — T1—086 56
   customs — 392.6
   law — 346.016
Coherent optics — 535.2
Cohesion
   chemical engineering — 660.293
   chemistry — 541.33
Cohomology theory — 514.23
Cohorts (Military units) — 355.31
Coimbra (Portugal :
   District) — T2—469 35
Coimbra da Luz, Carlos
   Brazilian history — 981.062
Coinage
   law — 343.032
   public revenue — 336.16
Coins — 332.404 2
   investment economics — 332.63
   monetary economics — 332.404 2
   numismatics — 737.4

Coir
textiles 677.18
*see also* Textiles
Cojedes (Venezuela : State) T2—874 6
Coke
chemical engineering 662.72
heating buildings 697.042
Coke County (Tex.) T2—764 723
Coke gases 665.772
Coke-oven gas 665.772
Cola
alkaloid crop 633.76
beverage 641.337 6
commercial processing 663.62
Colac (Vic.) T2—945 7
Colbert County (Ala.) T2—761 915
Colchagua (Chile :
Province) T2—833 3
Colchester (England :
Borough) T2—426 723
Colchester (N.S. : County) T2—716 12
Colchis 939.538
T2—395 38
Cold (Disease)
medicine 616.205
*see also* Respiratory tract
diseases — humans
Cold (Low temperature) 536.56
biophysics 571.464
humans 612.014 465
Cold adaptation 578.42
Cold-blooded vertebrates 597
culture 639.3
paleozoology 567
Cold climate
health 613.111
Cold dishes
cooking 641.79
Cold frames
gardening 635.048 3
manufacturing technology 681.763 1
Cold-molding glass powder 666.126
Cold sores
medicine 616.522
*see also* Skin diseases —
humans
Cold-storing foods 664.028 52
commercial preservation 664.028 52
home preservation 641.452
Cold weather
health 613.111
Cold-weather cooking 641.591 1

Cold-weather diseases
medicine 616.988 1
*see also* Environmental
diseases — humans
Cold-weather photography 778.75
Cold-working operations
metals 671.3
Coldwater River (B.C.) T2—711 72
Cole County (Mo.) T2—778 55
Coleman County (Tex.) T2—764 725
Colemanite
mineralogy 549.735
Coleoidea 594.5
Coleoptera 595.76
paleozoology 565.76
Coleraine (Northern
Ireland : Borough) T2—416 27
Coles County (Ill.) T2—773 72
Colesberg (South Africa :
District) T2—687 13
Colfax County (N.M.) T2—789 22
Colfax County (Neb.) T2—782 532
Colic
abdominal disorders 617.55
pediatrics 618.920 975 5
Coligny (South Africa :
District) T2—682 44
Coliiformes 598.75
paleozoology 568.7
Colima (Mexico : State) T2—723 6
Colinus 598.627 3
Colitis
medicine 616.344 7
*see also* Digestive system
diseases — humans
Collaborative indexing 025.487
Collaborative tagging 025.487
Collage 702.812
Collage painting 751.493
Collagen 572.67
biochemistry 572.67
human histology 611.018 2
medicine 616.77
*see also* Musculoskeletal
system; Proteins
Collagen diseases
medicine 616.77
*see also* Musculoskeletal
diseases — humans
Collards 641.353 47
cooking 641.653 47
food 641.353 47
garden crop 635.347

Collateral kinsmen 306.87
 T1—085
Collect-on-delivery mail 383.184
 *see also* Postal service
Collected biography 920
 T1—092 2
 *see Manual at* T1—0922;
  *also at* T1—0922 vs.
  T1—093–099; *also at*
  920.008 vs. 305–306, 362;
  *also at* 920.009, 920.03–.09
  vs. 909.09, 909.1–.8,
  930–990
Collectibles T1—075
 *see Manual at* 745.1
Collecting 069.4
 T1—075
 museology 069.4
 recreation 790.132
Collecting of accounts
 law 346.077
 management 658.88
Collection analysis
 library science 025.21
Collection development
 library science 025.21
Collection maintenance
 library operations 025.8
 library science 025.21
Collection management
 library science 025.21
Collections 069.5
 description T1—074
 fine arts 708
  temporary 707.4
  *see Manual at* 704.9 and
   753–758
 literature 808.8
  specific literatures T3B—08
  *see Manual at* T3B—08
   and T3B—09
  *see Manual at* 808.8
 museology 069.5
 of abstracts 080
  brief abstracts 011
 of texts 080
  *see Manual at* 080 vs. 800;
   *also at* 081–089
 preparation T1—075
Collective bargaining 331.89
 economics 331.89
 law 344.018 9
 personnel management 658.315 4
  public administration 352.68

Collective bargaining (continued)
 public administration 354.97
 women workers 331.479
Collective security 327.116
Collective settlements 307.77
Collectivism 335
 economics 335
 political ideology 320.53
 *see Manual at* 335 vs. 306.345,
  320.53
College administration 378.101
College administrators
 biography 378.009 2
 role and function 378.111
College admissions 378.161
College applications 378.161 6
College buildings 378.196
 architecture 727.3
 construction 690.73
 education 378.196
 institutional housekeeping 647.993
 interior decoration 747.873
College costs 378.38
College dropouts 378.169 13
College education 378
 *see also* Higher education
College enrollment 378.161 9
College entrance examinations 378.166 2
College entrance requirements 378.161 7
College extension 378.175
College graduates
 choice of vocation 331.702 35
 labor force 331.114 45
 social group 305.55
 unemployment 331.137 804
College-level accounting 657.044
College-level examinations 378.166 2
College libraries 027.7
 *see also* Academic libraries
College majors 378.241
College presidents
 biography 378.009 2
 role and function 378.111
College presses
 bibliographies of publications 011.54
 publishing 070.594
College readers (Reading
 comprehension textbooks)
 applied linguistics 418
 specific languages T4—86
College readers (Rhetoric
 textbooks) 808
 specific languages 808.04

| | |
|---|---|
| College sports | 796.043 |
| *see Manual at* 796.08 vs. 796.04 | |
| College students | |
| guides to religious life | |
| Christianity | 248.834 |
| pastoral care | |
| Christianity | 259.24 |
| College teachers | 378.12 |
| College teaching | 378.125 |
| College trustees | 378.101 1 |
| Colleges | 378.154 2 |
| | T1—071 1 |
| area planning | 711.57 |
| liability | 344.075 |
| *see also* Higher education | |
| Colleges without walls | 378.03 |
| *see also* Higher education | |
| Collembola | 595.725 |
| Colleton County (S.C.) | T2—757 95 |
| Collie (W.A.) | T2—941 2 |
| Collier County (Fla.) | T2—759 44 |
| Collies | 636.737 4 |
| Colligative properties | |
| chemical engineering | 660.294 15 |
| chemistry | 541.341 5 |
| Collin County (Tex.) | T2—764 556 |
| Collines-de-l'Outaouais | |
| (Quebec) | T2—714 223 |
| Collingsworth County | |
| (Tex.) | T2—764 831 |
| Collision prevention | |
| seamanship | 623.888 4 |
| Collisions (Physics) | |
| nuclear particles | 539.757 |
| solid-state physics | 530.416 |
| Colloid chemistry | 541.345 |
| applied | 660.294 5 |
| specific elements and | |
| compounds | 546 |
| Colloidal fuels | 662.82 |
| Colloids | 541.345 |
| specific elements and | |
| compounds | 546 |
| Colloquial language | 418 |
| specific languages | T4—8 |
| Collor de Mello, Fernando | |
| Affonso | |
| Brazilian history | 981.064 |
| Collotype printing | 686.232 5 |
| Collusion | 364.134 |
| law | 345.023 4 |
| Cologne (Germany) | T2—435 514 |

| | |
|---|---|
| Cologne (Germany : Regierungsbezirk) | T2—435 51 |
| Colom Caballeros, Álvaro | |
| Guatemalan history | 972.810 534 |
| Colombia | 986.1 |
| | T2—861 |
| Panamanian history | 972.870 3 |
| Colombian literature | 860 |
| Colombians | T5—688 61 |
| Colombo (Sri Lanka) | T2—549 3 |
| Colon | 573.379 |
| biology | 573.379 |
| human anatomy | 611.347 |
| human physiology | 612.36 |
| medicine | 616.34 |
| surgery | 617.554 7 |
| *see also* Digestive system | |
| Colón (Honduras : Dept.) | T2—728 313 |
| Colón (Panama : Province) | T2—728 732 |
| Colón, Archipiélago de | T2—866 5 |
| Colon cancer | |
| incidence | 614.599 943 47 |
| medicine | 616.994 347 |
| *see also* Cancer — humans | |
| Colon Classification | 025.435 |
| Colonia (Uruguay) | T2—895 11 |
| Colonial architecture | 724.1 |
| Colonial Heights (Va.) | T2—755 595 |
| Colonial military forces | 355.352 |
| Colonial Phoenician architecture | 722.32 |
| Colonialism | 325.3 |
| Colonic diseases | |
| medicine | 616.34 |
| *see also* Digestive system diseases — humans | |
| Colonies (Territories) | 321.08 |
| *see also* Non-self-governing territories | |
| Colonization | 325.3 |
| Colonnades | 721.2 |
| architecture | 721.2 |
| construction | 690.12 |
| Colonnettes | 721.3 |
| architecture | 721.3 |
| construction | 690.13 |
| Color | 535.6 |
| animal physiology | 573.5 |
| animals | 591.472 |
| arts | 701.85 |
| biological adaptation | 578.47 |
| drawing | 741.018 |
| interior decoration | 747.94 |
| mineralogy | 549.125 |
| painting | 752 |

Color (continued)
  physics — 535.6
  plants — 581.47
  religious significance — 203.7
    Christianity — 246.6
    *see also* Symbolism —
      religious significance
  technology — 667
  therapeutics — 615.831 2
Color (Sound) — 781.234
Color blindness
  incidence — 614.599 7
  ophthalmology — 617.759
  *see also* Eye diseases —
    humans
Color materials
  pottery — 666.42
    arts — 738.12
    technology — 666.42
Color perception
  psychology — 152.145
Color photography — 778.6
Color plants
  floriculture — 635.968
Color printing — 686.230 42
Color television — 621.388 04
Color therapy — 615.831 2
Color vision defects
  ophthalmology — 617.759
  *see also* Eye diseases —
    humans
Colorado — 978.8
    T2—788
Colorado County (Tex.) — T2—764 253
Colorado Desert (Calif. and
  Mexico) — T2—794 99
Colorado Plateau — T2—791 3
  Arizona — T2—791 3
  Colorado — T2—788 1
  Utah — T2—792 5
Colorado River (Colo.-
  Mexico) — T2—791 3
  Arizona — T2—791 3
  Colorado — T2—788 17
  Utah — T2—792 5
Colorado River (Tex.) — T2—764
Colorado Springs (Colo.) — T2—788 56
Colorado tick fever
  incidence — 614.588
  medicine — 616.918
  *see also* Communicable
    diseases — humans
Colorimetry — 543.55
Coloring oils and gases — 665.028 3

Coloring paper — 676.234
Colorless sulfur bacteria — 579.32
Colors (Flags) — 929.92
  armed forces — 355.15
Colossians (Biblical book) — 227.7
Colostomy — 617.554 7
Colquitt County (Ga.) — T2—758 975
Colubridae — 597.962
Colubroidea — 597.96
Colugos — 599.33
Columbia (S.C.) — T2—757 71
Columbia County (Ark.) — T2—767 59
Columbia County (Fla.) — T2—759 83
Columbia County (Ga.) — T2—758 635
Columbia County (N.Y.) — T2—747 39
Columbia County (Or.) — T2—795 47
Columbia County (Pa.) — T2—748 38
Columbia County (Wash.) — T2—797 46
Columbia County (Wis.) — T2—775 81
Columbia River — T2—797
  British Columbia — T2—711 6
  Oregon — T2—795 4
  Washington — T2—797
Columbia-Shuswap (B.C.) — T2—711 68
Columbiana County (Ohio) — T2—771 63
Columbiformes — 598.65
  paleozoology — 568.6
Columbines — 635.933 34
  botany — 583.34
  floriculture — 635.933 34
Columbium — 669.79
  chemistry — 546.524
  *see also* Chemicals; Niobium
Columbus (Ohio) — T2—771 57
Columbus, Christopher
  North American history — 970.015
  South American history — 980.013
Columbus County (N.C.) — T2—756 31
Columnar epithelia
  human histology — 611.018 7
Columns — 721.3
  architecture — 721.3
  construction — 690.13
  structural engineering — 624.177 25
    concrete — 624.183 425
Colusa County (Calif.) — T2—794 33
Colville Lake (N.W.T.) — T2—719 3
Colwyn (Wales) — T2—429 27
Colwyn Bay (Wales) — T2—429 27
Colydiidea — 595.769
Colymbiformes — 598.44
COM devices — 004.77
  manufacturing technology — 681.6

Coma
  medicine — 616.849
  *see also* Nervous system
    diseases — humans
Comal County (Tex.) — T2—764 887
Comanche County (Kan.) — T2—781 79
Comanche County (Okla.) — T2—766 48
Comanche County (Tex.) — T2—764 554
Comanche Indians — T5—974 572
Comanche language — 497.457 2
  — T6—974 572
Comayagua (Honduras :
  Dept.) — T2—728 372
Comb jellies — 593.8
Combat — 355.4
Combat aircraft — 358.418 3
  engineering — 623.746
  military equipment — 358.418 3
Combat disorders
  medicine — 616.852 12
  *see also* Mental disorders
Combat fatigue
  medicine — 616.852 12
  *see also* Mental disorders
Combat groups (Air force) — 358.413 1
Combat readiness — 355.033 2
Combat sports — 796.8
Combat squadrons (Air force) — 358.413 1
Combat units — 355.31
Combat vehicles — 355.83
  engineering — 623.74
  military equipment — 355.83
Combat zones
  living conditions — 355.129 4
Combatants
  law — 343.01
  law of war — 341.67
Combination of grades — 371.25
Combinations (Enterprises) — 338.8
  accounting — 657.96
  economics — 338.8
  law — 346.065
  management — 658.046
    initiation — 658.114 6
  *see also* International
    enterprises
  *see Manual at* 658.04 vs.
    658.114, 658.402
Combinations (Mathematics) — 511.64
Combinatorial analysis — 511.6
Combinatorial geometry — 516.13
Combinatorial optimization — 519.64
Combinatorial probabilities — 519.2
Combinatorial set theory — 511.322

Combinatorial topology — 514.22
Combinatorics — 511.6
Combinatory logic — 511.3
Combined operations (Armed
  forces) — 355.46
Combined sewers — 363.728 493
  social services — 363.728 493
  technology — 628.214
  *see also* Sewage treatment
Combines (Machines) — 633.104 5
  manufacturing technology — 681.763 1
Combing textiles — 677.028 21
  arts — 746.11
  manufacturing technology — 677.028 21
Combretaceae — 583.76
Combs — 646.724
  customs — 391.44
  *see also* Accessories
    (Clothing)
  manufacturing technology — 688.5
  personal appearance — 646.724
Combustion — 541.361
  chemical engineering — 660.296 1
  chemistry — 541.361
  diesel engines — 621.436 1
  heat engineering — 621.402 3
Combustion gases
  ecology — 577.276
  human toxicology — 615.91
  pollution — 363.738 7
  pollution technology — 628.532
  toxicology — 571.956
COMECON (Economic
  organization) — 341.242 7
  international commerce — 382.914 7
  international economics — 337.147
  law of nations — 341.242 7
Comedians — 792.702 809 2
Comedies (Drama) — 792.23
  literature — 808.825 23
    history and criticism — 809.252 3
    specific literatures — T3B—205 23
      individual authors — T3A—2
  motion pictures — 791.436 17
  radio programs — 791.446 17
  stage presentation — 792.23
  television programs — 791.456 17
Comedy
  arts — T3C—17
  literature — 808.801 7
    history and criticism — 809.917
    specific literatures — T3B—080 17
      history and
        criticism — T3B—091 7

| | | | |
|---|---|---|---|
| Comets | 523.6 | Commandments | |
| | T2—993 | Jewish law | 296.18 |
| Comfort equipment | | moral theology | 205 |
| aircraft | 629.134 42 | Christianity | 241.5 |
| automobile | 629.277 | Judaism | 296.36 |
| vehicles | 629.040 289 | Commando raids | 355.422 |
| Comfort stations | 363.729 4 | Commandos (Armed forces) | 356.167 |
| technology | 628.45 | Commelinales | 584.86 |
| *see also* Sanitation | | Commelinidae | 584.8 |
| Comfreys | 583.94 | Commemorations | 394.2 |
| floriculture | 635.933 94 | Holocaust, 1933–1945 | 940.531 862 |
| Comic books | 741.5 | *see also* Celebrations | |
| drawing | 741.51 | Commemorative medals | |
| genres | | numismatics | 737.222 |
| history, criticism, techniques | 741.53 | Commemorative stamps | 769.563 |
| geographic treatment | 741.593–.599 | Commencements | 371.291 2 |
| *see Manual at* 741.593–.599 | | customs | 394.2 |
| and 741.5693–.5699 | | Commensalism | 577.852 |
| *see Manual at* 741.5; *also at* | | Commentaries | |
| 741.56 | | journalism | 070.442 |
| Comic strips | 741.56 | Commerce | 381 |
| drawing | 741.51 | accounting | 657.839 |
| genres | | agent of social change | 303.482 |
| history, criticism, techniques | 741.53 | arts | 700.455 3 |
| geographic treatment | 741.569 3–.569 9 | | T3C—355 3 |
| *see Manual at* 741.593–.599 | | energy economics | 333.796 89 |
| and 741.5693–.5699 | | ethics | 174.4 |
| journalism | 070.444 | law | 343.08 |
| *see Manual at* 741.5; *also at* | | *see Manual at* 343.078 vs. | |
| 741.56 | | 343.08 | |
| Comic style | | literature | 808.803 553 |
| arts | T3C—17 | history and criticism | 809.933 553 |
| literature | 808.801 7 | specific literatures | T3B—080 355 3 |
| history and criticism | 809.917 | history and | |
| specific literatures | T3B—080 17 | criticism | T3B—093 553 |
| history and | | public administration | 354.73 |
| criticism | T3B—091 7 | sociology | 306.34 |
| Comics (Comic books) | 741.5 | *see Manual at* 380 | |
| Comics (Comic strips) | 741.56 | Commercial air conditioning | 697.931 6 |
| *see also* Comic strips | | Commercial airplanes | 387.733 404 23 |
| Cominform | 324.175 | engineering | 629.133 340 423 |
| Coming-of-age customs | 392.15 | piloting | 629.132 521 6 |
| etiquette | 395.24 | transportation services | 387.733 404 23 |
| Commagene | T2—393 6 | *see also* Aircraft | |
| Command and control systems | | Commercial areas | 307.333 |
| (Military) | 355.330 41 | area planning | 711.552 2 |
| Command economies | 330.124 | community sociology | 307.333 |
| Command functions (Armed | | land economics | 333.77 |
| forces) | 355.330 41 | Commercial art | 741.6 |
| Commandeering military | | Commercial artists | 741.609 2 |
| resources | 355.28 | Commercial aviation | 387.7 |
| Commander Islands | | *see also* Air transportation | |
| (Russia) | T2—577 | | |

| | |
|---|---|
| Commercial banks | 332.12 |
|   international operations | 332.15 |
|   law | 346.082 12 |
|   services | 332.17 |
|   *see also* Banks (Finance) | |
| Commercial bookbinding | 686.3 |
| Commercial buildings | |
|   architecture | 725.2 |
|   construction | 690.52 |
|   institutional housekeeping | 647.962 |
|   sale and rental | 333.338 7 |
|   theft from | 364.162 3 |
|     law | 345.026 23 |
| Commercial catalogs | 381.029 |
| | T1—029 |
|   *see Manual at* T1—025 vs. | |
|     T1—029; *also at* T1—074 | |
|     vs. T1—029 | |
| Commercial circulars | 381.029 |
| Commercial credit | 332.742 |
| Commercial crimes | 364.168 |
|   law | 345.026 8 |
| Commercial fishing | 338.372 7 |
|   economics | 338.372 7 |
|   technology | 639.2 |
|   *see also* Fisheries | |
| Commercial gardening | |
|   economics | 338.175 |
|   technology | 635 |
| Commercial general liability | |
|   insurance | 368.56 |
| Commercial insurance | 368.094 |
| Commercial land use | 333.77 |
|   community sociology | 307.333 |
|   economics | 333.77 |
| Commercial languages | 401.3 |
| Commercial law | 346.07 |
| Commercial leases | |
|   accounting | 657.75 |
|   buildings | 333.338 75 |
|   industrial lands | 333.336 5 |
|   law | 346.043 462 |
|   real property and equipment | |
|     financial management | 658.152 42 |
| Commercial liability insurance | 368.56 |
| Commercial miscellany | 381.029 |
| | T1—029 |
| Commercial multi-peril insurance | 368.094 |
| Commercial paper | 332.77 |
|   exchange medium | 332.55 |
| Commercial policy | 381.3 |
|   American Revolution cause | 973.311 2 |
|   international commerce | 382.3 |

| | |
|---|---|
| Commercial property | 333.77 |
|   taxation | 336.225 |
| Commercial property insurance | 368.12 |
| Commercial publishers | 070.592 |
| Commercial revenues | |
|   public finance | 336.1 |
| Commercial vehicles | |
|   (Automotive) | 388.34 |
|   engineering | 629.22 |
|   transportation services | 388.34 |
|   *see also* Automotive vehicles | |
| Commercials | 659.14 |
|   broadcast advertising | 659.14 |
|   radio performances | 791.443 |
|   television performances | 791.453 |
| Commewijne (Suriname : | |
|   District)    T2—883 7 | |
| Commission government | |
|   cities | 320.854 |
| Commissioned officers | 355.009 2 |
|   role and function | 355.332 |
| Commissioning | |
|   military personnel | 355.223 6 |
| Commissions (Governing boards) | 352.25 |
|   libraries | 021.82 |
| Committees | 302.34 |
|   legislative bodies | 328.365 |
|   social psychology | 302.34 |
| Commodities | 338.02 |
|   investment economics | 332.632 8 |
|   law | 346.092 2 |
|   production | 338.02 |
|   speculation | 332.632 8 |
| Commodity brokers | 332.62 |
|   public administration | 354.88 |
| Commodity exchanges | 332.644 |
|   architecture | 725.25 |
|   law | 343.08 |
|   public administration | 354.88 |
| Commodity futures | 332.632 8 |
| Commodity futures markets | 332.644 |
| Commodity options | 332.632 8 |
| Commodity options markets | 332.644 |
| Commodity standards (Money) | 332.42 |
| Commodores | 359.009 2 |
|   role and function | 359.331 |
| Common adder | 597.963 6 |
| Common beans | |
|   commercial processing | 664.805 652 |
|   field crop | 633.372 |
|   garden crop | 635.652 |
| Common carp | 641.392 |
|   *see also* Carp | |

Common carriers — 388.041
  law — 343.093
  sanitation services — 363.729 3
    public administration — 353.94
  truck — 388.324 3
  *see also* Freight services;
    Passenger services
Common cold
  medicine — 616.205
  *see also* Respiratory tract
    diseases — humans
Common dolphin — 599.532
Common herring — 597.452
Common lands — 333.2
  landscape architecture — 712.5
Common law — 340.57
*see Manual at* 340, 342–347 vs.
  340.57
Common-law marriage — 306.841
                T1—086 56
  law — 346.016
Common lectionary — 264.34
  preaching — 251.6
Common Market — 341.242 2
*see also* European Union
Common mice — 599.353
Common of the mass — 264.36
  music — 782.323 2
    choral and mixed voices — 782.532 32
    single voices — 783.093 232
Common partridge — 598.623 2
Common people
  customs — 390.24
  dress — 391.024
Common quail — 598.627 2
Common rats — 599.352
Common Slavic language — 491.8
                T6—918
Common stocks — 332.632 2
  speculation — 332.632 28
Common Worship — 264.03
Commons
  land economics — 333.2
  landscape architecture — 712.5
Commonwealth and Protectorate
  (Great Britain) — 941.063
Commonwealth of Independent — 947.086
  States — T2—47
Commonwealth of Nations — T2—171 241
Commonwealth of the
  Northern Mariana
  Islands — T2—967
Communal land — 333.2
Communal living — 307.774

Communalism — 302.14
Communauté régionale de
  l'Outaouais (Quebec) — T2—714 221
Communes — 307.774
  production economics — 338.7
Communicable diseases — 571.98
  agriculture — 632.3
  animals — 571.981
    veterinary medicine — 636.089 69
  biology — 571.98
  humans — 362.196 9
    geriatrics — 618.976 9
    law — 344.043 69
    medicine — 616.9
    nursing — 616.904 231
    pediatrics — 618.929
    pregnancy complications
      obstetrics — 618.36
    social services — 362.196 9
      public administration — 353.63
  plants — 571.982
    agriculture — 632.3
Communication — 302.2
                T1—014
  animals — 591.59
    physiology — 573.92
  ethics — 175
    religion — 205.65
      Christianity — 241.65
  management — 658.45
    military administration — 355.688 4
    public administration — 352.384
    *see Manual at* 658.45 vs.
      651.7, 808.06665
  office services — 651.7
    *see Manual at* 658.45 vs.
      651.7, 808.06665
  psychology — 153.6
  sociology — 302.2
Communication disorders — 362.196 855
  geriatrics — 618.976 855
  incidence — 614.598 55
  medicine — 616.855
  pediatrics — 618.928 55
  social services — 362.196 855
  special education — 371.914
Communication in management — 658.45
*see also* Communication —
  management
Communication in marketing
  management — 658.802
Communication in teaching — 371.102 2
Communication skills
  primary education — 372.6

| | |
|---|---|
| Communications | 384 |
| arts | T3C—355 8 |
| computer science | 004.6 |
| *see also* Computer communications | |
| engineering | 621.382 |
| *see also* Communications engineering | |
| law | 343.099 |
| literature | 808.803 558 |
| history and criticism | 809.933 558 |
| military science | 358.24 |
| air forces | 358.46 |
| land forces | 358.24 |
| naval forces | 359.983 |
| police services | 363.24 |
| public administration | 354.75 |
| social effects | 303.483 3 |
| *see Manual at* 380 | |
| Communications engineering | 621.382 |
| arts | T3C—356 |
| manned space flight | 629.457 |
| military | 623.73 |
| ships | 623.856 |
| space flight | 629.457 |
| spacecraft | 629.474 3 |
| unmanned space flight | 629.437 |
| unmanned spacecraft | 629.464 3 |
| Communications engineers | 621.382 092 |
| Communications equipment | |
| computer science | 004.64 |
| engineering | 621.398 1 |
| military equipment | 355.85 |
| Communications facilities | 384.042 |
| architecture | 725.23 |
| area planning | 711.8 |
| construction | 690.523 |
| military resources | 355.27 |
| misuse | 364.147 |
| railroads | 385.316 |
| Communications media | 302.23 |
| *see also* Mass media | |
| Communications network | |
| architecture | |
| communications engineering | 621.382 15 |
| computer science | 004.65 |
| engineering | 621.398 1 |
| Communications networks | |
| computer science | 004.6 |
| technology | 621.382 1 |
| Communications protocols | |
| communications engineering | 621.382 12 |
| computer science | 004.62 |

| | |
|---|---|
| Communications satellites | 384.51 |
| *see also* Satellite communication | |
| Communications services | 384.043 |
| air forces | 358.46 |
| armed forces | 358.24 |
| naval forces | 359.983 |
| police services | 363.24 |
| Communications workers | 384.092 |
| Communicative disorders | 362.196 855 |
| *see also* Communication disorders | |
| Communion (Part of service) | 264.36 |
| music | 782.323 5 |
| Communion of saints | 262.73 |
| Communion service | 264.36 |
| music | 782.323 |
| Communism | 335.4 |
| economics | 335.4 |
| political ideology | 320.532 |
| Communism and Christianity | 261.21 |
| Communism and Islam | 297.273 |
| Communist bloc | T2—171 7 |
| Communist ethics | 171.7 |
| Communist front organizations | |
| political science | 324.3 |
| Communist government | 321.92 |
| Communist Information Bureau | 324.175 |
| Communist International | 324.175 |
| Communist manifesto | 335.422 |
| Communist parties | 324.217 5 |
| international organizations | 324.175 |
| Communist Party of Australia | 324.294 097 5 |
| Communist Party of Austria | 324.243 607 5 |
| Communist Party of China | 324.251 075 |
| Communist Party of Germany | 324.243 075 |
| Communist Party of Japan | 324.252 075 |
| Communist Party of the Soviet Union | 324.247 075 |
| Communist Party of the United States of America | 324.273 75 |
| Communist Party of the United States of America (New York) | 324.274 707 5 |
| Communist Refoundation Party (Italy) | 324.245 075 |
| Communists | 335.409 2 |
| Marxist-Leninist | 335.430 92 |
| Communities | 307 |
| psychological influence | 155.94 |
| *see Manual at* 307 | |
| Community action (Social welfare) | 361.8 |
| public administration | 353.527 93 |

Community antenna television
   systems     384.554 6
  *see also* Television
Community banks     332.1
  *see also* Banks (Finance)
Community-based corrections     365.6
Community centers
  adult education     374.8
  architecture     727.9
  area planning     711.55
  recreation centers     790.068
Community chests     361.8
Community colleges (Two-year
   colleges)     378.154 3
Community development     307.14
  law     346.045
  public administration     354.279 3
Community ecology     577.82
  animals     591.782
  plants     581.782
Community health services     362.12
  *see also* Health services
Community information services
  libraries     021.28
Community mental health
  services     362.22
  *see also* Mental health services
Community nursing     610.734 3
Community of Christ     289.333
  *see also* Mormon Church
Community planning     307.12
  community sociology     307.12
  public administration     352.793
Community property     346.042
  divorce law     346.016 64
Community-school partnerships     371.19
  primary education     372.119
   reading     372.425
Community-school relations     306.432
  education     371.19
  higher education     378.103
  sociology     306.432
Community schools     371.03
Community service
  education     371.19
   higher education     378.103
   secondary education     373.119
  penology     364.68
Community suppers     642.4
Commutation of sentence     364.65
  law     345.077
  penology     364.65
Commutative algebras     512.44
Commutative groups     512.25

Commutative rings     512.44
Commutators (Generator parts)     621.316
Commuter services     388.042
  railroad
   engineering     625.4
  urban     388.4
   *see also* Urban transportation
  *see also* Passenger services
Como (Italy)     T2—452 31
  ancient     T2—372 264 1
Como (Italy : Province)     T2—452 3
  ancient     T2—372 264
Comorans     T5—969 694
Comoro Islands     969.4
    T2—694
Comoros     969.41
    T2—694 1
Comox-Strathcona (B.C.)     T2—711 2
Compact disc read-only memory     004.565
  *see also* CDs (Compact
   discs) — computer storage
Compact discs
  computer storage     004.565
  music     780
  recordings     384
   *see also* Sound recordings
  *see also* CDs (Compact discs)
Compact groups     512.55
Compact spaces     514.32
Companies     338.7
  law     346.066
  *see also* Business enterprises
Companies (Military units)     355.31
Companions of Muḥammad     297.648
Company law     346.066
Company meetings
  law     346.066 45
Company of New France
  Canadian history     971.016 2
Company records
  law     346.066 4
  records management     651.5
Company towns     307.767
Company unions     331.883 4
  *see also* Labor unions
Compaoré, Blaise
  Burkinan history     966.250 53
Comparable worth     331.215 3
  law     344.012 153
Comparative advantage
  economics     338.604 6
  international commerce     382.104 2
Comparative anatomy     571.3
Comparative education     370.9

| | |
|---|---|
| Comparative government | 320.3 |
| Comparative grammar | 415 |
| Comparative law | 340.2 |
| Comparative librarianship | 020.9 |
| Comparative linguistics | 410 |
| *see Manual at* 410 | |
| Comparative literature | 809 |
| Comparative physiology | 571.1 |
| Comparative psychology | 156 |
| Comparative religion | 200 |
| *see Manual at* 201–209 and | |
| 292–299 | |
| Comparison shopping | 381.33 |
| consumer products | 640.73 |
| Comparisons of products | |
| and services | T1—029 |
| Compass | 912.028 4 |
| manufacturing technology | 681.753 |
| Compatibility | |
| computer science | 004 |
| hardware | 004 |
| engineering | 621.39 |
| software | 005 |
| Compensation | 331.21 |
| economics | 331.21 |
| income distribution | 339.21 |
| personnel management | |
| armed forces | 355.64 |
| executives | 658.407 2 |
| public administration | 352.67 |
| public administration | 354.98 |
| Compensation (Legal remedy) | 347.077 |
| Compensation differentials | 331.22 |
| Compensation plans | 331.216 |
| personnel management | 658.322 |
| Compensation scales | 331.216 |
| personnel management | 658.322 2 |
| Compensatory education | 370.111 |
| Competition | 338.604 8 |
| communications industry | 384.041 |
| economics | 338.604 8 |
| law | 343.072 1 |
| price determination | 338.522 |
| transportation services | 388.049 |
| Competition (Biology) | 577.83 |
| Competition (Social) | 302.14 |
| Competition law | 343.072 1 |
| Competitions | T1—079 |
| recreation | 790.134 |
| research | 001.44 |
| use in advertising | 659.17 |
| Compilers (Computer programs) | 005.453 |
| Complaints (Civil procedure) | 347.053 |

| | |
|---|---|
| Complaints (Customer relations) | |
| marketing management | 658.812 |
| Complement (Immunology) | 571.968 8 |
| humans | 616.079 97 |
| Complement fixation | |
| human immunology | 616.079 97 |
| Complete fertilizers | 631.813 |
| chemical engineering | 668.62 |
| Completeness theorem | 511.3 |
| Complex analysis | 515.9 |
| Complex functions | 515.9 |
| Complex groups (Sociology) | 302.35 |
| Complex instruction set | |
| computing | 004.3 |
| *see also* Processing modes — | |
| computer science | |
| Complex multiplication | 516.35 |
| Complex numbers | 512.788 |
| Complex salts | |
| chemical engineering | 661.4 |
| Complex-valued functions | 515.7 |
| Complex-variable functions | 515.9 |
| Complexes (Topology) | 514.223 |
| Compline | 264.15 |
| music | 782.324 |
| Composers | 780.92 |
| *see Manual at* 780.92 | |
| Composing machines | 686.225 4 |
| manufacturing technology | 681.61 |
| use | 686.225 4 |
| Compositae | 583.99 |
| Composite current transmission | 621.319 15 |
| Composite materials | |
| furniture | 645.4 |
| manufacturing technology | 684.106 |
| *see also* Furniture | |
| handicrafts | 745.59 |
| materials science | 620.118 |
| Composite media | 709.040 7 |
| painting | 759.067 |
| Composite photography | 778.8 |
| Composite woods | 674.83 |
| Composites (Art) | |
| techniques | 702.81 |
| two-dimensional | 740 |
| Composition (Arts) | 701.8 |
| architectural design | 729.11 |
| drawing | 741.018 |
| Composition (Law) | 346.077 |
| Composition (Music) | 781.3 |
| computers | 781.34 |
| primary education | 372.874 |
| Composition (Printing) | 686.225 |

Composition (Writing)   808
   applied linguistics   418
    specific languages   T4—8
   primary education   372.623
   rhetoric   808
Composition of atmosphere   551.511
Composition of ocean floor   551.468 6
Compost   631.875
Compound bridges
   construction   624.2
Compound engines
   aircraft   629.134 352
Compound liquors   641.255
   commercial processing   663.55
Compound microscopes   502.823
   biology   570.282 3
Compound musical bows   787.93
   instrument   787.931 9
   music   787.93
   *see also* Stringed instruments
Compound words
   formation   415.92
    specific languages   T4—592
   usage (Applied linguistics)
    specific languages   T4—81
Compounds (Chemicals)   546
   chemical engineering   661
   chemistry   546
Comprehensive high schools   373.25
   *see also* Secondary education
Compressed air   621.51
Compressed-air transmission   621.53
Compressed workweek   331.257 22
   economics   331.257 22
   personnel management   658.312 1
Compressibility
   fluid mechanics   532.053 5
   gas mechanics   533.28
   liquid mechanics   532.58
Compressible flow
   aeronautics   629.132 323
Compression (Stress)
   materials science   620.112 42
Compromise of 1850   973.64
   Civil War (United States) cause   973.711 3
Compulsive behavior
   medicine   616.858 4
   *see also* Mental disorders
Compulsive eating
   medicine   616.852 6
   *see also* Mental disorders
Compulsive gambling   362.25
   medicine   616.858 41
   social welfare   362.25

Compulsive personality disorder
   medicine   616.858 1
   *see also* Mental disorders
Compulsive shopping
   medicine   616.858 4
   *see also* Mental disorders
Compulsory education   379.23
   law   344.079
Compulsory labor   331.117 3
Compulsory military service   355.223 63
   law   343.012 2
Compulsory welfare services   361.614
Computability   511.352
Computable functions   511.352
Computational complexity   511.352
Computational intelligence   006.3
Computational linguistics   006.35
   specific languages   T4—028 563 5
   *see Manual at* 006.35 vs.
    410.285
Computed tomography
   medicine   616.075 722
Computer access control   005.8
   management   658.478
Computer-aided design   620.004 202 85
Computer-aided design/
   computer-aided manufacture   670.285
Computer-aided manufacture   670.427
Computer-aided software
   engineering   005.102 85
Computer algorithms   005.1
Computer animated films   791.433 4
Computer animation   006.696
   computer art   776.6
Computer applications   T1—028 5
   *see Manual at* T1—0285
Computer architecture   004.22
   engineering   621.392
   *see Manual at* 004.21 vs.
    004.22, 621.392
Computer art   776
   *see Manual at* 776 vs. 006.5–.7
Computer-assisted instruction   371.334
   T1—078 5
   adult level   374.26
Computer-assisted printing   686.225 44
Computer communications   004.6
   T1—028 546
   communications services   384.3
   engineering   621.398 1
   law   343.099 44
   programming   005.711
   programs   005.713
   public administration   354.75

Computer communications (continued)
  sociology           302.231
  *see Manual at* 004.6 vs. 005.71;
    *also at* 004.6 vs. 384.3
Computer composition (Music)  781.34
Computer composition (Printing)  686.225 44
Computer control         629.89
Computer crimes         364.168
  law              345.026 8
Computer data security
  management       658.478
Computer engineering     621.39
  arts        T3C—356
  *see Manual at* 004–006 vs.
    621.39
Computer engineers      621.390 92
Computer games        794.8
Computer graphics       006.6
              T1—028 566
  engineering        621.399 6
  instructional use     371.334 66
              T1—078 566
Computer graphics programs  006.68
Computer hardware      004
  engineering        621.39
  *see Manual at* 004 vs. 005
Computer-human interaction  004.019
  engineering        621.398 4
Computer industry       338.470 04
Computer input devices    004.76
  engineering        621.398 6
Computer input-output devices  004.75
  engineering        621.398 5
Computer integrated
  manufacturing systems  670.285
Computer interfacing     004.6
  programming       005.711
  programs         005.713
  software          005.71
  *see Manual at* 004.6 vs. 005.71
Computer interfacing equipment  004.64
  engineering        621.398 1
Computer languages     005.13
  microprogramming    005.18
Computer literacy       004
  primary education    372.34
Computer mathematics    004.015 1
  *see Manual at* 004.0151 vs.
    511.1, 511.35
Computer mice         004.76
  engineering        621.398 6

Computer modeling       003.3
              T1—011 3
  instructional use     371.397
Computer music        786.76
Computer network resources  025.04
Computer network security  005.8
  certification        005.807 6
  *see also* Computer security
Computer networks      004.6
  certification        004.607 6
  communications services  384.3
  processing modes    004.3
    *see also* Processing modes —
      computer science
  security measures     005.8
  *see also* Computer
    communications
Computer-operated equipment
  printing composition    686.225 44
Computer organization    004.22
  engineering        621.392
Computer output devices    004.77
  engineering        621.398 7
Computer output microform
  devices
  manufacturing technology  681.6
Computer output printers
  manufacturing technology  681.62
Computer peripherals     004.7
  engineering        621.398 4
Computer power supply
  engineering        621.395
Computer printers       004.77
  engineering        621.398 7
Computer-processed accounts
  auditing           657.453
Computer programmers    005.109 2
Computer programming    005.1
              T1—028 551
  graphics          006.66
  multimedia systems   006.76
  *see Manual at* 005.1 vs. 005.3;
    *also at* 005.101; *also*
    *at* 005.268 vs. 005.265,
    005.269
Computer programs      005.3
              T1—028 553
  bibliographies      016.005 3
  *see Manual at* 011.39 vs.
    005.3029, 016.0053,
    025.0422
  cataloging         025.344
  coding            005.13
  graphics          006.68

Computer programs (continued)
  library treatment — 025.174
  multimedia systems — 006.78
  *see Manual at* T1—0285; *also at* 005.1 vs. 005.3; *also at* 005.3
Computer reliability — 004
  hardware — 004
    engineering — 621.39
  software — 005
Computer science — 004
        T1—028 5
  arts — T3C—39
  *see Manual at* T1—0285; *also at* 004–006 vs. 621.39; *also at* 510, T1—0151 vs. 004–006, T1—0285
Computer scientists — 004.092
Computer security — 005.8
  certification — 005.807 6
  data — 005.8
  management — 658.478
    armed services — 355.343 3
    public administration — 352.379
Computer simulation — 003.3
        T1—011 3
Computer software — 005.3
  *see also* Computer programs
  *see Manual at* 004 vs. 005
Computer software development — 005.1
Computer sorting — 005.741
  library catalogs — 025.317 7
Computer sound processing — 006.45
Computer sound synthesis — 006.5
        T1—028 565
Computer storage devices — 004.5
Computer systems — 004
  automobiles — 629.272
  embedded — 006.22
  engineering — 621.39
  networks
    processing modes — 004.3
      *see also* Processing modes — computer science
  programs — 005.3
Computer terminals — 004.75
  engineering — 621.398 5
Computer testing — 004.24
  engineering — 621.392
Computer theft — 364.162 800 4
  law — 345.026 280 04
Computer viruses — 005.84

Computer vision — 006.37
  engineering — 621.399 3
  *see Manual at* 006.37 vs. 006.42, 621.367, 621.391, 621.399
Computerized axial tomography
  medicine — 616.075 722
Computerized matching
  personnel selection — 658.311 2
Computerized office records — 651.59
Computerized process control — 629.895
  chemical engineering — 660.281 5
  engineering — 629.895
  manufacturing technology — 670.427 5
Computerized typesetting — 686.225 44
Computers — 004
  access control — 005.8
    management — 658.478
  engineering — 621.39
  instructional use — 371.334
    adult level — 374.26
    primary level — 372.133 4
  law — 343.099 9
  maintenance — 004.028 8
  music — 780.285
    musical instrument — 786.76
    *see also* Electrophones
  repair — 004.028 8
  social effects — 303.483 4
  theft of — 345.026 280 04
    law — 364.162 800 4
  *see Manual at* 004.1
Comtism — 146.4
Comum (Italy) — T2—372 264 1
Comunisti italiani (Political party) — 324.245 075
Conakry (Guinea) — T2—665 2
Concealed weapons — 364.143
  law — 345.024 3
Concealment
  military engineering — 623.77
Concentration
  psychology of learning — 153.153 2
Concentration camp inmates — T1—086 949
Concentration camps — 365.45
  Holocaust, 1933–1945 — 940.531 85
  penology — 365.45
  World War II — 940.531 7
  *see also* Internment camps; Penal institutions
Concentricycloidea — 593.93
Concepción (Chile : Province) — T2—833 9
Concepción (Paraguay) — T2—892 138

| | |
|---|---|
| Concepts | |
| epistemology | 121.4 |
| psychology | 153.23 |
| Conceptual art | 700 |
| fine arts | 709.040 75 |
| painting | 759.067 5 |
| sculpture | 735.230 475 |
| *see also* Arts | |
| Conceptualism | |
| philosophy | 149.1 |
| Concert halls | |
| architecture | 725.81 |
| music | 781.539 |
| Concert zithers | 787.75 |
| *see also* Stringed instruments | |
| Concertantes | 784.186 |
| Concerti grossi | 784.24 |
| Concertinas | 788.84 |
| instrument | 788.841 9 |
| music | 788.84 |
| *see also* Woodwind instruments | |
| Concertinos | 784.186 2 |
| Concertos | 784.23 |
| musical form | 784.186 |
| Concerts | 780.78 |
| Concho County (Tex.) | T2—764 71 |
| Conchostraca | 595.32 |
| Conciliation | |
| international politics | 327.17 |
| labor economics | 331.891 4 |
| law | 347.09 |
| Concord (N.H.) | T2—742 72 |
| Concord, Battle of, 1775 | 973.331 1 |
| Concordances | T1—03 |
| Concordia Parish (La.) | T2—763 73 |
| Concrete | 666.893 |
| architectural construction | 721.044 5 |
| building construction | 693.5 |
| building materials | 691.3 |
| foundation materials | 624.153 36 |
| materials science | 620.136 |
| ship design | 623.818 34 |
| ship hulls | 623.845 4 |
| shipbuilding | 623.820 7 |
| structural engineering | 624.183 4 |
| Concrete art | 709.040 56 |
| Concrete blocks | 666.894 |
| architectural construction | 721.044 4 |
| building construction | 693.4 |
| building materials | 691.3 |
| manufacturing technology | 666.894 |
| materials science | 620.139 |
| structural engineering | 624.183 2 |
| Concrete music | 786.75 |

| | |
|---|---|
| Concrete pavements | 625.84 |
| Concrete poetry | 808.814 |
| history and criticism | 809.14 |
| specific literatures | T3B—104 |
| individual authors | T3A—1 |
| Concurrent programming | 005.275 |
| Concussion idiophones | 786.87 |
| *see also* Percussion instruments | |
| Condemnation (Law) | 343.025 2 |
| Condemnation of Jesus Christ | 232.962 |
| Condensation (Chemical | |
| reaction) | 541.39 |
| chemical engineering | 660.284 4 |
| organic chemistry | 547.2 |
| Condensation (Liquefaction) | 536.44 |
| Condensation of moisture | |
| buildings | 693.893 |
| meteorology | 551.574 |
| Condensed matter | 530.41 |
| Condensed milk | 641.371 424 |
| cooking | 641.671 424 |
| food | 641.371 424 |
| processing | 637.142 4 |
| Condensers (Electrical) | 621.315 |
| radio engineering | 621.384 133 |
| Condensers (Steam) | 621.197 |
| Condiments | 641.338 2 |
| commercial processing | 664.5 |
| cooking with | 641.638 2 |
| food | 641.338 2 |
| Conditional equations | 515.25 |
| Conditional fees | |
| law | 347.057 2 |
| Conditional immortality | 236.23 |
| Conditional logic | 511.317 |
| mathematical logic | 511.317 |
| philosophical logic | 160.119 87 |
| Conditional probabilities | 519.2 |
| Conditional sales | |
| consumer credit | 332.743 |
| law | 346.074 |
| taxes | 343.055 2 |
| Conditioned reflexes | |
| comparative psychology | 156.232 24 |
| psychology | 152.322 4 |
| Conditions of employment | 331.2 |
| economics | 331.2 |
| law | 344.012 |
| public employees | 342.068 6 |
| personnel management | 658.312 |
| armed forces | 355.1 |
| public administration | 354.98 |
| *see also* Work environment | |
| Condominium apartments | 643.27 |

Condominiums   647.92
  architecture   728.314
  construction   690.831 4
  household management   647.92
  law   346.043 3
  *see also* Dwellings
Condoms
  health   613.943 5
    birth control   613.943 5
    disease prevention   613.95
  manufacturing technology   681.761
Condors   598.92
  conservation technology   639.978 92
  resource economics   333.958 92
Conduct of court proceedings   347.075
Conduct of life
  armed forces   355.133
  ethics   170.44
    religion   205
    *see also* Religious ethics
  etiquette   395
  parapsychology   131
  personal religion   204.4
    Buddhism   294.344 4
    Christianity   248.4
    Hinduism   294.544
    Islam   297.57
      Sufi   297.44
    Judaism   296.7
  psychology   158.1
Conducting   781.45
Conducting scores   780
  treatises   780.264
Conduction anesthesia
  surgery   617.964
Conductivity (Electrodynamics)
  crystals   548.85
Conductors (Music)   784.209 2
  chorus   782.509 2
  opera   782.109 2
  orchestra   784.209 2
Conduits
  road engineering   625.734
Condylarthra   569.62
Condylomata acuminata
  incidence   614.547
  medicine   616.951 8
  *see also* Communicable
    diseases — humans
Conecuh County (Ala.)   T2—761 263
Conejos County (Colo.)   T2—788 33
Cones   516.154
Confections   641.86

Confederal Democratic Union
  (Swiss political party)   324.249 408 2
Confederate States of America   973.713
                    T2—75
Confederate sympathizers
  United States history   973.718
Confederated Benedictines   255.11
  church history   271.11
Confederation of Arab
  Republics   T2—62
Confederation of the Rhine   943.06
Confederations   321.02
  law   342.042
  public administration   351
Conference calls   384.64
  *see also* Telephone
Conference committees
  legislative bodies   328.365 7
Conference on Data Systems
  Languages databases
  computer science   005.754
Conferences   060
Confession (Christian rite)   234.166
  public worship   265.62
  theology   234.166
Confession (Law)   345.06
Confessionals   247.1
  architecture   726.529 1
Confessions of faith   202
  Christianity   238
Confidence regions   519.54
Confidential communications   323.448
  civil right   323.448
  law   342.085 8
Confidentiality
  office services   651
Confinement (Childbirth)   392.12
  music   781.582
Confirmation (Religious rite)   203.8
  Christianity   234.162
    public worship   265.2
    theology   234.162
  etiquette   395.24
  Judaism   296.442 4
    liturgy   296.454 24
    women's   296.443 4
      liturgy   296.454 34
  music   781.583
Conflict   303.6
  international politics   327.16
  law   341.5
  social groups   305
  sociology   303.6

| | |
|---|---|
| Conflict management | 303.69 |
| business relationships | 650.13 |
| executive management | 658.405 3 |
| interpersonal relations | |
| personnel management | 658.314 5 |
| labor relations | |
| personnel management | 658.315 |
| Conflict of interest | |
| law | 342.068 4 |
| occupational ethics | 174 |
| political ethics | 172 |
| public administration | 353.46 |
| Conflict of laws | 340.9 |
| domestic | 342.042 |
| *see Manual at* 340.9 | |
| Conflict resolution | 303.69 |
| international relations | 327.17 |
| public safety | 363.321 5 |
| sociology | 303.69 |
| Conformal mapping | 516.36 |
| calculus | 515.9 |
| differential geometry | 516.36 |
| Conformal projections | 526.82 |
| Conformal transformations | 516.35 |
| Conformation (Biochemical | |
| structure) | 572.33 |
| Conformity | 303.32 |
| psychology | 153.854 |
| Confraternities | 267 |
| Confraternity Bible | 220.520 5 |
| Confucianism | 181.112 |
| art representation | 704.948 995 12 |
| arts | 700.482 995 12 |
| | T3C—382 995 12 |
| philosophy | 181.112 |
| religion | 299.512 |
| Confucianist holidays | |
| customs | 394.265 951 2 |
| Confucianists | |
| biography | 181.112 |
| religion | 299.512 092 |
| Congenital adrenal hyperplasia | |
| medicine | 616.45 |
| Congenital diseases | |
| humans | |
| medicine | 616.043 |
| pediatrics | 618.920 043 |
| Congenital heart defects | |
| medicine | 616.120 43 |
| *see also* Cardiovascular | |
| diseases — humans | |
| Congenital myxedema | |
| medicine | 616.858 848 043 |
| Congers | 597.43 |

| | |
|---|---|
| Congestion (Mathematics) | 519.82 |
| Congestive heart failure | |
| medicine | 616.129 |
| *see also* Cardiovascular | |
| diseases — humans | |
| Congleton (England : | |
| Borough) | T2—427 13 |
| Conglomerates (Enterprises) | 338.804 2 |
| *see also* Combinations | |
| (Enterprises) | |
| Congo (Brazzaville) | 967.24 |
| | T2—672 4 |
| Congo (Democratic Republic) | 967.51 |
| | T2—675 1 |
| Congo, French (Brazzaville) | T2—672 4 |
| Congo eels | 597.85 |
| Congo Free State | 967.510 22 |
| | T2—675 1 |
| Congo-Kordofanian languages | 496.3 |
| | T6—963 |
| Congo language | 496.393 1 |
| | T6—963 931 |
| Congo literature | 896.393 1 |
| Congo River | T2—675 1 |
| Congolese (Brazzaville) | T5—967 24 |
| Congolese (Kinshasa) | T5—967 51 |
| Congregational Christian | |
| Churches of the United States | 285.833 |
| *see also* Congregationalism | |
| Congregational Churches of the | |
| United States | 285.832 |
| *see also* Congregationalism | |
| Congregational Methodist | |
| Church | 287.2 |
| *see also* Methodist Church | |
| Congregational systems | |
| Christian ecclesiology | 262.4 |
| Congregationalism | 285.8 |
| church government | 262.058 |
| parishes | 254.058 |
| church law | 262.985 8 |
| doctrines | 230.58 |
| catechisms and creeds | 238.58 |
| general councils | 262.558 |
| guides to Christian life | 248.485 8 |
| missions | 266.58 |
| moral theology | 241.045 8 |
| public worship | 264.058 |
| religious associations | 267.185 8 |
| religious education | 268.858 |
| seminaries | 230.073 58 |
| theology | 230.58 |
| Congregationalists | |
| biography | 285.809 2 |

Congregations
  Christianity
    denominations — 280
    local church — 250
    papal administration — 262.136
  Judaism — 296.65
  religion — 206.5
Congress of Industrial
  Organizations (U.S.) — 331.883 309 73
Congress of Vienna, 1814–1815 — 940.271 4
Congresses (Legislative bodies) — 328
Congresses (Meetings) — 060
Congressional districts — 328.334 5
Congruences
  Euclidean geometry — 516.2
  number theory — 512.72
Conic sections — 516.152
  Euclidean geometry — 516.215 2
Conies (Hyraxes) — 599.68
Conies (Pikas) — 599.329
Coniferales — 585
  paleobotany — 561.5
  *see also* Conifers
Conifers — 585
  botany — 585
  forestry — 634.975
  ornamental arboriculture — 635.977 5
  ornamental gardening — 635.935
  paleobotany — 561.5
Conjoined twins
  medicine — 616.043
Conjugal rights of prisoners — 365.6
Conjugales — 579.837
Conjugated carbohydrates — 572.567
  *see also* Carbohydrates
Conjugated proteins — 572.68
  *see also* Proteins
Conjugation (Grammar) — 415.6
  specific languages — T4 56
Conjugation tables
  applied linguistics — 418
  specific languages — T4—82
Conjunctions (Grammar) — 415.7
  specific languages — T4—57
Conjunctival diseases
  ophthalmology — 617.77
    *see also* Eye diseases —
      humans
Conjunctivas
  human anatomy — 611.84
  human physiology — 612.841
  ophthalmology — 617.77

Conjunctivitis
  incidence — 614.599 7
  ophthalmology — 617.773
    *see also* Eye diseases —
      humans
Conjuring
  magic — 133.43
  recreation — 793.8
Connacht (Ireland) — T2—417 1
Connarales — 583.82
Connecticut — 974.6
  — T2—746
Connecticut River — T2—74
  Connecticut — T2—746
  Massachusetts — T2—744 2
  New Hampshire — T2—742
  Vermont — T2—743
Connecting rods — 621.827
  internal-combustion engines — 621.437
  machine engineering — 621.827
Connectionism
  artificial intelligence — 006.32
Connections (Mathematics) — 516.35
Connective tissue cells
  human cytology — 611.018 26
Connective tissue diseases
  medicine — 616.77
    *see also* Musculoskeletal
      diseases — humans
Connective tissues — 571.56
  biology — 571.56
  human anatomy — 611.74
  human histology — 611.018 2
  medicine — 616.77
  musculoskeletal system — 573.735 6
    human histology — 612.757
    human physiology — 612.757
  *see also* Musculoskeletal
    system
Connochaetes — 599.645 9
Conodonts — 562.2
Conrad I, Holy Roman Emperor
  German history — 943.022
Conscience — 170
  civil rights issues — 323.442
  ethical systems — 171.6
  religion — 205
    Buddhism — 294.35
    Christianity — 241.1
    Hinduism — 294.548
    Islam — 297.5
    Judaism — 296.36

| | |
|---|---|
| Conscientious objection | 355.224 |
|   ethics | 172.42 |
|     *see also* War — ethics | |
|   law | 343.012 6 |
|   social theology | 201.727 3 |
|     *see also* War — social theology | |
| Conscientious objectors | 355.224 |
|   *see also* Conscientious objection | |
| Conscious mental processes | 153 |
|   children | 155.413 |
|   comparative psychology | 156.3 |
|   educational psychology | 370.152 |
|   human physiology | 612.823 3 |
| Consciousness | 153 |
|   philosophy | 128.2 |
| Consciousness-raising groups | 305 |
| Conscription (Draft) | 355.223 63 |
|   law | 343.012 2 |
| Consecrations (Christian rites) | 265.92 |
| Consequential loss | |
|   insurance | 368.08 |
| Consequentialism | |
|   ethics | 171.5 |
| CONSER Project | 025.343 2 |
| Conservation (Maintenance and repair) | T1—028 8 |
|   arts | 069.53 |
|   bibliographic materials | 025.84 |
|   museology | 702.88 |
| Conservation of biodiversity | 333.951 6 |
| Conservation of energy (Physics) | 531.62 |
| Conservation of mass-energy | 530.11 |
| Conservation of natural resources | 333.72 |
|   economics | 333.72 |
|   law | 346.044 |
|   public administration | 354.334 |
|   social theology | 201.77 |
|     Christianity | 261.88 |
|   technology | 639.9 |
|   *see Manual at* 333.72 vs. 304.28, 320.58, 363.7; *also at* 333.7–.9 vs. 363.1, 363.73, 577 | |
| Conservation tillage | 631.451 |
| Conservationists | 333.720 92 |
|   of biological resources | 333.951 609 2 |
|   technologists | 639.909 2 |
| Conservatism | |
|   political ideology | 320.52 |
| Conservative Judaism | 296.834 2 |
|   liturgy | 296.450 47 |
| Conservative parties | 324.214 |
|   international organizations | 324.14 |
| Conservative Party (Great Britain) | 324.241 04 |
| Conservative Party (New York State) | 324.274 708 |
| Conservative Party of Canada | 324.271 04 |
| Conservatories (Botanical research buildings) | |
|   architecture | 727.558 |
| Conservatories (Greenhouses) | 631.583 |
|   architecture | 728.924 |
|   construction | 690.892 4 |
|   floriculture | 635.982 3 |
|   gardening | 635.048 3 |
| Consolatory devotions | 204.32 |
|   Christianity | 242.4 |
|   Judaism | 296.72 |
| Consolidated financial statements | 657.3 |
| Consolidation | |
|   land economics | 333.33 |
|   law | 346.043 6 |
|   management | 658.162 |
|   schools | 379.153 5 |
| Consonance | |
|   musical element | 781.238 |
| Consonants | 414 |
|   applied linguistics | |
|     specific languages | T4—813 |
|   specific languages | T4—15 |
| Consortia | |
|   higher education | 378.104 |
| Conspiracy | 364.1 |
|   law | 345.02 |
| Constance, Lake of | T2—434 62 |
|   Germany | T2—434 62 |
|   Switzerland | T2—494 597 |
| Constanța (Romania : Județ) | T2—498 3 |
| Constantine (Algeria : Province) | T2—655 |
| Constantinople | T2—496 18 |
|   ancient | T2—398 618 |
| Constantinopolitan Creed | 238.142 |
| Constellations | 523.8 |
| Constipation | |
|   medicine | 616.342 8 |
|   *see also* Digestive system diseases — humans | |
| Constituencies (Election districts) | 328.334 5 |
| Constituencies (Electoral politics) | 324.63 |
| Constituency services | 328.331 |
| Constitutional Act, 1791 | |
|   Canadian history | 971.028 |
| Constitutional amendments | 342.03 |

Constitutional Church 284.8
Constitutional conventions 342.029 2
Constitutional history 342.029
Constitutional law 342
Constitutional monarchs 352.233
Constitutional monarchy 321.87
Constitutional period (United
   States) 973.4
Constitutional reform 342.03
Constitutions 342.02
  organizations 060
Constraint databases
  computer science 005.753
Constraint programming 005.116
Construction 624
  government control 354.642 8
  military engineering 623.047
  underwater engineering 627.702
  *see Manual at* 624 vs. 690
Construction engineers 624.092
  *see also* Construction workers
Construction equipment
  manufacturing technology 681.76
Construction industry 338.476 24
  accounting 657.869
  energy economics 333.796 2
  enterprises 338.762 4
  law 343.078 624
  public administration 354.64
  restrictive practices 338.826 24
Construction noise 363.741
  *see also* Noise
Construction services (Military) 358.22
  land 358.22
  naval 359.982
Construction specifications 692.3
Construction toys 790.133
  manufacturing technology 688.725
Construction workers 624.092
  building trades 690.092
  civil engineering 624.092
  labor economics 331.762 4
  public administration 354.942 4
Constructions (Grammar) 415
  specific languages T4—5
Constructive accounting 657.1
Constructive mathematics 511.36
Constructivism
  fine arts 709.040 57
  painting 759.065 7
  sculpture 735.230 457
Constructivism (Philosophy) 149
Consular law 342.041 2
  law of nations 341.35

Consular service 327.2
  public administration 353.132 63
Consulate (France) 944.046
Consulate buildings
  architecture 725.17
Consultants 001
  management 658.46
    public administration 352.373
  marketing management 658.83
  physicians 362.172
Consultative bodies
  public administration 352.743
Consumer attitudes
  marketing research 658.834 3
Consumer behavior
  marketing research 658.834 2
Consumer complaints
  marketing management 658.812
Consumer cooperatives 334.5
  management 658.87
Consumer credit 332.743
  law 346.073
  marketing management 658.883
Consumer education 381.33
  home economics 640.73
Consumer finance institutions 332.35
Consumer food prices 338.19
Consumer income
  macroeconomics 339.22
Consumer information 381.33
  home economics 640.73
  public administration 352.746
Consumer information labeling 381.33
Consumer movements 381.32
Consumer preferences
  marketing research 658.834 3
Consumer price indexes 338.528
Consumer protection 381.34
  commerce 381.34
  law 343.071
  public administration 352.746
Consumer psychology
  marketing research 658.834 2
Consumer reports 381.33
              T1—029
  *see Manual at* T1—025 vs.
   T1—029
Consumer research
  marketing management 658.834
Consumer satisfaction
  customer relations
    marketing management 658.812
  marketing research 658.834 3
Consumerism 381.3

| | |
|---|---|
| Consumption | 339.47 |
| ethics | 178 |
| religion | 205.68 |
| Buddhism | 294.356 8 |
| Christianity | 241.68 |
| Hinduism | 294.548 68 |
| Islam | 297.568 |
| Judaism | 296.368 |
| *see also* Ethical problems | |
| macroeconomics | 339.47 |
| natural resources | 333.713 |
| sociology | 306.3 |
| Consumption-savings | |
| relationship | 339.43 |
| Contact allergies | |
| incidence | 614.599 33 |
| medicine | 616.973 |
| Contact dermatitis | |
| medicine | 616.51 |
| *see also* Skin diseases — | |
| humans | |
| Contact lenses | |
| manufacturing technology | 681.41 |
| optometry | 617.752 3 |
| Contact printing (Photography) | 771.44 |
| Contactors (Generator parts) | 621.316 |
| Contagious diseases | 571.98 |
| *see also* Communicable | |
| diseases | |
| Container gardening | 635.986 |
| houseplants | 635.965 |
| Container-ship operations | 387.544 2 |
| Containers | 688.8 |
| chemistry | 542.2 |
| earthenware | 666.68 |
| arts | 738.38 |
| technology | 666.68 |
| food board | 676.34 |
| glass | 666.19 |
| arts | 748.8 |
| technology | 666.19 |
| gold | |
| arts | 739.228 4 |
| handicrafts | 745.59 |
| ironwork | |
| arts | 739.48 |
| paper | 676.3 |
| paperboard | 676.3 |
| plastic technology | 668.497 |
| porcelain | 666.58 |
| arts | 738.28 |
| technology | 666.58 |

| | |
|---|---|
| Containers (continued) | |
| pottery | 666.3 |
| arts | 738 |
| technology | 666.3 |
| sculpture | 731.72 |
| silver | |
| arts | 739.238 4 |
| technology | 688.8 |
| warehouse management | 658.785 |
| wooden | 674.82 |
| Contamination control | 363.19 |
| *see also* Product safety | |
| Conte, Lansana | |
| Guinean history | 966.520 52 |
| Contemplation | 204.3 |
| Christianity | 248.34 |
| Contemplative religious orders | 255.01 |
| church history | 271.01 |
| women | 255.901 |
| church history | 271.901 |
| Contempt of court | 364.134 |
| law | 345.023 4 |
| Content-addressable memory | 004.5 |
| Content analysis | T1—014 |
| linguistics | 401.41 |
| specific languages | T4—014 1 |
| Content area reading | |
| primary education | 372.476 |
| Contested elections | |
| procedures | 324.65 |
| Contests | |
| advertising | 659.197 901 34 |
| recreation | 790.134 |
| use in advertising | 659.17 |
| Contextual theology | 202 |
| Christianity | 230 |
| Conthey (Switzerland : | |
| District) | T2—494 796 5 |
| Continental drift | 551.136 |
| Continental shelves | T2—141 |
| law | 346.046 918 |
| law of nations | 341.448 |
| resource economics | 333.918 |
| Continental wrestling | 796.812 2 |
| Continents | 551.41 |
| | T2—141 |
| geography | 910.914 1 |
| geomorphology | 551.41 |
| physical geography | 910.021 41 |
| Contingency | 123 |
| Contingent fees | |
| law | 347.057 2 |
| Continuation schools | 374.8 |

| | | | |
|---|---|---|---|
| Continued fractions | 515.243 | Contracting | 346.022 |
| number theory | 512.72 | *see also* Contracts | |
| Continuing care communities | 362.61 | Contracting out | 658.405 8 |
| Continuing care retirement | | | T1—068 4 |
| communities | 362.61 | armed forces | 355.621 2 |
| Continuing education | 374 | management | 658.405 8 |
| | T1—071 5 | public administration | 352.538 |
| *see also* Adult education | | Contraction (Effect of heat) | 536.41 |
| Continuity | 515.222 | Contractions | |
| Continuo | 781.47 | heart | 573.17 |
| Continuous bridges | | human physiology | 612.171 |
| construction | 624.21 | physiology | 573.17 |
| Continuous casting | | *see also* Cardiovascular | |
| metals | 671.256 | system | |
| Continuous functions | 515.222 | muscles | 573.75 |
| spaces | 515.73 | human physiology | 612.741 |
| Continuous processes | | *see also* Musculoskeletal | |
| production management | 658.533 | system | |
| Continuous radar systems | 621.384 85 | skin | 573.5 |
| Continuous-time systems | 003.8 | human physiology | 612.791 |
| Continuum hypothesis | 511.322 | *see also* Skin | |
| Continuum mechanics | 531 | Contractions (Linguistics) | 411 |
| Continuum physics | 530 | specific languages | T4—11 |
| theory | 530.14 | specific subjects | T1—014 8 |
| Contortion | | Contractors (Builders) | 690.092 |
| sports | 796.47 | Contracts | 346.022 |
| Contour farming | 631.455 | air forces | 358.416 212 |
| Contour surveying | 526.981 | armed forces | 355.621 2 |
| Contra Costa County | | civil rights issues | 323.46 |
| (Calif.) | T2—794 63 | collective bargaining | 331.891 |
| Contrabassoons | 788.59 | personnel management | 658.315 4 |
| instrument | 788.591 9 | public administration | 352.68 |
| music | 788.59 | construction | 692.8 |
| *see also* Woodwind instruments | | materials management | 658.723 |
| Contraception | 363.96 | | T1—068 7 |
| ethics | 176.3 | naval forces | 359.621 2 |
| *see also* Birth control | | public administration | 352.53 |
| Contraceptive drug implants | | Contractual liability insurance | 368.56 |
| health | 613.943 2 | Contradiction (Principle of) | 111 |
| medicine | 618.182 | Contradictions | |
| *see also* Birth control | | logic | 165 |
| Contraceptive drugs | | Contralto voices | 782.68 |
| health | 613.943 2 | children's | 782.78 |
| medicine | 618.182 | choral and mixed voices | 782.78 |
| *see also* Birth control | | single voices | 783.78 |
| Contract bridge | 795.415 | general works | 782.68 |
| Contract carriers | 388.041 | choral and mixed voices | 782.68 |
| truck | 388.324 3 | single voices | 783.68 |
| *see also* Freight services | | women's | 782.68 |
| Contract labor | 331.542 | choral and mixed voices | 782.68 |
| economics | 331.542 | single voices | 783.68 |
| penology | 365.65 | Contrapuntal forms | 784.187 |
| sociology | 306.363 | | |

| | |
|---|---|
| Contrastive linguistics | 410 |
| applied linguistics | 418 |
| *see Manual at* 410 | |
| Contraventions (Criminal law) | 345.02 |
| Contributory negligence | 346.032 |
| Contrition (Christian rite) | 234.166 |
| public worship | 265.61 |
| theology | 234.166 |
| Control | |
| executive management | 658.401 3 |
| military services | 355.685 |
| public administration | 352.35 |
| export trade | 382.64 |
| *see also* Export trade | |
| public administration | 352.8 |
| external control | 352.8 |
| internal control | 352.35 |
| social process | 303.33 |
| Control circuits | 621.381 537 |
| Control devices | |
| electrical engineering | 621.317 |
| heating buildings | 697.07 |
| transportation | 388.041 |
| engineering | 629.040 289 |
| transportation services | 388.041 |
| *see also* Signals | |
| Control line vehicles | 796.15 |
| Control mechanisms (Biology) | 571.7 |
| *see also* Endocrine system | |
| Control of usage | |
| natural resources | 333.717 |
| Control processes | |
| human physiology | 612.022 |
| Control rods | |
| nuclear reactors | 621.483 5 |
| Control theory | 003.5 |
| automation engineering | 629.831 2 |
| mathematics | 515.642 |
| systems | 003.5 |
| Controlled burning | |
| forestry | 634.955 |
| Controlled-environment | |
| agriculture | 631.583 |
| floriculture | 635.982 |
| gardening | 635.048 3 |
| Controlled subject vocabularies | 025.47 |
| Controlled transmission | |
| television | 384.556 |
| *see also* Television | |
| Controllers | |
| computer science | 004.64 |
| engineering | 621.398 1 |
| control engineering | 629.895 |

| | |
|---|---|
| Controllership | |
| executive management | 658.401 3 |
| financial management | 658.151 |
| Controversial knowledge | 001.9 |
| *see Manual at* 001.9 and 130 | |
| Contusions | |
| medicine | 617.13 |
| Contwoyto Lake (N.W.T. and Nunavut) | T2—719 55 |
| Conurbations | 307.764 |
| *see also* Metropolitan areas | |
| Conures | 598.71 |
| animal husbandry | 636.686 5 |
| Convalescent homes | 362.16 |
| *see also* Health care facilities | |
| Convalescents | 305.908 7 |
| | T1—087 7 |
| *see also* Sick people | |
| Convection-oven cooking | 641.58 |
| Convective heating | |
| buildings | 697.2 |
| Convenience foods | |
| home serving | 642.1 |
| Convenience stores | 381.147 |
| management | 658.87 |
| *see also* Commerce | |
| Convention centers | |
| architecture | 725.91 |
| institutional housekeeping | 647.969 1 |
| Convention for the Protection of Human Rights and Fundamental Freedoms, 1950 | 342.240 850 261 |
| Conventional houses | 643.1 |
| *see also* Dwellings | |
| Conventional war | 355.02 |
| Conventional weapons limitation | 327.174 3 |
| Conventions | |
| labor unions | 331.874 |
| political nominations | 324.56 |
| Conventions (Meetings) | 060 |
| Conventions (Treaties) | 341.37 |
| texts | 341.026 |
| Convents | 206.57 |
| architecture | 726.7 |
| Christianity | 255.9 |
| church history | 271.9 |
| religious significance of buildings | 246.97 |
| Conventuals | 255.37 |
| church history | 271.37 |
| Convergence | 515.24 |

Conversation
  ethics · 177.2
    religion · 205.672
      Christianity · 241.672
      Judaism · 296.367 2
    *see also* Ethical problems
  etiquette · 395.59
  literature · 808.856
    history and criticism · 809.56
    specific literatures · T3B—506
      individual authors · T3A—5
  rhetoric · 808.56
  social psychology · 302.346
Conversational language study · 418
  specific languages · T4—83
Converse County (Wyo.) · T2—787 16
Conversion (Law) · 346.036
Conversion (Religious
  experience) · 204.2
  Christianity · 248.24
  Islam · 297.574
  Judaism · 296.714
Conversion disorder
  medicine · 616.852 4
  *see also* Mental disorders
Conversion tables (Measurement) · 530.81
Conversion to metric system · 389.16
Converter substations
  electrical engineering · 621.312 6
Converters
  electrical engineering · 621.313
  electronic circuits · 621.381 532 2
Convertible tops · 629.26
Convertiplanes
  engineering · 629.133 35
Converts · 204.2
  Judaism · 296.714
    outreach activity for · 296.69
  missions for · 207.2
Convex analysis · 515.882
Convex functions · 515.882
Convex geometry · 516.08
Convex programming · 519.76
Convex sets
  geometry · 516.08
Convex surfaces · 516.362
Conveyancing · 346.043 8
Conveying equipment · 621.867
  mining · 622.66
  pneumatic engineering · 621.54
Conveyor belts · 621.867 5
  manufacturing technology · 678.36
  materials handling · 621.867 5

Convict labor · 365.65
  economics · 331.51
  law · 344.035 65
  penology · 365.65
Convicts · 365.6
  · T1—086 927
Convolutions
  cerebrum
    human physiology · 612.825
Convolutions (Functions) · 515.43
Convolvulaceae · 583.94
Convulsions
  medicine · 616.845
    *see also* Nervous system
      diseases — humans
Convulsive therapy
  psychiatry · 616.891 2
Conway County (Ark.) · T2—767 31
Conway Range National
  Park (Qld.) · T2—943 6
Conwy (Wales: County
  Borough) · T2—429 27
Cook, Joseph, Sir
  Australian history · 994.041
Cook County (Ga.) · T2—758 876
Cook County (Ill.) · T2—773 1
Cook County (Minn.) · T2—776 75
Cook Inlet (Alaska) · 551.461 434
  · T2—164 34
Cook Islands · T2—962 3
Cook Strait (N.Z.) · 551.461 478
  · T2—164 78
Cookbooks · 641.5
Cooke County (Tex.) · T2—764 533
Cookery · 641.5
  *see also* Cooking
Cookies · 641.865 4
  commercial processing · 664.752 5
  home preparation · 641.865 4
Cooking · 641.5
  customs · 392.37
  primary education · 372.373
Cooking for one · 641.561 1
Cooking for two · 641.561 2
Cooking greens · 641.354
  commercial processing · 664.805 4
  cooking · 641.654
  food · 641.354
  garden crop · 635.4
Cooking oils · 641.338 5
  cooking · 641.638 5
  food · 641.338 5
  food technology · 664.36

| | |
|---|---|
| Cooking utensils | 643.3 |
| manufacturing technology | 683.82 |
| Cookout cooking | 641.578 |
| Cooks | 641.509 2 |
| Cookstown (Northern Ireland : District) | T2—416 43 |
| Cool jazz | 781.655 |
| Coolants | 621.564 |
| nuclear engineering | 621.483 36 |
| refrigeration engineering | 621.564 |
| Coolgardie (W.A.) | T2—941 6 |
| Coolidge, Calvin | |
| United States history | 973.915 |
| Cooling coils | 621.56 |
| buildings | 697.932 2 |
| Cooling systems | |
| automotive | 629.256 |
| buildings | 697.93 |
| ships | 623.853 5 |
| Cooling towers | 621.197 |
| Cooloola National Park (Qld.) | T2—943 2 |
| Coon cat | 636.83 |
| Coonabarabran (N.S.W.) | T2—944 4 |
| Cooper County (Mo.) | T2—778 51 |
| Cooperage | 674.82 |
| Cooperation | 158 |
| social psychology | 302.14 |
| Cooperation in higher education | 378.104 |
| Cooperative apartment houses | 647.92 |
| architecture | 728.314 |
| construction | 690.831 4 |
| household management | 647.92 |
| law | 346.043 3 |
| *see also* Dwellings | |
| Cooperative apartments | 643.27 |
| *see also* Cooperative apartment houses | |
| Cooperative cataloging | 025.35 |
| Cooperative collection development | 025.21 |
| Cooperative education | 371.227 |
| higher education | 378.37 |
| secondary level | 373.28 |
| Cooperative information services | 025.523 |
| Cooperative learning | 371.36 |
| Cooperative marketing | 334.6 |
| Cooperatives | 334 |
| accounting | 657.97 |
| economics | 334 |
| law | 346.066 8 |
| property law | 346.043 3 |

| | |
|---|---|
| Cooperatives (continued) | |
| management | 658.047 |
| initiation | 658.114 7 |
| *see Manual at* 658.04 vs. 658.114, 658.402 | |
| sociology | 306.34 |
| Coopers Creek (Qld. and S. Aust.) | T2—942 37 |
| Coordinate constructions (Grammar) | 415 |
| specific languages | T4—5 |
| Coordinate indexing | 025.47 |
| Coordinate systems | |
| geometry | 516.16 |
| Coordination (Social process) | 303.3 |
| Coordination biochemistry | 572.51 |
| Coordination chemistry | 541.224 2 |
| Coordination of movement | |
| psychology | 152.385 |
| Coos County (N.H.) | T2—742 1 |
| Coos County (Or.) | T2—795 23 |
| Coosa County (Ala.) | T2—761 59 |
| Coosa River (Ga. and Ala.) | T2—761 6 |
| Cootamundra (N.S.W.) | T2—944 8 |
| Cooters | 597.925 94 |
| Coots | 598.32 |
| Copán (Honduras : Dept.) | T2—728 384 |
| Copeland (England) | T2—427 84 |
| Copenhagen (Denmark) | T2—489 13 |
| Copenhagen (Denmark : Amt) | T2—489 14 |
| Copepoda | 595.34 |
| Copepods | 595.34 |
| Copiah County (Miss.) | T2—762 52 |
| Copiapó (Chile : Province) | T2—831 45 |
| Copiers | 686.4 |
| *see also* Photocopying | |
| Copies | |
| arts | 702.872 |
| paintings | 751.5 |
| technical drawing | 604.25 |
| Copolymerization | |
| chemical engineering | 668.92 |
| chemistry | 547.28 |
| Copper | 669.3 |
| applied nutrition | 613.285 1 |
| architectural construction | 721.044 73 |
| biochemistry | 572.518 |
| humans | 612.015 24 |
| building construction | 693.73 |
| building material | 691.83 |
| chemical engineering | 661.065 2 |
| chemistry | 546.652 |
| decorative arts | 739.511 |

Copper (continued)
  economic geology — 553.43
  human toxicology — 615.925 652
  materials science — 620.182
  metabolism
    human physiology — 612.392 4
  metallography — 669.953
  metallurgy — 669.3
  metalworking — 673.3
  mining — 622.343
  organic chemistry — 547.056 52
    applied — 661.895
  physical metallurgy — 669.963
  structural engineering — 624.182 2
  *see also* Chemicals; Metals
Copper Age — 930.153
  T1—090 13
Copper-aluminum alloys — 669.3
  *see also* Copper
Copper-beryllium alloys — 669.3
  *see also* Copper
Copper soaps — 668.125
Copper sulfate water treatment — 628.166 2
Copperbelt Province
  (Zambia) — T2—689 4
Copperleaves (Plants) — 583.69
Coppermine (Nunavut) — T2—719 55
Copra — 665.355
Coptic Church — 281.72
  *see also* Eastern churches
Coptic language — 493.2
  T6—932
  Biblical texts — 220.49
Coptic literature — 893.2
Coptic people — T5—932
Coptic period — 932.023
Copts — T5—932
Copulation
  sociology — 306.77
Copying
  office use — 652.4
Copying machines — 686.4
  *see also* Photocopying
Copyright — 346.048 2
  law — 346.048 2
  library operations — 025.12
  public administration — 352.749
Copyright deposits
  library acquisitions — 025.26
Copyright infringement — 364.166 2
  criminal law — 345.026 62
Copyright piracy — 364.166 2
  law — 345.026 62
Coquet, River (England) — T2—428 87

Coquihalla River (B.C.) — T2—711 37
Coquimbo (Chile : Region) — T2—832 3
Coquitlam (B.C.) — T2—711 33
Cor pulmonale
  medicine — 616.12
  *see also* Cardiovascular
    diseases — humans
Cora Indians — T5—974 54
Cora language — 497.454
  T6—974 54
Coraciiformes — 598.78
  paleozoology — 568.7
Coracles — 386.229
  design — 623.812 9
  engineering — 623.829
  transportation services — 386.229
Coral fungi — 579.597
Coral Harbour (Nunavut) — T2—719 58
Coral reefs — 578.778 9
  T2—142
  biology — 578.778 9
  conservation technology — 639.973 6
  ecology — 577.789
  geography — 910.914 2
  physical geography — 910.021 42
  resource economics — 333.955 3
Coral Sea — 551.461 476
  T2—164 76
Coral Sea Islands — T2—948
Coral snakes — 597.964 4
Coralberry — 583.675
Corals — 593.6
  paleozoology — 563.6
Corby (England : Borough) — T2—425 51
Cordage
  ship gear — 623.862
  textiles — 677.71
Cordaitales — 561.59
Cordials — 641.255
  commercial processing — 663.55
Cordierite
  mineralogy — 549.64
Cordillera (Paraguay) — T2—892 135
Cordillera Occidental
  (Colombia) — T2—861 5
Cordite — 662.26
  military engineering — 623.452 6
Córdoba (Argentina :
  Province) — T2—825 4
Córdoba (Colombia : Dept.) — T2—861 12
Córdoba (Spain : Province) — T2—468 4
Cordoba caliphate — 946.02
Cords (Textiles) — 677.76
  textile arts — 746.27

| | |
|---|---|
| Corduroy | 677.617 |
| Cordylidae | 597.958 |
| Core curriculum | 375.002 |
| Core memory | 004.53 |
|   engineering | 621.397 3 |
| Core of earth | 551.112 |
| Corfu (Greece : Nome) | T2—495 5 |
| Coriariaceae | 583.77 |
| Corinth (Greece : Nome) | T2—495 22 |
|   ancient | T2—387 |
| Corinth, Isthmus of | |
|   (Greece) | T2—495 22 |
| Corinthia (Greece) | T2—495 22 |
|   ancient | T2—387 |
| Corinthians (Biblical books) | 227.2 |
| Corito (Italy) | T2—375 68 |
| Cork | 674.9 |
|   forestry | 634.985 |
| Cork (Ireland) | T2—419 56 |
| Cork (Ireland : County) | T2—419 5 |
| Cork oak | 583.46 |
| Cork trees (Rutaceae) | 635.977 377 |
|   botany | 583.77 |
|   ornamental arboriculture | 635.977 377 |
| Corkboard | |
|   materials science | 620.195 |
| Cormorants | 598.43 |
| Corms | 584.146 |
|   descriptive botany | 584.146 |
|   physiology | 575.496 |
| Corn | 641.331 5 |
|   botany | 584.92 |
|   cereal crop | 633.15 |
|   commercial processing | 664.724 |
|   cooking | 641.631 5 |
|   food | 641.331 5 |
|   forage crop | 633.255 |
|   garden crop | 635.67 |
| Corn earworm | 632.78 |
| Corn sugars | 641.336 |
|   commercial processing | 664.133 |
|   food | 641.336 |
|   *see also* Sugar | |
| Corn syrup | 641.336 |
|   commercial processing | 664.133 |
|   food | 641.336 |
|   *see also* Sugar | |
| Cornales | 583.84 |
| Corneal diseases | |
|   ophthalmology | 617.719 |
|     *see also* Eye diseases — | |
|       humans | |
| Corneas | |
|   human anatomy | 611.84 |
|   human physiology | 612.841 |
|   ophthalmology | 617.719 |
| Cornetists | 788.960 92 |
| Cornets | 788.96 |
|   instrument | 788.961 9 |
|   music | 788.96 |
|   *see also* Brass instruments | |
| Cornetts | 788.99 |
|   *see also* Brass instruments | |
| Cornflower | 583.99 |
| Cornices | 721.5 |
|   architecture | 721.5 |
|   construction | 690.15 |
| Cornish fowl | 636.587 2 |
|   food | 641.365 872 |
|   cooking | 641.665 872 |
| Cornish language | 491.67 |
| | T6—916 7 |
| Cornish literature | 891.67 |
| Cornish people | T5—916 7 |
| Cornishmen | T5—916 7 |
| Cornmeal | |
|   commercial processing | 664.724 |
| Corns (Disorder) | |
|   medicine | 616.544 |
|     *see also* Skin diseases — | |
|       humans | |
| Cornstalk pulp | 676.14 |
| Cornstarch | |
|   food technology | 664.22 |
| Cornwall (England : | |
|   County) | T2—423 7 |
| Cornwallis, Charles Cornwallis, | |
|   Marquess | |
|   Indian history | 954.031 1 |
|     1786–1793 | 954.031 1 |
|     1805 | 954.031 2 |
| Coromandel Peninsula | |
|   (N.Z.) | T2—933 23 |
| Corona of sun | 523.75 |
| Coronary arteriosclerosis | |
|   medicine | 616.123 2 |
|     *see also* Cardiovascular | |
|       diseases — humans | |
| Coronary artery bypass surgery | 617.412 |
| Coronary atherosclerosis | |
|   medicine | 616.123 2 |
|     *see also* Cardiovascular | |
|       diseases — humans | |

| | |
|---|---|
| Coronary care | 362.196 120 4 |
| coronary heart disease | |
| medicine | 616.123 028 |
| medicine | 616.120 28 |
| Coronary heart disease | |
| medicine | 616.123 |
| *see also* Cardiovascular | |
| diseases — humans | |
| Coronas (Electronics) | 537.52 |
| Coronatae | 593.53 |
| Coronations | |
| customs | 394.4 |
| Coroners | 614.109 2 |
| law | 347.016 |
| criminal law | 345.012 6 |
| Coronie (Suriname : | |
| District) | T2—883 2 |
| Corowa (N.S.W.) | T2—944 8 |
| Corozal District (Belize) | T2—728 21 |
| Corpora (Linguistics) | 410.188 |
| specific languages | T4—018 8 |
| Corpora quadrigemina | |
| human physiology | 612.826 4 |
| medicine | 616.8 |
| Corporal punishment | 364.67 |
| education | 371.542 |
| law | 345.077 3 |
| penology | 364.67 |
| Corporate bonds | 332.632 34 |
| Corporate crime | 364.168 |
| law | 345.026 8 |
| Corporate divestiture | |
| management | 658.164 |
| Corporate finance | 338.604 1 |
| management | 658.15 |
| Corporate governance | 658.4 |
| Corporate income tax | 336.243 |
| law | 343.052 67 |
| public administration | 352.44 |
| public finance | 336.243 |
| Corporate law | 346.066 |
| Corporate mergers | 338.83 |
| *see also* Mergers | |
| Corporate organization | 338.74 |
| economics | 338.74 |
| law | 346.066 2 |
| management | |
| initiation | 658.114 5 |
| internal organization | 658.402 |
| Corporate ownership | |
| land economics | 333.324 |
| Corporate planning | 658.401 2 |
| Corporate profits | |
| income distribution | 339.21 |

| | |
|---|---|
| Corporate reorganization | 338.74 |
| credit economics | 332.75 |
| law | 346.066 26 |
| management | 658.16 |
| production economics | 338.74 |
| Corporate retail chains | 381.12 |
| management | 658.870 2 |
| *see also* Commerce | |
| Corporate social responsibility | 174.4 |
| Corporate state (Government) | 321.94 |
| Corporate turnarounds | |
| executive management | 658.406 3 |
| Corporation directories | 338.740 25 |
| *see Manual at* T1—025 vs. | |
| T1—029 | |
| Corporation meetings | |
| law | 346.066 45 |
| management use | 658.456 |
| Corporation records | |
| law | 346.066 4 |
| records management | 651.5 |
| Corporation tax | 336.207 |
| law | 343.067 |
| Corporations | 338.74 |
| accounting | 657.95 |
| law | 346.066 48 |
| economics | 338.74 |
| income tax | 336.243 |
| law | 343.052 67 |
| law | 346.066 |
| tort law | 346.031 |
| management | 658.045 |
| initiation | 658.114 5 |
| law | 346.066 4 |
| *see Manual at* 658.04 vs. | |
| 658.114, 658.402 | |
| taxes | 336.207 |
| law | 343.067 |
| Corps (Military units) | 355.31 |
| Corps of engineers | 358.22 |
| Corpus Christi (Tex.) | T2—764 113 |
| Corpus iuris canonici | 262.923 |
| Corpus linguistics | 410.188 |
| specific languages | T4—018 8 |
| Corpus striatum | |
| human physiology | 612.825 |
| medicine | 616.8 |
| Corpuscular theory of light | 535.12 |
| Correctional institutions | 365 |
| *see also* Penal institutions | |
| Corrections (Astronomy) | 522.9 |
| Corrections (Penology) | 364.6 |
| public administration | 353.39 |
| Correlation analysis | 519.537 |

| | |
|---|---|
| Correspondence (Letters) | 383.122 |
| *see also* Letters | |
| (Correspondence) | |
| Correspondence analysis | 519.537 |
| Correspondence art | 709.040 84 |
| Correspondence courses | 371.356 |
| adult education | 374.4 |
| | T1—071 5 |
| higher education | 378.175 6 |
| Correspondence schools | 374.4 |
| | T1—071 5 |
| Corrèze (France : Dept.) | T2—446 7 |
| Corrientes (Argentina : | |
| Province) | T2—822 2 |
| Corrodentia | 595.732 |
| Corrosion | 620.112 23 |
| Corrosion control | |
| chemical process equipment | 660.283 04 |
| Corrosion-resistant construction | |
| ship hulls | 623.848 |
| Corrosive materials | 363.179 |
| public safety | 363.179 |
| technology | 604.7 |
| *see also* Hazardous materials | |
| Corrugated paperboard boxes | 676.32 |
| Corruption in government | 364.132 3 |
| law | 345.023 23 |
| government liability | 342.088 |
| public administration | 353.46 |
| Corryong (Vic.) | T2—945 5 |
| Cors anglais | 788.53 |
| instrument | 788.531 9 |
| music | 788.53 |
| *see also* Woodwind instruments | |
| Corsages | 745.923 |
| Corse (Region) | 944.99 |
| | T2—449 9 |
| ancient | 937.99 |
| | T2—379 9 |
| Corse-de-Sud (France) | T2—449 92 |
| ancient | T2—379 92 |
| Corsica (Region) | 944.99 |
| | T2—449 9 |
| ancient | 937.99 |
| | T2—379 9 |
| Corsican language | 459.984 |
| | T6—599 84 |
| Corsican literature | 859.984 |
| Corsicans | T5—599 84 |
| Corson County (S.D.) | T2—783 52 |
| Cortés (Honduras : Dept.) | T2—728 311 |
| Cortes Island (B.C.) | T2—711 1 |

| | |
|---|---|
| Cortex | |
| human anatomy | 611.81 |
| human physiology | 612.825 |
| medicine | 616.8 |
| Cortisone | |
| pharmacology | 615.364 |
| Cortland County (N.Y.) | T2—747 72 |
| Cortona (Italy) | |
| ancient | T2—375 68 |
| Çorum İli (Turkey) | T2—563 83 |
| ancient | T2—393 32 |
| Coruña (Spain : Province) | T2—461 1 |
| Corundum | 553.65 |
| gems | 553.84 |
| materials science | 620.198 |
| mineralogy | 549.523 |
| Corvidae | 598.864 |
| Corydalidae | 595.747 |
| Coryell County (Tex.) | T2—764 515 |
| Corynebacterium | 579.373 |
| Corythosaurus | 567.914 |
| Coryza | |
| medicine | 616.205 |
| *see also* Respiratory tract | |
| diseases — humans | |
| Cosenza (Italy : Province) | T2—457 85 |
| ancient | T2—377 85 |
| Cosets | 512.2 |
| Coshocton County (Ohio) | T2—771 65 |
| Cosmetic surgery | 617.952 |
| Cosmetics | 646.72 |
| customs | 391.63 |
| health | 613.488 |
| manufacturing technology | 668.55 |
| personal care | 646.72 |
| product safety | 363.196 |
| law | 344.042 3 |
| Cosmetologists | 646.720 92 |
| Cosmetology | 646.72 |
| Cosmic dust | 523.112 5 |
| Cosmic noise | |
| meteorology | 551.527 6 |
| Cosmic rays | 539.722 3 |
| biophysics | 571.459 |
| humans | 612.014 486 |
| meteorology | 551.527 6 |
| Cosmochemistry | 523.02 |
| Cosmogony | 523.12 |
| astronomy | 523.12 |
| philosophy | 113 |
| Cosmology | 523.1 |
| astronomy | 523.1 |
| philosophy | 113 |

Cosmology (continued)
  religion | 202.4
    Christianity | 231.765
    comparative religion | 202.4
    Hinduism | 294.524
    Islam | 297.242
    Judaism | 296.3
    philosophy of religion | 215.2
Cosmonauts | 629.450 092
Cosmos (Flowers) | 583.99
Cossacks | T5—917 14
Cost accounting | 657.42
Cost analysis | 658.155 2
Cost-benefit analysis | 658.155 4
  public administration | 352.43
Cost control | 658.155 2
  public administration | 352.85
Cost effectiveness
  financial management | 658.155 4
Cost of living | 339.42
Cost-output ratio | 338.06
  agricultural industries | 338.16
  economics | 338.06
  mineral industries | 338.26
  secondary industries | 338.45
Cost reduction | 658.155 2
Cost-volume-profit analysis | 658.155 4
Costa, Manuel Pinto da
  Sao Tomean history | 967.150 21
Costa e Silva, Arthur da
  Brazilian history | 981.063
Costa Region (Ecuador) | T2—866 3
Costa Rica | 972.86
  | T2—728 6
Costa Rican literature | 860
Costa Ricans | T5—687 286
Costaceae | 584.39
Costanoan Indians | T5—974 13
Costanoan language | 497.413
  | T6—974 13
Costilla County (Colo.) | T2—788 35
Costs | 338.51
  accounting | 657.42
  agricultural industries | 338.13
  economics | 338.51
  financial management | 658.155 2
  macroeconomics | 339.42
  mineral industries | 338.23
  secondary industries | 338.43
  transportation services | 388.049
Costume | 391
  arts | 700.456 4
  | T3C—356 4

Costume (continued)
  literature | 808.803 564
    history and criticism | 809.933 564
    specific literatures | T3B—080 356 4
     history and
      criticism | T3B—093 564
  *see Manual at* 391 vs. 646.3,
    746.92
Costume jewelry | 391.7
  customs | 391.7
  handicrafts | 745.594 2
  making | 688.2
Costume jewelry makers | 688.209 2
Costumes | 792.026
  commercial technology | 687.16
  customs | 391.48
  dramatic performances | 792.026
    motion pictures | 791.430 26
    stage | 792.026
    television | 791.450 26
  home sewing | 646.478
  *see also* Clothing
  *see Manual at* 391 vs. 646.3,
    746.92
Cot death
  pediatrics | 618.920 26
Côte d'Azur (France) | T2—449 4
Côte-de-Beaupré (Quebec) | T2—714 48
Côte-de-Gaspé (Quebec) | T2—714 793
Côte d'Ivoire | 966.68
  | T2—666 8
Côte-d'Or (France) | T2—444 2
Côte-Nord (Quebec) | T2—714 17
Côte-Nord (Quebec :
  Administrative region) | T2—714 17
Côte-Saint-Luc (Quebec) | T2—714 28
Côtes-d'Armor (France) | T2—441 2
Cotillions | 793.35
Cotingas | 598.822
Cotingidae | 598.822
Cotonou (Benin) | T2—668 3
Cotopaxi (Ecuador) | T2—866 14
Cotswold (England) | T2—424 17
Cotswold Hills (England) | T2—424 17
Cotswolds (England) | T2—424 17
Cottage cheese | 641.373 56
  cooking | 641.673 56
  food | 641.373 56
  processing | 637.356
Cottage industries | 338.634
  labor economics | 331.256 7
Cottages
  architecture | 728.37
  construction | 690.837

| | |
|---|---|
| Cottbus (Germany) | T2—431 51 |
| Cottbus (Germany : Bezirk) | T2—431 51 |
| Cotters | 621.883 |
| Cottle County (Tex.) | T2—764 751 |
| Cotton | |
| agricultural economics | 338.173 51 |
| botany | 583.685 |
| fiber crop | 633.51 |
| textiles | 677.21 |
| arts | 746.042 1 |
| *see also* Textiles | |
| Cotton County (Okla.) | T2—766 49 |
| Cotton grasses | 584.84 |
| Cotton rats | 599.357 2 |
| Cottonseed meal | 664.726 |
| Cottonseed oil | 641.335 1 |
| cooking | 641.635 1 |
| food | 641.335 1 |
| food technology | 664.363 |
| Cottontails | 599.324 |
| Cottonwood County (Minn.) | T2—776 28 |
| Cottonwoods | 583.65 |
| Coturnix | 598.627 2 |
| Cotylosauria | 567.92 |
| Couches | 645.4 |
| manufacturing technology | 684.12 |
| *see also* Furniture | |
| Couching | |
| arts | 746.44 |
| Coudres, Île aux (Quebec) | T2—714 492 |
| Cougar | 599.752 4 |
| conservation technology | 639.979 752 4 |
| resource economics | 333.959 752 4 |
| Cough remedies | |
| pharmacokinetics | 615.72 |
| Coulometers | 621.374 4 |
| Coulometry | 543.4 |
| Council for Mutual Economic | |
| Assistance | 341.242 7 |
| international commerce | 382.914 7 |
| international economics | 337.147 |
| law of nations | 341.242 7 |
| Council housing | 363.585 |
| law | 344.063 635 |
| *see also* Housing | |
| Council of Europe | T2—4 |
| law | 341.242 1 |
| Council of the European Union | 341.242 222 |
| Councils | |
| Christian ecclesiology | 262.5 |
| Councils of ministers | |
| public administration | 352.24 |
| Counseling | 361.06 |
| armed forces | 355.347 |
| crime prevention | 364.48 |
| education | 371.4 |
| law | 344.079 4 |
| employee programs | |
| personnel management | 658.385 |
| public administration | 352.67 |
| pastoral theology | |
| Christianity | 253.5 |
| Judaism | 296.61 |
| personal counseling | 361.06 |
| prisoner services | 365.661 |
| psychology | 158.3 |
| social work | 361.06 |
| older people | 362.66 |
| Counted thread embroidery | 746.443 |
| Counter displays | |
| advertising | 659.157 |
| Counter-Reformation | 270.6 |
| German history | 943.03 |
| Counterattacks (Military tactics) | 355.422 |
| Counterculture | 306.1 |
| Counterfactuals | 511.317 |
| mathematical logic | 511.317 |
| philosophical logic | 160.119 87 |
| Counterfeit cancellations | |
| philately | 769.562 |
| Counterfeit coins | |
| numismatics | 737.4 |
| Counterfeit covers | |
| philately | 769.562 |
| Counterfeit paper money | |
| arts | 769.55 |
| Counterfeit postage stamps | |
| philately | 769.562 |
| Counterfeiting | 364.133 4 |
| economics | 332.9 |
| law | 345.023 34 |
| merchandise | 364.166 8 |
| law | 345.026 68 |
| money | 364.133 4 |
| law | 345.023 34 |
| Counterglow (Astronomy) | 523.59 |
| Counterintelligence | 327.12 |
| armed forces | 355.343 3 |
| *see also* Unconventional warfare | |
| *see also* Espionage | |
| Countermining | 623.31 |
| Countermonopoly theory of unions | 331.880 1 |
| Counterpoint | 781.286 |

Counters
  numismatics — 737.3
Countersubjects
  musical element — 781.248
Countertenor voices — 782.86
  choral and mixed voices — 782.86
  single voices — 783.86
Countess of Huntingdon's
  Connexion — 285.23
Counties — 320.83
  government — 320.83
  public administration — 352.15
    support and control — 353.335
    *see Manual at* 351.3–.9 vs.
      352.13–.19
Counting — 513.211
Counting circuits — 621.381 534
Counting machines
  manufacturing technology — 681.14
Counting-out rhymes — 398.84
Counting rhymes — 398.84
Country and western music — 781.642
Country clubs
  landscape architecture — 712.7
Country music — 781.642
  songs — 782.421 642
Country musicians
  singers — 782.421 642 092
Country Party (Australia) — 324.294 04
Country singers — 782.421 642 092
County charters — 342.02
County courts — 347.02
County executives — 352.232 15
County government buildings
  architecture — 725.13
County planning
  civic art — 711.3
  economics — 338.9
Couples therapy
  psychiatry — 616.891 562
Coupling (Nuclear particles) — 539.75
Couplings — 621.825
  railroad engineering — 625.25
Coupons
  sales promotion — 658.82
Coups d'état — 321.09
  *see Manual at* 909, 930–990 vs.
    320.4, 321, 321.09
Courage
  ethics — 179.6
Courland (Duchy) — T2—479 6
Cournot, A. A. (Antoine
  Augustin)
  economic school — 330.154 3

Course in Miracles — 299.93
Courses of study — T1—071
Court calendars — 347.013
  criminal law — 345.012 3
Court clerks — 347.016
  criminal law — 345.012 6
Court costs
  judgments
    law — 347.077
  law — 347.057
Court decisions
  law of nations — 341.026 8
  texts — 348.044
    United States — 348.734 4
Court handball — 796.312
Court management — 347.013
  criminal law — 345.012 3
Court of First Instance of the
  European Communities — 341.242 228 2
Court of Justice of the European
  Communities — 341.242 228 4
Court records — 347.013
  criminal law — 345.012 3
  genealogy — 929.3
Court reporters — 347.016
  criminal law — 345.012 6
Court reporting
  shorthand — 653.18
Court rules — 347.051
  criminal law — 345.05
Court settings
  music — 781.536
Court tennis — 796.34
Courtesy
  ethics — 177.1
    *see also* Ethical problems
  etiquette — 395
Courthouses
  architecture — 725.15
Courtroom procedure — 347.075
  criminal law — 345.075
Courts (Law) — 347.01
  England — 347.420 1
  European Union — 341.242 228
  law of nations — 341.55
  Scotland — 347.411 01
  United States — 347.731
Courts-martial — 343.014 3
Courts of appeal — 347.03
  England — 347.420 3
  Scotland — 347.411 03
  United States — 347.732 4
Courts of first appeal — 347.033
  criminal law — 345.014 42

| | |
|---|---|
| Courts of first instance | 347.02 |
|   criminal law | 345.014 2 |
| Courts of last appeal | 347.035 |
|   criminal law | 345.014 44 |
| Courts of last resort | 347.035 |
|   criminal law | 345.014 44 |
| Courts of original jurisdiction | 347.02 |
|   criminal law | 345.014 2 |
| Courts of second appeal | 347.035 |
|   criminal law | 345.014 44 |
| Courts of second instance | 347.033 |
|   criminal law | 345.014 42 |
| Courts of third instance | 347.035 |
|   criminal law | 345.014 44 |
| Courtship | 306.734 |
|   customs | 392.4 |
|   ethics | 177.65 |
|     religion | 205.676 5 |
|       Christianity | 241.676 5 |
|       Judaism | 296.367 65 |
|     *see also* Ethical problems | |
|   life skills | 646.77 |
|   music | 781.586 |
|   sociology | 306.734 |
| Courtship (Animal behavior) | 591.562 |
| Courtyards | 721.84 |
| Cousins | 306.87 |
| | T1—085 |
| Couvade | 392.12 |
| Covasna (Romania : Judeţ) | T2—498 4 |
| Covenant relationship with God | |
|   Christianity | 231.76 |
|   Judaism | 296.311 72 |
| Coventry (England) | T2—424 98 |
| Cover crops | |
|   soil conservation | 631.452 |
| Cover letters | |
|   use in job hunting | 650.142 |
| Coverdale Bible | 220.520 1 |
| Covered bridges | 388.132 |
|   construction | 624.218 |
| Coverlets | |
|   manufacturing technology | 677.626 |
| Covers | |
|   bookbinding | 686.34 |
| Covers (Philately) | 769.565 |
| Covetousness | |
|   ethics | 179.8 |
| Covington (Va.) | T2—755 812 |
| Covington County (Ala.) | T2—761 27 |
| Covington County (Miss.) | T2—762 545 |
| Cowardice | |
|   ethics | 179.6 |
| Cowbirds | 598.874 |

| | |
|---|---|
| Cowboys | 636.213 092 |
| Cowbridge (Wales) | T2—429 89 |
| Coweta County (Ga.) | T2—758 423 |
| Cowfishes | 597.64 |
| Cowichan Valley (B.C.) | T2—711 2 |
| Cowley County (Kan.) | T2—781 89 |
| Cowlitz County (Wash.) | T2—797 88 |
| Cowlitz River (Wash.) | T2—797 82 |
| Cowpeas | 641.356 592 |
|   *see also* Black-eyed peas | |
| Cowpox | |
|   incidence | 614.521 |
|   medicine | 616.913 |
|     *see also* Communicable | |
|       diseases — humans | |
| Cowra (N.S.W.) | T2—944 5 |
| Cowries | 594.32 |
| Cows | 636.2 |
|   agricultural economics | 338.176 2 |
|   animal husbandry | 636.2 |
|   zoology | 599.642 2 |
| Coyote | 599.772 5 |
|   conservation technology | 639.979 772 5 |
|   predator control technology | 636.083 9 |
|   resource economics | 333.959 772 5 |
|   small game hunting | 799.259 772 5 |
| Coypu | 599.359 |
| CPM (Management) | 658.403 2 |
| CPR (Resuscitation) | |
|   medicine | 616.102 5 |
| CPU (Central processor) | 004 |
|   engineering | 621.39 |
| Crab culture | 639.66 |
| Crab fishing | 639.56 |
| Crabbing | 639.56 |
|   economics | 338.372 538 6 |
| Crabeater seal | 599.796 |
| Crabgrasses | 584.92 |
| Crabs | 595.386 |
|   conservation technology | 639.975 386 |
|   cooking | 641.695 |
|   fishing | 639.56 |
|   fishing industry | 338.372 538 6 |
|   food | 641.395 |
|     commercial processing | 664.94 |
|   paleozoology | 565.386 |
|   resource economics | 333.955 56 |
|   zoology | 595.386 |
| Cracidae | 598.64 |
| Crack abuse | 362.298 |
|   medicine | 616.864 7 |
|   personal health | 613.84 |
|   social welfare | 362.298 |
|   *see also* Substance abuse | |

| | | | |
|---|---|---|---|
| Crack resistance (Engineering) | | Crape myrtle | 635.977 376 |
| materials science | 620.112 6 | botany | 583.76 |
| Crackers | 641.815 | ornamental arboriculture | 635.977 376 |
| commercial processing | 664.752 | Crappies | 597.738 |
| cooking | 641.815 | sports fishing | 799.177 38 |
| Cracking processes | | Craps | 795.12 |
| petroleum | 665.533 | Crash injuries | |
| Cradle Mountain (Tas.) | T2—946 3 | incidence | 614.3 |
| Cradle Mountain-Lake | | medicine | 617.102 8 |
| Saint Clair National Park | | Crassulaceae | 583.72 |
| (Tas.) | T2—946 3 | Crater Lake National Park | |
| Cradock (South Africa : | | (Or.) | T2—795 915 |
| District) | T2—687 54 | Craters (Depressions) | 551.21 |
| Craft (Ships) | 387.2 | | T2—144 |
| *see also* Ships | | geography | 910.914 4 |
| Craft unions | 331.883 2 | geology | 551.21 |
| *see also* Labor unions | | physical geography | 910.021 44 |
| Crafts | 680 | Craters of the Moon | |
| arts | 745 | National Monument | |
| public administrative support | 353.77 | (Idaho) | T2—796 59 |
| sociology | 306.47 | Crates | |
| *see Manual at* 680 vs. 745.5 | | wooden | 674.82 |
| Craftsmen's marks | T1—027 8 | Craven (England) | T2—428 41 |
| Craig County (Okla.) | T2—766 98 | Craven County (N.C.) | T2—756 192 |
| Craig County (Va.) | T2—755 795 | Crawfishes | 595.384 |
| Craigavon (Northern | | *see also* Crayfishes | |
| Ireland : District) | T2—416 64 | Crawford County (Ark.) | T2—767 35 |
| Craighead County (Ark.) | T2—767 98 | Crawford County (Ga.) | T2—758 562 |
| Cranberries | 641.347 6 | Crawford County (Ill.) | T2—773 75 |
| botany | 583.66 | Crawford County (Ind.) | T2—772 28 |
| commercial processing | 664.804 76 | Crawford County (Iowa) | T2—777 45 |
| cooking | 641.647 6 | Crawford County (Kan.) | T2—781 98 |
| food | 641.347 6 | Crawford County (Mich.) | T2—774 77 |
| horticulture | 634.76 | Crawford County (Mo.) | T2—778 62 |
| Cranbrook (B.C.) | T2—711 65 | Crawford County (Ohio) | T2—771 27 |
| Crane County (Tex.) | T2—764 915 | Crawford County (Pa.) | T2—748 97 |
| Crane flies | 595.772 | Crawford County (Wis.) | T2—775 74 |
| Cranes (Birds) | 598.32 | Crawley (England) | T2—422 61 |
| conservation technology | 639.978 32 | Crawling | |
| resource economics | 333.958 32 | physiology | 573.79 |
| Cranes (Hoisting machinery) | 621.873 | Crayfish culture | 639.64 |
| Cranial nerve diseases | | Crayfishes | 595.384 |
| medicine | 616.856 | cooking | 641.695 |
| *see also* Nervous system | | culture | 639.64 |
| diseases — humans | | fishing | 639.54 |
| Cranial nerves | 573.85 | food | 641.395 |
| human physiology | 612.819 | sports fishing | 799.255 384 |
| medicine | 616.856 | zoology | 595.384 |
| *see also* Nervous system | | Crayfishing | 639.54 |
| Craniata | 596 | sports | 799.255 384 |
| Craniology | 599.948 | Crayon drawing | 741.23 |
| Craniotomy | | | |
| obstetrical surgery | 618.88 | | |
| Cranks (Mechanisms) | 621.827 | | |

| | |
|---|---|
| Cream | 641.371 48 |
| cooking | 641.671 48 |
| food | 641.371 48 |
| processing | 637.148 |
| Cream cheese | 641.373 52 |
| cooking | 641.673 52 |
| food | 641.373 52 |
| processing | 637.352 |
| Cream of tartar | |
| commercial processing | 664.68 |
| Cream puffs | 641.865 9 |
| commercial processing | 664.752 5 |
| home preparation | 641.865 9 |
| Creaming latex | 678.522 |
| Crease-resistant fabrics | 677.681 |
| *see also* Textiles | |
| Creation | |
| cosmogony | 523.12 |
| nuclear particles | 539.75 |
| philosophy | 113 |
| religion | 202.4 |
| Christianity | 231.765 |
| comparative religion | 202.4 |
| Islam | 297.242 |
| Judaism | 296.34 |
| philosophy of religion | 213 |
| Creation science | 231.765 2 |
| Creationism | 231.765 2 |
| biological evolution | 576.8 |
| public education | 379.28 |
| *see Manual at* 231.7652 vs. | |
| 213, 500, 576.8 | |
| Creative ability | 153.35 |
| business success | 650.1 |
| executives | 658.409 4 |
| *see also* Creativity | |
| Creative activities | |
| child care | 649.51 |
| education | 371.3 |
| Creative arts | 700 |
| primary education | 372.5 |
| Creative thinking | 153.42 |
| *see also* Creativity | |
| Creative writing | |
| primary education | 372.623 |
| Creativity | 153.35 |
| arts | 701.15 |
| educational objective | 370.118 |
| educational psychology | 370.157 |
| literature | 801.92 |
| promotion of | |
| personnel management | 658.314 |
| executives | 658.407 14 |
| public administration | 352.66 |

| | |
|---|---|
| Credibility | |
| Christian church | 262.72 |
| Credit | 332.7 |
| economics | 332.7 |
| law | 346.073 |
| public administration | 354.86 |
| Credit cards | 332.765 |
| banking services | 332.178 8 |
| credit economics | 332.765 |
| law | 346.073 |
| personal finance | 332.024 02 |
| Credit cooperatives | 334.2 |
| Credit institutions | 332.3 |
| public administration | 354.86 |
| *see also* Banks (Finance) | |
| Credit insurance | 368.87 |
| Credit investigations | |
| marketing management | 658.88 |
| Credit management | |
| marketing | 658.88 |
| Credit money | 332.42 |
| Credit restrictions | 332.75 |
| Credit unions | 334.22 |
| law | 346.066 8 |
| Creditors | |
| law | 346.077 |
| Credits (Education) | 371.218 |
| higher education | 378.161 8 |
| Credo | 264.36 |
| music | 782.323 2 |
| Cree Indians | T5—973 23 |
| Cree language | 497.323 |
| | T6—973 23 |
| Cree literature | 897.323 |
| Creeds | 202 |
| Christianity | 238 |
| Creek County (Okla.) | T2—766 84 |
| Creek Indians | T5—973 85 |
| Creek language | 497.385 |
| | T6—973 85 |
| Creep (Geology) | 551.307 |
| Creep (Materials science) | 620.112 33 |
| Creepers (Birds) | 598.82 |
| Creigiau (Cardiff, Wales) | T2—429 87 |
| Cremation | 363.75 |
| customs | 393.2 |
| social services | 363.75 |
| *see also* Undertaking | |
| (Mortuary) | |
| Crematoriums | 363.75 |
| architecture | 725.597 |
| Cremona (Italy) | T2—452 71 |
| Cremona (Italy : Province) | T2—452 7 |
| ancient | T2—373 15 |

| | |
|---|---|
| Crenshaw County (Ala.) | T2—761 36 |
| Creodonta | 569.7 |
| Creole cooking | 641.597 63 |
| Creoles | |
| linguistics | 417.22 |
| specific languages | T4—7 |
| *see Manual at* T4—7 | |
| Creosote bush | 583.79 |
| Crepe myrtle | 635.977 376 |
| botany | 583.76 |
| ornamental arboriculture | 635.977 376 |
| Crepes | 641.815 3 |
| Creping paper | 676.234 |
| Creping textiles | 677.028 25 |
| Cresses | 641.355 6 |
| botany | 583.64 |
| cooking | 641.655 6 |
| food | 641.355 6 |
| garden crop | 635.56 |
| Creston (B.C.) | T2—711 62 |
| Crests | 929.6 |
| Creswick (Vic.) | T2—945 3 |
| Cretaceous period | 551.77 |
| geology | 551.77 |
| paleontology | 560.177 |
| Crete (Greece) | 949.59 |
| | T2—495 9 |
| ancient | 939.18 |
| | T2—391 8 |
| Crete, Sea of (Greece) | 551.461 388 |
| | T2—163 88 |
| Creuse (France) | T2—446 8 |
| Creutzfeldt-Jakob disease | |
| medicine | 616.83 |
| *see also* Nervous system | |
| diseases — humans | |
| Crewe and Nantwich | |
| (England) | T2—427 12 |
| Crewelwork | 746.446 |
| Crib death | |
| pediatrics | 618.920 26 |
| Cribbage | 795.411 |
| Criblé engraving | 765.6 |
| Cricetidae | 599.35 |
| Cricetus | 599.356 |
| Cricket (Game) | 796.358 |
| Cricket players | 796.358 092 |
| Crickets | 595.726 |
| culture | 638.572 6 |
| Cries (Rhymes) | 398.87 |
| Crime | 364 |
| arts | 700.455 6 |
| | T3C—355 6 |
| correction | 364.6 |

| | |
|---|---|
| Crime (continued) | |
| folklore | 398.275 6 |
| history and criticism | 398.355 6 |
| law | 345 |
| literature | 808.803 556 |
| history and criticism | 809.933 556 |
| specific literatures | T3B—080 355 6 |
| history and | |
| criticism | T3B—093 556 |
| social theology | 201.764 |
| Christianity | 261.833 |
| Crime insurance | 368.82 |
| government-sponsored | |
| violent crimes | 368.48 |
| Crime prevention | 364.4 |
| criminology | 364.4 |
| public administration | 353.39 |
| management | 658.473 |
| penology | 364.601 |
| police services | 363.23 |
| public administration | 353.36 |
| school programs | 371.782 |
| Crime victims | 362.88 |
| | T1—086 949 |
| Crimea (Ukraine : Oblast) | T2—477 1 |
| Crimean Tatar language | 494.388 |
| | T6—943 88 |
| Crimean Tatar literature | 894.388 |
| Crimean Tatars | T5—943 88 |
| Crimean War, 1853–1856 | 947.073 8 |
| Crimes | 364.1 |
| *see also* Criminal offenses | |
| Crimes against humanity | 364.135 |
| law | 345.023 5 |
| Crimes against peace | 364.135 |
| law | 345.023 5 |
| Crimes against the state | 364.131 |
| law | 345.023 1 |
| Crimes without victims | 364.1 |
| law | 345.02 |
| Criminal abortion | 364.185 |
| law | 345.028 5 |
| Criminal anthropology | 364.2 |
| Criminal capacity | 345.04 |
| Criminal courts | 345.01 |
| England | 345.420 1 |
| Scotland | 345.411 01 |
| Criminal intent | 345.04 |
| Criminal investigation | 363.25 |
| armed forces | 355.133 23 |
| law | 345.052 |
| police services | 363.25 |
| Criminal jurisdiction | 345.012 2 |

Criminal justice                          364
  criminology                   364
  law                           345
  police services               363.2
  public administration         353.4
Criminal justice information
  systems                       025.063 64
Criminal law                              345
Criminal liability                        345.04
Criminal offenses                         364.1
  insurance against             368.82
  law                           345.02
    *see Manual at* 345.02 vs.
     346.03
  *see Manual at* 362–363 vs.
    364.1; *also at* 900
Criminal procedure                        345.05
  public administration         353.43
Criminal psychology                       364.3
Criminal responsibility                   345.04
Criminal trial practice                   345.075
Criminal trials                           345.07
Criminal usury                            364.168
  law                           345.026 8
Criminalistics                            363.25
  *see also* Criminal investigation
Criminally insane people                  364.38
  correctional institutions     365.46
    *see also* Penal institutions
Criminals                                 364.3
                                          T1—086 927
Criminologists                            364.092
Criminology                               364
Crinoidea                                 593.92
  paleozoology                  563.92
Crinozoa                                  593.92
  paleozoology                  563.92
Crioulo language                          T6—69
Crisis management                         658.405 6
Crisp County (Ga.)                        T2—758 893
Cristiani democratici uniti (Italian
  political party)              324.245 082
Criteria
  epistemology                  121.65
Critical care                             362.174
  medicine                      616.028
  nursing                       616.028
  social welfare                362.174
  *see also* Health services
Critical path method
  (Management)                   658.403 2
Critical pedagogy                         370.115
Critical phenomena                        530.474
  *see also* Phase transformations

Critical philosophy                       142
Critical points                           530.474
  fluid state                   530.424
  *see also* Phase transformations
Critical realism
  philosophy                     149.2
Critical size
  nuclear engineering           621.483 1
Critical thinking                         160
  educational psychology        370.152
  primary education
    reading            372.474
  psychology                     153.42
Criticism
  arts                          701.18
  fine arts
    specific subjects  704.94
  literature                     809
    specific literatures    T3B—09
     *see Manual at* T3B—08
     and T3B—09
  theory                        801.95
  *see Manual at* 800
Criticism of individuals                  T1—092
Crittenden County (Ark.)                  T2—767 94
Crittenden County (Ky.)                   T2—769 893
Cro-Magnons                               569.98
Croakers (Fishes)                         597.725
Croatia                                   949.72
                                          T2—497 2
  ancient                       939.872
                                          T2—398 72
Croatian language                         491.83
                                          T6—918 3
Croatian literature                       891.83
Croatians                                 T5—918 3
Croats                                    T5—918 3
Crocheted fabrics                         677.662
  arts                          746.434
  manufacturing technology      677.662
  *see also* Textiles
Crocheted laces                           677.662
  arts                          746.22
  manufacturing technology      677.662
Crocheted rugs
  arts                          746.73
Crocheting                                677.028 2
  arts                          746.434
  manufacturing technology      677.028 2
Crock-pot cooking                         641.588 4
Crockett County (Tenn.)                   T2—768 225
Crockett County (Tex.)                    T2—764 875

Crocodile River
  (Mpumalanga, South
  Africa)        T2—682 71
Crocodiles        597.982
  big game hunting        799.279 82
  conservation technology        639.977 982
  paleozoology        567.98
  resource economics        333.957 982
  zoology        597.982
Crocodilians        597.98
Crocodilidae        597.982
Crocodylus        597.982
Crocuses        635.934 38
  botany        584.38
  floriculture        635.934 38
Crohn disease
  medicine        616.344
    *see also* Digestive system
      diseases — humans
Cromwell, Oliver
  British history        941.064
  English history        942.064
  Scottish history        941.106 4
Cromwell, Richard
  British history        941.065
  English history        942.065
  Scottish history        941.106 5
Crook County (Or.)        T2—795 83
Crook County (Wyo.)        T2—787 13
Crop diversification
  agriculture        631.58
  economics        338.162
Crop-dusting        632.94
Crop-hail insurance        368.121
Crop insurance        368.121
Crop rotation
  cultivation technique        631.582
  economics        338.162
  soil conservation        631.452
Crop yields        338.1
  agricultural technology        631.558
  economics        338.1
  *see Manual at* 338.1 vs.
    631.558
Crops        630
  economics        338.1
  pathology        632
  plant physiology        571.2
  public administration        354.54
Croquet        796.354
Croquet players        796.354 092
Crosby County (Tex.)        T2—764 848
Crosier Fathers        255.19
  church history        271.19

Cross-country races
  humans        796.428
Cross-country skiing        796.932
Cross County (Ark.)        T2—767 93
Cross-cultural communication        303.482
Cross-cultural psychology        155.8
Cross dressing
  sexual practices        306.778
Cross-examination        347.075
  criminal law        345.075
Cross River languages        496.364
       T6—963 64
Cross River State (Nigeria)        T2—669 44
Cross-stitch        746.443
Crossbills        598.885
Crossbreeding
  agriculture        631.523
    animal husbandry        636.082
    plant cultivation        631.523
Crossdressing
  sexual practices        306.778
Crosses
  religious significance        246.558
Crossing over (Genetics)        572.877
Crossings (Railroad)        385.312
  engineering        625.163
  transportation services        385.312
Crossopterygii        597.39
  paleozoology        567.39
Crossroads (South Africa)        T2—687 35
Crossword puzzles        793.732
Crotalus        597.963 8
Crotone (Italy : Province)        T2—457 87
  ancient        T2—377 87
Crotons        635.933 69
  botany        583.69
  floriculture        635.933 69
Croup
  medicine        616.201
    *see also* Respiratory tract
      diseases — humans
  pediatrics        618.922 01
Crow Indians        T5—975 272
Crow language        497.527 2
       T6—975 272
Crow Wing County (Minn.)        T2—776 71
Crowbars        621.93
Crowberries        583.66
Crowd control        363.323
  public administration        353.36
Crowds        302.33
  public safety        363.323
Crowle (England)        T2—428 32
Crowley County (Colo.)        T2—788 94

| | | | |
|---|---|---|---|
| Crown lands | 333.1 | Crushing | |
| Crown of thorns (Plant) | 635.933 69 | chemical engineering | 660.284 22 |
| botany | 583.69 | ores | 622.73 |
| floriculture | 635.933 69 | Crushing tools | 621.914 |
| Crowns (Dentistry) | 617.692 2 | Crust of earth | 551.13 |
| Crows | 598.864 | compression | 551.82 |
| sports hunting | 799.248 864 | Crustacea | 595.3 |
| Crowsnest Pass (Alta.) | T2—712 34 | *see also* Crustaceans | |
| Croydon (London, England) | T2—421 91 | Crustaceans | 595.3 |
| Crozet Islands | 969.9 | conservation technology | 639.975 3 |
| | T2—699 | cooking | 641.695 |
| Cruciales | 583.64 | culture | 639.6 |
| Crucible steel | 669.142 9 | fishing | 639.5 |
| Crucibles | | fishing industry | 338.372 53 |
| chemistry | 542.2 | food | 641.395 |
| Cruciferae | 583.64 | commercial processing | 664.94 |
| Crucifixes | | paleozoology | 565.3 |
| religious significance | 246.558 | resource economics | 333.955 5 |
| Crucifixion of Jesus Christ | 232.963 | zoology | 595.3 |
| Crucifixion thorns | 583.64 | Crutches | |
| Crude drugs | | manufacturing technology | 681.761 |
| pharmacognosy | 615.321 | Cryobiology | 571.464 5 |
| Crude gelatin | 668.34 | humans | 612.014 467 |
| Cruelty | | Cryogenic engineering | 621.59 |
| ethics | 179 | Cryogenic engineers | 621.590 92 |
| *see also* Ethical problems | | Cryogenics | 536.56 |
| Cruelty to animals | | biophysics | 571.464 5 |
| criminology | 364.187 | humans | 612.014 467 |
| criminal law | 345.028 7 | engineering | 621.59 |
| ethics | 179.3 | materials science | 620.112 16 |
| *see also* Animals — | | Cryolite | |
| treatment of — ethics | | mineralogy | 549.4 |
| Cruisers | 359.835 3 | synthetic | 666.86 |
| design | 623.812 53 | Cryometry | 536.54 |
| engineering | 623.825 3 | Cryosurgery | 617.05 |
| naval equipment | 359.835 3 | Cryotherapy | |
| naval units | 359.325 3 | medicine | 615.832 9 |
| Crumhorns | 788.5 | Cryptanalysis | 652.8 |
| *see also* Woodwind instruments | | armed forces | 355.343 2 |
| Crusades | 909.07 | Cryptococcales | 579.55 |
| arts | T3C—358 207 | Cryptogamia | 586 |
| church history | 270.4 | paleobotany | 561.6 |
| European history | 940.18 | Cryptography | 652.8 |
| history | 909.07 | armed forces | 358.24 |
| 1096–1099 | 956.014 | computer science | 005.82 |
| 1147–1149 | 956.014 | recreation | 793.73 |
| 1189–1192 | 956.014 | Cryptophyta | 579.82 |
| 1202–1204 | 949.503 | Cryptozoic eon | 551.71 |
| 1212 | 944.023 | geology | 551.71 |
| Palestinian history | 956.940 32 | paleontology | 560.171 |
| Crushed stone pavements | 625.82 | Crystal conduction counters | |
| Crushers (Agricultural tools) | | nuclear physics | 539.776 |
| manufacturing technology | 681.763 1 | Crystal devices | |
| | | electronics | 621.381 52 |

Crystal gazing 133.322
Crystal growth 548.5
Crystal lattices 548.81
Crystalline lens
  human anatomy 611.84
  human physiology 612.844
  ophthalmology 617.742
Crystalline solids 530.413
Crystallization 548.5
  chemical engineering 660.284 298
  sugar production 664.115
Crystallograms 548.83
Crystallographers 548.092
Crystallographic mineralogy 549.18
Crystallographic properties
  materials science 620.112 99
Crystallography 548
  *see Manual at* 548 vs. 530.41;
    *also at* 549 vs. 548
Crystals 548
  occultism 133.254 8
    divination 133.322
Csongrád Megye (Hungary) T2—439 8
CSP (Austrian political party) 324.243 602 4
CSP (Swiss political party) 324.249 407
CSU (German political party) 324.243 04
CT (Tomography)
  medicine 616.075 722
Ctenophora 593.8
  paleozoology 563.8
Ctenostomata 594.676
Ctenothrissiformes 567.5
Cuaiquer Indians T5—982
Cuando Cubango (Angola) T2—673 5
Cuanza Norte (Angola) T2—673 2
Cuanza Sul (Angola :
  Province) T2—673 2
Cub Scouts 369.43
Cuba 972.91
  T2—729 1
Cuban campaign, 1898 973.893 3
Cuban communism 335.434 7
  economics 335.434 7
  political ideology 320.532 309 729 1
Cuban itch
  incidence 614.521
  medicine 616.913
  *see also* Communicable
    diseases — humans
Cuban literature 860
Cubans T5—687 291
Cubas Grau, Raúl
  Paraguayan history 989.207 43
Cubature 515.43

Cube-doubling 516.204
Cube root 513.23
Cubes 516.156
Cubic equations 512.942 2
  algebra 512.942 2
  calculus 515.252
Cubism 709.040 32
  painting 759.063 2
  sculpture 735.230 432
Cubomedusae 593.53
Cuckoo shrikes 598.8
Cuckoos 598.74
Cucujoidea 595.769
Cuculiformes 598.74
  paleozoology 568.7
Cucumber tree 583.22
Cucumbers 641.356 3
  botany 583.63
  commercial processing 664.805 63
  cooking 641.656 3
  food 641.356 3
  garden crop 635.63
Cucurbitales 583.63
Cued speech
  applied linguistics 418
    specific languages T4—895 5
Cuenca (Spain : Province) T2—464 7
Cuffs
  commercial technology 687.19
Cuitlateco language 497.9
  T6—979
Culberson County (Tex.) T2—764 94
Culicidae 595.772
Cullinan (South Africa :
  District) T2—682 29
Cullman County (Ala.) T2—761 73
Culpeper County (Va.) T2—755 392
Cultivated silk textiles 677.391
  *see also* Textiles
Cultivation 631.5
Cultivators 631.51
  manufacturing technology 681.763 1
Cults 209
  *see Manual at* 201–209 and
    292–299; *also at* 299.93
Cultural anthropologists 306.092
Cultural anthropology 306
Cultural centers
  architecture 725.804 2
  area planning 711.57
Cultural contact 303.482
Cultural ethnology 305.8

| | |
|---|---|
| Cultural exchanges | 303.482 |
| law | 344.08 |
| public administration | 353.7 |
| sociology | 303.482 |
| Cultural influence | |
| psychology | 155.92 |
| Cultural institutions | 306 |
| Cultural levels (Social | |
| classes) | T1—086 2 |
| Cultural pluralism | 305.8 |
| education | 370.117 |
| political science | 323.1 |
| sociology | 305.8 |
| Cultural programs | |
| libraries | 021.26 |
| Cultural property | |
| historic preservation | 363.69 |
| law | 344.094 |
| Cultural relations | 303.482 |
| law | 344.09 |
| Cultural Revolution | 951.056 |
| Culturally disadvantaged children | 305.230 869 4 |
| home care | 649.156 7 |
| psychology | 155.456 7 |
| social group | 305.230 869 4 |
| Culturally disadvantaged people | 305.56 |
| | T1—086 94 |
| Culture | 306 |
| law | 344.09 |
| public administrative support | 353.7 |
| sociology | 306 |
| *see Manual at* 306 vs. 305, 909, 930–990 | |
| Cultured cells | |
| experimental research | |
| medicine | 616.027 7 |
| Cultured skim milk | 641.371 476 |
| cooking | 641.671 476 |
| food | 641.371 476 |
| processing | 637.147 6 |
| Cultured whole milk | 641.371 46 |
| cooking | 641.671 46 |
| food | 641.371 46 |
| processing | 637.146 |
| Culverts (Drainage) | 625.734 2 |
| Cumacea | 595.376 |
| Cumae (Extinct city) | T2—377 252 |
| Cumberland (N.S. : County) | T2—716 11 |
| Cumberland, Lake (Ky.) | T2—769 63 |
| Cumberland County (Ill.) | T2—773 73 |
| Cumberland County (Ky.) | T2—769 683 |
| Cumberland County (Me.) | T2—741 91 |
| Cumberland County (N.C.) | T2—756 373 |
| Cumberland County (N.J.) | T2—749 94 |

| | |
|---|---|
| Cumberland County (Pa.) | T2—748 43 |
| Cumberland County (Tenn.) | T2—768 75 |
| Cumberland County (Va.) | T2—755 615 |
| Cumberland Mountains | T2—769 1 |
| Kentucky | T2—769 1 |
| Tennessee | T2—768 944 |
| Cumberland Plateau | T2—768 7 |
| Kentucky | T2—769 1 |
| Tennessee | T2—768 7 |
| Cumberland Presbyterian Church | 285.135 |
| *see also* Presbyterian Church | |
| Cumberland River (Ky. and Tenn.) | T2—768 5 |
| Cumbernauld and Kilsyth (Scotland) | T2—414 52 |
| Cumbria (England) | T2—427 8 |
| Cumbrian Mountains (England) | T2—427 8 |
| Cuming County (Neb.) | T2—782 232 |
| Cumnock and Doon Valley (Scotland) | T2—414 67 |
| Cumulative trauma disorders | |
| medicine | 617.172 |
| Cuna Indians (Panama) | T5—978 3 |
| Cuna language (Panama) | 497.83 |
| | T6—978 3 |
| Cuna literature (Panama) | 897.83 |
| Cundinamarca (Colombia) | T2—861 46 |
| Cunene Province (Angola) | T2—673 5 |
| Cuneo (Italy : Province) | T2—451 3 |
| ancient | T2—371 6 |
| Cunninghame (Scotland) | T2—414 61 |
| Cunoniaceae | 583.72 |
| Cup fungi | 579.57 |
| Cup games | |
| soccer | 796.334 64 |
| Cupedidae | 595.762 |
| Cupolas | 721.5 |
| architecture | 721.5 |
| construction | 690.15 |
| Cuprammonium rayon | 677.462 |
| *see also* Textiles | |
| Cupressaceae | 585.4 |
| paleobotany | 561.54 |
| Cuprite | |
| mineralogy | 549.522 |
| Cups | |
| paper | 676.34 |
| Curaçao | T2—729 86 |
| Curassows | 598.64 |
| Curbs | 625.888 |
| Curculionidae | 595.768 |
| Curculionoidea | 595.768 |
| agricultural pests | 632.768 |

Curfew
  crime prevention — 364.4
Curia Romana — 262.136
Curicó (Chile : Province) — T2—833 4
Curium — 546.442
  *see also* Chemicals
Curling (Sport) — 796.964
Currants — 641.347 21
  botany — 583.72
  cooking — 641.647 21
  food — 641.347 21
  horticulture — 634.721
Currency — 332.4
  *see also* Money
Currency convertibility — 332.456
Currency movements — 332.042 4
Currency paper — 676.282 6
Currency power (Legislative
  bodies) — 328.341 2
Currency question — 332.46
Current accounts (Checking
  accounts) — 332.175 22
Current assets
  accounting — 657.72
Current awareness services
  information science — 025.525
Current liabilities
  accounting — 657.74
Current transactions
  balance of payments
    international commerce — 382.17
Curricula — 375
  — T1—071
  adult education — 374.01
  higher education — 378.199
  law — 344.077
  primary education — 372.19
  public control — 379.155
  secondary education — 373.19
  special education — 371.904 4
Curriculum change — 375.006
Curriculum development — 375.001
Curriculum evaluation — 375.006
Curriculum libraries — 027.7
Curriculum planning — 375.001
Curriculum vitae — 650.142
Curriculums — 375
Currituck County (N.C.) — T2—756 132
Curry County (N.M.) — T2—789 27
Curry County (Or.) — T2—795 21
Curry powder — 641.338 4
  *see also* Hot spices
Curses
  folklore — 398.41

Curses (Occultism) — 133.44
Curtains — 645.32
  arts — 746.94
  commercial technology — 684.3
  home sewing — 646.21
  household management — 645.32
Curtin, John
  Australian history — 994.042
Curvature (Mathematics) — 516.362
Curve fitting — 511.42
Curves — 516.152
  algebraic geometry — 516.352
  differential geometry — 516.36
  integral geometry — 516.36
Curvilinear coordinate system — 516.16
Curzon, George Nathaniel
  Curzon, Marquis of
    Indian history — 954.035 5
Cuscatlán (El Salvador) — T2—728 424
Cuscuses — 599.232
Cuscutaceae — 583.94
Cush — 939.78
  — T2—397 8
Cush sovereignty — 932.015
Cushing syndrome
  medicine — 616.45
  *see also* Endocrine
    diseases — humans
Cushites — T5—935
Cushitic languages — 493.5
  — T6—935
Cushitic literatures — 893.5
Cushitic peoples — T5—935
Cusk eels — 597.63
Custard apples — 583.22
Custer County (Colo.) — T2—788 52
Custer County (Idaho) — T2—796 72
Custer County (Mont.) — T2—786 33
Custer County (Neb.) — T2—782 47
Custer County (Okla.) — T2—766 17
Custer County (S.D.) — T2—783 95
Custodial services
  schools — 371.68
Custody of children — 346.017 3
Custom production — 338.642
Customary law — 340.5
Customer clubs — 381.149
  management — 658.879
Customer relations
  marketing management — 658.812
Customer services
  marketing management — 658.812

| | |
|---|---|
| Customized vans | 388.343 4 |
| driving | 629.284 34 |
| engineering | 629.223 4 |
| repair | 629.287 34 |
| transportation services | 388.343 4 |
| *see also* Trucks | |
| Customizing automobiles | 629.287 |
| Customs (Practices) | 390 |
| arts | 700.455 9 |
| | T3C—355 9 |
| literature | 808.803 559 |
| history and criticism | 809.933 559 |
| specific literatures | T3B—080 355 9 |
| history and criticism | T3B—093 559 |
| music | 781.58 |
| social control | 303.372 |
| Customs (Tariff) | 382.7 |
| commerce | 382.7 |
| international agreements | 382.9 |
| law | 343.056 |
| public administration | 352.448 |
| public finance | 336.26 |
| Customs administration | 352.448 |
| Customs buildings | |
| architecture | 725.14 |
| Customs courts | 343.056 026 9 |
| Customs unions | 382.91 |
| Cut flowers | 745.92 |
| floriculture | 635.966 |
| Cut stock lumber | 674.28 |
| Cutaneous leishmaniasis | |
| incidence | 614.534 |
| medicine | 616.936 4 |
| *see also* Communicable diseases — humans | |
| Cutaneous perception | |
| psychology | 152.182 |
| Cutaneous sensory disorders | |
| medicine | 616.856 |
| *see also* Nervous system diseases — humans | |
| Cutlass fishes | 597.78 |
| Cutlery | 642.7 |
| manufacturing technology | 683.82 |
| table setting | 642.7 |
| Cuts | |
| road engineering | 625.733 |
| Cutting gems | 736.202 8 |
| Cutting glass | 666.12 |
| arts | 748.6 |
| technology | 666.12 |
| Cutting metals | 671.53 |
| decorative arts | 739.14 |
| machining process | 671.35 |
| sculpture | 731.41 |
| Cutting tools | 621.93 |
| Cuttings (Plant propagation) | 631.535 |
| Cuttlefish | 594.58 |
| Cutwork | |
| arts | 746.44 |
| Cutworms | 595.78 |
| agricultural pests | 632.78 |
| Cuyahoga County (Ohio) | T2—771 31 |
| Cuyahoga River (Ohio) | T2—771 31 |
| Cuyuni-Mazaruni Region (Guyana) | T2—881 9 |
| Cuzco (Peru : Dept.) | T2—853 7 |
| CVP (Swiss political party) | 324.249 404 |
| Cyanamide fertilizers | 631.841 |
| chemical engineering | 668.624 1 |
| Cyanastraceae | 584.35 |
| Cyanite | |
| mineralogy | 549.62 |
| Cyanobacteria | 579.39 |
| Cyanophyta | 579.39 |
| Cyberinfrastructure | 004 |
| Cybernetics | 003.5 |
| | T1—011 5 |
| Cyberterrorism | 363.325 |
| criminology | 364.168 |
| *see also* Terrorism | |
| Cycadales | 585.9 |
| paleobotany | 561.591 |
| Cycadeoidales | 561.592 |
| Cycadofilicales | 561.595 |
| Cycads | 585.9 |
| paleobotany | 561.591 |
| Cyclades (Greece) | T2—495 85 |
| ancient | T2—391 5 |
| Cyclamens | 635.933 675 |
| botany | 583.675 |
| floriculture | 635.933 675 |
| Cyclanthales | 584.62 |
| Cyclarhidae | 598.878 |
| Cycles (Periodicity) | |
| philosophy | 116 |
| Cycles (Vehicles) | 388.347 |
| engineering | 629.227 |
| repair | 629.287 7 |
| riding | 629.284 7 |
| sports | 796.6 |
| transportation services | 388.347 |
| Cyclic compounds | 547.5 |
| chemical engineering | 661.8 |
| Cyclic groups | 512.25 |

| | |
|---|---|
| Cyclical unemployment | 331.137 047 |
| Cycling | |
|   sports | 796.6 |
| Cycling paths | 388.12 |
|   *see also* Bicycle paths | |
| Cyclists | 796.609 2 |
| Cyclo-cross | 796.624 |
| Cyclo rubber | 678.68 |
| Cycloacetylenes | 547.513 |
|   chemical engineering | 661.815 |
| Cyclones (Low-pressure systems) | 551.551 3 |
| Cyclones (Tornadoes) | 551.553 |
| Cycloolefins | 547.512 |
|   chemical engineering | 661.815 |
| Cycloparaffins | 547.511 |
|   chemical engineering | 661.815 |
| Cyclopedias | 030 |
| Cyclopoida | 595.34 |
| Cyclops (Animals) | 595.34 |
| Cycloramas | 745.8 |
|   decorative arts | 745.8 |
|   painting | 751.74 |
| Cyclorrhapha | 595.774 |
| Cyclosilicates | |
|   mineralogy | 549.64 |
| Cyclostomata (Jawless fishes) | 597.2 |
|   paleozoology | 567.2 |
| Cyclotomy (Number theory) | 512.72 |
| Cyclotrons | 539.733 |
| Cygninae | 598.418 |
| Cygnus | 598.418 |
| Cylinder recordings | |
|   sound reproduction | 621.389 32 |
| Cylinders (Engine parts) | 621.437 |
| Cylinders (Shape) | 516.154 |
| Cylinders (Structural elements) | 624.177 2 |
|   concrete | 624.183 42 |
| Cylindrical bark beetles | 595.769 |
| Cymbals | 786.873 |
|   *see also* Percussion instruments | |
| Cymraeg literature | 891.66 |
| Cymric language | 491.66 |
| | T6—916 6 |
| Cymric literature | 891.66 |
| Cymry | T5—916 6 |
| Cynewulf | 829.4 |
| Cynic philosophy | 183.4 |
| Cynocephalidae | 599.33 |
| Cynocrambales | 583.5 |
| Cynomys | 599.367 |
| Cynon Valley (Wales) | T2—429 78 |
| Cyperales | 584.84 |
| Cypress Hills (Alta. and | |
|   Sask.) | T2—712 43 |
| Cypress pine | 585.4 |
| Cypresses | 585.4 |
|   forestry | 634.975 5 |
|   lumber | 674.144 |
| Cyprinidae | 597.482 |
| Cypriniformes | 597.48 |
|   paleozoology | 567.48 |
| Cyprinodontidae | 597.665 |
| Cyprinodontoidei | 597.66 |
| Cyprinus | 597.483 |
| Cypriot architecture | |
|   Phoenician | 722.32 |
| Cypriots | T5—895 |
| Cyprus | 956.93 |
| | T2—569 3 |
|   ancient | 939.37 |
| | T2—393 7 |
| Cyrenaic philosophy | 183.5 |
| Cyrenaica | T2—397 5 |
|   ancient | 939.75 |
| Cyrillic alphabet | 491.8 |
|   printing | 686.219 18 |
| Cyrillic calligraphy | 745.619 918 |
| Cyrrhestica | T2—393 6 |
|   southern | T2—394 32 |
| Cystic fibrosis | |
|   medicine | 616.372 |
|   *see also* Digestive system | |
|     diseases — humans | |
| Cystitis | |
|   medicine | 616.623 |
|   *see also* Urologic diseases — | |
|     humans | |
| Cystoidea | 563.95 |
| Cythera Island (Greece) | T2—495 2 |
| Cytinaceae | 583.2 |
| Cytochemistry | 572 |
| Cytodiagnosis | |
|   medicine | 616.075 82 |
| Cytogenetics | 572.8 |
|   humans | 611.018 16 |
| Cytokines | |
|   human immunology | 616.079 |
| Cytological examination | |
|   medicine | 616.075 82 |
| Cytology | 571.6 |
|   humans | 611.018 1 |
| Cytometry | |
|   diagnosis | |
|     medicine | 616.075 82 |
| Cytopathology | 571.936 |
|   humans | 611.018 15 |
| Cytoplasm | 571.65 |
| Cytoplasmic inheritance | 572.869 |

| | |
|---|---|
| Cytoplasmic membranes | 571.64 |
| Cytoskeleton | 571.654 |
| Cytotaxonomy | 578.012 |
| Cytotoxic T cells | 571.966 |
|   human immunology | 616.079 7 |
| Cyzicus (Extinct city) | T2—392 1 |
| Czech language | 491.86 |
| | T6—918 6 |
| Czech literature | 891.86 |
| Czech Republic | 943.71 |
| | T2—437 1 |
| Czechoslovak Republic | 943.703 2 |
| | T2—437 |
| Czechoslovakia | 943.703 |
| | T2—437 |
| Czechoslovaks | T5—918 6 |
| Czechs | T5—918 6 |
| Częstochowa (Poland : | |
|   Voivodeship) | T2—438 58 |

# D

| | |
|---|---|
| D region (Ionosphere) | 538.767 2 |
| Da capo form | 781.822 5 |
|   instrumental | 784.182 2 |
| Đà Nẵng (Vietnam) | T2—597 5 |
| Daba language | 493.7 |
| | T6—937 |
| Đắc Lắc (Vietnam) | T2—597 6 |
| Đắc Nông (Vietnam) | T2—597 6 |
| Dacca (Bangladesh : | |
|   Division) | T2—549 22 |
| Daces | 597.482 |
|   sports fishing | 799.174 82 |
| Dachau (Extermination camp) | 940.531 853 36 |
| Dachshund | 636.753 8 |
| Dacia | 939.88 |
| | T2—398 8 |
| Dacorum (England) | T2—425 84 |
| Dactylopteriformes | 597.64 |
| Dadaism | |
|   fine arts | 709.040 62 |
|   literature | 808.801 162 |
|     history and criticism | 809.911 62 |
|     specific literatures | T3B—080 116 2 |
|       history and | |
|         criticism | T3B—091 162 |
|   painting | 759.066 2 |
|   sculpture | 735.230 462 |
| Daddy longlegs | 595.43 |
| Dade County (Fla.) | T2—759 38 |
| Dade County (Ga.) | T2—758 342 |
| Dade County (Mo.) | T2—778 745 |

| | |
|---|---|
| Dādra and Nagar Haveli | |
|   (India) | T2—547 6 |
| Daendels, Herman Willem | |
|   Indonesian history | 959.802 22 |
| Daerah Khusus Ibukota | |
|   Jakarta (Indonesia) | T2—598 22 |
| Daffodils | 635.934 34 |
|   botany | 584.34 |
|   floriculture | 635.934 34 |
| Dagari (African people) | T5—963 5 |
| Dagari language | 496.35 |
| | T6—963 5 |
| Dagbani (African people) | T5—963 5 |
| Dagbani language | 496.35 |
| | T6—963 5 |
| Dagestan (Russia) | T2—475 2 |
| Dagestan languages | 499.964 |
| | T6—999 64 |
| Daggers | 623.441 |
|   art metalwork | 739.72 |
|   military engineering | 623.441 |
| Daggett County (Utah) | T2—792 15 |
| Daghestan languages | 499.964 |
| | T6—999 64 |
| Dagomba (African people) | T5—963 5 |
| Dagomba language | 496.35 |
| | T6—963 5 |
| Daguerreotype process | 772.12 |
| Dagur language | T6—942 |
| Dahlias | 635.933 99 |
|   botany | 583.99 |
|   floriculture | 635.933 99 |
| Dahme-Spreewald | |
|   (Germany : Landkreis) | T2—431 51 |
| Dahomeans | T5—966 83 |
| Dahomey | 966.83 |
| | T2—668 3 |
| Dahomey (African people) | T5—963 37 |
| Dahomey (Kingdom) | 966.830 18 |
| | T2—668 3 |
| Dahūk (Iraq : Province) | T2—567 2 |
| Dai language (Chad) | 493.7 |
| | T6—937 |
| Daic languages | 495.9 |
| | T6—959 |
| Daic literatures | 895.9 |
| Daic peoples | T5—959 |
| Da'īf (Hadith) | 297.125 22 |
| Daily devotions | 204.46 |
|   Christianity | 242.2 |
|   Judaism | 296.45 |
| Dairi Batak | T5—992 246 6 |
| Dairi language | 499.224 66 |
| | T6—992 246 6 |

Dairi literature 899.224 66
Dairy cattle
    animal husbandry 636.214 2
Dairy cooperatives 334.683 7
Dairy farmers 636.214 209 2
Dairy farming 636.214 2
Dairy industry 338.176 214 2
    law 343.076 621 42
    public administration 354.56
Dairy processing industry 338.476 37
Dairy products 641.37
    cooking 641.67
    food 641.37
    processing 637
    product safety 363.192 9
        *see also* Food — product
        safety
Dairy substitutes 641.302
    commercial processing 664.6
Dairymen 636.214 209 2
Daisies 583.99
    floriculture 635.933 99
Daisy (Italian political party) 324.245 05
Dajabón (Dominican
    Republic : Province) T2—729 345
Dak Lak (Vietnam) T2—597 6
Dak Nông (Vietnam) T2—597 6
Dakar (Senegal : Region) T2—663
Dakhla (Western Sahara) T2—648
Dakota County (Minn.) T2—776 56
Dakota County (Neb.) T2—782 224
Dakota Indians T5—975 243
Dakota language 497.524 3
    T6—975 243
Dakota languages 497.524
    T6—975 24
Dakota literature 897.524 3
Dalarnas län (Sweden) T2—487 8
Dalby (Qld.) T2—943 3
Dale County (Ala.) T2—761 33
Dale Hollow Lake (Tenn.
    and Ky.) T2—768 49
Dalhousie, James Andrew Broun
    Ramsay, Marquis
    Indian history 954.031 6
Dalits 305.568 8
    religion 200.869 4
        Hinduism 294.508 694
Dallam County (Tex.) T2—764 812
Dallas (Tex.) T2—764 281 2
Dallas County (Ala.) T2—761 45
Dallas County (Ark.) T2—767 67
Dallas County (Iowa) T2—777 57
Dallas County (Mo.) T2—778 813

Dallas County (Tex.) T2—764 281 1
Dalmatia (Croatia) T2—497 2
Dalmatian (Dog) 636.72
Dalmatian language (Romance) 457.949 72
    T6—57
Dalmatian literature (Romance) 850
Dalmatians (Romance
    people) T5—57
Dalsland landskap (Sweden) T2—486 7
Daly River (N.T.) T2—942 95
Dama (Fallow deer) 599.655
    animal husbandry 636.294 5
Damages (Law) 347.077
Daman and Diu (India) T2—547 7
Damascening 739.15
Damascus (Syria) T2—569 144
    ancient T2—394 344
Damascus (Syria : Province) T2—569 14
Damask 677.616
Damietta (Egypt : Province) T2—621
Dammar pines 585.3
    forestry 634.975 93
Damping
    aeronautics 629.132 364
Damping of sound
    physics 534.208
Dampness control
    construction
        buildings 693.893
Dams 627.8
    agricultural use 631.28
    ecology 577.272
    public administration 354.362 77
Damselfishes 597.72
Damselflies 595.733
Dan (African people) T5—963 4
Dan language 496.34
    T6—963 4
Dance 792.8
    primary education 372.868
        *see also* Dancing
Dance bands 784.48
Dance flies 595.773
Dance forms 784.188
Dance halls
    architecture 725.86
Dance injuries
    medicine 617.102 75
Dance music 781.554

| | |
|---|---|
| Dance of death | |
| arts | 700.454 8 |
| | T3C—354 8 |
| literature | 808.803 548 |
| history and literature | 809.933 548 |
| specific literatures | T3B—080 354 8 |
| history and | |
| criticism | T3B—093 548 |
| Dance orchestras | 784.48 |
| Dance therapy | |
| medicine | 615.851 55 |
| Dancers | 792.802 809 2 |
| *see Manual at* 780.92 and | |
| 791.092 | |
| Dances of the suite | 793.3 |
| music | 784.188 3 |
| Dancing | 792.8 |
| arts | 700.457 9 |
| | T3C—357 9 |
| customs | 394.3 |
| ethics | 175 |
| etiquette | 395.3 |
| literature | 808.803 579 |
| history and criticism | 809.933 579 |
| specific literatures | T3B—080 357 9 |
| history and | |
| criticism | T3B—093 579 |
| musical plays | 792.62 |
| religious significance | 203.7 |
| Christianity | 246.7 |
| *see also* Arts — religious | |
| significance | |
| sociology | 306.484 6 |
| Dancing games | 796.13 |
| Dancing injuries | |
| medicine | 617.102 75 |
| Dandelions | 583.99 |
| cooking | 641.655 1 |
| food | 641.355 1 |
| garden crop | 635.51 |
| Dandruff | |
| medicine | 616.546 |
| Dane County (Wis.) | T2—775 83 |
| Danes | T5—398 1 |
| Dangaleat language | 493.7 |
| | T6—937 |
| Dangerous animals | 591.65 |
| Dangerous goods | 363.17 |
| *see also* Hazardous materials | |
| Dani | T5—991 2 |
| Daniel (Biblical book) | 224.5 |
| Daniels County (Mont.) | T2—786 213 |
| Danios | 597.482 |
| Danish language | 439.81 |
| | T6—398 1 |
| Danish literature | 839.81 |
| Danish pastry | 641.865 9 |
| commercial processing | 664.752 5 |
| home preparation | 641.865 9 |
| Danish people | T5—398 1 |
| Dannhauser (South Africa : | |
| District) | T2—684 1 |
| Dano-Norwegian language | 439.82 |
| | T6—398 2 |
| Dano-Norwegian literature | 839.82 |
| Danube River | T2—496 |
| Austria | T2—436 12 |
| Germany | T2—433 |
| Danville (Va.) | T2—755 666 |
| Danzig (Germany) | T2—438 22 |
| Daphnes | 583.67 |
| Daqahlīyah (Egypt) | T2—621 |
| DAR (Patriotic society) | 369.135 |
| biography | 369.135 092 |
| Dar es Salaam (Tanzania : | |
| Region) | T2—678 232 |
| Darʻā (Syria : Province) | T2—569 14 |
| Dard (Indic people) | T5—914 99 |
| Dard languages | 491.499 |
| | T6—914 99 |
| Dard literatures | 891.499 |
| Dardanelles Strait (Turkey) | 551.461 389 |
| | T2—163 89 |
| Dardic languages | 491.499 |
| | T6—914 99 |
| Dardic literatures | 891.499 |
| Dardic peoples | T5—914 99 |
| Dare County (N.C.) | T2—756 175 |
| Darfur (Sudan) | T2—627 |
| Dargi language | 499.964 |
| | T6—999 64 |
| Dargwa language | 499.964 |
| | T6—999 64 |
| Dari language | 491.56 |
| | T6—915 6 |
| Dari literature | 891.56 |
| Darién (Panama : Province) | T2—728 778 |
| Darien, Gulf of (Colombia) | 551.461 365 |
| | T2—163 65 |
| Dārimī, ʻAbd Allāh ibn ʻAbd al- | |
| Raḥmān | |
| Hadith | 297.125 54 |
| Dark Ages | 940.12 |
| *see also* Early Middle Ages | |
| Dark matter (Astronomy) | 523.112 6 |
| Darke County (Ohio) | T2—771 47 |
| Darkling beetles | 595.769 |

| | |
|---|---|
| Darkroom practice | 771.44 |
| cinematography | 777.55 |
| negatives | 771.43 |
| photography | 771.44 |
| positives (photographs) | 771.44 |
| Darkrooms (Photography) | 771.1 |
| Darling Downs (Qld.) | T2—943 3 |
| Darling Range (W.A.) | T2—941 2 |
| Darlington (England : | |
| Borough) | T2—428 63 |
| Darlington County (S.C.) | T2—757 66 |
| Darmstadt (Germany) | T2—434 167 |
| Darmstadt (Germany : | |
| Regierungsbezirk) | T2—434 16 |
| Darmstadtium | |
| chemistry | 546.62 |
| Darned laces | |
| arts | 746.22 |
| Darning | 646.204 |
| Darom (Israel : District) | T2—569 49 |
| Dart, River (England) | T2—423 592 |
| Darters (Fishes) | 597.75 |
| Dartford (England : | |
| Borough) | T2—422 312 |
| Dartmoor (England) | T2—423 53 |
| Dartmouth (N.S.) | T2—716 225 |
| Darts | 794.3 |
| Darwin (N.T.) | T2—942 95 |
| Darwinism | 576.82 |
| Darwin's finches | 598.883 |
| Dascilloidea | 595.763 |
| Dassies | 599.68 |
| Dasycladales | 579.836 |
| Dasypodidae | 599.312 |
| Dasyuridae | 599.27 |
| DAT (Digital audio) | |
| sound reproduction | 621.389 3 |
| Data backup | 005.86 |
| Data banks | 025.04 |
| *see also* Databases | |
| Data bases | 025.04 |
| *see also* Databases | |
| Data cells (Computer storage) | 004.563 |
| engineering | 621.397 63 |
| Data collection | |
| descriptive research | 001.433 |
| | T1—072 3 |
| *see Manual at* | |
| T1—07201–07209 vs. | |
| T1—0721 | |
| Data communications | 004.6 |
| *see also* Computer | |
| communications | |
| Data compaction | 005.746 |

| | |
|---|---|
| Data compression | 005.746 |
| Data conversion | 005.72 |
| Data dictionaries | 005.742 |
| Data directories | 005.742 |
| Data encryption | |
| computer science | 005.82 |
| Data entry | 005.72 |
| Data files | 005.74 |
| *see Manual at* 025.04, 025.06 | |
| vs. 005.74 | |
| Data in computer systems | 005.7 |
| | T1—028 557 |
| Data mining | 006.312 |
| Data modeling | 005.743 |
| Data models | 005.743 |
| Data preparation | |
| computer science | 005.72 |
| Data processing | 004 |
| | T1—028 5 |
| management use | 658.05 |
| office services | 651.8 |
| *see Manual at* T1—0285; *also* | |
| *at* 004–006 vs. 621.39; | |
| *also at* 510, T1—0151 vs. | |
| 004–006, T1—0285 | |
| Data record formats | 005.72 |
| Data recovery | 005.86 |
| Data representation | 005.72 |
| Data security | 005.8 |
| | T1—028 558 |
| management | 658.478 |
| Data structures | 005.73 |
| Data tapes | 004.563 |
| computer engineering | 621.397 63 |
| Data transmission | 004.6 |
| *see also* Computer | |
| communications | |
| Data warehousing | 005.745 |
| Databanks | 025.04 |
| *see also* Databases | |
| Database architecture | 005.743 |
| Database design | 005.743 |
| Database management systems | 005.74 |
| Databases | 025.04 |
| civil rights issues | 323.448 3 |
| computer science | 005.74 |
| information science | 025.04 |
| law | 343.099 9 |
| management use | 658.403 801 1 |
| *see Manual at* 025.04, 025.06 | |
| vs. 005.74 | |
| Dataflow computation | 004.35 |
| Dates (Chronology) | 902.02 |

| | |
|---|---|
| Dates (Fruit) | 641.346 2 |
| agriculture | 634.62 |
| botany | 584.5 |
| commercial processing | 664.804 62 |
| cooking | 641.646 2 |
| food | 641.346 2 |
| Dating (Archaeological technique) | 930.102 85 |
| Dating (Social practice) | 306.73 |
| customs | 392.6 |
| life skills | 646.77 |
| sociology | 306.73 |
| Daturas | 583.952 |
| Daughters | 306.874 |
| | T1—085 4 |
| Daughters of the American Revolution | 369.135 |
| biography | 369.135 092 |
| Dauphin (Man.) | T2—712 72 |
| Dauphin County (Pa.) | T2—748 18 |
| Dauphiné (France) | T2—445 86 |
| Daur language | T6—942 |
| D'Autray (Quebec) | T2—714 43 |
| DAV (Veterans' organization) | 369.186 3 |
| Davao del Norte (Philippines) | T2—599 7 |
| Davao del Sur (Philippines) | T2—599 7 |
| Davao Oriental (Philippines) | T2—599 7 |
| Davenport (Iowa) | T2—777 69 |
| Davenport Range (N.T.) | T2—942 91 |
| Davenports | 645.4 |
| *see also* Furniture | |
| Daventry (England : District) | T2—425 56 |
| David, King of Israel | |
| Biblical leader | 222.409 2 |
| Palestinian history | 933.02 |
| David and Goliath story | 222.430 950 5 |
| Davidson County (N.C.) | T2—756 68 |
| Davidson County (Tenn.) | T2—768 55 |
| Davie County (N.C.) | T2—756 69 |
| Daviess County (Ind.) | T2—772 385 |
| Daviess County (Ky.) | T2—769 864 |
| Daviess County (Mo.) | T2—778 183 |
| Davis County (Iowa) | T2—777 97 |
| Davis County (Utah) | T2—792 27 |
| Davis Strait | 551.461 342 |
| | T2—163 42 |
| Davison County (S.D.) | T2—783 374 |
| Da'wah | 297.74 |
| Dawes County (Neb.) | T2—782 93 |

| | |
|---|---|
| Dawn | 525.7 |
| arts | T3C—33 |
| literature | 808.803 3 |
| history and criticism | 809.933 3 |
| specific literatures | T3B—080 33 |
| history and criticism | T3B—093 3 |
| Dawson (Yukon) | T2—719 1 |
| Dawson County (Ga.) | T2—758 263 |
| Dawson County (Mont.) | T2—786 24 |
| Dawson County (Neb.) | T2—782 46 |
| Dawson County (Tex.) | T2—764 854 |
| Dawson Creek (B.C.) | T2—711 87 |
| Day camps | 796.542 3 |
| Day care | 362.712 |
| law | 344.032 712 |
| preschool education | 372.21 |
| social welfare | 362.712 |
| Day County (S.D.) | T2—783 142 |
| Day language (Chad) | 493.7 |
| | T6—937 |
| Day lilies | 635.934 32 |
| botany | 584.32 |
| floriculture | 635.934 32 |
| Day of the Lord | |
| Christianity | 236.9 |
| Daydreams | 154.3 |
| Daylesford (Vic.) | T2—945 3 |
| Daylight saving time | 389.17 |
| law | 343.07 |
| Daylighting | 729.28 |
| Daymarks | 387.155 |
| navigation aids | 623.894 4 |
| transportation services | 387.155 |
| Dayr al-Zawr (Syria : Province) | T2—569 12 |
| Days | 529.1 |
| arts | T3C—33 |
| chronology | 529.1 |
| folklore | 398.236 |
| history and criticism | 398.33 |
| literature | 808.803 3 |
| history and criticism | 809.933 3 |
| specific literatures | T3B—080 33 |
| history and criticism | T3B—093 3 |
| music | 781.522 |
| Dayton (Ohio) | T2—771 73 |
| Daza (African people) | T5—965 |
| Daza language | 496.5 |
| | T6—965 |
| DBS systems | 384.552 |
| DDT (Insecticide) | 632.951 7 |

De Aar (South Africa :
   District)           T2—687 13
De Baca County (N.M.)     T2—789 44
De facto government
   law of nations        341.26
De facto relationships     306.841
                         T1—086 56
   law               346.016
De Kalb County (Ala.)     T2—761 66
De Kalb County (Ga.)      T2—758 225
De Kalb County (Ill.)      T2—773 28
De Kalb County (Ind.)     T2—772 77
De Kalb County (Mo.)     T2—778 153
De Kalb County (Tenn.)    T2—768 532
De Klerk, F. W. (Frederik
   Willem)
   South African history    968.064
De Menezes, Fradique Bandiera
   Melo
   Sao Tomean history      967.150 23
De Soto County (Fla.)     T2—759 59
De Soto County (Miss.)    T2—762 87
De Soto Parish (La.)      T2—763 63
De Witt County (Ill.)      T2—773 585
De Witt County (Tex.)     T2—764 259
Deaccessioning
   archives           025.281 4
Deacidification
   bibliographic materials   025.84
Deacons              270.092
   biography          270.092
      specific denominations  280
      *see Manual at* 230–280
   ecclesiology         262.14
   pastoral theology     253
   *see also* Clergy — Christian
Dead
   disposal           363.75
      customs         393
      music           781.588
      *see also* Undertaking
        (Mortuary)
   objects of worship     202.13
Dead animal disposal      363.78
Dead letter services      383.186
   *see also* Postal service
Dead nettles          583.96
Dead reckoning        629.045
   seamanship        623.892 3
Dead Sea (Israel and
   Jordan)           T2—569 4

Dead Sea Scrolls        296.155
   Old Testament works in   221.44
   pseudepigrapha       229.91
   Qumran community writings 296.155
Deaeration
   water supply treatment   628.165
Deaf-blind people       305.908 1
                       T1—087 1
   communication       419.4–.9
   *see also* Blind people
Deaf children          305.908 208 3
                       T1—087 2
   home care          649.151 2
   *see also* Hearing-impaired
     people
Deaf people           305.908 2
                       T1—087 2
   sign languages       419.4–.9
   *see also* Hearing-impaired
     people
Deaf Smith County (Tex.)  T2—764 835
Deaf workers          331.592
Deafness
   incidence          614.599 8
   medicine           617.8
      *see also* Ear diseases —
        humans
   social welfare        362.42
Deakin, Alfred
   Australian history      994.041
Dean, Forest of (England)  T2—424 13
Deans of students       371.4
Dearborn (Mich.)        T2—774 33
Dearborn County (Ind.)   T2—772 11
Death               306.9
   arts              700.454 8
                   T3C—354 8
   biology           571.939
   customs           393
   cytology          571.936
   demography       304.64
   ethics            179.7
     religion         205.697
       Buddhism      294.356 97
       Christianity     241.697
       Hinduism      294.548 697
       Judaism       296.369 7
   folklore          398.274 8
     history and criticism   398.354 8
   literature         808.803 548
     history and literature  809.933 548
     specific literatures   T3B—080 354 8
      history and
        criticism     T3B—093 548

| | |
|---|---|
| Death (continued) | |
| medical ethics | 179.7 |
| religion | 205.697 |
| medicine | 616.078 |
| music | 781.588 |
| philosophy | 113.8 |
| humans | 128.5 |
| psychology | 155.937 |
| religion | 202.3 |
| Christianity | 236.1 |
| Islam | 297.23 |
| Judaism | 296.33 |
| philosophy of religion | 218 |
| religious rites | 203.88 |
| Christianity | 265.85 |
| Islam | 297.385 |
| Judaism | 296.445 |
| liturgy | 296.454 5 |
| *see also* Rites — religion | |
| social services | 363.75 |
| *see also* Undertaking | |
| (Mortuary) | |
| sociology | 306.9 |
| Death adders | 597.964 |
| Death certificates | |
| public administration | 353.59 |
| Death of Jesus Christ | 232.963 |
| Death penalty | 364.66 |
| law | 345.077 3 |
| Death tax | 336.276 |
| law | 343.053 |
| public administration | 352.44 |
| Death Valley National Park | |
| (Calif. and Nev.) | T2—794 87 |
| Death watch beetles | 595.763 |
| Debarkation | 355.422 |
| Debaters | 809.53 |
| Debates | |
| literature | 808.853 |
| history and criticism | 809.53 |
| specific literatures | T3B—503 |
| individual authors | T3A—5 |
| rhetoric | 808.53 |
| Debating | 808.53 |
| Debit cards | 332.76 |
| banking services | 332.178 |
| credit economics | 332.76 |
| Debt collection | |
| law | 346.077 |
| management | 658.88 |
| Debt limits | |
| public finance | 336.346 |
| Debt management (Business) | 658.152 6 |
| Debt management (Personal) | 332.024 02 |

| | |
|---|---|
| Debt management (Public) | 336.36 |
| macroeconomic policy | 339.523 |
| public administration | 352.45 |
| public finance | 336.36 |
| Debtors | |
| law | 346.077 |
| Debtors' prisons | 365.4 |
| *see also* Penal institutions | |
| Debugging (Computer science) | 004.24 |
| engineering | 621.392 |
| programs | 005.14 |
| Deburring metals | 671.7 |
| Debuts | |
| customs | 392.15 |
| etiquette | 395.24 |
| music | 781.584 |
| Decalcomania | 745.74 |
| Decalogue | 222.16 |
| moral theology | |
| Christianity | 241.52 |
| Judaism | 296.36 |
| Decapoda (Crustaceans) | 595.38 |
| conservation technology | 639.975 38 |
| resource economics | 333.955 5 |
| Decapoda (Mollusks) | 594.58 |
| paleozoology | 564.58 |
| Decathlon | 796.42 |
| Decatur County (Ga.) | T2—758 993 |
| Decatur County (Ind.) | T2—772 16 |
| Decatur County (Iowa) | T2—777 875 |
| Decatur County (Kan.) | T2—781 143 |
| Decatur County (Tenn.) | T2—768 32 |
| Decay | |
| materials science | 620.112 2 |
| Decay (Sound) | |
| musical element | 781.235 |
| Decay schemes (Radioactivity) | 539.752 |
| Deccan (India) | T2—548 |
| Deceleration | |
| biophysics | |
| humans | 612.014 414 |
| extraterrestrial biophysics | |
| humans | 612.014 534 |
| Decentralization | |
| executive management | 658.402 |
| public administration | 352.283 |
| Deception | 001.95 |
| military operations | 355.41 |
| Decidability | 511.3 |
| Decimal fractions | 513.265 |
| Decimal numbers | 513.55 |
| Decimal system | 513.55 |
| Decision analysis | |
| management use | 658.403 54 |

Decision making
  executive management      658.403
                         T1—068 4
  military administration      355.683
  production management      658.503 6
  psychology      153.83
  public administration      352.33
  social psychology      302.3
Decision tables
  program design      005.120 28
Decision theory      003.56
                         T1—011 56
Decision theory (Mathematics)      519.542
Decks (Buildings)      721.84
  architecture      721.84
  construction      690.184
  domestic      728.93
    architecture      728.93
    construction      690.893
Declaration of Independence,
  1776      973.313
Declaration of intention      346.021
Declarative languages      005.13
Declaratory judgments      347.077
Declension (Grammar)      415.5
  specific languages      T4—55
Decoding skills (Reading)
  primary education      372.46
Decolonization      325.3
Decolorizing carbons      662.93
Decomposition
  materials science      620.112 2
Decomposition method      518
Decompression sickness
  medicine      616.989 4
  *see also* Environmental
     diseases — humans
Deconstruction
  philosophy      149.97
Decoration      745.4
  architecture      729
  arts      745.4
  automobile      629.262
Decorations (Awards)      929.81
  armed forces      355.134 2
  *see also* Military
     commemorations
  numismatics      737.223
Decorative arts      745
Decorative coloring      745.7
Decorative lettering      745.61
Decorative sculpture      731.72

Decorative treatment
  glass      748.6
  metals      739.15
  pottery      666.45
    arts      738.15
    technology      666.45
  sculpture      731.4
Decorative values      701.8
  drawing      741.018
Decoupage      745.546
Decoys
  handicrafts      745.593 6
Decubitus ulcers
  medicine      616.545
  *see also* Skin diseases —
     humans
Dedications (Christian rites)      265.92
Deduction (Logic)      162
  psychology      153.433
Deductive databases
  computer science      005.740 151 13
Deductive reasoning      162
  computer science      006.333
  logic      162
  psychology      153.433
Dee, River (Aberdeenshire,
  Scotland)      T2—412 4
Deeds      346.043 8
Deep-freezing foods      664.028 53
  commercial preservation      664.028 53
  home preservation      641.453
Deep sea biology      578.779
Deep sea cods      597.63
Deep-sea diving      627.72
Deep sea ecology      577.79
Deep-sea fishing      639.22
  commercial      639.22
  sports      799.16
Deep-sea hydrothermal vents
  biology      578.779 9
  ecology      577.799
Deer      599.65
  agricultural pests      632.696 5
  animal husbandry      636.294
  big game hunting      799.276 5
  commercial hunting      639.116 5
  conservation technology      639.979 65
  resource economics      333.959 65
  zoology      599.65
Deer Lodge County (Mont.)      T2—786 87
Deer mice      599.355
Deerflies      595.773

| | |
|---|---|
| Defamation | 364.156 |
| ethics | 177.3 |
| *see also* Ethical problems | |
| law | 345.025 6 |
| criminal law | 345.025 6 |
| torts | 346.034 |
| Default | 332.75 |
| Default logic | 511.31 |
| Defeasible logic | 511.31 |
| Defecation | |
| human physiology | 612.36 |
| Defendants | 347.052 |
| criminal law | 345.05 |
| Defense (Legal) | 347.05 |
| criminal law | 345.050 44 |
| Defense (Military operation) | 355.4 |
| engineering | 623.3 |
| Defense (National security) | 355.03 |
| law | 343.01 |
| Defense administration | 355.6 |
| Defense budgets | 355.622 8 |
| specific jurisdictions | 355.622 9 |
| Defense contracts | 355.621 2 |
| law | 346.023 |
| Defense departments | 355.6 |
| Defense industries | 338.473 55 |
| Defense mechanisms | |
| (Psychology) | 155.2 |
| Defense of home territory | 355.45 |
| Defense operations | 355.4 |
| Defenseless Mennonites | 289.73 |
| biography | 289.709 2 |
| *see also* Mennonite Church | |
| Defiance County (Ohio) | T2—771 14 |
| Defibrillation (Electric) | |
| medicine | 616.128 064 5 |
| Deficiency budgets (Public) | 352.48 |
| *see also* Budgets (Public) | |
| Deficiency diseases | |
| medicine | 616.39 |
| *see also* Digestive system | |
| diseases — humans | |
| Definite integrals | 515.43 |
| Definitive Treaty of Peace | |
| Between Great Britain and the | |
| United States | |
| United States history | 973.317 |
| Definitive Treaty of Peace with | |
| Spain, 1783 | |
| United States history | 973.317 |
| Defla (Algeria : Province) | T2—653 |
| Deflagrating explosives | 662.26 |
| Deflation (Economics) | 332.41 |

| | |
|---|---|
| Deflections | |
| structural analysis | 624.171 4 |
| Defluoridation | |
| water supply engineering | 628.166 3 |
| Defoid languages | 496.33 |
| | T6—963 3 |
| Deformation | 531.38 |
| crystals | 548.842 |
| geology | 551.8 |
| materials science | 620.112 3 |
| naval architecture | 623.817 6 |
| physics | 531.38 |
| structural analysis | 624.176 |
| Deformities | |
| biology | 571.976 |
| human teratology | 616.043 |
| psychological influence | 155.916 |
| Degeneration (Pathology) | 571.935 |
| cytology | 571.936 |
| humans | 616.07 |
| Deglutition disorders | |
| medicine | 616.323 |
| *see also* Digestive system | |
| diseases — humans | |
| Dehumidification | |
| chemical engineering | 660.284 29 |
| Dehumidifiers | |
| air conditioning | |
| buildings | 697.932 3 |
| Dehydrated foods | |
| cooking | 641.614 |
| Dehydrating foods | 664.028 4 |
| commercial preservation | 664.028 4 |
| home preservation | 641.44 |
| Dehydrogenases | 572.791 |
| *see also* Enzymes | |
| Dehydrogenation | |
| chemical engineering | 660.284 43 |
| Deinonychus | 567.912 |
| Deirochelys | 597.925 9 |
| Deism | 211.5 |
| Deists | 211.509 2 |
| Deities | 202.11 |
| *see also* Gods and goddesses | |
| Deixis | 401.456 |
| specific languages | T4—014 56 |
| Dek hockey | 796.356 4 |
| DeKalb County (Ga.) | T2—758 225 |
| Dekkan (India) | T2—548 |
| Del Norte County (Calif.) | T2—794 11 |
| Delagoa Bay | 551.461 524 |
| | T2—165 24 |
| Delareyville (South Africa : | |
| District) | T2—682 44 |

226

| | |
|---|---|
| Delaware | 975.1 |
| | T2—751 |
| Delaware Bay (Del. and N.J.) | 551.461 346 |
| | T2—163 46 |
| Delaware County (Ind.) | T2—772 65 |
| Delaware County (Iowa) | T2—777 385 |
| Delaware County (N.Y.) | T2—747 36 |
| Delaware County (Ohio) | T2—771 535 |
| Delaware County (Okla.) | T2—766 91 |
| Delaware County (Pa.) | T2—748 14 |
| Delaware Indians | T5—973 45 |
| Delaware language | 497.345 |
| | T6—973 45 |
| Delaware River (N.Y.-Del. and N.J.) | T2—749 |
| Delaware Water Gap (N.J. and Pa.) | T2—748 25 |
| Delegate counts | 324.5 |
| Delegated legislation | 348.025 |
| United States | 348.732 5 |
| Delegation of authority | 658.402 |
| public administration | 352.283 |
| Delémont (Switzerland) | T2—494 362 4 |
| Delémont (Switzerland : District) | T2—494 362 |
| Deleterious animals | 591.65 |
| Deleterious microorganisms | 579.165 |
| Deleterious organisms | 578.65 |
| Deleterious plants | 581.65 |
| Delft (Netherlands) | T2—492 38 |
| Delftware | 738.37 |
| Delhi (India : Union Territory) | T2—545 6 |
| Delicts | 346.03 |
| *see Manual at* 345.02 vs. 346.03 | |
| Déline (N.W.T.) | T2—719 3 |
| Delinquency in schools | 371.782 |
| Delinquent children | 364.36 |
| | T1—086 923 |
| Delinquent people | 305.906 92 |
| | T1—086 92 |
| Delinquent students | 371.93 |
| Delmarva Peninsula | T2—752 1 |
| Maryland | T2—752 1 |
| Virginia | T2—755 1 |
| Delmas (South Africa : District) | T2—682 77 |
| Delos Island (Greece) | T2—495 85 |
| Delphi (Greece) | T2—383 |
| Delphinapterus | 599.542 |
| Delphinidae | 599.53 |

| | |
|---|---|
| Delphiniums | 635.933 34 |
| botany | 583.34 |
| floriculture | 635.933 34 |
| Delphinus | 599.532 |
| Delsberg (Switzerland) | T2—494 362 4 |
| Delsberg (Switzerland : Bezirk) | T2—494 362 |
| Delta (B.C.) | T2—711 33 |
| Delta (Miss. : Region) | T2—762 4 |
| Delta Amacuro (Venezuela) | T2—876 2 |
| Delta County (Colo.) | T2—788 18 |
| Delta County (Mich.) | T2—774 94 |
| Delta County (Tex.) | T2—764 273 |
| Delta State (Nigeria) | T2—669 36 |
| Deltaplan (Netherlands) engineering | 627.549 094 92 |
| Deltas | 551.456 |
| | T2—146 |
| geography | 910.914 6 |
| geomorphology | 551.456 |
| physical geography | 910.021 46 |
| Delusions | 001.96 |
| Delyn (Wales) | T2—429 33 |
| Demai | 296.123 1 |
| Mishnah | 296.123 1 |
| Palestinian Talmud | 296.124 1 |
| Demand | |
| communications industry | 384.041 |
| forecasts | 338.02 |
| agricultural industries | 338.17 |
| production economics | 338.02 |
| secondary industries | 338.47 |
| labor economics | 331.123 |
| microeconomics | 338.521 2 |
| natural resources | 333.712 |
| transportation services | 388.049 |
| Demand deposits | 332.175 22 |
| Dematerialization (Spiritualism) | 133.92 |
| Dementia | |
| medicine | 616.83 |
| *see also* Nervous system diseases — humans | |
| Demerara-Mahaica Region (Guyana) | T2—881 5 |
| Demineralization | |
| sewage treatment | 628.358 |
| water supply treatment | 628.166 6 |
| Demmin (Germany : Landkreis) | T2—431 72 |
| Demobilization (Military science) | 355.29 |
| Democracy | 321.8 |
| educational objective | 370.115 |
| Democracy is Freedom-Daisy (Italian political party) | 324.245 05 |

| | | | |
|---|---|---|---|
| Democratic centralism | 335.43 | Demotic language (Egyptian) | 493.1 |
| economics | 335.43 | | T6—931 |
| political ideology | 320.532 2 | Demotic language (Modern | 489.3 |
| Democratic government | 321.8 | Greek) | T6—89 |
| Democratic Labor Party | | Demotic literature (Modern | |
| (Australia) | 324.294 06 | Greek) | 889 |
| Democratic Party (Italy) | 324.245 06 | Demotion | |
| Democratic Party (U.S.) | 324.273 6 | armed forces | 355.112 |
| Democratic Party of the Left | | personnel management | 658.314 4 |
| (Italy) | 324.245 07 | public administration | 352.66 |
| Democratic Republic of East | | Demythologizing (Bible) | 220.68 |
| Timor | 959.870 4 | Denali Borough (Alaska) | T2—798 6 |
| Democratic Republic of the | 967.51 | Denali National Park and | |
| Congo | T2—675 1 | Preserve (Alaska) | T2—798 3 |
| Democratic-Republican Party | | Denationalization | 338.925 |
| (U.S.) | 324.273 6 | Denbigh (Wales) | T2—429 37 |
| Democratic socialism | 335.5 | Denbighshire (Wales) | T2—429 37 |
| economics | 335.5 | Dendritic cells | |
| political ideology | 320.531 5 | human immunology | 616.079 |
| Democratici di sinistra (Italian | | Dendrobatidae | 597.877 |
| political party) | 324.245 07 | Dendrobiums | 584.4 |
| Democrats of the Left (Italian | | floriculture | 635.934 4 |
| political party) | 324.245 07 | Dendrochirotacea | 593.96 |
| Democrazia cristiana (Italian | | Dendrocolaptidae | 598.822 |
| political party) | 324.245 082 2 | Dendrologists | 582.160 92 |
| Democrazia è libertà-La | | Dendrology | 582.16 |
| Margherita (Italian political | | Dengue | |
| party) | 324.245 05 | incidence | 614.588 52 |
| Democritean philosophy | 182.7 | medicine | 616.918 52 |
| Demodulation | | *see also* Communicable | |
| electronics | 621.381 536 | diseases — humans | |
| Demodulators | | Dengue hemorrhagic fever | |
| electronic circuits | 621.381 536 | incidence | 614.588 52 |
| Demographic anthropology | 304.6 | medicine | 616.918 52 |
| Demography | 304.6 | *see also* Communicable | |
| Demolition (Military) | 623.27 | diseases — humans | |
| Demolition charges | | Denial | |
| military engineering | 623.454 5 | epistemology | 121.5 |
| Demolition operations (Military) | 358.23 | Denial of justice | 364.134 |
| underwater | 359.984 | law | 345.023 4 |
| Demoniac possession | 133.426 | Denial of rights | 364.132 2 |
| occultism | 133.426 | law | 345.023 22 |
| religion | 204.2 | government liability | 342.088 |
| Demonology | 133.42 | public administration | 353.46 |
| religion | 202.16 | Denis-Riverin (Quebec) | T2—714 791 |
| Demons | 133.42 | Denizli İli (Turkey) | T2—562 7 |
| religion | 202.16 | ancient | T2—392 4 |
| Christianity | 235.4 | Denjoy integrals | 515.43 |
| Demonstrations (Political | | Denman Island (B.C. : | |
| protests) | | Island) | T2—711 2 |
| public safety | 363.323 | Denmark | 948.9 |
| Demonstrative evidence | 347.064 | | T2—489 |
| Demospongiae | 593.46 | ancient | 936.89 |
| paleozoology | 563.4 | | T2—368 9 |

| | |
|---|---|
| Denmark Strait | 551.461 324 |
| | T2—163 24 |
| Denominations | 209 |
|   Christianity | 280 |
|   Judaism | 296.8 |
|   *see Manual at* 201–209 and | |
|     292–299 | |
| Dens | |
|   home economics | 643.58 |
| Density | 531.14 |
|   gas mechanics | 533.15 |
|   liquid mechanics | 532.4 |
|   solid mechanics | 531.54 |
| Density pumps | 621.699 |
| Dent County (Mo.) | T2—778 86 |
| Dental assistants | |
|   law | 344.041 3 |
|   role and function | 617.602 33 |
| Dental care | |
|   dentistry | 617.6 |
|   social services | 362.197 6 |
| Dental diseases | 573.356 39 |
|   *see also* Tooth diseases | |
| Dental enamel | |
|   dentistry | 617.634 |
| Dental hygiene | 617.601 |
| Dental implantation | |
|   dentistry | 617.693 |
| Dental implants | |
|   dentistry | 617.693 |
| Dental insurance | 368.382 3 |
| Dental pulp | |
|   dentistry | 617.634 2 |
| Dental pulp diseases | |
|   dentistry | 617.634 2 |
| Dental restoration | 617.69 |
| Dental surgery | 617.605 |
| Dental technicians | |
|   law | 344.041 3 |
|   role and function | 617.602 33 |
| Dentin | |
|   dentistry | 617.634 |
| Dentinal material products | 679.4 |
| Dentistry | 617.6 |
|   anesthesiology | 617.967 6 |
|   law | 344.041 3 |
|   pediatrics | 617.645 |
| Dentists | 617.609 2 |
|   law | 344.041 3 |
|   role and function | 617.602 32 |
| Dentition disorders | |
|   dentistry | 617.643 |
|   incidence | 614.599 6 |
| Denton County (Tex.) | T2—764 555 |
| D'Entrecasteaux Islands | |
|   (Papua New Guinea) | T2—954 1 |
| Dentures | |
|   dentistry | 617.692 |
| Denver (Colo.) | T2—788 83 |
| Denver County (Colo.) | T2—788 83 |
| Deodorants | |
|   pharmacokinetics | 615.778 |
| Deodorization | |
|   sewers | 628.23 |
| Deontic logic | 511.314 |
| Deontology | |
|   ethical systems | 171.2 |
| Deoxyribonucleic acid | 572.86 |
|   humans | 611.018 166 |
| Department heads | |
|   executive management | 658.43 |
|   public administration | 352.293 |
|   *see Manual at* 352–354 | |
| Department stores | 381.141 |
|   management | 658.871 |
|   *see also* Commerce | |
| Departments (Organizational | |
|   units) | |
|   management | 658.402 |
|   public administration | 351 |
| Departments (Territorial units) | 320.83 |
|   *see also* Counties | |
| Departments of agriculture | 354.5 |
| Departments of commerce | 354.73 |
| Departments of defense | 355.6 |
| Departments of education | 353.8 |
| Departments of energy | 354.4 |
| Departments of foreign affairs | 353.13 |
| Departments of health | 353.6 |
| Departments of housing | 353.55 |
| Departments of interior | 353.3 |
| Departments of justice | 353.4 |
| Departments of labor | 354.9 |
| Departments of natural resources | 354.3 |
| Departments of state | 351 |
| Departments of transportation | 354.76 |
| Departments of treasury | 352.4 |
| Dependence | |
|   personality trait | 155.232 |
| Dependency grammar | 415.018 4 |
|   specific languages | T4—501 84 |
| Dependent children | |
|   social welfare | 362.713 |
| Dependent personality disorder | |
|   medicine | 616.858 1 |
|   *see also* Mental disorders | |
| Dependent states | 321.08 |
|   *see also* Semisovereign states | |

Depletion allowance 336.243 16
  tax law 343.052 34
Deportation 364.68
  law 342.082
  penology 364.68
Deposit insurance 368.854
Deposition (Geology) 551.303
Depository libraries
  acquisitions 025.26
  government relations 021.8
Deposits (Bank) 332.175 2
  government guaranty 368.854
  public revenues 336.15
Depreciation
  accounting 657.73
  tax law 343.052 34
Depressant abuse 362.299
  medicine 616.86
  personal health 613.8
  social welfare 362.299
  *see also* Substance abuse
Depression (Mental state) 362.25
  medicine 616.852 7
  social welfare 362.25
  *see also* Mental disorders
Depressions (Economics)
  economic cycles 338.542
Depressions (Physiography) 551.44
    T2—144
  geography 910.914 4
  geomorphology 551.44
  physical geography 910.021 44
Depressive disorder
  medicine 616.852 7
  *see also* Mental disorders
Depressive psychoses
  medicine 616.895
  *see also* Mental disorders
Deputy chief executives
  executive management 658.42
  law 342.062
  public administration 352.239
Deputy heads of departments
  executive management 658.43
  public administration 352.293
Dera Ismāīl Khān
  (Pakistan : District) T2—549 124
Derby (England) T2—425 17
Derbyshire (England) T2—425 1
Derbyshire Dales (England) T2—425 13
Derivation (Morphology) 415.92
  specific languages T4—592
Derivational morphology 415.92
  specific languages T4—592

Derivatives (Speculation) 332.645 7
  multiple forms of investment 332.645 7
  securities 332.632
Derived spaces 514.32
Dermaptera 595.739
Dermatemydidae 597.926
Dermatitis
  medicine 616.51
  *see also* Skin diseases —
    humans
Dermatoglyphics 599.945
Dermatology 616.5
Dermatomycoses
  humans
    incidence 614.595 79
    medicine 616.579
  *see also* Skin diseases —
    humans
Dermestoidea 595.763
Dermochelyidae 597.928 9
Dermoptera 599.33
  paleozoology 569.33
Derricks 621.873
Derry (Northern Ireland) T2—416 21
Derry (Northern Ireland :
  County) T2—416 2
Derwent, River (Derbyshire,
  England) T2—425 1
Derwent, River (Yorkshire,
  England) T2—428 4
Derwentside (England) T2—428 68
Des Moines (Iowa) T2—777 58
Des Moines County (Iowa) T2—777 96
Des Moines River (Minn.
  and Iowa) T2—777
Des Plaines River (Wis. and
  Ill.) T2—773 2
Desai, Morarji Ranchodji
  Indian history 954.052
Desalinization 628.167
Descant recorders 788.364
  *see also* Woodwind instruments
Descant viols 787.62
  *see also* Stringed instruments
Descendants T1—085 4
  family relationships 306.874
Descent into hell of Jesus Christ 232.967
Deschutes County (Or.) T2—795 87
Deschutes River (Or.) T2—795 62

Description
  literature 808.802 2
    history and criticism 809.922
    specific literatures T3B—080 22
      history and
        criticism T3B—092 2
Description (Archives) 025.341 4
Description logics
  computer science 006.332
Descriptive bibliography 010.42
Descriptive biology 578
  animals 590
  microorganisms 579
  plants 580
  *see Manual at* 578 vs. 304.2,
    508, 910
Descriptive cataloging 025.32
Descriptive geometry 516.6
  applied 604.201 516 6
Descriptive government 320.4
Descriptive linguistics 410
  *see Manual at* 410
Descriptive metadata
  information science 025.3
Descriptive research 001.433
              T1—072 3
  public administrative support 352.75
  *see Manual at*
    T1—07201–07209
    vs. T1—0721; *also at*
    T1—07201–07209 vs.
    T1—0722–0724
Descriptive statistics 519.53
Descriptors (Terms) 025.47
Desegregation in education 379.263
Desert biology 578.754
Desert ecology 577.54
Desert plants 581.754
  floriculture 635.952 5
Desert Storm, Operation, 1991 956.704 424
Desert tactics 355.423
Deserters 355.133 4
  Algerian Revolution 965.046 8
  American Revolution 973.38
  Chaco War 989.207 168
  Civil War (England) 942.062 8
  Civil War (Spain) 946.081 8
  Civil War (United States) 973.78
  Crimean War 947.073 88
  Falkland Islands War 997.110 248
  Franco-German War 943.082 8
  Hundred Years' War 944.025 8
  Indo-Pakistan War, 1971 954.920 518
  Indochinese War 959.704 18

Deserters (continued)
  Iraq War, 2003– 956.704 438
  Iraqi-Iranian Conflict 955.054 28
  Korean War 951.904 28
  Mexican War 973.628
  Napoleonic Wars 940.278
  Persian Gulf War, 1991 956.704 428
  South African War 968.048 8
  Spanish-American War 973.898
  Thirty Years' War 940.248
  Vietnamese War 959.704 38
  War of the Pacific 983.061 68
  World War I 940.48
  World War II 940.548
Desertification 333.736
  geomorphology 551.415
Desertion (Domestic relations) 306.88
Desertion (Military) 355.133 4
  law 343.014
  *see also* Deserters
Deserts 551.415
              T2—154
  biology 578.754
  ecology 577.54
  *see also* Arid lands
Desha County (Ark.) T2—767 85
Design
  arts 745.4
  automotive 629.231
  engineering 620.004 2
  philosophy 124
  primary education 372.52
  road engineering 625.725
  structural engineering 624.177 1
Design anthropometry 620.82
Design protection 346.048 4
Designer drugs 362.299
  medicine 616.86
  personal health 613.8
  social welfare 362.299
  *see also* Substance abuse
Designs
  diagrammatic works T1—022 3
  pictorial works T1—022 2
  textiles 677.022
Désirade (Guadeloupe) T2—729 76
Desjardins (Quebec) T2—714 59
Desks
  decorative arts 749.3
  household management 645.4
  manufacturing technology 684.14
Desktop publishing
  composition 686.225 444 16
  computer software 005.52

| | |
|---|---|
| Desktop typesetting | 686.225 444 16 |
| Desmidiaceae | 579.837 |
| Desmids | 579.837 |
| Desmophyceae | 579.87 |
| Desmostylia | 569.5 |
| Desolation Sound Provincial | |
| Marine Park (B.C.) | T2—711 31 |
| Despotism | 321.9 |
| Dessau (Germany : | |
| Regierungsbezirk) | T2—431 86 |
| Desserts | 641.86 |
| Destiny | |
| philosophy | 123 |
| religion | 202.2 |
| Christianity | 234.9 |
| Destitute people | 305.569 |
| | T1—086 942 |
| *see also* Poor people | |
| Destroyer escorts | 359.835 4 |
| design | 623.812 54 |
| engineering | 623.825 4 |
| naval equipment | 359.835 4 |
| naval units | 359.325 4 |
| Destroyers | 359.835 4 |
| design | 623.812 54 |
| engineering | 623.825 4 |
| naval equipment | 359.835 4 |
| naval units | 359.325 4 |
| Destruction of universe | 523.19 |
| Destructors | |
| military engineering | 623.454 5 |
| Desulfurization | |
| coal technology | 662.623 |
| Detail drawings | |
| construction | 692.2 |
| Detail finishing | |
| buildings | 698 |
| Detailing automobiles | 629.287 |
| Detection | |
| electronics | 621.381 536 |
| Detection of crime | 363.25 |
| *see also* Criminal investigation | |
| Detection of particles | 539.77 |
| Detection of radioactivity | 539.77 |
| Detective films | 791.436 556 |
| Detective plays | |
| literature | 808.825 27 |
| history and criticism | 809.252 7 |
| specific literatures | T3B—205 27 |
| individual authors | T3A—2 |
| Detective programs | 791.446 556 |
| radio | 791.446 556 |
| television | 791.456 556 |

| | |
|---|---|
| Detective stories | 808.838 72 |
| history and criticism | 809.387 2 |
| specific literatures | T3B—308 72 |
| individual authors | T3A—3 |
| Detectives | 363.250 92 |
| Detectors (Demodulators) | 621.381 536 |
| Detectors (Sensors) | |
| manufacturing technology | 681.2 |
| Detention | 365 |
| Detention homes | 365.34 |
| *see also* Penal institutions | |
| Detergents | 668.14 |
| Deterioration | |
| materials science | 620.112 2 |
| Determinants | 512.943 2 |
| Determinative mineralogy | 549.1 |
| Determinism | 123 |
| literature | 808.801 2 |
| history and criticism | 809.912 |
| specific literatures | T3B—080 12 |
| history and | |
| criticism | T3B—091 2 |
| Deterministic systems | 003.7 |
| Deterrence (Nuclear strategy) | 355.021 7 |
| Detmold (Germany : | |
| Regierungsbezirk) | T2—435 65 |
| Detonators | 662.4 |
| military engineering | 623.454 2 |
| Detroit (Mich.) | T2—774 34 |
| Detroit River (Mich. and | |
| Ont.) | T2—774 33 |
| Deuel County (Neb.) | T2—782 913 |
| Deuel County (S.D.) | T2—783 25 |
| Deuterium | 546.212 |
| *see also* Chemicals | |
| Deuterium oxide | |
| chemical engineering | 661.08 |
| chemistry | 546.22 |
| Deuteromycetes | 579.55 |
| Deuteromycotina | 579.55 |
| Deuteronomy (Bible) | 222.15 |
| Deuterons | 539.723 2 |
| Deutsche Kommunistische Partei | 324.243 075 |
| Deutsche Nationalsozialistische | |
| Arbeiterpartei (Austria) | 324.243 602 38 |
| Deutsche Volksunion (Political | |
| party) | 324.243 03 |
| Deutsche Zentrumspartei | 324.243 025 |
| Deutscher Bund | 943.07 |
| Deutzias | 635.933 72 |
| botany | 583.72 |
| floriculture | 635.933 72 |

Deux-Montagnes (Quebec :
  Regional County
  Municipality)                    T2—714 252
Deux-Sèvres (France)               T2—446 2
Devaluation of currency            332.414 2
Devanagari alphabet                491.1
Developable surfaces               516.362
Developed regions                  T2—172 2
Developing (Photography)           771.44
  negatives                        771.43
  positives (photographs)          771.44
Developing apparatus
  photography                      771.44
Developing regions                 T2—172 4
Developing solutions
  photography                      771.54
Development
  biology                          571.8
    *see also* Developmental
      biology
  economics                        338.9
  natural resources                333.715
  sociology                        303.44
Development banks                  332.153
  domestic                         332.28
  international                     332.153
Developmental abnormalities        571.938
Developmental biology              571.8
  humans                           612.6
  microorganisms                   571.842 9
Developmental disabilities         571.938
  medicine                         616.858 8
  nursing                          616.858 802 31
  pediatrics                       618.928 588
Developmental disorders            571.938
  *see also* Developmental
    disabilities
Developmental genetics             571.85
Developmental immunology           571.963 8
Developmental linguistics          401.93
                                   T4—019
Developmental psychology           155
  comparative psychology           156.5
  *see Manual at* 155
Developmental reading              418.4
  specific languages               T4—843
Developmentally disabled people    305.908 5
                                   T1—087 5
  education                        371.92
  social group                     305.908 5
  social services                  362.196 8
    mental retardation             362.3
    physical illness               362.196 8

Developmentally disabled
  workers                          331.595
Deveron, River (Scotland)          T2—412 4
Deviation (Social)                 302.542
Device drivers                     005.71
  programming                      005.711
  programs                         005.713
Devil                              202.16
  art representation               704.948 7
  arts                             700.482 021 6
                                   T3C—382 021 6
  Christianity                     235.4
  Islam                            297.216
  Judaism                          296.316
  literature                       808.803 820 216
    history and criticism          809.933 820 216
    specific literatures           T3B—080 382 021 6
      history and
        criticism                  T3B—093 820 216
  occultism                        133.422
Devil worship                      202.16
  occultism                        133.422
Devolution, War of, 1667–1668      944.033
Devon (England)                    T2—423 5
Devon cattle                       636.226
Devonian period                    551.74
  geology                          551.74
  paleontology                     560.174
Devonport (Tas.)                   T2—946 5
Devotional calendars               242.2
Devotional literature              204.32
  Buddhism                         294.344 32
  Christianity                     242
  Hinduism                         294.543 2
  Islam                            297.382
    Sufi                           297.438 2
  Judaism                          296.72
Devotional theology                204
  Buddhism                         294.344
  Christianity                     240
  Hinduism                         294.54
  Islam                            297.57
    Sufi                           297.4
  Judaism                          296.7
Dew                                551.574 4
Dew points                         536.44
Dewberries                         641.347 17
  botany                           583.73
  cooking                          641.647 17
  food                             641.347 17
  horticulture                     634.717
Dewdney-Alouette (B.C)             T2—711 37
Dewetsdorp (South Africa :
  District)                        T2—685 6

Dewey County (Okla.)    T2—766 18
Dewey County (S.D.)    T2—783 54
Dewey Decimal Classification   025.431
Dewey shorthand system
   1936    653.428
Dexter cattle    636.225
Dextrans    572.566
   *see also* Carbohydrates
Dextrose    572.565
   *see also* Carbohydrates
Dhaka (Bangladesh :
   Division)    T2—549 22
Dhammapada    294.382 322
Dharma
   Hinduism    294.548
Dharmasastras    294.592 6
Dhegiha languages    497.525
   T6—975 25
Dhī Qār (Iraq : Province)   T2—567 5
Dhole    599.77
Diabetes    362.196 462
   medicine    616.462
   pregnancy complications
     obstetrics    618.364 6
   social services    362.196 462
   *see also* Endocrine diseases —
     humans
Diabetes insipidus
   medicine    616.47
   *see also* Endocrine
     diseases — humans
Diabetes mellitus    362.196 462
   cooking for    641.563 14
   medicine    616.462
   pediatrics    618.924 62
   pregnancy complications
     obstetrics    618.364 6
   social services    362.196 462
   *see also* Endocrine diseases —
     humans
Diabetes mellitus (Type 1)    362.196 462 2
   medicine    616.462 2
   pregnancy complications
     obstetrics    618.364 6
   social services    362.196 462 2
   *see also* Endocrine diseases —
     humans
Diabetes mellitus (Type 2)    362.196 462 4
   medicine    616.462 4
   pregnancy complications
     obstetrics    618.364 6
   social services    362.196 462 4
   *see also* Endocrine diseases —
     humans

Diabetic nephropathies
   medicine    616.61
   *see also* Urologic diseases —
     humans
Diabrotica    595.764 8
   agricultural pests    632.764 8
Diachronic linguistics    417.7
   specific languages    T4—7
   *see Manual at* 410
Diagenesis    552.03
Diagnosis
   medicine    616.075
Diagnostic cytology
   medicine    616.075 82
Diagnostic equipment
   manufacturing technology    681.761
Diagnostic graphology    155.282
   criminal investigation    363.256 5
   personnel selection    658.311 2
Diagnostic imaging
   medicine    616.075 4
Diagnostic magnetic resonance
   imaging
   medicine    616.075 48
Diagnostic radiology    616.075 7
Diagnostic services    362.177
   *see also* Health services
Diagnostic tests
   primary education
     reading    372.486
Diagnostic ultrasound
   medicine    616.075 43
Diagrams    T1—022 3
   *see Manual at* T1—0222 vs.
     T1—0223
Dial-a-message telephone calls    384.646
   *see also* Telephone
Dialectical materialism    146.32
   Marxian theory    335.411 2
   philosophy    146.32
Dialecticianism (Chinese
   philosophy)    181.115
Dialectology    417.2
   specific languages    T4—7
Dialects    417.2
   specific languages    T4—7
   *see Manual at* T4—1–5,
     T4—8 vs. T4—7; *also at*
     T4—7; *also at* 420–490
Dialing systems
   telephone communications
     services    384.65
     wireless    384.535

Dialogue
  literature     808.802 6
    history and criticism     809.926
    specific literatures     T3B—080 26
      history and
        criticism     T3B—092 6
Dialysis
  chemistry     542.6
Diamagnetism     538.42
Diamond-backed terrapin     597.925 9
Diamonds     553.82
  economic geology     553.82
  glyptics     736.23
  jewelry     739.27
  mineralogy     549.27
  mining     622.382
  synthetic     666.88
  *see also* Industrial diamonds
Dianetics     299.936
Diapause     571.785
Diapensiales     583.67
Diaphragm (Body part)     573.26
  biology     573.26
  human anatomy     611.26
  human physiology     612.25
  medicine     616.2
  surgery     617.547
  *see also* Respiratory system
Diaphragms (Birth control)
  health     613.943 5
  medicine     618.185
  *see also* Birth control
Diaporthales     579.567
Diapsida     567.9
Diaries     920
    T1—092
  biography     920
  literature     808.883
    history and criticism     809.983
    specific literatures     T3B—803
      individual authors     T3A—8
Diarrhea
  incidence     614.593 427
  medicine     616.342 7
  *see also* Digestive system
    diseases — humans
Diaspora (Jewish history)     909.049 24
Diaspore
  mineralogy     549.525
Diaspore clay     553.61
  *see also* Clay
Diastrophism     551.8
Diatessaron     226.1

Diathermy
  therapeutics     615.832 3
Diatomaceous earth     553.6
  economic geology     553.6
  mining     622.36
  petrology     552.5
Diatoms     579.85
Diatonicism     781.262
Diatrymiformes     568.3
Díaz, Porfirio
  Mexican history     972.081 4
Díaz Ordaz, Gustavo
  Mexican history     972.083 1
Diazepam
  pharmacokinetics     615.788 2
Diazines     547.593
  chemical engineering     661.894
Diazotization     547.27
  chemical engineering     660.284 4
Diazotype processes     773.7
Dibamidae     597.952
Dice games     795.1
Dichapetalaceae     583.69
Dichondras     583.94
Dickens County (Tex.)     T2—764 741
Dickenson County (Va.)     T2—755 745
Dickey County (N.D.)     T2—784 54
Dickinson County (Iowa)     T2—777 123
Dickinson County (Kan.)     T2—781 56
Dickinson County (Mich.)     T2—774 955
Dickson County (Tenn.)     T2—768 44
Dicotyledons     583
  forestry     634.972
  paleobotany     561.3
  *see Manual at* 583–584
Dictation (Office practice)     651.74
  shorthand     653.14
Dictators     321.9
  public administration     352.23
Dictatorship     321.9
Diction     418
  applied linguistics     418
    specific languages     T4—81
  rhetoric     808
Dictionaries     413
  specific languages     T4—3
    *see Manual at* T4—3 vs.
      T4—81
  specific subjects     T1—03
Dictionary catalogs     025.315
  bibliography     017
  library science     025.315
Dictyoptera     595.728

| | |
|---|---|
| Didactic poetry | 808.815 |
| history and criticism | 809.15 |
| specific literatures | T3B—105 |
| individual authors | T3A—1 |
| Didelphidae | 599.276 |
| Didjeridu | 783.99 |
| Dido language | 499.964 |
| | T6—999 64 |
| Didymelales | 583.43 |
| Die casting | 671.253 |
| Diefenbaker, John G. | |
| Canadian history | 971.064 2 |
| Diefenbaker, Lake (Sask.) | T2—712 42 |
| Dieffenbachias | 635.934 64 |
| botany | 584.64 |
| floriculture | 635.934 64 |
| Diegueño Indians | T5—975 72 |
| Dielectric materials | |
| materials science | 620.195 |
| Dielectrics | 537.24 |
| crystals | 548.85 |
| Dielsdorf (Switzerland : | |
| Bezirk) | T2—494 572 3 |
| Điện Biên (Vietnam : | |
| Province) | T2—597 1 |
| Diencephalon | |
| human anatomy | 611.81 |
| human physiology | 612.826 2 |
| medicine | 616.8 |
| Dies (Tools) | 621.984 |
| Diesel-electric locomotives | 385.366 2 |
| engineering | 625.266 2 |
| transportation services | 385.366 2 |
| *see also* Rolling stock | |
| Diesel engines | 621.436 |
| automotive | 629.250 6 |
| ships | 623.872 36 |
| Diesel fuel | 665.538 4 |
| Diesel-hydraulic locomotives | 385.366 4 |
| engineering | 625.266 4 |
| transportation services | 385.366 4 |
| *see also* Rolling stock | |
| Diesel locomotives | 385.366 |
| engineering | 625.266 |
| transportation services | 385.366 |
| *see also* Rolling stock | |
| Diesel submarines | 359.938 32 |
| design | 623.812 572 |
| engineering | 623.825 72 |
| naval equipment | 359.938 32 |
| Diet | |
| health | 613.2 |
| primary education | 372.373 |
| Diet cooking | 641.563 |

| | |
|---|---|
| Diet therapy | |
| medicine | 615.854 |
| Dietary laws | |
| Islam | 297.576 |
| Judaism | 296.73 |
| Dietary limitations | |
| cooking for | 641.563 |
| religion | 204.46 |
| Hinduism | 294.544 6 |
| Judaism | 296.73 |
| Dietary regimens | |
| health | 613.26 |
| Dietetic salts | |
| food technology | 664.4 |
| Dietetics | 613.2 |
| prenatal care | |
| obstetrics | 618.242 |
| *see Manual at* 363.8 vs. 613.2, | |
| 641.3 | |
| Dietikon (Switzerland : | |
| Bezirk) | T2—494 572 2 |
| Dieting (Weight loss) | |
| health | 613.25 |
| Difaqane | 968.041 |
| Difference algebras | 512.56 |
| Difference equations | 515.625 |
| Differentiable dynamical systems | 515.39 |
| Differentiable manifolds | 516.36 |
| Differentiable mappings | 514.72 |
| Differential algebras | 512.56 |
| Differential calculus | 515.33 |
| Differential diagnosis | |
| medicine | 616.075 |
| Differential-difference equations | 515.38 |
| Differential equations | 515.35 |
| Differential forms | 515.37 |
| Differential games | 519.32 |
| Differential gear | 621.833 |
| automotive engineering | 629.245 |
| Differential geometry | 516.36 |
| Differential inequalities | 515.36 |
| Differential invariants | 515.37 |
| Differential operators | 515.724 2 |
| Differential psychology | 155 |
| comparative psychology | 156.5 |
| education | 370.151 |
| *see Manual at* 155 | |
| Differential topology | 514.72 |
| Differentiated teacher staffing | 371.141 23 |
| Diffraction crystallography | 548.83 |
| Diffraction of light | 535.42 |
| Diffuse nebulas | 523.113 5 |

Diffusion                                   530.475
   analytical chemistry                     543.2
   chemical engineering                     660.294
   chemistry                                541.34
   gaseous-state physics                    530.435
   liquid-state physics                     530.425
   physics                                  530.475
   semiconductors                           537.622 5
   solid-state physics                      530.415
Diffusion coating
   metals                                   671.736
Diffusion processes
   (Mathematics)                            519.233
Diffusion welding                           671.529
Digambara (Jainism)                         294.493
Digby (N.S. : County)            T2—716 32
Digenea                                     592.48
Digestion                                   573.3
   human physiology                         612.3
   *see also* Digestive system
Digestive organs                            573.3
   human physiology                         612.3
   *see also* Digestive system
Digestive secretions                        573.337 9
Digestive system                            573.3
   biology                                  573.3
   diseases                                 573.339
      *see also* Digestive system
         diseases
   human anatomy                            611.3
   human histology                          612.304 5
   human physiology                         612.3
   medicine                                 616.3
   surgery                                  617.43
Digestive system diseases                   573.339
   anesthesiology                           617.967 43
   animals                                  573.339
      veterinary medicine                   636.089 63
   humans                                   362.196 3
      allergies                             362.196 975
         incidence                          614.599 35
         medicine                           616.975
         pediatrics                         618.929 75
         social services                    362.196 975
      anesthesiology                        617.967 43
         specific organs                    617.967 55
      cancer                                362.196 994 3
         incidence                          614.599 943
         medicine                           616.994 3
         social services                    362.196 994 3
         *see also* Cancer — humans
      geriatrics                            618.976 3
      incidence                             614.593
      medicine                              616.3
Digestive system diseases
   humans (continued)
      pediatrics                            618.923
      pharmacokinetics                      615.73
      social services                       362.196 3
      surgery                               617.43
Digests                              T1—020 2
Digests of cases                            348.046
   United States                            348.734 6
Digests of laws                             348.026
   United States                            348.732 6
Digital art                                 776
   *see Manual at* 776 vs. 006.5–.7
Digital audio technology
   computer science                         006.5
   sound reproduction                       621.389 3
Digital cameras                             771.3
Digital cinematography                      777
Digital circuits                            621.381 5
   computer engineering                     621.395
Digital codes (Computers)                   005.72
Digital communications                      384
   communications services                  384
   computer science                         004.6
   engineering                              621.382
   *see Manual at* 004.6 vs.
      621.382, 621.3981
Digital computers                           004
   *see also* Computers
Digital images                              740
   photography                              779
Digital instruments
   technology                               681.1
Digital libraries                           025.042
Digital literacy
   primary education                        372.34
Digital media                               302.231
   advertising                              659.144
   sociology                                302.231
Digital photography                         770
Digital preservation                        025.84
   office records                           651.59
Digital publications                        070.579 7
   bibliographies                           011.39
Digital rights management
   computer science                         005.8
Digital signatures
   computer science                         005.82
Digital subscriber lines                    621.387 8
Digital television                          621.388 07
Digital-to-analog converters
   computer engineering                     621.398 14
   computer science                         004.64
   electronic engineering                   621.381 59

| | |
|---|---|
| Digital video effects | 777.9 |
| Digital video technology | |
| computer science | 006.696 |
| Digital videography | 777 |
| Digitalis | |
| pharmacokinetics | 615.711 |
| Digitization | |
| office records | 651.59 |
| Digitizer tablets | 006.62 |
| computer engineering | 621.399 6 |
| Dignity of labor | 331.013 |
| Digraphs | 511.54 |
| Dihydroxy aromatics | 547.633 |
| Dijon (France) | T2—444 26 |
| Dik-diks | 599.646 |
| Dika | 583.79 |
| Dikes (Geology) | 551.88 |
| Dikes (Levees) | 627.42 |
| reclamation from sea | 627.549 |
| road engineering | 625.734 |
| Dilation | |
| heart | |
| human physiology | 612.171 |
| Dilation and curettage | |
| surgery | 618.145 8 |
| Dill | 641.338 2 |
| botany | 583.849 |
| *see also* Flavorings | |
| Dilleniales | 583.62 |
| Dilleniidae | 583.6 |
| Dillon County (S.C.) | T2—757 85 |
| Diluents | 661.807 |
| paint technology | 667.624 |
| Dimashq (Syria : Province) | T2—569 14 |
| Dîmboviţa (Romania : Judeţ) | T2—498 2 |
| Dimension stock lumber | 674.28 |
| Dimensional analysis | 530.8 |
| Dimensioning | |
| technical drawing | 604.243 |
| Dimensions | 530.81 |
| physics | 530.81 |
| standardization | 389.62 |
| Diminishing marginal returns | 338.512 |
| Diminishing marginal utility | 338.521 2 |
| Dimmit County (Tex.) | T2—764 455 |
| Dimorphism | |
| crystallography | 548.3 |
| Dimouts | |
| military engineering | 623.77 |
| Dinagat (Philippines) | T2—599 7 |
| Diné Indians | T5—972 6 |
| Diné language | 497.26 |
| | T6—972 6 |
| Diné literature | 897.26 |
| Dinefwr (Wales) | T2—429 65 |
| Diners (Restaurants) | 647.95 |
| *see also* Eating places | |
| Dingaan, King of the Zulus | |
| KwaZulu-Natal history | 968.404 1 |
| Dingo | 599.772 |
| predator control technology | 636.083 9 |
| Dining cars | 385.33 |
| engineering | 625.23 |
| *see also* Rolling stock | |
| Dining halls | |
| architecture | 727.38 |
| Dining rooms | 643.4 |
| home economics | 643.4 |
| interior decoration | 747.76 |
| Dinka (African people) | T5—965 |
| Dinka language | 496.5 |
| | T6—965 |
| Dinners | 642 |
| cooking | 641.54 |
| light meals | 641.53 |
| main meals | 641.54 |
| customs | 394.125 3 |
| light meals | 394.125 3 |
| main meals | 394.125 4 |
| Dinnerware | 642.7 |
| *see also* Tableware | |
| Dinocerata | 569.62 |
| Dinoflagellates | 579.87 |
| Dinophyceae | 579.87 |
| Dinornithiformes | 598.54 |
| paleozoology | 568.5 |
| Dinosaur National Monument (Colo. and Utah) | T2—788 12 |
| Dinosaurs | 567.9 |
| Dinwiddie County (Va.) | T2—755 582 |
| Dioceses | |
| Christian ecclesiology | 262.3 |
| Diodes | |
| semiconductor | 621.381 522 |
| Diola (African people) | T5—963 2 |
| Diola language | 496.32 |
| | T6—963 2 |
| Diomedeidae | 598.42 |
| Diophantine analysis | 512.74 |
| Diophantine approximations | 512.73 |
| Diophantine equations | 512.72 |
| Diopsidae | 595.774 |
| Dioramas | 745.8 |
| decorative arts | 745.8 |
| painting | 751.74 |

Diori, Hamani
  Nigerien (Niger) history    966.260 51
Diorite    552.3
Dioscoreaceae    584.357
Diouf, Abdou
  Senegalese history    966.305 1
Dioula (African people)    T5—963 45
Dioula language    496.345
   T6—963 45
Diourbel (Senegal : Region)   T2—663
Dioxin
  human toxicology    615.951 2
Diphenyl hydrocarbons    547.613
  chemical engineering    661.816
Diphenylmethane dyes    667.254
Diphtheria
  incidence    614.512 3
  medicine    616.931 3
  *see also* Communicable
    diseases — humans
Diphthongs (Phonology)    414.6
  specific languages    T4—16
Diplodocus    567.913
Diplomacy    327.2
  customs    399
  law of nations    341.33
Diplomas    371.291 2
  prints    769.5
Diplomatic causes of war    355.027 2
  World War I    940.311 2
  World War II    940.531 12
Diplomatic customs    399
Diplomatic history    327.09
  Algerian Revolution    965.046 2
  American Revolution    973.32
  Chaco War    989.207 162
  Civil War (England)    942.062 2
  Civil War (Spain)    946.081 2
  Civil War (United States)    973.72
    Confederate States of
      America    973.721
    United States    973.722
  Crimean War    947.073 82
  Falkland Islands War    997.110 242
  Franco-German War    943.082 2
  Hundred Years' War    944.025 2
  Indo-Pakistan War, 1971    954.920 512
  Indochinese War    959.704 12
  Iraq War, 2003–    956.704 432
  Iraqi-Iranian Conflict    955.054 22
  Korean War    951.904 22
  Mexican War    973.622
  Napoleonic Wars    940.272
  Persian Gulf War, 1991    956.704 422

Diplomatic history (continued)
  South African War    968.048 2
  Spanish-American War    973.892
  Thirty Years' War    940.242
  Vietnamese War    959.704 32
  War of 1812    973.522
  War of the Pacific    983.061 62
  World War I    940.32
  World War II    940.532
Diplomatic immunities    327.2
  law of nations    341.33
Diplomatic languages    401.3
Diplomatic law    342.041 2
  law of nations    341.33
Diplomatic privileges    327.2
  law of nations    341.33
Diplomatic service    327.2
  public administration    353.132 63
Diplomats    327.209 2
Diplopia
  ophthalmology    617.762
  *see also* Eye diseases —
    humans
Diplopoda    595.66
Diplura    595.724
Dipnoi    597.39
  paleozoology    567.39
Dipodomys    599.359 87
Dipole moments    537.243
Dipped latex    678.533
Dipped rubber    678.36
Dippers (Birds)    598.832
Dipperu National Park
  (Qld.)    T2—943 5
Dipping animals    636.083 3
Dipping latex    678.527
Diprotodontia    599.2
Dips (Appetizers)    641.812
Dips (Geology)    551.85
Dipsacales    583.92
Diptera    595.77
Dipterocarpaceae    583.624
Dīr District (Pakistan)    T2—549 122
Dirāyah    297.125 2
Dirē Dawa (Ethiopia :
  Administrative region)    T2—632
Dirē Dawa na Īsa na
  Gurgura Āwraja
  (Ethiopia)    T2—632
Direct advertising    659.133
Direct broadcast satellite systems    384.552
Direct-current machinery    621.313 2
Direct-current transmission    621.319 12

| | |
|---|---|
| Direct distance dialing | 384.64 |
| communications services | 384.64 |
| engineering | 621.385 7 |
| Direct-driven hoists | |
| mining | 622.67 |
| Direct energy conversion | |
| electrical engineering | 621.312 4 |
| Direct-fluid-pressure | |
| displacement pumps | 621.699 |
| Direct-mail advertising | 659.133 |
| Direct-mail marketing | 381.142 |
| management | 658.872 |
| Direct marketing | 381.1 |
| management | 658.872 |
| Direct-metal sculpture | 731.41 |
| Direct-positive processes | |
| photography | 772.1 |
| Direct processes | |
| color photography | 778.63 |
| Direct selling | 381.1 |
| management | 658.872 |
| Direct taxation | 336.294 |
| Direct-to-DVD motion pictures | 791.43 |
| Direct-to-video motion pictures | 791.43 |
| Directed graphs | 511.54 |
| Directed lighting | 621.321 4 |
| Direction (Drama) | 792.023 3 |
| motion pictures | 791.430 233 |
| radio | 791.440 233 |
| stage | 792.023 3 |
| television | 791.450 233 |
| Direction finders | |
| aircraft engineering | 629.135 1 |
| radio engineering | 621.384 191 |
| Direction finding | 629.045 |
| air navigation | 629.132 51 |
| marine navigation | 623.893 |
| radio engineering | 621.384 191 |
| Directional derivatives | 515.33 |
| geometry | 516.36 |
| Directional gyros | |
| aircraft | 629.135 2 |
| Directories | T1—025 |
| bibliographies | 011.7 |
| *see Manual at* T1—025 vs. | |
| T1—029; *also at* T1—025 | |
| vs. T1—0601–0609 | |
| Directors (Drama) | 792.023 309 2 |
| motion pictures | 791.430 233 092 |
| radio | 791.440 233 092 |
| stage | 792.023 309 2 |
| television | 791.450 233 092 |
| *see Manual at* 780.92 and | |
| 791.092 | |

| | |
|---|---|
| Directors of corporations | |
| executive management | 658.422 |
| law | 346.066 42 |
| Directors of religious education | 207.509 2 |
| biography | 207.509 2 |
| Christianity | 268.092 |
| biography | 268.092 |
| *see Manual at* 230–280 | |
| role and function | 268.3 |
| Judaism | 296.680 92 |
| biography | 296.680 92 |
| role and function | 296.68 |
| Directory (France) | 944.045 |
| Directory advertising | 659.132 |
| Dirichlet problem | 515.353 |
| Dirichlet series | 515.243 |
| Dirigibles | 387.732 4 |
| engineering | 629.133 24 |
| military engineering | 623.743 |
| piloting | 629.132 522 |
| transportation services | 387.732 4 |
| *see also* Aircraft | |
| Diriku language | 496.399 |
| | T6—963 99 |
| Dirks | 623.441 |
| art metalwork | 739.72 |
| military engineering | 623.441 |
| Dirouilles (Channel Islands) | T2—423 49 |
| Dirt roads | 388.12 |
| engineering | 625.74 |
| Disability | |
| arts | T3C—356 1 |
| literature | 808.803 561 |
| history and criticism | 809.933 561 |
| specific literatures | T3B—080 356 1 |
| history and | |
| criticism | T3B—093 561 |
| psychological influence | 155.916 |
| social welfare | 362.4 |
| Disability (Law) | 346.013 |
| Disability evaluation | |
| medicine | 616.075 |
| Disability income insurance | 368.386 |
| law | 346.086 386 |
| workers' compensation | 344.021 |
| Disability insurance | 368.382 |
| Disabled American Veterans | 369.186 3 |
| Disabled children | 305.908 083 |
| | T1—087 |
| home care | 649.151 |
| psychology | 155.45 |
| Disabled people | 305.908 |
| | T1—087 |
| architecture for | 720.87 |

Disabled people (continued)
  civil and human rights    323.3
  clothing
    home sewing    646.401
  collected biography    T1—092 7
  education    371.9
    law    344.079 11
  footwear for
    manufacturing technology    685.38
  government programs    353.539
  Holocaust, 1933–1945    940.531 808 7
  home care    649.8
  institutional buildings
    architecture    725.54
  legal status    346.013
    private law    346.013
  libraries for    027.663
    administration    025.197 663
    collection development    025.218 766 3
  museum services    069.17
  pastoral care
    Christianity    259.44
  publications for
    bibliographies    011.63
    reviews    028.163
  recreation    790.196
    indoor    793.019 6
    outdoor    796.087
  social group    305.908
  social welfare    362.4
    public administration
      health services    353.66
  sports    796.087
  *see Manual at* 796.08 vs.
    796.04
  *see Manual at* 362.1–.4 vs. 610
Disabled veterans    362.408 697
  legal status    343.011 6
  social welfare    362.408 697
Disabled workers    331.59
  economics    331.59
  government programs    354.908 7
  law    344.015 9
  personnel management    658.300 87
Disarmament    327.174
  ethics    172.4
    religion    205.624
      Christianity    241.624
    *see also* Political ethics
  international politics    327.174
  law    341.733

Disarmament (continued)
  social theology    201.727 3
    Christianity    261.87
    Judaism    296.382 7
Disassembling tools    621.93
Disaster insurance    368.122
Disaster nursing    610.734 9
Disaster preparedness
  library operations    025.82
Disaster relief    363.348
  law    344.053 48
  public administration    353.95
Disaster technology    628.92
Disasters    904
  law    344.053 4
  management of enterprises    658.477
  personal safety    613.69
  psychology    155.935
  social effects    303.485
  social services    363.34
    public administration    353.95
  *see Manual at* 900
Discarding
  library collections    025.216
  museology    069.51
Discharge (Military personnel)    355.114
Discharged offenders    364.8
  labor economics    331.51
Disciples of Christ    286.63
  *see also* Restoration movement
    (Christian movement)
Discipline
  armed forces    355.13
    law    343.014
  education    371.5
  home child care    649.64
  labor economics    331.259 8
  labor unions    331.873
  legislators    328.366
  personnel management    658.314
    public administration    352.66
      law    342.068 4
  prisons    365.643
Disco dancing    793.33
Discoglossoidea    597.86
Discographies    011.38
  music    016.780 266
Discomycetes    579.57
Discount    332.84
Discount brokers    332.62
Discount clubs    381.149
  management    658.879

| | |
|---|---|
| Discount rates | 332.84 |
| economics | 332.84 |
| central banking | 332.113 |
| macroeconomic policy | 339.53 |
| Discount stores | 381.149 |
| management | 658.879 |
| *see also* Commerce | |
| Discounts | |
| sales promotion | 658.82 |
| Discourse analysis | T1—014 1 |
| linguistics | 401.41 |
| language for special | |
| purposes | 401.47 |
| specific languages | T4—014 7 |
| specific languages | T4—014 1 |
| Discoveries in geography | 910.9 |
| *see Manual at* 913–919 | |
| Discoveries in natural history | 508 |
| Discoveries in science | 509 |
| Discovery | |
| archaeological technique | 930.102 82 |
| Discovery (Law) | 347.072 |
| criminal law | 345.072 |
| Discrete geometry | 516.11 |
| Discrete mathematics | 511.1 |
| *see Manual at* 004.0151 vs. | |
| 511.1, 511.35 | |
| Discrete-time systems | 003.83 |
| Discriminant analysis | 519.535 |
| Discriminants | |
| number theory | 512.74 |
| Discrimination | 305 |
| | T1—08 |
| ethics | 177.5 |
| religion | |
| Buddhism | 294.356 75 |
| Christianity | 241.675 |
| Islam | 297.567 5 |
| Judaism | 296.367 5 |
| *see also* Ethical problems | |
| religion | 200.8 |
| Christianity | 270.08 |
| Judaism | 296.08 |
| Discrimination (Psychology) | 152.1 |
| quantitative studies | 152.82 |
| Discrimination in education | 370.8 |
| law | 344.079 8 |
| Discrimination in employment | 331.133 |
| *see also* Equal employment | |
| opportunity | |
| Discrimination in housing | 363.51 |
| law | 344.063 635 1 |
| Discrimination in mortgage loans | 332.72 |

| | |
|---|---|
| Discrimination learning | |
| psychology | 153.152 8 |
| Discs (Recording devices) | 621.382 34 |
| sound reproduction | 621.389 32 |
| television | 384.558 |
| *see also* Video recordings | |
| Discus fishes | 597.74 |
| culture | 639.377 4 |
| Discus throwing | 796.435 |
| Discussion | |
| public | |
| literature | 808.853 |
| specific literatures | T3B—503 |
| individual | |
| authors | T3A—5 |
| rhetoric | 808.53 |
| teaching method | 371.37 |
| Discussion groups | |
| adult education | 374.22 |
| Discussion groups (Computer | |
| communications) | 004.693 |
| Discussion lists (Computer | |
| communications) | 004.693 |
| Disease carriers | |
| law | 344.043 |
| medicine | 614.43 |
| Disease control | 614.44 |
| law | 344.043 |
| public administration | 353.628 |
| public health | 614.44 |
| Disease prevention | |
| medicine | 613 |
| public health | 614.44 |
| Disease resistance | 571.96 |
| humans | 616.079 |
| Disease vectors | 571.986 |
| Diseases | 571.9 |
| agriculture | 632.3 |
| animals | 571.91 |
| conservation technology | 639.964 |
| veterinary medicine | 636.089 6 |
| *see Manual at* 571–575 vs. | |
| 630 | |
| humans | 362.1 |
| arts | T3C—356 1 |
| geriatrics | 618.97 |
| gynecology | 618.1 |
| incidence | 614.42 |
| literature | 808.803 561 |
| history and criticism | 809.933 561 |
| specific literatures | T3B—080 356 1 |
| history and | |
| criticism | T3B—093 561 |

Diseases
  humans (continued)
    medicine 616
      *see Manual at* 610 vs. 616;
        *also at* 616 vs. 612;
        *also at* 616 vs. 617.4;
        *also at* 616 vs. 618.92
    pastoral theology 206.1
      Christianity 259.41
    pediatrics 618.92
    prevalence 614.42
    psychological influence 155.916
    religious rites 203.8
      Christianity 265.82
    social services 362.1
    social theology 201.762 1
      Christianity 261.832 1
    sociology 306.461
    surgery 617
      *see Manual at* 617
      *see Manual at* 362.1–.4 and
        614.4–.5
  plants 571.92
    agriculture 632.3
    *see Manual at* 571–575 vs.
      630
Diseconomies of scale 338.514 4
Disfigurement
  psychological influence 155.916
Dishes 642.7
  *see also* Tableware
Dishwashers
  installation 696.184
  manufacturing technology 683.88
Disinfection
  public health 614.48
  sewage treatment 628.32
  water supply treatment 628.166 2
Disinformation activities
  international politics 327.14
Disk drives 004.563
  engineering 621.397 63
Disks (Computers) 004.563
  engineering 621.397 63
Disks (Geometrical shapes) 516.154
Disks (Recording devices) 621.382 34
Dislocation (Aftermath of war) 355.028
Dislocation (Crystallography) 548.842
Dislocations (Geology) 551.872
Dislocations (Injuries)
  medicine 617.16

Dismal Swamp (N.C. and
  Va.) T2—755 523
  North Carolina T2—756 135
  Virginia T2—755 523
Dismissal of employees
  economics 331.259 6
    unemployment 331.137
    worker security 331.259 6
  law 344.012 596
  personnel management 658.313
  public administration 352.69
Disordered solids 530.413
Disorderly conduct 364.143
  law 345.024 3
Disorders of sex development
  medicine 616.694
Dispatching 388.041
  production management 658.53
  *see also* Scheduling —
    transportation
Dispensaries 362.12
  armed forces 355.72
  *see also* Health care facilities
Dispensationalist theology 230.046 3
Dispensatories 615.13
Dispersion of light 535.4
Displaced persons 305.906 914
                T1—086 914
  law 342.083
  political science 325.21
  social welfare 362.87
  women
    social welfare 362.839 814
  young people
    social welfare 362.779 14
  *see also* Refugees
Display advertising 659.15
Display lighting 621.322 9
Display of merchandise
  advertising 659.15
Display screens (Computers) 004.77
  engineering 621.398 7
Disposable personal income 339.32
Disposal of dead 363.75
  *see also* Undertaking
    (Mortuary)
Disposal of government property 352.54
Disposal of military supplies 355.621 37
Disposal of public lands 333.16
  economics 333.16
  public administration 352.574

Dispute resolution 303.69
  international relations 327.17
  law 347.09
  sociology 303.69
Disruptive discharges 537.52
Dissent 303.484
  social action 361.23
Dissenters (Protestant churches) 280.4
  *see also* Protestantism
Dissertations (Academic) 378.242
  bibliographies 011.75
  rhetoric 808.066 378
  specific places 015
Dissociative disorders
  medicine 616.852 3
    *see also* Mental disorders
Dissolution of business
  enterprises 338.71
  management 658.166
Dissonance (Music) 781.239
Distance education 371.35
  adult level 374.4
    T1—071 5
  computers 371.334
  higher education 378.175
  radio 371.333 1
  television 371.335 8
Distance races 796.424
Distant prospection
  (Parapsychology) 133.323
Distillation
  alcoholic beverages 663.16
  chemistry 542.4
  desalinization 628.167 2
Distilled liquor 641.25
  commercial processing 663.5
  cooking with 641.625
  home preparation 641.874
Distomatosis
  incidence 614.553
  medicine 616.963
    *see also* Communicable
      diseases — humans
Distributed databases
  computer science 005.758
Distributed-parameter systems 003.78
Distributed processing 004.36
  communications 004.618 6
    programming 005.712 76
    programs 005.713 76
  interfacing
    programming 005.712 76
    programs 005.713 76
  multimedia-systems programs 006.787 6

Distributed processing (continued)
  operating systems 005.447 6
  programming 005.276
  programs 005.376
  *see also* Processing modes —
    computer science
Distribution channels 381.1
  marketing management 658.87
Distribution management 658.8
  T1—068 8
Distribution theory
  (Mathematics) 515.782
Distribution theory of prime
  numbers 512.73
Distributions
  functional analysis 515.782
  probabilities 519.24
Distributive justice
  ethics 172.2
  religion 205.622
    Buddhism 294.356 22
    Christianity 241.622
    Hinduism 294.548 622
    Islam 297.562 2
    Judaism 296.362 2
  law 340.115
Distributor brands
  sales promotion 658.827
District attorneys 345.012 62
District courts 347.02
  United States 347.732 2
District heating 697.03
  hot water 697.4
  resource economics 333.793
  steam 697.54
District nursing 610.734 3
District of Columbia 975.3
  T2—753
Districting (Legislatures) 328.334 5
  law 342.053
Districts (Local government
  units) 320.83
  *see also* Counties
Distrito Especial de Bogotá
  (Colombia) T2—861 48
Distrito Federal (Brazil) T2—817 4
Distrito Federal (Mexico) T2—725 3
Distrito Federal (Venezuela) T2—877
Distrito Nacional
  (Dominican Republic) T2—729 375
Ditches
  agriculture 631.62
  road engineering 625.734
Ditsobotla (South Africa) T2—682 44

Diuretics
  pharmacokinetics 615.761
Diurnal variations
  geomagnetism 538.742
Divehi language 491.489
                  T6—914 89
Divehi literature 891.489
Divers 627.720 92
  springboard sports 797.240 92
  underwater sports 797.230 92
  underwater technologists 627.720 92
Diversification
  production economics 338.6
  production management 658.503 8
Diversity in the workplace 331.133
  personnel management 658.300 8
Divertimentos 784.185 2
Divestment
  management 658.164
Divide County (N.D.) T2—784 71
Divided catalogs 025.315
Dividends 332.632 21
  accounting 657.76
  financial management 658.155
  income tax 336.242 6
    law 343.052 46
  law 346.092 2
Dividers
  road engineering 625.795
Divination 133.3
  religion 203.2
    African religions 299.613 2
Divinatory graphology 137
Divinatory signs 133.334
Divine law
  Christianity 241.2
Divine Light Mission 294
Divine office (Religion) 264.15
  Anglican 264.030 13
  music 782.324
    choral and mixed voices 782.532 4
    single voices 783.093 24
  Roman Catholic 264.020 15
    texts 264.024
Divine right of kings 321.6
Diving 627.72
  engineering 627.72
  sports 797.2
Diving medicine 616.980 22
Diving petrels 598.42
Divining rods 133.323
Divinity of Jesus Christ 232.8
Divinity schools 230.071 1
Divisibility 512.72

Division 512.92
  algebra 512.92
  arithmetic 513.214
Division algebras 512.4
Division of labor
  production economics 338.6
  sociology 306.368
Divisionism 709.034 5
  painting 759.055
Divisions (Army units) 355.31
Divisions (Naval units) 359.31
Divorce 306.89
  ethics 173
    religion 205.63
      Buddhism 294.356 3
      Christianity 241.63
      Hinduism 294.548 63
      Islam 297.563
      Judaism 296.363
  Judaism 296.444 4
  law 346.016 6
  psychology 155.93
  religion 204.41
  social theology 201.7
    Christianity 261.835 89
  social welfare 362.829 4
  *see also* Families — social
    welfare
  sociology 306.89
Divorced families 306.89
  social welfare 362.829 4
Divorced men 306.892
  guides to Christian life 248.842 3
  psychology 155.643 2
Divorced people 306.89
                T1—086 53
  Christian devotional literature 242.646
  family relationships 306.89
  guides to religious life
    Christianity 248.846
  legal status 346.016 6
  psychology 155.643
  social group 306.89
  social welfare 362.829 4
Divorced women 306.893
  guides to Christian life 248.843 3
  psychology 155.643 3
  social welfare 362.839 59
Dixie County (Fla.) T2—759 812
Dixiecrat Party (U.S.) 324.273 3
Dixieland jazz 781.653
Dixon County (Neb.) T2—782 223
Dixon Entrance (B.C. and 551.461 433
  Alaska) T2—164 33

Diyālá (Iraq)                      T2—567 4
Diyarbakır İli (Turkey)            T2—566 77
  ancient                T2—394 2
Dizziness
  medicine               616.841
   *see also* Nervous system
    diseases — humans
Djakarta (Indonesia)               T2—598 22
Djamena (Chad)                     T2—674 3
Djelfa (Algeria : Province)        T2—653
Djibouti                           967.71
                              T2—677 1
Djiboutians                        T5—967 71
Djirbal language                   499.15
                              T6—991 5
DNA (Genetics)                     572.86
  humans                 611.018 166
  *see Manual at* 576.5 vs. 572.8
DNA topology
  humans                 611.018 166 3
DNA virus infections
  incidence               614.581
  medicine                616.911
   *see also* Communicable
    diseases — humans
DNA viruses                        579.24
Dnepropetrovsk (Ukraine :
  Oblast)                 T2—477 4
Dnestr River (Ukraine and
  Moldova)                T2—477 9
Dnieper River                      T2—477
Dniester River (Ukraine and
  Moldova)                T2—477 9
Dnipropetrovs´ka oblast´
  (Ukraine)              T2—477 4
DNSAP (Austrian political party)   324.243 602 38
Do-it-yourself work                643.7
Dobby-weave fabrics                677.615
  *see also* Textiles
Doberai Peninsula
  (Indonesia)             T2—951 2
Doberman pinscher                  636.736
Dobruja (Romania and
  Bulgaria)               T2—498 3
  Bulgaria                T2—499 4
  Romania                 T2—498 3
Dobsonflies                        595.747
Dock (Plant)                       583.57
Docks (Port facilities)            387.15
  engineering             627.31
  *see also* Port facilities
Doctors                            610.92
  *see also* Physicians
Doctor's degree                    378.2

Doctrinal controversies
  Christian church history   273
Doctrinal theology                 202
  Buddhism                 294.342
  Christianity             230
  Hinduism                 294.52
  Islam                    297.2
   Sufi                297.41
  Judaism                  296.3
  philosophy of religion   210
Document delivery services         025.6
Document markup languages          006.74
Documentary evidence               347.064
  criminal investigation   363.256 5
  law                      347.064
Documentary films
  journalism               070.18
Documentary hypothesis
  (Pentateuchal criticism)  222.106 6
Documentary media
  journalism               070.1
Documentation                      025
  specific subjects        025.06
Dodders                            583.94
Doddridge County (W. Va.)   T2—754 56
Dodecanese                  T2—495 87
  ancient          T2—391 6
Dodecaphony                        781.268
Dōdekanēsos (Greece)        T2—495 87
  ancient          T2—391 6
Dodge County (Ga.)          T2—758 532
Dodge County (Minn.)        T2—776 153
Dodge County (Neb.)         T2—782 235
Dodge County (Wis.)         T2—775 82
Dodoma Region (Tanzania)    T2—678 26
Dodos                              598.65
Doe, Samuel K. (Samuel
  Kanyon)
  Liberian history         966.620 32
Dog breeds                         636.71
  *see Manual at* 636.72–.75
Dog family                         599.77
Dog pounds                         363.78
  *see also* Pest control
Dog racing                         798.8
Dog sled racing                    798.83
Dogbanes                           583.93
Dogfishes                          597.36
Dogmatism
  philosophy               148
Dogon (African people)      T5—963
Dogon language                     496.3
                       T6—963

| | | | |
|---|---|---|---|
| Dogs | 636.7 | Domestic animals | 636 |
| animal husbandry | 636.7 | Domestic architecture | 728 |
| predator control technology | 636.083 9 | Domestic arts | 640 |
| zoology | 599.772 | Domestic cats | 636.8 |
| Dogwoods | 635.977 384 | Domestic commerce | 381 |
| botany | 583.84 | law | 343.08 |
| ornamental arboriculture | 635.977 384 | public administration | 354.73 |
| Doilies | 642.7 | Domestic councils | |
| arts | 746.96 | public administration | 352.246 |
| home sewing | 646.21 | Domestic customs | 392.3 |
| table setting | 642.7 | Domestic employees | 640.46 |
| Dolerite | 552.3 | Domestic fowl | 636.5 |
| Dolgan language | 494.33 | agricultural economics | 338.176 5 |
| | T6—943 3 | zoology | 598.625 |
| Dolichopodidae | 595.773 | Domestic industries | 338.634 |
| Dolj (Romania) | T2—498 4 | Domestic investment | 332.6 |
| Doll clothing | 688.722 1 | Domestic law | |
| handicrafts | 745.592 21 | relation to law of nations | 341.04 |
| manufacturing technology | 688.722 1 | Domestic medicine | 616.024 |
| *see also* Toys | | Domestic order | |
| Doll furniture | 688.723 | public administration | 353.3 |
| handicrafts | 745.592 3 | Domestic partners | 306.841 |
| manufacturing technology | 688.723 | | T1—086 56 |
| *see also* Toys | | Domestic partnerships | 306.841 |
| Dollard-des-Ormeaux | | | T1—086 56 |
| (Quebec) | T2—714 28 | law | 346.016 |
| Dollhouses | 688.723 | Domestic relations (Family | |
| handicrafts | 745.592 3 | relations) | 306.8 |
| manufacturing technology | 688.723 | law | 346.015 |
| *see also* Toys | | Domestic safety | 363.13 |
| Dolls | 688.722 1 | public administration | 353.97 |
| ceramic arts | 738.83 | *see also* Safety | |
| handicrafts | 745.592 21 | Domestic sciences | 640 |
| manufacturing technology | 688.722 1 | Domestic settings | |
| *see also* Toys | | music | 781.535 |
| Dolly Varden trout | 597.554 | Domestic system | |
| Dolnośląskie Voivodeship | | economics | 338.634 |
| (Poland) | T2—438 52 | Domestic trade | 381 |
| Dolomite | 553.516 | law | 343.08 |
| economic geology | 553.516 | public administration | 354.73 |
| mineralogy | 549.782 | Domestic violence | 362.829 2 |
| petrology | 552.58 | *see also* Family violence | |
| Dolores County (Colo.) | T2—788 26 | Domestic wastes | 363.728 8 |
| Dolphinfishes | 597.72 | social services | 363.728 8 |
| Dolphins | 599.53 | technology | 628.4 |
| animal husbandry | 636.953 | water pollution engineering | 628.168 2 |
| conservation technology | 639.979 53 | *see also* Waste control | |
| resource economics | 333.959 53 | Domestic water supply | 363.61 |
| Domaine-du-Roy (Quebec) | T2—714 142 | economics | 333.912 2 |
| Domes | 721.46 | Domestication (Agriculture) | 631.52 |
| architecture | 721.46 | animals | 636.082 |
| construction | 690.146 | plants | 631.52 |
| structural engineering | 624.177 5 | | |
| concrete | 624.183 45 | | |

| | |
|---|---|
| Dominance | |
| applied psychology | 158.2 |
| social control | 303.33 |
| Dominica | 972.984 1 |
| | T2—729 841 |
| Dominican Republic | 972.93 |
| | T2—729 3 |
| Dominican Republic literature | 860 |
| Dominican Sisters | 255.972 |
| church history | 271.972 |
| Dominicans (Christian religious | |
| orders) | 255.2 |
| church history | 271.2 |
| women | 255.972 |
| church history | 271.972 |
| Dominicans (Dominican | |
| Republic people) | T5—687 293 |
| Dominion of Canada | 971.05 |
| | T2—71 |
| Dominion theology | 230.046 |
| Dominoes | 795.32 |
| Don, River (Scotland) | T2—412 4 |
| Don River (Russia) | T2—474 9 |
| Doña Ana County (N.M.) | T2—789 66 |
| Donations | |
| financial management | 658.153 |
| tax law | 343.052 32 |
| Donatism | 273.4 |
| Donbas (Ukraine and | |
| Russia) | T2—477 4 |
| Doncaster (England : | |
| Metropolitan Borough) | T2—428 27 |
| Donegal (Ireland : County) | T2—416 93 |
| Donets Basin (Ukraine and | |
| Russia) | T2—477 4 |
| Donets River (Russia and | |
| Ukraine) | T2—477 4 |
| Donets′k (Ukraine : Oblast) | T2—477 4 |
| Donets′ka oblast′ (Ukraine) | T2—477 4 |
| Đồng Nai (Vietnam : | |
| Province) | T2—597 7 |
| Đồng Tháp (Vietnam) | T2—597 8 |
| Doniphan County (Kan.) | T2—781 35 |
| Donkeys | 636.182 |
| conservation technology | 639.979 665 |
| resource economics | 333.959 665 |
| Donley County (Tex.) | T2—764 832 |
| Dooly County (Ga.) | T2—758 895 |
| Door County (Wis.) | T2—775 63 |
| Door furnishings | 645.3 |
| home sewing | 646.21 |
| household management | 645.3 |
| manufacturing technology | 684 |

| | |
|---|---|
| Door knockers | |
| artistic ironwork | 739.48 |
| Doors | 721.822 |
| architecture | 721.822 |
| automobiles | 629.26 |
| construction | 690.182 2 |
| interior decoration | 747.3 |
| sculpture | 731.542 |
| Doorstops | |
| rubber | 678.34 |
| Doorways | 721.822 |
| architecture | 721.822 |
| construction | 690.182 2 |
| Dopamine | |
| in nervous system | |
| human physiology | 612.804 2 |
| Doppelgänger | |
| literature | 808.802 7 |
| history and criticism | 809.927 |
| specific literatures | T3B—080 27 |
| history and | |
| criticism | T3B—092 7 |
| Doppler effect | 534.3 |
| Dorchester County (Md.) | T2—752 27 |
| Dorchester County (S.C.) | T2—757 94 |
| Dordogne (France) | T2—447 2 |
| Doris (Greece) | T2—383 |
| Dormancy (Biology) | 571.78 |
| Dormers | 721.5 |
| architecture | 721.5 |
| construction | 690.15 |
| Dormice | 599.359 6 |
| Dormitories | 371.871 |
| architecture | 727.38 |
| Dorneck (Switzerland) | T2—494 355 7 |
| Dorneck-Thierstein | |
| (Switzerland) | T2—494 355 |
| Dornoch Firth (Scotland) | T2—163 36 |
| Dorsal muscles | |
| human anatomy | 611.731 |
| Dorset (England) | T2—423 3 |
| Dortmund (Germany) | T2—435 633 |
| Dorval (Quebec) | T2—714 28 |
| Dosage determination | |
| pharmacology | 615.14 |
| Dosage forms | |
| pharmaceutical chemistry | 615.19 |
| Dosimetry | |
| biophysics | |
| humans | 612.014 480 287 |
| radiotherapy | 615.842 |
| Dothideales | 579.564 |
| Dotted swiss embroidery | 677.77 |
| Douala (Cameroon) | T2—671 1 |

| | |
|---|---|
| Douay Bible | 220.520 2 |
| Double basses | 787.5 |
|   instrument | 787.519 |
|   music | 787.5 |
|   *see also* Stringed instruments | |
| Double-bassists | 787.509 2 |
| Double bassoons | 788.59 |
|   instrument | 788.591 9 |
|   music | 788.59 |
|   *see also* Woodwind instruments | |
| Double cropping | 631.58 |
| Double helix | 572.863 3 |
| Double houses | |
|   architecture | 728.312 |
| Double jeopardy | 345.04 |
| Double mini-trampoline | 796.474 |
| Double-reed bagpipes | 788.49 |
|   *see also* Woodwind instruments | |
| Double-reed instruments | 788.5 |
|   *see also* Woodwind instruments | |
| Double salts | |
|   chemical engineering | 661.4 |
| Double stars | 523.841 |
| Double sulfides | |
|   mineralogy | 549.35 |
| Double taxation | 336.294 |
|   law | 343.052 6 |
|   public finance | 336.294 |
| Doubles (Literature) | 808.802 7 |
|   history and criticism | 809.927 |
|   specific literatures | T3B—080 27 |
|     history and criticism | T3B—092 7 |
| Doubles (Tennis) | 796.342 28 |
| Doubling the cube | 516.204 |
| Doubs (France : Dept.) | T2—444 6 |
| Doubs River (France and | |
|   Switzerland) | T2—444 6 |
|   France | T2—444 6 |
|   Switzerland | T2—494 36 |
| Doubt | |
|   epistemology | 121.5 |
| Dougherty County (Ga.) | T2—758 953 |
| Douglas County (Colo.) | T2—788 86 |
| Douglas County (Ga.) | T2—758 243 |
| Douglas County (Ill.) | T2—773 68 |
| Douglas County (Kan.) | T2—781 65 |
| Douglas County (Minn.) | T2—776 45 |
| Douglas County (Mo.) | T2—778 832 |
| Douglas County (Neb.) | T2—782 254 |
| Douglas County (Nev.) | T2—793 59 |
| Douglas County (Or.) | T2—795 29 |
| Douglas County (S.D.) | T2—783 383 |
| Douglas County (Wash.) | T2—797 31 |
| Douglas County (Wis.) | T2—775 11 |
| Douglas squirrel | 599.363 |
| Doukkala-Abda (Morocco) | T2—646 2 |
| Douro (Portugal : Region) | T2—469 15 |
| Douro Litoral (Portugal) | T2—469 15 |
| Dove, River (Derbyshire | |
|   and Staffordshire, | |
|   England) | T2—425 13 |
| Dovecotes | |
|   architecture | 728.927 |
|   construction | 690.892 7 |
| Dover (Del.) | T2—751 4 |
| Dover (England : District) | T2—422 352 |
| Dover, Strait of | 551.461 336 |
| | T2—163 36 |
| Doves | 598.65 |
|   conservation technology | 639.978 65 |
|   resource economics | 333.958 65 |
|   sports hunting | 799.246 5 |
| Dowayo (African people) | T5—963 61 |
| Dowayo language | 496.361 |
| | T6—963 61 |
| Down (Northern Ireland) | T2—416 5 |
| Down (Northern Ireland : | |
|   District) | T2—416 56 |
| Down syndrome | |
|   medicine | 616.858 842 |
|   pediatrics | 618.928 588 42 |
| Downhill ski racing | 796.935 |
| Downhill skiing | 796.935 |
| Downs (Qld. : District) | T2—943 3 |
| Downsizing of organizations | |
|   executive management | 658.406 |
|   personnel management | 658.313 4 |
|   production economics | 338.64 |
|   public administration | 352.367 |
|   worker security | 331.259 6 |
| Downtown | 307.333 16 |
|   area planning | 711.552 2 |
|   community redevelopment | 307.342 |
|   community sociology | 307.333 16 |
| Downy mildew | 579.546 |
| Dowry | 392.5 |
| Dowsing | 133.323 |
| Doxologies | |
|   Christian private prayer | 242.72 |
| Doyayo language | 496.361 |
| | T6—963 61 |
| DPI (Macroeconomics) | 339.32 |
| Dracaenas | 584.352 |
| Draco | 597.955 |
| Draft (Conscription) | 355.223 63 |
|   law | 343.012 2 |
| Draft animals | 636.088 2 |
| Draft horses | 636.15 |

| | |
|---|---|
| Draft registration | 355.223 6 |
| Draft resistance | 355.224 |
|   law | 343.012 2 |
| Drafted labor | 331.117 32 |
| Drafting (Drawing) | 604.2 |
| Drafting legislation | 328.373 |
| Drafts (Credit) | 332.77 |
|   exchange medium | 332.55 |
|   law | 346.096 |
| Draftsmen | 604.209 2 |
| Drag | |
|   aeronautics | 629.132 34 |
| Dragonfishes (Pegasiformes) | 597.64 |
| Dragonfishes (Stomiatoidei) | 597.5 |
| Dragonflies | 595.733 |
| Dragons | 398.245 4 |
|   *see also* Legendary animals | |
| Dragoons | 357.1 |
| Drainage | |
|   agriculture | 631.62 |
|   airport engineering | 629.136 35 |
|   engineering | 627.54 |
|   engineering geology | 624.151 36 |
|   mining | 622.5 |
|   road engineering | 625.734 |
| Drake Passage | 551.461 73 |
| | T2—167 3 |
| Drakensberg Mountains | T2—684 7 |
|   KwaZulu-Natal | T2—684 7 |
|   Mpumalanga | T2—682 7 |
| Drama (Greece : Nome) | T2—495 7 |
| Drama (Literature) | 808.82 |
|   criticism | 809.2 |
|     theory | 808.2 |
|   history | 809.2 |
|   rhetoric | 808.2 |
|   specific literatures | T3B—2 |
|     individual authors | T3A—2 |
|   *see Manual at* T3A—2, | |
|     T3B—2 vs. T3A—1, | |
|     T3B—102; *also at* T3B—2; | |
|     *also at* 808.82 vs. 791.437, | |
|     791.447, 791.457, 792.9 | |
| Drama (Theater) | 792 |
|   *see also* Theater | |
| Drama in Christian education | 268.67 |
| Dramatic monologues (Poetry) | 808.812 |
|   history and criticism | 809.12 |
|   specific literatures | T3B—102 |
|     individual authors | T3A—1 |
|   *see Manual at* T3A—2, | |
|     T3B—2 vs. T3A—1, | |
|     T3B—102 | |
| Dramatic music | 781.552 |
| Dramatic poetry | 808.812 |
|   history and criticism | 809.12 |
|   specific literatures | T3B—102 |
|     individual authors | T3A—1 |
|   *see Manual at* T3A—2, | |
|     T3B—2 vs. T3A—1, | |
|     T3B—102 | |
| Dramatic vocal forms | 782.1 |
|   music | 782.1 |
|   stage presentation | 792.5 |
|   *see Manual at* 782.1 vs. 792.5, | |
|     792.6 | |
| Dramatists | 809.2 |
|   collected biography | 809.2 |
|     specific literatures | T3B—200 9 |
|   individual biography | T3A—2 |
| Draped figures | 704.942 |
|   drawing | 743.4 |
|   painting | 757 |
| Draperies | 645.32 |
|   arts | 746.94 |
|   commercial technology | 684.3 |
|   drawing | 743.5 |
|   home sewing | 646.21 |
|   household management | 645.32 |
|   interior decoration | 747.5 |
| Draughts | 794.2 |
| Dravida languages | 494.81 |
| | T6—948 1 |
| Dravida literatures | 894.81 |
| Dravidian languages | 494.8 |
| | T6—948 |
| Dravidian literatures | 894.8 |
| Dravidians | T5—948 |
| Drawbacks | |
|   international commerce | 382.7 |
| Drawbridges | |
|   construction | 624.24 |
| Drawers (Artists) | 741.092 |
| Drawing (Delineating) | 741 |
|   arts | 741 |
|   primary education | 372.52 |
|   technology | 604.2 |
| Drawing glass | 666.124 |
| Drawing metals | 671.34 |
|   decorative arts | 739.14 |
|   sculpture | 731.41 |
| Drawing paper | 676.282 5 |
| Drawing rooms | 643.54 |
|   home economics | 643.54 |
|   interior decoration | 747.75 |
| Drawings | T1—022 2 |
|   arts | 741 |

Drawn work
  arts — 746.44
Dream books — 135.3
Dream interpretation — 154.63
Dreams — 154.63
  arts — T3C—353
  human physiology — 612.821
  literature — 808.803 53
    history and criticism — 809.933 53
    specific literatures — T3B—080 353
      history and
        criticism — T3B—093 53
  parapsychology — 135.3
  psychology — 154.63
Dred Scott decision, 1857
  Civil War (United States) cause — 973.711 5
Dredgers (Ships)
  design — 623.812 8
  engineering — 623.828
Dredging — 627.73
Dredging services
  ports — 387.168
Dredging spoil — 363.728 4
  engineering — 627.73
  social services — 363.728 4
  *see also* Waste control
Drenthe (Netherlands) — T2—492 15
Dresden (Germany) — T2—432 142
Dresden (Germany :
  Direktionsbezirk) — T2—432 14
Dresden (Germany :
  Regierungsbezirk) — T2—432 14
Dress accessories — 391.44
  *see also* Accessories (Clothing)
Dressage — 798.23
Dressers — 645.4
  manufacturing technology — 684.16
  *see also* Furniture
Dresses — 391.472
  commercial technology — 687.112
  customs — 391.472
  home economics — 646.34
  home sewing — 646.432
  *see also* Clothing
Dressing
  child training — 649.63
Dressing leather — 675.24
Dressmakers — 646.400 92
  commercial — 687.112 092
Dressmaking — 646.4
  commercial technology — 687.112
  home sewing — 646.4
Drew County (Ark.) — T2—767 825

Dried eggs — 641.375 4
  cooking — 641.675 4
  food — 641.375 4
  processing — 637.54
Dried foods
  commercial preservation — 664.028 4
  cooking — 641.614
  home preparation — 641.44
Dried milk — 641.371 43
  cooking — 641.671 43
  food — 641.371 43
  processing — 637.143
Dried plants
  botanical collections — 580.74
  flower arrangements — 745.925
Dried skim milk — 641.371 473
  cooking — 641.671 473
  food — 641.371 473
  processing — 637.147 3
Driers (Paints) — 667.622
Drift mining — 622.2
Driftwood arrangements — 745.925
Drill (Military training) — 355.54
Drilling
  gas wells — 622.338 1
  mining — 622.23
  oil wells — 622.338 1
  underwater engineering — 627.75
Drilling muds — 622.338 1
Drilling platforms — 627.98
  petroleum extraction — 622.338 19
Drilling ships
  design — 623.812 8
  engineering — 623.828
  petroleum extraction — 622.338 19
Drilling tools — 621.952
Drink driving — 364.147
  causes of accidents — 363.125 14
  law — 345.024 7
Drinking
  customs — 394.12
Drinking age — 363.41
  law — 344.054 1
Drinking glasses
  decorative arts — 748.83
Drinking places — 647.95
  architecture — 725.72
  household management — 647.95
  sanitation services — 363.729 6
    public administration — 353.94
Drinking water — 363.61
  economics — 333.912 2
  health — 613.287
  supply services — 363.61

Drinking water (continued)
  treatment engineering — 628.162
    nautical engineering — 623.854 2
  *see also* Water
Drinks — 641.2
  commercial processing — 663
  home preparation — 641.87
Drip-dry fabrics — 677.68
  *see also* Textiles
Drive shafts
  automotive engineering — 629.245
Driver information
  highway services — 388.312 4
    urban — 388.413 124
Drivers' licenses
  law — 343.094 6
  public administration — 354.765 284
Drives (Computer devices) — 004.563
  engineering — 621.397 63
Drives (Psychology) — 153.8
  physiological — 152.5
Driveways — 625.889
Driving belts — 621.852
  rubber technology — 678.36
Driving horses (Breeds) — 636.14
Driving horses (Recreation) — 798.6
Driving motor vehicles
  recreation — 796.7
Driving sports cars
  recreation — 796.72
Drogheda (Ireland) — T2—418 256
Drôme (France) — T2—445 87
Dromedaries — 636.295
  zoology — 599.636 2
Drones (Aircraft)
  control systems — 629.132 6
  military engineering — 623.746 9
Dronning Maud Land — T2—989
Dronten (Netherlands) — T2—492 2
Dropouts (Education) — 371.291 3
Drops — 530.427
  technology — 620.43
Droseraceae — 583.75
Drosophilidae — 595.774
Drought-resistant plants — 581.754
  floriculture — 635.952 5
Droughts
  agricultural economics — 338.14
  crop damage — 632.12
  effect on natural ecology — 577.22
  meteorology — 551.577 3
  social services — 363.349 29
    agricultural industries — 338.18

Drowning
  medicine — 617.18
Drug abuse — 362.29
  *see also* Substance abuse
Drug administration routes — 615.6
Drug adulteration — 363.194
  criminology — 364.142
  criminal law — 345.024 2
  *see also* Drugs
    (Pharmaceuticals) —
    product safety
Drug allergies
  incidence — 614.599 358
  medicine — 616.975 8
Drug compounding — 615.19
Drug culture — 306.1
Drug dependence — 362.29
  medicine — 616.86
  perinatal medicine — 618.326 86
  personal health — 613.8
  pregnancy complications
    obstetrics — 618.368 6
  social welfare — 362.29
  *see also* Substance abuse
Drug design — 615.19
Drug development — 615.19
Drug-herb interactions — 615.704 5
Drug incompatibilities
  pharmacokinetics — 615.704 5
  pharmacology — 615.14
Drug interactions
  pharmacokinetics — 615.704 5
Drug metabolism
  pharmacokinetics — 615.7
Drug-nutrient interactions — 615.704 52
Drug possession — 364.177
  law — 345.027 7
  *see also* Drug traffic
Drug resistance
  microorganisms — 616.904 1
Drug shock therapy
  psychiatry — 616.891 2
Drug side effects
  pharmacokinetics — 615.704 2
Drug smuggling — 364.133 65
  law — 345.023 365
Drug testing
  personnel management — 658.382 2
  personnel selection — 658.311 2
Drug therapy
  medicine — 615.58
  psychiatry — 616.891 8
Drug toxicity
  pharmacokinetics — 615.704

Drug traffic 363.45
  criminology 364.177
    law 345.027 7
  public administration 353.37
  school problem 371.784
  social problem 363.45
    law 344.054 5
Drug use 362.29
  *see also* Drug traffic; Substance
    abuse
Drugged driving 364.147
  causes of accidents 363.125 14
  law 345.024 7
Drugs (Narcotics)
  customs 394.14
  ethics 178.8
    *see also* Ethical problems
  pharmacokinetics 615.782 2
  smuggling 364.133 65
    law 345.023 365
Drugs (Pharmaceuticals) 615.1
  chemical analysis 615.190 1
  insurance 368.382 4
  manufacturing technology 615.19
  pharmacology 615.1
  preservation 615.18
  product safety 363.194
    criminology 364.142
      criminal law 345.024 2
    law 344.042 33
    public administration 353.998
  production economics 338.476 151
  *see Manual at* 615.1 vs.
    615.2–.3; *also at* 615.2–.3
    vs. 615.7
Druidism 299.16
Drum and bass 781.648
Drumheller (Alta.) T2—712 33
Drumlins 551.315
Drummers (Musicians) 786.909 2
Drumming (Signaling)
  social psychology 302.222
Drummond (Quebec :
  Regional County
  Municipality) T2—714 563
Drums (Computer devices) 004.563
  engineering 621.397 63
Drums (Fishes) 597.725
Drums (Music) 786.9
  instrument 786.919
  music 786.9
  *see also* Percussion instruments

Drunk driving 364.147
  causes of accidents 363.125 14
  law 345.024 7
Drunkenness 362.292
  criminology 364.173
    law 345.027 3
  *see also* Alcoholism
Drupaceous fruits 641.342
  botany 583.73
  cooking 641.642
  food 641.342
  orchard crops 634.2
Druzes (Islamic sect) 297.85
Dry cells (Batteries) 621.312 423
Dry cleaning 667.12
Dry-climate plants 581.754
  floriculture 635.952 5
Dry docks 623.83
Dry farming 631.586
Dry-weather photography 778.75
Dryers
  home laundry 648.1
    manufacturing technology 683.88
Drying clothes
  home economics 648.1
Drying coal 662.623
Drying foods 664.028 4
  commercial preservation 664.028 4
  home preservation 641.44
Drying lumber 674.38
Drying processes 660.284 26
Dryopoidea 595.764 5
Drypoint 767.3
Drywall 666.89
Drywall construction 693.6
DSL (Digital subscriber lines) 621.387 8
DTP (Publishing)
  composition 686.225 444 16
  computer software 005.52
Du Page County (Ill.) T2—773 24
Ḍuʿafāʾ (Hadith) 297.125 263
Dual-career families 306.872
Dual geometries 516.35
Dual nationality
  law 342.083
Dual personalities
  medicine 616.852 36
  *see also* Mental disorders
Duala (African people) T5—963 962
Duala language 496.396 2
   T6—963 962
Duala literature 896.396 2

| | |
|---|---|
| Dualism | |
| philosophy | 147.4 |
| Hindu | 181.484 |
| religion | 211.33 |
| classes of religions | 201.4 |
| Duality (Mathematics) | 515.782 |
| Duarte (Dominican Republic) | T2—729 367 |
| Duarte Frutos, Nicanor | |
| Paraguayan history | 989.207 45 |
| Dubai (United Arab Emirates : Emirate) | T2—535 7 |
| Dubawnt Lake (Nunavut and N.W.T.) | T2—719 58 |
| Dubayy (United Arab Emirates : Emirate) | T2—535 7 |
| Dubbo (N.S.W.) | T2—944 5 |
| Dublin (Ireland) | T2—418 35 |
| Dublin (Ireland : County) | T2—418 3 |
| Dublin Core | 025.3 |
| Dubnium | |
| chemistry | 546.52 |
| Dubois County (Ind.) | T2—772 37 |
| Dubuque County (Iowa) | T2—777 39 |
| Ducal Medici | 945.507 |
| Duchesne County (Utah) | T2—792 22 |
| Duck (Meat) | 641.365 97 |
| commercial processing | 664.93 |
| cooking | 641.665 97 |
| food | 641.365 97 |
| Duck-billed dinosaurs | 567.914 |
| Duck hunting | |
| sports | 799.244 |
| Duck River (Tenn.) | T2—768 434 |
| Ducks | 598.41 |
| animal husbandry | 636.597 |
| conservation technology | 639.978 41 |
| resource economics | 333.958 41 |
| sports hunting | 799.244 |
| Duckweeds | 584.64 |
| Duct flutes | 788.35 |
| *see also* Woodwind instruments | |
| Ductility | |
| materials science | 620.112 5 |
| Dude farming | 796.56 |
| Dude ranching | 796.56 |
| Dudley (England : Metropolitan Borough) | T2—424 93 |
| Due process of law | 347.05 |
| Dueling | 394.8 |
| customs | 394.8 |
| ethics | 179.7 |

| | |
|---|---|
| Duets | |
| chamber music | 785.12 |
| vocal music | 783.12 |
| Dufferin (Ont. : County) | T2—713 41 |
| Dufferin and Ava, Frederick Temple Blackwood, Marquis of | |
| Indian history | 954.035 4 |
| Dugong | 599.559 |
| Dugongidae | 599.559 |
| Duhalde, Eduardo Alberto | |
| Argentine history | 982.071 |
| Duikers | 599.64 |
| Duisburg (Germany) | T2—435 536 |
| Dukes County (Mass.) | T2—744 94 |
| Dukhobors | 289.9 |
| *see also* Christian denominations | |
| Dulcimers | 787.74 |
| *see also* Stringed instruments | |
| Duluth (Minn.) | T2—776 771 |
| Dumbarton (Scotland) | T2—414 32 |
| Dumbarton (Scotland : District) | T2—414 32 |
| Dumfries and Galloway (Scotland) | T2—414 7 |
| Dumping (Trade) | |
| law | 343.087 |
| Dumps (Solid waste) | 363.728 5 |
| technology | 628.445 62 |
| *see also* Waste control | |
| Dumyāṭ (Egypt : Province) | T2—621 |
| Dún Laoghaire (Ireland) | T2—418 38 |
| Dunaliellaceae | 579.832 |
| Dundee (Scotland) | T2—412 7 |
| Dundee (South Africa : District) | T2—684 1 |
| Dundy County (Neb.) | T2—782 86 |
| Dune buggies | |
| engineering | 629.222 |
| Dune stabilization | 631.64 |
| shore protection | 627.58 |
| Dunedin (N.Z.) | T2—939 2 |
| Dunedin City (N.Z.) | T2—939 2 |
| Dunes | 551.375 |
| *see also* Sand dunes | |
| Dunfermline (Scotland : District) | T2—412 9 |
| Dung beetles | 595.764 9 |
| Dung flies | 595.774 |
| Dungannon (Northern Ireland : District) | T2—416 45 |
| Dunkerque, Battle of, 1940 | 940.542 142 8 |

Dunkers    286.5
   *see also* Baptists
Dunkirk, Battle of, 1940    940.542 142 8
Dunklin County (Mo.)    T2—778 993
Dunn County (N.D.)    T2—784 82
Dunn County (Wis.)    T2—775 43
Dunoon (Scotland)    T2—414 2
Duodecimal system    513.5
Duodenal diseases
   medicine    616.34
   *see also* Digestive system
     diseases — humans
Duodenal ulcers
   medicine    616.343 3
   *see also* Digestive system
     diseases — humans
Duodenitis
   medicine    616.344
   *see also* Digestive system
     diseases — humans
Duodenum    573.378
   biology    573.378
   human anatomy    611.341
   human physiology    612.33
   medicine    616.34
   surgery    617.554 1
   *see also* Digestive system
DuPage County (Ill.)    T2—773 24
Duplex houses
   architecture    728.312
Duplex-process steel    669.142 3
Duplicating machines
   library services    025.12
   manufacturing technology    681.6
   office use    652.4
Duplin County (N.C.)    T2—756 382
Dupuit, Jules-Juvénal
   economic school    330.154 3
Durability engineering    620.004 54
Durable press fabrics    677.68
Durango (Mexico : State)    T2—721 5
Durazno (Uruguay : Dept.)    T2—895 24
Durban (South Africa :
   District)    T2—684 55
Durban-Pinetown industrial
   area    T2—684 55
Duress    345.04
Durham (England : City)    T2—428 65
Durham (England : County)    T2—428 6
Durham (Ont. : Regional
   municipality)    T2—713 56
Durham County (N.C.)    T2—756 563
Durham mission (Canadian
   history)    971.039

Duroc-Jersey swine    636.483
Düsseldorf (Germany)    T2—435 534
Düsseldorf (Germany :
   Regierungsbezirk)    T2—435 53
Dust
   meteorology    551.511 3
   technology    620.43
Dust control
   buildings    697.932 4
   mining    622.83
Dust diseases
   lungs
     medicine    616.244
     *see also* Respiratory tract
      diseases — humans
Dust storms    551.559
   social services    363.349 29
   *see also* Disasters
Dusting
   housecleaning    648.5
Dusting in agriculture    632.94
Dusting-on processes
   photographic printing    773.2
Dutch    T5—393 1
Dutch East India Company
   Indonesian history    959.802 1
Dutch East Indies    959.802 2
   T2—598
Dutch elm disease    635.977 345
Dutch language    439.31
   T6—393 1
Dutch literature    839.31
Dutch ovens
   use in cooking    641.589
Dutch Reformed Church in North
   America    285.732
   *see also* Reformed Church
     (American Reformed)
Dutch Republic    949.204
   T2—492
Dutch West Indies    T2—729 86
Dutchess County (N.Y.)    T2—747 33
Dutchman's breeches (Plant)    583.35
Duties (Tariff)    382.7
   *see also* Customs (Tariff)
Duties of citizens    323.65
Dutra, Eurico Gaspar
   Brazilian history    981.061
Duty
   religion    205
     Islam    297.5
Duty-free importation    382.78
Duval County (Fla.)    T2—759 12
Duval County (Tex.)    T2—764 463

Duvalier, François
  Haitian history      972.940 72
Duvalier, Jean-Claude
  Haitian history      972.940 72
Düzce İli (Turkey)      T2—563 4
  ancient      T2—393 15
Dvaita (Philosophy)      181.484 1
Dvaitādvaita (Philosophy)      181.484 3
DVDs      384.558
  computer storage      004.565
  engineering      621.397 67
  *see also* Video recordings
Dwarf pea      641.356 57
  *see also* Chick-peas
Dwarf potted trees      635.977 2
Dwarf sperm whales      599.547
Dwarfism (Pituitary)
  medicine      616.47
    *see also* Endocrine
      diseases — humans
Dwarfs
  physical anthropology      599.949
Dwellings      643.1
  architecture      728
  arts      700.456 4
          T3C—356 4
  construction      690.8
  customs      392.36
  folklore      398.276 4
    history and criticism      398.356 4
  health      613.5
  home economics      643.1
  interior decoration      747
  lighting      621.322 8
  literature      808.803 564
    history and criticism      809.933 564
    specific literatures    T3B—080 356 4
      history and
        criticism    T3B—093 564
  theft from      364.162 2
    law      345.026 22
  *see also* Housing
  *see Manual at* 363.5 vs. 643.1
Dwyfor (Wales)      T2—429 25
Dye lasers      621.366 4
Dye-producing plants
  agriculture      633.86
  economic botany      581.636
Dyeing      667.3
  home economics      648.1
  textile arts      746.6
Dyeing leather      675.25
Dyeing yarns
  arts      746.13

Dyer County (Tenn.)      T2—768 15
Dyerma language      496.5
          T6—965
Dyes      667.2
  chemistry      547.86
  technology      667.2
Dyfed (Wales)      T2—429 6
Dying      306.9
  music      781.588
  psychology      155.937
  social aspects      306.9
Dying patients      362.175
  pastoral theology      206.1
    Christianity      259.417 5
  social theology      201.762 175
    Christianity      261.832 175
  *see also* Terminal care
  *see Manual at* 362.1–.4 vs. 610
Dynamic logic      511.314
Dynamic oceanography      551.462
Dynamic programming      519.703
Dynamic psychology      150.193
Dynamic systems      003.85
Dynamical systems
  (Mathematics)      515.39
Dynamics      531.11
  air      533.62
    engineering      620.107 4
  atmosphere      551.515
  engineering      620.104
  fluids      532.05
    engineering      620.106 4
  gases      533.2
    engineering      620.107 4
  liquids      532.5
    engineering      620.106 4
  particles      531.163
    engineering      620.43
  physics      531.11
  solids      531.3
    engineering      620.105 4
Dynamism      146
Dynamite      662.27
  military engineering      623.452 7
Dynamos      621.313 2
Dysarthria
  medicine      616.855 2
    *see also* Communication
      disorders
Dysentery
  incidence      614.516
  medicine      616.935
    *see also* Communicable
      diseases — humans

Dysfunctional families
  pastoral theology      206.1
    Christianity      259.1
  social relationships      306.87
  social theology      201.7
    Christianity      261.835 85
Dyslexia
  medicine      616.855 3
  *see also* Communication
    disorders
  pediatrics      618.928 553
  special education      371.914 4
Dysmenorrhea
  gynecology      618.172
  *see also* Female genital
    diseases — humans
Dyspepsia
  medicine      616.332
  *see also* Digestive system
    diseases — humans
Dysphagia
  medicine      616.323
  *sec also* Digestive system
    diseases — humans
Dysphasia
  medicine      616.855 2
  *see also* Communication
    disorders
Dyspnea
  medicine      616.2
  *see also* Respiratory tract
    diseases — humans
Dysprosium
  chemistry      546.417
Dystocia
  obstetrics      618.5
Dystopias
  arts      T3C—372
  literature      808.803 72
    history and criticism      809.933 72
    specific literatures      T3B—080 372
      history and
        criticism      T3B—093 72
Dytikē Hellada (Greece)      T2—495 27
Dytikē Makedonia (Greece)      T2—495 62
Dytiscidae      595.762
Dyula (African people)      T5—963 45
Dyula language      496.345
     T6—963 45
Dzanani (South Africa :
  District)      T2—682 57
Dzongkha language      495.4
     T6—954

# E

E = mc²      530.11
E coli infections
  incidence      614.57
  medicine      616.926
  *see also* Communicable
    diseases — humans
E document (Biblical criticism)      222.106 6
E-flat horns      788.974
  *see also* Brass instruments
E-mail      004.692
  *see also* Electronic mail
E-mail lists      004.693
E region (Ionosphere)      538.767 3
Eagle County (Colo.)      T2—788 44
Eagles      598.942
  conservation technology      639.978 942
  resource economics      333.958 942
Ealing (London, England)      T2—421 84
Ear canal diseases
  medicine      617.83
  *see also* Ear diseases —
    humans
Ear diseases      573.893 9
  animals      573.893 9
  humans      362.197 8
    anesthesiology      617.967 8
    cancer
      incidence      614.599 948 5
      medicine      616.994 85
      *see also* Cancer —
        humans
    geriatrics      618.977 8
    incidence      614.599 8
    medicine      617.8
    pediatrics      618.920 978
    social services      362.197 8
    surgery      617.805 9
Ear ossicle diseases
  medicine      617.842
  *see also* Ear diseases —
    humans
Ear training (Music)      781.424
Eared seals      599.797
Earless monitor lizard      597.959 6
Earless seals      599.79
Early childhood education      372.21
Early Christian architecture      723.1
Early Christian art      709.021 2
  religious significance      246.2
Early Christian decoration      745.409 021
Early Christian painting      759.021 2
Early Christian philosophy      189

Early Christian sculpture 734.222
Early Church 270.1
   *see Manual at* 270, 230.11–.14
     vs. 230.15–.2, 281.5–.9,
     282
Early County (Ga.) T2—758 962
Early Middle Ages 940.12
  Italian history 945.02
  Lombardian history 945.202
  Piedmontese history 945.102
  Sardinian history 945.902
  Sicilian history 945.802
  Southern Italian history 945.702
  Tuscan history 945.502
  Venetian history 945.302
Early New High German
  language 437.02
Early school leavers 371.291 3
  secondary level 373.129 13
Earrings 391.7
  customs 391.7
  making 739.278
    costume jewelry 688.2
      handicrafts 745.594 2
    fine jewelry 739.278
Ears 573.89
  animal physiology 573.89
  descriptive zoology 591.44
    mammals 599.144
  diseases 573.893 9
    *see also* Ear diseases
  human anatomy 611.85
  human physiology 612.85
  medicine 617.8
  surgery 617.805 9
Earth 550
  astronomy 525
  extraterrestrial influences 001.94
  geologic history 551.7
  gravity 531.14
  internal structure 551.1
Earth currents (Geomagnetism) 538.748
Earth-fill dams 627.83
Earth roads 388.12
  engineering 625.74
Earth sciences 550
  information systems 025.065 5
  *see Manual at* 550 vs. 910
Earth-sheltered buildings 720.473
Earth-sheltered houses
  architecture 728.370 473
  construction 690.837 047 3
Earth temperature
  meteorological effect 551.523

Earthenware 666.6
  arts 738.3
  technology 666.6
Earthmoving machinery 621.865
Earthquake engineering 624.176 2
Earthquake insurance 368.122 6
Earthquake-resistant construction 624.176 2
  buildings 693.852
Earthquakes 551.22
  disaster services 363.349 5
  social effects 303.485
  *see also* Disasters
Earth's age 551.701
Earthwork 624.152
  dam engineering 627.81
  mining 622.2
  railroad engineering 625.12
  road engineering 625.73
Earthworks (Art style) 709.040 76
Earthworm culture 639.75
Earthworms 592.64
  culture 639.75
Earthy materials 553.6
  economic geology 553.6
  mining 622.36
Earthy minerals 553.6
  economic geology 553.6
  mining 622.36
  synthetic 666.86
Earwigs 595.739
Easements 346.043 5
  economics 333.323 4
  law of nations 341.4
Easington (England :
  District) T2—428 67
East 950
   T2—5
East Africa 967.6
   T2—676
East Anglia (England) T2—426
East Asia T2—5
East Asian languages 495
   T6—95
East Asian literatures 895
East Asian theater (World War II) 940.542 5
East Asians T5—95
East Avon River (England) T2—423 19
East Ayrshire (Scotland) T2—414 67
East Azerbaijan (Iran) T2—553
East Baton Rouge Parish
  (La.) T2—763 18
East Bengal (Pakistan) T2—549 2
East Berbice-Corentyne
  (Guyana) T2—881 7

East Berlin (Germany) T2—431 552
East Bird's Head languages T6—991 2
East Cambridgeshire
  (England) T2—426 56
East Carroll Parish (La.) T2—763 82
East China Sea 551.461 457
  T2—164 57
East Devon (England) T2—423 57
East Dorset (England) T2—423 34
East Dunbartonshire
  (Scotland) T2—414 36
East Equatoria (Sudan) T2—629 5
East Feliciana Parish (La.) T2—763 16
East Flanders (Belgium) T2—493 14
East Friesland (Germany) T2—435 917
East Frisian Islands
  (Germany) T2—435 917
East Germanic languages 439.9
  T6—399
East Germanic literatures 839.9
East Germany (Democratic 943.108 7
  Republic) T2—431
East Hampshire (England) T2—422 74
East Hertfordshire
  (England) T2—425 83
East India Company
  Indian history 954.031
East Indians T5—914
East Iranian languages (Ancient) 491.52
  T6—915 2
East Iranian literatures (Ancient) 891.52
East Java (Indonesia) T2—598 28
East Kalimantan (Indonesia) T2—598 38
East Kilbride (Scotland :
  District) T2—414 57
East Kootenay (B.C.) T2—711 65
East Lansing (Mich.) T2—774 27
East Lindsey (England) T2—425 32
East London (South Africa :
  District) T2—687 555
East Lothian (Scotland) T2—413 6
East Midlands (England) T2—425
East New Britain Province
  (Papua New Guinea) T2—958 5
East Northamptonshire
  (England) T2—425 54
East Nusa Tenggara
  (Indonesia) T2—598 68
East Orange (N.J.) T2—749 33
East Pakistan (Pakistan) T2—549 2
East Prussia (Poland and
  Russia) T2—438 32
  Poland T2—438 32
  Russia T2—472 4

East Punjab (India) T2—545 5
East Rand (South Africa) T2—682 24
East Redonda Island (B.C.) T2—711 1
East Renfrewshire
  (Scotland) T2—414 39
East Riding of Yorkshire
  (England) T2—428 39
East Scandinavian languages 439.5
  T6—395
East Scandinavian literatures 839.5
East Semites T5—921
East Semitic languages 492.1
  T6—921
East Semitic literatures 892.1
East Sepik Province (Papua
  New Guinea) T2—957 5
East Siberian Sea (Russia) 551.461 325
  T2—163 25
East Slavic languages 491.7
  T6—917
East Slavic literatures 891.7
East Slavs T5—917
East Staffordshire (England) T2—424 65
East Sussex (England) T2—422 5
East Texas T2—764 14
East Thurlow Island (B.C.) T2—711 1
East Timor 959.87
  T2—598 7
East York (Toronto, Ont.) T2—713 541
East Yorkshire (England) T2—428 39
Eastbourne (East Sussex,
  England) T2—422 58
Easter 263.93
  arts T3C—334
  customs 394.266 7
  devotional literature 242.36
  handicrafts 745.594 166 7
  sermons 252.63
Easter eggs 394.266 7
  customs 394.266 7
  handicrafts 745.594 4
Easter Island T2—961 8
Easter lily 635.934 32
  botany 584.32
  floriculture 635.934 32
Easter music 781.727
Easter Rebellion, 1916 941.508 21
Easter story 232.97
Eastern Algonquian languages 497.34
  T6—973 4
Eastern Alps (Austria) T2—436 4
Eastern Aramaic languages 492.3
  T6—923
Eastern Aramaic literatures 892.3

| | |
|---|---|
| Eastern Arctic Inuit language | 497.124 |
| | T6—971 24 |
| Eastern Canada | T2—713 |
| Eastern Canadian Inuit | T5—971 24 |
| Eastern Canadian Inuit language | 497.124 |
| | T6—971 24 |
| Eastern Canadian Inuktitut | T5—971 24 |
| Eastern Canadian Inuktitut | 497.124 |
| language | T6—971 24 |
| Eastern Canadian Inuktitut | |
| literature | 897.124 |
| Eastern Cape (South Africa) | 968.75 |
| | T2—687 5 |
| Eastern Catholic churches | 281.52 |
| *see also* Eastern churches | |
| Eastern churches | 281.5 |
| church government | 262.015 |
| parishes | 254.015 |
| church law | 262.981 5 |
| doctrines | 230.15 |
| general councils | 262.515 |
| guides to Christian life | 248.481 5 |
| liturgy | 264.015 |
| missions | 266.15 |
| monasticism | 255.81 |
| church history | 271.81 |
| women | 255.981 |
| church history | 271.981 |
| moral theology | 241.041 5 |
| public worship | 264.015 |
| religious associations | 267.181 5 |
| religious education | 268.815 |
| seminaries | 230.073 15 |
| theology | 230.15 |
| *see Manual at* 270, 230.11–.14 | |
| vs. 230.15–.2, 281.5–.9, 282 | |
| Eastern Desert (Egypt) | T2—623 |
| Eastern Empire | 949.501 3 |
| Eastern England | T2—426 |
| Eastern Europe | 947 |
| | T2—47 |
| Eastern Fijian languages | 499.59 |
| | T6—995 9 |
| Eastern Finland (Finland) | T2—489 75 |
| Eastern flying squirrel | 599.369 |
| Eastern France | T2—444 |
| Eastern front | |
| World War I | 940.414 7 |
| Eastern Hemisphere | T2—181 1 |
| Eastern Highlands Province | |
| (Papua New Guinea) | T2—956 9 |
| Eastern Himalayan languages | 495.49 |
| | '16—954 9 |
| Eastern Himalayan literatures | 895.49 |

| | |
|---|---|
| Eastern Himalayan peoples | T5—954 9 |
| Eastern Hindi languages | 491.492 |
| | T6—914 92 |
| Eastern Hindi literatures | 891.492 |
| Eastern languages (Adamawa- | 496.361 |
| Eastern phylum) | T6—963 61 |
| Eastern Macedonia and | |
| Thrace (Greece) | T2—495 7 |
| Eastern Malayo-Polynesian | |
| languages | 499.5 |
| | T6—995 |
| Eastern Malaysia | T2—595 3 |
| Eastern Mediterranean | |
| region | T2—182 24 |
| ancient | 938 |
| | T2—38 |
| Eastern Mediterranean Sea | 551.461 384 |
| | T2—163 84 |
| Eastern Ontario | T2—713 7 |
| Eastern Oregon | T2—795 5 |
| Eastern Orthodox Church | 281.9 |
| *see Manual at* 270, 230.11–.14 | |
| vs. 230.15–.2, 281.5–.9, | |
| 282 | |
| Eastern Orthodox sacred music | 781.711 9 |
| public worship | 782.322 19 |
| music | 782.322 19 |
| Eastern Panhandle (W. Va.) | T2—754 9 |
| Eastern Panjabi language | 491.42 |
| | T6—914 2 |
| Eastern philosophy | 181 |
| Eastern Province (Kenya) | T2—676 24 |
| Eastern Province (Zambia) | T2—689 4 |
| Eastern Region (China) | T2—512 |
| Eastern Region (Ecuador) | T2—866 4 |
| Eastern rite Catholics | 281.52 |
| *see also* Eastern churches | |
| Eastern rite churches | 281.5 |
| *see also* Eastern churches | |
| Eastern Roman Empire | 949.501 3 |
| Eastern Samar (Philippines) | T2—599 5 |
| Eastern Shore (Md. and Va.) | T2—752 1 |
| Eastern Siberia (Russia) | T2—575 |
| Eastern Townships | |
| (Quebec) | T2—714 6 |
| Eastern Turkic languages | 494.32 |
| | T6—943 2 |
| Eastern Washington | T2—797 1 |
| Eastertide | 263.93 |
| devotional literature | 242.36 |
| music | 781.727 |
| sermons | 252.63 |
| Eastland County (Tex.) | T2—764 547 |

Eastleigh (England :
  Borough)         T2—422 772
Eastwood (Scotland :
  District)         T2—414 39
Easy dishes (Cooking)    641.512
Eating
  animal physiology    573.35
  child training    649.63
  customs    394.12
  descriptive zoology    591.53
  human physiology    612.31
  sociology    306.461 3
Eating disorders
  medicine    616.852 6
  *see also* Mental disorders
Eating places    647.95
  accounting    657.837 5
  area planning    711.557
  household management    647.95
  meal service    642.5
  sanitation services    363.729 6
    public administration    353.94
Eaton County (Mich.)    T2—774 23
Eau Claire County (Wis.)    T2—775 45
Ebbw Vale (Wales)    T2—429 95
Ebenales    583.674
Ebla (Extinct city)    T2—394 33
Eblaite language    492.6
                T6—926
Eblaite literature    892.6
Ebonies
  botany    583.674
  forestry    634.973 674
Ebonyi State (Nigeria)    T2—669 47
Ebro River (Spain)    T2—465
EC (European Community)    341.242 2
  *see also* European Union
Ecbatana (Extinct city)    T2—357 52
Eccentrics (Mechanisms)    621.827
Ecclesiastes    223.8
Ecclesiastical law    262.9
Ecclesiasticus (Bible)    229.4
Ecclesiology
  Christianity    262
ECG (Medicine)    616.120 754 7
Echeverría, Luis
  Mexican history    972.083 2
Echidnas    599.29
Echinococcosis
  incidence    614.554
  medicine    616.964
  *see also* Communicable
    diseases — humans
Echinodera    592.55

Echinodermata    593.9
  paleozoology    563.9
Echinoidea    593.95
  paleozoology    563.95
Echinozoa    593.95
  paleozoology    563.95
Echiurida    592.3
  paleozoology    562.3
Echo-ranging devices
  geophysical prospecting    622.159 2
  marine navigation    623.893 8
Echocardiography
  medicine    616.120 754 3
Echoes
  physics    534.204
Echography
  medicine    616.075 43
Echoi    781.264
Echols County (Ga.)    T2—758 814
Echuca (Vic.)    T2—945 4
Eckankar    299.93
Eclairs    641.865 9
  commercial processing    664.752 5
  home preparation    641.865 9
Eclampsia
  obstetrics    618.361 32
Eclectic medicine
  therapeutic system    615.53
Eclecticism
  architecture    724.5
  philosophy    148
    ancient    186.3
Eclipses    523.99
  moon    523.38
  sun    523.78
Eclipsing binaries    523.844 4
Ecofeminism    304.208 2
Ecological anthropology    304.2
Ecological bioenergetics    577.13
Ecological chemistry    577.14
Ecological communities    577.82
Ecological genetics    576.58
Ecological heterogeneity    577
Ecological niches    577.82
Ecological pyramids    577.16
Ecological succession    577.18
Ecological toxicology    571.95
Ecologism    320.58
Ecology    577
  animals    591.7
  ethics    179.1
  religion    205.691
    Buddhism    294.356 91
    Christianity    241.691

Ecology
  ethics
    religion (continued)
      Hinduism ... 294.548 691
      Judaism ... 296.369 1
    microorganisms ... 579.17
    physical anthropology ... 599.95
    plants ... 581.7
    primary education ... 372.357
    social theology ... 201.77
      Christianity ... 261.88
      Judaism ... 296.38
    sociology ... 304.2
    specific environments ... 577
      *see Manual at 577.3–.7 vs.*
        *578.73–.77*
    *see Manual at 333.7–.9 vs.*
      *363.1, 363.73, 577; also at*
      *577.3–.7 vs. 579–590*
Econometrics ... 330.015 195
  management decision making ... 658.403 3
Economic aid
  international economics ... 338.91
Economic anthropology ... 306.3
Economic assistance
  international economics ... 338.91
  international politics ... 327.111
  law ... 343.074
  public administration ... 352.73
    foreign aid ... 353.132 73
Economic biology ... 578.6
Economic botany ... 581.6
Economic causes of war ... 355.027 3
  American Revolution ... 973.311
  World War I ... 940.311 3
  World War II ... 940.531 13
Economic classes ... 305.5
  T1—086 2
  civil rights ... 323.322
  customs ... 390.1
    dress ... 391.01
  relations with government ... 323.322
Economic concentration ... 338.8
Economic conditions ... 330.9
Economic cooperation
  international economics ... 337.1
  *see Manual at 337.3–.9 vs.*
    *337.1*
Economic development ... 338.9
  banking ... 332.153
    domestic ... 332.28
    international ... 332.153
  law ... 343.074

Economic development (continued)
  natural resources ... 333.715
    *see Manual at 333.7–.9 vs.*
      *363.1, 363.73, 577*
  production economics ... 338.9
  public administration ... 354.27
    *see Manual at 300, 320.6 vs.*
      *352–354*
  sociology ... 306.3
Economic ethics ... 174.4
Economic fluctuations ... 338.54
Economic forecasting ... 330.011 2
Economic geography ... 330.9
Economic geology ... 553
Economic growth ... 338.9
  macroeconomic policy ... 339.5
  production economics ... 338.9
Economic history ... 330.9
Economic integration
  international economics ... 337.1
Economic microbiology ... 579.16
Economic planning ... 338.9
Economic policy ... 338.9
Economic power (Legislative
    bodies) ... 328.341 3
Economic rent ... 333.012
Economic resources
  conservation ... 339.49
Economic rights ... 330
Economic services for workers ... 331.255
  personnel management ... 658.383
Economic situation ... 330.9
Economic sociology ... 306.3
Economic stabilization ... 339.5
  law ... 343.034
  macroeconomic policy ... 339.5
Economic systems ... 330.12
Economic zoology ... 591.6
Economics ... 330
  arts ... 700.455 3
    T3C—355 3
  information systems ... 025.063 3
  international politics ... 327.111
  literature ... 808.803 553
    history and criticism ... 809.933 553
    specific literatures ... T3B—080 355 3
      history and
        criticism ... T3B—093 553
  public administration ... 354
  social theology ... 201.73
    Christianity ... 261.85
    Islam ... 297.273
      *see Manual at 297.26–.27*

Economics
  social theology (continued)
    Judaism — 296.383
  *see Manual at* 330 vs. 650, 658
Economics libraries — 026.33
Economics of the firm — 338.5
Economies of scale — 338.514 4
Economists — 330.092
Ecosystems — 577
  *see Manual at* 333.7–.9 vs.
    363.1, 363.73, 577
Ecotones — 577
Ecotoxicology — 571.95
  ecology — 577.27
  pathology — 571.95
  *see Manual at* 363.73 vs.
    571.95, 577.27
Ecrehous (Channel Islands) — T2—423 49
Ecrins National Park
  (France) — T2—449 7
Ecstasy
  psychology — 152.42
Ectoparasitic infestations
  incidence — 614.558
  medicine — 616.968
Ectopic pregnancy
  obstetrics — 618.31
Ectoplasm — 133.92
Ectoprocta — 594.67
Ector County (Tex.) — T2—764 862
Ecuador — 986.6
  — T2—866
Ecuadorian literature — 860
Ecuadorians — T5—688 66
Ecumenical councils — 262.5
  Christian church history — 270.2
    modern period — 270.82
Ecumenical movement — 280.042
  *see Manual at* 280.042 vs.
    262.0011
Ecumenical Patriarchate of
  Constantinople — 281.949 61
Ecumenism — 262.001 1
  *see Manual at* 280.042 vs.
    262.0011
Eczema
  medicine — 616.51
  *see also* Skin diseases —
    humans
Eddies
  oceanography — 551.462
Eddy, Mary Baker
  Christian Science writings — 289.52
Eddy County (N.D.) — T2—784 512

Eddy County (N.M.) — T2—789 42
Eddy currents — 621.310 42
Eden (England) — T2—427 86
Eden (N.S.W.) — T2—944 7
Eden, River (Cumbria,
  England) — T2—427 86
Edenburg (South Africa :
  District) — T2—685 7
Edentata — 599.31
  paleozoology — 569.31
Edgar, King of England
  English history — 942.017 3
Edgar County (Ill.) — T2—773 69
Edgecombe County (N.C.) — T2—756 46
Edged weapons — 623.441
  art metalwork — 739.72
Edgefield County (S.C.) — T2—757 37
Edgings (Floriculture) — 635.963
Edible animals — 641.306
  agriculture — 636.088 3
  economic zoology — 591.63
  food source — 641.306
Edible bulbs — 641.352
  cooking — 641.652
  food — 641.352
  garden crops — 635.2
Edible mushrooms — 641.358
  biology — 579.616 32
  *see also* Mushrooms
Edible organisms — 641.3
  economic biology — 578.63
Edible plants — 641.303
  economic botany — 581.632
  food — 641.303
  *see Manual at* 583–585 vs. 600
Edible roots — 641.351
  cooking — 641.651
  food — 641.351
  garden crop — 635.1
Edinburgh (Scotland) — T2—413 4
Edirne (Turkey) — T2—496 14
Edirne İli (Turkey) — T2—496 14
Edisto River (S.C.) — T2—757 9
Editing — 808.027
  cinematography — 777.55
  journalism — 070.41
  videography — 777.55
Editing music — 780.149
Edition bookbinding — 686.303 4
Editorial cartoons — 070.442
Editorial policy — 070.41
Editorial techniques — 808.027
Editorials — 070.442

Editors
  publishing    070.510 92
Edmonson County (Ky.)    T2—769 752
Edmonton (Alta.)    T2—712 334
Edmund I, King of England
  English history    942.017 2
Edmund II, King of England
  English history    942.017 4
Edmunds County (S.D.)    T2—783 15
Edo (African people)    T5—963 3
Edo language    496.33
   T6—963 3
Edo period (Japan)    952.025
Edo State (Nigeria)    T2—669 32
Edoid languages    496.33
   T6—963 3
Edom    939.464
   T2—394 64
EDP (Computing)    004
Edred, King of England
  English history    942.017 2
EDU (Swiss political party)    324.249 408 2
Education    370
   T1—071
  arts    700.455 7
   T3C—355 7
  federal aid    379.121
  federal control    379.151
  intergovernmental
    organizations
    aid    379.128
    control    379.154
  international aid    379.129
  law    344.07
  library role    021.24
  literature    808.803 557
    history and criticism    809.933 557
    specific literatures    T3B—080 355 7
    history and
      criticism    T3B—093 557
  local control    379.153
  local support    379.123
  prisoner services    365.666
  psychological influence    370.158
  psychology    370.15
  public administrative support    353.8
    *see Manual at* 371 vs. 353.8,
      371.2, 379
  public policy    379
  public support    379.11
  sociology    306.43
  state aid    379.122
  state control    379.152

Education (continued)
  value    370.13
  *see also* Public education
  *see Manual at* 371.01–.8 vs.
    372–374, 378
Education and state    379
Education of employees    370.113
  *see also* Vocational education
Educational acceleration    371.28
Educational aid    379.11
  financial management    371.206
Educational anthropology    306.43
Educational areas
  area planning    711.57
Educational buildings    371.6
  architecture    727
  construction    690.7
  higher education    378.196
  institutional housekeeping    647.99
  interior decoration    747.87
  special education    371.904 5
Educational consortia
  higher education    378.104
Educational counseling    371.422
Educational equalization    379.26
Educational exchanges    370.116
  law    344.08
Educational exemptions
  customs duties    382.78
Educational facilities    371.6
  *see also* Educational buildings
Educational films
  instructional use    371.335 23
  journalism    070.18
Educational games    790.1
  instructional use    371.337
  recreation    790.1
Educational guidance    371.422
Educational institutions    371
  accounting    657.832 7
Educational law    344.07
Educational leave    331.257 63
  labor economics    331.257 63
  personnel management    658.312 2
Educational media    371.33
  journalism    070.1
Educational planning    371.207
Educational policy    379
  *see Manual at* 371 vs. 353.8,
    371.2, 379
Educational psychology    370.15
Educational research    370.72
Educational sociology    306.43

Educational technology 371.33
Educational tests 371.26
           T1—076
  *see Manual at* 371.262 vs.
    371.264
Educational therapy
  medicine 615.851 6
Educational toys 790.133
  instructional use 371.337
  manufacturing technology 688.725
  recreation 790.133
Educational vouchers 379.111
  private schools 379.32
Educationally disadvantaged
  students 371.826 94
Educators
  biography 370.92
  law 344.078
Eduyyot 296.123 4
  Babylonian Talmud 296.125 4
  Mishnah 296.123 4
  Palestinian Talmud 296.124 4
Edward, King of England, ca.
  963–978
  English history 942.017 3
Edward, King of England, ca.
  1003–1066
  English history 942.019
Edward, King of England, d. 924
  English history 942.016 5
Edward, the Confessor, King of
  England
  English history 942.019
Edward, the Elder, King of
  England
  English history 942.016 5
Edward, the Martyr, King of
  England
  English history 942.017 3
Edward I, King of England
  English history 942.035
Edward II, King of England
  English history 942.036
Edward III, King of England
  English history 942.037
Edward IV, King of England
  English history 942.044
Edward V, King of England
  English history 942.045
Edward VI, King of England
  English history 942.053

Edward VII, King of Great
  Britain
  British history 941.082 3
  English history 942.082 3
  Scottish history 941.108 23
Edward VIII, King of Great
  Britain
  British history 941.084
  English history 942.084
  Scottish history 941.108 4
Edwards County (Ill.) T2—773 791
Edwards County (Kan.) T2—781 782
Edwards County (Tex.) T2—764 882
Edwards Plateau (Tex.) T2—764 87
Edwy, King of England
  English history 942.017 2
EEC (Economic organization) 341.242 2
  *see also* European Union
Eelgrass 584.74
Eelpouts 597.63
Eels 597.43
Eels (Freshwater) 597.432
  commercial fishing 639.274 32
  cooking 641.692
  culture 639.374 32
  food 641.392
  sports fishing 799.174 32
Eelworms 592.57
  agricultural pests 632.625 7
Eerstehoek (South Africa :
  District) T2—682 72
Efes (Extinct city) T2—392 3
Effect
  philosophy 122
Efficiency
  agricultural industries 338.16
  communications industry 384.041
  economics 338.06
  military administration 355.687 5
  mineral industries 338.26
  promotion of
    personnel management 658.314
    production management 658.515
  public administration 352.375
  secondary industries 338.45
  transportation services 388.049
Effigial slabs 736.5
Effingham County (Ga.) T2—758 722
Effingham County (Ill.) T2—773 796
Efik (African people) T5—963 642
Efik language 496.364 2
           T6—963 642
Efik literature 896.364 2
EFP (Videography) 777.5

EFTA (Economic organization)   341.242
  international commerce   382.914 3
  international economics   337.143
  law of nations   341.242
Egadi Islands   T2—458 24
Egba (African people)   T5—963 33
Egba language   496.333
     T6—963 33
Egbert, King of England
  English history   942.016 1
Egg cells   571.845
Egg decorating   745.594 4
Egg-eating snakes   597.962
Egg production   636.514 2
Eggplants   641.356 46
  botany   583.952
  commercial processing   664.805 646
  cooking   641.656 46
  food   641.356 46
  garden crop   635.646
Eggs   591.468
  animal husbandry   636.514 2
  *see Manual at* 636.1–.8 vs.
    636.088
  cooking   641.675
  descriptive zoology   591.468
  food   641.375
  physiology   573.68
  processing   637.5
Eglise de Jésus-Christ sur la
  terre par le prophète Simon
  Kimbangu   289.93
  *see also* Christian
    denominations
Egmont National Park
  (N.Z.)   T2—934 82
Ego (Psychology)   155.2
  subconscious   154.2
Egoism
  ethical systems   171.9
Egrets   598.34
Egypt   962
     T2—62
  ancient   932
     T2—32
Egyptian language   493.1
     T6—931
Egyptian literature
  Arabic   892.7
  Egyptian   893.1
Egyptians (Ancient)   T5—931
Egyptians (Modern)   T5—927 62
Ehime-ken (Japan)   T2—523 2

Ehlers-Danlos syndrome
  medicine   616.77
  *see also* Musculoskeletal
    diseases — humans
Eichsfeld (Germany :
  Landkreis)   T2—432 24
Eiders   598.415
Eidetic imagery (Psychology)   153.32
Eidgenössisch-Demokratische
  Union (Swiss political party)   324.249 408 2
Eigenvalues   512.943 6
Eigenvectors   512.943 6
Figg (Scotland)   T2—411 54
Eighteenth century   909.7
     T1—090 33
Eighth century   909.1
     T1—090 21
Eilean Siar (Scotland)   T2—411 4
Eindhoven (Netherlands)   T2—492 45
Einsiedeln (Switzerland :
  Bezirk)   T2—494 752 4
Einstein geometry   516.374
Einsteinium   546.449
Eire   941.7
     T2—417
Eire (1937–1949)   941.708 22
Eisenach (Germany)   T2—432 26
Eisenhower, Dwight D. (Dwight
  David)
  United States history   973.921
EKG (Medicine)   616.120 754 7
Ekiti State (Nigeria)   T2—669 27
Ekurhuleni (South Africa)   T2—682 24
El Alamein, Battle of, 1942   940.542 321
El Asnam (Algeria :
  Province)   T2—653
El Beni (Bolivia)   T2—844 2
El Cocuy National Park
  (Colombia)   T2—861 44
El Dorado County (Calif.)   T2—794 41
El Loa (Chile)   T2—831 35
El Oro (Ecuador)   T2—866 31
El Paraíso (Honduras :
  Dept.)   T2—728 34
El Paso County (Colo.)   T2—788 56
El Paso County (Tex.)   T2—764 96
El Progreso (Guatemala :
  Dept.)   T2—728 153
El Salvador   972.84
     T2—728 4
El Seibo (Dominican
  Republic : Province)   T2—729 384
El Tuparro National Park
  (Colombia)   T2—861 92

| | |
|---|---|
| Elaeagnales | 583.82 |
| Elaeocarpaceae | 583.68 |
| Elam | 935.76 |
| | T2—357 64 |
| Elamite Kingdom | 935.760 1 |
| | T2—357 64 |
| Elamite language | 499.93 |
| | T6—999 3 |
| Elamites | T5—999 3 |
| Elands | 599.642 |
| Elapidae | 597.964 |
| Elasmobranchii | 597.3 |
| paleozoology | 567.3 |
| Elastic cartilage | 573.763 56 |
| human histology | 612.751 7 |
| *see also* Musculoskeletal | |
| system | |
| Elastic constants | 531.381 |
| Elastic deformation | 531.382 |
| *see also* Elasticity | |
| Elastic fibers | 677.55 |
| *see also* Textiles | |
| Elastic limit | 531.382 |
| materials science | 620.112 32 |
| Elastic tissues | |
| human histology | 611.018 2 |
| Elasticity | 531.382 |
| crystals | 548.842 |
| fluid mechanics | 532.053 5 |
| gas mechanics | 533.28 |
| liquid mechanics | 532.58 |
| materials science | 620.112 32 |
| muscles | 573.75 |
| human physiology | 612.741 |
| *see also* Musculoskeletal | |
| system | |
| solid mechanics | 531.382 |
| Elastomer industry workers | 678.092 |
| Elastomers | 678 |
| chemistry | 547.842 |
| manufacturing technology | 678 |
| equipment manufacture | 681.766 8 |
| materials science | 620.194 |
| structural engineering | 624.189 4 |
| Elastoplastics | 678.73 |
| Elateridae | 595.765 |
| Elateroidea | 595.765 |
| Elatinaceae | 583.624 |
| Elazığ İli (Turkey) | T2—566 76 |
| ancient | T2—394 2 |
| Elba (Italy) | T2—455 6 |
| Elbe-Elster (Germany : | |
| Landkreis) | T2—431 51 |
| Elbert County (Colo.) | T2—788 87 |
| Elbert County (Ga.) | T2—758 163 |
| Elbląg (Poland : | |
| Voivodeship) | T2—438 32 |
| Elbows | 612.97 |
| physiology | 612.97 |
| regional medicine | 617.574 |
| surgery | 617.574 |
| *see also* Upper extremities | |
| Elder abuse | 362.682 |
| criminology | 364.155 5 |
| criminal law | 345.025 55 |
| social welfare | 362.682 |
| Elder hostels | 910.466 |
| *see also* Lodging (Temporary | |
| housing) | |
| Elderberries | 641.347 4 |
| botany | 583.92 |
| cooking | 641.647 4 |
| food | 641.347 4 |
| horticulture | 634.74 |
| Elderly people | 305.26 |
| | T1—084 6 |
| *see also* Older people | |
| Elders (Plants) | 583.92 |
| Eleatic philosophy | 182.3 |
| Election (Christian doctrine) | 234 |
| Election campaigns | 324.9 |
| *see also* Campaigns (Politics) | |
| Election districts | 328.334 5 |
| Election fraud | 324.66 |
| criminology | 364.132 4 |
| criminal law | 345.023 24 |
| Election law | 342.07 |
| Election monitoring | 324.65 |
| Election offenses | 364.132 4 |
| law | 345.023 24 |
| Election officials | 324 65 |
| Election procedures | 324.6 |
| law | 342.07 |
| Election returns | 324.9 |
| Election sermons | |
| Christianity | 252.68 |
| Election systems | 324.6 |
| Electioneering | 324.7 |
| law | 342.078 |
| Elections | 324 |
| labor unions | 331.874 |
| Elective courses | 375.004 |
| higher education | 378.24 |
| Electoral colleges | 324.63 |
| Electoral districts | 328.334 5 |
| Electoral law | 342.07 |
| Electoral power (Legislative | |
| bodies) | 328.345 4 |

| | |
|---|---|
| Electoral systems | 324.63 |
| Electorates (Election districts) | 328.334 5 |
| Electrets | 537.24 |
| Electric arcs | 537.52 |
| Electric automobiles | 388.34 |
|   engineering | 629.229 3 |
|   transportation services | 388.34 |
| Electric charge | 537.21 |
| Electric circuits | 621.319 2 |
| Electric clocks | |
|   technology | 681.116 |
| Electric conductivity | 537.62 |
| Electric conductors | 537.62 |
| Electric control | 629.804 3 |
| Electric cooking | 641.586 |
| Electric countershock | |
|   medicine | 616.128 064 5 |
| Electric currents | |
|   measurement | 621.374 4 |
|   physics | 537.6 |
| Electric defibrillation | |
|   medicine | 616.128 064 5 |
| Electric eels | 597.48 |
| Electric energy | 333.793 2 |
|   *see also* Electric power | |
| Electric eyes | 621.381 542 |
| Electric furnace practice | 669.142 4 |
| Electric generators | 621.313 |
| Electric heating | 621.402 8 |
|   buildings | 697.045 |
| Electric injuries | |
|   medicine | 617.12 |
| Electric lighting | 621.32 |
|   mining | 622.474 |
|   ships | 623.852 |
| Electric locomotives | 385.363 |
|   engineering | 625.263 |
|   transportation services | 385.363 |
|   *see also* Rolling stock | |
| Electric meters | 621.373 |
|   watt-hour usage | 621.374 5 |
| Electric motors | 621.46 |
|   ships | 623.872 6 |
| Electric organs (Body parts) | 573.97 |
| Electric potential | 537.21 |
|   measurement | 621.374 3 |
| Electric power | 333.793 2 |
|   area planning | 711.8 |
|   economics | 333.793 2 |
|   engineering | 621.31 |
|   law | 343.092 9 |
|   measurement | 621.374 5 |
|   mining | 622.48 |
|   public administration | 354.49 |
| Electric power generation | 621.312 1 |
|   nuclear steam generation | 621.483 |
| Electric power measurement | 621.374 6 |
| Electric power systems | |
|   spacecraft | 629.474 45 |
| Electric propulsion | 621.46 |
|   automotive | 629.250 2 |
|   spacecraft | 629.475 5 |
| Electric railroads | 385 |
|   electrification | 621.33 |
| Electric resistance | 537.62 |
| Electric shavers | |
|   manufacturing technology | 688.5 |
| Electric shock therapy | |
|   psychiatry | 616.891 22 |
| Electric signs | |
|   advertising | 659.136 |
|   engineering | 621.322 9 |
| Electric slow cooking | 641.588 4 |
| Electric stimulation therapy | |
|   medicine | 615.845 |
| Electric submarines | 359.938 32 |
|   design | 623.812 572 |
|   engineering | 623.825 72 |
|   naval equipment | 359.938 32 |
| Electric trains | |
|   toys | 790.133 |
| Electric utilities | 333.793 2 |
|   law | 343.092 9 |
|   *see Manual at* 333.7–.9 vs. 363.6 | |
| Electric vehicles | |
|   engineering | 629.229 3 |
| Electric welding | 671.521 |
| Electrical appliances | 643.6 |
|   household equipment | 643.6 |
|   manufacturing technology | 683.83 |
| Electrical diagnosis | |
|   medicine | 616.075 47 |
| Electrical energy | 333.793 2 |
|   *see also* Electric power | |
| Electrical engineering | 621.3 |
|   military | 623.76 |
| Electrical engineers | 621.309 2 |
| Electrical equipment | |
|   public safety | 363.189 |
| Electrical machinery | 621.310 42 |
| Electrical power | 333.793 2 |
|   *see also* Electric power | |
| Electrical properties | |
|   crystals | 548.85 |
|   materials science | 620.112 97 |
| Electrical prospecting | 622.154 |

Electrical systems
  aircraft — 629.135 4
  automotive — 629.254
  ships — 623.850 3
Electrical toys — 790.133
  manufacturing technology — 688.728
  recreation — 790.133
Electrical zone melting — 669.028 4
Electricians (Interior wiring) — 621.319 240 92
Electricity — 333.793 2
  astrophysics — 523.018 7
  biophysics — 571.47
    humans — 612.014 42
  direct energy generation — 621.312 4
  economics — 333.793 2
  generation — 621.312 1
  meteorology — 551.563
  nuclear steam generation — 621.483
  physics — 537
  plant management — 658.26
  public administration — 354.49
  solar generation — 621.312 44
  therapeutic use — 615.845
Electrification — 333.793 2
  technology — 621.319
Electroacoustical
  communications
  engineering — 621.382 8
Electroacupuncture
  therapeutics — 615.892
Electrobiochemistry — 572.437
Electrocapillarity — 537.24
Electrocardiography
  medicine — 616.120 754 7
Electrochemical analysis — 543.4
Electrochemistry — 541.37
  biochemistry — 572.437
  chemical engineering — 660.297
  electrical engineering — 621.312 42
Electroconvulsive therapy
  psychiatry — 616.891 22
Electrodeposited latex — 678.538
Electrodeposited rubber — 678.36
Electrodeposition
  latex — 678.527
Electrodes — 541.372 4
  chemical engineering — 660.297 24
  chemistry — 541.372 4
Electrodiagnosis
  medicine — 616.075 47
Electrodialysis — 541.372
  chemical engineering — 660.297 2
Electrodynamics — 537.6
  engineering — 621.31

Electrodynamometers — 621.374 6
Electroencephalography
  medicine — 616.804 754 7
Electroforming metals — 671.4
Electroluminescence — 535.357
Electrolysis
  desalinization — 628.167 3
Electrolyte conductivity — 541.372
  chemical engineering — 660.297 2
Electrolyte-water imbalances — 571.937 5
  medicine — 616.399 2
    *see also* Digestive system
    diseases — humans
Electrolytic analysis — 543.4
Electrolytic balance — 571.75
  humans — 612.015 22
Electrolytic dissociation — 541.372 2
  chemical engineering — 660.297 22
Electrolytic solutions — 541.372
  chemical engineering — 660.297 2
Electromagnetic engineering — 621.3
Electromagnetic engineers — 621.309 2
Electromagnetic fields — 530.141
  effects in semiconductors — 537.622 6
Electromagnetic induction — 621.34
Electromagnetic interaction — 539.754 6
Electromagnetic radiation — 539.2
Electromagnetic spectrum — 539.2
Electromagnetic theory — 530.141
Electromagnetic theory of light — 535.14
Electromagnetic wave theory of
  matter — 530.141
Electromagnetic waves — 539.2
Electromagnetism — 537
  astrophysics — 523.018
  biophysics — 571.47
    humans — 612.014 42
  engineering — 621.3
Electromagnets — 621.34
  generator parts — 621.316
Electrometallurgy — 669.028 4
Electrometers — 621.374 3
Electromyography — 616.740 754 7
Electron arrangement
  crystallography — 548.81
  solid-state physics — 530.411
Electron beam welding — 671.521 4
Electron metallography — 669.950 282
Electron microscopes — 502.825
  biology — 570.282 5
  manufacturing technology — 681.413
Electron microscopy — 502.825
  biology — 570.282 5

Electron-nuclear double
  resonance 538.362
Electron optics
  physics 537.56
Electron paramagnetic resonance 538.364
Electron paramagnetic resonance
  spectroscopy 543.67
Electron spectroscopy 543.62
Electron spin resonance 538.364
Electron spin resonance
  spectroscopy 543.67
Electronic aids
  marine navigation 623.893
Electronic bands 784.6
Electronic books
  bibliographies 011.39
  publishing 070.573
Electronic bugging devices 621.389 28
Electronic bulletin boards 004.693
  communications services 384.33
  *see also* Computer
    communications
Electronic circuits 621.381 5
Electronic commerce 381.142
  law 343.081 142
  marketing management 658.872
Electronic communications
  engineering 621.382
Electronic components 621.381 5
Electronic computers 004
  *see also* Computers
Electronic control 629.89
Electronic data processing 004
  T1—028 5
  *see also* Data processing
Electronic digital computers 004
  *see also* Computers
Electronic distance education 371.358
  adult level 374.26
  higher education 378.175 8
Electronic eavesdropping devices 621.389 28
Electronic engineering 621.381
Electronic engineers 621.381 092
Electronic field production
  (Videography) 777.5
Electronic flash photography 778.72
Electronic fuel injection systems
  automobiles 629.253
Electronic funds transfers 332.178
  law 346.082 102 85
Electronic games 794.8
Electronic interference 621.382 24
Electronic journals T1—05
  *see also* Serials

Electronic mail 004.692
  communications services 384.34
  internal office communications 651.79
  *see also* Computer
    communications
Electronic mail lists 004.693
Electronic media 302.23
  advertising 659.14
  sociology 302.23
Electronic music 786.7
Electronic musical instruments 786.7
  *see also* Electrophones
Electronic news gathering 070.43
Electronic news services 070.435
Electronic noise 621.382 24
Electronic office machines 651.26
Electronic organs 786.59
  instrument 786.591 9
  music 786.59
  *see also* Keyboard instruments
Electronic programmed
  instruction 371.334
  adult education 374.26
Electronic properties
  crystals 548.85
  materials science 620.112 97
Electronic publications 070.579 7
  bibliographies 011.39
  sociology 302.231
  *see also* Electronic resources
Electronic reference services
  (Libraries) 025.52
Electronic resources 302.231
  bibliographies 011.39
    *see Manual at* 011.39 vs.
      005.3029, 016.0053,
      025.0422
  cataloging 025.344
  library treatment 025.174
  sociology 302.231
    *see Manual at* T1—0285
Electronic shopping 381.142
Electronic signatures
  computer science 005.8
Electronic spreadsheets 005.54
Electronic surveillance
  civil rights issue 323.448 2
  criminal investigation 363.252
  engineering 621.389 28
  law 345.052
Electronic systems
  aircraft 629.135 5
  automobiles 629.272
  automotive 629.254 9

Electronic systems (continued)
  internal-combustion engines 621.437
  ships 623.850 4
Electronic toys 790.133
  manufacturing technology 688.728
  recreation 790.133
Electronic tubes 621.381 51
Electronica 781.648
Electronics
  military engineering 623.043
  physics 537.5
  technology 621.381
Electrons 539.721 12
Electrooptical devices
  military communications
    engineering 623.731 4
Electrophones 786.7
  bands and orchestras 784
  chamber ensembles 785
    mixed 785.2–.5
    single type 785.67
  construction 786.719 23
    by hand 786.719 23
    by machine 681.867
  solo music 786.7
Electrophoresis 541.372
  analytical chemistry 543.4
  chemical engineering 660.297 2
Electrophotographic
  photocopying 686.44
Electrophotographic printing 686.233
Electrophysiology 572.437
  humans 612.014 27
  nerves 573.854 437
    human physiology 612.813
Electroplating 671.732
Electrorefining 669.028 4
Electroshock therapy
  psychiatry 616.891 22
Electrostatic photocopying 686.44
Electrostatic separation
  ores 622.77
Electrostatics 537.2
Electrostriction 537.24
Electrotherapeutics
  medicine 615.845
Electrotherapy
  medicine 615.845
Electrowinning 669.028 4
Elegies (Music) 784.189 64
Ēleia (Greece) T2—495 27
  ancient T2—388

Elementary education 372
  public administrative support 353.8
  *see also* Primary education
Elementary number theory 512.72
Elementary school buildings
  architecture 727.1
Elementary schools 372
  *see also* Primary education
Elements (Chemicals) 546
  chemistry 546
  mineralogy 549.2
Elephant Butte Reservoir
  (N.M.) T2—789 62
Elephant fishes 597.47
Elephant seals 599.794
Elephant shrews 599.337
Elephantiasis (Filarial)
  incidence 614.555 2
  medicine 616.965 2
  *see also* Communicable
    diseases — humans
Elephants 599.67
  animal husbandry 636.967
  big game hunting 799.276 7
  conservation technology 639.979 67
  resource economics 333.959 67
Elephant's ears (Plants) 584.64
Elephas 599.676
Eleuthera Island (Bahamas) T2—729 6
Eleutherodactylus 597.875 4
Elevated monorail systems
  engineering 625.44
Elevated rail transit systems 388.42
  engineering 625.44
  transportation services 388.42
  *see also* Local rail transit
    systems
Elevations (Physiography) 551.43
    T2—143
  *see also* Mountains
Elevator liability insurance 368.56
Elevators (Aircraft) 629.134 33
Elevators (Lifts)
  buildings 721.833
    architecture 721.833
    construction 690.183 3
  mining 622.68
Elevenses 642
  cooking 641.53
    light meals 641.53
    main meals 641.54
  customs 394.125 3
    light meals 394.125 3
    main meals 394.125 4

| | |
|---|---|
| Eleventh century | 909.1 |
| | T1—090 21 |
| Elgin (Ont. : County) | T2—713 34 |
| Elgin, James Bruce, Earl | |
| Indian history | 954.035 1 |
| Elgin, Victor Alexander Bruce, Earl of | |
| Indian history | 954.035 5 |
| Elian philosophy | 183.7 |
| Elis (Greece) | T2—495 27 |
| ancient | T2—388 |
| Elísa Piña (Dominican Republic : Province) | T2—729 343 |
| Elites | 305.52 |
| | T1—086 21 |
| Elitist systems of government | 321.5 |
| Elizabeth, Empress of Russia | |
| Russian history | 947.062 |
| Elizabeth I, Queen of England | |
| English history | 942.055 |
| Elizabeth II, Queen of Great Britain | |
| British history | 941.085 |
| English history | 942.085 |
| Scottish history | 941.108 5 |
| Elizabeth Islands (Mass.) | T2—744 94 |
| Elk (Moose) | 599.657 |
| big game hunting | 799.276 57 |
| conservation technology | 639.979 657 |
| Elk (Wapiti) | 599.654 2 |
| animal husbandry | 636.294 42 |
| big game hunting | 799.276 542 |
| conservation technology | 639.979 654 2 |
| Elk County (Kan.) | T2—781 915 |
| Elk County (Pa.) | T2—748 65 |
| Elk Island National Park (Alta.) | T2—712 33 |
| Elkhart County (Ind.) | T2—772 81 |
| Elko County (Nev.) | T2—793 16 |
| Elks (Fraternal order) | 366.5 |
| biography | 366.509 2 |
| Ellenborough, Edward Law, Earl of | |
| Indian history | 954.031 5 |
| Ellesmere Island (Nunavut) | T2—719 52 |
| Ellesmere Port and Neston (England) | T2—427 17 |
| Ellice Islands | T2—968 2 |
| Elliot (South Africa : District) | T2—687 57 |
| Elliotdale (South Africa : District) | T2—687 58 |
| Elliott County (Ky.) | T2—769 255 |
| Ellipses | 516.152 |
| Elliptic curves | 516.352 |
| Elliptic equations | 515.353 3 |
| Elliptic functions | 515.983 |
| Elliptic geometry | 516.9 |
| Elliptic operators | 515.724 2 |
| Ellis County (Kan.) | T2—781 19 |
| Ellis County (Okla.) | T2—766 155 |
| Ellis County (Tex.) | T2—764 281 5 |
| Ellisras (South Africa : District) | T2—682 53 |
| Ellsworth County (Kan.) | T2—781 535 |
| Ellsworth Land (Antarctic regions) | T2 –989 |
| Elmbridge (England) | T2—422 145 |
| Elminidae | 595.764 5 |
| Elmore County (Ala.) | T2—761 52 |
| Elmore County (Idaho) | T2—796 29 |
| Elms | 635.977 345 |
| botany | 583.45 |
| forestry | 634.972 8 |
| lumber | 674.142 |
| ornamental arboriculture | 635.977 345 |
| Elocution | 808.5 |
| Elopiformes | 597.43 |
| Elopomorpha | 597.43 |
| paleozoology | 567.43 |
| Elqui (Chile : Province) | T2—832 32 |
| Elves | 398.21 |
| *see also* Legendary beings | |
| Ely (England) | T2—426 56 |
| Ely, Isle of (England) | T2—426 53 |
| Emaciation | |
| medicine | 616.396 |
| *see also* Digestive system diseases — humans | |
| Emancipation of slaves | 326.8 |
| Emancipation Proclamation, 1863 | 973.714 |
| Emanuel County (Ga.) | T2—758 684 |
| Ēmathia (Greece) | T2—495 65 |
| Embalming | |
| customs | 393.3 |
| Embankments | |
| flood-control engineering | 627.42 |
| road engineering | 625.733 |
| structural engineering | 624.162 |
| Embargoes | |
| international commerce | 382.53 |
| *see also* Import trade | |
| law of nations | 341.582 |
| Embarrassment | 152.4 |
| Embassies | 327.2 |
| architecture | 725.17 |
| public administration | 353.13 |
| Embedded computer systems | 006.22 |

| | |
|---|---|
| Embellishments (Music) | 781.247 |
| Emberá (Panama) | T2—728 776 |
| Emberizidae | 598.883 |
| Emberizinae | 598.883 |
| Embezzlement | 364.162 4 |
| law | 345.026 24 |
| Embioptera | 595.737 |
| Embolisms | |
| arteries | |
| medicine | 616.135 |
| *see also* Cardiovascular | |
| diseases — humans | |
| lungs | |
| medicine | 616.249 |
| *see also* Respiratory tract | |
| diseases — humans | |
| medicine | 616.135 |
| *see also* Cardiovascular | |
| diseases — humans | |
| veins | |
| medicine | 616.145 |
| *see also* Cardiovascular | |
| diseases — humans | |
| Embossing leather | 675.25 |
| Embouchure | 784.193 4 |
| Embrithopoda | 569.62 |
| Embroidered rugs | |
| arts | 746.74 |
| Embroidery | |
| arts | 746.44 |
| Embryo | 571.86 |
| human physiology | 612.646 |
| Embryo transfer | |
| ethics | 176.2 |
| *see also* Reproduction — | |
| ethics | |
| surgery | 618.178 059 9 |
| Embryology | 571.86 |
| human physiology | 612.64 |
| Embryophyta | 580 |
| *see also* Plants | |
| Embryotomy | |
| obstetrical surgery | 618.88 |
| Embumbulu (South Africa : | |
| District) | T2—684 5 |
| Emden (Lower Saxony, | |
| Germany) | T2—435 917 |
| Emeralds | 553.86 |
| economic geology | 553.86 |
| jewelry | 739.27 |
| mining | 622.386 |
| Emergency care nursing | 616.025 |
| Emergency legislation | 343.01 |

| | |
|---|---|
| Emergency management | |
| management of enterprises | 658.477 |
| Emergency medical services | 362.18 |
| law | 344.032 18 |
| mental illness | 362.204 251 |
| Emergency medicine | 616.025 |
| injuries | 617.102 6 |
| Emergency planning | 363.345 25 |
| public administration | 353.95 |
| *see also* Disasters | |
| Emergency surgery | 617.026 |
| anesthesiology | 617.960 42 |
| Emergency telephone services | 384.64 |
| *see also* Telephone | |
| Emery County (Utah) | T2—792 57 |
| Emery wheels | 621.923 |
| Emigrant remittances | 332.042 46 |
| Emigration | 304.82 |
| Jews | |
| Holocaust, 1933–1945 | 940.531 814 2 |
| law | 342.082 |
| political science | 325.2 |
| sociology | 304.82 |
| Emigration from Mecca | 297.634 |
| Emilia-Romagna (Italy) | T2—454 |
| ancient | T2—372 6 |
| Eminent domain | 343.025 2 |
| land economics | 333.13 |
| Emission (Physics) | |
| solid-state physics | 530.416 |
| Emission control devices | |
| automotive | 629.252 8 |
| Emission of light | 535.3 |
| Emmanuel Philibert, Duke of | |
| Savoy | |
| Piedmontese history | 945.107 |
| Emmendingen (Germany : | |
| Landkreis) | T2—434 626 |
| Emmental (Switzerland) | T2—494 549 7 |
| Emmental-Oberaargau | |
| (Switzerland) | T2—494 549 |
| Emmet County (Iowa) | T2—777 125 |
| Emmet County (Mich.) | T2—774 88 |
| Emmons County (N.D.) | T2—784 78 |
| Emoticons | 004.601 48 |
| Emotional illness | 362.2 |
| social welfare | 362.2 |
| *see also* Mental health | |
| services | |
| *see also* Mental illness | |
| Emotional intelligence | 152.4 |
| Emotionally disturbed children | 305.908 408 3 |
| home care | 649.154 |

| | |
|---|---|
| Emotionally disturbed people | 305.908 4 |
| | T1—087 4 |
| *see also* Mentally ill people | |
| Emotions | 152.4 |
| adolescents | 155.512 4 |
| arts | T3C—353 |
| children | 155.412 4 |
| educational psychology | 370.153 4 |
| human physiology | 612.823 2 |
| literature | 808.803 53 |
| history and criticism | 809.933 53 |
| specific literatures | T3B—080 353 |
| history and | |
| criticism | T3B—093 53 |
| philosophy | 128.37 |
| Empangeni (South Africa) | T2—684 3 |
| Empathy | |
| psychology | 152.41 |
| Empedoclean philosophy | 182.5 |
| Emphysema | |
| medicine | 616.248 |
| *see also* Respiratory tract | |
| diseases — humans | |
| Empididae | 595.773 |
| Empires | 321.03 |
| | T2—171 2 |
| Empirical remedies | |
| therapeutics | 615.88 |
| Empiricism | 146.44 |
| ethics | 171.2 |
| Employee absenteeism | 331.259 88 |
| labor economics | 331.259 88 |
| personnel management | 658.314 |
| Employee assistance programs | |
| (Health and safety) | 331.255 |
| personnel management | 658.382 |
| Employee banks | 332.37 |
| credit unions | 334.22 |
| Employee benefits | 331.255 |
| economics | 331.255 |
| law | |
| public employees | 342.068 6 |
| personnel management | 658.325 |
| | T1—068 3 |
| executives | 658.407 25 |
| public administration | 352.67 |
| public administration | 354.98 |
| Employee development | 370.113 |
| *see also* Vocational education | |
| Employee discounts | 331.255 |
| economics | 331.255 |
| personnel management | 658.383 |

| | |
|---|---|
| Employee dismissal | |
| economics | 331.259 6 |
| employment security | 331.259 6 |
| unemployment | 331.137 |
| law | 344.012 596 |
| personnel management | 658.313 |
| public administration | 352.69 |
| Employee evaluation | |
| military personnel | 355.330 41 |
| personnel management | 658.312 5 |
| executives | 658.407 125 |
| libraries | 023.9 |
| public administration | 352.66 |
| Employee fringe benefits | 331.255 |
| *see also* Employee benefits | |
| Employee housing | 331.255 |
| personnel management | 658.383 |
| *see also* Employee benefits | |
| Employee malfeasance | |
| personnel management | 658.314 |
| Employee management | 658.3 |
| | T1—068 3 |
| *see also* Personnel management | |
| Employee morale | |
| personnel management | 658.314 |
| Employee motivation | |
| personnel management | 658.314 |
| executives | 658.407 14 |
| Employee organizations | 331.88 |
| economics | 331.88 |
| personnel management | 658.315 3 |
| military personnel | 355.33 |
| public administration | 352.68 |
| women workers | 331.478 |
| Employee orientation | |
| personnel management | 658.312 42 |
| Employee ownership | 338.69 |
| labor economics | 331.216 49 |
| personnel management | 658.322 59 |
| Employee participation in | |
| management | 331.011 2 |
| personnel management | 658.315 2 |
| public administration | 352.68 |
| Employee qualifications | 331.114 |
| *see also* Qualifications of | |
| employees | |
| Employee recognition | |
| personnel management | 658.314 2 |
| Employee representation in | |
| management | 331.011 2 |
| personnel management | 658.315 2 |
| Employee retention | |
| personnel management | 658.314 |

Employee rights | 331.011
  law | 344.010 1
Employee screening
  personnel management | 658.311 2
Employee selection
  personnel management | 658.311 2
               T1—068 3
    libraries | 023.9
    public administration | 352.65
Employee separation
  economics | 331.259 6
    employment security | 331.259 6
    unemployment | 331.137
  law | 344.012 596
  personnel management | 658.313
  public administration | 352.69
Employee share ownership plans
  personnel management | 658.322 59
Employee stock options | 331.216 49
  labor economics | 331.216 49
  personnel management | 658.322 59
  executives | 658.407 225 9
Employee stock ownership plans | 331.216 49
  labor economics | 331.216 49
  personnel management | 658.322 59
Employee theft | 364.162 3
  law | 345.026 23
  prevention
    management | 658.473
Employee training personnel
  personnel management | 658.312 404
Employee turnover | 331.126
  economics | 331.126
  personnel management | 658.314
Employee utilization
  personnel management | 658.312 8
  public administration | 352.66
Employees | 331.11
  bonding
    insurance | 368.83
  economics | 331.11
  household | 640.46
  journalism for | 070.486
  public administration | 354.9
  social class | 305.562
Employer-employee relationships
  personnel management | 658.315
    libraries | 023.9
    public administration | 352.68
  public administration | 354.97
Employer-supported services for
  workers | 331.255
  armed forces | 355.34
  economics | 331.255

Employer-supported services for workers
  (continued)
  personnel management | 658.38
               T1—068 3
    executives | 658.407 8
  public administration | 352.67
Employers' liability | 346.031
Employers' liability insurance | 368.56
Employment | 331.125
Employment agencies | 331.128
  *see also* Employment services
Employment conditions | 331.2
  *see also* Conditions of
    employment
Employment interviewing | 650.144
  job hunting | 650.144
  personnel selection | 658.311 24
Employment law | 344.01
Employment rights | 331.011
Employment security | 331.259 6
  law | 344.012 596
    public employees | 342.068 6
  public administration | 354.98
Employment services | 331.128
  economics | 331.128
  public administration | 354.96
  social services | 362.042 5
    disabled people | 362.404 84
    law | 344.032 042 5
    mentally disabled people | 362.384
    sick people | 362.178 6
Employment subsidies | 331.120 424
Employment tests
  personnel selection | 658.311 25
Emporia (Va.) | T2—755 573
Emu | 598.53
Emulsins | 572.756
  *see also* Enzymes
Emulsions | 541.345 14
  chemical engineering | 660.294 514
  pharmaceutical chemistry | 615.19
Emydidae | 597.925
Ena language | 496.394
               T6—963 94
Enactment of legislation | 328.37
  budgets | 352.48
  law | 342.057
  political science | 328.37
Enamel (Dental)
  dentistry | 617.634
Enameling
  ceramic arts | 738.4
  glass arts | 748.6

| | |
|---|---|
| Enamels | 666.2 |
| architectural decoration | 729.6 |
| ceramic arts | 738.4 |
| materials science | 620.146 |
| technology | 666.2 |
| Encampment | |
| military operations | 355.412 |
| military training | 355.544 |
| Encaustic painting | 751.46 |
| Encephalitis | |
| medicine | 616.832 |
| *see also* Nervous system | |
| diseases — humans | |
| Enclosures | |
| land economics | 333.2 |
| Encoding | |
| computer science | 005.72 |
| Encounter groups | |
| social psychology | 302.14 |
| social work | 361.06 |
| Encryption | 652.8 |
| computer science | 005.82 |
| Encyclicals | 262.91 |
| Encyclopedia yearbooks | 030 |
| | T1—03 |
| Encyclopedias | 030 |
| | T1—03 |
| Encyclopedists | |
| biography | 030.92 |
| End-blown flutes | 788.35 |
| *see also* Woodwind instruments | |
| End games (Chess) | 794.124 |
| End of the world | |
| controversial knowledge | 001.9 |
| religion | 202.3 |
| Christianity | 236.9 |
| End of universe | 523.19 |
| Endangered species | 333.952 2 |
| Enderby (B.C.) | T2—711 5 |
| Enderby Land (Antarctic | |
| regions) | T2—989 |
| Endive | 641.355 5 |
| botany | 583.99 |
| food | 641.355 5 |
| garden crop | 635.55 |
| Endocarditis | |
| medicine | 616.11 |
| *see also* Cardiovascular | |
| diseases — humans | |
| Endocardium | |
| human anatomy | 611.12 |
| human physiology | 612.17 |
| medicine | 616.11 |

| | |
|---|---|
| Endocardium diseases | |
| medicine | 616.11 |
| *see also* Cardiovascular | |
| diseases — humans | |
| Endocrine diseases | 573.439 |
| animals | 573.439 |
| veterinary medicine | 636.089 64 |
| humans | 362.196 4 |
| anesthesiology | 617.967 44 |
| cancer | 362.196 994 4 |
| incidence | 614.599 944 |
| medicine | 616.994 4 |
| social services | 362.196 994 4 |
| *see also* Cancer — humans | |
| geriatrics | 618.976 4 |
| incidence | 614.594 |
| medicine | 616.4 |
| pediatrics | 618.924 |
| pharmacokinetics | 615.74 |
| pregnancy complications | |
| obstetrics | 618.364 |
| social services | 362.196 4 |
| surgery | 617.44 |
| Endocrine drugs | |
| pharmacology | 615.36 |
| Endocrine glands | 573.4 |
| *see also* Endocrine system | |
| Endocrine gynecology | 618.1 |
| Endocrine secretions | 573.44 |
| human physiology | 612.4 |
| *see also* Endocrine system | |
| Endocrine system | 573.4 |
| anesthesiology | 617.967 44 |
| biology | 573.4 |
| diseases | 573.439 |
| *see also* Endocrine diseases | |
| human anatomy | 611.4 |
| human histology | 612.404 5 |
| human physiology | 612.4 |
| medicine | 616.4 |
| surgery | 617.44 |
| *see Manual at* 573.44 vs. | |
| 571.74 | |
| Endocrinology | 573.4 |
| medicine | 616.4 |
| Endocrinotherapy | 615.36 |
| Endodontics | 617.634 2 |
| Endogamy | 306.82 |
| Endometriosis | |
| gynecology | 618.1 |
| *see also* Female genital | |
| diseases — humans | |

Endometritis
  gynecology      618.142
  *see also* Female genital
    diseases — humans
Endomycetales      579.562
Endoparasitic diseases      571.999
  agriculture      632.623
  animals      571.999 1
    veterinary medicine      636.089 696 2
  humans
    incidence      614.552
    medicine      616.962
    *see also* Communicable
      diseases — humans
  plants      571.999 2
    agriculture      632.623
Endoplasmic reticulum      571.65
Endopterygota      595.7
  *see also* Insects
ENDOR (Physics)      538.362
Endoscopic surgery      617.057
Endoscopy
  medicine      616.075 45
  surgery      617.057
Endospore-forming gram-positive
  rods and cocci      579.36
Endosteum
  human histology      612.751 045
Endothelium      571.555
  human histology      611.018 7
Endothermic reactions      541.362
  chemical engineering      660.296 2
Endotoxins
  human toxicology      615.952 93
Endowment insurance      368.322
Endowments
  capital procurement      658.152 24
Endpapers
  handicrafts      745.54
Enemy sympathizers
  World War I      940.316 3
  World War II      940.531 63
Energism      146
Energy      333.79
  architectural consideration      720.472
  classical physics      531.6
  law      346.046 79
  philosophy      118
  physics      530
  plant management      658.26
  public administration      354.4
  quantum mechanics      530.12

Energy (continued)
  resource economics      333.79
  *see Manual at* 333.7–.9 vs.
    363.6
Energy budget (Nature)
  ecology      577.13
  meteorology      551.525
Energy conservation      333.791 6
  architectural consideration      720.472
  economics      333.791 6
  home economics      644
  housing program      363.583
  law      346.046 791 6
  management of enterprises      658.26
  public administration      354.43
  *see also* Energy
Energy development      333.791 5
  law      346.046 791 5
  public administration      354.427
  *see also* Energy
Energy engineering      621.042
  buildings      696
Energy flow (Nature)
  ecology      577.13
  meteorology      551.525
Energy levels (Nuclear physics)      539.725
Energy management      333.79
  business      658.26
        T1—068 2
  *see also* Energy
Energy metabolism      572.43
  human physiology      612.39
  *see also* Digestive system
Energy phenomena
  solid-state physics      530.416
Energy policy      333.79
  *see also* Energy
Energy production      333.79
Energy resources      333.79
  economic geology      553.2
  economics      333.79
  extraction      622.33
    economics      338.2
  law      346.046 79
  public administration      354.4
  *see also* Energy
Energy supply      333.791 1
  law      343.092
  *see also* Energy
Enets language      494.4
        T6—944
Enewetak Atoll (Marshall
  Islands)      T2—968 3
Enfield (London, England)      T2—421 89

| | |
|---|---|
| Enga language | 499.12 |
| | T6—991 2 |
| Enga Province (Papua New Guinea) | T2—956 3 |
| Engaged people | 306.734 |
| | T1—086 523 |
| Engagement (Betrothal) | 392.4 |
| customs | 392.4 |
| etiquette | 395.22 |
| music | 781.586 |
| social aspects | 306.734 |
| Engcobo (South Africa : District) | T2—687 58 |
| Engineering | 620 |
| accounting | 657.834 |
| effect on natural ecology | 577.272 |
| law | 343.078 62 |
| Engineering analysis structures | 624.17 |
| Engineering design | 620.004 2 |
| Engineering drawing | 604.2 |
| Engineering geology | 624.151 |
| dams | 627.81 |
| railroads | 625.122 |
| roads | 625.732 |
| Engineering graphics | 604.2 |
| Engineering installations (Armed forces) | 355.74 |
| Engineering materials | 620.11 |
| Engineering mechanics | 620.1 |
| Engineering optics | 621.36 |
| Engineering services (Armed forces) | 358.22 |
| air force | 358.47 |
| navy | 359.982 |
| Engineering systems ships | 623.85 |
| Engineers | 620.009 2 |
| Engines | 621.4 |
| air-cushion vehicles | 629.314 |
| aircraft | 629.134 35 |
| automotive | 629.25 |
| military aircraft | 623.746 049 |
| ships | 623.87 |
| spacecraft | 629.475 |
| England | 942 |
| | T2—42 |
| ancient | 936.2 |
| | T2—362 |
| *see Manual at* T2—41 and T2—42; *also at* 941 | |
| England, Eastern | T2—426 |
| England, Northern | T2—427 |
| England, Southern | T2—422 |

| | |
|---|---|
| English | T5—21 |
| *see Manual at* T5—201–209 vs. T5—2101–2109 | |
| English as a second language applied linguistics | |
| audio-lingual approach | 428.34 |
| formal approach | 428.24 |
| primary education | 372.652 1 |
| English billiards | 794.73 |
| English Channel | 551.461 336 |
| | T2—163 36 |
| English creole languages | 427.9 |
| | T6—217 |
| English folk music | 781.622 |
| English folk songs | 782.421 622 |
| English horns | 788.53 |
| instrument | 788.531 9 |
| music | 788.53 |
| *see also* Woodwind instruments | |
| English language | 420 |
| | T6—21 |
| primary education | 372.6 |
| rhetoric | 808.042 |
| English-language shorthand systems | 653.42 |
| English literature | 820 |
| English longhorn cattle | 636.226 |
| English peas | 641.356 56 |
| *see also* Peas (Pisum sativum) | |
| English Revised version Bible | 220.520 4 |
| English sparrow | 598.887 |
| English-speaking West Africa | T2—660 917 521 |
| English system (Measurement) | 530.813 |
| social aspects | 389.15 |
| English toy spaniel | 636.76 |
| Engraved seals numismatics | 737.6 |
| Engraved stamps numismatics | 737.6 |
| Engravers | 769.92 |
| Engraving | |
| gems | 736.202 8 |
| glass arts | 748.62 |
| graphic arts | 760 |
| Enhanced recovery oil extraction | 622.338 2 |
| Enhydra | 599.769 5 |
| Enigmas | 001.94 |
| Eniwetok Atoll (Marshall Islands) | T2—968 3 |
| Enjoyment | 152.42 |
| Enlargers photography | 771.44 |

Enlightenment
  European history    940.25
  religion    204.2
    Buddhism    294.344 2
    Hinduism    294.542
    Islam    297.57
Enlisted personnel    355.009 2
  role and function    355.338
Enlistment
  armed services    355.223
  law    343.012
Enna (Italy : Province)    T2—458 12
  ancient    T2—378 12
Enneagram    155.26
Enoch (Pseudepigrapha)    229.913
Enrollment
  higher education    378.161 9
Ensemble technique
  music    781.438
Enslaved people    306.362
Entablatures    721.2
  construction    690.12
  interior decoration    747.3
Entail    346.043 2
  land economics    333.323 4
Entailment
  linguistics    401.454
    specific languages    T4—014 54
Enteral nutrition
  medicine    615.854 82
Enteric fever
  incidence    614.511 2
  medicine    616.927 2
  *see also* Communicable
    diseases — humans
Enteritis
  medicine    616.344
  *see also* Digestive system
    diseases — humans
Enterobacteriaceae    579.34
Enterobiasis
  incidence    614.555 4
  medicine    616.965 4
  *see also* Communicable
    diseases — humans
Enteropneusta    593.99
  paleozoology    563.99
Entertainers    791.092
  *see Manual at* 780.92 and
    791.092
Entertaining    793.2
  etiquette    395.3
  indoor amusements    793.2
  meal service    642.4

Entertainment advertising    659.131
Entertainment equipment
  automobile    629.277
Entertainment films
  performing arts    791.43
Entertainment law    344.099
Entertainment media
  accounting    657.84
Entertainment programs
  radiobroadcasting
    performing arts    791.44
  television broadcasting
    performing arts    791.45
Entertainments (Parties)    793.2
  cooking    641.568
  etiquette    395.3
  indoor amusements    793.2
  interior decoration    747.93
  meal service    642.4
Entertainments (Performances)    790.2
  music    781.55
Enthusiasm
  psychology of learning    153.153 3
Entire functions    515.98
Entitlement spending    336.39
Entlebuch (Switzerland :
  Amt)    T2—494 551
Entombment    363.75
  customs    393.1
  *see also* Undertaking
    (Mortuary)
Entomologists    595.709 2
Entomology    595.7
  agriculture    632.7
  medicine    616.968
Entoprocta    594.66
  paleozoology    564.6
Entotrophi    595.724
Entrance examinations (Schools)    371.262
Entrance requirements (Schools)    371.217
Entre Douro e Minho
  (Portugal)    T2—469 1
Entre Ríos (Argentina)    T2—822 1
Entrées    641.82
  main dishes    641.82
  side dishes    641.81
Entremont (Switzerland)    T2—494 796 6
Entrepreneurial management    658.421
Entrepreneurs    338.040 92
    T1—086 22
  executive management    658.421
  social class    305.554
  *see Manual at* 300 vs. 600; *also*
    at 338.092

| | |
|---|---|
| Entrepreneurship | 338.04 |
| income distribution | 339.21 |
| management | 658.421 |
| production economics | 338.04 |
| Entropy | 536.73 |
| Enugu State (Nigeria) | T2—669 49 |
| Enumeration (Combinatorial analysis) | 511.62 |
| Enumerative geometry | 516.35 |
| Enuresis | |
| medicine | 616.849 |
| *see also* Nervous system diseases — humans | |
| pediatrics | 618.928 49 |
| Environment | 333.7 |
| architectural consideration | 720.47 |
| arts | 700.455 3 |
| | T3C—355 3 |
| economics | 333.7 |
| ethics | 179.1 |
| religion | 205.691 |
| Buddhism | 294.356 91 |
| Christianity | 241.691 |
| Hinduism | 294.548 691 |
| Judaism | 296.369 1 |
| literature | 808.803 553 |
| history and criticism | 809.933 553 |
| specific literatures | T3B—080 355 3 |
| history and criticism | T3B—093 553 |
| primary education | 372.357 |
| public administration | 354.3 |
| social theology | 201.77 |
| Christianity | 261.88 |
| Islam | 297.27 |
| Judaism | 296.38 |
| *see Manual at* 333.72 vs. 304.28, 320.58, 363.7; *also at* 333.7–.9 vs. 363.1, 363.73, 577 | |
| Environment versus heredity | |
| psychology | 155.7 |
| evolutionary psychology | 155.7 |
| individual psychology | 155.234 |
| Environmental abuse | 363.7 |
| social effects | 304.28 |
| social problem | 363.7 |
| social theology | 201.77 |
| Christianity | 261.88 |
| *see Manual at* 333.72 vs. 304.28, 320.58, 363.7 | |
| Environmental biology | 577 |
| Environmental biophysics | 571.49 |
| Environmental chemistry | 577.14 |

| | |
|---|---|
| Environmental control | |
| spacecraft | 629.477 |
| Environmental design | |
| arts | 711 |
| crime prevention | 364.49 |
| ergonomics | 620.82 |
| Environmental diseases | 571.95 |
| agriculture | 632.1 |
| animals | 571.951 |
| veterinary medicine | 636.089 698 |
| humans | 362.196 98 |
| geriatrics | 618.976 98 |
| incidence | 614.59 |
| medicine | 616.98 |
| pediatrics | 618.929 8 |
| social services | 362.196 98 |
| plants | 632.1 |
| *see Manual at* 363.73 vs. 571.95, 577.27 | |
| Environmental economics | |
| development policy | 338.927 |
| Environmental engineering | 628 |
| | T1—028 6 |
| buildings | 696 |
| sanitary engineering | 628 |
| work environment | 620.8 |
| Environmental engineers | 628.092 |
| Environmental factors | |
| genetics | 576.542 |
| physical ethnology | 599.972 |
| Environmental health | |
| personal health | 613.1 |
| Environmental health engineering | 628 |
| | T1—028 6 |
| Environmental impact studies | 333.714 |
| environmental protection | 363.7 |
| law | 344.046 |
| natural resources | 333.714 |
| *see Manual at* 333.7–.9 vs. 363.1, 363.73, 577 | |
| Environmental impairment | |
| liability insurance | 368.563 |
| Environmental law | 344.046 |
| Environmental medicine | 616.98 |
| Environmental monitoring | 363.706 3 |
| pollution | 363.736 3 |
| social services | 363.706 3 |
| *see Manual at* 333.7–.9 vs. 363.1, 363.73, 577 | |
| Environmental offenses | 364.145 |
| law | 345.024 5 |
| Environmental pollution | 363.73 |

Environmental protection 363.7
  engineering 628
    T1—028 6
  executive management 658.408 3
  law 344.046
  public administration 354.328
  social services 363.7
  *see also* Environment
  *see Manual at* 363 vs. 302–307,
    333.7, 570–590, 600
Environmental psychology 155.9
  adolescents 155.518 9
  children 155.418 9
  late adulthood 155.671 89
Environmental sanitation 363.72
Environmental studies 333.707
  primary education 372.357
  *see also* Environment
Environmental technology T1—028 6
  *see also* Green technology
Environmental toxicology 571.95
  ecology 577.27
  medicine 615.902
  pathology 571.95
Environmentalism 333.72
  politics 320.58
  *see Manual at* 333.72 vs.
    304.28, 320.58, 363.7
Environmentalist parties 324.218 7
  international organizations 324.187
Environmentalist political
  ideologies 320.58
Environmentalists 333.720 92
Environments (Art style) 709.040 74
Envoys 327.209 2
Envy 152.48
  ethics 179.8
    religion 205.698
    *see also* Vices
  psychology 152.48
Enya languages 496.394
    T6—963 94
Enzyme technology 660.634
Enzymes 572.7
  biochemistry 572.7
    humans 612.015 1
  pharmacology 615.35
Eocene epoch 551.784
  geology 551.784
  paleontology 560.178 4
Eolithic Age 930.124
    T1—090 12
Eosuchia 567.94
Eotheria 569.29

Epacridaceae 583.66
Epeirogeny 551.8
Ēpeiros (Greece) T2—495 3
Ephedrales 585.8
Ephedras 585.8
Ephedrine abuse 362.299 5
  medicine 616.864
  personal health 613.84
  social welfare 362.299 5
  *see also* Substance abuse
Ephemerides 528
  astrology 133.55
Ephemeroptera 595.734
Ephesians (Biblical book) 227.5
Ephesus (Extinct city) T2—392 3
Ephydridae 595.774
Epic poetry 808.813 2
  history and criticism 809.132
  specific literatures T3B—103 2
    individual authors T3A—1
Epicurean philosophy 187
Epidemic diarrhea
  incidence 614.593 427
  medicine 616.342 7
    *see also* Digestive system
      diseases — humans
Epidemic parotitis
  incidence 614.544
  medicine 616.313
    *see also* Digestive system
      diseases — humans
Epidemic typhus
  incidence 614.526 2
  medicine 616.922 2
    *see also* Communicable
      diseases — humans
Epidemics (Mathematics) 519.85
Epidemiology 614.4
  veterinary medicine 636.089 44
  *see Manual at* 614.4
Epidermis 573.5
  plants 575.451
  *see also* Skin
Epidote
  mineralogy 549.63
Epidural anesthesia
  surgery 617.964
Epiglottis 573.925
  human anatomy 611.22
  human physiology 612.233
  medicine 616.22
  surgery 617.533
  *see also* Respiratory system

Epiglottis diseases
  medicine      616.22
   *see also* Respiratory tract
    diseases — humans
Epigrams      808.882
  history and criticism      809.982
  specific literatures    T3B—802
    individual authors    T3A—8
Epigraphy      411.7
  specific languages    T4—11
Epilepsy
  medicine      616.853
   *see also* Nervous system
    diseases — humans
Epiphany      263.915
  devotional literature      242.335
  music      781.724
  sermons      252.615
Epirus (Greece)    T2—495 3
  ancient    T2—382
Epirus (Greece and Albania) T2—495 3
  Albania    T2—496 5
  Greece    T2—495 3
Epirus (Kingdom)    T2—382
Episcopacy      262.12
Episcopal Church      283.73
  church government      262.037 3
    parishes      254.037 3
  church law      262.983 73
  doctrines      230.3
    catechisms and creeds      238.3
  guides to Christian life      248.483
  liturgy      264.03
  missions      266.3
  moral theology      241.043
  religious associations      267.183 73
  religious education      268.837 3
  religious orders      255.83
    church history      271.83
    women      255.983
      church history      271.983
  seminaries      230.073 373
  theology      230.3
Episcopal palaces
  architecture      726.9
Episcopal systems
  Christian ecclesiology      262.3
Episcopalians
  biography      283.092
Episiotomy
  obstetrical surgery      618.85
Epistemic logic      511.314
Epistemology      121
Epistle of Jeremiah (Bible)      229.5

Epistles (Bible)      227
  pseudepigrapha      229.93
Epitaphs
  genealogy      929.5
Epithelial cells
  human cytology      611.018 76
Epithelial tissues      571.55
  human histology      611.018 7
Epithelium      571.55
  human histology      611.018 7
Epitomes    T1—020 2
Eponym dictionaries      412.03
  specific languages    T4—203
Epoxies      668.422 6
Epoxy resin      668.374
Epping Forest (England)    T2—426 74
EPR (Magnetic resonance)      538.364
Epsom and Ewell (England)   T2—422 15
Equal-area projections
  maps      526.85
Equal economic opportunity
  government programs      354.08
Equal educational opportunity      379.26
Equal employment opportunity      331.133
  economics      331.133
    labor unions      331.873 2
  government programs      354.908
  law      344.011 33
  personnel management      658.300 8
    government employees      352.608
Equal opportunity
  government programs      353.53
Equal pay for equal work      331.215 3
  economics      331.215 3
  law      344.012 153
Equal protection of the law      323.42
  law      340.11
  political science      323.42
Equal time (Election law)      342.078
Equality      305
  civil right      323.42
  political theory      320.011
  religion      200.8
    Christianity      270.08
    Judaism      296.08
  sociology      305
Équateur (Congo : Province) T2—675 13
Equation of exchange theory      332.401
Equation of time      529.1
Equations      511.326
  algebra      512.94
  calculus      515.25
Equatoria Region (Sudan)    T2—629 5

| | | | |
|---|---|---|---|
| Equatorial Guinea | 967.18 | Ergodic theory | 515.48 |
| | T2—671 8 | Ergonomics | 620.82 |
| Equatorial Guineans | T5—967 18 | computers | 004.019 |
| Equatorial Islands | 996.4 | engineering | 621.398 4 |
| | T2—964 | Erhard, Ludwig | |
| Equestrian performers | 791.320 92 | German history | 943.087 6 |
| Equestrian sculpture | 731.81 | Ericales | 583.66 |
| Equestrian sports | 798 | Erie, Lake | T2—771 2 |
| equipment technology | 688.78 | Ohio | T2—771 2 |
| Equestrians | 798.092 | Ontario | T2—713 3 |
| Equidae | 599.665 | Erie County (N.Y.) | T2—747 96 |
| animal husbandry | 636.1 | Erie County (Ohio) | T2—771 22 |
| Equilibrium | | Erie County (Pa.) | T2—748 99 |
| astronomy | 521 | Erik XIV, King of Sweden | |
| chemical engineering | 660.299 2 | Swedish history | 948.503 22 |
| macroeconomic policy | 339.5 | Erinaceidae | 599.332 |
| Equipment | T1—028 4 | Erinaceus | 599.332 2 |
| educational use | T1—078 | Eriocaulales | 584.87 |
| local Christian parishes | 254.7 | Eritrea | 963.5 |
| management | 658.27 | | T2—635 |
| | T1—068 2 | Eritrean Orthodox Church | 281.6 |
| public administration | 352.55 | *see also* Eastern churches | |
| office services | 651.2 | Eritreans | T5—928 9 |
| procurement | 658.72 | Erlangen (Germany) | T2—433 22 |
| teaching aids | 371.33 | Ermelo (South Africa : | |
| | T1—078 | District) | T2—682 78 |
| Equipment research | | Ermine | 599.766 2 |
| production management | 658.577 | Erodiums | 635.933 79 |
| Equipment sheds | | botany | 583.79 |
| agricultural use | 631.25 | floriculture | 635.933 79 |
| Equisetales | 587.2 | Erogeneity | 155.31 |
| paleobotany | 561.72 | Erosion | 551.302 |
| Equisetum | 587.2 | agriculture | 631.45 |
| Equitable remedies | 347.077 | by glaciers | 551.313 |
| Equity | 346.004 | by water | 551.352 |
| Equivalent projections | | by wind | 551.372 |
| maps | 526.85 | engineering | 627.5 |
| Equus | 599.665 | geology | 551.302 |
| Érable (Quebec) | T2—714 575 | *see Manual at* 551.302–.307 vs. | |
| Eragrosteae | 584.9 | 551.35 | |
| Erath County (Tex.) | T2—764 551 | Erotetic logic | 160.119 |
| Erbium | | Erotic literature | 808.803 538 |
| chemistry | 546.418 | history and criticism | 809.933 538 |
| Eremitical religious orders | 255.02 | specific literatures | T3B—080 353 8 |
| church history | 271.02 | history and criticism | T3B—093 538 |
| women | 255.902 | Erotic painting | 757.8 |
| church history | 271.902 | Erotica | |
| Erethizontidae | 599.359 74 | arts | 700.453 8 |
| Eretrian philosophy (Ancient) | 183.7 | | T3C—353 8 |
| Erewash (England) | T2—425 18 | literature | 808.803 538 |
| Erfurt (Germany) | T2—432 248 | history and criticism | 809.933 538 |
| Erfurt (Germany : Bezirk) | T2—432 24 | specific literatures | T3B—080 353 8 |
| Ergative constructions | 415 | history and | |
| specific languages | T4—5 | criticism | T3B—093 538 |

| | |
|---|---|
| Errachidia (Morocco : Province) | T2—645 |
| Error analysis (Mathematics) | 511.43 |
| Error-correcting codes | 005.717 |
| Error correctors automation engineering | 629.831 5 |
| Error detectors automation engineering | 629.831 5 |
| Errors | 001.96 |
| logic | 165 |
| psychology of perception | 153.74 |
| Errors and omissions insurance | 368.564 |
| Erudition | 001.2 |
| Eruptive variables | 523.844 6 |
| Eruvin | 296.123 2 |
| Babylonian Talmud | 296.125 2 |
| Mishnah | 296.123 2 |
| Palestinian Talmud | 296.124 2 |
| Erwinia | 579.34 |
| Erysipelas incidence | 614.595 23 |
| medicine | 616.523 |
| *see also* Skin diseases — humans | |
| Erysiphales | 579.567 |
| Erythroblastosis fetalis pediatrics | 618.921 5 |
| perinatal medicine | 618.326 1 |
| *see also* Cardiovascular diseases — humans | |
| Erythrocyte count human physiology | 612.111 2 |
| Erythrocyte disorders medicine | 616.151 |
| *see also* Cardiovascular diseases — humans | |
| Erythrocytes | 573.153 6 |
| human histology | 612.111 |
| human physiology | 612.111 |
| medicine | 616.151 |
| Erythroxylaceae | 583.79 |
| Erzgebirge (Czech Republic and Germany) | T2—437 15 |
| Czech Republic | T2—437 15 |
| Germany | T2—432 16 |
| Erzincan İli (Turkey) | T2—566 74 |
| ancient | T2—394 2 |
| Erzurum İli (Turkey) | T2—566 24 |
| ancient | T2—395 5 |
| Es Semara (Morocco : Province) | T2—648 |
| Esaki diodes | 621.381 522 |
| Escalators | 621.867 6 |
| architecture | 721.832 |
| building construction | 690.183 2 |
| Escalloniaceae | 583.72 |
| Escallonias | 583.72 |
| Escambia County (Ala.) | T2—761 265 |
| Escambia County (Fla.) | T2—759 99 |
| Escape equipment aircraft | 629.134 386 |
| military aircraft | 623.746 049 |
| Escapements clockwork | 681.112 |
| Escapes | 365.641 |
| Eschatology | 202.3 |
| Buddhism | 294.342 3 |
| Christianity | 236 |
| Hinduism | 294.523 |
| Islam | 297.23 |
| Judaism | 296.33 |
| philosophy of religion | 218 |
| Escherichia | 579.342 |
| Escherichia coli infections incidence | 614.57 |
| medicine | 616.926 |
| *see also* Communicable diseases — humans | |
| Eschrichtidae | 599.522 |
| Escrows | 346.043 73 |
| Escuintla (Guatemala : Dept.) | T2—728 163 |
| Esdras (Deuterocanonical book) | 229.1 |
| Eşfahān (Iran : Province) | T2—559 5 |
| Eshowe (South Africa : District) | T2—684 4 |
| Eskimo | T5—971 |
| Eskimo-Aleut languages | 497.1 |
| | T6—971 |
| Eskimo dogs | 636.73 |
| Eskimo languages | 497.1 |
| | T6—971 |
| Eskimo literature | 897.1 |
| Eskişehir İli (Turkey) | T2—563 5 |
| ancient | T2—392 6 |
| Esmeralda County (Nev.) | T2—793 35 |
| Esmeraldas (Ecuador : Province) | T2—866 35 |
| Esocidae | 597.59 |
| Esophageal diseases medicine | 616.32 |
| *see also* Digestive system diseases — humans | |
| Esophagus | 573.359 |
| biology | 573.359 |
| human anatomy | 611.32 |

Esophagus (continued)
  human physiology — 612.315
  medicine — 616.32
  surgery — 617.548
  *see also* Digestive system
Esoteric societies — 366
Esox — 597.59
ESP (Extrasensory perception) — 133.8
Espaillat (Dominican
    Republic : Province) — T2—729 362
Espartos — 584.9
Esperance (W.A.) — T2—941 7
Esperance National Park
  (W.A.) — T2—941 7
Esperanto language — 499.992
                  T6—999 92
Esperanto literature — 899.992
Espionage — 327.12
  armed forces — 355.343 2
  criminology — 364.131
    criminal law — 345.023 1
  ethics — 172.4
    *see also* Political ethics
  industrial management — 658.472
  international politics — 327.12
  labor economics — 331.894
  law of war — 341.63
  public administration — 353.17
  social theology — 201.727
    Christianity — 261.87
    *see also* International
      relations — social
      theology
Espírito Santo (Brazil :
    State) — T2—815 2
Esquimalt (B.C.) — T2—711 28
ESR (Magnetic resonance) — 538.364
Essaouira (Morocco :
    Province) — T2—646 4
Essayists (Literature) — 809.4
  collected biography — 809.4
    specific literatures — T3B—400 9
  individual biography — T3A—4
Essays — 080
  *see Manual at* 080 vs. 800; *also*
    *at* 081–089
Essays (Literature) — 808.84
  criticism — 809.4
    theory — 808.4
  history — 809.4
  rhetoric — 808.4
  specific literatures — T3B—4
    individual authors — T3A—4
Essen (Germany) — T2—435 538

Essence (Philosophy) — 111.1
Essences (Flavorings) — 641.338 2
  *see also* Flavorings
Essenes — 296.814
Essential hypertension
  medicine — 616.132
    *see also* Cardiovascular
      diseases — humans
Essential oils
  chemical engineering — 661.806
  chemistry — 547.71
Essequibo Islands-West
  Demerara Region
  (Guyana) — T2—881 3
Essex (England) — T2—426 7
Essex (Ont. : County) — T2—713 31
Essex County (Mass.) — T2—744 5
Essex County (N.J.) — T2—749 31
Essex County (N.Y.) — T2—747 53
Essex County (Va.) — T2—755 34
Essex County (Vt.) — T2—743 25
Essonne (France) — T2—443 65
Estate planning — 332.024 016
  law — 346.052
    tax law — 343.053
Estate sales — 381.19
Estate tax — 336.276
  law — 343.053
Estate wines — 641.22
  commercial processing — 663.2
Estates (Grounds)
  landscape architecture — 712.6
Estates (Inheritance)
  accounting — 657.47
  administration — 346.056
Estcourt (South Africa :
  District) — T2—684 7
Estelí (Nicaragua : Dept.) — T2—728 524
Esterases — 572.757
  *see also* Enzymes
Esterification — 547.27
  chemical engineering — 660.284 4
Esters — 547.038
  aromatic chemistry — 547.638
  chemical engineering — 661.83
Esther (Biblical book) — 222.9
Esther (Deuterocanonical book) — 229.27
Esthonian language — 494.545
                T6—945 45
Esthonian literature — 894.545
Esthonians — T5—945 45
Estill County (Ky.) — T2—769 59
Estimated budgets (Public) — 352.48
  *see also* Budgets (Public)

| | |
|---|---|
| Estimates | T1—029 |
| building construction | 692.5 |
| Estimation theory | 519.5 |
| probabilities | 519.287 |
| statistical mathematics | 519.544 |
| Estonia | 947.98 |
| | T2—479 8 |
| Estonian language | 494.545 |
| | T6—945 45 |
| Estonian literature | 894.545 |
| Estonians | T5—945 45 |
| Estrada, Joseph Ejercito | |
| Philippine history | 959.904 9 |
| Estremadura (Portugal) | |
| historic province | T2—469 4 |
| modern province | T2—469 42 |
| Estremadura (Portugal : | |
| Region) | T2—469 4 |
| Estremadura (Spain) | T2—462 6 |
| Estrie (Quebec) | T2—714 6 |
| Estrildidae | 598.886 |
| Estrith dynasty | 948.901 5 |
| Estuaries | 551.461 8 |
| biology | 578.778 6 |
| ecology | 577.786 |
| engineering | 627.124 |
| public administration | 354.36 |
| resource economics | 333.916 4 |
| *see Manual at* T2—162 | |
| Etchemins (Quebec) | T2—714 72 |
| Etching | |
| glass arts | 748.63 |
| graphic arts | 767.2 |
| Etelä-Suomen lääni | |
| (Finland) | T2—489 71 |
| Eternity | |
| philosophy | 115 |
| religion | 202.3 |
| Christianity | 236.21 |
| Islam | 297.23 |
| Judaism | 296.33 |
| Ethanol | |
| fuel | 662.669 2 |
| Ethelbald, King of England | |
| English history | 942.016 3 |
| Ethelbert, King of England | |
| English history | 942.016 3 |
| Ethelred I, King of England | |
| English history | 942.016 3 |
| Ethelred II, King of England | |
| English history | 942.017 4 |
| Ethelwulf, King of England | |
| English history | 942.016 2 |
| Ethers | 547.035 |
| aromatic chemistry | 547.635 |
| chemical engineering | 661.84 |
| human toxicology | 615.951 35 |
| Ethical education | 370.114 |
| Ethical problems | 172–179 |
| arts | T3C—353 |
| religion | 205.6 |
| Buddhism | 294.356 |
| Christianity | 241.6 |
| Hinduism | 294.548 6 |
| Islam | 297.56 |
| Judaism | 296.36 |
| Ethical systems | 171 |
| Ethical wills | |
| Judaism | 296.36 |
| Ethicists | 170.92 |
| Ethics | 170 |
| arts | T3C—353 |
| religion | 205 |
| Buddhism | 294.35 |
| Christianity | 241 |
| *see Manual at* 241 vs. | |
| 261.8 | |
| Hinduism | 294.548 |
| Islam | 297.5 |
| Sufi | 297.45 |
| Judaism | 296.36 |
| Ethics agencies | 352.88 |
| Ethics in government | 172.2 |
| law | 342.068 4 |
| Ethics of the Fathers | 296.123 47 |
| Ethiopia | 963 |
| | T2—63 |
| Ethiopia (Nubia) | 939.78 |
| | T2—397 8 |
| Ethiopian Church | 281.75 |
| *see also* Eastern churches | |
| Ethiopian languages | 492.8 |
| | T6—928 |
| Ethiopian literatures | 892.8 |
| Ethiopian Orthodox Tewahedo | |
| Church | 281.75 |
| *see also* Eastern churches | |
| Ethiopian War, 1895–1896 | 963.043 |
| Ethiopians | T5—928 |
| Ethiopic language | 492.81 |
| | T6—928 1 |
| Biblical texts | 220.46 |
| Ethiopic literature | 892.81 |
| Ethnic cleansing | |
| sociology | 304.663 |
| Ethnic clubs | 369.3 |
| Ethnic cooking | 641.592 |

Ethnic differences
  psychology      155.82
Ethnic groups      305.8
     T1—089
  civil and human rights      323.11
    law      342.087 3
    law of nations      341.485 3
  collected biography      T1—092 3
  criminology      364.34
  education      371.829
  geographic treatment      T1—089 009
    *see Manual at* T1—09 vs.
       T1—089
  government programs      353.533 9
    specific groups      353.534
  history      909.04
    specific places      930–990
  journalism for      070.484
  labor      331.6
    economics      331.6
    personnel management      658.300 89
  legal status      346.013
    constitutional law      342.087 3
    private law      346.013
  literature      808.898
    history and criticism      809.8
    specific literatures      T3B—080 8
      history and
        criticism      T3B—098
    *see Manual at* T3C—93–99,
       T3C—9174 vs. T3C—8
  military troops
    World War I      940.403
    World War II      940.540 4
  physical ethnology      599.97
  psychology      155.82
    *see Manual at* 155.89 vs.
       155.84
  relations with government      323.11
  religion      200.89
    Christianity      270.089
  social welfare      362.84
    public administration      353.533 9
    specific groups      353.534
  *see Manual at* Table 5
Ethnic minorities      305.8
Ethnic nationalism      320.54
Ethnic relations      305.8
Ethnobotany      581.63
Ethnographers      305.800 92
Ethnography      305.8
Ethnolinguistics      306.44
Ethnological jurisprudence      340.52
Ethnologists      305.800 92

Ethnology      305.8
  physical anthropology      599.97
Ethnomusicology      780.89
Ethnopsychology      155.82
  adolescents      155.508 9
  children      155.457
  late adulthood      155.670 89
Ethology (Animal behavior)      591.5
Etiology
  medicine      616.071
  *see Manual at* 616.1–.9
Etiquette      395
  armed forces      355.133 6
  arts      700.455 9
     T3C—355 9
Etna, Mount (Italy)      T2—458 13
Etobicoke (Toronto, Ont.)      T2—713 541
Etorofu Island      T2—524
Etowah County (Ala.)      T2—761 67
Etruria      T2—375
Etruria (Kingdom)      945.508 2
Etruscan architecture      722.62
Etruscan language      499.94
     T6—999 4
Etruscan sculpture      733.4
Etruscans      937.501
     T5—999 4
Ettrick and Lauderdale
  (Scotland)      T2—413 7
Études      784.189 49
Etymology      412
     T1—014
  dictionaries      412.03
  specific languages      T4—2
    dictionaries      T4—203
  *see Manual at* 401.43 vs.
     306.44, 401.45, 401.9, 412,
     415
EU (European Union)      341.242 2
  *see also* European Union
Eubacteriales      579.3
Eubalaena      599.527 3
Euboea (Greece : Nome)      T2—495 15
Euboea Island (Greece)      T2—495 15
  ancient      T2—384
Eucalyptus      583.766
  forestry      634.973 766
  medicinal crop      633.883 766
  ornamental arboriculture      635.977 376 6
Eucarida      595.38
Eucestoda      592.46

| | |
|---|---|
| Eucharist | 234.163 |
|   public worship | 264.36 |
|     Anglican | 264.030 36 |
|       texts | 264.03 |
|     Roman Catholic | 264.020 36 |
|       texts | 264.023 |
|   theology | 234.163 |
| Eucharistic Liturgy | 264.36 |
| Euclidean geometry | 516.2 |
|   metric differential | 516.37 |
| Eucommiales | 583.43 |
| Euechinoidea | 593.95 |
| Eugenics | 363.92 |
|   crime prevention | 364.4 |
|     *see also* Crime prevention | |
|   ethics | 176 |
|   health | 613.94 |
|   social services | 363.92 |
| Euglenida | 579.84 |
| Euglenoids | 579.84 |
| Euglenophyta | 579.84 |
| Eukaryotic cells | 571.6 |
| Eulerian integrals | 515.52 |
| Eumeces | 597.957 3 |
| Eumycetes | 579.5 |
| Eumycophyta | 579.5 |
| Eungella National Park | |
|   (Qld.) | T2—943 6 |
| Euphausiacea | 595.389 |
| Euphoniums | 788.975 |
|   instrument | 788.975 19 |
|   music | 788.975 |
|   *see also* Brass instruments | |
| Euphorbiales | 583.69 |
| Euphratensis (Roman | |
|   province) | T2—393 6 |
|   northern | T2—393 6 |
|   southern | T2—394 32 |
| Euphrates River | T2—567 4 |
| Eupteleales | 583.43 |
| Eurasia | T2—5 |
| Eurasian red squirrel | 599.362 |
| Eurasiatic languages | 410 |
| | T6—1 |
| Eure (France) | T2—442 42 |
| Eure-et-Loir (France) | T2—445 12 |
| Eureka County (Nev.) | T2—793 32 |
| Euro | 332.494 |
| Euroa (Vic.) | T2—945 5 |
| Eurobonds | 332.632 3 |
|   public finance | 336.31 |
| Eurocommunism | |
|   political ideology | 320.532 309 4 |
| Eurocurrency market | 332.456 094 |
| Eurodollar market | 332.456 094 |
| Europe | 940 |
| | T2—4 |
|   ancient | 936 |
| | T2—36 |
|   geography | 914 |
|   military operations | |
|     World War I | 940.414 |
|     World War II | 940.542 1 |
|   travel | 914.04 |
| Europe, Central eastern | 943.7 |
| | T2—437 |
| Europe, Eastern | 947 |
| | T2—47 |
| Europe, Northern | 948 |
| | T2—48 |
|   ancient | 936.8 |
| | T2—368 |
| Europe, Southeastern | 949.6 |
| | T2—496 |
|   ancient | 939.8 |
| | T2—398 |
| Europe, Southern | 940 |
| | T2—4 |
|   ancient | 938 |
| | T2—38 |
| Europe, Western | 940 |
| | T2—4 |
|   ancient | 936 |
| | T2—36 |
| European Arctic seawaters | 551.461 324 |
| | T2—163 24 |
| European bison | 599.643 |
| European Commission | 341.242 226 |
| European Common Market | 341.242 2 |
|   *see also* European Union | |
| European Community | 341.242 2 |
|   *see also* European Union | |
| European Convention on Human | |
|   Rights, 1950 | 342.240 850 261 |
| European Court of Human Rights | 342.240 850 269 |
| European Economic Community | 341.242 2 |
|   *see also* European Union | |
| European federation | 321.040 94 |
| European Free Trade Association | 341.242 |
|   international commerce | 382.914 3 |
|   international economics | 337.143 |
|   law of nations | 341.242 |
| European hedgehog | 599.332 2 |
| European Investment Bank | 332.153 4 |
| European Parliament | 341.242 224 |
|   legislative process | 328.4 |
| European philosophy | 190 |
| European polecat | 599.766 28 |

European theater (World War II)  940.542 1
European Union  341.242 2
  commerce  382.914 2
  economics  337.142
  law of nations  341.242 2
  public administration  352.114
European wildcat  599.752 6
Europeans  T5—09
Europium
  chemistry  546.415
Eurotiales  579.565
Euryapsida  567.93
Eurylaimidae  598.822
Eurypterida  565.493
Eurytania (Greece)  T2—495 15
  ancient  T2—383
Eurytanias Nomos (Greece)  T2—495 15
Eustachian tube diseases  617.86
  *see also* Ear diseases —
    humans
Eustachian tubes
  human anatomy  611.85
  human physiology  612.854
  medicine  617.86
Euthanasia
  ethics  179.7
    religion  205.697
    *see also* Death — ethics
  law  344.041 97
Eutheria  599
Eutrophication  577.631 58
Euvoia (Greece)  T2—495 15
Evaluation of employee training
  personnel management  658.312 404
Evaluation research  001.4
    T1—072
Evaluations of products and
  services  T1—029
Evangelical and Reformed
  Church  285.734
  *see also* Reformed Church
    (American Reformed)
Evangelical churches  289.95
Evangelical Congregational
  Church  289.9
  *see also* Christian
    denominations
Evangelical Free Church of
  America  289.95
  *see also* Christian
    denominations
Evangelical Lutheran Church  284.131 2
  *see also* Lutheran church

Evangelical Lutheran Church in
  America  284.135
  *see also* Lutheran church
Evangelical Lutheran Synodical
  Conference of North America  284.132
  *see also* Lutheran church
Evangelical theology  230.046 24
Evangelical United Brethren
  Church  289.9
  *see also* Christian
    denominations
Evangelicalism  270.82
  independent denominations  289.95
  Protestantism  280.4
Evangeline Parish (La.)  T2—763 57
Evangelische Kirche in
  Deutschland  284.094 3
  *see also* Lutheran church
Evangelische Volkspartei der
  Schweiz  324.249 408 2
Evangelism  269.2
Evangelistic sermons  252.3
Evangelistic writings  243
Evangelization  266
Evans County (Ga.)  T2—758 763
Evaporated foods
  cooking  641.614
Evaporated milk  641.371 422
  cooking  641.671 422
  food  641.371 422
  processing  637.142 2
Evaporating foods  664.028 4
  commercial preservation  664.028 4
  home preservation  641.44
Evaporation  536.44
  chemical engineering  660.284 26
  meteorology  551.572
Evaporation control
  water supply engineering  628.132
Evapotranspiration
  meteorology  551.572
Eve (Biblical person)
  Bible stories  222.110 950 5
Even language  494.1
    T6—941
Even-toed ungulates  599.63
Evening dress  391.486
  commercial technology  687.16
  customs  391.486
  home sewing  646.476
  *see also* Clothing
Evening prayer  264.15
  Anglican  264.030 15
    texts  264.034

| | |
|---|---|
| Evening prayer (continued) | |
| music | 782.326 |
| choral and mixed voices | 782.532 6 |
| single voices | 783.093 26 |
| Evening primroses | 635.933 76 |
| botany | 583.76 |
| floriculture | 635.933 76 |
| Evening schools | |
| adult education | 374.8 |
| higher education | 378.15 |
| Evenki (Asian people) | T5—941 |
| Evenki (Russia : Okrug) | T2—575 |
| Evenki language | 494.1 |
| | T6—941 |
| Evenskiĭ avtonomnyĭ okrug | |
| (Russia) | T2—575 |
| Evensong | 264.030 15 |
| music | 782.326 |
| texts | 264.034 |
| Eventing (Horsemanship) | 798.242 |
| Events | 900 |
| *see Manual at* 900 | |
| Events (Art style) | 709.040 74 |
| Everglades (Fla.) | T2—759 39 |
| Everglades National Park | |
| (Fla.) | T2—759 39 |
| Evergreen trees | 582.16 |
| ornamental arboriculture | 635.977 15 |
| Evergreen trees (Conifers) | 585 |
| ornamental arboriculture | 635.977 5 |
| Everlastings (Plants) | 635.973 |
| botany | 583.99 |
| floriculture | 635.973 |
| Everyday life | |
| art representation | 704.949 |
| arts | 700.455 |
| | T3C—355 |
| folklore | 398.275 |
| history and criticism | 398.355 |
| literature | 808.803 55 |
| history and criticism | 809.933 55 |
| specific literatures | T3B—080 355 |
| history and | |
| criticism | T3B—093 55 |
| Eviction | 346.043 4 |
| Evidence (Knowledge) | |
| epistemology | 121.65 |
| Evidence (Law) | 347.06 |
| criminal investigation | 363.25 |
| criminal law | 345.06 |
| law | 347.06 |
| preservation | 363.24 |
| procurement | 363.252 |
| Evil (Concept) | 111.84 |
| ethics | 170 |
| religion | 205 |
| Christianity | 241.3 |
| Islam | 297.5 |
| Judaism | 296.36 |
| religion | 202.118 |
| Christianity | 231.8 |
| freedom of choice | 233.7 |
| comparative religion | 202.118 |
| Islam | 297.211 8 |
| Judaism | 296.311 8 |
| philosophy of religion | 214 |
| Evil eye | 133.425 |
| Evil spirits | 133.423 |
| religion | 202.16 |
| *see also* Legendary beings | |
| Evolutes | 516.362 |
| Evolution | 576.8 |
| animals | 591.38 |
| biochemistry | 572.38 |
| biology | 576.8 |
| ethical systems | 171.7 |
| humans | 599.938 |
| microorganisms | 579.138 |
| molecular biology | 572.838 |
| philosophy | 116 |
| plants | 581.38 |
| *see Manual at* 576.8 vs. 560 | |
| Evolution (Mathematics) | 512.923 |
| Evolution (Social change) | 303.4 |
| Evolution of stars | 523.88 |
| Evolution versus creation | 202.4 |
| Christianity | 231.765 2 |
| *see Manual at* 231.7652 vs. | |
| 213, 500, 576.8 | |
| Judaism | 296.34 |
| philosophy of religion | 213 |
| Evolutionary cycles | 576.84 |
| Evolutionary genetics | 572.838 |
| Evolutionary psychology | 155.7 |
| Evolutionism | |
| philosophy | 146.7 |
| Evora (Portugal : District) | T2—469 52 |
| EVP (Swiss political party) | 324.249 408 2 |
| Evreĭskaia avtonomnaia | |
| oblast' (Russia) | T2—577 |
| Evritania (Greece) | T2—495 15 |
| Evros (Greece) | T2—495 7 |
| Ewe (African people) | T5—963 374 |
| Ewe language | 496.337 4 |
| | T6—963 374 |
| Ewe literature | 896.337 4 |
| Ewenki (Asian people) | T5—941 |

Ewondo language 496.396
T6—963 96
Ex-convicts 364.8
  labor economics 331.51
Examination of witnesses 347.075
  criminal investigation 363.254
  criminal law 345.075
Examinations (Educational tests) 371.26
T1—076
  teacher-prepared tests 371.271
  *see Manual at* 371.262 vs.
    371.264
Excavating machinery 621.865
Excavation 624.152
  archaeological technique 930.102 83
  mining 622.2
  road engineering 625.733
Excelsior 674.84
Excelsior (South Africa :
  District) T2—685 5
Exceptional children
  education 371.9
  home care 649.15
  psychology 155.45
Exceptional students 371.9
Excess liability insurance 368.5
Excess profits tax 336.243 2
  law 343.052 44
Exchange buildings
  architecture 725.25
Exchange rates
  foreign exchange 332.456
Exchanges
  library acquisitions 025.26
  library-government relations 021.8
Excise tax 336.271
  law 343.055 3
  public administration 352.44
  public finance 336.271
Excitation
  solid-state physics 530.416
Excited states
  solid-state physics 530.416
Excitons
  solid-state physics 530.416
Excluded classes 305.568
T1—086 94
Exclusionary rule 347.062
Excommunication
  Judaism 296.67
Excretion 573.49
  animals 573.49
  biology 573.49
  human physiology 612.46

Excretion (continued)
  plants 575.79
  *see also* Urinary system
Excretory organs 573.49
  *see also* Urinary system
Excretory system 573.49
  *see also* Urinary system
Exe, River (England) T2—423 5
Execution of wills 346.056
Executions of judgment 347.077
Executive ability 658.409
Executive advisory bodies 352.743
Executive agencies 351
  *see also* Administrative
    agencies
Executive branch of government 351
  control by legislature 328.345 6
  law 342.06
  sociology 306.24
Executive budgets 352.48
  *see also* Budgets (Public)
Executive buildings
  architecture 725.12
Executive councils
  public administration 352.24
Executive departments 351
Executive development
  personnel management 658.407 124
  public administration 352.39
Executive investigations
  official misconduct 353.463
Executive-judicial relations 320.404
  law 342.044
Executive leadership 658.409 2
  public administration 352.39
Executive-legislative relations 328.345 6
  law 342.044
Executive management 658.4
T1—068 4
  military administration 355.68
  public administration 352.3
  schools 371.207
    higher education 378.107
Executive mansions
  architecture 725.17
Executive messages
  public administration 352.238
Executive orders 348.025
  United States 348.732 5
Executive orders (Treatises) 342.060 263 6
Executive power 352.235
  law 342.06
Executive privilege 352.235
  law 342.06

| | |
|---|---|
| Executive recruiting | 658.407 111 |
| Executive secretaries | |
| office management | 651.3 |
| Executives | |
| personal aspects | 658.409 |
| personnel management | 658.407 |
| public administration | 352.39 |
| Exegesis | |
| sacred books | 208.2 |
| Bible | 220.6 |
| Hadith | 297.125 16 |
| Koran | 297.122 6 |
| Talmud | 296.120 6 |
| Exemptions | |
| customs duties | 382.78 |
| *see also* Customs (Tariff) | |
| Exercise | 613.71 |
| child care | 649.57 |
| human physiology | 612.044 |
| musculoskeletal system | 612.76 |
| physical fitness | 613.71 |
| prenatal care | |
| obstetrics | 618.244 |
| therapeutics | 615.82 |
| Exercise therapy | |
| medicine | 615.82 |
| Exercises (Problems) | T1—076 |
| Exeter (England) | T2—423 56 |
| Exhibit cases | |
| museology | 069.31 |
| Exhibition animals | |
| care and training | 636.081 1 |
| Exhibition buildings | |
| architecture | 725.91 |
| Exhibition catalogs | 069.52 |
| | T1—074 |
| *see Manual at* T1—074 vs. | |
| T1—029 | |
| Exhibitions | 907.4 |
| | T1—074 |
| advertising | 659.152 |
| civilization | 907.4 |
| commerce | 381.1 |
| customs | 394.6 |
| fine arts | 708 |
| temporary | 707.4 |
| *see Manual at* 704.9 and | |
| 753–758 | |
| management | 658.87 |
| public administrative support | 352.76 |
| technology | 607.34 |

| | |
|---|---|
| Exhibits | T1—074 |
| museology | 069.5 |
| preparation | T1—075 |
| *see also* Exhibitions | |
| Exile | |
| arts | 700.455 2 |
| | T3C—355 2 |
| literature | 808.803 552 |
| history and criticism | 809.933 552 |
| specific literatures | T3B—080 355 2 |
| history and | |
| criticism | T3B—093 552 |
| Exiles | 305.906 914 |
| | T1—086 914 |
| social welfare | 362.87 |
| women | |
| social welfare | 362.839 814 |
| young people | |
| social welfare | 362.779 14 |
| *see also* Refugees | |
| Existence | 111.1 |
| Existence of God | 212.1 |
| Christianity | 231 |
| comparative religion | 202.11 |
| Judaism | 296.311 |
| philosophy of religion | 212.1 |
| Existential psychology | 150.192 |
| Existentialism | 142.78 |
| arts | T3C—384 |
| ethics | 171.2 |
| literature | 808.803 84 |
| history and criticism | 809.933 84 |
| specific literatures | T3B—080 384 |
| history and | |
| criticism | T3B—093 84 |
| Existentialist theology | 230.046 |
| Exmoor (England) | T2—423 85 |
| Exobasidiales | 579.59 |
| Exocoetidae | 597.66 |
| Exocrine glands | 571.79 |
| human physiology | 612.4 |
| Exocrine secretions | |
| human physiology | 612.4 |
| Exodontics | 617.66 |
| Exodus (Bible) | 222.12 |
| Exogamy | 306.82 |
| Exogenous processes (Geology) | 551.3 |
| Exopterygota | 595.73 |
| Exorcism | |
| occultism | 133.427 |
| religious rite | 203.8 |
| Christianity | 265.94 |
| *see also* Rites — religion | |

Exorcists 200.92
  biography 200.92
  religious role and function 206.1
  *see Manual at* 200.92 and
    201–209, 292–299
Exoskeleton 591.477
  descriptive zoology 591.477
  physiology 573.77
Exothermic reactions 541.362
  chemical engineering 660.296 2
Exotic species 333.952 3
Expanding universe theories 523.18
Expanding vaults 721.45
  architecture 721.45
  construction 690.145
Expansion (Effect of heat) 536.41
Expansion of enterprises
  executive management 658.406
Expansions (Mathematics) 511.4
Expatriates 305.906 91
            T1—086 91
  social welfare 362.899 1
  women
    social welfare 362.839 81
  young people
    social welfare 362.779 1
Expatriation 323.64
Expectant mothers
  employment economics 331.44
Expectant parents' handbooks 649.102 42
  medicine 618.24
Expectation
  probabilities 519.287
  statistical mathematics 519.54
Expectorants
  pharmacokinetics 615.72
Expeditionary forces 355.352
Expense statements
  financial management 658.151 2
Expenses
  financial management 658.155
Experience
  philosophical anthropology 128.4
  religion 204.2
  *see also* Religious experience
Experiment in International
  Living 373.011 62
Experimental animals 616.027
  care and maintenance 636.088 5
  medicine 616.027
Experimental arts 700.411
            T3C—11
Experimental biology 570.724

Experimental biomedical
  research 610.724
Experimental design
  (Mathematics) 519.57
Experimental literary works 808.887
  history and criticism 809.987
  specific literatures   T3B—807
    individual authors   T3A—8
Experimental medicine 616.027
  ethics 174.28
  *see also* Medical ethics
Experimental research 001.434
            T1—072 4
  public administrative support 352.745
  *see Manual at*
    T1—07201–07209
    vs. T1—0721; *also at*
    T1—07201–07209 vs.
    T1—0722–0724
Experimental schools 371.04
  higher education 378.03
Experimentation on animals
  ethics 179.4
  *see also* Animals —
    treatment of — ethics
  medicine 616.027
Expert system shells 006.33
Expert systems 006.33
Expert testimony 347.067
  criminal law 345.067
Expert witnesses 347.067
  criminal law 345.067
Expertizing
  antiques 745.102 88
  arts 702.88
  ceramic arts 738.18
  paintings 751.62
Experts 001
  management use 658.46
Exploding wire phenomena 537.5
Explorations 910.9
  geography 910.9
  recreation 796.52
  science 508
  *see Manual at* 629.43, 629.45
    vs. 559.9, 919.904; *also at*
    913–919
Explorers 910.92
Explorers (Organization) 369.43
Explosion 541.361
  chemical engineering 660.296 1
  chemistry 541.361
Explosion insurance 368.12

| | |
|---|---|
| Explosions | |
| mine safety engineering | 622.82 |
| social services | 363.179 8 |
| Explosive technologists | 662.209 2 |
| Explosives | 662.2 |
| control | |
| public administration | 353.36 |
| law | 344.053 3 |
| military engineering | 623.452 |
| public safety | 363.179 8 |
| *see also* Hazardous materials | |
| Exponents | 512.922 |
| algebra | 512.922 |
| arithmetic | 513.22 |
| Export controls | 382.64 |
| law | 343.087 8 |
| Export credit | 332.742 |
| law | 346.073 |
| Export-Import Bank of the United States | 332.154 097 3 |
| Export licensing | 382.64 |
| law | 343.087 8 |
| Export marketing | 382.6 |
| commerce | 382.6 |
| management | 658.84 |
| Export policy | 382.63 |
| Export restrictions | 382.64 |
| Export subsidies | 382.63 |
| Export tax | 382.7 |
| public finance | 336.263 |
| *see also* Customs (Tariff) | |
| Export trade | 382.6 |
| commerce | 382.6 |
| law | 343.087 8 |
| management | 658.84 |
| promotion | 382.63 |
| public administration | 354.74 |
| Exposition (Rhetoric) | 808.066 |
| speaking | 808.5 |
| writing | 808.066 |
| Expositions | 907.4 |
| *see also* Exhibitions | |
| Expository writing | 808.066 |
| Exposure meters | 771.37 |
| Exposure of the dead | |
| customs | 393.4 |
| Express freight services | 388.044 |
| air | 387.744 |
| bus | 388.322 2 |
| canal | 386.404 24 |
| ferry | 386.6 |
| inland waterway | 386.244 |
| lake | 386.544 |
| marine | 387.544 |

| | |
|---|---|
| Express freight services (continued) | |
| railroad | 385.23 |
| special purpose | 385.5 |
| river | 386.354 |
| truck | 388.324 |
| Express mail | 383.18 |
| Expression | |
| drama | 792.028 |
| motion pictures | 791.430 28 |
| radio | 791.440 28 |
| stage | 792.028 |
| television | 791.450 28 |
| rhetoric of speech | 808.5 |
| Expressionism | |
| architecture | 724.6 |
| fine arts | 709.040 42 |
| literature | 808.801 15 |
| history and criticism | 809.911 5 |
| specific literatures | T3B—080 115 |
| history and criticism | T3B—091 15 |
| painting | 759.064 2 |
| sculpture | 735.230 442 |
| Expressive movements | 302.222 |
| psychology | 152.384 |
| *see also* Gestures | |
| Expressways | 388.122 |
| *see also* Roads | |
| Expropriation | 338.924 |
| land economics | 333.13 |
| law | 343.025 2 |
| law of war | 341.67 |
| production economics | 338.924 |
| Extemporaneous speaking | |
| rhetoric | 808.51 |
| Extemporization (Music) | 781.36 |
| Extended care facilities | 362.16 |
| mental illness | 362.23 |
| *see also* Mental health services | |
| physical illness | 362.16 |
| *see also* Health care facilities | |
| Extended coverage endorsement | 368.129 |
| *see also* Insurance | |
| Extended family | 306.857 |
| Extended school year | 371.236 |
| Extenders (Chemicals) | 661.807 |
| Extenders (Paints) | 667.623 |
| Extension cords | |
| electrical engineering | 621.319 24 |
| Extension services | 371.35 |
| | T1—071 5 |
| higher education | 378.175 |
| public libraries | 027.42 |

Extension theory   512.4
Exterior algebra   512.57
Exterior ballistics
  military engineering   623.514
Exterior lighting   621.322 9
Exterior painting
  buildings   698.12
Exterior wiring   621.319 25
Extermination camps
  European history   940.531 85
  Holocaust denial   940.531 818
  liberation   940.531 846
External affairs   327
  public administration   353.1
External ear diseases
  medicine   617.81
   *see also* Ear diseases —
   humans
External ears   573.89
  animal physiology   573.89
  descriptive zoology   591.44
  human anatomy   611.85
  human physiology   612.851
  medicine   617.81
  *see also* Ears
External storage
  computer science   004.56
  engineering   621.397 6
Exterritoriality
  law of nations   341.4
Extinct animals   560
  recently extinct   591.68
Extinct birds   568
  recently extinct   598.168
Extinct mammals   569
  recently extinct   599.168
Extinct plants   561
  recently extinct   581.68
Extinction (Biology)   576.84
  resource economics   333.952 2
Extortion   364.165
  law   345.026 5
Extortion insurance   368.82
Extrachromosomal DNA   572.869
Extraction (Chemical
  engineering)   660.284 2
  oils and gases   665.028 2
Extraction (Dentistry)   617.66
Extraction (Mining)   622
  petroleum   622.338
Extraction (Obstetrics)   618.82
Extractive industries   338

Extractive industry workers   331.794
  labor economics   331.794
  public administration   354.942 2
Extractive metallurgy   669
Extracts (Pharmaceuticals)
  pharmaceutical chemistry   615.19
Extracurricular activities   371.8
Extradition   345.052
Extralegislative powers
  (Legislative bodies)   328.345
Extramarital relations   306.736
  social problem   363.48
  social theology   201.7
   Christianity   261.835 736
  *see also* Sexual relations
Extrameridional instruments   522.2
Extranets (Computer networks)
  computer science   004.678
  online marketing   658.872 028 546
Extrasensory perception   133.8
Extrasensory perception of
  animals   133.89
Extrasolar planets   523.24
Extrasolar systems   523.24
Extraterrestrial biophysics   571.499
  humans   612.014 5
Extraterrestrial civilization   999
Extraterrestrial engineering   620.419
Extraterrestrial intelligence   999
Extraterrestrial life   576.839
Extraterrestrial rovers
  engineering   629.295
Extraterrestrial worlds   999
   T2—99
  earth sciences   559.9
  *see Manual at* 523 vs. 550
  *see Manual at* T2—99 vs.
   T2—19; *also at* 520 vs.
   500.5, 523.1, 530.1, 919.9
Extraterritoriality
  law of nations   341.4
Extrauterine pregnancy
  obstetrics   618.31
Extravehicular activity (Manned
  space flight)   629.458 4
Extremadura (Spain)   T2—462 6
Extremal combinatorics   511.66
Extreme environments
  biology   578.758
Extreme sports   796.046
Extreme unction   234.167
  public worship   265.7
  theology   234.167

| | |
|---|---|
| Extremities | |
| bones | |
| human anatomy | 611.718 |
| human physiology | 612.751 |
| medicine | 616.71 |
| surgery | 617.471 |
| fractures | |
| medicine | 617.158 |
| human anatomy | 611.98 |
| human physiology | 612.98 |
| joints | |
| medicine | 616.72 |
| surgery | 617.580 59 |
| muscles | |
| human anatomy | 611.738 |
| regional medicine | 617.58 |
| surgery | 617.580 59 |
| Extremophiles | 578.758 |
| Extrinsic variables (Stars) | 523.844 4 |
| Extroversion | 155.232 |
| Extruded latex | 678.538 |
| Extruded rubber | 678.35 |
| Extruding metals | 671.34 |
| decorative arts | 739.14 |
| sculpture | 731.41 |
| Extruding plastics | 668.413 |
| Extruding rubber | 678.27 |
| Eyadéma, Gnassingbé | |
| Togolese history | 966.810 42 |
| Eyak language | 497.2 |
| Eye banks | 362.178 3 |
| *see also* Health services | |
| Eye diseases | 573.883 9 |
| animals | 573.883 9 |
| veterinary medicine | 636.089 77 |
| humans | 362.197 7 |
| anesthesiology | 617.967 7 |
| cancer | |
| incidence | 614.599 948 4 |
| medicine | 616.994 84 |
| *see also* Cancer — | |
| humans | |
| diagnosis | 617.715 |
| geriatrics | 618.977 7 |
| incidence | 614.599 7 |
| nursing | 617.702 31 |
| ophthalmology | 617.7 |
| pediatrics | 618.920 977 |
| social services | 362.197 7 |
| surgery | 617.71 |
| Eyeballs | |
| human anatomy | 611.84 |
| human physiology | 612.84 |
| ophthalmology | 617.74 |

| | |
|---|---|
| Eyeglasses | |
| customs | 391.44 |
| manufacturing technology | 681.411 |
| optometry | 617.752 2 |
| Eyelid diseases | |
| ophthalmology | 617.771 |
| *see also* Eye diseases — | |
| humans | |
| Eyelids | |
| human physiology | 612.847 |
| ophthalmology | 617.771 |
| Eyes | 573.88 |
| anesthesiology | 617.967 7 |
| animal physiology | 573.88 |
| descriptive zoology | 591.44 |
| mammals | 599.144 |
| diseases | 573.883 9 |
| *see also* Eye diseases | |
| human anatomy | 611.84 |
| human physiology | 612.84 |
| injuries | 617.713 |
| ophthalmology | 617.7 |
| personal care | 646.726 |
| surgery | 617.71 |
| Eyre, Lake (S. Aust.) | T2—942 38 |
| Eyre Peninsula (S. Aust.) | T2—942 38 |
| Ezekiel (Biblical book) | 224.4 |
| Ezra (Biblical book) | 222.7 |

# F

| | |
|---|---|
| F region (Ionosphere) | 538.767 4 |
| Fabales | 583.74 |
| *see also* Legumes | |
| Fabian socialism | 335.14 |
| political ideology | 320.531 2 |
| Fables | |
| folklore | 398.24 |
| Fabliaux | 808.813 |
| history and criticism | 809.13 |
| specific literatures | T3B—103 |
| individual authors | T3A—1 |
| Fabric furnishings | 645.046 |
| commercial technology | 684.3 |
| *see also* Furnishings | |
| Fabricating equipment | 621.9 |
| Fabrics | 677.028 64 |
| home economics | 646.11 |
| home furnishings | 645.046 |
| home sewing | 646.11 |
| textile technology | 677.028 64 |
| *see also* Textiles | |
| Facades | |
| architectural design | 729.1 |

Face
  anthropometry 599.948
  human anatomy 611.92
  human physiology 612.92
  personal care 646.726
  regional medicine 617.52
  surgery 617.520 59
Face perception 153.758
Facelift 617.520 592
Facial bones
  fractures
    medicine 617.156
  human anatomy 611.716
  human physiology 612.751
  medicine 616.71
  surgery 617.471
Facility management 658.2
  *see also* Plant management
Facsimile transmission 384.14
  engineering 621.382 35
  postal service 383.141
    *see also* Postal service
  wireless 384.524
  *see also* Telegraphy
Facsimiles
  bibliographies 011.47
Fact books 030
Fact finding 001.4
               T1—072
  legislative activity 328.345 2
  public administration 352.743
    maladministration 353.46
  public safety 363.106 5
Factitious disorders
  medicine 616.858 6
    *see also* Mental disorders
Factor algebras 512.57
Factor analysis 519.535 4
Factor proportions
  economics 338.512
Factorial experiment designs 519.57
Factorial series 515.243
Factories
  architecture 725.4
  institutional housekeeping 647.964
  landscape architecture 712.7
  manufacturing industries 338.476 7
  manufacturing technology 670
  organization of production 338.65
Factoring 512.923
  *see also* Factorization

Factorization 512.923
  algebra 512.923
  arithmetic 513.23
  number theory 512.72
Factors (Mathematics) 512.923
  *see also* Factorization
Factors of production 338.01
  agricultural economics 338.14
  income distribution 339.21
  microeconomics 338.512
  mineral industries 338.26
  secondary industries 338.45
Factory management
  production management 658.5
Factory operations engineering 670.42
Factory outlets 381.15
  management 658.870 5
Factory ships 387.248
  design 623.812 48
  engineering 623.824 8
  transportation services 387.248
  *see also* Ships
Factory system
  economics 338.65
Facts (Philosophy) 111
Faculae 523.74
Facultatively anaerobic gram-
  negative rods 579.34
Faculty 371.1
  higher education 378.12
  *see also* Teachers
Faculty psychology 150.192
Fadden, Arthur (Arthur William),
  Sir
  Australian history 994.042
Faeroe Islands 949.15
               T2—491 5
Faeroes 949.15
               T2—491 5
Faeroese language 439.699
               T6—396 99
Faeroese literature 839.699
Faeroese people T5—396 9
Faesulae (Italy) T2—375 1
Fagales 583.46
Fagoideae 583.46
Fahs-Beni Makada
  (Morocco) T2—642
Faience 738.37
Failure (Materials science) 620.112
Failure time data analysis 519.546
Fair employment 331.133
  *see also* Equal employment
    opportunity

Fair linens
  arts    746.96
Fair organs    786.68
  *see also* Mechanical musical
    instruments
Fair trade    338.522
  law    343.07
Fairbanks North Star
  Borough (Alaska)    T2—798 6
Fairfax (Va.)    T2—755 292
Fairfax County (Va.)    T2—755 291
Fairfield County (Conn.)    T2—746 9
Fairfield County (Ohio)    T2—771 58
Fairfield County (S.C.)    T2—757 49
Fairgrounds
  area planning    711.552 2
  landscape architecture    712.5
Fairies    398.21
  *see also* Legendary beings
Fairness doctrine (Broadcasting)
  law    343.099 45
Fairs    907.4
     T1—074
  *see also* Exhibitions
Fairs (Street fairs)    381.186
Fairs (Trade fairs)    381.1
Fairways (Navigation)    387.1
  engineering    627.23
  *see also* Ports
Fairy chess    794.18
Fairy shrimps    595.32
Fairy tales    398.2
Faith    121.7
  epistemology    121.7
  religion    202.2
    Christianity    234.23
      knowledge of God    231.042
    Islam    297.22
    Judaism    296.32
    philosophy of religion    218
Faith and reason    210
  Christianity    231.042
  Judaism    296.311
  philosophy of religion    210
Faith healing
  medicine    615.852
  religion    203.1
    Christianity    234.131
  *see also* Spiritual healing —
    religion
Fal, River (England)    T2—423 7
Falangism    335.6
  economics    335.6
  political ideology    320.533

Falasha    T5—924
Falcón (Venezuela)    T2—872 4
Falconidae    598.96
Falconiformes    598.9
  paleozoology    568.9
Falconry    799.232
Falcons    598.96
  animal husbandry    636.686 9
  conservation technology    639.978 96
  resource economics    333.958 96
Faliscan languages    479.4
     T6—794
Falkirk (Scotland)    T2—413 18
Falkland Islands    997.11
     T2—971 1
Falkland Islands War    997.110 24
Fall    508.2
  music    781.524 6
  *see also* Seasons
Fall of humankind    233.14
Fall River County (S.D.)    T2—783 97
Fallacies    001.96
  logic    165
Falling bodies    531.14
  solid mechanics    531.5
Fallon County (Mont.)    T2—786 35
Fallopian tube diseases
  gynecology    618.12
  *see also* Female genital
    diseases — humans
Fallopian tubes
  gynecology    618.12
  human anatomy    611.65
  human physiology    612.625
Fallow deer    599.655
  animal husbandry    636.294 5
Fallowing    631.581 2
Falls Church (Va.)    T2—755 293
Falls County (Tex.)    T2—764 286
False arrest    346.033 4
False chameleons    597.954 8
False coral snake (Aniliidae)    597.967
False coral snakes (Colubridae)    597.962
False Dmitri I
  Russian history    947.045
False Dmitri II
  Russian history    947.045
False impersonation    364.163 3
  law    345.026 33
False imprisonment    346.033 4
False killer whales    599.53
False memory syndrome
  adult child abuse victims
    psychotherapy    616.858 223 906 51

False memory syndrome (continued)
  adult child sexual abuse
    victims
      psychotherapy    616.858 369 065 1
False scorpions    595.47
Falsetto voices    782.86
  choral and mixed voices    782.86
  single voices    783.86
Falster (Denmark)    T2—489 3
Families    306.85
  applied psychology    158.24
  government programs    353.533 1
  histories    929.2
    *see Manual at* 929.2
  influence on crime    364.253
  law    346.015
  psychological influence    155.924
  recreation    790.191
    indoor    793.019 1
    outdoor    796
  religion
    guides to life    204.41
      Christianity    248.4
      *see also* Family life —
        religion
    pastoral theology    206.1
      Christianity    259.1
    social theology    201.7
      Christianity    261.835 85
    worship    204.3
      Christianity    249
      Judaism    296.45
  social welfare    362.82
    law    344.032 82
    public administration    353.533 1
  sociology    306.85
Families of clergy
  Christianity
    pastoral theology    253.22
Family    306.85
  system of government    321.1
  *see also* Families
Family abuse    362.829 2
  sociology    306.87
  *see also* Family violence
Family behavior (Animals)    591.563
Family budgets
  macroeconomics    339.41
Family cars
  driving    629.283
  engineering    629.222
  repair    629.287 2
Family Compact    971.038

Family corporations    338.74
  law    346.066 8
  management    658.045
  *see also* Corporations
Family counseling    362.828 6
  Christian pastoral counseling    259.12
Family dissolution    306.88
Family Division of the High
  Court of Justice (Great
  Britain)    346.420 150 269
Family ethics    173
  religion    205.63
    Buddhism    294.356 3
    Christianity    241.63
    Hinduism    294.548 63
    Islam    297.563
    Judaism    296.363
Family histories    929.2
  *see Manual at* 929.2
Family law    346.015
Family leave    331.257 63
  personnel management    658.312 2
Family libraries    027.1
  catalogs    017.2
Family life    306.85
  applied psychology    158.24
  customs    392.3
  home economics    646.78
  primary education    372.374
  psychological influence    155.924
  religion    204.41
    Buddhism    294.344 41
    Christianity    248.4
    Hinduism    294.544 1
    Islam    297.577
    Judaism    296.74
Family meals    642.1
Family medicine    610
Family names    929.42
Family planning    363.96
  *see also* Birth control
Family psychotherapy
  psychiatry    616.891 56
Family purity
  Judaism    296.742
Family relationships    306.87
  home economics    646.78
Family rooms    643.55
  home economics    643.55
  interior decoration    747.791
Family size
  demography    304.63
Family socialization    303.323

| | |
|---|---|
| Family violence | 362.829 2 |
| criminology | 364.155 5 |
| criminal law | 345.025 55 |
| medicine | 616.858 22 |
| social theology | 201.762 829 2 |
| Christianity | 261.832 7 |
| social welfare | 362.829 2 |
| law | 344.032 829 2 |
| sociology | 306.87 |
| Famine | 363.8 |
| Fan-jet engines | |
| aircraft | 629.134 353 7 |
| Fan vaults | 721.45 |
| architecture | 721.45 |
| construction | 690.145 |
| Fanagalo | 496.398 6 |
| | T6—963 986 |
| Fanakalo | 496.398 6 |
| | T6—963 986 |
| Fancies (Music) | 784.187 6 |
| Fancy-weave fabrics | 677.61 |
| *see also* Textiles | |
| Fanfares | 784.189 24 |
| Fang (African people) | T5—963 96 |
| Fang language | 496.396 |
| | T6—963 96 |
| Fangs | 591.47 |
| Fannin County (Ga.) | T2—758 293 |
| Fannin County (Tex.) | T2—764 265 |
| Fans (Machinery) | 621.61 |
| Fans (Ornamental) | 391.44 |
| customs | 391.44 |
| handicrafts | 745.594 |
| *see also* Accessories (Clothing) | |
| Fantasias | 784.189 4 |
| Fantastic fiction | 808.838 766 |
| history and criticism | 809.387 66 |
| specific literatures | T3B—308 766 |
| individual authors | T3A—3 |
| Fantasy | 154.3 |
| arts | 700.415 |
| | T3C—15 |
| literature | 808.801 5 |
| history and criticism | 809.915 |
| specific literatures | T3B—080 15 |
| history and criticism | T3B—091 5 |
| motion pictures | 791.436 15 |
| psychology | 154.3 |
| radio programs | 791.446 15 |
| television programs | 791.456 15 |

| | |
|---|---|
| Fantasy fiction | 808.838 766 |
| history and criticism | 809.387 66 |
| specific literatures | T3B—308 766 |
| individual authors | T3A—3 |
| Fantasy games | 793.93 |
| *see Manual at* 793.932 vs. 794.822 | |
| Fante (African people) | T5—963 385 |
| Fante language | 496.338 5 |
| | T6—963 385 |
| Fante literature | 896.338 5 |
| Fanti (African people) | T5—963 385 |
| Fanti language | 496.338 5 |
| | T6—963 385 |
| Fanti literature | 896.338 5 |
| Far East | 950 |
| | T2—5 |
| Far East international organizations | 341.247 3 |
| Far North District (N.Z.) | T2—931 3 |
| Far Western Rand (South Africa) | T2—682 22 |
| Farallones de Cali National Park (Colombia) | T2—861 52 |
| Farces | 792.23 |
| literature | 808.825 232 |
| history and criticism | 809.252 32 |
| specific literatures | T3B—205 232 |
| individual authors | T3A—2 |
| stage presentation | 792.23 |
| Fareham (England : Borough) | T2—422 775 |
| Fares | |
| transportation services | 388.049 |
| Fargo (N.D.) | T2—784 13 |
| Faribault County (Minn.) | T2—776 22 |
| Farm accounting | 657.863 |
| Farm buildings | 631.2 |
| architecture | 725.37 |
| construction | 690.537 |
| use | 631.2 |
| Farm costs | 338.13 |
| Farm cottages | |
| architecture | 728.6 |
| Farm forestry | 634.99 |
| Farm income | 338.13 |
| Farm investment | 338.13 |
| Farm law | 343.076 |
| Farm loans | 332.71 |
| law | 346.073 |
| Farm manure | 631.861 |
| Farm-owner insurance | 368.096 |
| Farm pests | 632.6 |
| Farm prices | 338.13 |

Farm produce 338.17
  *see also* Agricultural products
Farm production quotas
  law 343.076 1
Farm profits 338.13
Farm property 333.76
  resource economics 333.76
  taxation 336.225
Farm roads
  use 631.28
Farm tenancy 333.335 53
  economics 333.335 53
  law 346.043 48
Farm tractors 629.225 2
Farm valuation
  tax economics 336.225
Farmers 630.92
 T1—088 63
  social class 305.963
Farmers' markets 381.41
Farmers parties 324.218
Farmhouses
  agriculture 631.21
  architecture 728.6
  construction 690.86
Farming 630
Farmowner-ranchowner
  insurance 368.096
Farms 630
  animal husbandry 636.01
Faro (Game) 795.42
Faro (Portugal : District) T2—469 6
Faroe Islands 949.15
 T2—491 5
Faroese language 439.699
 T6—396 99
Faroese literature 839.699
Faroese people T5—396 9
Farquhar Islands
  (Seychelles) T2—696
Fārs (Iran) T2—557 2
Farsi language 491.55
 T6—915 5
Farsi literature 891.55
Faruk I, King of Egypt
  Egyptian history 962.052
Fasciae
  human anatomy 611.74
  human physiology 612.75
  medicine 616.75
Fasciae diseases
  medicine 616.75
    *see also* Musculoskeletal
      diseases — humans

Fascioliasis
  medicine 616.362
    *see also* Digestive system
      diseases — humans
Fascism 335.6
  economics 335.6
  political ideology 320.533
Fascist government 321.94
Fascist parties
  after 1945 324.213 8
Fascist period (Italy) 945.091
Fascist Republican Party (Italy) 324.245 023 8
Fashion 391
  arts 746.92
  customs 391
    *see Manual at* 391 vs. 646.3,
      746.92
Fashion design 746.92
Fashion designers 746.920 92
Fashion drawing 741.672
Fashion modeling 746.92
  advertising 659.152
Fashion photography 778.997 469 2
Fast days 203.6
  Christianity 263.9
    cooking 641.566
    devotional literature 242.3
    sermons 252.6
  cooking 641.567
  customs 394.2
  Islam 297.53
  Judaism 296.43
    *see also* Holy days
Fast foods
  cooking 641.555
  home serving 642.1
Fasteners 621.88
  buildings 721.8
    architecture 721.8
    construction 690.18
  home sewing 646.19
Fastening equipment 621.97
Fasting
  health 613.25
  religious practice 204.47
    Buddhism 294.344 47
    Christianity 248.47
    Hinduism 294.544 7
    Islam 297.53
      Sufi 297.45
    Judaism 296.7
Fat cells
  human cytology 611.018 276
Fat-free cooking 641.563 84

| | |
|---|---|
| Fat-restricted diet | |
|   health | 613.284 3 |
| Fatalism | |
|   philosophy | 149.8 |
|   religion | 202.2 |
| Fate | |
|   philosophy | 123 |
| Father (God) | |
|   Christian doctrines | 231.1 |
|   Jewish doctrine | 296.311 2 |
| Father and child | 306.874 2 |
| Fatherhood | 306.874 2 |
| Fatherland Front (Austrian | |
|   political party) | 324.243 602 43 |
| Fathers | 306.874 2 |
| | T1—085 1 |
|   family relationships | 306.874 2 |
|   guides to Christian life | 248.842 1 |
|   psychology | 155.646 2 |
| Fatick (Senegal : Region) | T2—663 |
| Fatigue (Humans) | |
|   production management | 658.544 |
|   psychology | 152.188 6 |
| Fatigue (Materials) | 620.112 6 |
| Fatigue strength | 620.112 6 |
| Fats | 572.57 |
|   applied nutrition | 613.284 |
|   biochemistry | 572.57 |
|     humans | 612.015 77 |
|   chemistry | 547.77 |
|   food technology | 664.3 |
|   industrial | 665 |
|   metabolism | |
|     human physiology | 612.397 |
|   *see also* Lipids | |
| Fatty acids | 572.57 |
|   applied nutrition | 613.284 |
|   biochemistry | 572.57 |
|     humans | 612.015 77 |
|   metabolism | |
|     human physiology | 612.397 |
|   recovery from pulp | 676.5 |
|   *see also* Lipids | |
| Fatty-alcohol sulfates | 668.14 |
| Fatty tissues | 571.57 |
|   human histology | 611.018 27 |
| Faucets | 621.84 |
| Faulk County (S.D.) | T2—783 213 |
| Faulkner County (Ark.) | T2—767 74 |
| Fault-tolerant computing | 004.2 |
|   engineering | 621.392 |
|   firmware | 005.18 |
|   programming | 005.1 |
| Faults (Geology) | 551.872 |

| | |
|---|---|
| Fauna | 590 |
|   *see also* Animals | |
| Fauquier County (Va.) | T2—755 275 |
| Fauresmith (South Africa : | |
|   District) | T2—685 7 |
| Fauvism | 709.040 43 |
|   painting | 759.064 3 |
|   sculpture | 735.230 443 |
| Fava beans | 641.356 51 |
|   *see also* Broad beans | |
| Fax (Transmission) | 384.14 |
|   *see also* Facsimile transmission | |
| Fax directories | 910.25 |
|   *see Manual at* T1—025 vs. | |
|     T1—029 | |
| Fayette County (Ala.) | T2—761 87 |
| Fayette County (Ga.) | T2—758 426 |
| Fayette County (Ill.) | T2—773 797 |
| Fayette County (Ind.) | T2—772 623 |
| Fayette County (Iowa) | T2—777 35 |
| Fayette County (Ky.) | T2—769 47 |
| Fayette County (Ohio) | T2—771 813 |
| Fayette County (Pa.) | T2—748 84 |
| Fayette County (Tenn.) | T2—768 21 |
| Fayette County (Tex.) | T2—764 251 |
| Fayette County (W. Va.) | T2—754 71 |
| Faysal I, King of Iraq | |
|   Iraqi history | 956.704 1 |
| Faysal II, King of Iraq | |
|   Iraqi history | 956.704 2 |
| Fayyūm (Egypt : Province) | T2—622 |
| FDP.The Liberals (Swiss political | |
|   party) | 324.249 406 |
| Fear | 152.46 |
|   arts | T3C—353 |
|   literature | 808.803 53 |
|     history and criticism | 809.933 53 |
|     specific literatures | T3B—080 353 |
|     history and | |
|       criticism | T3B—093 53 |
|   social psychology | 302.17 |
| Fear of flying | |
|   medicine | 616.852 25 |
| Feast days | |
|   Christianity | 263.9 |
|     cooking | 641.566 |
|     devotional literature | 242.3 |
|     sermons | 252.6 |
|   cooking | 641.567 |
|   customs | 394.2 |
|   religion | 203.6 |
|   *see also* Holy days | |
| Feather products | |
|   manufacturing technology | 679.47 |

| | |
|---|---|
| Featherbedding | 331.889 6 |
| Feathers | 598.147 |
|   animal husbandry | 636.514 5 |
|     nonpoultry | 636.61 |
|   descriptive zoology | 598.147 |
|   physiology | 573.597 |
| Features | |
|   journalism | 070.44 |
| Fecal incontinence | |
|   medicine | 616.35 |
|   *see also* Digestive system | |
|       diseases — humans | |
| Feces | |
|   human physiology | 612.36 |
| Federal administration | 351 |
| Federal aid | |
|   education | 379.121 |
|   higher education | 379.121 4 |
|     law | 344.076 84 |
|   private schools | 379.32 |
| Federal aid to preschool | |
|   education | 379.121 22 |
| Federal aid to primary education | 379.121 2 |
| Federal and Islamic Republic of | 969.41 |
|   the Comoros    T2—694 1 | |
| Federal Capital Territory | |
|   (Nigeria)    T2—669 68 | |
| Federal cases | |
|   United States | 348.734 |
| Federal courts (United States) | 347.732 |
|   reports | 348.734 1 |
| Federal District (Brazil)  T2—817 4 | |
| Federal District (Mexico)  T2—725 3 | |
| Federal government | 321.02 |
|   law | 342.042 |
|   public administration | 351 |
| Federal law (Treatises) | 340 |
|   United States | 349.73 |
| Federal laws | 348.02 |
|   United States | 348.732 |
| Federal Party (U.S.) | 324.273 22 |
| Federal-provincial relations | 321.023 |
| Federal Register (United States) | 351.730 5 |
| Federal regulations | 348.025 |
|   United States | 348.732 5 |
| Federal regulations (Treatises) | 342.060 263 6 |
|   United States | 342.730 602 636 |
| Federal Republic of Germany | 943.087 |
|       T2—43 | |
| Federal Reserve System (U.S.) | 332.110 973 |
| Federal-state relations | 321.023 |
| Federal statutes | 348.02 |
|   United States | 348.732 |
| Federalism | 321.02 |

| | |
|---|---|
| Federalist Party (U.S.) | 324.273 22 |
| Federally Administered | |
|   Tribal Areas (Pakistan)  T2—549 11 | |
| Federation of Arab | |
|   Republics    T2—62 | |
| Federation of Independents | |
|   (Austrian political party) | 324.243 603 |
| Federation of Rhodesia and | 968.903 |
|   Nyasaland    T2—689 | |
| Federation of South Arabia  T2—533 5 | |
| Federation of the Greens (Italian | |
|   political party) | 324.245 087 |
| Federations | 321.02 |
|   law | 342.042 |
|   public administration | 351 |
| Federazione dei Verdi (Italian | |
|   political party) | 324.245 087 |
| Fee-based library services | 025.11 |
| Fee simple | 346.043 2 |
|   land economics | 333.323 2 |
| Fee splitting | |
|   medical ethics | 174.26 |
| Feed additives | 636.085 57 |
| Feedback circuits | |
|   electronics | 621.381 535 |
| Feedback control systems | 629.83 |
| Feeding animals | 636.084 |
| Feeding behavior (Animals) | 591.53 |
| Feeding-bottle nipples | |
|   latex technology | 678.533 |
| Feeding children | 649.3 |
| Feedlot runoff | 363.738 |
|   water pollution engineering | 628.168 46 |
| Feedlot wastes | |
|   animal husbandry | 636.083 8 |
| Feedlots | 636.084 3 |
| Feeds | 636.085 5 |
|   animal husbandry | 636.085 5 |
|   commercial processing | 664.66 |
|     grain and seeds | 664.76 |
|   industry | 338.476 646 6 |
| Feelings | 152.4 |
|   educational psychology | 370.153 4 |
|   human physiology | 612.823 2 |
| Fees | |
|   public administration | 352.44 |
|   public revenues | 336.16 |
| Feet | 612.98 |
|   physiology | 612.98 |
|   regional medicine | 617.585 |
|   surgery | 617.585 059 |
|   *see also* Lower extremities | |
| Fe'fe' (Cameroon people)  T5—963 6 | |

| | |
|---|---|
| Fe'fe' language | 496.36 |
| | T6—963 6 |
| Fejér Megye (Hungary) | T2—439 7 |
| Feldspar | |
| materials science | 620.198 |
| mineralogy | 549.68 |
| synthetic | 666.86 |
| Felidae | 599.75 |
| animal husbandry | 636.8 |
| paleozoology | 569.75 |
| Felis | 599.752 |
| Felling trees | 634.98 |
| Fellowships | 371.223 |
| | T1—079 |
| higher education | 378.33 |
| law | 344.079 5 |
| research | 001.44 |
| Feloidea | 599.74 |
| paleozoology | 569.74 |
| Felsite | 552.22 |
| Felt | 677.63 |
| *see also* Textiles | |
| Felting textiles | 677.028 24 |
| Female circumcision | |
| surgery | 618.160 59 |
| Female condoms | |
| health | 613.943 5 |
| medicine | 618.185 |
| Female genital diseases | |
| humans | 362.198 1 |
| anesthesiology | 617.968 1 |
| cancer | 362.196 994 65 |
| incidence | 614.599 946 5 |
| medicine | 616.994 65 |
| social services | 362.196 994 65 |
| *see also* Cancer — humans | |
| geriatrics | 618.978 |
| gynecology | 618.1 |
| incidence | 614.599 21 |
| medicine | 618.1 |
| nursing | 618.102 31 |
| pediatrics | 618.920 98 |
| social services | 362.198 1 |
| surgery | 618.105 9 |
| Female genital organs | 573.66 |
| Female genital system | 573.66 |
| anesthesiology | 617.968 1 |
| biology | 573.66 |
| gynecology | 618.1 |
| human anatomy | 611.65 |
| human physiology | 612.62 |
| surgery | 618.105 9 |
| Female goddesses | 202.114 |
| Female prostitution | 306.742 |

| | |
|---|---|
| Female reproductive system | 573.66 |
| animals | 573.66 |
| plants | 575.66 |
| *see also* Female genital system | |
| Female sexual disorders | |
| gynecology | 618.17 |
| *see also* Female genital diseases — humans | |
| Female spouses | |
| social welfare | 362.839 52 |
| Female-to-male transgender people | 306.768 |
| | T1—086 7 |
| social services | 362.897 |
| Female-to-male transgender young people | |
| social services | 362.785 |
| Females (Human) | 305.4 |
| | T1—082 |
| health | 613.042 4 |
| *see also* Women | |
| Femininity | 155.333 |
| Femininity of God | 202.114 |
| Christianity | 231.4 |
| Judaism | 296.311 2 |
| Feminism | 305.42 |
| political ideology | 320.562 2 |
| religion | 200.82 |
| Christianity | 270.082 |
| Judaism | 296.082 |
| social aspects | 305.42 |
| Feminist theology | 202.082 |
| Christianity | 230.082 |
| Judaism | 296.308 2 |
| Feminist views | T1—082 |
| Feminists | 305.42 |
| Femurs | |
| human anatomy | 611.718 |
| Fencers | 796.860 92 |
| Fences | 631.27 |
| agricultural use | 631.27 |
| landscape architecture | 717 |
| Fencing (Offense) | 364.162 7 |
| law | 345.026 27 |
| Fencing (Swordplay) | 796.86 |
| Fenders | |
| automobile | 629.26 |
| Feng shui | 133.333 7 |
| Fenians | 941.708 1 |
| Canadian history | 971.048 |
| Irish history | 941.708 1 |
| Fenland (England) | T2—426 53 |
| Fennec fox | 599.776 |
| Fens, The (England) | T2—426 |

Fentress County (Tenn.)        T2—768 69
Feral children
  psychology                   155.456 7
Feral livestock
  agricultural pests            632.696
  conservation technology       639.966
Ferdinand I, Holy Roman
  Emperor
  German history                943.032
Ferdinand II, Holy Roman
  Emperor
  German history                943.042
Ferdinand III, Holy Roman
  Emperor
  German history                943.043
Ferdinand V, King of Spain
  Spanish history               946.03
Ferdinand VI, King of Spain
  Spanish history               946.056
Ferdinand VII, King of Spain
  Spanish history               946.072
Fergus County (Mont.)         T2--786 292
Fermanagh (Northern
  Ireland)                     T2—416 3
Fermat's last theorem          512.74
Fermentation                   547.29
  alcoholic beverages           663.13
  biochemistry                  572.49
  chemical engineering          660.284 49
  food technology               664.024
Fermented cider
  commercial processing         663.29
Fermented soybean paste
  commercial processing         664.58
Fermions                       539.721
Fermium                        546.449
Fermo (Italy : Province)      T2—456 74
  ancient                      T2—374 7
Fernández de Kirchner, Cristina
  Argentine history             982.073
Fernando de Noronha
  (Brazil)                     T2—813 4
Fernando Po (Equatorial
  Guinea)                      T2—671 86
Ferns                          587.3
  floriculture                  635.937 3
Ferrara (Italy)               T2—454 51
Ferrara (Italy : Province)    T2—454 5
  ancient                      T2—372 65
Ferrets (Black-footed)         599.766 29
  conservation technology       639.979 766 29
  resource economics            333.959 766 29

Ferrets (Domestic polecat)     636.976 628
  animal husbandry              636.976 628
  zoology                       599.766 28
Ferrimagnetism                 538.45
Ferroalloying metals           669.73
  economic geology              553.46
  metallography                 669.957 3
  metallurgy                    669.73
  metalworking                  673.73
  physical metallurgy           669.967 3
Ferroconcrete                  624.183 41
  *see also* Reinforced concrete
Ferroelectricity               537.244 8
Ferromagnetism                 538.44
Ferrotype process              772.14
Ferrous metals                 669.1
  architectural construction    721.044 71
  building construction         693.71
  building materials            691.7
  decorative arts               739.4
  materials science             620.17
  metallography                 669.951
  metallurgy                    669.1
  metalworking                  672
  physical metallurgy           669.961
  ship design                   623.818 21
  shipbuilding                  623.820 7
  structural engineering        624.182 1
  *see also* Chemicals; Metals
Ferry County (Wash.)          T2—797 25
Ferry transportation           386.6
  public administration         354.78
  transportation services       386.6
Ferry transportation workers   386.609 2
Ferryboats                     386.223 4
  design                        623.812 34
  engineering                   623.823 4
  transportation services       386.223 4
  *see also* Ships
Fertility
  demography                    304.632
Fertility drugs
  pharmacokinetics              615.766
Fertilization (Biology)        571.864
Fertilization in vitro
  ethics                        176.2
  *see also* Reproduction —
    ethics
  medicine                      618.178 059 9
Fertilizer spreaders           631.816
  manufacturing technology      681.763 1
Fertilizers                    631.8
  agricultural economics        338.162
  chemical engineering          668.62

Fertilizers (continued)
  pollution 363.738
  use 631.8
  water pollution engineering 628.168 41
Fès-Boulemane (Morocco) T2—643 4
Fescues 633.28
  botany 584.9
Festivals 394.26
      T1—074
  customs 394.26
  performing arts 791.6
  religion 203.6
    Christianity 263
    Judaism 296.43
Festuca 633.28
  botany 584.9
Festuceae 584.9
Fetal alcohol syndrome
  perinatal medicine 618.326 861
Fetal death
  medicine 618.392
Fetal disorders
  incidence 614.599 232
  medicine 618.32
Fetal erythroblastosis
  pediatrics 618.921 5
  perinatal medicine 618.326 1
  *see also* Cardiovascular
    diseases — humans
Fetal tissue
  experimental research
    medicine 616.027
Fetal tissue transplantation
  surgery 617.954
Fetal version
  obstetrics 618.82
Fetishism
  religion 202.1
  sexual practices 306.77
Fetus
  human physiology 612.647
  law 342.085
Feudal Age
  European history 940.14
  Japanese history 952.02
Feudal law 340.55
Feudal tenure 321.3
  land economics 333.322
  political science 321.3
Feudalism 321.3
  land economics 333.322
  political science 321.3
Feuds
  influence on crime 364.256

Fever
  result of injury
    medicine 617.22
  symptom 616.047
Fever blisters
  medicine 616.522
  *see also* Skin diseases —
    humans
Few-bodies problem 530.14
Fez-Boulemane (Morocco) T2—643 4
Fez-Jdid Dar-Dbibegh
  (Morocco) T2—643 4
Fez-Medina (Morocco) T2—643 4
Fianarantsoa (Madagascar :
  Province) T2—691
Fiat money 332.42
Fiber (Diet)
  health 613.263
Fiber bundles 514.224
Fiber crops 633.5
Fiber glass 666.157
  materials science 620.144
  sculpture material 731.2
  ship design 623.818 38
  ship hulls 623.845 8
  shipbuilding 623.820 7
  textiles 677.52
    arts 746.045 2
  *see also* Textiles
Fiber-glass-reinforced plastic 668.494 2
Fiber optic sensors
  manufacturing technology 681.25
Fiber optics 621.369 2
Fiber spaces 514.224
Fiberboards 676.183
Fiberglass 666.157
  *see also* Fiber glass
Fiberglass-reinforced plastic 668.494 2
Fibers (Histology)
  humans 611.018 2
Fibers (Materials)
  materials science 620.197
  textile materials 677.028 32
Fibonacci numbers 512.72
Fibrin
  human physiology 612.115
Fibrinolytic agents
  pharmacokinetics 615.718
Fibrinoplastin
  human physiology 612.115
Fibrocartilage
  human histology 612.751 7

Fibromyalgia
  medicine    616.742
    *see also* Musculoskeletal
      diseases — humans
Fibrous cartilage
  human histology    612.751 7
Fibrous tunics
  human physiology    612.841
Fibulas
  human anatomy    611.718
Ficksburg (South Africa :
  District)    T2—685 1
Fiction    808.83
  criticism    809.3
    theory    808.3
  folklore    398.2
  history    809.3
  rhetoric    808.3
  specific literatures    T3B—3
    individual authors    T3A—3
  *see Manual at* T3B—3
Fiction writers    809.3
  collected biography    809.3
    specific literatures    T3B—300 9
  individual biography    T3A—3
Fictions
  logic    165
Ficus    583.45
Ficus elastica    635.933 45
  *see also* Rubber plant (Ficus)
Fida-Derb Soltane
  (Morocco)    T2—643 8
Fiddle makers    787.219 092
Fiddlers    787.209 2
Fiddles    787.2
  instrument    787.219
  music    787.2
  *see also* Stringed instruments
Fidelity bonds
  insurance    368.83
Fiduciary accounting    657.47
Fiduciary trusts    346.059
  income tax law    343.052 64
  tax law    343.064
Field artillery    358.128 2
  engineering    623.412
  military equipment    358.128 2
Field artillery forces    358.12
Field athletics    796.43
Field crops    633
  feeds    636.086
  public administration    354.54
  *see Manual at* 633–635
Field-effect transistors    621.381 528 4

Field effects
  solid-state physics    530.416
Field extensions
  number theory    512.74
Field glasses
  manufacturing technology    681.412 5
Field handball    796.327
Field hockey    796.355
Field hockey players    796.355 092
Field houses    796.068
  architecture    725.827
Field mice (Apodemus)    599.358 5
Field mice (Microtus)    599.354
Field offices
  public administration    352.288
Field peas    633.369
  botany    583.74
  field crop    633.369
Field theory (Mathematics)    512.3
Field theory (Physics)    530.14
Field theory (Psychological
  system)    150.198 4
Field training (Armed forces)    355.544
Field trips    371.384
  education    371.384
  museum services    069.15
Field work
  descriptive research    001.433
        T1—072 3
Fieldball    796.327
Fielding
  baseball    796.357 24
  cricket    796.358 23
Fields (Mathematics)    512.3
  number theory    512.74
Fiesole (Italy)
  ancient    T2—375 1
Fife (Scotland)    T2—412 9
Fifes    788.33
  instrument    788.331 9
  music    788.33
  *see also* Woodwind instruments
Fifteenth century    909.4
        T1—090 24
Fifth Republic (France)    944.083
Fighter-bombers    358.428 3
  engineering    623.746 3
  military equipment    358.428 3
Fighter forces (Air warfare)    358.43
Fighters (Aircraft)    358.438 3
  engineering    623.746 4
  military equipment    358.438 3
Fighting
  animal behavior    591.566

| | |
|---|---|
| Fighting animals | |
|   animal husbandry | 636.088 8 |
| Figs | 641.343 7 |
|   botany | 583.45 |
|   commercial processing | 664.804 37 |
|   cooking | 641.643 7 |
|   food | 641.343 7 |
|   orchard crop | 634.37 |
| Figueiredo, João Baptista de | |
|   Oliveira | |
|     Brazilian history | 981.063 |
| Figueres, José María | |
|   Costa Rican history | 972.860 523 |
| Figuig (Morocco : Province) | T2—643 3 |
| Figure skating | 796.912 |
| Figured bass | 781.47 |
| Figured madras fabrics | 677.615 |
|   *see also* Textiles | |
| Figures of speech | |
|   literature | 808.801 |
|     history and criticism | 809.91 |
|   rhetoric | 808.032 |
| Figurines | 666.68 |
|   ceramic arts | 738.82 |
|   ceramic technology | 666.68 |
|     earthenware | 666.68 |
|     porcelain | 666.58 |
|   glyptics | 736.224 |
| Figworts | 583.95 |
| Fiji | 996.11 |
| | T2—961 1 |
| Fiji Sea | 551.461 477 |
| | T2—164 77 |
| Fijian language | 499.59 |
| | T6—995 9 |
| Fijian literature | 899.59 |
| Fijians | T5—995 9 |
| Filamentous fungi | 579.5 |
| Filarial diseases | |
|   incidence | 614.555 2 |
|   medicine | 616.965 2 |
|   *see also* Communicable | |
|     diseases — humans | |
| Filariasis | |
|   incidence | 614.555 2 |
|   medicine | 616.965 2 |
|   *see also* Communicable | |
|     diseases — humans | |
| Filberts | 641.345 4 |
|   agriculture | 634.54 |
|   botany | 583.48 |
|   cooking | 641.645 4 |
|   food | 641.345 4 |

| | |
|---|---|
| File access methods | |
|   computer science | 005.741 |
| File cabinets | 651.54 |
|   manufacturing technology | 684.16 |
|   use in records management | 651.54 |
| File clerks | |
|   office services | 651.374 3 |
| File compression | 005.746 |
| File formats | |
|   computer science | 005.72 |
| File management systems | |
|   computer science | |
|     data file programs | 005.74 |
|     systems programs | 005.436 |
| File managers | |
|   computer science | |
|     data file programs | 005.74 |
|     systems programs | 005.436 |
| File organization | |
|   computer science | |
|     data files | 005.741 |
|     systems programs | 005.436 |
| File processing | |
|   databases | 005.74 |
| File structure | |
|   computer science | |
|     data files | 005.741 |
| File system management | |
|   computer science | |
|     systems programs | 005.436 |
| Filefishes | 597.64 |
| Filers (Clerks) | 651.374 3 |
| Files (Data) | |
|   computer science | 005.74 |
| Files (Tools) | 621.924 |
| Filicales | 587.3 |
|   paleobotany | 561.73 |
| Filicopsida | 587.3 |
|   paleobotany | 561.73 |
| Filing | |
|   library operations | 025.317 7 |
|   records management | 651.53 |
| Filing rules | |
|   library science | 025.317 7 |
| Filipino language | 499.211 |
| | T6—992 11 |
| Filipino literature | 899.211 |
| Filipinos | T5—992 1 |
| Fillers | |
|   plastic technology | 668.411 |
| Filling stations | |
|   architecture | 725.38 |
|   automotive engineering | 629.286 |

Fillings
  dentistry    617.675
Fillmore, Millard
  United States history    973.64
Fillmore County (Minn.)    T2—776 16
Fillmore County (Neb.)    T2—782 342
Fills
  road engineering    625.733
Film adaptations    791.436
Film cinematography    777
Film genres    791.436
  *see Manual at* T3B—102–107,
    T3B—205, T3B—308 vs.
    T3C—1, T3C—3
Film music    781.542
Film reviews    791.437 5
Films (Photographic material)    771.532 4
  cinematography    777.38
    development    777.55
  development    771.43
  photography    771.532 4
    development    771.43
Films (Photographic records)    791.43
  bibliographies    011.372
  cataloging    025.347 3
  library treatment    025.177 3
Filmscripts    791.437
  *see also* Screenplays
Filmstrips    779
  bibliographies    011.37
  cataloging    025.347 3
  instructional use    371.335 22
  library treatment    025.177 3
Filoviridae    579.256
Filters
  air conditioning
    buildings    697.932 4
  cameras    771.356
  chemistry    542.6
  electronic circuits    621.381 532 4
  radio engineering    621.384 12
Filtration
  chemical engineering    660.284 245
  sewage treatment    628.352
  water supply treatment    628.164
Fin whale    599.524 6
Final cause    124
Finance    332
  agricultural industries    338.13
  churches    262.006 81
    local church    254.8
  communications industry    384.041
  ethics    174.4
    *see also* Ethical problems

Finance (continued)
  insurance    368.01
  library operations    025.11
  management    658.15
    *see also* Financial
      management
  mineral industries    338.23
  production economics    338.604 1
  public administration    354.8
  secondary industries    338.43
  transportation services    388.049
  *see Manual at* 332, 336 vs. 339;
    *also at* 332 vs. 338, 658.15
Finance departments (Public
  administration)    352.4
Financial accounting    657
Financial administration    658.15
  *see also* Financial management
Financial aid (Welfare)    361.05
  crime prevention    364.44
Financial assistance
  public administration    352.73
    foreign aid    353.132 73
Financial clerks
  office services    651.37
Financial control
  management    658.151
  public administration    352.43
Financial crime    364.168
  law    345.026 8
Financial decision making
  management    658.15
Financial economics    332
  *see also* Finance
Financial futures    332.632
Financial independence (Personal
  finance)    332.024 01
Financial institutions    332.1
  public administration    354.8
  *see also* Banks (Finance)
Financial management    658.15
                T1—068 1
  armed services    355.622
  public administration    352.4
  schools    371.206
    higher education    378.106
  *see Manual at* 332 vs. 338,
    658.15
Financial patronage    T1—079
  research    001.44
Financial planning
  management    658.15
  personal finance    332.024

| | | | |
|---|---|---|---|
| Financial power (Legislative bodies) | 328.341 2 | Fingerprints | |
| | | anthropometry | 599.945 |
| Financial reports | 657.3 | criminal investigation | 363.258 |
| management use | 658.151 2 | Fingerspelling | 419 |
| *see also* Financial statements | | primary education | 372.6 |
| Financial security | | representing spoken language | 418 |
| personal finance | 332.024 01 | specific languages | T4—891 |
| Financial statements | 657.3 | special education | 371.912 46 |
| accounting | 657.3 | Finish carpentry | |
| law | 346.063 | construction | 694.6 |
| corporate law | 346.066 48 | Finished lumber | 674.4 |
| management use | 658.151 2 | Finishing leather | 675.25 |
| public administration | 352.43 | Finishing machines | |
| preparation | 657.32 | textile technology | 677.028 55 |
| Financial success | 650.12 | Finishing metals | 671.7 |
| Financial support | T1—079 | Finishing paper | 676.234 |
| research | 001.44 | Finishing textiles | 677.028 25 |
| Financial support by governments | | Finishing woodwork | |
| libraries | 021.83 | buildings | 698.3 |
| Financiers | 332.092 | Finistère (France) | T2—441 1 |
| Finback whale | 599.524 6 | Finite (Philosophy) | 111.6 |
| Finches | 598.88 | Finite Abelian groups | 512.25 |
| animal husbandry | 636.686 2 | Finite differences | 515.62 |
| Fine art museums | 708 | Finite element analysis | 518.25 |
| architecture | 727.7 | engineering | 620.001 518 25 |
| Fine arts | 700 | Finite geometry | 516.11 |
| auction catalogs | 702.9 | Finite groups | 512.23 |
| exhibitions | | Finite mathematics | 511.1 |
| auction catalogs | 707.4 | *see Manual at* 004.0151 vs. | |
| investment economics | 332.63 | 511.1, 511.35 | |
| public administrative support | 353.77 | Finite strip method | 518.25 |
| *see also* Arts | | Finite volume method | 518.25 |
| Fine bookbinding | 686.302 | Finland | 948.97 |
| Fine particle technology | 620.43 | | T2—489 7 |
| Fines | 364.68 | Finland, Gulf of | 551.461 334 |
| penology | 364.68 | | T2—163 34 |
| personnel management | 658.314 4 | Finlay River (B.C.) | T2—711 87 |
| public revenues | 336.16 | Finney County (Kan.) | T2—781 44 |
| Finger foods | | Finnic languages | 494.54 |
| appetizers | 641.812 | | T6—945 4 |
| Finger Lakes (N.Y.) | T2—747 8 | Finnic literatures | 894.54 |
| Finger painting | 751.49 | Finnic peoples | T5—945 4 |
| Finger rings | 391.72 | Finnish Evangelical Lutheran | |
| customs | 391.72 | Church | 284.133 4 |
| making | 739.278 2 | *see also* Lutheran church | |
| costume jewelry | 688.2 | Finnish language | 494.541 |
| handicrafts | 745.594 2 | | T6—945 41 |
| fine jewelry | 739.278 2 | Finnish literature | 894.541 |
| Finger spelling | 419 | Finnish spitz | 636.72 |
| *see also* Fingerspelling | | Finnmark fylke (Norway) | T2—484 6 |
| Finger techniques | | Finno-Ugrians | T5—945 |
| music | 784.193 68 | Finno-Ugric languages | 494.5 |
| Fingering (Music) | 784.193 68 | | T6—945 |
| Fingerprint files | 363.24 | Finno-Ugric literatures | 894.5 |

Finns T5—945 41
Finol Linares, José
  Brazilian history 981.061
Fins
  aircraft 629.134 33
Finsler geometry 516.375
Fiordland National Park
  (N.Z.) T2—939 6
Fipa language 496.394
  T6—963 94
Fipa-Mambwe languages 496.394
  T6—963 94
Fiqh 340.59
  religious law 297.14
  secular law 340.59
Fire
  folklore 398.26
    history and criticism 398.364
  literature 808.803 6
    history and criticism 809.933 6
    specific literatures T3B—080 36
      history and
        criticism T3B—093 6
  religious worship 202.12
Fire-bellied toads 597.86
Fire clays 553.67
  ceramic technology 666.72
  economic geology 553.67
  materials science 620.143
Fire control (Artillery)
  military gunnery 623.558
Fire detectors 628.922 5
Fire ecology 577.24
Fire engines 628.925 9
  construction 629.225
  use 628.925 9
Fire escapes 628.922
Fire fighters 363.370 92
Fire fighting 628.925
  forestry 634.961 8
  on ships 623.888 6
  social services 363.378
  *see also* Fire safety
Fire fighting equipment
  airport engineering 629.136 8
  military airport engineering 623.668
  ships 623.865
Fire hazards 363.37
  technology 628.92
  *see also* Fire safety
Fire insurance 368.11
  allied lines 368.12

Fire prevention 363.377
  law 344.053 77
  management of enterprises 658.477
  technology 628.922
Fire prevention equipment
  aircraft 629.134 43
Fire-resistant clothing
  commercial technology 687.162
Fire-resistant paints 667.69
Fire retardants 628.922 3
Fire safety 363.37
  law 344.053 7
  mining technology 622.82
  public administration 353.979
  social services 363.37
  technology 628.922
Fire stations 363.37
  architecture 725.19
  construction 690.519
Fire thorns 635.933 73
  botany 583.73
  floriculture 635.933 73
Firearms 683.4
  art metalwork 739.74
  military engineering 623.4
  *see also* Guns (Small arms)
Fireclays 553.67
  ceramic technology 666.72
  economic geology 553.67
  materials science 620.143
Fireflies 595.764 4
Fireless cooking 641.588
Firemen 363.370 92
Firenze (Italy) T2—455 11
  ancient T2—375 11
Firenze (Italy : Province) T2—455 1
  ancient T2—375 1
Fireplaces
  architecture 721.8
  construction 697.1
  furniture arts 749.62
  home economics 644.1
Fireproofing 628.922 3
  buildings 693.82
  ship hulls 623.848
Fires 363.37
  crop damage 632.18
  *see also* Fire safety
Firewalls (Computer security) 005.8
Fireweeds (Asteraceae) 583.99
Fireweeds (Onagraceae) 583.76
Fireworks 662.1
Firing artillery 623.558

| | |
|---|---|
| Firing clays | |
| arts | 730.28 |
| pottery | 666.443 |
| arts | 738.143 |
| technology | 666.443 |
| sculpture | 731.47 |
| Firing glass | 666.126 |
| Firing metallurgical furnaces | 669.83 |
| Firing of employees | |
| economics | 331.259 6 |
| employment security | 331.259 6 |
| unemployment | 331.137 |
| law | 344.012 596 |
| personnel management | 658.313 |
| public administration | 352.69 |
| Firmware | |
| hardware | 004 |
| engineering | 621.395 |
| microprograms | 005.18 |
| Firmware development | 005.18 |
| Firs | 585.2 |
| forestry | 634.975 4 |
| lumber | 674.144 |
| First aid | 362.18 |
| health services | 362.18 |
| injuries | |
| medicine | 617.102 62 |
| medicine | 616.025 2 |
| First aid stations | 362.18 |
| armed forces | 355.72 |
| First-class mail | 383.122 |
| *see also* Postal service | |
| First Crusade, 1096–1099 | 956.014 |
| First editions | 094.4 |
| First Empire (France) | 944.05 |
| First International | 324.17 |
| First names | 929.44 |
| First Nations peoples | T5—97 |
| *see also* American native | |
| peoples | |
| First-order logic | 511.3 |
| mathematical logic | 511.3 |
| philosophical logic | 160 |
| First Republic (Austria) | 943.605 1 |
| First Republic (France) | 944.042 |
| First Republic (Spain) | 946.073 |
| Firth of Clyde (Scotland) | 551.461 337 |
| | T2—163 37 |
| Firth of Forth (Scotland) | 551.461 336 |
| | T2—163 36 |
| Fiscal policy | 336.3 |
| law | 343.034 |
| macroeconomics | 339.52 |
| public finance | 336.3 |

| | |
|---|---|
| Fiscal tariffs | 382.72 |
| *see also* Customs (Tariff) | |
| Fischer-Tropsch processes | 662.662 3 |
| Fish | 597 |
| Fish culture | 639.3 |
| economics | 338.371 3 |
| enterprises | 338.763 93 |
| Fish farmers | 639.309 2 |
| Fish farming | 639.3 |
| freshwater | 639.31 |
| Fish hatcheries | 639.311 |
| Fish lice | 595.36 |
| Fish-liver oils | |
| pharmacology | 615.34 |
| Fish oil | 665.2 |
| Fish ponds | 639.31 |
| ecology | 577.636 |
| Fisher (Mammal) | 599.766 5 |
| Fisher, Andrew | |
| Australian history | 994.041 |
| Fisher County (Tex.) | T2—764 732 |
| Fisheries | 338.372 7 |
| economics | 338.372 7 |
| enterprises | 338.763 92 |
| law | 343.076 92 |
| products | 338.372 7 |
| commerce | 381.437 |
| public administration | 354.57 |
| technology | 639.2 |
| Fishermen | 639.209 2 |
| commercial | 639.209 2 |
| sports | 799.109 2 |
| Fishery law | 343.076 92 |
| Fishery technology | 639.2 |
| Fishes | 597 |
| arts | T3C—362 7 |
| conservation technology | 639.977 |
| cooking | 641.692 |
| culture | 639.3 |
| drawing | 743.67 |
| food | 641.392 |
| commercial processing | 664.94 |
| paleozoology | 567 |
| production economics | 338.372 7 |
| public administration | 354.57 |
| resource economics | 333.956 |
| law | 346.046 956 |
| sports fishing | 799.1 |
| zoology | 597 |
| Fishes as pets | 639.3 |
| Fishing | |
| commercial technology | 639.2 |
| economics | 338.372 7 |
| enterprises | 338.763 92 |

Fishing (continued)
  game laws                              346.046 956 9
  industrial law                         343.076 92
  public administration                  354.57
  sports                                 799.1
    public administrative support        353.78
Fishing boats
  engineering                            623.828 2
Fishing equipment
  sports
    technology                           688.791
Fishing industries                       338.372 7
  *see also* Fisheries
Fishponds                                639.31
  ecology                                577.636
Fishways                                 639.977
Fishworms
  culture                                639.75
Fission (Nuclear)                        539.762
Fission reactors                         621.483
Fissionable materials
  economic geology                       553.493
  nuclear engineering                    621.483 35
Fissipedia                               599.7
  paleozoology                           569.7
Fitting
  clothing                               646.408
    commercial tailoring                 687.044
    home sewing                          646.408
Fitzroy River (Qld.)          T2—943 5
Five Confucian Classics                  299.512 82
Five dynasties (China)                   951.018
Five Nations languages
  (Iroquoian)                            497.554
                              T6—975 54
Five pillars of Islam                    297.31
Five scrolls (Bible)                     221.044
Fixation
  microscopy                             502.82
  biology                                570.282 7
Fixatives
  painting material
    arts                                 751.2
Fixed assets                             332.041 4
  accounting                             657.73
  financial management                   658.152 42
Fixed capital                            332.041 4
  accounting                             657.73
  financial management                   658.152 42
Fixed costs                              338.514 2
  financial management                   658.155 3
Fixed exchange rates                     332.456 4
Fixed liabilities
  accounting                             657.75

Fixed rate securities                    332.632 044
Fixing solutions
  photography                            771.54
Fjord-du-Saguenay
  (Quebec)                    T2—714 165
Fjords                                   551.461 8
Flacourtiaceae                           583.625
Flag officers                            355.009 2
  role and function                      355.331
Flag presentations                       355.15
Flag signals
  military engineering                   623.731 2
  nautical engineering                   623.856 12
Flagella                                 571.67
Flagellates                              579.82
Flageolets                               788.35
  *see also* Woodwind instruments
Flagler County (Fla.)         T2—759 19
Flags                                    929.92
  armed forces                           355.15
  law                                    344.09
Flagstaff (South Africa :
  District)                   T2—687 59
Flagstones                               553.53
  economic geology                       553.53
  quarrying                              622.353
  road engineering                       625.81
Flame                                    541.361
Flame emission spectroscopy              543.52
Flame-resistant fabrics                  677.689
  *see also* Textiles
Flame throwers                           623.445
Flamenco                                 781.626 104 68
  dance                                  793.319 468
  music                                  781.626 104 68
    dance                                784.188 2
    songs                                782.421 626 104 68
    poetry                               861.009 946 8
Flameproof fabrics                       677.689
  *see also* Textiles
Flamingos                                598.35
Flammability testing                     628.922 2
Flammable materials                      363.179 8
  fire safety technology                 628.922 2
  public safety                          363.179 8
  technology                             604.7
  *see also* Hazardous materials
Flanders                      T2—493 1
Flanders (Belgium)            T2—493 1
Flanders (France)             T2—442 8
Flannel                                  677.624
  *see also* Textiles
Flap-footed lizards                      597.952
Flaps (Aircraft)                         629.134 33

| | |
|---|---|
| Flare stars | 523.844 6 |
| Flares | |
| nautical equipment | 623.86 |
| Flash drives | 004.568 |
| engineering | 621.397 68 |
| Flash welding | 671.521 3 |
| Flashbulb photography | 778.72 |
| Flashcards | |
| cataloging | 025.349 6 |
| library treatment | 025.179 6 |
| Flat-backed lutes | 787.85 |
| *see also* Stringed instruments | |
| Flat-file databases | |
| computer science | 005.75 |
| Flat racing | |
| horses | 798.4 |
| Flatcars | 385.34 |
| engineering | 625.24 |
| *see also* Rolling stock | |
| Flatfishes | 597.69 |
| sports fishing | 799.176 9 |
| Flathead County (Mont.) | T2—786 82 |
| Flathead Lake (Mont.) | T2—786 832 |
| Flats | 643.27 |
| *see also* Apartment houses | |
| Flattery | |
| ethics | 177.3 |
| *see also* Ethical problems | |
| Flatware | 642.7 |
| *see also* Tableware | |
| Flatworms | 592.4 |
| Flavivirus infections | |
| humans | |
| incidence | 614.588 5 |
| Flavorings | 641.338 2 |
| agriculture | 633.82 |
| commercial processing | 664.5 |
| cooking with | 641.638 2 |
| economic botany | 581.632 |
| food | 641.338 2 |
| Flax | |
| botany | 583.79 |
| fiber crop | 633.52 |
| textiles | 677.11 |
| arts | 746.041 1 |
| *see also* Textiles | |
| Flaxseed oil | 665.352 |
| Flea beetles | 595.764 8 |
| agricultural pests | 632.764 8 |
| Flea-borne typhus | |
| incidence | 614.526 2 |
| medicine | 616.922 2 |
| *see also* Communicable diseases — humans | |

| | | |
|---|---|---|
| Flea markets | | 381.192 |
| management | | 658.87 |
| *see also* Commerce | | |
| Fleabanes | | 583.99 |
| Fleas | | 595.775 |
| disease carriers | | |
| medicine | | 614.432 4 |
| Fleets (Naval units) | | 359.31 |
| Fleming County (Ky.) | T2—769 56 | |
| Flemings | T5—393 2 | |
| Flemish | T5—393 2 | |
| Flemish Brabant (Belgium) | T2—493 31 | |
| Flemish dialect | | 439.31 |
| | T6—393 1 | |
| Flemish literature | | 839.31 |
| Flesh flies | | 595.774 |
| Fleshing leather | | 675.22 |
| Fleshy-finned fishes | | 597.39 |
| Flevoland (Netherlands) | T2—492 2 | |
| Flexibilia | | 563.92 |
| Flexible algebras | | 512.4 |
| Flexible exchange rates | | 332.456 4 |
| Flexible hours of labor | | 331.257 24 |
| Flexible manufacturing systems | | 670.427 |
| Flexible polymers | | |
| chemistry | | 547.843 |
| Flexible scheduling | | 371.242 |
| Flexible work hours | | 331.257 24 |
| personnel management | | 658.312 1 |
| Flexure | | |
| effect on materials | | 620.112 44 |
| Flickers (Woodpeckers) | | 598.72 |
| Fliers | | 629.130 92 |
| Flies | | 595.77 |
| agricultural pests | | 632.77 |
| disease carriers | | 571.986 |
| medicine | | 614.432 2 |
| Flies (Houseflies) | | 595.774 |
| control technology | | 628.965 7 |
| Flight (Aeronautics) | | 629.13 |
| arts | T3C—356 | |
| literature | | 808.803 56 |
| history and criticism | | 809.933 56 |
| specific literatures | T3B—080 356 | |
| history and criticism | T3B—093 56 | |
| Flight (Animals) | | 573.798 |
| behavior | | 591.57 |
| physiology | | 573.798 |
| Flight attendants | | 387.742 092 |
| Flight crews | | 387.740 44 |
| Flight from Mecca | | 297.634 |
| Flight guides | | |
| aeronautics | | 629.132 54 |

Flight instrumentation
  aircraft 629.135 2
Flight into Egypt 232.92
Flight navigators 629.132 510 92
Flight operations systems
  spacecraft 629.474 2
  unmanned spacecraft 629.464 2
Flight simulators
  aeronautics 629.132 520 78
  manned space flight 629.450 078
Flight tests
  aircraft 629.134 53
Flightless birds 598.16
Flights (Air force units) 358.413 1
Flights (Naval air units) 359.943 4
Flin Flon (Man.) T2—712 72
Flinders Chase National
  Park (S. Aust.) T2—942 35
Flinders Island (Tas.) T2—946 7
Flinders Ranges (S. Aust.) T2—942 37
Flint 553.65
Flint (Mich.) T2—774 37
Flint River (Ga.) T2—758 9
Flintshire (Wales) T2—429 33
Floater insurance 368.2
Floating 532.25
Floating airports
  engineering 629.136 1
Floating dry docks 623.83
Floating exchange rates 332.456 2
Floating foundations 624.156
Floats (Parades)
  performing arts 791.6
Flocculation
  water supply treatment 628.162 2
Flood barriers 627.42
Flood control 363.349 36
  engineering 627.4
  public administration 354.362 7
  social services 363.349 36
Flood control facilities
  area planning 711.8
Flood control ponds 627.44
Flood insurance 368.122 2
Flood wreckage studies 627.4
Flooding
  military engineering 623.31
Floodlighting 621.321 4
  exterior 621.322 9
Floodplains 551.442
  biology 578.766
  ecology 577.66
  geography 910.914 4

Floodplains (continued)
  geomorphology 551.442
  physical geography 910.021 44
Floods
  crop damage 632.17
  engineering control 627.4
  hydrology 551.489
  social services 363.349 3
Floor (Gymnastic equipment) 796.442
Floor coverings 645.1
  building construction 698.9
  household management 645.1
Floorball 796.356 2
Floors 721.6
  architecture 721.6
  bridge engineering 624.283
  construction 690.16
  housecleaning 648.5
  interior decoration 747.4
Floppy disks 004.563
  engineering 621.397 63
Floral arts 745.92
Floral oils 668.542
  customs 391.63
Floral waters 668.542
  customs 391.63
Florence (City-state) 945.5
Florence (Italy) T2—455 11
  ancient T2—375 11
Florence (Italy : Province) T2—455 1
  ancient T2—375 1
Florence (Republic) 945.506
Florence County (S.C.) T2—757 84
Florence County (Wis.) T2—775 32
Florentia (Italy) T2—375 11
Flores (Uruguay) T2—895 26
Flores Facussé, Carlos
  Honduran history 972.830 536
Flores Island (Indonesia) T2—598 68
Flores Pérez, Francisco
  Salvadoran history 972.840 542
Flores Sea (Indonesia) 551.461 474
   T2—164 74
Floriculture 635.9
Florida 975.9
   T2—759
Florida (Uruguay : Dept.) T2—895 25
Florida, Straits of 551.461 363
   T2—163 63
Florida Keys (Fla.) T2—759 41
Florida Panhandle T2—759 9
Florideophycideae 579.89
Flórina (Greece : Nome) T2—495 62

| | |
|---|---|
| Flotation | |
| ores | 622.752 |
| Flotillas (Naval units) | 359.31 |
| Flounders | 597.69 |
| cooking | 641.692 |
| food | 641.392 |
| sports fishing | 799.176 9 |
| Flour | 641.331 |
| commercial processing | 664.720 7 |
| wheat | 664.722 72 |
| cooking | 641.631 |
| food | 641.331 |
| Flour beetles | 595.769 |
| Flow | |
| air mechanics | 533.62 |
| engineering | 620.106 4 |
| fluid mechanics | 532.051 |
| gas mechanics | 533.21 |
| liquid mechanics | 532.51 |
| Flow meters | |
| manufacturing technology | 681.28 |
| Flow-of-funds accounts | |
| macroeconomics | 339.26 |
| Flowcharting | |
| computer programming | 005.120 28 |
| Flower arrangements | 745.92 |
| Flower beds | 635.962 |
| Flower flies | 595.774 |
| Flower gardening | 635.9 |
| Flower language | 302.222 |
| Flowering plants | 580 |
| landscape architecture | 716 |
| *see Manual at* 580 vs. 582.13; | |
| *also at* 583–584 | |
| Flowering trees | 635.977 13 |
| botany | 582.16 |
| ornamental arboriculture | 635.977 13 |
| Flowers | 582.13 |
| art representation | 704.943 43 |
| arts | 700.464 213 |
| | T3C—364 213 |
| cooking | 641.659 |
| descriptive botany | 582.13 |
| drawing | 743.73 |
| dress customs | 391.44 |
| floral arts | 745.92 |
| food | 641.359 |
| gardening | 635.9 |
| literature | 808.803 642 13 |
| history and criticism | 809.933 642 13 |
| specific literatures | T3B—080 364 213 |
| history and | |
| criticism | T3B—093 642 13 |
| painting | 758.42 |

| | |
|---|---|
| Flowers (continued) | |
| physiology | 575.6 |
| *see Manual at* 580 vs. 582.13; | |
| *also at* 635.9 vs. 582.1 | |
| Flowmeters | |
| manufacturing technology | 681.28 |
| Floyd County (Ga.) | T2—758 35 |
| Floyd County (Ind.) | T2—772 19 |
| Floyd County (Iowa) | T2—777 26 |
| Floyd County (Ky.) | T2—769 22 |
| Floyd County (Tex.) | T2—764 841 |
| Floyd County (Va.) | T2—755 712 |
| Fluctuations (Mathematics) | 519.85 |
| Flues | |
| heating | |
| buildings | 697.8 |
| Flugelhorns | 788.97 |
| instrument | 788.971 9 |
| music | 788.97 |
| *see also* Brass instruments | |
| Fluid balance | 571.75 |
| humans | 612.015 22 |
| Fluid balance disorders | 571.937 5 |
| medicine | 616.399 2 |
| *see also* Digestive system | |
| diseases — humans | |
| Fluid mechanics | 532 |
| engineering | 620.106 |
| Fluid metabolism | |
| biochemistry | |
| humans | 612.015 22 |
| Fluid phases | |
| fluid-state physics | 530.424 |
| Fluid-power technology | 620.106 |
| Fluid-state lasers | 621.366 2 |
| Fluid-state physics | 530.42 |
| Fluidics | 629.804 2 |
| Fluidization | |
| chemical engineering | 660.284 292 |
| Fluidized-bed combustion | 621.402 3 |
| Fluidized nuclear reactors | 621.483 4 |
| Fluids | |
| biochemistry | |
| humans | 612.015 22 |
| heat transfer | 536.25 |
| state of matter | 530.42 |
| Fluke-caused diseases | |
| incidence | 614.553 |
| medicine | 616.963 |
| *see also* Communicable | |
| diseases — humans | |
| Flukes (Worms) | 592.48 |
| Fluorescence | 535.352 |
| mineralogy | 549.125 |

| | |
|---|---|
| Fluorescence spectroscopy | 543.56 |
| Fluorescent lighting | 621.327 3 |
| Fluoridation | 614.599 6 |
| dental disease prevention | 614.599 6 |
| water supply engineering | 628.166 3 |
| Fluorine | 553.95 |
| chemical engineering | 661.073 1 |
| chemistry | 546.731 |
| economic geology | 553.95 |
| organic chemistry | 547.02 |
| applied | 661.891 |
| *see also* Chemicals | |
| Fluorite | |
| mineralogy | 549.4 |
| Fluoroscopy | |
| medicine | 616.075 72 |
| Fluorspar | |
| mineralogy | 549.4 |
| Flute concertos | 784.283 2 |
| Flute family | 788.3 |
| *see also* Woodwind instruments | |
| Flutes | 788.32 |
| instrument | 788.321 9 |
| music | 788.32 |
| *see also* Woodwind instruments | |
| Flutists | 788.320 92 |
| Flutter | |
| aeronautics | 629.132 362 |
| Fluvanna County (Va.) | T2—755 47 |
| Flux (Metallurgy) | 669.84 |
| Fly fishing | 799.124 |
| Fly River Province (Papua New Guinea) | T2—954 9 |
| Fly tying (Fishing) | |
| technology | 688.791 24 |
| Flycatchers (New World) | 598.823 |
| Flycatchers (Old World) | 598.848 |
| Flying (Aeronautics) | 629.132 5 |
| sports | 797.5 |
| *see also* Flight (Aeronautics) | |
| Flying (Animals) | |
| behavior | 591.57 |
| physiology | 573.798 |
| Flying discs (Game) | 796.2 |
| Flying fishes | 597.66 |
| Flying foxes | 599.49 |
| Flying jeeps | |
| engineering | 629.133 35 |
| military engineering | 623.746 047 |
| Flying lemurs | 599.33 |
| Flying lizards | 597.955 |
| Flying reptiles | 567.918 |
| Flying saucers | 001.942 |
| Flying squirrels | 599.369 |
| FM radio stations | 384.545 3 |
| *see also* Radio stations | |
| FM radio systems | 621.384 152 |
| Foam glass | 666.157 |
| Foam latex | 678.532 |
| Foamed plastics | 668.493 |
| Foams | 541.345 14 |
| chemical engineering | 660.294 514 |
| Foard County (Tex.) | T2—764 748 |
| Foccacia | 641.815 |
| Focusing apparatus | 771.37 |
| Foehns (Winds) | 551.518 5 |
| Fog | 541.345 15 |
| colloid chemistry | 541.345 15 |
| applied | 660.294 515 |
| meteorology | 551.575 |
| Fog signals | 387.155 |
| navigation aids | 623.894 |
| Foggia (Italy : Province) | T2—457 57 |
| ancient | T2—377 53 |
| Foils | |
| use in cooking | 641.589 |
| Foix (France : County) | T2—447 35 |
| Fokís (Greece) | T2—495 15 |
| Folding boxes | 676.32 |
| Folds (Geology) | 551.875 |
| Foliage plants | 635.975 |
| Foliations | 514.72 |
| Folk arts | 745 |
| Folk beliefs | |
| folklore | 398.41 |
| Folk dancers | 793.319 2 |
| Folk dancing | 793.31 |
| Folk drama | 808.82 |
| literature | |
| specific literatures | T3B—2 |
| Folk high schools | 374.83 |
| Folk literature | 398.2 |
| *see also* Literature | |
| *see Manual at* 398.2; *also at* 398.2 vs. 201.3, 230, 270, 292–299; *also at* 398.2 vs. 398.3–.4; *also at* 800 vs. 398.2 | |
| Folk medicine | 610 |
| folklore | 398.276 1 |
| history and criticism | 398.356 1 |
| Folk music | 781.62 |
| modes | 781.263 |
| songs | 782.421 62 |

Folk music (continued)
  South Africa      781.629 68
  *see Manual at* 781.62 vs.
    780.89; *also at* 781.62 vs.
    781.63–.66
Folk musicians      781.620 092
  singers      782.421 620 092
Folk poetry      808.81
  specific literatures      T3B—1
Folk remedies
  therapeutics      615.88
Folk rock      781.66
Folk singers      782.421 620 092
Folk songs      782.421 62
Folklore      398
  arts      700.455 9
     T3C—355 9
  history and criticism      398.09
Folklorists      398.092
Folksonomies      025.487
Folkways      306
  sociology      390
Follicles
  hair
    human anatomy      611.78
    medicine      616.546
Fon (African people)      T5—963 37
Fon language      496.337
     T6—963 37
Fond du Lac County (Wis.)      T2—775 68
Fondues      641.81
Food      641.3
  armed forces supplies      355.81
  arts      700.456 4
     T3C—356 4
  commercial processing
    economics      338.476 64
    technology      664
  cooking      641.5
  customs      394.12
  folklore      398.276 4
    history and criticism      398.356 4
  health      613.2
  home economics      641.3
  home preservation      641.4
  literature      808.803 564
    history and criticism      809.933 564
    specific literatures      T3B—080 356 4
      history and
        criticism      T3B—093 564
  nutritional content      613.2
    public administration      353.997

Food (continued)
  preservation techniques      664.028
    commercial      664.028
    home      641.4
  primary education      372.373
  product safety      363.192
    criminology      364.142
      criminal law      345.024 2
    law      344.042 32
    public administration      353.997
  social welfare      361.05
    public administration      353.56
  *see Manual at* 363.8 vs. 613.2,
    641.3; *also at* 630 vs.
    579–590, 641.3
Food addiction      362.27
  medicine      616.852 6
  social welfare      362.27
Food additives      641.308
  commercial technology      664.06
    preservation      664.028 7
  home economics      641.308
  human toxicology      615.954
  law      344.042 32
  *see also* Food — product safety
Food adulteration      363.192
  criminology      364.142
    criminal law      345.024 2
  *see also* Food — product safety
Food allergies
  cooking for      641.563 18
  incidence      614.599 35
  medicine      616.975
Food and drink      641
  gastronomy      641.013
Food biotechnology      664.024
Food board      676.288
Food cartons      676.34
Food chains (Ecology)      577.16
Food colors
  commercial      664.062
Food demand
  economics      338.19
Food-drug interactions      615.704 52
Food guides      641.31
Food habits (Animals)      591.53
Food industry (Production)      338.19
  law      343.076
Food inspection      363.192 64
  *see also* Food — product safety
Food microbiology      664.001 579

Food plants                                        641.303
  agriculture                            630
  economic botany                        581.632
  food                                    641.303
Food poisons
  human toxicology                       615.954
Food processing industry                           338.476 64
Food processors
  use in cooking                         641.589 2
Food production                                    338.19
Food rationing                                     363.856
Food relief                                        363.883
  law                                    344.033
Food reserves
  economics                              338.19
Food safety                                        363.192
  *see also* Food — product safety
Food services
  sanitation services                    363.729 6
  schools                                371.716
Food services industry                             338.476 479 5
Food stamp programs                                363.882
Food stocks                                        363.8
  economics                              338.19
  *see also* Food supply
Food storage
  home economics                         641.48
Food storage (Plant physiology)                    575.78
Food supply                                        363.8
  economics                              338.19
  social welfare                         363.8
    law                         344.033
  spacecraft                             629.477 3
  *see Manual at* 363.5, 363.6,
    363.8 vs. 338; *also at* 363.8
    vs. 613.2, 641.3
Food taboos
  customs                                394.16
  religion                               204.46
    Hinduism                    294.544 6
    Islam                       297.576
    Judaism                     296.73
Food technologists                                 664.009 2
Food technology                                    664
  equipment manufacturing
    technology                  681.766 4
Food trade                                         381.456 413
Food webs (Ecology)                                577.16
Foodstuffs                                         641.3
  *see also* Food
Foot forces (Military)                             356
Foot warfare                                       356
Foot washing
  Christian rite                         265.9

Football                                           796.33
  electronic games                       794.863 3
  equipment technology                   688.763 3
Football cards                                     796.332 075
Football players                                   796.330 92
  American football                      796.332 092
  Australian football                    796.336 092
  Canadian football                      796.335 092
  rugby                                  796.333 092
  soccer                                 796.334 092
Football rattles                                   786.886
  *see also* Percussion instruments
Footings
  walls                                  721.2
    construction               690.12
Footpaths                                          388.12
  *see also* Pedestrian paths
Footwear                                           391.413
  commercial technology                  685.3
  customs                                391.413
  *see also* Clothing
For-hire carriers                                  388.041
  truck                                  388.324 3
  *see also* Freight services;
    Passenger services
Forage crops                                       633.2
  feeds                                  636.086
  *see Manual at* 583–585 vs. 600
Forage grasses                                     633.2
  agriculture                            633.2
  botany                                 584.9
Forage legumes                                     633.3
  botany                                 583.74
  feeds                                  636.086
Foraminifera                                       579.44
  paleontology                           561.994
Forbes (N.S.W.)                          T2—944 5
Forbs                                              582.12
Force (Energy)
  philosophy                             118
Force (International politics)                     327.117
Force and energy                                   531.6
Forced labor
  Holocaust, 1933–1945                   940.531 813 4
  World War II                           940.540 5
Forced loans                                       336.344
Forces (Mechanics)                                 531.113
Forcing (Plants)                                   631.583
  floriculture                           635.982
  gardening                              635.048 3
Forcipulata                                        593.93
  paleozoology                           563.93
Ford, Gerald R.
  United States history                  973.925

| | |
|---|---|
| Ford County (Ill.) | T2—773 62 |
| Ford County (Kan.) | T2—781 76 |
| Forde, Francis Michael | |
| Australian history | 994.042 |
| Forearm techniques | |
| music | 784.193 62 |
| Forebrain | |
| human physiology | 612.825 |
| medicine | 616.8 |
| Forecasting | 003.2 |
| | T1—011 2 |
| business | 338.544 |
| investments | 332.678 |
| management decision making | 658.403 55 |
| marketing management | 658.818 |
| occultism | 133.3 |
| social change | 303.49 |
| weather | 551.63 |
| Forecasting methods | |
| economics | 338.544 2 |
| Forecasts | 003.2 |
| | T1—011 2 |
| business | 338.544 3 |
| social change | 303.49 |
| Foreclosure | 346.043 64 |
| Forehand | |
| tennis | 796.342 22 |
| Foreign affairs | 327 |
| Foreign affairs departments | 353.13 |
| Foreign aid | 338.91 |
| economics | 338.91 |
| law | 343.074 8 |
| international relations | 327.111 |
| law | 342.041 2 |
| military science | 355.032 |
| public administration | 353.132 73 |
| social welfare | 361.26 |
| governmental | 361.6 |
| private | 361.77 |
| Foreign assistance | 338.91 |
| Foreign direct investment | 332.673 |
| Foreign economic assistance | 338.91 |
| Foreign economic policies | 337 |
| Foreign economic relations | 337 |
| Foreign enterprises | 338.88 |
| Foreign exchange | 332.45 |
| law | 343.032 5 |
| Foreign income | |
| tax economics | 336.24 |
| tax law | 343.052 48 |
| Foreign intelligence | 327.12 |
| *see also* Espionage | |

| | |
|---|---|
| Foreign investment | 332.673 |
| government policy | 332.673 2 |
| law | 346.092 |
| Foreign labor | 331.62 |
| law | 344.016 2 |
| Foreign language groups | |
| journalism for | 070.484 |
| Foreign languages | |
| primary education | 372.65 |
| Foreign legions | 355.359 |
| Foreign licensing | |
| management | 658.18 |
| Foreign loans | 336.343 5 |
| law | 346.073 |
| public finance | 336.343 5 |
| role of banks | 332.15 |
| Foreign merchants | 382.092 |
| Foreign missions | |
| Christianity | 266.023 |
| Foreign news | |
| journalism | 070.433 2 |
| Foreign-owned enterprises | 338.88 |
| *see also* International | |
| enterprises | |
| Foreign policy | 327.1 |
| Foreign relations | 327 |
| law | 342.041 2 |
| public administration | 353.13 |
| *see also* International relations | |
| Foreign service (Diplomatic | |
| service) | |
| public administration | 353.132 63 |
| Foreign shorthair cats | 636.82 |
| Foreign students | 371.826 91 |
| Foreign study | 370.116 |
| Foreign trade | 382 |
| commerce | 382 |
| law | 343.087 |
| marketing management | 658.84 |
| public administration | 354.74 |
| Foreign traders | 382.092 |
| Foreign words | 412 |
| specific languages | T4—24 |
| Foreigners | 305.906 91 |
| | T1—086 91 |
| social welfare | 362.899 1 |
| women | |
| social welfare | 362.839 81 |
| young people | |
| social welfare | 362.779 1 |
| Forenames | 929.44 |
| Forensic chemistry | |
| forensic medicine | 614.12 |
| Forensic dentistry | 614.18 |

| | |
|---|---|
| Forensic medicine | 614.1 |
| Forensic nursing | 614.1 |
| Forensic orations | 347.075 |
| Forensic osteology | |
|   forensic medicine | 614.17 |
| Forensic pathology | 614.1 |
| Forensic psychiatry | 614.15 |
| Forensic psychology | 347.066 019 |
|   criminal law | 345.066 019 |
|   forensic medicine | 614.15 |
| Forensic science | 363.25 |
|   *see also* Criminal investigation | |
| Forensic toxicology | 614.13 |
| Foreordination (Christian | |
|   doctrine) | 234.9 |
| Forest biology | 578.73 |
| Forest County (Pa.) | T2—748 68 |
| Forest County (Wis.) | T2—775 31 |
| Forest ecology | 577.3 |
| Forest fires | 363.379 |
|   forestry | 634.961 8 |
|   social services | 363.379 |
|   *see also* Fire safety | |
| Forest Heath (England) | T2—426 43 |
| Forest lands | 333.75 |
| | T2—152 |
|   biology | 578.73 |
|   ecology | 577.3 |
|   economics | 333.75 |
|     sale and rental | 333.335 7 |
|   geography | 910.915 2 |
|   landscape architecture | 719.33 |
|   law | 346.046 75 |
|   physical geography | 910.021 52 |
|   recreational resources | 333.784 |
| Forest management | 634.92 |
| Forest nurseries | 634.956 4 |
| Forest of Bowland | |
|   (England) | T2—427 685 |
| Forest of Dean (England) | T2—424 13 |
| Forest products | 634.98 |
|   agricultural economics | 338.174 98 |
| Forest reserves | 333.751 1 |
|   *see also* Forest lands | |
| Forest saltwater wetlands | |
|   biology | 578.769 7 |
|   ecology | 577.697 |
| Forest thinning | 634.953 |
| Forest wetlands | |
|   biology | 578.768 3 |
|   ecology | 577.683 |
| Forestation | 333.751 52 |
| Foresters | 634.909 2 |
| Forestry | 634.9 |
|   public administration | 354.55 |
| Forestry law | 346.046 75 |
|   industry | 343.076 49 |
|   protection | 346.046 75 |
| Forests | 333.75 |
| | T2—152 |
|   *see also* Forest lands | |
| Forfeit games | 793.5 |
| Forge welding | 671.529 |
| Forgeries | |
|   arts | 702.874 |
|   books | 098.3 |
|   financial instruments | 332.9 |
|   museology | 069.54 |
|   paintings | 751.58 |
| Forgery | 364.163 5 |
|   law | 345.026 35 |
| Forget-me-nots | 635.933 94 |
|   botany | 583.94 |
|   floriculture | 635.933 94 |
| Forgetting | 153.125 |
| Forging | 671.332 |
|   blacksmithing | 682 |
|   decorative arts | 739.14 |
|   sculpture | 731.41 |
| Forgiveness | |
|   psychology | 155.92 |
|     applied psychology | 158.2 |
|   religious doctrine | 202.2 |
|     Christianity | 234.5 |
| Forillon National Park | |
|   (Quebec) | T2—714 793 |
| Fork lifts | 621.863 |
| Forlì (Italy : Province) | T2—454 8 |
|   ancient | T2—372 68 |
| Forlì-Cesena (Italy : | |
|   Province) | T2—454 8 |
|   ancient | T2—372 68 |
| Form (Concept) | |
|   arts | 701.8 |
|     drawing | 741.018 |
|   philosophy | 117 |
| Form books | |
|   law | 347.055 |
| Form criticism | |
|   sacred books | 208.2 |
|     Bible | 220.663 |
|     Talmud | 296.120 663 |
| Form letters | |
|   office use | 651.752 |
| Form of juristic acts | 346.021 |

| | |
|---|---|
| Form perception | |
| visual | |
| psychology | 152.142 3 |
| Formal analysis | |
| music | 781.8 |
| Formal dress | 391.486 |
| commercial technology | 687.16 |
| customs | 391.486 |
| home sewing | 646.476 |
| *see also* Clothing | |
| Formal grammars | 511.3 |
| programming languages | 005.131 |
| Formal groups | 512.2 |
| Formal languages | 511.3 |
| programming languages | 005.131 |
| Formal logic | 511.3 |
| mathematical logic | 511.3 |
| philosophical logic | 160 |
| Formal usage (Language) | 418 |
| specific languages | T4—8 |
| Formaldehyde | |
| human toxicology | 615.951 36 |
| Format publishing | 686 |
| Formations | |
| sports | |
| American football | 796.332 22 |
| soccer | 796.334 22 |
| Formentera (Spain) | T2—467 56 |
| Former Yugoslav Republic of | 949.76 |
| Macedonia | T2—497 6 |
| Formicariidae | 598.822 6 |
| Formicidae | 595.796 |
| Formosa | 951.249 |
| | T2—512 49 |
| Formosa (Argentina : | |
| Province) | T2—823 5 |
| Formosa Strait | 551.461 457 |
| | T2—164 57 |
| Formosan native peoples | T5—992 5 |
| Forms (Documents) | |
| law | 347.055 |
| public administration | 352.387 |
| Forms (Mathematics) | 512.944 |
| Forms of address | |
| etiquette | 395.4 |
| Forms of music | 781.8 |
| instrumental | 784.18 |
| vocal | 782 |
| Formula feeds | 636.085 57 |
| commercial processing | 664.768 |
| Formula plans | |
| investments | 332.678 |
| Formularies | |
| pharmacology | 615.13 |

| | |
|---|---|
| Formulas | T1—021 2 |
| Forrest County (Miss.) | T2—762 18 |
| Forster (N.S.W.) | T2—944 2 |
| Forsyth County (Ga.) | T2—758 265 |
| Forsyth County (N.C.) | T2—756 67 |
| Forsythias | 635.933 87 |
| botany | 583.87 |
| floriculture | 635.933 87 |
| Fort Beaufort (South | |
| Africa : District) | T2—687 53 |
| Fort Bend County (Tex.) | T2—764 135 |
| Fort Franklin (N.W.T.) | T2—719 3 |
| Fort Gibson Lake (Okla.) | T2—766 87 |
| Fort Gibson Reservoir | |
| (Okla.) | T2—766 87 |
| Fort Lauderdale (Fla.) | T2—759 35 |
| Fort Loudon Lake (Tenn.) | T2—768 85 |
| Fort Macleod (Alta.) | T2—712 34 |
| Fort McMurray (Alta.) | T2—712 32 |
| Fort Nelson (B.C.) | T2—711 87 |
| Fort Nelson-Liard (B.C.) | T2—711 87 |
| Fort Nelson River (B.C.) | T2—711 87 |
| Fort Norman (N.W.T.) | T2—719 3 |
| Fort Peck Lake (Mont.) | T2—786 17 |
| Fort Qu'Appelle (Sask.) | T2—712 44 |
| Fort Simpson (N.W.T.) | T2—719 3 |
| Fort Smith (N.W.T.) | T2—719 3 |
| Fort Smith (N.W.T. : | |
| Region) | T2—719 3 |
| Fort St. John (B.C.) | T2—711 87 |
| Fort Wayne (Ind.) | T2—772 74 |
| Fort William (Scotland) | T2—411 56 |
| Fort Worth (Tex.) | T2—764 531 5 |
| Forth, Firth of (Scotland) | 551.461 336 |
| | T2—163 36 |
| Forth, River (Scotland) | T2—413 1 |
| Fortification | |
| military engineering | 623.1 |
| Fortifications | |
| basic training | 355.544 |
| Fortified wine | 641.222 6 |
| commercial processing | 663.226 |
| Fortress of Louisbourg | |
| National Historic Site | |
| (N.S.) | T2—716 955 |
| Fortresses | |
| architecture | 725.18 |
| military engineering | 623.1 |
| Forts | |
| architecture | 725.18 |
| military engineering | 623.1 |
| military installations | 355.7 |
| Fortune-tellers | 133.309 2 |
| Fortune-telling | 133.3 |

Forty Hours devotion
  Roman Catholic liturgy    264.027 4
Forums (Discussion and debate)
  rhetoric    808.53
Forward exchange    332.45
Forward Italy (Political party)    324.245 04
Forward play
  sports
    rugby    796.333 23
    soccer    796.334 23
Forza italia (Political party)    324.245 04
Fossa    599.742
Fossil animals    560
Fossil footprints    560.43
  vertebrates    566
Fossil fuels    553.2
  chemistry    547.82
  economic geology    553.2
  electric generation    621.312 132
  public administration    354.44
  resource economics    333.82
Fossil gums    553.29
  mining    622.339
Fossil resins    553.29
  mining    622.339
Fossilization    560.41
Fossils    560
Foster children    306.874
     T1—085 4
  family relationships    306.874
  home care    649.145
  psychology    155.445
  social welfare    362.733
Foster County (N.D.)    T2—784 516
Foster homes    362.733
  crime prevention    364.44
  social welfare    362.733
Foster parents    306.874
     T1—085
  family relationships    306.874
  social welfare    362.733
Fotonovelas    741.5
  genres
    history, criticism, techniques   741.53
  geographic treatment    741.593–.599
    *see Manual at* 741.593–.599
      and 741.5693–.5699
  techniques    741.51
  *see Manual at* 741.5; *also at*
    741.56
Foucault's pendulum    525.36
Found objects
  handicrafts    745.584
  sculpture material    731.2

Foundation engineering    624.15
Foundation soils    624.151
  railroad engineering    625.122
  road engineering    625.732
Foundations (Organizations)    060
  social welfare    361.763 2
    *see also* Charitable trusts
Foundations (Structures)    721.1
  architecture    721.1
  bridge engineering    624.284
  construction    690.11
  structural engineering    624.15
Founders of religions    206.3
Founding (Metalworking)    671.2
Fountain County (Ind.)    T2—772 47
Fountains    731.724
  architecture    725.9
  handicrafts    745.594 6
  landscape architecture    714
  sculpture    731.724
Fouquieriaceae    583.628
Four-color theorem    511.56
Four Corners Region    T2—792 59
Four-day week    331.257 22
Four-horned antelopes    599.642
Four-o'clock (Plant)    635.933 53
  botany    583.53
  floriculture    635.933 53
Four-year colleges    378.154 2
Fourier analysis    515.243 3
Fourier series    515.243 3
Fourier transform    515.723
Fourierism (Socialist school)
  economics    335.23
Fouriesburg (South Africa :
  District)    T2—685 1
Fourteenth century    909.3
     T1—090 23
Fourth-class mail    383.125
  *see also* Postal service
Fourth Crusade, 1202–1204    949.503
Fourth dimension    530.11
Fourth International    324.175
Fourth of July    394.263 4
Fourth Republic (France)    944.082
Fowling    799.24
Fowls    636.5
Fox hunting
  sports    799.259 775
Fox Indians    T5—973 14
Fox language    497.314
     T6—973 14
Fox Quesada, Vicente
  Mexican history    972.084 1

| | |
|---|---|
| Fox River (Wis.) | T2—775 6 |
| Fox squirrel | 599.362 |
| Fox trot | 793.33 |
| Foxes | 599.775 |
|   conservation technology | 639.979 775 |
|   resource economics | 333.959 775 |
|   small game hunting | 799.259 775 |
|   trapping | 639.117 75 |
| Foxgloves | 635.933 95 |
|   botany | 583.95 |
|   floriculture | 635.933 95 |
| FPÖ (Austrian political party) | 324.243 603 |
| FPS (Swiss political party) | 324.249 403 |
| Fractals | |
|   mathematics | 514.742 |
| Fractional calculus | 515.83 |
| Fractional distillation | |
|   chemical engineering | 660.284 25 |
|   petroleum | 665.532 |
| Fractionation | |
|   air | |
|     gas technology | 665.82 |
|   oils and gases | 665.028 3 |
| Fractions | 513.26 |
| Fracture | |
|   crystals | 548.842 |
|   mineralogy | 549.121 |
| Fracture mechanics | 620.112 6 |
| Fracture strength | |
|   materials science | 620.112 6 |
| Fractures | |
|   medicine | 617.15 |
| Fragile X syndrome | |
|   medicine | 616.858 841 |
|   pediatrics | 618.928 588 41 |
| Fragmented landscapes | 333.95 |
|   ecology | 577.27 |
| Fragrance plants | |
|   floriculture | 635.968 |
| Frame harps | 787.95 |
|   *see also* Stringed instruments | |
| Frame-shaped drums | 786.95 |
|   *see also* Percussion instruments | |
| Frame zithers | 787.73 |
|   *see also* Stringed instruments | |
| Framed soaps | 668.124 |
| Frames | |
|   naval architecture | 623.817 73 |
|   optical instruments | |
|     manufacturing technology | 681.43 |
|   structural engineering | 624.177 3 |
|   wood construction | 694.2 |

| | |
|---|---|
| France | 944 |
| | T2—44 |
|   ancient | 936.4 |
| | T2—364 |
| France. Assemblée nationale | |
|   constituante (1789–1791) | |
|   French history | 944.041 |
| France. Assemblée nationale | |
|   législative (1791–1792) | |
|   French history | 944.041 |
| France. Convention nationale | |
|   French history | 944.043 |
| France. Estates-General | |
|   French history | 944.041 |
| France. Etats généraux | |
|   French history | 944.041 |
| France. Legislative Assembly | |
|   (1791–1792) | |
|   French history | 944.041 |
| France. National Assembly | |
|   (1789–1791) | |
|   French history | 944.041 |
| France. National Convention | |
|   French history | 944.043 |
| France, Southern | T2—448 |
| Franche-Comté (France) | T2—444 5 |
| Franches-Montagnes | |
|   (Switzerland) | T2—494 368 |
| Francheville (Quebec) | T2—714 451 |
| Franchises | |
|   governmental | |
|     public revenue | 336.16 |
|   law | 346.048 |
|   retail | 381.13 |
|     management | 658.870 8 |
|   *see also* Commerce | |
| Francis I, Holy Roman Emperor | |
|   German history | 943.055 |
| Francis I, King of France | |
|   French history | 944.028 |
| Francis II, King of France | |
|   French history | 944.029 |
| Francis Case, Lake (S.D.) | T2—783 38 |
| Franciscans | 255.3 |
|   church history | 271.3 |
|   women | 255.973 |
|     church history | 271.973 |
| Francisco Morazán | |
|   (Honduras) | T2—728 371 |
| Francium | 669.725 |
|   chemistry | 546.386 |
|   metallurgy | 669.725 |
|   *see also* Chemicals | |

Franco, Francisco
  Spanish history      946.082
Franco, Itamar
  Brazilian history      981.064
Franco-German War, 1870–1871   943.082
Franco-Provençal language      449
                 T6—49
Franco-Provençal literature      849
Franco-Prussian War, 1870–1871   943.082
Francolins      598.623
Franconia (Germany)      T2—433
Franconian dialect      437.943 3
                 T6—32
Franconian emperors
  German history      943.023
Franconian Jura (Germany)      T2—433
Frankfort (Ky.)      T2—769 432
Frankfort (South Africa :
  District)      T2—685 1
Frankfurt am Main
  (Germany)      T2—434 164
Frankfurt an der Oder
  (Germany)      T2—431 532
Frankfurt an der Oder
  (Germany : Bezirk)      T2—431 53
Frankia      579.37
Franking privileges      383.120 2
  *see also* Postal service
Franklin (Nunavut and
  N.W.T.)      T2—719 52
Franklin (State)      976.803
                 T2—768
Franklin (Va.)      T2—755 553
Franklin County (Ala.)      T2—761 913
Franklin County (Ark.)      T2—767 34
Franklin County (Fla.)      T2—759 91
Franklin County (Ga.)      T2—758 135
Franklin County (Idaho)      T2—796 42
Franklin County (Ill.)      T2—773 94
Franklin County (Ind.)      T2—772 15
Franklin County (Iowa)      T2—777 28
Franklin County (Kan.)      T2—781 66
Franklin County (Ky.)      T2—769 432
Franklin County (Mass.)      T2—744 22
Franklin County (Me.)      T2—741 72
Franklin County (Miss.)      T2—762 27
Franklin County (Mo.)      T2—778 63
Franklin County (N.C.)      T2—756 54
Franklin County (N.Y.)      T2—747 55
Franklin County (Neb.)      T2—782 377
Franklin County (Ohio)      T2—771 56
Franklin County (Pa.)      T2—748 44
Franklin County (Tenn.)      T2—768 63
Franklin County (Tex.)      T2—764 213

Franklin County (Va.)      T2—755 68
Franklin County (Vt.)      T2—743 13
Franklin County (Wash.)      T2—797 33
Franklin D. Roosevelt Lake
  (Wash.)      T2—797 23
Franklin District (N.Z.)      T2—933 1
  Auckland Region      T2—932 7
  Waikato Region      T2—933 1
Franklin Parish (La.)      T2—763 77
Franz Josef Land (Russia)      T2—985
Fraser, Malcolm
  Australian history      994.063
Fraser Canyon (B.C.)      T2—711 37
Fraser-Cheam (B.C.)      T2—711 37
Fraser-Fort George (B.C.)      T2—711 82
Fraser Island (Qld.)      T2—943 2
Fraser Plateau (B.C.)      T2—711 75
Fraser River (B.C.)      T2—711 3
Fraser Valley (B.C.)      T2—711 37
Fraserburg (South Africa :
  District)      T2—687 17
Fraternal benefit societies      334.7
  economics      334.7
  insurance      368.3
    *see also* Insurance
Fraternal insurance      368.363
Fraternal organizations      369
Fraternities
  education      371.855
Fraud      364.163
  criminology      364.163
  law      345.026 3
  occultism      130
  prevention
    management      658.473
Fraudulent claims      364.163
  criminology      364.163
  insurance      368.014
  law      345.026 3
Fraudulent elections      324.66
  criminology      364.132 4
    criminal law      345.023 24
Frauenfeld (Switzerland)      T2—494 591 8
Frauenfeld (Switzerland :
  Bezirk)      T2—494 591
Frazil ice      551.344
Freaks (Circuses)      791.35
Fréchet algebras      512.55
Frederick, the Great
  German history      943.053
Frederick I, Holy Roman
  Emperor
  German history      943.024

Frederick II, Holy Roman
  Emperor
  German history             943.025
Frederick II, King of Prussia
  German history             943.053
Frederick III, Emperor of
  Germany
  German history             943.028
Frederick III, German Emperor
  German history             943.084
Frederick Barbarossa, Holy
  Roman Emperor
  German history             943.024
Frederick County (Md.)     T2—752 87
Frederick County (Va.)     T2—755 992
Fredericksburg (Va.)       T2—755 366
Fredericton (N.B.)         T2—715 515
Frederiksberg (Denmark)   T2—489 13
Frederiksborg (Denmark)   T2—489 1
Fredholm equations          515.45
Fredrik I, King of Sweden
  Swedish history         948.503 62
Free aerophones           788.29
  *see also* Wind instruments
Free algebras             512.4
Free assistance (Social welfare)   361.02
  *see also* Welfare services
Free balloons
  engineering           629.133 22
  military engineering     623.742
Free choice of employment     331.013
Free Church of Scotland      285.234
Free churches            280.4
  *see also* Protestantism
Free Democratic Party
  (Germany)            324.243 06
Free enterprise          330.122
  economics           330.122
  sociology            306.342
Free labor              331.117 2
Free land              333.16
Free mail              383.120 2
  *see also* Postal service
Free market price determination   338.522
Free materials
  bibliographies         011.03
Free Methodist Church of North
  America             287.2
  *see also* Methodist Church
Free-piston engines       621.433 5
Free ports             387.13
  *see also* Ports
Free press and fair trial     347.05

Free products
  catalogs            T1—029
Free radicals (Chemicals)     541.224
Free reeds             788.8
  *see also* Woodwind instruments
Free schools (Alternative
  schools)            371.04
Free services
  catalogs            T1—029
Free Soil Party (U.S.)       324.273 2
Free State (South Africa)     968.5
                       T2—685
Free television           384.554
Free thought            211.4
Free time
  sociology            306.481 2
Free trade             382.71
  *see also* Customs (Tariff)
Free universities (Alternative
  higher education)      378.03
  *see also* Higher education
Free will
  philosophy           123.5
  religion             202.2
    Christianity         233.7
      soteriology       234.9
    Islam            297.227
    Judaism          296.32
Freeborn County (Minn.)   T2—776 18
Freedmen's Bureau
  United States history     973.714
Freedom
  philosophy           123.5
Freedom of action        323.44
Freedom of association     323.47
Freedom of conscience     323.442
Freedom of contract       323.46
Freedom of expression     323.44
  law              342.085
  *see also* Civil rights
Freedom of information     323.445
  law              342.085 3
Freedom of publication     323.445
  law              342.085 3
Freedom of religion       323.442
  *see also* Religious freedom
Freedom of speech        323.443
  law              342.085 3
Freedom of the press      323.445
  law              342.085 3
Freedom Party of Austria    324.243 603
Freedom Party of Switzerland   324.249 403
Freemasonry           366.1

Freemasons 366.1
  biography 366.109 2
Freesias 635.934 38
  botany 584.38
  floriculture 635.934 38
Freestone County (Tex.) T2—764 232
Freestyle skiing 796.937
Freestyle snowboarding 796.939
Freestyle wrestling 796.812 3
Freetown (Sierra Leone) T2—664
Freeways 388.122
  *see also* Roads
Freewill Baptists 286.2
  *see also* Baptists
Freeze-dried foods
  cooking 641.614
Freeze-drying foods 664.028 45
  commercial preservation 664.028 45
  home preservation 641.44
Freezers 621.57
  kitchen appliances 641.453 028 4
  low-temperature engineering 621.57
Freezing 536.42
Freezing foods 664.028 53
  commercial preservation 664.028 53
  home preservation 641.453
Fregatidae 598.43
Frei Montalva, Eduardo
  Chilean history 983.064 5
Frei Ruiz-Tagle, Eduardo
  Chilean history 983.066 2
Freiberge (Switzerland) T2—494 368
Freiburg (Germany :
  Regierungsbezirk) T2—434 62
Freiburg (Switzerland) T2—494 535 4
Freiburg (Switzerland :
  Canton) T2—494 53
Freiburg im Breisgau
  (Germany) T2—434 626 2
Freie Demokratische Partei
  (Germany) 324.243 06
Freight and freightage 388.044
  *see also* Freight services
Freight cars 385.34
  engineering 625.24
  *see also* Rolling stock
Freight insurance 368.2
Freight services 388.044
  air 387.744
    airport services 387.736 4
    law 343.097 8
  automobile 388.321

Freight services (continued)
  bus 388.322 2
    law 343.094 82
    terminal services 388.33
  canal 386.404 24
  ferries 386.6
  ground 388.044
    law 343.093 2
  inland waterway 386.244
    law 343.096 8
    port services 386.864
  lake 386.544
    law 343.093 2
  marine 387.544
    law 343.096 8
    port services 387.164
  port services 387.164
    engineering 623.888 1
  public administration 354.764
  railroad 385.24
    law 343.095 8
    public administration 354.767 4
    special purpose 385.5
    terminal services 385.264
  river 386.354
  truck 388.324
    law 343.094 83
    terminal services 388.33
  urban 388.413 24
    terminal services 388.473
Freight terminals 388.044
  architecture 725.3
  area planning 711.7
  construction 690.53
  inland waterway 386.853
  ports 387.153
Freighters (Ships) 387.245
  engineering 623.824 5
  *see also* Ships
Freiheitliche Partei Österreichs 324.243 603
Freiheits-Partei der Schweiz 324.249 403
Freisinnig-Demokratische Partei
  der Schweiz 324.249 406
Fremantle (W.A.) T2—941 1
Fremont County (Colo.) T2—788 53
Fremont County (Idaho) T2—796 56
Fremont County (Iowa) T2—777 77
Fremont County (Wyo.) T2—787 63
French T5—41
French and Indian War,
  1756–1763 940.253 4
  North American history 973.26
French Broad River (N.C.
  and Tenn.) T2—768 895

| | |
|---|---|
| French bulldog | 636.72 |
| French Cameroons | T2—671 1 |
| French-Canadian literature | 840 |
| French Canadians | T5—114 |
| *see Manual at* T5—112, | |
| T5—114 vs. T5—2, | |
| T5—41 | |
| French Communist Party | 324.244 075 |
| French Community | T2—171 244 |
| French Congo (Brazzaville) | T2—672 4 |
| French creole languages | 447.9 |
| | T6—417 |
| French Equatorial Africa | 967.203 |
| | T2—672 |
| Central African history | 967.410 3 |
| Chadian history | 967.430 2 |
| Congolese history | 967.240 3 |
| Gabonese history | 967.210 2 |
| French Flanders | T2—442 8 |
| French folk music | 781.624 1 |
| French folk songs | 782.421 624 1 |
| French Guiana | 988.2 |
| | T2—882 |
| French Guinea | 966.520 3 |
| | T2—665 2 |
| French horns | 788.94 |
| instrument | 788.941 9 |
| music | 788.94 |
| *see also* Brass instruments | |
| French Indochina | 959.703 |
| | T2—597 |
| Cambodian history | 959.603 |
| Laotian history | 959.403 |
| Vietnamese history | 959.703 |
| French invasions of Italy, | |
| 1494–1559 | 945.06 |
| French Island (Vic.) | T2—945 2 |
| French language | 440 |
| | T6—41 |
| French literature | 840 |
| French pastry | 641.865 9 |
| commercial processing | 664.752 5 |
| home preparation | 641.865 9 |
| French Polynesia | T2—962 |
| French Revolution | 944.04 |
| French Riviera (France) | T2—449 4 |
| French Sign Language | 419.44 |
| French Somaliland | 967.710 32 |
| | T2—677 1 |
| French-speaking West | |
| Africa | T2—660 917 541 |
| French Sudan | 966.230 3 |
| | T2—662 3 |

| | |
|---|---|
| French Territory of the Afars and | 967.710 34 |
| Issas | T2—677 1 |
| French Togoland | 966.810 3 |
| | T2—668 1 |
| French West Indies | T2—729 76 |
| Frenchmans Cap National | |
| Park (Tas.) | T2—946 6 |
| Frequency allocation | |
| radio | 384.545 24 |
| television | 384.552 1 |
| Frequency bridges | |
| electric engineering | 621.374 7 |
| Frequency distributions | 519.532 |
| Frequency meters | |
| electric engineering | 621.374 7 |
| Frequency-modulation radio | |
| systems | 621.384 152 |
| Frequency modulators | |
| electronic circuits | 621.381 536 3 |
| Frequency synthesizers | 621.381 548 6 |
| Fresco painting | 751.44 |
| Frescoes | 751.73 |
| Fresh water | 553.7 |
| | T2—169 |
| economic geology | 553.7 |
| hydrology | 551.48 |
| Freshwater animals | 591.76 |
| Freshwater aquariums | 639.34 |
| Freshwater biological resources | 333.952 8 |
| Freshwater biology | 578.76 |
| *see Manual at* 578.76–.77 vs. | |
| 551.46, 551.48 | |
| Freshwater ecology | 577.6 |
| Freshwater eels | 597.432 |
| Freshwater fishes | 597.176 |
| culture | 639.31 |
| Freshwater fishing | 639.21 |
| commercial | 639.21 |
| sports | 799.11 |
| Freshwater hatchetfishes | 597.48 |
| Freshwater hydrology | 551.48 |
| *see Manual at* 578.76–.77 vs. | |
| 551.46, 551.48 | |
| Freshwater lagoons | 551.482 |
| | T2—169 2 |
| biology | 578.763 |
| ecology | 577.63 |
| Freshwater phytoplankton | 579.817 6 |
| Freshwater plants | 581.76 |
| Freshwater zebra fishes | 597.482 |
| Freshwater zooplankton | 592.176 |
| Fresno (Calif.) | T2—794 83 |
| Fresno County (Calif.) | T2—794 82 |
| Freudian psychology | 150.195 2 |

Freycinet National Park
  (Tas.)      T2—946 4
Friaries
  architecture      726.7
  church history      271
  religious significance of
    buildings      246.97
Fribourg (Switzerland)      T2—494 535 4
Friction      531.113 4
  fluid mechanics      532.053 3
  gas mechanics      533.28
  liquid mechanics      532.58
  machine engineering      621.89
  solid mechanics      531.4
Friction drums      786.98
  *see also* Percussion instruments
Friction idiophones      786.86
  set      786.86
  single      786.888
  *see also* Percussion instruments
Friction resistance
  materials science      620.112 92
Frictional unemployment      331.137 045
Friday
  Islamic observance      297.36
Friedel-Crafts reaction
  chemical engineering      660.284 4
Friedreich ataxia
  medicine      616.83
    *see also* Nervous system
      diseases — humans
Friendly fire casualties (Military
  science)      355.422
Friendly Islands      996.12
       T2—961 2
Friendly occupation
  law of nations      341.722
Friendly societies      334.7
  economics      334.7
  insurance      368.3
Friends (Religious society)      289.6
  biography      289.609 2
  *see also* Society of Friends
Friends of the library
  organizations      021.7
Friendship      177.62
  applied psychology      158.25
  arts      T3C—353
  ethics      177.62
    religion      205.676 2
  folklore      398.273
    history and criticism      398.353

Friendship (continued)
  literature      808.803 53
    history and criticism      809.933 53
    specific literatures      T3B—080 353
    history and
      criticism      T3B—093 53
  psychological influence      155.925
  social psychology      302.34
  *see also* Ethical problems
Friesian language      439.2
       T6—392
Friesians      T5—392
Friesland (Germany)      T2—435 917
Friesland (Netherlands)      T2—492 13
Frieze (Fabric)      677.617
  *see also* Textiles
Frigate birds      598.43
Frigid zones      T2—11
  biology      578.091 1
  diseases
    medicine      616.988 1
    *see also* Environmental
      diseases — humans
  ecology      577.091 1
  health      613.111
Frigidity
  medicine      616.858 32
Fringe benefits      331.255
  *see also* Employee benefits
Fringes
  arts      746.27
Fringes (Judaism)      296.461
Fringillidae      598.883
Frio County (Tex.)      T2—764 442
Frisian language      439.2
       T6—392
Frisian literature      839.2
Friuli-Venezia Giulia (Italy)      945.39
       T2—453 9
  ancient      T2—373 8
Friulian language      459.92
       T6—599 2
Friulian literature      859.92
Friulians      T5—599 2
Frobisher Bay (Nunavut)      T2—719 52
Frogbits      584.73
Frogfishes      597.62
Frogmen (Navy)      359.984
Frogmouths      598.99

| | |
|---|---|
| Frogs (Animals) | 597.89 |
| agriculture | 639.378 9 |
| food | 641.396 |
| commercial processing | 664.95 |
| cooking | 641.696 |
| home preservation | 641.495 |
| zoology | 597.89 |
| Frogs (Track crossings) | 625.163 |
| Fromm, Erich | |
| psychological system | 150.195 7 |
| Fronds (Plants) | 581.48 |
| descriptive botany | 581.48 |
| physiology | 575.57 |
| Front axles | |
| automotive engineering | 629.247 |
| Front-end systems | 025.04 |
| computer science | 005.758 |
| information science | 025.04 |
| Front Range (Colo. and Wyo.) | T2—788 6 |
| Front yards | |
| landscape architecture | 712.6 |
| Frontenac (Ont.) | T2—713 71 |
| Frontier County (Neb.) | T2—782 835 |
| Frontier defense | 355.45 |
| Frontier troops | 355.351 |
| Frontiers | 320.12 |
| *see also* Boundaries | |
| Fronts (Meteorology) | 551.551 2 |
| Frosinone (Italy : Province) | T2—456 22 |
| ancient | T2—376 7 |
| Frost | 551.38 |
| cold spell | 551.525 3 |
| weather forecasting | 551.642 53 |
| weather modification | 551.682 53 |
| geologic agent | 551.38 |
| hydrometeorology | 551.574 4 |
| Frost injury to crops | 632.11 |
| Frostbite | |
| medicine | 616.58 |
| *see also* Skin diseases — humans | |
| Froths | 541.345 14 |
| chemical engineering | 660.294 514 |
| Frottole | 782.43 |
| Frozen desserts | 641.862 |
| commercial processing | 637.4 |
| home preparation | 641.862 |
| Frozen dinners | |
| commercial processing | 664.65 |
| home serving | 642.1 |
| Frozen foods | |
| cooking | 641.615 3 |
| Frozen human embryos | 346.017 |

| | |
|---|---|
| Frozen seawater | |
| geology | 551.343 |
| Frozen yogurt | 641.862 |
| commercial processing | 637.4 |
| home preparation | 641.862 |
| Fructose | 572.565 |
| *see also* Carbohydrates | |
| Fruit | 581.464 |
| *see also* Fruits | |
| Fruit arrangements | 745.924 |
| Fruit bats (Phyllostomidae) | 599.45 |
| Fruit bats (Pteropodidae) | 599.49 |
| Fruit culture | 634 |
| Fruit drinks | 641.875 |
| commercial processing | 663.6 |
| home preparation | 641.875 |
| Fruit flies | 595.774 |
| agricultural pests | 634.049 774 |
| Fruit growers | 634.092 |
| Fruit juices | 641.34 |
| commercial processing | 663.63 |
| cooking with | 641.64 |
| food | 641.34 |
| home preparation | 641.875 |
| Fruits | 581.464 |
| art representation | 704.943 4 |
| arts | T3C—364 |
| commercial preservation | 664.8 |
| cooking | 641.64 |
| descriptive botany | 581.464 |
| drawing | 743.7 |
| food | 641.34 |
| forest products | 634.987 |
| home preservation | 641.4 |
| orchard crop | 634 |
| paleobotany | 561.14 |
| physiology | 575.67 |
| product safety | 363.192 9 |
| *see also* Food — product safety | |
| Frustration | 152.47 |
| Frutigen-Niedersimmental (Switzerland) | T2—494 541 5 |
| Frying | 641.77 |
| Fthiótis (Greece) | T2—495 15 |
| Fu'ād I, King of Egypt | |
| Egyptian history | 962.051 |
| Fucales | 579.888 |
| Fuchsias | 635.933 76 |
| botany | 583.76 |
| floriculture | 635.933 76 |
| Fucus | 579.888 |
| Fuel alcohols | 662.669 2 |
| Fuel cells | 621.312 429 |

Fuel element materials
  nuclear reactors — 621.483 35
Fuel engineers — 662.609 2
Fuel industry — 338.476 626
Fuel oils — 665.538 4
Fuel resources
  economics — 333.82
  extraction
    economics — 338.2
    law — 346.046 82
    public administration — 354.4
Fuel systems
  automotive — 629.253
Fueling — 388.041
  aircraft — 387.736 4
  boats — 387.168
  buses — 388.33
    urban — 388.473
  ships — 387.168
  trains — 385.26
  trucks — 388.33
    urban — 388.473
Fuels — 662.6
  aircraft — 629.134 351
  automotive — 629.253 8
  chemical engineering — 662.6
  economic geology — 553.2
  heat engineering — 621.402 3
  heating buildings — 697.04
  marine engines — 623.874
  metallurgical furnaces — 669.81
  military supplies — 355.83
  nuclear reactors — 621.483 35
  production economics — 338.476 626
  public administration — 354.4
  resource economics — 333.82
  spacecraft — 629.475
  steam engineering — 621.182
  unmanned spacecraft — 629.465
Fuelwood — 333.953 97
Fugitive slaves
  Civil War (United States) cause 973.711 5
Fugues — 784.187 2
Fujairah (United Arab
  Emirates : Emirate) — T2—535 7
Fujayrah (United Arab
  Emirates : Emirate) — T2—535 7
Fuji, Mount (Japan) — T2—521 66
Fuji-san (Japan) — T2—521 66
Fujian Sheng (China) — T2—512 45
Fujimori, Alberto
  Peruvian history — 985.064 3
Fujiyama (Japan) — T2—521 66
Fukien Province (China) — T2—512 45

Fukui-ken (Japan) — T2—521 55
Fukuoka-ken (Japan) — T2—522 2
Fukushima-ken (Japan) — T2—521 17
Fula language — 496.322
  — T6—963 22
Fula literature — 896.322
Fulah (African people) — T5—963 22
Fulah language — 496.322
  — T6—963 22
Fulah literature — 896.322
Fulani (African people) — T5—963 22
Fulani Empire — 966.950 1
  — T2—669 5
Fulani language — 496.322
  — T6—963 22
Fulani literature — 896.322
Fulfulde language — 496.322
  — T6—963 22
Fulfulde literature — 896.322
Full-employment policy — 331.120 424
  macroeconomics — 339.5
  *see Manual at* 331.120424 vs.
    331.1377
Full orchestras — 784.2
Full-scale plants
  chemical engineering — 660.280 73
Full scores — 780
  treatises — 780.264
Full-text databases — 025.04
  computer science — 005.759
  information science — 025.04
Full-text indexing — 025.486
Full-year school — 371.236
Fuller's earth — 553.61
  economic geology — 553.61
  mining — 622.361
Fulmars — 598.42
Fulton County (Ark.) — T2—767 22
Fulton County (Ga.) — T2—758 23
Fulton County (Ill.) — T2—773 48
Fulton County (Ind.) — T2—772 87
Fulton County (Ky.) — T2—769 99
Fulton County (N.Y.) — T2—747 47
Fulton County (Ohio) — T2—771 115
Fulton County (Pa.) — T2—748 72
Fumariaceae — 583.35
Fumaroles — 551.23
Fumes (Pollutants) — 363.738 7
  *see also* Pollution
Fumigants — 632.95
  agricultural use — 632.950 4
  chemical engineering — 668.65

Fumigation
agricultural pest control 632.94
public health 614.48
Fumitories (Plants) 583.35
Function
architectural design 729.2
Function theory 515
Functional analysis 515.7
Functional equations 515.75
Functional foods
health 613.2
Functional organization
executive management 658.402
Functional programming 005.114
Functionalism
architecture 724.6
fine arts 709.040 2
linguistics 410.18
specific languages T4—018
painting 759.062
psychology 150.193
sculpture 735.230 42
Functionals 515.7
Functions (Mathematics) 511.326
calculus 515.25
number theory 512.73
Functions of complex variables 515.9
Functions of one complex
variable 515.93
Functions of real variables 515.8
Functions of several complex
variables 515.94
Functions of several real
variables 515.84
Functor theory 515.7
Functors 512.62
Fund raising 658.152 24
T1—068 1
capital procurement 658.152 24
local Christian church 254.8
social welfare 361.706 81
study and teaching T1—079
Fundamental education 370.111
adult level 374.012
Fundamental interactions
(Nuclear physics) 539.754
Fundamental particles 539.72
Fundamental theology
(Christianity) 230.01
Fundamentalism
Christianity 270.82
independent denominations 289.95
Protestantism 280.4

Fundamentalism (continued)
Islam
political science 320.557
religion 297.09
Fundamentalist theology 230.046 26
Fundy, Bay of 551.461 345
T2—163 45
Funeral homes 363.75
*see also* Undertaking
(Mortuary)
Funeral music 781.588
Funeral sermons
Christianity 252.1
Funerals 393.93
Buddhist rites 294.343 88
Christian rites 265.85
customs 393.93
etiquette 395.23
flower arrangements 745.926
Hindu rites 294.538 8
Islamic rites 297.385
Jewish rites 296.445
liturgy 296.454 5
religious rites 203.88
Funes, Carlos Mauricio
Salvadoran history 972.840 544
Fungal diseases 571.995
*see also* Mycoses
Fungal skin diseases
humans
incidence 614.595 79
medicine 616.579
Fungal viruses 579.27
Fungi 579.5
medical microbiology 616.969 01
paleontology 561.92
physiology 571.295
Fungi Imperfecti 579.55
Fungicides 632.952
agricultural use 632.952
chemical engineering 668.652
Fungus diseases 571.995
*see also* Mycoses
Fungus weevils 595.768
Funicular railroads 385.6
engineering 625.32
transportation services 385.6
Funj Sultanate 962.402 3
T2—624
Funnies 741.56
*see also* Comic strips
Fur 599.714 7
descriptive zoology 599.714 7
physiology 573.58

Fur-bearing animals — 599.7
  animal husbandry — 636.97
  conservation technology — 639.979 7
  resource economics — 333.959 7
  small game hunting — 799.259 7
  trapping — 639.117
  zoology — 599.7
Fur clothing — 391
  commercial technology — 685.24
  customs — 391
  home sewing — 646.4
  *see also* Clothing
Fur farming — 636.97
Fur goods
  commercial technology — 685
Fur processing — 675.3
  economics — 338.476 753
Fur seals — 599.797 3
  conservation technology — 639.979 797 3
  resource economics — 333.959 797 3
Fur trapping — 639.117
  economics — 338.372 97
Furans — 547.592
  chemical engineering — 661.8
Furloughs
  armed forces — 355.113
  penology — 365.643
Furnaces
  heat engineering — 621.402 5
  heating buildings — 697.07
    steam — 697.507
  steam engineering — 621.183
Furnariidae — 598.822 5
Furnas County (Neb.) — T2—782 384
Furneaux Islands (Tas.) — T2—946 7
Furnishings — 645
  commercial technology — 684
  customs — 392.36
  home cleaning — 648.5
  household management — 645
  interior decoration — 747
  libraries
    management — 022.9
  schools — 371.63
Furniture — 645.4
  cleaning — 648.5
  customs — 392.36
  decorative arts — 749
  household management — 645.4
  libraries
    management — 022.9
  manufacturing technology — 684.1
  office services — 651.23
  ships — 623.866

Furniture arrangement — 645.4
Furniture covers — 645.4
  home sewing — 646.21
  household management — 645.4
  textile arts — 746.95
Furniture designers — 749.092
Furniture makers — 684.100 92
Furriers — 675.309 2
Furs
  handicrafts — 745.537
  home sewing materials — 646.1
  processing — 675.3
  products
    commercial technology — 685
Further education — 374
  — T1—071 5
  *see also* Adult education
Furuncles
  medicine — 616.523
  *see also* Skin diseases — humans
Furunculosis
  medicine — 616.523
  *see also* Skin diseases — humans
Fusarium — 579.567 7
Fused aromatic compounds — 547.615
  chemical engineering — 661.816
Fused heterocyclic compounds — 547.596
Fuselages
  aircraft — 629.134 34
Fuses (Detonators) — 662.4
  military engineering — 623.454 2
Fuses (Electrical) — 621.317
Fusibility
  crystals — 548.86
Fusion (Melting) — 536.42
Fusion (Thermonuclear) — 539.764
Fusion power plants — 621.484
Fusion reactors — 621.484
Future interests (Law) — 346.042
Future life
  occultism — 133.901 3
  philosophy — 129
  religion — 202.3
    Buddhism — 294.342 3
    Christianity — 236.2
    Hinduism — 294.523
    Islam — 297.23
    Judaism — 296.33
Future punishment — 202.3
Futures — 332.645 2

| | |
|---|---|
| Futurism | |
| fine arts | 709.040 33 |
| literature | 808.801 14 |
| history and criticism | 809.911 4 |
| specific literatures | T3B—080 114 |
| history and criticism | T3B—091 14 |
| painting | 759.063 3 |
| sculpture | 735.230 433 |
| Futurology | 003.2 |
| occultism | 133.3 |
| social change | 303.49 |
| Fuzzy logic | 511.313 |
| Fuzzy mathematics | 511.313 |
| Fuzzy sets | 511.322 3 |
| Fuzzy systems | 511.313 |
| Fylde (England) | T2—427 662 |
| Fylde (England : Borough) | T2—427 662 |
| Fyn (Denmark) | T2—489 4 |
| Fyns amt (Denmark) | T2—489 4 |
| Fyodor I, Czar of Russia | |
| Russian history | 947.044 |
| Fyodor III, Czar of Russia | |
| Russian history | 947.049 |

# G

| | |
|---|---|
| Gã (African people) | T5—963 378 |
| Gã language | 496.337 8 |
| | T6—963 378 |
| Gã literature | 896.337 8 |
| Gabbro | 552.3 |
| Gables | 721.5 |
| architecture | 721.5 |
| construction | 690.15 |
| Gabon | 967.21 |
| | T2—672 1 |
| Gabonese | T5—967 21 |
| Gaborone (Botswana) | T2—688 3 |
| Gadaba (Dravidian people) | T5—948 2 |
| Gadaba (Munda people) | T5—959 5 |
| Gadaba language (Dravidian) | 494.82 |
| | T6—948 2 |
| Gadaba language (Munda) | 495.95 |
| | T6—959 5 |
| Gadba (Dravidian people) | T5—948 2 |
| Gadba (Munda people) | T5—959 5 |
| Gadba language (Dravidian) | 494.82 |
| | T6—948 2 |
| Gadba language (Munda) | 495.95 |
| | T6—959 5 |
| Gadidae | 597.632 |
| Gadiformes | 597.63 |
| paleozoology | 567.63 |

| | |
|---|---|
| Gadolinium | |
| chemistry | 546.416 |
| Gadsden County (Fla.) | T2—759 925 |
| Gadus | 597.633 |
| Gaelic football | 796.33 |
| Gaelic languages | 491.6 |
| | T6—916 |
| Irish | 491.62 |
| | T6—916 2 |
| Scottish | 491.63 |
| | T6—916 3 |
| Gaelic literatures | 891.6 |
| Irish | 891.62 |
| Scottish | 891.63 |
| Gaels | T5—916 |
| Gaetulia | 939.77 |
| | T2—397 7 |
| Gagauz language | 494.36 |
| | T6—943 6 |
| Gage County (Neb.) | T2—782 286 |
| Gagnon (Quebec) | T2—714 117 |
| Gain sharing | 331.216 47 |
| labor economics | 331.216 47 |
| personnel management | 658.322 5 |
| Gaines County (Tex.) | T2—764 855 |
| Gaining weight diet | |
| health | 613.24 |
| Gairdner, Lake (S. Aust.) | T2—942 38 |
| Gaitas | 788.49 |
| *see also* Woodwind instruments | |
| Galagos | 599.83 |
| Galapagos Islands | T2—866 5 |
| Galapagos tortoise | 597.924 6 |
| Galaţi (Romania : Judeţ) | T2—498 1 |
| Galatia | T2—393 2 |
| Galatia Salutaris | T2—393 2 |
| Galatians (Biblical book) | 227.4 |
| Galax | 583.67 |
| Galax (Va.) | T2—755 715 |
| Galaxies | 523.112 |
| *see Manual at* 520 vs. 523.1, 523.112, 523.8 | |
| Galbulidae | 598.72 |
| Galcha language | 491.57 |
| | T6—915 7 |
| Galcha literature | 891.57 |
| Galchah language | 491.57 |
| | T6—915 7 |
| Galchah literature | 891.57 |
| Galena | |
| mineralogy | 549.32 |
| Galerkin method | 518.63 |
| Galibi language | 498.422 |
| | T6—984 22 |

| | |
|---|---|
| Galicia (Poland and Ukraine) | T2—438 6 |
| Poland | T2—438 6 |
| Ukraine | T2—477 9 |
| Galicia (Spain : Region) | T2—461 |
| Galician language | 469.9 |
| | T6—699 |
| Galician literature | 869.9 |
| Galicians | T5—699 |
| Galilee (Israel) | T2—569 45 |
| ancient | T2—334 5 |
| Gall bladder | 573.38 |
| *see also* Gallbladder | |
| Galla (African people) | T5—935 5 |
| Galla language | 493.55 |
| | T6—935 5 |
| Galla literature | 893.55 |
| Gallatin County (Ill.) | T2—773 97 |
| Gallatin County (Ky.) | T2—769 365 |
| Gallatin County (Mont.) | T2—786 662 |
| Gallbladder | 573.38 |
| biology | 573.38 |
| human anatomy | 611.36 |
| human physiology | 612.35 |
| medicine | 616.365 |
| surgery | 617.556 5 |
| *see also* Digestive system | |
| Gallbladder diseases | |
| medicine | 616.365 |
| *see also* Digestive system diseases — humans | |
| Gallegan language | 469.9 |
| | T6—699 |
| Gallegan literature | 869.9 |
| Galleons | 387.22 |
| design | 623.812 2 |
| engineering | 623.822 |
| transportation services | 387.22 |
| *see also* Ships | |
| Galleries (Museums) | 069 |
| | T1—074 |
| Galleys (Ships) | 387.21 |
| design | 623.812 1 |
| engineering | 623.821 |
| handling | 623.882 1 |
| transportation services | 387.21 |
| *see also* Ships | |
| Galli | 598.6 |
| Gallia Cisalpina | T2—372 |
| Gallia Cispadana | T2—372 6 |
| Gallia County (Ohio) | T2—771 89 |
| Gallia Transalpina | T2—364 |
| Gallia Transpadana | T2—372 2 |

| | |
|---|---|
| Galliards | 793.3 |
| music | 784.188 2 |
| Gallican schismatic churches | 284.8 |
| *see also* Old Catholic churches | |
| Galliformes | 598.6 |
| paleozoology | 568.6 |
| sports hunting | 799.246 |
| Gallinules | 598.32 |
| Gallipoli Campaign, 1915 | 940.426 |
| Gallipoli peninsula (Turkey) | T2—496 12 |
| Gallium | 669.79 |
| chemical engineering | 661.067 5 |
| chemistry | 546.675 |
| metallurgy | 669.79 |
| *see also* Chemicals | |
| Gallo-Roman period | 936.402 |
| Galloway cattle | 636.223 |
| Galls | |
| agriculture | 632.2 |
| Gallus domesticus | 636.5 |
| zoology | 598.625 |
| Galois theory | 512.32 |
| Galops | 793.3 |
| music | 784.188 4 |
| Galvanometers | 621.374 4 |
| Galveston County (Tex.) | T2—764 139 |
| Galway (Ireland) | T2—417 45 |
| Galway (Ireland : County) | T2—417 4 |
| Gama grass | 584.9 |
| Gambai dialect | 496.5 |
| | T6—965 |
| Gambēla Āstedader Ākababī (Ethiopia) | T2—633 |
| Gambella Federal State (Ethiopia) | T2—633 |
| Gambel's quail | 598.627 |
| Gambia | 966.51 |
| | T2—665 1 |
| Gambia River | T2—665 1 |
| Gambians | T5—966 51 |
| Gambier Island (B.C.) | T2—711 31 |
| Gambier Islands (French Polynesia) | T2—962 2 |
| Gamblers | 795.092 |
| Gambling | 306.482 |
| criminology | 364.172 |
| criminal law | 345.027 2 |
| customs | 394.3 |
| ethics | 175 |
| *see also* Recreation — ethics | |
| horse racing | 798.401 |
| law | 344.099 |
| mathematics | 519.27 |
| occupational ethics | 174.6 |

| | |
|---|---|
| Gambling (continued) | |
| public control | 363.42 |
| law | 344.054 2 |
| public administration | 353.37 |
| recreation | 795 |
| sociology | 306.482 |
| Game animals | 591.63 |
| animal husbandry | 636.088 8 |
| conservation technology | 639.9 |
| economic zoology | 591.63 |
| food | 641.391 |
| cooking | 641.691 |
| mammals | 599.163 |
| theft of | 364.162 859 9 |
| law | 345.026 285 99 |
| resource economics | 333.954 9 |
| theft of | 364.162 859 1 |
| law | 345.026 285 91 |
| Game birds | 598.163 |
| animal husbandry | 636.63 |
| conservation technology | 639.978 163 |
| economic zoology | 598.163 |
| food | 641.391 |
| cooking | 641.691 |
| resource economics | 333.958 29 |
| sports hunting | 799.24 |
| theft of | 364.162 859 8 |
| law | 345.026 285 98 |
| Game fishes | 597.163 |
| conservation technology | 639.977 163 |
| resource economics | 333.956 9 |
| sports fishing | 799.12 |
| theft of | 364.162 859 7 |
| law | 345.026 285 97 |
| Game fishes (Salmonids) | 597.55 |
| conservation technology | 639.977 55 |
| resource economics | 333.956 55 |
| sports fishing | 799.175 5 |
| Game fishing | 799.12 |
| Game laws | 346.046 954 9 |
| Game protection | 333.954 916 |
| technology | 639.9 |
| Game reserves | 333.954 916 |
| conservation technology | 639.95 |
| Game theory | 519.3 |
| Gamekeepers | 639.909 2 |
| Games | 790.1 |
| camp sports | 796.545 |
| cataloging | 025.349 6 |
| customs | 394.3 |
| ethics | 175 |
| folk literature | 398.8 |
| indoor | 793 |
| library treatment | 025.179 6 |

| | |
|---|---|
| Games (continued) | |
| management decision making | 658.403 53 |
| outdoor | 796 |
| sociology | 306.487 |
| use in child care | 649.55 |
| *see also* Recreation | |
| Games of chance | 795 |
| equipment technology | 688.75 |
| probabilities | 519.27 |
| *see Manual at* 795.015192 vs. | |
| 519.27 | |
| Games of skill | 790.1 |
| indoor | 794 |
| mathematics | 519.3 |
| outdoor | 796 |
| Gamete intrafallopian transfer | |
| surgery | 618.178 059 9 |
| Gametes | 571.845 |
| Gametogenesis | 571.845 |
| Gaming | 306.482 |
| *see also* Gambling | |
| Gamka River (South Africa) | T2—687 38 |
| Gamma decay | 539.752 4 |
| Gamma functions | 515.52 |
| Gamma particles | 539.722 2 |
| biophysics | 571.459 |
| humans | 612.014 486 |
| physics | 539.722 2 |
| Gamma-ray astronomy | 522.686 2 |
| Gamma-ray electronics | 537.535 |
| Gamma-ray photography | |
| engineering | 621.367 3 |
| Gamma-ray spectroscopes | |
| manufacturing technology | 681.414 8 |
| Gamma-ray spectroscopy | 543.6 |
| analytical chemistry | 543.6 |
| engineering | 621.361 |
| physics | 537.535 2 |
| Gamma rays | 539.722 2 |
| biophysics | 571.459 |
| humans | 612.014 486 |
| physics | 539.722 2 |
| Gan dialects (China) | 495.172 22 |
| | T6—951 7 |
| Ganapataism | 294.551 5 |
| Ganda (African people) | T5—963 957 |
| Ganda language | 496.395 7 |
| | T6—963 957 |
| Ganda literature | 896.395 7 |
| Gandhi, Indira | |
| Indian history | 954.045 |
| 1966–1971 | 954.045 |
| 1971–1977 | 954.051 |
| 1980–1984 | 954.052 |

| | |
|---|---|
| Gandhi, Rajiv | |
|   Indian history | 954.052 |
| Ganges River (India and | |
|   Bangladesh) | T2—541 |
| Ganglia | |
|   basal | |
|     medicine | 616.83 |
|     human anatomy | 611.83 |
|     human physiology | 612.81 |
|   non-basal | |
|     medicine | 616.856 |
| Gangrene | |
|   medicine | 616.047 |
| Gangs | |
|   criminology | 364.106 6 |
|   social psychology | 302.34 |
| Gangsterism | 364.106 6 |
| Ganoidei | 597.42 |
| Gansu Sheng (China) | T2—514 5 |
| Ganyesa (South Africa : | |
|   District) | T2—682 46 |
| Gaols | 365.34 |
|   *see also* Penal institutions | |
| Gaonim | 296.120 092 |
| GAR (Organization) | 369.15 |
| Garage sales | 381.195 |
|   management | 658.87 |
|   *see also* Commerce | |
| Garages | |
|   architecture | 725.38 |
|   automotive engineering | 629.286 |
|   construction | 690.538 |
|   domestic | |
|     architecture | 728.98 |
|     construction | 690.898 |
|     theft from | 364.162 2 |
|     law | 345.026 22 |
| Garamond type | 686.224 7 |
| Garavance | 641.356 57 |
|   *see also* Chick-peas | |
| Garbage collection | 363.728 8 |
|   technology | 628.442 |
| Garbage disposal | 363.728 8 |
|   technology | 628.445 |
|   use as fertilizer | 631.875 |
|   *see also* Waste control | |
| Garbage-disposal units | |
|   installation | 696.184 |
|   manufacturing technology | 683.88 |
| Garbanzo | 641.356 57 |
|   *see also* Chick-peas | |
| García, Alan | |
|   Peruvian history | 985.064 5 |

| | |
|---|---|
| Garcia, Carlos | |
|   Philippine history | 959.904 4 |
| Garcinias | 583.624 |
| Gard (France) | T2—448 3 |
| Garda, Lake (Italy) | T2—452 6 |
| Garden County (Neb.) | T2—782 915 |
| Garden crops | 635 |
|   *see Manual at* 633–635 | |
| Garden eggs | 641.356 46 |
|   *see also* Eggplants | |
| Garden furniture | 645.8 |
|   *see also* Outdoor furniture | |
| Garden legumes | 641.356 5 |
|   horticulture | 635.65 |
| Garden lighting | 621.322 9 |
| Garden peas | 641.356 56 |
|   *see also* Peas (Pisum sativum) | |
| Garden Route (South | |
|   Africa) | T2—687 37 |
| Garden sculpture | 731.72 |
| Gardeners | 635.092 |
| Gardenias | 635.933 93 |
|   botany | 583.93 |
|   floriculture | 635.933 93 |
| Gardening | 635 |
|   landscape architecture | 712 |
|   therapeutic use | 615.851 5 |
| Gardens | 635 |
|   arts | 700.464 |
| | T3C—364 |
|   biology | 578.755 4 |
|   ecology | 577.554 |
|   landscape architecture | 712 |
|   literature | 808.803 64 |
|     history and criticism | 809.933 64 |
|     specific literatures | T3B—080 364 |
|     history and | |
|       criticism | T3B—093 64 |
| Garfield, James A. (James | |
|   Abram) | |
|   United States history | 973.84 |
| Garfield County (Colo.) | T2—788 16 |
| Garfield County (Mont.) | T2—786 27 |
| Garfield County (Neb.) | T2—782 764 |
| Garfield County (Okla.) | T2—766 28 |
| Garfield County (Utah) | T2—792 52 |
| Garfield County (Wash.) | T2—797 44 |
| Garfish | 597.66 |
| Gargoyles | |
|   architectural decoration | 729.5 |
| Garhwali language | 491.496 |
| | T6—914 96 |
| Garibaldi (Fish) | 597.72 |

| | |
|---|---|
| Garibaldi Provincial Park | |
| (B.C.) | T2—711 31 |
| Garífuna language | 497.92 |
| | T6—979 2 |
| Garland County (Ark.) | T2—767 41 |
| Garlic | 641.352 6 |
| botany | 584.33 |
| cooking | 641.652 6 |
| food | 641.352 6 |
| garden crop | 635.26 |
| pharmacology | 615.324 33 |
| Garment workers | 687.092 |
| Garments | 391 |
| *see also* Clothing | |
| Garnets | 553.87 |
| mineralogy | 549.62 |
| *see also* Semiprecious stones | |
| Garnishes | 641.819 |
| Garnishment | 347.077 |
| civil procedure | 347.077 |
| commercial law | 346.077 |
| Garo language | 495.4 |
| | T6—954 |
| Garonne River (Spain and | |
| France) | T2—447 |
| Garrard County (Ky.) | T2—769 525 |
| Garrett County (Md.) | T2—752 97 |
| Garrison Reservoir (N.D.) | T2—784 75 |
| Garrya | 583.84 |
| Gars | 597.41 |
| Garvin County (Okla.) | T2—766 56 |
| Gary (Ind.) | T2—772 99 |
| Garza County (Tex.) | T2—764 852 |
| Gas abuse | 362.299 3 |
| Gas appliances | |
| chemistry | 542.7 |
| household appliances | 643.6 |
| manufacturing technology | 683.88 |
| Gas chromatography | 543.85 |
| chemical engineering | 660.284 23 |
| Gas-detection prospecting | 622.159 |
| Gas dynamics | 533.2 |
| Gas engineering | 665.7 |
| equipment manufacturing | |
| technology | 681.766 5 |
| Gas engineers | 665.709 2 |
| Gas equipment | |
| chemistry | 542.7 |
| household appliances | 643.6 |
| manufacturing technology | 683.88 |
| Gas exchange | |
| human physiology | 612.22 |
| *see also* Respiratory system | |

| | |
|---|---|
| Gas fitting | |
| buildings | 696.2 |
| Gas heating | |
| buildings | 697.043 |
| Gas lighting | 621.324 |
| Gas mechanics | 533 |
| engineering | 620.107 |
| Gas oil | 665.538 4 |
| Gas pipes | |
| buildings | 696.2 |
| Gas supply facilities | |
| area planning | 711.8 |
| Gas tubes | |
| electronics | 621.381 513 |
| Gas-turbine engines | 621.433 |
| aircraft | 629.134 353 |
| automotive | 629.250 3 |
| ships | 623.872 33 |
| Gas-turbine locomotives | 385.362 |
| engineering | 625.262 |
| transportation services | 385.362 |
| *see also* Rolling stock | |
| Gas welding | 671.522 |
| Gascogne (France) | T2—447 3 |
| Gascon dialect (Occitan | |
| language) | T6—491 |
| Gasconade County (Mo.) | T2—778 61 |
| Gascony (France) | T2—447 3 |
| Gascoyne River (W.A.) | T2—941 3 |
| Gaseous-state lasers | 621.366 3 |
| Gaseous-state physics | 530.43 |
| Gaseous wastes | 363.728 |
| social services | 363.728 |
| technology | 628.53 |
| *see also* Waste control | |
| Gases | |
| chemical engineering | 660.043 |
| expansion and contraction | 536.412 |
| heat transfer | 536.25 |
| pneumatics | 533 |
| sound transmission | 534.24 |
| specific heat | 536.65 |
| state of matter | 530.43 |
| Gases (Fuels) | 665.7 |
| cooking | 641.584 |
| dowsing | 133.323 7 |
| mine safety engineering | 622.82 |
| natural | 553.285 |
| *see also* Natural gas | |
| plant management | 658.26 |
| public administration | 354.46 |
| public safety | 363.179 8 |
| public utilities | 363.63 |
| *see also* Hazardous materials | |

Gases (Noxious)
  human toxicology    615.91
  mine safety engineering    622.82
  pollution    363.738 7
  *see also* Pollution
Gases in atmosphere    551.511 2
Gasohol    662.669 2
Gasoline    665.538 27
  public safety    363.179 8
  *see also* Hazardous materials
Gasoline engines    621.434
Gašparovič, Ivan
  Slovak history    943.730 513
Gaspé Peninsula (Quebec)    T2—714 77
Gaspée (Ship), Burning of, 1772    973.311 2
Gaspésie (Quebec)    T2—714 77
Gaspésie-Îles-de-la-
  Madeleine (Quebec)    T2—714 77
Gaspésie National Park
  (Quebec)    T2—714 791
Gasteromycetes    579.599
Gasteropelecidae    597.48
Gasterosteidae    597.672
Gasterosteiformes    597.67
  paleozoology    567.67
Gaston County (N.C.)    T2—756 773
Gastric analysis
  diagnosis
    general disease    616.075 63
Gastric secretions    573.363 79
  human physiology    612.32
  medicine    616.332
  *see also* Digestive system
Gastric ulcers
  medicine    616.334
  *see also* Digestive system
    diseases — humans
Gästrikland landskap
  (Sweden)    T2—488 1
Gastritis
  medicine    616.333
  *see also* Digestive system
    diseases — humans
Gastroenteritis
  medicine    616.33
  *see also* Digestive system
    diseases — humans
Gastroenterology    616.33
Gastroesophageal reflux
  medicine    616.324
  *see also* Digestive system
    diseases — humans
Gastrointestinal agents
  pharmacokinetics    615.73

Gastrointestinal diseases
  medicine    616.33
  *see also* Digestive system
    diseases — humans
Gastrointestinal organs    573.36
  human anatomy    611.33
  human physiology    612.32
  *see also* Digestive system
Gastronomy    641.013
Gastropoda    594.3
  paleozoology    564.3
Gastrotricha    592.53
Gastrulation    571.865
Gataga River (B.C.)    T2—711 85
Gatehouses
  architecture    728.9
  construction    690.89
Gates
  canal engineering    627.135 2
  dam engineering    627.882
Gates County (N.C.)    T2—756 153
Gates of the Arctic National
  Park and Preserve
  (Alaska)    T2—798 6
Gateshead (England :
  Metropolitan Borough)    T2—428 73
Gateways
  architecture    725.96
  landscape architecture    717
Gathas    295.82
Gatineau (Quebec)    T2—714 221
Gatineau Park (Quebec)    T2—714 223
Gatineau River (Quebec)    T2—714 224
GATT (Commerce)    382.92
  law    343.087 026 1
Gäu (Switzerland)    T2—494 353 3
Gauge fields
  physics    530.143 5
Gaul    936.4
    T2—364
Gauley River (W. Va.)    T2—754 69
Gaulish language    491.6
    T6—916
Gaulish literature    891.6
Gauls    T5—916
Gauntlets
  manufacturing technology    685.43
Gaur    599.642 2
Gauss geometry    516.9
Gaussian processes    519.23
Gautama Buddha    294.363
  art representation    704.948 943 63
  arts    700.482 943 63
    T3C—382 943 63

| | | | |
|---|---|---|---|
| Gauteng (South Africa) | 968.22 | Gaziantep İli (Turkey) | T2—564 9 |
| | T2—682 2 | ancient | T2—393 6 |
| Gavial | 597.98 | GB (Swiss political party) | 324.249 408 7 |
| Gaviiformes | 598.442 | Gbagbo, Laurent | |
| paleozoology | 568.4 | Ivorian history | 966.680 53 |
| Gävleborg (Sweden) | T2—488 1 | Gbandi (Liberian people) | T5—963 48 |
| Gavottes | 793.319 44 | Gbandi language | 496.348 |
| music | 784.188 3 | | T6—963 48 |
| Gawler (S. Aust.) | T2—942 32 | Gbaya (African people) | T5—963 61 |
| Gay liberation movement | 306.766 | Gbaya language | 496.361 |
| Gay marriage | 306.848 | | T6—963 61 |
| law | 346.016 8 | Gbe languages | 496.337 |
| Gay men | 306.766 2 | | T6—963 37 |
| | T1—086 642 | GCSE (Educational tests) | 373.126 2 |
| psychology | 155.344 2 | Gdańsk (Poland : | |
| social welfare | 362.896 4 | Voivodeship) | T2—438 22 |
| Gay parents | 306.874 086 64 | GDP (Macroeconomics) | 339.31 |
| Gay rights | 323.326 4 | GDVP (Austrian political party) | 324.243 602 3 |
| law | 342.087 | Gê Indians | T5—984 |
| Gay teenagers | 306.766 083 5 | Gê language | 498.4 |
| psychology | 155.508 66 | | T6—984 |
| social welfare | 362.786 6 | Gear-cutting tools | 621.944 |
| Gay women | 306.766 3 | Gear-driven hoists | |
| | T1—086 643 | mining | 622.67 |
| | | Gears | 621.833 |
| *see also* Lesbians | | clockwork | 681.112 |
| Gay workers | 331.53 | Geary County (Kan.) | T2—781 29 |
| Gays | 306.766 | Geauga County (Ohio) | T2—771 336 |
| | T1—086 64 | Geckos | 597.952 |
| civil and human rights | 323.326 4 | GED tests | 373.126 2 |
| female | 306.766 3 | Gedling (England) | T2—425 28 |
| | T1—086 643 | Geelong (Vic.) | T2—945 2 |
| psychology | 155.344 3 | Geelvink Bay languages | T6—991 2 |
| Holocaust, 1933–1945 | 940.531 808 664 | Geese | 598.417 |
| labor economics | 331.53 | animal husbandry | 636.598 |
| male | 306.766 2 | conservation technology | 639.978 417 |
| | T1—086 642 | resource economics | 333.958 417 |
| psychology | 155.344 2 | sports hunting | 799.244 7 |
| psychology | 155.344 | Ge'ez language | 492.81 |
| religion | 200.866 4 | | T6—928 1 |
| Christianity | 270.086 64 | Biblical texts | 220.46 |
| pastoral theology | 259.086 64 | Ge'ez literature | 892.81 |
| social welfare | 362.896 4 | Gegenschein | 523.59 |
| Gaza (Mozambique : | | Geiger-Müller counters | |
| Province) | T2—679 2 | nuclear physics | 539.774 |
| Gaza Strip | 953.1 | Geisel, Ernesto | |
| | T2—531 | Brazilian history | 981.063 |
| ancient | 939.47 | Geishas | 792.702 809 52 |
| | T2—394 8 | Gekkonidae | 597.952 |
| Gazankulu (South Africa) | T2—682 59 | Gekkonidea | 597.952 |
| Gazehounds | 636.753 2 | Gela (Italy) | |
| Gazella | 599.646 9 | ancient | T2—378 21 |
| Gazelles | 599.646 9 | Gelatin | |
| Gazetteers | 910.3 | commercial processing | 664.26 |
| Gazettes (Official publications) | 351.05 | | |

| | |
|---|---|
| Gelatin desserts | 641.864 2 |
| Gelatin process | |
| printing | 686.232 5 |
| Gelderland (Netherlands) | T2—492 18 |
| Gelibolu (Turkey) | T2—496 12 |
| Gels | 541.345 13 |
| chemical engineering | 660.294 513 |
| Gelsenkirchen (Germany) | T2—435 618 |
| Gem County (Idaho) | T2—796 27 |
| Gemini (Zodiac) | 133.526 4 |
| Gemini project | 629.454 |
| Gempylidae | 597.78 |
| Gems | 553.8 |
| carving | 736.2 |
| economic geology | 553.8 |
| jewelry | 739.27 |
| materials science | 620.198 |
| mining | 622.38 |
| occultism | 133.255 38 |
| divination | 133.322 |
| prospecting | 622.188 |
| synthetic | 666.88 |
| Gen-Gbe language | 496.337 |
| | T6—963 37 |
| Gen language | 496.337 |
| | T6—963 37 |
| Gender identity | 305.3 |
| | T1—081 |
| arts | 700.452 1 |
| | T3C—352 1 |
| labor economics | 331.56 |
| literature | |
| specific literatures | T3B—080 352 1 |
| history and | |
| criticism | T3B—093 521 |
| psychology | 155.33 |
| adolescents | 155.53 |
| children | 155.43 |
| Gender identity disorders | |
| medicine | 616.858 3 |
| Gender role | 305.3 |
| | T1—081 |
| arts | 700.452 1 |
| | T3C—352 1 |
| labor economics | 331.56 |
| literature | |
| specific literatures | T3B—080 352 1 |
| history and | |
| criticism | T3B—093 521 |
| Gene activation | 572.865 |
| Gene expression | 572.865 |
| Gene mapping | 572.863 3 |
| humans | 611.018 166 3 |
| Gene pools | 576.58 |
| Gene silencing | 572.865 |
| Gene splicing | |
| biotechnology | 660.65 |
| Gene therapy | |
| law | 344.041 96 |
| therapeutics | 615.895 |
| Genealogical registers | 929.3 |
| Genealogists | 929.109 2 |
| Genealogy | 929.1 |
| General accounting offices | 352.43 |
| audit reports | 352.439 |
| General Agreement on Tariffs | |
| and Trade (1947) | 382.92 |
| law | 343.087 026 1 |
| General anesthesia | |
| surgery | 617.962 |
| General Carrera (Chile : | |
| Province) | T2—836 25 |
| General catalogs | 025.31 |
| bibliography | 011 |
| library science | 025.31 |
| General certificate of education | |
| examination (United | |
| Kingdom) | 371.262 |
| A level | 378.166 2 |
| GCSE | 373.126 2 |
| General Conference Mennonite | |
| Church | 289.73 |
| *see also* Mennonite Church | |
| General educational development | |
| tests | 373.126 2 |
| General services agencies | 352.5 |
| General Society of Colonial Wars | |
| (U.S.) | 369.12 |
| General Society of Mayflower | |
| Descendants | 369.12 |
| General staffs | 355.330 42 |
| General stores | 381.14 |
| *see also* Commerce | |
| General strikes | 322.2 |
| economics | 331.892 5 |
| *see also* Strikes (Work | |
| stoppages) | |
| General topology | 514.322 |
| Generalized functions | 515.782 |
| Generalized system of preference | 382.753 |
| *see also* Customs (Tariff) | |
| Generals | 355.009 2 |
| role and function | 355.331 |
| Generating electricity | 621.312 1 |
| Generating functions | 515.55 |
| Generating machinery | |
| electrical engineering | 621.313 |
| Generating steam | 621.18 |

| | | | |
|---|---|---|---|
| Generation gap | 305.2 | Genetic transcription | 572.884 5 |
| family relationships | 306.874 | Genetic transduction | 571.964 8 |
| Generation of sound | | Genetic transformation | 571.964 8 |
| physics | 534.1 | Genetic translation | 572.645 |
| Generative grammar | 415.018 2 | Geneticists | 576.509 2 |
| specific languages | T4—501 82 | Genetics | 576.5 |
| Generative organs | 573.6 | animal husbandry | 636.082 1 |
| *see also* Genital system | | animals | 591.35 |
| Genes | 572.86 | humans | 599.935 |
| humans | 611.018 166 | sociology | 304.5 |
| Genesee County (Mich.) | T2—774 37 | microorganisms | 579.135 |
| Genesee County (N.Y.) | T2—747 92 | plants | 581.35 |
| Genesee River (Pa. and | | sociology | 304.5 |
| N.Y.) | T2—747 88 | *see Manual at* 576.5 vs. 572.8 | |
| Genesis (Bible) | 222.11 | Genets | 599.742 |
| Genetic algorithms | | Geneva (Switzerland : | |
| computer science | 005.1 | Canton) | T2—494 51 |
| artificial intelligence | 006.31 | Geneva, Lake (Switzerland | |
| mathematics | 519.625 | and France) | T2—494 52 |
| Genetic code | 572.863 3 | France | T2—445 84 |
| humans | 611.018 166 3 | Switzerland | T2—494 52 |
| Genetic disorders | 571.948 | Geneva Conventions | 341.65 |
| animals | 571.948 1 | Geneva County (Ala.) | T2—761 292 |
| humans | 362.196 042 | Genève (Switzerland) | T2—494 516 |
| medicine | 616.042 | Genève (Switzerland : | |
| social services | 362.196 042 | Canton) | T2—494 51 |
| Genetic engineering | 660.65 | Genf (Switzerland) | T2—494 516 |
| agriculture | 631.523 3 | Genf (Switzerland : Canton) | T2—494 51 |
| pest resistance | 632.9 | Genghis Khan | |
| animal husbandry | 636.082 1 | Asian history | 950.21 |
| cells | | Geniculate bodies | |
| research | | human physiology | 612.826 2 |
| medicine | 616.027 7 | Genital diseases | 573.639 |
| ethics | 174.2 | animals | 573.639 |
| *see also* Ethical problems | | veterinary medicine | 636.089 665 |
| law | 344.095 7 | humans | 362.196 65 |
| medical | 344.041 96 | anesthesiology | 617.967 46 |
| tissue | | cancer | 362.196 994 6 |
| research | | incidence | 614.599 946 |
| medicine | 616.027 | medicine | 616.994 6 |
| Genetic evolution | 572.838 | social services | 362.196 994 6 |
| Genetic factors | | *see also* Cancer — humans | |
| influence on crime | 364.24 | geriatrics | 618.976 65 |
| physical ethnology | 599.972 | incidence | 614.596 5 |
| Genetic makeup | 576.53 | medicine | 616.65 |
| Genetic recombination | 572.877 | pediatrics | 618.926 5 |
| Genetic regulation | 572.865 | pharmacokinetics | 615.766 |
| Genetic replication | 572.864 5 | social services | 362.196 65 |
| Genetic resources | 333.953 4 | surgery | 617.46 |
| animals | 333.954 | *see also* Urogenital diseases | |
| economics | 333.953 4 | | |
| plants | 333.953 4 | | |
| Genetic screening | 362.196 042 07 | | |
| crime prevention | 364.41 | | |

Genital herpes
  incidence — 614.547
  medicine — 616.951 8
  *see also* Communicable
    diseases — humans
Genital organs — 573.6
  *see also* Genital system
Genital system — 573.6
  anesthesiology — 617.967 46
  animals — 573.6
  diseases — 573.639
    *see also* Genital diseases
  human anatomy — 611.6
  human histology — 612.604 5
  human physiology — 612.6
  medicine — 616.65
  surgery — 617.46
  *see also* Female genital system;
    Male genital system
Genital warts
  incidence — 614.547
  medicine — 616.951 8
    *see also* Communicable
    diseases — humans
Genitalia — 573.6
  *see also* Genital system
Genitourinary system — 573.6
  human physiology — 612.46
  *see also* Genital system;
    Urinary system
Geniuses — 305.908 9
  T1—087 9
  psychology — 153.98
Genoa (Italy) — T2—451 821
  ancient — T2—371 21
Genoa (Italy : Province) — T2—451 82
  ancient — T2—371 2
Genoa (Republic) — 945.18
  T2—451 8
Genocide — 364.151
  ethics — 179.7
    *see also* Ethical problems
  law — 345.025 1
  sociology — 304.663
Genome mapping — 572.863 3
  humans — 611.018 166 3
Genomes — 572.86
  humans — 611.018 166
Genotype-environment
  interaction — 576.85
Genotypes — 576.53
Genova (Italy) — T2—451 821
  ancient — T2—371 21

Genova (Italy : Province) — T2—451 82
  ancient — T2—371 2
Genre paintings — 754
Gent (Belgium) — T2—493 142
Gentianales — 583.93
Gentians — 583.93
Gentleness — 179.9
  *see also* Virtues
Gentry County (Mo.) — T2—778 145
Genua (Italy) — T2—371 21
Geobotanical prospecting — 622.12
Geochelone — 597.924 6
Geochemical prospecting — 622.13
Geochemistry — 551.9
Geodesics
  geometry — 516.362
Geodesists — 526.109 2
Geodesy — 526.1
Geodetic astronomy — 526.6
Geodetic coordinates — 526.6
  spherical astronomy — 522.7
Geodetic surveying — 526.3
Geographers — 910.92
Geographic information systems — 910.285
  T1—028 5
  mathematical geography — 526.028 5
Geographic myths — 398.234
  *see also* Legendary places
Geographic positions
  geodetic astronomy — 526.64
Geographic subjects
  painting — 758.991
Geographic treatment — T1—09
  fine arts — 709
    *see Manual at* 704.9
    and 753–758; *also*
    at 709.012–.015,
    709.02–.05 vs. 709.3–.9
  *see Manual at* T1—09; *also at*
    380
Geography — 910
  arts — 700.42
    T3C—32
  Bible — 220.91
  literature — 808.803 2
    history and criticism — 809.933 2
  motion pictures — 791.436 2
  primary education — 372.891
  *see Manual at* 578 vs. 304.2,
    508, 910; *also at* 909,
    930–990 vs. 910
Geologic time — 551.701
Geological age measurements — 551.701
Geological ages — 551.7

Geological instruments
  manufacturing technology    681.755
Geological prospecting    622.12
Geological surveys
  public administration    354.39
  specific areas    554–559
Geologists    551.092
Geology    551
  law    344.095 5
  specific areas    554–559
Geomagnetic reversals    538.727
Geomagnetism    538.7
Geomancy    133.333
Geometric abstractionism    709.040 52
  painting    759.065 2
  sculpture    735.230 452
Geometric design    709.040 3
  painting    759.063
  sculpture    735.230 43
Geometric number theory    512.75
Geometric probability    519.2
Geometric progressions    515.24
Geometric shapes    516.15
Geometrical crystallography    548.81
Geometrical optics    535.32
Geometries over algebras    516.18
Geometries over rings    516.18
Geometroidea    595.78
Geometry    516
  famous problems    516.204
  primary education    372.76
Geometry of numbers    512.75
Geomorphologists    551.410 92
Geomorphology    551.41
Geomyidae    599.359 9
Geonavigation
  nautical    623.892
Geonavigation aids
  marine navigation    623.893
Geonim    296.120 092
Geophysical prospecting    622.15
Geophysics    550
  *see Manual at* 550 vs. 910
Geopolitics    320.12
  international relations    327.101
George (South Africa :
  District)    T2—687 37
George, Henry
  economic school    330.155
George, Lake (N.Y.)    T2—747 51
George I, King of Great Britain
  British history    941.071
  English history    942.071
  Scottish history    941.107 1

George II, King of Great Britain
  British history    941.072
  English history    942.072
  Scottish history    941.107 2
George III, King of Great Britain
  British history    941.073
  English history    942.073
  Scottish history    941.107 3
George IV, King of Great Britain
  British history    941.074
  English history    942.074
  Scottish history    941.107 4
George V, King of Great Britain
  British history    941.083
  English history    942.083
  Scottish history    941.108 3
George VI, King of Great Britain
  British history    941.084
  English history    942.084
  Scottish history    941.108 4
George County (Miss.)    T2—762 165
Georgetown (Guyana)    T2—881 5
Georgetown County (S.C.)    T2—757 89
Georgia    975.8
     T2—758
Georgia (Republic)    947.58
     T2—475 8
  ancient    939.536
     T2—395 36
Georgia, Strait of (B.C.)    551.461 433
     T2—164 33
Georgian architecture    724.19
Georgian Bay (Ont. : Bay)    T2—713 15
Georgian language    499.969
     T6—999 69
Georgian literature    899.969
Georgians
  (Transcaucasians)    T5—999 69
Geotectonics    551.8
Geothermal energy    333.88
  economics    333.88
  public administration    354.48
Geothermal engineering    621.44
Geothermal prospecting    622.159
Gera (Germany)    T2—432 22
Gera (Germany : Bezirk)    T2—432 22
Geraldton (W.A.)    T2—941 2
Geraniales    583.79
Geraniums (Pelargoniums)    635.933 79
  botany    583.79
  floriculture    635.933 79
Gerberas    583.99
  floriculture    635.933 99

Gerbils 636.935 83
 animal husbandry 636.935 83
 zoology 599.358 3
GERD (Disease)
 medicine 616.324
  *see also* Digestive system
   diseases — humans
Geriatric cardiology 618.976 12
Geriatric disorders 362.198 97
 incidence 614.599 297
 medicine 618.97
 social services 362.198 97
Geriatric nursing 618.970 231
Geriatric preventive measures 613.043 8
Geriatric surgery 617.97
Geriatric therapeutics 615.547
Geriatricians 618.970 092
 role and function 618.970 232
Geriatrics 618.97
 *see Manual at* 618.977 vs. 617
Germ cells 571.845
Germ plasm 333.953 4
 agriculture 631.523
  animal breeding 636.082 1
  plant cultivation 631.523
 resource economics 333.953 4
  animals 333.954
  plants 333.953 4
Germ warfare 358.38
 *see also* Biological warfare
German Center Party 324.243 025
German Communist Party 324.243 075
German Confederation 943.07
German Democratic Republic 943.108 7
  T2—431
German Empire 943.083
  T2—43
German folk music 781.623 1
German folk songs 782.421 623 1
German Green Party 324.243 087
German historical school
 (Economics) 330.154 2
German language 430
  T6—31
German literature 830
German measles
 incidence 614.524
 medicine 616.916
  *see also* Communicable
   diseases — humans
 pediatrics 618.929 16
German National Socialist Labor
 Party (Austria) 324.243 602 38

German New Guinea 995.302 1
  T2—953
German People's Union (Political
 party) 324.243 03
German police dog 636.737 6
German Pomerania T2—431 78
German Reformed Church (U.S.) 285.733
 *see also* Reformed Church
  (American Reformed)
German shepherd dog 636.737 6
Germania Inferior T2—369 2
Germania Magna T2—363
Germania Superior T2—364 39
Germanic languages 430
  T6—3
Germanic literatures 830
Germanic people T5—3
Germanic regions 943
  T2—43
 ancient 936.3
  T2—363
 Netherlands 949.2
  T2—492
  ancient 936.921
   T2—369 21
 Switzerland 949.4
  T2—494 7
  ancient 936.947
   T2—369 47
Germanic religion 293
Germanium
 chemical engineering 661.068 4
 chemistry 546.684
 metallurgy 669.79
Germans T5—31
Germans (Dances) 793.35
Germany 943
  T2—43
 ancient 936.3
  T2—363
Germany (East) 943.108 7
  T2—431
Germany (West) 943.087
  T2—43
Germination 571.862
Germiston (South Africa :
 District) T2—682 25
Germplasm 333.953 4
 *see also* Germ plasm
Gerona (Spain : Province) T2—467 1
Gerontology 305.26
 human physiology 612.67
 social aspects 305.26
 social welfare 362.6

Gerrymandering 328.334 55
Gers (France) T2—447 7
Gersau (Switzerland :
  Bezirk) T2—494 752 8
Gerunds 415.54
  specific languages T4—554
Gesneriaceae 583.95
Gestalt psychology 150.198 2
Gestalt therapy
  psychiatry 616.891 43
Gestational diabetes
  pregnancy complications
    obstetrics 618.364 6
Gestures 302.222
  drama 792.028
    motion pictures 791.430 28
    stage 792.028
    television 791.450 28
  preaching 251.03
  psychology 153.69
    expressive movements 152.384
    nonverbal communication 153.69
  rhetoric of speech 808.5
  social psychology 302.222
Gettysburg, Battle of, 1863 973.734 9
Geysers 551.23
Gezira (Sudan : State) T2—626 4
Ghana 966.7
  T2—667
Ghana Empire 966.101 6
  T2—661
Ghanaians T5—966 7
Gharb al-Istiwā'īyah
  (Sudan) T2—629 5
Gharb Baḥr al Ghazāl
  (Sudan) T2—629 4
Gharb-Chrarda-Béni Hsen
  (Morocco) T2—643 5
Gharb Dārfūr (Sudan :
  State) T2—627
Gharb Kurdufān (Sudan) T2—628
Gharbīyah (Egypt) T2—621
Ghardaia (Algeria :
  Province) T2—657
Gharīb
  Hadith 297.125 24
Ghazi I, King of Iraq
  Iraqi history 956.704 2
Ghazni dynasty 954.022 3
Ghent (Belgium) T2—493 142
Ghettos 307.336 6
  Holocaust, 1933–1945 940.531 85
Ghor dynasty 954.022 5
Ghost pipefishes 597.67

Ghost sharks 597.38
Ghosts 133.1
  arts 700.475
    T3C—375
  fiction 808.838 733
    history and criticism 809.387 33
    specific literatures T3B—308 733
      individual authors T3A—3
  folklore 398.25
    history and criticism 398.47
  literature 808.803 75
    history and criticism 809.933 75
    specific literatures T3B—080 375
      history and
        criticism T3B—093 75
  occultism 133.1
Gia Lai (Vietnam) T2—597 6
Giant ferns 587.33
Giant forest hog 599.633
Giant otter 599.769
Giant panda 599.789
  conservation technology 639.979 789
  resource economics 333.959 789
Giant perches 597.72
Giant schnauzer 636.73
Giant slalom skiing 796.935
Giant stars 523.88
Giants
  physical anthropology 599.949
Giant's Castle Game
  Reserve (South Africa) T2—684 7
Giardiasis
  medicine 616.34
    *see also* Digestive system
      diseases — humans
Gibbons 599.882
Gibbs' phase rule
  thermochemistry 541.363
Gibraltar 946.89
  T2—468 9
Gibraltar, Strait of 551.461 381
  T2—163 81
Gibraltar Range National
  Park (N.S.W.) T2—944 3
Gibson County (Ind.) T2—772 35
Gibson County (Tenn.) T2—768 23
Gibson Desert (W.A.) T2—941 5
Giessen (Germany :
  Regierungsbezirk) T2—434 14
Gift revenues
  public finance 336.16

| | |
|---|---|
| Gift tax | 336.276 |
| law | 343.053 5 |
| public administration | 352.44 |
| public finance | 336.276 |
| Gift wrappings | 745.54 |
| Gifted children | 305.908 908 3 |
| home care | 649.155 |
| psychology | 155.455 |
| special education | 371.95 |
| Gifted people | 305.908 9 |
| | T1—087 9 |
| collected biography | T1—092 7 |
| special education | 371.95 |
| Gifts | |
| financial management | 658.153 |
| library acquisitions | 025.26 |
| library-government relations | 021.8 |
| military rewards | 355.134 9 |
| sales promotion | 658.82 |
| Gifts of the Holy Spirit | 234.13 |
| Gifu-ken (Japan) | T2—521 62 |
| Gigantism (Pituitary) | |
| medicine | 616.47 |
| *see also* Endocrine | |
| diseases — humans | |
| Giglio Island (Italy) | T2—455 7 |
| Gila County (Ariz.) | T2—791 55 |
| Gila monster | 597.959 52 |
| Gila River (N.M. and Ariz.) | T2—791 7 |
| Gīlān (Iran) | T2—551 4 |
| Gilbert Islands | T2—968 1 |
| Gilchrist County (Fla.) | T2—759 78 |
| Gilding | |
| bookbinding | 686.36 |
| decorative arts | 745.75 |
| Giles County (Tenn.) | T2—768 61 |
| Giles County (Va.) | T2—755 782 |
| Gilgandra (N.S.W.) | T2—944 5 |
| Gill fungi | 579.6 |
| Gilles de la Tourette syndrome | |
| medicine | 616.83 |
| *see also* Nervous system | |
| diseases — humans | |
| Gillespie County (Tex.) | T2—764 65 |
| Gilliam County (Or.) | T2—795 65 |
| Gillingham (Kent, England) | T2—422 32 |
| Gills | 573.28 |
| descriptive zoology | 591.4 |
| physiology | 573.28 |
| Gilmer County (Ga.) | T2—758 295 |
| Gilmer County (W. Va.) | T2—754 27 |
| Gilpin County (Colo.) | T2—788 62 |
| Gilt-edged securities | 332.632 044 |
| *see Manual at* 332.632044 vs. | |
| 332.6323 | |
| Gilwern (Wales) | T2—429 98 |
| Gilyak | T5—946 |
| Gilyak language | 494.6 |
| | T6—946 |
| Gimps | 677.76 |
| Gin | 641.255 |
| commercial processing | 663.55 |
| Gin rummy | 795.418 |
| Ginger | 641.338 3 |
| botany | 584.39 |
| *see also* Spices | |
| Ginger ales | |
| commercial processing | 663.62 |
| Ginger lily | |
| botany | 584.39 |
| Gingival diseases | |
| dentistry | 617.632 |
| incidence | 614.599 6 |
| Gingivitis | |
| dentistry | 617.632 |
| Ginkgo tree | 635.977 57 |
| botany | 585.7 |
| ornamental arboriculture | 635.977 57 |
| Ginkgoales | 585.7 |
| paleobotany | 561.57 |
| Ginning cotton | 677.212 1 |
| Ginsengs | |
| botany | 583.84 |
| medicinal crops | 633.883 84 |
| pharmacology | 615.323 84 |
| Gippsland (Vic.) | T2—945 6 |
| Giraffe | 599.638 |
| Giraffidae | 599.638 |
| Girder bridges | |
| construction | 624.21 |
| Girders | 624.177 23 |
| naval architecture | 623.817 723 |
| structural engineering | 624.177 23 |
| Girdle-tailed lizards | 597.958 |
| Giresun İli (Turkey) | T2—565 7 |
| ancient | T2—393 37 |
| Girl Guides | 369.463 |
| Girl Scout camps | 796.542 2 |
| Girl Scouts | 369.463 |
| Girls | 305.230 82 |
| | T1—083 |
| criminal offenders | 364.36 |
| education | 371.822 |
| health | 613.042 42 |
| home care | 649.133 |
| journalism for | 070.483 27 |

Girls (continued)
| | |
|---|---|
| psychology | 155.433 |
| publications for | |
|   bibliographies | 011.624 2 |
| recreation | 790.194 |
|   indoor | 793.019 4 |
|   outdoor | 796.083 |
| sex hygiene | 613.955 |
| social aspects | 305.230 82 |

*see also* Children

| | |
|---|---|
| Girls' clubs | 369.46 |
| Girls' societies | 369.46 |
| Gironde (France) | T2—447 14 |
| GIS (Geographic information | |
|   systems) | 910.285 |
| | T1—028 5 |
|   mathematical geography | 526.028 5 |
| Gisborne District (N.Z.) | T2—934 4 |
| Gisborne Region (N.Z.) | T2—934 4 |
| Gisu (African people) | T5—963 95 |
| Gisu language | 496.395 |
| | T6—963 95 |
| Gittin | 296.123 3 |
|   Babylonian Talmud | 296.125 3 |
|   Mishnah | 296.123 3 |
|   Palestinian Talmud | 296.124 3 |
| Giudicati | 945.903 |
| Giurgiu (Romania : Județ) | T2—498 2 |
| Given names | 929.44 |
| Giyani (South Africa : | |
|   District) | T2—682 59 |
| Giza (Egypt) | T2—622 |
|   ancient | T2—322 |
| Gjoa Haven (Nunavut) | T2—719 55 |
| Glacial action | 551.313 |
| Glacial drift (Geologic | |
|   landforms) | 551.315 |
| Glacial drift (Geologic material) | 551.314 |
| Glacier Bay National Park | |
|   and Preserve (Alaska) | T2—798 2 |
| Glacier County (Mont.) | T2—786 52 |
| Glacier National Park (B.C.) | T2—711 68 |
| Glacier National Park | |
|   (Mont.) | T2—786 52 |
| Glaciers | 551.312 |
|   biology | 578.758 6 |
|   ecology | 577.586 |
| Glaciology | 551.31 |
| Glades County (Fla.) | T2—759 51 |
| Gladiolus | 635.934 38 |
|   botany | 584.38 |
|   floriculture | 635.934 38 |
| Gladstone (Qld.) | T2—943 5 |

| | |
|---|---|
| Gladwin County (Mich.) | T2—774 72 |
| Glamorgan, Vale of (Wales) | T2—429 89 |
| Gland diseases | |
|   medicine | 616.4 |

  *see also* Endocrine
    diseases — humans

| | |
|---|---|
| Glanders | |
|   incidence | 614.564 |
|   medicine | 616.954 |

  *see also* Communicable
    diseases — humans

| | |
|---|---|
| Glands | 571.79 |
|   biology | 571.79 |
|     endocrine system | 573.4 |
|   human anatomy | 611.4 |
|   human physiology | 612.4 |
|   medicine | 616.4 |

*see also* Endocrine system

| | |
|---|---|
| Glâne (Switzerland) | T2—494 532 |
| Glanford (England) | T2—428 32 |
| Glaris (Switzerland : | |
|   Canton) | T2—494 74 |
| Glarner Alps (Switzerland) | T2—494 74 |
| Glarus (Switzerland) | T2—494 744 |
| Glarus (Switzerland : | |
|   Canton) | T2—494 74 |
| Glascock County (Ga.) | T2—758 666 |
| Glasgow (Scotland) | T2—414 4 |
| Glass | 666.1 |
|   architectural construction | 721.044 96 |
|   building construction | 693.96 |
|   building materials | 691.6 |
|   decorative arts | 748 |
|   materials science | 620.144 |
|   optical components | |
|     manufacturing technology | 681.42 |
|   sculpture material | 731.2 |
|   ship design | 623.818 38 |
|   ship hulls | 623.845 8 |
|   shipbuilding | 623.820 7 |
|   structural engineering | 624.183 8 |
|   technology | 666.1 |
| Glass artists | 748.092 |
| Glass beads | 748.85 |
| Glass breakage insurance | 368.6 |
| Glass fibers | 666.157 |
| Glass harmonicas | 786.866 |

  *see also* Percussion instruments

| | |
|---|---|
| Glass insurance | 368.6 |
| Glass lizards | 597.959 2 |
| Glass painting | 748.502 82 |
| Glass-reinforced plastic | 668.494 2 |
| Glass sand | 553.622 |
| Glass sponges | 593.44 |

| | |
|---|---|
| Glass staining | 748.502 82 |
| Glass underpainting | 751.76 |
| Glassblowing | 666.122 |
| decorative arts | 748.202 82 |
| Glasscock County (Tex.) | T2—764 872 |
| Glassfibers | 666.157 |
| Glassware | 642.7 |
| decorative arts | 748 |
| biography | 748.092 |
| manufacturing technology | 666.19 |
| table setting | 642.7 |
| tableware | |
| decorative arts | 748.2 |
| biography | 748.209 2 |
| Glaucoma | |
| incidence | 614.599 7 |
| ophthalmology | 617.741 |
| see also Eye diseases — | |
| humans | |
| Glaucomys | 599.369 |
| Glauconite | |
| mineralogy | 549.67 |
| Glaze (Meteorology) | 551.574 4 |
| Glazes | |
| pottery | 666.427 |
| arts | 738.127 |
| technology | 666.427 |
| Glaziers | 698.509 2 |
| Glazing | |
| arts | 730.28 |
| leather | 675.25 |
| pottery | 666.444 |
| arts | 738.144 |
| technology | 666.444 |
| sculpture | 731.4 |
| windows | 698.5 |
| Glen Canyon National Recreation Area (Utah and Ariz.) | T2—792 59 |
| Glen Innes (N.S.W.) | T2—944 4 |
| Glencoe (South Africa : District) | T2—684 1 |
| Glenn County (Calif.) | T2—794 31 |
| Gliders (Aircraft) | 387.733 3 |
| engineering | 629.133 33 |
| piloting | 629.132 523 |
| transportation services | 387.733 3 |
| see also Aircraft | |
| Gliding | |
| aeronautics | 629.132 31 |
| sports | 797.55 |
| Gliridae | 599.359 6 |
| Global analysis | 514.74 |
| Global differential geometry | 516.362 |
| Global positioning systems | 910.285 |
| | T1—028 5 |
| mathematical geography | 526.640 285 |
| radio engineering | 621.384 191 |
| Global warming | 363.738 74 |
| see also Greenhouse effect | |
| Globes | |
| cataloging | 025.346 |
| library treatment | 025.176 |
| Globular clusters | 523.855 |
| Globulins | 572.66 |
| see also Proteins | |
| Glockenspiels | 786.843 |
| see also Percussion instruments | |
| Glomerulonephritis | |
| medicine | 616.612 |
| see also Urologic diseases — humans | |
| Gloria | 264.36 |
| music | 782.323 2 |
| Glossaries | |
| applied linguistics | 418 |
| specific languages | T4—81 |
| Glossinidae | 595.774 |
| Glossolalia | 234.132 |
| Glossopteris | 561.597 |
| Glottis | 573.925 |
| human anatomy | 611.22 |
| human physiology | 612.233 |
| medicine | 616.22 |
| see also Respiratory system | |
| Glottis diseases | |
| medicine | 616.22 |
| Gloucester (England) | T2—424 14 |
| Gloucester (N.B.) | T2—715 12 |
| Gloucester (N.S.W.) | T2—944 2 |
| Gloucester County (N.J.) | T2—749 81 |
| Gloucester County (Va.) | T2—755 32 |
| Gloucestershire (England) | T2—424 1 |
| Glove compartments | |
| automobile | 629.277 |
| Glove makers | 685.409 2 |
| Gloves | 391.412 |
| commercial technology | 685.4 |
| customs | 391.412 |
| home economics | 646.3 |
| home sewing | 646.48 |
| see also Clothing | |
| Glowworms | 595.764 4 |
| Gloxinias | 635.933 95 |
| botany | 583.95 |
| floriculture | 635.933 95 |
| Glucose | 572.565 |
| see also Carbohydrates | |

| | | | |
|---|---|---|---|
| Glue | 668.3 | Goats | 636.39 |
| *see also* Adhesives | | animal husbandry | 636.39 |
| Glue abuse | 362.299 3 | zoology | 599.648 |
| medicine | 616.86 | Goat's milk | 641.371 7 |
| personal health | 613.8 | cooking | 641.671 7 |
| social welfare | 362.299 3 | food | 641.371 7 |
| *see also* Substance abuse | | processing | 637.17 |
| Gluing | | Goatsuckers | 598.99 |
| bookbinding | 686.35 | Gobi Desert (Mongolia and | |
| Gluttony | 178 | China) | T2—517 3 |
| *see also* Consumption — ethics | | Gobies | 597.7 |
| Glycemic index | | Gobiesociformes | 597.62 |
| applied nutrition | 613.283 | God | 211 |
| human physiology | 612.396 | art representation | 704.948 |
| Glycerin | 668.2 | arts | 700.482 11 |
| Glycogen | 572.566 | | T3C—382 11 |
| *see also* Carbohydrates | | Buddhism | 294.342 11 |
| Glycoproteins | 572.68 | Christianity | 231 |
| *see also* Proteins | | comparative religion | 202.11 |
| Glycosides | 572.567 | Hinduism | 294.521 1 |
| *see also* Carbohydrates | | Islam | 297.211 |
| Glyndŵr (Wales) | T2—429 37 | Judaism | 296.311 |
| Glynn County (Ga.) | T2—758 742 | literature | 808.803 821 1 |
| Glyptics | 736.2 | history and criticism | 809.933 821 1 |
| Glyptographers | 736.209 2 | specific literatures | T3B—080 382 11 |
| Gmelina | 583.96 | history and | |
| forestry | 634.973 96 | criticism | T3B—093 821 1 |
| Gnassingbé, Faure | | philosophy of religion | 211 |
| Togolese history | 966.810 43 | Goddess religions | 201.43 |
| Gnats | 595.772 | Goddesses | 202.114 |
| Gneiss | 552.4 | arts | 700.482 021 14 |
| Gnetales | 585.8 | | T3C—382 021 14 |
| Gneticae | 585.8 | literature | 808.803 820 211 4 |
| paleobotany | 561.58 | history and criticism | 809.933 820 211 4 |
| Gnetum | 585.8 | specific literatures | T3B—080 382 021 14 |
| Gnosticism | 299.932 | history and | |
| Christian heresy | 273.1 | criticism | T3B—093 820 211 4 |
| GNP (Macroeconomics) | 339.31 | *see also* Gods and goddesses | |
| Gnus | 599.645 9 | Gödel's theorem | 511.3 |
| Go (Game) | 794.4 | Gods | 202.11 |
| Goa (India : State) | T2—547 8 | male | 202.113 |
| Goa, Daman and Diu (India) | T2—547 8 | Gods and goddesses | 202.11 |
| Goajiro Indians | T5—983 9 | African | 299.612 11 |
| Goalkeeping | | art representation | 704.948 |
| ice hockey | 796.962 27 | arts | 700.482 021 1 |
| soccer | 796.334 26 | | T3C—382 021 1 |
| Goat (Meat) | 641.363 9 | Australian | 299.921 5 |
| commercial processing | 664.92 | Buddhist | 294.342 11 |
| cooking | 641.663 9 | Celtic | 299.161 211 |
| food | 641.363 9 | Chinese | 299.511 211 |
| Goat hair textiles | 677.33 | classical | 292.211 |
| *see also* Textiles | | folklore | 398.21 |
| Goatfishes | 597.7 | history and criticism | 398.45 |
| | | Germanic | 293.211 |

Gods and goddesses (continued)
  Greek   292.211
  Hawaiian   299.924 202 11
  Hindu   294.521 1
  literature   808.803 820 211
    history and criticism   809.933 820 211
    specific literatures   T3B—080 382 021 1
    history and
      criticism   T3B—093 820 211
  Native American   299.712 11
    North American   299.712 11
    South American   299.812 11
  Norse   293.211
  Polynesian   299.924 021 1
  Roman   292.211
  Scandinavian   293.211
  Semitic   299.2
  Shinto   299.561 211
Goedelic languages   491.6
    T6—916
Goedelic literatures   891.6
Goethite
  mineralogy   549.525
Gogebic County (Mich.)   T2—774 983
Gogo languages   496.391
    T6—963 91
Goh, Chok Tong
  Singaporean history   959.570 52
Goiás (Brazil : State)   T2—817 3
Goidelic languages   491.6
    T6—916
Goidelic literatures   891.6
Going public (Securities)   658.152 24
  corporate law   346.066 2
  financial management   658.152 24
  investment economics   332.632 2
Goiter
  medicine   616.442
  *see also* Endocrine
    diseases — humans
  surgery   617.539
Gökçeada (Turkey)   T2—562 2
Gold   669.22
  chemical engineering   661.065 6
  chemistry   546.656
  economic geology   553.41
  materials science   620.189 22
  metallography   669.952 2
  metallurgy   669.22
  metalworking   673.22
  mining   622.342 2
  monetary law   343.032
  physical metallurgy   669.962 2
  production economics   338.274 1

Gold (continued)
  prospecting   622.184 1
  *see also* Chemicals; Metals
Gold Coast   966.703
    T2—667
Gold coins   332.404 2
  investment economics   332.63
  monetary economics   332.404 2
  numismatics   737.43
Gold standard   332.422 2
  foreign exchange   332.452
Golden (B.C.)   T2—711 68
Golden algae   579.86
Golden eagle   598.942 3
Golden Ears Provincial Park
  (B.C.)   T2—711 37
Golden Gate Highlands
  National Park (South
  Africa)   T2—685 1
Golden hamsters   599.356
Golden Rule
  Christianity   241.54
  Judaism   296.36
Golden Valley County
  (Mont.)   T2—786 311
Golden Valley County
  (N.D.)   T2—784 95
Goldeneyes   598.415
Goldenrods   583.99
Goldfinches   598.885
Goldfish   639.374 84
  culture   639.374 84
  zoology   597.484
Goldi   T5—941
Goldi language   494.1
    T6—941
Golds   T5—941
Goldsmithing   739.22
Goldsmiths   739.220 92
Golestān (Iran : Province)   T2—552 2
Golf   796.352
  equipment technology   688.763 52
Golf courses   796.352 068
Golfe-du-Saint-Laurent
  (Quebec)   T2—714 179
Golfers   796.352 092
Golgi apparatus   571.656
Goliad County (Tex.)   T2—764 123
Gombe State (Nigeria)   T2—669 84
Gomel' (Belarus : Oblast)   T2—478 1
Gómez, Juan Vicente
  Venezuelan history   987.063 13
Goms (Switzerland)   T2—494 794 1

Göncz, Árpád
  Hungarian history    943.905 41
Gond (Dravidian people)    T5—948 23
Gondi language    494.823
     T6—948 23
Gondi literature    894.823
Gondola cars    385.34
  engineering    625.24
  *see also* Rolling stock
Gonga (African people)    T5—935 9
Gongola State (Nigeria)    T2—669 88
Gongs    786.884 3
  *see also* Percussion instruments
Gonorhynchiformes    597.5
Gonorrhea
  incidence    614.547 8
  medicine    616.951 5
    *see also* Communicable
      diseases — humans
Gonystylus    583.68
  forestry    634.973 68
Gonzales County (Tex.)    T2—764 257
González Macchi, Luis Angel
  Paraguayan history    989.207 44
Goochland County (Va.)    T2—755 455
Good and evil    111.84
  ethics    170
    religion    205
      Christianity    241
      Islam    297.5
      Judaism    296.36
  religion    202.118
    Christianity    231.8
      freedom of choice    233.7
    comparative religion    202.118
    Islam    297.2
      freedom of choice    297.227
      theodicy    297.211 8
    Judaism    296.311 8
      freedom of choice    296.32
    philosophy of religion    214
Good Friday    263.925
  devotional literature    242.35
  music    781.726
  sermons    252.625
Good Hope, Cape of (South
  Africa : Cape)    T2—687 35
Good luck charms    133.443
Good luck spells    133.443
Good News Bible    220.520 82
Good spirits    202.15
Goodeniaceae    583.98
Goodhue County (Minn.)    T2—776 14
Gooding County (Idaho)    T2—796 36

Goodness-of-fit tests    519.56
Goodness of God    214
  Christianity    231.8
  comparative religion    202.112
  Islam    297.211 2
  Judaism    296.311 2
  philosophy of religion    214
Goodwood (South Africa :
  District)    T2—687 35
Goole (England)    T2—428 39
Goose hunting
  sports    799.244 7
Gooseberries    641.347 25
  botany    583.72
  cooking    641.647 25
  food    641.347 25
  horticulture    634.725
Goosefishes    597.62
Goosefoots (Plants)    583.53
Gophers (Ground squirrels)    599.365
Gophers (Pocket gophers)    599.359 9
Gorbachev, Mikhail Sergeevich
  Russian history    947.085 4
Gordioida    592.59
Gordon (Scotland : District)    T2—412 4
Gordon County (Ga.)    T2—758 362
Gordonia (South Africa :
  District)    T2—687 12
Gore District (N.Z.)    T2—939 7
Gorge walking    796.524
Gorges    551.442
     T2—144
  geography    910.914 4
  geomorphology    551.442
  physical geography    910.021 44
Gorgonzola cheese    641.373 53
  cooking    641.673 53
  food    641.373 53
  processing    637.353
Gorilla    599.884
  big game hunting    799.278 84
  conservation technology    639.979 884
  resource economics    333.959 884
Gorizia (Italy : Province)    T2—453 92
  ancient    T2—373 82
Gorj (Romania)    T2—498 4
Gorno-Altay (Russia)    T2—573
Gorno-Badakhshan
  Autonomous Oblast
  (Tajikistan)    T2—586
Goroka (Papua New
  Guinea)    T2—956 9
Gorontalo (Indonesia)    T2—598 43

Gorton, John, Sir
  Australian history    994.061
Gorzów Wielkopolski
  (Poland : Voivodeship)  T2—438 12
Gor'ki (Russia : Oblast)  T2—474 1
Gor'kovskaĩa oblast'
  (Russia)  T2—474 1
Gosford (N.S.W.)  T2—944 2
Gösgen (Switzerland :
  Bezirk)  T2—494 351 3
Goshen County (Wyo.)  T2—787 18
Gospel music  782.254
  choral and mixed voices  782.525 4
  single voices  783.092 54
Gospel stories retold  226.095 05
Gospels (Bible)  226
  pseudepigrapha  229.8
Gosper County (Neb.)  T2—782 387
Gosport (England)  T2—422 78
Gossip
  ethics  177.2
    religion  205.672
      Christianity  241.672
      Judaism  296.367 2
    *see also* Ethical problems
  social psychology  302.24
Götaland (Sweden)  T2—486
Göteborgs och Bohus län
  (Sweden)  T2—486 7
Gotha (Germany :
  Landkreis)  T2—432 24
Gothic architecture  723.5
Gothic art  709.022
  religious significance  246.1
Gothic calligraphy  745.619 75
Gothic decoration  745.409 021
Gothic fiction  808.838 729
  history and criticism  809.387 29
  specific literatures  T3B—308 729
    individual authors  T3A—3
Gothic language  439.9
      T6—399
  literature  839.9
Gothic music  780.902
Gothic novels  808.838 729
  history and criticism  809.387 29
  specific literatures  T3B—308 729
    individual authors  T3A—3
Gothic painting  759.022
Gothic revival architecture  724.3
Gothic sculpture  734.25
Gothic tracery  729.5
Gothic type  686.224 7

Goths (Germanic people)  T5—39
  Italian history  945.01
  Sicilian history  945.801
Gotland landskap (Sweden)  T2—486 9
Gotlands län (Sweden)  T2—486 9
Gouache  751.422
Goulart, João Belchior Marques
  Brazilian history  981.062
Goulburn (N.S.W.)  T2—944 7
Goulburn River (Vic.)  T2—945 4
Gouled Aptidon, Hassan
  Djiboutian history  967.710 41
Gourds  583.63
  floriculture  635.933 63
Gourmet cooking  641.514
Gout
  medicine  616.399 9
    *see also* Digestive system
      diseases — humans
Gove County (Kan.)  T2—781 152
Governing boards
  executive management  658.422
      T1—068 4
  hospitals  362.110 684
  libraries  021.82
  public administration  352.25
Government  320
  ethics  172.2
    *see also* Political ethics
  *see Manual at* 320.9, 320.4 vs.
    351
Government accounting  657.835
  law  343.034
Government advisory boards  352.743
Government agencies  351
  *see also* Administrative
    agencies
Government audit procedures  657.835 045
Government bills  332.632 32
  *see also* Government securities
Government bonds  332.632 32
  *see also* Government securities
Government buildings
  architecture  725.1
  area planning  711.551
Government business enterprises  338.749
Government certificates  332.632 32
  *see also* Government securities
Government cities
  area planning  711.45
Government contracts  352.53
  armed forces  355.621 2
  law  346.023

Government corporations 338.749
  law 346.067
  production economics 338.749
  public administration 352.266
  public revenue source 336.19
Government employees 352.63
  *see also* Government workers
Government expenditures 336.39
  *see also* Public expenditures
Government farm policies 338.18
Government gazettes 351.05
Government grants
  production economics 338.922
Government information services
  international relations 327.11
    libraries 027.5
    public administration 353.132 74
Government institutions
  sociology 306.2
Government investment 332.672 52
  international 332.673 12
Government liability
  law 342.088
  public administration 352.885
Government loans
  credit economics 332.7
  economic development 338.922
  law 343.074 2
  public revenues 336.15
Government notes 332.632 32
  *see also* Government securities
Government of Ireland Act, 1920 941.608 21
Government ownership
  land economics 333.1
Government policy 320.6
Government procurement 352.53
  armed forces 355.621 2
Government property
  land economics 333.1
  law 343.02
  management 352.5
Government publications
  bibliographies 011.53
  cataloging 025.343 4
  library treatment 025.173 4
Government publishers 070.595
Government savings banks 332.21
Government securities 332.632 32
  flotation 336.344
  income tax 336.242 6
    law 343.052 46
  investment economics 332.632 32
  law 346.092 2
  public administration 352.45

Government securities (continued)
  public finance 336.31
  purchase
    central banking 332.114
  *see Manual at* 332.632044 vs.
    332.6323
Government service 352.63
Government spending 336.39
  *see also* Public expenditures
Government-sponsored insurance 368.4
  law 344.02
  public administration 353.54
Government subsidies
  production economics 338.922
Government work force 352.63
Government workers 352.63
  administrative law 342.068
  biography 351.092
  labor economics 331.795
    labor force 331.119 042
    labor market 331.129 042
  pensions 331.252 913 51
    public administration 353.549
  public administration 352.63
  social class 305.553
Governmental investigations
  official misconduct 353.463
Governmental organizations 351
  *see also* Administrative
    agencies
Governmental social action 361.6
Governments-in-exile
  World War II 940.533 6
Governors (Control devices)
  internal-combustion engines 621.437
Governors (Executives) 352.23
  public administration 352.232 13
Governors-general
  (Commonwealth of Nations)
  public administration 352.233
GPS (Global positioning
  systems) 910.285
                T1—028 5
  mathematical geography 526.640 285
  radio engineering 621.384 191
GPS (Swiss political party) 324.249 408 7
GPS receivers
  marine navigation 623.893 3
  radio engineering 621.384 191
Graaff-Reinet (South
  Africa : District) T2—687 54
Grace (Religious doctrine) 202.2
  Christianity 234

Gracias a Dios (Honduras : Dept.)   T2—728 32
Grackles   598.874
Grade repetition   371.285
Grade schools   372
  *see also* Primary education
Grade separations (Roads)   388.13
Grades (Military ranks)   355.33
Grading (Earthwork)   624.152
  foundation engineering   624.152
  road engineering   625.733
Grading (Students)   371.272
Grading clothing
  commercial technology   687.042
Grading crops   631.567
Grading lumber   674.5
Gradual   264.36
  music   782.323 5
Graduate Record Examination   378.166 2
Graduate schools   378.155
Graduations (Commencements)   371.291 2
  customs   394.2
Grady County (Ga.)   T2—758 986
Grady County (Okla.)   T2—766 54
Graffiti   080
  literature   808.882
    history and criticism   809.982
    specific literatures   T3B—802
      individual authors   T3A—8
  painting   751.73
Graft (Crime)   364.132 3
  law   345.023 23
  public administration   353.46
Grafting (Plant propagation)   631.541
  equipment manufacturing
    technology   681.763 1
  fruit crops   634.044 1
  ornamental plants   635.915 41
Grafting (Surgery)   617.954
Grafton (N.S.W.)   T2—944 3
Grafton County (N.H.)   T2—742 3
Graham County (Ariz.)   T2—791 54
Graham County (Kan.)   T2—781 163
Graham County (N.C.)   T2—756 97
Grain (Cereal)   641.331
  animal feed
    commercial processing   664.762
    commercial processing   664.7
  *see also* Cereals
Grain amaranths   641.331
  *see also* Amaranths
Grain beetles   633.104 976
Grain elevators   633.104 68
Grain legumes   633.3

Grain sorghums   633.174
Grainger County (Tenn.)   T2—768 932
Graining (Woodwork)
  buildings   698.32
Gram-negative aerobic rods and
  cocci   579.33
Gram-negative bacterial
  infections
  humans
    incidence   614.57
    medicine   616.92
    *see also* Communicable
      diseases — humans
Gram-positive bacterial
  infections
  humans
    incidence   614.579
    medicine   616.929
    *see also* Communicable
      diseases — humans
Gram-positive cocci   579.35
Graminales   584.9
  paleobotany   561.49
Gramineae   584.9
Grammar   415
  applied linguistics   418
    specific languages   T4—82
  primary education   372.61
  specific languages   T4—5
  *see Manual at* 401.43 vs.
    306.44, 401.45, 401.9, 412,
    415
Grammar checkers (Computer
  programs)   005.52
Grammar schools (Primary
  schools)   372
  *see also* Primary education
Grammar schools (Secondary
  schools)   373.241
  *see also* Secondary education
Grammarians   415.092
Grammatical categories   415
  specific languages   T4—5
Grammatical relations   415
  specific languages   T4—5
Grammatidae   597.73
Grampian (Scotland)   T2—412 4
Grampian Mountains
  (Scotland)   T2—411 58
Grampians (Scotland)   T2—411 58
Gran Colombia   986.104
     T2—861
  Colombian history   986.104
  Ecuadorian history   986.604

Gran Colombia (continued)
  Panamanian history      972.870 3
  Venezuelan history      987.05
Granada (Nicaragua : Dept.)  T2—728 515
Granada (Spain : Province)  T2—468 2
Granadillas      583.626
Granadine Confederation      986.105 3
  Colombian history      986.105 3
  Panamanian history      972.870 3
Granaries      633.104 68
Granby River (B.C.)  T2—711 62
Grand Alliance, War of the,
  1688–1697      940.252 5
Grand Army of the Republic      369.15
Grand Bahama (Bahamas)  T2—729 6
Grand Bahama Island  T2—729 6
Grand Banks of Newfoundland      551.461 344
      T2—163 44
Grand Canyon National
  Park (Ariz.)  T2—791 32
Grand Casablanca
  (Morocco)  T2—643 8
Grand County (Colo.)  T2—788 65
Grand County (Utah)  T2—792 58
Grand Forks (B.C.)  T2—711 62
Grand Forks County (N.D.)  T2—784 16
Grand Isle County (Vt.)  T2—743 12
Grand jury      345.072
Grand Lake (Ohio)  T2—771 415
Grand Manan Island (N.B.)  T2—715 33
Grand Prairie (Tex.)  T2—764 51
Grand Rapids (Mich.)  T2—774 56
Grand River (Iowa and Mo.)  T2—778 2
Grand River (Mich.)  T2—774 15
Grand Staircase-Escalante
  National Monument
  (Utah)  T2—792 51
Grand Teton National Park
  (Wyo.)  T2—787 55
Grand Traverse Bay (Mich.)  T2—774 64
Grand Traverse County
  (Mich.)  T2—774 64
Grand unified theory      530.142
Grand'Anse (Haiti : Dept.)  T2—729 466
Grandchildren      306.874 5
      T1—085 4
Grande Prairie (Alta.)  T2—712 31
Grande Terre (Guadeloupe)  T2—729 76
Grandmothers
  social welfare      362.839 55
Grandparents      306.874 5
      T1—085 3

Grandstands
  architecture      725.827
Granit (Quebec)  T2—714 69
Granite      553.52
  building material      691.2
  economic geology      553.52
  petrology      552.3
  quarrying      622.352
Granite Belt National Park
  (Qld.)  T2—943 3
Granite County (Mont.)  T2—786 88
Granite mosses      588.2
Granma (Cuba)  T2—729 163
Grant, Ulysses S. (Ulysses
  Simpson)
  United States history      973.82
Grant County (Ark.)  T2—767 71
Grant County (Ind.)  T2—772 69
Grant County (Kan.)  T2—781 723
Grant County (Ky.)  T2—769 395
Grant County (Minn.)  T2—776 44
Grant County (N.D.)  T2—784 87
Grant County (N.M.)  T2—789 692
Grant County (Neb.)  T2—782 783
Grant County (Okla.)  T2—766 23
Grant County (Or.)  T2—795 78
Grant County (S.D.)  T2—783 24
Grant County (W. Va.)  T2—754 92
Grant County (Wash.)  T2—797 32
Grant County (Wis.)  T2—775 77
Grant Parish (La.)  T2—763 67
Grants
  capital procurement      658.152 24
  education      379.11
      T1—079
    financial management      371.206
    public policy      379.11
    student aid      371.223
      higher education      378.33
      law      344.079 5
  production economics      338.922
  public administration      352.73
  research      001.44
      T1—079
  students  T1—079
Grants-in-aid (Government)      336.185
  law      343.034
  public administration      352.73
  public finance      336.185
Granulocytes      571.968
  human immunology      616.079 9
Granville County (N.C.)  T2—756 535
Grape ferns      587.33

| | |
|---|---|
| Grape wine | 641.22 |
| commercial processing | 663.2 |
| cooking with | 641.622 |
| home preparation | 641.872 |
| Grapefruit | 641.343 2 |
| commercial processing | 664.804 32 |
| cooking | 641.643 2 |
| food | 641.343 2 |
| orchard crop | 634.32 |
| Grapes | 641.348 |
| botany | 583.86 |
| commercial processing | 664.804 8 |
| cooking | 641.648 |
| food | 641.348 |
| viticulture | 634.8 |
| Graph coloring | 511.56 |
| Graph theory | 511.5 |
| Graphic artists | 740.92 |
| Graphic arts | 740 |
| Graphic arts paper | 676.282 |
| Graphic calculators | 510.284 |
| Graphic design | |
| arts | 741.6 |
| Graphic designers | 741.609 2 |
| Graphic expressions | |
| psychology | 152.384 5 |
| Graphic methods | 518.23 |
| Graphic novelists | |
| biography | 741.593–.599 |
| *see Manual at* 741.593–.599 | |
| and 741.5693–.5699 | |
| Graphic novels | 741.5 |
| | T1—022 2 |
| drawing | 741.51 |
| genres | |
| history, criticism, techniques | 741.53 |
| geographic treatment | 741.593–.599 |
| *see Manual at* 741.593–.599 | |
| and 741.5693 .5699 | |
| humor | T1—020 7 |
| *see Manual at* 741.5; *also at* | |
| 741.56 | |
| Graphic representation | 604.2 |
| Graphic statics | |
| mechanics | 531.12 |
| solids | 531.2 |
| structural analysis | 624.171 2 |
| Graphical user interfaces | |
| systems programs | 005.437 |
| Graphics | |
| computer science | 006.6 |
| | T1—028 566 |
| engineering | 621.399 6 |
| Graphics programming languages | 006.663 |
| Graphics terminals | 006.62 |
| Graphics utilities | 006.68 |
| Graphite | 553.26 |
| chemical engineering | 662.92 |
| economic geology | 553.26 |
| materials science | 620.198 |
| mineralogy | 549.27 |
| mining | 622.336 |
| synthetic | 666.86 |
| Graphitic anthracite coal | |
| properties | 662.622 5 |
| Graphology | 155.282 |
| criminal investigation | 363.256 5 |
| divination | 137 |
| personnel selection | 658.311 2 |
| Graphs | 511.5 |
| | T1—022 |
| Graptemys | 597.925 9 |
| Graptolitoidea | 563.55 |
| Grass carp | 597.482 |
| Grass owls | 598.97 |
| Grass skiing | 796.2 |
| Grass wax | 665.12 |
| Grass wetlands | |
| biology | 578.768 4 |
| ecology | 577.684 |
| Grasses | 584.9 |
| botany | 584.9 |
| cereal crops | 633.1 |
| floriculture | 635.964 |
| forage crops | 633.2 |
| ornamental gardening | 635.934 9 |
| paleobotany | 561.49 |
| Grasshoppers | 595.726 |
| agricultural pests | 632.726 |
| culture | 638.572 6 |
| Grasslands | 333.74 |
| | T2—153 |
| animal husbandry | 636.084 5 |
| biology | 578.74 |
| ecology | 577.4 |
| economics | 333.74 |
| geography | 910.915 3 |
| geomorphology | 551.453 |
| physical geography | 910.021 53 |
| Gratiot County (Mich.) | T2—774 49 |
| Gratitude | 179.9 |
| *see also* Virtues | |
| Grau (Peru : Region) | T2—851 2 |
| Graubünden (Switzerland) | T2—494 73 |
| Graupel | 551.578 7 |

| | |
|---|---|
| Gravel | 553.626 |
|   economic geology | 553.626 |
|   materials science | 620.191 |
|   quarrying | 622.362 6 |
| Gravel pavements | 625.82 |
| Graves County (Ky.) | T2—769 93 |
| Graves' disease | |
|   medicine | 616.443 |
|   *see also* Endocrine | |
|     diseases — humans | |
| Graves registration service | |
|   (Armed forces) | 355.699 |
| Gravesham (England) | T2—422 315 |
| Gravestone inscriptions | |
|   genealogy | 929.5 |
| Gravimetric analysis | 543.2 |
| Gravitation | 531.14 |
|   *see also* Gravity | |
| Gravitational interaction | 539.754 |
| Gravitational prospecting | 622.152 |
| Gravitational waves | 539.754 |
| Gravity | 531.14 |
|   astromechanics | 629.411 1 |
|   biophysics | 571.435 |
|     humans | 612.014 412 |
|   celestial mechanics | 521.1 |
|   extraterrestrial biophysics | |
|     humans | 612.014 532 |
|   mechanics | 531.14 |
|   solid mechanics | 531.5 |
| Gravity concentration of ores | 622.751 |
| Gravity determinations | |
|   geodesy | 526.7 |
| Gravity planes | |
|   mining | 622.66 |
| Gravity waves | 551.515 |
| Gray County (Kan.) | T2—781 74 |
| Gray County (Tex.) | T2—764 827 |
| Gray fox | 599.776 |
| Gray kangaroos | 599.222 |
| Gray partridge | 598.623 2 |
| Gray seal | 599.793 |
| Gray squirrel | 599.362 |
| Gray whale | 599.522 |
|   conservation technology | 639.979 522 |
|   resource economics | 333.959 522 |
| Gray wolf | 599.773 |
| Graylings | 597.559 |
| Grays Harbor County | |
|   (Wash.) | T2—797 95 |
| Graysby | 597.736 |
| Grayson County (Ky.) | T2—769 842 |
| Grayson County (Tex.) | T2—764 557 |
| Grayson County (Va.) | T2—755 717 |
| Graz (Austria) | T2—436 55 |
| Grazing | 591.54 |
|   animal husbandry | 636.084 5 |
|   descriptive zoology | 591.54 |
| Grazing lands | 333.74 |
|   *see also* Grasslands | |
| GRE (Graduate Record | |
|   Examination) | 378.166 2 |
| Great apes | 599.88 |
| Great Australian Bight (W.A. and | 551.461 576 |
|   S. Aust.) | T2—165 76 |
| Great Barrier Island (N.Z.) | T2—932 4 |
| Great Barrier Reef (Qld.) | T2—943 |
| Great Basin | 979 |
| | T2—79 |
| Great Basin National Park | T2—793 15 |
| Great Bear Lake (N.W.T.) | T2—719 3 |
| Great Belt (Denmark) | 551.461 334 |
| | T2—163 34 |
| Great blue shark | 597.34 |
| Great Britain | 941 |
| | T2—41 |
|   ancient | 936.1 |
| | T2—361 |
|   *see Manual at* 941 | |
| Great Britain. Attorney-General | 345.420 1 |
| Great Britain. County Court | 347.420 21 |
| Great Britain. Court of Appeal | 347.420 32 |
| Great Britain. Court of Appeal. | |
|   Civil Division | 347.420 35 |
| Great Britain. Court of Appeal. | |
|   Criminal Division | 345.420 18 |
| Great Britain. Crown Court | 345.420 14 |
| Great Britain. Director of Public | |
|   Prosecutions | 345.420 1 |
| Great Britain. High Court of | |
|   Justice | 347.420 25 |
| Great Britain. High Court of | |
|   Justice. Chancery Division | 347.420 26 |
| Great Britain. High Court of | |
|   Justice. Family Division | 346.420 150 269 |
| Great Britain. High Court | |
|   of Justice. King's Bench | |
|   Division | 347.420 27 |
| Great Britain. High Court of | |
|   Justice. Queen's Bench | |
|   Division | 347.420 27 |
| Great Britain. High Court of | |
|   Justice. Queen's Bench | |
|   Division. Divisional Court | 345.420 16 |
| Great Britain. House of Lords | |
|   (Court of last resort) | 347.420 39 |
| Great Britain. Magistrates Court | 345.420 12 |

Great Britain. Magistrates Court.
  Domestic Court                347.420 23
Great Britain. Privy Council.
  Judicial Committee            347.420 4
Great Britain. Supreme Court of
  Judicature                    347.420 29
Great Dane                      636.73
Great Dividing Range            T2—94
Great Earthquake, 1692          972.920 32
Great Glen (Scotland)           T2—411 56
Great grandchildren             306.874 5
                                T1—085 4
Great grandparents              306.874 5
                                T1—085 3
Great Grimsby (England)         T2—428 34
Great Indian Desert (India
  and Pakistan)                 T2—544
Great Island (Argentina and
  Chile)                        T2—827 6
Great Karoo (South Africa)      T2—687 39
Great Kei River (South
  Africa)                       T2—687 58
Great Lake (Tas.)               T2—946 3
Great Lakes                     T2—77
  Canada                        T2—713
  United States                 T2—77
Great liverworts                588.3
Great Moravian Empire           943.702 1
                                T2—437
Great Northern War, 1700–1721   947.05
Great Ouse, River (England)     T2—426
Great Plains                    T2—78
  Colorado                      T2—788 7
  Montana                       T2—786 1
  New Mexico                    T2—789 2
  Texas                         T2—764 8
  Wyoming                       T2—787 1
Great Pyrenee (Dog)             636.73
Great Rift Valley               T2—676
Great Salt Lake (Utah)          T2—792 42
Great Salt Lake Desert
  (Utah)                        T2—792 43
Great Sand Dunes National
  Park and Preserve
  (Colo.)                       T2—788 49
Great Sandy Desert (W.A.)       T2—941 5
Great schism, 1054              270.38
Great Slave Lake (N.W.T.)       T2—719 3
Great Smoky Mountains
  (N.C. and Tenn.)              T2—768 89
  North Carolina                T2—756 96
  Tennessee                     T2—768 89

Great Smoky Mountains
  National Park (N.C. and
  Tenn.)                        T2—768 89
Great Trek, 1835–1838           968.042
Great Valley (Calif.)           T2—794 5
Great Victoria Desert
  (W.A.)                        T2—941 5
Great War, 1914–1918            940.3
Great whales                    599.5
Great White Brotherhood         299.93
Great white shark               597.33
Great Yarmouth (England :
  Borough)                      T2—426 18
Greater Anchorage Area
  Borough (Alaska)              T2—798 35
Greater Antilles                T2—729
Greater Manchester
  (England)                     T2—427 3
Greater Saint Lucia Wetland
  Park (South Africa)           T2—684 3
Greater Sudbury (Ont.)          T2—713 133
Greater Vancouver (B.C.)        T2—711 33
Grebes                          598.443
Grebo language                  496.33
                                T6—963 3
Greco-Roman wrestling           796.812 2
Greco-Turkish War, 1896–1897    949.507 2
Greece                          949.5
                                T2—495
  ancient                       938
                                T2—38
Greed                           178
  moral theology                205.68
  see also Vices
Greek architecture              722.8
Greek calligraphy               745.619 8
Greek language                  480
                                T6—8
  Biblical texts                220.48
  printing                      686.218
Greek language (Modern)         489.3
                                T6—89
Greek law
  ancient                       340.538
Greek-letter societies          371.85
                                T1—06
Greek literature                880
Greek literature (Modern)       889
Greek philosophy                180
  modern                        199.495
Greek religion                  292.08
Greek revival architecture      724.23
Greek sculpture                 733.3

| | | | |
|---|---|---|---|
| Greeks (Ethnic group) | T5—8 | Greene County (Pa.) | T2—748 83 |
| ancient | T5—81 | Greene County (Tenn.) | T2—768 91 |
| modern | T5—89 | Greene County (Va.) | T2—755 375 |
| Greeks (National group) | T5—893 | Greenhouse effect | 363.738 74 |
| Greeley County (Kan.) | T2—781 413 | crop damage | 632.1 |
| Greeley County (Neb.) | T2—782 49 | ecology | 577.276 |
| Green algae | 579.83 | meteorology | 551.525 3 |
| Green Alliance (Swiss political | | pollution aspects | 363.738 74 |
| party) | 324.249 408 7 | social effects | 304.28 |
| Green bacteria | 579.38 | weather forecasting | 551.642 5 |
| Green Bay (Wis.) | T2—775 61 | Greenhouse gardening | 635.048 3 |
| Green Bay (Wis. and Mich.) | T2—775 63 | floriculture | 635.982 3 |
| Green County (Ky.) | T2—769 695 | Greenhouses | 631.583 |
| Green County (Wis.) | T2—775 86 | agriculture | 631.583 |
| Green fodder | | architecture | 725.37 |
| forage crop | 633.2 | construction | 690.537 |
| Green integral | 515.43 | domestic | |
| Green Lake County (Wis.) | T2—775 59 | architecture | 728.924 |
| Green manures | 631.874 | construction | 690.892 4 |
| Green marketing | | floriculture | 635.982 3 |
| management | 658.802 | gardening | 635.048 3 |
| Green monkeys | 599.862 | Greenland | 998.2 |
| Green Mountains (Vt.) | T2—743 | | T2—982 |
| Green movement | 320.58 | Greenland cod | 597.633 |
| Green parties | 324.218 7 | Greenland halibut | 597.694 |
| Green Party (Germany) | 324.243 087 | Greenland right whale | 599.527 6 |
| Green Party of Switzerland | 324.249 408 7 | Greenland Sea | 551.461 324 |
| Green peppers | 641.356 43 | | T2—163 24 |
| *see also* Sweet peppers | | Greenlandic Inuit | T5—971 2 |
| Green politics | 320.58 | Greenlandic Inuit language | 497.12 |
| Green River (Ky. : River) | T2—769 8 | | T6—971 2 |
| Green River (Wyo.-Utah) | T2—792 5 | Greenlandic Inuktitut language | 497.12 |
| Utah | T2—792 5 | | T6—971 2 |
| Wyoming | T2—787 85 | Greenlandic language | 497.12 |
| Green seaweeds | 579.83 | | T6—971 2 |
| Green technology | T1—028 6 | Greenlee County (Ariz.) | T2—791 51 |
| architecture | 720.47 | Greenlets | 598.878 |
| construction | 690.028 6 | Greens (Austrian political party) | 324.243 608 7 |
| engineering | 628 | Greens (German political party) | 324.243 087 |
| Green turtle | 597.928 | Greensands | |
| Greenbrier County (W. Va.) | T2—754 88 | petrology | 552.5 |
| Greenbrier River (W. Va.) | T2—754 88 | Greensville County (Va.) | T2—755 572 |
| Greenbriers | 584.356 | Greenup County (Ky.) | T2—769 293 |
| Greene County (Ala.) | T2—761 42 | Greenville County (S.C.) | T2—757 27 |
| Greene County (Ark.) | T2—767 993 | Greenwich (London, | |
| Greene County (Ga.) | T2—758 612 | England) | T2—421 62 |
| Greene County (Ill.) | T2—773 84 | Greenwood (B.C.) | T2—711 62 |
| Greene County (Ind.) | T2—772 42 | Greenwood County (Kan.) | T2—781 913 |
| Greene County (Iowa) | T2—777 466 | Greenwood County (S.C.) | T2—757 33 |
| Greene County (Miss.) | T2—762 173 | Greer County (Okla.) | T2—766 443 |
| Greene County (Mo.) | T2—778 78 | Greeting card verse | 808.81 |
| Greene County (N.C.) | T2—756 393 | history and criticism | 809.1 |
| Greene County (N.Y.) | T2—747 37 | specific literatures | T3B—1 |
| Greene County (Ohio) | T2—771 74 | individual authors | T3A—1 |

| | |
|---|---|
| Greeting cards | |
| handicrafts | 745.594 1 |
| illustration | 741.684 |
| Greetings | |
| etiquette | 395.4 |
| Gregg County (Tex.) | T2—764 189 |
| Gregg shorthand systems | 653.427 |
| Gregorian calendar | 529.43 |
| Gregorian chants | 782.322 2 |
| Gregory VII, Pope | |
| Corsican history | 944.990 2 |
| Gregory County (S.D.) | T2—783 59 |
| Greifswald (Germany) | T2—431 78 |
| Greiz (Germany : | |
| Landkreis) | T2—432 22 |
| Grenada | 972.984 5 |
| | T2—729 845 |
| Grenada County (Miss.) | T2—762 635 |
| Grenades | 623.451 14 |
| Grenadiers (Fishes) | 597.63 |
| Grenadiers (Troops) | 356.162 |
| Grenadine (Textile) | 677.652 |
| Grenadines | T2—729 844 |
| Grenoble (France) | T2—445 865 |
| Grevena (Greece : Nome) | T2—495 62 |
| Grevilleas | 635.933 89 |
| botany | 583.89 |
| floriculture | 635.933 89 |
| Grey (Ont. : County) | T2—713 18 |
| Grey Cup | 796.335 648 |
| Grey District (N.Z.) | T2—937 2 |
| Greyerz (Switzerland : | |
| Bezirk) | T2—494 533 |
| Greyhound | 636.753 4 |
| Greyhound racing | 798.85 |
| Greylag goose | 598.417 3 |
| Grid computing | 004.36 |
| Gridiron street patterns | |
| area planning | 711.41 |
| Gridirons (American football) | 796.332 068 |
| Grief | 152.4 |
| at death | 155.937 |
| Christianity | |
| pastoral theology | 259.6 |
| personal religion | 248.866 |
| prayers and meditations | 242.4 |
| psychology | 155.937 |
| Grievances (Labor) | 331.889 66 |
| economics | 331.889 66 |
| law | 344.018 896 |
| personnel management | 658.315 5 |
| public administration | 352.68 |
| Grievances against government | |
| public administration | 352.885 |
| Griffith (N.S.W.) | T2—944 8 |
| Griggs County (N.D.) | T2—784 34 |
| Grilling (Cooking) | 641.76 |
| Grills (Cooking equipment) | |
| outdoor cooking | 641.578 4 |
| Grills (Screens) | |
| ironwork | |
| arts | 739.48 |
| Grimes County (Tex.) | T2—764 243 |
| Grimoire | 133.43 |
| Grimsby (England) | T2—428 34 |
| Grinding | |
| chemical engineering | 660.284 22 |
| coal | 662.623 |
| metals | 671.35 |
| ores | 622.73 |
| Grinding tools | 621.92 |
| Grindstones | 621.923 |
| Griqualand East (South | |
| Africa) | T2—684 6 |
| Grise Fiord (Nunavut) | T2—719 52 |
| Grisons (Animals) | 599.766 |
| Grisons (Switzerland) | T2—494 73 |
| Grizzly bear | 599.784 |
| conservation technology | 639.979 784 |
| resource economics | 333.959 784 |
| Groblersdal (South Africa : | |
| District) | T2—682 75 |
| Grocery trade | 381.456 413 |
| Grodno (Belarus : Oblast) | T2—478 8 |
| Groined arches | 721.44 |
| architecture | 721.44 |
| construction | 690.144 |
| Groined vaults | 721.44 |
| architecture | 721.44 |
| construction | 690.144 |
| Groningen (Netherlands : | |
| Province) | T2—492 12 |
| Grooming | 646.7 |
| child training | 649.63 |
| Grooming behavior (Animals) | 591.563 |
| Grooming of animals | 636.083 3 |
| Groote Eylandt (N.T.) | T2—942 95 |
| Gros-de-Vaud (Switzerland) | T2—494 522 7 |
| Gros Ventre language | 497.354 |
| | T6—973 54 |
| Grosbeaks | 598.883 |
| Gross domestic product | 339.31 |
| Gross national product | 339.31 |
| Grossdeutsche Volkspartei | |
| (Austria) | 324.243 602 3 |
| Grosse Île (Montmagny, | |
| Quebec) | T2—714 735 |

| | |
|---|---|
| Grosseto (Italy : Province) | T2—455 7 |
| ancient | T2—375 64 |
| Grossulariaceae | 583.72 |
| Grotesque | |
| arts | T3C—15 |
| literature | 808.801 5 |
| history and criticism | 809.915 |
| specific literatures | T3B—080 15 |
| history and | |
| criticism | T3B—091 5 |
| Grottoes | 551.447 |
| | T2—144 |
| *see also* Caves | |
| Ground bass | 781.827 |
| instrumental | 784.182 7 |
| Ground beetles | 595.762 |
| Ground cover | 635.964 |
| floriculture | 635.964 |
| landscape architecture | 716 |
| Ground-effect machines | |
| engineering | 629.3 |
| Ground forces (Military science) | 355 |
| Ground inspections | |
| aircraft | 629.134 52 |
| Ground ivy | 583.96 |
| Ground operations (Armed | |
| forces) | 355.4 |
| Ground photogrammetry | 526.982 5 |
| Ground squirrels | 599.365 |
| Ground substances (Histology) | |
| humans | 611.018 2 |
| Ground surveying | 526.9 |
| Ground testing facilities | |
| spacecraft | 629.478 |
| Ground tests | |
| aircraft | 629.134 52 |
| Ground transportation | 388 |
| engineering | 629.049 |
| law | 343.093 |
| military engineering | 623.61 |
| public administration | 354.76 |
| safety | 363.12 |
| *see also* Transportation safety | |
| transportation services | 388 |
| urban | 388.4 |
| *see also* Urban | |
| transportation | |
| Ground transportation facilities | |
| area planning | 711.7 |
| Ground warfare | 355.02 |
| Ground wood process | 676.122 |
| Ground zithers | 787.73 |
| *see also* Stringed instruments | |
| Groundhog | 599.366 |

| | |
|---|---|
| Grounding devices | 621.317 |
| radio engineering | 621.384 133 |
| Grounding prevention | |
| seamanship | 623.888 4 |
| Groundnuts (Peanuts) | 641.356 596 |
| *see also* Peanuts | |
| Grounds | |
| landscape architecture | 712 |
| prisons | 365.5 |
| Grounds management | 658.2 |
| | T1—068 2 |
| libraries | 022.1 |
| museums | 069.21 |
| public administration | 352.57 |
| schools | 371.61 |
| Groundsels | 583.99 |
| Groundwater | 553.79 |
| | T2—169 8 |
| artificial recharge | 627.56 |
| economic geology | 553.79 |
| economics | 333.910 4 |
| hydrology | 551.49 |
| public administration | 354.36 |
| water supply engineering | 628.114 |
| Group 1 elements | 546.38 |
| Group 2 elements | 546.39 |
| Group 3 elements | 546.4 |
| Group 4 elements | 546.51 |
| Group 5 elements | 546.52 |
| Group 6 elements | 546.53 |
| Group 7 elements | 546.54 |
| Group 8 elements | 546.62 |
| Group 9 elements | 546.62 |
| Group 10 elements | 546.62 |
| Group 11 elements | 546.65 |
| Group 12 elements | 546.66 |
| Group 13 elements | 546.67 |
| Group 14 elements | 546.68 |
| Group 15 elements | 546.71 |
| Group 16 elements | 546.72 |
| Group 17 elements | 546.73 |
| Group 18 elements | 546.75 |
| Group behavior | 302.3 |
| Group counseling | 158.35 |
| Group decision making | |
| management use | 658.403 6 |
| Group dynamics | 302.3 |
| Group homes | 363.59 |
| chronically ill people | 362.16 |
| *see also* Health care facilities | |
| disabled people | 362.404 85 |
| homeless people | 362.5 |
| maladjusted young people | 362.74 |
| mentally disabled people | 362.385 |

Group homes (continued)
  mentally ill people     362.223
    *see also* Mental health
      services
  older people     362.61
  *see also* Halfway houses
Group identity     305
    T1—08
Group insurance     368.3
Group practice
  medicine     610.65
Group problem solving
  management use     658.403 6
Group psychotherapy
  prisoner services     365.667 2
  psychiatry     616.891 52
Group relations training
  social psychology     302.14
Group representations     512.22
Group sex     306.77
Group teaching     371.395
Group work
  education     371.36
  social welfare     361.4
Groupers     597.736
Grouping of students     371.25
Groupoids     512.28
Groups (Air force)     358.413 1
Groups (Mathematics)     512.2
Groups (Naval air force)     359.943 4
Groups of human figures
  art representation     704.942 6
  painting     757.6
Groupware     005.376
Grouse     598.63
  conservation technology     639.978 63
  resource economics     333.958 63
  sports hunting     799.246 3
Growing layers (Plants)     575.48
Growing points (Plants)     575.48
Growlers (Ice formations)     551.342
Growth     571.8
  animals     571.81
  cells     571.849
  developmental biology     571.8
  human physiology     612.6
  microorganisms     571.849 29
  plants     571.82
Growth (Social development)     303.44
Growth hormones     571.837 4
Growth regulators
  agriculture     631.89
  chemical engineering     668.6
Grues, Île aux (Quebec)     T2—714 735

Grues Island (Quebec)     T2—714 735
Gruidae     598.32
Gruiformes     598.32
  paleozoology     568.3
Grundy County (Ill.)     T2—773 265
Grundy County (Iowa)     T2—777 537
Grundy County (Mo.)     T2—778 215
Grundy County (Tenn.)     T2—768 78
Grünen (German political party)     324.243 087
Grünen (Swiss political party)     324.249 408 7
Grünen - Die Grüne Alternative
  (Austrian political party)     324.243 608 7
Grünes Bündnis (Swiss political
  party)     324.249 408 7
Grunts (Fishes)     597.7
Gruyère (Switzerland :
  District)     T2—494 533
Grylloblattodea     595.726
GSP (Tariff)     382.753
  *see also* Customs (Tariff)
Guadalajara (Spain :
  Province)     T2—464 9
Guadalcanal (Solomon
  Islands)     T2—959 33
Guadalcanal, Battle of,
  1942–1943     940.542 659 33
Guadalquivir River (Spain)     T2—468
Guadalupe County (N.M.)     T2—789 25
Guadalupe County (Tex.)     T2—764 34
Guadalupe Mountains
  National Park (Tex.)     T2—764 94
Guadalupe River (Tex.)     T2—764 12
Guadeloupe     972.976
    T2—729 76
Guahiban languages     498.9
    T6—989
Guaicuru languages     498.7
    T6—987
Guainía (Colombia)     T2—861 67
Guairá (Paraguay)     T2—892 128
Guajira (Colombia : Dept.)     T2—861 17
Guam     T2—967
Guanacaste (Costa Rica :
  Province)     T2—728 66
Guanaco     599.636 7
  animal husbandry     636.296 6
Guanaco wool textiles     677.32
  *see also* Textiles
Guanajuato (Mexico : State)     T2—724 1
Guanche language     493.3
    T6—933
Guangdong Sheng (China)     T2—512 7
Guangxi Zhuangzu Zizhiqu
  (China)     T2—512 8

Guangzhou (China)    T2—512 75
Guano
   agricultural use    631.866
Guans    598.64
Guantánamo (Cuba :
   Province)    T2—729 167
Guaraní Indians    T5—983 822
Guaraní language    498.382 2
   T6—983 822
Guaranteed annual wage    331.236
Guaranteed minimum income    362.582
   law    344.032 582
   public administration    353.54
Guaranteed wages    331.23
Guarantees (Insurance)    368.85
Guarantees (Law)    343.08
Guaranty (Suretyship)    346.074
Guard animals    636.088 6
Guard dogs    636.73
Guarda (Portugal : District)    T2—469 32
Guardian and ward    346.018
Guards (Safety equipment)    621.992
Guárico (Venezuela : State)    T2—874 7
Guatemala    972.81
   T2—728 1
Guatemala (Guatemala :
   Dept.)    T2—728 11
Guatemalan literature    860
Guatemalans    T5—687 281
Guavas    641.344 21
   botany    583.765
   commercial processing    664.804 421
   cooking    641.644 21
   food    641.344 21
   orchard crop    634.421
Guaviare (Colombia)    T2—861 66
Guayama (P.R. : District)    T2—729 58
Guayaquil, Gulf of    551.461 41
   T2—164 1
Guayas (Ecuador :
   Province)    T2—866 32
Guayule    583.99
Guebuza, Armando Emílio
   Mozambican history    967.905 3
Guelleh, Ismail Omar
   Djiboutian history    967.710 42
Guelma (Algeria : Province)    T2—655
Guelmim (Morocco :
   Province)    T2—646 8
Guelmim-Es Semara
   (Morocco)    T2—646 8
Guelph (Ont.)    T2—713 43
Guenons    599.862
Guernsey (Channel Islands)    T2—423 42

Guernsey cattle    636.224
Guernsey County (Ohio)    T2—771 92
Guernsey lily    635.934 34
Guerrero (Mexico : State)    T2—727 3
Guerrilla tactics    355.425
Guerrilla troops    356.15
Guerrilla warfare    355.021 8
Guerrillas    322.42
Guests
   seating at table    642.6
Guevara, Ernesto
   Cuban communism    335.434 7
GUI (User interface)
   systems programs    005.437
Guiana    988
   T2—88
Guidance
   crime prevention    364.48
   education    371.4
   manned space flight    629.453
   social welfare    361.06
     older people    362.66
   space flight    629.41
   unmanned space flight    629.433
Guidance systems
   spacecraft    629.474 2
   unmanned spacecraft    629.464 2
Guidebooks    910.202
   *see Manual at* 913–919; *also at*
     913–919 vs. 796.51
Guidebooks of exhibits    T1—074
Guided aircraft
   control systems    629.132 6
   military engineering    623.746 9
Guided-light communication    621.382 75
Guided missile forces    358.17
   in space    358.8
   navy    359.981 7
Guided missiles    358.171 82
   engineering    623.451 9
   military equipment    358.171 82
Guided missiles in space    358.882
   engineering    623.451 98
   military equipment    358.882
Guided-way systems    388.42
   engineering    625.4
   *see also* Local rail transit
     systems
Guides to religious life    204.4
   Buddhism    294.344 4
   Christianity    248.4
   Hinduism    294.544

Guides to religious life (continued)
  Islam 297.57
    Sufi 297.44
  Judaism 296.7
Guiding equipment (Tools) 621.992
Guild socialism 335.15
Guild system 338.632
Guildford (England :
  Borough) T2—422 162
Guilford County (N.C.) T2—756 62
Guillain-Barré syndrome
  medicine 616.856
    *see also* Nervous system
      diseases — humans
Guilt
  psychology 152.44
  religion 202.2
    Christianity 233.4
    Judaism 296.32
Guilt (Law) 345.04
Guinea 966.52
  T2—665 2
Guinea, Gulf of 551.461 373
  T2—163 73
Guinea-Bissau 966.57
  T2—665 7
Guinea-Bissauans T5—966 57
Guinea fowl 636.593
  animal husbandry 636.593
  zoology 598.64
Guinea pigs 636.935 92
  animal husbandry 636.935 92
  experimental animals
    medicine 616.027 33
    zoology 599.359 2
Guineans T5—966 52
Guipúzcoa (Spain) T2—466 1
Guiros 786.886
  *see also* Percussion instruments
Guitar concertos 784.278 7
Guitarfishes 597.35
Guitarists 787.870 92
Guitars 787.87
  instrument 787.871 9
  music 787.87
    *see also* Stringed instruments
Guizhou Sheng (China) T2—513 4
Gujar T5—914 79
Gujarat (India) T2—547 5
Gujarati T5—914 71
Gujarati language 491.47
  T6—914 71
Gujarati literature 891.47

Gulches 551.442
  T2—144
  geography 910.914 4
  geomorphology 551.442
  physical geography 910.021 44
Gulf Coast (U.S.) 976
  T2—76
Gulf County (Fla.) T2—759 947
Gulf Islands (B.C.) T2—711 28
Gulf languages (North American
  native languages) 497.9
  T6—979
Gulf of Aden 551.461 532
  T2—165 32
Gulf of Alaska (Alaska) 551.461 434
  T2—164 34
Gulf of Aqaba 551.461 533
  T2—165 33
Gulf of Bothnia 551.461 334
  T2—163 34
Gulf of California (Mexico) 551.461 41
  T2—164 1
Gulf of Darien (Colombia) 551.461 365
  T2—163 65
Gulf of Finland 551.461 334
  T2—163 34
Gulf of Guayaquil 551.461 41
  T2—164 1
Gulf of Guinea 551.461 373
  T2—163 73
Gulf of Honduras 551.461 365
  T2—163 65
Gulf of Lions (France) 551.461 382
  T2—163 82
Gulf of Martaban (Burma) 551.461 565
  T2—165 65
Gulf of Mexico 551.461 364
  T2—163 64
Gulf of Oman 551.461 536
  T2—165 36
Gulf of Panama (Panama) 551.461 41
  T2—164 1
Gulf of Paria (Venezuela and 551.461 366
  Trinidad and Tobago) T2—163 66
Gulf of Riga (Latvia and Estonia) 551.461 334
  T2—163 34
Gulf of Saint Lawrence 551.461 344
  T2—163 44
Gulf of Siam 551.461 472
  T2—164 72
Gulf of Suez 551.461 533
  T2—165 33
Gulf of Taranto (Italy) 551.461 386
  T2—163 86

| | | | |
|---|---|---|---|
| Gulf of Tehuantepec (Mexico) | 551.461 41 | Gunma-ken (Japan) | T2—521 33 |
| | T2—164 1 | Gunmetal | 669.3 |
| Gulf of Thailand | 551.461 472 | materials science | 620.182 |
| | T2—164 72 | metallography | 669.953 |
| Gulf of Urabá (Colombia) | 551.461 365 | metallurgy | 669.3 |
| | T2—163 65 | metalworking | 673.3 |
| Gulf of Venice (Italy) | 551.461 385 | physical metallurgy | 669.963 |
| | T2—163 85 | Gunneras | 635.933 82 |
| Gulf Province (Papua New | | botany | 583.82 |
| Guinea) | T2—954 7 | floriculture | 635.933 82 |
| Gulf Stream | 551.462 131 | Gunnery | 623.55 |
| Gulf War, 1980–1988 | 955.054 2 | Gunnison County (Colo.) | T2—788 41 |
| Gulf War, 1991 | 956.704 42 | Gunpowder | 662.26 |
| Gulfs | | military engineering | 623.452 6 |
| resource economics | 333.916 4 | Guns (Artillery) | 355.821 |
| Gulistān (Iran : Province) | T2—552 2 | *see also* Artillery | |
| Gullah dialect | 427.975 799 | Guns (Small arms) | 683.4 |
| | T6—217 | art metalwork | 739.744 2 |
| Gulls | 598.338 | civil rights issues | 323.43 |
| Gum-bichromate processes | 773.5 | control | 363.33 |
| Gum diseases | | law | 344.053 3 |
| dentistry | 617.632 | manufacturing technology | 683.4 |
| incidence | 614.599 6 | military engineering | 623.442 |
| Gum trees (Eucalypti) | 583.766 | military equipment | 355.824 2 |
| *see also* Eucalyptus | | military training | 355.547 |
| Gumatj language | 499.15 | shooting game | 799.213 |
| | T6—991 5 | sports | 799.202 83 |
| Gumma-ken (Japan) | T2—521 33 | target shooting | 799.31 |
| Gums (Mouth parts) | | Gunshot wounds | |
| animal physiology | 573.35 | medicine | 617.145 |
| descriptive zoology | 596.14 | Gunsmithing | 683.4 |
| human anatomy | 611.31 | Gunsmiths | 683.400 92 |
| human physiology | 612.31 | Guntersville Lake (Ala. and | |
| Gums (Substances) | 572.567 2 | Tenn.) | T2—761 94 |
| biochemistry | 572.567 2 | Guppies | 597.667 |
| chemistry | 547.78 | culture | 639.376 67 |
| commercial processing | 668.37 | Gupta dynasty | 934.06 |
| fossil | 553.29 | Gur languages | 496.35 |
| materials science | 620.192 4 | | T6—963 5 |
| *see also* Carbohydrates | | Gur literatures | 896.35 |
| Gümüşhane İli (Turkey) | T2—565 7 | Gurage (African people) | T5—928 |
| ancient | T2—393 37 | Gurage language | 492.8 |
| Gun control | 363.33 | | T6—928 |
| civil rights issues | 323.43 | Gurage literature | 892.8 |
| law | 344.053 3 | Gurma (African people) | T5—963 5 |
| public administration | 353.36 | Gurma language | 496.35 |
| public safety | 363.33 | | T6—963 5 |
| Gun mounts | 623.43 | Gurnards | 597.68 |
| Gun salutes | | Guru Granth | 294.682 |
| armed forces | 355.134 9 | Gurung language | 495.4 |
| Guncotton | 662.26 | | T6—954 |
| military engineering | 623.452 6 | | |
| Gundis | 599.359 | | |
| Gundogs | 636.752 | | |

Gurus 200.92
  biography 200.92
  Buddhist 294.309 2
    biography 294.309 2
      specific sects 294.39
      role and function 294.361
  Hindu 294.509 2
    biography 294.509 2
      specific sects 294.55
      role and function 294.561
  role and function 206.1
  Sikh 294.609 2
    biography 294.609 2
    role and function 294.663
  *see Manual at* 200.92 and
    201–209, 292–299
Gusii (African people) T5—963 95
Gusii language 496.395
  T6—963 95
Gustation 573.878
  *see also* Taste (Sense)
Gustatory organs 573.878
Gustatory perception
  psychology 152.167
Gustav I Vasa, King of Sweden
  Swedish history 948.503 21
Gustav II Adolf, King of Sweden
  Swedish history 948.503 41
Gustav III, King of Sweden
  Swedish history 948.503 81
Gustav IV Adolf, King of
  Sweden
  Swedish history 948.503 82
Gustav V, King of Sweden
  Swedish history 948.505 1
Gustav VI Adolf, King of
  Sweden
  Swedish history 948.505 3
Gustavian Period 948.503 8
Güstrow (Germany :
  Landkreis) T2—431 74
Guthrie, Edwin R. (Edwin Ray)
  psychological system 150.194 34
Guthrie County (Iowa) T2—777 49
Gutters
  road engineering 625.734
Guttiferae 583.624
Guyana 988.1
  T2—881
Guyandotte River (W. Va.) T2—754 4
Guyane 988.2
  T2—882
Guyanese T5—914 1
Guyenne (France) T2—447

Guysborough (N.S. :
  County) T2—716 21
Guzmán Blanco, Antonio
  Venezuelan history 987.062 8
Gwaun-cae-Gurwen (Wales) T2—429 85
Gwent (Wales) T2—429 9
Gwich'in Indians T5—972
Gwinnett County (Ga.) T2—758 223
Gwydir River (N.S.W.) T2—944 4
Gwynedd (Wales) T2—429 25
Gwynedd (Wales : County) T2—429 2
Gymnascales 579.565
Gymnasiums (Secondary
  schools) 373.241
  *see also* Secondary education
Gymnasiums (Sports) 796.406 8
  architecture 725.85
  sports 796.406 8
Gymnastic exercises 613.714
Gymnastics 796.44
  child care 649.57
Gymnasts 796.440 92
Gymnolaemata 594.676
Gymnophiona 597.82
  paleozoology 567.8
Gymnosomata 594.34
Gymnosperms 585
  forestry 634.975
  paleobotany 561.5
Gymnotidae 597.48
Gympie (Qld.) T2—943 2
Gynecologic cancer
  incidence 614.599 946 5
  medicine 616.994 65
  *see also* Cancer — humans
Gynecologic disorders 362.198 1
  *see also* Female genital
    diseases — humans
Gynecologic nursing 618.102 31
Gynecologic surgery 618.105 9
Gynecologists 618.100 92
  law 344.041 2
  role and function 618.102 32
Gynecology 618.1
  anesthesiology 617.968 1
  geriatrics 618.978
  pediatrics 618.920 98
  surgery 618.105 9
Gynoplasty 618.105 92
Győr-Moson-Sopron Megye
  (Hungary) T2—439 7
Gypsies T5—914 97
  Holocaust, 1933–1945 940.531 808 991 497
  social aspects 305.891 497

| | |
|---|---|
| Gypsum | 553.635 |
| economic geology | 553.635 |
| mineralogy | 549.755 |
| mining | 622.363 5 |
| petrology | 552.5 |
| Gypsum plasters | 666.92 |
| Gypsy language | 491.497 |
| | T6—914 97 |
| Gypsy literature | 891.497 |
| Gypsy moth | |
| agricultural pests | 634.049 78 |
| Gyrinidae | 595.762 |
| Gyrocompasses | |
| aircraft engineering | 629.135 1 |
| Gyrodynamics | 531.34 |
| Gyrohorizons | 629.135 2 |
| Gyropilots | 629.135 2 |
| Gyroscopes | |
| manufacturing technology | 681.753 |

# H

| | |
|---|---|
| Hà Giang (Vietnam : Province) | T2—597 1 |
| Hà Nam (Vietnam : Province) | T2—597 3 |
| Hà Tây (Vietnam : Province) | T2—597 3 |
| Hà Tĩnh (Vietnam : Province) | T2—597 4 |
| Haakon County (S.D.) | T2—783 56 |
| Haar integral | 515.43 |
| Haarlem (Netherlands) | T2—492 35 |
| Habad Lubavitch Hasidism | 296.833 22 |
| Habakkuk (Biblical book) | 224.95 |
| Habeas corpus | 347.05 |
| criminal law | 345.056 |
| Habersham County (Ga.) | T2—758 125 |
| Habibie, B. J. (Bacharuddin Jusuf) | |
| Indonesian history | 959.804 1 |
| Habit breaking | 152.33 |
| Habitat improvement (Wildlife) | |
| technology | 639.92 |
| Habitat surveys | 333.95 |
| Habitations | |
| animals | 591.564 |
| Habits | |
| child training | 649.6 |
| customs | 390 |
| psychology | 152.33 |
| Habituations | 362.29 |
| *see also* Substance abuse | |

| | |
|---|---|
| Habré, Hissein | |
| Chadian history | 967.430 43 |
| Habsburg, House of | 943.603 |
| Austrian history | 943.603 |
| Dutch history | 949.202 |
| genealogy | 929.736 |
| German history | 943.03 |
| Hungarian history | 943.904 2 |
| Spanish history | 946.04 |
| Habyarimana, Juvénal | |
| Rwandan history | 967.571 042 |
| Hackberries | 583.45 |
| Hackensack River (N.Y. and N.J.) | T2—749 21 |
| Hackney (London, England) | T2—421 44 |
| Hackney horse | 636.14 |
| Hadal zone | |
| biology | 578.779 |
| ecology | 577.79 |
| Haddocks | 641.392 |
| cooking | 641.692 |
| food | 641.392 |
| zoology | 597.632 |
| Hades | 202.3 |
| *see also* Hell | |
| Hadith | 297.125 |
| Hadith Qudsi | 297.125 8 |
| Hadith stories | 297.125 12 |
| Ḥadj | 297.352 |
| Hadrons | 539.721 6 |
| Hadrosauridae | 567.914 |
| Haematopodidae | 598.33 |
| Haemodoraceae | 584.354 |
| Hafnium | 669.79 |
| chemical engineering | 661.051 4 |
| chemistry | 546.514 |
| metallurgy | 669.79 |
| *see also* Chemicals | |
| Hagen (Germany) | T2—435 635 |
| Hagfishes | 597.2 |
| Haggadah (Passover) | 296.453 71 |
| Haggai (Biblical book) | 224.97 |
| Ḥagigah | 296.123 2 |
| Babylonian Talmud | 296.125 2 |
| Mishnah | 296.123 2 |
| Palestinian Talmud | 296.124 2 |
| Hagiographa (Bible) | 223 |
| Hague (Netherlands) | T2—492 382 |
| Hahnium | |
| chemistry | 546.52 |
| Hải Dương (Vietnam : Province) | T2—597 3 |
| Haida Gwaii (B.C.) | T2—711 12 |
| Haida Indians | T5—972 8 |

| | | | |
|---|---|---|---|
| Haida language | 497.28 | Hair dyeing | |
| | T6—972 8 | personal care | 646.724 |
| Haida literature | 897.28 | Hair follicle diseases | |
| Haidallah, Khouna Ould | | medicine | 616.546 |
| Mauritanian history | 966.105 2 | *see also* Skin diseases — | |
| Haifa (Israel : District) | T2—569 46 | humans | |
| Haiku | 808.814 1 | Hair follicles | |
| history and criticism | 809.141 | medicine | 616.546 |
| specific literatures | T3B—104 1 | Hair removal | |
| individual authors | T3A—1 | surgery | 617.477 9 |
| Hail | 551.578 7 | Hair seals | 599.79 |
| crop damage | 632.14 | Hair transplantation | 617.477 905 92 |
| weather forecasting | 551.647 87 | Haircutting | 646.724 |
| Hail insurance | 368.122 | Hairdressers | 646.724 092 |
| crops | 368.121 | Hairdressing | 646.724 |
| Hail Mary | 242.74 | customs | 391.5 |
| Haile Selassie I, Emperor of | | Hairstyles | 646.724 |
| Ethiopia | | customs | 391.5 |
| Ethiopian history | 963.055 | Hairstyling | 646.724 |
| as emperor | 963.055 | Hairweaving | 646.724 |
| as regent and king | 963.054 | Hairworms | 592.59 |
| Hailstones | 551.578 7 | Haiti | 972.94 |
| Hailstorms | 551.554 | | T2—729 4 |
| social services | 363.349 24 | Haitian Creole | 447.972 94 |
| *see also* Disasters | | | T6—417 |
| Hainan Sheng (China) | T2—512 9 | Haitian literature | 840 |
| Hainaut (Belgium) | T2—493 42 | Haitians | T5—969 729 4 |
| Haines (Alaska : Borough) | T2—798 2 | Hajdú-Bihar Megye | |
| Haiphong (Vietnam) | T2—597 3 | (Hungary) | T2—439 9 |
| Hair | 599.147 | Hajeb (Morocco : Province) | T2—645 |
| animal husbandry | 636.088 45 | Ḥajj | 297.352 |
| animal physiology | 573.58 | Hakeas | 583.89 |
| descriptive zoology | 599.147 | Hakes | 641.392 |
| dramatic performances | 792.027 | cooking | 641.692 |
| motion pictures | 791.430 27 | food | 641.392 |
| stage | 792.027 | zoology | 597.632 |
| television | 791.450 27 | Hakka (Chinese people) | T5—951 7 |
| human anatomy | 611.78 | Hakka dialects | 495.172 |
| human physiology | 612.799 | | T6—951 7 |
| medicine | 616.546 | Hakkâri İli (Turkey) | T2—566 28 |
| personal care | 646.724 | ancient | T2—395 5 |
| surgery | 617.477 9 | Hala | 584.66 |
| Hair analysis | | Ḥalab (Syria : Province) | T2—569 13 |
| criminal investigation | 363.256 2 | Halakhah | 296.18 |
| Hair diseases | | Midrash | 296.141 |
| humans | | Talmud | 296.127 4 |
| geriatrics | 618.976 546 | Haldimand (Ont. : County) | T2—713 37 |
| incidence | 614.595 46 | Haldimand-Norfolk (Ont.) | T2—713 36 |
| medicine | 616.546 | Hale County (Ala.) | T2—761 43 |
| *see also* Skin diseases — | | Hale County (Tex.) | T2—764 842 |
| humans | | Half-life (Nuclear physics) | 539.752 |
| pediatrics | 618.925 46 | Halfback play | |
| pharmacokinetics | 615.779 | rugby | 796.333 24 |
| | | soccer | 796.334 24 |

| | |
|---|---|
| Halfbeaks | 597.66 |
| Halfmoons | 597.7 |
| Halfpipe snowboarding | 796.939 |
| Halftone cuts | |
| printing | 686.232 7 |
| Halfway houses | 365.34 |
| corrections | 365.34 |
| juvenile offenders | 365.42 |
| maladjusted young people | 362.74 |
| *see also* Group homes; Penal | |
| institutions | |
| Halh Mongolian language | 494.23 |
| | T6—942 3 |
| Halh Mongolian literature | 894.23 |
| Halh Mongols | T5—942 3 |
| Haliaeetus leucocephalus | 598.943 |
| Haliburton (Ont. : County) | T2—713 61 |
| Halibuts | 641.392 |
| conservation technology | 639.977 695 |
| cooking | 641.692 |
| fishing | 639.276 95 |
| food | 641.392 |
| resource economics | 333.956 695 |
| zoology | 597.695 |
| Halicarnassus (Extinct city) | T2—392 4 |
| Halichoerus | 599.793 |
| Halides | |
| mineralogy | 549.4 |
| Halifax (N.S.) | T2—716 225 |
| Halifax (N.S. : Regional | |
| municipality) | T2—716 22 |
| Halifax, Edward Frederick | |
| Lindley Wood, Earl of | |
| Indian history | 954.035 8 |
| Halifax County (N.C.) | T2—756 48 |
| Halifax County (Va.) | T2—755 661 |
| Halifax Metropolitan Area | |
| (N.S.) | T2—716 225 |
| Halite | 553.632 |
| mineralogy | 549.4 |
| *see also* Salt (Sodium chloride) | |
| Hall Beach (Nunavut) | T2—719 52 |
| Hall County (Ga.) | T2—758 272 |
| Hall County (Neb.) | T2—782 41 |
| Hall County (Tex.) | T2—764 753 |
| Hall effects in semiconductors | 537.622 6 |
| Ḥallah | 296.123 1 |
| Mishnah | 296.123 1 |
| Palestinian Talmud | 296.124 1 |
| Halland landskap (Sweden) | T2—486 6 |
| Hallands län (Sweden) | T2—486 6 |
| Halle (Germany) | T2—431 848 |
| Halle (Germany : | |
| Regierungsbezirk) | T2—431 84 |

| | |
|---|---|
| Halley's comet | 523.642 |
| Hallmarks | 929.9 |
| | T1—027 8 |
| Halloween | 394.264 6 |
| handicrafts | 745.594 164 6 |
| Hallucinations | |
| psychology | 154.4 |
| Hallucinogen abuse | 362.294 |
| medicine | 616.863 4 |
| personal health | 613.83 |
| social welfare | 362.294 |
| *see also* Substance abuse | |
| Hallucinogens | |
| pharmacokinetics | 615.788 3 |
| Halmahera (Indonesia) | T2—598 56 |
| Halobacteriaceae | 579.321 |
| Halocarbons | 547.02 |
| *see also* Organohalogen | |
| compounds | |
| Halogen gases | |
| technology | 665.83 |
| Halogen salts | |
| chemical engineering | 661.42 |
| Halogenated compounds | |
| aromatic chemistry | 547.62 |
| chemical engineering | 661.891 |
| human toxicology | 615.951 2 |
| organic chemistry | 547.02 |
| Halogenated rubber | 678.68 |
| Halogenation | 547.27 |
| chemical engineering | 660.284 4 |
| Halogens | |
| biochemistry | 572.556 |
| chemical engineering | 661.073 |
| chemistry | 546.73 |
| organic chemistry | 547.02 |
| applied | 661.891 |
| Halophilic bacteria | 579.321 |
| Haloragales | 583.82 |
| Hälsingland landskap | |
| (Sweden) | T2—488 1 |
| Halton (Cheshire, England) | T2—427 18 |
| Halton (Ont.) | T2—713 533 |
| Ham | 641.364 |
| *see also* Pork | |
| Ham radio | |
| engineering | 621.384 16 |
| Hamadān (Iran : Province) | T2—555 2 |
| Ḥamāh (Syria : Province) | T2—569 13 |
| Hamamelidales | 583.44 |
| Hamamelididae | 583.4 |
| Hamber Provincial Park | |
| (B.C.) | T2—711 68 |
| Hamblen County (Tenn.) | T2—768 923 |

Hambleton (England)    T2—428 49
Hamburg (Germany)    T2—435 15
Häme (Finland : Lääni)    T2—489 73
Hämeen lääni (Finland)    T2—489 73
Hamilton (N.Z.)    T2—933 4
Hamilton (Ont.)    T2—713 52
Hamilton (Scotland :
   District)    T2—414 57
Hamilton (Vic.)    T2—945 7
Hamilton City (N.Z.)    T2—933 4
Hamilton County (Fla.)    T2—759 84
Hamilton County (Ill.)    T2—773 95
Hamilton County (Ind.)    T2—772 56
Hamilton County (Iowa)    T2—777 52
Hamilton County (Kan.)    T2—781 415
Hamilton County (N.Y.)    T2—747 52
Hamilton County (Neb.)    T2—782 354
Hamilton County (Ohio)    T2—771 77
Hamilton County (Tenn.)    T2—768 82
Hamilton County (Tex.)    T2—764 549
Hamilton-Wentworth (Ont.)    T2—713 52
Hamiltonian systems    515.39
Hamitic languages    493
   T6—93
Hamitic literatures    893
Hamitic peoples    T5—93
Hamito-Semitic languages    492
   T6—92
Hamito-Semitic literatures    892
Hamlin County (S.D.)    T2—783 26
Hammering metals
   sculpture    731.41
Hammers    621.973
Hammersmith and Fulham
   (London, England)    T2—421 33
Hammurabi, King of Babylonia
   Mesopotamian history    935.502
Hampden County (Mass.)    T2—744 26
Hampshire (England)    T2—422 7
Hampshire County (Mass.)    T2—744 23
Hampshire County (W. Va.)    T2—754 95
Hampshire swine    636.484
Hampstead (Quebec)    T2—714 28
Hampton (Va.)    T2—755 412
Hampton County (S.C.)    T2—757 97
Hampton Roads, Battle of, 1862    973.752
Hamsters    636.935 6
   animal husbandry    636.935 6
   experimental animals
     medicine    616.027 33
   zoology    599.356
Han Chinese    T5—951
Han dynasty    931.04
Hanafites (Islamic sect)    297.811

Hanbalites (Islamic sect)    297.814
Hancock County (Ga.)    T2—758 623
Hancock County (Ill.)    T2—773 43
Hancock County (Ind.)    T2—772 58
Hancock County (Iowa)    T2—777 24
Hancock County (Ky.)    T2—769 862
Hancock County (Me.)    T2—741 45
Hancock County (Miss.)    T2—762 14
Hancock County (Ohio)    T2—771 19
Hancock County (Tenn.)    T2—768 946
Hancock County (W. Va.)    T2—754 12
Hand bells    786.884 85
   instrument    786.884 851 9
   music    786.884 85
   *see also* Percussion instruments
Hand bookbinding    686.302
Hand composition
   printing    686.225 3
Hand County (S.D.)    T2—783 282
Hand-forged tools
   manufacturing technology    682.4
Hand grenades    623.451 14
Hand haulage
   mining    622.65
Hand muscles
   human anatomy    611.737
Hand production
   paper    676.22
Hand-propelled boats    387.29
   design    623.812 9
   engineering    623.829
   transportation services    387.29
   *see also* Ships
Hand pumps    621.64
Hand sewing    646.204 2
   bookbinding    686.35
   home economics    646.204 2
Hand techniques
   music    784.193 65
Hand tools    621.908
   use in home woodworking    684.082
Handbags    391.44
   customs    391.44
   home sewing    646.48
   manufacturing technology    685.51
   *see also* Accessories (Clothing)
Handball (Court handball)    796.312
Handball (Team handball)    796.327
Handbill paper    676.286
Handcars    385.32
   engineering    625.22
   transportation services    385.32
   *see also* Rolling stock

Handedness
- educational psychology 370.155
- psychology 152.335

Handguns 683.43
- manufacturing technology 683.43
- military engineering 623.443

Handheld computing devices 004.167
- engineering 621.391 67
- programming 005.25
- *see also* Personal computers

Handicapped people 305.908
- T1—087
- *see also* Disabled people

Handicraft industries
- arts economics 338.477 455
- economics 338.476 8
- production organization 338.642 5

Handicrafters 745.509 2

Handicrafts 680
- arts 745.5
- primary education 372.55
- *see Manual at* 680 vs. 745.5

Handkerchiefs 391.44
- *see also* Accessories (Clothing)

Handreading 133.6

Hands 612.97
- physiology 612.97
- regional medicine 617.575
- surgery 617.575 059
- *see also* Upper extremities

Handwork
- textile arts 746.4

Handwriting 652.1
- primary education 372.634

Handwriting analysis 155.282
- criminal investigation 363.256 5
- divination 137
- personnel selection 658.311 2

Handwriting recognition
- computer science 006.425

Hang gliders
- engineering 629.14

Hang gliding
- engineering 629.14
- sports 797.55

Hangars 387.736 2
- architecture 725.39
- *see also* Airports

Hangings 645.2
- commercial technology 684.3
- home sewing 646.21
- household management 645.2
- interior decoration 747.3
- textile arts 746.3

Hankel functions 515.53

Hankey (South Africa : District) T2—687 51

Hannover (Germany) T2—435 954

Hannover (Germany : Regierungsbezirk) T2—435 95

Hannover (Germany : Region) T2—435 954

Hanoi (Vietnam) T2—597 3

Hanover (South Africa : District) T2—687 13

Hanover, House of 941.07
- British history 941.07
- English history 942.07
- genealogy 929.72
- Scottish history 941.107

Hanover County (Va.) T2—755 462

Hansen's disease
- incidence 614.546
- medicine 616.998
- *see also* Communicable diseases — humans

Hansford County (Tex.) T2—764 814

Hanson County (S.D.) T2—783 373

Hantavirus infections
- incidence 614.588
- medicine 616.918
- *see also* Communicable diseases — humans

Hants (England) T2—422 7

Hants (N.S.) T2—716 35

Hanukkah 296.435
- customs 394.267
- liturgy 296.453 5

Haouz (Morocco : Province) T2—646 4

Haploid cells 571.845

Haplosclerida 593.46

Haplotaxida 592.64

Happenings (Art style) 709.040 74

Happiness 152.42
- applied psychology 158
- children 155.419
- arts T3C—353
- hedonism 171.4
- literature 808.803 53
- history and criticism 809.933 53
- specific literatures T3B—080 353
- history and criticism T3B—093 53
- parapsychology 131
- psychology of emotions 152.42
- virtue ethics 171.3

Hapsburg, House of 943.603
- *see also* Habsburg, House of

| | |
|---|---|
| Haptophyceae | 579.86 |
| Harakmbet language | 498.9 |
| | T6—989 |
| Haralson County (Ga.) | T2—758 38 |
| Harare (Zimbabwe) | T2—689 1 |
| Harari (African people) | T5—928 |
| Harari language | 492.8 |
| | T6—928 |
| Harari literature | 892.8 |
| Harassment | 364.15 |
| social welfare | 362.88 |
| Harbor patrols | 363.286 |
| Harbor piloting | 623.892 9 |
| Harbor police | 363.286 |
| Harbor porpoises | 599.539 |
| Harbor seal | 599.792 3 |
| Harborough (England) | T2—425 44 |
| Harbors | 387.1 |
| engineering | 627.2 |
| *see also* Ports | |
| Hard bop | 781.655 |
| Hard cheeses | |
| processing | 637.354 |
| Hard disk management | 004.563 |
| systems programs | 005.436 |
| Hard disks (Computers) | 004.563 |
| engineering | 621.397 63 |
| Hard fiber crops | 633.57 |
| Hard rock | 781.66 |
| Hardanger | |
| arts | 746.44 |
| Hardanger fiddles | 787.6 |
| *see also* Stringed instruments | |
| Hardball hockey | 796.356 64 |
| Hardecanute, King of England | |
| English history | 942.018 3 |
| Hardee County (Fla.) | T2—759 57 |
| Hardeman County (Tenn.) | T2—768 28 |
| Hardeman County (Tex.) | T2—764 747 |
| Hardening metals | 671.36 |
| Hardin County (Ill.) | T2—773 98 |
| Hardin County (Iowa) | T2—777 535 |
| Hardin County (Ky.) | T2—769 845 |
| Hardin County (Ohio) | T2—771 44 |
| Hardin County (Tenn.) | T2—768 31 |
| Hardin County (Tex.) | T2—764 157 |
| Harding, Warren G. (Warren Gamaliel) | |
| United States history | 973.914 |
| Harding County (N.M.) | T2—789 24 |
| Harding County (S.D.) | T2—783 42 |
| Hardinge, Henry Hardinge, Viscount | |
| Indian history | 954.031 5 |

| | |
|---|---|
| Hardinge of Penshurst, Charles Hardinge, Baron | |
| Indian history | 954.035 6 |
| Hardness | |
| crystals | 548.842 |
| materials science | 620.112 6 |
| mineralogy | 549.121 |
| Hardware | 683 |
| Hardware (Computers) | 004 |
| engineering | 621.39 |
| *see Manual at* 004 vs. 005 | |
| Hardware description languages | 621.392 |
| Hardwicke Island (B.C. : Island) | T2—711 1 |
| Hardwoods | |
| forestry | 634.972 |
| lumber | 674.142 |
| Hardy County (W. Va.) | T2—754 93 |
| Harelip | |
| surgery | 617.522 |
| Hārerī Hizb kelel (Ethiopia) | T2—632 |
| Hares | 599.328 |
| animal husbandry | 636.932 8 |
| Harford County (Md.) | T2—752 74 |
| Harghita (Romania) | T2—498 4 |
| Hariana (India) | T2—545 58 |
| Haringey (London, England) | T2—421 88 |
| Härjedalen landskap (Sweden) | T2—488 3 |
| Harlan County (Ky.) | T2—769 154 |
| Harlan County (Neb.) | T2— 782 382 |
| Harlem jazz | 781.653 |
| Harlow (England) | T2—426 73 |
| Harmful animals | 591.65 |
| Harmful microorganisms | 579.165 |
| Harmful organisms | 578.65 |
| Harmful plants | 581.65 |
| Harmon County (Okla.) | T2—766 445 |
| Harmonic analysis | 515.243 3 |
| abstract | 515.785 |
| Harmonic functions | 515.53 |
| Harmonic organization | 781.25 |
| Harmonic rhythm | 781.256 |
| Harmonicas (Mouth organs) | 788.82 |
| instrument | 788.821 9 |
| music | 788.82 |
| *see also* Woodwind instruments | |
| Harmonicas (Musical glasses) | 786.866 |
| *see also* Percussion instruments | |
| Harmonies of Bible | 220.65 |
| Harmonies of Gospels | 226.1 |

| | | | |
|---|---|---|---|
| Harmoniums | 786.55 | Harrison County (Ind.) | T2—772 21 |
| instrument | 786.551 9 | Harrison County (Iowa) | T2—777 47 |
| music | 786.55 | Harrison County (Ky.) | T2—769 413 |
| *see also* Keyboard instruments | | Harrison County (Miss.) | T2—762 13 |
| Harmonization | 781.434 | Harrison County (Mo.) | T2—778 17 |
| Harmony | | Harrison County (Ohio) | T2—771 68 |
| arts | 701.8 | Harrison County (Tex.) | T2—764 192 |
| musical element | 781.25 | Harrison County (W. Va.) | T2—754 57 |
| Harness horses | 636.14 | Harrison Lake (Fraser- | |
| Harness makers | 685.109 2 | Cheam, B.C.) | T2—711 37 |
| Harness racehorses | 636.175 | Harrisonburg (Va.) | T2—755 921 |
| Harness racing | 798.46 | Harrogate (England : | |
| equipment technology | 688.78 | Borough) | T2—428 42 |
| Harnesses | 636.108 37 | Harrow (London, England) | T2—421 86 |
| animal husbandry | 636.083 7 | Harrows | |
| horse rearing | 636.108 37 | manufacturing technology | 681.763 1 |
| manufacturing technology | 685.1 | Harsha | |
| Harnett County (N.C.) | T2—756 362 | Indian history | 934.07 |
| Harney County (Or.) | T2—795 95 | Hart (England) | T2—422 723 |
| Harold I, King of England | | Hart County (Ga.) | T2—758 155 |
| English history | 942.018 2 | Hart County (Ky.) | T2—769 715 |
| Harold II, King of England | | Hartebeests | 599.645 |
| English history | 942.019 | Hartford (Conn.) | T2—746 3 |
| Harp-lutes | 787.98 | Hartford County (Conn.) | T2—746 2 |
| *see also* Stringed instruments | | Hartlepool (England : | |
| Harp seal | 599.792 9 | Borough) | T2—428 57 |
| Harp zithers | 787.73 | Hartley County (Tex.) | T2—764 823 |
| *see also* Stringed instruments | | Harts River (South Africa) | T2—687 11 |
| Harpacticoida | 595.34 | Hartswater (South Africa : | |
| Harper, Stephen | | District) | T2—687 11 |
| Canadian history | 971.073 | Hartz Mountains National | |
| Harper County (Kan.) | T2—781 845 | Park (Tas.) | T2—946 2 |
| Harper County (Okla.) | T2—766 153 | Harvest mice | 599.35 |
| Harpists | 787.909 2 | Harvest music | 781.524 6 |
| Harps | 787.9 | Harvesting | 631.55 |
| *see also* Stringed instruments | | equipment manufacturing | |
| Harpsichordists | 786.409 2 | technology | 681.763 1 |
| Harpsichords | 786.4 | production efficiency | 338.163 |
| instrument | 786.419 | Harvestmen (Arachnids) | 595.43 |
| music | 786.4 | Harvey County (Kan.) | T2—781 85 |
| *see also* Keyboard instruments | | Haryana (India) | T2—545 58 |
| Harquebuses | | Harz Mountains (Germany) | T2—431 82 |
| art metalwork | 739.744 25 | Ḥasakah (Syria : Province) | T2—569 12 |
| Harrier (Dog) | 636.753 6 | Hasan (Hadith) | 297.125 21 |
| Harriers (Birds) | 598.94 | Hashing (Computer science) | 005.741 |
| Harris County (Ga.) | T2—758 466 | Hashish | |
| Harris County (Tex.) | T2—764 141 | agriculture | 633.79 |
| Harrisburg (Pa.) | T2—748 18 | Hashish abuse | 362.295 |
| Harrismith (South Africa : | | medicine | 616.863 5 |
| District) | T2—685 1 | personal health | 613.835 |
| Harrison, Benjamin | | social welfare | 362.295 |
| United States history | 973.86 | *see also* Substance abuse | |
| Harrison, William Henry | | Hasidism | 296.833 2 |
| United States history | 973.58 | liturgy | 296.450 44 |

Haskell County (Kan.)          T2—781 732
Haskell County (Okla.)         T2—766 77
Haskell County (Tex.)          T2—764 736
Hasmonean period               933.04
Hassan II, King of Morocco
  Moroccan history   964.052
Hassium
  chemistry          546.62
Hastings (England)             T2—422 59
Hastings (Ont. : County)       T2—713 585
Hastings, Battle of, 1066      942.021
Hastings, Francis Rawdon-
  Hastings, Marquess of
  Indian history      954.031 3
Hastings, Warren
  Indian history      954.029 8
Hastings District (N.Z.)       T2—934 65
Hatay İli (Turkey)             T2—564 8
  ancient             939.431
                               T2—394 31
Hatcheries
  fish culture        639.311
Hatchetfishes (Freshwater)     597.48
Hatchetfishes (Marine)         597.5
Hate                           179.8
  psychology          152.4
  *see also* Vices
Hate crimes                    364.15
  law                 345.025
Hatha yoga
  health              613.704 6
Hato Mayor (Dominican
  Republic : Province) T2—729 381
Hatred                         179.8
  psychology          152.4
  *see also* Vices
Hats                           391.43
  *see also* Headwear
Hattah Lakes National Park
  (Vic.)              T2—945 9
Hatteras, Cape (N.C.)          T2—756 175
Hatters                        646.502 092
Hậu Giang (Vietnam)            T2—597 9
Haulage
  mining              622.6
Haunted places                 133.12
Hauraki District (N.Z.)        T2—933 27
Hausa (African people)         T5—937
Hausa language                 493.72
                               T6—937 2
Hausa literature               893.72
Hausa states                   966.970 1
Haut-Rhin (France)             T2—443 93
Haut-Richelieu (Quebec)        T2—714 38

Haut-Saint-François
  (Quebec)            T2—714 68
Haut-Saint-Laurent
  (Quebec)            T2—714 31
Haut-Saint-Maurice
  (Quebec)            T2—714 459
Haute-Corse (France)           T2—449 96
  ancient             T2—379 96
Haute-Côte-Nord (Quebec)       T2—714 172
Haute-Garonne (France)         T2—447 36
Haute-Gaspésie (Quebec)        T2—714 791
Haute-Loire (France)           T2—445 95
Haute-Marne (France)           T2—443 32
Haute-Normandie (France)       T2—442 4
Haute-Saône (France)           T2—444 53
Haute-Savoie (France)          T2—445 84
Haute-Vienne (France)          T2—446 62
Haute-Yamaska (Quebec)         T2—714 63
Hautes-Alpes (France)          T2—449 7
Hautes-Pyrénées (France)       T2—447 8
Hauts-de-Seine (France)        T2—443 64
Havana (Cuba)                  T2—729 123
Havana (Cuba : Province)       T2—729 124
Havant (England : Borough)     T2—422 795
Havasupai Indians              T5—975 724
Havasupai-Walapai-Yavapai      497.572 4
  language            T6—975 724
Havel, Václav
  Czech history       943.710 511
Havelland (Germany :
  Landkreis)          T2—431 54
Havelland-Fläming
  (Germany :
  Raumordnungsregion) T2—431 54
Havering (London,
  England)            T2—421 74
Havu language                  496.394
                               T6—963 94
Hawaii                         996.9
                               T2—969
Hawaii County (Hawaii)         T2—969 1
Hawaii Island (Hawaii)         T2—969 1
Hawaiian language              499.42
                               T6—994 2
Hawaiian literature            899.42
Hawaiian religion              299.924 2
Hawaiians (Native people)      T5—994 2
Hawea, Lake (N.Z.)             T2—939 5
Hawfinches                     598.885
Hawke, Bob
  Australian history  994.064
Hawke's Bay Region (N.Z.)      T2—934 6
Hawkesbury River (N.S.W.)      T2—944 2
Hawkins County (Tenn.)         T2—768 95

| | |
|---|---|
| Hawks | 598.944 |
| animal husbandry | 636.686 9 |
| Hawksbill turtle | 597.928 |
| Hawthorns | 583.73 |
| Hay | |
| animal feed | 636.086 |
| forage crop | 633.2 |
| Hay (South Africa : District) | T2—687 11 |
| Hay fever | |
| incidence | 614.599 3 |
| medicine | 616.202 |
| *see also* Respiratory tract | |
| diseases — humans | |
| Hay Mohamed-Aïn Sebaâ | |
| (Morocco : Prefecture) | T2—643 8 |
| Hay River (N.W.T.) | T2—719 3 |
| Haya-Jita languages | 496.395 |
| | T6—963 95 |
| Hayes, Rutherford Birchard | |
| United States history | 973.83 |
| Hayes County (Neb.) | T2—782 832 |
| Hays County (Tex.) | T2—764 888 |
| Haythamī, Nūr al-Dīn 'Alī ibn | |
| Abī Bakr | 297.125 64 |
| Haywood County (N.C.) | T2—756 94 |
| Haywood County (Tenn.) | T2—768 223 |
| Hazardous machinery | 363.18 |
| law | 344.047 2 |
| public administration | 353.99 |
| *see also* Safety | |
| Hazardous materials | 363.17 |
| effect on natural ecology | 577.27 |
| public administration | 353.993 |
| public safety | 363.17 |
| law | 344.047 2 |
| technology | 604.7 |
| *see Manual at* 604.7 vs. | |
| 660.2804 | |
| transportation | 388.044 |
| law | 343.093 22 |
| technology | 604.7 |
| transportation services | 388.044 |
| Hazardous wastes | 363.728 7 |
| law | 344.046 22 |
| public administration | 353.994 |
| social services | 363.728 7 |
| technology | 628.42 |
| *see also* Waste control | |
| Hazelnuts | 641.345 4 |
| *see also* Filberts | |
| Hazelton (B.C.) | T2—711 85 |
| Hazelton Mountains (B.C.) | T2—711 85 |
| Hazing | |
| education | 371.58 |

| | |
|---|---|
| HDTV (High-definition | |
| television) | 621.388 06 |
| Head | 591.44 |
| animal physiology | 573.995 |
| anthropometry | 599.948 |
| descriptive zoology | 591.44 |
| human anatomy | 611.91 |
| human physiology | 612.91 |
| regional medicine | 617.51 |
| surgery | 617.510 59 |
| Head lice | |
| medicine | 616.572 |
| *see also* Skin diseases — | |
| humans | |
| Head muscles | |
| human anatomy | 611.732 |
| Head scarves | 391.43 |
| *see also* Headwear | |
| Head start (Education) | 372.21 |
| Head teachers | 371.1 |
| biography | 371.100 92 |
| public control | 379.157 |
| Headaches | |
| medicine | 616.849 1 |
| *see also* Nervous system | |
| diseases — humans | |
| Headgear | 391.43 |
| *see also* Headwear | |
| Headings (Cataloging) | 025.322 |
| Headmasters | |
| biography | 371.200 92 |
| public control | 379.157 |
| role and function | 371.201 2 |
| Heads of government | 352.23 |
| Heads of state | 352.23 |
| Headscarves | 391.43 |
| *see also* Headwear | |
| Headstanders | 597.48 |
| Headwear | 391.43 |
| commercial technology | 687.4 |
| customs | 391.43 |
| home economics | 646.3 |
| home sewing | 646.5 |
| *see also* Clothing | |
| Healesville (Vic.) | T2—945 2 |
| Healing | |
| religion | 203.1 |
| *see also* Spiritual healing — | |
| religion | |
| *see Manual at* 615.852 vs. | |
| 203.1, 234.131, 292–299 | |
| therapeutics | 615.5 |
| Healing touch | |
| medicine | 615.852 |

| Health | 613 |
|---|---|
| arts | T3C—356 1 |
| child care | 649.4 |
| literature | 808.803 561 |
|   history and criticism | 809.933 561 |
|   specific literatures | T3B—080 356 1 |
|    history and | |
|     criticism | T3B—093 561 |
| medicine | 613 |
| primary education | 372.37 |
| social theology | 201.762 1 |
|   Christianity | 261.832 1 |
|   Judaism | 296.38 |
| sociology | 306.461 |
| *see Manual at* 613 vs. 612, | |
|  615.8 | |
| Health care | 362.1 |
| arts | T3C—356 1 |
| literature | 808.803 561 |
|   history and criticism | 809.933 561 |
|   specific literatures | T3B—080 356 1 |
|    history and | |
|     criticism | T3B—093 561 |
| *see also* Health services | |
| Health care facilities | 362.1 |
| accounting | 657.832 2 |
| architecture | 725.51 |
| cooking | 641.579 |
| law | 344.032 1 |
| meal service | 642.56 |
| public administration | 353.68 |
| safety | 363.15 |
| sanitation services | 363.729 7 |
|   public administration | 353.94 |
| social welfare | 362.1 |
| *see also* Health services | |
| Health centers | 362.12 |
| *see also* Health care facilities | |
| Health cooking | 641.563 |
| Health ethics | 174.2 |
| Health foods | 641.302 |
| cooking | 641.563 7 |
| food | 641.302 |
| Health insurance | 368.382 |
| government-sponsored | 368.42 |
|   law | 344.022 |
| labor economics | 331.255 4 |
|   law | 346.086 382 |
| public administration | 353.69 |
| Health maintenance organizations | 362.104 258 4 |
| insurance | 368.382 |
| law | 344.032 104 258 4 |
| *see also* Health services | |

| Health promotion | |
|---|---|
| medicine | 613 |
| public administration | 353.627 4 |
| Health protection service | |
| public administration | 353.628 |
| Health resorts | |
| personal health | 613.122 |
| Health services | 362.1 |
| Algerian Revolution | 965.046 7 |
| American Revolution | 973.375 |
| armed forces | 355.345 |
| Chaco War | 989.207 167 |
| Civil War (England) | 942.062 7 |
| Civil War (Spain) | 946.081 7 |
| Civil War (United States) | 973.775 |
| Crimean War | 947.073 87 |
| employee programs | |
|   personnel management | 658.382 |
|   public administration | 352.67 |
| Falkland Islands War | 997.110 247 |
| Franco-German War | 943.082 7 |
| Hundred Years' War | 944.025 7 |
| Indo-Pakistan War, 1971 | 954.920 517 |
| Indochinese War | 959.704 17 |
| Iraq War, 2003– | 956.704 437 |
| Iraqi-Iranian Conflict | 955.054 27 |
| Korean War | 951.904 27 |
| labor economics | 331.255 4 |
| law | 344.032 1 |
| Napoleonic Wars | 940.277 |
| pastoral theology | 206.1 |
|   Christianity | 259.41 |
| Persian Gulf War, 1991 | 956.704 427 |
| prisoner services | 365.667 |
| public administration | 353.6 |
| social theology | 201.762 1 |
|   Christianity | 261.832 1 |
| social welfare | 362.1 |
| South African War | 968.048 7 |
| student welfare | 371.71 |
| Thirty Years' War | 940.247 |
| Vietnamese War | 959.704 37 |
| War of the Pacific | 983.061 67 |
| World War I | 940.475 |
| World War II | 940.547 5 |
| *see also* Health care facilities | |
| *see Manual at* 362.1–.4 vs. | |
|  610; *also at* 362.1–.4 and | |
|  614.4–.5 | |
| Health surveys | 614.42 |

| | |
|---|---|
| Health visitors | 610.734 3 |
|   medicine | 610.734 3 |
|   social welfare | 362.14 |
|    *see also* Health services | |
|   *see also* Nursing | |
| Heard County (Ga.) | T2—758 422 |
| Hearing | 573.89 |
|   human physiology | 612.85 |
|   psychology | 152.15 |
|   *see also* Ears | |
| Hearing aids | |
|   audiology | 617.89 |
| Hearing devices | |
|   audiology | 617.89 |
| Hearing disorders | |
|   medicine | 617.8 |
|    *see also* Ear diseases — | |
|     humans | |
| Hearing examiners (Law) | 342.066 4 |
| Hearing-impaired children | 305.908 208 3 |
| | T1—087 2 |
|   home care | 649.151 2 |
|   *see also* Hearing-impaired | |
|    people | |
| Hearing-impaired people | 305.908 2 |
| | T1—087 2 |
|   education | 371.912 |
|   library services | 027.663 |
|   social group | 305.908 2 |
|   social welfare | 362.42 |
| Hearing impairment | |
|   medicine | 617.8 |
|    *see also* Ear diseases — | |
|     humans | |
| Hearings | |
|   legislative | 328.345 |
| Hearsay evidence | 347.064 |
| Heart | 573.17 |
|   animals | 573.17 |
|   human anatomy | 611.12 |
|   human biochemistry | 612.173 |
|   human biophysics | 612.171 |
|   human metabolism | 612.173 |
|   human physiology | 612.17 |
|   medicine | 616.12 |
|   physiology | 573.17 |
|   surgery | 617.412 |
|   *see also* Cardiovascular system | |
| Heart attacks | |
|   medicine | 616.123 025 |
|    myocardial infarction | 616.123 7 |
|    *see also* Cardiovascular | |
|     diseases — humans | |

| | |
|---|---|
| Heart depressants | |
|   pharmacokinetics | 615.716 |
| Heart diseases | |
|   cooking for | 641.563 11 |
|   medicine | 616.12 |
|    *see also* Cardiovascular | |
|     diseases — humans | |
|   pediatrics | 618.921 2 |
|   surgery | 617.412 |
| Heart failure | |
|   medicine | 616.129 |
|    *see also* Cardiovascular | |
|     diseases — humans | |
| Heart pacers (Electronic) | |
|   medicine | 617.412 064 5 |
| Heart stimulants | |
|   pharmacokinetics | 615.711 |
| Heart surgery | 617.412 |
| Heart transplants | 617.412 059 2 |
|   *see also* Organ transplants | |
| Heart valve diseases | |
|   medicine | 616.125 |
|    *see also* Cardiovascular | |
|     diseases — humans | |
| Heartburn | |
|   medicine | 616.324 |
|    *see also* Digestive system | |
|     diseases — humans | |
| Heat | 536 |
|   astrophysics | 523.013 |
|   biophysics | 571.467 |
|    humans | 612.014 462 |
|   crop damage | 632.12 |
|   effect on matter | 536.4 |
|   pathological effect | 571.934 67 |
|    medicine | 616.989 |
|   physics | 536 |
| Heat absorption | 536.3 |
| Heat capacity | 536.6 |
| Heat conduction | 536.23 |
|   engineering | 621.402 23 |
| Heat conduction in fluids | 536.25 |
| Heat conductivity | |
|   materials science | 620.112 96 |
| Heat convection | 536.25 |
|   engineering | 621.402 25 |
| Heat distribution systems | 621.402 8 |
| Heat engineering | 621.402 |
| Heat engineers | 621.402 092 |
| Heat engines | 621.402 5 |
| Heat exchange | |
|   engineering | 621.402 2 |
|   metallurgical furnaces | 669.85 |
| Heat exchangers | 621.402 5 |

Heat exhaustion
  medicine 616.989
  *see also* Environmental
    diseases — humans
Heat loss
  electric circuits 621.319 21
Heat of fusion 536.42
Heat of vaporization 536.44
Heat perception 152.182 2
HEAT projectiles
  engineering 623.451 7
Heat pumps 621.402 5
  refrigeration engineering 621.563
Heat radiation 536.3
  engineering 621.402 27
Heat-resistant glass 666.155
Heat scattering 536.3
Heat storage 621.402 8
  solar engineering 621.471 2
Heat stress disorders 571.934 67
  humans
    medicine 616.989
    *see also* Environmental
      diseases — humans
Heat transfer 536.2
  chemical engineering 660.284 27
  engineering 621.402 2
  physics 536.2
Heat treatment
  metals 671.36
Heat weapons 623.446
Heaters
  buildings 697.07
Heathcote (Vic.) T2—945 3
Heather 583.66
  floriculture 635.933 66
Heaths (Ericaceae) 583.66
Heaths (Shrublands)
  biology 578.738
  ecology 577.38
Heating
  aircraft 629.134 42
  automobile 629.277 2
  buildings 697
    customs 392.36
  chemistry 542.4
  household management 644.1
  library buildings 697.978
    plant management 022.8
  museums 069.29
  plant management 658.25
  vehicles 629.040 289
Heating coils
  air conditioning buildings 697.932 2

Heating engineers 697.009 2
Heating equipment 621.402 5
  air conditioning buildings 697.932 2
  furniture arts 749.62
  installation in buildings 697.07
  ships 623.853 7
Heating from central stations 697.03
  resource economics 333.793
Heating oil 665.538 4
Heaven 202.3
  Christianity 236.24
  Islam 297.23
  Judaism 296.33
Heavenly bodies 520
  folklore 398.26
    history and criticism 398.362
Heavier-than-air aircraft 387.733
  engineering 629.133 3
  military engineering 623.746
  transportation services 387.733
  *see also* Aircraft
Heavy equipment
  capital procurement 658.152 42
  household appliances 643.6
    manufacturing technology 683.88
Heavy ions 539.723 4
Heavy metal (Music) 781.66
Heavy spar 553.662
Heavy water
  chemical engineering 661.08
  chemistry 546.22
Hebei Sheng (China) T2 —511 52
Hebrew language 492.4
   T6—924
  Biblical texts 220.44
  Midrashic texts 296.140 4
  printing 686.219 24
  Talmudic texts 296.120 4
Hebrew literature 892.4
Hebrew schools 296.680 83
Hebrews T5—924
Hebrews (Biblical book) 227.87
Hebrides (Scotland) T2—411 4
Hebron district (West Bank) T2—569 51
Hecate Strait (B.C.) 551.461 433
   T2—164 33
Hedge laurels 583.72
Hedgehogs 599.332
Hedgerows
  biology 578.755 5
  ecology 577.555
Hedges
  agricultural use 631.27
  floriculture 635.976

Hedging (Finance) 332.645 24
Hedmark fylke (Norway) T2—482 4
Hedonism
  ethical systems 171.4
Heel-and-toe races 796.429
Hegirah 297.634
Hei-Lung Chiang (China
  and Russia) T2—577
Heidelberg (Cape of Good
  Hope, South Africa :
  District) T2—687 36
Heidelberg (Gauteng, South
  Africa : District) T2—682 23
Heidelberg (Germany) T2—434 645 4
Heidelberg man 569.97
Heilbron (South Africa :
  District) T2—685 2
Heilongjiang Sheng (China) T2—518 4
Heilungkiang Province
  (China) T2—518 4
Heimatblock (Austrian political
  party) 324.243 602 4
Heisei period 952.049
Heisenberg representation 530.122
Hejaz (Saudi Arabia) T2—538
Helena (Mont.) T2—786 615
Helenopontus T2—393 32
Helensburgh (Scotland) T2—414 2
Helicobacter 579.323
Helicobacter infections
  medicine 616.330 14
  *see also* Digestive system
    diseases — humans
Heliconiaceae 584.39
Heliconias 584.39
  floriculture 635.934 39
Helicopter accidents 363.124 93
  *see also* Air safety
Helicopters 387.733 52
  engineering 629.133 352
  military engineering 623.746 047
  piloting 629.132 525 2
  transportation services 387.733 52
  *see also* Aircraft
Heliographs
  military engineering 623.731 2
  nautical engineering 623.856 12
Heliotherapy
  medicine 615.831 4
Heliothis 595.78
  agricultural pests 632.78
Heliotropes (Plants) 583.94

Heliports 387.736
  engineering 629.136 16
  military engineering 623.661 6
  *see also* Airports
Helium 553.971
  chemistry 546.751
  economic geology 553.971
  gas technology 665.822
  *see also* Chemicals
Helium extraction 665.73
Hell 202.3
  art representation 704.948 9
    Christianity 704.948 2
  arts T3C—382 023
  Christianity 236.25
  Islam 297.23
  literature 808.803 820 23
    history and criticism 809.933 820 23
    specific literatures T3B—080 382 023
    history and
      criticism T3B—093 820 23
Hellbender (Salamander) 597.85
Hellebores 583.34
  floriculture 635.933 34
Hellenic languages 480
             T6—8
Hellenic literatures 880
Hellenic sculpture 733.3
Hellenistic Greek language 487.4
             T6—87
Hellenistic movement (Judaism) 296.81
Hellenistic period
  Egyptian history 932.021
  Greek history 938.08
  Mesopotamian history 935.06
  Middle Eastern history 939.404
  Palestinian history 933.03
Hellenistic World 938
             T2—38
Hellespontus (Roman
  province) T2—392 1
Helmets (Armor) 623.441
  art metalwork 739.75
Helmets (Headwear) 391.43
  *see also* Headwear
Helminthologists 592.309 2
Helminthology 592.3
  agriculture 632.623
  medicine 616.962
  plant crops 632.623
  veterinary medicine 636.089 696 2
Heloderma 597.959 5
Helodermatidae 597.959 5
Helotiales 579.57

| | | | |
|---|---|---|---|
| Help facilities (Computers) | 005.3 | Hematuria | |
| development | 005.15 | medicine | 616.63 |
| Help-wanted advertising | 659.193 311 24 | *see also* Urologic diseases — | |
| Helping behavior | 158.3 | humans | |
| Helsinki (Finland) | T2—489 71 | Hemiascomycetes | 579.562 |
| Helvetia | T2—369 43 | Hemic disorders | |
| Helvetic Republic | 949.405 | medicine | 616.15 |
| | T2—494 | *see also* Cardiovascular | |
| Hemangiomas | | diseases — humans | |
| medicine | 616.993 13 | Hemichordata | 593.99 |
| Hemapheresis | | paleozoology | 563.99 |
| pharmacology | 615.39 | Hemimetabola | 595.73 |
| Hematheia (Greece) | T2—495 65 | Hemiprocnidae | 598.762 |
| Hematite | | Hemiptera | 595.754 |
| mineralogy | 549.523 | Hemispheres | T2—181 |
| Hematologic agents | | Hemlocks | 585.2 |
| pharmacokinetics | 615.718 | forestry | 634.975 3 |
| Hematologic diseases | | lumber | 674.144 |
| medicine | 616.15 | ornamental arboriculture | 635.977 52 |
| *see also* Cardiovascular | | Hemoconia | |
| diseases — humans | | human physiology | 612.117 |
| Hematologic neoplasms | | Hemodialysis | |
| incidence | 614.599 941 8 | medicine | 617.461 059 |
| medicine | 616.994 18 | Hemoglobin | |
| *see also* Cancer — humans | | human physiology | 612.111 1 |
| Hematology | 616.15 | medicine | 616.151 |
| diagnosis | | Hemoglobin disorders | |
| general disease | 616.075 61 | medicine | 616.151 |
| Hematopoiesis | 573.155 | *see also* Cardiovascular | |
| *see also* Hematopoietic system | | diseases — humans | |
| Hematopoietic system | 573.155 | Hemolytic anemia | |
| animals | 573.155 | medicine | 616.152 |
| diseases | 573.155 39 | *see also* Cardiovascular | |
| *see also* Hematopoietic | | diseases — humans | |
| system diseases | | Hemolytic disease of the | |
| human anatomy | 611.41 | newborn | |
| human physiology | 612.41 | pediatrics | 618.921 5 |
| medicine | 616.41 | perinatal medicine | 618.326 1 |
| Hematopoietic system diseases | 573.155 39 | *see also* Cardiovascular | |
| animals | 573.155 39 | diseases — humans | |
| humans | 362.196 41 | Hemophilia | |
| cancer | 362.196 994 41 | medicine | 616.157 2 |
| incidence | 614.599 944 1 | *see also* Cardiovascular | |
| medicine | 616.994 41 | diseases — humans | |
| social services | 362.196 994 41 | pediatrics | 618.921 572 |
| *see also* Cancer — humans | | Hemopoiesis | 573.155 |
| geriatrics | 618.976 41 | *see also* Hematopoietic system | |
| incidence | 614.594 1 | Hemopoietic system | 573.155 |
| medicine | 616.41 | *see also* Hematopoietic system | |
| pediatrics | 618.924 1 | Hemorheology | |
| pharmacokinetics | 615.718 | humans | 612.118 1 |
| social services | 362.196 41 | | |

Hemorrhage
  medicine    616.157
    *see also* Cardiovascular
      diseases — humans
Hemorrhagic diseases
  medicine    616.157
    *see also* Cardiovascular
      diseases — humans
Hemorrhoids
  medicine    616.352
    *see also* Digestive system
      diseases — humans
Hemp (Agavaceae)    584.352
Hemp (Apocynaceae)    583.93
Hemp (Cannabaceae)    583.45
Hemp (Fiber)    677.12
  botany    583.45
  crop    633.53
  textiles    677.12
    arts    746.041 2
    *see also* Textiles
Hemp (Musaceae)    584.39
Hemp pulp    676.14
Hemphill County (Tex.)    T2—764 817
Hempstead County (Ark.)    T2—767 54
Henan Sheng (China)    T2—511 8
Henbanes    583.952
Henderson County (Ill.)    T2—773 413
Henderson County (Ky.)    T2—769 87
Henderson County (N.C.)    T2—756 92
Henderson County (Tenn.)    T2—768 263
Henderson County (Tex.)    T2—764 227
Henderson Island (Pitcairn
  Island)    T2—961 8
Hendricks County (Ind.)    T2—772 53
Hendry County (Fla.)    T2—759 46
Hennenman (South Africa :
  District)    T2—685 3
Hennepin County (Minn.)    T2—776 57
Henophidia    597.967
Henrico County (Va.)    T2—755 453
Henry I, King of England
  English history    942.023
Henry I, King of France
  French history    944.021
Henry II, King of England
  English history    942.031
Henry II, King of France
  French history    944.028
Henry III, King of England
  English history    942.034
Henry III, King of France
  French history    944.029

Henry IV, King of England
  English history    942.041
Henry IV, King of France
  French history    944.031
Henry V, King of England
  English history    942.042
Henry VI, King of England
  English history    942.043
Henry VII, King of England
  English history    942.051
Henry VIII, King of England
  English history    942.052
Henry County (Ala.)    T2—761 31
Henry County (Ga.)    T2—758 435
Henry County (Ill.)    T2—773 38
Henry County (Ind.)    T2—772 64
Henry County (Iowa)    T2—777 95
Henry County (Ky.)    T2—769 385
Henry County (Mo.)    T2—778 462
Henry County (Ohio)    T2—771 15
Henry County (Tenn.)    T2—768 34
Henry County (Va.)    T2—755 692
Hepatic encephalopathy
  medicine    616.83
    *see also* Nervous system
      diseases — humans
Hepaticae    588.3
Hepatidae    588.3
Hepatitis
  medicine    616.362 3
    *see also* Digestive system
      diseases — humans
Hepatopsida    588.3
Heptarchy    942.015
Heptathlon    796.42
Heraclitean philosophy    182.4
Hērakleion (Greece : Nome)  T2—495 9
Heraldic design    929.6
  decorative arts    745.66
  insignia    929.6
Heraldry    929.6
Hérault (France)    T2—448 4
Herb gardens    635.7
Herb teas    641.357
  agriculture    635.7
  commercial processing    663.96
  cooking with    641.657
  food    641.357
  home preparation    641.877
Herbaceous plants    582.12
  landscape architecture    716
Herbaceous vines    582.189
Herbal medicine    615.321

Herbals
  pharmacognosy      615.321
    *see Manual at* 615.1 vs.
      615.2–.3
Herbariums      580.74
Herbert (South Africa :
  District)      T2—687 11
Herbicides      632.954
  agricultural use      632.954
  chemical engineering      668.654
Herbivorous animals      591.54
Herbivorous Saurischia      567.913
Herbs      581.63
  botany      581.63
  commercial processing      664.805 7
  cooking with      641.657
  food      641.357
  garden crop      635.7
  pharmacognosy      615.321
    *see Manual at* 615.1 vs.
      615.2–.3
Herculaneum (Extinct city)      T2—377 256 4
Herdbooks      636.082 2
Herders (People)      636.084 509 2
Herders (Work animals)
  care and training      636.088 6
Herding (Animal husbandry)      636.084 5
Herding dogs      636.737
Heredia (Costa Rica :
  Province)      T2—728 64
Hereditary diseases      571.948
Hereditary metabolic disorders
  medicine      616.390 42
    *see also* Digestive system
      diseases — humans
Hereditary societies      369.2
  biography      369.209 2
  United States      369.1
Heredity      576.5
  animals      591.35
  humans      599.935
  influence on crime      364.24
  plants      581.35
  psychology      155.7
    evolutionary psychology      155.7
    individual psychology      155.234
Heredity versus environment
  psychology      155.7
    evolutionary psychology      155.7
    individual psychology      155.234
Hereford (England)      T2—424 2
Hereford and Worcester
  (England)      T2—424 4
Hereford cattle      636.222

Herefordshire (England)      T2—424 2
Hérens (Switzerland)      T2—494 796 3
Herero (African people)      T5—963 99
Herero language      496.399
      T6—963 99
Heresy
  Christianity      262.8
    church history      273
    polemics      239
  criminology      364.188
  Judaism      296.67
    polemics      296.35
    religious authority      296.67
  law      345.028 8
Herisau (Switzerland)      T2—494 712 6
Herkimer County (N.Y.)      T2—747 61
Herm Island (Channel
  Islands)      T2—423 46
Hermanus (South Africa :
  District)      T2—687 36
Hermaphroditism      571.886
  biology      571.886
  humans
    medicine      616.694
    *see also* Genital
      diseases — humans
Hermeneutics      121.686
  philosophy      121.686
  sacred books      208.2
    Bible      220.601
    Hadith      297.125 160 1
    Koran      297.122 601
    Talmud      296.120 601
Hermetism      135.45
Hermit crabs      595.387
  culture      639.67
Hermite polynomials      515.55
Hermitian spaces      515.73
Hernandiaceae      583.23
Hernando County (Fla.)      T2—759 71
Hernando Island (B.C.)      T2—711 31
Hernias (Abdominal region)
  regional medicine      617.559
  surgery      617.559 059
Heroes
  arts      T3C—352
  literature      808.803 52
    history and criticism      809.933 52
    specific literatures      T3B—080 352
      history and
      criticism      T3B—093 52
  objects of worship      202.13

# Dewey Decimal Classification

| | |
|---|---|
| Heroin abuse | 362.293 |
|   medicine | 616.863 2 |
|   personal health | 613.83 |
|   social welfare | 362.293 |
|   *see also* Substance abuse | |
| Heroism | |
|   arts | T3C—353 |
|   literature | 808.803 53 |
|     history and criticism | 809.933 53 |
|     specific literatures | T3B—080 353 |
|     history and criticism | T3B—093 53 |
| Herons | 598.34 |
| Herpes genitalis | |
|   incidence | 614.547 |
|   medicine | 616.951 8 |
|   *see also* Communicable diseases — humans | |
| Herpes labialis | |
|   medicine | 616.522 |
|   *see also* Skin diseases — humans | |
| Herpes simplex type 1 | |
|   medicine | 616.522 |
|   *see also* Skin diseases — humans | |
| Herpes simplex type 2 | |
|   incidence | 614.547 |
|   medicine | 616.951 8 |
|   *see also* Communicable diseases — humans | |
| Herpes zoster | |
|   medicine | 616.522 |
|   *see also* Skin diseases — humans | |
| Herpesviridae | 579.243 4 |
| Herpesvirus diseases | |
|   incidence | 614.581 2 |
|   medicine | 616.911 2 |
|   *see also* Communicable diseases — humans | |
| Herpetologists | 597.909 2 |
| Herpetology | 597.9 |
| Herrera (Panama : Province) | T2—728 724 |
| Herring (Clupea harengus) | 641.392 |
|   conservation technology | 639.977 452 |
|   cooking | 641.692 |
|   fishing | 639.274 52 |
|   food | 641.392 |
|   resource economics | 333.956 452 |
|   zoology | 597.452 |
| Herring family | 597.45 |
| Herschel (South Africa : District) | T2—687 56 |
| Hertford County (N.C.) | T2—756 155 |
| Hertfordshire (England) | T2—425 8 |
| Hertsmere (England) | T2—425 895 |
| Hertzog, James Barry Munnik | |
|   South African history | 968.054 |
| Hesperioidea | 595.788 |
| Hesperonesian languages | 499.2 |
| | T6—992 |
| Hesperornithiformes | 568.23 |
| Hesse (Germany) | T2—434 1 |
| Hetero nitrogen compounds | 547.593 |
|   chemical engineering | 661.894 |
| Hetero oxygen compounds | 547.592 |
|   chemical engineering | 661.8 |
| Hetero sulfur compounds | 547.594 |
|   chemical engineering | 661.896 |
| Heterobasidiomycetes | 579.59 |
| Heterocyclic compounds | 547.59 |
|   chemical engineering | 661.8 |
| Heterogeneous grouping of students | 371.252 |
| Heterogenesis | 571.884 |
| Heteromyidae | 599.359 8 |
| Heterophony | 781.283 |
| Heteroptera | 595.754 |
| Heterosexuality | 306.764 |
| Heterosexuals | 306.764 |
| | T1—086 62 |
|   psychology | 155.34 |
|   social welfare | 362.896 2 |
| Heterosomata | 597.69 |
| Hettinger County (N.D.) | T2—784 86 |
| Heveas | 583.69 |
|   rubber crop | 633.895 2 |
| Heves Megye (Hungary) | T2—439 8 |
| Hewu (South Africa : District) | T2—687 55 |
| Hexacorallia | 593.6 |
| Hexactinellida | 593.44 |
|   paleozoology | 563.4 |
| Hexadecimal system | 513.5 |
| Hexagonal chess | 794.18 |
| Hexapoda | 595.7 |
|   *see also* Insects | |
| Hexateuch (Bible) | 222.1 |
| Hi-fi | |
|   sound reproduction systems | 621.389 332 |
| Hiatal hernia | |
|   regional medicine | 617.559 |
| Hibernation | 591.565 |
|   behavior | 591.565 |
|   physiology | 571.787 |
| Hibiscuses | 583.685 |
|   floriculture | 635.933 685 |

| | |
|---|---|
| Hickman County (Ky.) | T2—769 98 |
| Hickman County (Tenn.) | T2—768 434 |
| Hickories | 583.49 |
| Hickory County (Mo.) | T2—778 496 |
| Hidalgo (Mexico : State) | T2—724 6 |
| Hidalgo County (N.M.) | T2—789 693 |
| Hidalgo County (Tex.) | T2—764 492 |
| Hidatsa Indians | T5—975 274 |
| Hidatsa language | 497.527 4 |
| | T6—975 274 |
| Hide-and-seek (Game) | 796.14 |
| Hides | |
| animal husbandry | 636.088 44 |
| descriptive zoology | 599.614 7 |
| physiology | 573.519 6 |
| processing | 675.2 |
| Hierarchical databases | |
| computer science | 005.755 |
| Hierarchical systems | 003.7 |
| Hierarchy | |
| armed forces | 355.33 |
| organizational behavior | 302.35 |
| Hieroglyphic Hittite language | 491.998 |
| | T6—919 98 |
| Hieroglyphics | |
| Egyptian language | 493.111 |
| Hierotherapy | |
| medicine | 615.852 |
| High altitude | |
| biophysics | 571.49 |
| High-altitude plants | |
| floriculture | 635.952 8 |
| High-alumina cement | 666.95 |
| High Atlas Mountains | |
| (Morocco) | T2—644 |
| High bar (Gymnastic equipment) | 796.442 |
| High blood cholesterol | 616.399 7 |
| *see also* Digestive system | |
| diseases — humans | |
| High blood pressure | |
| medicine | 616.132 |
| *see also* Cardiovascular | |
| diseases — humans | |
| High-calorie cooking | 641.563 |
| High-calorie diet | |
| health | 613.24 |
| High-compression-ignition | |
| engines | 621.436 |
| automotive | 629.250 6 |
| High-contrast photography | 778.8 |
| High-definition television | 621.388 06 |
| High-energy forming | 671.3 |
| High-energy physics | 539.76 |

| | |
|---|---|
| High-explosive ammunition | |
| engineering | 623.451 7 |
| High explosives | 662.27 |
| High-fat cooking | 641.563 8 |
| High-fat diet | |
| health | 613.284 |
| High-fiber cooking | 641.563 |
| High-fiber diet | |
| health | 613.263 |
| High-fidelity systems | |
| sound reproduction | 621.389 332 |
| High Holy Days | 296.431 |
| liturgy | 296.453 1 |
| High jump | 796.432 |
| High-level languages | 005.13 |
| High Middle Ages | 940.18 |
| High-octane-rating gasoline | 665.538 25 |
| High Peak (England) | T2—425 11 |
| High polymers | |
| chemistry | 547.84 |
| High-protein cooking | 641.563 8 |
| High-protein diet | |
| health | 613.282 |
| High-rise buildings | 720.483 |
| *see also* Tall buildings | |
| High school administration | 373.12 |
| High school dropouts | 373.129 13 |
| High school enrollment | 373.121 9 |
| High school equivalency | |
| certificate | 373.126 2 |
| High school equivalency | |
| programs | 373.238 |
| High school graduates | |
| choice of vocation | 331.702 33 |
| labor force | 331.114 43 |
| unemployment | 331.137 804 |
| High school postgraduate | |
| programs | 373.238 |
| High school students | 373.18 |
| High school teachers | 373.11 |
| High school teaching | 373.110 2 |
| High schools | 373 |
| | T1—071 2 |
| *see also* Secondary education | |
| High seas | 551.46 |
| law of nations | 341.45 |
| *see Manual at* 341.45 vs. | |
| 343.0962 | |
| *see also* Oceans | |
| High-speed cinematography | 777.6 |
| High-speed local networks | 004.68 |
| *see also* Computer | |
| communications | |
| High-speed photography | 778.37 |

| | |
|---|---|
| High-speed videography | 777.6 |
| High-styrene resins | 678.73 |
| High-temperature biology | |
| humans | 612.014 462 |
| High-temperature injury | 571.934 67 |
| humans | |
| medicine | 617.11 |
| High temperatures | 536.57 |
| biophysics | 571.467 |
| chemical engineering | 660.296 87 |
| chemistry | 541.368 7 |
| effect on materials | 620.112 17 |
| physics | 536.57 |
| High-tension electric | |
| transmission | 621.319 13 |
| High Veld (South Africa) | T2—682 |
| High-velocity armor-piercing | |
| ammunition | 623.451 8 |
| High voice | 783.3 |
| High-voltage accelerators | 539.732 |
| High-yield bonds | 332.632 34 |
| Higher criticism | |
| Bible | 220.66 |
| Higher education | 378 |
| | T1—071 1 |
| federal aid | 379.121 4 |
| law | 344.074 |
| public administrative support | 353.88 |
| public support | 379.118 |
| law | 344.076 84 |
| special education | 371.904 74 |
| Higher-order logic | 511.3 |
| Highland (Scotland) | T2—411 5 |
| Highland cattle | 636.223 |
| Highland County (Ohio) | T2—771 845 |
| Highland County (Va.) | T2—755 89 |
| Highland Region (Scotland) | T2—411 5 |
| Highland Rim | T2—768 4 |
| Kentucky | T2—769 6 |
| Tennessee | T2—768 4 |
| Highlands (Papua New Guinea) | 995.6 |
| | T2—956 |
| Highlands (Scotland) | T2—411 5 |
| Highlands County (Fla.) | T2—759 55 |
| Highly volatile petroleum | |
| products | 665.538 2 |
| Highveld (South Africa) | T2—682 |
| Highveld Ridge (South | |
| Africa : District) | T2—682 77 |
| Highway accidents | 363.125 |
| *see also* Highway safety | |
| Highway engineers | 625.709 2 |
| Highway maps | 912 |
| Highway patrol | 363.233 2 |

| | |
|---|---|
| Highway post offices | 383.42 |
| *see also* Postal service | |
| Highway safety | 363.125 |
| engineering | 625.702 89 |
| law | 343.094 |
| public administration | 353.98 |
| social services | 363.125 |
| Highway transportation | 388.31 |
| *see also* Road transportation | |
| Highways | 388.1 |
| engineering | 625.7 |
| transportation services | 388.1 |
| *see also* Roads | |
| Hijacking | 364.155 2 |
| law | 345.025 52 |
| Hijrah | 297.634 |
| Hikers | 796.510 92 |
| Hiking | 796.51 |
| Hilbert spaces | 515.733 |
| Hilbert transform | 515.723 |
| Hildburghausen (Germany : | |
| Landkreis) | T2—432 26 |
| Hildebrand, Bruno | |
| economic school | 330.154 2 |
| Hildesheim (Germany) | T2—435 95 |
| Hill climbing | 796.522 |
| Hill County (Mont.) | T2—786 14 |
| Hill County (Tex.) | T2—764 283 |
| Hillingdon (London, | |
| England) | T2—421 83 |
| Hills | 551.436 |
| | T2—143 |
| *see also* Mountains | |
| Hillsboro County (N.H.) | T2—742 8 |
| Hillsborough County (Fla.) | T2—759 65 |
| Hillsborough County (N.H.) | T2—742 8 |
| Hillsdale County (Mich.) | T2—774 29 |
| Himachal Pradesh (India) | T2—545 2 |
| Himalaya Mountains | T2—549 6 |
| Himalayan cat | 636.83 |
| Himalayish languages | 495.4 |
| | T6—954 |
| Ḥimṣ (Syria : Province) | T2—569 12 |
| Hinayana Buddhism | 294.391 |
| Hinchinbrook Island | |
| National Park (Qld.) | T2—943 6 |
| Hinckley and Bosworth | |
| (England) | T2—425 49 |
| Hindi language | 491.43 |
| | T6—914 31 |
| Hindi literature | 891.43 |
| Hindi-speaking peoples | T5—914 3 |
| Hindis | T5—914 3 |
| Hinds County (Miss.) | T2—762 51 |

| | | | |
|---|---|---|---|
| Hindu architecture | 720.954 | Hips | 612.98 |
| Hindu calendar | 529.324 5 | medicine | 616.72 |
| religion | 294.536 | physiology | 612.98 |
| Hindu education | 294.575 | regional medicine | 617.581 |
| Hindu ethics | 294.548 | surgery | 617.581 059 |
| Hindu holidays | 294.536 | *see also* Lower extremities | |
| customs | 394.265 45 | Hiring halls | 331.889 6 |
| *see also* Holidays | | Hiring of employees | |
| Hindu Kush Mountains | | personnel management | 658.311 2 |
| (Afghanistan and | | public administration | 352.65 |
| Pakistan) | T2—581 | Hiroshima-ken (Japan) | T2—521 95 |
| Hindu philosophy | 181.4 | Hiroshima-shi (Japan) | T2—521 954 |
| Hindu sacred music | 781.745 | Hirudinea | 592.66 |
| public worship | 782.345 | Hirundinidae | 598.826 |
| music | 782.345 | Hispania | |
| religion | 294.538 | ancient | T2—366 |
| religion | 294.537 | Hispanic Americans | T5—68 |
| Hindu sculpture | 730.954 | Hispanic Americans (U.S.) | T5—680 73 |
| Hindu temples and shrines | 294.535 | education | 371.829 680 73 |
| architecture | 726.145 | Hispaniola | T2—729 3 |
| Hinduism | 294.5 | Histeroidea | 595.763 |
| art representation | 704.948 945 | Histochemical examination | |
| arts | 700.482 945 | medicine | 616.075 83 |
| | T3C—382 945 | Histochemistry | 572 |
| Islamic polemics | 297.294 | Histogenesis | 571.835 |
| Hinduism and Islam | 294.515 | humans | 611.018 |
| Hindu view | 294.515 | Histological examination | |
| Islamic view | 297.284 5 | medicine | 616.075 83 |
| Hindus | T1—088 294 5 | Histology | 571.5 |
| biography | 294.509 2 | humans | 611.018 |
| social group | 305.694 5 | Histones | 572.66 |
| Hinsdale County (Colo.) | T2—788 39 | *see also* Proteins | |
| Hinterrhein (Switzerland) | T2—494 735 4 | Histopathology | 571.9 |
| Hinwil (Switzerland : | | humans | 611.018 |
| Bezirk) | T2—494 574 3 | *see also* Pathology | |
| Hip bones | | Histophysiology | 571.5 |
| human anatomy | 611.718 | humans | 611 018 |
| Hip-hop (Music) | 781.649 | Historians | 907.202 |
| Hip muscles | | Historians of religion | 200.92 |
| human anatomy | 611.738 | Historic buildings | |
| Hippies | 305.568 | law | 344.094 |
| | T1—086 9 | preservation | 363.69 |
| Hippoboscidae | 595.774 | technology | 720.288 |
| Hippocampus | 597.679 8 | Historic political parties | 324.212 |
| Hippocastanaceae | 583.78 | Historic preservation | 363.69 |
| Hippocrateaceae | 583.85 | law | 344.094 |
| Hippocratic oath | 174.22 | public administrative support | 353.77 |
| Hippocratic theory of | | social services | 363.69 |
| temperaments | 155.262 | *see Manual at* 930–990 | |
| Hippoglossus | 597.695 | Historical atlases | 911 |
| Hippopotamidae | 599.635 | Historical bibliography | 002 |
| Hippopotamuses | 599.635 | Historical books (Old Testament) | 222 |
| Hippotraginae | 599.645 | Historical books | |
| Hippuridales | 583.82 | (Pseudepigrapha) | 229.911 |

| | |
|---|---|
| Historical criticism | |
| sacred books | 208.2 |
| Bible | 220.67 |
| Koran | 297.122 67 |
| Talmud | 296.120 67 |
| Historical drama | 792.14 |
| literature | 808.825 14 |
| history and criticism | 809.251 4 |
| specific literatures | T3B—205 14 |
| individual authors | T3A—2 |
| stage presentation | 792.14 |
| Historical events | 900 |
| art representation | 704.949 9 |
| arts | 700.458 |
| | T3C—358 |
| literature | 808.803 58 |
| history and criticism | 809.933 58 |
| specific literatures | T3B—080 358 |
| history and | |
| criticism | T3B—093 58 |
| *see Manual at* 900 | |
| Historical fiction | 808.838 1 |
| history and criticism | 809.381 |
| specific literatures | T3B—308 1 |
| individual authors | T3A—3 |
| Historical geography | 911 |
| Historical geology | 551.7 |
| *see Manual at* 551.7 vs. 560 | |
| Historical linguistics | 417.7 |
| specific languages | T4—7 |
| *see Manual at* 410 | |
| Historical materialism | |
| Marxian theory | 335.411 9 |
| Historical novels | 808.838 1 |
| history and criticism | 809.381 |
| specific literatures | T3B—308 1 |
| individual authors | T3A—3 |
| Historical pageants | |
| performing arts | 791.624 |
| Historical periods | 909 |
| | T1—090 1–090 5 |
| specific places | 930–990 |
| *see Manual at* T1—0901–0905 | |
| Historical remedies | |
| therapeutics | 615.88 |
| Historical research | 907.2 |
| | T1—072 2 |
| public administrative support | 352.744 |
| *see Manual at* | |
| T1—07201–07209 | |
| vs. T1—0721; *also at* | |
| T1—07201–07209 vs. | |
| T1—0722–0724 | |
| Historical school (Economics) | 330.154 2 |

| | |
|---|---|
| Historical themes | |
| arts | 700.458 |
| | T3C—358 |
| folklore | 398.278 |
| history and criticism | 398.358 |
| literature | 808.803 58 |
| history and criticism | 809.933 58 |
| specific literatures | T3B—080 358 |
| history and | |
| criticism | T3B—093 58 |
| painting | 758.99 |
| Historical treatment | T1—09 |
| *see also* History | |
| Historicism | |
| philosophy | 149 |
| philosophy of history | 901 |
| Historicity of Jesus Christ | 232.908 |
| Historiographers | 907.202 |
| Historiography | 907.2 |
| | T1—072 2 |
| History | 900 |
| | T1—09 |
| Biblical events | 220.95 |
| art representation | 704.948 4 |
| arts | 700.482 2 |
| | T3C—382 2 |
| primary education | 372.89 |
| specific places | 930–990 |
| *see Manual at* 930–990 vs. | |
| 355.009, 355–359 | |
| world | 909 |
| *see Manual at* T1—09; *also at* | |
| 306 vs. 305, 909, 930–990; | |
| *also at* 900; *also at* 909, | |
| 930–990 vs. 320 | |
| History (Theology) | 202.117 |
| Christianity | 231.76 |
| Islam | 297.211 4 |
| Judaism | 296.311 7 |
| Histrionic personality disorder | |
| medicine | 616.858 1 |
| *see also* Mental disorders | |
| Hit-and-run tactics | 355.422 |
| Hitchcock County (Neb.) | T2—782 845 |
| Hitler, Adolf | |
| German history | 943.086 |
| Hittite language | 491.998 |
| | T6—919 98 |
| Hittite literature | 891.998 |
| Hittites | T5—919 9 |
| HIV (Viruses) | |
| medical microbiology | 616.979 201 |

HIV infections
  incidence — 614.599 392
  medicine — 616.979 2
  *see also* Communicable
    diseases — humans
Hives (Disease)
  medicine — 616.517
  *see also* Skin diseases —
    humans
Hixkaryana language — 498.42
    T6—984 2
Hlabisa (South Africa :
  District) — T2—684 3
Hlanganani (South Africa :
  District) — T2—682 57
Hluhluwe Game Reserve
  (South Africa) — T2—684 3
Hmong — T5—959 72
Hmong language — 495.972
    T6—959 72
Hmong literature — 895.972
Hmong-Mien languages — 495.97
    T6—959 7
HMOs (Managed care providers) — 362.104 258 4
  insurance — 368.382
  *see also* Health services
Ho Chi Minh City — T2—597 7
Ho language (Munda) — 495.95
    T6—959 5
Hòa Bình (Vietnam :
  Province) — T2—597 1
Hoarding food (Animal behavior) — 591.53
Hoarfrost — 551.574 4
Hoatzin — 598.74
Hoaxes — 001.95
  books — 098.3
Hobart (Tas.) — T2—946 1
Hobbies — 790.13
    T1—023
  recreation — 790.13
  sociology — 306.487
  *see also* Recreation
Hobgoblins — 133.14
Hoboes — 305.569
    T1—086 942
Hoceïma (Morocco :
  Province) — T2—643 2
Hochdorf (Switzerland :
  Amt) — T2—494 559
Hochrhein — T2—494 564
Hockey — 796.356
Hockey (Field sports) — 796.355
Hockey (Ice sports) — 796.962
  electronic games — 794.869 62

Hockey cards — 796.962 075
Hockey players (Ice sports) — 796.962 092
Hocking County (Ohio) — T2—771 835
Hocking River (Ohio) — T2—771 97
Hockley County (Tex.) — T2—764 846
Hodge theory — 514.74
Hodgeman County (Kan.) — T2—781 47
Hodgkin disease
  medicine — 616.994 46
  *see also* Cancer — humans
Hoedowns — 793.34
  music — 784.188 7
Hoëveldrif (South Africa :
  District) — T2—682 77
Höfe (Switzerland) — T2—494 752 3
Hofmeyr (South Africa :
  District) — T2—687 56
Hog plums (Anacardiaceae) — 583.77
Hog plums (Rosaceae) — 583.73
Hogs — 636.4
Hohenstaufen, House of
  Sicilian history — 945.804
  Southern Italian history — 945.704
Hohenstaufen dynasty — 943.024
  Sicilian history — 945.804
  Southern Italian history — 945.704
Hohenzollern (Germany) — T2—434 73
Hoisting
  mining — 622.6
Hoisting equipment — 621.862
Hokan languages — 497.57
    T6—975 7
Hoke County (N.C.) — T2—756 365
Hokkaido (Japan) — T2—524
Hokuriku Region (Japan) — T2—521 5
Holderness (England) — T2—428 39
Holding companies — 338.86
  economics — 338.86
  law — 346.066 8
  *see also* Combinations
    (Enterprises)
Holding equipment — 621.992
Holguín (Cuba : Province) — T2—729 164
Holiday work — 331.257 4
  economics — 331.257 4
  personnel management — 658.312 1
Holidays — 394.26
  cooking — 641.568
  customs — 394.26
  flower arrangements — 745.926
  folklore — 398.236
    history and criticism — 398.33
  handicrafts — 745.594 16
  interior decoration — 747.93

| | |
|---|---|
| Holidays (continued) | |
| labor economics | 331.257 6 |
| law | 344.091 |
| literature | 808.803 34 |
| history and criticism | 809.933 34 |
| specific literatures | T3B—080 334 |
| history and | |
| criticism | T3B—093 34 |
| personnel management | 658.312 2 |
| religion | 203.6 |
| Buddhism | 294.343 6 |
| Christianity | 263.9 |
| devotional literature | 242.3 |
| sermons | 252.6 |
| Hinduism | 294.536 |
| Islam | 297.36 |
| Judaism | 296.43 |
| liturgy | 296.453 |
| sociology | 306.481 25 |
| Holiness | 202.2 |
| Christian church attribute | 262.72 |
| Christian doctrine | 234.8 |
| Holistic medicine | 610 |
| health | 613 |
| therapeutics | 615.5 |
| Holistic psychology | 150.193 |
| Holland | 949.2 |
| | T2—492 |
| ancient | 936.92 |
| | T2—369 2 |
| Holland (England : County) | T2—425 39 |
| Holland (Kingdom) | 949.205 |
| | T2—492 |
| Hollies | 635.977 385 |
| botany | 583.85 |
| ornamental arboriculture | 635.977 385 |
| Hollow blocks | 666.894 |
| architectural construction | 721.044 4 |
| building construction | 693.4 |
| ceramic technology | 666.894 |
| Hollow ware | |
| rubber | 678.34 |
| Hollyhocks | 635.933 685 |
| botany | 583.685 |
| floriculture | 635.933 685 |
| Holman (N.W.T.) | T2—719 3 |
| Holmes County (Fla.) | T2—759 965 |
| Holmes County (Miss.) | T2—762 625 |
| Holmes County (Ohio) | T2—771 64 |
| Holmium | |
| chemistry | 546.417 |
| Holocaust, 1933–1945 | 940.531 8 |
| arts | 700.458 405 318 |
| | T3C—358 405 318 |

| | |
|---|---|
| Holocaust, 1933–1945 (continued) | |
| biography | 940.531 809 2 |
| Christian theology | 231.76 |
| European history | 940.531 8 |
| interreligious relations | 261.26 |
| Jewish theology | 296.311 74 |
| literature | 808.803 584 053 18 |
| Holocaust denial | 940.531 818 |
| Holocene epoch | 551.793 |
| geology | 551.793 |
| paleontology | 560.179 3 |
| Holocephali | 597.38 |
| paleozoology | 567.38 |
| Holographic images | 774 |
| Holography | 774 |
| arts | 774 |
| engineering | 621.367 5 |
| Holometabola | 595.7 |
| *see also* Insects | |
| Holomorphic functions | 515.98 |
| Holostei | 597.41 |
| paleozoology | 567.41 |
| Holothurioidea | 593.96 |
| paleozoology | 563.96 |
| Holstein-Friesian cattle | 636.234 |
| Holt, Harold | |
| Australian history | 994.061 |
| Holt County (Mo.) | T2—778 115 |
| Holt County (Neb.) | T2—782 745 |
| Holu languages | 496.393 |
| | T6—963 93 |
| Holy, The | 211 |
| Holy Communion | 234.163 |
| public worship | 264.36 |
| Anglican | 264.030 36 |
| texts | 264.03 |
| Roman Catholic | 264.020 36 |
| texts | 264.023 |
| theology | 234.163 |
| Holy day work | 331.257 4 |
| economics | 331.257 4 |
| personnel management | 658.312 1 |
| Holy days | 203.6 |
| Buddhism | 294.343 6 |
| Christianity | 263.9 |
| devotional literature | 242.3 |
| sermons | 252.6 |
| customs | 394.265 |
| *see Manual at* 203.6, | |
| 263.9, 292–299 vs. | |
| 394.265–.267 | |
| Hinduism | 294.536 |
| Islam | 297.36 |

Holy days (continued)
    Judaism      296.43
       liturgy      296.453
    *see also* Holidays
Holy Family      232.92
    art representation      704.948 56
    arts      T3C—382 329 2
Holy Ghost      231.3
Holy Hours      264.7
Holy Orders      234.164
    public worship      265.4
    theology      234.164
Holy places      203.5
    *see also* Sacred places
Holy Roman Empire      943.02
        T2—43
    church history      270
    German history      943.02
Holy See
    acts      262.91
Holy Shroud      232.966
Holy Spirit      231.3
    baptism in      234.13
Holy war (Islam)      297.72
Holy Week      263.925
    devotional literature      242.35
    music      781.726
    Roman Catholic liturgy      264.027 2
    sermons      252.625
Homalozoa      563.92
Home affairs departments      353.3
Home and school associations      371.192 06
Home aquariums      639.34
Home-based enterprises
    management      658.041 2
       initiation      658.114 12
Home brewing      641.873
Home buying      643.12
Home care services      362.14
    mental illness      362.24
    *see also* Mental health
       services
    *see also* Health services
Home computers      004.16
    *see also* Personal computers
Home Counties (England)      T2—422
Home defense (Military science)      355.45
Home departments      353.3
Home economics      640
    arts      700.456 4
        T3C—356 4
    customs      392.3

Home economics (continued)
    literature      808.803 564
       history and criticism      809.933 564
    primary education      372.37
Home economists      640.92
Home finance      332.722
Home furnishings      645
    home sewing      646.21
    household management      645
    manufacturing technology      684
Home gardens      635
    landscape architecture      712.6
Home guards      355.37
    active units      355.351
    reserve units      355.37
Home improvement      690.802 86
    home economics      643.7
    *see Manual at* 690 vs. 643.7
Home inspection      643.12
Home instruction by educational
    personnel      371.39
Home labor      331.256 7
Home libraries (Rooms)      643.58
    home economics      643.58
    interior decoration      747.73
Home loan associations      332.32
    law      346.082 32
    public administration      354.86
Home management      640
    arts      T3C—356 4
    customs      392.3
    green technology      640.286
    literature
       history and criticism      809.933 564
    primary education      372.37
Home meals      642.1
Home medicine      616.024
Home missions      266.022
Home movies      791.433
Home nursing
    by professionals      610.734 3
       health services      362.14
       medicine      610.734 3
Home ownership      363.583
    public administrative support      353.55
Home remedies
    therapeutics      615.88
Home repairs      690.802 88
    home economics      643.7
    *see Manual at* 690 vs. 643.7
Home reserves (Armed forces)      355.37
Home rule
    law      342.042
    local government      320.8

| | |
|---|---|
| Home safety | 363.13 |
| *see also* Safety | |
| Home schooling | 371.042 |
| primary education | 372.104 242 |
| Home schools | 371.042 |
| Home selection | 643.12 |
| Home shopping | 381.142 |
| Home sites | |
| selection | 643.12 |
| Home video systems | 777 |
| engineering | 621.388 |
| videography | 777 |
| Home workshops | 684.08 |
| Homeland Bloc (Austrian | |
| political party) | 324.243 602 4 |
| Homelands (South Africa) | 968.29 |
| | T2—682 9 |
| Cape of Good Hope | T2—687 5 |
| Natal | T2—684 |
| Orange Free State | T2—685 1 |
| Homeless children | |
| social group | 305.230 869 42 |
| social welfare | 362.775 692 |
| Homeless families | 362.592 3 |
| Homeless people | 305.569 2 |
| | T1—086 942 |
| social theology | 201.762 5 |
| Christianity | 261.832 5 |
| social welfare | 362.592 |
| *see also* Poor people | |
| Homeless shelters | 362.592 82 |
| Homeless women | |
| social group | 305.484 42 |
| social welfare | 362.839 85 |
| Homeless youth | |
| social welfare | 362.775 692 |
| Homel´ (Belarus : Voblasts) | T2—478 1 |
| Homel´skaĩa voblasts´ | |
| (Belarus) | T2—478 1 |
| Homemakers | 640.92 |
| | T1—088 64 |
| legal status | 346.016 3 |
| Homemaking | 640 |
| Homeomorphisms | 514 |
| Homeopathy | |
| therapeutic system | 615.532 |
| Homeostasis | |
| biology | 571.75 |
| human physiology | 612.022 |
| Homeowner's insurance | 368.096 |
| liability | 368.56 |

| | |
|---|---|
| Homes | 640 |
| home economics | 640 |
| social services | 363.5 |
| older people | 362.61 |
| *see also* Group homes | |
| *see also* Dwellings | |
| Homework | 371.302 81 |
| Homicidal behavior | |
| medicine | 616.858 44 |
| Homicide | 364.152 |
| ethics | 179.7 |
| law | 345.025 2 |
| Homiletic illustrations | |
| Christianity | 251.08 |
| Homiletics | |
| Christianity | 251 |
| Homilies | 204.3 |
| Christianity | 252 |
| Homing | |
| manned space flight | 629.453 |
| space flight | 629.41 |
| unmanned space flight | 629.433 |
| Homing pigeons | |
| animal husbandry | 636.596 |
| Homing systems | |
| spacecraft | 629.474 2 |
| unmanned spacecraft | 629.464 2 |
| Hominidae | 599.88 |
| paleozoology | 569.88 |
| Hominoidea | 599.88 |
| paleozoology | 569.88 |
| Homo (Genus) | |
| paleozoology | 569.9 |
| Homo erectus | 569.97 |
| Homo neanderthalis | 569.986 |
| Homo sapiens | |
| paleontology | 569.98 |
| zoology | 599.9 |
| Homo sapiens neanderthalis | 569.986 |
| Homobasidiomycetes | 579.59 |
| Homogeneous coordinate system | 516.16 |
| Homogeneous equations | |
| calculus | 515.253 |
| Homogeneous grouping of | |
| students | 371.254 |
| Homogeneous spaces | 514 |
| Homogenization | |
| milk processing | 637.141 |
| Homoiothermy | 571.76 |
| Homological algebra | 512.64 |
| Homology theory | 514.23 |
| Homonym dictionaries | 413.1 |
| specific languages | T4—31 |
| Homophobia | 306.766 |

| | |
|---|---|
| Homophony | 781.285 |
| Homoplasy | 576.8 |
| Homoptera | 595.752 |
| Homosexuality | 306.766 |
| arts | 700.453 |
| | T3C—353 |
| ethics | 176.4 |
| religion | 205.66 |
| *see also* Sexual relations — | |
| ethics | |
| literature | 808.803 53 |
| history and criticism | 809.933 53 |
| specific literatures | T3B—080 353 |
| history and | |
| criticism | T3B—093 53 |
| medicine | 616.858 3 |
| *see Manual at* 616.8583 | |
| psychology | 155.344 |
| religion | 200.866 4 |
| Christianity | 270.086 64 |
| social problem | 363.49 |
| Homosexuals | 306.766 |
| | T1—086 64 |
| civil and human rights | 323.326 4 |
| female | 306.766 3 |
| | T1—086 643 |
| psychology | 155.344 3 |
| Holocaust, 1933–1945 | 940.531 808 664 |
| labor economics | 331.53 |
| male | 306.766 2 |
| | T1—086 642 |
| psychology | 155.344 2 |
| psychology | 155.344 |
| religion | 200.866 4 |
| Christianity | 270.086 64 |
| pastoral theology | 259.086 64 |
| social welfare | 362.896 4 |
| Homotopy theory | 514.24 |
| Honan Province (China) | T2—511 8 |
| Honduran literature | 860 |
| Hondurans | T5—687 283 |
| Honduras | 972.83 |
| | T2—728 3 |
| Honduras, Gulf of | 551.461 365 |
| | T2—163 65 |
| Honecker, Erich | |
| German history | 943.108 77 |
| Honesty | 179.9 |
| moral theology | 205.699 |
| *see also* Virtues | |
| Honey | 641.38 |
| cooking | 641.68 |
| food | 641.38 |
| processing | 638.16 |
| Honey bush | 583.78 |
| Honey eaters | 598.8 |
| conservation technology | 639.978 8 |
| resource economics | 333.958 8 |
| Honey guides | 598.72 |
| Honey wine | 641.23 |
| commercial processing | 663.4 |
| Honeybees | 638.1 |
| apiculture | 638.1 |
| zoology | 595.799 |
| Honeycomb structures | |
| naval architecture | 623.817 79 |
| structural engineering | 624.177 9 |
| Honeydew melon | 641.356 117 |
| cooking | 641.656 117 |
| food | 641.356 117 |
| garden crop | 635.611 7 |
| Honeymoons | |
| customs | 392.5 |
| Honeysuckles | 635.933 92 |
| botany | 583.92 |
| floriculture | 635.933 92 |
| Honeyworts | 583.94 |
| Hong Kong | 951.250 4 |
| | T2—512 5 |
| Hong Kong (China) | 951.25 |
| | T2—512 5 |
| Honolulu (Hawaii) | T2—969 31 |
| Honolulu County (Hawaii) | T2—969 3 |
| Honor rolls (Military) | 355.134 |
| World War I | 940.467 |
| World War II | 940.546 7 |
| *see also* Military | |
| commemorations | |
| Honor societies | |
| education | 371.852 |
| Honor system | |
| education | 371.51 |
| higher education | 378.195 1 |
| Honorary degrees | 378.25 |
| Honorary insignia | |
| armed forces | 355.134 2 |
| Honorary titles | T1—079 |
| Honorias | T2—393 15 |
| Honors | T1—079 |
| orders and decorations | 929.81 |
| research | 001.44 |
| Honors work | 371.394 2 |
| Honshū (Japan) | T2—521 |
| Honsyū (Japan) | T2—521 |
| Hood, Mount (Or.) | T2—795 61 |
| Hood County (Tex.) | T2—764 522 |
| Hood River County (Or.) | T2—795 61 |
| Hooded seal | 599.796 |

| | |
|---|---|
| Hoofed mammals | 599.6 |
| *see also* Ungulates | |
| Hookahs | 688.4 |
| Hooked rugs | |
| arts | 746.74 |
| Hooker County (Neb.) | T2—782 777 |
| Hooke's law | 531.382 |
| Hookworm infections | |
| medicine | 616.965 4 |
| *see also* Communicable | |
| diseases — humans | |
| Hoops (Gymnastic equipment) | 796.443 |
| Hoopstad (South Africa : | |
| District) | T2—685 3 |
| Hoover, Herbert | |
| United States history | 973.916 |
| Hop, step, and jump | 796.432 |
| Hop tree | 635.977 377 |
| botany | 583.77 |
| ornamental arboriculture | 635.977 377 |
| Hopbushes | 583.78 |
| Hope | |
| Christianity | 234.25 |
| psychology | 152.4 |
| Hope (B.C.) | T2—711 37 |
| Hope Island (B.C.) | T2—711 2 |
| Hopefield (South Africa : | |
| District) | T2—687 32 |
| Hopeh Province (China) | T2—511 52 |
| Hopetown (South Africa : | |
| District) | T2—687 13 |
| Hopewell (Va.) | T2—755 586 |
| Hopf algebras | 512.55 |
| Hopi Indians | T5—974 58 |
| Hopi language | 497.458 |
| | T6—974 58 |
| Hopi literature | 897.458 |
| Hopkins County (Ky.) | T2—769 823 |
| Hopkins County (Tex.) | T2—764 274 |
| Hoplocarida | 595.379 6 |
| Hoppers (Insects) | 595.752 |
| agricultural pests | 632.752 |
| Hoppers (Railroad cars) | 385.34 |
| engineering | 625.24 |
| *see also* Rolling stock | |
| Hops | 641.23 |
| agriculture | 633.82 |
| botany | 583.45 |
| brewing additive | 641.23 |
| Horary astrology | 133.56 |
| Horayot | 296.123 4 |
| Babylonian Talmud | 296.125 4 |
| Mishnah | 296.123 4 |
| Palestinian Talmud | 296.124 4 |

| | |
|---|---|
| Hordaland fylke (Norway) | T2—483 6 |
| Hordeeae | 584.9 |
| Horehounds | 583.96 |
| Horgen (Switzerland : | |
| Bezirk) | T2—494 572 8 |
| Horizontal bars (Gymnastic | |
| equipment) | 796.442 |
| Horizontal combinations | |
| (Enterprises) | 338.804 2 |
| *see also* Combinations | |
| (Enterprises) | |
| Horizontal property | |
| law | 346.043 3 |
| Hormic psychology | 150.193 |
| Hormones | 571.74 |
| animal physiology | 573.44 |
| biochemistry | 571.74 |
| humans | 612.405 |
| chemistry | 547.7 |
| human physiology | 612.405 |
| pharmacology | 615.36 |
| *see also* Endocrine system | |
| *see Manual at* 573.44 vs. | |
| 571.74 | |
| Hormozgān (Iran) | T2—557 5 |
| Hormuz, Strait of | 551.461 535 |
| | T2—165 35 |
| Horn carving | 736.6 |
| Horn concertos | 784.289 4 |
| Horn of Africa | T2—63 |
| Horn players | 788.940 92 |
| Hornbeams | 583.48 |
| Hornbills | 598.78 |
| Hornby Island (B.C.) | T2—711 2 |
| Horned dinosaurs | 567.915 |
| Horned liverworts | 588.3 |
| Horney, Karen | |
| psychological system | 150.195 7 |
| Horns | 788.94 |
| English | 788.53 |
| instrument | 788.531 9 |
| music | 788.53 |
| *see also* Woodwind | |
| instruments | |
| French | 788.94 |
| instrument | 788.941 9 |
| music | 788.94 |
| *see also* Brass instruments | |
| instrument | 788.941 9 |
| music | 788.94 |
| *see also* Brass instruments | |
| Horns (Animals) | 591.47 |
| descriptive zoology | 591.47 |
| physiology | 573.59 |

Hornworts (Anthocerotidae) 588.3
Hornworts (Ceratophyllaceae) 583.29
Horology 529.7
Horoscopes 133.54
Horowhenua District (N.Z.) T2—935 9
Horror
  arts 700.416 4
                    T3C—164
  literature 808.801 64
    history and criticism 809.916 4
    specific literatures T3B—080 164
      history and
        criticism T3B—091 64
  motion pictures 791.436 164
  psychology 152.4
  radio programs 791.446 164
  television programs 791.456 164
Horror fiction 808.838 738
  history and criticism 809.387 38
  specific literatures T3B—308 738
    individual authors T3A—3
Horry County (S.C.) T2—757 87
Hors d'oeuvres 641.812
Horse cavalry 357.1
Horse chestnuts 583.78
Horse-drawn streetcars 388.46
  engineering 625.66
  transportation services 388.46
Horse racers 798.400 92
Horse racing 798.4
  electronic games 794.884
  equipment technology 688.78
  law 344.099
Horse shows 798.24
Horse sports 798
Horse stealing 364.162 863 61
  law 345.026 286 361
Horseflies 595.773
Horsefly River (B.C.) T2—711 75
Horsehair worms 592.59
Horsemanship
  sports 798.2
  therapeutic use 615.851 581
Horseradish 641.338 4
  *see also* Hot spices
Horses 636.1
  animal husbandry 636.1
  remount services 357.2
  theft of 364.162 863 61
    law 345.026 286 361
  therapeutic use 615.851 581
  zoology 599.665 5
Horseshoe crabs 595.492
  paleozoology 565.492

Horseshoe shrimps 595.36
Horseshoe worms 592.3
Horseshoeing 682.1
Horseshoes (Game) 796.24
Horsetails (Plants) 587.2
Horsham (England :
  District) T2—422 64
Horsham (Vic.) T2—945 8
Horticulture 635
Horticulturists 635.092
Hose (Clothing) 391.423
  *see also* Hosiery
Hosea (Biblical book) 224.6
Hoses
  rubber 678.36
Hosiery 391.423
  commercial technology 687.3
  customs 391.423
  home economics 646.3
  home sewing 646.42
  *see also* Clothing
Hospices (Terminal care
  facilities) 362.175 6
  pastoral theology 206.1
    Christianity 259.417 56
  social theology 201.762 175 6
    Christianity 261.832 175 6
  social welfare 362.175 6
  *see also* Health care facilities
Hospital chaplaincy 206.1
  Christianity 259.411
Hospital cooking 641.579
Hospital insurance 368.382 7
  public administration 353.69
Hospital libraries 027.662
  administration 025.197 662
  collection development 025.218 766 2
Hospital ships 359.836 4
  design 623.812 64
  military
    engineering 623.826 4
  naval equipment 359.836 4
  naval units 359.326 4
Hospital ward management 362.173 068
Hospitalers of St. John of
  Jerusalem 255.791 2
  church history 271.791 2
Hospitality
  ethics 177.1
    *see also* Ethical problems
  etiquette 395.3

Hospitality industry | 338.479 1
  accounting | 657.837
  economics | 338.479 1
  household management | 647.94
Hospitals | 362.11
  accounting | 657.832 2
  American Revolution | 973.376
  animal husbandry | 636.083 21
  architecture | 725.51
  armed forces | 355.72
  Civil War (United States) | 973.776
  construction | 690.551
  energy economics | 333.796 4
  institutional housekeeping | 647.965 1
  landscape architecture | 712.7
  law | 344.032 11
  liability law | 346.031
  meal service | 642.56
  pastoral theology | 206.1
    Christianity | 259.411
  social theology | 201.762 11
    Christianity | 261.832 11
  social welfare | 362.11
  World War I | 940.476
  World War II | 940.547 6
  *see also* Health services
Host-parasite relationships | 577.857
Host-virus relationships
  medical microbiology | 616.910 1
Hostage taking
  criminology | 364.154
    criminal law | 345.025 4
Hostas | 635.934 32
  botany | 584.32
  floriculture | 635.934 32
Hostels | 910.466
  *see also* Lodging (Temporary
    housing)
Hostile environments
  biology | 578.758
  ecology | 577.58
Hostile work environments | 331.133
Hot air balloons
  engineering | 629.133 22
  sports | 797.51
Hot-air heating
  buildings | 697.3
Hot cake mixes | 664.753
Hot cakes | 641.815 3
Hot lines (Counseling services) | 361.06
  mental illness | 362.204 251
  suicide | 362.288 1
Hot-metal dipping | 671.733

Hot peppers | 641.338 4
  *see also* Hot spices
Hot rods | 796.72
  driving | 629.284 86
  engineering | 629.228 6
  repair | 629.287 86
  sports | 796.72
Hot spices | 641.338 4
  agriculture | 633.84
  commercial processing | 664.54
  cooking with | 641.638 4
  economic botany | 581.632
  food | 641.338 4
Hot Spring County (Ark.) | T2—767 42
Hot springs | 551.23
Hot Springs County (Wyo.) | T2—787 43
Hot Springs National Park
  (Ark.) | T2—767 41
Hot-water bottles
  rubber | 678.34
Hot-water heating
  buildings | 697.4
Hot-water pipes
  buildings | 696.6
Hot-water supply
  buildings | 696.6
  household management | 644.6
Hot weather
  health | 613.113
Hot-weather cooking | 641.591 3
Hot-weather photography | 778.75
Hot-working operations
  metals | 671.3
Hotbeds | 631.583
  floriculture | 635.982
  gardening | 635.048 3
  manufacturing technology | 681.763 1
Hotel cooking | 641.572
Hotel industry | 338.476 479 4
  law | 343.078 647 94
Hotel management | 647.940 68
Hotel meal service | 642.5
Hotelkeepers | 647.940 92
Hotels | 910.46
  accounting | 657.837 4
  architecture | 728.5
  area planning | 711.557
  arts | T3C—32
  household management | 647.94
  landscape architecture | 712.7
  management | 647.940 68
  sanitation services | 363.729 8
    law | 344.046 4
  travel | 910.46

| | |
|---|---|
| Hotlines (Counseling services) | 361.06 |
| mental illness | 362.204 251 |
| suicide | 362.288 1 |
| Hottentot language | 496.1 |
| | T6—961 |
| Hottentots | T5—961 |
| Houghton County (Mich.) | T2—774 993 |
| Hounds | 636.753 |
| *see Manual at 636.72–.75* | |
| Hound's tongues | 583.94 |
| Hounslow (London, England) | T2—421 82 |
| Houphouët-Boigny, Félix | |
| Ivorian history | 966.680 51 |
| Hourglasses | |
| technology | 681.111 |
| Hours of work | 331.257 |
| economics | 331.257 |
| personnel management | 658.312 1 |
| public administration | 352.67 |
| House bats | 599.47 |
| House churches | 250 |
| House mouse | 599.353 |
| House music | 781.648 |
| House organs | T1—05 |
| journalism | 070.486 |
| management use | 658.455 |
| House painting | 698.1 |
| House plants | 635.965 |
| House selling | 333.338 3 |
| House sparrow | 598.887 |
| House-to-house fighting | 355.426 |
| Houseboating | |
| sports | 797.129 |
| Houseboats | 643.2 |
| architecture | 728.78 |
| construction | 690.878 |
| home economics | 643.2 |
| Housebound people | 305.908 7 |
| | T1—087 7 |
| *see also* Sick people | |
| Housecleaning | 648.5 |
| Houseflies | 595.774 |
| control technology | 628.965 7 |
| Household appliance makers | 683.809 2 |
| Household appliances | 643.6 |
| manufacturing technology | 683.8 |
| product safety | 363.19 |
| Household biology | 578.755 4 |
| Household budgets | |
| macroeconomics | 339.41 |
| Household ecology | 577.554 |

| | |
|---|---|
| Household employees | 640.46 |
| home economics | 640.46 |
| public households | 647.2 |
| hours and duties | 647.6 |
| Household equipment | 643 |
| Household finances | 332.024 |
| Household furnishings | 645 |
| household management | 645 |
| manufacturing technology | 684 |
| Household garbage | |
| use as fertilizer | 631.875 |
| Household income | |
| macroeconomics | 339.22 |
| Household management | 640 |
| public households | 647 |
| Household pests | |
| control technology | 628.96 |
| Household sanitation | 648 |
| Household security | 643.16 |
| Household utilities | 644 |
| Household wastes | 363.728 8 |
| *see also* Waste control | |
| Household water supply | 363.61 |
| economics | 333.912 2 |
| Househusbands | 640.92 |
| | T1—088 64 |
| legal status | 346.016 3 |
| social group | 305.336 4 |
| Housekeepers | 640.92 |
| Housekeeping | 648 |
| public households | 647 |
| Houseleeks | 583.72 |
| Houseparents | 362.732 |
| Houseplants | 635.965 |
| interior decoration | 747.98 |
| Houses | 643.1 |
| architecture | 728.37 |
| construction | 690.837 |
| *see also* Dwellings | |
| Houses (Astrology) | 133.530 42 |
| Housewives | 640.92 |
| | T1—088 64 |
| legal status | 346.016 3 |
| social group | 305.436 4 |
| Housing | 363.5 |
| animal husbandry | 636.083 1 |
| armed forces | 355.12 |
| economics | 333.338 |
| energy economics | 333.796 3 |
| home economics | 643.1 |
| psychological influence | 155.945 |
| public administration | 353.55 |
| sanitation services | 363.729 8 |
| social services | 363.5 |

Housing (continued)
 sociology 307.336
 *see Manual at* 363.5, 363.6,
  363.8 vs. 338; *also at* 363.5
  vs. 307.336, 307.34; *also at*
  363.5 vs. 643.1
Housing allowances 363.582
 armed forces 355.12
 *see also* Housing
Housing conditions 363.51
 *see also* Housing
Housing cooperatives 334.1
Housing renewal
 area planning 711.59
 community sociology 307.34
Housing succession 307.336
Houston (Tex.) T2—764 141 1
Houston County (Ala.) T2—761 295
Houston County (Ga.) T2—758 515
Houston County (Minn.) T2—776 11
Houston County (Tenn.) T2—768 36
Houston County (Tex.) T2—764 235
Hove (England) T2—422 56
Hover flies 595.774
Hovercraft
 engineering 629.3
Howard, John
 Australian history 994.066
 1996–1999 994.066
 2000–2007 994.071
Howard County (Ark.) T2—767 483
Howard County (Ind.) T2—772 85
Howard County (Iowa) T2—777 312
Howard County (Md.) T2—752 81
Howard County (Mo.) T2—778 285
Howard County (Neb.) T2—782 43
Howard County (Tex.) T2—764 858
Howden (England) T2—428 39
Howe Sound (B.C.) T2—711 31
Howell County (Mo.) T2—778 85
Howitzers 355.822
 engineering 623.42
 military equipment 355.822
Howland Island T2—969 9
Howler monkeys 599.855
Hrodzen (Belarus :
 Voblasts) T2—478 8
Hrodzenskaia voblasts'
 (Belarus) T2—478 8
Hsiang dialects 495.172 15
  T6—951 7
Hualapai Indians T5—975 724
Hualapai language 497.572 4
  T6—975 724

Huambo (Angola :
 Province) T2—673 4
Huancavelica (Peru : Dept.) T2—852 8
Huang He (China) T2—511
Huánuco (Peru : Dept.) T2—852 2
Huasco (Chile : Province) T2—831 48
Huastec Indians T5—974 2
Huastec language 497.42
  T6—974 2
Huave Indians T5—979
Huavean languages 497.9
  T6—979
Hubbard County (Minn.) T2—776 85
Hubei Sheng (China) T2—512 12
Huckaback fabrics 677.615
Huckleberries 641.347 32
 botany 583.66
 cooking 641.647 32
 food 641.347 32
 horticulture 634.732
Hudson Bay 551.461 327
  T2—163 27
Hudson Bay Region T2—714 111
Hudson County (N.J.) T2—749 26
Hudson River (N.Y. and
 N.J.) T2—747 3
Hudspeth County (Tex.) T2—764 95
Huehuetenango
 (Guatemala : Dept.) T2—728 171
Huelva (Spain : Province) T2—468 7
Huerfano County (Colo.) T2—788 51
Huerta, Adolfo de la
 Mexican history 972.082 1
Huesca (Spain : Province) T2—465 55
Hugh Capet, King of France
 French history 944.021
Hughes, William Morris
 Australian history 994.041
Hughes County (Okla.) T2—766 72
Hughes County (S.D.) T2—783 29
Hugoniaceae 583.79
Huguenots 284.5
 biography 284.509 2
 persecution of 272.4
Huichol Indians T5—974 544
Huichol language 497.454 4
  T6—974 544
Huichol literature 897.454 4
Huíla (Angola) T2—673 5
Huila (Colombia : Dept.) T2—861 39
Huku language 496.394
  T6—963 94
Hull (England) T2—428 37

Hull, Clark Leonard  
  psychological system    150.194 34  
Hullin    296.123 5  
  Babylonian Talmud    296.125 5  
  Mishnah    296.123 5  
Hulls (Ships)  
  engineering    623.84  
Humacao (P.R. : District)    T2—729 59  
Human-alien encounters    001.942  
Human anatomy    611  
  arts    T3C—356 1  
  literature    808.803 561  
    history and criticism    809.933 561  
    specific literatures    T3B—080 356 1  
      history and  
        criticism    T3B—093 561  
  *see Manual at* 599.94 vs. 611;  
    *also at* 612 vs. 611  
Human behavior  
  psychology    150  
  social psychology    302  
Human body  
  arts    T3C—356 1  
  folklore    398.276 1  
    history and criticism    398.353  
  literature    808.803 561  
    history and criticism    809.933 561  
    specific literatures    T3B—080 356 1  
      history and  
        criticism    T3B—093 561  
Human capital  
  accounting    657.4  
Human characteristics  
  arts    700.453  
    T3C—353  
  literature    808.803 53  
    history and criticism    809.933 53  
    specific literatures    T3B—080 353  
      history and  
        criticism    T3B—093 53  
Human chromosome  
  abnormalities  
  medicine    616.042  
Human cloning  
  ethics    176.22  
    *see also* Reproduction —  
      ethics  
Human-computer interaction    004.019  
  engineering    621.398 4  

Human ecology    304.2  
  biology    599.95  
  social theology    201.77  
    Christianity    261.88  
    Judaism    296.38  
  *see Manual at* 578 vs. 304.2,  
    508, 910  
Human embryo    612.646  
  experimental research    616.027  
    medical ethics    174.28  
  physiology    612.646  
  transplantation  
    ethics    176.2  
      *see also* Reproduction —  
        ethics  
    surgery    618.178 059 9  
Human engineering    620.82  
Human evolution    599.938  
Human experimentation in  
  medicine  
  clinical trials    615.507 24  
  ethics    174.28  
    *see also* Medical ethics  
  law    344.041 96  
Human factors engineering    620.82  
  computers    621.39  
Human figures  
  art representation    704.942  
  arts    700.456 1  
    T3C—356 1  
  drawing    743.4  
  literature    808.803 561  
    history and criticism    809.933 561  
    specific literatures    T3B—080 356 1  
      history and  
        criticism    T3B—093 561  
  painting    757  
Human genetics    599.935  
Human geography    304.2  
Human immunodeficiency  
  viruses  
  medical microbiology    616.979 201  
Human information processing    153  
Human life  
  folklore    398.27  
    history and criticism    398.35  
    persons    398.22  
  origin  
    religion    202.2  
      Christianity    233.11  
      Islam    297.221  
      Judaism    296.32  
      philosophy of religion    213  
    philosophy    128

Human life (continued)
  respect for
    ethics 179.7
Human milk diet 613.269
Human papillomavirus infections
  incidence 614.581
  medicine 616.911
    *see also* Communicable
      diseases — humans
Human physiology 612
  arts T3C—356 1
  literature 808.803 561
    history and criticism 809.933 561
  specific literatures T3B—080 356 1
    history and
      criticism T3B—093 561
  *see Manual at* 612 vs. 611; *also*
    *at* 612.1–.8; *also at* 613 vs.
    612, 615.8; *also at* 616 vs.
    612
Human pigmentation
  physical anthropology 599.95
Human qualities
  folklore 398.27
    history and criticism 398.353
Human races 305.8
  physical ethnology 599.97
  *see also* Ethnic groups
Human relations
  applied psychology 158.2
  business 650.13
  personnel management 658.314 5
    executives 658.407 145
  public administration 352.66
Human relations training
  personnel management 658.312 44
    executives 658.407 124 4
  public administration 352.669
Human reproduction 612.6
  *see also* Genital system
Human reproductive technology
  ethics 176.2
    *see also* Reproduction —
      ethics
  health 613.94
  infertility
    gynecology 618.178 06
    medicine 616.692 06
Human resource development 370.113
  *see also* Vocational education
Human resource management 658.3
                          T1—068 3
  *see also* Personnel management

Human resources 331.11
  accounting 657.4
  armed forces 355.22
  economics 331.11
  utilization
    economics 331.125
Human resources management 658.3
                          T1—068 3
  *see also* Personnel management
Human rights 323
  law of nations 341.48
    *see Manual at* 342.085 vs.
      341.48
  social welfare 361.614
  *see also* Civil rights
Human sacrifice
  religion 203.42
Human services 361
  *see also* Welfare services
Human settlement 307.14
Human smuggling 364.137
  law 345.023 7
Human variation
  physical anthropology 599.94
Humane law 344.049
Humanism
  arts T3C—384
  ethics 171.2
  literature 808.803 84
    history and criticism 809.933 84
  specific literatures T3B—080 384
    history and
      criticism T3B—093 84
  philosophy 144
  philosophy of religion 211.6
Humanistic education 370.112
Humanistic Judaism 296.834
Humanistic psychology 150.198 6
Humanitarian intervention
  law of nations 341.584
Humanitarian law 341.67
Humanitarians 361.740 92
Humanities 001.3
  law 344.097
  public administrative support 353.77
Humanities policy (Government
  policy) 001.3

| Humanity | | |
|---|---|---|
| arts | 700.45 | |
| | T3C—35 | |
| literature | 808.803 5 | |
| history and criticism | 809.933 5 | |
| specific literatures | T3B—080 35 | |
| history and criticism | T3B—093 5 | |
| Humanity of Jesus Christ | 232.8 | |
| Humankind | 301 | |
| *see also* Humans | | |
| Humans | 301 | |
| anthropology | 301 | |
| effect on natural ecology | 577.27 | |
| paleozoology | 569.9 | |
| philosophy | 128 | |
| physical anthropology | 599.9 | |
| physiology | 612 | |
| religion | 202.2 | |
| Buddhism | 294.342 2 | |
| Christianity | 233 | |
| Hinduism | 294.522 | |
| Islam | 297.22 | |
| Judaism | 296.32 | |
| philosophy of religion | 218 | |
| sociology | 301 | |
| zoology | 599.9 | |
| Humansdorp (South Africa : District) | T2—687 51 | |
| Humayun, Emperor of Hindustan | | |
| Indian history | 954.025 3 | |
| Humber, River (England) | T2—428 3 | |
| Humberside (England) | T2—428 3 | |
| Humboldt County (Calif.) | T2—794 12 | |
| Humboldt County (Iowa) | T2—777 272 | |
| Humboldt County (Nev.) | T2—793 54 | |
| Humboldt Current | 551.462 141 | |
| Humboldt River (Nev.) | T2—793 16 | |
| Humeri | | |
| human anatomy | 611.717 | |
| Humidification | | |
| chemical engineering | 660.284 293 | |
| Humidifiers | | |
| air conditioning | | |
| buildings | 697.932 3 | |
| Humidistats | | |
| air conditioning | | |
| buildings | 697.932 3 | |
| Humidity | | |
| health | 613.11 | |
| meteorology | 551.571 | |

| Humidity control | | |
|---|---|---|
| air conditioning | | |
| buildings | 697.932 3 | |
| spacecraft | 629.477 5 | |
| Humility | 179.9 | |
| moral theology | 205.699 | |
| *see also* Virtues | | |
| Humiriaceae | 583.79 | |
| Hummingbirds | 598.764 | |
| conservation technology | 639.978 764 | |
| resource economics | 333.958 764 | |
| Humor | 152.43 | |
| journalism | 070.444 | |
| literary criticism | 809.7 | |
| theory | 808.7 | |
| literary history | 809.7 | |
| literature | 808.87 | |
| specific literatures | T3B—7 | |
| psychology | 152.43 | |
| rhetoric | 808.7 | |
| sociology | 306.481 | |
| specific subjects | T1—020 7 | |
| *see Manual at* T1—0207 vs. T3B—7, T3A—8 + 02, T3B—802, T3B—8 + 02, T3A—8 + 07, T3B—807, T3B—8 + 07 | | |
| Humorists | 809.7 | |
| collected biography | 809.7 | |
| specific literatures | T3B—700 9 | |
| Humorous fiction | 808.839 17 | |
| Humorous poetry | 808.817 | |
| history and criticism | 809.17 | |
| specific literatures | T3B—107 | |
| specific literatures | T3A—1 | |
| Humors (Psychology) | 155.262 | |
| Humpback whale | 599.525 | |
| Humpbacked flies | 595.774 | |
| Humphreys County (Miss.) | T2—762 48 | |
| Humphreys County (Tenn.) | T2—768 37 | |
| Humus | | |
| soil science | 631.417 | |
| Hunan Sheng (China) | T2—512 15 | |
| Hundred Days, 1815 | 944.05 | |
| Hundred Years' War, 1337–1453 | 944.025 | |
| Hunedoara (Romania : Judeţ) | T2—498 4 | |
| Hưng Yên (Vietnam : Province) | T2—597 3 | |
| Hungana language | 496.393 | |
| | T6—963 93 | |
| Hungarian language | 494.511 | |
| | T6—945 11 | |
| Hungarian literature | 894.511 | |

| | |
|---|---|
| Hungarian partridge | 598.623 2 |
| Hungarians | T5—945 11 |
| Hungary | 943.9 |
| | T2—439 |
|   ancient | 936.39 |
| | T2—363 9 |
| Hunger | |
|   human physiology | 612.391 |
|   psychology | 152.188 6 |
|   social theology | 201.763 8 |
|     Christianity | 261.832 6 |
|   social welfare | 363.8 |
| Hunger strikes | |
|   social conflict | 303.61 |
| Hunt County (Tex.) | T2—764 272 |
| Hunter River (N.S.W.) | T2—944 2 |
| Hunterdon County (N.J.) | T2—749 71 |
| Hunters | |
|   commercial | 639.109 2 |
|   sports | 799.292 |
| Hunting | 799.2 |
|   arts | T3C—357 9 |
|   commercial | 639.1 |
|     production economics | 338.372 9 |
|     public administration | 354.349 |
|   ethics | 179.3 |
|     *see also* Animals — | |
|       treatment of — ethics | |
|   game laws | 346.046 954 9 |
|   painting | 758.3 |
|   products | 338.372 9 |
|     commerce | 381.432–.439 |
|   public administration | 354.349 |
|   sports | 799.2 |
|     public administrative support | 353.78 |
| Hunting and gathering societies | 306.364 |
| Hunting animals | |
|   animal husbandry | 636.088 8 |
| Hunting dogs | 636.75 |
|   sports | 799.234 |
| Hunting lodges | |
|   architecture | 728.7 |
| Huntingdon County (Pa.) | T2—748 73 |
| Huntingdonshire (England) | T2—426 54 |
| Huntington County (Ind.) | T2—772 71 |
| Huntington disease | |
|   medicine | 616.851 |
|   *see also* Nervous system | |
|     diseases — humans | |
| Huntsville (Ala.) | T2—761 97 |
| Huon pine | 585.3 |
|   forestry | 634.975 93 |
| Hupa Indians | T5—972 |

| | |
|---|---|
| Hupa language | 497.2 |
| | T6—972 |
| Hupeh Province (China) | T2—512 12 |
| Hurdlers | 796.426 092 |
| Hurdles (Race) | |
|   horses | 798.45 |
|   humans | 796.426 |
| Hurdy-gurdies | 787.69 |
|   instrument | 787.691 9 |
|   music | 787.69 |
|   *see also* Stringed instruments | |
| Hurling (Game) | 796.35 |
| Huron (Ont. : County) | T2—713 22 |
| Huron, Lake (Mich. and | |
|   Ont.) | T2—774 |
|   Michigan | T2—774 |
|   Ontario | T2—713 2 |
| Huron County (Mich.) | T2—774 44 |
| Huron County (Ohio) | T2—771 25 |
| Huron Indians | T5—975 55 |
| Huron language | 497.555 |
| | T6—975 55 |
| Hurrian languages | 499.9 |
| | T6—999 |
| Hurricanes | 551.552 |
|   meteorology | 551.552 |
|   social services | 363.349 22 |
|   weather forecasting | 551.645 2 |
|   weather modification | 551.685 2 |
|   *see also* Disasters | |
| Hurunui District (N.Z.) | T2—938 1 |
|   Canterbury Region | T2—938 1 |
|   Nelson-Marlborough | |
|     Region | T2—937 9 |
| Husband and wife | 306.872 |
|   law | 346.016 3 |
| Husbands | 306.872 2 |
| | T1—086 55 |
|   social welfare | 362.820 865 5 |
|   *see also* Married men | |
| Huskers | |
|   manufacturing technology | 681.763 1 |
| Huskies | 636.73 |
| Husking | 631.56 |
| Hussein, Saddam | |
|   Iraqi history | 956.704 4 |
| Hussein Onn, Datuk | |
|   Malaysian history | 959.505 3 |
| Hussite Wars, 1419–1436 | 943.702 24 |
| Hussites | 284.3 |
| Hutchinson County (S.D.) | T2—783 384 |
| Hutchinson County (Tex.) | T2—764 821 |
| Hutias | 599.359 |

Hutterite Brethren 289.73
  biography 289.709 2
  *see also* Mennonite Church
Hutu (African people) T5—963 946 1
HVAC (Building systems) 697
HVAP ammunition 623.451 8
Hwang Ho (China) T2—511
Hyacinths 635.934 32
  botany 584.32
  floriculture 635.934 32
Hyaenidae 599.743
Hyaline cartilage
  human histology 612.751 7
Hyalospongiae 593.44
  paleozoology 563.4
Hybrid computers 004.19
  architecture 004.259
  communications 004.619
    programming 005.712 9
    programs 005.713 9
  engineering 621.391 9
  graphics programming 006.679
  graphics programs 006.689
  interfacing 004.619
    programming 005.712 9
    programs 005.713 9
  multimedia-systems
    programming 006.779
  multimedia-systems programs 006.789
  operating systems 005.449
  performance evaluation 004.190 29
    for improvement and design 004.259
  programming 005.29
  programs 005.39
  systems analysis 004.259
  systems design 004.259
Hybrid photography 770
Hybrids
  agriculture 631.523
    animal husbandry 636.082
    plant cultivation 631.523
Hydatid diseases
  incidence 614.554
  medicine 616.964
  *see also* Communicable
    diseases — humans
Hyde County (N.C.) T2—756 184
Hyde County (S.D.) T2—783 283
Hyderabad (India : State) T2—548 4
Hyderabad (Pakistan :
  District) T2—549 182
Hydnaceae 579.6
Hydrangeaceae 583.72

Hydrangeas 635.933 72
  botany 583.72
  floriculture 635.933 72
Hydras 593.55
Hydraulic control 629.804 2
Hydraulic engineering 627
Hydraulic engineers 627.092
Hydraulic fluids 621.204 24
Hydraulic machinery 621.2
Hydraulic mining 622.292 7
Hydraulic-power engineering 621.2
Hydraulic-power engineers 621.209 2
Hydraulic pumps 621.252
Hydraulic rams 621.27
Hydraulic structures 627
Hydraulic transmission 621.26
Hydraulic turbines 621.24
Hydraulics 532
  engineering 620.106
  hydraulic engineering 627
  physics 532
Hydrides
  chemical engineering 661.08
Hydrobatidae 598.42
Hydrocarbons 547.01
  alicyclic chemical engineering 661.815
  alicyclic chemistry 547.51
  aliphatic chemical engineering 661.814
  aliphatic chemistry 547.41
  aromatic chemical engineering 661.816
  aromatic chemistry 547.61
  chemical engineering 661.81
  human toxicology 615.95
Hydrocephalus
  medicine 616.858 843
  pediatrics 618.928 588 43
Hydrocharitales 584.73
Hydrochloric acid
  chemical engineering 661.23
Hydrodynamics 532.5
Hydroelectric power 333.914
  *see also* Water power
Hydroelectric power plants 621.312 134
Hydroelectricity 333.914
  *see also* Water power
Hydrofoils 387.204 4
  engineering 623.820 4
  transportation services 387.204 4
  *see also* Ships
Hydrogen 553.92
  biochemistry 572
  chemical engineering 661.08
  chemistry 546.2
  economic geology 553.92

Hydrogen (continued)

| | |
|---|---|
| gas technology | 665.81 |
| organic chemistry | 547 |

see also Chemicals

| | |
|---|---|
| Hydrogen embrittlement | 620.162 3 |
| Hydrogen-ion concentration | 541.372 8 |
| chemical engineering | 660.297 28 |

Hydrogen sulfide

| | |
|---|---|
| gas technology | 665.89 |
| human toxicology | 615.91 |
| Hydrogenation | 547.23 |
| carbonaceous gas technology | 662.662 3 |
| chemical engineering | 660.284 43 |
| coal technology | 662.662 2 |
| petroleum distillates | 665.533 |

Hydrographic currents

| | |
|---|---|
| navigation tables | 623.894 9 |
| Hydrographic surveying | 526.99 |
| Hydrography | 551.46 |
| Hydroida | 593.55 |
| Hydroids | 593.55 |
| Hydrolases | 572.793 |

see also Enzymes

| | |
|---|---|
| Hydrological cycle | 551.48 |
| Hydrology (Fresh waters) | 551.48 |

see Manual at 578.76–.77 vs.
   551.46, 551.48

| | |
|---|---|
| Hydrolysis | 541.39 |
| chemical engineering | 660.284 4 |
| organic chemistry | 547.2 |
| Hydromechanics | 532 |
| engineering | 620.106 |
| hydraulic engineering | 627 |
| physics | 532 |
| soil physics | 631.432 |
| Hydrometallurgy | 669.028 3 |
| Hydrometeorology | 551.57 |
| Hydrophiidae | 597.965 |
| Hydrophiloidea | 595.763 |
| Hydrophyllaceae | 583.94 |
| Hydroplanes | 387.231 4 |
| engineering | 623.823 14 |
| transportation services | 387.231 4 |

see also Ships

| | |
|---|---|
| Hydroponics | 631.585 |
| Hydroquinones | 547.633 |
| Hydroscaphidae | 595.762 |
| Hydrosols | 541.345 14 |
| chemical engineering | 660.294 514 |
| Hydrosphere | 551.46 |
| Hydrostatics | 532.2 |
| Hydrosulfides | 547.063 |

Hydrosulfites

| | |
|---|---|
| chemical engineering | 661.896 |

Hydrotherapy

| | |
|---|---|
| medicine | 615.853 |

Hydrothermal vents

| | |
|---|---|
| biology | 578.779 9 |
| ecology | 577.799 |

Hydrous sulfates

| | |
|---|---|
| mineralogy | 549.755 |

Hydroxides

| | |
|---|---|
| mineralogy | 549.53 |
| Hydroxy compounds | 547.03 |
| aliphatic chemistry | 547.43 |
| aromatic chemistry | 547.63 |
| chemical engineering | 661.8 |
| Hydroxyketone dyes | 667.256 |
| Hydrozoa | 593.55 |
| Hyenas | 599.743 |
| Hyeniales | 561.72 |
| Hygiene | 613 |
| customs | 391.64 |
| personal | 613 |
| primary education | 372.37 |
| veterinary medicine | 636.089 3 |
| Hygienists | 613.092 |
| Hyla | 597.878 2 |
| Hylidae | 597.878 |
| Hylobates | 599.882 |
| Hylobatidae | 599.882 |

Hymen

| | |
|---|---|
| gynecology | 618.1 |
| human anatomy | 611.67 |
| human physiology | 612.628 |

Hymen diseases

| | |
|---|---|
| gynecology | 618.1 |

see also Female genital
   diseases — humans

| | |
|---|---|
| Hymenoptera | 595.79 |
| Hymenostomatida | 579.495 |
| Hymns | 782.27 |
| choral and mixed voices | 782.527 |
| religion | 203.8 |
| Christianity | 264.23 |
| Judaism | 296.462 |
| private devotions | 204.3 |
| single voices | 783.092 7 |
| Hyndburn (England) | T2—427 625 |
| Hyōgo-ken (Japan) | T2—521 87 |

Hyperactive children

| | |
|---|---|
| home care | 649.154 |
| Hyperactive students | 371.94 |

Hyperactivity

| | |
|---|---|
| medicine | 616.858 9 |
| pediatrics | 618.928 589 |

Hyperadrenalism
  medicine       616.45
    *see also* Endocrine
      diseases — humans
Hyperbaric oxygenation
  therapeutics    615.836
Hyperbola    516.152
Hyperbolic equations    515.353 5
Hyperbolic geometry    516.9
Hyperboloids    516.154
Hyperborean languages    494.6
             T6—946
Hyperborean literatures    894.6
Hypercholesteremia
  medicine    616.399 7
    *see also* Digestive system
      diseases — humans
Hypercholesterolemia
  medicine    616.399 7
    *see also* Digestive system
      diseases — humans
Hypercubes    516.158
Hyperfunctions    515.9
Hypergeometric polynomials    515.55
Hypericaceae    583.624
Hyperkinesia
  medicine    616.858 9
  pediatrics    618.928 589
Hyperlipidemia
  medicine    616.399 7
    *see also* Digestive system
      diseases — humans
Hypermarkets    381.149
  management    658.879
Hypermedia    006.7
Hyperons    539.721 64
Hyperopia
  optometry    617.755
    *see also* Eye diseases —
      humans
Hyperparathyroidism
  medicine    616.445
    *see also* Endocrine
      diseases — humans
Hyperpinealism
  medicine    616.48
    *see also* Endocrine
      diseases — humans
Hypersensitivity
  incidence    614.599 3
  medicine    616.97
Hypersonic flow    533.276
  air mechanics    533.62
  aeronautics    629.132 306

Hypertension
  medicine    616.132
    *see also* Cardiovascular
      diseases — humans
  pregnancy complications
    obstetrics    618.361 32
Hypertext    006.7
Hypertext databases
  computer science    005.759
Hyperthyroidism
  medicine    616.443
    *see also* Endocrine
      diseases — humans
Hypertrichosis
  medicine    616.546
    *see also* Skin diseases —
      humans
Hypertrophies
  skin
    medicine    616.544
    *see also* Skin diseases —
      humans
Hyperventilation
  medicine    616.208
    *see also* Respiratory tract
      diseases — humans
Hyphochytridiomycetes    579.53
Hyphomycetes    579.55
Hypnosis    154.7
Hypnotherapy
  medicine    615.851 2
Hypnotic phenomena    154.77
Hypnotic regression
  occultism    133.901 35
Hypnotics
  pharmacokinetics    615.782
Hypnotism    154.7
  parapsychology    133.89
Hypoadrenalism
  medicine    616.45
    *see also* Endocrine
      diseases — humans
Hypochondria
  medicine    616.852 5
    *see also* Mental disorders
Hypochondriasis
  medicine    616.852 5
    *see also* Mental disorders
Hypocreales    579.567 7
Hypoglycemia
  medicine    616.466
    *see also* Endocrine
      diseases — humans

| | |
|---|---|
| Hypoparathyroidism | |
|   medicine | 616.445 |
|   *see also* Endocrine | |
|     diseases — humans | |
| Hypopituitarism | |
|   medicine | 616.47 |
|   *see also* Endocrine | |
|     diseases — humans | |
| Hypostatic union | 232.8 |
| Hypothalamus | 573.459 |
|   biology | 573.459 |
|   human anatomy | 611.81 |
|   human physiology | 612.826 2 |
|   medicine | 616.8 |
|   *see also* Nervous system | |
| Hypothermia | |
|   medicine | 616.989 |
|   *see also* Environmental | |
|     diseases — humans | |
|   therapeutics | 615.832 9 |
| Hypotheses | |
|   logic | 167 |
|   mathematics | 511.3 |
| Hypothesis testing (Statistics) | 519.56 |
| Hypothyroidism | |
|   medicine | 616.444 |
|   *see also* Endocrine | |
|     diseases — humans | |
| Hypoxidaceae | 584.354 |
| Hypsilophodon | 567.914 |
| Hyracoidea | 599.68 |
| Hyraxes | 599.68 |
| Hyrcania | T2—396 |
| Hyssop | 583.96 |
| Hysterectomies | |
|   surgery | 618.145 3 |
| Hysteresis (Magnetism) | 538.3 |
| Hysteria | |
|   medicine | 616.852 4 |
|   *see also* Mental disorders | |
| Hystricidae | 599.359 7 |
| Hystricomorpha | 599.359 |

# I

| | |
|---|---|
| ÎAkutiîa (Russia) | T2—575 |
| Ialomiţa (Romania) | T2—498 2 |
| ÎAroslavskaîa oblast′ | |
|   (Russia) | T2—473 2 |
| Iaşi (Romania : Judeţ) | T2—498 1 |
| Iatrogenic diseases | |
|   medicine | 615.5 |
| Ibadan (Nigeria) | T2—669 25 |

| | |
|---|---|
| Ibadites | 297.833 |
|   Hadith | 297.125 933 |
| Ibaraki-ken (Japan) | T2—521 31 |
| Iberia (Kingdom) | 939.536 |
| | T2—395 36 |
| Iberia Parish (La.) | T2—763 49 |
| Iberian Peninsula | 946 |
| | T2—46 |
|   ancient | 936.6 |
| | T2—366 |
| Iberville (Quebec : County) | T2—714 38 |
| Iberville Parish (La.) | T2—763 44 |
| Ibexes | 599.648 |
| Ibibio (African people) | T5—963 64 |
| Ibibio language | 496.364 |
| | T6—963 64 |
| Ibis | 598.34 |
| Ibiza Island (Spain) | T2—467 56 |
| Ibizan hound | 636.753 2 |
| Ibn Abī Shaybah, ʻAbd Allāh ibn | |
|   Muḥammad | |
|   Hadith | 297.125 56 |
| Ibn Bābawayh al-Qummī, | |
|   Muḥammad ibn ʻAli | |
|   Hadith | 297.125 921 2 |
| Ibn Ḥanbal, Aḥmad ibn | |
|   Muḥammad | |
|   Hadith | 297.125 612 |
| Ibn Mājah, Muḥammad ibn Yazīd | |
|   Hadith | 297.125 52 |
| Ibo (African people) | T5—963 32 |
| Ibo language | 496.332 |
| | T6—963 32 |
| Ibo literature | 896.332 |
| Ibrāhīm (Patriarch) | |
|   Islam | 297.246 3 |
| Ica (Peru : Province) | T2—852 7 |
| Icacinaceae | 583.85 |
| Icarianism (Socialist school) | 335.2 |
| ICBM (Missiles) | 358.175 482 |
|   engineering | 623.451 954 |
|   military equipment | 358.175 482 |
| Ice | 551.31 |
|   building construction | 693.91 |
|   economic geology | 553.7 |
|   geology | 551.31 |
|   manufacturing technology | 621.58 |
|   mineralogy | 549.522 |
| Ice age | 551.792 |
|   geology | 551.792 |
|   paleontology | 560.179 2 |
| Ice bugs | 595.726 |
| Ice carving | 736.94 |

Ice control
  road engineering — 625.763
Ice cream — 641.862
  commercial processing — 637.4
  home preparation — 641.862
Ice crossings
  railroad engineering — 625.147
  road engineering — 625.792
Ice dancing — 796.912
Ice fishing — 799.122
Ice formation
  aeronautics — 629.132 4
Ice games — 796.96
Ice hockey — 796.962
  electronic games — 794.869 62
Ice hockey players — 796.962 092
Ice milk — 641.862
  commercial processing — 637.4
  home preparation — 641.862
Ice plants (Sea figs) — 583.53
Ice roads — 388.12
  engineering — 625.792
Ice skaters — 796.910 92
Ice skates
  manufacturing technology — 688.769 1
Ice skating — 796.91
Ice sports — 796.9
  equipment technology — 688.769
Ice storms — 551.556
  social services — 363.349 26
Ice wine — 641.222
  commercial processing — 663.22
Icebergs — 551.342
Iceboating — 796.97
Icebreakers — 387.28
  design — 623.812 8
  engineering — 623.828
  *see also* Ships
Icebreaking services — 387.54
İçel İli (Turkey) — T2—564 6
  ancient — T2—393 5
Iceland — 949.12
  — T2—491 2
Iceland pony — 636.16
Icelanders — T5—396 1
Icelandic language — 439.69
  — T6—396 91
Icelandic literature — 839.69
Icelandic people — T5—396 1
Ices — 641.863
  commercial processing — 637.4
  home preparation — 641.863
Ichneumonoidea — 595.79
Ichneumons — 595.79

Ichnology — 560.43
  vertebrates — 566
Ichthyologists — 597.092
Ichthyology — 597
Ichthyornithiformes — 568.23
Ichthyosauria — 567.937
Ichthyosis
  medicine — 616.544
  *see also* Skin diseases —
    humans
Iconography
  drawing — 743.9
  fine arts — 704.9
    *see Manual at* 704.9 and
      753–758
  painting — 753–758
    *see Manual at* 704.9 and
      753–758
  use in advertising — 659.104 5
Icons
  fine arts — 704.948
    Christianity — 704.948 2
  religious significance — 203.7
    Christianity — 246.53
    *see also* Symbolism —
      religious significance
Ictaluridae — 597.492
Ictalurus — 597.492
Icteridae — 598.874
Id (Psychology) — 154.2
'Īd al-Aḍḥā — 297.36
'Īd al-Fiṭr — 297.36
Ida County (Iowa) — T2—777 422
Idaho — 979.6
  — T2—796
Idaho County (Idaho) — T2—796 82
Ideal states — 321.07
  *see also* Utopias
Idealism — 141
  arts — T3C—13
  education — 370.12
  literature — 808.801 3
    history and criticism — 809.913
    specific literatures — T3B—080 13
      history and
        criticism — T3B—091 3
Ideals (Mathematics) — 512.42
  algebra — 512.42
  number theory — 512.74
Ideas
  epistemology — 121.4
  psychology — 153.2

Ideation
  epistemology    121
  psychology    153.2
Idée fixe
  musical element    781.248
Identification
  arts    702.87
Identification cards    929.9
Identification marks    929.9
     T1—027
Identification of criminals    363.258
Identity
  philosophy    111.82
    humans    126
  psychology    155.2
Identity theft    364.163 3
  law    345.026 33
  prevention    332.024
Ideographs    411
  specific languages    T4—11
Ideologies (Political science)    320.5
  party programs    324.23
Ideology    140
  philosophical system    145
Idioms    418
  dictionaries    413.1
    specific languages    T4—313
  specific languages    T4—8
Idiophones    786.82
  *see also* Percussion instruments
Idlib (Syria : Province)    T2—569 13
Idolatry    202.18
Idols    202.18
Idoma (African people)    T5—963 3
Idoma language    496.33
     T6—963 3
Idomoid languages    496.33
     T6—963 3
Idris I, King of Libya
  Libyan history    961.204 1
Idutywa (South Africa :
  District)    T2—687 58
Ife (Kingdom)    966.928 01
     T2—669 28
Ifrane (Morocco : Province)    T2—645
Ifugao (Philippines)    T2—599 1
Ig (Immunoglobulin)    571.967
  humans    616.079 8
Igala (African people)    T5—963 33
Igbo (African people)    T5—963 32
Igbo language    496.332
     T6—963 32
Igbo literature    896.332

Igboid languages    496.33
     T6—963 3
Iğdır İli (Turkey)    T2—566 26
  ancient    T2—395 5
Igloolik (Nunavut)    T2—719 52
Igloos
  construction    693.91
Igluligaarjuk (Nunavut)    T2—719 58
Iglulik (Nunavut)    T2—719 52
Igneous rocks    552.1
Ignition    541.361
  chemical engineering    660.296 1
  chemistry    541.361
Ignition systems
  automotive    629.254
  internal-combustion engines    621.437
Iguanas    597.954 2
Iguanidae    597.954
Iguanodon    567.914
Ijo (African people)    T5—963
Ijo language    496.3
     T6—963
Ijoid languages    496.3
     T6—963
IJssel Lake (Netherlands)    T2—492 2
IJssel River (Netherlands)    T2—492 18
Ikaluktutiak (Nunavut)    T2—719 55
Ikhnaton, King of Egypt
  Egyptian history    932.014
Īlām (Iran : Province)    T2—555 8
Ilamba-Irangi languages    496.394
     T6—963 94
Île aux Coudres (Quebec)    T2—714 492
Île aux Grues (Quebec)    T2—714 735
Ile-de-France (France)    T2—443 6
Ile de la Tortue (Haiti)    T2—729 42
Île-d'Orléans (Quebec)    T2—714 476
Île-Dorval (Quebec)    T2—714 28
Île Verte (Quebec)    T2—714 764
Ileal diseases
  medicine    616.34
    *see also* Digestive system
      diseases — humans
Ileitis
  medicine    616.344 5
    *see also* Digestive system
      diseases — humans
Ileostomy    617.554 1
Îles-de-la-Madeleine
  (Quebec)    T2—714 797
Ileum    573.378
  biology    573.378
  human anatomy    611.341
  medicine    616.34

Ileum (continued)
surgery 617.554 1
*see also* Digestive system
Ilía (Greece) T2—495 27
ancient T2—388
Ilium (Extinct City) T2—392 1
Ill people 305.908 7
T1—087 7
*see also* Sick people
Ille-et-Vilaine (France) T2—441 5
Illecillewaet River (B.C.) T2—711 68
Illegal immigration 364.137
law 345.023 7
Illegitimacy 306.874
law 346.017
Illegitimate children 306.874
T1—086 945
*see also* Children of unmarried
parents
Illiciales 583.3
Illicit distilling 364.133 2
law 345.023 32
Illinois 977.3
T2—773
Illinois Indians T5—973 15
Illinois language 497.315
T6—973 15
Illinois River (Ill.) T2—773 5
Illiteracy 302.224 4
*see also* Literacy
Illiterate people 305.56
T1—086 94
Illizi (Algeria : Province) T2—657
Illness 362.1
medicine 616
*see also* Diseases — humans
Illocutionary acts 401.452
specific languages T4—014 52
Illuminating engineering 621.32
*see also* Lighting
Illumination 621.32
*see also* Lighting
Illumination (Decorative arts) 745.67
Illuminations (Performing arts) 791.6
Illusions 001.96
psychology of perception 153.74
sensory perception 152.1
Illustration
arts 741.6
*see Manual at* 741.6 vs. 800
Illustrations T1—022
notable books 096.1
*see Manual at* T1—0222 vs.
T1—0223

Illustrators 741.609 2
Illyria 939.87
T2—398 7
Illyrian languages (Ancient Indo- 491.993
European) T6—919 93
Illyricum 939.87
T2—398 7
Ilm-Kreis (Germany :
Landkreis) T2—432 26
Ilmenite
mineralogy 549.523
ILO (Labor office) 354.921 1
law 344.01
Ilocos Norte (Philippines) T2—599 1
Ilocos Sur (Philippines) T2—599 1
Iloilo (Philippines :
Province) T2—599 5
Iloko language 499.21
T6—992 1
Ilorin (Nigeria) T2—669 57
Image manipulation
computer science 006.6
digital photography 771.44
Image processing 621.367
computer science 006.42
engineering 621.399 4
*see Manual at* 006.37 vs.
006.42, 621.367, 621.391,
621.399
Imagery (Psychology) 153.32
Images
fine arts 704.9
religious significance 203.7
Christianity 246.53
*see also* Symbolism —
religious significance
religious worship 202.18
Imaginary numbers 512.788
Imaginary wars
military analysis 355.48
Imagination 153.3
educational psychology 370.157
philosophy 128.3
Imaging
medical diagnosis 616.075 4
Imamate 297.61
Imams 297.092
biography 297.092
specific sects 297.8
role and function 297.61
*see Manual at* 297.092
Imbabura (Ecuador) T2—866 12
Imbibition processes 773.3

Imboden (Switzerland :
  Bezirk)           T2—494 735 6
Imbros Island         T2—562 2
  ancient            T2—391 1
IMF (Fund)            332.152
  law              346.082 152
Imidazoles           547.593
  chemical engineering   661.894
Imitation furs         675.3
Imitation-leather covers
  bookbinding        686.343
Imitation leathers      675.4
Imitative learning
  psychology         153.152 3
Immaculate Conception of Mary  232.911
Immigrants          305.906 912
                T1—086 912
  labor economics     331.62
  social welfare      362.899 12
  women
    social welfare     362.839 812
  young people
    social welfare     362.779 12
Immigration          304.82
  illegal            364.137
    law            345.023 7
  influence on crime    364.256
  law              342.082
  political science     325.1
  public administration   353.484
  sociology         304.82
Immorality           170
  religion           205
  *see also* Moral theology
Immortality
  philosophy         129
  religion           202.3
    Christianity      236.22
    Islam           297.23
    Judaism        296.33
    philosophy of religion  218
Immune deficiency diseases  571.974
  animals          571.974
    veterinary medicine   636.089 697 9
  humans          362.196 979
    incidence       614.599 39
    medicine        616.979
    social services    362.196 979
Immune gamma globulins
  pharmacology      615.37
Immune reactions     571.964 6
  humans          616.079 5
Immune recognition    571.964 6
  human immunology   616.079 5

Immune response      571.964 6
  humans          616.079 5
Immune serums
  pharmacology      615.37
Immune system       571.96
  humans          616.079
Immune system diseases  571.963
  humans
    medicine        616.97
Immunity            571.96
  humans          616.079
Immunity of legislators   328.348
Immunization
  disease control     614.47
  law              344.043
Immunoassays
  medicine         616.075 6
Immunochemistry     571.964
  medicine         616.079
    diagnosis       616.075 6
Immunocytochemistry   571.964
  medicine         616.079
Immunodiagnosis
  medicine         616.075 6
Immunogenetics      571.964 8
  medicine         616.079 6
Immunoglobulins      571.967
  humans          616.079 8
  pharmacology      615.37
Immunologic diseases
  medicine         616.97
Immunologic drugs
  pharmacology      615.37
Immunology          571.96
  humans          616.079
Immunotherapy       615.37
Imo State (Nigeria)     T2—669 46
Impact strength
  materials science    620.112 5
Impact studies (Environmental)  333.714
Impala             599.646
Impatiens           583.79
Impeachment        342.068
  chief executives    342.062
  judges           347.014
Impeachment power (Legislative
  bodies)           328.345 3
Impendle (South Africa :
  District)         T2—684 7
Imperia (Italy : Province)  T2—451 87
  ancient            T2—371 4
Imperial County (Calif.)   T2—794 99
Imperial system (Measurement)  530.813
  social aspects      389.15

Imperial Valley (Calif. and
  Mexico)      T2—794 99
Imperialism      325.32
  international relations      327.1
Impersonation      792.028
  illegal      364.163 3
    law      345.026 33
  motion pictures      791.430 28
  radio      791.440 28
  stage      792.028
  television      791.450 28
Impetigo
  medicine      616.523
  *see also* Skin diseases —
    humans
Implant-supported dentures
  dentistry      617.693
Implication
  linguistics      401.454
    specific languages      T4—014 54
Import quotas      382.52
  *see also* Import trade
Import tax      382.7
  public finance      336.264
  *see also* Customs (Tariff)
Import trade      382.5
  law      343.087 7
  public administration      354.74
Imposition
  printing      686.225 6
Impotence
  drug therapy      616.692 206 1
  medicine      616.692 2
  *see also* Male genital
    diseases — humans
  neurotic
    medicine      616.858 32
Impoverished people      305.569
     T1—086 942
  *see also* Poor people
Impressing equipment      621.984
Impression
  printing      686.23
Impressionism
  fine arts      709.034 4
  literature      808.801 1
    history and criticism      809.911
    specific literatures      T3B—080 11
      history and
        criticism      T3B—091 1
  music      780.904
  painting      759.054
Imprisonment      365
Impromptus      784.189 4

Improper integrals      515.43
Improvisation (Drama)      792.028
  motion pictures      791.430 28
  radio      791.440 28
  stage      792.028
  television      791.450 28
Improvisation (Music)      781.36
Improvisatory forms      784.189 4
Impulse control disorders
  medicine      616.858 4
  *see also* Mental disorders
Impulsive personality
  medicine      616.858 4
  *see also* Mental disorders
İmroz Island      T2—562 2
In-house training      331.259 2
  personnel management      658.312 43
  *see also* Vocational education
In-laws      306.87
     T1—085
In-line skating      796.21
In-service training      331.259 2
     T1—071 55
  libraries      020.715 5
  museums      069.63
  *see also* Vocational education
In-situ processing      622.22
  *see Manual at* 622.22, 622.7 vs.
    662.6, 669
In vitro fertilization
  ethics      176.2
    *see also* Reproduction —
      ethics
  medicine      618.178 059 9
Inactive files (Records
  management)
  storage      651.56
Inadunata      563.92
Inanda (South Africa :
  District)      T2—684 4
Inari Saami language      494.576
     T6—945 76
Inari Sámi language      494.576
     T6—945 76
Inaudible sound      534.5
Inaugural addresses
  public administration      352.238 6
Inaugurations
  customs      394.4
  music      781.57
Inboard motorboats      387.231 4
  design      623.812 314
  engineering      623.823 14

Inboard motorboats (continued)
  transportation services — 387.231 4
  *see also* Ships
Inboard motors — 623.872 3
Inboard-outboard motorboats — 387.231 5
  design — 623.812 315
  engineering — 623.823 15
  transportation services — 387.231 5
  *see also* Ships
Inborn errors of metabolism
  medicine — 616.390 42
    *see also* Digestive system
      diseases — humans
Inbreeding — 576.544
  agriculture — 631.523
    animal husbandry — 636.082
    plant cultivation — 631.523
  genetics — 576.544
  sociology — 306.82
Inca (Peru : Region) — T2—853 7
Inca period — 985.019
Incandescent lighting — 621.326
Incantations (Occultism) — 133.44
Incarcerated people — 365.6
  — T1—086 927
Incarnation
  philosophy — 129
Incarnation of Jesus Christ — 232.1
Incas — T5—983 23
Incendiary weapons — 623.451 6
Incense cedars — 585.4
Incense trees — 583.77
Incentive payments
  labor economics — 331.216 4
  personnel management — 658.322 5
    executives — 658.407 225
    public administration — 352.67
Incentives
  labor economics — 331.216 4
  personnel management — 658.314 2
    executives — 658.407 142
  research — 001.44
  social control — 303.35
Incest — 306.877
  criminology — 364.153 6
    criminal law — 345.025 36
  medicine — 616.858 36
  sociology — 306.877
Incidence geometry — 516.12
Incidental music — 781.552
Incineration
  sewage sludge disposal — 628.37
  waste disposal — 363.728
  waste technology — 628.445 7

Incisions (Wounds)
  medicine — 617.143
Inclined railroads — 385.6
  engineering — 625.3
  transportation services — 385.6
Inclines
  canal engineering — 627.135 3
Inclosures
  land economics — 333.2
Inclusive education — 371.904 6
Income — 339.32
  accounting — 657.7
  agricultural industries — 338.13
  financial management — 658.155 4
  increase
    personal finance — 332.024 01
  labor economics — 331.21
  macroeconomics — 339.32
  mineral industries — 338.23
  secondary industries — 338.43
  transportation services — 388.049
Income accounts
  (Macroeconomics) — 339.32
Income-consumption relations
  macroeconomics — 339.41
Income distribution — 339.2
Income maintenance — 362.582
  public administration — 353.54
  social welfare — 362.582
Income redistribution
  macroeconomic policy — 339.52
Income statements
  financial management — 658.151 2
Income tax — 336.24
  law — 343.052
  public administration — 352.44
  public finance — 336.24
Income theory
  monetary economics — 332.401
Incomes policy — 339.5
  inflation control — 332.415
Incompatibilities
  philosophical logic — 160
Incompressible airflow
  aeronautics — 629.132 322
Incorporated banks — 332.122
Incorporation
  law — 346.066 22
  local government — 320.85
  management — 658.114 5
  public administration — 352.84
Incrustation
  architectural decoration — 729.6

Incubi     133.423
    *see also* Legendary beings
Incunabula     093
    bibliographies     011.42
Indecent exposure     364.153
    law     345.025 3
Indemnification
    Holocaust, 1933–1945     940.531 814 4
    law of war     341.66
Indentured labor
    sociology     306.363
Independence County (Ark.)     T2—767 26
Independence Day (United
    States)     394.263 4
Independence days     394.26
    *see also* Holidays
Independencia (Dominican
    Republic)     T2—729 325
Independent agencies
    public administration     352.264
Independent Fundamental
    Churches of America     289.95
    *see also* Christian
       denominations
Independent Fundamentalist and
    Evangelical churches     289.95
Independent Methodists     287.533
    *see also* Methodist Church
Independent Order of Odd
    Fellows     366.3
    biography     366.309 2
Independent reading
    primary education     372.454
Independent regulatory agencies     352.8
Independent retail stores     381.1
    *see also* Commerce
Independent schools     371.02
    secondary education     373.222
    *see also* Private schools
Independent study     371.394 3
Indeterminacy composition     781.32
Indeterminate equations     515.253
Indeterminate sentence     364.62
Indeterminism     123
Index librorum prohibitorum     098.11
Index theorems     514.74
Indexing     025.3
    computer science     005.741
    information science     025.3
    museology     069.52
    subject cataloging     025.47

India     954
    T2—54
    ancient     934
    T2—34
India-Pakistan Conflict, 1971     954.920 51
India rubber tree     635.933 45
    *see also* Rubber plant (Ficus)
Indian corn     641.331 5
Indian elephant     599.676
    conservation technology     639.979 676
    resource economics     333.959 676
Indian hemp     583.93
Indian languages (American)     497
    T6—97
    South America     498
    T6—98
Indian literatures (American)     897
    South America     898
Indian literatures (South Asian)
    Dravidian     894.8
    English     820
    Indic     891.1
Indian National Congress
    (Political party)     324.254 083
Indian Ocean     551.461 5
    T2—165
    *see Manual at* T2—163 and
       T2—164, T2—165
Indian Ocean region     T2—182 4
Indian Orthodox Church     281.6
    *see also* Eastern churches
Indian pipe (Plant)     583.66
Indian River County (Fla.)     T2—759 28
Indian sarsaparilla     583.93
Indian Territory (Okla.)     T2—766 5
Indian tobacco     583.98
Indiana     977.2
    T2—772
Indiana County (Pa.)     T2—748 89
Indianapolis (Ind.)     T2—772 52
Indians (National group)     T5—914 11
Indians of Central America     T5—970 728
Indians of North America     T5—97
Indians of South America     T5—98
Indians of the West Indies     T5—970 729
Indic languages     491.1
    T6—911
Indic literatures     891.1
Indic people     T5—914
Indic religions     294
    art representation     704.948 94
    arts     700.482 94
       T3C—382 94

Indic religions (continued)
| | |
|---|---|
| Islamic polemics | 297.294 |

*see Manual at* 200.9 vs. 294, 299.5

| | |
|---|---|
| Indic religions and Islam | 294 |
| Indic view | 294 |
| Islamic view | 297.284 |
| Indic rugs | |
| arts | 746.754 |
| Indicator species | |
| ecology | 577.27 |
| Indicatoridae | 598.72 |
| Indictment | 345.072 |
| Indie rock | 781.66 |
| Indigenous peoples | 305.8 |
| Australia | T5—991 5 |
| Central America | T5—970 728 |
| civil and human rights | 323.11 |
| law | 342.087 2 |
| law of nations | 341.485 2 |
| Hawaii | T5—994 2 |
| legal status | 346.013 |
| constitutional law | 342.087 2 |
| private law | 346.013 |
| legal systems | 340.52 |

*see Manual at* 340.52

| | |
|---|---|
| North America | T5—97 |
| South America | T5—98 |
| Tasmania | T5—991 59 |
| West Indies | T5—970 729 |
| Indigestion | |
| medicine | 616.332 |

*see also* Digestive system diseases — humans

| | |
|---|---|
| Indigo dyes | 667.26 |
| Indigo plants | 583.74 |
| Indigoid dyes | 667.257 |
| Indirect taxation | 336.294 |
| Indium | 669.79 |
| chemical engineering | 661.067 7 |
| chemistry | 546.677 |
| economic geology | 553.499 |
| metallurgy | 669.79 |
| physical metallurgy | 669.967 9 |

*see also* Chemicals

| | |
|---|---|
| Individual freedom | 323 |

*see also* Civil rights

| | |
|---|---|
| Individual fulfillment | |
| educational goal | 370.119 |
| Individual income tax | 336.242 |
| law | 343.052 62 |
| public administration | 352.44 |
| public finance | 336.242 |

| | |
|---|---|
| Individual land tenure | |
| economics | 333.323 |
| Individual proprietorships | 338.72 |

*see also* Proprietorships

| | |
|---|---|
| Individual psychology | 155.2 |
| children | 155.418 2 |
| late adulthood | 155.671 82 |
| Individual retirement accounts | 332.024 014 5 |
| tax law | 343.052 33 |
| Individualism | |
| economics | 330.153 |
| philosophy | 141.4 |
| political ideology | 320.512 |
| social psychology | 302.54 |
| Individuality | 155.2 |
| children | 155.418 2 |
| Individualized instruction | 371.394 |
| Individualized reading instruction | |
| primary education | 372.417 |
| Indo-Aryan languages | 491.1 |
| | T6—911 |
| Indo-Aryan literatures | 891.1 |
| Indo-Aryan period | 934.02 |
| Indo-Aryans | T5—914 |
| Indo-European languages | 410 |
| | T6—1 |
| Indo-European literatures | 800 |
| Indo-Europeans | T5—09 |
| Indo-Germanic languages | 410 |
| | T6—1 |
| Indo-Hittite languages | 410 |
| | T6—1 |
| Indo-Iranian languages | 491.1 |
| | T6—911 |
| Indo-Iranian literatures | 891.1 |
| Indo-jazz | 781.657 |
| Indo-Pakistan War, 1965 | 954.904 5 |
| Indo-Pakistan War, 1971 | 954.920 51 |
| Indochina (French Indochina) | T2—597 |
| Indochina (Southeast peninsula of Asia) | 959 T2—59 |
| Indochinese War, 1946–1954 | 959.704 1 |
| Indochinese War, 1961–1975 | 959.704 3 |
| Indonesia | 959.8 |
| | T2—598 |
| Indonesian language (Bahasa Indonesia) | 499.221 T6—992 21 |
| Indonesian languages | 499.22 |
| | T6—992 2 |
| Indonesian literature (Bahasa Indonesia) | 899.221 |
| Indonesian literatures | 899.22 |
| Indonesians | T5— 992 2 |

Indoor air pollution
  health                 613.5
Indoor air quality
  health                 613.5
Indoor amusements      793
Indoor climbing      796.522 4
Indoor field hockey      796.355
Indoor games      793
Indoor gardening
  floriculture      635.965
Indoor music      781.534
Indoor photography      778.72
Indoor recreation centers      790.068
  architecture      725.84
Indoor temperatures
  health      613.5
Indre (France : Dept.)      T2—445 51
Indre-et-Loire (France)      T2—445 4
Indri      599.83
Inductance meters      621.374 2
Induction (Logic)
  philosophical logic      161
  psychology      153.432
Induction accelerators      539.734
Induction heating      621.402
Induction of employees
  armed forces      355.223
  personnel management      658.312 42
  public administration      352.66
Induction of hypnosis      154.76
Induction welding      671.521 5
Inductive reasoning      161
  philosophical logic      161
  psychology      153.432
Inductors
  radio engineering      621.384 133
Indulgences (Christian rite)      265.66
Indus River      T2—549 1
Indus script      494.899
                T6—948 99
Industrial accidents      363.11
  insurance      368.56
    government-sponsored      368.41
  *see also* Industrial safety
Industrial advertising      659.131 5
Industrial air conditioning      697.931 6
Industrial arbitration      331.891 43
  law      344.018 914 3
  personnel management      658.315 4
Industrial archaeology
  economic aspects      338.09
  historical aspects      900
  technological aspects      609

Industrial areas
  area planning      711.552 4
Industrial art      745.2
Industrial arts      600
  primary education      372.358
  *see also* Technology
Industrial biochemistry      660.63
Industrial biology      660.6
Industrial botany      581.636
Industrial buildings
  architecture      725.4
  construction      690.54
  institutional housekeeping      647.964
  landscape architecture      712.7
  lighting      621.322 54
  sale and rental      333.338 7
Industrial casualty insurance      368.7
Industrial chemicals      661
  human toxicology      615.902
Industrial chemistry      660
Industrial chemists      660.092
Industrial cities      307.766
  area planning      711.45
Industrial concentration      338.8
Industrial conditions      338.09
Industrial conflict
  sociology      306.34
Industrial costs      338.51
  financial management      658.155 2
  *see also* Costs
Industrial credit      332.742
Industrial democracy      331.011 2
  theory of union role      331.880 1
Industrial design      745.2
Industrial development      338.9
  *see also* Economic development
Industrial development banks      332.153
  domestic      332.28
  international      332.153
Industrial diamonds      553.65
  economic geology      553.65
  mining      622.365
  *see also* Diamonds
Industrial diseases
  health      613.62
  medicine      616.980 3
  *see also* Environmental
    diseases — humans
Industrial disputes      331.89
Industrial drawing      604.2
Industrial economics      338
Industrial engineering      670
Industrial engineering
  (Production management)      658.5

| | |
|---|---|
| Industrial equipment | |
|   capital procurement | 658.152 42 |
| Industrial espionage | 364.16 |
|   ethics | 174.4 |
|   law | 343.072 |
|   management | 658.472 |
| Industrial fats | 665 |
| Industrial gases | 665.7 |
|   equipment manufacturing | |
|     technology | 681.766 5 |
| Industrial hazards | 363.11 |
|   *see also* Industrial safety | |
| Industrial health | 613.62 |
| Industrial insurance | 368.3 |
|   accident | 368.56 |
|     government-sponsored | 368.41 |
|   life | 368.362 |
| Industrial land use | |
|   community sociology | 307.332 |
| Industrial lands | 333.77 |
|   economics | 333.77 |
|     sale and rental | 333.336 |
| Industrial law | 343.07 |
| Industrial libraries | 027.69 |
| Industrial life insurance | 368.362 |
| Industrial management | 658 |
| Industrial marketing | |
|   management | 658.804 |
| Industrial medicine | 616.980 3 |
| Industrial microbiology | 660.62 |
| Industrial-military complex | 355.021 3 |
|   economics | 338.473 55 |
|   military science | 355.021 3 |
|   sociology | 306.27 |
| Industrial minerals | 553.6 |
| Industrial mobilization | 355.26 |
|   law | 343.01 |
| Industrial noise | 363.741 |
|   *see also* Noise | |
| Industrial nursing | 610.734 6 |
| Industrial oils | 665 |
| Industrial organization | 338.6 |
|   economics | 338.6 |
|   executive management | 658.402 |
| Industrial parks | |
|   area planning | 711.552 4 |
| Industrial pollution | 363.731 |
|   social welfare | 363.731 |
|   technology | 628.5 |
|   *see also* Pollution | |
| Industrial procurement | 658.72 |
| Industrial productivity | 338.06 |
|   economics | 338.06 |
|   mineral industries | 338.26 |

| | |
|---|---|
| Industrial productivity (continued) | |
|   promotion of | |
|     production management | 658.515 |
|   secondary industries | 338.45 |
| Industrial project management | 658.404 |
| Industrial property | 346.048 |
| Industrial psychology | 158.7 |
| Industrial railroads | 385.54 |
| Industrial relations | 331 |
|   *see also* Labor relations | |
| Industrial research | |
|   production management | 658.57 |
|   technology | 607.2 |
| Industrial resources | 338.09 |
|   economics | 338.09 |
|   military science | 355.26 |
| Industrial revolution | 909.81 |
|   economic history | 330.903 4 |
| Industrial robots | 629.892 |
|   engineering | 629.892 |
|   factory operations engineering | 670.427 2 |
| Industrial sabotage | 364.164 |
|   law | 345.026 4 |
| Industrial safety | 363.11 |
|   engineering | 620.86 |
|   law | 344.046 5 |
|   personal health | 613.62 |
|   public administration | 353.96 |
|   social services | 363.11 |
|   *see also* Safety | |
| Industrial sanitation | 363.729 5 |
|   engineering | 628.51 |
|   law | 344.046 5 |
|   *see also* Sanitation | |
| Industrial schools (Correctional | |
|   institutions) | 365.42 |
|   *see also* Penal institutions | |
| Industrial sociology | 306.36 |
| Industrial stoichiometry | 660.7 |
| Industrial surveys | 338.09 |
| Industrial towns | 307.766 |
|   area planning | 711.45 |
| Industrial toxicology | |
|   medicine | 615.902 |
| Industrial trusts | 338.8 |
|   *see also* Combinations | |
|     (Enterprises) | |
| Industrial unions | 331.883 3 |
|   *see also* Labor unions | |
| Industrial wastes | 363.728 |
|   pollution technology | 628.5 |
|   social services | 363.728 |
|   technology | 628.4 |

Industrial wastes (continued)
  water pollution engineering  628.168 3
  *see also* Waste control
Industrial water supply  363.61
  economics  333.912 3
Industrial workers  331.794
  labor economics  331.794
  public administration  354.93
Industrial Workers of the World  331.886 097 3
Industrial yellow pages  T1—029
  *see Manual at* T1—025 vs.
    T1—029
Industrialization  338.9
Industries  338
  *see also* Industry
Industry  338
  art representation  704.949 6
  arts  700.455 3
    T3C—355 3
  economics  338
  energy economics  333.796 5
  law  343.07
  literature  808.803 553
    history and criticism  809.933 553
    specific literatures  T3B—080 355 3
      history and
        criticism  T3B—093 553
  location
    economic rationale  338.604 2
    production  338.09
  public administration  354
  relations with government  322.3
Industry-school relations  371.195
  higher education  378.103 5
Indwe (South Africa :
  District)  T2—687 57
Inequalities
  algebra  512.97
  calculus  515.26
  geometry  516.1
Inequality  305
  religion  200.8
    Christianity  270.08
  sociology  305
Inerrancy (Bible)  220.132
Inert gases
  chemistry  546.75
  economic geology  553.97
  technology  665.822
Inertia  531.12
  aeronautics  629.132 364
  fluids  532.02
  gases  533.12
  liquids  532.2

Inezgane-Aït Melloul
  (Morocco)  T2—646 6
Infallibility
  Christian church  262.72
  pope  262.131
Infancy  305.232
  music  781.582
  *see also* Infants
Infancy of Jesus Christ  232.92
Infant baptism  234.161 2
  music  781.582
  public worship  265.12
  theology  234.161 2
Infant betrothal
  customs  392.4
Infant schools (Primary schools)  372.241
  *see also* Primary education
Infanticide
  customs  392.12
  demographic effect  304.668
Infantry  356.1
Infants  305.232
    T1—083 2
  cooking for  641.562 22
  development
    physiology  612.654
    health  613.043 2
    home care  649.122
  legal status  346.013 5
    constitutional law  342.087 72
    private law  346.013 5
  pediatrics  618.920 2
  psychology  155.422
  reading
    library science  028.532
  social aspects  305.232
Infections  571.98
  humans
    medicine  616.9
    result of injury  617.22
  *see also* Communicable
    diseases
Infectious diseases  571.98
  *see also* Communicable
    diseases
Infectious mononucleosis
  incidence  614.581 2
  medicine  616.911 22
  *see also* Communicable
    diseases — humans
Inference
  philosophical logic  160
  psychology  153.432
  statistical mathematics  519.54

| | |
|---|---|
| Infertility | |
| gynecology | 618.178 |
| *see also* Female genital | |
| diseases — humans | |
| medicine | 616.692 |
| men | 616.692 1 |
| *see also* Male genital | |
| diseases — humans | |
| *see also* Genital diseases — | |
| humans | |
| Infield play | |
| baseball | 796.357 24 |
| Infiltration (Military tactics) | 355.422 |
| Infinite (Philosophy) | 111.6 |
| Infinite processes | 515.24 |
| Infinite series | 515.243 |
| Infinitesimal calculus | 515.33 |
| Infinitesimal geometry | 516.36 |
| Infinitives | 415.6 |
| specific languages | T4—56 |
| Infirmaries | 362.11 |
| armed forces | 355.72 |
| *see also* Health care facilities | |
| Infixes | 415.92 |
| specific languages | T4—592 |
| Inflammable materials | 363.179 8 |
| fire safety technology | 628.922 2 |
| public safety | 363.179 8 |
| technology | 604.7 |
| *see also* Hazardous materials | |
| Inflammation | |
| result of injury | |
| medicine | 617.22 |
| symptom | 616.047 3 |
| Inflammatory bowel diseases | |
| medicine | 616.344 |
| *see also* Digestive system | |
| diseases — humans | |
| Inflation (Economics) | 332.41 |
| accounting | 657.48 |
| personal finance | 332.024 |
| Inflection (Grammar) | 415.95 |
| specific languages | T4—595 |
| Inflection (Phonology) | 414.6 |
| specific languages | T4—16 |
| Inflection tables (Grammar) | |
| applied linguistics | 418 |
| specific languages | T4—82 |
| Influence | |
| psychology | 155.9 |
| children | 155.418 9 |
| social psychology | 302.13 |

| | |
|---|---|
| Influence peddling | 364.132 3 |
| law | 345.023 23 |
| public administration | 353.46 |
| Influenza | |
| incidence | 614.518 |
| medicine | 616.203 |
| *see also* Respiratory tract | |
| diseases — humans | |
| Informal logic | 160 |
| Informatics | |
| computer science | 004 |
| information science | 020 |
| Information | |
| civil rights issues | 323.445 |
| sociology | 306.42 |
| Information and referral services | 025.52 |
| Information architecture | 006.7 |
| Information centers | 027 |
| *see also* Libraries | |
| Information control | 363.31 |
| *see also* Censorship | |
| Information display systems | |
| electronic engineering | 621.381 542 |
| Information exchange | |
| law | 344.09 |
| Information gathering | |
| executive management | 658.403 8 |
| Information literacy | |
| primary education | 372.34 |
| Information management | |
| executive management | 658.403 8 |
| military administration | 355.688 |
| office services | 651 |
| production management | 658.503 6 |
| public administration | 352.38 |
| Information policy | 338.926 |
| *see Manual at* 338.926 vs. | |
| 352.745, 500 | |
| Information retrieval | |
| information science | 025.524 |
| Information science | 020 |
| Information scientists | 020.92 |
| Information security | |
| management | 658.472 |
| Information services | 025.52 |
| public administration | 352.74 |
| Information sources | |
| use | 028.7 |
| Information storage and retrieval | |
| systems | 025.04 |
| computer science | 005.74 |
| law | 343.099 9 |
| management use | 658.403 801 1 |
| specific subjects | 025.06 |

| | |
|---|---|
| Information technology | |
| computer science | 004 |
| social effects | 303.483 3 |
| Information theory | 003.54 |
| | T1—011 54 |
| communications engineering | 621.382 2 |
| Informational programs | |
| management use | 658.455 |
| Informed consent | 344.041 2 |
| Informers | |
| criminal investigation | 363.252 |
| Infrared astronomy | 522.683 |
| Infrared cinematography | 777.6 |
| Infrared photography | 778.34 |
| arts | 778.34 |
| engineering | 621.367 2 |
| Infrared radiation | 535.012 |
| biophysics | 571.454 |
| humans | 612.014 482 |
| chemical effect | 541.353 2 |
| chemical engineering | 660.295 32 |
| engineering | 621.362 |
| military engineering | 623.042 |
| physics | 535.012 |
| Infrared spectroscopes | |
| manufacturing technology | 681.414 2 |
| Infrared spectroscopy | 543.57 |
| analytical chemistry | 543.57 |
| engineering | 621.361 |
| physics | 535.842 |
| Infrared technology | 621.362 |
| *see also* Infrared radiation | |
| Infrared videography | 777.6 |
| Ingenika River (B.C.) | T2—711 87 |
| Ingestion | 573.35 |
| animal physiology | 573.35 |
| human physiology | 612.31 |
| *see also* Digestive system | |
| Ingestion disorders | |
| incidence | 614.593 |
| medicine | 616.31 |
| *see also* Digestive system | |
| diseases — humans | |
| Ingham (Qld.) | T2—943 6 |
| Ingham County (Mich.) | T2—774 26 |
| Inglenooks | |
| furniture arts | 749.62 |
| Inglewood (Vic.) | T2—945 4 |
| Ingolstadt (Germany) | T2—433 62 |
| Ingot iron | 669.142 3 |
| Ingrian language | 494.54 |
| | T6—945 4 |
| Ingroups | 302.4 |

| | |
|---|---|
| Inguinal hernia | |
| regional medicine | 617.559 |
| surgery | 617.559 059 |
| Ingush | T5—999 641 |
| Ingush language | 499.964 1 |
| | T6—999 641 |
| Ingushetia (Russia) | T2—475 2 |
| Ingushetiia (Russia) | T2—475 2 |
| Ingwavuma (South Africa : | |
| District) | T2—684 3 |
| Inhalant abuse | 362.299 3 |
| medicine | 616.86 |
| personal health | 613.8 |
| social welfare | 362.299 3 |
| *see also* Substance abuse | |
| Inhalation | |
| human physiology | 612.21 |
| Inhalation anesthesia | |
| surgery | 617.962 |
| Inhalation drug administration | 615.6 |
| Inhalation therapy | |
| medicine | 615.836 |
| Inhalation toxicology | |
| medicine | 615.91 |
| Inhambane (Mozambique : | |
| Province) | T2—679 3 |
| Inheritance law | 346.052 |
| Inheritance of acquired | |
| characteristics | 576.827 |
| Inheritance tax | 336.276 |
| law | 343.053 |
| Iniidae | 599.538 |
| Inini (French Guiana) | T2—882 |
| Initial public offerings | |
| (Securities) | 658.152 24 |
| corporate law | 346.066 2 |
| financial management | 658.152 24 |
| investment economics | 332.632 2 |
| Initial-value problems | 515.35 |
| Initiation of business enterprises | 338.71 |
| economics | 338.71 |
| management | 658.11 |
| | T1—068 1 |
| *see Manual at* 338.091–.099 | |
| vs. 332.67309, 338.6042; | |
| *also at* 658.04 vs. 658.114, | |
| 658.402 | |
| Initiation rites | |
| Christianity | 234.161 |
| public worship | 265.1 |
| theology | 234.161 |
| customs | 392.14 |
| etiquette | 395.24 |

| | |
|---|---|
| Initiation rites (continued) | |
| music | 781.57 |
| religion | 203.82 |
| Initiative (Human trait) | |
| psychology | 155.232 |
| Initiative (Legislation) | 328.22 |
| Injection molding of plastics | 668.412 |
| Injections | |
| administering | 615.6 |
| Injunctions | 347.077 |
| labor economics | 331.893 |
| law | 344.018 93 |
| management measure | 331.894 |
| Injuries | |
| anesthesiology | 617.967 1 |
| biology | 571.975 |
| incidence | 614.3 |
| medicine | 617.1 |
| Injurious animals | 591.65 |
| Injurious microorganisms | 579.165 |
| Injurious organisms | 578.65 |
| Injurious plants | 581.65 |
| Ink drawing | 741.26 |
| Ink painting | 751.425 |
| Inka | T5—983 23 |
| Inka period | 985.019 |
| Inks | 667.4 |
| Inland marine insurance | 368.23 |
| Inland revenue | 336.2 |
| law | 343.04 |
| Inland Sea (Japan) | 551.461 455 |
| | T2—164 55 |
| Inland seas | 551.482 9 |
| | T2—168 |
| biology | 578.763 9 |
| ecology | 577.639 |
| law of nations | 341.444 |
| Inland water transportation | 386 |
| engineering | 629.048 |
| waterways | 627.1 |
| law | 343.096 4 |
| public administration | 354.78 |
| transportation services | 386 |
| Inland water transportation | |
| workers | 386.092 |
| Inland waterway mail | 383.143 |
| Inland waterway security services | 363.287 2 |
| Inland waterways | 386 |
| engineering | 627.1 |
| hydrology | 551.48 |
| land economics | 333.915 |
| *see also* Inland water | |
| transportation | |

| | |
|---|---|
| Inlay trim | |
| furniture arts | 749.5 |
| wood handicrafts | 745.512 |
| Inlays | |
| dentistry | 617.675 |
| Inline hockey | 796.356 62 |
| Inline skater hockey | 796.356 6 |
| Inmates (Prisoners) | 365.6 |
| | T1—086 927 |
| labor economics | 331.51 |
| legal status | 344.035 6 |
| Inn (Switzerland) | T2—494 732 7 |
| Inn River | T2—436 42 |
| Austria | T2—436 42 |
| Switzerland | T2—494 732 7 |
| Innate ideas | 121.4 |
| Innate reflexes | |
| psychology | 152.322 3 |
| Innate virtues (Christian doctrine) | 234 |
| Innatism | 149.7 |
| Inner cities | |
| community redevelopment | 307.342 |
| Inner-city residents | |
| government programs | 353.533 3 |
| Inner ears | 573.89 |
| human physiology | 612.858 |
| *see also* Ears | |
| Inner Hebrides (Scotland) | T2—411 54 |
| Inner Mongolia (China) | T2—517 7 |
| Inner Mongolia | |
| Autonomous Region | |
| (China) | T2—517 7 |
| Inner product spaces | 515.733 |
| Inner tubes | 678.35 |
| Innervation | 573.85 |
| human heart | 612.178 |
| human muscles | 612.743 |
| human physiology | 612.81 |
| human respiratory system | 612.28 |
| human skin | 612.798 |
| muscles | 573.752 8 |
| *see also* Nervous system | |
| Innisfail (Qld.) | T2—943 6 |
| Innkeepers | 647.940 92 |
| Innocent passage | 341.4 |
| Innomines | 784.187 6 |
| Innovation | |
| agent of social change | 303.484 |
| executive management | 658.406 3 |
| Inns | 910.46 |
| *see also* Hotels | |
| Innsbruck (Austria) | T2—436 424 |
| Inoculation | |
| disease control | 614.47 |

İnönü, İsmet
  Turkish history … 956.102 5
Inorganic biochemistry … 572.51
  humans … 612.015 24
Inorganic chemistry … 546
  applied … 660
  *see Manual at* 541 vs. 546; *also*
    at 549 vs. 546
Inorganic drugs
  pharmacology … 615.2
Inorganic poisons
  human toxicology … 615.92
Inorganic substances
  metabolism … 572.514
    human physiology … 612.392
    *see also* Digestive system
Inosilicates
  mineralogy … 549.66
Input-output analysis … 339.23
Input-output peripherals … 004.75
  engineering … 621.398 5
Input peripherals … 004.76
  computer engineering … 621.398 6
Inquiry
  epistemology … 121.6
Inquisition (Church history) … 272.2
Insanity … 362.2
  folklore … 398.276 1
    history and criticism … 398.356 1
  legal defense … 345.04
  *see also* Mental illness
Inscriptions
  architectural design … 729.19
  prints … 769.5
  stone … 736.5
Insect control … 363.78
  environmental engineering … 628.965 7
  household sanitation … 648 7
  social welfare … 363.78
  technology
    agriculture … 632.7
  *see also* Pest control
Insect culture … 638
Insect culturists … 638.092
Insect venom
  human toxicology … 615.942
Insect waxes … 665.13
Insecta … 595.7
  *see also* Insects
Insecticide-producing plants
  agriculture … 633.898
  economic botany … 581.636

Insecticides … 632.951 7
  agricultural economics … 338.162
  agricultural use … 632.951 7
  chemical engineering … 668.651
Insectivora … 599.33
  paleozoology … 569.33
Insectivorous plants … 583.75
  *see also* Carnivorous plants
Insects … 595.7
  agricultural pests … 632.7
  arts … T3C—362 57
  coevolution with plants … 576.875
  conservation technology … 639.975 7
  control technology … 628.965 7
  disease carriers
    medicine … 614.432
  drawing … 743.657
  food … 641.396
    commercial processing … 664.95
    cooking … 641.696
  paleozoology … 565.7
  resource economics … 333.955 7
  zoology … 595.7
Inside Passage … 551.461 433
    T2—164 33
Insider trading in securities … 364.168
  law … 345.026 8
Insignia … 929.9
  armed forces … 355.134 2
    rank and service … 355.14
  religious significance … 203.7
    Christianity … 246.56
Insolvency … 332.75
Insomnia
  medicine … 616.849 82
  *see also* Nervous system
    diseases — humans
Inspection
  engineering … 620.004 4
  military administration … 355.685
  production management … 658.568
  public administration … 352.83
    external control … 352.83
    internal control … 352.35
Inspection technology … 670.425
Inspectors general
  military administration … 355.685
Inspiration
  Bible … 220.13
Instabilities in semiconductors … 537.622 6
Installations (Armed forces) … 355.7
Installations (Art style) … 709.040 74

Installment sales
  consumer credit — 332.743
  law — 346.074
   taxes — 343.055 2
Instant cameras — 771.32
Instant messaging — 004.692
Instant photography — 770
Instantaneous systems — 003.8
Instinct
  animals — 591.512
Instinctive movements
  psychology — 152.324
Institutes (Adult education) — T1—071 5
Institutes (Roman law) — 340.54
Institutional care — 361.05
  children — 362.732
  older people — 362.61
Institutional cooking — 641.57
Institutional economics
  (Economic school) — 330.155 2
Institutional grounds
  landscape architecture — 712.7
Institutional households
  household management — 647.96
Institutional housekeeping — 647
  *see Manual at* 647.068, 658.2,
   T1—0682
Institutional investment — 332.672 53
  international — 332.673 14
Institutional investors — 332.672 53
  international — 332.673 14
Institutional nursing — 610.733
Institutional publishers — 070.594
Institutionalized children
  psychology — 155.446
Institutions (Sociology) — 306
  *see Manual at* 302–307 vs. 320
Instruction services
  museology — 069.15
Instructional materials — 371.33
  primary education — 372.133
   reading — 372.412
  public control — 379.156
Instructional materials centers — 027.7
  college libraries — 027.7
  school libraries — 027.8
Instructional supervision — 371.203
Instructional technology — 371.33
Instructions to juries — 347.075 8
  criminal law — 345.075
Instrument flying — 629.132 521 4
Instrumental ensembles — 784
Instrumental forms — 784.18
Instrumentalism — 144.5

Instrumentation — T1—028 4
  aircraft — 629.135
  analytical chemistry — 543.19
  physics — 530.7
  weather reporting — 551.635
Instruments — T1—028 4
Instruments (Music) — 784.19
  *see also* Musical instruments
Insulating materials
  building materials — 691.95
  materials science — 620.195
Insulation
  building construction — 693.83
  electrical circuits — 621.319 37
  heat engineering — 621.402 4
  steam engineering — 621.185
Insulators
  electrical circuits — 621.319 37
Insulin — 572.565
  biochemistry — 572.565
  human physiology — 612.34
  pharmacology — 615.365
  *see also* Digestive system;
   Endocrine system
Insulin-dependent diabetes — 362.196 462 2
  medicine — 616.462 2
  pregnancy complications
   obstetrics — 618.364 6
  social services — 362.196 462 2
  *see also* Endocrine diseases —
   humans
Insulin therapy
  psychiatry — 616.891 2
Insurance — 368
  accounting — 657.73
  financial management — 658.153
  labor economics — 331.255
  law — 346.086
  malpractice — 346.086 02
  personnel management — 658.325 4
  public administration — 354.85
Insurance agents — 368.009 2
Insurance companies — 368.006 5
  accounting — 657.836
  credit functions — 332.38
  investment by — 332.672 532
  investment in — 332.672 2
Insurance law — 346.086
Insurance rates — 368.011
Insured mail — 383.182
  *see also* Postal service
Insurgency (Warfare) — 355.021 8
Insurgent warfare — 355.021 8
Intaglio printing — 765

| | |
|---|---|
| Intaglios | 736.223 |
| Intangible property | 346.048 |
| Intangible property risks | 368.063 |
| Integer programming | 519.77 |
| Integers | 512.72 |
| Integral calculus | 515.43 |
| Integral domains | 512.4 |
| Integral equations | 515.45 |
| numerical solutions | 518.66 |
| Integral geometry | 516.362 |
| Integral inequalities | 515.46 |
| Integral operators | 515.723 |
| Integral transforms | 515.723 |
| Integrals | 515.43 |
| Integrated circuits | 621.381 5 |
| computer engineering | 621.395 |
| Integrated development | |
| environments | 005.1 |
| Integrated optics | 621.369 3 |
| Integrated pest management | 632.9 |
| Integrated programs | 005.5 |
| Integrated services digital | |
| networks | 384 |
| engineering | 621.382 |
| Integration (Mathematics) | 515.43 |
| Integration in education | 379.263 |
| Integration theory | 515.42 |
| Integro-differential equations | 515.38 |
| Integument | 573.5 |
| animal physiology | 573.5 |
| descriptive zoology | 591.47 |
| human anatomy | 611.77 |
| human physiology | 612.79 |
| medicine | 616.5 |
| Integument diseases | |
| medicine | 616.5 |
| *see also* Skin diseases — | |
| humans | |
| Integumentary system | |
| human physiology | 612.79 |
| Intellect | 153.9 |
| philosophy | 128.3 |
| psychology | 153.9 |
| Intellectual disability | 362.3 |
| *see also* Mental retardation | |
| Intellectual freedom | 323.44 |
| library policies | 025.213 |
| Intellectual history | 001.09 |
| Intellectual life | 001.1 |
| sociology | 306.42 |
| Intellectual processes | 153 |
| children | 155.413 |
| Intellectual property | 346.048 |
| public administration | 352.749 |

| | |
|---|---|
| Intellectual property infringement | 364.166 |
| criminal law | 345.026 6 |
| Intellectualism | 149.7 |
| Intellectuals | 305.552 |
| | T1—086 222 |
| civil rights | 323.323 1 |
| relations with government | 323.323 1 |
| Intelligence | 153.9 |
| comparative psychology | 156.39 |
| educational psychology | 370.152 9 |
| evolutionary psychology | 155.7 |
| human physiology | 612.823 39 |
| philosophy | 128.3 |
| psychology | 153.9 |
| Intelligence (Animals) | 591.513 |
| Intelligence (Information) | 327.12 |
| armed forces | 355.343 2 |
| executive management | 658.472 |
| public administration | 352.379 |
| international relations | 327.12 |
| public administration | 353.17 |
| military technology | 623.71 |
| *see also* Espionage | |
| Intelligence levels | 153.9 |
| Intelligence tests | 153.93 |
| Intelligent agents (Computer | |
| software) | 006.3 |
| Intelligent road transportation | |
| systems | 388.312 |
| engineering | 625.794 |
| Intelligent vehicle-highway | |
| system | 388.312 |
| engineering | 625.794 |
| Intelligentsia | 305.552 |
| | T1—086 222 |
| Intensifying solutions | |
| photography | 771.54 |
| Intensity of light | 535.22 |
| Intensive care | 362.174 |
| medicine | 616.028 |
| nursing | 616.028 |
| social welfare | 362.174 |
| *see also* Health services | |
| Intentionality | |
| philosophy | 128.2 |
| psychology | 153.8 |
| Inter-American Development | |
| Bank | 332.153 8 |
| Interactive multimedia | 006.7 |
| cataloging | 025.344 |
| computer art | 776.7 |
| Interactive processing | 004 |
| Interactive television | |
| engineering | 621.388 |

| | |
|---|---|
| Interactive video | 006.7 |
| computer science | 006.7 |
| instructional use | 371.334 67 |
| | T1—078 567 |
| library treatment | 025.174 |
| performing arts | 791.45 |
| Interactive videotex | 004.69 |
| *see also* Computer communications | |
| Interamerican Development Bank | 332.153 8 |
| Interception of communication | |
| civil rights issue | 323.448 2 |
| Interceptor missiles | 358.174 82 |
| engineering | 623.451 94 |
| military equipment | 358.174 82 |
| Intercession of Jesus Christ | 232.8 |
| Interchangeability engineering | 620.004 5 |
| Interchangeability standards | |
| commerce | 389.62 |
| Intercoastal routes | 387.522 |
| Intercollegiate sports | 796.043 |
| Intercom systems | |
| office use | 651.79 |
| Intercontinental ballistic missiles | 358.175 482 |
| engineering | 623.451 954 |
| military equipment | 358.175 482 |
| Intercultural communication | 303.482 |
| Intercultural education | 370.117 |
| adult level | 374.017 |
| Intercultural marriage | 306.845 |
| Interdenominational cooperation | 280.042 |
| Interdependence | |
| economics | 338.9 |
| Interdisciplinary approach to knowledge | 001 |
| primary education | 372.3 |
| Interest (Income) | 332.8 |
| financial economics | 332.8 |
| central banking | 332.113 |
| law | 346.073 |
| macroeconomics | 339.21 |
| public administration | 354.86 |
| tax | 336.242 6 |
| corporations | 336.243 |
| Interest (Psychology) | |
| learning | 153.153 3 |
| Interest groups (Political science) | 322.4 |
| political process | 324.4 |
| relations with government | 322.4 |
| Interest rate futures | 332.632 3 |
| Interest rate options | 332.632 3 |
| Interface description language | 005.71 |
| Interfaces (Chemistry) | 541.33 |
| Interfacial tension | |
| chemical engineering | 660.293 |
| Interfacing (Computers) | 004.6 |
| | T1—028 546 |
| engineering | 621.398 1 |
| programming | 005.711 |
| programs | 005.713 |
| software | 005.71 |
| *see Manual at* 004.6 vs. 005.71 | |
| Interfacing protocols | |
| computer science | 004.62 |
| Interfaith marriage | 306.843 |
| Judaism | 296.444 3 |
| religion | 204.41 |
| social theology | 201.7 |
| Christianity | 261.835 843 |
| Interfaith relations | 201.5 |
| *see also* Interreligious relations | |
| Interference | |
| communications engineering | 621.382 24 |
| electronic engineering | 621.382 24 |
| microwave electronics | 621.381 31 |
| radio engineering | 621.384 11 |
| television engineering | 621.388 1 |
| Interference eliminators | |
| electronic circuits | 621.381 532 |
| radio engineering | 621.384 12 |
| Interference of light | 535.47 |
| Interferometry | 535.470 287 |
| analytical chemistry | 543.59 |
| Interferons | 571.964 4 |
| human immunology | 616.079 1 |
| pharmacology | 615.37 |
| Intergalactic matter | 523.112 5 |
| Intergovernmental administration | 353.33 |
| Intergovernmental fiscal relations | 336 |
| economics | 336 |
| law | 343.034 |
| public administration | 352.73 |
| Intergovernmental grants | 336.185 |
| law | 343.034 |
| public administration | 352.73 |
| public finance | 336.185 |
| Intergovernmental organizations | 341.2 |
| | T1—060 1 |
| bibliographies of publications | 011.52 |
| economic cooperation | 337.1 |
| *see Manual at* 337.3–.9 vs. 337.1 | |
| law of nations | 341.2 |
| public administration | 352.11 |
| Intergovernmental publishers | 070.595 |
| Intergovernmental revenues | |
| public finance | 336.18 |

| | |
|---|---|
| Intergovernmental tax relations | 336.2 |
| law | 343.04 |
| Interindustry analysis | 339.23 |
| Interior architecture | 729 |
| Interior arrangement | |
| architectural design | 729.24 |
| Interior ballistics | |
| military engineering | 623.513 |
| Interior decoration | 747 |
| arts | 747 |
| home economics | 645 |
| Interior decorators | 747.092 |
| Interior departments | 353.3 |
| Interior design | 729 |
| *see Manual at* 729 | |
| Interior furnishings | |
| arts | 747 |
| household management | 645 |
| textile arts | 746.9 |
| Interior lighting | 621.322 |
| Interior of earth | 551.11 |
| Interior painting | |
| buildings | 698.14 |
| Interior Salish languages | 497.943 |
| | T6—979 43 |
| Interior wiring | 621.319 24 |
| Interjections (Grammar) | 415.7 |
| specific languages | T4—57 |
| Interlake Region (Man.) | T2—712 72 |
| Interlaken-Oberhasli | |
| (Switzerland) | T2—494 541 8 |
| Interlibrary loans | 025.62 |
| Interlingua language | 499.993 |
| | T6—999 93 |
| Interlocking directorates | 338.87 |
| *see also* Combinations | |
| (Enterprises) | |
| Interludes (Drama) | |
| literature | 808.824 1 |
| history and criticism | 809.241 |
| specific literatures | T3B—204 1 |
| individual authors | T3A—2 |
| Interludes (Music) | 784.189 3 |
| Intermediate appellate courts | 347.033 |
| criminal law | 345.014 42 |
| Intermediate forms (Music) | 784.189 3 |
| Intermediate logic | 511.3 |
| Intermediate primary grades | 372.242 |
| Intermediate-range ballistic | |
| missiles | 358.175 382 |
| engineering | 623.451 953 |
| military equipment | 358.175 382 |
| Intermediate schools | 372.242 |
| Intermediate service (Penalty) | 364.68 |
| Intermediate state (Christian | |
| doctrine) | 236.4 |
| Intermetallic compounds | |
| metallurgy | 669.94 |
| Intermezzos | 784.189 3 |
| Intermolecular forces | |
| chemistry | 541.226 |
| Internal auditing | 657.458 |
| Internal-combustion engines | 621.43 |
| automotive | 629.25 |
| electric generation | 621.312 133 |
| ships | 623.872 3 |
| Internal commerce | 381 |
| law | 343.08 |
| public administration | 354.73 |
| Internal ear diseases | |
| medicine | 617.882 |
| *see also* Ear diseases — | |
| humans | |
| Internal ears | 573.89 |
| human anatomy | 611.85 |
| human physiology | 612.858 |
| medicine | 617.882 |
| *see also* Ears | |
| Internal friction | |
| solid-state physics | 530.416 |
| Internal management auditing | 658.401 3 |
| public administration | 352.43 |
| Internal management audits | 658.401 3 |
| public administration | 352.439 |
| Internal medicine | 616 |
| Internal migration | 304.809 |
| community sociology | 307.2 |
| Internal organization | 658.402 |
| | T1—068 4 |
| education | 371.207 |
| public administration | 352.28 |
| *see Manual at* 658.04 vs. | |
| 658.114, 658.402 | |
| Internal respiration | |
| human physiology | 612.26 |
| *see also* Respiratory system | |
| Internal revenue | 336.2 |
| law | 343.04 |
| Internal storage (Computers) | 004.53 |
| engineering | 621.397 3 |
| International administration | 352.11 |
| International agencies | |
| law | 341.2 |
| International arbitration | 327.17 |
| international politics | 327.17 |
| law of nations | 341.522 |

International assistance
  economics 338.91
  social welfare 361.26
    governmental 361.6
International Association of
  Rebekah Assemblies 366.38
  biography 366.380 92
International Bank for
  Reconstruction and
  Development 332.153 2
  law 346.082 153 2
International banking 332.15
  law 346.082 15
International banks 332.15
International borrowing 336.343 5
  public administration 352.45
  public finance 336.343 5
International business enterprises 338.88
International claims
  public administration 353.44
International commerce 382
  *see also* Foreign trade
International Committee of the
  Red Cross 361.772
International Communist
  Congress 324.175
International conflict 327.16
  law 341.5
  *see also* Wars
International cooking 641.59
International cooperation 327.17
  law 341.7
International Court of Justice 341.552
International courts 341.55
International crimes 364.135
  law 345.023 5
International Criminal Police
  Organization 363.206 01
  law 345.052
International debt 336.343 5
  public administration 352.45
  public finance 336.343 5
International development
  economics 338.91
International Development
  Association 332.153
International disputes 327.16
  law 341.5
International economic assistance 338.91
International economic
  cooperation 337

International economic
  development 338.91
  role of multinational
    enterprises 338.883
International economic law 343.07
International economic
  organizations
  law 343.07
International economic planning 337
International economic relations 337
International economics 337
International education 370.116
International enterprises 338.88
  accounting 657.96
  financial management 658.159 9
  management 658.049
    initiation 658.114 9
    organization 658.18
  taxes 336.207
International farm policies 338.181
International Federation of Red
  Cross and Red Crescent
  Societies 361.772
International finance 332.042
  law 343.03
International Finance Corporation 332.153
International forces (Military) 355.357
International governmental
  organizations 341.2
  *see also* Intergovernmental
    organizations
International grants
  public finance 336.188
International investment 332.673
  government policy 332.673 2
International labor mobility 331.127 91
International Labour Office 354.921 1
  law 344.01
International languages 401.3
International law 341
  relation to domestic law 341.04
  *see Manual at* 341 vs. 327
International legal personality 341.2
International migration 304.82
  political science 325
International Monetary Fund 332.152
  law 346.082 152
International monetary policy 332.456 6
International monetary reform 332.456 6
International monetary system 332.45
International news
  journalism 070.433 2
International offenses 364.135
  law 345.023 5

International Order of Job's
  Daughters 366.108 352
International Order of the
  Rainbow for Girls 366.108 352
International organizations 060
                T1—060 1
  bibliographies of publications 011.52
  *see also* Intergovernmental
    organizations
International party organizations 324.1
International planning
  civic art 711.2
  social services 361.26
    governmental 361.6
International politics 327.1
  history 900
International postal conventions 383.41
  law 343.099 2
International Red Cross
  Committee 361.772
International relations 303.482
  ethics 172.4
    religion 205.624
      Christianity 241.624
      Islam 297.562 4
    *see also* Political ethics
  law of nations 341.3
  legislative control 328.346
  political science 327
  public administration 353.13
  social theology 201.727
    Christianity 261.87
    Islam 297.272
    Judaism 296.382 7
  sociology 303.482
  *see Manual at* 341 vs. 327
International security forces
  law 341.72
International Serials Data
  Program 025.343 2
International settlements
  (Banking) 332.155
International social services 361.26
International Socialist Congress 324.174
International societies 369.21
International Society for Krishna
  Consciousness 294.551 2
International Standard Book
  Number 025.3
International Standard Serial
  Number 025.343 2
International style of architecture 724.6
International territories 321
  public administration 353.159

International trade 382
International trusteeships 321.08
  *see also* Semisovereign states
International understanding
  educational objective 370.116
International unions 331.880 91
  *see also* Labor unions
International welfare services
  governmental 361.6
Internationalism
  international relations 327.17
  political ideology 320.548
Internationals (Political party
  organizations) 324.1
Internet 004.678
  films 791.43
  information systems 025.042
  radio programs 791.44
  sociology 302.231
  television programs 791.45
  *see Manual at* 004.678 vs.
    006.7, 025.042, 384.33
Internet acronyms 004.601 48
Internet addiction
  medicine 616.858 4
Internet advertising 659.144
Internet auctions 381.177
  management 658.877 7
Internet banking 332.170 285 467 8
Internet marketing 381.142
  management 658.872
Internet programming 006.76
Internet publishing 070.579 73
Internet resources 025.042 2
Internet searching 025.042 5
Internet shopping 381.142
Internet telephony 384.6
  computer science 004.695
Internet voting 324.650 285 467 8
Internetworking (Computer
  networks) 004.6
Internment (Military)
  service status 355.113
Internment camp inmates T1—086 949
Internment camps 365.45
  Civil War (United States) 973.71
  Holocaust, 1933–1945 940.531 85
  Mexican War 973.621
  penology 365.45
  South African War 968.048 1
  Spanish-American War 973.891
  Vietnamese War 959.704 31
  World War I 940.317

Internment camps (continued)
 World War II  940.531 7
 *see also* Penal institutions
Interoccupational mobility 305.9
Interoceanic canals 386.42
 engineering 627.137
 law 343.096 4
 transportation services 386.42
Interoperability (Computers) 004.6
Interparliamentary unions 328.060 1
Interpersonal communication
 psychology 153.6
Interpersonal relations 302
 applied psychology 158.2
 business 650.13
 executive management 658.409 5
 personnel management 658.314 5
  executives 658.407 145
  public administration 352.66
 primary education 372.374
 sociology 302
Interplanetary matter 523.5
Interpol 363.206 01
 law 345.052
Interpolation 511.422
Interpretation
 archaeological technique 930.102 85
 linguistics 418.02
  specific languages T4—802
  specific subjects 418.03
   specific languages T4—803
 musical technique 781.46
 philosophy 121.686
 sacred books
  Hadith 297.125 16
Interpretation of tongues 234.13
Interpreters (Computer programs)
 programming languages 005.452
Interpreters (Translators) 418.020 92
 specific languages T4—802 092
Interpreting
 linguistics 418.02
  specific languages T4—802
  specific subjects 418.03
   specific languages T4—803
Interpretive dancing 792.8
Interprocess communications 005.71
Interproduct price competition 338.522
Interprovincial relations
 law 342.042
 public administration 352.133
Interracial marriage 306.846
Interregional commerce 381.5
 *see also* Commerce

Interregnum, 1254–1273 943.025
Interreligious marriage 306.843
 *see also* Interfaith marriage
Interreligious relations 201.5
 Buddhism 294.335
 Christianity 261.2
 Hinduism 294.515
 Islam 297.28
 Judaism 296.39
Interrogation
 criminal investigation 363.254
 law 345.052
Intersections (Mathematics) 516.35
Intersections (Roads) 388.13
 engineering 625.7
 transportation services 388.13
 urban 388.411
Intersex people 306.768 5
     T1—086 75
 labor economics 331.5
 psychology 155.33
 social services 362.897
 young people
  social services 362.785
Intersexuality 306.768 5
 medicine 616.694
Interstate agreements 342.042
 public administration 352.133
Interstate banking 332.16
Interstate commerce 381.5
 law 343.081 5
 *see also* Commerce
Interstate planning
 civic art 711.3
 economics 338.9
Interstate relations (Federal
 systems)
 law 342.042
 public administration 352.133
Interstellar matter 523.112 5
 Milky Way 523.113 5
Interstitial nerve tissues
 human histology 612.810 45
Intertidal biology 578.769 9
Intertidal ecology 577.699
Interurban railroads 388.46
 engineering 625.6
 transportation services 388.46
Interval analysis (Mathematics) 511.42
Intervals (Music) 781.237
Intervention (Law of nations) 341.584
Interventionism
 economics 330.126

Interviewing | 158.39
  applied psychology | 158.39
  descriptive research | 001.433
   | T1—072 3
  job hunting | 650.144
  marketing research | 658.83
  personnel selection | 658.311 24
    public administration | 352.65
  social work | 361.322
Interviews | 080
Intestinal diseases
  medicine | 616.34
  *see also* Digestive system
    diseases — humans
Intestinal obstructions
  medicine | 616.342
  *see also* Digestive system
    diseases — humans
  surgery | 617.554
Intestinal secretions | 573.373 79
  human physiology | 612.33
  *see also* Digestive system
Intestine | 573.37
  biology | 573.37
  human anatomy | 611.34
  human physiology | 612.33
  medicine | 616.34
  surgery | 617.554
  *see also* Digestive system
Intibucá (Honduras : Dept.) | T2—728 381
Intimacy
  applied psychology | 158.2
Intonation (Linguistics) | 414.6
  specific languages | T4—16
Intoxication | 362.29
  medicine | 616.86
  social welfare | 362.29
  *see also* Substance abuse
Intractable pain
  medicine | 616.047 2
Intrafamily relationships | 306.87
Intragovernmental revenues
  public finance | 336.18
Intramural college sports | 796.043
Intramural sports | 796.042
Intranets | 004.682
  computer science | 004.682
  office use | 651.792
Intraocular lenses
  ophthalmology | 617.752 4
Intraoperative care
  surgery | 617.919
Intraoperative complications
  surgery | 617.919

Intrauterine contraceptives
  health | 613.943 5
  medicine | 618.185 2
  *see also* Birth control
Intravenous anesthesia
  surgery | 617.962
Intravenous feeding
  medicine | 615.854 84
Intravenous medication
  administering | 615.6
Intravenous therapy
  medicine | 615.855
Intrinsic variables (Stars) | 523.844 2
Introduced species | 333.952 3
Introductory forms (Music) | 784.189 2
Introit | 264.36
  music | 782.323 5
Introversion | 155.232
Intrusions (Geology) | 551.88
Intuition | 153.44
  epistemology | 121.3
  ethical systems | 171.2
  psychology | 153.44
Intuitionism | 143
Intuitionistic logic
  mathematical logic | 511.36
Intuitionistic mathematics | 511.36
Inuit | T5—971 2
Inuit languages | 497.12
   | T6—971 2
Inuit literatures | 897.12
Inuktitut | T5—971 2
Inuktitut (Eastern Canada) | T5—971 24
Inuktitut language (Eastern | 497.124
  Canada) | T6—971 24
Inuktitut languages | 497.12
   | T6—971 2
Inuktitut literature (Eastern
  Canada) | 897.124
Inuktitut literatures | 897.12
Inupiat | T5—971 2
Inupiatun language | T6—971 2
Inupik language | 497.12
   | T6—971 2
Inuvik (N.W.T.) | T2—719 3
Inuvik (N.W.T. : Region) | T2—719 3
Invariant theory | 512.74
  algebra | 512.944
Invariants | 512.5
Invasion
  engineering defense | 623.31

| | |
|---|---|
| Invasion of privacy | 323.448 |
|   criminology | 364.156 |
|   law | 345.025 6 |
|     criminal law | 345.025 6 |
|     torts | 346.033 |
|   political science | 323.448 |
| Invasive species | 333.952 3 |
| Inventions | 600 |
| Inventions (Musical form) | 784.187 4 |
| Inventories (Lists) | T1—021 6 |
| Inventors | 609.2 |
| Inventory | |
|   accounting | 657.72 |
|   financial economics | 332.041 2 |
|   financial management | 658.152 44 |
|   government property | 352.54 |
|   library operations | 025.82 |
|   materials management | 658.787 |
|   military supplies | 355.621 32 |
| Inventory (Mathematics) | 519.83 |
| Invercargill District (N.Z.) | T2—939 8 |
| Inverclyde (Scotland) | T2—414 31 |
| Inverell (N.S.W.) | T2—944 4 |
| Invermere (B.C.) | T2—711 65 |
| Inverness (N.S. : County) | T2—716 91 |
| Inverness (Scotland) | T2—411 56 |
| Inverness (Scotland : District) | T2—411 56 |
| Inverse problems (Differential equations) | 515.357 |
| Inversion (Genetics) | 572.877 |
| Inversions (Mathematics) | 511.33 |
| Inversive geometry | 516.9 |
| Invertebrate viruses | 579.23 |
| Invertebrates | 592 |
|   agricultural pests | 632.62 |
|   conservation technology | 639.972 |
|   harvest and culture | 639.4 |
|   paleozoology | 562 |
|   resource economics | 333.955 |
|   zoology | 592 |
| Inverters | |
|   electronic circuits | 621.381 532 2 |
| Investigation (Research) | 001.4 |
| | T1—072 |
| Investigative power (Legislative bodies) | 328.345 2 |
| Investment | 332.6 |
|   *see also* Investments | |
| Investment advisers | 332.62 |
| Investment banking | 332.66 |
|   law | 346.066 2 |
| Investment banks | 332.66 |
| Investment casting | |
|   metals | 671.255 |
| Investment company securities | 332.632 7 |
| Investment counselors | 332.62 |
|   law | 346.092 6 |
| Investment guarantees | 368.853 |
|   *see also* Insurance | |
| Investment guides | 332.678 |
| Investment income | |
|   financial management | 658.155 4 |
|   income tax | 336.242 6 |
|   law | 343.052 46 |
| Investment law | 346.092 |
| Investment manuals | 332.678 |
| Investment prospectuses | 332.6 |
| Investment tax credit | 336.241 6 |
|   law | 343.052 37 |
| Investment trusts | 332.632 7 |
| Investments | 332.6 |
|   banking services | 332.175 4 |
|   capital formation | 332.041 5 |
|   economics | 332.6 |
|   financial management | 658.152 |
|   law | 346.092 |
|   macroeconomics | 339.43 |
|   public administration | 354.88 |
|   public revenues | 336.15 |
| Invitations | |
|   etiquette | 395.4 |
| Involuntary movement | |
|   psychology | 152.32 |
| Involuntary muscle tissues | |
|   human histology | 612.740 45 |
| Involuntary sterilization | 363.97 |
|   *see also* Sterilization (Birth control) | |
| Involutes | 516.362 |
| Involution | 512.922 |
| Involutional psychoses | |
|   medicine | 616.895 |
|   *see also* Mental disorders | |
| Inyo County (Calif.) | T2—794 87 |
| Iōannina (Greece : Nome) | T2—495 3 |
| Iodine | 553.6 |
|   chemical engineering | 661.073 4 |
|   chemistry | 546.734 |
|   economic geology | 553.6 |
|   organic chemistry | 547.02 |
|   applied | 661.891 |
|   *see also* Chemicals | |
| Ion exchange | 541.372 3 |
|   chemical engineering | 660.297 23 |
| Ion-exchange chromatography | 543.82 |

| | | | |
|---|---|---|---|
| Ion implantation | | IQ tests | 153.93 |
| solid-state physics | 530.416 | Iqaluit (Nunavut) | T2—719 52 |
| Ion optics | | Iquique (Chile : Province) | T2—831 27 |
| physics | 537.56 | IRA (Retirement account) | 332.024 014 5 |
| Ion propulsion | 621.46 | tax law | 343.052 33 |
| spacecraft | 629.475 5 | Iran | 955 |
| Ion transport | | | T2—55 |
| physiology | 572.3 | ancient | 935.7 |
| Ionia | T2—392 3 | | T2—357 |
| Ionia County (Mich.) | T2—774 54 | Iran-Iraq War, 1980–1988 | 955.054 2 |
| Ionian Islands (Greece) | T2—495 5 | Irangi (African people) | T5—963 94 |
| ancient | T2—382 | Irangi language | 496.394 |
| Ionian Sea | 551.461 386 | | T6—963 94 |
| | T2—163 86 | Iranian-Iraqi Conflict, 1980–1988 | 955.054 2 |
| Ionic equilibriums | 541.372 3 | Iranian languages | 491.5 |
| chemical engineering | 660.297 23 | | T6—915 |
| Ionic philosophy | 182.1 | Iranian literatures | 891.5 |
| Ionioi Nēsoi (Greece) | T2—495 5 | Iranian Plateau | |
| Ionization | 530.444 | ancient | 935.7 |
| chemical engineering | 660.297 22 | | T2—357 |
| chemistry | 541.372 2 | Iranians (National group) | T5—915 5 |
| meteorology | 551.561 | Iraq | 956.7 |
| plasma physics | 530.444 | | T2—567 |
| Ionization chambers | | ancient | 935 |
| nuclear physics | 539.772 | | T2—35 |
| Ionization of gases | 530.444 | Iraq-Kuwait Crisis, 1990–1991 | 956.704 42 |
| electronic physics | 537.532 | Iraq War, 2003– | 956.704 43 |
| Ionized gases | 530.44 | Iraqi-Iranian Conflict, 1980–1988 | 955.054 2 |
| Ionizing radiation | 539.722 | Iraqis | T5—927 567 |
| biophysics | 571.459 | Irbid (Jordan : Province) | T2—569 542 |
| Ionosphere | 538.767 | Irbīl (Iraq : Province) | T2—567 2 |
| | T2—161 4 | IRBM (Missiles) | 358.175 382 |
| meteorology | 551.514 5 | engineering | 623.451 953 |
| Ionospheric probes | | military equipment | 358.175 382 |
| unmanned | 629.435 2 | Iredell County (N.C.) | T2—756 793 |
| Ions | | Ireland | 941.7 |
| chemical engineering | 660.297 2 | | T2—417 |
| electrochemistry | 541.372 | ancient | 936.17 |
| Iosco County (Mich.) | T2—774 74 | | T2—361 7 |
| Iowa | 977.7 | *see Manual at* 941 | |
| | T2—777 | Ireland (Island) | 941.5 |
| Iowa County (Iowa) | T2—777 653 | | T2—415 |
| Iowa County (Wis.) | T2—775 78 | ancient | 936.15 |
| Iowa Indians | T5—975 2 | | T2—361 5 |
| Iowa language | 497.52 | Irian Barat | 995.1 |
| | T6—975 2 | | T2—951 |
| Iowa River (Iowa) | T2—777 6 | Irian Jaya (Indonesia) | 995.1 |
| IPM (Pest management) | 632.9 | | T2—951 |
| IPOs (Securities) | 658.152 24 | Irian Jaya Barat (Indonesia) | T2—951 2 |
| corporate law | 346.066 2 | Iridales | 584.38 |
| financial management | 658.152 24 | Iridium | 669.7 |
| investment economics | 332.632 2 | chemical engineering | 661.064 3 |
| Ipswich (England) | T2—426 49 | chemistry | 546.643 |
| Ipswich (Qld.) | T2—943 2 | metallography | 669.957 |

Iridium (continued)
metallurgy 669.7
physical metallurgy 669.967
*see also* Chemicals
Iringa Region (Tanzania) T2—678 25
Irion County (Tex.) T2—764 874
Iris diseases
ophthalmology 617.72
*see also* Eye diseases —
humans
Irises (Eyes)
human physiology 612.842
ophthalmology 617.72
Irises (Plants) 635.934 38
botany 584.38
floriculture 635.934 38
Irish T5—916 2
Irish Free State 941.708 22
T2—417
Irish Gaelic language 491.62
T6—916 2
Irish Gaelic literature 891.62
Irish Gaels T5—916 2
Irish harps 787.95
*see also* Stringed instruments
Irish language 491.62
T6—916 2
Irish literature
English 820
Gaelic 891.62
Irish Sea 551.461 337
T2—163 37
Irish wolfhounds 636.753 5
Irkutsk (Russia : Oblast) T2—575
Irkutskaĩa oblast' (Russia) T2—575
Iron 669.141
applied nutrition 613.285 1
architectural construction 721.044 71
biochemistry 572.517
humans 612.015 24
building construction 693.71
building material 691.7
chemical engineering 661.062 1
chemistry 546.621
economic geology 553.3
materials science 620.17
metabolism
human physiology 612.392 4
metallography 669.951 41
metallurgy 669.141
metalworking 672
mining 622.341
organic chemistry 547.056 21
applied 661.895

Iron (continued)
physical metallurgy 669.961 41
prospecting 622.183
ship design 623.818 21
shipbuilding 623.820 7
structural engineering 624.182 1
*see also* Chemicals; Metals
Iron Age 930.16
T1—090 14
Iron County (Mich.) T2—774 975
Iron County (Mo.) T2—778 883
Iron County (Utah) T2—792 47
Iron County (Wis.) T2—775 22
Iron-deficiency anemia
medicine 616.152
*see also* Cardiovascular
diseases — humans
Iron industry 338.273
metallurgy 338.476 691
mining 338.273
Iron law of wages 331.210 1
Iron soaps 668.125
Iron truss bridges
construction 624.217
Iron workers 669.109 2
metallurgy 669.109 2
metalworking 672.092
Ironbarks (Eucalypti) 583.766
*see also* Eucalyptus
Ironing
home economics 648.1
Irons (Golf equipment) 796.352 33
Ironwoods 583.48
Ironwoods (Betulaceae) 583.48
Ironwoods (Hamamelidaceae) 583.44
Ironwoods (Rhamnaceae) 583.86
Ironwork
blacksmithing 682.4
decorative arts 739.4
Irony
literature 808.801 8
history and criticism 809.918
specific literatures T3B—080 18
history and
criticism T3B—091 8
Iroquoian Indians T5—975 5
Iroquoian languages 497.55
T6—975 5
Iroquois County (Ill.) T2—773 64
Iroquois Indians T5—975 5
Irradiating foods 664.028 8
Irregular street patterns
area planning 711.41
Irregular troops 356.15

Irreligion
  religious attitude toward   201.5
    Christianity   261.21
Irrigation   333.913
  agriculture   631.587
  engineering   627.52
  land economics   333.913
  law   346.046 913
  public administration   354.367
  sewage effluent technology   628.362 3
  water pollution engineering   628.168 41
Irrigation canals
  engineering   627.52
Irritability   573.85
  cytology   571.67
  muscles   573.752 8
    human physiology   612.741
    *see also* Musculoskeletal
      system
  nerves   573.85
    human physiology   612.816
    *see also* Nervous system
  plants   575.98
  sense of touch   573.875
  sensory functions
    human physiology   612.88
  skin   573.5
    human physiology   612.791
    *see also* Skin
Irritable bowel syndrome
  medicine   616.342
    *see also* Digestive system
      diseases — humans
Irritable colon
  medicine   616.342
    *see also* Digestive system
      diseases — humans
Irwin County (Ga.)   T2—758 855
Isaac (Biblical patriarch)   222.110 92
Isabel (Solomon Islands)   T2—959 36
Isabela (Philippines :
  Province)   T2—599 1
Isabella I, Queen of Spain
  Spanish history   946.03
Isabella II, Queen of Spain
  Spanish history   946.072
Isabella County (Mich.)   T2—774 51
Isagogics
  Bible   220.61
Isaiah (Biblical book)   224.1
Isanti County (Minn.)   T2—776 64
Isauria   T2—393 5
ISBD (Bibliographic description)   025.324
ISBN (Standard book number)   025.3

Ischemic heart diseases
  medicine   616.123
  *see also* Cardiovascular
    diseases — humans
Ischia Island (Italy)   T2—457 3
ISDN (Digital networks)   384
  engineering   621.382
ISDP (Program)   025.343 2
Isère (France)   T2—445 86
Isernia (Italy : Province)   T2—457 194
  ancient   T2—377 33
Işfahān (Iran : Province)   T2—559 5
Ishikawa-ken (Japan)   T2—521 54
Isiswazi language   496.398 7
           T6—963 987
Isla de la Juventud   T2—729 125
Isla Gorge National Park
  (Qld.)   T2—943 5
Isla Grande de Tierra del
  Fuego (Argentina and
  Chile)   T2—827 6
Islam   297
  art representation   704.948 97
  arts   700.482 97
          T3C—382 97
Islam and Buddhism   294.335
  Buddhist view   294.335
  Islamic view   297.284 3
Islam and Christianity   261.27
  Christian view   261.27
  Islamic view   297.283
Islam and Hinduism   294.515
  Hindu view   294.515
  Islamic view   297.284 5
Islam and Indic religions   294
  Indic view   294
  Islamic view   297.284
Islam and Judaism   296.397
  Islamic view   297.282
  Jewish view   296.397
Islam and occultism   297.261
Islam and Sikhism   294.615
  Islamic view   297.284 6
  Sikh view   294.615
Islāmābād (Pakistan)   T2—549 149
Islāmābād Capital Territory
  (Pakistan)   T2—549 149
Islamic calendar   529.327
Islamic education   297.77
  *see Manual at* 207.5, 268 vs.
    200.71, 230.071, 292–299
Islamic ethics   297.5

Islamic fundamentalism
   political science — 320.557
   religion — 297.09
Islamic holidays — 297.36
   customs — 394.265 7
   *see also* Holidays
Islamic ideologies
   political science — 320.557
Islamic law — 340.59
   religion — 297.14
Islamic legends — 297.18
Islamic philosophy — 181.07
Islamic regions — T2—176 7
Islamic schools (General
   education) — 371.077
Islamic shrines — 297.35
   architecture — 726.2
Islamism
   political science — 320.557
   *see Manual at* 320.557 vs.
      297.09, 297.272, 322.1
Island Carib Indians — T5—979 2
Island County (Wash.) — T2—797 75
Island of Skye (Scotland) — T2—411 54
Islands — 551.42
       T2—142
   biology — 578.752
   ecology — 577.52
   geography — 910.914 2
   geomorphology — 551.42
   physical geography — 910.021 42
Islands authorities
   (Scotland) — T2—411 3
Islands of Langerhans — 573.377
   biology — 573.377
   human anatomy — 611.37
   human physiology — 612.34
   medicine — 616.46
   surgery — 617.557
   *see also* Digestive system;
      Endocrine system
Islands of Langerhans diseases
   medicine — 616.46
   *see also* Endocrine
      diseases — humans
Islands of the Arctic — T2—98
   Canada — T2—719 52
Islands of the Atlantic — 997
       T2—97
Islands of the Pacific — 990
       T2—9
Islas de la Bahía (Honduras) — T2—728 315
Islas Malvinas — 997.11
       T2—971 1

Isle of Anglesey (Wales) — T2—429 21
Isle of Axholme (England) — T2—428 32
Isle of Capri (Italy) — T2—457 3
Isle of Ely (England) — T2—426 53
Isle of Man — T2—427 9
Isle of Orléans (Quebec) — T2—714 476
Isle of Rhum (Scotland) — T2—411 54
Isle of Rum (Scotland) — T2—411 54
Isle of Skye (Scotland) — T2—411 54
Isle of Wight (England) — T2—422 8
Isle of Wight County (Va.) — T2—755 54
Isle of Youth — T2—729 125
Isle Royale (Mich.) — T2—774 997
Isle Royale National Park
   (Mich.) — T2—774 997
Isles of Scilly (England) — T2—423 79
Islet (Quebec : Regional
   County Municipality) — T2—714 74
Isleta Indians — T5—974 97
Isleta language — 497.497
       T6—974 97
Islets of Langerhans — 573.377
   *see also* Islands of Langerhans
Islington (London, England) — T2—421 43
Islwyn (Wales) — T2—429 76
Ismailia (Egypt : Province) — T2—621 5
Ismaïlia (Morocco :
   Prefecture) — T2—645
Ismailis (Islamic sect) — 297.822
Ismailites
   Hadith — 297.125 922
Isobutylene rubber — 678.72
Isoetales — 587.9
   paleobotany — 561.79
Isolation
   disease control — 614.45
   social psychology — 302.545
Isomerases — 572.79
   *see also* Enzymes
Isomers — 547.122 52
   inorganic chemistry — 541.225 2
   organic chemistry — 547.122 52
Isometric exercises — 613.714 9
Isometric projection
   technical drawing — 604.245
Isomorphism — 511.326
   crystallography — 548.3
   mathematics — 511.326
Isonitriles — 547.044
   chemical engineering — 661.894
Isopoda — 595.372
Isoptera — 595.736
Isotope structure — 539.74

Isotopes
  chemical engineering    660.298 8
  radiochemistry    541.388
Isparta İli (Turkey)    T2—564 3
  ancient    T2—392 7
Isrā'    297.633
Israel    956.94
    T2—569 4
  ancient    933.4
    T2—334
  Biblical geography and history  220.9
  Christian theology    231.76
  Jewish theology    296.311 73
Israel-Arab War, 1948–1949    956.042
Israel-Arab War, 1967    956.046
Israel-Arab War, 1973    956.048
Israel-Lebanon-Syria Conflict,
  1982–1985    956.052
Israelis    T5—924
Israelites    T5—924
Issaquena County (Miss.)    T2—762 412
ISSN (Standard serial number)    025.343 2
Issuing houses    332.66
Istanbul (Turkey)    T2—496 18
  ancient    T2—398 618
İstanbul İli (Turkey)    T2—496 18
  Asia    T2—563 2
    ancient    T2—393 13
  Europe    T2—496 18
Isthmus of Corinth (Greece)  T2—495 22
Isthmus of Suez (Egypt)    T2—621 5
Istiophoridae    597.78
Istria (Croatia)    T2—497 2
  ancient    T2—373 9
Isuridae    597.33
Itä-Suomen lääni (Finland)  T2—489 75
Itala Game Preserve (South
  Africa)    T2—684 2
Italian Communist Party    324.245 075 2
Italian Democratic Socialist Party
  (1952–1995)    324.245 072 2
Italian Democratic Socialist Party
  (2004– )    324.245 072
Italian folk music    781.625 1
Italian folk songs    782.421 625 1
Italian greyhound    636.76
Italian language    450
    T6—51
Italian Liberal Party (1943–1994)  324.245 04
Italian Liberal Party (2004– )    324.245 04
Italian literature    850

Italian Peninsula    945
    T2—45
  ancient    937
    T2—37
Italian Popular Party
  (1919–1926)    324.245 028 2
Italian Popular Party
  (1994–2002)    324.245 082
Italian Republican Party    324.245 05
Italian Riviera (Italy)    T2—451 8
Italian Social Movement
  (Political party)    324.245 038
Italian Social Movement-Right
  National (Political party)    324.245 038
Italian Socialist Party    324.245 074 2
Italian Somaliland    T2—677 3
Italian Wars, 1494–1559    945.06
Italianate revivals
  architecture    724.52
Italians    T5—51
Italic calligraphy    745.619 77
Italic languages    470
    T6—7
Italic literatures    870
Italic peoples    T5—4
Italic type    686.224 7
Italo-Ethiopian War, 1935–1936  963.056
Italy    945
    T2—45
  ancient    937
    T2—37
Italy (Kingdom)    945.082
Italy, Central    945.6
    T2—456
Italy, Northern    945.1
    T2—451
Italy, Southern    945.7
    T2 —457
  ancient    T2—377
Itapúa (Paraguay)    T2—892 126
Itasca County (Minn.)    T2—776 78
Itawamba County (Miss.)    T2—762 982
Iterative methods    518.26
Ithaca (N.Y.)    T2—747 71
Ithaca Island (Greece)    T2—495 5
  ancient    T2—383
Ithna Asharites (Islamic sect)    297.821
  Hadith    297.125 921
Itzá Indians    T5—974 27
Itzá language    497.427
    T6—974 27

IUD (Contraceptive)
health 613.943 5
medicine 618.185 2
*see also* Birth control
Iudaea T2—334 9
Ivan, the Terrible
Russian history 947.043
Ivan III, Grand Duke of Russia
Russian history 947.041
Ivan IV, Czar of Russia
Russian history 947.043
Ivan VI, Emperor of Russia
Russian history 947.061
Ivano-Frankivs´k (Ukraine :
Oblast) T2—477 9
Ivano-Frankivs´ka oblast´
(Ukraine) T2—477 9
Ivanovo (Russia : Oblast) T2—473 3
Ivanovskaĩa oblast´ (Russia) T2—473 3
Ivies 635.933 84
botany 583.84
floriculture 635.933 84
Ivoirians T5—966 68
Ivorians T5—966 68
Ivory
manufacturing technology 679.43
Ivory carving 736.62
Ivory Coast 966.68
T2—666 8
Ivory Coast people T5—966 68
Ivrea (Margravate) 945.103
Iwate-ken (Japan) T2—521 14
IWW (Labor) 331.886 097 3
Ixonanthaceae 583.79
Ixopo (South Africa :
District) T2—684 7
Izabal (Guatemala : Dept.) T2—728 131
Izard County (Ark.) T2—767 27
İzmir İli (Turkey) T2—562 5
ancient T2—392 3
İzmit (Turkey) T2—563 3

# J

J document (Biblical criticism) 222.106 6
Jacamars 598.72
Jacanas 598.33
Jacanidae 598.33
Jack County (Tex.) T2—764 544
Jack-in-the-pulpits 584.64
Jackals 599.772

Jackets (Clothing) 391.46
commercial technology 687.14
indoor garments 687.113
outdoor garments 687.14
customs 391.46
indoor garments 391.473
outdoor garments 391.46
home sewing 646.45
indoor garments 646.433
outdoor garments 646.45
*see also* Clothing
Jackrabbits 599.328
Jacks (Fishes) 597.72
Jacks (Lifting mechanisms) 621.877
Jackson (Miss.) T2—762 51
Jackson, Andrew
United States history 973.56
Jackson County (Ala.) T2—761 95
Jackson County (Ark.) T2—767 97
Jackson County (Colo.) T2—788 66
Jackson County (Fla.) T2—759 93
Jackson County (Ga.) T2—758 145
Jackson County (Ill.) T2—773 994
Jackson County (Ind.) T2—772 23
Jackson County (Iowa) T2—777 64
Jackson County (Kan.) T2—781 335
Jackson County (Ky.) T2—769 183
Jackson County (Mich.) T2—774 28
Jackson County (Minn.) T2—776 235
Jackson County (Miss.) T2—762 12
Jackson County (Mo.) T2—778 41
Jackson County (N.C.) T2—756 95
Jackson County (Ohio) T2—771 85
Jackson County (Okla.) T2—766 45
Jackson County (Or.) T2—795 27
Jackson County (S.D.) T2—783 572
Jackson County (Tenn.) T2—768 51
Jackson County (Tex.) T2—764 127
Jackson County (W. Va.) T2—754 31
Jackson County (Wis.) T2—775 51
Jackson Parish (La.) T2—763 92
Jacksonville (Fla.) T2—759 12
Jacob (Biblical patriarch) 222.110 92
Jacobi polynomials 515.55
Jacobite Church 281.63
*see also* Eastern churches
Jacobite Patriarchate of Antioch 281.63
*see also* Eastern churches
Jacob's ladders (Plants)
botany 583.94
Jacobsdal (South Africa :
District) T2—685 8
Jacquard-weave fabrics 677.616
*see also* Textiles

Jacquard-weave rugs
  arts    746.72
Jacques-Cartier (Quebec)    T2—714 474
Jacques-Cartier National
  Park (Quebec)    T2—714 48
Jacques-Cartier River
  (Quebec)    T2—714 474
Jade    553.876
  economic geology    553.876
  glyptics    736.24
  jewelry    739.27
  materials science    620.198
  mining    622.387 6
  occultism    133.255 387 6
    divination    133.322
  prospecting    622.188 76
Jadīda (Morocco : Province)    T2—646 2
Jadite    553.876
  *see also* Jade
Jaegers    598.338
Jaén (Spain : Province)    T2—468 3
Jagan, Cheddi
  Guyanese history    988.103 31
Jagan, Janet
  Guyanese history    988.103 32
Jagdeo, Bharrat
  Guyanese history    988.103 33
Jagellon dynasty    943.802 3
Jagersfontein (South
  Africa : District)    T2—685 7
Jaguar    599.755
  big game hunting    799.277 55
  conservation technology    639.979 755
  resource economics    333.959 755
Jahangir, Emperor of Hindustan
  Indian history    954.025 6
Jahn-Teller effect (Physics)    530.416
Jail breaks    365.641
Jails    365.34
  *see also* Penal institutions
Jain architecture    720.954
Jain philosophy    181.044
Jain sculpture    730.954
Jain temples and shrines    294.435
  architecture    726.144
Jainism    294.4
  art representation    704.948 944
  arts    700.482 944
     T3C—382 944
Jains
  biography    294.409 2
Jaipuri dialect    491.479 7
     T6—914 79
Jaipuri literature    891.479

Jakarta (Indonesia)    T2—598 22
Jakun (Malaysian people)    T5—992 8
Jakun language    499.28
     T6—992 8
Jalapa (Guatemala : Dept.)    T2—728 142
Jalisco (Mexico)    T2—723 5
Jamaica    972.92
     T2—729 2
Jamaica bayberry    583.765
Jamaican literature    810
Jamaicans    T5—969 729 2
Jambi (Indonesia)    T2—598 15
James (Biblical book)    227.91
James, William
  personality theory    155.264
James I, King of England
  British history    941.061
  English history    942.061
  Scottish history    941.106 1
James I, King of Scotland
  Scottish history    941.104
James II, King of England
  British history    941.067
  English history    942.067
  Scottish history    941.106 7
James II, King of Scotland
  Scottish history    941.104
James III, King of Scotland
  Scottish history    941.104
James IV, King of Scotland
  Scottish history    941.104
James V, King of Scotland
  Scottish history    941.104
James VI, King of Scotland
  Scottish history    941.106 1
  1567–1603    941.105
  1603–1625    941.106 1
James Bay Region (Ont. and
  Quebec)    T2—714 115
James City County (Va.)    T2—755 425 1
James River (N.D. and S.D.)    T2—783 3
  North Dakota    T2—784 5
  South Dakota    T2—783 3
James River (Va.)    T2—755 4
Jameson raid, 1895–1896    968.204 75
Jammeh, A. J. J.
  Gambian history    966.510 32
Jammu and Kashmir (India)    T2—546
Jams    641.852
  commercial processing    664.152
  home preparation    641.852
Jämtland landskap (Sweden)    T2—488 3
Jämtlands län (Sweden)    T2—488 3
Jan Mayen Island    T2—983

| | |
|---|---|
| Jansenism | 273.7 |
| denominations | 284.84 |
| Jansenville (South Africa : District) | T2—687 51 |
| Janūb Dārfūr (Sudan : State) | T2—627 |
| Janūb Kurdufān (Sudan) | T2—628 |
| Janūb Sīnā' (Egypt) | T2—531 |
| Japan | 952 |
| | T2—52 |
| Japan, Sea of | 551.461 454 |
| | T2—164 54 |
| Japan Current | 551.462 145 |
| Japanese | T5—956 |
| Japanese beetles | 595.764 9 |
| agricultural pests | 632.764 9 |
| Japanese calendar | 529.329 56 |
| Japanese cedar | 585.5 |
| Japanese chess | 794.18 |
| Japanese chin | 636.76 |
| Japanese Communist Party | 324.252 075 |
| Japanese flower arrangements | 745.922 52 |
| Japanese flowering cherry | 635.977 373 |
| Japanese ink painting | 751.425 2 |
| Japanese language | 495.6 |
| | T6—956 |
| Japanese literature | 895.6 |
| Japanese macaque | 599.864 4 |
| Japanese medlars | 641.341 6 |
| *see also* Loquats | |
| Japanese quail | 598.627 2 |
| Japanese religions | 299.56 |
| Japanese river fever | |
| incidence | 614.526 4 |
| medicine | 616.922 4 |
| *see also* Communicable diseases — humans | |
| Japanese spaniel | 636.76 |
| Japanning | |
| decorative arts | 745.726 |
| technology | 667.75 |
| Jar cutting | |
| decorative arts | 748.202 86 |
| Jarai | T5—992 2 |
| Jarash (Jordan : Province) | T2—569 548 |
| Jardins-de-Napierville (Quebec) | T2—714 35 |
| Jargon | 417.2 |
| specific languages | T4—7 |
| Jarḥ wa al-Ta'dīl (Hadith) | 297.125 26 |
| Jars | 688.8 |
| glass | 666.192 |
| decorative arts | 748.82 |
| technology | 666.192 |
| *see also* Containers | |
| Jasmines | 583.87 |
| botany | 583.87 |
| floriculture | 635.933 87 |
| perfume crop | 633.81 |
| Jasper County (Ga.) | T2—758 583 |
| Jasper County (Ill.) | T2—773 74 |
| Jasper County (Ind.) | T2—772 977 |
| Jasper County (Iowa) | T2—777 594 |
| Jasper County (Miss.) | T2—762 575 |
| Jasper County (Mo.) | T2—778 72 |
| Jasper County (S.C.) | T2—757 98 |
| Jasper County (Tex.) | T2—764 159 |
| Jasper National Park (Alta.) | T2—712 332 |
| Jász-Nagykun-Szolnok Megye (Hungary) | T2—439 8 |
| Jatakas | 294.382 325 |
| Jaundice | |
| medicine | 616.362 5 |
| *see also* Digestive system diseases — humans | |
| Java (Indonesia) | T2—598 2 |
| Java man | 569.97 |
| Java Sea | 551.461 474 |
| | T2—164 74 |
| Java War, 1825–1830 | 959.802 23 |
| Javan pig | 599.633 2 |
| Javanese | T5—992 22 |
| Javanese language | 499.222 |
| | T6—992 22 |
| Javanese literature | 899.222 |
| Javelin hurling | 796.435 |
| Jawa (Indonesia) | T2—598 2 |
| Jawa Barat (Indonesia) | T2—598 24 |
| Jawa Tengah (Indonesia) | T2—598 26 |
| Jawa Timur (Indonesia) | T2—598 28 |
| Jawāmi' | |
| Hadith | 297.125 4 |
| Jawara, Dawda Kairaba | |
| Gambian history | 966.510 31 |
| Jawless fishes | 597.2 |
| Jaws | |
| fractures | |
| medicine | 617.156 |
| human anatomy | 611.92 |
| human physiology | 612.92 |
| regional medicine | 617.522 |
| surgery | 617.522 |
| Jay County (Ind.) | T2—772 67 |
| Jays | 598.864 |
| conservation technology | 639.978 864 |
| resource economics | 333.958 864 |
| Jaza'ir (Algeria : Province) | T2—653 |
| Jazīrah (Sudan : State) | T2—626 4 |

| | |
|---|---|
| Jazz | 781.65 |
| songs | 782.421 65 |
| Jazz bands | 784.416 5 |
| Jazz dancing | 793.3 |
| Jazz ensembles | 785.065 |
| Jazz musicians | 781.650 92 |
| singers | 782.421 650 92 |
| Jazz pianists | 786.216 509 2 |
| Jazz saxophonists | 788.716 509 2 |
| Jazz singers | 782.421 650 92 |
| Jazz trumpeters | 788.921 650 92 |
| Jazz vocals | 782.421 65 |
| Jealousy | 152.48 |
| ethics | 179.8 |
| religion | 205.698 |
| psychology | 152.48 |
| *see also* Vices | |
| Jean I, King of France | |
| French history | 944.024 |
| Jean II, King of France | |
| French history | 944.025 |
| Jeep cavalry | 357.54 |
| Jeeps | 388.342 |
| driving | 629.283 |
| engineering | 629.222 |
| military engineering | 623.747 22 |
| repair | 629.287 2 |
| transportation services | 388.342 |
| *see also* Automobiles | |
| Jeff Davis County (Ga.) | T2—758 827 |
| Jeff Davis County (Tex.) | T2—764 934 |
| Jefferson, Thomas | |
| United States history | 973.46 |
| 1801–1805 | 973.46 |
| 1805–1809 | 973.48 |
| Jefferson City (Mo.) | T2—778 55 |
| Jefferson County (Ala.) | T2—761 78 |
| Jefferson County (Ark.) | T2—767 79 |
| Jefferson County (Colo.) | T2—788 84 |
| Jefferson County (Fla.) | T2—759 87 |
| Jefferson County (Ga.) | T2—758 663 |
| Jefferson County (Idaho) | T2—796 58 |
| Jefferson County (Ill.) | T2—773 793 |
| Jefferson County (Ind.) | T2—772 13 |
| Jefferson County (Iowa) | T2—777 94 |
| Jefferson County (Kan.) | T2—781 37 |
| Jefferson County (Ky.) | T2—769 44 |
| Jefferson County (Miss.) | T2—762 283 |
| Jefferson County (Mo.) | T2—778 67 |
| Jefferson County (Mont.) | T2—786 67 |
| Jefferson County (N.Y.) | T2—747 57 |
| Jefferson County (Neb.) | T2—782 332 |
| Jefferson County (Ohio) | T2—771 69 |
| Jefferson County (Okla.) | T2—766 52 |
| Jefferson County (Or.) | T2—795 85 |
| Jefferson County (Pa.) | T2—748 62 |
| Jefferson County (Tenn.) | T2—768 924 |
| Jefferson County (Tex.) | T2—764 145 |
| Jefferson County (W. Va.) | T2—754 99 |
| Jefferson County (Wash.) | T2—797 98 |
| Jefferson County (Wis.) | T2—775 85 |
| Jefferson Davis County (Miss.) | T2—762 543 |
| Jefferson Davis Parish (La.) | T2—763 55 |
| Jefferson Parish (La.) | T2—763 38 |
| Jehovah's Witnesses | 289.92 |
| biography | 289.920 92 |
| Holocaust, 1933–1945 | 940.531 808 828 992 |
| *see also* Christian denominations | |
| Jejunal diseases | |
| medicine | 616.34 |
| *see also* Digestive system diseases — humans | |
| Jejunitis | |
| medicine | 616.344 |
| *see also* Digestive system diseases — humans | |
| Jejunum | 573.378 |
| biology | 573.378 |
| human anatomy | 611.341 |
| medicine | 616.34 |
| surgery | 617.554 1 |
| *see also* Digestive system | |
| Jelenia Góra (Poland : Voivodeship) | T2—438 52 |
| Jellies (Gelatin desserts) | 641.864 2 |
| commercial processing | 664.26 |
| home preparation | 641.864 2 |
| Jellies (Preserves) | 641.852 |
| commercial processing | 664.152 |
| home preparation | 641.852 |
| Jelly fungi | 579.59 |
| Jellyfishes | 593.53 |
| Jellying agents | |
| commercial processing | 664.25 |
| Jena (Germany) | T2—432 22 |
| Jenkins County (Ga.) | T2—758 693 |
| Jenkins' Ear, War of, 1739–1741 | 946.055 |
| Jennings County (Ind.) | T2—772 17 |
| Jerada (Morocco : Province) | T2—643 3 |
| Jerauld County (S.D.) | T2—783 32 |
| Jerboas | 599.35 |
| Jeremiah (Biblical book) | 224.2 |
| Jerome County (Idaho) | T2—796 35 |
| Jersey (Channel Islands) | T2—423 41 |
| Jersey cattle | 636.224 |
| Jersey City (N.J.) | T2—749 27 |

| | | | |
|---|---|---|---|
| Jersey County (Ill.) | T2—773 855 | Jet planes (continued) | |
| Jerusalem | T2—569 442 | transportation services | 387.733 49 |
| ancient | T2—334 42 | *see also* Aircraft | |
| sacred place | | Jet pumps | 621.691 |
| Christianity | 263.042 569 442 | Jet skiing | 797.37 |
| Judaism | 296.482 | Jet streams (Meteorology) | 551.518 3 |
| Jerusalem artichoke sugar | 641.336 | Jethou (Channel Islands) | T2—423 47 |
| commercial processing | 664.139 | Jetties | |
| food | 641.336 | engineering | 627.24 |
| *see also* Sugar | | Jevons, William Stanley | |
| Jerusalem artichoke syrup | 641.336 | economic school | 330.157 |
| commercial processing | 664.139 | Jewelers | 739.270 92 |
| food | 641.336 | Jewell County (Kan.) | T2—781 22 |
| *see also* Sugar | | Jewelry | 391.7 |
| Jerusalem artichokes | 641.352 4 | customs | 391.7 |
| agriculture | 635.24 | making | 739.27 |
| cooking | 641.652 4 | costume jewelry | 688.2 |
| food | 641.352 4 | handicrafts | 745.594 2 |
| Jerusalem Bible | 220.520 7 | fine jewelry | 739.27 |
| Jerusalem district (Israel) | T2—569 44 | theft of | 364.162 873 927 |
| Jerusalem district (West | | law | 345.026 287 392 7 |
| Bank) | T2—569 52 | Jewelweeds | 583.79 |
| Jerusalem Talmud | 296.124 | Jewish apocalypses | |
| Jessamine County (Ky.) | T2—769 483 | pseudepigrapha | 229.913 |
| Jessamines | 583.87 | Jewish architecture | |
| *see also* Jasmines | | ancient | 722.33 |
| Jestbooks | 808.882 | Jewish Autonomous Region | |
| *see also* Jokes | | (Russia) | T2—577 |
| Jests | 808.882 | Jewish Bible | 221 |
| *see also* Jokes | | *see Manual at* 221 | |
| Jesuits | 255.53 | Jewish calendar | 529.326 |
| church history | 271.53 | religion | 296.43 |
| Jesus Christ | 232 | Jewish-Christian dialogue | 261.26 |
| art representation | 704.948 53 | Christian theology | 261.26 |
| arts | 700.482 32 | Jewish theology | 296.396 |
| | T3C—382 32 | Jewish Christians (Sects) | 289.9 |
| biography | 232.901 | Jewish cooking | 641.567 6 |
| Gospel text and criticism | 226 | Jewish day schools | 371.076 |
| *see Manual at* 230–280 | | Jewish education | 296.68 |
| Islam | 297.246 5 | *see Manual at* 207.5, 268 vs. | |
| Jewish interpretations | 232.906 | 200.71, 230.071, 292–299 | |
| rationalistic interpretations | 232.9 | Jewish holidays | 296.43 |
| Jésus Island (Quebec) | T2—714 271 | customs | 394.267 |
| Jesus prayer | 242.72 | liturgy | 296.453 |
| Jet (Precious stone) | 553.87 | *see also* Holidays | |
| *see also* Semiprecious stones | | Jewish law | 340.58 |
| Jet engines | 621.435 2 | religion | 296.18 |
| aircraft | 629.134 353 | Jewish philosophy | 181.06 |
| Jet fuel | 665.538 25 | Jewish Publication Society Bible | 221.520 8 |
| Jet planes | 387.733 49 | Jewish religious schools | 296.680 83 |
| engineering | 629.133 349 | Jewish sacred music | 781.76 |
| military engineering | 623.746 044 | public worship | 782.36 |
| military equipment | 358.418 3 | music | 782.36 |
| | | religion | 296.462 |

| | | | |
|---|---|---|---|
| Jewish sculpture | 732.3 | Jivaroan languages | 498.37 |
| Jews | T5—924 | | T6—983 7 |
| civilization | 909.049 24 | Jizah (Egypt) | |
| Holocaust, 1933–1945 | 940.531 8 | ancient | T2—322 |
| social aspects | 305.892 4 | Jīzah (Egypt : Province) | T2—622 |
| Jews (Religious group) | T1—088 296 | Jnana yoga | 294.543 6 |
| biography | 296.092 | Jo Daviess County (Ill.) | T2—773 343 |
| specific denominations | 296.8 | Joachim, Saint | 232.933 |
| role of leaders | 296.61 | private prayers to | 242.75 |
| social aspects | 305.696 | Job (Biblical book) | 223.1 |
| Jew's harps | 786.887 | Job analysis | 658.306 |
| *see also* Percussion instruments | | military personnel | 355.614 |
| Jharkhand (India : State) | T2—541 27 | personnel management | 658.306 |
| Jiangsu Sheng (China) | T2—511 36 | public administration | 352.64 |
| Jiangxi dialects | 495.172 22 | Job applications | 650.142 |
| | T6—951 7 | Job banks | 331.128 |
| Jiangxi Sheng (China) | T2—512 22 | Job burnout | 158.723 |
| Jicarilla Apache language | 497.25 | Job classification | 658.306 |
| | T6—972 5 | military personnel | 355.614 |
| Jicarilla Indians | T5—972 5 | personnel management | 658.306 |
| Jig saws | 621.934 | public administration | 352.64 |
| wood handicrafts | 745.513 | Job control languages | 005.434 |
| Jigawa State (Nigeria) | T2—669 77 | Job creation | 331.120 424 |
| Jigs (Tools) | 621.992 | government policy | 331.120 424 |
| Jigsaw puzzles | 793.73 | *see Manual at* 331.120424 | |
| Jihad | 297.72 | vs. 331.1377 | |
| Jihlavský kraj (Czech | | public administration | 354.927 |
| Republic) | T2—437 22 | Job description | 658.306 |
| Jihočeský kraj (Czech | | military personnel | 355.614 |
| Republic) | T2—437 13 | personnel management | 658.306 |
| Jihomoravský kraj (Czech | | libraries | 023.7 |
| Republic) | T2—437 24 | public administration | 352.64 |
| Jijel (Algeria : Province) | T2—655 | Job enrichment | |
| Jījil (Algeria : Province) | T2—655 | personnel management | 658.314 23 |
| Jilin Sheng (China) | T2—518 8 | Job evaluation | |
| Jim Hogg County (Tex.) | T2—764 482 | personnel management | 658.306 |
| Jim Wells County (Tex.) | T2—764 465 | Job hunting | 650.14 |
| Jimi River (Papua New | | Job information | 331.128 |
| Guinea) | T2—956 5 | Job mobility | 331.127 |
| Jimsonweed | 583.952 | Job openings | 331.124 |
| Jin dynasty | 931.04 | Job opportunities | 331.124 |
| Jindjibandji language | 499.15 | Job rights | 331.011 |
| | T6—991 5 | law | 344.010 1 |
| Jingpho-Konyak-Bodo languages | 495.4 | Job satisfaction | 331.012 |
| | T6—954 | labor economics | 331.012 |
| Jinn | 297.217 | personnel management | 658.314 22 |
| Jinnah, Mahomed Ali | | public administration | 352.66 |
| Pakistani history | 954.904 2 | psychology | 158.7 |
| Jinotega (Nicaragua : Dept.) | T2—728 522 | Job security | 331.259 6 |
| Jipijapa | 584.62 | law | 344.012 596 |
| Jita language | 496.395 | public employees | 342.068 6 |
| | T6—963 95 | public administration | 354.98 |
| Jitterbug | 793.33 | Job sharing | 331.257 277 |

| | |
|---|---|
| Job stress | 158.72 |
| executive management | 658.409 5 |
| labor economics | 331.256 |
| Job training | 370.113 |
| *see also* Vocational education | |
| Job vacancies | 331.124 |
| Jobbers (Wholesalers) | |
| commerce | 381.2 |
| Jobs | |
| openings | 331.124 |
| personal success | 650.14 |
| Jockeys | 798.400 92 |
| Joel (Biblical book) | 224.7 |
| Jogging | 613.717 2 |
| Johannesburg (South Africa : District) | T2—682 21 |
| John (Biblical books) | 226.5 |
| Epistles | 227.94 |
| gospel | 226.5 |
| Revelation | 228 |
| John, King of England | |
| English history | 942.033 |
| John, the Baptist, Saint | 232.94 |
| John I, King of France | |
| French history | 944.024 |
| John II, King of France | |
| French history | 944.025 |
| John III, King of Sweden | |
| Swedish history | 948.503 23 |
| John IV, Negus of Ethiopia | |
| Eritrean history | 963.504 2 |
| Ethiopian history | 963.042 |
| John Brown's Raid, 1859 | |
| Civil War (United States) cause | 973.711 6 |
| John Dories | 597.64 |
| Johnson, Andrew | |
| United States history | 973.81 |
| Johnson, Lyndon B. (Lyndon Baines) | |
| United States history | 973.923 |
| Johnson County (Ark.) | T2—767 33 |
| Johnson County (Ga.) | T2—758 676 |
| Johnson County (Ill.) | T2—773 996 |
| Johnson County (Ind.) | T2—772 515 |
| Johnson County (Iowa) | T2—777 655 |
| Johnson County (Kan.) | T2—781 675 |
| Johnson County (Ky.) | T2—769 245 |
| Johnson County (Mo.) | T2—778 455 |
| Johnson County (Neb.) | T2—782 276 |
| Johnson County (Tenn.) | T2—768 99 |
| Johnson County (Tex.) | T2—764 524 |
| Johnson County (Wyo.) | T2—787 35 |
| Johnson-Sirleaf, Ellen | |
| Liberian history | 966.620 34 |
| Johnston County (N.C.) | T2—756 41 |
| Johnston County (Okla.) | T2—766 68 |
| Johnston Island | T2—969 9 |
| Johor | T2—595 1 |
| Joinery | 684.08 |
| construction | 694.6 |
| ship hulls | 623.844 |
| woodworking | 684.08 |
| Joining equipment | 621.97 |
| Joining metals | 671.5 |
| decorative arts | 739.14 |
| sculpture | 731.41 |
| Joint chiefs of staff | 355.330 42 |
| Joint committees | |
| legislative bodies | 328.365 7 |
| Joint custody | 346.017 3 |
| Joint diseases | 573.783 9 |
| animals | 573.783 9 |
| humans | |
| medicine | 616.72 |
| *see also* Musculoskeletal diseases — humans | |
| Joint operations (Armed forces) | 355.46 |
| Joint stock companies | 338.7 |
| *see also* Business enterprises; Unincorporated business enterprises | |
| Joint tenancy | 346.042 |
| Joint ventures | 338.7 |
| law | 346.068 2 |
| management of enterprises | 658.044 |
| initiation | 658.114 4 |
| *see Manual at* 658.04 vs. 658.114, 658.402 | |
| *see also* Business enterprises | |
| Joints (Body parts) | 573.78 |
| diseases | 573.783 9 |
| extremities | |
| surgery | 617.580 59 |
| human anatomy | 611.72 |
| human physiology | 612.752 |
| medicine | 616.72 |
| surgery | 617.472 |
| *see also* Musculoskeletal system | |
| Joints (Geology) | 551.84 |
| Jokebooks | 808.882 |
| *see also* Jokes | |

| | |
|---|---|
| Jokes | 808.882 |
|   folk literature | 398.7 |
|   literature | 808.882 |
|     history and criticism | 809.982 |
|     specific literatures   T3B—802 | |
|       individual authors   T3A—8 | |
|   *see Manual at* T1—0207 vs. | |
|     T3B—7, T3A—8 + 02, | |
|     T3B—802, T3B—8 + 02, | |
|     T3A—8 + 07, T3B—807, | |
|     T3B—8 + 07 | |
| Joliette (Quebec : Regional | |
|   County Municipality)   T2—714 42 | |
| Jonah (Biblical book) | 224.92 |
| Jonathan, Leabua | |
|   Lesotho history | 968.850 31 |
| Jones County (Ga.)   T2—758 567 | |
| Jones County (Iowa)   T2—777 63 | |
| Jones County (Miss.)   T2—762 55 | |
| Jones County (N.C.)   T2—756 21 | |
| Jones County (S.D.)   T2—783 577 | |
| Jones County (Tex.)   T2—764 733 | |
| Jönköpings län (Sweden)   T2—486 4 | |
| Jonquière (Saguenay, | |
|   Quebec)   T2—714 162 | |
| Jonquils | 635.934 34 |
|   botany | 584.34 |
|   floriculture | 635.934 34 |
| Jordan | 956.95 |
| | T2—569 5 |
|   ancient | 933.5 |
| | T2—335 |
| Jordan algebras | 512.48 |
| Jordan River   T2—569 4 | |
| Jordanians   T5—927 569 5 | |
| Jos (Nigeria)   T2—669 52 | |
| Joseph (Son of Jacob) | 222.110 92 |
| Joseph, Saint | 232.932 |
|   private prayers to | 242.75 |
| Joseph I, Emperor of Germany | |
|   German history | 943.051 |
| Joseph II, Holy Roman Emperor | |
|   German history | 943.057 |
| Joseph Bonaparte, King of Spain | |
|   Spanish history | 946.06 |
| Josephine County (Or.)   T2—795 25 | |
| Josephson effect (Physics) | 530.416 |
| Joshua (Biblical book) | 222.2 |
| Joshua Tree National Park | |
|   (Calif.)   T2—794 97 | |
| Joual | 447.971 4 |
| | T6—41 |
| Joubertina (South Africa : | |
|   District)   T2—687 51 | |
| Joule's law | 536.71 |
| Journalism | 070.4 |
|   arts   T3C—39 | |
|   civil rights issues | 323.445 |
|   sociology | 302.23 |
| Journalists | 070.92 |
|   occupational ethics | 174.907 |
| Journals (Diaries) | 920 |
| | T1—092 |
| Journals (Mechanisms) | 621.821 |
| Journals (Serials) | 050 |
| | T1—05 |
|   *see also* Serials | |
| Joy | 152.42 |
| Joysticks (Computers) | 004.76 |
|   engineering | 621.398 6 |
| Ju-chen (Manchurian | |
|   people)   T5—941 | |
| Ju-chen language | 494.1 |
| | T6—941 |
| Juab County (Utah)   T2—792 44 | |
| Juan Carlos I, King of Spain | |
|   Spanish history | 946.083 |
| Juan de Fuca Strait (B.C. and | 551.461 432 |
|   Washington)   T2—164 32 | |
| Juárez, Benito | |
|   Mexican history | 972.07 |
| Jubilees | |
|   customs | 394.4 |
| Judaea   T2—334 9 | |
| Judah   T2—334 9 | |
| Judaism | 296 |
|   art representation | 704.948 96 |
|   arts | 700.482 96 |
| | T3C—382 96 |
|   Christian polemics | 239.2 |
|   Islamic polemics | 297.292 |
| Judaism and Christianity | 261.26 |
|   Christian view | 261.26 |
|   Jewish view | 296.396 |
| Judaism and Islam | 296.397 |
|   Islamic view | 297.282 |
|   Jewish view | 296.397 |
| Judaism and occultism | 296.371 |
| Judas's betrayal of Jesus Christ | 232.961 |
| Jude (Biblical book) | 227.97 |
| Judeo-Arabic language | 492.77 |
| | T6—927 |
| Judeo-Arabic literature | 892.7 |
| Judeo-German language | 439.1 |
| | T6—391 |
| Judeo-German literature | 839.1 |
| Judeo-Spanish language | 467.949 6 |
| | T6—67 |

| | |
|---|---|
| Judeo-Spanish literature | 860 |
| Judges (Biblical book) | 222.32 |
| Judges (Jurists) | 347.014 |
|   criminal courts | 345.012 4 |
|   occupational ethics | 174.3 |
| Judges (Rulers) | |
|   Palestinian history | 933.02 |
| Judging competitions | T1—079 |
| Judging livestock | 636.081 1 |
| Judgment | |
|   epistemology | 121 |
|   psychology | 153.46 |
| Judgment Day | 202.3 |
|   Christianity | 236.9 |
|   Islam | 297.23 |
| Judgments (Law) | 347.077 |
| Judicial administration | 347.013 |
|   criminal law | 345.012 3 |
| Judicial assistance | 345.052 |
| Judicial branch of government | 347 |
| Judicial cooperation | 347.012 |
|   criminal law | 345.012 2 |
| Judicial discretion | 347.012 |
|   criminal law | 345.012 2 |
| Judicial error | 347.012 |
|   criminal law | 345.012 2 |
| Judicial-executive relations | 320.404 |
|   law | 342.044 |
| Judicial institutions | |
|   sociology | 306.25 |
| Judicial-legislative relations | 320.404 |
|   law | 342.044 |
| Judicial power | 347.012 |
|   chief executives | 352.235 |
|   legislatures | 328.345 3 |
| Judicial process | 347.05 |
| Judicial review | 347.012 |
|   criminal law | 345.012 2 |
| Judicial statistics | 347.013 |
| Judith (Deuterocanonical book) | 229.24 |
| Judith Basin County (Mont.) | T2—786 62 |
| Judo | 796.815 2 |
| Juggling | 793.87 |
| Juglandales | 583.49 |
| Jugnauth, Aneerood | |
|   Mauritian history | 969.820 42 |
| Juices (Beverages) | 641.34 |
|   commercial processing | 663.63 |
|   home preparation | 641.875 |
| Jujitsu | 796.815 2 |
| Jujubes | 641.342 |
|   botany | 583.86 |
|   cooking | 641.642 |

| | |
|---|---|
| Jujubes (continued) | |
|   food | 641.342 |
|   orchard crop | 634.2 |
| Jujuy (Argentina : Province) | T2—824 1 |
| Jukeboxes | 621.389 33 |
| Jula language | 496.345 |
| | T6—963 45 |
| Julian calendar | 529.42 |
| Juliana, Queen of the Netherlands | |
|   Dutch history | 949.207 2 |
| July Monarchy | 944.063 |
| Jum'ah | 297.36 |
| Jumble sales | 381.195 |
| Jump rope rhymes | 398.8 |
| Jumpers (Athletes) | 796.432 092 |
| Jumping | |
|   field sports | 796.432 |
|   horses | 798.25 |
|   skiing | 796.933 |
| Jumping mice | 599.35 |
| Juncaginaceae | 584.74 |
| Juncales | 584.82 |
| Juncos | 598.883 |
| Junction diodes | 621.381 522 |
| Junction transistors | 621.381 528 2 |
| Juncture (Linguistics) | 414.6 |
|   specific languages | T4—16 |
| June beetles | 595.764 9 |
| June bugs | 595.764 9 |
| Juneau (Alaska) | T2—798 2 |
| Juneau County (Wis.) | T2—775 55 |
| Juneberries | 641.347 4 |
|   botany | 583.73 |
|   cooking | 641.647 4 |
|   food | 641.347 4 |
|   horticulture | 634.74 |
| Junee (N.S.W.) | T2—944 8 |
| Jungermanniales | 588.3 |
| Jungian psychology | 150.195 4 |
|   personality theory | 155.264 4 |
| Jungle diseases | |
|   medicine | 616.988 3 |
|   *see also* Environmental | |
|     diseases — humans | |
| Jungle fowl | 598.625 |
| Jungle tactics | 355.423 |
| Jungles | 333.75 |
| | T2—152 |
|   biology | 578.734 |
|   ecology | 577.34 |
|   *see also* Forest lands | |
| Juniata County (Pa.) | T2—748 47 |
| Juniata River (Pa.) | T2—748 45 |
| Junín (Peru : Dept.) | T2—852 4 |

| | | | | |
|---|---|---|---|---|
| Junior colleges (Two-year | | Justice | | |
| colleges) | 378.154 3 | arts | T3C—353 | |
| Junior high schools | 373.236 | ethics | 172.2 | |
| *see also* Secondary education | | religion | 205.622 | |
| Junior schools (Primary schools) | 372 | Buddhism | 294.356 22 | |
| *see also* Primary education | | Christianity | 241.622 | |
| Junipers | 585.4 | Hinduism | 294.548 622 | |
| Junk bonds | 332.632 34 | Islam | 297.562 2 | |
| Junqalī (Sudan : State) | T2—629 3 | Judaism | 296.362 2 | |
| Jupiter (Planet) | 523.45 | law | 340.114 | |
| | T2—992 5 | literature | 808.803 53 | |
| astrology | 133.536 | history and criticism | 809.933 53 | |
| unmanned flights to | 629.435 45 | specific literatures | T3B—080 353 | |
| Jura (France) | T2—444 7 | history and | | |
| Jura (Switzerland) | T2—494 36 | criticism | T3B—093 53 | |
| Jura Mountains (France and | | political science | 320.011 | |
| Switzerland) | T2—494 3 | public administration | 353.4 | |
| France | T2—444 5 | social theology | 201.76 | |
| Switzerland | T2—494 3 | Christianity | 261.8 | |
| Jura-Nord Vaudois | | Islam | 297.27 | |
| (Switzerland) | T2—494 522 5 | Judaism | 296.38 | |
| Jurassic period | 551.766 | Justice of God | 214 | |
| geology | 551.766 | *see also* Theodicy | | |
| paleontology | 560.176 6 | Justices of the peace | 347.016 | |
| Jurchen (Manchurian | | occupational ethics | 174.3 | |
| people) | T5—941 | Justification (Christian doctrine) | 234.7 | |
| Jurchen language | 494.1 | Jute | 677.13 | |
| | T6—941 | agricultural economics | 338.173 54 | |
| Juries | 347.075 2 | botany | 583.68 | |
| criminal law | 345.075 | fiber crop | 633.54 | |
| Jurisdiction | | textiles | 677.13 | |
| courts | 347.012 | arts | 746.041 3 | |
| criminal law | 345.012 2 | economics | 338.476 771 3 | |
| *see Manual at* 347 | | *see also* Textiles | | |
| government | 342.041 | Jute pulp | 676.14 | |
| law of nations | 341.4 | Jutiapa (Guatemala : Dept.) | T2—728 143 | |
| persons (legal concept) | 342.08 | Jutland (Denmark) | T2—489 5 | |
| territory | 342.041 3 | Juvenile correctional institutions | 365.42 | |
| Jurisprudence | 340 | *see also* Penal institutions | | |
| Juristic acts | 346.02 | Juvenile courts | 345.081 | |
| Juristic persons | 346.013 | Juvenile delinquency | 364.36 | |
| Jurists (Judges) | 347.014 092 | school problem | 371.782 | |
| Jurists (Lawyers) | 340.092 | Juvenile delinquents | 364.36 | |
| Jury ethics | 174.3 | | T1—086 923 | |
| Jury instructions | 347.075 8 | home care | 649.153 | |
| Jury selection | 347.075 2 | law | 345.03 | |
| criminal law | 345.075 | pastoral care | | |
| Jury trial | 347.052 | Christianity | 259.5 | |
| criminal law | 345.056 | penal institutions | 365.42 | |
| Just war theory | | *see also* Penal institutions | | |
| ethics | 172.42 | Juvenile justice | 364.36 | |
| religion | 205.624 2 | criminology | 364.36 | |
| Christianity | 241.624 2 | law | 345.08 | |

Juvenile literature 808.899 282
  history and criticism 809.892 82
  reviews 028.162
  rhetoric 808.068
  specific literatures T3B—080 928 2
   history and criticism T3B—099 282
Juvenile procedure 345.08

# K

K-mesons 539.721 62
K-theory 512.66
  algebra 512.66
  topology 514.23
Kabardian language 499.962 4
  T6—999 624
Kabardino-Balkaria (Russia) T2—475 2
Kabardino-Balkariĩa
  (Russia) T2—475 2
Kabbalah 296.16
*see also* Cabala
Kabuki theater 792.095 2
Kabwe man 569.98
Kabyle language 493.34
  T6—933 4
Kabyle literature 893.34
Kabyles T5—933
Kacem (Morocco :
  Province) T2—643 5
Kachin language 495.4
  T6—954
Kaczyński, Lech
  Polish history 943.805 73
Kadai languages 495.9
  T6—959
Kadai literatures 895.9
Kadai peoples T5—959
Kadarites (Islamic sect) 297.835
Kaduna State (Nigeria) T2—669 73
Kaffraria T2—687 5
Kafiri languages 491.49
  T6—914 9
Kafiri literatures 891.49
Kafirs (Afghanistan people) T5—914 9
Kafr al-Shaykh (Egypt) T2—621
Kagawa-ken (Japan) T2—523 5
Kagera Region (Tanzania) T2—678 27
Kagoshima-ken (Japan) T2—522 6
Kahoolawe (Hawaii) T2—969 22
Kahramanmaraş İli (Turkey) T2—565 3
  ancient T2—393 6
Kaikoura District (N.Z.) T2 937 8
Kainah Indians T5—973 52
Kaipara District (N.Z.) T2—931 8

Kaka languages 496.396
  T6—963 96
Kakapo 598.71
  conservation technology 639.978 71
  resource economics 333.958 71
Kako languages 496.396
  T6—963 96
Kala-azar
  incidence 614.534
  medicine 616.936 4
  *see also* Communicable
   diseases — humans
Kalahari Desert T2—688 3
  Botswana T2—688 3
  South Africa T2—687 11
Kalahari Gemsbok National
  Park (South Africa) T2—687 12
Kalām (Islam) 297.2
Kalam District (Pakistan) T2—549 122
Kalamazoo County (Mich.) T2—774 17
Kalanga language (Tanzania and
  Congo) 496.394
  T6—963 94
Kalāt District (Pakistan) T2—549 153
Kalâtdlisut language 497.12
  T6—971 2
Kalawao County (Hawaii) T2—969 24
Kalbarri National Park
  (W.A.) T2—941 2
Kale 641.353 47
  cooking 641.653 47
  food 641.353 47
  garden crop 635.347
Kalenjin language 496.5
  T6—965
Kalgoorlie (W.A.) T2—941 6
Kalimantan (Indonesia) T2—598 3
Kalimantan Barat
  (Indonesia) T2—598 32
Kalimantan Island T2—598 3
Kalimantan Selatan
  (Indonesia) T2—598 36
Kalimantan Tengah
  (Indonesia) T2—598 34
Kalimantan Timur
  (Indonesia) T2—598 38
Kalinga-Apayao
  (Philippines) T2—599 1
Kalinin (Russia : Oblast) T2—472 8
Kaliningrad (Russia :
  Oblast) T2—472 4
Kaliningradskaĩa oblast'
  (Russia) T2—472 4

Kalininskaĩa oblast'
  (Russia)      T2—472 8
Kalispel Indians      T5—979 435
Kalispel literature      897.943 5
Kalispel-Pend d'Oreille language   497.943 5
     T6—979 435
Kalisz (Poland :
  Voivodeship)      T2—438 49
Kalkaska County (Mich.)      T2—774 65
Kallitype processes      772.16
Kalmar län (Sweden)      T2—486 3
Kalmar Union      948.03
  Danish history      948.902
  Norwegian history      948.101
  Swedish history      948.501 82
Kalmias      583.66
Kalmuck language      494.2
     T6—942
Kalmyk      T5—942
Kalmyk language      494.2
     T6—942
Kalmyk-Oirat language      T6—942
Kalmykia (Russia)      T2—474 8
Kalmykiĩa (Russia)      T2—474 8
Kaluga (Russia : Oblast)      T2—472 6
Kaluzhskaĩa oblast' (Russia)   T2—472 6
Kam-Sui languages      495.9
     T6—959
Kam-Sui literatures      895.9
Kam-Sui peoples      T5—959
Kamakura period      952.021
Kamba (African people)      T5—963 953
Kamba language      496.395 3
     T6—963 953
Kamchatka (Russia : Oblast)   T2—577
Kamchatskaĩa oblast'
  (Russia)      T2—577
Kamerun      967.110 2
     T2—671 1
Kames      551.315
Kamhlushwa (South Africa :
  District)      T2—682 72
Kamloops (B.C.)      T2—711 72
Kamouraska (Quebec :
  Regional County
  Municipality)      T2—714 75
Kampala (Uganda)      T2—676 1
Kampuchea      959.604 2
     T2—596
Kan dialects      495.172 22
     T6—951 7
Kanabec County (Minn.)      T2—776 63
Kanagawa-ken (Japan)      T2—521 36
Kananaskis Country (Alta.)   T2—712 332

Kanaq (Malaysian people)   T5—992 8
Kanarese      T5—948 14
Kanarese language      494.814
     T6—948 14
Kanarese literature      894.814
Kanawha County (W. Va.)   T2—754 37
Kanawha River (W. Va.)      T2—754 3
Kandh (Dravidian people)   T5—948 24
Kandh language      494.824
     T6—948 24
Kandh literature      894.824
Kandiyohi County (Minn.)   T2—776 48
Kane County (Ill.)      T2—773 23
Kane County (Utah)      T2—792 51
Kanem (Kingdom)      967.430 1
     T2—674 3
Kanem-Bornu (Kingdom)      966.980 1
Kanem-Bornu Empire      T2—669 8
Kanembu (African people)   T5—965
Kanembu language      496.5
     T6—965
Kangaroo Island (S. Aust.)   T2—942 35
Kangaroo mice      599.359 8
Kangaroo rats      599.359 87
Kangaroos      599.222
  big game hunting      799.272 22
  conservation technology   639.979 222
  resource economics      333.959 222
Kangiqsliniq (Nunavut)      T2—719 58
KaNgwane (South Africa)   T2—682 72
Kankakee County (Ill.)      T2—773 63
Kankan (Guinea)      T2—665 2
Kannada language      494.814
     T6—948 14
Kannada literature      894.814
Kano State (Nigeria)      T2—669 78
Kansa Indians      T5—975 25
Kansas      978.1
     T2—781
Kansas City (Kan.)      T2—781 39
Kansas City (Mo.)      T2—778 411
Kansas City jazz      781.653
Kansas River (Kan.)      T2—781 3
Kansu Province (China)      T2—514 5
Kantianism      142.3
Kantō Region (Japan)      T2—521 3
Kanuri language      496.5
     T6—965
Kaolack (Senegal : Region)   T2—663
Kaolin      553.61
  economic geology      553.61
  mining      622.361
Kaolinite
  mineralogy      549.67

| | | | |
|---|---|---|---|
| Kaonde language | 496.393 | Karen languages | 495 |
| | T6—963 93 | | T6—95 |
| Kaons | 539.721 62 | Kari languages (Bantu) | 496.394 |
| Kapadokya (Turkey) | T2—564 1 | | T6—963 94 |
| Kapiti Coast District (N.Z.) | T2—936 1 | Karlovarský kraj (Czech | |
| Kapok | | Republic) | T2—437 15 |
| botany | 583.68 | Karlsruhe (Germany) | T2—434 643 6 |
| fiber crop | 633.56 | Karlsruhe (Germany : | |
| materials science | 620.195 | Landkreis) | T2—434 643 |
| textiles | 677.23 | Karlsruhe (Germany : | |
| *see also* Textiles | | Regierungsbezirk) | T2—434 64 |
| Kaposi's sarcoma | | Karma | 202.2 |
| incidence | 614.599 947 7 | Buddhism | 294.342 2 |
| medicine | 616.994 77 | Hinduism | 294.522 |
| *see also* Cancer — humans | | Karma yoga | 294.543 6 |
| Kara-Kalpak language | 494.34 | Karnak (Egypt) | T2—323 |
| | T6—943 4 | Karnataka (India) | T2—548 7 |
| Kara Sea | 551.461 325 | Karnes County (Tex.) | T2—764 444 |
| | T2—163 25 | Kärnten (Austria) | T2—436 6 |
| Karachaevo-Cherkesiīa | | Karo, Joseph ben Ephraim | |
| (Russia) | T2—475 2 | Jewish legal codes | 296.182 |
| Karachay-Balkar language | 494.38 | Karoo (South Africa) | T2—687 39 |
| | T6—943 8 | Karoo, Great (South Africa) | T2—687 39 |
| Karachay-Cherkessia | | Karoo, Little (South Africa) | T2—687 38 |
| (Russia) | T2—475 2 | Karoo, Northern (South | |
| Karachi (Pakistan : District) | T2—549 183 | Africa) | T2—687 13 |
| Karagwe (Kingdom) | 967.610 1 | Karoo, Upper (South | |
| | T2—676 1 | Africa) | T2—687 13 |
| Karaim language | 494.38 | Karoo National Park (South | |
| | T6—943 8 | Africa) | T2—687 39 |
| Karaites | 296.81 | Karpathos Island (Greece) | T2—495 87 |
| Karak (Jordan : Province) | T2—569 563 | ancient | T2—391 7 |
| Karakalpak (Uzbekistan) | T2—587 | Kars İli (Turkey) | T2—566 26 |
| Karakalpak language | 494.34 | ancient | T2—395 5 |
| | T6—943 4 | Karsts | 551.447 |
| Karakoram Range | T2—546 | | T2—144 |
| Karaman İli (Turkey) | T2—564 5 | *see also* Caves | |
| ancient | T2—392 7 | Karting | 796.76 |
| Karanga (African people) | T5—963 975 | Karts (Racing cars) | 796.76 |
| Karanga kingdoms | 968.910 1 | driving | 629.284 8 |
| Karanga language | 496.397 5 | engineering | 629.228 |
| | T6—963 975 | repair | 629.287 8 |
| Karate | 796.815 3 | sports | 796.76 |
| physical fitness | 613.714 8 | Kartvelian languages | 499.968 |
| Karbalā' (Iraq : Province) | T2—567 5 | | T6—999 68 |
| Karbük İli (Turkey) | T2—563 7 | Kasaï-Occidental (Congo) | T2—675 123 |
| Karditsa (Greece : Nome) | T2—495 4 | Kasaï-Oriental (Congo) | T2—675 126 |
| Karelia (Region) | T2—471 5 | Kascm language | 496.35 |
| Karelia (Russia) | T2—471 5 | | T6—963 5 |
| Karelian language | 494.54 | Kasena language | 496.35 |
| | T6—945 4 | | T6—963 5 |
| Karelian literature | 894.54 | Kashmir | T2—546 |
| Karelians | T5—945 4 | India | T2—546 |
| Karen | T5—95 | Pakistan | T2—549 13 |

Kashmiri language 491.499
    T6—914 99
Kashmiri literature 891.499
Kashmiris T5—914 99
Kashrut 296.73
Kashubian language 491.85
    T6—918 5
Kashubian literature 891.85
Kashubians T5—918 5
Kashubs T5—918 5
Kassalā (Sudan : State) T2—625
Kassel (Germany) T2—434 124
Kassel (Germany :
    Regierungsbezirk) T2—434 12
Kastamonu İli (Turkey) T2—563 7
    ancient T2—393 17
Kastoria (Greece : Nome) T2—495 62
Katanga (Congo) T2—675 18
Katanning (W.A.) T2—941 2
Katharevusa language (Modern 489.3
    Greek) T6—89
Katharevusa literature (Modern
    Greek) 889
Katherine (N.T.) T2—942 95
Katherine Gorge National
    Park (N.T.) T2—942 95
Kativik Regional
    Administration (Quebec) T2—714 111
Katmai National Park and
    Preserve (Alaska) T2—798 4
Katoomba (N.S.W.) T2—944 5
Katowice (Poland :
    Voivodeship) T2—438 58
Katsina State (Nigeria) T2—669 76
Katsura tree 583.43
Kattang language 499.15
    T6—991 5
Kattegat (Denmark and Sweden) 551.461 334
    T2—163 34
Katukinan languages 498.9
    T6—989
Katydids 595.726
Kauai (Hawaii) T2—969 41
Kauai County (Hawaii) T2—969 4
Kaufman County (Tex.) T2—764 277
Kaunda, Kenneth D. (Kenneth
    David)
    Zambian history 968.940 41
Kauris 585.3
    forestry 634.975 93
Kavala (Greece : Nome) T2—495 7
Kavieng (Papua New
    Guinea) T2—958 3

Kavirondo language (Nilotic) 496.5
    T6—965
Kaw River (Kan.) T2—781 3
Kawar T5—914 92
Kawartha Lakes (Ont.) T2—713 64
Kawartha Lakes (Ont. :
    Lakes) T2—713 67
Kawau Island (N.Z. : Island) T2—932 1
Kawerau (N.Z.) T2—934 26
Kawerau District (N.Z.) T2—934 26
Kay County (Okla.) T2—766 24
Kayaking 797.122 4
Kayseri İli (Turkey) T2—564 12
    ancient T2—393 4
Kazak language 494.345
    T6—943 45
Kazak literature 894.345
Kazakh language 494.345
    T6—943 45
Kazakh literature 894.345
Kazakhs T5—943 45
Kazakhstan 958.45
    T2—584 5
Kazaks T5—943 45
Kazoo 783.99
Kearney County (Neb.) T2—782 394
Kearny County (Kan.) T2—781 425
Kearsarge and Alabama, Battle
    of, 1864 973.754
Keating, Paul
    Australian history 994.065
Keats Island (B.C. : Island) T2—711 31
Kebbi State (Nigeria) T2—669 63
Kechika River (B.C.) T2—711 85
Kechua Indians T5—983 23
Kechua language 498.323
    T6—983 23
Kechua literature 898.323
Kechuan Indians T5—983 23
Kechuan languages 498.323
    T6—983 23
Kedah T2—595 1
Keeling Islands 969.9
    T2—699
Keene's cement 666.92
Keeshond 636.72
Keewatin (Nunavut) T2—719 58
Keffa (Ethiopia) T2—633
Kegs
    wooden 674.82
Keiskammahoek (South
    Africa : District) T2—687 55
Keith County (Neb.) T2—782 89

Kejimkujik National Park
  (N.S.)    T2—716 33
Kekchí Indians    T5—974 2
Kekchí language    497.42
   T6—974 2
Kelaa des Srarhna
  (Morocco : Province)    T2—646 4
Kelâat Es-Sraghna
  (Morocco : Province)    T2—646 4
Kelantan    T2—595 1
Kele languages (Democratic    496.396
  Republic of Congo)    T6—963 96
Kele languages (Gabon)    496.396
   T6—963 96
Kelim    296.123 6
Kelowna (B.C.)    T2—711 5
Kelps    579.887
  resource economics    333.953 8
Kemerovo (Russia : Oblast)    T2—573
Kemerovskaĩa oblast′
  (Russia)    T2—573
Kemper County (Miss.)    T2—762 683
Kempo    796.815 9
Kempsey (N.S.W.)    T2—944 3
Kempton Park (South
  Africa : District)    T2—682 25
Kenaf
  botany    583.685
  fiber crop    633.56
Kenai Fjords National Park
  (Alaska)    T2—798 3
Kenai Peninsula (Alaska)    T2—798 3
Kenai Peninsula Borough
  (Alaska)    T2—798 3
Kendall County (Ill.)    T2—773 263
Kendall County (Tex.)    T2—764 886
Kendo    796.86
Kenedy County (Tex.)    T2—764 473
Kenhardt District (South
  Africa)    T2—687 12
Kénitra (Morocco :
  Province)    T2—643 5
Kennebec County (Me.)    T2—741 6
Kennebec River (Me.)    T2—741 22
Kennedy, John F. (John
  Fitzgerald)
  United States history    973.922
Kennelly-Heaviside layers    538.767 3
Kennels (Dog housing)    636.708 31
Kennet (England)    T2—423 17
Kenora (Ont. : District)    T2—713 112
  Patricia Portion    T2—713 1
Kenosha County (Wis.)    T2—775 98

Kensington and Chelsea
  (London, England)    T2—421 34
Kent (England)    T2—422 3
Kent (N.B. : County)    T2—715 22
Kent (Ont. : County)    T2—713 33
Kent County (Del.)    T2—751 4
Kent County (Md.)    T2—752 36
Kent County (Mich.)    T2—774 55
Kent County (R.I.)    T2—745 4
Kent County (Tex.)    T2—764 738
Kentani (South Africa :
  District)    T2—687 58
Kenton County (Ky.)    T2—769 35
Kentrikē Makedonia
  (Greece)    T2—495 65
Kentucky    976.9
   T2—769
Kentucky Lake (Ky. and
  Tenn.)    T2—769 895
Kentucky River    T2—769 3
Kenya    967.62
   T2—676 2
Kenyans    T5—967 62
Kenyatta, Jomo
  Kenyan history    967.620 41
Keogh plans    332.024 014 5
  tax law    343.052 33
Keokuk County (Iowa)    T2—777 91
Kephallēnia (Greece)    T2—495 5
Kepler's laws    521.3
Kepulauan Bangka Belitung
  (Indonesia)    T2—598 196
Kepulauan Riau (Indonesia)    T2—598 192
Kerala (India)    T2—548 3
Keratin    572.67
  *see also* Proteins
Keratinous material products    679.4
Keratosis
  medicine    616.544
  *see also* Skin diseases —
    humans
Kerbs    625.888
Kérékou, Mathieú
  Beninese history    966.830 51
  1972–1991    966.830 51
  1996–2006    966.830 53
Kerensky, Aleksandr
  Fyodorovich
  Russian history    947.084 1
Keres language    497.9
   T6—979
Keresan Indians    T5—979
Kerguelen Islands    969.9
   T2—699

| | |
|---|---|
| Keritot | 296.123 5 |
| Babylonian Talmud | 296.125 5 |
| Mishnah | 296.123 5 |
| Kerkyra (Greece : Nome) | T2—495 5 |
| Kermadec Islands | T2—939 9 |
| Kermān (Iran : Province) | T2—558 2 |
| Kermānshāhān (Iran : Province) | T2—555 6 |
| Kern County (Calif.) | T2—794 88 |
| Kerosene | 665.538 3 |
| Kerosene lamps | 621.323 |
| *see also* Lighting | |
| Kerr County (Tex.) | T2—764 884 |
| Kerrier (England) | T2—423 7 |
| Kerry (Ireland) | T2—419 6 |
| Kershaw County (S.C.) | T2—757 61 |
| Keski-Suomen lääni (Finland) | T2—489 73 |
| Keski-Suomi (Finland) | T2—489 73 |
| Kesteven (England) | T2—425 35 |
| Kestrels | 598.96 |
| Ket | T5—946 |
| Ket language | 494.6 |
| | T6—946 |
| Ketchikan Gateway Borough (Alaska) | T2—798 2 |
| Ketchup | 641.814 |
| commercial processing | 664.58 |
| home preparation | 641.814 |
| Kete language | 496.393 |
| | T6—963 93 |
| Kethubim | 223 |
| Ketones | 547.036 |
| aromatic chemistry | 547.636 |
| chemical engineering | 661.85 |
| Kettering (England : Borough) | T2—425 52 |
| Kettle River (B.C. and Wash.) | T2—711 62 |
| Kettle-shaped drums | 786.93 |
| *see also* Percussion instruments | |
| Kettledrums | 786.93 |
| *see also* Percussion instruments | |
| Kettles (Geologic landforms) | 551.315 |
| Ketubbot | 296.123 3 |
| Babylonian Talmud | 296.125 3 |
| Mishnah | 296.123 3 |
| Palestinian Talmud | 296.124 3 |
| Ketuvim | 223 |
| Keuka Lake (N.Y.) | T2—747 82 |
| Kewa language | 499.12 |
| | T6—991 2 |
| Kewaunee County (Wis.) | T2—775 62 |
| Keweenaw County (Mich.) | T2—774 995 |
| Keweenaw Peninsula (Mich.) | T2—774 99 |
| Key accounts | |
| marketing management | 658.804 |
| sales personnel organization | 658.810 2 |
| Key West (Fla.) | T2—759 41 |
| Key word indexing | 025.486 |
| Keya Paha County (Neb.) | T2—782 725 |
| Keyboard bands | 784.6 |
| Keyboard electrophones | 786.59 |
| *see also* Keyboard instruments | |
| Keyboard idiophones | 786.83 |
| *see also* Percussion instruments | |
| Keyboard instruments | 786 |
| bands and orchestras | 784 |
| chamber ensembles | 785 |
| mixed | 785.2 |
| single type | 785.62–.65 |
| construction | 786.192 3 |
| by hand | 786.192 3 |
| by machine | 681.86 |
| solo music | 786 |
| Keyboard stringed instruments | 786 |
| *see also* Keyboard instruments | |
| Keyboard wind instruments | 786.5 |
| *see also* Keyboard instruments | |
| Keyboarding | 652.3 |
| Keyboards (Computers) | 004.76 |
| engineering | 621.398 6 |
| Keynesian economics | 330.156 |
| Keys | 683.32 |
| Keyword indexing | 025.486 |
| Kgalagadi Transfrontier Park | T2—687 12 |
| Khabarovsk (Russia : Kray) | T2—577 |
| Khabarovskiĭ kraĭ (Russia) | T2—577 |
| Khairpūr District (Pakistan) | T2—549 17 |
| Khakassia (Russia) | T2—575 |
| Khakasskaia respublika (Russia) | T2—575 |
| Khalaj language (Turkic) | 494.36 |
| | T6—943 6 |
| Khalji dynasty | 954.023 4 |
| Khalkha | T5—942 3 |
| Khalkha Mongolian language | 494.23 |
| | T6—942 3 |
| Khalkha Mongolian literature | 894.23 |
| Khama, Seretse | |
| Botswana history | 968.830 31 |
| Khama, Seretse Khama Ian | |
| Botswana history | 968.830 34 |
| Khamti | T5—959 19 |

Khánh Hòa (Vietnam :
  Province)             T2—597 5
Khantia-Mansia (Russia)   T2—573
Khanty                T5—945 1
Khanty language         494.51
                      T6—945 1
Khanty literature        894.51
Khanty-Mansiĭskiĭ
  avtonomnyĭ okrug
  (Russia)              T2—573
Kharia language         495.95
                      T6—959 5
Kharias                T5—959 5
Kharijites            297.83
Kharkiv (Ukraine : Oblast)   T2—477 5
Kharkivs´ka oblast´
  (Ukraine)           T2—477 5
Khartoum (Sudan : State)   T2—626 2
Kharṭūm (Sudan : State)   T2—626 2
Khasi                 T5—959 3
Khasi language          495.93
                      T6—959 3
Khaskovo (Bulgaria :
  Oblast)             T2—499 6
Khaskovska oblast
  (Bulgaria)          T2—499 6
Khat
  alkaloidal crop        633.7
  botany             583.85
Khātamī, Muḥammad
  Iranian history       955.054 4
Khémisset (Morocco :
  Province)             T2—643 6
Khenchela (Algeria :
  Province)             T2—655
Khénifra (Morocco :
  Province)             T2—645
Kherson (Ukraine : Oblast)   T2—477 3
Khersons´ka oblast´
  (Ukraine)           T2—477 3
Khmel´nyts´ka oblast´
  (Ukraine)           T2—477 8
Khmel´nyts´kyy (Ukraine :
  Oblast)              T2—477 8
Khmer                T5—959 32
Khmer Empire          959.602
                      T2—596
Khmer language         495.932
                      T6—959 32
Khmer literature        895.932
Khmer Republic       959.604 2
                      T2—596
Khoi-Khoi language       496.1
                      T6—961

Khoi language           496.1
                      T6—961
Khoikhoi (African people)   T5—961
Khoikhoi language        496.1
                      T6—961
Khoisan (African people)   T5—961
Khoisan languages        496.1
                      T6—961
Khoisan literatures       896.1
Khomeini, Ruhollah
  Iranian history       955.054 2
Khond (Dravidian people)   T5—948 24
Khond language         494.824
                      T6—948 24
Khond literature        894.824
Khorāsān (Iran)         T2—559 2
Khorāsān-e Jonūbī (Iran)   T2—559 2
Khorāsān-e Razavī (Iran)   T2—559 2
Khorāsān-e Shomālī (Iran)   T2—559 2
Khotanese language      491.53
                      T6—915 3
Khotanese literature      891.53
Khouribga (Morocco :
  Province)             T2—643 9
Khowar language        491.499
                      T6—914 99
Khowar literature        891.499
Khrushchev, Nikita Sergeevich
  Russian history       947.085 2
Khuddakanikāya       294.382 32
Khulna (Bangladesh :
  Division)            T2—549 25
Khuṭbah              297.37
Khūzestān (Iran)        T2—556 4
Khyber-Pakhtunkhwa
  (Pakistan)          T2—549 12
Kiangsi dialects       495.172 22
                      T6—951 7
Kiangsi Province (China)   T2—512 22
Kiangsu Province (China)   T2—511 36
Kibaki, Mwai
  Kenyan history       967.620 43
Kibbutzim            307.776
Kickapoo Indians       T5—973 12
Kickapoo language      497.312
                      T6—973 12
Kicking
  American football     796.332 27
Kidder County (N.D.)     T2—784 57
Kiddushin           296.123 3
  Babylonian Talmud    296.125 3
  Mishnah           296.123 3
  Palestinian Talmud     296.124 3
Kidnap insurance        368.82

Kidnapping 364.154
  law 345.025 4
  prevention 364.4
    self-defense 613.66
Kidney beans 641.356 52
  botany 583.74
  cooking 641.656 52
  food 641.356 52
Kidney dialysis
  medicine 617.461 059
Kidney diseases
  medicine 616.61
    *see also* Urologic diseases —
      humans
  pediatrics 618.926 1
  surgery 617.461
Kidney failure
  medicine 616.614
    *see also* Urologic diseases —
      humans
Kidney stones
  medicine 616.622
    *see also* Urologic diseases —
      humans
Kidneys 573.496
  biology 573.496
  human anatomy 611.61
  human physiology 612.463
  medicine 616.61
  surgery 617.461
  *see also* Urinary system
Kiel (Germany) T2—435 123
Kielce (Poland :
  Voivodeship) T2—438 45
Kiên Giang (Vietnam) T2—597 9
Kiesinger, Kurt Georg
  German history 943.087 6
Kiev (Ukraine : Oblast) T2—477 7
Kievan Rus 947.7
  Belarussian history 947.8
  Russian history 947.02
  Ukrainian history 947.7
Kigali (Rwanda) T2—675 71
Kigoma Region (Tanzania) T2—678 28
Kikongo languages 496.393 1
  T6—963 931
Kikuyu (African people) T5—963 954
Kikuyu-Kamba languages 496.395 3
  T6—963 953
Kikuyu language 496.395 4
  T6—963 954
Kikuyu literature 896.395 4
Kikwete, Jakaya Khalfan Mrisho
  Tanzanian history 967.804 4

Kilayim 296.123 1
  Mishnah 296.123 1
  Palestinian Talmud 296.124 1
Kildare (Ireland : County) T2—418 5
Kildin Saami language 494.576
  T6—945 76
Kildin Sámi language 494.576
  T6—945 76
Kilimanjaro, Mount
  (Tanzania) T2—678 26
Kilimanjaro National Park
  (Tanzania) T2—678 26
Kilimanjaro Region
  (Tanzania) T2—678 26
Kilis İli (Turkey) T2—564 9
  ancient T2—393 6
Kilkenny (Ireland : County) T2—418 9
Kilkis (Greece : Nome) T2—495 65
Killarney (Ireland) T2—419 65
Killer cells 571.968
  human immunology 616.079 9
Killer whale 599.536
  conservation technology 639.979 536
  resource economics 333.959 536
Killifishes 597.665
Kilmarnock and Loudoun
  (Scotland) T2—414 67
Kiln drying lumber 674.384
Kilns 666.436
  decorative arts 738.136
  sculpture 731.3
  technology 666.436
Kim, Chŏng-il
  North Korean history 951.930 51
Kim, Dae Jung
  South Korean history 951.950 5
Kim, Il-sŏng
  North Korean history 951 930 43
Kimbala languages 496.393
  T6—963 93
Kimball County (Neb.) T2—782 973
Kimberley (B.C.) T2—711 65
Kimberley (South Africa :
  District) T2—687 11
Kimberley (W.A.) T2—941 4
Kimble County (Tex.) T2—764 878
Kimbundu language 496.393 2
  T6—963 932
Kimbundu literature 896.393 2
Kimchi 641.81
Kin recognition (Animals) 591.563
Kinbasket Lake (B.C.) T2—711 68
Kincardine (Scotland) T2—411 52

Kincardine and Deeside
  (Scotland)       T2—412 4
Kindergarten       372.218
  *see also* Primary education
Kindergarten teachers       372.11
Kindergarten teaching       372.110 2
Kindness
  ethics       177.7
    *see also* Love — ethics
Kinematics       531.112
  fluids       532.05
  gases       533.2
  liquid mechanics       532.5
  meteorology       551.515 1
  solids       531.3
Kinesiology
  health       613.7
Kinesthesis       152.188 2
  human physiology       612.88
  psychology       152.188 2
Kinesthetic perception       152.188 2
Kinetic art       709.040 7
  sculpture       735.230 473
Kinetic energy       531.6
Kinetic theories (Statistical
  mechanics)       530.136
Kinetic theory of gases       533.7
Kinetics       531.113
  fluids       532.05
  gases       533.2
  liquid mechanics       532.5
  physical chemistry       541.394
    biochemistry       572.44
    enzymes       572.744
  solids       531.3
King, William Lyon Mackenzie
  Canadian history       971.062 2
  1921–1930       971.062 2
  1935–1948       971.063 2
King and Queen County
  (Va.)       T2—755 352
King County (Tex.)       T2—764 742
King County (Wash.)       T2—797 77
King crabs       595.387
  fishing       639.57
King George County (Va.)       T2—755 25
King George's War, 1740–1748   940.253 2
  North American history       973.26
King James version (Bible)       220.520 3
King Philip's War, 1675–1676     973.24
King vulture       598.92
King William County (Va.)       T2—755 355
King William Island
  (Nunavut)       T2—719 55

King William's Town
  (South Africa : District)   T2—687 55
King William's War, 1688–1697   940.252 5
  North American history       973.25
Kinga language       496.391
             T6—963 91
Kingaok (Nunavut)       T2—719 55
Kingaroy (Qld.)       T2—943 2
Kingdom of God       231.72
  eschatology       236
Kingdom of the Two Sicilies   945.708 3
  Sicilian history       945.808 3
  Southern Italian history       945.708 3
Kingfish       597.725
Kingfisher County (Okla.)   T2—766 32
Kingfishers       598.78
Kinglake National Park
  (Vic.)       T2—945 2
Kinglets       598.843
Kingman County (Kan.)   T2—781 843
Kings (Biblical books)       222.5
Kings (Chessmen)       794.147
Kings (N.B.)       T2—715 41
Kings (N.S. : County)       T2—716 34
Kings (P.E.I.)       T2—717 7
Kings (Rulers)       352.23
  *see also* Monarchs; Royalty
Kings Canyon National Park
  (Calif.)       T2—794 82
Kings County (Calif.)       T2—794 85
Kings County (N.Y.)       T2—747 23
King's Lynn and West
  Norfolk (England)       T2—426 13
Kingsburgh (South Africa)   T2—684 55
Kingsbury County (S.D.)   T2—783 273
Kingship of Jesus Christ       232.8
Kingston (Ont.)       T2—713 72
Kingston (Tas.)       T2—946 2
Kingston upon Hull
  (England)       T2—428 37
Kingston upon Thames
  (London, England)       T2—421 94
Kingswood (England :
  Borough)       T2—423 91
Kinkajou       599.763
Kinki Region (Japan)       T2—521 8
Kinney County (Tex.)       T2—764 433
Kinngait (Nunavut)       T2—719 52
Kinnim       296.123 5
Kinorhyncha       592.55
Kinosternidae       597.923
Kinosternon       597.923
Kinsei period       952.025
Kinshasa (Congo)       T2—675 112

Kinship                                       306.83
  genealogy                         929.2
  system of descent                 306.83
Kinsmen                                       306.87
                                     T1—085
Kinyarwanda language                          496.394 61
                                     T6—963 946 1
Kinyarwanda literature                        896.394 61
Kiowa Apache Indians                          T5—972 5
Kiowa Apache language                         497.25
                                     T6—972 5
Kiowa County (Colo.)                          T2—788 93
Kiowa County (Kan.)                           T2—781 785
Kiowa County (Okla.)                          T2—766 47
Kiowa Indians                                 T5—974 92
Kiowa language                                497.492
                                     T6—974 92
Kiowa literature                              897.492
Kiowa Tanoan Indians                          T5—974 9
Kiowa-Tanoan languages                        497.49
Kiowa Tanoan languages                        T6—974 9
Kiranti languages                             495.49
                                     T6—954 9
Kiranti literatures                           895.49
Kirantish languages                           495.49
                                     T6—954 9
Kirchner, Néstor
  Argentine history                  982.072
Kirghiz                                        T5—943 47
Kirghiz language                              494.347
                                     T6—943 47
Kirghiz literature                            894.347
Kirghizia                                     T2—584 3
Kiribati                                      996.81
                                     T2—968 1
Kırıkkale İli (Turkey)                        T2—563 8
  ancient                            T2—393 2
Kirin Province (China)                        T2—518 8
Kiritimati (Kiribati)                         T2—964
Kirkcaldy (Scotland :
  District)                          T2—412 9
Kirkintilloch (Scotland)                      T2—414 36
Kirkland (Quebec)                             T2—714 28
Kırklareli İli (Turkey)                       T2—496 15
Kirklees (England)                            T2—428 13
Kirkwood (South Africa :
  District)                          T2—687 53
Kirlian photography                           778.3
  parapsychology                     133.892
Kirov (Russia : Oblast)                       T2—474 2
Kirovohrad (Ukraine :
  Oblast)                            T2—477 6
Kirovohrads´ka oblast´
  (Ukraine)                          T2—477 6

Kirovskaĩa oblast´ (Russia)                   T2—474 2
Kırşehir İli (Turkey)                         T2—564 1
  ancient                            T2—393 4
Kirstenbosch Botanic
  Gardens (South Africa)            T2—687 355
Kirundi language                              496.394 65
                                     T6—963 946 5
Kirundi literature                            896.394 65
Kisangani (Congo)                             T2—675 15
Kissi (African people)                        T5—963 2
Kissi language                                496.32
                                     T6—963 2
Kissimmee River (Fla.)                        T2—759 53
Kissing
  customs                            394
Kiswahili language                            496.392
                                     T6—963 92
Kiswahili literature                          896.392
Kit Carson County (Colo.)                     T2—788 91
Kitchen utensils                              643.3
  manufacturing technology          683.82
Kitchener (Ont.)                              T2—713 45
Kitchens                                      643.3
  construction                       690.44
  home economics                     643.3
  plumbing                           696.184
  residential interior decoration    747.797
Kites (Aircraft)                              629.133 32
  recreation                         796.158
Kites (Birds)                                 598.945
  conservation technology            639.978 945
  resource economics                 333.958 945
Kitikmeot (Nunavut)                           T2—719 55
Kitimat (B.C.)                                T2—711 1
Kitimat-Stikine (B.C.)                        T2—711 1
Kitsap County (Wash.)                         T2—797 76
Kitsch                                        709.034 8
  painting                           759.058
Kittens                                       636.807
Kittitas County (Wash.)                       T2—797 57
Kittson County (Minn.)                        T2—776 99
Kituba language                               496.393 1
                                     T6—963 931
Kivallik (Nunavut)                            T2—719 58
Kivu, Lake (Congo and
  Rwanda)                            T2—675 17
  Congo                              T2—675 17
  Rwanda                             T2—675 71
Kiwi (Fruit)                                  641.344
  botany                             583.66
  cooking                            641.644
  food                               641.344
  horticulture                       634.4
Kiwis (Birds)                                 598.54

| | |
|---|---|
| Kiyaka languages | 496.393 |
| | T6—963 93 |
| Klamath County (Or.) | T2—795 91 |
| Klamath Indians | T5—974 122 |
| Klamath-Modoc language | 497.412 2 |
| | T6—974 122 |
| Klamath Mountains (Calif. and Or.) | T2—795 2 |
| California | T2—794 21 |
| Oregon | T2—795 2 |
| Klaus, Václav | |
| Czech history | 943.710 512 |
| Kleberg County (Tex.) | T2—764 472 |
| Kleptomania | 362.27 |
| medicine | 616.858 42 |
| social welfare | 362.27 |
| Klerk, F. W. de (Frederik Willem) | |
| South African history | 968.064 |
| Klerksdorp (South Africa : District) | T2—682 43 |
| Klickitat County (Wash.) | T2—797 53 |
| Klinefelter's syndrome | |
| medicine | 616.680 42 |
| *see also* Male genital diseases — humans | |
| Klingon (Artificial language) | T6—999 9 |
| Klip River (South Africa : District) | T2—684 7 |
| Kliprivier (South Africa : District) | T2—684 7 |
| Klystrons | 621.381 333 |
| Knapp, Georg Friedrich | |
| economic school | 330.154 2 |
| Kneelers | |
| home sewing | 646.21 |
| household management | 645.4 |
| textile arts | 746.95 |
| Knees | 612.98 |
| physiology | 612.98 |
| regional medicine | 617.582 |
| surgery | 617.582 059 |
| *see also* Lower extremities | |
| Knies, Karl | |
| economic school | 330.154 2 |
| Knife combat | |
| military training | 355.548 |
| Knifefishes | 597.48 |
| Knighthood | |
| genealogy | 929.7 |
| Knighthood orders | 929.71 |
| Christian religious orders | 255.791 |
| church history | 271.791 |

| | |
|---|---|
| Knights (Chessmen) | 794.144 |
| Knights Hospitalers of St. John of Jerusalem | 255.791 2 |
| church history | 271.791 2 |
| Knights of Labor | 331.883 309 73 |
| Knights of Malta | 255.791 2 |
| church history | 271.791 2 |
| Maltese history | 945.850 2 |
| Knights of Pythias | 366.2 |
| biography | 366.209 2 |
| Knights Templars | 255.791 3 |
| church history | 271.791 3 |
| Knitted fabrics | 677.661 |
| *see also* Textiles | |
| Knitted laces | |
| arts | 746.226 |
| Knitted rugs | |
| arts | 746.73 |
| Knitting | 677.028 245 |
| arts | 746.432 |
| manufacturing technology | 677.028 245 |
| Knives | 621.932 |
| art metalwork | 739.72 |
| military engineering | 623.441 |
| Knob celery | 641.351 28 |
| *see also* Celeriac | |
| Knobs region (Ky.) | T2—769 5 |
| Knockers | |
| artistic ironwork | 739.48 |
| Knossos (Extinct city) | T2—391 8 |
| Knots (Mathematics) | 514.224 2 |
| Knott County (Ky.) | T2—769 165 |
| Knotted fabrics | 677.66 |
| *see also* Textiles | |
| Knotting (Seamanship) | 623.888 2 |
| Knotting textiles | 677.028 2 |
| arts | 746.422 |
| manufacturing technology | 677.028 2 |
| Know-Nothing Party (U.S.) | 324.273 2 |
| Knowability of God | 212.6 |
| *see also* Knowledge of God | |
| Knowledge | 001 |
| psychology | 153.4 |
| public administrative support | 352.74 |
| sociology | 306.42 |
| theory of | 121 |
| Knowledge acquisition | |
| computer science | 006.331 |
| Knowledge-based systems | 006.33 |
| Knowledge engineering | |
| computer science | 006.332 |

Knowledge of God 212.6
  Christianity 231.042
  comparative religion 202.11
  philosophy of religion 212.6
Knowledge representation
  computer science 006.332
Knowsley (England) T2—427 54
Knox County (Ill.) T2—773 49
Knox County (Ind.) T2—772 39
Knox County (Ky.) T2—769 125
Knox County (Me.) T2—741 53
Knox County (Mo.) T2—778 315
Knox County (Neb.) T2—782 59
Knox County (Ohio) T2—771 52
Knox County (Tenn.) T2—768 85
Knox County (Tex.) T2—764 743
Knoxville (Tenn.) T2—768 85
Knysna (South Africa :
  District) T2—687 37
Knysna Lakes National Park
  (South Africa) T2—687 37
Knysna National Lake Area
  (South Africa) T2—687 37
Koala 599.25
Koasati Indians T5—973 8
Koasati language 497.38
  T6—973 8
Kōbe-shi (Japan) T2—521 874
København (Denmark) T2—489 13
Københavns amt (Denmark) T2—489 14
Koblenz (Germany) T2—434 323
Koblenz (Germany :
  Regierungsbezirk) T2— 434 32
Kobuk Valley National Park
  (Alaska) T2—798 6
Kocaeli İli (Turkey) T2—563 3
  ancient T2—393 13
Kōchi-ken (Japan) T2—523 3
Kodashim 296.123 5
  Babylonian Talmud 296.125 5
  Mishnah 296.123 5
  Palestinian Talmud 296.124 5
Kodiak Island (Alaska) T2—798 4
Kodiak Island Borough
  (Alaska) T2—798 4
Koffiefontein (South
  Africa : District) T2—685 8
Kogi State (Nigeria) T2—669 56
Kohelet 223.8
Kohistani language 491.499
  T6—914 99
Kohistani literature 891.499
Kohistanis T5—914 99

Kohkīlūyeh va Boyer
  Ahmadī (Iran) T2—556 8
Kohl, Helmut
  German history 943.087 8
  1982–1990 943.087 8
  1990–1998 943.088 1
Kohlrabi 641.353 47
  cooking 641.653 47
  food 641.353 47
Koi 639.374 83
Koine (Greek language) 487.4
  T6—87
Koksilah River (B.C.) T2—711 2
Kola Peninsula (Russia) T2—471 3
Kola trees 583.68
  alkaloidal crop 633.76
Kolda (Senegal : Region) T2—663
Kolingba, André
  Central African history 967.410 52
Köln (Germany) T2—435 514
Köln (Germany :
  Regierungsbezirk) T2—435 51
Komandorski Islands
  (Russia) T2—577
Komárom-Esztergom
  Megye (Hungary) T2—439 7
Komati River T2—679 1
  Mozambique T2—679 1
  South Africa T2—682 72
  Swaziland T2—688 7
Komga (South Africa :
  District) T2—687 55
Komi T5—945 3
Komi (Russia) T2—474 3
Komi language 494.53
  T6—945 3
Komi literature 894.53
Komi-Permiak (Russia) T2—474 3
Komi-Permiatskiĭ
  avtonomnyĭ okrug
  (Russia) T2—474 3
Kominform 324.175
Kommunisticheskaia partiia
  Sovetskogo Soiuza 324.247 075
Kommunistische Partei
  Deutschlands 324.243 075
Kommunistische Partei
  Österreichs 324.243 607 5
Komodo dragon 597.959 68
Komondor 636.73
Komorowski, Bronisław
  Polish history 943.805 74
Kon Tum (Vietnam) T2—597 6

| | | | |
|---|---|---|---|
| Konaré, Alpha Oumar | | Korea Strait | 551.461 454 |
| Malian history | 966.230 52 | | T2—164 54 |
| Konde language | 496.391 | Korean language | 495.7 |
| | T6—963 91 | | T6—957 |
| Kongo (African people) | T5—963 931 | Korean literature | 895.7 |
| Kongo (Kingdom) | 967.511 401 | Korean War, 1950–1953 | 951.904 2 |
| | T2—675 114 | societies | 369.2 |
| Kongo language | 496.393 1 | United States | 369.186 |
| | T6—963 931 | Koreans | T5—957 |
| Kongo literature | 896.393 1 | Koriak (Russia : Okrug) | T2—577 |
| Konin (Poland : | | Koriakskiĭ avtonomnyĭ | |
| Voivodeship) | T2—438 49 | okrug (Russia) | T2—577 |
| Konjo languages | 496.394 | Korinthia (Greece) | T2—495 22 |
| | T6—963 94 | ancient | T2—387 |
| Konkani | T5—914 69 | Kos Island (Greece) | T2—495 87 |
| Konkani language | 491.469 | Kosciusko County (Ind.) | T2—772 82 |
| | T6—914 69 | Kosciusko National Park | |
| Konkani literature | 891.469 | (N.S.W.) | T2—944 7 |
| Kono (African people) | T5—963 4 | Kosher cooking | 641.567 6 |
| Kono language | 496.34 | Kosher observance | 296.73 |
| | T6—963 4 | Košický kraj (Slovakia) | T2—437 35 |
| Konya İli (Turkey) | T2—564 2 | Kosovo Civil War, 1998–1999 | 949.710 315 |
| ancient | T2—392 7 | Kosovo i Metohija (Serbia) | T2—497 1 |
| Konzo languages | 496.394 | Kosrae (Micronesia) | T2—966 |
| | T6—963 94 | Kossuth County (Iowa) | T2—777 21 |
| Koochiching County | | Koster (South Africa : | |
| (Minn.) | T2—776 79 | District) | T2—682 42 |
| Koongo language | 496.393 1 | Kostroma (Russia : Oblast) | T2—473 3 |
| | T6—963 931 | Kostromskaĭa oblast' | |
| Koongo literature | 896.393 1 | (Russia) | T2—473 3 |
| Kootenai County (Idaho) | T2—796 94 | Kosygin, Aleksey Nikolayevich | |
| Kootenai River | T2—711 65 | Russian history | 947.085 3 |
| Kootenay Boundary (B.C.) | T2—711 62 | Koszalin (Poland : | |
| Kootenay Lake (B.C.) | T2—711 62 | Voivodeship) | T2—438 16 |
| Kootenay National Park | | Kota language (Dravidian) | 494.81 |
| (B.C.) | T2—711 65 | | T6—948 1 |
| Kootenay River | T2—711 65 | Kota literature (Dravidian) | 894.81 |
| Kopparbergs län (Sweden) | T2—487 8 | Kountché, Seyni | |
| Koppies (South Africa : | | Nigerien (Niger) history | 966.260 52 |
| District) | T2—685 2 | Kováč, Michal | |
| Koran | 297.122 | Slovak history | 943.730 511 |
| Koran stories | 297.122 2 | Koyukon Indians | T5—972 |
| Koras | 787.98 | Koyukon language | 497.2 |
| *see also* Stringed instruments | | | T6—972 |
| Kordestān (Iran) | T2—555 4 | Kozanē (Greece : Nome) | T2—495 62 |
| Kordofan (Sudan) | T2—628 | Kpelle (African people) | T5—963 4 |
| Kordofanian languages | 496.3 | Kpelle language | 496.34 |
| | T6—963 | | T6—963 4 |
| Korea | 951.9 | KPÖ (Austrian political party) | 324.243 607 5 |
| | T2—519 | Kraft process | 676.126 |
| Korea (North) | 951.93 | Kraft wrapping paper | 676.287 |
| | T2—519 3 | Kraków (Poland : | |
| Korea (South) | 951.95 | Voivodeship) | T2—438 62 |
| | T2—519 5 | | |

Královéhradecký kraj
  (Czech Republic)      T2—437 18
Kranskop (South Africa :
  District)      T2—684 7
Krasnodar (Russia : Kray)    T2—475 2
Krasnodarskiĭ kraĭ (Russia)    T2—475 2
Krasnoīarskiĭ kraĭ (Russia)    T2—575
Krasnoyarsk (Russia : Kray)   T2—575
Krebs cycle      572.475
Krefeld (Germany)      T2—435 535 7
Krētē (Greece)      T2—495 9
  ancient      T2—391 8
Kretschmer, Ernst
  personality theory      155.264
Kreuzlingen (Switzerland :
  Bezirk)      T2—494 597
Kriel (South Africa :
  District)      T2—682 77
Krill      595.389
Krio language      427.966 4
     T6—217
Kristallnacht, 1938      940.531 842
Kristianstads län (Sweden)   T2—486 1
Kronobergs län (Sweden)    T2—486 5
Kroonstad (South Africa :
  District)      T2—685 2
Krosno (Poland :
  Voivodeship)      T2—438 66
Kru (African people)      T5—963 3
Kru languages      496.33
     T6—963 3
Kruger National Park (South
  Africa)      T2—682 71
Krugersdorp (South Africa :
  District)      T2—682 22
Krymskaīa oblast′ (Ukraine) T2—477 1
Krypton
  chemistry      546.754
  gas technology      665.822
Ku Klux Klan      322.420 973
Ku-ring-gai Chase National
  Park (N.S.W.)      T2—944 1
Kuala Lumpur (Malaysia)   T2—595 1
Kuando Kubango Province
  (Angola)      T2—673 5
Kuba (Kingdom)      967.512 601
     T2—675 126
Kuba languages      496.396
     T6—963 96
Kubitschek, Juscelino
  Brazilian history      981.062
Kublai Khan
  Asian history      950.22

Kuchean language      491.994
     T6—919 94
Kudumane (South Africa :
  District)      T2—682 46
Kudus      599.642 3
Kudzu      583.74
Kufuor, John Agyekum
  Ghanaian history      966.705 3
Kugluktuk (Nunavut)      T2—719 55
Kui (Dravidian people)    T5—948 24
Kui language (Dravidian)      494.824
     T6—948 24
Kui literature (Dravidian)      894.824
Kuĭbyshev (Russia : Oblast)   T2—474 4
Kuĭbyshevskaīa oblast′
  (Russia)      T2—474 4
Kuils River (South Africa :
  District)      T2—687 35
Kuiper belt objects      523.492
Kujawsko-Pomorskie
  Voivodeship (Poland)   T2—438 26
Kuki-Chin languages      495.4
     T6—954
Kuki-Chin Naga languages    495.4
     T6—954
Kulaynī, Muḥammad ibn Yaʻqūb
  Hadith      297.125 921 1
Kulm (Switzerland)      T2—494 562 3
Kumamoto-ken (Japan)    T2—522 5
Kumasi (Ghana)      T2—667
Kumquats      641.343 4
  cooking      641.643 4
  food      641.343 4
  orchard crop      634.34
Kuna de Madungandí
  (Panama)      T2—728 773
Kuna de Wargandi
  (Panama)      T2—728 774
Kuna Indians (Panama)    T5—978 3
Kuna language (Panama)      497.83
     T6—978 3
Kuna literature (Panama)      897.83
Kuna Yala (Panama)      T2—728 772
Kunashiri Island
  (R.S.F.S.R.)      T2—524
Kundalini yoga
  comparative religion      204.36
  Hinduism      294.543 6
Kunene Province (Angola)   T2—673 5
Kung fu      796.815 9
Kuopio (Finland)      T2—489 75
Kurdi language      491.597
     T6—915 97
Kurdi literature      891.597

Kurdish Autonomous
    Region (Iraq)         T2—567 2
    ancient              T2—352
Kurdish language         491.597
                      T6—915 97
Kurdish literature        891.597
Kurdish nationalism      320.540 956 67
Kurdistan               T2—566 7
    Iran                 T2—555 4
    Iraq                 T2—567 2
    Turkey             T2—566 7
    ancient             T2—394 2
Kurds                  T5—915 97
Kurgan (Russia : Oblast)   T2—573
Kurganskaîa oblast′
    (Russia)           T2—573
Kuria (African people)    T5—963 95
Kuria languages         496.395
                      T6—963 95
Kuril Islands (Russia)     T2—577
Kurland (Duchy)         T2—479 6
Kurmanji language       491.597
                      T6—915 97
Kurmanji literature      891.597
Kursk (Russia : Oblast)    T2—473 5
Kurskaîa oblast′ (Russia)   T2—473 5
Kurukh                T5—948 3
Kurukh language         494.83
                      T6—948 3
Kurukh literature        894.83
Kuruman (South Africa :
    District)           T2—687 11
Kurux                 T5—948 3
Kurux language          494.83
                      T6—948 3
Kush                  939.78
                      T2—397 8
Kushans              T5—915
Kuskokwim River (Alaska)   T2—798 4
Küssnacht (Switzerland :
    Bezirk)            T2—494 752 9
Kūt (Iraq : Province)     T2—567 5
Kütahya (Turkey : İli)    T2—562 8
    ancient             T2—392 6
Kutchin Indians         T5—972
Kutchin language        497.2
Kutenai Indians         T5—979 92
Kutenai language        497.992
                      T6—979 92
Kuvasz (Dog)           636.73
Kuwait                953.67
                      T2—536 7
    ancient             939.49
                      T2—394 9

Kuwait-Iraq Crisis, 1990–1991   956.704 42
Kuwaitis              T5—927 536 7
Kven                 T5—945 4
Kven Finnish           494.54
                      T6—945 4
Kven Finnish literature    894.54
Kwa languages          496.337
                      T6—963 37
Kwa literatures         896.337
Kwa Zulu (South Africa)   T2—684
Kwajalein Atoll (Marshall
    Islands)           T2—968 3
Kwakiutl Indians       T5—979 53
Kwakiutl language       497.953
                      T6—979 53
Kwamhlanga (South
    Africa : District)      T2—682 75
KwaNdebele (South Africa)   T2—682 75
Kwangsi Chuang
    Autonomous Region
    (China)            T2—512 8
Kwangtung Province
    (China)            T2—512 7
Kwangwa languages     496.399
                      T6—963 99
Kwanzaa             394.261 2
Kwara State (Nigeria)     T2—669 57
Kwashiorkor
    medicine           616.396
       *see also* Digestive system
           diseases — humans
Kwaśniewski, Aleksander
    Polish history        943.805 72
KwaZulu (South Africa)   T2—684
KwaZulu-Natal (South Africa)   968.4
                      T2—684
Kweichow Province (China)   T2—513 4
Kwese language         496.393
                      T6—963 93
KWIC indexing         025.486
KWOC indexing       025.486
Kwomtari-Baibai languages   T6—991 2
Kyabram (Vic.)         T2—945 4
Kyanite
    mineralogy         549.62
Kyffhäuserkreis (Germany :
    Landkreis)        T2—432 24
Kyïvs′ka oblast′ (Ukraine)   T2—477 7
Kyklades (Greece)      T2—495 85
Kyle and Carrick (Scotland)   T2—414 64
Kymen lääni (Finland)    T2—489 71
Kymi (Finland : Lääni)    T2—489 71
Kyogle (N.S.W.)         T2—944 3
Kyoto (Japan)          T2—521 864

Kyoto (Japan : Prefecture)     T2—521 86
Kyrgyz                         T5—943 47
Kyrgyz language                494.347
                               T6—943 47
Kyrgyz literature              894.347
Kyrgyzstan                     958.43
                               T2—584 3
Kyrie                          264.36
  music                        782.323 2
Kythēra Island (Greece)        T2—495 2
Kyūshū Island (Japan)          T2—522
Kyūshū Region (Japan)          T2—522
Kyusyu Island (Japan)          T2—522
Kyusyu Region (Japan)          T2—522

# L

L-functions                    512.73
La Altagracia (Dominican
  Republic : Province)         T2—729 385
La Bostonnais (Quebec)         T2—714 459
La Chaux-de-Fonds
  (Switzerland : District)     T2—494 381
La Coruña (Spain :
  Province)                    T2—461 1
La Côte-de-Beaupré
  (Quebec)                     T2—714 48
La Côte-de-Gaspé (Quebec)      T2—714 793
La Crosse County (Wis.)        T2—775 71
La Guajira (Colombia :
  Dept.)                       T2—861 17
La Habana (Cuba)               T2—729 123
La Habana (Cuba :
  Province)                    T2—729 124
La Haute-Côte-Nord
  (Quebec)                     T2—714 172
La Haute-Gaspésie
  (Quebec)                     T2—714 791
La Haute-Yamaska
  (Quebec)                     T2—714 63
La Jacques-Cartier (Quebec)    T2—714 474
La Libertad (El Salvador :
  Dept.)                       T2—728 422
La Libertad (Peru : Dept.)     T2—851 6
La Libertad (Peru : Region)    T2—851 6
La Mancha (Spain)              T2—464
La Matapédia (Quebec :
  Regional County
  Municipality)                T2—714 778
La Mauricie National Park
  (Quebec)                     T2—714 453
La Mitis (Quebec)              T2—714 773
La Moure County (N.D.)         T2—784 53

La Nouvelle-Beauce
  (Quebec)                     T2—714 718
La Pampa (Argentina :
  Province)                    T2—821 3
La Paz (Bolivia : Dept.)       T2—841 2
La Paz (El Salvador : Dept.)   T2—728 425
La Paz (Honduras : Dept.)      T2—728 36
La Paz County (Ariz.)          T2—791 72
La Perouse Strait              551.461 453
                               T2—164 53
La Plata County (Colo.)        T2—788 29
La Porte County (Ind.)         T2—772 91
La Région-Sherbrookoise
  (Quebec)                     T2—714 66
La Rioja (Argentina :
  Province)                    T2—824 6
La Rioja (Spain)               T2—463 54
La Rivière-du-Nord
  (Quebec)                     T2—714 246
La Rochelle (France)           T2—446 42
La Romana (Dominican
  Republic : Province)         T2—729 383
La Salle County (Ill.)         T2—773 27
La Salle County (Tex.)         T2—764 453
La Salle Parish (La.)          T2—763 75
La Spezia (Italy : Province)   T2—451 83
  ancient                      T2—371 1
La Tuque (Quebec)              T2—714 459
La Unión (El Salvador :
  Dept)                        T2—728 434
La Union (Philippines)         T2—599 1
La Vallée-de-la-Gatineau
  (Quebec)                     T2—714 224
La Vallée-du-Richelieu
  (Quebec)                     T2—714 365
La Vega (Dominican
  Republic)                    T2—729 369 7
La Vérendrye Wildlife
  Reserve (Quebec)             T2—714 224
Laadi language                 496.393 1
                               T6—963 931

Laâyoune (Morocco :
  Province)                    T2—648
Laâyoune-Bojador-Sakia El-
  Hamra (Morocco)              T2—648
Labanotation                   792.82
Labeling
  library materials            025.7
  production management        658.564
  regulation                   343.082
Labels
  illustration                 741.692
  stamps
    prints                     769.57

| | | | |
|---|---|---|---|
| Labette County (Kan.) | T2—781 96 | Labor leaders | 331.880 92 |
| Labiatae | 583.96 | biography | 331.880 92 |
| Labor | 331 | role and function | 331.873 3 |
| arts | 700.455 3 | Labor-management bargaining | 331.89 |
| | T3C—355 3 | *see also* Collective bargaining | |
| economics | 331 | Labor market | 331.12 |
| ethics | 174 | maladjustments | 331.13 |
| religion | 205.64 | Labor mobility | 331.127 |
| Christianity | 241.64 | Labor movements | 331.8 |
| Judaism | 296.364 | economics | 331.8 |
| *see also* Ethical problems | | relations with government | 322.2 |
| income distribution | 339.21 | Labor need | 331.123 |
| law | 344.01 | Labor parties | 324.217 |
| literature | 808.803 553 | international organizations | 324.17 |
| history and criticism | 809.933 553 | Labor Party (Australia) | 324.294 07 |
| specific literatures | T3B—080 355 3 | Labor productivity | 331.118 |
| history and | | economics | 331.118 |
| criticism | T3B—093 553 | promotion of | |
| psychology | 158.7 | personnel management | 658.314 |
| public administration | 354.9 | Labor relations | 331 |
| religion | 201.73 | economics | 331 |
| Christianity | 261.85 | law | 344.01 |
| guides to life | 248.88 | personnel management | 658.315 |
| Judaism | 296.383 | | T1—068 3 |
| social aspects | 306.36 | military personnel | 355.33 |
| *see also* Working class | | public administration | 352.68 |
| Labor (Obstetrics) | 618.4 | public administration | 354.9 |
| complications | 618.5 | sociology | 306.34 |
| Labor banks | 332.37 | Labor requirements | 331.123 |
| Labor conditions | 331.2 | Labor rights | 331.011 |
| Labor contracts | 331.891 | law | 344.010 1 |
| *see also* Collective bargaining | | Labor shortages | 331.136 |
| Labor costs | | Labor supply | 331.11 |
| financial management | 658.155 3 | Labor surpluses | 331.137 |
| production economics | 338.512 | Labor systems | |
| Labor demand | 331.123 | economics | 331.117 |
| Labor discipline | | sociology | 306.36 |
| labor economics | 331.259 8 | Labor theory of value | |
| personnel management | 658.314 | Marxian theory | 335.412 |
| Labor disputes | 331.89 | Labor turnover | 331.126 |
| Labor economics | 331 | economics | 331.126 |
| Labor estimates | T1—029 | personnel management | 658.314 |
| building construction | 692.5 | Labor unions | 331.88 |
| Labor exchanges | 331.128 | accounting | 657.861 |
| Labor force | 331.11 | benefits | 331.873 5 |
| Labor grievances | 331.889 66 | elections | 331.874 |
| *see also* Grievances (Labor) | | law | 344.018 8 |
| Labor groups | | membership | 331.873 2 |
| relations with government | 322.2 | organization | 331.87 |
| Labor injunctions | | personnel management | 658.315 3 |
| economics | 331.893 | public administration | 352.68 |
| law | 344.018 93 | public administration | 354.97 |
| Labor law | 344.01 | relations with government | 322.2 |

462

Labor unions (continued)
  social welfare                        361.766
  women workers                         331.478
Labor use
  agricultural industries               338.16
Labor violence
  economics                             331.893
Laboratories                            001.4
  architecture                          727.5
  chemistry                             542.1
  institutional housekeeping            647.995
  interior decoration                   747.875
  school facilities                     371.623
Laboratory animals                      616.027
  care and maintenance                  636.088 5
  medicine                              616.027
Laboratory diagnosis
  medicine                              616.075 6
Laboratory manuals          T1—078
  research                  T1—072 1
Laboratory method                       371.382
Laboratory mice                         616.027 333
  animal husbandry                      636.935 3
  medicine                              616.027 333
Laboratory rats                         616.027 33
  animal husbandry                      636.935 2
  medicine                              616.027 33
Laborers                                331.11
  public administration                 354.9
  social class                          305.562
                            T1—086 24
Laboring class                          305.562
                            T1—086 23
  *see also* Working class
Laboulbeniales                          579.567
Labour Party (Great Britain)            324.241 07
Labrador (N.L.)                         971.82
                            T2—718 2
Labrador Current                        551.462 134
Labrador Sea                            551.461 343
                            T2—163 43
Labuan                      T2—595 3
Labyrinth diseases
  medicine                              617.882
  *see also* Ear diseases —
    humans
Labyrinth fishes                        597.7
Labyrinthodontia                        567.8
Labyrinths (Ears)
  human anatomy                         611.85
  human physiology                      612.858
  medicine                              617.882
Lac (Switzerland)           T2—494 538
Lac-Édouard (Quebec)        T2—714 459

Lac la Biche (Alta.)        T2—712 33
Lac qui Parle County
  (Minn.)                   T2—776 38
Lac-Saint-Jean-Est
  (Quebec : Regional
  County Municipality)      T2—714 148
Lac-Saint-Jean Region
  (Quebec)                  T2—714 14
Lacalle Herrera, Luis Alberto
  Uruguayan history                     989.506 72
Lacandón Indians            T5—974 27
Lacandón language                       497.427
                            T6—974 27
Laccadive, Minicoy, and
  Amindivi Islands (India)  T2—548 1
Laccadive Sea                           551.461 537
                            T2—165 37
Laccoliths                              551.88
Lacerations (Wounds)
  medicine                              617.13
Lacertidae                              597.958
Laces                                   677.653
  arts                                  746.22
  manufacturing technology              677.653
Lacewings                               595.747
Lachlan River (N.S.W.)      T2—944 9
Lacings                                 677.76
Lackawanna County (Pa.)     T2—748 36
Laclede County (Mo.)        T2—778 815
Laconia (Greece)            T2—495 22
  ancient                   T2—389
Lacquering                              667.75
  decorative arts                       745.726
  furniture arts                        749.5
  woodwork
    buildings                           698.34
Lacrimal apparatus
  human physiology                      612.847
  ophthalmology                         617.764
Lacrimal apparatus diseases
  ophthalmology                         617.764
  *see also* Eye diseases —
    humans
Lacrosse (Game)                         796.347
Lacrosse players                        796.347 092
Lactation                               573.679
  biology                               573.679
  human physiology                      612.664
  obstetrics                            618.71
Lactic acid bacteria                    579.35
Lactobacillus                           579.37
Lactococcus                             579.355
Lactose                                 572.565
  *see also* Carbohydrates

Lactose intolerance
  medicine             616.399 8
  *see also* Digestive system
    diseases — humans
Ladin language           459.94
              T6—599 4
Ladin literature         859.94
Ladino language       467.949 6
              T6—67
Ladino literature        860
Ladins                T5—599 4
Ladismith (South Africa :
  District)           T2—687 38
Ladoga Lake (Russia)    T2—471 5
Lady Frere (South Africa :
  District)           T2—687 58
Lady Grey (South Africa :
  District)           T2—687 56
Ladybrand (South Africa :
  District)           T2—685 5
Ladybugs           595.769
  culture           638.576 9
Lae (Papua New Guinea)   T2—957 1
Lafayette County (Ark.)    T2—767 57
Lafayette County (Fla.)    T2—759 816
Lafayette County (Miss.)   T2—762 83
Lafayette County (Mo.)    T2—778 453
Lafayette County (Wis.)    T2—775 79
Lafayette Parish (La.)     T2—763 47
Lafourche Parish (La.)    T2—763 39
Lag b'Omer          296.439
  liturgy            296.453 9
Laghouat (Algeria :
  Province)          T2—657
Lagomorpha         599.32
  paleozoology       569.32
Lagoons           551.461 8
              T2—168
  biology           578.778
  ecology           577.78
  freshwater biology    578.763
  freshwater ecology    577.63
  freshwater hydrology   551.482
  oceanography       551.461 8
Lagopus           598.633
Lagos (Chile : Region)    T2—835
Lagos Escobar, Ricardo
  Chilean history      983.066 3
Lagos State (Nigeria)    T2—669 1
LaGrange County (Ind.)   T2—772 79
Lagrange polynomials    515.55
Laguerre polynomials    515.55
Laguna (Philippines :
  Province)          T2—599 1

Lahn River (Germany)   T2—434 14
Lahnda language       491.419
              T6—914 19
Lahnda literature      891.419
Lahore District (Pakistan)   T2—549 143
Lai Châu (Vietnam :
  Province)          T2—597 1
Laingsburg (South Africa :
  District)           T2—687 39
Laissez-faire economics   330.153
Laity (Church members)   262.15
              T1—088 28
  biography         270.092
    specific denominations   280
  church government    262.15
  pastoral theology     253
  social group        305.6
Lajemmerais (Quebec)   T2—714 362
Lak-Dargwa languages   499.964
              T6—999 64
Lak language         499.964
              T6—999 64
Lake Abitibi (Ont. and
  Quebec)           T2—713 142
Lake and Peninsula
  Borough (Alaska)     T2—798 4
Lake Athabasca (Sask. and
  Alta.)             T2—712 41
Lake Barkley (Ky. and
  Tenn.)            T2—769 79
Lake Champlain      T2—747 54
  New York         T2—747 54
  Vermont          T2—743 1
Lake Champlain, Battle of, 1814    973.525 6
Lake Clark National Park
  and Preserve (Alaska)   T2—798 6
Lake Constance      T2—434 62
  Germany          T2—434 62
  Switzerland        T2—494 597
Lake County (Calif.)    T2—794 17
Lake County (Colo.)    T2—788 46
Lake County (Fla.)     T2—759 22
Lake County (Ill.)      T2—773 21
Lake County (Ind.)     T2—772 99
Lake County (Mich.)    T2—774 68
Lake County (Minn.)    T2—776 76
Lake County (Mont.)    T2—786 832
Lake County (Ohio)    T2—771 334
Lake County (Or.)      T2—795 93
Lake County (S.D.)     T2—783 35
Lake County (Tenn.)    T2—768 12
Lake Cumberland (Ky.)   T2—769 63
Lake Diefenbaker (Sask.)   T2—712 42
Lake District (England)   T2—427 8

| | |
|---|---|
| Lake Erie | T2—771 2 |
| Ohio | T2—771 2 |
| Ontario | T2—713 3 |
| Lake Erie, Battle of, 1813 | 973.525 4 |
| Lake Eyre (S. Aust.) | T2—942 38 |
| Lake Francis Case (S.D.) | T2—783 38 |
| Lake Gairdner (S. Aust.) | T2—942 38 |
| Lake Garda (Italy) | T2—452 6 |
| Lake Geneva (Switzerland | |
| and France) | T2—494 52 |
| France | T2—445 84 |
| Switzerland | T2—494 52 |
| Lake George (N.Y.) | T2—747 51 |
| Lake Hawea (N.Z.) | T2—939 5 |
| Lake Huron (Mich. and | |
| Ont.) | T2—774 |
| Michigan | T2—774 |
| Ontario | T2—713 2 |
| Lake ice | 551.345 |
| Lake Kivu (Congo and | |
| Rwanda) | T2—675 17 |
| Congo | T2—675 17 |
| Rwanda | T2—675 71 |
| Lake Ladoga (Russia) | T2—471 5 |
| Lake liners | 386.224 36 |
| design | 623.812 436 |
| engineering | 623.824 36 |
| *see also* Ships | |
| Lake Lucerne (Switzerland) | T2—494 557 |
| Lake Lugano (Switzerland | |
| and Italy) | T2—494 785 |
| Lake Maggiore (Italy and | |
| Switzerland) | T2—451 65 |
| Italy | T2—451 65 |
| Switzerland | T2—494 788 |
| Lake Mälar (Sweden) | T2—487 2 |
| Lake Malawi | T2—689 7 |
| Lake Manapouri (N.Z.) | T2—939 6 |
| Lake Manitoba (Man.) | T2—712 72 |
| Lake Maracaibo | |
| (Venezuela) | T2—872 3 |
| Lake Martin (Ala.) | T2—761 53 |
| Lake Maurepas (La.) | T2—763 32 |
| Lake Mead (Ariz. and Nev.) | T2—793 12 |
| Lake Mead National | |
| Recreation Area (Ariz. | |
| and Nev.) | T2—793 12 |
| Lake Michigan | T2—774 |
| Lake Mweru (Congo and | |
| Zambia) | T2—675 18 |
| Lake Nasser (Egypt and | |
| Sudan) | T2—623 |
| Lake Nicaragua (Nicaragua) | T2—728 517 |
| Lake Nipissing (Ont.) | T2—713 147 |
| Lake Nyasa | T2—689 7 |
| Lake Oahe (S.D. and N.D.) | T2—783 5 |
| Lake of Constance | T2—434 62 |
| Germany | T2—434 62 |
| Switzerland | T2—494 597 |
| Lake of Lugano | |
| (Switzerland and Italy) | T2—494 785 |
| Lake of the Ozarks (Mo.) | T2—778 493 |
| Lake of the Woods | T2—776 81 |
| Canada | T2—713 11 |
| Minnesota | T2—776 81 |
| Lake of the Woods County | |
| (Minn.) | T2—776 81 |
| Lake of Thun (Switzerland) | T2—494 541 5 |
| Lake of Zurich | |
| (Switzerland) | T2—494 572 |
| Lake Ohau (N.Z.) | T2—938 97 |
| Lake Okeechobee (Fla.) | T2—759 39 |
| Lake Onega (Russia) | T2—471 5 |
| Lake Ontario (N.Y. and | |
| Ont.) | T2—747 9 |
| New York | T2—747 9 |
| Ontario | T2—713 5 |
| Lake Pedder National Park | |
| (Tas.) | T2—946 2 |
| Lake Pontchartrain (La.) | T2—763 34 |
| Lake Powell (Utah and | |
| Ariz.) | T2—792 59 |
| Lake Pukaki (N.Z.) | T2—938 8 |
| Lake Rudolf (Kenya and | |
| Ethiopia) | T2—676 27 |
| Lake Saint Clair (Mich. and | |
| Ont.) | T2—774 39 |
| Michigan | T2—774 39 |
| Ontario | T2—713 31 |
| Lake Saint Clair (Tas.) | T2—946 3 |
| Lake Saint Clair National | |
| Park (Tas.) | T2—946 3 |
| Lake Saint Marys (Ohio) | T2—771 415 |
| Lake Sakakawea (N.D.) | T2—784 75 |
| Lake States | 977 |
| | T2—77 |
| Lake Superior | T2—774 9 |
| Michigan | T2—774 9 |
| Ontario | T2—713 12 |
| Lake Tahoe (Calif. and | |
| Nev.) | T2—794 38 |
| California | T2—794 38 |
| Nevada | T2—793 57 |
| Lake Tanganyika | T2—678 28 |
| Lake Taupo (N.Z.) | T2—933 9 |
| Lake Te Anau (N.Z.) | T2—939 6 |
| Lake Texoma (Okla. and | |
| Tex.) | T2—766 61 |

| | |
|---|---|
| Lake Titicaca (Peru and Bolivia) | T2—841 2 |
| Bolivia | T2—841 2 |
| Peru | T2—853 6 |
| Lake transportation | 386.5 |
| *see also* Inland water transportation | |
| Lake trout | 597.554 |
| Lake Turkana (Kenya and Ethiopia) | T2—676 27 |
| Lake Väner (Sweden) | T2—486 7 |
| Lake Vättern (Sweden) | T2—486 4 |
| Lake Victoria | T2—678 27 |
| Lake Wakatipu (N.Z.) | T2—939 5 |
| Lake Wallenpaupack (Pa.) | T2—748 23 |
| Lake Wanaka (N.Z.) | T2—939 5 |
| Lake Winnebago (Wis.) | T2—775 64 |
| Lake Winnipeg (Man.) | T2—712 72 |
| Lake Winnipegosis (Man.) | T2—712 72 |
| Lake Winnipesaukee (N.H.) | T2—742 4 |
| Lake Zug (Switzerland) | T2—494 756 |
| Lakes | 551.482 |
| | T2—169 2 |
| biology | 578.763 |
| ecology | 577.63 |
| engineering | 627.14 |
| hydrology | 551.482 |
| influence on precipitation | 551.577 5 |
| interactions with atmosphere | 551.524 8 |
| landscape architecture | 714 |
| law | 346.046 916 3 |
| law of nations | 341.444 |
| recreational resources | 333.784 4 |
| recreational use | 797 |
| resource economics | 333.916 3 |
| water supply engineering | 628.112 |
| Lakes (Sudan) | T2—629 4 |
| Lakes Entrance (Vic.) | T2—945 6 |
| Lakōnia (Greece) | T2—495 22 |
| ancient | T2—389 |
| Lakota Indians | T5—975 244 |
| Lakota language | 497.524 4 |
| | T6—975 244 |
| Lakshadweep (India) | T2—548 1 |
| Lâm Đồng (Vietnam) | T2—597 6 |
| Lama (Genus) | 599.636 7 |
| Lamaism | 294.392 3 |
| Lamar County (Ala.) | T2—761 86 |
| Lamar County (Ga.) | T2—758 446 |
| Lamar County (Miss.) | T2—762 19 |
| Lamar County (Tex.) | T2—764 263 |
| Lamarckism | 576.827 |

| | |
|---|---|
| Lamb (Meat) | 641.363 |
| commercial processing | 664.92 |
| cooking | 641.663 |
| food | 641.363 |
| Lamb County (Tex.) | T2—764 843 |
| Lamba language | 496.391 |
| | T6—963 91 |
| Lambayeque (Peru : Dept.) | T2—851 4 |
| Lambda calculus | 511.35 |
| Lambeth (London, England) | T2—421 65 |
| Lambton (Ont.) | T2- 713 27 |
| Lamé | 677.616 |
| Lamellibranchia | 594.4 |
| Lamellicornia | 595.764 9 |
| Lamentations (Bible) | 224.3 |
| Lamiales | 583.96 |
| L'Amiante (Quebec) | T2—714 712 |
| Laminar flow | 532.052 5 |
| air mechanics | 533.62 |
| gas mechanics | 533.215 |
| liquid mechanics | 532.515 |
| Laminariales | 579.887 |
| Laminated fabrics | 677.69 |
| *see also* Textiles | |
| Laminated glass | 666.154 |
| Laminated plastic | 668.492 |
| Laminated wood | 674.835 |
| *see also* Wood | |
| Laminating plastics | 668.414 |
| Lamington National Park (Qld.) | T2—943 2 |
| Lammermuir Hills (Scotland) | T2—413 6 |
| Lamnidae | 597.33 |
| Lamniformes | 597.3 |
| Lamoille County (Vt.) | T2—743 35 |
| Lamp shells | 594.68 |
| paleozoology | 564.68 |
| Lampasas County (Tex.) | T2—764 513 |
| Lampblack | 662.93 |
| Lampedusa (Italy) | T2—458 22 |
| Lampreys | 597.2 |
| Lampridiformes | 597.64 |
| Lamps | 621.32 |
| ceramic arts | 738.8 |
| furniture arts | 749.63 |
| manufacturing technology | 683.83 |
| mining | 622.473 |
| *see also* Lighting | |
| Lampshades | |
| handicrafts | 745.593 2 |
| Lampung | T5—992 248 |
| Lampung (Indonesia) | T2—598 18 |

Lampung language 499.224 8
    T6—992 248
Lampung literature 899.224 8
Lampyridae 595.764 4
Lamut T5—941
Lamut language 494.1
    T6—941
LAN (Computer network) 004.68
  *see also* Computer
    communications
Lanai (Hawaii) T2—969 23
Lanao del Norte
  (Philippines) T2—599 7
Lanao del Sur (Philippines) T2—599 7
Lanark (Ont. : County) T2—713 82
Lanaudière Region
  (Quebec) T2—714 41
Lancashire (England) T2—427 6
Lancaster (England : City) T2—427 69
Lancaster, House of 942.04
  English history 942.04
  Irish history 941.504
Lancaster County (Neb.) T2—782 293
Lancaster County (Pa.) T2—748 15
Lancaster County (S.C.) T2—757 45
Lancaster County (Va.) T2—755 22
Lancelets 596.4
Lancers (Cavalry) 357.1
Lances 623.441
Lancewoods
  botany 583.22
  forestry 634.973 22
L'Ancienne-Lorette
  (Quebec) T2—714 471
Land 333
    T2—14
  economics 333
    *see Manual at* 333.73–.78 vs.
      333, 333.1–.5
  financial management 658.152 42
  income distribution 339.21
  investment economics 332.632 42
  military reservations 355.79
  property law 346.043
  public administration 354.34
    public land 352.57
  resource economics 333.73
  taxes 336.22
    law 343.054
    public administration 352.44
    public finance 336.22
Land appraisal 333.332
Land art 709.040 76

Land-atmosphere interactions 551.523
  microclimatology 551.66
Land banks 332.31
Land Between the Lakes
  (Ky. and Tenn.) T2—769 79
Land birds 598
Land breezes 551.518 5
Land carnivores 599.7
Land conservation 333.731 6
  law 346.046 731 6
Land development 333.731 5
Land economics 333
Land forces (Military science) 355
Land gift 333.333
Land-grant universities 378.05
Land grants
  economics 333.16
  law 343.025 3
Land gunnery 623.551
Land management (Plant
  management) 658.2
  public land 352.57
Land nationalization 333.14
  economics 333.14
  law 343.025 2
Land operations 355.4
  Algerian Revolution 965.046 42
  American Revolution 973.33
  Chaco War 989.207 164 2
  Civil War (England) 942.062 42
  Civil War (Spain) 946.081 42
  Crimean War 947.073 842
  Falkland Islands War 997.110 244 2
  Franco-German War 943.082 42
  Hundred Years' War 944.025 42
  Indo-Pakistan War, 1971 954.920 514 2
  Indochinese War 959.704 142
  Iraq War, 2003– 956.704 434 2
  Iraqi-Iranian Conflict 955.054 242
  Korean War 951.904 242
  military analysis 355.48
  Napoleonic Wars 940.274 2
  Persian Gulf War, 1991 956.704 424 2
  South African War 968.048 4
  Spanish-American War 973.893
  Thirty Years' War 940.244 2
  Vietnamese War 959.704 342
  War of 1812 973.523
  War of the Pacific 983.061 642
  World War I 940.41
  World War II 940.541
Land ownership 333.3
Land policy (Government policy) 333.73

| | |
|---|---|
| Land reclamation | 333.731 53 |
| agriculture | 631.6 |
| effect on natural ecology | 577.272 |
| hydraulic engineering | 627.5 |
| from the sea | 627.549 |
| law | 346.046 731 53 |
| revegetation | 631.64 |
| Land redistribution | |
| economics | 333.31 |
| Land reform | |
| economics | 333.31 |
| law | 346.044 |
| Land resettlement | |
| economics | 333.31 |
| Land resources | 333.73 |
| economics | 333.73 |
| public administration | 354.34 |
| *see Manual at* 333.73–.78 vs. | |
| 333, 333.1–.5 | |
| Land sailing | 796.68 |
| Land sale | 333.333 |
| Land settlement | |
| economics | 333.31 |
| Land slugs | 594.38 |
| Land snails | 594.38 |
| *see also* Snails (Land) | |
| Land subdivision | 333.3 |
| law | 346.043 77 |
| public administration | 354.34 |
| Land surveys | 333.08 |
| economics | 333.08 |
| public land | 333.18 |
| technology | 526.9 |
| Land tenure | 333.3 |
| agricultural sociology | 306.349 |
| economics | 333.3 |
| law | 346.043 2 |
| sociology | 306.32 |
| *see Manual at* 333.73–.78 vs. | |
| 333, 333.1–.5 | |
| Land titles | 346.043 8 |
| Land transfer | 333.33 |
| economics | 333.33 |
| law | 346.043 6 |
| Land transportation | 388 |
| engineering | 629.049 |
| military engineering | 623.61 |
| *see also* Ground transportation | |
| Land trusts | |
| law | 346.068 |
| Land use | 333.731 3 |
| agricultural surveys | 631.47 |
| community sociology | 307.33 |
| economics | 333.731 3 |

| | |
|---|---|
| Land use (continued) | |
| law | 346.045 |
| *see Manual at* 333.73–.78 vs. | |
| 333, 333.1–.5 | |
| Land use planning | |
| arts | 711 |
| Land valuation | 333.332 |
| Land value taxation | 336.225 |
| Land vehicles | 388.34 |
| engineering | 629.049 |
| transportation services | 388.34 |
| *see also* Automotive vehicles | |
| Land vertebrates | 596 |
| Landbund (Austrian political | |
| party) | 324.243 602 3 |
| Landed gentry | 305.523 2 |
| | T1—086 21 |
| genealogy | 929.2 |
| Lander County (Nev.) | T2—793 33 |
| Landes (France : Dept.) | T2—447 15 |
| Landesring der Unabhängigen | |
| (Swiss political party) | 324.249 408 |
| Landforms | 551.41 |
| | T2—14 |
| geography | 910.914 |
| geomorphology | 551.41 |
| physical geography | 910.021 4 |
| Landing | |
| aeronautics | 629.132 521 3 |
| manned space flight | 629.458 8 |
| Landing (Military tactics) | 355.422 |
| Landing accidents | 363.124 92 |
| *see also* Air safety | |
| Landing craft | 359.835 6 |
| design | 623.812 56 |
| engineering | 623.825 6 |
| naval equipment | 359.835 6 |
| naval units | 359.325 6 |
| Landing fields | 387.736 |
| *see also* Airports | |
| Landing lights | 629.135 1 |
| Landing systems | |
| aircraft | 629.134 381 |
| spacecraft | 629.474 2 |
| unmanned spacecraft | 629.464 2 |
| Landkreise | 320.83 |
| *see also* Counties | |
| Landlord and tenant | 333.54 |
| law | 346.043 4 |
| Landlord-tenant relations | 333.54 |
| law | 346.043 4 |
| Landlords' liability insurance | 368.56 |
| Landowners | 333.009 2 |

Landowning classes   305.523 2
  T1—086 21
Landquart (Switzerland :
  Bezirk)   T2—494 732 1
Landsailing   796.68
Landscape architects   712.092
Landscape architecture   712
  engineering aspects   624
Landscape design   712
Landscapes
  art representation   704.943 6
  arts   700.46
    T3C—36
  drawing   743.836
  literature   808.803 6
    history and criticism   809.933 6
    specific literatures   T3B—080 36
    history and
      criticism   T3B—093 6
  painting   758.1
Landshut (Germany)   T2—433 58
Landslides   551.307
Landsmål language   439.82
    T6—398 2
Landsmål literature   839.82
Lane County (Kan.)   T2—781 45
Lane County (Or.)   T2—795 31
Lạng Sơn (Vietnam :
  Province)   T2—597 1
Langbaurgh-on-Tees
  (England)   T2—428 54
Langeland (Denmark)   T2—489 4
Langi language   496.394
    T6—963 94
Langlade County (Wis.)   T2—775 354
Langley (B.C.)   T2—711 33
Language   400
    T1—014
  animal communication   591.59
  arts   T3C—34
  education   407.1
    prescriptive approach   418.007 1
    specific languages   T4—800 71
    *see Manual at* T1—407.1
  law   344.09
  philosophy   401
  sociology   306.44
Language acquisition   401.93
  specific languages   T4—019
  *see Manual at* T1—407.1
Language arts
  primary education   372.6

Language disorders
  medicine   616.855
  *see also* Communication
    disorders
Language experience approach
  primary education   372.62
  reading
    primary education   372.475
Language for special purposes   401.47
  specific languages   T4—014 7
Language groups
  sociology   305.7
Language laboratories
  applied linguistics   418.007 8
    specific languages   T4—800 78
Language planning   306.449
Language policy   306.449
Language programs
  public administration   353.7
Language regions   T2—175
Language textbooks
  audio-lingual approach   T4—83
    for nonnative speakers   T4—834
  formal approach   T4—82
    for nonnative speakers   T4—824
Language usage   418
  primary education   372.61
  specific languages   T4—8
Languages   400
    T6—1–9
  *see also* Language
  *see Manual at* Table 6
Langue d'oc   449
    T6—491
Langue d'oc literature   849
Languedoc (France)   T2—448
Languedoc-Roussillon
  (France)   T2—448
Languedocien dialect
  (Occitan language)   T6—491
Lanier County (Ga.)   T2—758 817
Laniidae   598.862
Lanolin   665.13
Lansdowne, Henry Charles Keith
  Petty-FitzMaurice, Marquess
  of
  Indian history   954.035 4
Länsi-Suomen lääni
  (Finland)   T2—489 73
Lansing (Mich.)   T2—774 27
Lantern-eyed fishes   597.64
Lantern fishes   597.61

Lanthanide series
  chemistry 546.41
  economic geology 553.494
  metallurgy 669.291
Lanthanotidae 597.959 6
Lanthanum
  chemistry 546.411
Lanuvian language 479.4
  T6—794
Lao (Tai people) T5—959 191
Lào Cai (Vietnam :
  Province) T2—597 1
Lao language 495.919 1
  T6—959 191
Lao literature 895.919 1
Laoighis (Ireland) T2—418 7
Laois (Ireland) T2—418 7
Laos 959.4
  T2—594
Lap robes
  manufacturing technology 677.626
Laparoscopic surgery 617.550 597
Laparoscopy
  diagnosis 617.550 754 5
    gynecology 618.107 545
  surgery 617.550 597
Lapeer County (Mich.) T2—774 42
Lapidary work 736.202 8
Lapin lääni (Finland) T2—489 77
Laplace functions 515.53
Laplace transform 515.723
Lapland T2—489 77
Lapp languages 494.57
  T6—945 7
Lapp literatures 894.57
Lappet embroidery 677.77
Lappi (Finland : Lääni) T2—489 77
Lapping tools 621.922
Lappish languages 494.57
  T6—945 7
Lappish literatures 894.57
Lappland landskap
  (Sweden) T2—488 8
Laprairie (Quebec : County) T2—714 34
Lapse
  insurance 368.016
Laptev Sea (Russia) 551.461 325
  T2—163 25
Laptop computers 004.16
  *see also* Personal computers
Lapwings 598.33
L'Aquila (Italy : Province) T2—457 11
  ancient T2—377 34
Lara (Venezuela) T2—872 5

Larache (Morocco :
  Province) T2—642
Laramie County (Wyo.) T2—787 19
Laramie Mountains (Wyo.
  and Colo.) T2—787 9
Larceny 364.162
  *see also* Theft
Larceny insurance 368.82
Larches 585.2
  forestry 634.975 7
  lumber 674.144
  ornamental arboriculture 635.977 52
Lard
  food technology 664.34
Large business 338.644
  economics 338.644
  management 658.023
  personnel management 658.303
Large format cameras 771.32
Large fruit flies 595.774
Large industry 338.644
Large intestine 573.379
  biology 573.379
  human anatomy 611.347
  human physiology 612.36
  medicine 616.34
  surgery 617.554 7
  *see also* Digestive system
Large-print publications
  bibliographies 011.63
  cataloging 025.349
  library treatment 025.179
Large-scale digital computers 004.12
  *see also* Mainframe computers
Large-scale systems 003.71
Large-type publications
  cataloging 025.349
  library treatment 025.179
Largemouth bass 597.738 8
  culture 639.377 388
  sports fishing 799.177 388
Lari 598.338
Laridae 598.338
Larimer County (Colo.) T2—788 68
Larisa (Greece : Nome) T2—495 4
Larks 598.825
Larkspurs 635.933 34
  botany 583.34
  floriculture 635.933 34
Larne (Northern Ireland :
  Borough) T2—416 16
Larue County (Ky.) T2—769 713
Larvacea 596.2

Larvae 571.876
  descriptive zoology 591.392
  physiology 571.876
Laryngeal diseases
  medicine 616.22
    *see also* Respiratory tract
      diseases — humans
Laryngeal muscles
  human anatomy 611.22
Laryngitis
  medicine 616.22
    *see also* Respiratory tract
      diseases — humans
Laryngology 616.22
Larynx 573.925
  biology 573.925
  human anatomy 611.22
  human physiology 612.233
    speech 612.78
  medicine 616.22
  surgery 617.533
  *see also* Respiratory system
Las Animas County (Colo.) T2—788 96
Las Palmas (Canary
  Islands : Province) T2—649
Las Tunas (Cuba : Province) T2—729 162
Las Vegas (Nev.) T2—793 135
Laser coagulation
  surgery 617.058
Laser communications
  engineering 621.382 7
Laser microsurgery 617.058
Laser optical discs 384.558
  *see also* Video recordings
Laser printing 686.233
Laser surgery 617.058
Laser warfare 358.39
Laser weapons
  engineering 623.446
Laser welding 671.52
Lasers 621.366
Lashley, Karl Spencer
  psychological system 150.194 32
Lasithi (Greece) T2—495 9
Lasqueti Island (B.C.) T2—711 31
Lassen County (Calif.) T2—794 26
Lassen Volcanic National
  Park (Calif.) T2—794 24
L'Assomption (Quebec :
  Regional County
  Municipality) T2—714 416
Lassos
  sports 799.202 82

Last Judgment
  Christianity 236.9
Last Supper 232.957
Latah County (Idaho) T2—796 86
Latakia (Syria : Province) T2—569 13
Latches 683.31
Late Middle Ages 940.19
  Italy 945.04
  Lombardian history 945.205
  Piedmontese history 945.104
  Sardinian history 945.903
  Sicilian history 945.804
  Tuscan history 945.504
  Venetian history 945.304
Latent heat 536.4
  chemical engineering 660.296 2
  evaporation and condensation 536.44
  fusion and solidification 536.42
  thermochemistry 541.362
Latent structure analysis 519.535
Later Prophets (Biblical books) 224
Laterality
  psychology 152.335
Latex biscuits 678.522
Latex paints 667.63
Latexes
  chemistry 547.842 5
  manufacturing technology 678.5
Lathers 541.345 14
  chemical engineering 660.294 514
  colloid chemistry 541.345 14
Lathes 621.942
Lathing 693.6
  architectural construction 721.044 6
Latidae 597.72
Latimer County (Okla.) T2—766 76
Latin America 980
               T2 8
Latin American literature 860
Latin American Spanish dialects 467.98
               T6—61
Latin Americans T5—68
Latin calligraphy 745.619 7
Latin language 470
               T6—71
  Biblical texts 220.47
  *see Manual at* 471–475, 478 vs.
    477
Latin literature 870
Latin peoples T5—4
Latin squares 511.64
Latina (Italy : Province) T2—456 23
  ancient T2—376 5

Latinian languages 479.4
 T6—794
Latinos T5—68
Latinos (U.S.) T5—680 73
Latitude 526.61
 celestial navigation 527.1
Latium (Italy)
 ancient T2—376
Latter-Day Saints
 biography 289.309 2
Latter-Day Saints Church 289.3
 *see also* Mormon Church
Lattice dynamics
 solid-state physics 530.411
Lattice plant 584.74
Lattice point geometry 516.35
Lattices (Crystals) 548.81
Lattices (Mathematics) 511.33
Latvia 947.96
 T2—479 6
Latvian language 491.93
 T6—919 3
Latvian literature 891.93
Latvians T5—919 3
Lauderdale County (Ala.) T2—761 99
Lauderdale County (Miss.) T2—762 676
Lauderdale County (Tenn.) T2—768 16
Lauds 264.15
 music 782.324
Laufen (Switzerland :
 Bezirk) T2—494 331
Laufenburg (Switzerland :
 Bezirk) T2—494 564 5
Laughter
 psychology 152.43
Launceston (Tas.) T2—946 5
Launch complexes
 guided missiles 623.451 9
 spacecraft 629.478
Launch vehicles
 guided missiles 623.451 9
Launching
 manned space flight 629.452
 space flight 629.41
 unmanned space flight 629.432
Laundering 667.13
 home economics 648.1
Laundries 667.13
 construction 690.43
 plumbing 696.183
 sanitation services 363.729 9
Laurales 583.23
Laurel County (Ky.) T2—769 143
Laurel wax 665.12

Laurels 583.23
Laurels (Ericaceae) 583.66
Laurels (Lauraceae) 583.23
Laurels (Saxifragales) 583.72
Laurens County (Ga.) T2—758 535
Laurens County (S.C.) T2—757 31
Laurentian Mountains
 (Quebec) T2—714 4
 Laurentians region T2—714 24
Laurentian Plateau T2—714
 Ontario T2—713 1
 Quebec T2—714
Laurentians (Quebec) T2—714 24
Laurentides (Quebec) T2—714 242
Laurentides (Quebec :
 Region) T2—714 24
Laurentides Provincial Park
 (Quebec) T2—714 48
Laurentides Wildlife
 Reserve (Quebec) T2—714 48
Laurier, Wilfrid, Sir
 Canadian history 971.056
Lausanne (Switzerland) T2—494 524 14
Lausanne (Switzerland :
 District) T2—494 524 1
Lausitz-Spreewald
 (Germany :
 Raumordnungsregion) T2—431 51
Lava 552.22
Lava Beds National
 Monument (Calif.) T2—794 21
Lavaca County (Tex.) T2—764 255
Laval (Quebec) T2—714 271
Lavalieres 391.7
 customs 391.7
 making 739.278
  costume jewelry 688.2
   handicrafts 745.594 2
  fine jewelry 739.278
Lavalleja (Uruguay : Dept.) T2—895 21
Lavatories (Bathrooms) 643.52
 construction 690.42
 home economics 643.52
 plumbing 696.182
Lavaux-Oron (Switzerland) T2—494 524 5
Lavenders (Plants) 583.96
Law 340
 arts 700.455 4
 T3C—355 4
 information systems 025.063 4

Law (continued)
  literature                              808.803 554
    history and criticism       809.933 554
    specific literatures     T3B—080 355 4
      history and
        criticism                   T3B—093 554
  religious                         208.4
    *see also* Religious law
  specific jurisdictions     349.4–.9
    *see Manual at* 340.02–.09 vs.
      349; *also at* 342–349
  specific socioeconomic regions 349.1
  *see Manual at* 363 vs.
    344.02–.05, 353–354
Law (Theology)
  Christianity                   241.2
  Judaism                     296.18
Law and ethics              340.112
Law and gospel            241.2
Law and morality        340.112
Law and society          340.115
Law codification          348.004
  law of nations          341.026 7
  United States          348.730 4
Law enforcement        363.23
  armed forces          355.133 23
  law                       345.052
  public administration   353.36
  *see Manual at* 363 vs.
    344.02–.05, 353–354
Law libraries             026.34
Law of falling bodies    531.5
Law of God
  Christianity                   241.2
Law of nations            341
  relation to domestic law 341.04
  *see Manual at* 341 vs. 327
Law of supply and demand 338.521
Law of the sea           341.45
  *see Manual at* 341.45 vs.
    343.0962
Law reform               340.3
Law reports             348.04
  national                 348.041
  provincial             348.043
  regional               348.042
  state                   348.043
Law schools             340.071 1
Lawn bowling           796.315
Lawn tennis             796.342
Lawns
  floriculture           635.964 7
  landscape architecture 712.6

Lawrence, John Laird Mair,
  Baron
  Indian history         954.035 1
Lawrence County (Ala.)   T2—761 92
Lawrence County (Ark.)   T2—767 25
Lawrence County (Ill.)    T2—773 76
Lawrence County (Ind.)   T2—772 26
Lawrence County (Ky.)    T2—769 26
Lawrence County (Miss.)  T2—762 536
Lawrence County (Mo.)   T2—778 75
Lawrence County (Ohio)  T2—771 88
Lawrence County (Pa.)    T2—748 93
Lawrence County (S.D.)  T2—783 91
Lawrence County (Tenn.)  T2—768 42
Lawrencium            546.449
Laws                       348.02
  enactment and repeal   328.37
  United States          348.732
Laws of thermodynamics  536.71
Lawsuits               347.053
  procedure             347.050 4
Lawyers                340.092
  fees
    law                   347.057 2
  malpractice          347.050 41
  occupational ethics    174.3
  practice              347.050 4
  role and function    340.023
Laxatives
  pharmacokinetics     615.732
Lay brothers
  religious orders       255.093
    church history      271.093
Lay ministry            253
  ecclesiology          262.15
  pastoral theology     253
Lay notaries            347.016
Lay sisters
  religious orders       255.909 3
  church history       271.909 3
Layering (Plant propagation) 631.534
Laying on of hands (Christian
  rite)                    265.9
Laylat al-Barā'ah      297.36
Laylat al-Mi'rāj       297.36
Laylat al-Qadr        297.362
Laymen (Church members) 262.15
  *see also* Laity (Church
    members)
Layoffs of employees
  economics             331.259 6
    employment security 331.259 6
    unemployment      331.137
    union control       331.889 6

Layoffs of employees (continued)
  law      344.012 596
  personnel management      658.313 4
    public administration      352.69
Layout
  plant management      658.23
  typesetting      686.225 2
Laz language      499.968
     T6—999 68
Lazarists      255.77
  church history      271.77
Lazio (Italy)      T2—456 2
  ancient      T2—376
LB (Austrian political party)      324.243 602 3
LdU (Swiss political party)      324.249 408
Le Bas-Richelieu (Quebec)      T2—714 39
Le Centre-de-la-Mauricie
  (Quebec)      T2—714 453
Le Domaine-du-Roy
  (Quebec)      T2—714 142
Le Fjord-du-Saguenay
  (Quebec)      T2—714 165
Le Flore County (Okla.)      T2—766 79
Le Golfe-du-Saint-Laurent
  (Quebec)      T2—714 179
Le Granit (Quebec)      T2—714 69
Le Haut-Richelieu (Quebec)      T2—714 38
Le Haut-Saint-François
  (Quebec)      T2—714 68
Le Haut-Saint-Laurent
  (Quebec)      T2—714 31
Le Haut-Saint-Maurice
  (Quebec)      T2—714 459
Le Locle (Switzerland :
  District)      T2—494 388
Le Rocher-Percé (Quebec)      T2—714 795
Le Sueur County (Minn.)      T2—776 553
Le Val-Saint-François
  (Quebec)      T2—714 65
Lea County (N.M.)      T2—789 33
Leach mining wells      622.22
Lead      669.4
  architectural construction      721.044 74
  building construction      693.74
  building material      691.84
  chemical engineering      661.068 8
  chemistry      546.688
  decorative arts      739.54
  economic geology      553.44
  human toxicology      615.925 688
  materials science      620.183
  metallography      669.954
  metallurgy      669.4
  metalworking      673.4

Lead (continued)
  mining      622.344
  organic chemistry
    applied      661.895
  physical metallurgy      669.964
  pollution      363.738 492
  *see also* Pollution
  public safety      363.179 1
  *see also* Hazardous materials
  *see also* Chemicals; Metals
Lead soldiers
  handicrafts      745.592 82
Leaded glass
  arts      748.5
Leadership      303.34
  armed forces      355.330 41
  Christian church      262.1
    local church      253
  executive management      658.409 2
    public administration      352.39
  political parties      324.22
  psychology      158.4
  schools      371.201 1
  social control      303.34
Leadership role of chief
  executives      658.409 2
  public administration      352.236
Leading windows
  buildings      698.5
Leadworts      583.5
Leaf beetles      595.764 8
  agricultural pests      632.764 8
Leaf frogs      597.87
Leaf insects      595.729
Leaf miner flies      595.774
Leaf miners
  agricultural pests      632.7
Leafhoppers      595.752
  agricultural pests      632.752
League of Arab States      341.247 7
  finance      336.091 68
League of Augsburg, War of the,
  1688–1697      940.252 5
  North American history      973.25
League of Nations      341.22
  finance      336.091 62
  law of nations      341.22
  public administration      352.112
League of Nations treaties series      341.026 1
League soccer      796.334 63
Leake County (Miss.)      T2—762 653
Leapfrog (Game)      796.14

| | |
|---|---|
| Learned societies | 060 |
| libraries | 027.68 |
| *see also* Nonprofit organizations | |
| Learned society buildings | |
| architecture | 727.9 |
| Learning | 153.15 |
| animal behavior | 591.514 |
| comparative psychology | 156.315 |
| educational psychology | 370.152 3 |
| psychology | 153.15 |
| children | 155.413 15 |
| Learning (Scholarship) | 001.2 |
| Learning ability | 153.9 |
| Learning curves | 153.158 |
| Learning disabilities | 371.9 |
| medicine | 616.858 89 |
| pediatrics | 618.928 588 9 |
| Learning-disabled people | T1—087 |
| education | 371.9 |
| social group | 305.908 4 |
| Learning disorders | |
| medicine | 616.858 89 |
| pediatrics | 618.928 588 9 |
| Lease system | |
| penology | 365.65 |
| Leases | |
| accounting | 657.75 |
| equipment | |
| financial management | 658.152 42 |
| personal property | |
| law | 346.047 |
| real property | 333.5 |
| economics | 333.5 |
| financial management | 658.152 42 |
| law | 346.043 46 |
| public | 333.16 |
| Least squares | 511.42 |
| Leather | 675 |
| handicrafts | 745.531 |
| home sewing material | 646.1 |
| Leather clothing | 391 |
| commercial technology | 685.22 |
| customs | 391 |
| home sewing | 646.4 |
| *see also* Clothing | |
| Leather covers | |
| bookbinding | 686.342 |
| Leather fungi | 579.6 |
| Leather goods | |
| commercial technology | 685 |
| Leather goods makers | 685.092 |
| Leather workers | 675.209 2 |
| Leatherback turtle | 597.928 9 |
| Leatherjackets (Crane fly larvae) | 595.772 |
| agricultural pests | 633.104 977 2 |
| Leave (Absence) | 331.257 6 |
| armed forces | 355.113 |
| labor economics | 331.257 6 |
| law | 344.012 576 |
| public employees | 342.068 6 |
| personnel management | 658.312 2 |
| public administration | 352.67 |
| Leavening agents | 664.68 |
| Leavenworth County (Kan.) | T2—781 38 |
| Leaves (Plants) | 581.48 |
| descriptive botany | 581.48 |
| paleobotany | 561.15 |
| physiology | 575.57 |
| Lebanese | T5—927 569 2 |
| Lebanese adder | 597.963 6 |
| Lebanon | 956.92 |
| | T2—569 2 |
| ancient | 939.44 |
| | T2—394 4 |
| Lebanon Conflict, 1982–1985 | 956.052 |
| Lebanon County (Pa.) | T2—748 19 |
| Lebanon War, 2006 | 956.920 452 |
| Lebel-sur-Quévillon (Quebec) | T2—714 115 |
| Lebern (Switzerland) | T2—494 357 3 |
| Lebesgue integral | 515.43 |
| Lebombo Mountains | T2—682 71 |
| Lebowa (South Africa) | T2—682 55 |
| Lecce (Italy : Province) | T2—457 53 |
| ancient | T2—377 65 |
| Lecco (Italy : Province) | T2—452 37 |
| ancient | T2—372 265 |
| Lecterns | |
| church architecture | 726.529 2 |
| Lectionaries (Public worship) | 264.34 |
| Anglican | 264.030 34 |
| texts | 264.032 |
| preaching | 251.6 |
| Roman Catholic | 264.020 34 |
| texts | 264.029 |
| Lecture method | 371.396 |
| Christian religious education | 268.632 |
| Lectures | 080 |
| museum services | 069.15 |
| Lecturing | |
| rhetoric | 808.51 |
| Lecythidaceae | 583.76 |
| LED (Diodes) | 621.381 522 |
| Ledbury (England) | T2—424 2 |
| Lee, Charles | |
| treason | 973.383 |

Lee, Hsien Loong
  Singaporean history     959.570 53
Lee, Kuan Yew
  Singaporean history     959.570 51
Lee County (Ala.)     T2—761 55
Lee County (Ark.)     T2—767 89
Lee County (Fla.)     T2—759 48
Lee County (Ga.)     T2—758 943
Lee County (Ill.)     T2—773 36
Lee County (Iowa)     T2—777 99
Lee County (Ky.)     T2—769 185
Lee County (Miss.)     T2—762 935
Lee County (N.C.)     T2—756 355
Lee County (S.C.)     T2—757 67
Lee County (Tex.)     T2—764 247
Lee County (Va.)     T2—755 735
Leeaceae     583.86
Leeches     592.66
Leeds (England : City)     T2—428 19
Leeds and Grenville (Ont.)     T2—713 73
Leeks     641.352 6
  botany     584.33
  cooking     641.652 6
  food     641.352 6
  garden crop     635.26
Leelanau County (Mich.)     T2—774 635
Leer (Germany : Landkreis)     T2—435 917
Lee's invasion of Maryland, 1862     973.733 6
Leeton (N.S.W.)     T2—944 8
Leeward Islands (West Indies)     972.97
    T2—729 7
Leflore County (Miss.)     T2—762 46
Left, The (German political
  party)     324.243 074
Left and right (Psychology)     152.335
Left-hand techniques
  music     784.193 66
Left-handedness
  psychology     152.335
Left May languages     T6—991 2
Leftist parties     324.217
  international organizations     324.17
Leftovers (Cooking)     641.552
Leg bones
  human anatomy     611.718
  human physiology     612.751
Leg exercises     613.718 88
Leg muscles
  human anatomy     611.738
Leg techniques
  music     784.193 8
Lega dei Ticinesi (Swiss political
  party)     324.249 408 4

Lega-Kalanga languages     496.394
    T6—963 94
Lega nord (Italian political party)     324.245 084
Legal accounting     657.834
Legal aid     362.586
  law     347.017
    criminal law     345.012 7
    welfare law     344.032 58
  social services     362.586
Legal codes     348.023
  United States     348.732 3
Legal costs
  law     347.057
Legal counsel
  management use     658.12
Legal education     340.07
Legal ethics     174.3
Legal fees
  judgments
    law     347.077
  law     347.057
Legal keyboarding     652.326
Legal malpractice     347.050 41
Legal officers     347.016
  criminal courts     345.012 6
Legal personnel     340.092
  fees
    law     347.057 2
  role and function     340.023
Legal positivism     340.112
Legal procedure     347.05
Legal process     347.05
Legal profession     340.023
Legal reasoning     340.11
Legal responsibility     346.022
Legal services     347
Legal systems     340.5
Legal tender     332.42
Legal writing     808.066 34
  *see Manual at* 340 vs.
    808.06634
Legalism (Chinese philosophy)     181.115
Legations     327.2
  architecture     725.17
  public administration     353.13
Legendary animals     398.245 4
  art representation     704.947
  arts     700.474
    T3C—374
  folklore     398.245 4
    history and criticism     398.469

| | |
|---|---|
| **Legendary animals** (continued) | |
| literature | 808.803 74 |
| history and criticism | 809.933 74 |
| specific literatures | T3B—080 374 |
| history and criticism | T3B—093 74 |
| mysteries | 001.944 |
| **Legendary beings** | 398.21 |
| art representation | 704.947 |
| arts | 700.475 |
| | T3C—375 |
| folklore | 398.21 |
| history and criticism | 398.45 |
| literature | 808.803 75 |
| history and criticism | 809.933 75 |
| specific literatures | T3B—080 375 |
| history and criticism | T3B—093 75 |
| **Legendary persons** | 398.22 |
| art representation | 704.947 |
| arts | 700.451 |
| | T3C—351 |
| folklore | 398.22 |
| history and criticism | 398.352 |
| literature | 808.803 51 |
| history and criticism | 809.933 51 |
| specific literatures | T3B—080 351 |
| history and criticism | T3B—093 51 |
| **Legendary places** | 398.234 |
| art representation | 704.947 |
| arts | 700.472 |
| | T3C—372 |
| folklore | 398.234 |
| history and criticism | 398.42 |
| literature | 808.803 72 |
| history and criticism | 809.933 72 |
| specific literatures | T3B—080 372 |
| history and criticism | T3B—093 72 |
| mysteries | 001.94 |
| **Legendre function** | 515.53 |
| **Legendre polynomials** | 515.55 |
| **Legendre transform** | 515.723 |
| **Legends** | |
| art representation | 704.947 |
| arts | 700.47 |
| | T3C—37 |
| folklore | 398.2 |
| *see Manual at* 398.2 vs. | |
| 201.3, 230, 270, 292–299 | |

| | |
|---|---|
| **Legends** (continued) | |
| literature | 808.803 7 |
| history and criticism | 809.933 7 |
| specific literatures | T3B—080 37 |
| history and criticism | T3B—093 7 |
| paintings | 753.7 |
| **Leghorn (Poultry)** | 636.55 |
| **Legionella** | 579.33 |
| **Legionnaires' disease** | |
| medicine | 616.241 |
| *see also* Respiratory tract diseases — humans | |
| **Legions (Military units)** | 355.31 |
| **Legislation (Enactment and repeal)** | 328.37 |
| law | 342.057 |
| **Legislation (Laws and statutes)** | 348.02 |
| **Legislative bodies** | 328 |
| bibliographies of publications | 011.532 |
| law | 342.05 |
| *see Manual at* 909, 930–990 vs. 320 | |
| **Legislative branch** | 328 |
| law | 342.05 |
| **Legislative budgets** | 352.48 |
| *see also* Budgets (Public) | |
| **Legislative buildings** | |
| architecture | 725.11 |
| **Legislative calendars** | 328.4–.9 |
| **Legislative districts** | 328.334 5 |
| **Legislative drafting** | 328.373 |
| **Legislative duties** | 328.34 |
| law | 342.052 |
| **Legislative-executive relations** | 328.345 6 |
| law | 342.044 |
| **Legislative functions** | 328.34 |
| law | 342.052 |
| **Legislative hearings** | 328.345 |
| law | 348.01 |
| United States | 348.731 |
| *see Manual at* 300–330, 355– 390 vs. 342–347, 352–354 | |
| **Legislative historics** | 348.01 |
| United States | 348.731 |
| **Legislative immunity** | 328.348 |
| **Legislative institutions** | |
| sociology | 306.23 |
| **Legislative investigation** | 328.345 2 |
| **Legislative journals** | 328.4–.9 |
| **Legislative-judicial relations** | 320.404 |
| law | 342.044 |
| **Legislative lobbying** | 328.38 |
| law | 342.05 |

| | |
|---|---|
| Legislative organization | 328.36 |
|   law | 342.057 |
| Legislative oversight | 328.345 6 |
| Legislative powers | 328.34 |
|   chief executives | 352.235 |
|   law | 342.052 |
| Legislative privileges | 328.347 |
| Legislative procedures | 328.1 |
|   law | 342.057 |
| Legislative process | 328 |
| Legislative reference bureaus | 027.65 |
| Legislative reform | 328.304 |
| Legislative reporting | 328.1 |
| Legislative representation | 328.334 |
| Legislators | |
|   biography | 328.092 |
|   law | 342.055 |
|   personal privileges | 328.347 |
|   role and function | 328.33 |
| Legitimacy of government | 320.011 |
| Legitimation | |
|   family law | 346.017 5 |
| Legnica (Poland : | |
|   Voivodeship) | T2—438 52 |
| Legs | 591.479 |
|   animal physiology | 573.79 |
|   descriptive zoology | 591.479 |
|   human anatomy | 611.98 |
|   human physiology | 612.98 |
|   regional medicine | 617.58 |
|   surgery | 617.580 59 |
| Legumes | 583.74 |
|   botany | 583.74 |
|   commercial processing | 664.805 65 |
|   cooking | 641.656 5 |
|   edible fruits | 641.344 6 |
|     cooking | 641.644 6 |
|     food | 641.344 6 |
|     orchard crop | 634.46 |
|   field crop | 633.3 |
|   food | 641.356 5 |
|   garden crop | 635.65 |
|   *see Manual at* 633–635 | |
| Leguminales | 583.74 |
|   *see also* Legumes | |
| Lehigh County (Pa.) | T2—748 27 |
| Lehurutshe (South Africa : | |
|   District) | T2—682 48 |
| Leicester (England) | T2—425 42 |
| Leicestershire (England) | T2—425 4 |
| Leiden (Netherlands) | T2—492 38 |
| Leinster (Ireland) | T2—418 |
| Leiopelmatidae | 597.86 |
| Leipzig (Germany) | T2—432 122 |

| | |
|---|---|
| Leipzig (Germany : | |
|   Direktionsbezirk) | T2—432 12 |
| Leipzig (Germany : | |
|   Regierungsbezirk) | T2—432 12 |
| Leiria (Portugal : District) | T2—469 41 |
| Leishmaniasis | |
|   incidence | 614.534 |
|   medicine | 616.936 4 |
|   *see also* Communicable | |
|     diseases — humans | |
| Leisure | 790.1 |
|   educational objective | 370.119 |
|   ethics | 175 |
|   influence on crime | 364.25 |
|   recreational arts | 790.1 |
|   sociology | 306.481 2 |
| Leitmotif | 781.248 |
| Leitneriales | 583.43 |
| Leitrim (Ireland) | T2—417 6 |
| Leix (Ireland) | T2—418 7 |
| Lelystad (Netherlands) | T2—492 2 |
| Léman Lake (Switzerland | |
|   and France) | T2—494 52 |
|   France | T2—445 84 |
|   Switzerland | T2—494 52 |
| Lemhi County (Idaho) | T2—796 78 |
| Lemmings | 599.358 2 |
| Lemmus | 599.358 2 |
| Lemnaceae | 584.64 |
| Lemnos Island (Greece) | T2—495 82 |
|   ancient | T2—391 1 |
| Lemon shark | 597.34 |
| Lemons | 641.343 34 |
|   commercial processing | 664.804 334 |
|   cooking | 641.643 34 |
|   food | 641.343 34 |
|   orchard crop | 634.334 |
| Lempira (Honduras) | T2—728 382 |
| Lemuridae | 599.83 |
| Lemurs | 599.83 |
|   conservation technology | 639.979 83 |
|   resource economics | 333.959 83 |
| Lenape Indians | T5—973 45 |
| Lenawee County (Mich.) | T2—774 31 |
| Lenca Indians | T5—979 |
| Lenca language | 497.9 |
| | T6—979 |
| Lending institutions | 332.1 |
|   law | 346.082 |
|   public administration | 354.86 |
|   *see also* Banks (Finance) | |
| Lending power (Legislative | |
|   bodies) | 328.341 2 |

Lenin, Vladimir Il'ich
  Russian history    947.084 1
Leningrad (Russia : Oblast)  T2—472 1
Leningradskaĭa oblast'
  (Russia)    T2—472 1
Leninism    335.43
  economics    335.43
  political ideology    320.532 2
Lenje-Tonga languages    496.391
    T6—963 91
Lenni Lenape Indians  T5—973 45
Lenni Lenape language    497.345
    T6—973 45
Lennox and Addington
  (Ont.)  T2—713 59
Lennox Hills (Scotland)  T2—413 12
Leno-weave fabrics    677.652
  *see also* Textiles
Lenoir County (N.C.)  T2—756 385
Lens diseases
  ophthalmology    617.742
    *see also* Eye diseases —
      humans
Lenses
  cameras    771.352
  manufacturing technology    681.423
Lent    263.92
  devotional literature    242.34
  sermons    252.62
Lenten cooking    641.566
Lenten music    781.725
Lentibulariaceae    583.95
Lentils    641.356 58
  botany    583.74
  commercial processing    664.805 658
  cooking    641.656 58
  field crop    633.37
  food    641.356 58
  garden crop    635.658
Lenzburg (Switzerland :
  Bezirk)  T2—494 562 5
Leo (Cat genus)    599.755
Leo (Zodiac)    133.526 6
Leominster (England :
  District)  T2—424 2
León (Nicaragua : Dept.)  T2—728 512
León (Spain : Province)  T2—462 1
León (Spain : Region)  T2—462
Leon County (Fla.)  T2—759 88
Leon County (Tex.)  T2—764 233
Leopard seal    599.796
Leopards    599.755 4
  conservation technology    639.979 755 4
  resource economics    333.959 755 4

Leopold I, Holy Roman Emperor
  German history    943.044
Léopold III, King of the Belgians
  Belgian history    949.304 2
Lepcha language    495.4
    T6—954
Lephlale (South Africa :
  District)  T2—682 53
Lepidodendrales    561.79
Lepidoptera    595.78
  agricultural pests    632.78
Lepidosauria    597.94
  paleozoology    567.94
Lepontine Alps (Italy and
  Switzerland)  T2—494 78
Leporidae    599.32
Lepospondyli    597.8
  paleozoology    567.8
Leprosy
  incidence    614.546
  medicine    616.998
    *see also* Communicable
      diseases — humans
Leptis Magna (Extinct city)  T2—397 4
Leptodactylidae    597.875
Leptolepis    567
Leptons    539.721 1
Leptostraca    595.379 2
Leptotyphlopidae    597.969
Leptureae    584.9
Lepus    599.328
L'Érable (Quebec)  T2—714 575
Lérida (Spain : Province)  T2—467 4
Lernaeopodoida    595.34
Les Appalaches (Quebec)  T2—714 712
Les Basques (Quebec)  T2—714 766
Les Chenaux (Quebec)  T2—714 455
Les Chutes-de-la-Chaudière
  (Quebec)  T2—714 59
Les Collines-de-l'Outaouais
  (Quebec)  T2—714 223
Les Etchemins (Quebec)  T2—714 72
Les Îles-de-la-Madeleine
  (Quebec)  T2—714 797
Les Jardins-de-Napierville
  (Quebec)  T2—714 35
Les Laurentides (Quebec)  T2—714 242
Les Maskoutains (Quebec)  T2—714 523
Les Moulins (Quebec)  T2—714 412
Les Pays-d'en-Haut
  (Quebec)  T2—714 244
Les Saintes Islands
  (Guadeloupe)  T2—729 76
Les Sources (Quebec)  T2—714 573

| | |
|---|---|
| Lesbianism | 306.766 3 |
| religion | 200.866 43 |
| Christianity | 270.086 643 |
| *see also* Homosexuality | |
| Lesbians | 306.766 3 |
| | T1—086 643 |
| psychology | 155.344 3 |
| religion | 200.866 43 |
| Christianity | 270.086 643 |
| pastoral theology | 259.086 643 |
| social welfare | 362.839 66 |
| Lesbos (Greece) | T2—495 82 |
| Lesbos Island (Greece) | T2—495 82 |
| ancient | T2—391 2 |
| Leslie County (Ky.) | T2—769 152 |
| Lesotho | 968.85 |
| | T2—688 5 |
| Lesotho people | T5—968 85 |
| Lespedezas | 633.364 |
| botany | 583.74 |
| forage crop | 633.364 |
| Less developed countries | T2—172 4 |
| Lesser Antilles | T2—729 |
| Lesser celandine | 583.34 |
| Lesser panda | 599.763 |
| Lesser Slave Lake (Alta.) | T2—712 31 |
| Lesser Sunda Islands | |
| (Indonesia) | T2—598 6 |
| Lesson plans | 371.302 8 |
| Lesvos (Greece) | T2—495 82 |
| Leszno (Poland : | |
| Voivodeship) | T2—438 49 |
| Letaba (South Africa) | T2—682 59 |
| Letcher County (Ky.) | T2—769 163 |
| Lethal gases | |
| human toxicology | 615.91 |
| Lethbridge (Alta.) | T2—712 345 |
| Lethrinidae | 597.72 |
| Letsie III, King of Lesotho | |
| Lesotho history | 968.850 32 |
| Lettering | |
| architectural design | 729.19 |
| bookbinding | 686.36 |
| decorative arts | 745.61 |
| prints | 769.5 |
| stone | 736.5 |
| technical drawing | 604.243 |
| Letterpress | |
| mechanical printing technique | 686.231 2 |
| Letters (Correspondence) | 383.122 |
| biography | 920 |
| | T1—092 |
| direct advertising | 659.133 |
| etiquette | 395.4 |
| Letters (Correspondence) (continued) | |
| office services | 651.75 |
| rhetoric | 808.066 651 |
| postal handling | 383.122 |
| *see also* Postal service | |
| Letters (Literature) | 808.86 |
| criticism | 809.6 |
| theory | 808.6 |
| history | 809.6 |
| rhetoric | 808.6 |
| specific literatures | T3B—6 |
| individual authors | T3A—6 |
| Letters of credit | 332.77 |
| law | 346.096 |
| Letters rogatory | 347.012 |
| criminal law | 345.012 2 |
| Lettish language | 491.93 |
| | T6—919 3 |
| Lettish literature | 891.93 |
| Letts | T5—919 3 |
| Lettuce | 641.355 2 |
| botany | 583.99 |
| commercial processing | 664.805 52 |
| cooking | 641.655 2 |
| food | 641.355 2 |
| garden crop | 635.52 |
| Lëtzeburgesch dialect | 437.949 35 |
| | T6—32 |
| Leucite | |
| mineralogy | 549.68 |
| Leucocytes | 571.96 |
| *see also* Leukocytes | |
| Leuk (Switzerland : Bezirk) | T2—494 794 8 |
| Leukas (Greece) | T2—495 5 |
| Leukemia | 362.196 994 19 |
| incidence | 614.599 941 9 |
| medicine | 616.994 19 |
| social services | 362.196 994 19 |
| *see also* Cancer — humans | |
| Leukocyte count | |
| human physiology | 612.112 7 |
| Leukocyte disorders | |
| cancer | 362.196 994 19 |
| incidence | 614.599 941 9 |
| medicine | 616.994 19 |
| social services | 362.196 994 19 |
| *see also* Cancer — humans | |
| medicine | 616.154 |
| *see also* Cardiovascular | |
| diseases — humans | |
| Leukocytes | 571.96 |
| human biochemistry | 612.112 1 |
| human histology | 612.112 |
| human immunology | 616.079 |

Leukocytes (continued)
  human physiology — 612.112
  medicine — 616.154
  physiology — 571.96
  *see also* Cardiovascular system
Leukocytosis
  medicine — 616.154
  *see also* Cardiovascular
    diseases — humans
Leukopenia
  medicine — 616.154
  *see also* Cardiovascular
    diseases — humans
Leukorrhea
  gynecology — 618.15
  *see also* Female genital
    diseases — humans
Levant — T2—56
Levees (Flood barriers) — 627.42
Leveling (Surveying) — 526.36
Levels of education — 372–374
  *see Manual at* 371.01–.8 vs.
    372–374, 378; *also at*
    372.24 and 373.23
Leventina (Switzerland) — T2—494 781
Lévis (Quebec) — T2—714 59
Levitation (Spiritualism) — 133.92
Leviticus — 222.13
Levy County (Fla.) — T2—759 77
Lewes (England : District) — T2—422 57
Lewis and Clark County
  (Mont.) — T2—786 615
Lewis County (Idaho) — T2—796 84
Lewis County (Ky.) — T2—769 295
Lewis County (Mo.) — T2—778 345
Lewis County (N.Y.) — T2—747 59
Lewis County (Tenn.) — T2—768 432
Lewis County (W. Va.) — T2—754 61
Lewis County (Wash.) — T2—797 82
Lewisham (London,
  England) — T2—421 63
Lexicographers — 413.092
Lexicography — 413.028
   — T1—03
  specific languages — T4—302 8
Lexicology — 401.4
  specific languages — T4—014
Lexington (Ky.) — T2—769 47
Lexington (Mass.) — T2—744 4
Lexington (Va.) — T2—755 853
Lexington, Battle of, 1775 — 973.331 1
Lexington County (S.C.) — T2—757 73
Leyte (Philippines) — T2—599 5
Leyte Island (Philippines) — T2—599 5

Lezghi language — 499.964
   — T6—999 64
Lezghian language — 499.964
   — T6—999 64
Lhasa apso — 636.72
Lhomi language — 495.4
   — T6—954
Liability — 346.022
  government — 342.088
  schools — 344.075
Liability for environmental
  damages — 344.046
Liability insurance — 368.5
  law — 346.086 5
Liability of states
  law of nations — 341.26
Liability risks — 368.08
Liaoning Sheng (China) — T2—518 2
Liard River — T2—711 87
Libel — 364.156
  law — 345.025 6
    criminal law — 345.025 6
    torts — 346.034
Liberal Catholic Church — 284.8
  *see also* Old Catholic churches
Liberal-Conservative Party
  (Canada) — 324.271 04
Liberal Democrats (British
  political party) — 324.241 06
Liberal education — 370.112
Liberal Forum (Austrian political
  party) — 324.243 606
Liberal parties — 324.216
  international organizations — 324.16
Liberal Party (Great Britain) — 324.241 06
Liberal Party of Australia — 324.294 05
Liberal Party of Canada — 324.271 06
Liberal Party of New York State — 324.274 708
Liberal theology — 230.046
Liberale Partei der Schweiz — 324.249 406
Liberale Parteien (Austrian
  political party) — 324.243 602 6
Liberales Forum (Austrian
  political party) — 324.243 606
Liberalism
  philosophy — 148
  political ideology — 320.51
Liberality
  ethics — 177.7
Liberation theology — 230.046 4
  political aspects — 261.7
  Roman Catholic — 230.2
  socioeconomic aspects — 261.8

Liberecký kraj (Czech
  Republic)    T2—437 17
Liberia    966.62
   T2—666 2
Liberians    T5—966 62
Libertad (El Salvador :
  Dept.)    T2—728 422
Libertad (Peru : Dept.)    T2—851 6
Libertad (Peru : Region)    T2—851 6
Libertador General
  Bernardo O'Higgins
  (Chile)    T2—833 2
Libertadores Wari (Peru)    T2—852 7
Libertarian parties    324.218
  international organizations    324.18
Libertarian Party (U.S.)    324.273 8
Libertarianism    320.512
Liberty (Personal freedom)    323.44
  philosophy    123.5
  *see also* Civil rights
Liberty (Political theory)    320.011
Liberty County (Fla.)    T2—759 923
Liberty County (Ga.)    T2—758 733
Liberty County (Mont.)    T2—786 13
Liberty County (Tex.)    T2—764 155
Libido    155.31
Libode (South Africa :
  District)    T2—687 58
Libra (Zodiac)    133.527 2
Librarians    020.92
  library operations
    role and function    023.2
Libraries    027
  accounting    657.832
  armed forces    355.346
  law    344.092
  operations    025
  political aspects    021.8
  public administrative support    352.744
  publications for
    bibliographies    011.67
    reviews    028.167
  publishing    070.594
  relationships    021
  residential interior decoration    747.73
Libraries and museums    021.3
Library acquisitions    025.2
Library administration    025.1
Library aides    023.3
Library and state    021.8
Library assistants    023.3
Library boards    021.82
Library bookbinding    686.303 2

Library buildings
  architecture    727.8
  area planning    711.57
  institutional housekeeping    647.998
  lighting    621.322 78
    plant management    022.7
  planning    022.3
Library catalogs    025.31
  library science    025.31
  maintenance    025.317
Library clerks    023.3
Library collections
  maintenance    025.8
Library commissions    021.82
Library-community relations    021.2
Library consortia    021.65
Library consultants    023.2
Library cooperation    021.64
Library equipment
  management    022.9
Library extension
  public libraries    027.42
Library-government relations    021.8
Library information networks    021.65
Library materials
  preservation    025.84
  selection policy    025.21
Library networks    021.65
Library of Congress    027.573
Library of Congress
  Classification    025.433
Library orientation    025.56
Library outreach programs
  public libraries    027.42
Library paraprofessionals    023.3
Library policy (Government
  policy)    021.8
Library regulations    025.56
Library science    020
  arts    T3C—39
Library signs    025.56
Library systems
  cooperation    021.65
  operations    025
Library systems analysts    023.2
Library technicians    023.3
Library trustees    021.82
Library use studies    025.58
Librettos    780
  treatises    780.268
Libreville (Gabon)    T2—672 1

| | |
|---|---|
| Libya | 961.2 |
| | T2—612 |
| ancient | 939.74 |
| | T2—397 4 |
| Libyan Desert | T2—612 |
| Libyans | T5—927 612 |
| Lice | 595.756 |
| disease carriers | 571.986 |
| medicine | 614.432 4 |
| Lice infestations | |
| medicine | 616.572 |
| License agreements | 343.07 |
| License fees | |
| public revenues | 336.16 |
| License plates | 929.9 |
| Licensing | 352.84 |
| economic law | 343.07 |
| enforcement | 363.233 |
| export trade | 382.64 |
| *see also* Export trade | |
| import trade | 382.54 |
| *see also* Import trade | |
| intangible property law | 346.048 |
| public administration | 352.84 |
| Lichees | 641.346 |
| *see also* Litchis | |
| Lichens | 579.7 |
| Lichfield (England : | |
| District) | T2—424 68 |
| Lichtenburg (South Africa : | |
| District) | T2—682 44 |
| Licking County (Ohio) | T2—771 54 |
| Lie algebras | 512.482 |
| Lie detectors | 363.254 |
| civil rights | 323.448 |
| criminal investigation | 363.254 |
| law of privacy | 342.085 8 |
| law of self-incrimination | 345.056 |
| personnel management | 658.314 |
| selection procedures | 658.311 2 |
| Lie groups | 512.482 |
| Liechtenstein | 943.648 |
| | T2—436 48 |
| ancient | 936.364 8 |
| | T2—363 648 |
| Lieder | 782.421 68 |
| Liège (Belgium : Province) | T2—493 46 |
| Liens | |
| law | 346.074 |
| Liesegang rings | 541.348 5 |
| Liestal (Switzerland) | T2—494 335 4 |
| Liestal (Switzerland : | |
| Bezirk) | T2—494 335 |

| | |
|---|---|
| Lieutenant governors | |
| public administration | 352.239 |
| LiF (Austrian political party) | 324.243 606 |
| Life | |
| biological nature | 570.1 |
| civil rights issues | 323.43 |
| medical ethics | 179.7 |
| origin | 576.83 |
| *see also* Origin of life | |
| philosophy | 113.8 |
| respect for | |
| ethics | 179.1 |
| religion | 205.691 |
| Buddhism | 294.356 91 |
| Christianity | 241.691 |
| Hinduism | 294.548 691 |
| Judaism | 296.369 1 |
| Life after death | |
| occultism | 133.901 3 |
| philosophy | 129 |
| religion | 202.3 |
| Christianity | 236.2 |
| Islam | 297.23 |
| Judaism | 296.33 |
| philosophy of religion | 218 |
| Life care communities | 362.61 |
| *see also* Health care facilities | |
| Life cycle | 571.8 |
| animal behavior | 591.56 |
| animal physiology | 571.81 |
| animals | 591.56 |
| arts | T3C—354 |
| customs | 392 |
| developmental biology | 571.8 |
| etiquette | 395.2 |
| folklore | 398.274 |
| history and criticism | 398.354 |
| literature | 808.803 54 |
| history and criticism | 809.933 54 |
| specific literatures | T3B—080 354 |
| history and | |
| criticism | T3B—093 54 |
| microorganisms | 571.842 9 |
| music | 781.58 |
| physiology | 571.8 |
| plants | 571.82 |
| Life estates | 346.043 2 |
| land economics | 333.323 4 |
| Life expectancy | 304.645 |
| human physiology | 612.68 |
| Life insurance | 368.32 |
| law | 346.086 32 |
| tax law | 343.052 4 |
| Life on other planets | 576.839 |

| | |
|---|---|
| Life rafts | |
| aircraft | 629.134 43 |
| Life sciences | 570 |
| Life sciences and religion | 201.657 |
| Christianity | 261.55 |
| philosophy of religion | 215.7 |
| Life skills | 646.7 |
| primary education | 372.37 |
| Life-support systems | |
| spacecraft | 629.477 |
| Lifeboats | 387.29 |
| design | 623.812 9 |
| engineering | 623.829 |
| transportation services | 387.29 |
| *see also* Ships | |
| Lifelong education | 374 |
| | T1—071 5 |
| *see also* Adult education | |
| Lifesaving equipment | |
| aircraft | 629.134 43 |
| ships | 623.865 |
| Liffey, River (Ireland) | T2—418 3 |
| Lift (Aeronautics) | 629.132 33 |
| Lift systems | |
| air-cushion vehicles | 629.313 |
| Lifts (Canal engineering) | 627.135 3 |
| Lifts (Elevators) | 621.877 |
| *see also* Elevators (Lifts) | |
| Liga veneta (Italian political | |
| party) | 324.245 308 4 |
| Ligament diseases | |
| medicine | 616.77 |
| *see also* Musculoskeletal | |
| diseases — humans | |
| Ligaments | 573.783 56 |
| biology | 573.783 56 |
| human anatomy | 611.72 |
| human physiology | 612.752 |
| medicine | 616.77 |
| *see also* Musculoskeletal | |
| system | |
| Ligands | 541.224 2 |
| Ligases | 572.79 |
| *see also* Enzymes | |
| Light | 535 |
| arts | 701.8 |
| drawing | 741.018 |
| astrophysics | 523.015 |
| biophysics | 571.455 |
| humans | 612.014 44 |
| chemical effect | 541.353 3 |
| chemical engineering | 660.295 33 |
| engineering | 621.36 |
| health | 613.19 |

| | |
|---|---|
| Light (continued) | |
| meteorology | 551.565 |
| military engineering | 623.042 |
| physics | 535 |
| therapeutics | 615.831 |
| Light absorption | 535.326 |
| meteorology | 551.566 |
| Light beacons | |
| navigation aids | 623.894 4 |
| Light-emitting diodes | 621.381 522 |
| Light harness horses | 636.17 |
| Light lists | |
| navigation aids | 623.894 5 |
| Light meals | 642 |
| cooking | 641.53 |
| customs | 394.125 3 |
| Light metals | 669.72 |
| economic geology | 553.492 |
| metallography | 669.957 2 |
| metallurgy | 669.72 |
| metalworking | 673.72 |
| physical metallurgy | 669.967 2 |
| Light microscopy | |
| biology | 570.282 3 |
| Light orchestras | 784.4 |
| Light pens | |
| bar-code scanners | 006.42 |
| engineering | 621.399 4 |
| computer graphics | 006.62 |
| engineering | 621.399 6 |
| computer input devices | 004.76 |
| engineering | 621.398 6 |
| Light rail transit systems | 388.46 |
| engineering | 625.6 |
| transportation services | 388.46 |
| Light spectroscopy | |
| engineering | 621.361 |
| physics | 535.843 |
| Light trucks | 388.343 |
| driving | 629.284 3 |
| engineering | 629.223 |
| repair | 629.287 3 |
| transportation services | 388.343 |
| *see also* Trucks | |
| Light verse | 808.817 |
| history and criticism | 809.17 |
| specific literatures | T3B—107 |
| individual authors | T3A—1 |
| Lighter-than-air aircraft | 387.732 |
| engineering | 629.133 2 |
| military engineering | 623.741 |
| sports flying | 797.51 |
| transportation services | 387.732 |
| *see also* Aircraft | |

Lighters (Ships) 387.245
  towed 387.29
  *see also* Ships
Lighthouses 387.155
  engineering 623.894 2
  transportation services 387.155
Lighting 621.32
  airport engineering 629.136 5
  architectural design 729.28
  automobile 629.271
  cinematography 777.52
  customs 392.36
  dramatic performances 792.025
    motion pictures 791.430 25
    stage 792.025
    television 791.450 25
  engineering 621.32
  household management 644.3
  interior decoration 747.92
  library buildings 621.322 78
    plant management 022.7
  mining 622.47
  museums 069.29
  photography 778.7
  plant management 658.24
  public areas 628.95
  religious significance 203.7
    Christianity 246.6
  *see also* Symbolism —
    religious significance
  road transportation 388.312
  videography 777.52
Lighting fixtures 621.32
  ceramic arts 738.8
  church architecture 726.529 8
  furniture arts 749.63
  household management 645.5
  manufacturing technology 683.83
Lightning 551.563 2
  crop damage 632.15
Lightning arresters 621.317
Lightning protection
  buildings 693.898
Lightships 387.28
  engineering 623.894 3
  *see also* Ships
Lignin
  recovery from pulp 676.5
Lignin-derived plastics 668.45
Lignite 553.22
  economic geology 553.22
  mining 622.332
  properties 662.622 2
Lignum vitaes 583.79

Liguria (Italy) 945.18
   T2—451 8
  ancient T2—371
Ligurian language 491.993
   T6—919 93
Ligurian Republic 945.180 82
Ligurian Riviera (Italy) T2—451 8
Ligurian Sea 551.461 382
   T2—163 82
Lihou (Channel Islands) T2—423 49
Lihoumel (Channel Islands) T2—423 49
Lij Yasu, Negus of Ethiopia
  Ethiopian history 963.053
Lilacs 635.933 87
  botany 583.87
  floriculture 635.933 87
Lilaeaceae 584.74
L'Île-d'Orléans (Quebec) T2—714 476
L'Île-Dorval (Quebec) T2—714 28
Liliaceae 584.32
  floriculture 635.934 32
Liliales 584.3
Lilies 584.3
  floriculture 635.934 3
Liliidae 584.3
Liliopsida 584
  *see Manual at* 583–584
Lille (France) T2—442 84
Lille Bælt (Denmark) 551.461 334
   T2—163 34
Lillooet (B.C.) T2—711 31
Lillooet Lake (B.C.) T2—711 31
Lillooet River (B.C.) T2—711 3
Lilongwe (Malawi) T2—689 7
Lily of the valley 635.934 32
  botany 584.32
  floriculture 635.934 32
Lima (Peru : Dept.) T2—852 5
Lima beans 641.356 53
  botany 583.74
  commercial processing 664.805 653
  cooking 641.656 53
  field crop 633.37
  food 641.356 53
  garden crop 635.653
Limarí (Chile : Province) T2—832 35
Limavady (Northern
  Ireland : District) T2—416 25
Limbo 236.4
Limbu language 495.49
   T6—954 9
Limburg (Belgium :
  Province) T2—493 24
Limburg (Netherlands) T2—492 48

| | | | |
|---|---|---|---|
| Limburger cheese | 641.373 53 | Limousines (continued) | |
| cooking | 641.673 53 | transportation services | 388.342 32 |
| food | 641.373 53 | *see also* Automobiles | |
| processing | 637.353 | Limpets | 594.32 |
| Lime | 553.68 | Limpopo (South Africa) | 968.25 |
| economic geology | 553.68 | | T2—682 5 |
| use as soil conditioner | 631.821 | Limpopo River | T2—679 2 |
| Lime mortars | 666.93 | Mozambique | T2—679 2 |
| Limerick (Ireland) | T2—419 45 | South Africa | T2—682 5 |
| Limerick (Ireland : County) | T2—419 4 | Linaceae | 583.79 |
| Limericks | 808.817 5 | Linares (Chile : Province) | T2—833 7 |
| history and criticism | 809.175 | Linares, José Finol | |
| specific literatures | T3B—107 5 | Brazilian history | 981.061 |
| individual authors | T3A—1 | Lincoln (England) | T2—425 34 |
| Limes (Fruit) | 641.343 37 | Lincoln (Neb.) | T2—782 293 |
| commercial processing | 664.804 337 | Lincoln (Ont. : County) | T2—713 38 |
| cooking | 641.643 37 | Lincoln, Abraham | |
| food | 641.343 37 | United States history | 973.7 |
| orchard crop | 634.337 | Lincoln County (Ark.) | T2—767 823 |
| Limes (Lindens) | | Lincoln County (Colo.) | T2—788 89 |
| botany | 583.68 | Lincoln County (Ga.) | T2—758 165 |
| forestry | 634.972 77 | Lincoln County (Idaho) | T2—796 34 |
| Limestone | 553.516 | Lincoln County (Kan.) | T2—781 532 |
| building material | 691.2 | Lincoln County (Ky.) | T2—769 625 |
| economic geology | 553.516 | Lincoln County (Me.) | T2—741 57 |
| petrology | 552.58 | Lincoln County (Minn.) | T2—776 365 |
| quarrying | 622.351 6 | Lincoln County (Miss.) | T2—762 534 |
| Limestone County (Ala.) | T2—761 98 | Lincoln County (Mo.) | T2—778 37 |
| Limestone County (Tex.) | T2—764 285 | Lincoln County (Mont.) | T2—786 81 |
| Liming leather | 675.22 | Lincoln County (N.C.) | T2—756 782 |
| Limit | 515.222 | Lincoln County (N.M.) | T2—789 64 |
| Limitation of actions | 347.052 | Lincoln County (Neb.) | T2—782 82 |
| Limitation of rights | 323.49 | Lincoln County (Nev.) | T2—793 14 |
| Limited companies | 338.74 | Lincoln County (Okla.) | T2—766 35 |
| law | 346.066 8 | Lincoln County (Or.) | T2—795 33 |
| *see also* Corporations | | Lincoln County (S.D.) | T2—783 391 |
| Limited editions | 094.4 | Lincoln County (Tenn.) | T2—768 624 |
| publishing | 070.573 | Lincoln County (W. Va.) | T2—754 43 |
| Limited government | 320.512 | Lincoln County (Wash.) | T2—797 35 |
| Limited monarchies | 321.87 | Lincoln County (Wis.) | T2—775 27 |
| Limited war | 355.021 5 | Lincoln County (Wyo.) | T2—787 82 |
| Limnocharitaceae | 584.72 | Lincoln Heath (England) | T2—425 3 |
| Limnology | 551.48 | Lincoln National Park (S. | |
| biology | 577.6 | Aust.) | T2—942 38 |
| Limoges (France) | T2—446 624 | Lincoln Parish (La.) | T2—763 91 |
| Limón (Costa Rica : | | Lincoln Sea | 551.461 327 |
| Province) | T2—728 61 | | T2—163 27 |
| Limousin (France) | T2—446 6 | Lincoln Wolds (England) | T2—425 32 |
| Limousine services | 388.321 | Lincolnshire (England) | T2—425 3 |
| urban | 388.413 214 | Lindens | |
| Limousines | 388.342 32 | botany | 583.68 |
| driving | 629.283 32 | forestry | 634.972 7 |
| engineering | 629.222 32 | Lindi Region (Tanzania) | T2—678 24 |
| repair | 629.287 232 | | |

Lindley (South Africa : District) T2—685 1
Lindsey (England : County) T2—425 31
Line and staff organization 658.402
  armed forces 355.330 4
  public administration 352.283
Line cuts
  printing 686.232 7
Line dancing 793.36
Line engraving 765.2
Line geometry 516.183
Line integrals 515.43
Line Islands 996.4
  T2—964
Line-outs 796.333 23
Line play
  American football 796.332 23
Linear A 492.6
  T6—926
  *see Manual at* T6—926
Linear accelerators 539.733
Linear algebra 512.5
Linear B 487.1
  T6—87
Linear closed-loop systems
  automation engineering 629.832
Linear differential equations 515.354
Linear equations 515.252
Linear logic 511.31
Linear operators 515.724 6
Linear programming 519.72
Linear systems 003.74
Linear topological spaces 515.73
Linen textiles 677.11
  *see also* Textiles
Lines (Electrical) 621.319 2
Lines (Mathematics) 516.152
Lineups (Criminal investigation) 363.258
Lingala language 496.396 86
  T6—963 968 6
Lingala literature 896.396 86
Lingayats 294.551 3
Lingerie 391.423 082
  commercial technology 687.22
  customs 391.423 082
  home economics 646.34
  home sewing 646.420 4
  *see also* Undergarments
Lingga Islands (Indonesia) T2—598 192
Lingua francas 401.3
Linguatula 592.76
Linguistic analysis
  philosophy 149.94

Linguistic change 417.7
  specific languages T4—7
Linguistic disorders
  medicine 616.855
  *see also* Communication disorders
  special education 371.914
Linguistic groups
  sociology 305.7
Linguistic philosophies 149.94
Linguistics 410
  *see Manual at* 410
Linguists
  language specialists
    specific languages T4—092
  linguistics specialists 410.92
    specific languages T4—092
  philologists 409.2
    specific languages T4—092
Linin network 571.66
Linkage editors 005.43
Linkers (Computer programs) 005.43
Links (Mathematics) 514.224
Linlithgow, Victor Alexander John Hope, Marquess of
  Indian history 954.035 9
Linn County (Iowa) T2—777 62
Linn County (Kan.) T2—781 69
Linn County (Mo.) T2—778 24
Linn County (Or.) T2—795 35
Linoleum 645.1
  building construction 698.9
  household management 645.1
Linoleum-block printing 761.3
Linotype
  manufacturing technology 681.61
Linotype composition
  automatic 686.225 44
  manual 686.225 42
Linsangs 599.742
Linseed oil 665.352
Linters
  plastic technology 668.411
Linz (Austria) T2—436 24
Lion 599.757
  big game hunting 799.277 57
  conservation technology 639.979 757
  resource economics 333.959 757
Lions, Gulf of (France) 551.461 382
  T2—163 82
Lions Bay (B.C.) T2—711 33
Lions International 369.5
Lions River (South Africa : District) T2—684 7

| | |
|---|---|
| Lip diseases | |
| medicine | 616.31 |
| Lip-reed instruments | 788.9 |
| *see also* Brass instruments | |
| Lipari Islands (Italy) | T2—458 11 |
| Lipases | 572.757 |
| *see also* Enzymes | |
| Lipectomy | 617.952 |
| Lipetsk (Russia : Oblast) | T2—473 5 |
| Lipetskaia oblast' (Russia) | T2—473 5 |
| Lipid membranes | 572.577 |
| Lipids | 572.57 |
| biochemistry | 572.57 |
| humans | 612.015 77 |
| chemistry | 547.77 |
| metabolic disorders | 571.945 7 |
| medicine | 616.399 7 |
| *see also* Digestive system | |
| diseases — humans | |
| metabolism | 572.574 |
| human physiology | 612.397 |
| *see also* Digestive system | |
| Lipizzaner horse | 636.138 |
| Lipolytic enzymes | 572.757 |
| *see also* Enzymes | |
| Lipoproteins | 572.68 |
| *see also* Proteins | |
| Lipostraca | 565.32 |
| Liposuction | 617.952 |
| Lipotyphla | 599.33 |
| Lippe River | T2—435 6 |
| Lippizaner horse | 636.138 |
| Lippmann process | 778.63 |
| Lipreading | 418 |
| applied linguistics | 418 |
| specific languages | T4—895 4 |
| education | 418 |
| | T4—895 4 |
| primary education | 372.6 |
| special education | 371.912 46 |
| Lips | 591.44 |
| descriptive zoology | 591.44 |
| human anatomy | 611.317 |
| human physiology | 612.31 |
| speech | 612.78 |
| medicine | 616.31 |
| personal care | 646.726 |
| physiology | 573.355 |
| surgery | 617.522 |
| *see also* Digestive system | |
| Lipscomb County (Tex.) | T2—764 816 |
| Lipspeaking | |
| applied linguistics | 418 |
| specific languages | T4—895 |

| | |
|---|---|
| Liquefaction of air | |
| technology | 665.82 |
| Liquefaction of coal | |
| technology | 662.662 2 |
| Liquefaction of gases | |
| heat physics | 536.44 |
| Liqueurs | 641.255 |
| commercial processing | 663.55 |
| Liquid chromatography | 543.84 |
| Liquid crystal displays | 621.381 542 2 |
| Liquid crystals | 530.429 |
| Liquid-drop model (Nuclear | |
| physics) | 539.742 |
| Liquid dynamics | 532.5 |
| Liquid-gas interface | 530.427 |
| Liquid-in-glass thermometry | 536.51 |
| Liquid mechanics | 532 |
| engineering | 620.106 |
| hydraulic engineering | 627 |
| physics | 532 |
| Liquid particle technology | 620.43 |
| Liquid phases | |
| liquid-state physics | 530.424 |
| Liquid polymers | |
| liquid-state physics | 530.429 |
| Liquid propellants | 662.26 |
| aircraft | 629.134 351 |
| military engineering | 623.452 6 |
| spacecraft | 629.475 22 |
| Liquid soaps | 668.124 |
| Liquid-state lasers | 621.366 2 |
| Liquid-state physics | 530.42 |
| Liquid statics | 532.2 |
| Liquid wastes | 363.728 4 |
| social services | 363.728 4 |
| technology | 628.43 |
| *see also* Waste control | |
| Liquidation of corporations | |
| law | 346.066 2 |
| management | 658.1 |
| Liquids | |
| chemical engineering | 660.042 |
| expansion and contraction | 536.413 |
| heat transfer | 536.25 |
| sound transmission | 534.23 |
| specific heat | 536.63 |
| state of matter | 530.42 |
| Liquor laws | 344.054 1 |
| Liquor traffic | 363.41 |
| law | 344.054 1 |
| public administration | 353.37 |
| social problem | 363.41 |
| Lisboa (Portugal : District) | T2—469 42 |
| Lisbon (Portugal : District) | T2—469 42 |

Lisburn (Northern Ireland :
  District)    T2 —416 19
L'Islet (Quebec : Regional
  County Municipality)   T2—714 74
Lismore (N.S.W.)   T2—944 3
Listening   302.224 2
  applied linguistics   418
    specific languages   T4—83
  child care   649.58
  music training method   781.424
  primary education   372.69
  psychology
    communication   153.68
    perception   153.733
  recreation   790.138
  social interaction   302.224 2
Listeria   579.37
Lists   T1—021 6
Litanies   264.13
  music   782.292
  Roman Catholic   264.027 4
Litchfield County (Conn.)   T2—746 1
Litchis   641.346
  botany   583.78
  cooking   641.646
  food   641.346
  orchard crop   634.6
Literacy   302.224 4
  adult education   374.012 4
  educational policy   379.24
  linguistics   418.4
    T4—84
  primary education   372.6
  sociology   302.224 4
  training
    personnel management   658.312 44
Literacy programs   379.24
  adult education   374.012 4
Literary agents
  publishing   070.52
Literary criticism   809
  sacred books   208.2
    Bible   220.66
    Talmud   296.120 66
  specific literatures   T3B—09
    see Manual at T3B—08 and
      T3B—09
  theory   801.95
  see Manual at 800
Literary forgeries   098.3

Literary forms   808.81–.88
  criticism   809.1–.7
    theory   808.1–.7
    see Manual at 808.81–.88
      and 809.1–.7
  history   809.1–.7
    see Manual at 808.81–.88
      and 809.1–.7
  rhetoric   808.1–.7
    children's literature   808.068 1–.068 7
  specific literatures   T3B—1–8
    individual authors   T3A—1–8
  translating   418.041–.048
    specific languages   T4—804 1–804 8
  see Manual at 800; also at
    808.81–.88 and 809.1–.7
Literary genres   808.81–.88
  sacred books   208.2
    Bible   220.66
    Talmud   296.120 66
  specific literatures   T3B—1–8
    see Manual at
      T3B—102–107,
      T3B—205, T3B—308 vs.
      T3C—1, T3C—3
  see also Literary forms
Literary hoaxes   098.3
Literary movements   808.801
  history and criticism   809.91
  specific literatures   T3B—080 1
    history and criticism   T3B—091
Literary style   800
  criticism   809
    specific literatures   T3B—09
  rhetoric   808
Literary themes
  arts   700.457
    T3C—357
  folklore   398.277
    history and criticism   398.357
  literature   808.803 57
    history and criticism   809.933 57
    specific literatures   T3B—080 357
      history and
        criticism   T3B—093 57
Literature   800
  geographic treatment   T3C—93–99
    see Manual at T3C—93–99;
      also at T3C—93–99,
      T3C—9174 vs. T3C—8
  history and criticism   809
    specific literatures   T3B—09
  influence on crime   364.254
  primary education   372.64

Literature (continued)
| | |
|---|---|
| translating | 418.04 |
| specific languages | T4—804 |

*see also* Arts

*see Manual at* 741.6 vs. 800;
  *also at* 800; *also at* 800 vs.
  398.2

| | |
|---|---|
| Literature (Black authors, African | |
|   origin) | 808.898 96 |
|   history and criticism | 809.889 6 |
|   specific literatures | T3B—080 896 |
|     history and criticism | T3B—098 96 |
| Literature and religion | 201.68 |
|   Christianity | 261.58 |
| Lithgow (N.S.W.) | T2—944 5 |
| Lithium | 669.725 |
|   chemical engineering | 661.038 1 |
|   chemistry | 546.381 |
|   economic geology | 553.499 |
|   metallurgy | 669.725 |
|   physical metallurgy | 669.967 25 |

*see also* Chemicals

| | |
|---|---|
| Lithography | 686.231 5 |
|   graphic arts | 763 |
| Lithology | 552 |
| Lithops | 583.53 |
| Lithosphere | 551 |
| Lithuania | 947.93 |
| | T2—479 3 |
| Lithuanian language | 491.92 |
| | T6—919 2 |
| Lithuanian literature | 891.92 |
| Lithuanians | T5—919 2 |
| Litopterna | 569.62 |
| Little Barrier Island (N.Z.) | T2—932 4 |
| Little Belt (Denmark) | 551.461 334 |
| | T2—163 34 |
| Little Big Horn, Battle of the, | |
|   1876 | 973.82 |
| Little brown bats | 599.472 |
| Little Church of France | 284.8 |
| Little Colorado River (N.M. | |
|   and Ariz.) | T2—791 33 |
| Little Kanawha River (W. | |
|   Va.) | T2—754 2 |
| Little Karoo (South Africa) | T2—687 38 |
| Little league (Baseball) | 796.357 62 |
| Little River County (Ark.) | T2—767 55 |
| Little Rock (Ark.) | T2—767 73 |
| Little Sisters of the Poor | 255.95 |
|   church history | 271.95 |
| Little theater | 792.022 3 |
| Liturgical dance | 246.7 |

| | |
|---|---|
| Liturgical drama | |
|   music | 782.298 |
|     choral and mixed voices | 782.529 8 |
|     single voices | 783.092 98 |
| Liturgical music | 782.29 |
|   instrumental forms | 784.189 93 |
|   vocal forms | 782.29 |
|     choral and mixed voices | 782.529 |
|     single voices | 783.092 9 |
| Liturgical objects | 203.7 |
|   Christianity | 247 |
|   Judaism | 296.461 |
| Liturgical renewal | 264.001 |
| Liturgical year | 263.9 |
|   devotional literature | 242.3 |
|   sermons | 252.6 |
| Liturgy | 203.8 |

*see also* Public worship

| | |
|---|---|
| Liturgy of the hours | 264.15 |
|   Anglican | 264.030 15 |
|   Roman Catholic | 264.020 15 |
|   texts | 264.024 |
| Live-bearers | 597.667 |
|   culture | 639.376 67 |
| Live-forevers (Plants) | 583.72 |
| Live Oak County (Tex.) | T2—764 447 |
| Liver | 573.38 |
|   biology | 573.38 |
|   human anatomy | 611.36 |
|   human physiology | 612.352 |
|   medicine | 616.362 |
|   surgery | 617.556 2 |

*see also* Digestive system

| | |
|---|---|
| Liver diseases | |
|   medicine | 616.362 |

  *see also* Digestive system
    diseases — humans

| | |
|---|---|
| Liverpool (England) | T2—427 53 |
| Liverworts | 588.3 |
| Livestock | 636 |
| Livestock exhibition | 636.081 1 |
| Livestock feeding | 636.084 |
| Livestock feeds | 636.085 5 |

*see also* Feeds

| | |
|---|---|
| Livestock judging | 636.081 1 |
| Livestock liability insurance | 368.56 |
| Livestock workers | 636.009 2 |
| Living Bible | 220.520 83 |
| Living chess | 794.17 |
| Living conditions | |
|   armed forces | 355.12 |
| Living fossils | 576.8 |

Living rooms 643.54
  home economics 643.54
  interior decoration 747.75
Living standard
  macroeconomics 339.47
Living stones 583.53
Living together 306.841
  T1—086 56
  law 346.016
Livingston County (Ill.) T2—773 61
Livingston County (Ky.) T2—769 895
Livingston County (Mich.) T2—774 36
Livingston County (Mo.) T2—778 223
Livingston County (N.Y.) T2—747 85
Livingston Parish (La.) T2—763 14
Livonia T2—479 8
Livonian language 494.54
  T6—945 4
Livonian literature 894.54
Livonian War, 1557–1582 947.043
Livonians T5—945 4
Livorno (Italy : Province) T2—455 6
  ancient T2—375 62
Lizard fishes 597.61
Lizards 597.95
  resource economics 333.957 94
Lizards as pets 639.395
Lizard's-tail (Plant) 583.25
Llama wool textiles 677.32
  *see also* Textiles
Llamas 636.296 6
Llandrindod Wells (Wales) T2—429 51
Llanelli (Wales : Borough) T2—429 65
Llangollen (Wales) T2—429 37
Llano County (Tex.) T2—764 62
Llano Estacado T2—764 8
  New Mexico T2—789 3
  Texas T2—764 8
Llanquihue (Chile :
  Province) T2—835 4
Llantrisant (Wales) T2—429 78
Llanwrtyd Wells (Wales) T2—429 56
Lliw Valley (Wales) T2—429 82
Lloydminster (Sask. and
  Alta.) T2—712 42
Lloyds of London 368.012 060 421 2
Loa (Chile) T2—831 35
Loaches 597.48
Loaders (Computer programs) 005.43
Loading equipment
  port engineering 627.34
  ships 623.867

Loading operations
  materials management 658.788 5
  ships 623.888 1
Loads
  bridge engineering 624.252
  structural analysis 624.172
Loan brokers 332.3
Loan collections
  museology 069.56
Loan guarantees
  public administration 352.736
Loan services
  library science 025.6
  museology 069.13
Loan words 412
  specific languages T4—24
Loans 332.7
  capital management 658.152 24
  economics 332.7
    banking services 332.175 3
    central banking 332.113
  law 346.073
    economic assistance 343.074 2
  public administrative support 352.736
  public revenues 336.15
    administration 352.45
Loasaceae 583.94
Lobachevski geometry 516.9
Lobbying 324.4
  law 342.05
  legislative bodies 328.38
  public relations 659.293 244
Lobeliaceae 583.98
Lobi (African people) T5—963 5
Lobi language 496.35
  T6—963 5
Lobster culture 639.64
Lobster fishing 639.54
Lobsters 641.395
  conservation technology 639.975 384
  cooking 641.695
  culture 639.64
  fishing 639.54
  fishing industry 338.372 538 4
  food 641.395
    commercial processing 664.94
  resource economics 333.955 54
  zoology 595.384
Local anesthesia
  surgery 617.966
Local-area networks 004.68
  *see also* Computer
    communications
Local bibliographies 015

| | |
|---|---|
| Local Christian church | 250 |
|   ecclesiology | 262.2 |
|   specific denominations | 280 |
|   *see Manual at* 260 vs. 251–254, 259 | |
| Local courts | 347.02 |
|   criminal law | 345.014 2 |
|   Great Britain | 347.420 2 |
|   Scotland | 347.411 02 |
|   United States | 347.734 |
| Local finance | 336.014 |
|   law | 343.03 |
|   public administration | 352.421 4 |
|   public finance | 336.014 |
| Local government | 320.8 |
|   grants-in-aid | 336.185 |
|     public administration | 352.734 4 |
|   law | 342.09 |
|   public administration | 352.14 |
|     support and control | 353.334 |
|   *see Manual at* 351.3–.9 vs. 352.13–.19 | |
| Local government buildings | |
|   architecture | 725.13 |
| Local heating | |
|   buildings | 697.02 |
| Local laws | 348.02 |
| Local Malay languages | 499.22 |
| | T6—992 2 |
| Local news | |
|   journalism | 070.433 |
| Local planning | 307.12 |
|   civic art | 711.4 |
|   community sociology | 307.12 |
|   law | 346.045 |
| Local rail transit stations | |
|   architecture | 725.31 |
| Local rail transit systems | 388.42 |
|   engineering | 625.4 |
|   law | 343.098 3 |
|   public administration | 354.769 |
|   transportation services | 388.42 |
| Local railroads | 388.42 |
|   engineering | 625.4 |
|   *see also* Local rail transit systems | |
| Local religious organizations | 206.5 |
| Local support of education | 379.123 |
| Local taxation | 336.201 4 |
|   law | 343.043 |
|   public administration | 352.442 14 |
| Local telephone service | 384.64 |
|   *see also* Telephone | |
| Local transportation | 388.4 |
|   *see also* Urban transportation | |
| Local wind systems | 551.518 5 |
| Locality pay | 331.216 6 |
|   personnel management | 658.322 2 |
| Localization (Auditory perception) | |
|   psychology | 152.158 |
| Locally compact groups | 512.55 |
| Locals (Unions) | 331.872 |
|   *see also* Labor unions | |
| Locarno (Switzerland : Distretto) | T2—494 788 |
| Location of business enterprises | 338.09 |
|   *see also* Business enterprises — location | |
|   *see Manual at* 338.091–.099 vs. 332.67309, 338.6042 | |
| Location of plants | |
|   management | 658.21 |
|   *see also* Business enterprises — location; Plant location — management | |
| Loch Broom (Scotland) | T2—163 37 |
| Loch Lomond (Scotland) | T2—414 2 |
| Loch Ness (Scotland) | T2—411 56 |
| Loch Ness monster | 001.944 |
| Lochaber (Scotland) | T2—411 56 |
| Lockouts | 331.894 |
|   economics | 331.894 |
|   law | 344.018 94 |
| Locks (Canals) | |
|   engineering | 627.135 2 |
| Locks (Fasteners) | 683.32 |
| Locksmithing | 683.3 |
| Locksmiths | 683.309 2 |
| Lockup (Printing) | 686.225 6 |
| Locle (Switzerland : District) | T2—494 388 |
| Locomotion | 573.79 |
|   animal physiology | 573.79 |
|   human physiology | 612.76 |
|   *see also* Musculoskeletal system | |
|   physical adaptation | 591.479 |
|   psychology | 152.382 |
| Locomotives | 385.36 |
|   engineering | 625.26 |
|   mining | 622.66 |
|   transportation services | 385.36 |
|     special purpose | 385.5 |
|   *see also* Rolling stock | |

Locomotor ataxia
  medicine — 616.83
  *see also* Nervous system
    diseases — humans
Locoweeds — 583.74
Locris (Greece) — T2—495 15
  ancient — T2—383
Loculoascomycetes — 579.564
Locusts (Animals) — 595.726
  agricultural pests — 632.726
Locusts (Plants) — 583.74
  forestry — 634.973 74
Lodes — 553.19
Lodges (Resort hotels) — 910.462
  *see also* Resorts
Lodging (Temporary housing) — 910.46
  accounting — 657.837
  architecture — 728
  area planning — 711.557
  household management — 647.94
  landscape architecture — 712.7
  management — 647.940 68
  sanitation services — 363.729 8
    law — 344.046 4
  travel — 910.46
Lodi (Italy : Province) — T2—452 19
  ancient — T2—372 28
Lodi dynasty — 954.024 5
Łódź (Poland :
  Voivodeship) — T2—438 47
Łódź Ghetto — 940.531 853 847
Łódzkie Voivodeship
  (Poland) — T2—438 47
Lofoten (Norway) — T2—484 4
Lofoten Islands (Norway) — T2—484 4
Lofting
  ship hulls — 623.842
Logan County (Ark.) — T2—767 37
Logan County (Colo.) — T2—788 75
Logan County (Ill.) — T2—773 57
Logan County (Kan.) — T2—781 135
Logan County (Ky.) — T2—769 76
Logan County (N.D.) — T2—784 56
Logan County (Neb.) — T2—782 795
Logan County (Ohio) — T2—771 463
Logan County (Okla.) — T2—766 33
Logan County (W. Va.) — T2—754 44
Loganberries — 641.347 14
  cooking — 641.647 14
  food — 641.347 14
  horticulture — 634.714
Loganiaceae — 583.93

Logarithms — 512.922
  algebra — 512.922
  arithmetic — 513.22
Logbooks
  aeronautics — 629.132 54
Loggers — 634.980 92
Logging — 634.98
Logic (Reasoning) — 160
Logic circuits — 621.395
Logic databases
  computer science — 005.740 151 13
Logic design
  computer circuits — 621.395
Logic operators — 511.3
  mathematical logic — 511.3
  philosophical logic — 160
Logic programming — 005.115
  artificial intelligence — 006.3
Logical atomism — 146.5
Logical positivism — 146.42
Logistics
  management — 658.5
  military operations — 355.411
Logooli language — 496.395
  — T6—963 95
Logos — 232.2
Logroño (Spain) — T2—463 54
Loir-et-Cher (France) — T2—445 3
Loire (France : Dept.) — T2—445 81
Loire-Atlantique (France) — T2—441 67
Loire River (France) — T2—445
Loiret (France) — T2—445 2
Loja (Ecuador : Province) — T2—866 25
Lokāyata — 181.46
Lolland (Denmark) — T2—489 3
Lollards — 284.3
Lolo languages — 495.4
  — T6—954
Loloish languages — 495.4
  — T6—954
Lombardia (Italy) — 945.2
  — T2—452
  ancient — T2—372 2
Lombards
  Italian history — 945.01
  Southern Italian history — 945.701
Lombardy (Italy) — 945.2
  — T2—452
  ancient — T2—372 2
Lombok (Indonesia) — T2—598 65
Lomé (Togo) — T2—668 1
Lomond, Loch (Scotland) — T2—414 2
Łomża (Poland :
  Voivodeship) — T2—438 36

London (England)    T2—421
London (Ont.)    T2—713 26
Londonderry (Northern
   Ireland)    T2—416 21
Londonderry (Northern
   Ireland : County)    T2—416 2
Loneliness    155.92
   applied psychology    158.2
Long An (Vietnam :
   Province)    T2—597 8
Long County (Ga.)    T2—758 762
Long-distance service    384.64
   *see also* Telephone
Long-haired cats    636.83
Long-horned flies    595.772
Long Island (N.Y.)    T2—747 21
Long Island Sound (N.Y. and    551.461 346
   Conn.)    T2—163 46
Long jump    796.432
Long-legged flies    595.773
Long-necked lutes    787.8
   *see also* Stringed instruments
Long-period variable stars    523.844 26
Long-range ballistic missiles    358.175 482
   engineering    623.451 954
   military equipment    358.175 482
Long-range weather forecasting    551.636 5
Long-service leave
   personnel management    658.312 2
Long-span bridges
   construction    624.2
Long-tailed shrews    599.336 2
Long-term capital    332.041 4
   accounting    657.73
   financial management    658.152 42
Long-term care health insurance    368.382
   government-sponsored    368.42
   law    344.022
Long-term care nursing    610.736
Long-term loans receivable
   financial management    658.152 42
Long track speed skating    796.914
Long-wave electronics
   physics    537.534 2
Long-wave radio systems    621.384 153
Long waves (Economics)    338.54
Longevity    571.879
   human physiology    612.68
Longevity pay    331.216 6
   personnel management    658.322 2
Longford (Ireland : County)    T2—418 12
Longhair cats    636.83
Longitude    526.62
   celestial navigation    527.2

Longreach (Qld.)    T2—943 5
Longueuil (Quebec)    T2—714 373
Longueuil (Quebec : Urban
   agglomeration)    T2—714 37
Lonoke County (Ark.)    T2—767 78
Looking
   psychology    153.733
Lookout Mountain
   (Appalachian
   Mountains)    T2—768 82
   Georgia    T2—758 342
   Tennessee    T2—768 82
Lookout towers
   forestry    634.93
Looms
   textile technology    677.028 54
Loons    598.442
Loosestrifes (Lythraceae)    583.76
Loosestrifes (Primulaceae)    583.675
Looting    364.16
   law    345.026
López Contreras, Eleazar
   Venezuelan history    987.063 14
López Mateos, Adolfo
   Mexican history    972.082 9
López Portillo, José
   Mexican history    972.083 3
Lophiiformes    597.62
Lopseed    583.96
Loquats    641.341 6
   botany    583.73
   cooking    641.641 6
   food    641.341 6
   orchard crop    634.16
L'Or-Blanc (Quebec)    T2—714 573
Lorain County (Ohio)    T2—771 23
Loran
   marine navigation    623.893 2
   radio engineering    621.384 191
Loranthaceae    583.88
Lord Howe Island (N.S.W.)    T2—948 1
Lord's Prayer    226.96
   music    782.295
   private devotions    242.722
Lord's Supper    234.163
   public worship    264.36
   theology    234.163
Lorestān (Iran)    T2—556 2
Loreto (Peru : Dept.)    T2—854 4
Loricata    597.98
Lories (Parrots)    598.71
   animal husbandry    636.686 5
Lorises    599.83
Lorisidae    599.83

Lorraine (France)  T2—443 8
Lorraine, House of
  Tuscan history  945.507
  1737–1801  945.507
  1814–1860  945.508 3
Lorries  388.344
  engineering  629.224
  *see also* Trucks
Los Alamos County (N.M.)  T2—789 58
Los Andes (Chile :
  Province)  T2—832 42
Los Angeles (Calif.)  T2—794 94
Los Angeles County (Calif.)  T2—794 93
Los Lagos (Chile : Region)  T2—835
Los Libertadores Wari
  (Peru)  T2—852 7
Los Picahos National Park
  (Colombia)  T2—861 94
Los Ríos (Ecuador)  T2—866 33
Los Santos (Panama :
  Province)  T2—728 723
Losengo language  496.396 86
  T6—963 968 6
Losengo literature  896.396 86
Loss (Financial management)  658.155
Loss (Psychology)  155.93
Loss of citizenship  323.6
  penology  364.68
Loss of territory  320.12
Loss of vote  324.62
  penology  364.68
Lost-wax casting
  metals  671.255
  sculpture  731.456
Lot (France)  T2—447 33
Lot-et-Garonne (France)  T2—447 18
Lotbinière (Quebec :
  Regional County
  Municipality)  T2—714 58
Lothair II, Holy Roman Emperor
  German history  943.023
Lothian (Scotland)  T2—413 3
Lotteries  795.38
  advertising  659.197 953 8
  occupational ethics  174.6
  use in advertising  659.17
Lottery income
  public administration  352.44
  public finance  336.17
Lotto  795.38
Lotuses  635.933 3
  botany  583.3
  floriculture  635.933 3

Loudness
  acoustical engineering  620.21
Loudon County (Tenn.)  T2—768 863
Loudoun County (Va.)  T2—755 28
Louga (Senegal : Region)  T2—663
Lough Neagh (Northern
  Ireland)  T2—416
Louis VI, King of France
  French history  944.022
Louis VII, King of France
  French history  944.022
Louis VIII, King of France
  French history  944.023
Louis IX, King of France
  French history  944.023
Louis X, King of France
  French history  944.024
Louis XI, King of France
  French history  944.027
Louis XII, King of France
  French history  944.027
Louis XIII, King of France
  French history  944.032
Louis XIV, King of France
  French history  944.033
Louis XV, King of France
  French history  944.034
Louis XVI, King of France
  French history  944.035
  1774–1789  944.035
  1789–1792  944.041
Louis XVIII, King of France
  French history  944.061
  1814–1815  944.05
  1815–1824  944.061
Louis Philippe, King of the
  French
  French history  944.063
Louisa County (Iowa)  T2—777 926
Louisa County (Va.)  T2—755 465
Louisbourg (N.S.)  T2—716 955
Louisiana  976.3
  T2—763
Louisiana French Creole  447.976 3
  T6—417
Louisville (Ky.)  T2—769 44
Lounge cars  385.33
  engineering  625.23
  *see also* Rolling stock
Loungewear  391.426
  commercial technology  687.165
  customs  391.426
  home economics  646.3

Loungewear (continued)
  home sewing                    646.475
  *see also* Clothing
Loup County (Neb.)               T2—782 767
Louse-borne typhus
  incidence                      614.526 2
  medicine                       616.922 2
    *see also* Communicable
    diseases — humans
Louse flies                      595.774
Louth (Ireland : County)         T2—418 25
Love
  arts                           700.454 3
                                 T3C—354 3
  ethics                         177.7
    religion                     205.677
      Buddhism                   294.356 77
      Christianity               241.4
      Hinduism                   294.548 677
      Islam                      297.567 7
      Judaism                    296.367 7
  folklore                       398.274 3
    history and criticism        398.354 3
  God's love                     212.7
    Christianity                 231.6
    comparative religion         202.112
    philosophy of religion       212.7
  literature                     808.803 543
    history and criticism        809.933 543
    specific literatures         T3B—080 354 3
      history and
        criticism                T3B—093 543
  philosophy                     128.46
  psychology                     152.41
  social interaction             302.3
Love charms                      133.442
Love County (Okla.)              T2—766 59
Love feasts
  Christian rite                 265.9
Love spells                      133.442
Love stories                     808.838 5
  history and criticism          809.385
  specific literatures           T3B—308 5
    individual authors           T3A—3
Lovebirds (Agapornis)            636.686 5
  animal husbandry               636.686 5
  zoology                        598.71
Lovebirds (Budgerigars)          636.686 4
  animal husbandry               636.686 4
  zoology                        598.71
Lovech (Bulgaria : Oblast)       T2—499 2
Lovers (Extramarital
  relationships)                 306.736
Loveshka oblast (Bulgaria)       T2—499 2

Loving County (Tex.)             T2—764 912
Loving cups                      739.228 4
Low Archipelago                  T2—963 2
Low birth weight
  pediatrics                     618.920 11
Low budget cooking               641.552
Low budget interior decorating   747.1
Low-calorie cooking              641.563 5
Low-calorie diet
  health                         613.25
Low-calorie food                 641.302
  technology                     664.63
Low-carbohydrate cooking         641.563 83
Low-carbohydrate diet
  health                         613.283 3
Low-cholesterol cooking          641.563 847
Low-cholesterol diet
  health                         613.284 32
Low-cost housing
  architecture                   728.1
  construction                   690.81
Low Countries                    949.2
                                 T2—492
  ancient                        936.92
                                 T2—369 2
Low-dimensional topology         514.22
Low-fat cooking                  641.563 84
Low-fat diet
  health                         613.284 3
Low-fiber cooking                641.563
Low-fiber diet
  health                         613.263
Low German language              439.4
                                 T6—394
Low German literature            839.4
Low Germanic languages           439
                                 T6—39
Low Germanic literatures         839
Low-income people                305.569
                                 T1—086 24
    *see also* Poor people
Low power television stations    384.55
Low-protein cooking              641.563 8
Low-protein diet
  health                         613.282
Low-salt cooking                 641.563 23
Low-salt diet
  health                         613.285 223
Low-sodium cooking               641.563 23
Low-sodium diet
  health                         613.285 223
Low-temperature biology
  humans                         612.014 465
Low-temperature technology       621.56

Low temperatures 536.56
  biophysics 571.464
  chemical engineering 660.296 86
  chemistry 541.368 6
  effect on materials 620.112 16
  physics 536.56
Low veld (South Africa) T2—682 59
Low voice 783.5
Lowell (Mass.) T2—744 4
Lower Arrow Lake (B.C.) T2—711 62
Lower Austria (Austria) T2—436 12
Lower Avon River
  (England) T2—423 9
Lower Bavaria (Germany) T2—433 5
Lower California (Mexico) T2—722
Lower Canada 971.03
  Quebec 971.402
Lower chambers (Legislative
  bodies) 328.32
Lower classes 305.56
  T1—086 24
  social welfare 362.892
Lower criticism
  Bible 220.404 6
Lower Egypt T2—621
Lower extremities 612.98
  anatomy 611.98
  bones 612.751
    anatomy 611.718
    medicine 616.71
    physiology 612.751
    surgery 617.471
  fractures
    medicine 617.158
  joints
    medicine 616.72
    surgery 617.580 59
  muscles
    anatomy 611.738
  physiology 612.98
  regional medicine 617.58
  surgery 617.580 59
Lower Franconia (Germany) T2—433 3
Lower Guinea 967.1
  T2—671
Lower houses (Legislative
  bodies) 328.32
Lower Hutt City (N.Z.) T2—936 4
Lower legs
  regional medicine 617.584
  surgery 617.584
Lower Lusatia (Germany) T2—431 51
Lower Mamberamo languages 499.1
  T6—991

Lower Mesopotamia T2—567 5
  ancient 935.5
  T2—355
Lower middle class 305.55
  T1—086 23
Lower Paleolithic Age 930.124
Lower Peninsula (Mich.) T2—774
Lower primary grades 372.241
Lower Saxony (Germany) T2—435 9
Lower Tugela (South
  Africa : District) T2—684 4
Lower Umfolozi (South
  Africa : District) T2—684 3
Lowland game birds 598.41
  conservation technology 639.978 41
  resource economics 333.958 41
  sports hunting 799.244
Lowlands (Scotland) T2—413
Lowndes County (Ala.) T2—761 465
Lowndes County (Ga.) T2—758 864
Lowndes County (Miss.) T2—762 973
Lowveld (South Africa) T2—682 59
Loxodonta 599.674
Loxton (S. Aust.) T2—942 33
Loyalty Islands (New
  Caledonia) T2—959 7
Loyalty oaths 323.65
  law 342.068 4
  obligation of citizens 323.65
  public personnel management 352.65
Loyalty of citizens 323.65
Lozère (France : Dept.) T2—448 1
Lozi (African people) T5—963 99
Lozi language 496.399
  T6—963 99
$L^p$ spaces 515.73
LPS (Swiss political party) 324.249 406
LPTV stations 384.55
LSD abuse 362.294
  medicine 616.863 4
  personal health 613.83
  social welfare 362.294
  *see also* Substance abuse
LSP (Special-purpose language) 401.47
  specific languages T4—014 7
Luanda (Angola : Province) T2—673 2
Luapula Province (Zambia) T2—689 4
Luba (African people) T5—963 93
Luba (Kingdom) 967.518 01
  T2—675 18
Luba languages 496.393
  T6—963 93
Lubavitch Hasidism 296.833 22
Lubbock County (Tex.) T2—764 847

| | |
|---|---|
| Lübeck (Germany) | T2—435 125 |
| Lubelskie Voivodeship (Poland) | T2—438 43 |
| Lublin (Poland : Voivodeship) | T2—438 43 |
| Lubricants | |
| automobiles | 629.255 |
| plastic technology | 668.411 |
| Lubricating grease | 665.538 5 |
| Lubricating oil | 665.538 5 |
| Lubrication | 621.89 |
| Lubumbashi (Congo) | T2—675 18 |
| Lubuskie Voivodeship (Poland) | T2—438 12 |
| Lucania (Italy) | T2—457 7 |
| ancient | T2—377 7 |
| Lucanidae | 595.764 9 |
| Lucas County (Iowa) | T2—777 863 |
| Lucas County (Ohio) | T2—771 12 |
| Lucazi language | 496.399 |
| | T6—963 99 |
| Lucca (Italy : Province) | T2—455 3 |
| ancient | T2—375 3 |
| Luce County (Mich.) | T2—774 925 |
| Lucerne (Plant) | 633.31 |
| botany | 583.74 |
| forage crop | 633.31 |
| Lucerne (Switzerland) | T2—494 557 4 |
| Lucerne (Switzerland : Amt) | T2—494 557 |
| Lucerne (Switzerland : Canton) | T2—494 55 |
| Lucerne Lake (Switzerland) | T2—494 557 |
| Luchazi language | 496.399 |
| | T6—963 99 |
| Luchu Islands | T2—522 9 |
| Lucifer | |
| Christianity | 235.47 |
| Lucioperca | 597.758 |
| Ludwigshafen am Rhein (Germany) | T2—434 353 2 |
| Ludwigslust (Germany : Landkreis) | T2—431 76 |
| Luganda language | 496.395 7 |
| | T6—963 957 |
| Luganda literature | 896.395 7 |
| Lugano (Switzerland : Distretto) | T2—494 785 |
| Lugano, Lake (Switzerland and Italy) | T2—494 785 |
| Lugbara (African people) | T5—965 |
| Lugbara language | 496.5 |
| | T6—965 |
| Lugdunensis | T2—364 5 |
| Lugeing | 796.954 |
| Luggage | |
| manufacturing technology | 685.51 |
| Lugo (Spain : Province) | T2—461 3 |
| Lugo Méndez, Fernando | |
| Paraguayan history | 989.207 46 |
| Luhans´k (Ukraine : Oblast) | T2—477 4 |
| Luhans´ka oblast´ (Ukraine) | T2—477 4 |
| Luhya language | 496.395 |
| | T6—963 95 |
| Luiseño Indians | T5—974 5 |
| Luiseño language | 497.45 |
| | T6—974 5 |
| Luke (Gospel) | 226.4 |
| Lula | |
| Brazilian history | 981.065 |
| Lula da Silva, Luiz Inácio | |
| Brazilian history | 981.065 |
| Lule Saami language | 494.574 3 |
| | T6—945 743 |
| Lule Saami literature | 894.574 3 |
| Lule Sámi language | 494.574 3 |
| | T6—945 743 |
| Lule Sámi literature | 894.574 3 |
| Lule-Vilela languages | 498.7 |
| | T6—987 |
| Lulekani (South Africa : District) | T2—682 59 |
| Lullabies | 781.582 |
| folk literature | 398.8 |
| music | 781.582 |
| songs | 782.421 582 |
| Lumbee Indians | T5—973 |
| Lumbee language | 497.3 |
| | T6—973 |
| Lumber | 674 |
| Lumber industry | 338.476 74 |
| law | 343.078 674 |
| Lumber industry workers | 674.092 |
| Lumbering | 634.98 |
| Lumbermen | 634.980 92 |
| Lumberyards | 674.32 |
| Lumbriculida | 592.64 |
| Luminescence | 535.35 |
| materials science | 620.112 95 |
| mineralogy | 549.125 |
| Luminescence spectroscopy | 543.56 |
| Luminism | 709.034 4 |
| painting | 759.054 |
| Luminous paints | 667.69 |
| Luminous-tube lighting | 621.327 |
| Lumped-parameter systems | 003.7 |
| Lumpkin County (Ga.) | T2—758 273 |
| Luna County (N.M.) | T2—789 68 |

| | | | |
|---|---|---|---|
| Lunar flights | 629.454 | Luo (African people) | T5—965 |
| manned | 629.454 | Luo language (Africa) | 496.5 |
| unmanned | 629.435 3 | | T6—965 |
| Lunch periods | | Luorawetlin languages | 494.6 |
| labor economics | 331.257 6 | | T6—946 |
| personnel management | 658.312 2 | Lupines | 583.74 |
| Lunchbox cooking | 641.53 | field crop | 633.367 |
| Luncheons | 642 | floriculture | 635.933 74 |
| cooking | 641.53 | Lupus erythematosus | |
| light meals | 641.53 | medicine | 616.772 |
| main meals | 641.54 | *see also* Musculoskeletal | |
| customs | 394.125 3 | diseases — humans | |
| light meals | 394.125 3 | Luristān (Iran) | T2—556 2 |
| main meals | 394.125 4 | Lusaka (Zambia) | T2—689 4 |
| Lunches | 642 | Lusaka Province (Zambia) | T2—689 4 |
| cooking | 641.53 | Lusatia (Germany) | T2—431 51 |
| light meals | 641.53 | Lusatian language | 491.88 |
| main meals | 641.54 | | T6—918 8 |
| customs | 394.125 3 | Lusatian literature | 891.88 |
| light meals | 394.125 3 | Lusatians | T5—918 8 |
| main meals | 394.125 4 | Lusengo language | 496.396 86 |
| Lunchrooms | 647.95 | | T6—963 968 6 |
| *see also* Eating places | | Lusengo literature | 896.396 86 |
| Lunda (Kingdom) | 967.340 1 | Lusikisiki (South Africa : | |
| | T2—673 4 | District) | T2—687 59 |
| Lunda languages | 496.393 | Lusitania | T2—366 9 |
| | T6—963 93 | Lust | |
| Lunda Norte (Angola) | T2—673 4 | ethics | 176.4 |
| Lunda Sul (Angola) | T2—673 4 | religion | 205.66 |
| Lundu-Balong languages | 496.396 | Christianity | 241.3 |
| | T6—963 96 | Lute family | 787 |
| Lüneburg (Germany : | | *see also* Stringed instruments | |
| Regierungsbezirk) | T2—435 93 | Lutes | 787.83 |
| Lunenburg (N.S. : County) | T2—716 23 | instrument | 787.831 9 |
| Lunenburg County (Va.) | T2—755 643 | music | 787.83 |
| Lung cancer | | *see also* Stringed instruments | |
| incidence | 614.599 942 4 | Lutetium | |
| medicine | 616.994 24 | chemistry | 546.419 |
| *see also* Cancer — humans | | Lutheran church | 284.1 |
| Lung diseases | | church government | 262.041 |
| medicine | 616.24 | parishes | 254.041 |
| *see also* Respiratory tract | | church law | 262.984 1 |
| diseases — humans | | doctrines | 230.41 |
| Lungfishes | 597.39 | catechisms and creeds | 238.41 |
| Lungless salamanders | 597.859 | general councils | 262.541 |
| Lungs | 573.25 | guides to Christian life | 248.484 1 |
| biology | 573.25 | missions | 266.41 |
| human anatomy | 611.24 | moral theology | 241.044 1 |
| human physiology | 612.24 | public worship | 264.041 |
| medicine | 616.24 | religious associations | 267.184 1 |
| surgery | 617.542 | religious education | 268.841 |
| *see also* Respiratory system | | seminaries | 230.073 41 |
| Lungu language | 496.394 | theology | 230.41 |
| | T6—963 94 | | |

| | |
|---|---|
| Lutheran Church in America | 284.133 |
|   *see also* Lutheran church | |
| Lutheran Church—Missouri | |
|   Synod | 284.132 2 |
|   *see also* Lutheran church | |
| Lutheran Free Church | 284.131 4 |
|   *see also* Lutheran church | |
| Lutheran sacred music | 781.714 1 |
|   public worship | 782.322 41 |
|     music | 782.322 41 |
|     religion | 264.041 02 |
| Lutherans | |
|   biography | 284.109 2 |
| Lutjanidae | 597.72 |
| Luton (England) | T2—425 67 |
| Lutra | 599.769 2 |
| Lutrinae | 599.769 |
| Lutselk'e (N.W.T.) | T2—719 3 |
| Luwian language | 491.998 |
| | T6—919 98 |
| Luxembourg | 949.35 |
| | T2—493 5 |
|   ancient | 936.935 |
| | T2—369 35 |
| Luxembourg (Belgium) | T2—493 48 |
| Luxembourgeois dialect | 437.949 35 |
| | T6—32 |
| Luxembourgers | T5—3 |
| Luxembourgian dialect | 437.949 35 |
| | T6—32 |
| Luxemburg, House of | 943.702 24 |
|   Czechoslovakian history | 943.702 24 |
|   German history | 943.027 |
| Luxor (Egypt) | T2—323 |
| Luxury tax | 336.271 |
|   law | 343.055 |
|   public administration | 352.44 |
|   public finance | 336.271 |
| Luyana languages | 496.399 |
| | T6—963 99 |
| Luyia language | 496.395 |
| | T6—963 95 |
| Luzern (Switzerland) | T2—494 557 4 |
| Luzern (Switzerland : Amt) | T2—494 557 |
| Luzern (Switzerland : | |
|   Canton) | T2—494 55 |
| Luzerne County (Pa.) | T2—748 32 |
| Luzon (Philippines) | T2—599 1 |
| Luzon Strait (Philippines) | 551.461 458 |
| | T2—164 58 |
| Lwo languages (Africa) | 496.5 |
| | T6—965 |
| Lyases | 572.79 |
|   *see also* Enzymes | |
| Lycaonia | T2—392 7 |
| Lycées (Secondary schools) | 373.241 |
|   *see also* Secondary education | |
| Lycia | T2—392 8 |
| Lycian language | 491.998 |
| | T6—919 98 |
| Lycidae | 595.764 4 |
| Lycoming County (Pa.) | T2—748 51 |
| Lycoperdales | 579.599 |
| Lycopodiales | 587.9 |
| Lycopsida | 587.9 |
| Lydenburg (South Africa : | |
|   District) | T2—682 71 |
| Lydia (Kingdom) | T2—392 2 |
| Lydian language | 491.998 |
| | T6—919 98 |
| Lygeeae | 584.9 |
| Lyginopteridaceae | 561.595 |
| Lying | |
|   ethics | 177.3 |
|   *see also* Ethical problems | |
| Lyman County (S.D.) | T2—783 58 |
| Lyme disease | |
|   incidence | 614.574 6 |
|   medicine | 616.924 6 |
|   *see also* Communicable | |
|     diseases — humans | |
| Lymexyloidea | 595.763 |
| Lymph | 573.16 |
|   biology | 573.16 |
|   human histology | 612.420 45 |
|   human physiology | 612.42 |
| Lymphatic diseases | 573.163 9 |
|   animals | 573.163 9 |
|   humans | 362.196 42 |
|     cancer | 362.196 994 42 |
|       glands | |
|         incidence | 614.599 944 6 |
|         medicine | 616.994 46 |
|       incidence | 614.599 944 2 |
|       medicine | 616.994 42 |
|       social services | 362.196 994 42 |
|     *see also* Cancer — humans | |
|     geriatrics | 618.976 42 |
|     incidence | 614.594 2 |
|     medicine | 616.42 |
|     pediatrics | 618.924 2 |
|     pharmacokinetics | 615.74 |
|     social services | 362.196 42 |
|     surgery | 617.44 |
| Lymphatic glands | |
|   human anatomy | 611.46 |
|   human physiology | 612.42 |
|   medicine | 616.42 |

Lymphatic system     573.16
  biology     573.16
  diseases     573.163 9
   *see also* Lymphatic diseases
  human anatomy     611.42
   glands     611.46
  human histology     612.420 45
  human physiology     612.42
  medicine     616.42
  surgery     617.44
Lymphocytes     571.96
  human cytology     612.420 46
  human immunology     616.079
Lymphogranuloma venereum
  incidence     614.547
  medicine     616.951 8
   *see also* Communicable
     diseases — humans
Lymphoid tissue
  human histology     612.420 45
Lymphokines
  human immunology     616.079
Lymphomas
  incidence     614.599 944 6
  medicine     616.994 46
   *see also* Cancer — humans
Lynchburg (Va.)     T2—755 671
Lynching     364.134
  law     345.023 4
Lynn County (Tex.)     T2—764 851
Lynx     599.753
  conservation technology     639.979 753
  resource economics     333.959 753
Lyon (France)     T2—445 823
Lyon County (Iowa)     T2—777 114
Lyon County (Kan.)     T2—781 62
Lyon County (Ky.)     T2—769 813
Lyon County (Minn.)     T2—776 363
Lyon County (Nev.)     T2—793 58
Lyonnais (France)     T2—445 82
Lyons, J. A. (Joseph Aloysius)
  Australian history     994.042
Lyrebirds     598.822
Lyres     787.78
  instrument     787.781 9
  music     787.78
  *see also* Stringed instruments
Lyric poetry     808.814
  history and criticism     809.14
  specific literatures     T3B—104
   individual authors     T3A—1
Lyrics     780
  treatises     780.268

Lysergic acid diethylamide abuse   362.294
  medicine     616.863 4
  personal health     613.83
  social welfare     362.294
  *see also* Substance abuse
Lysosomes     571.655
Lyssavirus     579.256 6
Lythraceae     583.76
Lytton (B.C.)     T2—711 72
Lytton, Edward Robert Bulwer
  Lytton, Earl of
  Indian history     954.035 3
Lzhedmitriĭ I, Czar of Russia
  Russian history     947.045
Lzhedmitriĭ II
  Russian history     947.045
L'viv (Ukraine : Oblast)     T2—477 9
L'vivs'ka oblast' (Ukraine)     T2—477 9

# M

Ma'ājim     297.125 63
Ma'ān (Jordan : Province)     956.957 7
    T2—569 577
Maas River     T2—492 4
  Belgium     T2—493 46
  Netherlands     T2—492 4
Maasai language     496.5
    T6—965
Ma'aser Sheni (Tractate)     296.123 1
  Mishnah     296.123 1
  Palestinian Talmud     296.124 1
Ma'aserot (Tractate)     296.123 1
  Mishnah     296.123 1
  Palestinian Talmud     296.124 1
Maastricht (Netherlands)     T2—492 48
Maastricht Treaty on European
  Union, 1992     341.242 202 65
Macaca     599.864
Macadam pavements     625.86
Macadamia nuts     641.345
  agriculture     634.5
  botany     583.89
  cooking     641.645
  food     641.345
Macao     951.260 4
    T2—512 6
Macao (China)     951.26
    T2—512 6
Macapagal, Diosdado
  Philippine history     959.904 5
Macaques     599.864

Macaroni 641.822
  commercial processing 664.755
  home preparation 641.822
Macau 951.260 4
  T2—512 6
Macau (China) 951.26
  T2—512 6
Macaws 598.71
  animal husbandry 636.686 5
Maccabean period 933.04
Maccabees (Biblical books) 229.7
Macclesfield (England :
  Borough) T2—427 16
MacDonald, John Alexander, Sir
  Canadian history 971.051
    1867–1873 971.051
    1878–1891 971.054
Mace (Spice) 641.338 3
  *see also* Spices
Macedonia (Region) T2—495 6
  ancient 938.1
    T2—381
  Bulgaria T2—499 8
  Greece T2—495 6
  Macedonia (Republic) T2—497 6
Macedonia (Republic) 949.76
  T2—497 6
  ancient 939.876
    T2—398 76
Macedonian language 491.819
  T6—918 19
Macedonian literature 891.819
Macedonian supremacy 938.07
Macedonians (Slavic
  people) T5—918 19
Macerata (Italy : Province) T2—456 73
  ancient T2—374 6
Maces (Weapons) 623.441
Mach number
  aeronautics 629.132 32
Machel, Samora
  Mozambican history 967.905 1
Machine composition
  printing 686.225 4
Machine design 621.815
Machine embroidery 677.77
  arts 746.440 28
  manufacturing technology 677.77
Machine engineering 621.8
Machine gunners 356.162
Machine guns 355.824 24
  military engineering 623.442 4
  military equipment 355.824 24
    infantry 356.162

Machine laces 677.653
Machine languages 005.136
Machine learning 006.31
Machine parts 621.82
Machine-readable catalog records
  format 025.316
  maintenance 025.317
  retrospective conversion 025.317 3
Machine-Readable Cataloging
  format 025.316
Machine-readable data
  representation 005.72
Machine-readable materials 302.231
  *see also* Electronic resources
Machine sewing
  home economics 646.204 4
Machine sheds
  agricultural use 631.25
Machine-shop practice 670.423
  agriculture 631.304
Machine shorthand 653.3
Machine theory
  computer engineering 621.39
  computer science 004
  mathematics 511.35
Machine tools 621.902
Machine translating
  linguistics 418.020 285 635
    specific languages T4—802 028 563 5
Machinery 621.8
Machinery insurance 368.7
Machines in industry 338.06
Machining metals 671.35
  decorative arts 739.14
  sculpture 731.41
Machmeters 629.135 2
Machynlleth (Wales) T2—429 51
Macías Nguema, Francisco
  Equatorial Guinean history 967.180 31
Mackay (Qld.) T2—943 6
Mackenzie (B.C.) T2—711 82
Mackenzie (N.W.T. and
  Nunavut) T2—719 3
Mackenzie, Alexander
  Canadian history 971.052
MacKenzie District (N.Z.) T2—938 8
Mackenzie King Island
  (N.W.T. and Nunavut) T2—719 3
Mackenzie Mountains
  (N.W.T. and Yukon) T2—719 3
Mackenzie River (N.W.T.) T2—719 3
Mackerel 641.392
  cooking 641.692
  fishing 639.277 82

Mackerel (continued)
  food      641.392
  zoology      597.782
Mackerel sharks      597.33
Mackinac, Straits of (Mich.)   T2—774 923
Mackinac County (Mich.)   T2—774 923
Maclear (South Africa :
  District)      T2—687 57
Macleay River (N.S.W.)   T2—944 3
Macomb County (Mich.)   T2—774 39
Macon (Ga.)   T2—758 552
Macon County (Ala.)   T2—761 49
Macon County (Ga.)   T2—758 513
Macon County (Ill.)   T2—773 582
Macon County (Mo.)   T2—778 27
Macon County (N.C.)   T2—756 982
Macon County (Tenn.)   T2—768 484
Macoupin County (Ill.)   T2—773 83
Macpherson, John, Sir
  Indian history      954.031 1
Macquarie perch      597.73
Macramé      746.422 2
Macro-Gê languages      498.4
                  T6—984
Macro processors      005.45
Macrobiotic diet
  health      613.264
Macrocystis      579.887
Macroeconomic policy      339.5
Macroeconomics      339
  *see Manual at* 332, 336 vs. 339
Macrofungi      579.6
Macroinstructions
  programming      005.13
  programs      005.3
Macromolecules      572
  biochemistry      572
  chemistry      547.7
Macrophages      571 968 5
  human immunology      616.079 95
Macropodidae      599.22
Macropus      599.222
Macroscelidea      599.337
  paleozoology      569.337
Macrosudanic languages      496.5
                  T6—965
Macrotonality      781.265
Macrouridae      597.63
Macrura      595.384
Macruronidae      597.632
Ma'dabā (Jordan : Province)   T2—569 562
Madagascar      969.1
                  T2—691

Madang Province (Papua
  New Guinea)   T2—957 3
Madawaska (N.B. : County)   T2—715 54
Madders      583.93
Made-for-television movies      791.43
  *see Manual at* 791.43 vs.
    791.45
Madeira Islands   T2—469 8
Madeira vine      583.53
Madeleine, Îles-de-la-
  (Quebec)   T2—714 797
Madera County (Calif.)   T2—794 81
Madhvāchārya (Philosophy)      181.484 1
Madhya Pradesh (India)   T2—543
Madhyamika Buddhism      294.392
Madikwe (South Africa :
  District)   T2—682 48
Madison (Wis.)   T2—775 83
Madison, James
  United States history      973.51
Madison County (Ala.)   T2—761 97
Madison County (Ark.)   T2—767 15
Madison County (Fla.)   T2—759 85
Madison County (Ga.)   T2—758 152
Madison County (Idaho)   T2—796 55
Madison County (Ill.)   T2—773 86
Madison County (Ind.)   T2—772 57
Madison County (Iowa)   T2—777 81
Madison County (Ky.)   T2—769 53
Madison County (Miss.)   T2—762 623
Madison County (Mo.)   T2—778 91
Madison County (Mont.)   T2—786 663
Madison County (N.C.)   T2—756 875
Madison County (N.Y.)   T2—747 64
Madison County (Neb.)   T2—782 54
Madison County (Ohio)   T2—771 55
Madison County (Tenn.)   T2—768 27
Madison County (Tex.)   T2—764 237
Madison County (Va.)   T2—755 38
Madison Parish (La.)   T2—763 81
Mádl, Ferenc
  Hungarian history      943.905 42
Madness      362.2
  individual interactions      302.542
  *see also* Mental illness
Madonna and Child
  art representation      704.948 55
  arts   T3C—382 329 2
Madras (India : State)   T2—548 2
Madre de Dios (Peru :
  Dept.)   T2—854 2
Madrid (Spain : Province)   T2—464 1
Madrid Hurtado, Miguel de la
  Mexican history      972.083 4

| | |
|---|---|
| Madrigals | 782.43 |
| choral and mixed voices | 782.543 |
| single voices | 783.094 3 |
| Madriz (Nicaragua) | T2—728 523 |
| Madtoms | 597.492 |
| Madura (Indonesia) | T2—598 28 |
| Madura language | 499.223 4 |
| | T6—992 234 |
| Madura literature | 899.223 4 |
| Madurese | T5—992 234 |
| Madurese language | 499.223 4 |
| | T6—992 234 |
| Madurese literature | 899.223 4 |
| Maduro, Ricardo | |
| Honduran history | 972.830 537 |
| Mafia | 364.106 |
| Mafraq (Jordan : Province) | T2—569 597 |
| ancient | T2—335 97 |
| Magadan (Russia : Oblast) | T2—577 |
| Magadanskaĩa oblast' | |
| (Russia) | T2—577 |
| Magahi language | 491.454 7 |
| | T6—914 54 |
| Magahi literature | 891.454 |
| Magallanes (Chile : | |
| Province) | T2—836 44 |
| Magallanes y Antártica | |
| Chilena (Chile) | T2—836 4 |
| Magari language | 495.49 |
| | T6—954 9 |
| Magazine illustration | 741.652 |
| Magazines | 050 |
| | T1—05 |
| *see also* Serials | |
| Magdalen Islands (Quebec) | T2—714 797 |
| Magdalena (Colombia : | |
| Dept.) | T2—861 16 |
| Magdalena River | |
| (Colombia) | T2—861 |
| Magdeburg (Germany) | T2—431 822 |
| Magdeburg (Germany : | |
| Regierungsbezirk) | T2—431 82 |
| Magellan, Strait of (Chile and | 551.461 74 |
| Argentina) | T2—167 4 |
| Maggiore, Lake (Italy and | |
| Switzerland) | T2—451 65 |
| Italy | T2—451 65 |
| Switzerland | T2—494 788 |
| Maggots | 595.771 392 |
| agricultural pests | 632.77 |
| Magherafelt (Northern | |
| Ireland : District) | T2—416 29 |
| Maghreb | T2—61 |
| Magi (Christian doctrines) | 232.923 |

| | |
|---|---|
| Magic | 133.43 |
| arts | T3C—377 |
| folklore | 398.2 |
| history and criticism | 398.4 |
| literature | 808.803 77 |
| history and criticism | 809.933 77 |
| specific literatures | T3B—080 377 |
| history and | |
| criticism | T3B—093 77 |
| recreation | 793.8 |
| religious practice | 203 |
| sociology | 306.4 |
| Magic squares | 511.64 |
| Magicians (Occultists) | 133.430 92 |
| *see also* Legendary beings | |
| Magicians (Performers) | 793.809 2 |
| Magicians (Religious leaders) | 200.92 |
| biography | 200.92 |
| role and function | 206.1 |
| *see Manual at* 200.92 and | |
| 201–209, 292–299 | |
| Magicians' manuals | 133.43 |
| Magisterium | 262.8 |
| Magma | 551.13 |
| Magna Graecia | 937.7 |
| | T2—377 |
| Magnēsia (Greece) | T2—495 4 |
| Magnesia ad Maeandrum | |
| (Extinct city) | T2—392 3 |
| Magnesia cement | 666.95 |
| Magnesite | |
| mineralogy | 549.782 |
| Magnesium | 669.723 |
| applied nutrition | 613.285 2 |
| biochemistry | 572.523 92 |
| humans | 612.015 24 |
| chemical engineering | 661.039 2 |
| chemistry | 546.392 |
| economic geology | 553.492 9 |
| materials science | 620.187 |
| metabolism | 572.523 92 |
| human physiology | 612.392 4 |
| metallography | 669.957 23 |
| metallurgy | 669.723 |
| metalworking | 673.723 |
| mining | 622.349 29 |
| organic chemistry | 547.053 92 |
| applied | 661.895 |
| physical metallurgy | 669.967 23 |
| *see also* Chemicals; Metals | |
| Magnesium soaps | 668.125 |
| Magnet schools | 373.241 |
| Magnetic bubble memory | 004.563 |
| engineering | 621.397 63 |

| | |
|---|---|
| Magnetic-core memory | 004.53 |
|   engineering | 621.397 3 |
| Magnetic currents (Earth) | 538.748 |
| Magnetic diagnosis | |
|   medicine | 616.075 48 |
| Magnetic disks (Computers) | 004.563 |
|   engineering | 621.397 63 |
| Magnetic drums | 004.563 |
|   engineering | 621.397 63 |
| Magnetic engineering | 621.34 |
| Magnetic engineers | 621.340 92 |
| Magnetic fields (Earth) | 538.7 |
| Magnetic induction | 538.4 |
| Magnetic ink character | |
|   recognition | 006.4 |
|   engineering | 621.399 4 |
| Magnetic levitation trains | 388.42 |
|   *see also* Local rail transit | |
|     systems | |
| Magnetic observations (Earth) | 538.79 |
| Magnetic phenomena | 538.3 |
| Magnetic properties | 538.3 |
|   crystals | 548.85 |
|   materials science | 620.112 97 |
| Magnetic prospecting | 622.153 |
| Magnetic relaxation | 538.3 |
| Magnetic resonance | 538.36 |
| Magnetic resonance imaging | |
|   medicine | 616.075 48 |
| Magnetic resonance | |
|   spectroscopes | |
|   manufacturing technology | 681.414 8 |
| Magnetic resonance spectroscopy | |
|   engineering | 621.361 |
| Magnetic separation | |
|   ores | 622.77 |
| Magnetic storms (Earth) | 538.744 |
| Magnetic stripe encoding | |
|   computer science | 006.24 |
| Magnetic substances | 538.4 |
| Magnetic surveys (Earth) | 538.78 |
| Magnetic tapes | |
|   computer storage | 004.563 |
|     engineering | 621.397 63 |
|   music | 786.75 |
|     *see also* Electrophones | |
|   recordings | |
|     engineering | 621.382 34 |
| Magnetic testing | |
|   materials science | 620.112 78 |
| Magnetic variations | |
|   (Geomagnetism) | 538.74 |
| Magnetism | 538 |
|   astrophysics | 523.018 8 |
|   biophysics | 571.47 |
|     humans | 612.014 42 |
|   physics | 538 |
|   therapeutic use | 615.845 4 |
| Magnetite | |
|   mineralogy | 549.526 |
| Magnetochemistry | 541.378 |
|   chemical engineering | 660.297 8 |
| Magnetohydrodynamic | |
|   generation | 621.312 45 |
| Magnetohydrodynamic power | |
|   systems | |
|   spacecraft | 629.474 45 |
| Magnetohydrodynamic | |
|   propulsion | |
|   spacecraft | 629.475 5 |
| Magnetohydrodynamics | 538.6 |
| Magnetosphere | 538.766 |
|   meteorology | 551.514 |
| Magnetostriction | 538.3 |
| Magnetotherapy | |
|   medicine | 615.845 4 |
| Magnetrons | 621.381 334 |
| Magnets | 538.4 |
|   artificial | 621.34 |
|   natural | 538.4 |
| Magnifying glasses | |
|   biology | 570.282 3 |
| Magnolia vine | 583.3 |
| Magnoliales | 583.22 |
| Magnolias | 635.977 322 |
|   botany | 583.22 |
|   ornamental arboriculture | 635.977 322 |
| Magnoliidae | 583.2 |
| Magnoliopsida | 583 |
|   *see Manual at* 583–584 | |
| Magoffin County (Ky.) | T2—769 215 |
| Magpie larks | 598.8 |
| Magpies | 598.864 |
| Magsaysay, Ramon | |
|   Philippine history | 959.904 3 |
| Magyar language | 494.511 |
| | T6—945 11 |
| Magyar literature | 894.511 |
| Magyars | T5—945 11 |
| Mah jong | 795.34 |
| Mahabharata | 294.592 3 |
| Mahaica-Berbice Region | |
|   (Guyana) | T2—881 6 |
| Mahajanga (Madagascar : | |
|   Province) | T2—691 |

| | |
|---|---|
| Mahakiranti languages | 495.49 |
| | T6—954 9 |
| Mahakiranti literatures | 895.49 |
| Maharashtra (India) | T2—547 9 |
| Mahasanghika Buddhism | 294.391 |
| Mahaska County (Iowa) | T2—777 84 |
| Mahathir bin Mohamad | |
| Malaysian history | 959.505 4 |
| Mahayana Buddhism | 294.392 |
| Mahé Island (Seychelles) | T2—696 |
| Mahilioŭ (Belarus : | |
| Voblasts) | T2—478 2 |
| Mahilioŭskaia voblasts' | |
| (Belarus) | T2—478 2 |
| Mahnomen County (Minn.) | T2—776 94 |
| Mahoganies | |
| botany | 583.77 |
| forestry | 634.973 77 |
| Mahomet, Prophet | 297.63 |
| Mahoning County (Ohio) | T2—771 39 |
| Mahoning River (Ohio and | |
| Pa.) | T2—771 39 |
| Mahratta | T5—914 61 |
| Mahri | T5—929 |
| Mahri language | 492.9 |
| | T6—929 |
| Mahri literature | 892.9 |
| Mahzorim | 296.453 |
| Maiasaura | 567.914 |
| Maidenhair ferns | 587.3 |
| Maidenhair tree | 635.977 57 |
| botany | 585.7 |
| ornamental arboriculture | 635.977 57 |
| Maidstone (England : | |
| Borough) | T2—422 375 |
| Maidu Indians | T5—974 1 |
| Maidu language | 497.41 |
| | T6—974 1 |
| Maiduguri (Nigeria) | T2—669 85 |
| Mail | 383 |
| *see also* Postal service | |
| Mail art | 709.040 84 |
| Mail cars | 385.33 |
| engineering | 625.23 |
| *see also* Rolling stock | |
| Mail collection | 383.145 |
| Mail delivery | 383.145 |
| Mail fraud | 364.136 |
| law | 345.023 6 |
| Mail handling | 383.1 |
| office services | 651.759 |
| Mail-order catalogs | 381.142 029 |
| | T1—029 |
| direct advertising | 659.133 |
| Mail-order houses | 381.142 |
| management | 658.872 |
| *see also* Commerce | |
| Mail service | 383.1 |
| *see also* Postal service | |
| Mailboxes | 383.145 |
| Mailing lists (Computer | |
| communications) | 004.693 |
| Maimonides, Moses | |
| Jewish legal writings | 296.181 |
| Main dishes (Cooking) | 641.82 |
| Main meals | 642 |
| cooking | 641.54 |
| customs | 394.125 4 |
| Main memory (Computers) | 004.53 |
| engineering | 621.397 3 |
| Main River (Germany) | T2—434 |
| Main-sequence stars | 523.88 |
| Maine | 974.1 |
| | T2—741 |
| Maine (France) | T2—441 6 |
| Maine, Gulf of | 551.461 345 |
| | T2—163 45 |
| Maine coon cat | 636.83 |
| Maine-et-Loire (France) | T2—441 8 |
| Mainframe computers | 004.12 |
| architecture | 004.252 |
| communications | 004.612 |
| programming | 005.712 2 |
| programs | 005.713 2 |
| engineering | 621.391 2 |
| graphics programming | 006.672 |
| graphics programs | 006.682 |
| interfacing | 004.612 |
| programming | 005.712 2 |
| programs | 005.713 2 |
| multimedia-systems | |
| programming | 006.772 |
| multimedia-systems programs | 006.782 |
| operating systems | 005.442 |
| performance evaluation | 004.120 29 |
| for design and improvement | 004.252 |
| programming | 005.22 |
| programs | 005.32 |
| systems analysis | 004.252 |
| systems design | 004.252 |
| *see Manual at* 004.11–.16 | |
| Mainstream jazz | 781.654 |
| Mainstreaming | |
| education | 371.904 6 |
| gifted students | 371.952 |
| grouping of students | 371.252 |
| library services | 027.663 |
| Maintainability engineering | 620.004 5 |

| | |
|---|---|
| Maintenance | 620.004 6 |
| | T1—028 8 |
| plant management | 658.202 |
| | T1—068 2 |
| public administration | 352.564 |
| public administration | 352.54 |
| Maintenance (Domestic relations) | 346.016 63 |
| Maintenance facilities | |
| spacecraft | 629.478 |
| Mainz (Rhineland- | |
| Palatinate, Germany) | T2—434 351 |
| Maipuran languages | 498.39 |
| | T6—983 9 |
| Maithili language | 491.454 7 |
| | T6—914 54 |
| Maithili literature | 891.454 |
| Maitland (N.S.W.) | T2—944 2 |
| Maize | 641.331 5 |
| Majingai dialect | 496.5 |
| | T6—965 |
| Majolica | 738.372 |
| Major County (Okla.) | T2—766 29 |
| Major medical insurance | 368.382 8 |
| law | 346.086 382 8 |
| Major Prophets (Biblical books) | 224 |
| Majorca (Spain) | T2—467 54 |
| Majority (Age) | |
| customs | 392.15 |
| etiquette | 395.24 |
| law | 346.013 5 |
| music | 781.584 |
| Makaa-Njem languages | 496.396 |
| | T6—963 96 |
| Makah Indians | T5—979 54 |
| Makah language | 497.954 |
| | T6—979 54 |
| Makasar | T5—992 264 |
| Makasar language | 499.226 4 |
| | T6—992 264 |
| Makasar literature | 899.226 4 |
| Makasar Strait | 551.461 473 |
| | T2—164 73 |
| Make-ahead meals | |
| cooking | 641.555 |
| Makedonia (Greece : | |
| Periphereia) | T2—495 6 |
| Makeup | 646.72 |
| dramatic performances | 792.027 |
| motion pictures | 791.430 27 |
| stage | 792.027 |
| television | 791.450 27 |
| *see also* Cosmetics | |
| Makhshirin | 296.123 6 |
| Makira and Ulawa | |
| (Solomon Islands) | T2—959 38 |
| Makkot | 296.123 4 |
| Babylonian Talmud | 296.125 4 |
| Mishnah | 296.123 4 |
| Palestinian Talmud | 296.124 4 |
| Mako sharks | 597.33 |
| Makonde (African people) | T5—963 97 |
| Makonde language | 496.397 |
| | T6—963 97 |
| Maku languages | 498.9 |
| | T6—989 |
| Makua languages | 496.397 |
| | T6—963 97 |
| Makurdi (Nigeria) | T2—669 54 |
| Malabar Independent Syrian | |
| Church | 281.54 |
| *see also* Eastern churches | |
| Malabo (Equatorial Guinea) | T2—671 86 |
| Malabsorption syndromes | |
| medicine | 616.399 |
| *see also* Digestive system | |
| diseases — humans | |
| Malacca (State) | T2—595 1 |
| Malacca, Strait of | 551.461 565 |
| | T2—165 65 |
| Malachi (Biblical book) | 224.99 |
| Malachite | |
| mineralogy | 549.785 |
| Malaclemys | 597.925 9 |
| Malacology | 594 |
| Malacostraca | 595.37 |
| paleozoology | 565.37 |
| Maladjusted students | 371.93 |
| Maladjusted young people | |
| delinquent | 364.36 |
| | T1—086 923 |
| mentally ill | 305.908 408 3 |
| | T1—087 4 |
| predelinquent | 305.230 869 23 |
| | T1—086 923 |
| social welfare | 362.74 |
| Málaga (Spain : Province) | T2—468 5 |
| Malagasy | T5—993 |
| Malagasy language | 499.3 |
| | T6—993 |
| Malagasy literature | 899.3 |
| Malagasy Republic | T2—691 |
| Malaita (Solomon Islands) | T2—959 37 |
| Malamulele (South Africa : | |
| District) | T2—682 57 |
| Malan, D. F. (Daniel François) | |
| South African history | 968.056 |
| Malanje (Angola) | T2—673 4 |

| | | | |
|---|---|---|---|
| Mälar, Lake (Sweden) | T2—487 2 | Maldivian language | 491.489 |
| Mälaren (Sweden) | T2—487 2 | | T6—914 89 |
| Malaria | | Maldivian literature | 891.489 |
|   incidence | 614.532 | Maldivians | T5—914 89 |
|   medicine | 616.936 2 | Maldon (England : District) | T2—426 756 |
|   *see also* Communicable | | Maldon (Vic.) | T2—945 3 |
|     diseases — humans | | Maldonado (Uruguay : | |
| Malas Zénāwi | |   Dept.) | T2—895 15 |
|   Ethiopian history | 963.072 1 | Male breast | |
| Malaspina Peninsula (B.C.) | T2—711 31 |   medicine | 616.49 |
| Malatya İli (Turkey) | T2—565 4 |   surgery | 617.549 |
|   ancient | T2—393 6 | Male genital diseases | |
| Malawi | 968.97 |   humans | 362.196 65 |
| | T2—689 7 |     anesthesiology | 617.967 463 |
| Malawi (Kingdom) | 968.970 1 |     cancer | 362.196 994 63 |
| | T2—689 7 |       incidence | 614.599 946 3 |
| Malawi, Lake | T2—689 7 |       medicine | 616.994 63 |
| Malawi people | T5—968 97 |       social services | 362.196 994 63 |
| Malawians | T5—968 97 |       *see also* Cancer — humans | |
| Malay Archipelago | T2—598 |     incidence | 614.596 5 |
| Malay Archipelago inner seas | 551.461 473 |     medicine | 616.65 |
| | T2—164 73 |     social services | 362.196 65 |
| Malay language | 499.28 |     surgery | 617.463 |
| | T6—992 8 | Male genital system | 573.65 |
| Malay languages | 499.22 |   anesthesiology | 617.967 463 |
| | T6—992 2 |   biology | 573.65 |
| Malay literature | 899.28 |   human anatomy | 611.63 |
| Malay Peninsula | T2—595 1 |   human physiology | 612.61 |
| Malay-Polynesian languages | 499.2 |   medicine | 616.65 |
| | T6—992 |   surgery | 617.463 |
| Malaya | T2—595 1 | Male gods | 202.113 |
| Malayalam language | 494.812 | Male infertility | |
| | T6—948 12 |   medicine | 616.692 1 |
| Malayalam literature | 894.812 |   *see also* Male genital | |
| Malayalis | T5—948 12 |     diseases — humans | |
| Malayan languages | 499.22 | Male prostitution | 306.743 |
| | T6—992 2 | Male reproductive system | 573.65 |
| Malayan literatures | 899.2 |   animals | 573.65 |
| Malayic languages | 499.22 |   plants | 575.65 |
| | T6—992 2 |   *see also* Male genital system | |
| Malayo-Polynesian languages | 499.2 | Male sex disorders | |
| | T6—992 |   medicine | 616.69 |
| Malayo-Polynesian languages of | 499.224 |   *see also* Male genital | |
|   Sumatra | T6—992 24 |     diseases — humans | |
| Malayo-Polynesians | T5—992 | Male sexual disorders | |
| Malays (Asian people) | T5—992 8 |   medicine | 616.69 |
| Malaysia | 959.5 |   *see also* Male genital | |
| | T2—595 |     diseases — humans | |
| Malaysia, East | T2—595 3 | Male-to-female transgender | |
| Malaysians | T5—992 8 |   people | 306.768 |
| Malcolm Island (B.C.) | T2—711 2 | | T1—086 7 |
| Maldive Islands | T2—549 5 |   social services | 362.897 |
| Maldives | 954.95 | | |
| | T2—549 5 | | |

Male-to-female transgender
  young people
    social services    362.785
Malecite-Passamaquoddy    497.34
  language    T6—973 4
Malenkov, Georgi
  Russian history    947.085 2
Males (Human)    305.31
     T1—081 1
  health    613.042 3
  *see also* Men
Malfeasance by employees
  labor economics    331.259 8
  personnel management    658.314
Malfeasance in office    364.132
  law    345.023 2
  public administration    353.46
Malheur County (Or.)    T2—795 97
Mali    966.23
     T2—662 3
Mali Empire    966.201 7
     T2—662
Malians    T5—966 23
Malicious mischief insurance    368.12
Malicious prosecution    346.033 4
Malignant neoplasms    571.978
  *see also* Cancer
Malignant tumors    571.978
  incidence    614.599 9
  medicine    616.994
  *see also* Cancer
Mālik ibn Anas    297.125 58
Malikites (Islamic sect)    297.813
Malinke (African people)    T5—963 45
Malinke language    496.345
     T6—963 45
Malis (Greece)    T2—383
Mallard    598.413 4
Malleability
  materials science    620.112 5
Malleco (Chile)    T2—834 5
Mallee (Vic. : District)    T2—945 9
Mallet games    796.35
Mallophaga    595.757
Mallorca (Spain)    T2—467 54
Mallows    583.685
Malls (Shopping centers)    381.11
  *see also* Shopping centers
Malmesbury (South Africa :
  District)    T2—687 32
Malmöhus län (Sweden)    T2—486 1

Malnutrition
  humans    362.196 39
    incidence    614.593 9
    medicine    616.39
    social services    362.196 39
Malnutrition surveys    614.593 9
Maloggia (Switzerland :
  Distretto)    T2—494 732 8
Maloja (Switzerland :
  Bezirk)    T2—494 732 8
Małopolskie Voivodeship
  (Poland)    T2—438 62
Malpighiaceae    583.79
Malpractice    346.033
Malpractice insurance    368.564
Malta    945.85
     T2—458 5
  ancient    937.85
     T2—378 5
Maltases    572.756
  *see also* Enzymes
Malted alcoholic beverages    641.23
  commercial processing    663.3
  home preparation    641.873
Malted nonalcoholic beverages    641.26
  commercial processing    663.6
  home preparation    641.875
Maltese    T5—927 9
Maltese (Dog)    636.76
Maltese language    492.79
     T6—927 9
Maltese literature    892.79
Malthusian economic school    330.153
Malto language    494.83
     T6—948 3
Malto literature    894.83
Maltose    572.565
  *see also* Carbohydrates
Maluku (Indonesia : islands)    T2—598 5
Maluku (Indonesia :
  province)    T2—598 52
Maluku Utara (Indonesia)    T2—598 56
Maluti (South Africa :
  District)    T2—687 59
Malvaceae    583.685
Malvales    583.68
Malvern (England)    T2—424 47
Malvern Hills (England)    T2—424 47
Malvinas Islands    997.11
     T2—971 1
Malware    005.84
Mam Indians    T5—974 2
Mam language    497.42
     T6—974 2

| | |
|---|---|
| Mambwe language | 496.394 |
| | T6—963 94 |
| Mamelukes | 962.024 |
| Egyptian history | 962.024 |
| Palestinian history | 956.940 33 |
| Mammal nest beetles | 595.764 2 |
| Mammalia | 599 |
| *see also* Mammals | |
| Mammalogists | 599.092 |
| Mammals | 599 |
| agricultural pests | 632.69 |
| animal husbandry | 636 |
| arts | T3C—362 9 |
| big game hunting | 799.26 |
| commercial hunting | 639.11 |
| conservation technology | 639.9 |
| control technology | 628.969 |
| agriculture | 632.69 |
| drawing | 743.69 |
| experimental animals | |
| medicine | 616.027 3 |
| paleozoology | 569 |
| resource economics | 333.954 |
| small game hunting | 799.259 |
| zoology | 599 |
| *see Manual at* 599 | |
| Mammaplasty | 618.190 592 |
| Mammary glands | 573.679 |
| biology | 573.679 |
| gynecology | 618.19 |
| human anatomy | 611.49 |
| human cancer | |
| incidence | 614.599 944 9 |
| medicine | 616.994 49 |
| *see also* Cancer — humans | |
| human physiology | 612.664 |
| surgery | 618.190 59 |
| Mammee apple | 583.624 |
| Mammography | |
| medicine | 618.190 757 2 |
| Mammoplasty | 618.190 592 |
| Mammoth Cave National | |
| Park (Ky.) | T2—769 754 |
| Man | 301 |
| *see also* Humans | |
| Man, Isle of | T2—427 9 |
| Man-machine ratios | |
| production management | 658.514 |
| Man-machine systems | |
| ergonomics | 620.82 |
| computer science | 004.019 |
| cngineering | 621.398 4 |

| | |
|---|---|
| Man-made environments | |
| biology | 578.755 |
| ecology | 577.55 |
| Man-made fibers | |
| paper | 676.7 |
| textiles | 677.4 |
| arts | 746.044 |
| *see also* Textiles | |
| Manabí (Ecuador) | T2—866 34 |
| Managed care plans | 362.104 258 |
| insurance | 368.382 |
| Managed currency | 332.46 |
| Managed floating exchange rates | 332.456 4 |
| Management | 658 |
| | T1—068 |
| armed forces | 355.6 |
| arts | 700.455 3 |
| | T3C—355 3 |
| literature | 808.803 553 |
| history and criticism | 809.933 553 |
| personal aspects | 658.409 |
| public administration | 351 |
| sociology | 302.35 |
| *see Manual at* T1—068; *also at* | |
| T1—068 vs. 353–354; *also* | |
| *at* 330 vs. 650, 658 | |
| Management accounting | 658.151 1 |
| public administration | 352.43 |
| Management auditing | 658.401 3 |
| public administration | 352.43 |
| Management audits | 658.401 3 |
| public administration | 352.439 |
| Management by objectives | 658.401 2 |
| public administration | 352.36 |
| Management consultants | 658.46 |
| public administration | 352.373 |
| Management environment | 658.409 5 |
| public administration | 352.39 |
| Management for legal | |
| compliance | 658.12 |
| Managerial accounting | 658.151 1 |
| public administration | 352.43 |
| Managerial finance | 658.15 |
| *see also* Financial management | |
| Managerial occupations | 331.761 658 |
| Managerial success | 658.409 |
| Managers | 338.092 |
| | T1—086 22 |
| labor economics | 331.761 658 |
| social class | 305.554 |
| Managing change | 658.406 |
| military administration | 355.686 7 |
| public administration | 352.367 |
| Managing your boss | 650.13 |

Managua (Nicaragua : Dept.) T2—728 513
Manakins 598.822
Manapouri, Lake (N.Z.) T2—939 6
Manassas (Va.) T2—755 273 4
Manassas Park (Va.) T2—755 273 6
Manatee County (Fla.) T2—759 62
Manatees 599.55
  conservation technology 639.979 55
  resource economics 333.959 55
Manawatu District (N.Z.) T2—935 6
Manawatu-Wanganui
  Region (N.Z.) T2—935
Mancha T2—464
Manche 551.461 336
  T2—163 36
Manche (France) T2—442 12
Manchester (England) T2—427 33
Manchester (N.H.) T2—742 8
Manchester terrier (Standard dog) 636.755
Manchester terrier (Toy dog) 636.76
Manchineels 583.69
Manchu T5—941
Manchu dynasty 951.03
Manchu languages 494.1
  T6—941
Manchu literatures 894.1
Manchuria T2—518
Manda languages 496.391
  T6—963 91
Mandab, Strait of 551.461 532
  T2—165 32
Mandalas 203.7
  Buddhism 294.343 7
  Hinduism 294.537
Mandan Indians T5—975 22
Mandan language 497.522
  T6—975 22
Mandarin Chinese language 495.1
  T6—951 1
Mandarin duck 598.412
Mandates 321.08
  establishment
    World War I 940.314 26
    World War II 940.531 426
  *see also* Semisovereign states
Mande (African people) T5—963 45
Mande languages 496.34
  T6—963 4
Mande literatures 896.34
Mandeb, Bab el 551.461 532
  T2—165 32
Mandekan languages 496.345
  T6—963 45

Mandela, Nelson
  South African history 968.065
Manding languages 496.345
  T6—963 45
Manding-Mokole languages 496.345
  T6—963 45
Mandingo (African people) T5—963 45
Mandingo languages 496.345
  T6—963 45
Mandinka (African people) T5—963 45
Mandinka languages 496.345
  T6—963 45
Mandolins 787.84
  instrument 787.841 9
  music 787.84
  *see also* Stringed instruments
Mandrakes
  botany 583.952
  medicinal crop 633.883 952
Mandrakes (Mayapples) 583.34
Maneuvers (Military) 355.4
  training 355.52
Manga 741.595 2
  drawing 741.51
Manganese 669.732
  chemical engineering 661.054 1
  chemistry 546.541
  economic geology 553.462 9
  human toxicology 615.925 541
  materials science 620.189 32
  metallography 669.957 32
  metallurgy 669.732
  metalworking 673.732
  mining 622.346 29
  organic chemistry 547.055 41
    applied 661.895
  physical metallurgy 669.967 32
  *see also* Chemicals; Metals
Manganese group
  chemical engineering 661.054
  chemistry 546.54
Mangbetu language 496.5
  T6—965
Mange
  animals
    veterinary medicine 636.089 657 3
  humans
    medicine 616.573
    *see also* Skin diseases —
     humans
Mangoes 641.344 4
  botany 583.77
  cooking 641.644 4

| | |
|---|---|
| Mangoes (continued) | |
| food | 641.344 4 |
| orchard crop | 634.44 |
| Mangosteens | 641.346 55 |
| agriculture | 634.655 |
| botany | 583.624 |
| cooking | 641.646 55 |
| food | 641.346 55 |
| Mangrove swamps | 577.698 |
| biology | 578.769 8 |
| ecology | 577.698 |
| *see also* Wetlands | |
| Mangroves | 583.763 |
| Arecaceae | 584.5 |
| Myrtales | 583.763 |
| Verbenaceae | 583.96 |
| Mangue Indians | T5—976 |
| Manguindanao (Philippines) | T2—599 7 |
| Manhattan (New York, N.Y.) | T2—747 1 |
| Manholes | |
| sewers | 628.25 |
| Manhwa | 741.595 19 |
| drawing | 741.51 |
| Manic-depressive illness | |
| medicine | 616.895 |
| *see also* Mental disorders | |
| Manic psychoses | |
| medicine | 616.895 |
| *see also* Mental disorders | |
| Manica (Mozambique : Province) | T2—679 4 |
| Manicaland Province (Zimbabwe) | T2—689 1 |
| Manicheism | 299.932 |
| Christian heresy | 273.2 |
| Manicouagan (Quebec : Regional County Municipality) | T2—714 174 |
| Manicure tools | |
| manufacturing technology | 688.5 |
| Manicuring | 646.727 |
| Maniema (Congo) | T2—675 17 |
| Manifold topology | 514.34 |
| Manifolds (Mathematics) | |
| geometry | 516.07 |
| topology | 514.34 |
| Manihiki Atoll (Cook Islands) | T2—962 4 |
| Manila (Philippines) | T2—599 16 |
| Manila hemp | |
| botany | 584.39 |
| fiber crop | 633.571 |
| Manila paper | 676.287 |

| | |
|---|---|
| Manioc | 641.336 82 |
| *see also* Cassava | |
| Manipulators (Mechanism) | 629.893 3 |
| Manipur (India) | T2—541 7 |
| Manisa İli (Turkey) | T2—562 4 |
| ancient | T2—392 2 |
| Manistee County (Mich.) | T2—774 62 |
| Manitoba | 971.27 |
| | T2—712 7 |
| Manitoba, Lake (Man.) | T2—712 72 |
| Manitoulin (Ont.) | T2—713 135 |
| Manitowoc County (Wis.) | T2—775 67 |
| Manjimup (W.A.) | T2—941 2 |
| Mankind | 301 |
| *see also* Humans | |
| Mankwe (South Africa : District) | T2—682 48 |
| Manned space flight | |
| engineering | 629.45 |
| Manned spacecraft | |
| engineering | 629.47 |
| Manners | 390 |
| child training | 649.6 |
| etiquette | 395 |
| Mannheim (Germany) | T2—434 645 2 |
| Manning Provincial Park (B.C.) | T2—711 5 |
| Manor houses | |
| architecture | 728.8 |
| Manpower | |
| armed forces | 355.22 |
| civilians | 355.23 |
| military law | 343.012 |
| Manpower planning | |
| management | 658.301 |
| Manpower shortages | 331.136 |
| Mansel Island (Nunavut) | T2—719 52 |
| Mansfield (England : District) | T2—425 23 |
| Mansi | T5—945 1 |
| Mansi language | 494.51 |
| | T6—945 1 |
| Mansi literature | 894.51 |
| Mansions | |
| architecture | 728.8 |
| Manslaughter | 364.152 5 |
| law | 345.025 25 |
| Mantels | |
| furniture arts | 749.62 |
| Mantis shrimps | 595.379 6 |
| Mantises | 595.727 |
| culture | 638.572 7 |
| Mantle of earth | 551.116 |
| Mantodea | 595.727 |

| | |
|---|---|
| Mantova (Italy) | T2—452 81 |
| ancient | T2—373 181 |
| Mantova (Italy : Province) | T2—452 8 |
| ancient | T2—373 18 |
| Mantras | 203.7 |
| Buddhism | 294.343 7 |
| Hinduism | 294.537 |
| Mantua (Italy) | T2—452 81 |
| ancient | T2—373 181 |
| Mantua (Italy : Province) | T2—452 8 |
| ancient | T2—373 18 |
| Manual alphabet | 419 |
| representing spoken language | 418 |
| specific languages | T4—891 |
| Manual arts | |
| primary education | 372.5 |
| Manual of arms | 355.547 |
| Manually coded language | 418 |
| specific languages | T4—891 |
| Manufactured gases | 665.7 |
| Manufacturers | 338.476 709 2 |
| directories | 338.767 025 |
| Manufacturers' outlets | 381.15 |
| management | 658.870 5 |
| Manufactures | 338.476 7 |
| Manufacturing | |
| ethics | 174.4 |
| production management | 658.5 |
| taxes | 336.207 |
| technology | 670 |
| *see Manual at* 671–679 vs. 680 | |
| Manufacturing industries | 338.476 7 |
| accounting | 657.867 |
| public administration | 354.66 |
| Manufacturing wastes | |
| water pollution engineering | 628.168 37 |
| Manufacturing workers | 670.92 |
| labor economics | 331.767 |
| public administration | 354.947 |
| Manukau City (N.Z.) | T2—932 5 |
| Manures | 631.86 |
| animal husbandry | 636.083 8 |
| Manus | T5—991 2 |
| Manus Province (Papua New Guinea) | T2—958 1 |
| Manuscript editing | 808.027 |
| publishing | 070.51 |
| Manuscript illumination | 745.67 |
| Manuscript selection | |
| publishing | 070.51 |
| Manuscripts | 091 |
| bibliographies | 011.31 |
| cataloging | 025.341 2 |
| Manuscripts (continued) | |
| library treatment | 025.171 2 |
| music | 780 |
| treatises | 780.262 |
| Manx | T5—916 4 |
| Manx cat | 636.822 |
| Manx language | 491.64 |
| | T6—916 4 |
| Manx literature | 891.64 |
| Manxmen | T5—916 4 |
| Many-bodies problem | 530.144 |
| astronomy | 521 |
| Many-valued logic | 511.312 |
| Mao, Zedong | |
| Chinese history | 951.05 |
| Maoism | 335.434 5 |
| economics | 335.434 5 |
| political ideology | 320.532 309 51 |
| Maori | T5—994 42 |
| Maori language | 499.442 |
| | T6—994 42 |
| Maori literature | 899.442 |
| Maori Wars, 1843–1847 | 993.021 |
| Maori Wars, 1860–1870 | 993.022 |
| Map coloring | 511.56 |
| Map drawing | 526 |
| Map makers | 526.092 |
| Map making | 526 |
| military engineering | 623.71 |
| military intelligence service | 355.343 2 |
| Map projections | 526.8 |
| Map reading | 912.014 |
| Map thefts | 364.162 891 2 |
| law | 345.026 289 12 |
| Map turtles | 597.925 9 |
| Maple Ridge (B.C.) | T2—711 33 |
| Maple sugar | 641.336 4 |
| agriculture | 633.64 |
| biochemistry | 572.565 |
| commercial processing | 664.132 |
| cooking | 641.636 4 |
| food | 641.336 4 |
| *see also* Carbohydrates | |
| Maple syrup | 641.336 4 |
| agriculture | 633.64 |
| commercial processing | 664.132 |
| cooking | 641.636 4 |
| food | 641.336 4 |
| *see also* Carbohydrates | |
| Maples | 583.78 |
| forestry | 634.972 2 |
| lumber | 674.142 |
| ornamental arboriculture | 635.977 378 |
| Maplewood (N.J.) | T2—749 33 |

Mappings (Mathematics) 511.326
  topology 514
Maps 912
  T1—022 3
  aeronautics 629.132 54
  cartography 526
    military engineering 623.71
  cataloging 025.346
  geography 912
  library treatment 025.176
  printing 686.283
  publishing 070.579 3
  theft of 364.162 891 2
  law 345.026 289 12
Maps (Functions) 511.326
Mapuche Indians T5—987 2
Mapuche language 498.72
  T6—987 2
Mapuche literature 898.72
Mapudungu Indians T5—987 2
Mapudungun language 498.72
  T6—987 2
Mapudungun literature 898.72
Mapulaneng (South Africa :
  District) T2—682 59
Mapumulu (South Africa :
  District) T2—684 4
Maputaland (South Africa) T2—684 3
Maputo (Mozambique :
  Province) T2—679 1
Maputo River T2—684 2
  Mozambique T2—679 1
  South Africa T2—684 2
Maqtū' 297.125 21
Maqurrah (Kingdom) 962.502 2
  T2—625
Mar Thoma Church 281.54
  *see also* Eastern churches
Mar Thoma Syrian Church 281.54
  *see also* Eastern churches
Mara Region (Tanzania) T2—678 27
Maracaibo, Gulf of (Colombia 551.461 365
  and Venezuela) T2—163 65
Maracaibo Lake
  (Venezuela) T2—872 3
Maracas 786.885
  *see also* Percussion instruments
Marakwet (African people) T5—965
Marakwet language 496.5
  T6—965
Maramureş (Romania :
  Judeţ) T2—498 4
Maranhão (Brazil) T2—812 1
Marañón (Peru : Region) T2—851 4

Marantaceae 584.39
Maraş İli (Turkey) T2—565 3
Maratha T5—914 61
Marathi language 491.46
  T6—914 61
Marathi literature 891.46
Marathon (Ancient site) T2—385
Marathon County (Wis.) T2—775 29
Marathon races 796.425 2
Marattiales 587.33
  paleobotany 561.73
Marble 553.512
  building material 691.2
  economic geology 553.512
  petrology 552.4
  quarrying 622.351 2
Marbled polecat 599.766
Marbles (Game) 796.2
Marbling (Paper)
  bookbinding 686.36
Marbling (Woodwork)
  buildings 698.32
MARC format 025.316
Marcgraviaceae 583.624
March (Switzerland) T2—494 752 1
March flies 595.772
March flies (Bibionidae) 595.772
March flies (Tabanidae) 595.773
Marchantiales 588.3
Marche (France : Province) T2—446 8
Marche (Italy) T2—456 7
  ancient T2—374 5
Marches 784.189 7
Marches (Italy) T2—456 7
  ancient T2—374 5
Marching bands 784.83
Marcos, Ferdinand E. (Ferdinand
  Edralin)
  Philippine history 959.904 6
Mardi Gras 394.25
  customs 394.25
  recreation 791.6
Mardin İli (Turkey) T2—566 78
  ancient T2—394 2
Mareeba (Qld.) T2—943 6
Maremma (Italy) T2—455 7
Marengo County (Ala.) T2—761 392
Mare's tails (Plants) 583.82
Marfan syndrome
  medicine 616.773
  *see also* Musculoskeletal
    diseases — humans
Marfū' 297.125 21

Margarine
  food technology — 664.32
Margay — 599.752
Margherita (Italian political
  party) — 324.245 05
Margiana — T2—396
Margin — 332.645
  multiple forms of investment — 332.645
  stocks — 332.632 28
Marginal costs — 338.514 2
  management — 658.155 3
Marginal productivity theory
  land economics — 333.012
  wages — 331.210 1
Marginal revenue — 338.516
Marginal utility school
  (Economics) — 330.157
Marginalist school (Economics) — 330.157
Mari — T5—945 6
Mari El (Russia) — T2—474 6
Mari language — 494.56
   — T6—945 6
Mari literature — 894.56
Maria-Chapdelaine
  (Quebec) — T2—714 145
Maria Island National Park
  (Tas.) — T2—946 4
María Trinidad Sánchez
  (Dominican Republic :
  Province) — T2—729 364
Mariana Islands — 996.7
   — T2—967
Mariátegui (Peru : Region) — T2—853 4
Marico (South Africa :
  District) — T2—682 48
Marico River (South Africa
  and Botswana) — T2—682 48
Maricopa County (Ariz.) — T2—791 73
Maricopa Indians — T5—975 72
Maricopa language — 497.572
   — T6—975 72
Mariculture — 639.8
Marie Galante — T2—729 76
Maries County (Mo.) — T2—778 592
Marigolds — 635.933 99
  botany — 583.99
  floriculture — 635.933 99
Marijuana
  agriculture — 633.79
  botany — 583.45
  customs — 394.14
  human toxicology — 615.952 345
  pharmacokinetics — 615.782 7
  pharmacology — 615.323 45

Marijuana abuse — 362.295
  medicine — 616.863 5
  personal health — 613.835
  social welfare — 362.295
  *see also* Substance abuse
Marimbas — 786.843
  *see also* Percussion instruments
Marin County (Calif.) — T2—794 62
Marinas — 387.15
  engineering — 627.38
  *see also* Port facilities
Marinduque (Philippines) — T2—599 1
Marine animals — 591.77
Marine aquariums — 597.177 073
  fish culture — 639.342
Marine archaeology — 930.102 804
Marine architecture — 623.81
Marine biological resources
  public administration — 354.57
  resource economics — 333.956
Marine biology — 578.77
  *see Manual at* 578.76–.77 vs.
    551.46, 551.48
Marine botany — 579.177
Marine carnivores — 599.79
Marine cooking — 641.575 3
Marine ecology — 577.7
Marine engineering — 623.87
Marine fishes — 597.177
  culture — 639.32
Marine forces (Military service) — 359.96
Marine geology — 551.468
Marine hatchetfishes — 597.5
Marine insurance — 368.2
Marine invertebrates — 592.177
  resource economics — 333.955
Marine lizards (Mosasauridae) — 567.95
Marine mammals — 599.5
  paleozoology — 569.5
  resource economics — 333.959 5
Marine microorganisms — 579.177
Marine navigation — 623.89
Marine organisms — 578.77
Marine pollution — 363.739 4
  *see also* Water pollution
Marine reptiles (Paleontological
  grouping) — 567.937
Marine resources — 333.916 4
  public administration — 354.369
Marine safety technology — 623.888
Marine scenes
  art representation — 704.943 7
  painting — 758.2

Marine science    551.46
   *see also* Oceans
Marine snakes    597.965
Marine transportation    387.5
   *see also* Ocean transportation
Marine transportation facilities    387.15
   *see also* Port facilities
Marine transportation safety    363.123
   *see also* Water transportation —
     safety
Marine transportation workers    387.509 2
Marine waters    551.46
   *see also* Oceans
Marine zebra fishes    597.68
Marine zoology    591.77
Mariner project    629.435 4
Marines (Armed forces)    359.96
Marinette County (Wis.)    T2—775 33
Maring (Papua New Guinea
   people)    T5—991 2
Mariology (Christian doctrines)    232.91
Marion County (Ala.)    T2—761 89
Marion County (Ark.)    T2—767 193
Marion County (Fla.)    T2—759 75
Marion County (Ga.)    T2—758 482
Marion County (Ill.)    T2—773 794
Marion County (Ind.)    T2—772 52
Marion County (Iowa)    T2—777 83
Marion County (Kan.)    T2—781 57
Marion County (Ky.)    T2—769 51
Marion County (Miss.)    T2—762 21
Marion County (Mo.)    T2—778 353
Marion County (Ohio)    T2—771 514
Marion County (Or.)    T2—795 37
Marion County (S.C.)    T2—757 86
Marion County (Tenn.)    T2—768 79
Marion County (Tex.)    T2—764 193
Marion County (W. Va.)    T2—754 54
Marionettes    791.53
   making
     handicrafts    745.592 24
   *see also* Puppets
Mariopteris    561.597
Mariotype process    773.1
Mariposa County (Calif.)    T2—794 46
Marital property    346.042
   divorce law    346.016 64
Marital psychotherapy
   psychiatry    616.891 562
Marital rights    346.016 3
Marital status    306.81
Maritime (Russia: Kray)    T2—577

Maritime law    343.096
   *see Manual at* 341.45 vs.
     343.0962
Maritime Provinces    971.5
   T2—715
Marjoram    641.357
   botany    583.96
   *see also* Herbs
Mark (Gospel)    226.3
Markazī (Iran)    T2—552 7
Marker drawing    741.26
Markerwaard (Netherlands)    T2—492 2
Market analysis procedure
   management    658.83
     T1—068 8
Market analysis reports    381
Market economy    330.122
Market research procedure
   management    658.83
     T1—068 8
Market research reports    381
Market segmentation
   management    658.802
Market study procedure
   management    658.83
     T1—068 8
Market study reports    381
Marketing    381
   ethics    174.4
   law    343.08
   management    658.8
     T1—068 8
   *see also* Commerce
Marketing channels    381.1
   management    658.87
Marketing cooperatives    334.6
Marketing firms    381
Marketing management    658.8
     T1—068 8
Marketing survey procedure
   management    658.83
     T1—068 8
Marketing survey reports    381
Markets    381
   area planning    711.552 2
   marketing management    658.87
   retail    381.1
     management    658.87
   *see also* Commerce
Markham River (Papua New
   Guinea)    T2—957 1
Marking (Students)    371.272
Märkisch-Oderland
   (Germany : Landkreis)    T2—431 53

| | |
|---|---|
| Markov chains | 519.233 |
| Markov processes | 519.233 |
| Markov risk | 519.287 |
| Marks of identification | 929.9 |
| | T1—027 |
| Markup languages | 006.74 |
| Marl | 553.68 |
| Marlboro County (S.C.) | T2—757 64 |
| Marlborough District (N.Z.) | T2—937 5 |
| Marlins | 597.78 |
| sports fishing | 799.177 8 |
| Marmalades | 641.852 |
| commercial processing | 664.152 |
| home preparation | 641.852 |
| Marmara, Sea of (Turkey) | 551.461 389 |
| | T2—163 89 |
| Marmarica | T2—397 6 |
| ancient | 939.76 |
| Marmosets | 599.84 |
| Marmota | 599.366 |
| Marmots | 599.366 |
| Marne (France) | T2—443 2 |
| Marne River (France) | T2—443 |
| Maronites | 281.52 |
| *see also* Eastern churches | |
| Maronites (Religious order) | 255.18 |
| church history | 271.18 |
| Marowijne (Suriname : | |
| District) | T2—883 8 |
| Marquard (South Africa : | |
| District) | T2—685 5 |
| Marquesan language | 499.42 |
| | T6—994 2 |
| Marquesas Islands | T2—963 1 |
| Marquesic languages | 499.42 |
| | T6—994 2 |
| Marquetry | |
| furniture arts | 749.5 |
| wood handicrafts | 745.512 |
| Marquette County (Mich.) | T2—774 96 |
| Marquette County (Wis.) | T2—775 58 |
| Marquisettes | 677.652 |
| Marrakech-Médina | |
| (Morocco) | T2—646 4 |
| Marrakech-Ménara | |
| (Morocco) | T2—646 4 |
| Marrakech-Tensift-El | |
| Haouz (Morocco) | T2—646 4 |
| Marriage | 306.81 |
| arts | 700.454 3 |
| | T3C—354 3 |
| customs | 392.5 |

| | | |
|---|---|---|
| Marriage (continued) | | |
| ethics | 173 | |
| religion | 205.63 | |
| Buddhism | 294.356 3 | |
| Christianity | 241.63 | |
| Hinduism | 294.548 63 | |
| Islam | 297.563 | |
| Judaism | 296.363 | |
| folklore | 398.274 3 | |
| history and criticism | 398.354 3 | |
| law | 346.016 | |
| literature | 808.803 543 | |
| history and criticism | 809.933 543 | |
| specific literatures | T3B—080 354 3 | |
| history and | | |
| criticism | T3B—093 543 | |
| music | 781.587 | |
| personal religion | 204.41 | |
| Buddhism | 294.344 41 | |
| Christianity | 248.4 | |
| Hinduism | 294.544 1 | |
| Islam | 297.577 | |
| Judaism | 296.74 | |
| religion | 204.41 | |
| Christianity | 248.4 | |
| Islam | 297.577 | |
| Judaism | 296.74 | |
| religious doctrine | 202.2 | |
| Christianity | 234.165 | |
| religious law | 208.4 | |
| Christianity | 262.9 | |
| Judaism | 296.444 | |
| rites | 203.85 | |
| Christianity | 265.5 | |
| Judaism | 296.444 | |
| liturgy | 296.454 4 | |
| *see also* Public worship | | |
| social theology | 201.7 | |
| Christianity | 261.835 81 | |
| Marriage counseling | | |
| pastoral theology | 206.1 | |
| Christianity | 259.14 | |
| Judaism | 296.61 | |
| psychotherapy | 616.891 562 | |
| social welfare | 362.828 6 | |
| Married men | 306.872 2 | |
| | T1—086 55 | |
| family relationships | 306.872 2 | |
| home economics | 646.782 | |
| guides to Christian life | 248.842 5 | |
| psychology | 155.645 2 | |
| social welfare | 362.820 865 5 | |

| | | | |
|---|---|---|---|
| Married people | 306.872 | Marshes | 551.417 |
| T1—086 55 | | biology | 578.768 |
| Christian devotional literature | 242.644 | ecology | 577.68 |
| family relationships | | *see also* Wetlands | |
| home economics | 646.782 | Marsian language | 479.7 |
| guides to religious life | 204.41 | T6—797 | |
| Christianity | 248.844 | Marsiliales | 587.3 |
| Islam | 297.577 | Marsupial cats | 599.27 |
| Judaism | 296.74 | Marsupial mice | 599.27 |
| *see also* Marriage — personal | | Marsupial moles | 599.27 |
| religion | | Marsupial rats | 599.27 |
| law | 346.016 3 | Marsupialia | 599.2 |
| psychology | 155.645 | Marsupials | 599.2 |
| social group | 306.872 | conservation technology | 639.979 2 |
| social welfare | 362.820 865 5 | paleozoology | 569.2 |
| Married women | 306.872 3 | resource economics | 333.959 2 |
| T1—086 55 | | Marsupicarnivora | 599.27 |
| Christian devotional literature | 242.643 5 | Martaban, Gulf of (Burma) | 551.461 565 |
| family relationships | 306.872 3 | T2—165 65 | |
| home economics | 646.782 | Martens | 599.766 5 |
| guides to Christian life | 248.843 5 | Martes | 599.766 5 |
| labor economics | 331.43 | Martha's Vineyard (Mass.) | T2—744 94 |
| psychology | 155.645 3 | Martial artists | 796.809 2 |
| social welfare | 362.839 52 | Martial arts | 796.8 |
| Marrucinian language | 479.7 | physical fitness | 613.714 8 |
| T6—797 | | Martial law | 342.062 8 |
| Mars (Planet) | T2—992 3 | Martigny (Switzerland : | |
| astrology | 133.535 | District) | T2—494 796 7 |
| manned flights to | 629.455 3 | Martin, Lake (Ala.) | T2—761 53 |
| unmanned flights to | 629.435 43 | Martin, Paul | |
| Marsá Maṭrūḥ (Egypt) | T2—621 | Canadian history | 971.072 |
| Marseille (France) | T2—449 12 | Martin County (Fla.) | T2—759 31 |
| Marseilles | T2—449 12 | Martin County (Ind.) | T2—772 382 |
| Marsh flies | 595.774 | Martin County (Ky.) | T2—769 243 |
| Marsh rabbit | 599.324 | Martin County (Minn.) | T2—776 232 |
| Marshall County (Ala.) | T2—761 94 | Martin County (N.C.) | T2—756 45 |
| Marshall County (Ill.) | T2—773 515 | Martin County (Tex.) | T2—764 857 |
| Marshall County (Ind.) | T2—772 88 | Martinelli Berrocal, Ricardo | |
| Marshall County (Iowa) | T2—777 55 | Alberto | |
| Marshall County (Kan.) | T2—781 31 | Panamanian history | 972.870 543 |
| Marshall County (Ky.) | T2—769 91 | Martingales | 519.236 |
| Marshall County (Minn.) | T2—776 97 | Martinicans | T5—969 729 82 |
| Marshall County (Miss.) | T2—762 88 | Martiniquais | T5—969 729 82 |
| Marshall County (Okla.) | T2—766 61 | Martinique | 972.982 |
| Marshall County (S.D.) | T2—783 13 | T2—729 82 | |
| Marshall County (Tenn.) | T2—768 585 | Martins | 598.826 |
| Marshall County (W. Va.) | T2—754 16 | Martinsville (Va.) | T2—755 693 |
| Marshall Islands | 996.83 | Martyrs | 200.92 |
| T2—968 3 | | biography | 200.92 |
| Marshallese language | 499.52 | Christian | 272.092 |
| T6—995 2 | | *see Manual at* 230–280 | |
| Marshals (Law) | 347.016 | role and function | 206.1 |
| criminal law | 345.012 6 | *see Manual at* 200.92 and | |
| Marshals (Police) | 363.282 | 201–209, 292–299 | |

| | | | |
|---|---|---|---|
| Marwari language | 491.479 7 | Masers | 621.381 336 |
| | T6—914 79 | Maseru (Lesotho) | T2—688 5 |
| Marwari literature | 891.479 | Mashhūr (Hadith) | 297.125 24 |
| Marxian parties | 324.217 | Mashona (African people) | T5—963 975 |
| international organizations | 324.17 | Mashonaland Central | |
| Marxian socialism | 335.4 | Province (Zimbabwe) | T2—689 1 |
| economics | 335.4 | Mashonaland East Province | |
| political ideology | 320.531 5 | (Zimbabwe) | T2—689 1 |
| Marxism | 335.4 | Mashonaland West Province | |
| economics | 335.4 | (Zimbabwe) | T2—689 1 |
| political ideology | 320.531 5 | Masire, Ketumile, Sir | |
| Marxism-Leninism | 335.43 | Botswana history | 968.830 32 |
| economics | 335.43 | Maskinongé (Quebec : | |
| political ideology | 320.532 2 | Regional County | |
| Marxist-Christian dialogue | | Municipality) | T2—714 44 |
| Christian theology | 261.21 | Maskoutains (Quebec) | T2—714 523 |
| Marxist-Leninists | 335.430 92 | Masks | 391.434 |
| Marxists | 335.409 2 | commercial technology | 687.4 |
| *see Manual at* 230–280 | | customs | 391.434 |
| Mary, Blessed Virgin, Saint | 232.91 | home construction | 646.478 |
| art representation | 704.948 55 | *see also* Clothing | |
| arts | T3C—351 | Masks (Sculpture) | 731.75 |
| private prayers to | 242.74 | Masochism | |
| Mary, Queen of Scots | | medicine | 616.858 35 |
| Scottish history | 941.105 | *see also* Mental disorders | |
| Mary I, Queen of England | | sociology | 306.776 |
| English history | 942.054 | Mason County (Ill.) | T2—773 553 |
| Mary II, Queen of England | | Mason County (Ky.) | T2—769 323 |
| British history | 941.068 | Mason County (Mich.) | T2—774 61 |
| English history | 942.068 | Mason County (Tex.) | T2—764 66 |
| Scottish history | 941.106 8 | Mason County (W. Va.) | T2—754 33 |
| Mary Tudor, Queen of England | | Mason County (Wash.) | T2—797 97 |
| English history | 942.054 | Masonry | 693.1 |
| Maryborough (Qld.) | T2—943 2 | Masonry (Secret order) | 366.1 |
| Maryborough (Vic.) | T2—945 3 | Masonry adhesives | 666.9 |
| Maryland | 975.2 | building materials | 691.5 |
| | T2—752 | materials science | 620.135 |
| Masaba-Luyia languages | 496.395 | Masonry arch bridges | |
| | T6—963 95 | construction | 624.225 |
| Masai (African people) | T5—965 | Masonry dams | 627.82 |
| Masai language | 496.5 | Masonry materials | |
| | T6—965 | architectural construction | 721.044 1 |
| Masai literature | 896.5 | materials science | 620.13 |
| Masānīd | 297.125 61 | structural engineering | 624.183 |
| Masaya (Nicaragua : Dept.) | T2—728 514 | Masons | 693.109 2 |
| Masbate (Philippines : | | Masons (Secret order) | 366.1 |
| Province) | T2—599 5 | Masques | 782.15 |
| Mascara (Algeria : | | literature | 808.825 |
| Province) | T2—651 | history and criticism | 809.25 |
| Mascarene Islands | T2—698 | specific literatures | T3B—205 |
| Mascoian languages | 498.9 | individual authors | T3A—2 |
| | T6—989 | music | 782.15 |
| Mascots (Occultism) | 133.44 | stage presentation | 792.6 |
| Masculinity | 155.332 | | |

| | |
|---|---|
| Mass (Christian rite) | 264.36 |
| Anglican | 264.030 36 |
| texts | 264.03 |
| music | 782.323 |
| choral and mixed voices | 782.532 3 |
| single voices | 783.093 23 |
| Roman Catholic | 264.020 36 |
| texts | 264.023 |
| Mass (Substance) | 531.14 |
| air mechanics | 533.6 |
| gas mechanics | 533.15 |
| liquid mechanics | 532.4 |
| solid mechanics | 531.5 |
| Mass communication | 302.2 |
| communications services | 384 |
| law | 343.099 |
| social aspects | 302.2 |
| Mass culture | 306 |
| Mass deacidification | |
| bibliographic materials | 025.84 |
| Mass-energy equivalence | 530.11 |
| Mass hysteria | 302.17 |
| Mass media | 302.23 |
| accounting | 657.84 |
| election campaigns | 324.73 |
| influence on crime | 364.254 |
| instructional use | 371.358 |
| adult level | 374.26 |
| higher education | 378.175 8 |
| law | 343.099 |
| religion | 201.7 |
| Christianity | 261.52 |
| evangelism | 269.26 |
| use by local Christian | |
| church | 253.78 |
| administration | 254.3 |
| Judaism | 296.37 |
| sociology | 302.23 |
| Mass media music | 781.54 |
| Mass movement (Geology) | 551.307 |
| Mass murder | 364.152 34 |
| law | 345.025 234 |
| Mass murderers | 364.152 34 |
| biography | 364.152 340 92 |
| Mass spectrometry | 543.65 |
| analytical chemistry | 543.65 |
| physics | 539.602 87 |
| Mass spectroscopy | 543.65 |
| analytical chemistry | 543.65 |
| physics | 539.602 87 |
| Mass transfer | 530.475 |
| chemical engineering | 660.284 23 |
| gaseous-state physics | 530.435 |
| liquid-state physics | 530.425 |

| | | |
|---|---|---|
| Mass transfer (continued) | | |
| physics | | 530.475 |
| semiconductors | | 537.622 5 |
| solid-state physics | | 530.415 |
| Mass transit | | 388.4 |
| *see also* Urban transportation | | |
| Mass transport (Physics) | | 530.475 |
| *see also* Mass transfer | | |
| Mass transportation | | 388.042 |
| law | | 343.093 3 |
| transportation services | | 388.042 |
| urban | | 388.4 |
| *see also* Urban transportation | | |
| *see also* Passenger services | | |
| Mass wasting (Geology) | | 551.307 |
| Massa-Carrara (Italy : | | |
| Province) | T2—455 4 | |
| ancient | T2—375 4 | |
| Massa e Carrara (Italy : | | |
| Province) | T2—455 4 | |
| ancient | T2—375 4 | |
| Massac County (Ill.) | T2—773 997 | |
| Massachuset language | | 497.348 |
| | T6—973 48 | |
| Massachusetts | | 974.4 |
| | T2—744 | |
| Massachusetts Bay (Mass.) | | 551.461 345 |
| | T2—163 45 | |
| Massacre of innocents | | 232.92 |
| Massage | | 615.822 |
| physical fitness | | 613.72 |
| therapeutics | | 615.822 |
| Massif Central (France) | T2—445 9 | |
| Massively parallel | | |
| supercomputers | | 004.35 |
| Mast cell disease | | |
| medicine | | 616.77 |
| *see also* Musculoskeletal | | |
| diseases — humans | | |
| Mast cells | | |
| human cytology | | 611.018 26 |
| Mastectomy | | 616.994 490 59 |
| Master and servant | | |
| law | | 346.024 |
| Master's degree | | 378.2 |
| Masters Golf Tournament | | 796.352 66 |
| Masterton District (N.Z.) | T2—936 8 | |
| Mastication | | |
| human physiology | | 612.311 |
| rubber | | 678.22 |
| Mastiffs | | 636.73 |
| Mastigomycotina | | 579.53 |

Mastocytosis
  medicine 616.77
  *see also* Musculoskeletal
    diseases — humans
Mastoid process diseases
  medicine 617.87
  *see also* Ear diseases —
    humans
Mastoid processes
  human anatomy 611.85
  human physiology 612.854
  medicine 617.87
Masts 623.862
Masturbation
  sociology 306.772
Masvingo Province
  (Zimbabwe) T2—689 1
Mặt trận dân tộc giải phóng miền
  nam Việt Nam 959.704 332 2
Matabeleland North
  Province (Zimbabwe) T2—689 1
Matabeleland South
  Province (Zimbabwe) T2—689 1
Mataco-Guaicuru languages 498.7
  T6—987
Matagalpa (Nicaragua :
  Dept.) T2—728 525
Matagalpan Indians T5—978
Matagami (Quebec) T2—714 115
Matagorda County (Tex.) T2—764 132
Matamata Piako District
  (N.Z.) T2—933 53
Matane (Quebec : Regional
  County Municipality) T2—714 775
Matanuska-Susitna Borough
  (Alaska) T2—798 3
Matanzas (Cuba : Province) T2—729 13
Matapédia (Quebec :
  Regional County
  Municipality) T2—714 778
Matawinie (Quebec) T2—714 418
Match-cover advertising 659.131
Match covers 741.694
Matches 662.5
Matching numbers contests 790.134
Matching theory 511.66
Maté 641.337 7
  agriculture 633.77
  beverage 641.337 7
  botany 583.85
  commercial processing 663.96
  cooking with 641.637 7
  home preparation 641.877

Mate selection
  customs 392.4
  life skills 646.77
  sociology 306.82
Matera (Italy : Province) T2—457 72
  ancient T2—377 73
Materia medica 615.1
  *see also* Drugs
    (Pharmaceuticals)
Material culture 306.46
Material remains 930.1
Materialism 146.3
  Christian polemics 239.7
  Indian philosophy 181.46
  Islamic polemics 297.298
Materialization (Spiritualism) 133.92
Materials T1—028 4
  architectural construction 721.04
  building construction 691
  engineering 620.11
  foundation engineering 624.153
  manufacturing technology 670
  nuclear reactors 621.483 3
  standards and specifications
    production management 658.562
  structural engineering 624.18
Materials costs
  financial management 658.155 3
Materials engineers 620.110 92
Materials estimates T1—029
  building construction 692.5
Materials handling
  materials management 658.781
Materials-handling equipment 621.86
  ships 623.867
Materials management 658.7
  T1—068 7
  public administration 352.55
  schools 371.67
Materials science 620.11
Matériel (Armed forces) 355.8
Maternal behavior (Animals) 591.563
Maternal deaths
  incidence 614.599 279
  obstetrics 618.79
Maternally acquired antibodies 571.963 8
Maternity garments 392
  commercial technology 687.16
  customs 392
  home economics 646.34
  home sewing 646.47
  *see also* Clothing
Maternity insurance 368.424
  law 344.022 4

| | |
|---|---|
| Maternity leave | 331.44 |
|   economics | 331.44 |
|   personnel management | 658.312 2 |
| Maternity services | 362.198 2 |
|   *see also* Health services | |
| Mathematical analysis | 515 |
| Mathematical crystallography | 548.7 |
| Mathematical economics | 330.015 1 |
|   economic school | 330.154 3 |
| Mathematical games | 793.74 |
| Mathematical geography | 526 |
| Mathematical linguistics | 410.151 |
| Mathematical logic | 511.3 |
|   computer programming | |
|     languages | 005.131 |
| Mathematical models | 511.8 |
| | T1—015 118 |
|   systems | 003 |
| | T1—011 |
| Mathematical optimization | 519.6 |
|   *see also* Optimization | |
| Mathematical physics | 530.15 |
| Mathematical programming | 519.7 |
|   management decision making | 658.403 3 |
| Mathematical recreations | 793.74 |
| Mathematical school | |
|   (Economics) | 330.154 3 |
| Mathematical shortcuts | 513.9 |
| Mathematical statistics | 519.5 |
| Mathematicians | 510.92 |
| Mathematics | 510 |
| | T1—015 1 |
|   arts | T3C—36 |
|   primary education | 372.7 |
|   *see Manual at* 510; *also at* | |
|     510, T1—0151 vs. 003, | |
|     T1—011; *also at* 510, | |
|     T1—0151 vs. 004–006, | |
|     T1—0285 | |
| Mathews County (Va.) | T2—755 31 |
| Mathieu functions | 515.54 |
| Mating | 591.562 |
| Matins | 264.15 |
|   Anglican | 264.030 15 |
|   texts | 264.033 |
|   music | 782.324 |
|     Anglican church | 782.325 |
| Mato Grosso (Brazil : State) | T2—817 2 |
| Mato Grosso do Sul (Brazil) | T2—817 1 |
| Matriarchal family | 306.859 |
| Matriarchy (System of | |
|   government) | 321.1 |
| Matrices | 512.943 4 |
| Matriculation | 371.21 |

| | |
|---|---|
| Matrilineal kinship | 306.83 |
| Matrimony | 306.81 |
|   sacrament | 234.165 |
|   public worship | 265.5 |
|   theology | 234.165 |
|   *see also* Marriage | |
| Matrix algebra | 512.943 4 |
| Matrix mechanics | 530.122 |
| Matroids | 511.6 |
| Maṭrūḥ (Egypt) | T2—621 |
| Mats | 642.7 |
|   arts | 746.96 |
|   home sewing | 646.21 |
|   table setting | 642.7 |
| MATS (Air transportation) | 358.44 |
| Matter | 530 |
|   philosophy | 117 |
|   physics | 530 |
|   structure | 539.1 |
| Matter at high temperatures | 536.57 |
| Matter at low temperatures | 536.56 |
| Matthew (Gospel) | 226.2 |
| Matthias, Holy Roman Emperor | |
|   German history | 943.035 |
| Matthiola | 583.64 |
| Matting | |
|   arts | 746.41 |
| Mattresses | 645.4 |
|   manufacturing technology | 684.15 |
|   *see also* Furniture | |
| Matumbi languages | 496.397 |
| | T6—963 97 |
| Maturation | 571.87 |
|   developmental psychology | 155 |
|   human physiology | 612.6 |
| Maturity | |
|   developmental psychology | |
|     adulthood | 155.6 |
|   human physiology | 612.663 |
|   individual psychology | |
|     character development | 155.25 |
| Maui (Hawaii) | T2—969 21 |
| Maui County (Hawaii) | T2—969 2 |
| Maule (Chile : Region) | T2—833 5 |
| Maumee River (Ind. and | |
|   Ohio) | T2—771 1 |
| Maundy Thursday | 263.925 |
|   devotional literature | 242.35 |
|   music | 781.726 |
|   sermons | 252.625 |
| Maurelle Island (B.C.) | T2—711 1 |
| Maurepas, Lake (La.) | T2—763 32 |
| Mauretania | 939.71 |
| | T2—397 1 |

| | |
|---|---|
| Mauretania (Kingdom) | 939.710 3 |
| | T2—397 1 |
| Moroccan history | 939.712 03 |
| Mauretania Caesariensis | 939.714 |
| | T2—397 14 |
| Mauretania Tingitana | 939.712 |
| | T2—397 12 |
| Mauricie National Park | |
| (Quebec) | T2—714 453 |
| Mauricie Region (Quebec) | T2—714 45 |
| Mauritania | 966.1 |
| | T2—661 |
| Mauritanians | T5—966 1 |
| Mauritians | T5—914 1 |
| Mauritius | 969.82 |
| | T2—698 2 |
| Maury County (Tenn.) | T2—768 59 |
| Maurya dynasty | 934.04 |
| Maverick County (Tex.) | T2—764 435 |
| Mawḍu' (Hadith) | 297.125 225 |
| Mawlid al-Nabī | 297.36 |
| Mawqūf | 297.125 21 |
| Mawṣilī, Abū Ya'lá Aḥmad ibn | |
| 'Ali | |
| Hadith | 297.125 613 |
| Maxamed Siyaad Barre | |
| Somali history | 967.730 52 |
| Maxima | |
| combinatorics | 511.66 |
| Maximilian, Emperor of Mexico | |
| Mexican history | 972.07 |
| Maximilian I, Holy Roman | |
| Emperor | |
| German history | 943.029 |
| Maximilian II, Emperor of | |
| Germany | |
| German history | 943.033 |
| Maxims | 398.9 |
| Maximum-security prisons | 365.33 |
| *see also* Penal institutions | |
| Maxwell's equations (Physics) | 530.141 |
| Maxwell's thermodynamic | |
| formulas | 536.71 |
| May Day | 394.262 7 |
| Maya Indians | 972.81 |
| | T5—974 2 |
| Guatemala | 972.81 |
| Mexico | 972.6 |
| Maya Indians (Yucatecan | |
| Maya) | T5—974 27 |
| Maya language | 497.427 |
| | T6—974 27 |
| Maya literature | 897.427 |
| Mayaguana Island | |
| (Bahamas) | T2—729 6 |
| Mayagüez (P.R. : District) | T2—729 56 |
| Mayan calendar | 529.329 784 27 |
| Mayan languages | 497.42 |
| | T6—974 2 |
| Mayan period | 972.810 16 |
| Mayans | T5—974 2 |
| Mayans (Yucatecan Maya) | T5—974 27 |
| Mayapple | 583.34 |
| Mayas | T5—974 2 |
| Mayas (Yucatecan Maya) | T5—974 27 |
| Maydeae | 584.92 |
| Mayenne (France : Dept.) | T2—441 62 |
| Mayes County (Okla.) | T2—766 93 |
| Mayflies | 595.734 |
| Mayflower | 583.34 |
| Mayo (Ireland : County) | T2—417 3 |
| Mayo, Richard Southwell | |
| Bourke, Earl of | |
| Indian history | 954.035 2 |
| Mayonnaise | 641.814 |
| food technology | 664.37 |
| home preparation | 641.814 |
| Mayor-council government | 320.854 |
| Mayors | 320.854 |
| public administration | 352.232 16 |
| Mayotte | 969.45 |
| | T2—694 5 |
| Maypop | 583.626 |
| Maysān (Iraq) | T2—567 5 |
| Māzandarān (Iran) | T2—552 3 |
| ancient | 939.6 |
| | T2—396 |
| Mazatec Indians | T5—976 |
| Mazdaism | 295 |
| Maze puzzles | 793.738 |
| Mazowieckie Voivodeship | |
| (Poland) | T2—438 41 |
| Mazurkas | 793.319 438 |
| music | 784.188 4 |
| Mbabane (Swaziland) | T2—688 7 |
| Mbai language (Moissala) | 496.5 |
| | T6—965 |
| Mbala (Congolese people, | |
| Bandundu region) | T5—963 93 |
| Mbam languages | T6—963 96 |
| Mbasogo, Teodoro Obiang | |
| Nguema | |
| Equatorial Guinean history | 967.180 32 |
| Mbeki, Thabo | |
| South African history | 968.066 |
| Mbere languages | 496.396 |
| | T6—963 96 |

| | |
|---|---|
| Mbete languages | 496.396 |
| | T6—963 96 |
| Mbeya Region (Tanzania) | T2—678 28 |
| Mbibana (South Africa : | |
| District) | T2—682 75 |
| MBO (Management by | |
| objectives) | 658.401 2 |
| public administration | 352.36 |
| Mbole-Ena languages | 496.394 |
| | T6—963 94 |
| Mboshi languages | 496.396 |
| | T6—963 96 |
| Mbosi language | 496.396 |
| | T6—963 96 |
| Mbukushu language | 496.399 |
| | T6—963 99 |
| Mbum language | 496.361 |
| | T6—963 61 |
| Mbundu (Angolan people, | |
| Benguela Province) | T5—963 99 |
| Mbundu (Angolan people, | |
| Luanda Province) | T5—963 932 |
| Mbundu language (Benguela | 496.399 |
| Province, Angola) | T6—963 99 |
| Mbundu language (Luanda | 496.393 2 |
| Province, Angola) | T6—963 932 |
| Mbundu literature (Luanda | |
| Province, Angola) | 896.393 2 |
| McBride (B.C.) | T2—711 82 |
| McClain County (Okla.) | T2—766 55 |
| McCone County (Mont.) | T2—786 26 |
| McCook County (S.D.) | T2—783 372 |
| McCormick County (S.C.) | T2—757 36 |
| McCracken County (Ky.) | T2—769 95 |
| McCreary County (Ky.) | T2—769 135 |
| McCulloch County (Tex.) | T2—764 67 |
| McCurtain County (Okla.) | T2—766 64 |
| McDonald County (Mo.) | T2—778 736 |
| McDonough County (Ill.) | T2—773 42 |
| McDowell County (N.C.) | T2—756 89 |
| McDowell County (W. Va.) | T2—754 49 |
| McDuffie County (Ga.) | T2—758 632 |
| McEwen, John, Sir | |
| Australian history | 994.061 |
| McGregor River (B.C.) | T2—711 82 |
| McHenry County (Ill.) | T2—773 22 |
| McHenry County (N.D.) | T2—784 62 |
| McIntosh County (Ga.) | T2—758 737 |
| McIntosh County (N.D.) | T2—784 55 |
| McIntosh County (Okla.) | T2—766 74 |
| McKean County (Pa.) | T2—748 63 |
| McKenzie County (N.D.) | T2—784 81 |
| McKinley, William | |
| United States history | 973.88 |

| | |
|---|---|
| McKinley County (N.M.) | T2—789 83 |
| McLean County (Ill.) | T2—773 59 |
| McLean County (Ky.) | T2—769 826 |
| McLean County (N.D.) | T2—784 75 |
| McLennan County (Tex.) | T2—764 284 |
| McLeod County (Minn.) | T2—776 52 |
| McMahon, William | |
| Australian history | 994.061 |
| McMinn County (Tenn.) | T2—768 865 |
| McMullen County (Tex.) | T2—764 452 |
| McNairy County (Tenn.) | T2—768 29 |
| McNaughton Lake (B.C.) | T2—711 68 |
| McPherson County (Kan.) | T2—781 55 |
| McPherson County (Neb.) | T2—782 793 |
| McPherson County (S.D.) | T2—783 16 |
| Mdantsane (South Africa : | |
| District) | T2—687 55 |
| Mdutjana (South Africa : | |
| District) | T2—682 75 |
| Mead | 641.23 |
| commercial processing | 663.4 |
| Mead, Lake (Ariz. and | |
| Nev.) | T2—793 12 |
| Meade County (Kan.) | T2—781 75 |
| Meade County (Ky.) | T2—769 852 |
| Meade County (S.D.) | T2—783 44 |
| Meadow beauties | 583.76 |
| Meadow mice | 599.354 |
| Meadowlarks | 598.874 |
| Meadows | 333.74 |
| biology | 578.746 |
| ecology | 577.46 |
| *see also* Grasslands | |
| Meagher County (Mont.) | T2—786 612 |
| Meal (Milling products) | |
| commercial processing | 664.720 7 |
| wheat | 664.722 73 |
| Meals | 642 |
| customs | 394.125 |
| transportation services | 388.042 |
| *see also* Passenger services | |
| Mealworms | 595.769 |
| Mean | 519.533 |
| Mean value theorems | 515.33 |
| Meaning | |
| epistemology | 121.68 |
| linguistics | 401.43 |
| specific languages | T4—014 3 |
| *see Manual at* 401.43 vs. | |
| 306.44, 401.45, 401.9, | |
| 412, 415 | |

Mcasles
  incidence — 614.523
  medicine — 616.915
    *see also* Communicable
      diseases — humans
  pediatrics — 618.929 15
Measure theory — 515.42
Measurement — 530.8
    T1—028 7
  chemistry — 542.3
Measurement systems — 530.81
  physics — 530.81
  social aspects — 389.15
Measurement theory — 530.801
Measures — 530.81
  *see also* Weights and measures
Measuring instruments
  electric measurement — 621.37
  electronics — 621.381 548
  manufacturing technology — 681.2
  physics — 530.7
Meat — 641.36
  commercial preservation
    technology — 664.902 8
  commercial processing
    economics — 338.476 649
    technology — 664.9
  cooking — 641.66
  food — 641.36
  home preservation — 641.49
  product safety — 363.192 9
    *see also* Food — product
      safety
Meat cutting — 664.902 9
Meat loaf — 641.824
  commercial processing — 664.92
  home preparation — 641.824
Meat pies
  commercial processing — 664.92
  home preparation — 641.824
Meat processing industry — 338.476 649
Meath (Ireland) — T2—418 22
Meatless high-protein foods
  technology — 664.64
Meats — 641.36
  *see also* Meat
Mecca (Saudi Arabia) — T2—538
  Islamic religion — 297.352
Mechanical bands — 784.6
Mechanical barriers
  military engineering — 623.31
Mechanical chess players — 794.17
Mechanical conveyer systems
  office services — 651.79

Mechanical deformation
  materials science — 620.112 3
Mechanical drawing — 604.2
Mechanical engineering — 621
  military applications — 623.045
Mechanical engineers — 621.092
Mechanical forces — 530
  biophysics — 571.43
    humans — 612.014 41
  extraterrestrial biophysics
    humans — 612.014 53
  materials science — 620.112 3
Mechanical musical instruments — 786.6
  bands and orchestras — 784
  chamber ensembles — 785
    single type — 785.66
  construction — 786.619 23
    by hand — 786.619 23
    by machine — 681.866
  solo music — 786.6
Mechanical pencils
  manufacturing technology — 681.6
Mechanical processes
  printing — 686.231
  pulp to paper — 676.2
  wood pulp — 676.122
Mechanical properties
  materials science — 620.112 92
Mechanical separation
  ores — 622.75
Mechanical stokers
  steam engineering — 621.183
Mechanical systems
  ships — 623.850 1
Mechanical toys — 790.133
  manufacturing technology — 688.728
  recreation — 790.133
Mechanical working
  metals — 671.3
Mechanics — 530
  atmosphere — 551.515
  classical physics — 531
  engineering — 620.1
  foundation soils — 624.151 36
  physics — 530
  quantum physics — 530.12
  structures — 624.17
Mechanics' liens — 346.024
Mechanics of materials — 620.112 3
Mechanics of particles
  classical physics — 531.16
Mechanics of points — 531.1
Mechanism (Philosophy) — 146.6

Mechanisms
  engineering 621.8
Mechanization
  agricultural economics 338.161
  control engineering 629.8
  economics 338.064
  factory operations engineering 670.427
  mineral industries 338.26
  production management 658.514
  secondary industries 338.45
  social effects 303.483
Mechanized bells 786.64
  *see also* Mechanical musical
    instruments
Mechanized cavalry 357.5
Mechanotherapy
  medicine 615.82
Mechitarists 255.17
  church history 271.17
Méchouar de Casablanca
  (Morocco) T2—643 8
Mecklenburg (Germany :
  State) T2—431 7
Mecklenburg County (N.C.) T2—756 76
Mecklenburg County (Va.) T2—755 645
Mecklenburg-Strelitz
  (Germany : Landkreis) T2—431 72
Mecklenburg-Vorpommern
  (Germany) T2—431 7
Mecoptera 595.744
Mecosta County (Mich.) T2—774 52
Medal of Honor Legion (U.S.) 369.11
Medallions
  numismatics 737.22
Medals
  armed forces 355.134 2
  numismatics 737.22
  religious significance 203.7
  *see also* Symbolism —
    religious significance
  research incentive 001.44
Médéa (Algeria : Province) T2—653
Medelpad landskap
  (Sweden) T2—488 5
Media 302.23
  *see also* Mass media
Media (Ancient area) 935.75
  T2—357 5
Media centers 027
  *see also* Libraries
Media ethics 175
Media kits
  cataloging 025.349 6
  library treatment 025.179 6

Media production
  primary education 372.672
Median 519.533
Median Empire 935.750 4
  T2—357 5
Mediastinal diseases
  medicine 616.27
  *see also* Respiratory tract
    diseases — humans
Mediastinum
  human anatomy 611.27
  human physiology 612.25
  medicine 616.27
  surgery 617.545
Mediation
  labor economics 331.891 42
    public administration 354.97
  law 347.09
  law of nations 341.52
  personnel management 658.315 4
    public administration 352.68
  social conflict 303.69
Medicaid 368.420 097 3
  law 344.730 22
  public administration 353.690 973
Medicaid fraud 364.163
  law 345.730 263
Medical accounting 657.834
Medical anthropology 306.461
Medical assistants 610.737 092
  role and function 610.737 069
  services 610.737
Medical astrology 133.586 1
Medical bacteriology 616.920 1
Medical care 362.1
  *see also* Health services
Medical care facilities
  area planning 711.555
Medical chemistry 615.19
Medical climatology 616.988
Medical economics 338.473 621
Medical emergencies 362.18
  medicine 616.025
  social services 362.18
Medical entomology 616.968
Medical ethics 174.2
  religion 205.642
    Buddhism 294.356 42
    Christianity 241.642
    Hinduism 294.548 642
    Islam 297.564 2
    Judaism 296.364 2
Medical examinations 616.075

| | |
|---|---|
| Medical examiners | 614.109 2 |
| law | 347.016 |
| criminal law | 345.012 6 |
| Medical genetics | 616.042 |
| law | 344.041 96 |
| Medical geography | 614.42 |
| Medical gymnastics | |
| therapeutics | 615.82 |
| Medical helminthology | 616.962 |
| Medical history taking | 616.075 1 |
| Medical installations (Armed | |
| forces) | 355.72 |
| Medical instruments | 610.284 |
| manufacturing technology | 681.761 |
| product safety | 363.19 |
| public administration | 353.99 |
| Medical insurance | 368.382 2 |
| public administration | 353.69 |
| Medical jurisprudence | 614.1 |
| Medical keyboarding | 652.326 |
| Medical law | 344.041 |
| Medical libraries | 026.61 |
| Medical machinery | |
| manufacturing technology | 681.761 |
| Medical malpractice | |
| torts | 344.041 1 |
| Medical malpractice insurance | 368.564 2 |
| Medical meteorology | 616.988 |
| Medical microbiology | 616.904 1 |
| *see Manual at* 579.165 vs. | |
| 616.9041; *also at* 616.1–.9 | |
| Medical missionaries | |
| Christian | 266.009 2 |
| role and function | 610.69 |
| Medical missions | 362.1 |
| Christian | 266 |
| social welfare | 362.1 |
| *see also* Health services | |
| Medical mycology | 616.969 01 |
| Medical office buildings | |
| architecture | 725.23 |
| Medical parasitology | 616.96 |
| Medical personnel | 610.92 |
| law | 344.041 |
| malpractice | 344.041 1 |
| role and function | 610.69 |
| *see Manual at* 362.1–.4 vs. 610 | |
| Medical physics | 610.153 |
| Medical protozoology | 616.936 01 |
| Medical radiology | 616.075 7 |
| Medical records management | 651.504 261 |
| Medical rehabilitation | 617.03 |
| Medical schools | 610.711 |
| Medical sciences | 610 |
| information systems | 025.066 1 |
| Medical screening | 362.177 |
| public administration | 353.628 |
| *see also* Health services | |
| Medical services | 362.1 |
| armed forces | 355.345 |
| *see also* Health services | |
| Medical shorthand | 653.18 |
| Medical social work | 362.104 25 |
| Medical supplies | 610.284 |
| armed forces | 355.88 |
| product safety | 363.19 |
| public administration | 353.99 |
| Medical technicians | 610.737 092 |
| role and function | 610.737 069 |
| services | 610.737 |
| Medical virology | 616.910 1 |
| Medical wastes | 363.728 8 |
| law | 344.046 22 |
| Medicare (Australia) | 368.420 099 4 |
| law | 344.940 22 |
| public administration | 353.690 994 |
| Medicare (United States) | 368.426 009 73 |
| law | 344.730 226 |
| public administration | 353.690 973 |
| Medicare fraud | 364.163 |
| law | 345.730 263 |
| Medicare supplement insurance | 368.382 |
| Medication methods | 615.6 |
| Medications | 615.1 |
| *see also* Drugs | |
| (Pharmaceuticals) | |
| Médici, Emílio Garrastazu | |
| Brazilian history | 981.063 |
| Medici, House of | |
| Tuscan history | 945.505 |
| 1348–1494 | 945.505 |
| 1512–1527 | 945.506 |
| 1531–1737 | 945.507 |
| Medicinal plants | 615.321 |
| agriculture | 633.88 |
| economic botany | 581.634 |
| pharmacognosy | 615.321 |
| *see Manual at* 583–585 vs. 600 | |
| Medicinal teas | |
| pharmacognosy | 615.321 |
| Medicine | 610 |
| applied science | 610 |
| arts | 700.456 1 |
| | T3C—356 1 |
| economics | 338.473 621 |
| folklore | 398.276 1 |
| history and criticism | 398.356 1 |

Medicine (continued)
  law    344.041
  literature    808.803 561
    history and criticism    809.933 561
    specific literatures    T3B—080 356 1
    history and
      criticism    T3B—093 561
  sociology    306.461
  *see Manual at* 610 vs. 616
Medicine and religion    201.661
  Christianity    261.561
  Judaism    296.376
Medicine Bow Mountains
  (Colo. and Wyo.)    T2—787 86
Medicine Hat (Alta.)    T2—712 34
Medicine shows    791.1
Medicines    615.1
  *see also* Drugs
    (Pharmaceuticals)
Medieval architecture    723
Medieval art    709.02
Medieval church modes    781.263
Medieval law    340.55
Medieval metrical romances    808.813 3
  history and criticism    809.133
  specific literatures    T3B—103 3
    individual authors    T3A—1
Medieval music    780.902
Medieval painting    759.02
Medieval period    909.07
       T1—090 2
  Austrian history    943.602
  church history    270.3
  Danish history    948.901
  English history    942.03
  European history    940.1
  French history    944.02
  German history    943.02
  Italian history    945.01
  Japanese history    952.02
  Lombardian history    945.201
  Norwegian history    948.101
  Sardinian history    945.902
  Scandinavian history    948.02
  Sicilian history    945.801
  Southern Italian history    945.701
  specific centuries    909.1–.4
  Swedish history    948.501
  Tuscan history    945.501
  Venetian history    945.301
  *see Manual at* T1—0940902 vs.
    T1—0902

Medieval philosophy
  eastern    181
  western    189
Medieval remedies
  therapeutics    615.880 902
Medieval sculpture    734
Medigap    368.382
  *see also* Insurance
Medina (England)    T2—422 8
Medina (Saudi Arabia)    T2—538
  Islamic religion    297.355 38
Medina Angarita, Isaías
  Venezuelan history    987.063 15
Medina County (Ohio)    T2—771 35
Medina County (Tex.)    T2—764 42
Medio Campidano (Italy :
  Province)    T2—459 6
  ancient    T2—379 6
Mediolanum (Italy)    T2—372 271
Meditation    158.12
  religion    204.35
    Buddhism    294.344 35
    Christianity    248.34
    Hinduism    294.543 5
    Islam    297.382
      Sufi    297.438 2
    Judaism    296.72
Meditations    158.128
  religion    204.32
    Buddhism    294.344 32
    Christianity    242
    Hinduism    294.543 2
    Islam    297.382 4
      Sufi    297.438 24
    Judaism    296.72
Meditations (Music)    784.189 6
Mediterranean Region    T2—182 2
  ancient    937
       T2—37
Mediterranean Sea    551.461 38
       T2—163 8
Mediterranean-type ecosystems    577.38
  biology    578.738
Mediterranean-type plants    581.738
Mediterranean vegetation    581.738
Medium-security prisons    365.33
  *see also* Penal institutions
Mediums of exchange    332.4
Mediumship (Spiritualism)    133.91
Medlars    641.341 5
  botany    583.73
  cooking    641.641 5
  food    641.341 5
  orchard crop    634.15

| | |
|---|---|
| Medulla oblongata | |
| human anatomy | 611.81 |
| human physiology | 612.828 |
| medicine | 616.8 |
| Medullosaceae | 561.595 |
| Medusae (Jellyfishes) | 593.53 |
| Medvedev, Dmitry | |
| Russian history | 947.086 3 |
| Medway (England) | T2—422 32 |
| Meeker County (Minn.) | T2—776 49 |
| Meerkat | 599.742 |
| Meetings | 060 |
| management use | 658.456 |
| Megachiroptera | 599.49 |
| paleozoology | 569.4 |
| Megaloptera | 595.747 |
| Megalopteris | 561.597 |
| Megapodiidae | 598.64 |
| Megaptera | 599.525 |
| Megaric philosophy | 183.6 |
| Megaris (Greece) | T2—384 |
| Megasporangia | 575.665 |
| Megaspores | 571.845 2 |
| Meghalaya (India) | T2—541 64 |
| Megillah (Tractate) | 296.123 2 |
| Babylonian Talmud | 296.125 2 |
| Mishnah | 296.123 2 |
| Palestinian Talmud | 296.124 2 |
| Megillot (Bible) | 221.044 |
| Mehedinți (Romania) | T2—498 4 |
| Meighen, Arthur | |
| Canadian history | 971.061 3 |
| 1920–1921 | 971.061 3 |
| 1926 | 971.062 2 |
| Mcigs County (Ohio) | T2—771 99 |
| Meigs County (Tenn.) | T2—768 836 |
| Meiji period | 952.031 |
| Meʻilah | 296.123 5 |
| Babylonian Talmud | 296.125 5 |
| Mishnah | 296.123 5 |
| Meilen (Switzerland : | |
| Bezirk) | T2—494 572 9 |
| Meiosis | 571.845 |
| Meirionnydd (Wales) | T2—429 25 |
| Meitnerium | |
| chemistry | 546.62 |
| Mékinac (Quebec) | T2—714 457 |
| Meknès-El Menzeh | |
| (Morocco) | T2—645 |
| Meknès-Tafilalt (Morocco) | T2—645 |
| Mekong River | T2—59 |
| Mekong River Delta | |
| (Vietnam and Cambodia) | T2—597 8 |
| Melaka (State) | T2—595 1 |
| Melamines | 668.422 4 |
| Melancholy | |
| arts | T3C—353 |
| literature | 808.803 53 |
| history and criticism | 809.933 53 |
| specific literatures | T3B—080 353 |
| history and | |
| criticism | T3B—093 53 |
| Melanconiales | 579.55 |
| Melanesia | 995 |
| | T2—95 |
| Melanesian languages | 499.5 |
| | T6—995 |
| Melanesian literatures | 899.5 |
| Melanesians | T5—995 |
| Melanoma | |
| incidence | 614.599 947 7 |
| medicine | 616.994 77 |
| *see also* Cancer — humans | |
| Melanommatales | 579.564 |
| Melastomataceae | 583.76 |
| Melatonin | |
| human physiology | 612.492 |
| Melayu Asli languages | 499.28 |
| | T6—992 8 |
| Melbourne (Vic.) | T2—945 1 |
| Meleagrididae | 598.645 |
| Meleagris gallopavo | 598.645 |
| Meles | 599.767 2 |
| Meliaceae | 583.77 |
| Melilla (Spain) | T2—641 |
| ancient | T2—397 12 |
| Melilotus | 633.366 |
| botany | 583.74 |
| forage crop | 633.366 |
| Melinae | 599.767 |
| Meliorism | |
| philosophy | 149.5 |
| Mellette County (S.D.) | T2—783 63 |
| Mellivorinae | 599.767 |
| Melmoth (South Africa) | T2—684 3 |
| Melodeons | 788.863 |
| instrument | 788.863 19 |
| music | 788.863 |
| *see also* Woodwind instruments | |
| Melodrama | 792.27 |
| literature | 808.825 27 |
| history and criticism | 809.252 7 |
| specific literatures | T3B—205 27 |
| individual authors | T3A—2 |
| stage presentation | 792.27 |
| Melody | 781.24 |
| Meloidea | 595.769 |

| | |
|---|---|
| Melons | 641.356 1 |
| botany | 583.63 |
| commercial processing | 664.805 61 |
| cooking | 641.656 1 |
| food | 641.356 1 |
| garden crop | 635.61 |
| Melos Island (Greece) | T2—495 85 |
| Melting | 536.42 |
| chemical engineering | 660.284 296 |
| metals | 671.24 |
| Melton (England : Borough) | T2—425 46 |
| Melville (Sask.) | T2—712 44 |
| Melville Peninsula | |
| (Nunavut) | T2—719 52 |
| Membership lists | T1—06 |
| directories | T1—025 |
| Membrane lipids | 572.577 |
| Membrane processes | |
| chemical engineering | 660.284 24 |
| desalinization | 628.167 4 |
| water supply treatment | 628.164 |
| Membrane proteins | 572.696 |
| Membranes | |
| cytology | 571.64 |
| Membranophones | 786.9 |
| *see also* Percussion instruments | |
| Memoirs | 920 |
| | T1—092 |
| Memorabilia | T1—075 |
| Memorandums | |
| office use | 651.755 |
| Memorial buildings | 725.94 |
| Memorials | 394.4 |
| Holocaust, 1933–1945 | 940.531 864 |
| *see also* Military | |
| commemorations | |
| Memorizing | |
| music training method | 781.426 |
| Memory | 153.12 |
| educational psychology | 370.152 2 |
| human physiology | 612.823 312 |
| philosophy | 128.3 |
| Memory (Computers) | 004.5 |
| engineering | 621.397 |
| Memory cards | 004.568 |
| engineering | 621.397 68 |
| Memory disorders | |
| medicine | 616.83 |
| *see also* Nervous system | |
| diseases — humans | |
| Memory management | 005.435 |
| Memphis (Extinct city) | T2—322 |
| Memphis (Tenn.) | T2—768 19 |
| Memphrémagog (Quebec) | T2—714 64 |

| | |
|---|---|
| Memphrémagog Lake | |
| (Quebec) | T2—714 64 |
| Men | 305.31 |
| | T1—081 1 |
| art representation | 704.942 3 |
| arts | 700.452 11 |
| | T3C—352 11 |
| biography | 920.71 |
| criminal offenders | 364.373 |
| drawing | 743.43 |
| education | 371.821 1 |
| etiquette | 395.142 |
| fine arts | 704.041 |
| grooming | 646.704 4 |
| health | 613.042 34 |
| journalism for | 070.483 46 |
| labor economics | 331.561 |
| literature | 808.803 521 1 |
| history and criticism | 809.933 521 1 |
| specific literatures | T3B—080 352 11 |
| history and | |
| criticism | T3B—093 521 1 |
| painting | 757.3 |
| physical fitness | 613.704 49 |
| psychology | 155.332 |
| recreation | 790.194 |
| indoor | 793.019 4 |
| outdoor | 796.0811 |
| religion | 200.811 |
| Christianity | 270.081 1 |
| devotional literature | 242.642 |
| guides to Christian life | 248.842 |
| guides to life | 204.408 11 |
| sex hygiene | 613.952 |
| social aspects | 305.31 |
| *see Manual at* T1—081 *and* | |
| T1—08351, T1—08352, | |
| T1—08421, T1—08422 | |
| Menabe (Kingdom) | 969.101 |
| | T2—691 |
| Menaḥot | 296.123 5 |
| Babylonian Talmud | 296.125 5 |
| Mishnah | 296.123 5 |
| Menarche | |
| human physiology | 612.662 |
| Menard County (Ill.) | T2—773 555 |
| Menard County (Tex.) | T2—764 877 |
| Mende (African people) | T5—963 48 |
| Mende-Bandi languages | 496.348 |
| | T6—963 48 |
| Mende language | 496.348 |
| | T6—963 48 |
| Mende literature | 896.348 |
| Mendelevium | 546.449 |

| | |
|---|---|
| Mendel's laws | 576.52 |
| Mendicant religious orders | 255.06 |
| church history | 271.06 |
| Mending books | 025.7 |
| Mending textiles | |
| home economics | 646.2 |
| clothes | 646.6 |
| Mendip (England) | T2—423 83 |
| Mendip Hills (England) | T2—423 83 |
| Mendocino County (Calif.) | T2—794 15 |
| Mendoza (Argentina : Province) | T2—826 4 |
| Mendrisio (Switzerland : Distretto) | T2—494 786 |
| Menelik II, Negus of Ethiopia | |
| Ethiopian history | 963.043 |
| Menger, Carl | |
| economic school | 330.157 |
| Mengistu Haile-Mariam | |
| Ethiopian history | 963.071 |
| Menhadens | 597.45 |
| fishing | 639.274 5 |
| Meniere's disease | |
| medicine | 617.882 |
| *see also* Ear diseases — humans | |
| Menifee County (Ky.) | T2—769 583 |
| Menindee Lake (N.S.W.) | T2—944 9 |
| Meningeal diseases | |
| medicine | 616.82 |
| *see also* Nervous system diseases — humans | |
| Meninges | 573.862 5 |
| human anatomy | 611.81 |
| human histology | 612.820 45 |
| human physiology | 612.82 |
| medicine | 616.82 |
| *see also* Nervous system | |
| Meningitis | |
| medicine | 616.82 |
| *see also* Nervous system diseases — humans | |
| Meningoencephalitis | |
| medicine | 616.832 |
| *see also* Nervous system diseases — humans | |
| Menispermaceae | 583.34 |
| Mennonite Church | 289.7 |
| church government | 262.097 |
| parishes | 254.097 |
| church law | 262.989 7 |
| doctrines | 230.97 |
| catechisms and creeds | 238.97 |
| general councils | 262.597 |
| Mennonite Church (continued) | |
| guides to Christian life | 248.489 7 |
| missions | 266.97 |
| moral theology | 241.049 7 |
| public worship | 264.097 |
| religious associations | 267.189 7 |
| religious education | 268.897 |
| seminaries | 230.073 97 |
| theology | 230.97 |
| Mennonite cooking | 641.566 |
| Mennonites | |
| biography | 289.709 2 |
| Menominee County (Mich.) | T2—774 953 |
| Menominee County (Wis.) | T2—775 356 |
| Menominee Indians | T5—973 13 |
| Menomini Indians | T5—973 13 |
| Menomini language | 497.313 |
| | T6—973 13 |
| Menopause | |
| disorders | |
| gynecology | 618.175 |
| *see also* Female genital diseases — humans | |
| human physiology | 612.665 |
| Menorca (Spain) | T2—467 52 |
| Menorrhagia | |
| gynecology | 618.172 |
| *see also* Female genital diseases — humans | |
| Men's clothing | 391.1 |
| commercial technology | 687.081 1 |
| customs | 391.1 |
| home economics | 646.32 |
| home sewing | 646.402 |
| *see also* Clothing | |
| Men's liberation movement | 305.32 |
| Men's prisons | 365.44 |
| *see also* Penal institutions | |
| Men's voices | 782.8 |
| choral and mixed voices | 782.8 |
| single voices | 783.8 |
| Menstruation | |
| human physiology | 612.662 |
| Menstruation disturbances | |
| gynecology | 618.172 |
| Mensuration | 530.8 |
| | T1—028 7 |
| forestry | 634.928 5 |
| geometry | 516.15 |
| Mental arithmetic | 513.9 |
| Mental disorders | 362.2 |
| geriatrics | 618.976 89 |
| nursing | 616.890 231 |
| pediatrics | 618.928 9 |

Mental disorders (continued)
  pregnancy complications
    obstetrics                  618.368
    psychiatry                 616.89
  puerperal diseases
    medicine                  618.76
  social welfare            362.2
    *see also* Mental health
      services
  therapy                  616.891
  *see also* Mental illness
Mental disorders diagnosed in
  childhood
  pediatrics             618.928 588
Mental healing (Psychic healing)
  medicine                615.852 8
Mental health
  social welfare           362.2
Mental health facilities      362.21
  architecture           725.52
  *see also* Mental health services
Mental health insurance     368.382 5
Mental health law         344.044
Mental health personnel     616.890 092
  law                   344.044
  role and function      616.890 23
Mental health services      362.2
  employee programs
    personnel management   658.382
      public administration   352.67
  law                   344.044
  pastoral theology       206.1
    Christianity           259.42
  prisoner services       365.667 2
  public administration     353.64
  social theology         201.762 2
    Christianity          261.832 2
  students               371.713
  *see also* Health services
Mental illness             362.2
  arts            T3C—356 1
  Christian religious guidance   248.862
  folklore              398.276 1
    history and criticism     398.356 1
  geriatrics            618.976 89
  influence on crime      364.24
  literature           808.803 561
    history and criticism     809.933 561
    specific literatures   T3B—080 356 1
    history and
      criticism      T3B—093 561
  nursing             616.890 231
  pastoral theology       206.1
    Christianity          259.42

Mental illness (continued)
  pediatrics            618.928 9
  pregnancy complications
    obstetrics            618.368
    psychiatry           616.89
  puerperal diseases
    medicine            618.76
  social theology        201.762 2
    Christianity          261.832 2
  social welfare          362.2
    *see also* Mental health
      services
  therapy              616.891
Mental retardation        362.3
  arts            T3C—356 1
  geriatrics           618.976 858 8
  literature          808.803 561
    history and criticism   809.933 561
    specific literatures   T3B—080 356 1
    history and
      criticism      T3B—093 561
  medicine           616.858 8
  nursing           616.858 802 31
  pediatrics          618.928 588
  social welfare       362.3
    public administration   353.65
Mental tests            153.93
Mentally disabled children   305.908 408 3
                  T1—087 4
  education           371.92
  home care          649.152 8
Mentally disabled people    305.908 4
                  T1—087 4
  civil and human rights   323.3
  education           371.92
    law                344.079 12
  institutional buildings
    architecture         725.53
  legal status          346.013 8
    constitutional law    342.087
    private law         346.013 8
  social group         305.908 4
  social welfare        362.3
Mentally ill people        305.908 4
                  T1—087 4
  civil and human rights   323.3
  criminal offenders     364.38
    correctional institutions  365.46
    *see also* Penal institutions
  education           371.94
    law                344.079 14
  guides to Christian life   248.862
  Holocaust, 1933–1945    940.531 808 74

Mentally ill people (continued)
  legal status      346.013 8
    private law      346.013 8
  social group      305.908 4
  social welfare      362.2
    law      344.044
  *see also* Mental health
    services
  *see Manual at* 362.1–.4 vs. 610
Mentoring
  education      371.102
  personnel management      658.312 4
Menu cookbooks      642
Menuridae      598.822
Menus      642
Menzies, Robert, Sir
  Australian history      994.05
    1939–1941      994.042
    1949–1966      994.05
Mephitinae      599.768
Meprobamate
  pharmacokinetics      615.788 2
Merbein (Vic.)      T2—945 9
Mercantile credit      332.742
  marketing management      658.882
Mercantilism (Economic school)      330.151 3
Mercantour National Park
  (France)      T2—449 4
Mercator projection      526.82
Merced County (Calif.)      T2—794 58
Mercedarians      255.45
  church history      271.45
Mercenary troops      355.354
  American Revolution      973.342
Mercer County (Ill.)      T2—773 395
Mercer County (Ky.)      T2—769 485
Mercer County (Mo.)      T2—778 213
Mercer County (N.D.)      T2—784 83
Mercer County (N.J.)      T2—749 65
Mercer County (Ohio)      T2—771 415
Mercer County (Pa.)      T2—748 95
Mercer County (W. Va.)      T2—754 74
Mercerizing textiles      677.028 25
Merchandisers      381.092
Merchandising      381
  management      658.8
Merchant marine      387.5
  *see also* Ocean transportation
Merchant mariners      387.509 2
  technologists      623.880 92
Merchant ships      387.2
  design      623.812
  engineering      623.82

Merchant ships (continued)
  freight services      387.544
  power-driven      387.24
    design      623.812 4
    engineering      623.824
    transportation services      387.24
  transportation services      387.2
  wind-driven      387.224
    design      623.812 24
    engineering      623.822 4
    handling      623.882 24
    transportation services      387.224
  *see also* Ships
Merchants      381.092
Mercia supremacy      942.015 7
Mercuries (Plants)      583.69
Mercury (Element)      669.71
  chemical engineering      661.066 3
  chemistry      546.663
  economic geology      553.454
  human toxicology      615.925 663
  metallurgy      669.71
  mining      622.345 4
  organic chemistry      547.056 63
    applied      661.895
  physical metallurgy      669.967 1
  toxicology      571.954 663
  *see also* Chemicals; Metals
Mercury (Planet)      523.41
     T2—992 1
  astrology      133.533
  unmanned flights to      629.435 41
Mercury fulminate      662.27
Mercury project      629.454
Mercury-vapor lighting      621.327 4
Mergansers      598.415
Merge sort (Computer science)      005.741
Mergers      338.83
  accounting      657.96
  banks      332.16
  economics      338.83
  law      346.066 26
  management      658.162
Merging data      005.741
Mergini      598.415
Mérida (Spain)      T2—462 7
Mérida (Venezuela : State)      T2—871 3
Meridian (Miss.)      T2—762 677
Meridional instruments      522.2
Merina (Kingdom)      969.101
     T2—691
Merino sheep      636.36
Meristem      575.48
Merit (Christian doctrine)      234

| | |
|---|---|
| Merit awards | |
| personnel management | 658.322 5 |
| Merit pay | 331.216 4 |
| labor economics | 331.216 4 |
| personnel management | 658.322 5 |
| Merit system (Civil service) | 352.63 |
| Meriwether County (Ga.) | T2—758 455 |
| Merkaz (Israel : District) | T2—569 47 |
| Merkcl, Angela | |
| German history | 943.088 3 |
| Merlucciid hakes | 597.632 |
| Merlucciidae | 597.632 |
| Mermaids | 398.21 |
| *see also* Legendary beings | |
| Mermen | 398.21 |
| *see also* Legendary beings | |
| Meromorphic functions | 515.982 |
| Meropidae | 598.78 |
| Merostomata | 595.49 |
| Merovingian dynasty | 944.013 |
| French history | 944.013 |
| German history | 943.013 |
| Merreden (W.A.) | T2—941 2 |
| Merrick County (Neb.) | T2—782 423 |
| Merrimac, Battle of Monitor and, 1862 | 973.752 |
| Merrimack County (N.H.) | T2—742 72 |
| Merrimack River (N.H. and Mass.) | T2—742 72 |
| Merritt (B.C.) | T2—711 72 |
| Mersey, River (England) | T2—427 5 |
| Merseyside (England) | T2—427 5 |
| Mersin İli (Turkey) | T2—564 6 |
| ancient | T2—393 5 |
| Merthyr Tydfil (Wales : County Borough) | T2—429 75 |
| Merton (London, England) | T2—421 93 |
| Mesa County (Colo.) | T2—788 17 |
| Mesa Verde National Park (Colo.) | T2—788 27 |
| Mesabi Range (Minn.) | T2—776 77 |
| Mescal | 641.25 |
| commercial processing | 663.5 |
| Mescalero-Chiricahua Apache language | 497.256 |
| | T6—972 56 |
| Mescalero Indians | T5—972 56 |
| Mescaline abuse | 362.294 |
| medicine | 616.863 4 |
| personal health | 613.83 |
| social welfare | 362.294 |
| *see also* Substance abuse | |
| Mesencephalon | |
| human anatomy | 611.81 |
| human physiology | 612.826 4 |
| medicine | 616.8 |
| Mesentery | |
| human anatomy | 611.38 |
| human physiology | 612.33 |
| medicine | 616.38 |
| surgery | 617.558 |
| Mesilinka River (B.C.) | T2—711 87 |
| Mesmerism | 154.7 |
| Meso-American native languages | 497 |
| | T6—97 |
| Meso-American native literatures | 897 |
| Meso-American native peoples | T5—970 72 |
| Mesocricetus | 599.356 |
| Mesogastropoda | 594.32 |
| Mesolithic Age | 930.13 |
| Mesons | 539.721 62 |
| Mesopotamia | 956.7 |
| | T2—567 |
| ancient | 935 |
| | T2—35 |
| Mesopotamian architecture | 722.51 |
| Mesopotamian sculpture | 732.5 |
| Mesosauria | 567.937 |
| Mesosphere | 551.514 |
| Mesozoic era | 551.76 |
| geology | 551.76 |
| paleontology | 560.176 |
| Mesquakie language | 497.314 |
| | T6—973 14 |
| Mesquite | 583.748 |
| Mess services (Armed forces) | 355.341 |
| Message passing | 005.71 |
| Messana (Italy) | T2—378 111 |
| Messapian language | 491.993 |
| | T6—919 93 |
| Messenger services | |
| internal office communication | 651.79 |
| office services | 651.374 3 |
| Messēnia (Greece) | T2—495 22 |
| ancient | T2—389 |
| Messiahs | |
| Christianity | 232.1 |
| Judaism | 296.336 |
| role and function | 206.1 |
| Messianic Judaism | 289.9 |
| Messianic prophecies | |
| Christianity | 232.12 |
| Judaism | 296.336 |
| Messianism | 202.3 |
| Judaism | 296.336 |

| | | | |
|---|---|---|---|
| Messina (Italy) | T2—458 111 | Metalinguistics | 410.1 |
| ancient | T2—378 111 | | T4—01 |
| Messina (Italy : Province) | T2—458 11 | Metallic compounds | 546.3 |
| ancient | T2—378 11 | chemical engineering | 661.03 |
| Messina (South Africa : | | Metallic fillings | |
| District) | T2—682 57 | dentistry | 617.675 |
| Messina, Strait of (Italy) | 551.461 386 | Metallic glass | 669.94 |
| | T2—163 86 | Metallic inlays | |
| Meta (Colombia) | T2—861 94 | dentistry | 617.675 |
| Metabolic diseases | 571.944 | Metallic salt processes | |
| humans | 362.196 39 | photography | 772 |
| incidence | 614.593 9 | Metallic soaps | 668.125 |
| medicine | 616.39 | Metallic solids | 530.413 |
| social services | 362.196 39 | Metallic wood-boring beetles | 595.763 |
| *see also* Digestive system | | Metallizing | 671.734 |
| diseases — humans | | Metallography | 669.95 |
| Metabolism | 572.4 | Metallurgical furnaces | 669.8 |
| animals | 572.41 | Metallurgists | 669.092 |
| bone diseases | | Metallurgy | 669 |
| medicine | 616.716 | equipment manufacturing | |
| *see also* Musculoskeletal | | technology | 681.766 9 |
| diseases — humans | | Metals | 669 |
| human physiology | 612.39 | applied nutrition | 613.285 1 |
| inborn errors | | architectural construction | 721.044 7 |
| medicine | 616.390 42 | architectural decoration | 729.6 |
| medicine | 616.39 | biochemistry | 572.51 |
| pharmacokinetics | 615.739 | humans | 612.015 24 |
| plants | 572.42 | building construction | 693.7 |
| *see also* Digestive system | | building materials | 691.8 |
| Metacarpals | | chemistry | 546.3 |
| human anatomy | 611.717 | decorative arts | 739 |
| Metadata | | dowsing | 133.323 3 |
| information science | 025.3 | economic geology | 553.4 |
| format | 025.316 | foundation materials | 624.153 6 |
| Metaethics | 170.42 | handicrafts | 745.56 |
| Metagenesis | 571.884 | human toxicology | 615.925 3 |
| Metal engraving | 765 | materials science | 620.16 |
| Metal forming | 671.3 | metabolism | 572.514 |
| Metal furniture | 645.4 | human physiology | 612.392 4 |
| manufacturing technology | 684.105 | metallography | 669.95 |
| *see also* Furniture | | military resources | 355.242 |
| Metal intaglio engraving | 765 | mineralogy | 549.23 |
| Metal manufacturing equipment | | mining | 622.34 |
| manufacturing technology | 681.767 1 | organic chemistry | 547.05 |
| Metal-oxide-semiconductor | | aliphatic | 547.45 |
| memory | 004.53 | applied | 661.895 |
| engineering | 621.397 32 | prospecting | 622.184 |
| Metal products | 671.8 | sculpture material | 731.2 |
| Metal relief engraving | 761.8 | ship design | 623.818 2 |
| Metal spraying | 671.734 | shipbuilding | 623.820 7 |
| Metal-work | 671 | structural engineering | 624.182 |
| *see also* Metalworking | | textiles | 677.53 |
| Metalanguage | 410.1 | *see also* Textiles | |
| | T4—01 | | |

Metals (continued)
  toxicology — 571.954 3
  *see also* Chemicals
Metalworkers — 669.092
  metallurgy — 669.092
  metalworking — 671.092
Metalworking — 671
  home workshops — 684.09
  production economics — 338.476 71
  ship hulls — 623.843
  technology — 671
Metamathematics — 510.1
Metamorphic rocks — 552.4
Metamorphosis (Biology) — 571.876
Metaphor — 808.032
  literature — 808.801 5
    history and criticism — 809.915
Metaphysics — 110
Metaponto (Italy) — T2—457 72
  ancient — T2—377 73
Metatarsals
  human anatomy — 611.718
Metatheria — 599.2
  paleozoology — 569.2
Metcalfe, Charles Theophilus
  Metcalfe, Baron
  Indian history — 954.031 4
Metcalfe County (Ky.) — T2—769 693
Metchosin (B.C.) — T2—711 28
Meteor showers — 523.53
Meteorite craters — 551.397
Meteorites — 523.51
  mineralogy — 549.112
  petrology — 549.112
Meteoroids — 523.51
  — T2—993
  effect on space flight — 629.416
Meteorologists — 551.509 2
Meteorology — 551.5
  — T1—015 515
  aeronautics — 629.132 4
  agriculture — 630.251 5
  law — 344.095 5
  *see Manual at* 551.5 vs. 551.6
Meteors — 523.51
Meter (Music) — 781.226
Meter (Prosody) — 808.1
Methamphetamine abuse — 362.299 5
Methane
  biogas technology — 665.776
Methane producing bacteria — 579.321
Methanogenic bacteria — 579.321

Methodist Church — 287
  church government — 262.07
    parishes — 254.07
  church law — 262.987
  doctrines — 230.7
    catechisms and creeds — 238.7
  guides to Christian life — 248.487
  missions — 266.7
  moral theology — 241.047
  public worship — 264.07
  religious associations — 267.187
  religious education — 268.87
  seminaries — 230.073 7
  theology — 230.7
Methodist Church (U.S.) — 287.631
  *see also* Methodist Church
Methodist Church of Great
  Britain — 287.536
Methodist Episcopal Church — 287.632
  *see also* Methodist Church
Methodist Episcopal Church,
  South — 287.633
  *see also* Methodist Church
Methodist New Connexion — 287.53
  *see also* Methodist Church
Methodist Protestant Church — 287.7
  *see also* Methodist Church
Methodist sacred music — 781.717
  public worship — 782.322 7
    music — 782.322 7
    religion — 264.070 2
Methodists
  biography — 287.092
Methodology (Principles) — T1—01
Metric differential geometries — 516.37
Metric geometry — 516.1
  Euclidean — 516.2
Metric spaces — 514.325
Metric system — 530.812
  law — 343.075
  social aspects — 389.15
Metric topology — 514.3
Metrical romances — 808.813 3
  history and criticism — 809.133
  specific literatures — T3B—103 3
    individual authors — T3A—1
Metrication — 389.16
Metro Vancouver (B.C.) — T2—711 33
Metrology
  commerce — 389.1
Metronomes
  technology — 681.118
Metropolitan-area networks — 004.67

Metropolitan areas    307.764
   area planning    711.43
   government    320.85
   public administration    352.167
Metropolitana (Chile)    T2—833 1
Metz (France)    T2—443 853
Meurthe-et-Moselle
   (France)    T2—443 82
Meuse (France)    T2—443 81
Meuse River    T2—492 4
   Belgium    T2—493 46
   Netherlands    T2—492 4
Mevleviyeh    297.482
Mexican-American Border
   Region    T2—721
Mexican Americans    T5—687 207 3
Mexican Hairless    636.76
Mexican literature    860
Mexican Revolution, 1910–1917    972.081 6
Mexican War, 1845–1848    973.62
Mexicans    T5—687 2
Mexico    972
   T2—72
Mexico (Mexico)    T2—725 2
Mexico, Gulf of    551.461 364
   T2—163 64
Mexico, Valley of (Mexico)    T2—725
Mexico City (Mexico)    T2—725 3
Mezereum    583.67
Mezuzot    296.461
Mezzo-soprano voices    782.67
   children's    782.77
     choral and mixed voices    782.77
     single voices    783.77
   general works    782.67
     choral and mixed voices    782.67
     single voices    783.67
   women's    782.67
     choral and mixed voices    782.67
     single voices    783.67
Mezzotinting    766.2
Mfecane    968.041
Mgeni River (South Africa)    T2—684 7
Mhala (South Africa :
   District)    T2—682 59
Mhlabatini (South Africa :
   District)    T2—684 3
Miami (Fla.)    T2—759 381
Miami Beach (Fla.)    T2—759 381
Miami County (Ind.)    T2—772 84
Miami County (Kan.)    T2—781 68
Miami County (Ohio)    T2—771 48
Miami Indians    T5—973 15

Miami language (Algic)    497.315
   T6—973 15
Miami River (Ohio)    T2—771 7
Miao    T5—959 72
Miao language    495.972
   T6—959 72
Miao literature    895.972
Miao-Yao languages    495.97
   T6—959 7
MIAs    355.113
   *see also* Missing in action
Mica    553.674
   economic geology    553.674
   mineralogy    549.67
   mining    622.367 4
   synthetic    666.86
   technology    666.72
Micah (Biblical book)    224.93
Mice (Computers)    004.76
   engineering    621.398 6
Mice (Muridae)    599.35
   *see also* Rodents
Mice (Mus)    599.353
   agricultural pests    632.693 53
   animal husbandry    636.935 3
   experimental animals
     medicine    616.027 333
   household sanitation    648.7
Michael, Czar of Russia
   Russian history    947.047
Michael the Brave (Wallachia)
   Romanian history    949.801 5
Michelias    635.977 322
   botany    583.22
   ornamental arboriculture    635.977 322
Michif language    497.323
   T6—973 23
Michigan    977.4
   T2—774
Michigan, Lake    T2—774
Michoacán (Mexico : State)    T2—723 7
Michoacán de Ocampo
   (Mexico)    T2—723 7
Micmac Indians    T5—973 43
Micmac language    497.343
   T6—973 43
MICR (Computer science)    006.4
   engineering    621.399 4
Microanalysis (Chemistry)    543.22
Microascales    579.565
Microassembly languages    005.18
Microbes    579
   *see also* Microorganisms

Microbial diseases 571.98
  *see also* Communicable
    diseases
Microbiologists 579.092
Microbiology 579
  applied 660.62
  medicine 616.904 1
  *see Manual at* 579.165
    vs. 616.9041; *also at*
    616.1–.9
Microbiotheriidae 599.27
Microcephaly
  medicine 616.858 844
Microchemical analysis 543.22
Microchemistry 543.22
Microchiroptera 599.4
  paleozoology 569.4
Microcircuits 621.381 5
Microclimatology 551.66
  ecology 577.22
Microcode 005.18
Microcomputer workstations 004.16
  *see also* Personal computers
Microcomputers 004.16
  *see also* Personal computers
  *see Manual at* 004.11–.16
Microcoryphia 595.723
Microeconomics 338.5
Microelectronic circuits 621.381 5
Microelectronics 621.381
  social effects 303.483 4
Microfiche 302.23
  *see also* Microforms
Microfilaments 571.654
Microfilms 302.23
  bibliographies 011.36
  *see also* Microforms
Microform catalogs 025.313
Microforms 302.23
  bibliographies 011.36
  cataloging 025.349 4
  library treatment 025.179 4
  production
    office records 651.58
    technology 686.43
  publishing 070.579 5
Microfossils 560.47
Microhylidae 597.89
Microlithography
  electronics 621.381 531
Micrometeorology 551.66
  ecology 577.22
Micronesia T2—965

Micronesia (Federated
    States) T2—966
Micronesian languages 499.52
  T6—995 2
Micronesians T5—995 2
Micronutrients 572.515
  *see also* Trace elements
Microorganisms 579
  air pollution control 628.536
  cell biology 571.629
  *see Manual at* 571.629 vs.
    571.29
  cell culture 571.638 29
  food technology 664.024
  medical microbiology 616.904 1
  paleontology 561.9
  physiology 571.29
  *see Manual at* 571.629 vs.
    571.29
  resource economics 333.953
Micropaleontology 560.47
Micropedology 631.433
Microphones 621.382 84
  radio engineering 621.384 133
Microphotography
  technology 686.43
Microprocessors 004.16
  *see also* Personal computers
Microprogramming 005.18
  T1—028 551 8
Microprograms 005.18
  T1—028 551 8
Micropterus 597.738 8
Microreproductions 302.23
  bibliographies 011.36
  *see also* Microforms
Microscopes 502.82
  biology 570.282
  manufacturing technology 681.413
Microscopic analysis
  chemistry 543.22
Microscopic metallography 669.950 282
Microscopic objects
  photography 778.31
Microscopic petrology 552.8
Microscopy 502.82
  biology 570.282
  medical diagnosis 616.075 8
  natural sciences 502.82
Microsporangia 575.65
Microsporida 579.48
Microstructure
  materials science 620.112 99
Microsurgery 617.05

Microtechnique 502.82
  biology 570.282 7
Microtomy 502.82
  biology 570.282 7
Microtonality 781.269
Microtubules 571.654
Microtus 599.354
Microwave aids
  marine navigation 623.893 3
Microwave cooking 641.588 2
Microwave dinners
  home serving 642.1
Microwave electronics
  engineering 621.381 3
  physics 537.534 4
Microwave spectroscopes
  manufacturing technology 681.414 8
Microwave spectroscopy 543.6
  analytical chemistry 543.6
  engineering 621.361
  physics 537.534 4
Microwaves 537.534 4
  biophysics 571.453
    humans 612.014 481
Micrurus 597.964 4
Mid Bedfordshire (England) T2—425 63
Mid Devon (England) T2—423 54
Mid Glamorgan (Wales) T2—429 7
Mid Suffolk (England) T2—426 45
Mid Sussex (England) T2—422 65
Mid Wales T2—429 5
Mid-Western State (Nigeria) T2—669 3
Midair collisions 363.124 92
  *see also* Air safety
Midbrain
  human anatomy 611.81
  human physiology 612.826 4
  medicine 616.8
Middelburg (Eastern Cape,
  South Africa : District) T2 —687 54
Middelburg (Mpumalanga,
  South Africa : District) T2—682 76
Middle age 305.244
Middle-aged men 305.244 1
Middle-aged people 305.244
  T1—084 4
  civil rights 323.353
  guides to Christian life 248.84
  guides to religious life
    Judaism 296.708 44
  health 613.043 4
  labor economics 331.394
  psychology 155.66
  relations with government 323.353

Middle-aged people (continued)
  religion 200.844
    Christianity 270.084 4
  social aspects 305.244
Middle-aged women 305.244 2
Middle-aged workers 331.394
Middle Ages 909.07
  T1—090 2
  *see also* Medieval period
Middle America 972
  T2—72
Middle American native 497
  languages T6—97
Middle American native
  literatures 897
Middle American native
  peoples T5—970 72
Middle Atlantic States 974
  T2—74
Middle class 305.55
  T1—086 22
  customs 390.1
  dress 391.01
  social welfare 362.892
Middle Congo 967.240 3
  T2—672 4
Middle-distance races 796.423
Middle ear diseases
  medicine 617.84
  *see also* Ear diseases —
    humans
Middle ears
  human anatomy 611.85
  human physiology 612.854
  medicine 617.84
Middle East 956
  T2—56
  ancient 939.4
  T2—394
Middle East theater (World War
  II) 940.542 4
Middle Eastern people T5—94
Middle Egypt T2—622
Middle English language 427.02
  T6—219
Middle Franconia
  (Germany) T2—433 2
Middle French language 447.02
  T6—41
Middle games (Chess) 794.123
Middle High German language 437.02
  T6—31
Middle-income classes 305.55
  T1—086 22

| | |
|---|---|
| Middle Indic languages | 491.3 |
| | T6—913 |
| Middle Indic literatures | 891.3 |
| Middle Indo-Aryan languages | 491.3 |
| | T6—913 |
| Middle Iranian languages | 491.53 |
| | T6—915 3 |
| Middle Iranian literatures | 891.53 |
| Middle Italian language | 457.02 |
| | T6—51 |
| Middle kingdom (Egypt) | 932.013 |
| Middle latitude zones | T2—12 |
| Middle management | 658.43 |
| public administration | 352.284 |
| Middle Norwegian language | 439.827 02 |
| Middle Paleolithic Age | 930.126 |
| Middle Persian language | 491.53 |
| | T6—915 3 |
| Middle Persian literature | 891.53 |
| Middle Portuguese language | 469.702 |
| | T6—69 |
| Middle Russian language | 491.770 2 |
| | T6—917 1 |
| Middle schools | 373.236 |
| *see also* Secondary education | |
| Middle Spanish language | 467.02 |
| | T6—61 |
| Middle Stone Age | 930.13 |
| Middle voice | 783.4 |
| Middle Volga languages | 494.56 |
| | T6—945 6 |
| Middle Volga literatures | 894.56 |
| Middle West | T2—77 |
| Middledrift (South Africa : District) | T2—687 55 |
| Middlesbrough (England) | T2—428 53 |
| Middlesex (England) | T2—421 8 |
| Middlesex (Ont.) | T2—713 25 |
| Middlesex County (Conn.) | T2—746 6 |
| Middlesex County (Mass.) | T2—744 4 |
| Middlesex County (N.J.) | T2—749 41 |
| Middlesex County (Va.) | T2—755 33 |
| Middleware | 005.3 |
| distributed systems | 005.376 |
| Middot | 296.123 5 |
| Midges | 595.772 |
| agricultural pests | 632.772 |
| Midget car racing | 796.76 |
| MIDI (Musical instrument digital interface) | 784.190 285 46 |
| Midi-Pyrénées (France) | T2—447 3 |
| Midland County (Mich.) | T2—774 48 |
| Midland County (Tex.) | T2—764 861 |
| Midlands (England) | T2—424 |

| | |
|---|---|
| Midlands Avon River (England) | T2—424 4 |
| Midlands Province (Zimbabwe) | T2—689 1 |
| Midlothian (Scotland) | T2—413 5 |
| Midrange computers | 004.14 |
| architecture | 004.254 |
| communications | 004.614 |
| programming | 005.712 4 |
| programs | 005.713 4 |
| engineering | 621.391 4 |
| graphics programming | 006.674 |
| graphics programs | 006.684 |
| interfacing | 004.614 |
| programming | 005.712 4 |
| programs | 005.713 4 |
| multimedia-systems programming | 006.774 |
| multimedia-systems programs | 006.784 |
| operating systems | 005.444 |
| performance evaluation | 004.140 29 |
| for design and improvement | 004.254 |
| programming | 005.24 |
| specific computers | 005.245 |
| programs | 005.34 |
| systems analysis | 004.254 |
| systems design | 004.254 |
| *see Manual at* 004.11–.16 | |
| Midrash | 296.14 |
| Midway, Battle of, 1942 | 940.542 669 9 |
| Midway Islands | T2—969 9 |
| Midwest | T2—77 |
| Midwife toads | 597.86 |
| Midwifery | |
| law | 344.041 5 |
| medicine | 618.2 |
| Midwives | |
| law | 344.041 5 |
| role and function | 618.202 33 |
| Mie-ken (Japan) | T2—521 81 |
| Mifepristone | |
| medicine | 618.29 |
| pharmacokinetics | 615.766 |
| Mifflin County (Pa.) | T2—748 46 |
| Mignonettes | 635.933 64 |
| botany | 583.64 |
| floriculture | 635.933 64 |
| Migraine | |
| medicine | 616.849 12 |
| *see also* Nervous system diseases — humans | |
| Migrant agricultural workers | |
| economics | 331.544 |
| social class | 305.563 |

Migrant workers | 331.544
  | T1—086 24
  economics | 331.544
  social class | 305.562
  social welfare | 362.85
Migration | 304.8
  political science | 325
Migration (Animals) | 591.568
Migratory animals | 591.568
Migratory birds | 598.156 8
Mihai II, Viteazul, Voivode of
  Wallachia
  Romanian history | 949.801 5
Mikasuki Indians | T5—973 8
Mikasuki language | 497.38
  | T6—973 8
Mikkeli (Finland) | T2—489 75
Mikkelin lääni (Finland) | T2—489 75
Mikva'ot (Tractate) | 296.123 6
Mikveh | 296.75
Mila (Algeria : Province) | T2—655
Milam County (Tex.) | T2—764 288
Milan (Italy) | T2—452 11
  ancient | T2—372 271
Milan (Italy : Province) | T2—452 1
  ancient | T2—372 27
Milano (Italy) | T2—452 11
  ancient | T2—372 271
Milano (Italy : Province) | T2—452 1
  ancient | T2—372 27
Mildew | 579.53
  agricultural disease | 632.43
  materials science | 620.112 23
Mildura (Vic.) | T2—945 9
Miletus | T2—392 3
Milieu therapy
  psychiatry | 616.891 44
Militarism | 355.021 3
  ethics | 172.42
    *see also* War — ethics
  social theology | 201.727 3
    *see also* War — social
    theology
  sociology | 303.66
Military accounting | 657.835
Military administration | 355.6
Military air transportation service | 358.44
Military aircraft | 358.418 3
  armed forces equipment | 358.418 3
  engineering | 623.746
Military alliances | 355.031
  armed forces | 355.356
Military arts | 355

Military assistance | 355.032
  law | 342.041 2
Military attachés | 355.032
Military bands | 784.84
Military bases | 355.7
  law | 343.015 7
Military buildings
  architecture | 725.18
Military camps | 355.7
Military capability | 355.033 2
Military commemorations | 355.16
  Algerian Revolution | 965.046 6
  American Revolution | 973.36
  Chaco War | 989.207 166
  Civil War (England) | 942.062 6
  Civil War (Spain) | 946.081 6
  Civil War (United States) | 973.76
  Crimean War | 947.073 86
  Falkland Islands War | 997.110 246
  Franco-German War | 943.082 6
  Hundred Years' War | 944.025 6
  Indo-Pakistan War, 1971 | 954.920 516
  Indochinese War | 959.704 16
  Iraq War, 2003– | 956.704 436
  Iraqi-Iranian Conflict | 955.054 26
  Korean War | 951.904 26
  Mexican War | 973.626
  Napoleonic Wars | 940.276
  Persian Gulf War, 1991 | 956.704 426
  South African War | 968.048 6
  Spanish-American War | 973.896
  Thirty Years' War | 940.246
  Vietnamese War | 959.704 36
  War of 1812 | 973.526
  War of the Pacific | 983.061 66
  World War I | 940.46
  World War II | 940.546
Military consultants | 355.687 3
Military contracts | 355.621 2
Military cooking | 641.57
Military courts | 343.014 3
Military customs | 355.1
Military dependents
  living conditions | 355.12
  social services | 355.34
Military deserters | 355.133 4
  *see also* Deserters
Military discipline | 355.13
  law | 343.014
Military districts | 355.31
Military engineering | 623
  arts | T3C—356
Military engineers | 623.092
Military equipment | 355.8

| | |
|---|---|
| Military geography | 355.47 |
| Military government | 355.49 |
| Military history | 355.009 |
|   Algerian Revolution | 965.046 4 |
|   American Revolution | 973.33 |
|   Chaco War | 989.207 164 |
|   Civil War (England) | 942.062 4 |
|   Civil War (Spain) | 946.081 4 |
|   Civil War (United States) | 973.73 |
|   Crimean War | 947.073 84 |
|   Falkland Islands War | 997.110 244 |
|   Franco-German War | 943.082 4 |
|   Hundred Years' War | 944.025 4 |
|   Indo-Pakistan War, 1971 | 954.920 514 |
|   Indochinese War | 959.704 14 |
|   Iraqi-Iranian Conflict | 955.054 24 |
|   Korean War | 951.904 24 |
|   Napoleonic Wars | 940.274 |
|   Persian Gulf War, 1991 | 956.704 424 |
|   South African War | 968.048 4 |
|   Spanish-American War | 973.893 |
|   Thirty Years' War | 940.244 |
|   Vietnamese War | 959.704 34 |
|   War of 1812 | 973.523 |
|   War of the Pacific | 983.061 64 |
|   World War I | 940.4 |
|   World War II | 940.54 |
|   *see Manual at* 930–990 vs. 355.009, 355–359 | |
| Military housing | 355.12 |
|   American Revolution | 973.311 3 |
| Military hygiene | 355.345 |
|   engineering | 623.75 |
| Military-industrial complex | 355.021 3 |
|   economics | 338.473 55 |
|   military science | 355.021 3 |
|   sociology | 306.27 |
| Military intelligence | 355.343 2 |
|   technology | 623.71 |
|   *see also* Unconventional warfare | |
| Military law | 343.01 |
| Military life | 355.1 |
|   Algerian Revolution | 965.046 8 |
|   American Revolution | 973.38 |
|   Chaco War | 989.207 168 |
|   Civil War (England) | 942.062 8 |
|   Civil War (Spain) | 946.081 8 |
|   Civil War (United States) | 973.783 |
|     Confederate States of America | 973.784 |
|     United States | 973.783 |
|   Crimean War | 947.073 88 |
|   Falkland Islands War | 997.110 248 |

| | |
|---|---|
| Military life (continued) | |
|   Franco-German War | 943.082 8 |
|   Hundred Years' War | 944.025 8 |
|   Indo-Pakistan War, 1971 | 954.920 518 |
|   Indochinese War | 959.704 18 |
|   Iraq War, 2003– | 956.704 438 |
|   Iraqi-Iranian Conflict | 955.054 28 |
|   Korean War | 951.904 28 |
|   law | 343.013 |
|   Mexican War | 973.628 |
|   Napoleonic Wars | 940.278 |
|   Persian Gulf War, 1991 | 956.704 428 |
|   South African War | 968.048 8 |
|   Spanish-American War | 973.898 |
|   Thirty Years' War | 940.248 |
|   Vietnamese War | 959.704 38 |
|   War of the Pacific | 983.061 68 |
|   World War I | 940.483 |
|   World War II | 940.548 3 |
| Military mail | 355.693 |
| Military maneuvers | 355.4 |
|   training | 355.52 |
| Military medals | 355.134 2 |
|   numismatics | 737.223 |
| Military medicine | 616.980 23 |
| Military missions | 355.032 |
|   law | 342.041 2 |
| Military models | 355.48 |
|   handicrafts | 745.592 82 |
|   war games | 355.48 |
| Military music | 781.599 |
|   songs | 782.421 599 |
| Military occupation | 355.028 |
|   law of war | 341.66 |
|   operations | 355.49 |
| Military offenses (Law) | 343.014 3 |
| Military operations | 355.4 |
|   World War I | 940.41 |
|   World War II | 940.541 |
| Military Order of Foreign Wars of the United States | 369.11 |
| Military pacts | 355.031 |
| Military penology | 365.48 |
|   law | 343.014 6 |
| Military pensions | 331.252 913 55 |
|   law | 343.011 2 |
| Military personnel | 355.009 2 |
|   law | 343.01 |
|     civil rights | 342.085 |
|   law of war | 341.67 |
|   role and function | 355.33 |
| Military personnel missing in action | 355.113 |
|   *see also* Missing in action | |

| | | | |
|---|---|---|---|
| Military police | 355.133 23 | Military transportation | 358.25 |
| Military policy | 355.033 5 | air forces | 358.44 |
| Military prisons | 365.48 | engineering | 623.6 |
| law | 344.035 48 | land forces | 358.25 |
| penology | 365.48 | naval forces | 359.985 |
| *see also* Penal institutions | | Military transports (Ships) | 359.985 83 |
| Military procurement | 355.621 2 | *see also* Transports (Ships) | |
| Military records management | 355.688 7 | Military units | 355.31 |
| Military relations | 355.031 | American Revolution | 973.34 |
| Military religious orders | 255.791 | Civil War (United States) | 973.74 |
| church history | 271.791 | Confederate States of America | 973.742 |
| Military resources | 355.2 | France | |
| law | 343.013 | American Revolution | 973.347 |
| Military schools (Higher | | Great Britain | |
| education) | 378.4–.9 | American Revolution | 973.341 |
| *see Manual at* 378.4–.9 vs. | | War of 1812 | 973.524 1 |
| 355.00711 | | Poland | |
| Military schools (Secondary | | American Revolution | 973.346 |
| education) | 373.243 | Spain | |
| *see also* Secondary education | | American Revolution | 973.346 |
| Military schools (Service | | Spanish-American War | 973.894 |
| academies) | 355.007 11 | states of United States | |
| *see Manual at* 378.4–.9 vs. | | Civil War (United States) | 973.744–.749 |
| 355.00711 | | Sweden | |
| Military science | 355 | American Revolution | 973.346 |
| arts | 700.458 1 | United States | |
| | T3C—358 1 | American Revolution | 973.344–.345 |
| literature | 808.803 581 | Civil War (United States) | 973.741 |
| history and criticism | 809.933 581 | War of 1812 | 973.524 4–.524 7 |
| Military sealift commands | 359.985 | War of 1812 | 973.524 |
| Military service (Conditions of | | World War I | 940.412–.413 |
| work) | 355.1 | World War II | 940.541 2–.541 3 |
| Military service (Manpower | | *see Manual at* 930–990 | |
| procurement) | 355.223 | Militia | 355.37 |
| ethics | 172.42 | Milk | 641.371 |
| *see also* War — ethics | | animal husbandry | 636.088 42 |
| law | 343.012 | cow's milk | 636.214 2 |
| Military services | 355 | *see Manual at* 636.1–.8 vs. | |
| *see also* Armed services | | 636.088 | |
| Military situation | 355.03 | cooking | 641.671 |
| Military societies | 369.2 | food | 641.371 |
| biography | 369.209 2 | physiology | 573.679 |
| United States | 369.1 | processing | 637.1 |
| Military sociology | 306.27 | Milk-free diet | |
| Military songs | 782.421 599 | health | 613.26 |
| Military supplies | 355.8 | Milk River (Mont. and | |
| Military supply ships | 359.985 83 | Alta.) | T2—786 1 |
| design | 623.812 65 | Milk substitutes | |
| engineering | 623.826 5 | commercial processing | 663.64 |
| naval equipment | 359.985 83 | Milkfish | 641.392 |
| naval units | 359.985 3 | cooking | 641.692 |
| Military surgery | 617.99 | culture | 639.375 |
| Military training | 355.5 | food | 641.392 |
| | | zoology | 597.5 |

| | |
|---|---|
| Milking | 637.124 |
| Milkweeds | 583.93 |
| Milkworts | 583.82 |
| Milky Way | 523.113 |
| Mill, John Stuart | |
|   economic school | 330.153 |
| Millard County (Utah) | T2—792 45 |
| Mille Lacs County (Minn.) | T2—776 68 |
| Milled soaps | 668.124 |
| Millennium | |
|   Christianity | 236.9 |
| Milleporina | 593.55 |
| Miller County (Ark.) | T2—767 56 |
| Miller County (Ga.) | T2—758 964 |
| Miller County (Mo.) | T2—778 56 |
| Millets | 641.331 71 |
|   botany | 584.92 |
|   commercial processing | 664.72 |
|   cooking | 641.631 71 |
|   food | 641.331 71 |
|   food crop | 633.171 |
|   forage crop | 633.257 1 |
| Milliammeters | 621.374 4 |
| Milliners | 646.504 092 |
| Millinery | 646.504 |
|   commercial technology | 687.42 |
|   home construction | 646.504 |
| Milling grains | 664.72 |
| Milling metals | 671.35 |
| Milling plants | |
|   ore dressing | 622.79 |
| Milling tools | 621.91 |
| Millipedes | 595.66 |
| Millmerran (Qld.) | T2—943 3 |
| Mills | |
|   architecture | 725.4 |
|   construction | 690.54 |
| Mills County (Iowa) | T2—777 74 |
| Mills County (Tex.) | T2—764 512 |
| Milne Bay Province (Papua | |
|   New Guinea) | T2—954 1 |
| Milos | |
|   botany | 584.92 |
| Milton Keynes (England) | T2—425 91 |
| Milwaukee (Wis.) | T2—775 95 |
| Milwaukee County (Wis.) | T2—775 94 |
| Mimamsa (Philosophy) | 181.42 |
| Mime | 792.3 |
| Mimicry (Biology) | 578.47 |
|   animals | 591.473 |
|   plants | 581.47 |
| Mimidae | 598.844 |
| Mimosa | 583.748 |
| Mimosaceae | 583.748 |

| | |
|---|---|
| Mimosas | 583.748 |
|   ornamental arboriculture | 635.977 374 8 |
| Mina (African people) | T5—963 37 |
| Minangkabau | T5—992 244 |
| Minangkabau language | 499.224 4 |
| | T6—992 244 |
| Minangkabau literature | 899.224 4 |
| Minarets | 297.351 |
|   architecture | 726.2 |
| Minas Gerais (Brazil) | T2—815 1 |
| Mind | 128.2 |
|   philosophy | 128.2 |
|   psychology | 150 |
| Mind reading | 133.82 |
| Mindanao Island | |
|   (Philippines) | T2—599 7 |
| Mindoro (Philippines) | T2—599 3 |
| Mindoro Occidental | |
|   (Philippines) | T2—599 3 |
| Mindoro Oriental | |
|   (Philippines) | T2—599 3 |
| Mine clearing | 355.4 |
|   civilian operations | 363.349 88 |
|   military engineering | 623.26 |
|   operations | 355.4 |
| Mine drainage | 622.5 |
|   water pollution engineering | 628.168 32 |
| Mine health | 363.119 622 |
|   social services | 363.119 622 |
|   technology | 622.8 |
| Mine laying (Military) | 623.26 |
| Mine railroads | 622.66 |
| Mine roof control | 622.28 |
| Mine safety | 363.119 622 |
|   social services | 363.119 622 |
|   technology | 622.8 |
|   *see also* Safety | |
| Mine shafts | 622.25 |
| Mine surveys | 622.14 |
| Mine timbering | 622.28 |
| Mined lands | 333.765 |
|   economics | 333.765 |
|   reclamation technology | 631.64 |
| Minelayers | 359.836 2 |
|   design | 623.812 62 |
|   engineering | 623.826 2 |
|   naval equipment | 359.836 2 |
|   naval units | 359.326 2 |
| Miner County (S.D.) | T2—783 34 |
| Mineral commodities | 338.27 |
|   investment economics | 332.644 2 |
| Mineral County (Colo.) | T2—788 38 |
| Mineral County (Mont.) | T2—786 84 |
| Mineral County (Nev.) | T2—793 51 |

Mineral County (W. Va.)    T2—754 94
Mineral drugs
  pharmacology    615.2
Mineral fertilizers    631.8
  economic geology    553.64
  *see also* Fertilizers
Mineral industries    338.2
  enterprises    338.762 2
  law    343.077
  products    338.27
    commerce    381.42
  public administration    354.39
Mineral oils
  processing    665.4
Mineral pigments    553.662
Mineral resources
  land economics    333.85
  law    346.046 85
  military science    355.242
  public administration    354.39
Mineral rights
  law    346.043
    private ownership    346.043
    public control    346.046 85
  public revenue    336.12
  sale and rental    333.339
Mineral springs
  health resorts    613.122
  therapeutics    615.853
Mineral surveys
  prospecting    622.13
Mineral waters    553.73
  commercial processing    663.61
  economic geology    553.73
  health    613.287
  therapeutics    615.853
Mineral waxes
  processing    665.4
Mineralized beverages    641.26
  commercial processing    663.62
Mineralogists    549.092
Mineralogy    549
  *see Manual at* 549 vs. 546; *also*
    *at* 549 vs. 548
Minerals    553
  applied nutrition    613.285
    animal husbandry    636.085 27
  biochemistry    572.51
    humans    612.015 24
  economic geology    553
  economics    338.2
    resources    333.85

Minerals (continued)
  folklore    398.26
    history and criticism    398.365
      legendary    398.465
      real    398.365
  metabolism    572.514
    human physiology    612.392
  mineralogy    549
  synthetic    666.86
Miners    622.092
  labor economics    331.762 2
  public administration    354.942 2
Mines (Excavations)    622.2
  environment technology    622.4
  psychological influence    155.964
  public administration    354.39
Mines (Weapons)    355.825 115
  engineering    623.451 15
  laying and clearing    623.26
  military equipment    355.825 115
Minesweepers    359.836 2
  design    623.812 62
  engineering    623.826 2
  naval equipment    359.836 2
  naval units    359.326 2
Ming dynasty    951.026
Minganie (Quebec)    T2—714 178
Mingo County (W. Va.)    T2—754 48
Minho (Portugal)    T2—469 12
Minho (Portugal : Region)    T2—469 12
Mini-series
  television programs    791.45
    *see Manual at* 791.43 vs.
      791.45
  video recordings    791.45
    *see Manual at* 791.43 vs.
      791.45
Miniature aircraft    629.133 1
  military engineering    623.746 022 8
Miniature automobiles    629.221 2
Miniature books    099
Miniature cameras    771.32
Miniature dachshund    636.76
Miniature golf    796.352 2
Miniature paintings    751.77
Miniature pinscher    636.76
Miniature portraits
  painting    757.7
Miniature railroads    625.19
Miniature schnauzer    636.755
Miniature scores    780
  treatises    780.265
Miniature trains    625.19
Miniature trees    635.977 2

| | |
|---|---|
| Miniatures | 688.1 |
| | T1—022 8 |
| handicrafts | 745.592 8 |
| *see Manual at* 745.5928 | |
| manufacturing technology | 688.1 |
| Miniaturization | |
| electronics | 621.381 52 |
| Minibikes | 388.347 5 |
| engineering | 629.227 5 |
| *see also* Motorcycles | |
| Minicomputers | 004.14 |
| *see also* Midrange computers | |
| *see Manual at* 004.11–.16 | |
| Minidoka County (Idaho) | T2—796 33 |
| Minima | |
| combinatorics | 511.66 |
| Minimal brain dysfunction | |
| medicine | 616.858 9 |
| pediatrics | 618.928 589 |
| Minimal curves | 516.362 |
| Minimal surfaces | 516.362 |
| Minimalism (Art style) | 709.040 58 |
| Minims (Religious order) | 255.49 |
| church history | 271.49 |
| Minimum-security prisons | 365.33 |
| *see also* Penal institutions | |
| Minimum tillage | 631.581 |
| Minimum wage | 331.23 |
| Mining | 622 |
| engineering | 622 |
| enterprises | 338.762 2 |
| accounting | 657.862 |
| labor economics | 331.762 2 |
| law | 343.077 |
| production economics | 338.2 |
| public administration | 354.39 |
| Mining bureaus | 354.39 |
| Mining engineers | 622.092 |
| Mining equipment | |
| manufacturing technology | 681.76 |
| Mining law | 343.077 |
| Mining towns | 307.766 |
| Ministates | 321.06 |
| Ministerial authority | 262.8 |
| Ministers (Christian clergy) | 270.092 |
| ecclesiology | 262.14 |
| *see also* Clergy — Christian | |
| Ministers of justice | |
| advisory opinions | 348.05 |
| public administration | 353.422 93 |
| Ministers of state | 352.293 |
| Ministries of state | 351 |
| Minivans | |
| engineering | 629.222 |

| | |
|---|---|
| Minke whale | 599.524 |
| Minkowski geometry | 516.374 |
| Minks | 599.766 27 |
| animal husbandry | 636.976 627 |
| conservation technology | 639.979 766 27 |
| resource economics | 333.959 766 27 |
| trapping | 639.117 662 7 |
| zoology | 599.766 27 |
| Minna (Nigeria) | T2—669 65 |
| Minneapolis (Minn.) | T2—776 579 |
| Minneapolis Metropolitan | |
| Area (Minn.) | T2—776 579 |
| Minnedosa (Man.) | T2—712 73 |
| Minnehaha County (S.D.) | T2—783 371 |
| Minnesang (Poetry) | 808.814 |
| history and criticism | 809.14 |
| specific literatures | T3B—104 |
| individual authors | T3A—1 |
| Minnesota | 977.6 |
| | T2—776 |
| Minnesota River (S.D. and | |
| Minn.) | T2—776 3 |
| Minnows | 597.482 |
| Minoan architecture | 722.61 |
| Minoan Linear A | 492.6 |
| | T6—926 |
| *see Manual at* T6—926 | |
| Minoan Linear B | 487.1 |
| | T6—87 |
| Minoans | 939.18 |
| Minor arts | 745 |
| Minor Clerks Regular | 255.56 |
| church history | 271.56 |
| Minor Prophets (Bible) | 224.9 |
| Minor surgery | 617.024 |
| obstetrics | 618.85 |
| Minor tractates (Talmud) | 296.123 7 |
| Minorca (Spain) | T2—467 52 |
| Minorities | 305 |
| | T1—08 |
| bibliographies of works by | 011.8 |
| civil rights | 323.1 |
| education | 371.82 |
| government programs | 353.53 |
| legal status | 346.013 |
| libraries for | 027.63 |
| relations with government | 323.1 |
| social welfare | 362 |
| public administration | 353.53 |
| *see Manual at* T1—08 and | |
| 306.2–.6 | |
| Minorities (Ethnic and national) | 305.8 |
| | T1—089 |
| psychology | 155.8 |

Minorities (Ethnic and national) (continued)
  social welfare    362.84
  *see also* Ethnic groups
Minority enterprises    338.642 2
  economics    338.642 2
  financial management    658.159 208
  management    658.022 08
Minority groups (Ethnic and    305.8
  national)    T1—089
  psychology    155.8
  social welfare    362.84
Minors    305.23
  *see also* Young people
Minquiers (Channel Islands)  T2—423 48
Minsk (Belarus : Oblast)    T2—478 6
Minskaïa voblastsʹ
  (Belarus)    T2—478 6
Minstrel shows    791.12
Mint (Herb)    641.338 2
  botany    583.96
  *see also* Flavorings
Minting policies    332.46
Minto, Gilbert Elliot, Earl of
  Indian history    954.031 3
Minto, Gilbert John Murray
  Kynynmond Elliot, Earl of
  Indian history    954.035 6
Minuets    793.3
  music    784.188 35
Minūfīyah (Egypt)    T2—621
Minutes
  office records    651.77
Minyā (Egypt : Province)    T2—622
Miocene epoch    551.787
  geology    551.787
  paleontology    560.178 7
Mirabel (Quebec)    T2—714 254
Miracle plays
  literature    808.825 16
    history and criticism    809.251 6
    specific literatures    T3B—205 16
      individual authors  T3A—2
  stage presentation    792.16
Miracles    202.117
  Christianity    231.73
    of Jesus Christ    232.955
      Gospels    226.7
    of Mary    232.917
    spiritual gift    234.13
  Judaism    296.311 6
  philosophy of religion    212
Mirages    551.565
Miʿrāj    297.633

Miramichi River (N.B.)  T2—715 21
Miranda (Venezuela : State)  T2—873 5
Mirliton    783.99
Mirounga    599.794
Mirrors
  automobile    629.276
  decorative arts    748.8
  furniture    645.4
    decorative arts    749.3
    *see also* Furniture
  manufacturing technology    681.428
Misamis Occidental
  (Philippines)    T2—599 7
Misamis Oriental
  (Philippines)    T2—599 7
Misappropriation of funds    364.132 3
  law    345.023 23
  public administration    353.46
Miscarriage
  obstetrics    618.392
Miscegenation    306.846
Miscellaneous facts
  books    030
Misconduct by employees
  labor economics    331.259 8
  personnel management    658.314
Misconduct in office    364.132
  law    345.023 2
  public administration    353.46
Mishnah    296.123
Mishnaic period    956.940 2
Mishneh Torah    296.181 2
Misinformation campaigns
  international politics    327.14
Misiones (Argentina)  T2—822 3
Misiones (Paraguay)  T2—892 125
Mískito Indians  T5—978 82
Mískito language    497.882
      T6—978 82
Miso
  commercial processing    664.58
Missals    264.36
  Anglican    264.030 36
    texts    264.03
  Roman Catholic    264.020 36
    texts    264.023
Missaukee County (Mich.)  T2—774 66
Missile forces    358.17
Missile-hurling weapons
  art metalwork    739.73
Missiles    358.171 82
  military engineering    623.451
  military equipment    358.171 82
Missing children    362.829 7

| | | | |
|---|---|---|---|
| Missing in action | 355.113 | Mississippi River | T2—77 |
| Algerian Revolution | 965.046 8 | Arkansas | T2—767 8 |
| American Revolution | 973.38 | Tennessee | T2—768 1 |
| Chaco War | 989.207 168 | Mississippi River Delta | |
| Civil War (England) | 942.062 8 | (La.) | T2—763 3 |
| Civil War (Spain) | 946.081 8 | Mississippian period | 551.751 |
| Civil War (United States) | 973.78 | geology | 551.751 |
| Crimean War | 947.073 88 | paleontology | 560.175 1 |
| Falkland Islands War | 997.110 248 | Missoula County (Mont.) | T2—786 85 |
| Franco-German War | 943.082 8 | Missouri | 977.8 |
| Hundred Years' War | 944.025 8 | | T2—778 |
| Indo-Pakistan War, 1971 | 954.920 518 | Missouri Compromise, 1820 | 973.54 |
| Indochinese War | 959.704 18 | Civil War (United States) cause | 973.711 3 |
| Iraq War, 2003– | 956.704 438 | Missouri River | T2—78 |
| Iraqi-Iranian Conflict | 955.054 28 | Missouri | T2—778 |
| Korean War | 951.904 28 | Montana | T2—786 |
| Mexican War | 973.628 | Nebraska | T2—782 2 |
| Napoleonic Wars | 940.278 | North Dakota | T2—784 7 |
| Persian Gulf War, 1991 | 956.704 428 | South Dakota | T2—783 3 |
| South African War | 968.048 8 | Missouri Valley Siouan | |
| Spanish-American War | 973.898 | languages | 497.527 |
| Thirty Years' War | 940.248 | | T6—975 27 |
| Vietnamese War | 959.704 38 | Mist | 541.345 15 |
| War of the Pacific | 983.061 68 | colloid chemistry | 541.345 15 |
| World War I | 940.48 | applied | 660.294 515 |
| World War II | 940.548 | meteorology | 551.575 |
| Missing persons | | Mistletoes | 583.88 |
| police searches | 363.233 6 | Mistresses (Extramarital | |
| Mission (B.C.) | T2—711 37 | relationships) | 306.736 |
| Mission buildings | | Misty Fjords National | |
| architecture | 726.9 | Monument (Alaska) | T2—798 2 |
| Mission control | | Misumalpan languages | 497.88 |
| manned space flight | 629.453 | | T6—978 8 |
| unmanned space flight | 629.433 | Mitanni (Ancient kingdom) | 935.402 |
| Mission schools | 371.07 | | T2—354 |
| Missionaries | 207.209 2 | Mitchell (Qld.) | T2—943 4 |
| Christian | 266.009 2 | Mitchell County (Ga.) | T2—758 973 |
| occupational ethics | 241.641 | Mitchell County (Iowa) | T2—777 234 |
| *see Manual at* 230–280 | | Mitchell County (Kan.) | T2—781 23 |
| occupational ethics | 174.1 | Mitchell County (N.C.) | T2—756 865 |
| religion | 205.641 | Mitchell County (Tex.) | T2—764 729 |
| Missionaries of Charity | 255.97 | Mitchell's Plain (South | |
| church history | 271.97 | Africa : District) | T2—687 35 |
| Missionary stories | | Mite infestations | |
| Christianity | 266 | humans | |
| Missions (Religion) | 207.2 | medicine | 616.573 |
| Christianity | 266 | *see also* Skin diseases — | |
| Islam | 297.74 | humans | |
| Mississippi | 976.2 | Mites | 595.42 |
| | T2—762 | agricultural pests | 632.654 2 |
| Mississippi County (Ark.) | T2—767 95 | disease carriers | |
| Mississippi County (Mo.) | T2—778 983 | medicine | 614.433 |
| | | Mithraism | 299.15 |
| | | Mitis (Quebec) | T2—714 773 |

| | |
|---|---|
| Mitochondria | 571.657 |
| Mitochondrial DNA | 572.869 |
| Mitosis | 571.844 |
| Mitral valve diseases | |
|   medicine | 616.125 |
|   *see also* Cardiovascular | |
|     diseases — humans | |
| Mitral valves | |
|   human anatomy | 611.12 |
|   human physiology | 612.17 |
|   medicine | 616.125 |
| Mittelfranken (Germany) | T2—433 2 |
| Mittelland (Switzerland) | T2—494 5 |
| Mitten makers | 685.409 2 |
| Mittens | 391.412 |
|   commercial technology | 685.4 |
|   customs | 391.412 |
|   home economics | 646.3 |
|   home sewing | 646.48 |
|   *see also* Clothing | |
| Mittimatalik (Nunavut) | T2—719 52 |
| Mittlerer Oberrhein | |
|   (Germany : Region) | T2—434 643 |
| Mitzvot | |
|   Jewish ethics | 296.36 |
|   Jewish law | 296.18 |
| Miwok Indians | T5—974 133 |
| Miwok language | 497.413 3 |
| | T6—974 133 |
| Mixe Indians | T5—974 3 |
| Mixe-Zoque languages | 497.43 |
| | T6—974 3 |
| Mixed ability grouping in | |
|   education | 371.252 |
| Mixed-bloods (People) | T5—05 |
| Mixed descent | T5—05 |
| Mixed drinks | 641.874 |
|   commercial processing | 663.1 |
| Mixed economies | 330.126 |
| Mixed equations | 515.38 |
| Mixed languages | 417.22 |
|   specific languages | T4—7 |
| Mixed-level classrooms | 371.25 |
| Mixed marriage | 306.84 |
| Mixed-media arts | |
|   techniques | 702.81 |
|   two-dimensional | 740 |
| Mixed voices | 782.5 |
| Mixes (Pastry) | 664.753 |
| Mixing | |
|   chemical engineering | 660.284 292 |
|   oceanography | 551.462 |
| Mixing paints | |
|   buildings | 698.102 83 |
| Mixtec Indians | T5—976 3 |
| Mixtec language | 497.63 |
| | T6—976 3 |
| Mixtecan languages | 497.63 |
| | T6—976 3 |
| Miyagi-ken (Japan) | T2—521 15 |
| Miyazaki-ken (Japan) | T2—522 7 |
| Mizoram (India) | T2—541 66 |
| Mizzī, Yūsuf ibn al-Zakī 'Abd al- | |
|   Raḥmān | |
|   Hadith | 297.125 62 |
| Mkapa, Benjamin W. (Benjamin | |
|   William) | |
|   Tanzanian history | 967.804 3 |
| Mkobola (South Africa : | |
|   District) | T2—682 75 |
| Mkuze Game Reserve | |
|   (South Africa) | T2—684 3 |
| Mnemonics | 153.14 |
| Moab (Kingdom) | 939.462 |
| | T2—394 62 |
| Moabite language | 492.6 |
| | T6—926 |
| Moas | 568.5 |
| Moats | |
|   architecture | 725.98 |
|   military engineering | 623.31 |
| Moba language | 496.35 |
| | T6—963 5 |
| Mobile computing | 004 |
| Mobile County (Ala.) | T2—761 22 |
| Mobile home parks | 647.92 |
| Mobile homes | 643.29 |
|   architecture | 728.79 |
|   automotive engineering | 629.226 |
|   construction | 690.879 |
|   economics | 333.338 |
|   home economics | 643.29 |
|   law | 346.043 |
|   property tax | 336.23 |
|   travel | 910 |
|   *see also* Dwellings | |
|   *see Manual at* 643.29, 690.879, | |
|     728.79 vs. 629.226 | |
| Mobile libraries | |
|   public library use | 027.42 |
| Mobile radio stations | 621.384 5 |
| Mobile River (Ala.) | T2—761 22 |
| Mobile robots | 629.893 2 |
| Mobile tactics | 355.422 |
| Mobiles | 731.55 |
| Mobility-impaired children | 305.908 308 3 |
|   home care | 649.151 6 |

| | |
|---|---|
| Mobility-impaired people | 305.908 3 |
| | T1—087 3 |
| education | 371.916 |
| social group | 305.908 3 |
| social welfare | 362.43 |
| Mobilization | 355.28 |
| World War I | 940.402 |
| World War II | 940.540 2 |
| Mobs (Organized crime) | 364.106 |
| Mobs (Temporary groups) | 302.33 |
| Mobutu Sese Seko | |
| Congolese history | 967.510 33 |
| Mock oranges | 583.72 |
| Mockingbirds | 598.844 |
| Modal logic | 511.314 |
| mathematical logic | 511.314 |
| philosophical logic | 160.119 84 |
| Modality | |
| linguistics | 415.6 |
| specific languages | T4—56 |
| philosophical logic | 160 |
| Mode | 519.533 |
| Model aircraft | 629.133 1 |
| military engineering | 623.746 022 8 |
| recreation | 796.154 |
| *see Manual at* 796.15 vs. | |
| 629.0460228 | |
| Model airplanes | 629.133 134 |
| military engineering | 623.746 022 8 |
| recreation | 796.154 |
| *see Manual at* 796.15 vs. | |
| 629.0460228 | |
| Model automobiles | 629.221 2 |
| recreation | 796.156 |
| *see Manual at* 796.15 vs. | |
| 629.0460228 | |
| Model boats | 623.820 1 |
| recreation | 796.152 |
| *see Manual at* 796.15 vs. | |
| 629.0460228 | |
| Model cars | 629.221 2 |
| recreation | 796.156 |
| *see Manual at* 796.15 vs. | |
| 629.0460228 | |
| Model land vehicles | 629.221 |
| military engineering | 623.747 022 8 |
| recreation | 796.156 |
| *see Manual at* 796.15 vs. | |
| 629.0460228 | |
| Model makers | 688.109 2 |
| Model ships | 623.820 1 |
| recreation | 796.152 |
| *see Manual at* 796.15 vs. | |
| 629.0460228 | |

| | |
|---|---|
| Model theory | 511.34 |
| Model trains | 625.19 |
| recreation | 790.133 |
| *see Manual at* 796.15 vs. | |
| 629.0460228 | |
| Model vehicles | 629.046 022 8 |
| recreation | 796.15 |
| *see Manual at* 796.15 vs. | |
| 629.0460228 | |
| Modeling | |
| plastic arts | 730.28 |
| pottery | 666.442 |
| arts | 738.142 |
| technology | 666.442 |
| primary education | 372.53 |
| sculpture | 731.42 |
| use in child care | 649.51 |
| Modeling (Fashion design) | 746.92 |
| Modeling (Simulation) | 003 |
| | T1—011 |
| Models (Fashion) | 746.920 92 |
| Models (Molds) | |
| sculpture | 731.43 |
| Models (Representations) | 688.1 |
| | T1—022 8 |
| arts | 702.8 |
| cataloging | 025.349 6 |
| educational use | T1—078 |
| handicrafts | 745.592 8 |
| *see Manual at* 745.5928 | |
| library treatment | 025.179 6 |
| manufacturing technology | 688.1 |
| Models (Simulations) | 003 |
| | T1—011 |
| management decision making | 658.403 52 |
| Modems | 004.64 |
| engineering | 621.398 14 |
| Modena (Italy) | T2—454 21 |
| ancient | T2—372 621 |
| Modena (Italy : Province) | T2—454 2 |
| ancient | T2—372 62 |
| Moderators | |
| nuclear engineering | 621.483 37 |
| Modern algebra | 512 |
| Modern architecture | 724 |
| Modern art | 709.04 |
| religious significance | 203.7 |
| Christianity | 246.4 |
| Modern dance | 792.8 |
| Modern dance performers | 792.802 809 2 |
| Modern decoration | 745.409 04 |
| Modern differential geometry | 516.362 |
| Modern geometry | 516.04 |

| | | | |
|---|---|---|---|
| Modern Greek language | 489.3 | Modular arithmetic | 513.6 |
| | T6—89 | Modular coordination | |
| Modern Greek literature | 889 | architectural design | 729.23 |
| Modern history | 909.08 | Modular design | 729.2 |
| | T1—090 3 | Modular forms (Mathematics) | 512.73 |
| arts | T3C—358 208 | Modular functions | 515.982 |
| specific centuries | 909.4–.8 | Modular geometry | 516.18 |
| Modern Indic languages | 491.4 | Modular houses | 643.2 |
| | T6—914 | *see also* Dwellings | |
| Modern Indic literatures | 891.4 | Modular programming | 005.112 |
| Modern Indo-Aryan languages | 491.4 | Modulation | |
| | T6—914 | electronics | 621.381 536 |
| Modern jazz | 781.655 | Modulation circuits | |
| Modern languages | 410 | radio engineering | 621.384 12 |
| Modern Latin peoples | T5—4 | Modulators | |
| Modern literature | 808.800 3 | electronic circuits | 621.381 536 |
| history and criticism | 809.03 | Modules | |
| Modern music | 780.903 | algebra | 512.42 |
| Modern paganism | 299.94 | electronics | 621.381 52 |
| Modern painting | 759.06 | Modulus of rigidity | 531.381 |
| Modern pentathlon | 796 | Moe (Vic.) | T2—945 6 |
| Modern philosophy | 190 | Mo'ed (Order) | 296.123 2 |
| eastern | 181 | Babylonian Talmud | 296.125 2 |
| western | 190 | Mishnah | 296.123 2 |
| Modern physics | 539 | Palestinian Talmud | 296.124 2 |
| Modern Prakrit languages | 491.4 | Mo'ed Katan | 296.123 2 |
| | T6—914 | Babylonian Talmud | 296.125 2 |
| Modern Prakrit literatures | 891.4 | Mishnah | 296.123 2 |
| Modern sculpture | 735 | Palestinian Talmud | 296.124 2 |
| Modern standard Arabic | 492.7 | Moësa (Switzerland) | T2—494 735 2 |
| Modern standard Arabic literature | 892.7 | Moesia | 939.89 |
| Modern world | T2—4–9 | | T2—398 9 |
| Modernism | | Moffat County (Colo.) | T2—788 12 |
| arts | 700.411 2 | Mogadishu (Kingdom) | 967.730 1 |
| | T3C—112 | | T2—677 3 |
| church history | 273.9 | Mogadishu (Somalia) | T2—677 3 |
| literature | 808.801 12 | Mogae, Festus Gontebanye | |
| history and criticism | 809.911 2 | Botswana history | 968 830 33 |
| specific literatures | T3B—080 112 | Mogalakwena River (South | |
| history and | | Africa) | T2—682 53 |
| criticism | T3B—091 12 | Mogilev (Belarus : Oblast) | T2—478 2 |
| Modernization | | Mogilevskaïa oblast' | |
| executive management | 658.406 | (Belarus) | T2—478 2 |
| military administration | 355.686 7 | Mogul Empire | 954.025 |
| public administration | 352.367 | | T2—54 |
| production management | 658.514 | Mogul skiing | 796.937 |
| Modes (Music) | 781.263 | Mohammed, Prophet | 297.63 |
| Modesty | 179.9 | Mohammed VI, King of Morocco | |
| moral theology | 205.699 | Moroccan history | 964.053 |
| *see also* Virtues | | Mohammed Reza Pahlavi, Shah | |
| Modoc County (Calif.) | T2—794 23 | of Iran | |
| Modoc Indians | T5—974 122 | Iranian history | 955.053 |
| Modoc language | 497.412 2 | Mohammedia (Morocco : | |
| | T6—974 122 | Prefecture) | T2—643 8 |

Mohave County (Ariz.) T2—791 59
Mohave Desert (Calif.) T2—794 95
Mohave Indians T5—975 722
Mohave language 497.572 2
T6—975 722
Mohawk Indians T5—975 542
Mohawk language 497.554 2
T6—975 542
Mohawk River (N.Y.) T2—747 6
Mohegan Indians T5—973 44
Mohegan-Montauk-Narragansett
language 497.344
T6—973 44
Mohism (Chinese philosophy) 181.115
Moi, Daniel Arap
Kenyan history 967.620 42
Moism (Chinese philosophy) 181.115
Moisture
meteorology 551.57
soil physics 631.432
Moistureproof construction
buildings 693.893
Mojave Desert (Calif.) T2—794 95
Mokerong (South Africa :
District) T2—682 53
Mokole languages 496.345
T6—963 45
Mokopane (South Africa :
District) T2—682 53
Molasses 641.336
commercial processing 664.118
cooking with 641.636
food 641.336
Moldavia T2—498 1
Moldova T2—476
Romania T2—498 1
Moldavia (Principality) 949.801 4
T2—498 1
Moldavian language 459
T6—591
Moldavians T5—591
Molded pulp 676.182
Molded rubber 678.34
Molding
arts 730.28
ceramic arts 738.142
sculpture 731.43
Molding glass 666.125
Molding latex 678.527
Molding plastics 668.412
Molding rubber 678.27
Moldmaking
metal casting 671.23

Moldova 947.6
T2—476
ancient 939.88
T2—398 8
Molds (Fungi) 579.53
agricultural diseases 632.43
Molds (Tools) 621.984
Mole rats 599.35
Mole salamanders 597.858
Mole Valley (England) T2—422 165
Molecular biology 572.8
humans 611.018 16
Molecular botany 572.82
Molecular electronics 621.381
Molecular evolution 572.838
Molecular genetics 572.8
humans 611.018 16
Molecular physics 539.6
astronomy 523.019 6
Molecular properties
materials science 620.112 99
Molecular spectra 539.6
Molecular spectroscopy 543.54
Molecular structure 541.22
biochemistry 572.33
chemistry 541.22
physics 539.12
Molecular weights 541.222
Molecules
chemistry 541.22
physics 539.6
Moles (Animals) 599.335
agricultural pests 632.693 35
Moles (Disorder)
medicine 616.55
*see also* Skin diseases —
humans
Molinism 273.7
persecution of 272.5
Molise (Italy : Region) T2—457 19
ancient T2—377 33
Mollicutes 579.328
Mollies 597.667
Mollusca 594
*see also* Mollusks
Molluscoidea 594.6
paleozoology 564.6
Mollusks 594
conservation technology 639.974
control technology 628.964
cooking 641.694
culture 639.4
fishing 639.4
fishing industry 338.372 4

Mollusks (continued)
food                                641.394
  commercial processing             664.94
paleozoology                        564
resource economics                  333.955 4
zoology                             594
Molokai (Hawaii)                   T2—969 24
Molopo (South Africa :
  District)                        T2—682 47
Molteno (South Africa :
  District)                        T2—687 55
Molucca Sea                         551.461 473
                                   T2—164 73
Moluccas                           T2—598 5
Molybdates
  mineralogy                        549.74
Molybdenite
  mineralogy                        549.32
Molybdenum                          669.734
  chemical engineering              661.053 4
  chemistry                         546.534
  economic geology                  553.464 6
  materials science                 620.189 34
  metallography                     669.957 34
  metallurgy                        669.734
  metalworking                      673.734
  mining                            622.346 46
  organic chemistry                 547.055 34
    applied                         661.895
  physical metallurgy               669.967 34
  *see also* Chemicals; Metals
Momase region (Papua New            995.7
  Guinea)                          T2—957
Mombasa (Kenya)                    T2—676 23
Moment distribution method
  structural analysis               624.171 5
Moments of inertia
  aeronautics                       629.132 364
Momentum                            531.6
Momentum transfer
  chemical engineering              660.284 292
Momoh, Joseph Saidu
  Sierra Leonean history            966.404 3
Momoyama period                     952.024
Mon-Khmer languages                 495.93
                                   T6—959 3
Mon-Khmer literatures               895.93
Mon-Khmer peoples                  T5—959 3
Mon language                        495.93
                                   T6—959 3
Monachus                            599.795
Monaco                              944.949
                                   T2—449 49

Monads
  ontology                          111
Monagas (Venezuela :
  State)                           T2—875 6
Monaghan (Ireland :
  County)                          T2—416 97
Monarchist parties                  324.213
  international organizations       324.13
Monarchs                            352.23
  customs                           390.22
  dress                             391.022
  folklore                          398.22
    history and criticism           398.352
  objects of worship                202.13
  political science
    absolute monarchy               321.6
    constitutional monarchy         321.87
  public administration             352.23
Monashee Mountains (B.C.) T2—711 62
Monasteries                         206.57
  architecture                      726.7
  Buddhism                          294.365 7
  Christianity                      255
    church history                  271
    religious significance of
      buildings                     246.97
Monastic schools                    371.07
Monastic sign languages             419.1
                                   T6—999 8
Monasticism                         206.57
  Buddhism                          294.365 7
  Christianity                      255
    church history                  271
    personal religion               248.894
Monazite
  mineralogy                        549.72
Mönchengladbach
  (Germany)                        T2—435 535 3
Moncton (N.B.)                     T2—715 235
Monera                              579.3
Monetarism                          330.155 3
Monetary law                        343.032
Monetary policy                     332.46
  economics                         332.46
    central banking                 332.112
    international                    332.456 6
  law                               343.032 6
  macroeconomics                    339.53
Monetary reform
  international                      332.456 6
Monetary stabilization              332.415
  international banking              332.152
Monetary standards                  332.42
Monetary theory                     332.401

| | |
|---|---|
| Money | 332.4 |
| arts | 737.4 |
| economics | 332.4 |
| law | 343.032 |
| public administration | 354.84 |
| Money market funds | 332.632 7 |
| Money orders | 332.76 |
| law | 346.096 |
| Money-saving cooking | 641.552 |
| Money-saving interior decorating | 747.1 |
| Money supply | 332.4 |
| effect on value of money | 332.414 |
| Mong language | 495.972 |
| | T6—959 72 |
| Mong literature | 895.972 |
| Mongkut, King of Siam | |
| Thai history | 959.303 4 |
| Mongo (African people) | T5—963 96 |
| Mongo languages | 496.396 |
| | T6—963 96 |
| Mongol dynasty | 951.025 |
| Mongol Empire | 950.2 |
| | T2—5 |
| Mongolia | 951.73 |
| | T2—517 3 |
| Mongolia (Region) | 951.7 |
| | T2—517 |
| Mongolian language | 494.23 |
| | T6—942 3 |
| Mongolian languages | 494.2 |
| | T6—942 |
| Mongolian literature | 894.23 |
| Mongolian literatures | 894.2 |
| Mongolian People's Republic | 951.73 |
| | T2—517 3 |
| Mongolians | T5—942 3 |
| Mongoloid race | T5—95 |
| Mongols | T5—942 |
| Mongooses | 599.742 |
| Monifieth (Scotland) | T2—412 6 |
| Moniliales | 579.55 |
| Moniligastrida | 592.64 |
| Monimiaceae | 583.23 |
| Monism | |
| philosophy | 147.3 |
| Moniteau County (Mo.) | T2—778 52 |
| Monito del monte | 599.27 |
| Monitor and Merrimac, Battle of, 1862 | 973.752 |
| Monitor lizards | 597.959 6 |
| Monitorial system of education | 371.39 |
| Monitoring (Social control) | 361.25 |
| *see also* Environmental monitoring | |

| | |
|---|---|
| Monitors (Computers) | |
| control programs | 005.43 |
| firmware | 005.18 |
| video display screens | 004.77 |
| engineering | 621.398 7 |
| Monitors (Disciplinarians) | |
| student discipline | 371.59 |
| Monk seals | 599.795 |
| Monkeys | 599.8 |
| animal husbandry | 636.98 |
| experimental animals | |
| medicine | 616.027 38 |
| *see also* Primates | |
| Monkeys (New World) | 599.85 |
| Monkeys (Old World) | 599.86 |
| Monklands (Scotland) | T2—414 52 |
| Monks | 206.57 |
| Buddhist | 294.365 7 |
| Christian | 255 |
| biography | 271.009 2 |
| *see Manual at* 230–280 | |
| ecclesiology | 262.24 |
| guides to Christian life | 248.894 2 |
| Monkshoods | 583.34 |
| Monmouth (Wales : District) | T2—429 98 |
| Monmouth County (N.J.) | T2—749 46 |
| Monmouthshire (Wales) | T2—429 9 |
| Monmouthshire (Wales : County) | T2—429 98 |
| Mono County (Calif.) | T2—794 48 |
| Mono Indians | T5—974 57 |
| Mono language | 497.457 |
| | T6—974 57 |
| Monochromatic photography | 778.62 |
| Monoclonal antibodies | |
| human immunology | 616.079 8 |
| Monocotyledons | 584 |
| forestry | 634.974 |
| paleobotany | 561.4 |
| *see Manual at* 583–584 | |
| Monocycles | |
| engineering | 629.227 1 |
| repair | 629.287 71 |
| riding | 629.284 71 |
| Monodon | 599.543 |
| Monodontidae | 599.542 |
| Monody | 781.282 |
| Monogamy | 306.842 2 |
| Monogenea | 592.44 |
| Monographs | 002 |
| *see also* Books | |
| Monohydric hydroxy aromatics | 547.632 |
| Monolithic circuits (Electronics) | 621.381 5 |

Monologues (Drama)
  literature    808.824 5
    history and criticism    809.245
      specific literatures    T3B—204 5
        individual authors    T3A—2
Monometallic standards    332.422
Monomotapas (Kingdom)    968.910 1
        T2—689 1
Monona County (Iowa)    T2—777 44
Monongahela River (W. Va.
  and Pa.)    T2—748 8
  Pennsylvania    T2—748 8
  West Virginia    T2—754 5
Monongalia County (W.
  Va.)    T2—754 52
Mononucleosis
  incidence    614.581 2
  medicine    616.911 22
  *see also* Communicable
    diseases — humans
Monophonic electrophones    786.73
  *see also* Electrophones
Monophysite churches    281.6
  *see also* Eastern churches
Monoplacophora    594.2
Monopoly    338.82
  economics    338.82
  international economics    338.884
  law    343.072
Monopulse radar systems
  engineering    621.384 85
Monorail railroads    388.42
  engineering    625.44
  transportation services    388.42
Monorail rolling stock    388.42
  engineering    625.44
  transportation services    388.42
Monorail tracks    625.44
Monosaccharides    572.565
  *see also* Carbohydrates
Monosodium glutamate
  food technology    664.4
Monotheism    211.34
  Christianity    231
  comparative religion    202.11
  Islam    297.211
  Judaism    296.311
  philosophy of religion    211.34
Monotheistic religions    201.4
Monotony studies
  production management    658.544
Monotremata    599.29
  paleozoology    569.29
Monotropaceae    583.66

Monotype
  manufacturing technology    681.61
Monotype composition
  automatic    686.225 44
  manual    686.225 42
Monroe, James
  United States history    973.54
Monroe County (Ala.)    T2—761 25
Monroe County (Ark.)    T2—767 87
Monroe County (Fla.)    T2—759 41
Monroe County (Ga.)    T2—758 563
Monroe County (Ill.)    T2—773 91
Monroe County (Ind.)    T2—772 255
Monroe County (Iowa)    T2—777 865
Monroe County (Ky.)    T2—769 685
Monroe County (Mich.)    T2—774 32
Monroe County (Miss.)    T2—762 975
Monroe County (Mo.)    T2—778 325
Monroe County (N.Y.)    T2—747 88
Monroe County (Ohio)    T2—771 96
Monroe County (Pa.)    T2—748 25
Monroe County (Tenn.)    T2—768 883
Monroe County (W. Va.)    T2—754 78
Monroe County (Wis.)    T2—775 54
Monrovia (Liberia)    T2—666 2
Monseñor Nouel
  (Dominican Republic :
  Province)    T2—729 369 3
Monserrat    972.975
Monsoons    551.518 4
Monster flower    583.2
Monsteras    584.64
Monsters
  arts    700.47
      T3C—37
  literature    808.803 7
    history and criticism    809.933 7
      specific literatures    T3B 080 37
      history and
        criticism    T3B—093 7
  unexplained phenomena    001.944
Monstrilloida    595.34
Mont-Royal (Quebec)    T2—714 28
Mont-Tremblant National
  Park (Quebec)    T2—714 418
Montage    702.813
Montagnais Indians    T5—973 2
Montagnais language    497.32
      T6—973 2
Montagnards (Vietnamese
  people)    T5—959 3
Montagu (South Africa :
  District)    T2—687 33
Montague County (Tex.)    T2—764 541

| | |
|---|---|
| Montana | 978.6 |
| | T2—786 |
| Montana (Bulgaria : Oblast) | T2—499 1 |
| Montauk language | 497.344 |
| | T6—973 44 |
| Montcalm (Quebec : Regional County Municipality) | T2—714 415 |
| Montcalm County (Mich.) | T2—774 53 |
| Monte-Carlo (Monaco) | T2—449 49 |
| Monte Carlo method | 518.282 |
| Monte Cristi (Dominican Republic : Province) | T2—729 352 |
| Monte Plata (Dominican Republic : Province) | T2—729 377 |
| Monteiro, António Mascarenhas Cape Verdean history | 966.580 32 |
| Montenegrins | T5—918 29 |
| Montenegro | 949.745 |
| | T2—497 45 |
| ancient | 939.874 5 |
| | T2—398 745 |
| Montérégie (Quebec) | T2—714 3 |
| Monterey Bay (Calif.) | 551.461 432 |
| | T2—164 32 |
| Monterey County (Calif.) | T2—794 76 |
| Montessori method | 371.392 |
| Montevideo (Uruguay : Dept.) | T2—895 13 |
| Montezuma County (Colo.) | T2—788 27 |
| Montgomery (Wales : District) | T2—429 51 |
| Montgomery County (Ala.) | T2—761 47 |
| Montgomery County (Ark.) | T2—767 43 |
| Montgomery County (Ga.) | T2—758 832 |
| Montgomery County (Ill.) | T2—773 82 |
| Montgomery County (Ind.) | T2—772 48 |
| Montgomery County (Iowa) | T2—777 75 |
| Montgomery County (Kan.) | T2—781 93 |
| Montgomery County (Ky.) | T2—769 553 |
| Montgomery County (Md.) | T2—752 84 |
| Montgomery County (Miss.) | T2—762 642 |
| Montgomery County (Mo.) | T2—778 382 |
| Montgomery County (N.C.) | T2—756 74 |
| Montgomery County (N.Y.) | T2—747 46 |
| Montgomery County (Ohio) | T2—771 72 |
| Montgomery County (Pa.) | T2—748 12 |
| Montgomery County (Tenn.) | T2—768 45 |
| Montgomery County (Tex.) | T2—764 153 |
| Montgomery County (Va.) | T2—755 785 |
| Monthey (Switzerland : District) | T2—494 796 9 |
| Months | 529.2 |
| Montmagny (Quebec : Regional County Municipality) | T2—714 735 |
| Montmorency County (Mich.) | T2—774 83 |
| Monto (Qld. : Shire) | T2—943 5 |
| Montour County (Pa.) | T2—748 39 |
| Montpelier (Vt.) | T2—743 4 |
| Montpellier (France) | T2—448 42 |
| Montréal (Quebec) | T2—714 28 |
| Montréal (Quebec : Urban agglomeration) | T2—714 28 |
| Montréal-Est (Quebec) | T2—714 28 |
| Montréal Island (Quebec) | T2—714 28 |
| Montréal Metropolitan Community (Quebec) | T2—714 27 |
| Montréal-Ouest (Quebec) | T2—714 28 |
| Montréal Region (Quebec) | T2—714 27 |
| Montrose County (Colo.) | T2—788 19 |
| Montserrat | T2—729 75 |
| Monumental brasses arts | 739.522 |
| Monumental reliefs | 731.549 |
| Monuments | 725.94 |
| architecture | 725.94 |
| law | 344.094 |
| sculpture | 731.76 |
| World War I | 940.465 |
| World War II | 940.546 5 |
| *see also* Military commemorations | |
| Monza-Brianza province (Italy : Province) | T2—452 28 |
| ancient | T2—372 262 |
| Mood (Grammar) | 415.6 |
| specific languages | T4—56 |
| Mood disorders medicine | 616.852 7 |
| *see also* Mental disorders | |
| Moods | 152.4 |
| Moody County (S.D.) | T2—783 36 |
| Mooi River (South Africa : District) | T2—684 7 |
| Mooirivier (South Africa : District) | T2—684 7 |
| Moon | 523.3 |
| | T2—991 |
| astrology | 133.532 |
| gravity | 523.3 |
| law of nations | 341.47 |
| manned flights to | 629.454 |
| unmanned flights to | 629.435 3 |
| Moon cars engineering | 629.295 |

Moonfishes (Citharinidae) 597.48
Moonfishes (Perciformes) 597.7
Moons 523.98
Moonseeds 583.34
Moonworts 587.33
Mooré (African people) T5—963 5
Moore County (N.C.) T2—756 352
Moore County (Tenn.) T2—768 627
Moore County (Tex.) T2—764 822
Mooré language 496.35
    T6—963 5
Mooring areas 387.15
  engineering 627.22
  *see also* Port facilities
Mooring structures 387.15
  engineering 627.32
  *see also* Port facilities
Moorish architecture 723.3
Moorish period
  Spanish history 946.02
Moorreesburg (South
  Africa : District) T2—687 32
Moors
  biology 578.768 7
  ecology 577.687
Moors (Bogs)
  biology 578.768 7
  ecology 577.687
Moors (Heaths)
  biology 578.738
  ecology 577.38
Moose 599.657
  big game hunting 799.276 57
  conservation technology 639.979 657
  resource economics 333.959 657
Moose Jaw (Sask.) T2—712 44
Moosehead Lake (Me.) T2—741 2
Mopán language 497.427
  T6—974 27
Mopeds 388.347 5
  engineering 629.227 5
  *see also* Motorcycles
Mops 679.6
Moquegua (Peru : Dept.) T2—853 4
Mora County (N.M.) T2—789 54
Morab horse 636.13
Moraceae 583.45
  edible fruits 641.343 6
    cooking 641.643 6
    orchard crop 634.36
Moraines (Geologic landforms) 551.315
Moraines (Geologic material) 551.314
Moral anti-realism 170.42

Moral determinants
  individual psychology 155.234
Moral development
  psychology 155.25
Moral education 370.114
Moral judgment 170
  psychology 155.232
Moral offenses
  criminology 364.17
    criminal law 345.027
  social control 363.4
Moral philosophers 170.92
  *see Manual at* 170.92 vs. 171
Moral philosophy 170
Moral realism 170.42
Moral Rearmament 267.16
Moral renewal (Christianity) 248.25
Moral sense
  ethical systems 171.2
Moral theology 205
  Buddhism 294.35
  Christianity 241
    *see Manual at* 241 vs. 261.8
  Hinduism 294.548
  Islam 297.5
    Sufi 297.45
  Judaism 296.36
Moral training
  home child care 649.7
Morale
  armed forces 355.123
  personnel management 658.314
  public administration 352.66
Morales Ayma, Evo
  Bolivian history 984.054 2
Morality 170
  public control 363.4
    criminology 364.17
      criminal law 345.027
    public administration 353.37
  religion 205
    *see also* Moral theology
Morality plays
  literature 808.825 16
    history and criticism 809.251 6
    specific literatures T3B—205 16
      individual authors T3A—2
  stage presentation 792.16
Morat, Lake of
  (Switzerland) T2—494 538
Moravia (Czech Republic) 943.72
  T2—437 2

| | |
|---|---|
| Moravian Church | 284.6 |
| *see also* Christian | |
| denominations | |
| Moravian dialects | 491.867 |
| | T6—918 6 |
| Moravian literature | 891.86 |
| Moravians (Ethnic group) | T5—918 6 |
| Moravians (Religious group) | |
| biography | 284.609 2 |
| Moravskoslezský kraj | |
| (Czech Republic) | T2—437 28 |
| Moray (Scotland) | T2—412 2 |
| Morays | 597.43 |
| Morazán (El Salvador) | T2—728 433 |
| Morbid obesity | |
| medicine | 616.398 |
| *see also* Digestive system | |
| diseases — humans | |
| surgery | 617.43 |
| Morbihan (France) | T2—441 3 |
| Mordell conjecture | 516.352 |
| Mordellidae | 595.769 |
| Mordoviĩa (Russia) | T2—474 6 |
| Mordvin | T5—945 6 |
| Mordvin language | 494.56 |
| | T6—945 6 |
| Mordvin literature | 894.56 |
| Mordvinia (Russia) | T2—474 6 |
| Moré (African people) | T5—963 5 |
| Moré language | 496.35 |
| | T6—963 5 |
| Møre og Romsdal fylke | |
| (Norway) | T2—483 9 |
| Morehouse Parish (La.) | T2—763 84 |
| Morelos (Mexico) | T2—724 9 |
| Morels | 579.578 |
| Mores | 306 |
| customs | 390 |
| sociology | 306 |
| Moretele I (South Africa : | |
| District) | T2—682 41 |
| Moretele II (South Africa : | |
| District) | T2—682 75 |
| Morgan County (Ala.) | T2—761 93 |
| Morgan County (Colo.) | T2—788 74 |
| Morgan County (Ga.) | T2—758 595 |
| Morgan County (Ill.) | T2—773 463 |
| Morgan County (Ind.) | T2—772 513 |
| Morgan County (Ky.) | T2—769 253 |
| Morgan County (Mo.) | T2—778 53 |
| Morgan County (Ohio) | T2—771 94 |
| Morgan County (Tcnn.) | T2—768 74 |
| Morgan County (Utah) | T2—792 26 |
| Morgan County (W. Va.) | T2—754 96 |

| | |
|---|---|
| Morgan horse | 636.177 |
| Morges (Switzerland : | |
| District) | T2—494 522 3 |
| Morgues | 363.75 |
| architecture | 725.597 |
| Morice Lake (B.C.) | T2—711 82 |
| Morice River (B.C.) | T2—711 82 |
| Moridae | 597.63 |
| Moringaceae | 583.64 |
| Mormon Church | 289.3 |
| church government | 262.093 |
| parishes | 254.093 |
| church law | 262.989 3 |
| doctrines | 230.93 |
| catechisms and creeds | 238.93 |
| general councils | 262.593 |
| guides to Christian life | 248.489 3 |
| missions | 266.93 |
| moral theology | 241.049 3 |
| public worship | 264.093 |
| religious associations | 267.189 3 |
| religious education | 268.893 |
| seminaries | 230.073 93 |
| temples | 246.958 93 |
| theology | 230.93 |
| Mormon tea | 585.8 |
| Mormons | |
| biography | 289.309 2 |
| Mormyriformes | 597.47 |
| Morning after pills | |
| health | 613.943 2 |
| medicine | 618.182 5 |
| *see also* Birth control | |
| Morning-blooming plants | |
| floriculture | 635.953 |
| Morning glories | 635.933 94 |
| botany | 583.94 |
| floriculture | 635.933 94 |
| Morning prayer | 264.15 |
| Anglican | 264.030 15 |
| texts | 264.033 |
| music | 782.325 |
| choral and mixed voices | 782.532 5 |
| single voices | 783.093 25 |
| Mornington (Vic.) | T2—945 2 |
| Morobe Province (Papua | |
| New Guinea) | T2—957 1 |
| Moroccans | T5—927 64 |
| Morocco | 964 |
| | T2—64 |
| ancient | 939.712 |
| | T2—397 12 |
| Morocco (Spanish zone) | T2—642 |

Morogoro Region
  (Tanzania)      T2—678 25
Morona-Santiago (Ecuador)   T2—866 43
Morone      597.732
Moroni (Comoros)      T2—694 1
Moronidae      597.732
Morphine abuse      362.293
  medicine      616.863 2
  personal health      613.83
  social welfare      362.293
  *see also* Substance abuse
Morphing
  computer graphics      006.696
Morphisms (Mathematics)      512.62
Morphogenesis      571.833
Morphology (Biology)      571.3
Morphology (Grammar)      415.9
  specific languages      T4—59
Morphophonemics      414
  specific languages      T4—15
Morphophonology      414
  specific languages      T4—15
Morphosyntax      415
  specific languages      T4—5
Morrill County (Neb.)      T2—782 95
Morris County (Kan.)      T2—781 58
Morris County (N.J.)      T2—749 74
Morris County (Tex.)      T2—764 217
Morrison County (Minn.)      T2—776 69
Morrison plan      371.39
Morrow County (Ohio)      T2—771 516
Morrow County (Or.)      T2 795 67
Morse code telegraphy      384.14
  wireless      384.524
  *see also* Telegraphy
Mortal sin      241.31
Mortality
  demography      304.64
Mortar (Material)      666.9
  building material      691.5
  materials science      620.135
Mortars (Weapons)      355.822
  engineering      623.42
  military equipment      355.822
Mortgage banks      332.32
  law      346.082 32
  public administration      354.86
Mortgage bonds      332.632 3
Mortgage certificates      332.632 3
Mortgage defaults      332.72
Mortgage delinquencies      332.72
Mortgage insurance      368.852
  law      346.086 852
    economic assistance      343.074 2

Mortgages      332.72
  accounting      657.75
  credit economics      332.72
  investment economics      332.632 44
  law      346.043 64
  public administration      354.86
Morton County (Kan.)      T2—781 715
Morton County (N.D.)      T2—784 85
Morton National Park
  (N.S.W.)      T2—944 6
Mortuary chapels
  architecture      726.8
Mortuary practice      363.75
  *see also* Undertaking
    (Mortuary)
Moruya (N.S.W.)      T2—944 7
Morwell (Vic.)      T2—945 6
MOS memory      004.53
  engineering      621.397 32
Mosaic diseases
  agriculture      632.8
Mosaic glass
  arts      748.5
Mosaic law (Bible)      222.1
Mosaics      738.5
  architectural decoration      729.7
Mosasauridae      567.95
Moscoso, Mireya
  Panamanian history      972.870 541
Moscow (Russia : Oblast)      T2—473 1
Moscow Patriarchate      281.947
Moselle (France)      T2—443 85
Moselle River      T2—434 3
Moses
  Biblical leader      222.109 2
  Islam      297.246
Mosetenan languages      498.9
       T6 989
Moshavim      307.776
Moshoeshoe II, King of Lesotho
  Lesotho history      968.850 31
    1966–1990      968.850 31
    1995–1996      968.850 32
Mosisili, Pakalitha Bethuel
  Lesotho history      968.850 32
Moskovskaîa oblast'
  (Russia)      T2—473 1
Mosques      297.351
  architecture      726.2
  organization      297.65
Mosquito control      363.78
  social welfare      363.78
  technology      628.965 7
  *see also* Pest control

| | | |
|---|---|---|
| Mosquito Indians | T5—978 82 | |
| Mosquito language | 497.882 | |
| | T6—978 82 | |
| Mosquitoes | 595.772 | |
| disease carriers | 571.986 | |
| medicine | 614.432 3 | |
| Moss animals | 594.67 | |
| Mössbauer spectroscopy | | |
| physics | 537.535 2 | |
| Mossel Bay (South Africa : District) | T2—687 37 | |
| Mosselbaai (South Africa : District) | T2—687 37 | |
| Mosses | 588.2 | |
| paleobotany | 561.8 | |
| Mossi (African people) | T5—963 5 | |
| Mossi (Kingdom) | 966.250 1 | |
| | T2—662 5 | |
| Mossi languages | 496.35 | |
| | T6—963 5 | |
| Mostaganem (Algeria : Province) | T2—651 | |
| Mosul (Iraq) | T2—567 4 | |
| Motacillidae | 598.854 | |
| Motazilites | 297.834 | |
| Motelkeepers | 647.940 92 | |
| Motels | 910.46 | |
| *see also* Hotels | | |
| Motets | 782.26 | |
| choral and mixed voices | 782.526 | |
| single voices | 783.092 6 | |
| Moth flies | 595.772 | |
| Mother and child | 306.874 3 | |
| Mother of God | | |
| Christian doctrine | 232.91 | |
| Motherhood | 306.874 3 | |
| Mothering Sunday | 394.262 8 | |
| Mothers | 306.874 3 | |
| | T1—085 2 | |
| Christian devotional literature | 242.643 1 | |
| family relationships | 306.874 3 | |
| guides to Christian life | 248.843 1 | |
| psychology | 155.646 3 | |
| social welfare | 362.839 53 | |
| Mother's Day | 394.262 8 | |
| Motherwell (Scotland : District) | T2—414 52 | |
| Moths | 595.78 | |
| agricultural pests | 632.78 | |
| culture | 638.578 | |
| Motility | | |
| cytology | 571.67 | |
| microorganisms | 571.672 9 | |

| | | |
|---|---|---|
| Motion | | |
| celestial bodies | 521 | |
| philosophy | 116 | |
| physics | 531.11 | |
| stars | 523.83 | |
| Motion picture advertising | 659.14 | |
| Motion picture directors | 791.430 233 092 | |
| Motion picture music | 781.542 | |
| Motion picture photography | 777 | |
| Motion picture plays | 791.437 | |
| *see also* Screenplays | | |
| Motion picture projection | 777.57 | |
| Motion picture scripts | 791.437 | |
| rhetoric | 808.066 791 | |
| Motion picture theaters | | |
| architecture | 725.823 | |
| Motion pictures | 791.43 | |
| accounting | 657.84 | |
| cataloging | 025.347 3 | |
| communications services | 384.8 | |
| ethics | 175 | |
| influence on crime | 364.254 | |
| instructional use | 371.335 23 | |
| adult level | 374.26 | |
| journalism | 070.18 | |
| library treatment | 025.177 3 | |
| performing arts | 791.43 | |
| *see Manual at* 791.43, 791.45 vs. 777 | | |
| public administration | 354.75 | |
| sociology | 302.234 3 | |
| use in advertising | 659.152 | |
| *see Manual at* 384.54, 384.55, 384.8 vs. 791.4 | | |
| Motion sickness | | |
| medicine | 616.989 2 | |
| *see also* Environmental diseases — humans | | |
| Motion studies | | |
| production management | 658.542 3 | |
| psychology | 152.3 | |
| Motions (Law) | 347.052 | |
| Motivation | 153.8 | |
| armed forces | 355.123 | |
| education | | |
| gifted students | 371.956 | |
| educational psychology | 370.154 | |
| learning psychology | 153.153 4 | |
| personnel management | 658.314 | |
| executives | 658.407 14 | |
| public administration | 352.66 | |
| primary education | | |
| reading | 372.42 | |

Motivation research
  marketing management   658.834 2
Motlanthe, Kgalema
  South African history   968.067
Motley County (Tex.)   T2—764 752
Motocross   796.756
Motor bicycles   388.347 5
  engineering   629.227 5
  *see also* Motorcycles
Motor functions
  human physiology   612.7
    localization in brain   612.825 2
  psychology   152.3
Motor homes   388.346
  architecture   728.79
  camper cooking   641.575
  driving   629.284 6
  engineering   629.226
  repair   629.287 6
  transportation services   388.346
  travel   910
  *see also* Automotive vehicles
  *see Manual at* 643.29, 690.879,
    728.79 vs. 629.226
Motor horns
  music   786.99
    *see also* Percussion
      instruments
Motor land vehicles   388.34
  engineering   629.2
  transportation services   388.34
  *see also* Automotive vehicles
Motor learning
  psychology   152.334
Motor nerves
  human physiology   612.811
Motor organs   573.7
  *see also* Musculoskeletal
    system
Motor scooter racing   796.75
Motor skills
  educational psychology   370.155
Motor system   573.7
  *see also* Musculoskeletal
    system
Motor vehicle engineers   629.209 2
Motor vehicle insurance   368.092
  inland marine   368.232
  liability   368.572
Motor vehicle racing   796.7
Motor vehicle registration plates   929.9

Motor vehicle transportation
  facilities
  architecture   725.38
  area planning   711.73
Motor vehicles   388.34
  engineering   629.2
  transportation services   388.34
  *see also* Automotive vehicles
Motor yachting   797.125 6
Motor yachts   387.231 4
  engineering   623.823 14
  transportation services   387.231 4
  *see also* Ships
Motorboat racing   797.14
Motorboating
  sports   797.125
Motorboats   387.231
  design   623.812 31
  engineering   623.823 1
  handling   623.882 31
  transportation services   387.231
  *see also* Ships
Motorcycle accidents   363.125 9
  *see also* Highway safety
Motorcycle racers   796.750 92
Motorcycle racing   796.75
Motorcycle theft   364.162 862 922 75
  law   345.026 286 292 275
Motorcycle transportation
  facilities
  area planning   711.73
Motorcycle troops (Armed
  forces)   357.53
Motorcycles   388.347 5
  engineering   629.227 5
  repair   629.287 75
  riding   629.284 75
  sports   796.75
  theft of   364.162 862 922 75
  law   345.026 286 292 275
  transportation services   388.347 5
  *see also* Automotive vehicles
  *see Manual at* 629.046 vs. 388
Motorized homes   388.346
  *see also* Motor homes
Motorized infantry   356.16
Motors   621.4
Motorscooters   388.347 5
  engineering   629.227 5
  repair   629.287 75
  *see also* Motorcycles
Motorways   388.122
  *see also* Roads
Moulins (Quebec)   T2—714 412

| | |
|---|---|
| Moultrie County (Ill.) | T2—773 675 |
| Mound builders (Birds) | 598.64 |
| Mount Aspiring National Park (N.Z.) | T2—937 1 |
| Mount Athos (Greece) | T2—495 65 |
| Mount Ayliff (South Africa : District) | T2—687 59 |
| Mount Buffalo National Park (Vic.) | T2—945 5 |
| Mount Cook National Park (N.Z.) | T2—938 8 |
| Mount Currie (South Africa : District) | T2—684 6 |
| Mount Desert Island (Me.) | T2—741 45 |
| Mount Elliott National Park (Qld.) | T2—943 6 |
| Mount Etna (Italy) | T2—458 13 |
| Mount Field National Park (Tas.) | T2—946 2 |
| Mount Fletcher (South Africa : District) | T2—687 59 |
| Mount Frere (South Africa : District) | T2—687 59 |
| Mount Fuji (Japan) | T2—521 66 |
| Mount Gambier (S. Aust.) | T2—942 34 |
| Mount Hood (Or.) | T2—795 61 |
| Mount Isa (Qld.) | T2—943 7 |
| Mount Kaputar National Park (N.S.W.) | T2—944 4 |
| Mount Kilimanjaro (Tanzania) | T2—678 26 |
| Mount Lofty Ranges (S. Aust.) | T2—942 32 |
| Mount McKinley National Park (Alaska) | T2—798 3 |
| Mount Rainier National Park (Wash.) | T2—797 782 |
| Mount Revelstoke National Park (B.C.) | T2—711 68 |
| Mount Robson Provincial Park (B.C.) | T2—711 82 |
| Mount Spec National Park (Qld.) | T2—943 6 |
| Mount Waddington (B.C.) | T2—711 2 |
| Mount Whitney (Calif.) | T2—794 86 |
| Mountain ashes | 583.73 |
| Mountain biking | 796.63 |
| Mountain building | 551.82 |
| Mountain climbing | 796.522 |
| equipment technology | 688.765 22 |
| Mountain goat | 599.647 5 |
| conservation technology | 639.979 647 5 |
| resource economics | 333.959 647 5 |
| Mountain laurel | 583.66 |

| | |
|---|---|
| Mountain lion | 599.752 4 |
| conservation technology | 639.979 752 4 |
| resource economics | 333.959 752 4 |
| Mountain Province (Philippines) | T2—599 1 |
| Mountain railroads | 385.6 |
| engineering | 625.3 |
| transportation services | 385.6 |
| Mountain sickness | |
| medicine | 616.989 3 |
| *see also* Environmental diseases — humans | |
| Mountain tactics | 355.423 |
| Mountain troops | 356.164 |
| Mountain tunnels | |
| construction | 624.192 |
| Mountain winds | 551.518 5 |
| Mountain Zebra National Park (South Africa) | T2—687 54 |
| Mountaineering | 796.522 |
| Mountaineers | 796.522 092 |
| Mountains | 551.432 |
| | T2—143 |
| biology | 578.753 |
| ecology | 577.53 |
| geography | 910.914 3 |
| geomorphology | 551.432 |
| health | 613.12 |
| land economics | 333.73 |
| physical geography | 910.021 43 |
| recreational resources | 333.784 |
| recreational use | 796.522 |
| Mountbatten of Burma, Louis Mountbatten, Earl | |
| Indian history | 954.035 9 |
| Mounted forces | 357 |
| Mountrail County (N.D.) | T2—784 74 |
| Mourne Mountains (Northern Ireland) | T2—416 58 |
| Mourning | 393.9 |
| music | 781.588 |
| religion | |
| Christianity | |
| devotional literature | 242.4 |
| religious guidance | 248.866 |
| rites | 265.85 |
| devotional literature | 204.32 |
| Islam | |
| rites | 297.385 |
| Judaism | |
| rites | 296.445 |
| liturgy | 296.454 5 |
| religious guidance | 204.42 |
| rites | 203.88 |

Mouse deer | 599.63
Mousebirds | 598.75
Mousterian culture | 930.126
Mouth | 591.44
  animal physiology | 573.35
  descriptive zoology | 591.44
    mammals | 599.144
  human anatomy | 611.31
  human physiology | 612.31
    speech | 612.78
  medicine | 616.31
  surgery | 617.522
  *see also* Digestive system
Mouth-breeding frogs | 597.87
Mouth diseases
  medicine | 616.31
  *see also* Digestive system
    diseases — humans
Mouth organs | 788.82
  instrument | 788.821 9
  music | 788.82
  *see also* Woodwind instruments
Moutse (South Africa :
  District) | T2—682 75
Movable bridges
  construction | 624.24
Movable dams | 627.84
Movable property
  law | 346.047
    private ownership | 346.047
    public ownership | 343.023
Movement | 573.7
  animal behavior | 591.5
  animal physiology | 573.7
  arts | 701.8
    drawing | 741.018
  cytology | 571.67
  human physiology | 612.04
    musculoskeletal system | 612.7
  plants | 575.97
  psychology | 152.3
  *see also* Musculoskeletal
    system
Movement disorders
  medicine | 616.83
  *see also* Nervous system
    diseases — humans
Movement education
  primary education | 372.868
Movement perception
  human physiology | 612.88
    visual perception | 612.84
  psychology | 153.754
    visual perception | 152.142 5

Movies | 791.43
  *see also* Motion pictures
Movimento sociale italiano
  (Political party) | 324.245 038
Movimento sociale italiano-
  Destra nazionale (Political
  party) | 324.245 038
Moving and storage industry | 388.044
  law | 343.093 2
Moving household goods | 648.9
  freight services | 388.044
  personnel management | 658.383
Moving sidewalks | 388.41
Moving targets
  gun sports | 799.313
  physics | 531.112
Mower County (Minn.) | T2—776 17
Mowing | 631.55
Moxibustion
  therapeutics | 615.892
Moxico (Angola : Province) | T2—673 4
Moyle (Northern Ireland) | T2—416 15
Mozambicans | T5—967 9
Mozambique | 967.9
  | T2—679
Mozambique Channel | 551.461 525
  | T2—165 25
MP (Military Police) | 355.133 23
Mpendle (South Africa :
  District) | T2—684 7
Mpofu (South Africa :
  District) | T2—687 55
Mpongwe language | 496.396
  | T6—963 96
Mpumalanga (South Africa) | 968.27
  | T2—682 7
Mqanduli (South Africa :
  District) | T2—687 58
MRI (Imaging)
  medicine | 616.075 48
MSG (Food additive)
  food technology | 664.4
M'Sila (Algeria : Province) | T2—655
Msinga (South Africa :
  District) | T2—684 7
Mswati III, King of Swaziland
  Swazi history | 968.870 3
Mthatha (South Africa :
  District) | T2—687 58
Mthethwa (Kingdom) | 968.403 8
  | T2—684
Mtonjaneni (South Africa :
  District) | T2—684 3

Mtunzini (South Africa : District) — T2—684 4
Mtwara Region (Tanzania) — T2—678 24
Mu-mesons — 539.721 14
Mu'allaq (Hadith) — 297.125 22
Mubārak, Muḥammad Ḥusnī
  Egyptian history — 962.055
Mucilage — 668.33
Muck (Scotland) — T2—411 54
Mucocutaneous leishmaniasis
  incidence — 614.534
  medicine — 616.936 4
  *see also* Communicable
    diseases — humans
Mucous membranes
  human histology — 611.018 7
Mud flows — 551.307
Mud fuels — 662.82
Mud puppies — 597.85
Mud turtles — 597.923
Mu'ḍal (Hadith) — 297.125 22
Mudéjar architecture — 720.946 090 2
Mudgee (N.S.W.) — T2—944 5
Mudīrīyat al-Sharqīyah
  (Egypt) — T2—621
Mudminnows — 597.5
Muffin mixes — 664.753
Muffins — 641.815 7
Mufflers (Automobile part) — 629.252
Muffs — 391.44
  commercial technology — 687.19
  fur — 685.24
  customs — 391.44
  *see also* Accessories (Clothing)
Mugabe, Robert Gabriel
  Zimbabwean history — 968.910 51
Mugilidae — 597.7
Muğla İli (Turkey) — T2—562 7
  ancient — T2—392 4
Muḥammad, Prophet — 297.63
Muhammad, Zahir Shah
  Afghan history — 958.104 3
Muḥammad V, King of Morocco
  Moroccan history — 964.04
    1927–1956 — 964.04
    1956–1961 — 964.051
Muhlenberg County (Ky.) — T2—769 832
Muirhead (North
  Lanarkshire, Scotland) — T2—414 52
Mujica Cordano, José Alberto
  Uruguayan history — 989.506 76
Mukhara (Kingdom) — 962.502 2
  — T2—625

Mukurra (Kingdom) — 962.502 2
  — T2—625
Mulberries — 583.45
  botany — 583.45
  cooking — 641.643 8
  food — 641.343 8
  orchard crop — 634.38
  ornamental arboriculture — 635.977 345
Mulch tillage — 631.451
Mule deer — 599.653
  big game hunting — 799.276 53
  conservation technology — 639.979 653
  resource economics — 333.959 653
Mules — 636.183
Mülheim an der Ruhr
  (Germany) — T2—435 537 3
Mulhouse (France) — T2—443 933
Mulleins — 583.95
Mullets — 641.392
  cooking — 641.692
  culture — 639.377
  food — 641.392
  zoology — 597.7
Mullica River (N.J.) — T2—749 61
Mulroney, Brian
  Canadian history — 971.064 7
Multān District (Pakistan) — T2—549 14
Multi-agent systems
  artificial intelligence — 006.3
Multi-peril real property
  insurance — 368.096
Multiagent systems
  artificial intelligence — 006.3
Multicultural education — 370.117
  adult level — 374.017
Multiculturalism
  political ideology — 320.561
  sociolinguistics — 306.446
  sociology — 305.8
Multidimensional algebra — 512.5
Multiform functions — 515.22
Multigraded classes — 371.25
Multilateral agreements
  international economics — 337.1
Multilateral economic
  cooperation — 337.1
  *see Manual at* 337.3–.9 vs.
    337.1
Multilateral trade agreements — 382.91
  Eastern Europe — 382.914 7
Multilateral treaties — 341.37
  sources of law of nations — 341.1
  texts — 341.026 5

Multilevel marketing
  management — 658.872
Multilinear algebra — 512.5
Multilinear forms
  algebraic geometry — 516.35
Multilingual phrase books — 418.07
Multilingual shorthand systems — 653.41
Multilingualism — 306.446
  linguistics — 404.2
    specific languages — T4—042
  sociology — 306.446
Multimedia authoring software — 006.78
Multimedia systems
  cataloging — 025.344
  computer art — 776.7
  computer science — 006.7
  instructional use — 371.334 67
      T1—078 567
  library treatment — 025.174
Multinational enterprises — 338.88
Multinational forces (Military) — 355.356
  internationally controlled — 355.357
Multiphase flow
  liquid mechanics — 532.56
Multiple access systems
  computer communications — 004.6
  *see also* Computer
    communications
  processing modes — 004.3
  *see also* Processing modes —
    computer science
Multiple art — 709.040 7
  sculpture — 735.230 478
Multiple birth
  obstetrics — 618.25
Multiple column tariffs — 382.753
  *see also* Customs (Tariff)
Multiple cropping — 631.58
Multiple deficiency states
  medicine — 616.399
  *see also* Digestive system
    diseases — humans
Multiple dwellings
  architecture — 728.31
Multiple flutes — 788.37
  *see also* Woodwind instruments
Multiple intelligences — 153.9
  educational psychology — 370.152 9
  psychology — 153.9
Multiple-line insurance coverage — 368.09
Multiple-loop systems
  automation engineering — 629.833

Multiple myeloma
  incidence — 614.599 941 8
  medicine — 616.994 18
  *see also* Cancer — humans
Multiple organ failure
  medicine — 616.047 5
Multiple personality disorder
  medicine — 616.852 36
  *see also* Mental disorders
Multiple pregnancy
  obstetrics — 618.25
Multiple-purpose buildings — 720.49
Multiple sclerosis — 362.196 834
  medicine — 616.834
  social services — 362.196 834
  *see also* Nervous system
    diseases — humans
Multiple stars — 523.841
Multiple-valued logic — 511.312
Multiplexers
  communications engineering — 621.382 16
  computer communications — 004.66
  engineering — 621.398 1
Multiplexing
  communications engineering — 621.382 16
  computer communications — 004.66
  engineering — 621.398 1
Multiplication — 512.92
  algebra — 512.92
  arithmetic — 513.213
Multiplicative properties — 512.73
Multiplier (Economics) — 339.43
Multiprocessing — 004.35
  communications — 004.618 5
  programming — 005.275
  programs — 005.375
  *see also* Processing modes —
    computer science
Multiprocessors — 004.35
  engineering — 621.391
  *see also* Processing modes —
    computer science
Multiprogramming — 005.434
  computer hardware — 004.3
  systems programs — 005.434
  *see also* Processing modes —
    computer science
Multistage programming — 519.703
Multistory buildings — 720.483
  *see also* Tall buildings
Multistory houses
  architecture — 728.372

| | |
|---|---|
| Multitasking (Computer science) | 005.434 |
| computer hardware | 004.3 |
| *see also* Processing modes — | |
| computer science | |
| Multitrophic interactions | |
| (Ecology) | 577.16 |
| Multiuser processing (Computer | |
| science) | 004.3 |
| Multivariate analysis | 519.535 |
| Multnomah County (Or.) | T2—795 49 |
| Muluzi, Bakili | |
| Malawian history | 968.970 42 |
| Mumbai (India) | T2—547 92 |
| Mummies | |
| customs | 393.3 |
| Mumps | |
| incidence | 614.544 |
| medicine | 616.313 |
| *see also* Digestive system | |
| diseases — humans | |
| pediatrics | 618.923 13 |
| Munchausen syndrome | |
| medicine | 616.858 6 |
| *see also* Mental disorders | |
| Munchausen syndrome by proxy | |
| medicine | 616.858 223 |
| *see also* Child abuse | |
| München (Germany) | T2—433 64 |
| Münchwilen (Switzerland : | |
| Bezirk) | T2—494 593 |
| Muncie (Ind.) | T2—772 65 |
| Munda | T5—959 5 |
| Munda languages | 495.95 |
| | T6—959 5 |
| Munda literatures | 895.95 |
| Mundane astrology | 133.5 |
| Mundari language | 495.95 |
| | T6—959 5 |
| Mundari literature | 895.95 |
| Munich (Germany) | T2—433 64 |
| Municipal annexation | 320.859 |
| law | 342.041 3 |
| Municipal bankruptcy | 336.368 |
| Municipal bonds | 332.632 33 |
| law | 346.092 2 |
| Municipal charters | 342.02 |
| Municipal colleges | 378.052 |
| *see also* Higher education | |
| Municipal contracts | 352.532 14 |
| Municipal corporations | 320.85 |
| law | 342.09 |
| Municipal courts | 347.02 |
| Municipal engineering | 628 |
| Municipal engineers | 628.092 |

| | |
|---|---|
| Municipal finance | 336.014 |
| law | 343.03 |
| public administration | 352.421 4 |
| public finance | 336.014 |
| Municipal franchises | |
| public revenue | 336.16 |
| Municipal government | |
| law | 342.09 |
| Municipal incorporation | 320.85 |
| Municipal theater | 792.022 |
| Municipal universities | 378.052 |
| *see also* Higher education | |
| Municipal wastes | 363.728 |
| *see also* Waste control | |
| Municipal water supply | 363.61 |
| engineering | 628.1 |
| Municipalities | 320.85 |
| law | 342.09 |
| *see Manual at* T2—713 and | |
| T2—714 | |
| Munqati' (Hadith) | 297.125 22 |
| Munsee Indians | T5—973 45 |
| Munsee language | 497.345 |
| | T6—973 45 |
| Münster (Germany : | |
| Regierungsbezirk) | T2—435 61 |
| Munster (Ireland) | T2—419 |
| Münster (Westphalia, | |
| Germany) | T2—435 614 |
| Münsterland (Germany) | T2—435 61 |
| Muntjacs | 599.65 |
| Muntz metal | 669.3 |
| materials science | 620.182 |
| metallography | 669.953 |
| metallurgy | 669.3 |
| metalworking | 673.3 |
| physical metallurgy | 669.963 |
| Muong | T5—959 2 |
| Muong language | 495.92 |
| | T6—959 2 |
| Muons | 539.721 14 |
| Mura languages | 498.9 |
| | T6—989 |
| Mural paintings | 751.73 |
| Murcia (Spain : Region) | T2—467 7 |
| Murder | 364.152 3 |
| law | 345.025 23 |
| Murderers | 364.152 3 |
| biography | 364.152 309 2 |
| Mureş (Romania) | T2—498 4 |
| Muri (Switzerland : Bezirk) | T2—494 566 7 |
| Muriatic acid | |
| chemical engineering | 661.23 |
| Muridae | 599.35 |

Murine typhus
  incidence 614.526 2
  medicine 616.922 2
  *see also* Communicable
    diseases — humans
Müritz (Germany :
  Landkreis) T2—431 72
Murjiites (Islamic sect) 297.837
Murmansk (Russia : Oblast) T2—471 3
Murmanskaîa oblast'
  (Russia) T2—471 3
Muromachi period 952.023
Murray Bridge (S. Aust.) T2—942 32
Murray County (Ga.) T2—758 31
Murray County (Minn.) T2—776 27
Murray County (Okla.) T2—766 57
Murray River (B.C.) T2—711 87
Murray River (N.S.W.-S.
  Aust.) T2—944
Murraysburg (South Africa :
  District) T2—687 39
Murres 598.33
  conservation technology 639.978 33
  resource economics 333.958 33
  sports hunting 799.248 33
Murrumbidgee River
  (N.S.W.) T2—944 8
Mursal (Hadith) 297.125 222
Murua Island (Papua New
  Guinea) T2—954 1
Murui language 498.9
   T6—989
Murwillumbah (N.S.W.) T2—944 3
Mus 599.353
Muş İli (Turkey) T2—566 72
  ancient T2—394 2
Musā
  Islam 297.246
Musaceae 584.39
Musannafat 297.125 56
Muscat and Oman T2—535 3
Muscatine County (Iowa) T2—777 68
Musci 588.2
Muscicapidae 598.848
Muscidae 595.774
Muscle fatigue
  human biochemistry 612.744
Muscles 573.75
  biology 573.75
  drawing
    animals 743.6
    humans 743.47
  human anatomy 611.73
  human biochemistry 612.744

Muscles (continued)
  human biophysics 612.741
  human physiology 612.74
  injuries 617.473 044
  medicine 616.74
  pharmacokinetics 615.773
  surgery 617.473
Muscogee County (Ga.) T2—758 473
Muscular diseases
  medicine 616.74
  *see also* Musculoskeletal
    diseases — humans
Muscular dystrophy 362.196 748
  medicine 616.748
  pediatrics 618.927 48
  social services 362.196 748
  *see also* Musculoskeletal
    diseases — humans
Muscular rheumatism
  medicine 616.742
  *see also* Musculoskeletal
    diseases — humans
Muscular tissue
  human histology 612.740 45
Musculoskeletal diseases 573.739
  animals 573.739
    veterinary medicine 636.089 67
  humans 362.196 7
    anesthesiology 617.967 47
    cancer 362.196 994 7
      incidence 614.599 947
      medicine 616.994 7
      social services 362.196 994 7
      *see also* Cancer — humans
    geriatrics 618.976 7
    incidence 614.597
    medicine 616.7
    pediatrics 618.927
    pharmacokinetics 615.77
    social services 362.196 7
    surgery 617.47
Musculoskeletal system 573.7
  anesthesiology 617.967 47
  animals 573.7
  diseases 573.739
    *see also* Musculoskeletal
      diseases
  dislocations
    medicine 617.16
  fractures
    medicine 617.15
  human anatomy 611.7
  human histology 612.704 5
  human physiology 612.7

Musculoskeletal system (continued)
 injuries 617.470 44
 medicine 616.7
 sprains
  medicine 617.17
  surgery 617.47
Museologists 069.092
Museology 069
  T1—075
 arts T3C—39
Museum activities 069
  T1—075
Museum catalogs 069.52
  T1—074
Museum collections 069.5
  T1—074
Museum documentation 069.52
  T1—075
Museum equipment 069.3
Museum furnishings
 plant management 069.3
Museum furniture
 museology 069.33
Museum guidebooks T1—074
Museum labels 069.53
Museum libraries 027.68
Museum objects
 circulation 069.132
 selection 069.51
Museum policy (Government
 policy) 069
Museum registration methods 069.52
  T1—075
Museum science 069
Museum services 069.1
  T1—075
Museums 069
  T1—074
 architecture 727.6
 area planning 711.57
 fine arts 708
  *see Manual at* 704.9 and
   753–758
 institutional housekeeping 647.996
 law 344.093
 public administrative support 352.76
 publishing 070.594
Museveni, Yoweri
 Ugandan history 967.610 44
Mushrooms 579.6
 agriculture 635.8
 commercial processing 664.805 8
 cooking 641.658

Mushrooms (continued)
 food 641.358
 human toxicology 615.952 96
Music 780
 arts T3C—357 8
 ethics 175
  religion
   Christianity 241.65
  *see also* Recreation — ethics
 folklore 398.277 8
  history and criticism 398.357 8
 primary education 372.87
 printing 686.284
 public administrative support 353.77
 publishing 070.579 4
 religion 203.7
  attitude toward secular music 201.678
  Buddhism 294.343 7
  Christianity 246.75
   attitude toward secular
    music 261.578
  Hinduism 294.537
  Jainism 294.437
  Judaism 296.462
  public worship 203.8
   Christianity 264.2
   Judaism 296.462
  *see also* Public worship
 research 780.72
 sociology 306.484 2
 use in child care 649.51
 *see Manual at* 780
Music appreciation 781.17
 primary education 372.872
Music boxes 786.65
 *see also* Mechanical musical
  instruments
Music dictionaries 780.3
Music editing 780.149
Music education 780.7
Music hall presentations 792.7
Music halls
 architecture 725.81
Music instruction 780.7
Music libraries 026.78
Music theory 781
Music therapy
 medicine 615.851 54
Musical aptitude tests 153.947 8
Musical bows 787.92
 instrument 787.921 9
 music 787.92
 *see also* Stringed instruments
Musical chairs (Recreation) 793.4

Musical elements 781.2
Musical forms 781.8
  instrumental 784.18
  vocal 782
Musical glasses 786.866
  *see also* Percussion instruments
Musical instrument digital
    interface 784.190 285 46
Musical instrument makers 784.190 92
  craft producers 784.190 92
  mass producers 681.809 2
  *see Manual at* 784–788
Musical instruments 784.19
  construction 784.192 3
    by hand 784.192 3
    by machine 681.8
Musical notation 780.148
Musical pitch 781.232
Musical plays 782.14
  music 782.14
  stage presentation 792.6
  *see Manual at* 782.1 vs. 792.5,
    792.6
Musical saws 786.888
  *see also* Percussion instruments
Musical sound 781.23
Musical temperament 784.192 8
Musical traditions 781.6
Musicals 782.14
  music 782.14
  stage presentation 792.6
  *see Manual at* 782.1 vs. 792.5,
    792.6
Musicians 780.92
  *see Manual at* 780.92; *also at*
    780.92 and 791.092; *also at*
    781.6; *also at* 784–788
Musicology 780.721
Musina (South Africa :
    District) T2—682 57
Musique concrète 786.75
Musk turtles 597.923
Muskegon County (Mich.) T2—774 57
Muskellunge 597.59
  sports fishing 799.175 9
Muskets
  art metalwork 739.744 25
  military engineering 623.442 5
Muskhogean Indians T5—973 8
Muskie 597.59
  sports fishing 799.175 9
Muskingum County (Ohio) T2—771 91
Muskingum River (Ohio) T2—771 91

Muskmelons 641.356 11
  cooking 641.656 11
  food 641.356 11
  garden crop 635.611
Muskogean Indians T5—973 8
Muskogean languages 497.38
  T6—973 8
Muskogee County (Okla.) T2—766 82
Muskogee language 497.385
  T6—973 85
Muskoka (Ont. : District
    municipality) T2—713 16
Muskox 599.647 8
Muskrats 599.357 9
  conservation technology 639.979 357 9
  resource economics 333.959 357 9
  trapping 639.113 579
Muslim ibn al-Ḥajjāj al-Qushayrī
  Hadith 297.125 42
Muslims 297.092
  T1—088 297
  biography 297.092
    specific sects 297.8
  social group 305.697
  *see Manual at* 297.092
Musophagidae 598.74
Mussel shrimps 595.33
Mussels 641.394
  cooking 641.694
  fishing 639.42
  food 641.394
    commercial processing 664.94
  zoology 594.4
Musselshell County (Mont.) T2—786 312
Mussolini, Benito
  Italian history 945.091
Mustache shrimps 595.36
Mustaches 646.724
  care 646.724
  customs 391.5
Mustadrākāt 297.125 45
Mustakhrajat 297.125 7
Muṣṭalaḥ al-Ḥadīth 297.125 2
Mustang 636.13
  zoology 599.665 5
Mustard 641.338 4
  botany 583.64
  *see also* Hot spices
Mustela 599.766 2
Mustelidae 599.766
  conservation technology 639.979 766
  resource economics 333.959 766
Mustelinae 599.766
Muswellbrook (N.S.W.) T2—944 2

| | |
|---|---|
| Mutagenesis | 572.838 |
| Mutagens | |
| biology | 576.542 |
| medicine | 616.042 |
| Mutale (South Africa : | |
| District) | T2—682 57 |
| Mu'talif wa-al-mukhtalif | |
| Hadith | 297.125 264 2 |
| Mutation (Genetics) | 576.549 |
| Mutawātir (Hadith) | 297.125 23 |
| Mutazilites | 297.834 |
| Mute swan | 598.418 7 |
| Muthanná (Iraq : Province) | T2—567 5 |
| Mutharika, B. W. T. | |
| Malawian history | 968.970 43 |
| Mutina (Italy) | T2—372 621 |
| Mutiny | 355.133 4 |
| Muttafiq wa-al-muftariq | 297.125 264 |
| Muttaṣil (Hadith) | 297.125 21 |
| Mutton | 641.363 |
| commercial processing | 664.92 |
| cooking | 641.663 |
| food | 641.363 |
| Mutual-aid groups | 361.43 |
| Mutual aid societies | 334.7 |
| economics | 334.7 |
| insurance | 368.3 |
| Mutual funds | 332.632 7 |
| law | 346.092 2 |
| Mutual savings banks | 332.21 |
| Mutual security pacts | 355.031 |
| law | 341.72 |
| Mutualism (Biology) | 577.852 |
| Muwaṭṭa'āt | 297.125 58 |
| Mwanawasa, Levy P. | |
| Zambian history | 968.940 43 |
| Mwanza Region (Tanzania) | T2—678 27 |
| Mweru, Lake (Congo and | |
| Zambia) | T2—675 18 |
| Mwinyi, Ali Hassan | |
| Tanzanian history | 967.804 2 |
| Myalgia | |
| medicine | 616.742 |
| *see also* Musculoskeletal | |
| diseases — humans | |
| Myalgic encephalomyelitis | |
| medicine | 616.047 8 |
| Myanmar | 959.1 |
| | T2—591 |
| Myasthenia gravis | |
| medicine | 616.744 2 |
| *see also* Musculoskeletal | |
| diseases — humans | |
| Mycelia Sterilia | 579.55 |

| | |
|---|---|
| Mycenae (Extinct city) | T2—388 |
| Mycenaean architecture | 722.61 |
| Mycenaean Greek language | 487.1 |
| | T6—87 |
| Mycenaean Linear B | 487.1 |
| | T6—87 |
| Mycetozoa | 579.52 |
| Mycobacteria | 579.374 |
| Mycobacterium infections | |
| incidence | 614.579 |
| medicine | 616.929 4 |
| *see also* Communicable | |
| diseases — humans | |
| Mycologists | 579.509 2 |
| Mycology | 579.5 |
| medicine | 616.969 01 |
| Mycoplasma infections | |
| incidence | 614.57 |
| medicine | 616.92 |
| *see also* Communicable | |
| diseases — humans | |
| Mycoplasmas | 579.328 |
| Mycoses | 571.995 |
| agriculture | 632.4 |
| animals | 571.995 11 |
| veterinary medicine | 636.089 696 9 |
| biology | 571.995 |
| humans | 362.196 969 |
| incidence | 614.559 |
| medicine | 616.969 |
| *see also* Communicable | |
| diseases — humans | |
| social services | 362.196 969 |
| plants | |
| plant crops | 632.4 |
| Mycota | 579.5 |
| Mycotoxins | |
| human toxicology | 615.952 95 |
| Mycrothyriales | 579.564 |
| Myctophiformes | 597.61 |
| Mydas flies | 595.773 |
| Myelin sheaths | |
| human cytology | 612.810 46 |
| human histology | 612.810 45 |
| Myene language | 496.396 |
| | T6—963 96 |
| Myers-Briggs personality | |
| inventory | 155.283 |
| Myers-Briggs typology | |
| personality theory | 155.264 4 |
| Mykolaïvs'ka oblast' | |
| (Ukraine) | T2—477 3 |
| Mykolayiv (Ukraine : | |
| Oblast) | T2—477 3 |

Mykonos Island (Greece)   T2—495 85
Mynas   598.863
  animal husbandry   636.68
Myocardial depressants
  pharmacokinetics   615.716
Myocardial diseases
  medicine   616.124
    *see also* Cardiovascular
      diseases — humans
Myocardial infarction
  medicine   616.123 7
    *see also* Cardiovascular
      diseases — humans
Myocardial ischemia
  medicine   616.123
    *see also* Cardiovascular
      diseases — humans
Myocarditis
  medicine   616.124
    *see also* Cardiovascular
      diseases — humans
Myocardium
  human anatomy   611.12
  human physiology   612.17
  medicine   616.124
Myodocopa   595.33
  paleozoology   565.33
Myomorpha   599.35
Myopia
  optometry   617.755
    *see also* Eye diseases —
      humans
Myoporaceae   583.95
Myositis
  medicine   616.743
    *see also* Musculoskeletal
      diseases — humans
Myotis   599.472
Myoxidae   599.359 6
Myriangiales   579.564
Myriapoda   595.6
  paleozoology   565.6
Myricales   583.43
Myristicaceae   583.22
Myrmecophagidae   599.314
Myrsinaceae   583.675
Myrtaceae   583.765
  edible fruits   641.344 2
    cooking   641.644 2
    food   641.344 2
    orchard crop   634.42
Myrtales   583.76
Myrtle wax   665.12

Myrtles   635.933 765
  botany   583.765
  floriculture   635.933 765
Myrtles (Oregon myrtle)   583.23
Myrtles (Wax myrtles)   583.43
Mysia (Turkey)   939.21
     T2—392 1
Mysidacea   595.375
Mysore (India : State)   T2—548 7
Mystacocarida   595.36
Mysteries
  occultism   135
  unexplained phenomena   001.94
Mystery films   791.436 556
Mystery games   793.93
  *see Manual at* 793.932 vs.
    794.822
Mystery plays (Religious)
  literature   808.825 16
    history and criticism   809.251 6
    specific literatures   T3B—205 16
      individual authors   T3A—2
  stage presentation   792.16
Mystery plays (Suspense)   792.27
  literature   808.825 27
    history and criticism   809.252 7
    specific literatures   T3B—205 27
      individual authors   T3A—2
  stage presentation   792.27
Mystery programs   791.446 556
  radio   791.446 556
  television   791.456 556
Mystery stories   808.838 72
  history and criticism   809.387 2
  specific literatures   T3B—308 72
    individual authors   T3A—3
Mystical body of Christ   262.77
Mystical Judaism   296.833
Mysticeti   599.5
  paleozoology   569.5
Mysticism   204.22
  Buddhism   294.344 22
  Christianity   248.22
  comparative religion   204.22
  Hinduism   294.542 2
  Islam   297.4
  Judaism   296.712
  philosophy   149.3
    medieval western   189.5
Myth   398.2
  arts   700.415
     T3C—15
  *see Manual at* T3C—37 vs.
    T3C—15

Myth (continued)
  literature — 808.801 5
    history and criticism — 809.915
    specific literatures — T3B—080 15
      history and
        criticism — T3B—091 5
  *see also* Mythology
Mythical animals — 398.245 4
  *see also* Legendary animals
Mythological interpretation
  Bible — 220.68
Mythologists — 201.309 2
Mythology — 398.2
  African religions — 299.611 3
  art representation — 704.947
  arts — 700.47
    T3C—37
    *see Manual at* T3C—37 vs.
      T3C—15
  Australian religion — 299.921 5
  Buddhism — 294.333
  Celtic religion — 299.161 13
  Chinese religions — 299.511 13
  Christianity — 230
  classical religion — 292.13
  folklore — 398.2
  Germanic religion — 293.13
  Greek religion — 292.13
  Hawaiian religion — 299.924 201 3
  Hinduism — 294.513
  literature — 808.803 7
    history and criticism — 809.933 7
    specific literatures — T3B—080 37
      history and
        criticism — T3B—093 7
  Native American religions — 299.711 3
    North American — 299.711 3
    South American — 299.811 3
  Norse religion — 293.13
  paintings — 753.7
  Polynesian religion — 299.924 013
  religion — 201.3
    sources — 208
  Roman religion — 292.13
  Scandinavian religion — 293.13
  Semitic religions — 299.2
  Shinto — 299.561 13
  *see Manual at* 398.2 vs. 201.3,
    230, 270, 292–299
Myxedema
  medicine — 616.858 848
Myxobacteria — 579.32
Myxogastromycetidae — 579.52
Myxomycetes — 579.52

Myxomycophyta — 579.52
Myxomycota — 579.52
Myxomycotina — 579.52
Myxophaga — 595.762
Myzostomida — 592.62

# N

NA (Swiss political party) — 324.249 403
Na-Dene languages — 497.2
  T6—972
Naâma (Algeria : Province) — T2—657
Naan — 641.815
Nablus district (West Bank) — T2—569 53
Nacogdoches County (Tex.) — T2—764 182
Nador (Morocco : Province) — T2—643 3
Naga languages — 495.4
  T6—954
Nāgāland (India) — T2—541 65
Nagano-ken (Japan) — T2—521 63
Nagar Haveli (India) — T2—547 6
Nagasaki-ken (Japan) — T2—522 4
Nagasaki-shi (Japan) — T2—522 44
Nagorno-Karabakh
  (Azerbaijan) — T2—475 4
Nagoya-shi (Japan) — T2—521 674
Naguib, Mohammed
  Egyptian history — 962.053
Nahanni National Park
  (N.W.T.) — T2—719 3
Nahatlatch River (B.C.) — T2—711 37
Nahr an Nīl (Sudan) — T2—625
Nahuas — T5—974 52
Nahuatl language — 497.452
  T6—974 52
Nahuatl literature — 897.452
Nahum (Biblical book) — 224.94
Naiads (Plants) — 584.74
Nail-care tools
  manufacturing technology — 688.5
Nail diseases
  humans
    geriatrics — 618.976 547
    incidence — 614.595 47
    medicine — 616.547
    *see also* Skin diseases —
      humans
    pediatrics — 618.925 47
    pharmacokinetics — 615.779
    surgery — 617.477
Nails (Body parts) — 599.814 7
  animal physiology — 573.59
  descriptive zoology — 599.814 7
  human anatomy — 611.78

Nails (Body parts) (continued)
  human physiology — 612.799
  medicine — 616.547
  personal care — 646.727
  surgery — 617.477
  *see also* Skin
Nails (Fasteners) — 621.884
  arts — 739.48
Nairn (Scotland : District) — T2—411 58
Nairobi (Kenya) — T2—676 25
Nais — 788.37
  *see also* Woodwind instruments
Naja — 597.964 2
Najadales — 584.74
Najaf (Iraq : Province) — T2—567 5
Najd (Saudi Arabia) — T2—538
Najib Tun Razak, Datuk
  Malaysian history — 959.506 2
Nakers — 786.93
  *see also* Percussion instruments
Nakh languages — 499.964 1
  — T6—999 641
Nakhichevan (Azerbaijan) — T2—475 4
Nakho-Daghestan languages — 499.964
  — T6—999 64
Nam Định (Vietnam :
  Province) — T2—597 3
Nama language — 496.1
  — T6—961
Namakgale (South Africa :
  District) — T2—682 59
Namaqualand (South
  Africa) — T2—687 19
Nambiquaran languages — 498.4
  — T6—984
Namboku period — 952.022
Name cards
  prints — 769.5
Names — 929.97
  cataloging — 025.322
  customs — 392.12
  divination — 133.33
  etymology — 412
    specific languages — T4—2
  geographic — 910.014
    gazetters — 910.3
  personal — 929.4
    law — 346.012
Names of God
  Islam — 297.211 2
  Judaism — 296.311 2
Namibe Province (Angola) — T2—673 5
Namibia — 968.81
  — T2—688 1

Namibians — T5—968 81
Naming ceremonies
  Judaism — 296.443
Nampula (Mozambique) — T2—679 7
Namur (Belgium : Province) — T2—493 44
Nanai (Asian people) — T5—941
Nanai language — 494.1
  — T6—941
Nanaimo (B.C. : Regional
  District) — T2—711 2
Nance County (Neb.) — T2—782 425
Nancy (France) — T2—443 823
Nande (Zairian people) — T5—963 94
Nande languages — 496.394
  — T6—963 94
Nandi (East African people) — T5—965
Nandi (Zairian people) — T5—963 94
Nandi language (Bantu) — 496.394
  — T6—963 94
Nandi languages (Nilotic) — 496.5
  — T6—965
Nanggroe Aceh Darussalam
  (Indonesia) — T2—598 11
Nangklao, King of Siam
  Thai history — 959.303 3
Nanjing (Jiang Sheng,
  China) — T2—511 36
Nanking (China) — T2—511 36
Nannofossils — 561.9
Nanoporous materials
  materials science — 620.116
Nanostructured materials
  materials science — 620.115
Nanotechnology — 620.5
Nantes (France) — T2—441 675
Nantucket County (Mass.) — T2—744 97
Nantucket Island (Mass.) — T2—744 97
Nantucket Sound (Mass.) — 551.461 346
  — T2—163 46
Napa County (Calif.) — T2—794 19
Naphthalenes — 547.615
  chemical engineering — 661.816
Naphthas — 665.538 24
Naphuno (South Africa :
  District) — T2—682 59
Napier City (N.Z.) — T2—934 67
Napkin folding — 642.79
Napkins — 642.7
  arts — 746.96
  home sewing — 646.21
  table setting — 642.7
Naples (Italy) — T2—457 31
  ancient — T2—377 251

Naples (Italy : Province)   T2—457 3
  ancient   T2—377 25
Naples (Kingdom)   945.7
Napo (Ecuador : Province)   T2—866 416
Napoleon I, Emperor of the
  French
  French history   944.05
Napoleon III, Emperor of the
  French
  French history   944.07
Napoleonic Wars   940.27
Napoli (Italy)   T2—457 31
  ancient   T2—377 251
Napoli (Italy : Province)   T2—457 3
  ancient   T2—377 25
Nappes (Geology)   551.872
Naqara   786.93
  *see also* Percussion instruments
Naqshabandiyah   297.48
Nara-ken (Japan)   T2—521 84
Narasimha Rao, P. V.
  Indian history   954.052
Narbonensis   T2—364 8
Narcissistic personality disorder
  medicine   616.858 54
  *see also* Mental disorders
Narcissus   635.934 34
  botany   584.34
  floriculture   635.934 34
Narcolepsy
  medicine   616.849 8
  *see also* Nervous system
    diseases — humans
Narcotic antagonists
  pharmacokinetics   615.782 2
Narcotics   362.29
  customs   394.14
  ethics   178.8
  *see also* Ethical problems
  pharmacokinetics   615.782 2
  smuggling   364.133 65
  law   345.023 365
  *see also* Drug traffic; Substance
    abuse
Narcotics abuse   362.293
  medicine   616.863 2
  personal health   613.83
  social welfare   362.293
  *see also* Substance abuse
Narcotics agents   363.45
Narcotics traffic   363.45
  *see also* Drug traffic
Nardeae   584.9
Nariño (Colombia : Dept.)   T2—861 58

Närke landskap (Sweden)   T2—487 6
Narooma (N.S.W.)   T2—944 7
Narragansett Bay (R.I.)   551.461 346
     T2—163 46
Narragansett Indians   T5—973 44
Narragansett language   497.344
     T6—973 44
Narration
  literature   808.802 3
    history and criticism   809.923
    specific literatures   T3B— 080 23
    history and
      criticism   T3B—092 3
  rhetoric   808.036
Narrative
  literature   808.802 3
    history and criticism   809.923
    specific literatures   T3B—080 23
    history and
      criticism   T3B—092 3
Narrative poetry   808.813
  history and criticism   809.13
  specific literatures   T3B—103
  individual authors   T3A—1
Narrogin (W.A. : Shire)   T2—941 2
Narrow-gage railroads   385.52
Narwhal   599.543
Nasā'ī, Aḥmad ibn Shu'ayb
  Hadith   297.125 53
Nasal sinus diseases
  medicine   616.212
  *see also* Respiratory tract
    diseases — humans
Nasal sinuses   573.26
  biology   573.26
  human anatomy   611.21
  human physiology   612.232
  medicine   616.212
  *see also* Respiratory system
Nash County (N.C.)   T2—756 47
Nashim   296.123 3
  Babylonian Talmud   296.125 3
  Mishnah   296.123 3
  Palestinian Talmud   296.124 3
Nashville (Tenn.)   T2—768 55
Nāsikh wa-al-mansūkh
  Hadith   297.125 163
Naskapi Indians   T5—973 2
Naskapi language   497.32
     T6—973 2
Nasopharynx
  human anatomy   611.32
  human physiology   612.31
  medicine   616.21

Nasopharynx diseases
  medicine       616.21
   *see also* Respiratory tract
    diseases — humans
Nass River (B.C.)   T2—711 85
Nassarawa State (Nigeria)   T2—669 53
Nassau (Bahamas)   T2—729 6
Nassau County (Fla.)   T2— 759 11
Nassau County (N.Y.)   T2—747 245
Nasser, Gamal Abdel
  Egyptian history   962.053
Nasser, Lake (Egypt and
  Sudan)   T2—623
Nasturtiums (Brassicaceae)   583.64
Nasturtiums (Tropaeolaceae)   635.933 79
  botany   583.79
  floriculture   635.933 79
Natal (South Africa)   968.405
        T2—684
Natal Drakensberg Park
  (South Africa)   T2—684 7
Natalia   968.404 2
Natantia   595.388
Natchez (Miss.)   T2—762 26
Natchez Indians   T5—979
Natchitoches Parish (La.)   T2—763 65
Nathalia (Vic.)   T2—945 4
Nation of Islam   297.87
  political science   320.558
Nation River (B.C.)   T2—711 82
Nation-states   321.05
National Action for People and
  Homeland (Swiss political
  party)   324.249 403
National advertising   659.131 2
National Alliance (Italian
  political party)   324.245 04
National Alliance of
  Independents (Swiss political
  party)   324.249 408
National anthems   782.421 599
National bankruptcy   336.368
National banks   332.122 3
National Baptist Convention of
  America   286.134
  *see also* Baptists
National Baptist Convention of
  the United States of America   286.133
  *see also* Baptists
National bibliographies   015
National borrowing   336.343 3
  *see also* National debt
National Botanic Gardens of
  South Africa   T2—687 355

National Capital (Papua
  New Guinea)   T2—954 5
National Capital Region
  (Ont. and Quebec)   T2—713 84
  Ontario   T2—713 84
  Quebec   T2—714 221
National cemeteries   363.75
  landscape architecture   718.8
National characteristics   305.8
  psychology   155.89
National conferences of bishops   262.12
National Council of the Churches
  of Christ in the United States
  of America   277.308 206
National Country Party
  (Australia)   324.294 04
National dances   793.31
National debt   336.343 3
  law   343.037
  macroeconomic policy   339.523
  public administration   352.45
  public finance   336.343 3
National Democratic Party
  (Austria)   324.243 603 8
National Democratic Party of
  Germany   324.243 03
National Fascist Party (Italy)   324.245 023 8
National flags   929.92
National forests   333.75
  *see also* Forest lands
National Front (Colombia)   986.106 33
National groups   305.8
        T1—089
  literature   808.898
   *see Manual at* T3C—93–99,
    T3C—9174 vs. T3C—8
  *see also* Ethnic groups
National guards   355.37
National health insurance   368.42
  law   344.022
National Hunt racing   798.45
National income   339.32
  distribution   339.2
National income theory of wages   331.210 1
National Liberation Front of
  South Viet Nam   959.704 332 2
National-local relations   320.404 9
  law   342.042
  public administration   353.334
National Merit Scholarship
  Qualifying Test   378.166 2
National minorities   305.8
  *see also* Ethnic groups

National parks 363.68
  conservation of natural
    resources 333.72
  *see also* Parks
  *see Manual at* 333.7–.9 vs. 508,
    913–919, 930–990
National Party of Australia 324.294 04
National Performance Review
  (United States) 352.3
National planning
  civic art 711.2
  economics 338.9
National product
  (Macroeconomics) 339.31
National-provincial relations 320.404 9
  law 342.042
  public administration 353.333
National psychology 155.89
  *see Manual at* 155.89 vs.
    155.84
National Republican Party (U.S.) 324.273 23
National resources
  conservation 339.49
National security 355.03
  law 343.01
    police powers 342.041 8
  public administration 353.1
National security councils 353.122 4
National self-determination 320.15
National service (Selective
  service) 355.223 63
  law 343.012 2
National Service Life Insurance 368.364
National socialism 335.6
  economics 335.6
  political ideology 320.533
National Socialist German Labor
  Party (Austria) 324.243 602 38
National Socialist German Labor
  Party (Germany) 324.243 023 8
National Socialist Labor Party
  (Austria) 324.243 602 38
National Socialist White People's
  Party (U.S.) 324.273 38
National Society of the Colonial
  Dames of America 369.12
National songs 782.421 599
National-state relations 320.404 9
  law 342.042
  public administration 353.333
National states 321.05
National states (South Africa) 968.29
      T2—682 9

National taxation 336.201 2
  law 343.043
  public finance 336.201 2
National territory 320.12
  law of nations 341.42
National unions 331.872
  *see also* Labor unions
National universities 378.05
  *see also* Higher education
National wealth 339.3
  conservation 339.49
Nationaldemokratische Partei
  (Austrian) 324.243 603 8
Nationaldemokratische Partei
  Deutschlands 324.243 03
Nationale Aktion für Volk und
  Heimat (Swiss political party) 324.249 403
Nationalism 320.54
  arts 700.458 1
      T3C—358 1
  folklore 398.278 1
    history and criticism 398.358 1
  literature 808.803 581
    history and criticism 809.933 581
    specific literatures T3B—080 358 1
    history and
      criticism T3B—093 581
  music 780.903 4
  social theology 201.72
    Christianity 261.7
Nationalist China T2—512 49
Nationalist parties 324.218 3
  international organizations 324.183
Nationality (Citizenship) 323.6
  *see also* Citizenship
Nationality clubs 369.2
Nationalization of alien property
  law 343.025 2
Nationalization of industry 338.924
  law 343.07
Nationalization of property 333.14
  land economics 333.14
  law 343.025 2
Nationals, The (Australian
  political party) 324.294 04
Nationalsozialistische
  Arbeiterpartei (Austria) 324.243 602 38
Nationalsozialistische Deutsche
  Arbeiter-Partei (Austria) 324.243 602 38
Nationalsozialistische Deutsche
  Arbeiter-Partei (Germany) 324.243 023 8

Native American languages 497
T6—97
  South America 498
T6—98
Native American literatures 897
  South America 898
Native American peoples T5—97
  South America T5—98
  *see also* American native
    peoples
Native American religions 299.7
  North America 299.7
  South America 299.8
Native elements 549.2
  *see also* Chemicals
Native metals 549.23
  *see also* Metals
Native peoples 305.8
  legal status 346.013
    constitutional law 342.087 2
    private law 346.013
  *see also* Indigenous peoples
Native plants
  floriculture 635.951
  resource economics 333.953 3
Nativism 149.7
Nativity of Jesus Christ 232.92
NATO (Alliance) 355.031 091 821
  law 341.72
Natrona County (Wyo.) T2—787 93
Natuna Islands (Indonesia) T2—598 192
Natural areas 333.951 6
  biological resource
    conservation 333.951 6
  land conservation 333.731 6
  wildlife conservation 333.954 16
  *see also* Wildlife reserves
Natural childbirth
  obstetrics 618.45
Natural communities 577.82
Natural dyes
  technology 667.26
Natural environments
  health 613.1
Natural family planning
  health 613.943 4
  medicine 618.184
  *see also* Birth control
Natural foods 641.302
Natural gas 553.285
  economic geology 553.285
  extraction 622.338 5
  extractive economics 338.272 85
    law 343.077 2

Natural gas (continued)
  pipeline transportation 388.56
    engineering 665.744
    law 343.093 96
  prospecting 622.182 85
  public administration 354.46
  public utilities 363.63
    law 343.092 6
  resource economics 333.823 3
    law 346.046 823 3
  technology 665.7
    economics 338.476 657
  *see also* Petroleum
Natural gas vehicles 388.34
  engineering 629.220 43
  repair 629.287 043
  transportation services 388.34
  *see also* Automotive vehicles
Natural history 508
  animals 590
  biology 578
  microorganisms 579
  plants 580
  *see Manual at* 578 vs. 304.2,
    508, 910; *also at* 579–590
    vs. 571–575
Natural landscapes
  landscape architecture 719
Natural language indexing
  subject cataloging 025.48
Natural language processing
  computer science 006.35
Natural law
  ethical systems 171.2
    Christianity 241.2
  law 340.112
Natural leather 675.2
Natural magnets 538.4
Natural monuments
  landscape architecture 719.32
Natural numbers 513.2
  number theory 512.72
Natural phenomena 508
  *see also* Nature
Natural radioactivity 539.752
Natural religion 210
Natural resource management 333.7
  *see Manual at* 333.7–.9 vs.
    363.1, 363.73, 577
Natural resources 333.7
  conservation 333.72
  *see Manual at* 333.72 vs.
    304.28, 320.58, 363.7

Natural resources (continued)
  economics 333.7
    *see Manual at* 333.73–.78 vs.
      333, 333.1–.5
  ethics 178
    religion 205.68
      Christianity 241.68
    *see also* Ethical problems
  law 346.044
  law of nations 341.4
  public administration 354.3
  restoration 333.715 3
  social theology 201.77
    Christianity 261.88
  *see Manual at* 333.7–.9 vs.
    363.1, 363.73, 577; *also at*
    333.7–.9 vs. 363.6
Natural rights 323.01
  law 340.112
Natural sciences 500
  *see also* Science
Natural selection 576.82
Natural stone 553.5
  *see also* Stone
Natural theology 210
Naturalism 146
  ethics 171.2
  fine arts 709.034 3
  literature 808.801 2
    history and criticism 809.912
    specific literatures T3B—080 12
      history and
        criticism T3B—091 2
  painting 759.053
Naturalists 508.092
Naturalization 323.623
  law 342.083
  public administration 353.484
Naturalized species 333.952 3
Nature 508
  art representation 704.943
  arts 700.46
      T3C—36
  Christian doctrine 231.7
  folklore 398.24
    history and criticism 398.36
    living 398.24
    nonliving 398.26
  literature 808.803 6
    history and criticism 809.933 6
    specific literatures T3B—080 36
      history and
        criticism T3B—093 6
  painting 758

Nature (continued)
  philosophy 113
  primary education 372.357
  religious worship 202.12
  respect for
    ethics 179.1
      religion 205.691
        Christianity 241.691
    *see also* Ethical problems
Nature reserves
  biological resource
    conservation 333.951 6
Nature study
  primary education 372.357
Nature versus nurture
  psychology
    evolutionary psychology 155.7
    individual psychology 155.234
Natures of Jesus Christ 232.8
Naturopathy
  therapeutic system 615.535
Naujaat (Nunavut) T2—719 58
Nauru 996.85
      T2—968 5
Nautical almanacs 528
Nautical charts 623.892 2
Nautical engineering 623.8
Nautical engineers 623.809 2
Nautical facilities 387.15
  *see also* Port facilities
Nautical health 613.68
Nautical instruments 623.863
Nautiloidea 594.52
  paleozoology 564.52
Navajo County (Ariz.) T2—791 35
Navajo Indians T5—972 6
Navajo language 497.26
      T6—972 6
Navajo literature 897.26
Navajo rugs
  arts 746.72
Naval air forces 359.94
Naval aircraft 359.948 34
  military engineering 623.746
  naval equipment 359.948 34
Naval architecture 623.81
Naval artillery 359.981 282
  engineering 623.418
  naval equipment 359.981 282
Naval artillery services 359.981 2
Naval aviation 359.94

Naval bases
  military engineering 623.64
  World War I 940.453
  World War II 940.545 3
Naval cooking 641.575 3
Naval defense 359.03
Naval design 623.81
Naval disarmament 327.174 3
Naval engineering 623.8
Naval engineers 623.809 2
Naval forces 359
  Confederate States of America 973.757
  United States
    Civil War (United States) 973.758
Naval gunnery 623.553
Naval health 613.68
Naval maneuvers 359.4
  training 359.52
  *see also* Naval operations
Naval medicine 616.980 24
Naval officers 359.009 2
  role and function 359.332
Naval operations 359.4
  Algerian Revolution 965.046 45
  American Revolution 973.35
  Civil War (England) 942.062 45
  Civil War (Spain) 946.081 45
  Civil War (United States) 973.75
  Crimean War 947.073 845
  Falkland Islands War 997.110 244 5
  Hundred Years' War 944.025 45
  Indo-Pakistan War, 1971 954.920 514 5
  Indochinese War 959.704 145
  Iraq War, 2003– 956.704 434 5
  Iraqi-Iranian Conflict 955.054 245
  Korean War 951.904 245
  Napoleonic Wars 940.274 5
  Persian Gulf War, 1991 956.704 424 5
  Spanish-American War 973.895
  Thirty Years' War 940.244 5
  Vietnamese War 959.704 345
  War of 1812 973.525
  World War I 940.45
  World War II 940.545
Naval ordnance 359.8
  engineering 623.825 1
  naval equipment 359.8
Naval personnel 359.009 2
Naval reserves 359.37
Naval schools (Secondary
  education) 373.243
  *see also* Secondary education
Naval stores 665.33
Naval warfare 359

Naval weapons 359.8
  engineering 623.8
  naval equipment 359.8
Navarra (Spain) T2—465 2
Navarro County (Tex.) T2—764 282
Naves 726.592
Navigable waters
  land economics 333.915
Navigation 629.045
  air transportation 629.132 51
    law 343.097 6
  animal physiology 573.87
  aquatic sports 797.1
  engineering 629.045
  maritime transportation 623.89
    law 343.096 6
  space flight 629.453
Navigation Acts
  United States history 973.311 2
Navigation aids 387.155
  marine navigation 623.893
  transportation services 387.155
Navigation instrumentation
  aircraft engineering 629.135 1
Navigation systems
  spacecraft 629.474 2
  unmanned spacecraft 629.464 2
Navigators 629.045 092
Navy beans 641.356 52
  *see also* Kidney beans
Navy life 359.1
Naxi T5—954
Naxi language 495.4
    T6—954
Naxos Island (Greece) T2—495 85
  ancient T2—391 5
Nayarit (Mexico) T2—723 4
Nāys 788.35
  *see also* Woodwind instruments
Nazi government 321.94
Nazi parties
  after 1945 324.213 8
Nazi Party (Germany) 324.243 023 8
Nazir 296.123 3
  Babylonian Talmud 296.125 3
  Mishnah 296.123 3
  Palestinian Talmud 296.124 3
Nazism 335.6
  economics 335.6
  political ideology 320.533
Nazko River (B.C.) T2—711 75
Ndebele (South Africa) T2—682 75
Ndebele (South African
  people) T5—963 989

Ndebele (Zimbabwean
  people)          T5—963 98
Ndebele language (South Africa)  496.398 9
                  T6—963 989
Ndebele language (Zimbabwe)    496.398
                  T6—963 98
Ndebele literature (South Africa)  896.398 9
Ndembu (African people)      T5—963 93
Ndonga languages           496.399
                  T6—963 99
NDP (Austrian political party)   324.243 603 8
Ndumu Game Reserve
  (South Africa)        T2—684 3
Ndwanwe (Kingdom)      968.403 8
                  T2—684
Ndwedwe (South Africa :
  District)          T2—684 4
Neagh, Lough (Northern
  Ireland)         T2—416
Neamț (Romania)       T2—498 1
Neanderthals          569.986
Neapolis (Italy)        T2—377 251
Near-death experience
  occultism         133.901 3
Near drowning
  medicine         617.18
Near East          956
              T2—56
  ancient         939.4
              T2—394
Near-space exploration
  unmanned      629.435 2
Nearshore biology      578.778
Nearshore ecology      577.78
Neath (Wales : District)   T2—429 85
Neath Port Talbot (Wales)  T2—429 85
Neat's-foot oil        665.2
Nebaliacea         595.379 2
Nebiim           224
Nebo (South Africa :
  District)         T2—682 55
Nebraska          978.2
              T2—782
Nebraska Panhandle    T2—782 9
Nebuchadnezzar II, King of
  Babylonia
    Mesopotamian history   935.04
Necessity
  philosophy        123.7
Nechako Plateau (B.C.)   T2—711 82
Nechako Reservoir (B.C.)  T2—711 82
Nechako River (B.C.)    T2—711 82
Neches River (Tex.)     T2—764 15

Neck
  fractures
    medicine         617.151
    human anatomy    611.93
    human physiology   612.93
    regional medicine   617.53
    surgery         617.530 59
Neck muscles
  human anatomy      611.733
Neckar-Odenwald-Kreis
  (Germany : Landkreis)  T2—434 645
Neckar River (Germany)  T2—434 645
Necklaces          391.7
  customs         391.7
  making          739.278
    costume jewelry    688.2
      handicrafts      745.594 2
    fine jewelry       739.278
Necks (Geology)       551.88
Neckwear          391.41
  *see also* Accessories (Clothing)
Necrologies         920
Necromancy         133.9
Necropneumonia
  medicine         616.245
  *see also* Respiratory tract
      diseases — humans
Necrotizing fasciitis
  incidence        614.579 8
  medicine         616.929 8
  *see also* Communicable
      diseases — humans
Necrotizing ulcerative gingivitis
  medicine         616.312
  *see also* Digestive system
      diseases — humans
Nectarines         641.342 57
  cooking         641.642 57
  food           641.342 57
  orchard crop      634.257
Nectria          579.567 7
Nedarim          296.123 3
  Babylonian Talmud   296.125 3
  Mishnah         296.123 3
  Palestinian Talmud   296.124 3
Nederlandsche Oost-Indische
  Compagnie
    Indonesian history    959.802 1
Needlefishes        597.66
Needlepoint         746.442
Needlepoint laces     677.653
  arts           746.224
  manufacturing technology  677.653

Needles
  home sewing   646.19
Needlestick injuries
  medicine   617.143
Needlework
  primary education   372.54
  textile arts   746.4
Ñeembucú (Paraguay :
  Dept.)   T2—892 124
Nefertiti, Queen of Egypt
  Egyptian history   932.014
Nega'im   296.123 6
Negation
  philosophical logic   160
Negative income tax   362.582
  law   344.032 582
Negatives (Photography)   771.43
  distribution   771.48
  manipulation   771.43
  organization   771.48
  preparation   771.43
  preservation   771.45
  storage   771.45
Negeri Sembilan   T2—595 1
Negev (Israel)   T2—569 49
Neglected children
  social welfare   362.76
  *see also* Child abuse
Negligence (Law)   346.032
Negotiable instruments   332.76
  law   346.096
Negotiable order of withdrawal
  accounts   332.175 22
Negotiation   302.3
  collective bargaining   331.891 2
  executive management   658.405 2
  psychology   158.5
  social psychology   302.3
Negro Methodist churches   287.8
  *see also* Methodist Church
Negros Island (Philippines)   T2—599 5
Negros Occidental
  (Philippines)   T2—599 5
Negros Oriental
  (Philippines)   T2—599 5
Nehemiah (Biblical book)   222.8
Nehru, Jawaharlal
  Indian history   954.042
Nei Monggol Zizhiqu
  (China)   T2—517 7
Neighborhood centers
  recreation centers   790.068
Neighborhoods   307.336 2

Neighbors
  applied psychology   158.25
  psychological influence   155.925
Neisseria   579.33
Nejd (Saudi Arabia)   T2—538
Nelson (B.C.)   T2—711 62
Nelson and Hay National
  Park (W.A.)   T2—941 2
Nelson City (N.Z.)   T2—937 6
Nelson County (Ky.)   T2—769 495
Nelson County (N.D.)   T2—784 35
Nelson County (Va.)   T2—755 493
Nelson Lakes National Park
  (N.Z.)   T2—937 4
Nelson Mandela Bay
  Municipality (South
  Africa)   T2—687 52
Nelson-Marlborough
  Region (N.Z.)   T2—937 5
Nelson River (Man.)   T2—712 71
Nelspruit (South Africa :
  District)   T2—682 73
Nelumbonales   583.3
Nemaha County (Kan.)   T2—781 332
Nemaha County (Neb.)   T2—782 278
Nemata   592.57
Nemathelminthes   592.5
Nematocera   595.772
Nematoda   592.57
  agricultural pests   632.625 7
  paleozoology   562.57
Nematode infections   571.999
  agriculture   632.625 7
  animals   571.999
    veterinary medicine   636.089 696 5
  humans
    incidence   614.555
    medicine   616.965
  plants   571.999
    agriculture   632.625 7
  *see also* Communicable
    diseases
Nematomorpha   592.59
Nemertea   592.32
  paleozoology   562.32
Nemertina   592.32
Nene, River (England)   T2—425 5
Nenets Autonomous District
  (Russia)   T2—471 1
Nenets language   494.4
    T6—944
Nenetskiĭ avtonomnyĭ okrug
  (Russia)   T2—471 1
Neo-Aristotelianism   149.91

| | |
|---|---|
| Neo-Babylonian Empire | 935.04 |
| | T2—35 |
| Neo-Confucianism | 181.112 |
| Neo-impressionism | 709.034 5 |
| painting | 759.055 |
| Neo-Kantianism | 142.3 |
| Neo-Nazi parties | 324.213 8 |
| Neo-Nazism | 335.6 |
| economics | 335.6 |
| political ideology | 320.533 |
| Neo-Persian Empire | 935.07 |
| | T2—35 |
| Neo-scholasticism | 149.91 |
| Neo-Thomism | 149.91 |
| Neobehaviorism | 150.194 34 |
| Neocene period | 551.786 |
| geology | 551.786 |
| paleontology | 560.178 6 |
| Neoclassical architecture | 724.2 |
| Neoclassical economics | 330.157 |
| Neoclassical school (Economics) | 330.157 |
| Neoclassicism | |
| music | 780.904 |
| painting | 759.051 |
| Neodymium | |
| chemistry | 546.413 |
| Neofascist parties | 324.213 8 |
| Neofiber | 599.357 9 |
| Neogastropoda | 594.32 |
| Neogene period | 551.786 |
| geology | 551.786 |
| paleontology | 560.178 6 |
| Neolithic Age | 930.14 |
| Neon | |
| chemistry | 546.752 |
| gas technology | 665.822 |
| Neon lighting | 621.327 5 |
| Neonatal development | |
| humans | 612.652 |
| Neonatal medicine | 618.920 1 |
| Neonates | |
| pediatrics | 618.920 1 |
| Neonatology | 618.920 1 |
| Neopaganism | 299.94 |
| Neoplasms | 571.978 |
| humans | |
| incidence | 614.599 9 |
| medicine | 616.994 |
| *see also* Cancer | |
| Neoplastic diseases | |
| incidence | 614.599 9 |
| medicine | 616.994 |
| *see also* Cancer — humans | |

| | |
|---|---|
| Neoplasticism | 709.040 52 |
| painting | 759.065 2 |
| sculpture | 735.230 452 |
| Neoplatonism | 186.4 |
| ancient | 186.4 |
| Christian polemics | 239.4 |
| modern | 141.2 |
| Neopsychoanalytic systems | 150.195 7 |
| Neorealism | |
| philosophy | 149.2 |
| Neornithes | 598 |
| paleozoology | 568 |
| Neosho County (Kan.) | T2—781 95 |
| Neotoma | 599.357 3 |
| Neotropical fruit bats | 599.45 |
| Nepal | 954.96 |
| | T2—549 6 |
| Nepalese | T5—914 95 |
| Nepali | T5—914 95 |
| Nepali language | 491.495 |
| | T6—914 95 |
| Nepali literature | 891.495 |
| Nepean River (N.S.W.) | T2—944 6 |
| Nepenthales | 583.75 |
| Nephews | 306.87 |
| | T1—085 |
| Nephrite | 553.876 |
| *see also* Jade | |
| Nephritis | |
| medicine | 616.612 |
| *see also* Urologic diseases — | |
| humans | |
| Nephrology | 616.61 |
| Neptune (Planet) | 523.48 |
| | T2—992 8 |
| astrology | 133.539 1 |
| Neptunium | 546.432 |
| *see also* Chemicals | |
| Nerve compression syndromes | |
| medicine | 616.856 |
| *see also* Nervous system | |
| diseases — humans | |
| Nerve fibers | 573.85 |
| human physiology | 612.81 |
| Nerve tissues | 573.85 |
| human histology | 612.810 45 |
| *see also* Nervous system | |
| Nerves | 573.85 |
| biology | 573.85 |
| human anatomy | 611.83 |
| human biochemistry | 612.814 |
| human biophysics | 612.813 |
| human physiology | 612.81 |
| medicine | 616.856 |

Nerves (continued)
  surgery   617.483
  *see also* Nervous system
Nervous system   573.8
  anesthesiology   617.967 48
  biology   573.8
  diseases   573.839
    *see also* Nervous system
      diseases
  human anatomy   611.8
  human biophysics   612.804 3
  human histology   612.8
  human physiology   612.8
  medicine   616.8
  pediatrics   618.928
  perinatal medicine   618.326 8
  pharmacokinetics   615.78
  pregnancy complications
    obstetrics   618.368
  surgery   617.48
  *see also* Innervation
Nervous system diseases   573.839
  animals   573.839
    veterinary medicine   636.089 68
    veterinary pharmacokinetics   636.089 578
  humans   362.196 8
    anesthesiology   617.967 48
    cancer   362.196 994 8
      incidence   614.599 948
      medicine   616.994 8
      social services   362.196 994 8
      *see also* Cancer — humans
    geriatrics   618.976 8
    incidence   614.598
    medicine   616.8
    social services   362.196 8
    surgery   617.481
    symptoms   616.84
Neshoba County (Miss.)   T2—762 685
Nesosilicates
  mineralogy   549.62
Ness, Loch (Scotland)   T2—411 56
Ness County (Kan.)   T2—781 46
Nesting   591.564
Nestorian churches   281.8
  *see also* Eastern churches
Nests   591.564
Net national product   339.32
Net-winged beetles   595.764 4
Net worth
  personal finance   332.024 01
Netball   796.324
Netball players   796.324 092

Netbook computers   004.16
  *see also* Personal computers
Netherlanders   T5—393 1
Netherlandish languages   439.3
      T6—393
Netherlandish literatures   839.3
Netherlandish peoples   T5—393
Netherlands   949.2
      T2—492
  ancient   936.92
      T2—369 2
Netherlands Antilles   T2—729 86
Netherlands New Guinea   T2—951
Neto, António Agostinho
  Angolan history   967.304 1
Nets (Devices)
  fishing   639.202 84
    sports   799.13
  hunting
    sports   799.202 82
Nets (Mathematics)
  topology   514.223
Nets (Surveying)   526.33
Netsukes   736.68
Netted fabrics   677.664
  *see also* Textiles
Netting
  arts   746.422 4
Nettles   583.45
Network affiliates
  television   384.550 65
Network analysis
  management   658.403 2
  telephony   621.385 1
Network architecture
  communications engineering   621.382 15
  computer science   004.65
Network databases
  computer science   005.754
Network operating systems   005.447 6
Network programs   791.443
  radio performances   791.443
  television performances   791.453
Network protocols
  communications engineering   621.382 12
  computer science   004.62
Network theory   003.72
Network topology
  communications engineering   621.382 15
  computer science   004.65
Networks (Communications)   384.540 65
  enterprises   384.540 65
  facilities   384.545 5
  performing arts   791.44

Networks (Electrical)   621.319 2
Networks (Systems)   003.72
Neubrandenburg (Germany)   T2—431 72
Neubrandenburg
  (Germany : Bezirk)   T2—431 72
Neuchâtel (Switzerland)   T2—494 384 4
Neuchâtel (Switzerland :
  Canton)   T2—494 38
Neuchâtel (Switzerland :
  District)   T2—494 384
Neuchâtel, Lake of
  (Switzerland)   T2—494 384
Neuenburg (Switzerland)   T2—494 384 4
Neuenburg (Switzerland :
  Bezirk)   T2—494 384
Neuenburg (Switzerland :
  Canton)   T2—494 38
Neuenburger See
  (Switzerland)   T2—494 384
Neufchâtel cheese   641.373 53
  cooking   641.673 53
  food   641.373 53
  processing   637.353
Neumann function   515.53
Neumes   780.148
Neuquén (Argentina :
  Province)   T2—827 2
Neural computers   006.32
Neural nets (Computer science)   006.32
Neural networks (Computer
  science)   006.32
Neuralgias
  medicine   616.856
  *see also* Nervous system
    diseases — humans
Neurasthenia
  medicine   616.852 8
  *see also* Mental disorders
Neurilemma
  human cytology   612.810 46
Neuritis
  medicine   616.856
  *see also* Nervous system
    diseases — humans
Neuroanatomy   573.833
  humans   611.8
Neurobiology   573.8
  humans   612.8
Neuroblastoma
  pediatrics   618.929 948
Neurochemistry   573.84
  human physiology   612.804 2

Neurofibromatosis
  incidence   614.599 9
  medicine   616.993 83
Neuroglia
  human cytology   612.810 46
Neurolinguistics
  disorders
    medicine   616.855
  human physiology   612.823 36
Neurological diseases   573.839
  *see also* Nervous system
    diseases
Neurological language disorders
  medicine   616.855 2
  *see also* Communication
    disorders
Neurological nursing   616.804 231
Neurology
  medicine   616.8
Neuromuscular diseases
  medicine   616.744
  *see also* Musculoskeletal
    diseases — humans
Neuronal ceroid-lipofuscinosis
  medicine   616.83
  *see also* Nervous system
    diseases — humans
Neurons   573.853 6
  human cytology   612.810 46
  *see also* Nervous system
Neuropharmacology   615.78
Neurophysics
  human physiology   612.804 3
Neurophysiology   573.8
  humans   612.8
Neuropsychiatry   616.8
Neuropsychological tests   616.804 75
Neuropsychology   612.8
Neuropsychopharmacology   615.78
Neuroptera   595.747
Neuropteris   561.597
Neuroses   362.25
  medicine   616.852
  social welfare   362.25
Neurosurgery   617.48
Neurosyphilis
  medicine   616.83
  *see also* Nervous system
    diseases — humans
Neurotic disorders
  medicine   616.852
  *see also* Mental disorders
Neuse River (N.C.)   T2—756 19
Neuston   592.176

| | |
|---|---|
| Neutral countries | T2—171 83 |
| law of war | 341.64 |
| World War I | 940.335 |
| diplomatic history | 940.325 |
| World War II | 940.533 5 |
| diplomatic history | 940.532 5 |
| Neutralist blocs | T2—171 6 |
| Neutrality | |
| law of war | 341.64 |
| Neutrinos | 539.721 5 |
| Neutron radiation | |
| biophysics | 571.459 |
| humans | 612.014 486 |
| Neutron stars | 523.887 4 |
| Neutrons | 539.721 3 |
| Neutrophils | |
| human immunology | 616.079 |
| Nevada | 979.3 |
| | T2—793 |
| Nevada County (Ark.) | T2—767 52 |
| Nevada County (Calif.) | T2—794 37 |
| Nevado del Huila National | |
| Park (Colombia) | T2—861 39 |
| Nevi | |
| medicine | 616.55 |
| *see also* Skin diseases — | |
| humans | |
| Nevi'im | 224 |
| Nevi'im aḥaronim | 224 |
| Nevi'im rishonim | 222 |
| Nevis | T2—729 73 |
| Nevşehir İli (Turkey) | T2—564 14 |
| ancient | T2—393 4 |
| New Academy (Philosophy) | 186.2 |
| New Age movement | 299.93 |
| Christian polemics | 239.93 |
| occultism | 130 |
| Christian viewpoint | 261.513 |
| parapsychology | 130 |
| religion | 299.93 |
| *see Manual at* 299.93 | |
| New Age religions | 299.93 |
| *see Manual at* 299.93 | |
| New American Bible | 220.520 5 |
| New Britain Island (Papua | |
| New Guinea) | T2—958 5 |
| New Brunswick | 971.51 |
| | T2—715 1 |
| New Brunswick (N.J.) | T2—749 42 |
| New business enterprises | |
| management | 658.11 |
| New Caledonia | 995.97 |
| | T2—959 7 |

| | |
|---|---|
| New Caledonia (Canada) | 971.102 |
| | T2—711 |
| New Castile (Spain) | T2—464 |
| New Castle County (Del.) | T2—751 1 |
| New Century Bible | 220.520 8 |
| New Delhi (India) | T2—545 6 |
| New England | 974 |
| | T2—74 |
| New England National Park | |
| (N.S.W.) | T2—944 4 |
| New English Bible | 220.520 6 |
| New Forest (England : | |
| District) | T2—422 75 |
| New France, Company of | |
| Canadian history | 971.016 2 |
| New Glasgow (N.S.) | T2—716 13 |
| New Granada | 986.102 |
| | T2—861 |
| Colombian history | 986.102 |
| Ecuadorian history | 986.602 |
| Panamanian history | 972.870 2 |
| Venezuelan history | 987.03 |
| New Granada (Republic) | 986.105 2 |
| | T2—861 |
| Colombian history | 986.105 2 |
| Panamanian history | 972.870 3 |
| New Guinea | 995 |
| | T2—95 |
| New Guinea (Territory) | 995.302 2 |
| | T2—953 |
| New Guinea plateless turtle | 597.926 |
| New Hampshire | 974.2 |
| | T2—742 |
| New Hanover (South | |
| Africa : District) | T2—684 7 |
| New Hanover County | |
| (N.C.) | T2—756 27 |
| New Haven (Conn.) | T2—746 8 |
| New Haven County (Conn.) | T2—746 7 |
| New Hebrides | T2—959 5 |
| New International version (Bible) | 220.520 81 |
| New Ireland Province | |
| (Papua New Guinea) | T2—958 3 |
| New Jersey | 974.9 |
| | T2—749 |
| New Jerusalem Bible | 220.520 7 |
| New Jerusalemites | |
| biography | 289.409 2 |
| New Kent County (Va.) | T2—755 43 |
| New King James Bible | 220.520 8 |
| New Kingdom (Egypt) | 932.014 |
| New left | 320.53 |
| New Living Translation (Bible) | 220.520 83 |

New London County
(Conn.)    T2—746 5
New Madrid County (Mo.)    T2—778 985
New Mexico    978.9
   T2—789
New nations
   establishment
     World War I    940.314 25
     World War II    940.531 425
New Norfolk (Tas.)    T2—946 2
New Norse language    439.82
   T6—398 2
New Norwegian literature    839.82
New Orleans (La.)    T2—763 35
New Orleans, Battle of, 1815    973.523 9
New Orleans jazz    781.653
New Plymouth District
(N.Z.)    T2—934 82
New product development
   management    658.575
New Providence Island
(Bahamas)    T2—729 6
New Quebec (Quebec)    T2—714 11
New religious movements    209
   *see Manual at* 201–209 and
     292–299
New Revised Standard version
   Bible    220.520 43
New River (N.C.-W. Va.)    T2—754 7
   North Carolina    T2—756 83
   Virginia    T2—755 7
   West Virginia    T2—754 7
New Siberian Islands
   (Russia)    T2—988
New South Wales    T2—944
New Southwest    979
   T2—79
New Stone Age    930.14
New Testament    225
New Testament Greek language    487.4
   T6—87
New Testament pseudepigrapha    229.92
New Testament theology    230.041 5
New Thought    299.93
   Christian    289.98
New towns    307.768
   area planning    711.45
New Westminster (B.C.)    T2—711 33
New World blackbirds    598.874
New World chameleons    597.954 8
New World flycatchers    598.823
New World fruit bats    599.45
New World monkeys    599.85
New World pitcher plants    583.36

New World polecats    599.768
New World porcupines    599.359 74
New World runners (Lizards)    597.958 2
New World seedeaters    598.883
New World vultures    598.92
New World warblers    598.872
New Year    394.261 4
   customs    394.261 4
   Jewish    394.267
   Jewish    296.431 5
   liturgy    296.453 15
New York (N.Y.)    T2—747 1
New York (State)    974.7
   T2—747
New York Bay (N.Y.)    551.461 346
   T2—163 46
New York County (N.Y.)    T2—747 1
New York jazz    781.653
New York Metropolitan
   Area    T2—747 1
New Zealand    993
   T2—93
   *see Manual at* T2—93
New Zealand literature    820
New Zealand red pine    585.3
New Zealand Wars, 1843–1847    993.021
New Zealand Wars, 1860–1870    993.022
New Zealanders    T5—23
Newar    T5—954 9
Newari language    495.49
   T6—954 9
Newari literature    895.49
Newark (N.J.)    T2—749 32
Newark and Sherwood
   (England)    T2—425 24
Newaygo County (Mich.)    T2—774 58
Newberry County (S.C.)    T2—757 39
Newborn infants
   pediatrics    618.920 1
Newbury (England :
   District)    T2—422 91
Newcastle (N.S.W.)    T2—944 2
Newcastle (South Africa :
   District)    T2—684 1
Newcastle-under-Lyme
   (England : Borough)    T2—424 62
Newcastle upon Tyne
   (England)    T2—428 76
Newfoundland    971.8
   T2—718
Newfoundland (Dog)    636.73
Newfoundland, Island of
   (N.L.)    T2—718

Newfoundland and Labrador 971.8
    T2—718
Newham (London, England) T2—421 76
Newport (R.I.) T2—745 7
Newport (Wales : County
    Borough) T2—429 91
Newport County (R.I.) T2—745 6
Newport News (Va.) T2—755 416
Newry and Mourne
    (Northern Ireland) T2—416 58
News agencies 070.435
News gathering 070.43
News media 070.1
News programs 070.43
News sources
    journalism 070.431
Newsgroups (Computer
    communications) 004.693
Newsletters 050
    journalism 070.175
    *see also* Serials
Newspaper columns
    journalism 070.44
Newspaper illustration 741.65
Newspapers 070
    T1—05
    bibliographies 011.35
    journalism 070.172
    postal handling 383.123
    *see also* Postal service
    publishing 070.572 2
    sociology 302.232 2
Newsprint 676.286
Newsreel journalism 070.43
Newsreel photography 777.890 7
Newton County (Ark.) T2—767 16
Newton County (Ga.) T2—758 593
Newton County (Ind.) T2—772 9/4
Newton County (Miss.) T2—762 672
Newton County (Mo.) T2—778 732
Newton County (Tex.) T2—764 162
Newton Mearns (Scotland) T2—414 39
Newtonian mechanics 531
Newtown (Powys, Wales) T2—429 51
Newtownabbey (Northern
    Ireland) T2—416 18
Newts 597.85
Nez Perce County (Idaho) T2—796 85
Nez Percé Indians T5—974 124
Nez Percé language 497.412 4
    T6—974 124

Nezikin 296.123 4
    Babylonian Talmud 296.125 4
    Mishnah 296.123 4
    Palestinian Talmud 296.124 4
Ngaanyatjara language 499.15
    T6—991 5
Ngala language 496.396 86
    T6—963 968 6
Ngambai dialect 496.5
    T6—965
Nganasan language 494.4
    T6—944
Ngando languages 496.396
    T6—963 96
Nghệ An (Vietnam) T2—597 4
Ngo language 496.36
    T6—963 6
Ngöbe Buglé (Panama) T2—728 717
Ngombe languages 496.396
    T6—963 96
Ngonde (African people) T5—963 91
Ngonde language 496.391
    T6—963 91
Ngondi languages 496.396
    T6—963 96
Ngoni (Tanzania-Malawi
    people) T5—963 91
NGOs (International agencies) 060
    social welfare 361.77
Ngotshe (South Africa :
    District) T2—684 2
Ngqeleni (South Africa :
    District) T2—687 58
Nguema, Francisco Macías
    Equatorial Guinean history 967.180 31
Ngundi languages 496.396
    T6—963 96
Nguni (African people) T5—963 98
Nguni kingdoms 968.403 8
Nguni languages 496.398
    T6—963 98
Ngurus 788.38
    *see also* Woodwind instruments
Nhengatu language 498.383 2
    T6—983 832
Nhengatu literature 898.383 2
NI (Macroeconomics) 339.32
Niagara (Ont. : Regional
    municipality) T2—713 38
Niagara County (N.Y.) T2—747 98
Niagara Escarpment T2—713
Niagara Falls (N.Y.) T2—747 98

Niagara Falls (N.Y. and
  Ont.)      T2—713 39
  New York      T2—747 99
  Ontario      T2—713 39
Niagara Falls (Ont.)      T2—713 38
Niagara Peninsula (Ont.)      T2—713 38
Niagara River (N.Y. and
  Ont.)      T2—713 38
  New York      T2—747 98
  Ontario      T2—713 38
Niamey (Niger)      T2—662 6
Niassa (Mozambique :
  Province)      T2—679 9
Nicaragua      972.85
     T2—728 5

Nicaragua, Lake
  (Nicaragua)      T2—728 517
Nicaragua Canal      386.445
Nicaraguan literature      860
Nicaraguans      T5—687 285
Nice (County)      T2—449 4
Nice (France)      T2—449 41
Nicene Creed      238.142
Niceno-Constantinopolitan Creed    238.142
Niches (Architectural element)    721.48
  architecture      721.48
  construction      690.148
Niches (Ecology)      577.82
Nichiren Shoshu      294.392 8
Nicholas I, Emperor of Russia
  Russian history      947.073
Nicholas II, Emperor of Russia
  Russian history      947.083
Nicholas County (Ky.)      T2—769 417
Nicholas County (W. Va.)    T2—754 69
Nickel      669.733 2
  biochemistry      572.526 25
  building construction      693.773 32
  building material      691.873 32
  chemical engineering      661.062 5
  chemistry      546.625
  decorative arts      739.56
  economic geology      553.485
  human toxicology      615.925 625
  materials science      620.188
  metallography      669.957 332
  metallurgy      669.733 2
  metalworking      673.733 2
  mining      622.348 5
  physical metallurgy      669.967 332
  *see also* Chemicals; Metals
Nickerie (Suriname :
  District)      T2—883 1
Nicola River (B.C.)      T2—711 72

Nicolet-Yamaska (Quebec)    T2—714 54
Nicollet County (Minn.)      T2—776 32
Nicomedia (Turkey)      T2—563 3
Nicotine
  human toxicology      615.952 395 2
Niddah (Tractate)      296.123 6
  Babylonian Talmud      296.125 6
  Mishnah      296.123 6
  Palestinian Talmud      296.124 6
Niddah practice      296.742
Nidulariales      579.599
Nidwald (Switzerland)      T2—494 762
Nidwalden (Switzerland)    T2—494 762
Nieces      306.87
     T1—085
Niederbayern (Germany)    T2—433 5
Niederösterreich (Austria)    T2—436 12
Niedersachsen (Germany)    T2—435 9
Nielim language      496.361
     T6—963 61
Nielloing
  decorative arts      739.15
Nièvre (France)      T2—444 16
Niğde İli (Turkey)      T2—564 1
  ancient      T2—393 4
Nigei Island (B.C.)      T2—711 2
Nigel (South Africa :
  District)      T2—682 24
Niger      966.26
     T2—662 6
Niger-Congo languages      496.3
     T6—963
Niger-Kordofanian languages    496.3
     T6—963
Niger people      T5—966 26
Niger River      T2—662
Niger State (Nigeria)      T2—669 65
Nigeria      966.9
     T2—669
Nigerians      T5—966 9
Nigeriens (People of Niger)    T5—966 26
Night-blooming plants
  floriculture      635.953
Night crawlers      592.64
  culture      639.75
Night flying      629.132 521 4
Night journey of Muḥammad    297.633
Night lizards      597.959 8
Night photography      778.719
Night schools
  adult education      374.8
  higher education      378.15
Night skies
  meteorology      551.566

| | | | |
|---|---|---|---|
| Night tactics | 355.423 | Nineteen seventies | 909.827 |
| Night work | 331.257 4 | | T1—090 47 |
| personnel management | 658.312 1 | Nineteen sixties | 909.826 |
| Nightclothes | 391.426 | | T1—090 46 |
| see also Clothing | | Nineteen tens | 909.821 |
| Nightclub presentations | 792.7 | | T1—090 41 |
| Nighthawks | 598.99 | Nineteen thirties | 909.823 |
| Nightingales | 598.842 | | T1—090 43 |
| Nightjars | 598.99 | Nineteen twenties | 909.822 |
| Nightmares | 154.632 | | T1—090 42 |
| Nightshades | 583.952 | Nineteenth century | 909.81 |
| Nihali language | T6—948 9 | | T1—090 34 |
| Nihali-speaking people | T5—948 9 | Nineveh (Extinct city) | T2—354 |
| Nihilism | | Nineveh (Iraq : Province) | T2—567 4 |
| arts | T3C—384 | Ningsia Hui Autonomous | |
| literature | 808.803 84 | Region (China) | T2—517 5 |
| history and criticism | 809.933 84 | Ningxia Hui Zizhiqu | |
| specific literatures | T3B—080 384 | (China) | T2—517 5 |
| history and | | Ningxia Huizu Zizhiqu | |
| criticism | T3B—093 84 | (China) | T2—517 5 |
| philosophy | 149.8 | Ninh Bình (Vietnam : | |
| Niigata-ken (Japan) | T2—521 52 | Province) | T2—597 3 |
| Niihau (Hawaii) | T2—969 42 | Ninh Thuận (Vietnam : | |
| Nijmegen (Netherlands) | T2—492 18 | Province) | T2—597 5 |
| Nika language | 496.395 | Ninth century | 909.1 |
| | T6—963 95 | | T1—090 21 |
| Nīl (Sudan) | T2—625 | Ninth of Av | 296.439 |
| Nīl al-Abyaḍ (Sudan) | T2—626 4 | Niobium | 669.79 |
| Nīl al Azraq (Sudan) | T2—626 4 | chemical engineering | 661.052 4 |
| Nile River | T2—62 | chemistry | 546.524 |
| Nile River Delta | T2—621 | economic geology | 553.499 |
| Nilo-Hamitic peoples | T5—965 | metallurgy | 669.79 |
| Nilo-Saharan languages | 496.5 | physical metallurgy | 669.967 9 |
| | T6—965 | see also Chemicals | |
| Nilotic-Kavirondo language | 496.5 | Niobrara County (Wyo.) | T2—787 15 |
| | T6—965 | Niobrara River (Wyo. and | |
| Nilotic languages | 496.5 | Neb.) | T2—782 7 |
| | T6—965 | Nipa palm | 584.5 |
| Nilotic peoples | T5—965 | Nipissing (Ont. : District) | T2—713 147 |
| Nimbarka (Philosophy) | 181.484 3 | Nipissing, Lake (Ont.) | T2—713 147 |
| Nîmes (France) | T2—448 37 | Nirvana | |
| Nīnawá (Iraq : Province) | T2—567 4 | Buddhism | 294.342 3 |
| Ninepins | 794.6 | Hinduism | 294.523 |
| Nineteen eighties | 909.828 | Niska Indians | T5—974 12 |
| | T1—090 48 | Niter | 553.64 |
| Nineteen fifties | 909.825 | mineralogy | 549.732 |
| | T1—090 45 | Nith, River (Scotland) | T2—414 7 |
| Nineteen forties | 909.824 | Nithsdale (Scotland) | T2—414 7 |
| | T1—090 44 | Nitidulidae | 595.769 |
| Nineteen hundreds (Decade) | 909.821 | Nitrate fertilizers | 631.842 |
| | T1—090 41 | chemical engineering | 668.624 2 |
| Nineteen nineties | 909.829 | Nitrates | 553.64 |
| | T1—090 49 | chemical engineering | 661.65 |
| | | economic geology | 553.64 |

| | |
|---|---|
| Nitrates (continued) | |
| mineralogy | 549.732 |
| mining | 622.364 |
| Nitration | 547.27 |
| chemical engineering | 660.284 4 |
| Nitriansky kraj (Slovakia) | T2—437 33 |
| Nitric acid | |
| chemical engineering | 661.24 |
| Nitrides | |
| chemical engineering | 661.65 |
| Nitrification | 572.545 |
| Nitrifying bacteria | |
| agricultural use | 631.847 |
| Nitrifying crops | 631.847 |
| Nitriles | 547.044 |
| chemical engineering | 661.894 |
| Nitrites | |
| chemical engineering | 661.65 |
| Nitro compounds | 547.041 |
| chemical engineering | 661.894 |
| Nitro dyes | 667.252 |
| Nitrocellulose | 662.26 |
| textiles | 677.461 |
| *see also* Textiles | |
| Nitrocellulose glue | 668.33 |
| Nitrogen | 553.93 |
| animal nutrition | 572.544 1 |
| animal husbandry | 636.085 21 |
| biochemistry | 572.54 |
| chemical engineering | 661.071 1 |
| chemistry | 546.711 |
| economic geology | 553.93 |
| gas technology | 665.824 |
| organic chemistry | 547.04 |
| aliphatic | 547.44 |
| applied | 661.894 |
| aromatic | 547.64 |
| *see also* Chemicals | |
| Nitrogen cycle | |
| (Biogeochemistry) | 577.145 |
| Nitrogen fertilizers | 631.84 |
| chemical engineering | 668.624 |
| Nitrogen fixation | 572.545 |
| Nitrogen removal | |
| sewage treatment | 628.357 |
| Nitrogen salts | |
| chemical engineering | 661.65 |
| Nitroglycerin | |
| military engineering | 623.452 7 |
| Nitrosation | 547.27 |
| chemical engineering | 660.284 4 |
| Nitroso compounds | 547.041 |
| chemical engineering | 661.894 |
| Nitroso dyes | 667.252 |

| | |
|---|---|
| Nitrous oxide abuse | 362.299 3 |
| medicine | 616.86 |
| personal health | 613.8 |
| social welfare | 362.299 3 |
| *see also* Substance abuse | |
| Niue | T2—962 6 |
| Niue language | 499.484 |
| | T6—994 84 |
| Niue literature | 899.484 |
| Niuean language | 499.484 |
| | T6—994 84 |
| Niuean literature | 899.484 |
| Niueans | T5—994 84 |
| Nivation | 551.38 |
| Nivkh | T5—946 |
| Nivkh language | 494.6 |
| | T6—946 |
| Nixon, Richard M. (Richard Milhous) | |
| United States history | 973.924 |
| Niyazov, Saparmurad | |
| Turkmenistan history | 958.508 61 |
| Nizhegorod (Russia : Oblast) | T2—474 1 |
| Nizhegorodskaia oblast' (Russia) | T2—474 1 |
| Nizhniy Novgorod (Russia : Oblast) | T2—474 1 |
| Njabi languages | 496.396 |
| | T6—963 96 |
| Njebi languages | 496.396 |
| | T6—963 96 |
| Njem language | 496.396 |
| | T6—963 96 |
| Nkandla (South Africa : District) | T2—684 7 |
| Nkomazi (South Africa : District) | T2—682 72 |
| Nkoya languages | 496.393 |
| | T6—963 93 |
| Nkrumah, Kwame | |
| Ghanaian history | 966.705 1 |
| Nkundo language | 496.396 |
| | T6—963 96 |
| Nkundu language | 496.396 |
| | T6—963 96 |
| NMR (Physics) | 538.362 |
| NMR imaging | |
| medicine | 616.075 48 |
| NMSQT (Merit scholarship test) | 378.166 2 |
| NNP (Macroeconomics) | 339.32 |
| Nō | |
| literature | 895.620 51 |
| theater | 792.095 2 |

No-fault insurance   368.5
   law   346.086 5
No-fault motor vehicle insurance   368.572 8
   law   346.086 572 8
No-tillage   631.581 4
Noah (Biblical person)
   Bible stories   222.110 950 5
Nobatia (Kingdom)   962.502 2
    T2—625
Nobelium   546.449
Nobility (Social class)   305.522
    T1—086 21
   customs   390.23
    dress   391.023
   genealogy   929.7
Noble County (Ind.)   T2—772 76
Noble County (Ohio)   T2—771 95
Noble County (Okla.)   T2—766 27
Noble gases
   chemistry   546.75
   economic geology   553.97
   technology   665.822
Nobles County (Minn.)   T2—776 24
Nobles of the Mystic Shrine   366.16
   biography   366.160 92
Nocardia   579.37
Noctuoidea   595.78
Nocturnal animals   591.518
Nocturnal behavior (Animals)   591.518
Nocturnes   784.189 66
Nodaway County (Mo.)   T2—778 124
Nodes (Plant stems)   575.454
Nofretete, Queen of Egypt
   Egyptian history   932.014
Nogai language   494.34
    T6—943 4
Nógrád Megye (Hungary)   T2—439 8
Noh
   literature   895.620 51
   theater   792.095 2
Noise   363.74
   communications engineering   621.382 24
   electronic engineering   621.382 24
   engineering   620.23
   law   344.046 38
   psychology   152.15
    environmental psychology   155.911 5
   public administration   354.338
   social welfare   363.74
Noise control equipment
   plant management   658.28
Nola (Italy)
   ancient   T2—377 255
Nolan County (Tex.)   T2—764 728

Nolanaceae   583.95
Nomads   305.906 918
    T1—086 918
   social welfare   362.899 1
   women
    social welfare   362.839 818
   young people
    social welfare   362.779 18
Nomenclature   T1—014
Nominal groups (Grammar)   415.5
   specific languages   T4—55
Nominalism   149.1
Nominals (Nouns)   415.54
   specific languages   T4—554
Nominating conventions
   (Political parties)   324.56
Nomination (Political parties)   324.5
Nomination hearings   352–354
   legislative function   328.345 5
   *see Manual at* 300, 320.6 vs.
    352–354
Nomography   518.23
Non-Austronesian languages of   499.1
   Oceania   T6—991
Non-Chalcedonian churches   281.6
   *see also* Eastern churches
Non-Euclidean geometry   516.9
Non-insulin-dependent diabetes   362.196 462 4
   medicine   616.462 4
   pregnancy complications
    obstetrics   618.364 6
   social services   362.196 462 4
   *see also* Endocrine diseases —
    humans
Non-self-governing territories   321.08
    T2—171 9
   law of nations   341.28
   public administration   353.15
    specific territories   351.3–.9
Non-Trinitarian concepts
   Christianity
    God   231.044
    Jesus   232.9
Nonaffiliated commercial
   television   384.550 65
Nonalcoholic beverages   641.26
   commercial processing   663.6
   cooking with   641.62
   home preparation   641.875
Nonalcoholic brewed beverages   641.877
   commercial processing   663.9
   home preparation   641.877
Nonaqueous solutions   541.342 3
Nonaqueous solvents   541.348 2

| | |
|---|---|
| Nonassociative algebras | 512.48 |
| Nonassociative rings | 512.48 |
| Nonbeing | 111.5 |
| Nonbook materials | |
| cataloging | 025.34 |
| library treatment | 025.17 |
| Nonclassical logic | 511.31 |
| mathematical logic | 511.31 |
| philosophical logic | 160.119 8 |
| Noncombat services (Armed forces) | 355.34 |
| Noncombatants | |
| law of war | 341.67 |
| World War I | 940.316 1 |
| World War II | 940.531 61 |
| Noncommercial radio | 384.54 |
| Noncommercial television | 384.554 |
| Noncommissioned officers | 355.009 2 |
| role and function | 355.338 |
| Noncommissioned officers' clubs | 355.346 |
| Noncommunicable diseases | 571.9 |
| humans | |
| incidence | 614.59 |
| medicine | 616.98 |
| Noncommutative algebras | 512.46 |
| Noncommutative rings | 512.46 |
| Nonconformists (British churches) | 280.4 |
| *see also* Protestantism | |
| Nonconsequentialism | 171.2 |
| Noncrystalline solids | 530.413 |
| Nondairy coffee whiteners | |
| commercial processing | 663.64 |
| Nondestructive testing | |
| materials science | 620.112 7 |
| Nondifferentiable functions | 515.8 |
| Nondomesticated animals | |
| culture | 639 |
| Nondominant groups | 305.56 |
| | T1—086 93 |
| *see also* Minorities | |
| Nondramatic vocal forms | 782.2 |
| choral and mixed voices | 782.52 |
| None (Divine office) | 264.15 |
| music | 782.324 |
| Nonelectronic data processing | 004.9 |
| Nonets | |
| chamber music | 785.19 |
| vocal music | 783.19 |
| Nonexplosive ammunition | |
| military engineering | 623.459 |
| Nonferrous metals | 669 |
| architectural construction | 721.044 7 |
| building construction | 693.72–.77 |

| | |
|---|---|
| Nonferrous metals (continued) | |
| building materials | 691.8 |
| economic geology | 553.4 |
| materials science | 620.18 |
| metallography | 669.95 |
| metallurgy | 669 |
| metalworking | 673 |
| mining | 622.34 |
| physical metallurgy | 669.96 |
| ship design | 623.818 2 |
| shipbuilding | 623.820 7 |
| structural engineering | 624.1822–.1829 |
| *see also* Chemicals; Metals | |
| Nongoma (South Africa : District) | T2—684 3 |
| Nongovernmental organizations (International agencies) | 060 |
| | T1—060 1 |
| social welfare | 361.77 |
| Nongraded schools | 371.255 |
| Nonimpact printing | 686.233 |
| Nonlinear analysis | |
| functional analysis | 515.724 8 |
| Nonlinear closed-loop systems | |
| automation engineering | 629.836 |
| Nonlinear differential equations | 515.355 |
| Nonlinear equations | 515.252 |
| Nonlinear functional analysis | 515.724 8 |
| Nonlinear operators | 515.724 8 |
| Nonlinear optics | 535.2 |
| engineering | 621.369 4 |
| Nonlinear programming | 519.76 |
| Nonlinear systems | 003.75 |
| Nonlinguistic communication | 302.222 |
| | T1—014 |
| Nonliterate people | 305.56 |
| | T1—086 94 |
| Nonliterate societies | 301.7 |
| government | 321.1 |
| religion | 201.4 |
| Nonloom weaving | |
| arts | 746.42 |
| Nonmechanized data processing | 004.9 |
| Nonmetals | |
| biochemistry | 572 |
| chemistry | 546.7 |
| materials science | 620.193 |
| mineralogy | 549.27 |
| solid-state physics | 530.413 |
| Nonmonotonic logic | 511.31 |
| Nonmotor land vehicles | 388.341 |
| manufacturing technology | 688.6 |
| transportation services | 388.341 |

Nonnative animals    333.954 3
   biology    591.62
   resource economics    333.954 3
Nonnative plants    333.953 3
   biology    581.62
   resource economics    333.953 3
Nonnative species    333.952 3
   biology    578.62
   resource economics    333.952 3
Nonobjectivity (Art style)    709.040 56
   painting    759.065 6
   sculpture    735.230 456
Nonoptical spectroscopy    543.6
Nonoscine Passeriformes    598.822
Nonparametric inference    519.54
Nonparametric statistical
   methods    519.5
Nonprescription drugs    615.1
   *see also* Drugs
     (Pharmaceuticals)
Nonprocedural languages    005.13
Nonprofit organizations    060
   accounting    657.98
   financial management    658.159
   law    346.064
   libraries    027.68
   management    658.048
     initiation    658.114 8
   publishing    070.594
   social welfare    361.763
Nonrenewable fuels    553.2
   *see also* Fossil fuels
Nonrigid airships    387.732 7
   engineering    629.133 27
   military engineering    623.743 7
   transportation services    387.732 7
Nonrigid materials
   architectural construction    721.044 98
   building construction    693.98
Nonsporting dogs    636.72
Nonstriated muscle tissues
   human histology    612.740 45
Nontariff trade barriers    382.5
   international agreements    382.9
Nontax revenues    336.1
   public administration    352.44
   public finance    336.1
Nontheistic religions    201.4
Nonverbal communication    302.222
     T1—014
   psychology    153.69
   social psychology    302.222

Nonviolence    303.61
   ethics    179.7
   religion    205.697
     Buddhism    294.356 97
     Christianity    241.697
     Hinduism    294.548 697
     Islam    297.569 7
     Judaism    296.369 7
   social conflict    303.61
Nonwestern art music    781.69
Nonwoven fabrics    677.6
   *see also* Textiles
Noodles    641.822
   commercial processing    664.755
   home preparation    641.822
Noord-Brabant
   (Netherlands)    T2—492 45
Noord-Holland
   (Netherlands)    T2—492 35
Nootka Indians    T5—979 55
Nootka language    497.955
     T6—979 55
Nor Oriental del Marañón
   (Peru)    T2—851 4
Nord (France : Dept.)    T2—442 8
Nord (Haiti : Dept.)    T2—729 432
Nord-du-Québec (Quebec)    T2—714 11
Nord-Est (Haiti : Dept.)    T2—729 436
Nord-Kivu (Congo)    T2—675 17
Nord-Norge    T2—484 3
Nord-Ouest (Haiti)    T2—729 42
Nord-Pas-de-Calais (France)    T2—442 7
Nord-Trøndelag fylke
   (Norway)    T2—484 2
Norddeutscher Bund    943.081
     T2—43
Nordhausen (Germany :
   Landkreis)    T2—432 24
Nordic combination (Skiing)    796.932
Nordic languages    439.5
     T6—395
Nordic literatures    839.5
Nordic people (North
   Germanic)    T5—395
Nordic skiing    796.932
Nordjyllands amt
   (Denmark)    T2—489 5
Nordland fylke (Norway)    T2—484 4
Nordrhein-Westfalen
   (Germany)    T2—435 5
Nordvorpommern
   (Germany : Landkreis)    T2—431 78
Nordwestmecklenburg
   (Germany : Landkreis)    T2—431 76

| | | | |
|---|---|---|---|
| Nore River (Ireland) | T2—418 9 | North American native | |
| Norfolk (England) | T2—426 1 | peoples | T5—97 |
| Norfolk (Ont. : County) | T2—713 36 | North American red squirrels | 599.363 |
| Norfolk (Va.) | T2—755 521 | North American wood warblers | 598.872 |
| Norfolk Broads (England) | T2—426 17 | North Americans | T5—1 |
| Norfolk County (Mass.) | T2—744 7 | North Atlantic Ocean | 551.461 31 |
| Norfolk Island | T2—948 2 | | T2—163 1 |
| Noricum | 936.36 | North Atlantic Treaty | |
| | T2—363 6 | Organization | 355.031 091 821 |
| Norite | 552.3 | law | 341.72 |
| Norman architecture | 723.4 | North Ayrshire (Scotland) | T2—414 61 |
| Norman County (Minn.) | T2—776 93 | North Battleford (Sask.) | T2—712 42 |
| Normandie (France) | T2—442 | North Borneo | T2—595 3 |
| Normandy (France) | T2—442 | North Brabant (Netherlands) | T2—492 45 |
| Normandy Invasion, 1944 | 940.542 142 1 | North Calotte | T2—48 |
| Normans | T5—395 | North Canadian River | |
| Southern Italian history | 945.703 | (Okla.) | T2—766 1 |
| Normative ethics | 170.44 | North Carolina | 975.6 |
| Normed linear spaces | 515.732 | | T2—756 |
| Nornalup National Park | | North Cascades National | |
| (W.A.) | T2—941 2 | Park (Wash.) | T2—797 73 |
| Norrbotten landskap | | North Caucasian languages | 499.96 |
| (Sweden) | T2—488 8 | | T6—999 6 |
| Norrbottens län (Sweden) | T2—488 8 | North central Caucasian | 499.964 1 |
| Norris Lake (Tenn.) | T2—768 935 | languages | T6—999 641 |
| Norrland (Sweden) | T2—488 | North Central State | |
| Norse religion | 293 | (Nigeria) | T2—669 73 |
| Norseman (W.A.) | T2—941 7 | North Central States | 977 |
| Norte de Santander | | | T2—77 |
| (Colombia) | T2—861 24 | North Channel (Huron, | |
| North Africa | 961 | Lake, Mich. and Ont.) | T2—713 132 |
| | T2—61 | North Channel (Ireland and | 551.461 337 |
| ancient | 939.7 | Scotland) | T2—163 37 |
| | T2—397 | North Coast (South Africa) | T2—684 4 |
| North Africans | T5—927 61 | North Cornwall (England) | T2—423 7 |
| North America | 970 | North Cotabato | |
| | T2—7 | (Philippines) | T2—599 7 |
| Chinese explorations | 970.012 | North Dakota | 978.4 |
| English explorations | 970.017 | | T2—784 |
| French explorations | 970.018 | North Devon (England) | T2—423 52 |
| geography | 917 | North Dorset (England) | T2—423 32 |
| Norse explorations | 970.013 | North Down (Northern | |
| pre-Columbian claims | 970.011 | Ireland) | T2—416 53 |
| Spanish and Portuguese | | North Downs (England) | T2—422 3 |
| explorations | 970.016 | North Dravidian languages | 494.83 |
| travel | 917.04 | | T6—948 3 |
| Welsh explorations | 970.014 | North Dravidian literatures | 894.83 |
| *see Manual at* T2—73 vs. | | North Dravidians | T5—948 3 |
| T2—71 | | North East Derbyshire | |
| North American box turtles | 597.925 | (England) | T2—425 14 |
| North American catfishes | 597.492 | North East Fife (Scotland) | T2—412 9 |
| North American native languages | 497 | North East Frontier Agency, | |
| | T6—97 | India | T2—541 63 |
| North American native literatures | 897 | | |

North East Lincolnshire
  (England)           T2—428 34
North East Polder        T2—492 16
North-Eastern Province
  (Kenya)             T2—676 22
North-Eastern Region
  (China)              T2—518
North Friesland (Germany)  T2—435 12
North frigid zone         T2—113
North Frisian Islands
  (Denmark and Germany)  T2—435 12
North German Confederation   943.081
                        T2—43
North Germanic languages     439.5
                        T6—395
North Germanic literatures    839.5
North Germanic people     T5—395
North Hertfordshire
  (England)           T2—425 81
North Holland
  (Netherlands)      T2—492 35
North Island (N.Z.)     T2—931
North Kesteven (England)  T2—425 35
North Khorāsān (Iran)    T2—559 2
North Korea            951.93
                        T2—519 3
North Korean communism    335.434 6
North Lanarkshire
  (Scotland)          T2—414 52
North Land (Russia)    T2—987
North Lincolnshire
  (England)           T2—428 32
North Maluku (Indonesia)  T2—598 56
North Norfolk (England)   T2—426 12
North Okanagan (B.C.)   T2—711 5
North Ossetia (Russia)   T2—475 2
North Pacific Ocean     551.461 44
                        T2—164 4
North Platte River      T2—787 16
North Polar Sea         551.461 32
                        T2—163 2
North Pole             T2—163 2
North Queensland tick typhus
  incidence            614.526 3
  medicine            616.922 3
   *see also* Communicable
     diseases — humans
North Rhine-Westphalia
  (Germany)          T2—435 5
North Saami language     494.574 5
                        T6—945 745
North Saami literature    894.574 5
North Saanich (B.C.)    T2—711 28

North Sámi language      494.574 5
                        T6—945 745
North Sámi literature     894.574 5
North Saskatchewan River
  (Alta. and Sask.)    T2—712 33
North Sea           551.461 336
                        T2—163 36
North Shore City (N.Z.)  T2—932 2
North Shropshire (England) T2—424 53
North Slope Borough
  (Alaska)            T2—798 7
North Solomons Province (Papua  995.92
  New Guinea)        T2—959 2
North Somerset (England)  T2—423 96
North Sulawesi (Indonesia)  T2—598 42
North Sumatra (Indonesia)  T2—598 12
North temperate zone    T2—123
North Thompson River
  (B.C.)               T2—711 72
North Tyneside (England)  T2—428 79
North Vancouver (B.C.)   T2—711 33
North Vietnam (1954–1975)   959.730 43
                        T2—597 3
North Wales           T2—429 1
North Warwickshire
  (England)          T2—424 81
North-West (South Africa)   968.24
                        T2—682 4
North-West Frontier
  Province (Pakistan)   T2—549 12
North West Leicestershire
  (England)          T2—425 48
North-Western Province
  (Zambia)           T2—689 4
North-Western Region
  (China)              T2—514
North Wiltshire (England)  T2—423 12
North York (Toronto, Ont.)  T2—713 541
North Yorkshire (England)  T2—428 4
North Yorkshire Moors
  (England)          T2—428 46
Northam (W.A.)       T2—941 2
Northampton (England)  T2—425 57
Northampton County (N.C.) T2—756 49
Northampton County (Pa.)  T2—748 22
Northampton County (Va.)  T2—755 15
Northampton Uplands
  (England)          T2—425 56
Northamptonshire (England) T2—425 5
Northavon (England)    T2—423 91
Northbrook, Thomas George
  Baring, Earl of
  Indian history        954.035 2

Northeast Caucasian languages 499.964
  T6—999 64
Northeast Turkic languages 494.33
  T6—943 3
Northeastern India T2—541
Northeastern States 974
  T2—74
Northern Aegean (Greece) T2—495 82
Northern Areas (Pakistan) T2—549 132
Northern Australia T2—942 9
Northern Bahr al Ghazal
  (Sudan) T2—629 4
Northern Bantu languages 496.394
  T6—963 94
Northern Baptists 286.131
  *see also* Baptists
Northern Britain 941.1
  T2—411
  ancient 936.11
  T2—361 1
Northern Cape (South Africa) 968.71
  T2—687 1
Northern coastal region (Papua 995.7
  New Guinea) T2—957
Northern Darfur (Sudan :
  State) T2—627
Northern dynasties
  Chinese history 951.015
Northern England T2—427
Northern Europe 948
  T2—48
  ancient 936.8
  T2—368
Northern France T2—442 7
Northern fur seal 599.797 3
Northern Hemisphere T2—181 3
Northern Ireland 941.6
  T2—416
  ancient 936.16
  T2—361 6
  *see Manual at* T2—41 and
    T2—42
Northern Italy 945.1
  T2—451
Northern Karoo (South
  Africa) T2—687 13
Northern Kordofan (Sudan) T2—628
Northern League (Italian political
  party) 324.245 084
Northern lights 538.768
Northern Mariana Islands T2—967
Northern Min dialects 495.172 45
  T6—951 7
Northern Neck (Va.) T2—755 2

Northern Norway T2—484 3
Northern Ontario T2—713 1
Northern Paiute Indians T5—974 577
Northern Paiute language 497.457 7
  T6—974 577
Northern Panhandle (W.
  Va.) T2—754 1
Northern Province (Papua
  New Guinea) T2—954 2
Northern Province (Zambia) T2—689 4
Northern Region (China) T2—511
Northern Rhodesia 968.940 2
  T2—689 4
Northern Rockies (B.C.) T2—711 87
Northern Samar
  (Philippines) T2—599 5
Northern Sotho language 496.397 71
  T6—963 977 1
Northern Sotho literature 896.397 71
Northern Sporades (Greece) T2—495 4
  ancient T2—391 1
Northern State (Sudan) T2—625
Northern territories 971.9
  T2—719
Northern Territory T2—942 9
Northern Tiwa Indians T5—974 96
Northern Tiwa language 497.496
  T6—974 96
Northern Turkic languages 494.33
  T6—943 3
Northern Vietnam T2—597 3
Northern Yemen T2—533 2
Northern Yemenis T5—927 533 2
Northland Region (N.Z.) T2—931 3
Northmen T5—395
Northumberland (England) T2—428 8
Northumberland (N.B.) T2—715 21
Northumberland (Ont.) T2—713 57
Northumberland County
  (Pa.) T2—748 31
Northumberland County
  (Va.) T2—755 21
Northumbria supremacy 942.015 3
Northumbrian pipes 788.49
  *see also* Woodwind instruments
Northwest, Old 977
  T2—77
Northwest, Pacific T2—795
Northwest Arctic Borough
  (Alaska) T2—798 6
Northwest Caucasian languages 499.962
  T6—999 62
Northwest Malayo-Polynesian 499.225
  languages T6—992 25

Northwest Rebellion, 1885 971.054
Northwest Semitic languages 492
  T6—92
Northwest Semitic literatures 892
Northwest Territories 971.93
  T2—719 3
Northwest Territories 971.92
 (1870–1999) T2—719 2
Northwest Turkic languages 494.38
  T6—943 8
Northwestern Bantu languages 496.396
  T6—963 96
Norton (Va.) T2—755 744
Norton County (Kan.) T2—781 155
Norton Sound (Alaska) 551.461 434
  T2—164 34
Norway 948.1
  T2—481
 ancient 936.81
  T2—368 1
Norway rat 599.352
Norwegian elkhound 636.753
Norwegian language 439.82
  T6—398 2
Norwegian literature 839.82
Norwegian Sea 551.461 324
  T2—163 24
Norwegians T5—398 2
Norwich (England) T2—426 15
Nose 599.144
 animal physiology 573.26
 descriptive zoology 599.144
 fractures
  medicine 617.156
 human anatomy 611.21
 human physiology 612.232
  smelling 612.86
  speech 612.78
 medicine 616.21
 surgery 617.523
Nose diseases
 medicine 616.21
 *see also* Respiratory tract
  diseases — humans
Nose flutes 788.3
 *see also* Woodwind instruments
Nostocales 579.39
Nostratic hypothesis 417.7
  T6—1
Notacanthiformes 597.43
Notaries (Lay notaries) 347.016
Notaries (Legally trained
 notaries) 346.002 3
Notaspidea 594.34

Notched flutes 788.35
 *see also* Woodwind instruments
Note rows 781.268
Note-taking (Study technique) 371.302 81
Notebook computers 004.16
 *see also* Personal computers
Notebooks
 literature 808.883
  history and criticism 809.983
  specific literatures T3B—803
  individual authors T3A—8
Notes payable 657.74
 accounting 657.74
 financial management 658.152 6
Nothingness 111.5
Nothosauria 567.937
Notio Aigaio (Greece) T2—495 85
Notions 646.19
 commercial technology 687.8
 home sewing 646.19
Notodelphyoida 595.34
Notostraca 595.32
Notoungulata 569.62
Notre-Dame-des-Anges
 (Quebec) T2—714 471
Notre-Dame Mountains
 (Quebec) T2—714 7
Nottingham (England) T2—425 27
Nottingham Island
 (Nunavut) T2—719 52
Nottinghamshire (England) T2—425 2
Nottoway County (Va.) T2—755 637
Noturus 597.492
Nouakchott (Mauritania) T2—661
Noun phrases 415.5
 specific languages T4—55
Nouns 415.54
 specific languages T4—554
Noupoort (South Africa :
 District) T2—687 13
Nouveau-Québec (Quebec) T2—714 11
Nouvelle-Beauce (Quebec) T2—714 718
Nova Scotia 971.6
  T2—716
Novaĩa Zemlĩa (Russia) T2—986
Novara (Italy : Province) T2—451 6
 ancient T2—372 24
Novas 523.844 6
Novaya Zemlya (Russia) T2—986
Novelettes 808.83
 history and criticism 809.3
 specific literatures T3B—3
 individual authors T3A—3

Novelists 809.3
  collected biography 809.3
    specific literatures T3B—300 9
    individual biography T3A—3
Novellas 808.83
  history and criticism 809.3
    specific literatures T3B—3
    individual authors T3A—3
Novels 808.83
  history and criticism 809.3
    specific literatures T3B—3
    individual authors T3A—3
Novelties
  manufacturing technology 688.726
Novenas 264.7
Novgorod (Russia : Oblast) T2—472 2
Novitiate (Monastic life) 248.894 25
  women 248.894 35
Novo Estado (Portugal) 946.904 2
Novogrodskaĭa oblast'
  (Russia) T2—472 2
Novosibirsk (Russia :
  Oblast) T2—573
Novosibirskaĭa oblast'
  (Russia) T2—573
NOW accounts 332.175 22
Nowata County (Okla.) T2—766 97
Nowra (N.S.W.) T2—944 7
Nowy Sącz (Poland :
  Voivodeship) T2—438 62
Noxubee County (Miss.) T2—762 955
Noyon, Treaty of, 1516 945.306
NP-complete problems 511.352
Nqamakwe (South Africa :
  District) T2—687 58
NQR (Physics) 538.362
Nqutu District of KwaZulu
  (South Africa) T2—684 2
NSAP (Austrian political party) 324.243 602 38
NSDAP (Austrian political party) 324.243 602 38
Nsikazi (South Africa :
  District) T2—682 71
Ntabethemba (South
  Africa : District) T2—687 55
Ntcham language 496.35
   T6—963 5
Ntomba language 496.396 8
   T6—963 968
Nubia 939.78
   T2—397 8
Nubian languages 496.5
   T6—965
Nubians T5—965
Ñuble (Chile) T2—833 8

Nuckolls County (Neb.) T2—782 372
Nuclear accidents 363.179 9
  public safety 363.179 9
  technology 621.483 5
  *see also* Hazardous materials
Nuclear activation analysis 543.63
Nuclear activities 539.75
  *see Manual at* 530.416 vs.
    539.75
Nuclear chemistry 541.38
  applied 660.298
Nuclear disarmament 327.174 7
  law of nations 341.734
Nuclear energy 333.792 4
  economics 333.792 4
  law 343.092 5
  physics 539.7
  public administration 354.47
Nuclear energy industry 333.792 4
Nuclear energy insurance 368.7
Nuclear engineering 621.48
  military applications 623.044
Nuclear engineers 621.480 92
Nuclear envelope 571.66
Nuclear family 306.855
Nuclear fission 539.762
Nuclear forces 355.021 7
Nuclear fuels
  economic geology 553.493
  engineering 621.483 35
  public administration 354.47
  resource economics 333.854 93
Nuclear fusion 539.764
Nuclear hazards insurance 368.7
Nuclear heating
  buildings 697.79
Nuclear interactions 539.75
  *see Manual at* 530.416 vs.
    539.75
Nuclear liability insurance 368.7
Nuclear magnetic resonance 538.362
  imaging
    medicine 616.075 48
Nuclear magnetic resonance
  spectroscopy 543.66
Nuclear medicine 616.075 75
Nuclear membrane 571.66
Nuclear missile forces 358.17
Nuclear missiles 358.171 82
  engineering 623.451 9
  military equipment 358.171 82
Nuclear models 539.74
Nuclear nonproliferation 327.174 7
  law of nations 341.734

| | | | |
|---|---|---|---|
| Nuclear physicists | 539.709 2 | Nucleic acids | 572.8 |
| Nuclear physics | 539.7 | biochemical genetics | 572.8 |
| astronomy | 523.019 7 | chemistry | 547.7 |
| Nuclear power plants | 621.483 | humans | 611.018 16 |
| law | 343.092 5 | Nucleolus | 571.66 |
| Nuclear power systems | | Nucleons | 539.721 2 |
| auxiliary systems | | Nucleoplasm | 571.66 |
| spacecraft | 629.474 43 | Nucleoproteins | 572.84 |
| propulsion | 621.485 | *see also* Proteins | |
| *see also* Nuclear propulsion | | Nucleosides | 572.85 |
| Nuclear-powered automobiles | | Nucleosomes | 572.87 |
| engineering | 629.229 6 | Nucleotide sequences | 572.863 3 |
| Nuclear-powered submarines | 359.938 34 | humans | 611.018 166 3 |
| design | 623.812 574 | Nucleotides | 572.85 |
| engineering | 623.825 74 | humans | 611.018 16 |
| naval equipment | 359.938 34 | Nucleus (Cells) | 571.66 |
| Nuclear propulsion | 621.485 | Nuclide structure | 539.74 |
| aircraft | 629.134 355 | Nuda | 593.8 |
| automotive | 629.250 9 | Nudes | |
| ships | 623.872 8 | art representation | 704.942 1 |
| spacecraft | 629.475 3 | drawing | 743.4 |
| Nuclear quadrupole resonance | 538.362 | painting | 757.2 |
| Nuclear reactions | 539.76 | Nudibranchia | 594.36 |
| Nuclear reactors | 621.483 | Nudism | |
| Nuclear safety | 363.179 9 | health | 613.194 |
| public administration | 353.999 | Nudity | |
| public safety | 363.179 9 | arts | 700.456 1 |
| technology | 621.483 5 | | T3C—356 1 |
| *see also* Hazardous materials | | literature | 808.803 561 |
| Nuclear spectroscopy | 543.6 | history and criticism | 809.933 561 |
| Nuclear structure | 539.74 | specific literatures | T3B—080 356 1 |
| Nuclear terrorism | 363.325 5 | history and | |
| *see also* Terrorism | | criticism | T3B—093 561 |
| Nuclear warfare | 355.021 7 | Nueces County (Tex.) | T2—764 113 |
| civil defense | 363.35 | Nueces River (Tex.) | T2—764 11 |
| ethics | 172.422 | Nuer (African people) | T5—965 |
| religion | 205.624 22 | Nuer language | 496.5 |
| Christianity | 241.624 22 | | T6 965 |
| *see also* War — ethics | | Nueva Ecija (Philippines : | |
| operations | 355.43 | Province) | T2—599 1 |
| social theology | 201.727 5 | Nueva Esparta (Venezuela) | T2—875 4 |
| Christianity | 261.873 2 | Nueva Segovia (Nicaragua) | T2—728 521 |
| Judaism | 296.382 7 | Nueva Vizcaya | |
| *see also* Disasters | | (Philippines) | T2—599 1 |
| Nuclear weapons | 355.825 119 | Nuevo León (Mexico : | |
| control | 327.174 7 | State) | T2—721 3 |
| law of nations | 341.734 | Nuisance (Law) | 346.036 |
| engineering | 623.451 19 | Nujoma, Sam | |
| military equipment | 355.825 119 | Namibian history | 968.810 41 |
| *see also* Nuclear warfare | | Nukuoro language | 499.46 |
| Nuclei as particles | 539.723 2 | | T6—994 6 |
| Nucleic-acid hybridization | 572.84 | Nullification movement | |
| Nucleic acid-protein interactions | 572.84 | United States history | 973.561 |

| | |
|---|---|
| Numayrī, Ja'far Muḥammad | |
| Sudanese history | 962.404 2 |
| Numbat | 599.27 |
| Number (Grammar) | 415.5 |
| specific languages | T4—55 |
| Number (Quantity) | |
| philosophy | 119 |
| Number systems | 513.5 |
| Number theoretic functions | 512.73 |
| Number theory | 512.7 |
| Numbers | 513.5 |
| fortune-telling | 133.335 4 |
| number theory | 512.72 |
| Numbers (Biblical book) | 222.14 |
| Numeracy | 513 |
| primary education | 372.72 |
| Numeration systems | 513.5 |
| Numerical algebra | 518.42 |
| Numerical analysis | 518 |
| Numerical approximation | 518.5 |
| Numerical calculations | |
| applied mathematics | 518 |
| Numerical control | |
| machine tools | 621.902 3 |
| Numerical differentiation | 518.53 |
| Numerical integration | 518.54 |
| Numerical interpretation | |
| Bible | 220.68 |
| Koran | 297.122 68 |
| Numerical mathematics | 518 |
| Numerical taxonomy | 578.012 |
| Numerology | 133.335 |
| Numic Indians | T5—974 57 |
| Numic languages | 497.457 |
| | T6—974 57 |
| Numidia | 939.72 |
| | T2—397 2 |
| Numidia (Kingdom) | 939.720 3 |
| | T2—397 2 |
| Numididae | 598.64 |
| Numismatics | 737 |
| Numismatists | 737.092 |
| Nunavik (Quebec) | T2—714 111 |
| Nunavut | 971.95 |
| | T2—719 5 |
| Nuneaton and Bedworth | |
| (England) | T2—424 83 |
| Nunggubuyu language | 499.15 |
| | T6—991 5 |
| Nuns | 206.57 |
| Buddhist | 294.365 7 |
| Christian | 255.9 |
| biography | 271.900 2 |
| *see Manual at* 230–280 | |

| | |
|---|---|
| Nuns | |
| Christian (continued) | |
| ecclesiology | 262.24 |
| guides to Christian life | 248.894 3 |
| Nuoro (Italy : Province) | T2—459 2 |
| ancient | T2—379 2 |
| Nuove musiche | 780.903 2 |
| Nupe (African people) | T5—963 3 |
| Nupe language | 496.33 |
| | T6—963 3 |
| Nupoid languages | 496.33 |
| | T6—963 3 |
| Nuremberg (Germany) | T2—433 24 |
| Nuremberg laws | |
| Holocaust, 1933–1945 | 940.531 842 |
| Nuremberg war crimes trials | 341.690 268 |
| Nuri (Afghanistan people) | T5—914 9 |
| Nuristani (Asian people) | T5—914 9 |
| Nuristani languages | 491.49 |
| | T6—914 9 |
| Nuristani literatures | 891.49 |
| Nürnberg (Germany) | T2—433 24 |
| Nurse and patient | 610.730 699 |
| Nurse and physician | 610.730 699 |
| Nurse practitioners | 610.730 92 |
| role and function | 610.730 692 |
| Nurseries (Children's rooms) | 643.530 83 |
| home economics | 643.530 83 |
| interior decoration | 747.77 |
| Nurseries (Plant culture) | 631.52 |
| floriculture | 635.915 2 |
| forestry | 634.956 4 |
| Nursery catalogs | 631.520 29 |
| Nursery practice | 631.52 |
| floriculture | 635.915 2 |
| forestry | 634.956 4 |
| Nursery rhymes | 398.8 |
| Nursery schools | 372.21 |
| Nurses | 610.730 92 |
| role and function | 610.730 69 |
| *see also* Nursing | |
| Nurses' aides | 610.730 92 |
| role and function | 610.730 698 |
| Nursing | 610.73 |
| health services | 362.173 |
| law | 344.041 4 |
| malpractice | 344.041 4 |
| medicine | 610.73 |
| school programs | 371.712 |
| Nursing (Breast feeding) | 649.33 |
| child rearing | 649.33 |
| health | 613.269 |
| human physiology | 612.664 |

Nursing assessment
  medicine 616.075
Nursing assistants 610.730 92
  role and function 610.730 698
Nursing care plans 610.73
Nursing diagnosis
  medicine 616.075
Nursing homes 362.16
  cooking 641.579
  meal service 642.56
  mental illness 362.23
  physical illness 362.16
  *see also* Health care facilities;
    Mental health services
Nursing interventions 610.73
Nursing orders (Christianity) 255.07
  church history 271.07
  women 255.907
    church history 271.907
Nursing process 610.73
Nusa Tenggara (Indonesia) T2—598 6
Nusa Tenggara Barat
  (Indonesia) T2—598 65
Nusa Tenggara Timur
  (Indonesia) T2—598 68
Nutation
  celestial mechanics 521.9
Nuthatches 598.82
Nutmeg 641.338 3
  botany 583.22
  *see also* Spices
Nutria 599.359
Nutrition 363.8
  animal husbandry 636.085 2
  animal physiology 572.41
  biology 572.4
    requirements 572.39
  health 613.2
  human physiology 612.3
  plants 572.42
    nutrient absorption 575.76
  prenatal care
    obstetrics 618.242
  primary education 372.373
  social welfare 363.8
    law 344.033
  *see also* Digestive system
  *see Manual at* 363.8 vs. 613.2,
    641.3
Nutrition disorders
  humans 362.196 39
    incidence 614.593 9
    medicine 616.39
    pediatrics 618.923 9

Nutrition disorders
  humans (continued)
    social services 362.196 39
    *see also* Digestive system
     diseases — humans
Nutrition support
  medicine 615.854 8
Nutrition surveys 363.82
Nutrition therapy
  medicine 615.854
Nutritional diseases
  humans 362.196 39
    *see also* Nutrition
     disorders — humans
Nutritional requirements 572.39
Nutritional services
  health services 362.176
  public administration 353.56
  schools 371.716
Nutritionists 363.809 2
Nutritive organs 573.3
  *see also* Digestive system
Nuts 581.464
  commercial processing 664.804 5
  cooking 641.645
  descriptive botany 581.464
  food 641.345
  forest products 634.987
  orchard crop 634.5
  physiology 575.67
Nuts (Fasteners) 621.882
Nuweveld Range (South
  Africa) T2—687 17
Nyakyusa-Ngonde language 496.391
   T6—963 91
Nyalas 599.642 3
Nyamwezi (African people) T5—963 94
Nyamwezi language 496.394
   T6—963 94
Nyanga language 496.394
   T6—963 94
Nyanja (African people) T5—963 918
Nyanja language 496.391 8
   T6—963 918
Nyanja literature 896.391 8
Nyankore language 496.395 6
   T6—963 956
Nyanza Province (Kenya) T2—676 29
Nyasa, Lake T2—689 7
Nyasaland 968.970 2
   T2—689 7
Nyaya (Philosophy) 181.43
Nyctaginaceae 583.53
Nyctibiidae 598.99

| | |
|---|---|
| Nye County (Nev.) | T2—793 34 |
| Nyerere, Julius K. (Julius Kambarage) | |
| Tanzanian history | 967.804 1 |
| Nyika (Nika) language | 496.395 |
| | T6—963 95 |
| Nyika-Safwa languages | 496.391 |
| | T6—963 91 |
| Nyika-Taita languages | 496.395 |
| | T6—963 95 |
| Nyilamba-Langi languages | 496.394 |
| | T6—963 94 |
| Nylons (Plastics) | 668.423 5 |
| textiles | 677.473 |
| *see also* Textiles | |
| Nymphaeales | 583.29 |
| Nymphomania | |
| medicine | 616.858 33 |
| Nyngan (N.S.W.) | T2—944 9 |
| Nynorsk language | 439.82 |
| | T6—398 2 |
| Nynorsk literature | 839.82 |
| Nyon (Switzerland : District) | T2—494 522 1 |
| Nyoro-Ganda languages | 496.395 6 |
| | T6—963 956 |
| Nytrils | |
| textiles | 677.474 4 |
| *see also* Textiles | |
| Nyunga | T5—991 5 |
| Nyungar dialects | 499.15 |
| | T6—991 5 |
| Nzima (African people) | T5—963 38 |
| Nzima language | 496.338 |
| | T6—963 38 |

# O

| | |
|---|---|
| Oadby and Wigston (England) | T2—425 43 |
| Oahe, Lake (S.D. and N.D.) | T2—783 5 |
| Oahu (Hawaii) | T2—969 3 |
| Oak Bay (B.C.) | T2—711 28 |
| Oakey (Qld.) | T2—943 3 |
| Oakland (Calif.) | T2—794 66 |
| Oakland County (Mich.) | T2—774 38 |
| Oaks | 583.46 |
| forestry | 634.972 1 |
| lumber | 674.142 |
| Oarfishes | 597.64 |
| OAS (Alliance) | 341.245 |
| Oatlands (Tas.) | T2—946 3 |

| | |
|---|---|
| Oats | 641.331 3 |
| botany | 584.9 |
| commercial processing technology | 664.72 |
| cooking | 641.631 3 |
| food | 641.331 3 |
| food crop | 633.13 |
| forage crop | 633.253 |
| Oaxaca (Mexico) | T2—727 4 |
| Ob-Ugric languages | 494.51 |
| | T6—945 1 |
| Obadiah (Biblical book) | 224.91 |
| Obama, Barack | |
| United States history | 973.932 |
| Oban (Scotland) | T2—414 2 |
| Obasanjo, Olusegun | |
| Nigerian history | 966.905 4 |
| OBE (Parapsychology) | 133.95 |
| Obedience | |
| home child care | 649.64 |
| Obedience (Christian doctrine) | 234.6 |
| Obedience training (Pets) | 636.088 7 |
| Oberaargau (Switzerland) | T2—494 549 3 |
| Oberbayern (Germany) | T2—433 6 |
| Oberfranken (Germany) | T2—433 1 |
| Oberhausen (Germany) | T2—435 537 7 |
| Oberhavel (Germany : Landkreis) | T2—431 54 |
| Oberholzer (South Africa : District) | T2—682 22 |
| Oberösterreich (Austria) | T2—436 2 |
| Oberpfalz (Germany) | T2—433 4 |
| Obersimmental-Saanen (Switzerland) | T2—494 541 2 |
| Oberspreewald-Lausitz (Germany : Landkreis) | T2—431 51 |
| Obesity | |
| low-calorie cooking | 641.563 5 |
| medicine | 616.398 |
| *see also* Digestive system diseases — humans | |
| Obiang Nguema Mbasogo, Teodoro | |
| Equatorial Guinean history | 967.180 32 |
| Obion County (Tenn.) | T2—768 13 |
| Obituaries | 920 |
| Obituary sermons | |
| Christianity | 252.9 |
| Object-oriented databases | |
| computer science | 005.757 |
| Object-oriented programming | 005.117 |
| Object-relational databases | |
| computer science | 005.756 |
| Objective knowledge | 121.4 |

Objectivism 149
Objectivity
  epistemology 121.4
Oblates 255.76
  church history 271.76
  women 255.97
    church history 271.97
Obligations of citizens 323.65
Oblong books 099
Oboe concertos 784.285 2
Oboes 788.52
  instrument 788.521 9
  music 788.52
  *see also* Woodwind instruments
Obote, A. Milton (Apollo Milton)
  Ugandan history 967.610 41
    1962–1971 967.610 41
    1980–1985 967.610 43
Obregón, Alvaro
  Mexican history 972.082 2
O'Brien County (Iowa) T2—777 14
Obscenity
  criminology 364.174
    law 345.027 4
  ethics 176.7
    religion 205.667
      Christianity 241.667
  law 344.054 7
  postal handling 383.120 5
  social problem 363.47
Obscenity in speech 179.5
Observation
  descriptive research 001.433
        T1—072 3
Observatories
  architecture 727.5
  astronomy 522.1
Obsessive-compulsive disorder
  medicine 616.852 27
  *see also* Mental disorders
Obsidian 552.22
  glyptics 736.28
Obstacle courses (Military
  training) 355.544
Obstetrical disorders
  incidence 614.599 22
  medicine 618.2
Obstetrical nursing 618.202 31
Obstetrical surgery 618.8
Obstetricians 618.200 92
  law 344.041 2
  malpractice 344.041 21
  role and function 618.202 32

Obstetrics 618.2
  anesthesiology 617.968 2
  veterinary medicine 636.089 82
Obstructions
  intestine
    medicine 616.342
    *see also* Digestive system
      diseases — humans
    surgery 617.554
Obstructive pulmonary disease
  medicine 616.24
  *see also* Respiratory tract
    diseases — humans
Obwalden (Switzerland) T2—494 764
Ocarinas 788.38
  *see also* Woodwind instruments
Occasional sermons
  Christianity 252.6
Occasionalism 147
Occident 909.098 21
        T2—182 1
Occidental Mindoro
  (Philippines) T2—599 3
Occidental region
  (Paraguay) T2—892 2
Occitan language 449
        T6—491
Occlusion disorders
  dentistry 617.643
  incidence 614.599 6
Occult sciences 130
  *see Manual at* 130 vs. 200
Occultations 523.99
Occultism 130
  arts T3C—37
  literature 808.803 7
    history and criticism 809.933 7
    specific literatures T3B—080 37
    history and
      criticism T3B—093 7
  religious practice 203
  *see Manual at* 001.9 and 130;
    *also at* 130 vs. 200
Occultism and religion 201.613
  Christianity 261.513
  Islam 297.261
  Judaism 296.371
Occultists 130.92
Occupational aptitude tests 153.94
Occupational diseases
  health 613.62
  law 344.043 698 03

Occupational diseases (continued)
  medicine    616.980 3
    *see also* Environmental
      diseases — humans
  workers' compensation law    344.021 8
Occupational ethics    174
  religion    205.64
  *see also* Ethical problems
Occupational groups    305.9
        T1—088
  customs    390.4
  dress    391.04
  journalism for    070.486
  religion
    Christianity
      guides to life    248.88
  *see Manual at* 305.9 vs. 305.5
Occupational guidance    331.702
  *see also* Vocational guidance
Occupational health    613.62
Occupational health nursing    610.734 6
Occupational health services
  personnel management    658.382
  public administration    352.67
Occupational licensing    354.928 4
  law    344.017
  public administration    354.928 4
Occupational medicine    616.980 3
Occupational mobility    305.9
  economics    331.127 2
Occupational requirements
  personnel selection    658.311 2
Occupational safety    363.11
  *see also* Industrial safety
Occupational specialties    331.702
        T1—023
  *see also* Vocational guidance
Occupational stress    158.72
Occupational therapy
  medicine    615.851 5
Occupational training    370.113
        T1—071 5
  *see also* Vocational education
Occupations    331.7
        T1—023
  active employment    331.125
  collective bargaining    331.890 4
  compensation    331.28
  demand    331.123
  economics    331.7
  employment conditions    331.204
  folklore    398.275 3
    history and criticism    398.355 3

Occupations (continued)
  industrial relations    331.04
  labor force    331.119
  labor market    331.129
  labor unions    331.881
  pensions    331.252 9
  public administration    354.9
  social groups    305.9
  sociology of production    306.36
  strikes (work stoppages)    331.892 8
  unemployment    331.137 8
  works for    T1—024
Occupied countries    355.49
  aftermath of war    355.028
  World War I    940.33
  World War II    940.533 6
  *see Manual at* 930–990
Occupied territory    355.49
Ocean-atmosphere interactions    551.524 6
Ocean basins    T2—182
Ocean bottom    551.468
  law of nations    341.455
  *see also* Ocean floor
Ocean bottom vehicles
  engineering    629.292
Ocean circulation    551.462
Ocean color    551.465 5
Ocean County (N.J.)    T2—749 48
Ocean currents    551.462
Ocean dumping    363.728
  law    344.046 26
  *see also* Waste control
Ocean engineering    620.416 2
Ocean Falls (B.C.)    T2—711 1
Ocean floor    551.468
  biology    578.777
  ecology    577.77
  oceanography    551.468
Ocean floor mining    622.295
Ocean floor vehicles
  engineering    629.292
Ocean liners    387.243 2
  design    623.812 432
  engineering    623.824 32
  *see also* Ships
Ocean marine insurance    368.22
Ocean marine war risk insurance    368.22
Ocean sunfishes    597.64
Ocean temperatures    551.465 3
  meteorological effect    551.524 6
Ocean thermal power conversion    333.914

Ocean transportation 387.5
  law 343.096 2
    *see Manual at* 341.45 vs.
    343.0962
  public administration 354.78
  transportation services 387.5
Ocean travel 910.45
  arts T3C—321 62
Ocean waters 551.46
  *see also* Oceans
Oceana County (Mich.) T2—774 59
Oceania 995
  T2—95
Oceanic languages 499.5
  T6—995
Oceanographers 551.460 92
Oceanography 551.46
  law 344.095 5
  *see Manual at* 578.76–.77 vs.
  551.46, 551.48
Oceans 551.46
  T2—162
  biology 578.77
  ecology 577.7
  geologic agent 551.36
  influence on precipitation 551.577 5
  interactions with atmosphere 551.524 6
  law of nations 341.45
    *see Manual at* 341.45 vs.
    343.0962
  physical geology 551.46
  public administration 354.369
  resource economics 333.916 4
  *see Manual at* T2—162
Ocelot 599.752
  animal husbandry 636.89
Ochil Hills (Scotland) T2—412 8
Ochiltree County (Tex.) T2—764 815
Ochnaceae 583.624
Ochotona 599.329
Ochotonidae 599.329
Oconee County (Ga.) T2—758 193
Oconee County (S.C.) T2—757 21
Oconee River (Ga.) T2—758 6
Oconto County (Wis.) T2—775 37
Ocotepeque (Honduras :
  Dept.) T2—728 383
Ocotillo 583.628
OCR (Computer science) 006.424
Octal system (Numeration) 513.5
Octets
  chamber music 785.18
  vocal music 783.18

Octopoda 594.56
  paleozoology 564.56
Octopuses 594.56
  cooking 641.694
  food 641.394
    commercial processing 664.94
Ocular motility disorders
  ophthalmology 617.762
    *see also* Eye diseases —
    humans
Ocular neuromuscular
  mechanism
  human physiology 612.846
  ophthalmology 617.762
Odd Fellows 366.3
  biography 366.309 2
Odd-toed ungulates 599.66
Odendaalsrus (South
  Africa : District) T2—685 3
Oder-Spree (Germany :
  Landkreis) T2—431 53
Oderland-Spree (Germany :
  Raumordnungsregion) T2—431 53
Odes 808.814 3
  history and criticism 809.143
  specific literatures T3B—104 3
    individual authors T3A—1
Odes of Solomon 229.912
Odessa (Ukraine : Oblast) T2—477 2
Odes´ka oblast´ (Ukraine) T2—477 2
Odi (South Africa : District) T2—682 41
ODL (Open and distance
  learning) 371.35
  adult education 374.4
  higher education 378.175
Odobenidae 599.799
Odocoileus 599.652
Odocoileus hemionus 599.653
Odonata 595.733
Odontoceti 599.5
  paleozoology 569.5
Odontopteris 561.597
Oea (Libya) T2—397 4
Oestridae 595.774
Off-road biking 796.63
Off-road vehicles 388.34
  driving 629.283 042
  engineering 629.220 42
  military engineering 623.747
  repair 629.287 042
  transportation services 388.34
  *see also* Automotive vehicles
Offaly (Ireland) T2—418 6

| | |
|---|---|
| Offenbach am Main (Germany) | T2—434 163 |
| Offenders | 364.3 |
| | T1—086 927 |
| criminology | 364.3 |
| law | 345.03 |
| pastoral care | |
| Christianity | 259.5 |
| punishment | 364.6 |
| welfare services | 364.6 |
| Offenses against military discipline | 355.133 4 |
| Offenses against property | 364.16 |
| Holocaust, 1933–1945 | 940.531 813 2 |
| restitution | 940.531 814 4 |
| law | 345.026 |
| Offenses against public morals | 364.17 |
| law | 345.027 |
| Offenses against public safety | 364.142 |
| law | 345.024 2 |
| Offenses against religion | 364.188 |
| law | 345.028 8 |
| Offenses against the person | 364.15 |
| law | 345.025 |
| Offensive arms | |
| art metalwork | 739.7 |
| customs | 399 |
| Offerings (Religion) | 203.4 |
| Christianity | 248.6 |
| Judaism | 296.492 |
| Offertory | 264.36 |
| music | 782.323 5 |
| Office buildings | |
| architecture | 725.23 |
| construction | 690.523 |
| health | 613.5 |
| institutional housekeeping | 647.962 3 |
| lighting | 621.322 523 |
| Office employees | 651.309 2 |
| *see also* Office workers | |
| Office equipment | |
| armed forces | 355.81 |
| manufacturing technology | 681.6 |
| office services | 651.2 |
| procurement | 658.72 |
| | T1—068 7 |
| Office etiquette | 395.52 |
| Office furniture | |
| manufacturing technology | 684 |
| office services | 651.23 |
| procurement | 658.72 |
| Office hours (Religion) | 264.15 |
| Anglican | 264.030 15 |
| music | 782.324 |

| | |
|---|---|
| Office hours (Religion) (continued) | |
| Roman Catholic | 264.020 15 |
| texts | 264.024 |
| Office layout | |
| plant management | 658.23 |
| Office management | 651.3 |
| Office of chief executive | |
| management | 658.42 |
| public administration | 352.237 |
| Office practice | 651.374 |
| Office security | |
| office services | 651 |
| public administration | 352.379 |
| Office services | 651 |
| Office suites (Computer software) | 005.5 |
| Office supplies | |
| armed forces | 355.81 |
| office services | 651.29 |
| procurement | 658.72 |
| Office workers | 651.309 2 |
| labor economics | 331.761 651 3 |
| personnel management | 651.306 83 |
| public administration | 352.63 |
| social class | 305.965 13 |
| Officers (Armed forces) | 355.009 2 |
| role and function | 355.332 |
| Officers' clubs | 355.346 |
| Officers of corporations | |
| executive management | 658.4 |
| law | 346.066 42 |
| Officers' training (Armed forces) | 355.55 |
| Official ceremonies and observances | 394.4 |
| armed forces | 355.17 |
| customs | 394.4 |
| Official gazettes | 351.05 |
| *see also* Serials | |
| Official languages | |
| primary education | 372.65 |
| Official residences | |
| architecture | 725.17 |
| Official secrets | 342.068 4 |
| Offline processing | 004.3 |
| *see also* Processing modes — computer science | |
| Offset printing | 686.231 5 |
| Offshore mining | 622.295 |
| Offshore petroleum drilling | 622.338 19 |
| Offshore structures | 627.98 |
| Offspring | 306.874 |
| | T1—085 4 |
| Ogaden War, 1977–1978 | 963.071 |
| Ogasawara-guntō (Japan) | T2—528 |

Ogeechee River (Ga.)           T2—758 6
Ogemaw County (Mich.)          T2—774 75
Oglala Indians                 T5—975 244
Ogle County (Ill.)             T2—773 32
Oglethorpe County (Ga.)        T2—758 175
Ogliastra (Italy : Province)   T2—459 28
  ancient                      T2—379 28
Ogres                          398.21
  *see also* Legendary beings
Ogun State (Nigeria)           T2—669 23
Ogwr (Wales)                   T2—429 71
Ohau, Lake (N.Z.)              T2—938 97
Ohio                           977.1
                               T2—771
Ohio County (Ind.)             T2—772 123
Ohio County (Ky.)              T2—769 835
Ohio County (W. Va.)           T2—754 14
Ohio River                     T2—77
  Kentucky                     T2—769
  West Virginia                T2—754 1
Ohmmeters                      621.374 2
Oholot                         296.123 6
Oil (Petroleum)                553.282
  economic geology             553.282
  extraction                   622.338 2
  extractive economics         338.272 82
    law                        343.077 2
  pipeline technology          665.544
  processing                   665.5
    economics                  338.476 655
    enterprises                338.766 55
  prospecting                  622.182 82
  public administration        354.45
  public utilities             363.6
    law                        343.092 6
  resource economics           333.823 2
    law                        346.046 823 2
  *see also* Petroleum
Oil beetles                    595.769
Oil depletion allowance        336.243 16
  tax law                      343.052 34
Oil gas                        665.773
Oil heating
  buildings                    697.044
Oil lamps                      621.323
  *see also* Lighting
Oil painting                   751.45
Oil palms                      633.851
  agriculture                  633.851
  botany                       584.5
Oil pollution                  363.738 2
  law                          344.046 332
  water supply engineering     628.168 33
  *see also* Pollution

Oil processes
  photographic printing        773.8
Oil-producing plants
  agriculture                  633.85
Oil sands                      553.283
  *see also* Tar sands
Oil shale                      553.283
  economic geology             553.283
  mining                       622.338 3
    law                        343.077 2
  processing                   665.4
Oil-soluble paint              667.62
Oil spills                     363.738 2
  law                          344.046 332
  water pollution engineering  628.168 33
Oil well flooding              622.338 2
Oil wells                      622.338 2
Oilbird                        598.99
Oiling
  woodwork
    buildings                  698.33
Oils
  applied nutrition            613.284
  food technology              664.3
  hydraulic-power technology   621.204 24
  industrial                   665
  materials science            620.198
  metabolism
    human physiology           612.397
  paint technology             667.622
Oilseed plants
  agriculture                  633.85
Ointments
  pharmaceutical chemistry     615.19
Oirat                          T5—942
Oirat-Kalmyk language          494.2
                               T6—942
Oise (France)                  T2—442 64
Ōita-ken (Japan)               T2—522 8
Ojibwa Indians                 T5—973 33
Ojibwa language                497.333
                               T6—973 33
Ojibwa languages               497.33
                               T6—973 3
Ojibwa literature              897.333
Ojibway Indians                T5—973 33
Okaloosa County (Fla.)         T2—759 982
Okanagan Lake (B.C.)           T2—711 5
Okanagan-Similkameen
  (B.C.)                       T2—711 5
Okanogan County (Wash.)        T2—797 28
Okapi                          599.638
Okayama-ken (Japan)            T2—521 94
Okeechobee, Lake (Fla.)        T2—759 39

| | | | |
|---|---|---|---|
| Okeechobee County (Fla.) | T2—759 53 | Old Catholic churches (continued) | |
| Okefenokee Swamp (Ga. | | moral theology | 241.044 8 |
| and Fla.) | T2—758 752 | public worship | 264.048 |
| Okfuskee County (Okla.) | T2—766 73 | religious education | 268.848 |
| Okhotsk, Sea of | 551.461 453 | theology | 230.48 |
| | T2—164 53 | Old Catholics | |
| Okinawa Island (Japan) | T2—522 94 | biography | 284.8 |
| Okinawa-ken (Japan) | T2—522 9 | Old Church Slavic language | 491.817 01 |
| Oklahoma | 976.6 | | T6—918 17 |
| | T2—766 | Old Danish language | 439.817 01 |
| Oklahoma City (Okla.) | T2—766 38 | Old English language | 429 |
| Oklahoma County (Okla.) | T2—766 38 | | T6—29 |
| Oklahoma Panhandle | | Old English literature | 829 |
| (Okla.) | T2—766 13 | Old French language | 447.01 |
| Oklahoma Territory | T2—766 1 | | T6—41 |
| Okmulgee County (Okla.) | T2—766 83 | Old Frisian language | 439.2 |
| Oko languages | 496.33 | | T6—392 |
| | T6—963 3 | Old Frisian literature | 839.2 |
| Okpe language | 496.33 | Old-growth forests | 333.75 |
| | T6—963 3 | *see also* Forest lands | |
| Okra | 641.356 48 | Old High German language | 437.01 |
| botany | 583.685 | | T6—31 |
| commercial processing | 664.805 648 | Old Icelandic language | 439.6 |
| cooking | 641.656 48 | | T6—396 1 |
| food | 641.356 48 | Old Icelandic literature | 839.6 |
| garden crop | 635.648 | Old Indic language | 491.29 |
| Oktibbeha County (Miss.) | T2—762 953 | | T6—912 9 |
| Oktoberfest | 394.264 4 | Old Indic literature | 891.29 |
| Olacaceae | 583.88 | Old Italian language | 457.01 |
| Olancho (Honduras) | T2—728 33 | | T6—51 |
| Öland (Sweden) | T2—486 3 | Old Kingdom (Egypt) | 932.012 |
| Öland (Sweden : Island) | T2—486 3 | Old Latin language | 477 |
| Olbia-Tempio (Italy : | | | T6—71 |
| Province) | T2—459 37 | Old Low Franconian language | 439.31 |
| ancient | T2—379 37 | | T6—393 1 |
| Old age | 305.26 | Old Low Franconian literature | 839.31 |
| Old-age and survivors' insurance | 368.3 | Old Low German language | 439.4 |
| government-sponsored | 368.43 | | T6—394 |
| law | 344.023 | Old Low German literature | 839.4 |
| Old age homes | 362.61 | Old Low Germanic languages | 439 |
| Old age pensions | 331.252 | | T6—39 |
| *see also* Pensions | | Old Low Germanic literatures | 839 |
| Old Bulgarian language | 491.817 01 | Old Norse language | 439.6 |
| | T6—918 17 | | T6—396 1 |
| Old Bulgarian literature | 891.81 | Old Norse literature | 839.6 |
| Old Castile (Spain) | T2—463 5 | Old Northwest | 977 |
| Old Catholic churches | 284.8 | | T2—77 |
| church government | 262.048 | Old people | 305.26 |
| parishes | 254.048 | | T1—084 6 |
| church law | 262.984 8 | *see also* Older people | |
| doctrines | 230.48 | Old Persian language | 491.51 |
| catechisms and creeds | 238.48 | | T6—915 1 |
| guides to Christian life | 248.484 8 | Old Persian literature | 891.51 |
| missions | 266.48 | | |

Old Portuguese language — 469.701
  T6—69
Old Prussian language — 491.91
  T6—919 1
Old Prussian literature — 891.91
Old Russian language — 491.770 1
  T6—917 1
Old Saxon language — 439.4
  T6—394
Old Saxon literature — 839.4
Old School Baptists — 286.4
  *see also* Baptists
Old Southwest — 976
  T2—76
Old Spanish language — 467.01
  T6—61
Old Stone Age — 930.12
Old Swedish language — 439.770 1
Old Testament — 221
  *see Manual at* 221
Old Testament Apocrypha — 229
Old Testament pseudepigrapha — 229.91
Old Testament theology
  Christianity — 230.041 1
Old Turkic language — 494.31
  T6—943 1
Old World badger — 599.767 2
Old World flycatchers — 598.848
Old World fruit bats — 599.49
Old World monkeys — 599.86
Old World pitcher plants — 583.75
Old World polecats — 599.766 2
Old World porcupines — 599.359 7
Old World rabbit — 599.322
Old World runners (Lizards) — 597.958
Old World vultures — 598.94
Old World warblers — 598.843
Oldenburg (Germany) — T2—435 914
Older men — 305.261
Older minorities (Ethnic and
  national)
  social welfare — 362.699
Older people — 305.26
  T1—084 6
  accident insurance
    government-sponsored — 368.426
    law — 344.022 6
  architecture for — 720.846
  civil rights — 323.354
  cooking for — 641.562 7
  customs — 390.084 6
  etiquette — 395.126
  geriatrics — 618.97
  government programs — 353.537

Older people (continued)
  health — 613.043 8
  health insurance
    government-sponsored — 368.426
    law — 344.022 6
  home care — 649.808 46
  institutional buildings
    architecture — 725.56
  institutional care — 362.61
  labor economics — 331.398
  legal status — 346.013
    constitutional law — 342.087 74
    private law — 346.013
  libraries for — 027.622
  life skills — 646.79
  material assistance — 362.63
  physical fitness — 613.704 46
  physiology — 612.67
  psychology — 155.67
  recreation — 790.192 6
    indoor — 793.019 26
    outdoor — 796.084 6
  relations with government — 323.354
  religion — 200.846
    Christianity — 270.084 6
      devotional literature — 242.65
      guides to life — 248.85
      pastoral care — 259.3
    guides to life — 204.408 46
  residential care — 362.61
  social aspects — 305.26
  social welfare — 362.6
    law — 344.032 6
    public administration — 353.537
Older women — 305.262
Older workers — 331.398
  *see also* Older people
Oldham (England :
  Metropolitan Borough) — T2—427 393
Oldham County (Ky.) — T2—769 383
Oldham County (Tex.) — T2—764 824
Oleales — 583.87
Oleanders — 635.933 93
  botany — 583.93
  floriculture — 635.933 93
Oleasters — 635.933 82
  botany — 583.82
  floriculture — 635.933 82
Olefins — 547.412
  chemical engineering — 661.814
  textiles — 677.474 5
    *see also* Textiles

| | | | |
|---|---|---|---|
| Oleomargarine | | Olympic Games | 796.48 |
| food technology | 664.32 | summer | 796.48 |
| Olfaction | 573.877 | winter | 796.98 |
| human physiology | 612.86 | Olympic Mountains (Wash.) | T2—797 94 |
| Olfactory nerves | 573.877 | Olympic National Park | |
| human physiology | 612.86 | (Wash.) | T2—797 98 |
| medicine | 616.856 | Olympic Peninsula (Wash.) | T2—797 94 |
| Olfactory organs | 573.877 | Olyreae | 584.9 |
| human anatomy | 611.86 | Omagh (Northern Ireland : | |
| human physiology | 612.86 | District) | T2—416 47 |
| *see also* Nervous system | | Omaha (Neb.) | T2—782 254 |
| Olfactory perception | | Omaha Indians | T5—975 253 |
| psychology | 152.166 | Omaha language | 497.525 3 |
| Oligarchy | 321.5 | | T6—975 253 |
| Oligocene epoch | 551.785 | Oman | 953.53 |
| geology | 551.785 | | T2—535 3 |
| paleontology | 560.178 5 | ancient | 939.49 |
| Oligochaeta | 592.64 | | T2—394 9 |
| Oligomenorrhea | | Oman, Gulf of | 551.461 536 |
| gynecology | 618.172 | | T2—165 36 |
| *see also* Female genital | | Omanis | T5—927 535 3 |
| diseases — humans | | Ombudsmen | 352.88 |
| Oligopoly | 338.82 | law | 342.066 7 |
| economics | 338.82 | legislative branch | 328.345 2 |
| international economics | 338.884 | military administration | 355.685 |
| Oligosaccharides | 572.565 | public administration | 352.88 |
| *see also* Carbohydrates | | agency ombudsmen | 352.35 |
| Olive oil | 641.346 3 | Omens | 133.334 |
| cooking with | 641.646 3 | religion | 203.2 |
| food | 641.346 3 | Omentum | |
| food technology | 664.362 | human anatomy | 611.38 |
| Oliver County (N.D.) | T2—784 843 | human physiology | 612.33 |
| Olives | 641.346 3 | medicine | 616.38 |
| agriculture | 634.63 | surgery | 617.558 |
| botany | 583.87 | Omineca Mountains (B.C.) | T2—711 85 |
| commercial processing | 664.804 63 | Omineca River (B.C.) | T2—711 82 |
| cooking | 641.646 3 | Omissions insurance | 368.564 |
| food | 641.346 3 | Omnipotence of God | 212.7 |
| Olivetans | 255.13 | *see also* Attributes of God | |
| church history | 271.13 | Omniscience of God | 212.7 |
| women | 255.97 | *see also* Attributes of God | |
| church history | 271.97 | Omotic languages | 493.59 |
| Olmsted County (Minn.) | T2—776 155 | | T6—935 9 |
| Olomoucký kraj (Czech | | Omotic peoples | T5—935 9 |
| Republic) | T2—437 27 | Omsk (Russia : Oblast) | T2—573 |
| Olsztyn (Poland : | | Omskaĩa oblast' (Russia) | T2—573 |
| Voivodeship) | T2—438 32 | On-the-job training | 331.259 2 |
| Olt (Romania) | T2—498 2 | | T1—071 55 |
| Olten (Switzerland : Bezirk) | T2—494 351 7 | *see also* Vocational education | |
| Olten-Gösgen (Switzerland) | T2—494 351 | Ona Indians | T5—987 |
| Oltenia (Romania) | T2—498 4 | Onagraceae | 583.76 |
| Olympia (Greece : Ancient | | | |
| sanctuary) | T2—388 | | |
| Olympia (Wash.) | T2—797 79 | | |

Onchocerciasis
  incidence    614.555 2
  medicine    616.965 2
    *see also* Communicable
      diseases — humans
Oncogenes
  medicine    616.994 042
Oncogenic viruses    579.256 9
Oncology    616.994
Oncopods    592.7
  paleozoology    562.7
Oncorhynchus    597.56
Oncoviruses    579.256 9
Ondatra    599.357 9
Ondes martenot    786.73
  *see also* Electrophones
Ondo State (Nigeria)    T2—669 28
One-act plays
  literature    808.824 1
    history and criticism    809.241
    specific literatures    T3B—204 1
      individual authors    T3A—2
One-dish cooking    641.82
One old cat    796.357 8
One-person corporations    338.74
  management    658.045
  *see also* Corporations
One-person enterprises
  management    658.041
  initiation    658.114 1
One-room schools    372.125
Onega Lake (Russia)    T2—471 5
Oneida County (Idaho)    T2—796 41
Oneida County (N.Y.)    T2—747 62
Oneida County (Wis.)    T2—775 25
Oneida Indians    T5—975 543
Oneida Lake (N.Y.)    T2—747 62
Oneida language    497.554 3
   T6—975 543
Onions    641.352 5
  botany    584.33
  commercial processing    664.805 25
  cooking    641.652 5
  food    641.352 5
  garden crop    635.25
Onionskin paper    676.282 3
Online advertising    659.144
Online auctions    381.177
  management    658.877 7
Online catalogs    025.313 2
Online chat groups    004.693
Online etiquette    395.5
Online help facilities    005.3
  development    005.15

Online information systems    025.04
  *see also* Information storage
    and retrieval systems
Online marketing    381.142
  management    658.872
Online processing    004
Online shopping    381.142
  law    343.081 142
Online social networks
  computer science    006.754
Only children    306.874
   T1—085 4
  family relationships    306.874
  home care    649.142
  psychology    155.442
Onomastics    929.97
  etymology    412
    specific languages    T4—2
  geographic names    910.014
    gazetters    910.3
  personal names    929.4
Onondaga County (N.Y.)    T2—747 65
Onondaga Indians    T5—975 54
Onondaga language    497.554
   T6—975 54
Onslow County (N.C.)    T2—756 23
Ontario    971.3
   T2—713
  *see Manual at* T2—713 and
    T2—714
Ontario, Lake (N.Y. and
  Ont.)    T2—747 9
  New York    T2—747 9
  Ontario    T2—713 5
Ontario, Northern    T2—713 1
Ontario County (N.Y.)    T2—747 86
Ontologies    006.332
Ontology    111
Ontonagon County (Mich.)    T2—774 985
Onychophora    592.74
Onygenales    579.565
Onyx    553.87
  *see also* Semiprecious stones
Onyx marble    553.55
  economic geology    553.55
  quarrying    622.355
O'Odham Indians    T5—974 552
O'Odham language    497.455 2
   T6—974 552
Oolite    552.58
Oomycetes    579.54
Oort cloud objects    523.497
Oost-Vlaanderen (Belgium)    T2—493 14

| | |
|---|---|
| Op art | 709.040 72 |
| painting | 759.067 2 |
| sculpture | 735.230 472 |
| Op-ed pages | 070.442 |
| Opah | 597.64 |
| Opals | 553.873 |
| mineralogy | 549.68 |
| *see also* Semiprecious stones | |
| Open air schools | 371.384 |
| Open and distance learning | 371.35 |
| adult education | 374.4 |
| higher education | 378.175 |
| Open classroom grouping | 371.256 |
| Open classroom instruction | 371.394 1 |
| Open clusters (Stars) | 523.852 |
| Open-cut mining | 622.292 |
| Open economy | 330.122 |
| Open-end mutual funds | 332.632 7 |
| Open-field system | |
| land economics | 333.2 |
| Open fires | |
| heating buildings | 697.1 |
| Open-hearth furnace practice | 669.142 2 |
| Open learning | |
| adult education | 374.4 |
| Open-loop systems | |
| automation engineering | 629.82 |
| Open-market operations | 332.114 |
| central banking | 332.114 |
| macroeconomic policy | 339.53 |
| Open-pit mining | 622.292 |
| Open plan schools | 371.256 |
| instruction | 371.394 1 |
| Open shop | 331.889 2 |
| Open stacks | 025.81 |
| Open Systems Interconnection | 004.62 |
| Open universities (Alternative | |
| higher education) | 378.03 |
| *see also* Higher education | |
| Openings (Buildings) | 721.82 |
| architecture | 721.82 |
| construction | 690.182 |
| Openings (Chess) | 794.122 |
| Openings (Physiography) | T2—144 |
| Openwork fabrics | 677.65 |
| Opera glasses | |
| manufacturing technology | 681.412 5 |
| Opera houses | |
| architecture | 725.822 |
| history | 792.509 |
| Opera reviews | 792.545 |
| Opera singers | 782.109 2 |
| Operant conditioning | 153.152 6 |

| | |
|---|---|
| Operas | 782.1 |
| music | 782.1 |
| stage presentation | 792.5 |
| *see Manual at* 782.1 vs. 792.5, | |
| 792.6 | |
| Operating budgets (Public) | 352.48 |
| *see also* Budgets (Public) | |
| Operating rooms (Surgery) | 617.917 |
| Operating systems | 005.43 |
| certification | 005.430 76 |
| graphics programming | 006.678 2 |
| graphics programs | 006.688 2 |
| multimedia-systems | |
| programming | 006.778 2 |
| multimedia-systems programs | 006.788 2 |
| programming | 005.42 |
| Operation Desert Storm, 1991 | 956.704 424 |
| Operational amplifiers | 621.395 |
| Operational audits | 658.401 3 |
| public administration | 352.439 |
| Operational calculus | 515.72 |
| Operations (Mathematics) | 511.33 |
| number theory | 512.72 |
| Operations income | |
| financial management | 658.155 4 |
| Operations research | 003 |
| | T1—011 |
| management decision making | 658.403 4 |
| Operative gynecology | 618.105 9 |
| Operative surgery | 617.91 |
| Operator algebras | 512.556 |
| Operator errors | 363.120 1 |
| *see also* Transportation safety | |
| Operator theory | 515.724 |
| Operators (Mathematics) | 515.724 |
| Operettas | 782.12 |
| music | 782.12 |
| stage presentation | 792.5 |
| Ophicleides | 788.99 |
| *see also* Brass instruments | |
| Ophidiidae | 597.63 |
| Ophioglossales | 587.33 |
| paleobotany | 561.73 |
| Ophiurida | 593.94 |
| Ophiuroidea | 593.94 |
| paleozoology | 563.94 |
| Ophthalmic nursing | 617.702 31 |
| Ophthalmologists | 617.709 2 |
| role and function | 617.702 32 |
| Ophthalmology | 617.7 |
| anesthesiology | 617.967 7 |
| geriatrics | 618.977 7 |
| nursing | 617.702 31 |
| pediatrics | 618.920 977 |

Opiliaceae 583.88
Opilioacariformes 595.42
Opiliones 595.43
Opisthobranchia 594.34
Opisthocomidae 598.74
Opium
　pharmacokinetics 615.782 2
　pharmacology 615.323 35
Opium abuse 362.293
　medicine 616.863 2
　personal health 613.83
　social welfare 362.293
　*see also* Substance abuse
Opium War, 1840–1842 951.033
Opole (Poland :
　Voivodeship) T2—438 55
Opolskie Voivodeship
　(Poland) T2—438 55
Opossum shrimps 595.375
Opossums 599.276
Opossums (America) 599.276
Opossums (Australasia) 599.23
Opotiki District (N.Z.) T2—934 28
Oppland fylke (Norway) T2—482 5
Opposition parties (Legislatures) 328.369
Optic nerve diseases
　incidence 614.599 7
　ophthalmology 617.732
　*see also* Eye diseases —
　　humans
Optic nerves 573.882 8
　animal physiology 573.882 8
　human anatomy 611.84
　human physiology 612.843
　ophthalmology 617.732
　*see also* Eyes
Optical art 709.040 72
　painting 759.067 2
　sculpture 735.230 472
Optical binaries 523.841
Optical character recognition 006.424
　computer engineering 621.399 4
Optical communications
　engineering 621.382 7
Optical components
　cameras 771.35
Optical computers
　engineering 621.391
　　*see Manual at* 006.37
　　　vs. 006.42, 621.367,
　　　621.391, 621.399
Optical crystallography 548.9

Optical data processing 621.367
　computer science 006.42
　engineering 621.399 6
　*see Manual at* 006.37 vs.
　　006.42, 621.367, 621.391,
　　621.399
Optical detectors
　manufacturing technology 681.25
Optical diagnosis
　medicine 616.075 45
Optical digital discs 004.565
　engineering 621.397 67
Optical disc technology 621.382 7
Optical engineering 621.36
　military engineering 623.042
Optical-fiber cable
　computer science 004.64
　engineering 621.398 1
Optical-fiber communication 621.382 75
Optical glass 666.156
Optical illusions 152.148
Optical instruments
　manufacturing technology 681.4
Optical metallography 669.950 282
Optical pattern recognition
　computer science 006.42
　engineering 621.399 4
　　*see Manual at* 006.37
　　　vs. 006.42, 621.367,
　　　621.391, 621.399
Optical properties
　materials science 620.112 95
Optical rotation
　chemistry 541.7
Optical scanning
　computer science 006.42
　engineering 621.399 4
Optical spectroscopes
　manufacturing technology 681.414
Optical spectroscopy 543.5
　analytical chemistry 543.5
　physics 535.84
Optical storage devices 004.565
　engineering 621.397 67
Optical surgery 617.71
Opticianry 617.752
Opticians 681.409 2
Optics 535
　*see also* Light
Optimal control
　automation engineering 629.831 2
　mathematics 515.642
Optimism
　philosophy 149.5

| | |
|---|---|
| Optimization | |
| mathematics | 519.6 |
| systems | 003 |
| | T1—011 |
| Options (Finance) | 332.645 3 |
| Optoacoustic communications | |
| engineering | 621.382 8 |
| Optoelectronic devices | 621.381 52 |
| Optoelectronics | 621.381 045 |
| Optometry | 617.75 |
| Oqsuqtooq (Nunavut) | T2—719 55 |
| Or-Blanc (Quebec) | T2—714 573 |
| Oracles | 133.324 8 |
| religion | 203.2 |
| Oral communication | 302.224 2 |
| management use | 658.452 |
| office services | 651.73 |
| rhetoric | 808.5 |
| Oral contraceptives | |
| health | 613.943 22 |
| medicine | 618.182 2 |
| *see also* Birth control | |
| pharmacokinetics | 615.766 |
| Oral history (Research method) | 907.2 |
| | T1—072 2 |
| Oral hygiene | |
| dentistry | 617.601 |
| Oral interpretation (Lipspeaking) | |
| applied linguistics | 418 |
| specific languages | T4—895 |
| Oral interpretation (Reading | |
| aloud) | 808.54 |
| Oral interpretation of poetry | 808.545 |
| Oral medication | |
| administering | 615.6 |
| Oral presentations | |
| primary education | 372.66 |
| Oral reading | |
| primary education | 372.452 |
| Oral region | |
| medicine | 617.522 |
| surgery | 617.522 059 |
| Oral sex | |
| sociology | 306.774 |
| Oral surgery | 617.522 059 |
| dentistry | 617.605 |
| Oral traditions | |
| folklore | 398.2 |
| religion | 208.3 |
| Bible | 220.663 |
| Buddhism | 294.383 |
| Hinduism | 294.593 |
| Islam | 297.1 |
| Judaism | 296.1 |

| | |
|---|---|
| Oran (Algeria : Province) | T2—651 |
| Orang Kanaq language | T6—992 8 |
| Orang Seletar language | T6—992 8 |
| Orange (N.J.) | T2—749 33 |
| Orange (N.S.W.) | T2—944 5 |
| Orange County (Calif.) | T2—794 96 |
| Orange County (Fla.) | T2—759 24 |
| Orange County (Ind.) | T2—772 27 |
| Orange County (N.C.) | T2—756 565 |
| Orange County (N.Y.) | T2—747 31 |
| Orange County (Tex.) | T2—764 147 |
| Orange County (Va.) | T2—755 372 |
| Orange County (Vt.) | T2—743 63 |
| Orange Free State | 968.504 5 |
| | T2—685 |
| Orange Free State (South Africa) | 968.505 |
| | T2—685 |
| Orange jessamine | 635.977 377 |
| botany | 583.77 |
| ornamental arboriculture | 635.977 377 |
| Orange River | T2—687 1 |
| Orange River Colony | 968.504 9 |
| | T2—685 |
| Orange River Sovereignty | 968.504 2 |
| | T2—685 |
| Orange roughy | 597.64 |
| Orange Walk District | |
| (Belize) | T2—728 26 |
| Orangeburg County (S.C.) | T2—757 79 |
| Oranges | 641.343 1 |
| botany | 583.77 |
| commercial processing | 664.804 31 |
| cooking | 641.643 1 |
| food | 641.343 1 |
| orchard crop | 634.31 |
| Orangutan | 599.883 |
| Oraon | T5—948 3 |
| Oraon language | 494.83 |
| | T6—948 3 |
| Oraon literature | 894.83 |
| Oratories (Chapels) | |
| architecture | 726.595 |
| Oratorios | 782.23 |
| choral and mixed voices | 782.523 |
| Orators | 809.5 |
| collected biography | 809.5 |
| specific literatures | T3B—500 9 |
| individual biography | T3A—5 |
| Oratory | 808.51 |
| Orbital diseases | |
| ophthalmology | 617.78 |
| *see also* Eye diseases — | |
| humans | |

Orbital flights
  manned     629.454
Orbitals (Quantum chemistry)     541.28
Orbits (Astromechanics)     521.3
  astronautics     629.411 3
  astronomy     521.3
    comets     523.63
    earth     525.3
    moon     523.33
Orbits (Eye sockets)
  human anatomy     611.84
  ophthalmology     617.78
Orbits (Nuclear particles)     539.725
Orcaella     599.538
Orchard grass     633.22
  botany     584.9
Orchards     634
Orchestra conductors     784.209 2
Orchestral harps     787.95
  *see also* Stringed instruments
Orchestral music     784.2
Orchestras     784.2
Orchestras with solo instruments     784.23
Orchestras with toy instruments     784.46
Orchestras with vocal parts     784.22
Orchestration     781.374
Orchidales     584.4
Orchids     584.4
  floriculture     635.934 4
Orcinus     599.536
Ord River (W.A. : River)     T2—941 4
Order
  philosophy     117
Order of DeMolay for Boys     366.108 351
Order of the Eastern Star     366.18
  biography     366.180 92
Order statistics     519.5
Ordered algebraic structures     511.33
Ordered solids     530.413
Ordered topological spaces     514.32
Ordering
  library acquisitions     025.23
  materials management     658.72
Orders (Awards)     929.81
  armed forces     355.134 2
  numismatics     737.223
Orders (Societies)     369
Orders of knighthood     929.71
Ordinances     348.02
Ordinary differential equations     515.352
  numerical solutions     518.63
Ordinary differentiation     515.33
Ordinary language philosophy     149.94

Ordinary of the mass     264.36
  music     782.323 2
Ordination of clergy     206.1
  Christianity     262.14
    ecclesiology     262.14
    sacrament     234.164
      public worship     265.4
      theology     234.164
  Judaism     296.61
Ordination of women     206.108 2
  Christianity     262.14
  Judaism     296.610 82
Ordnance     355.8
  engineering     623.4
    air ordnance     623.746 1
    naval ordnance     623.825 1
  military equipment     355.8
    air ordnance     358.418
    naval ordnance     359.8
  *see Manual at* 355–359 vs. 623
Ordos
  Roman Catholic liturgy     264.021
Ordovician period     551.731
  geology     551.731
  paleontology     560.173 1
Ordu İli (Turkey)     T2—565 6
  ancient     T2—393 37
Orduña (Spain)     T2—466 9
Ore dressing     622.7
  *see Manual at* 622.22, 622.7 vs.
    662.6, 669
Ore processing     622.7
Oreamnos     599.647 5
Örebro län (Sweden)     T2—487 6
Oregano     641.357
  *see also* Herbs
Oregon     979.5
    T2—795
Oregon County (Mo.)     T2—778 875
Oregon myrtle     583.23
Orel (Russia : Oblast)     T2—473 5
Orenburg (Russia : Oblast)     T2—474 3
Orenburgskaia oblast'
  (Russia)     T2—474 3
Orense (Spain : Province)     T2—461 5
Ores     553
Oresund (Denmark and Sweden)     551.461 334
    T2—163 34
Organ banks     362.178 3
  *see also* Health services
Organ builders     786.519 092
Organ cases
  church architecture     726.529 7
Organ concertos     784.265

| | |
|---|---|
| Organ culture | 571.538 |
| humans | 612.028 |
| Organ donation | 362.178 3 |
| law | 344.041 94 |
| Organ transplants | 362.197 95 |
| law | 344.041 94 |
| medical ethics | 174.297 954 |
| *see also* Medical ethics | |
| social services | 362.197 95 |
| surgery | 617.954 |
| Organelles | 571.65 |
| Organic chemicals | |
| chemical engineering | 661.8 |
| Organic chemistry | 547 |
| analytical chemistry | 543.17 |
| applied | 661.8 |
| Organic compounds | 547 |
| biochemistry | 572 |
| humans | 612.015 7 |
| human toxicology | 615.95 |
| pollution | |
| ecology | 577.278 |
| toxicology | 571.957 |
| Organic drugs | |
| pharmacology | 615.3 |
| Organic evolution | 576.8 |
| Organic farming | 631.584 |
| Organic fertilizers | 631.86 |
| chemical engineering | 668.63 |
| Organic gardening | 635.048 4 |
| floriculture | 635.987 |
| Organic geochemistry | 553.2 |
| Organic materials | |
| materials science | 620.117 |
| Organic poisons | 363.179 1 |
| human toxicology | 615.95 |
| public safety | 363.179 1 |
| *see also* Hazardous materials | |
| Organic solids | 530.413 |
| Organically grown foods | 641.302 |
| agriculture | 631.584 |
| home economics | 641.302 |
| Organismic psychology | 150.193 |
| Organists | 786.509 2 |
| Organization (Management) | 658.1 |
| T1—068 1 | |
| executive | 658.402 |
| production | 658.51 |
| public administration | 352.2 |
| *see Manual at* 658.04 vs. | |
| 658.114, 658.402 | |
| Organization of African Unity | 341.249 |
| public administration | 352.116 |

| | |
|---|---|
| Organization of American States | 341.245 |
| public administration | 352.117 |
| Organization of production | 338.6 |
| economics | 338.6 |
| management | 658.51 |
| T1—068 5 | |
| Organizational behavior | 302.35 |
| management | 658 |
| Organizational change | |
| executive management | 658.406 |
| public administration | 352.367 |
| Organizations | 060 |
| T1—06 | |
| business enterprises | 338.7 |
| law | 346.06 |
| organizational behavior | 302.35 |
| religious | 206.5 |
| *see also* Religious | |
| organizations | |
| social | 369 |
| *see Manual at* T1—025 vs. | |
| T1—0601–0609; *also* | |
| *at* T1—0601–0609; | |
| *also at* T1—072 vs. | |
| T1—0601–0609 | |
| Organized crime | 364.106 |
| law | 345.02 |
| Organohalogen compounds | 547.02 |
| alicyclic chemistry | 547.52 |
| aliphatic chemistry | 547.42 |
| biochemistry | 572.556 |
| human toxicology | 615.951 2 |
| Organometallic compounds | 547.05 |
| aliphatic chemistry | 547.45 |
| biochemistry | 572.51 |
| chemical engineering | 661.895 |
| human toxicology | 615.951 5 |
| Organonitrogen compounds | 547.04 |
| aliphatic chemistry | 547.44 |
| aromatic chemistry | 547.64 |
| Organophosphorus compounds | 547.07 |
| aliphatic chemistry | 547.47 |
| Organosilicon compounds | 547.08 |
| aliphatic chemistry | 547.48 |
| Organosulfur compounds | 547.06 |
| aliphatic chemistry | 547.46 |
| aromatic chemistry | 547.66 |
| Organotherapy | |
| pharmacology | 615.36 |
| Organs (Musical instruments) | 786.5 |
| instrument | 786.519 |
| music | 786.5 |
| *see also* Keyboard instruments | |

Oribi Gorge Nature Reserve
  (South Africa) — T2—684 5
Orient — 950
   — T2—5
Oriental (Morocco) — T2—643 3
Oriental architecture — 720.95
  ancient — 722.1
Oriental arts — 709.5
Oriental churches — 281.6
  *see also* Eastern churches
Oriental horses — 636.11
Oriental languages — 490
   — T6—9
Oriental Mindoro
  (Philippines) — T2—599 3
Oriental Orthodox churches — 281.6
  *see also* Eastern churches
Oriental philosophy — 181
Oriental region (Paraguay) — T2—892 1
Oriental rugs
  arts — 746.750 95
Oriental sculpture — 730.95
  ancient — 732.7
Oriental shorthair cats — 636.82
Oriental sores
  incidence — 614.534
  medicine — 616.936 4
    *see also* Communicable
    diseases — humans
Orientale (Congo :
  Province) — T2—675 15
Orientation (Geography) — 912.014
Orientation of employees
  personnel management — 658.312 42
  public administration — 352.66
Orientational perception
  psychology — 152.188 2
Oriente (Ecuador) — T2—866 4
Orienteering — 796.58
Origami — 736.982
Origin of legislation — 328.372
Origin of life — 576.83
  philosophy — 113.8
  religion — 202.4
    Christianity — 231.765
    philosophy of religion — 213
Origin of races
  physical ethnology — 599.972
Origin of the state — 320.11
Origin of universe — 523.12
  philosophy — 113
  religion — 202.4
    Christianity — 231.765
    philosophy of religion — 213

Original sin — 233.14
Orinoco River (Venezuela) — T2—87
Orinoquia Region
  (Colombia) — T2—861 9
Orioles — 598.874
Orissa (India) — T2—541 33
Oristano (Italy : Province) — T2—459 4
  ancient — T2—379 4
Oriya — T5—914 56
Oriya language — 491.456
   — T6—914 56
Oriya literature — 891.456
Orkney (Scotland) — T2—411 32
Orkney Islands (Scotland) — T2—411 32
Orlah — 296.123 1
  Mishnah — 296.123 1
  Palestinian Talmud — 296.124 1
Orléanais (France) — T2—445 1
Orléans (France) — T2—445 27
Orléans, Île-de (Quebec) — T2—714 476
Orléans, Isle of (Quebec) — T2—714 476
Orleans County (N.Y.) — T2—747 91
Orleans County (Vt.) — T2—743 23
Orleans Parish (La.) — T2—763 35
Orléansville (Algeria :
  Province) — T2—653
Orlicz spaces — 515.73
Orlovskaĩa oblast′ (Russia) — T2—473 5
Ormiston Gorge National
  Park (N.T.) — T2—942 91
Ornamental birds — 636.68
  economic zoology — 598.163
  *see also* Birds
Ornamental bookbinding — 686.36
Ornamental fans
  decorative arts — 736.7
  dress customs — 391.44
Ornamental fishes — 639.3
Ornamental glass
  architectural decoration — 729.8
Ornamental nails
  ironwork — 739.48
Ornamental plants — 635.9
  economic botany — 581.636
  *see Manual at* 583–585 vs. 600;
    *also at* 633–635; *also at*
    635.9 vs. 582.1
Ornamental woodwork
  furniture arts — 749.5
  handicrafts — 745.51

| | |
|---|---|
| Ornaments | |
| arts | 745 |
| glass | 748.8 |
| stone | 736.5 |
| wood | 736.4 |
| handicrafts | 745.594 |
| manufacturing technology | 688.726 |
| Ornaments (Music) | 781.247 |
| Orne (France) | T2—442 3 |
| Ornithischia | 567.914 |
| Ornithologists | 598.092 |
| Ornithology | 598 |
| Ornithopoda | 567.914 |
| Ornithopters | |
| engineering | 629.133 36 |
| Ornithorhynchidae | 599.29 |
| Oro (Ecuador) | T2—866 31 |
| Oro Province (Papua New Guinea) | T2—954 2 |
| Orobanchaceae | 583.95 |
| Orogeny | 551.82 |
| Oromiyā kelel (Ethiopia) | T2—632 |
| Oromo (African people) | T5—935 5 |
| Oromo language | 493.55 |
| | T6—935 5 |
| Oromo literature | 893.55 |
| Orphanages | 362.732 |
| Orphans | 305.230 869 45 |
| | T1—086 945 |
| social group | 305.230 869 45 |
| social services | 362.73 |
| Orpines | 583.72 |
| Ortega, Daniel | |
| Nicaraguan history | 972.850 53 |
| 1985–1990 | 972.850 53 |
| 2007– | 972.850 544 |
| Ortenaukreis (Germany : Landkreis) | T2—434 626 |
| Orthochromatic photography | 778.62 |
| Orthodontics | 617.643 |
| Orthodox cathedrals | |
| architecture | 726.63 |
| Orthodox Christians | |
| biography | 281.909 2 |
| Orthodox Church | 281.9 |
| church government | 262.019 |
| parishes | 254.019 |
| church law | 262.981 9 |
| doctrines | 230.19 |
| catechisms and creeds | 238.19 |
| general councils | 262.519 |
| guides to Christian life | 248.481 9 |
| liturgy | 264.019 |
| missions | 266.19 |

| | |
|---|---|
| Orthodox Church (continued) | |
| monasticism | 255.819 |
| church history | 271.819 |
| women | 255.981 9 |
| church history | 271.981 9 |
| moral theology | 241.041 9 |
| public worship | 264.019 |
| | 267.181 9 |
| religious education | 268.819 |
| seminaries | 230.073 19 |
| theology | 230.19 |
| *see Manual at* 270, 230.11 .14 vs. 230.15–.2, 281.5–.9, 282 | |
| Orthodox Church of Greece | 281.949 5 |
| Orthodox Eastern Church | 281.9 |
| Orthodox Judaism | 296.832 |
| Orthodox sacred music | |
| public worship | |
| religion | 264.019 02 |
| Orthogonal polynomials | 515.55 |
| Orthogonal series | 515.243 |
| Orthographic projection | |
| technical drawing | 604.245 |
| Orthography | 411 |
| applied linguistics | 418 |
| specific languages | T4—813 |
| specific subjects | T1—014 |
| linguistics | 411 |
| specific languages | T4—152 |
| primary education | 372.632 |
| Orthomorphic projections | 526.82 |
| Orthopedic appliances | |
| manufacturing technology | 681.761 |
| Orthopedic equipment | 617.9 |
| Orthopedic nursing | 616.702 31 |
| Orthopedic shoes | |
| manufacturing technology | 685.38 |
| Orthopedic surgery | 617.47 |
| Orthopedics | 616.7 |
| Orthoptera | 595.726 |
| Orthopters | |
| engineering | 629.133 36 |
| Orthoptics | 617.762 |
| Orthorrhapha | 595.773 |
| Ortiz Rubio, Pascual | |
| Mexican history | 972.082 43 |
| Oruro (Bolivia : Dept.) | T2—841 3 |
| Orvieto (Italy) | |
| ancient | T2—375 76 |
| Oryctolagus | 599.322 |
| Oryx | 599.645 |
| conservation technology | 639.979 645 |
| resource economics | 333.959 645 |
| Oryzeae | 584.9 |

| | | | |
|---|---|---|---|
| Osage County (Kan.) | T2—781 643 | Osmium (continued) | |
| Osage County (Mo.) | T2—778 58 | metallography | 669.957 |
| Osage County (Okla.) | T2—766 25 | metallurgy | 669.7 |
| Osage Indians | T5—975 254 | physical metallurgy | 669.967 |
| Osage language | 497.525 4 | *see also* Chemicals | |
| | T6—975 254 | Osmosis | 530.425 |
| Osage orange | 583.45 | physics | 530.425 |
| Osaka (Japan) | T2—521 834 | water supply treatment | 628.164 |
| Osaka (Japan : Prefecture) | T2—521 83 | Osmotic pressure | 541.341 5 |
| Osborne County (Kan.) | T2—781 215 | Osnabrück (Germany) | T2—435 911 |
| Oscan language | 479.9 | Osorno (Chile : Province) | T2—835 3 |
| | T6—799 | Osoyoos (B.C.) | T2—711 5 |
| Oscans | T5—79 | Osprey | 598.93 |
| Oscar I, King of Sweden and | | Osroene | T2—394 2 |
| Norway | | Osseous tissues | |
| Swedish history | 948.504 1 | human histology | 612.751 045 |
| Oscar II, King of Sweden | | Ossete language | 491.59 |
| Swedish history | 948.504 2 | | T6—915 9 |
| Osceola County (Fla.) | T2—759 25 | Ossete literature | 891.59 |
| Osceola County (Iowa) | T2—777 116 | Ossetic language | 491.59 |
| Osceola County (Mich.) | T2—774 69 | | T6—915 9 |
| Oscillations | | Ossetic literature | 891.59 |
| solid-state physics | 530.416 | Ossets | T5—915 9 |
| solids | 531.32 | Ossicle diseases | |
| Oscillatoriales | 579.39 | medicine | 617.842 |
| Oscillators | | *see also* Ear diseases — | |
| electronic circuits | 621.381 533 | humans | |
| radio engineering | 621.384 12 | Ossicles | |
| Oscillographs | 621.374 7 | human anatomy | 611.85 |
| electronic engineering | 621.381 548 3 | human physiology | 612.854 |
| Oscilloscopes | 621.381 548 3 | medicine | 617.842 |
| Oscines | 598.8 | Ostariophysi | 597.48 |
| *see Manual at* 598.824–.88 | | Osteichthyes | 597 |
| Osco-Umbrian languages | 479.9 | *see also* Fishes | |
| | T6—799 | Osteitis | |
| Osco-Umbrian literatures | 879.9 | medicine | 616.712 |
| Osco-Umbrians | T5—79 | *see also* Musculoskeletal | |
| Oscoda County (Mich.) | T2—774 78 | diseases humans | |
| Osee (Biblical book) | 224.6 | Osteitis deformans | |
| Osetin language | 491.59 | medicine | 616.712 |
| | T6—915 9 | *see also* Musculoskeletal | |
| Osetin literature | 891.59 | diseases — humans | |
| Oshkosh (Wis.) | T2—775 64 | Osteoarthritis | |
| OSI (Computer communication) | 004.62 | medicine | 616.722 3 |
| Osilinka River (B.C.) | T2—711 85 | *see also* Musculoskeletal | |
| Oslo fylke (Norway) | T2—482 1 | diseases — humans | |
| Osmaniye İli (Turkey) | T2—564 7 | Osteochondritis | |
| ancient | T2—393 5 | medicine | 616.712 |
| Osmanli language | 494.35 | *see also* Musculoskeletal | |
| | T6—943 5 | diseases — humans | |
| Osmanli literature | 894.35 | Osteoglossomorpha | 597.47 |
| Osmium | 669.7 | paleozoology | 567.47 |
| chemical engineering | 661.064 1 | | |
| chemistry | 546.641 | | |

| | | | |
|---|---|---|---|
| Osteomyelitis | | Oto Indians | T5—975 2 |
| medicine | 616.715 | Oto language (Siouan) | 497.52 |
| *see also* Musculoskeletal | | | T6—975 2 |
| diseases — humans | | Oto-Manguean languages | 497.6 |
| Osteopathic physicians | 610.92 | | T6—976 |
| Osteopathy | 610 | Otoe County (Neb.) | T2—782 273 |
| therapeutic system | 615.533 | Otolaryngology | 617.51 |
| Osteoporosis | | Otologists | 617.809 2 |
| medicine | 616.716 | role and function | 617.802 32 |
| *see also* Musculoskeletal | | Otology | 617.8 |
| diseases — humans | | anesthesiology | 617.967 8 |
| Östergötland landskap | | geriatrics | 618.977 8 |
| (Sweden) | T2—486 8 | pediatrics | 618.920 978 |
| Östergötlands län (Sweden) | T2—486 8 | surgery | 617.805 9 |
| Österreichische Volkspartei | 324.243 604 | Otomí Indians | T5—976 |
| Østfold fylke (Norway) | T2—482 3 | Otomí language | 497.6 |
| Ostia (Italy) | T2—456 3 | | T6—976 |
| ancient | T2—376 3 | Otorohanga District (N.Z.) | T2—933 7 |
| Ostinato | 781.827 | Otsego County (Mich.) | T2—774 84 |
| instrumental | 784.182 7 | Otsego County (N.Y.) | T2—747 74 |
| Østlandet (Norway) | T2—482 | Ottawa (Ont.) | T2—713 84 |
| Östlich Raron (Switzerland) | T2—494 794 2 | Ottawa-Carleton (Ont.) | T2—713 84 |
| Ostprignitz-Ruppin | | Ottawa County (Kan.) | T2—781 26 |
| (Germany : Landkreis) | T2—431 54 | Ottawa County (Mich.) | T2—774 15 |
| Ostracoda | 595.33 | Ottawa County (Ohio) | T2—771 212 |
| paleozoology | 565.33 | Ottawa County (Okla.) | T2—766 99 |
| Ostravský kraj (Czech | | Ottawa Indians | T5—973 36 |
| Republic) | T2—437 28 | Ottawa language | 497.336 |
| Ostriches | 598.524 | | T6—973 36 |
| animal husbandry | 636.694 | Ottawa River (Quebec and | |
| Ostrołęka (Poland : | | Ont.) | T2—713 8 |
| Voivodeship) | T2—438 41 | Ontario | T2—713 8 |
| Ostropales | 579.57 | Quebec | T2—714 2 |
| Ostvorpommern (Germany : | | Otter shrews | 599.33 |
| Landkreis) | T2—431 78 | Otter Tail County (Minn.) | T2—776 89 |
| Ostyak language | 494.51 | Otterhound | 636.753 6 |
| | T6—945 1 | Otters | 599.769 |
| Ostyak literature | 894.51 | animal husbandry | 636.976 9 |
| Ostyak Samoyed language | 494.4 | conservation technology | 639.979 769 |
| | T6—944 | resource economics | 333.959 769 |
| Ostyaks | T5—945 1 | small game hunting | 799.259 769 |
| Osun State (Nigeria) | T2—669 26 | Otters (River otters) | 599.769 2 |
| Oswego County (N.Y.) | T2—747 67 | animal husbandry | 636.976 92 |
| Oswestry (England : | | conservation technology | 639.979 769 2 |
| Borough) | T2—424 51 | resource economics | 333.959 769 2 |
| Otago Region (N.Z.) | T2—939 1 | small game hunting | 799.259 769 2 |
| Otariidae | 599.797 | Ottoman Empire | 956.015 |
| Otariinae | 599.797 5 | | T2—56 |
| OTC market | 332.643 | Algerian history | 965.024 |
| Otero County (Colo.) | T2—788 95 | Arabian history | 953.03 |
| Otero County (N.M.) | T2—789 65 | Balkan Peninsula | 949.603 |
| Other minds | | Egyptian history | 962.03 |
| epistemology | 121.2 | Iraqi history | 956.703 |
| Otididae | 598.32 | Jordanian history | 956.950 3 |

Ottoman Empire (continued)
  Lebanese history    956.920 34
  Libyan history    961.202 4
  North African history    961.023
  Palestinian history    956.940 34
  Syrian history    956.910 3
  Tunisian history    961.103
  Turkish history    956.101 5
  Yemeni history    953.303
Ottoman Turkish language    494.35
    T6—943 5
Ottoman Turkish literature    894.35
Ouachita County (Ark.)    T2—767 66
Ouachita Mountains (Okla.
  and Ark.)    T2—766 6
  Arkansas    T2—767 4
  Oklahoma    T2—766 6
Ouachita Parish (La.)    T2—763 87
Ouachita River (Ark. and
  La.)    T2—763 7
Ouagadougou (Burkina
  Faso)    T2—662 5
Ouargla (Algeria : Province)    T2—657
Ouarzazate (Morocco :
  Province)    T2—646 6
Ouds    787.82
  *see also* Stringed instruments
Oudtshoorn (South Africa :
  District)    T2—687 38
Oued (Algeria : Province)    T2—657
Oued Eddahab-Lagouira
  (Morocco)    T2—648
Ouest (Haiti : Dept.)    T2—729 452
Ouest lausannois
  (Switzerland)    T2—494 522 9
Ouija board    133.932 5
Oujda-Angad (Morocco)    T2—643 3
Ould Daddah, Mokhtar
  Mauritanian history    966.105 1
Oulu (Finland)    T2—489 76
Oulun lääni (Finland)    T2—489 76
Oum el Bouaghi (Algeria :
  Province)    T2—655
Ounce (Snow leopard)    599.755 5
Ouray County (Colo.)    T2—788 22
Ouse, River (Yorkshire,
  England)    T2—428 4
Out-of-body experience    133.95
Outagamie County (Wis.)    T2—775 39
Outaouais (Quebec :
  Administrative region)    T2—714 22
Outaouais Region (Quebec)    T2—714 22

Outaouais Regional
  Community (Quebec)    T2—714 221
Outboard motorboats    387.231 3
  design    623.812 313
  engineering    623.823 13
  transportation services    387.231 3
  *see also* Ships
Outboard motors    623.872 34
Outcrops (Geology)    551.85
Outdoor advertising    659.134 2
Outdoor cooking    641.578
Outdoor education    371.384
Outdoor furniture    645.8
  cleaning    648.5
  customs    392.36
  decorative arts    749.8
  household management    645.8
  manufacturing technology    684.18
Outdoor games    796
Outdoor life    796.5
  equipment technology    688.765
Outdoor markets    381.18
  management    658.87
  *see also* Commerce
Outdoor music    781.532
Outdoor photography    778.71
Outdoor recreation centers    790.068
Outdoor safety
  public administration    353.97
Outdoor sports    796
  equipment technology    688.76
Outer Banks (N.C.)    T2—756 1
Outer ears    573.89
  animal physiology    573.89
  descriptive zoology    591.44
  human physiology    612.851
  medicine    617.81
  *see also* Ears
Outer Hebrides (Scotland)    T2—411 4
Outer London (England)    T2—421 7
Outer Mongolia    951.73
    T2—517 3
Outer space    520
    T2—19
  astronomy    520
  law of nations    341.47
  resource economics    333.94
  *see Manual at* 520 vs. 500.5,
    523.1, 530.1, 919.9
Outerwear    391.46
  commercial technology    687.14
    fur    685.24
    leather    685.22
  customs    391.46

Outerwear (continued)
home economics 646.3
home sewing 646.45
*see also* Clothing
Outfield play
baseball 796.357 25
Outgroups 302.4
Outlet stores 381.15
management 658.870 5
*see also* Commerce
Outlets
electrical engineering 621.319 24
Outlines T1—020 2
Outpatient departments 362.12
*see also* Health services
Outpatient surgery 617.024
Output peripherals 004.77
computer engineering 621.398 7
Outsider art 709.040 9
Outsourcing 658.405 8
Ovarian diseases
gynecology 618.11
*see also* Female genital
diseases — humans
Ovaries 573.665
biology 573.665
gynecology 618.11
human anatomy 611.65
human physiology 612.625
plants 575.665
Ovenbirds 598.822 5
Ovens River (Vic.) T2—945 5
Over-the-counter drugs 615.1
*see also* Drugs
(Pharmaceuticals)
Over-the-counter markets 332.643
Overberg (South Africa) T2—687 36
Overcoats 391.46
*see also* Clothing
Overflows
sewer systems 628.21
Overglaze painting 666.45
arts 738.15
technology 666.45
Overhead costs
financial management 658.155 3
Overhead electrical lines 621.319 22
Overijssel (Netherlands) T2—492 16
Overindulgence
ethics 178
Overland air-cushion vehicles
engineering 629.322
military engineering 623.748 2

Overland mail 383.143
*see also* Postal service
Overpopulation 363.91
Overseas service 384.64
*see also* Telephone
Oversewing
bookbinding 686.35
Overshoes 678.33
Oversight 658.401 3
legislative function 328.345 6
management 658.401 3
military administration 355.685
public administration 352.35
independent agencies 352.88
Overtime pay 331.216 2
personnel management 658.322 2
Overtime work 331.257 2
personnel management 658.312 1
Overton County (Tenn.) T2—768 684
Overtures 784.189 26
musical form 784.189 26
orchestral music 784.218 926
Overuse injuries
medicine 617.172
Overwater air-cushion vehicles 387.2
engineering 629.324
military engineering 623.748 4
transportation services 387.2
inland water 386.22
ocean 387.2
Overweight people
cooking for 641.563 5
reducing diet 613.25
Ovibos 599.647 8
Oviducts
gynecology 618.12
Oviedo (Spain) T2—461 9
Ovimbundu (African
people) T5—963 99
Oviraptor 567.912
Ovis 599.649
Ovis canadensis 599.649 7
ÖVP (Austrian political party) 324.243 604
Ovulation detection method
health 613.943 4
medicine 618.184
*see also* Birth control
Owen County (Ind.) T2—772 43
Owen County (Ky.) T2—769 393
Owenism 335.12
Owensboro (Ky.) T2—769 864
Owl Creek Mountains
(Wyo.) T2—787 43

Owls 598.97
  conservation technology 639.978 97
  resource economics 333.958 97
Owners' liability insurance 368.56
Ownership
  communications industry 384.041
  land economics 333.3
  real property law 346.043 2
  transportation services 388.049
Ownership equity
  accounting 657.76
Ownership flags 929.92
Ownership marks 929.9
                  T1—027 7
  animal husbandry 636.081 2
Ownership of land 333.3
Owsley County (Ky.) T2—769 176
Owyhee County (Idaho) T2—796 21
Oxalidaceae 583.79
Oxazines 547.595
Oxazoles 547.592
  chemical engineering 661.8
Oxdiazines 547.595
Oxdiazoles 547.595
Oxen 599.642 2
  animal husbandry 636.216
Oxford (England) T2—425 74
Oxford (Ont. : County) T2—713 46
Oxford County (Me.) T2—741 75
Oxfordshire (England) T2—425 7
Oxidases 572.791
  *see also* Enzymes
Oxidation 541.393
Oxidation ditches 628.351
Oxidation ponds 628.351
Oxidation-reduction reaction 541.393
  biochemistry 572.53
  chemical engineering 660.284 43
  organic chemistry 547.23
Oxides
  mineralogy 549.5
Oxidizing enzymes 572.791
  *see also* Enzymes
Oxidoreductases 572.791
  *see also* Enzymes
Oxpeckers 598.863
Oxy compounds 547.03
  aliphatic chemistry 547.43
  aromatic chemistry 547.63
  chemical engineering 661.8
Oxygen
  biochemistry 572.53
    human physiology 612.22
  chemical engineering 661.072 1

Oxygen (continued)
  chemistry 546.721
  economic geology 553.94
  gas technology 665.823
  organic chemistry 547.03
    applied 661.8
  therapeutics 615.836
Oxygen inhalation therapy
  medicine 615.836
Oxygen supply
  human physiology 612.22
  *see also* Respiratory system
Oxynotidae 597.36
Oyo (Kingdom) 966.925 01
                T2—669 25
Oyo State (Nigeria) T2—669 25
Oystercatchers 598.33
Oysters 641.394
  conservation technology 639.974 4
  cooking 641.694
  fishing 639.41
  fishing industry 338.372 44
  food 641.394
    commercial processing 664.94
  resource economics 333.955 41
  zoology 594.4
Ozark County (Mo.) T2—778 835
Ozark Mountains T2—767 1
  Arkansas T2—767 1
  Missouri T2—778 8
  Oklahoma T2—766 8
Ozark Plateau T2—767 1
Ozarks T2—767 1
Ozarks, Lake of the (Mo.) T2—778 493
Ozaukee County (Wis.) T2—775 92
Ozobrome process 773.1
Ozokerite 553.27
  *see also* Asphalt
Ozone
  gas technology 665.89
Ozone layer 551.514 2
Ozone layer depletion 363.738 75
  ecology 577.276
  meteorology 551.514 2
  pollution aspects 363.738 75
Ozone treatment
  water supply engineering 628.166 2
Ozotype process 773.1

## P

P-adic numbers 512.74
P document (Biblical criticism) 222.106 6

Paarl (South Africa :
  District)      T2—687 34
Pabok (Quebec)      T2—714 795
Pacas      599.359
Pacemakers (Electronic cardiac)
  medicine      617.412 064 5
Pacers (Horses)      636.175
Pacheco, Abel
  Costa Rican history      972.860 525
Pachycephalosaurus      567.914
Pacific, War of the, 1879–1883      983.061 6
Pacific Area      T2—182 3
Pacific Coast (B.C.)      T2—711 1
Pacific Coast (North America)      979
     T2—79
Pacific Coast Region
  (Colombia)      T2—861 5
Pacific cod      597.633
Pacific County (Wash.)      T2—797 92
Pacific fur seal      599.797 3
Pacific intergovernmental
  organizations      341.246
Pacific Islanders      T5—995
Pacific Islands (Trust Territory)      996.5
     T2—965
Pacific Northwest      T2—795
Pacific Ocean      551.461 4
     T2—164
  *see Manual at* T2—163 and
     T2—164, T2—165
Pacific Ocean islands      990
     T2—9
  geography      919
  travel      919.04
Pacific Ocean theater (World
  War II)      940.542 6
Pacific region      T2—182 3
Pacific Rim National Park
  (B.C.)      T2—711 2
Pacific settlement of disputes      303.69
  international relations      327.17
  law of nations      341.52
  sociology      303.69
Pacifism      303.66
  ethics      172.42
  *see also* Peace — ethics
  international politics      327.172
  social theology      201.727 3
  *see also* Peace — social
     theology
  sociology      303.66
Pacifists      303.66
  biography
    international politics      327.172 092

Pacifists (continued)
  World War I      940.316 2
  World War II      940.531 62
Pack animals (Beasts of burden)      636.088 2
Packaging      658.564
  drugs (pharmaceuticals)
    preservation      615.18
  electronics      621.381 046
  engineering      688.8
  law      343.075
  production management      658.564
  sales promotion      658.823
Packers (Agricultural tools)
  manufacturing technology      681.763 1
Packet switching (Data
  transmission)
  communications engineering      621.382 16
  computer communications      004.66
  computer engineering      621.398 1
Packing clothes
  home economics      646.6
Packing crops      631.56
Packing for shipment
  materials management      658.788 4
PACs (Action committees)      324.4
  law      342.078
Padded toys
  making      688.724
    handicrafts      745.592 4
    technology      688.724
Paddle tennis      796.34
Paddlefishes      597.42
Paddy rice      641.331 8
  *see also* Rice
Padova (Italy)      T2—453 21
  ancient      T2—373 41
Padova (Italy : Province)      T2—453 2
  ancient      T2—373 4
Padre Island (Tex.)      T2—764 47
Padua (Italy)      T2—453 21
  ancient      T2—373 41
Padua (Italy : Province)      T2—453 2
  ancient      T2—373 4
Paelignian language      479.7
     T6—797
Paeoniales      583.62
Paestum (Extinct city)      T2—377 773
Paez language      498.2
     T6—982
Pagalu (Equatorial Guinea)      T2—671 86
Paganism      292
  Christian polemics      239.3
Page, Earle, Sir
  Australian history      994.042

| | |
|---|---|
| Page County (Iowa) | T2—777 78 |
| Page County (Va.) | T2—755 94 |
| Page design | |
|   typesetting | 686.225 2 |
| Pageantry | |
|   performing arts | 791.6 |
| Pageants | 394.5 |
|   customs | 394.5 |
|   performing arts | 791.62 |
| Paget disease of bone | |
|   medicine | 616.712 |
|     *see also* Musculoskeletal | |
|       diseases — humans | |
| Paging systems | |
|   engineering | 621.389 2 |
| Pahang | T2—595 1 |
| Pahari | T5—914 96 |
| Pahari languages | 491.496 |
| | T6—914 96 |
| Pahari literatures | 891.496 |
| Pahlavi language | 491.53 |
| | T6—915 3 |
| Pahlavi literature | 891.53 |
| Paid assistance (Social welfare) | 361.04 |
|   *see also* Welfare services | |
| Paid vacations | 331.257 6 |
|   labor economics | 331.257 6 |
|   personnel management | 658.312 2 |
| Pails | |
|   manufacturing technology | 683.82 |
| Pain | |
|   human physiology | 612.88 |
|   symptom | 616.047 2 |
|     nervous system diseases | 616.849 |
|       *see also* Nervous system | |
|         diseases — humans | |
| Pain perception | |
|   psychology | 152.182 4 |
| Paint | 667.6 |
|   architectural decoration | 729.4 |
|   household management | 645.2 |
| Paint horse | 636.13 |
| Paint removers | 667.6 |
| Paint thinners | 667.624 |
| Painted Desert (Ariz.) | T2—791 33 |
| Painted glass | |
|   arts | 748.5 |
| Painted turtle | 597.925 92 |
| Painters (Building trades) | 698.109 2 |
| Painting | 667.6 |
|   art | 750 |
|   buildings | 698.1 |
|     woodwork | 698.35 |
|   decorative arts | 745.723 |
| Painting (continued) | |
|   folklore | 398.277 |
|     history and criticism | 398.357 |
|   interior decoration | 747.3 |
|   literature | 808.803 57 |
|     history and criticism | 809.933 57 |
|     specific literatures | T3B—080 357 |
|       history and | |
|         criticism | T3B—093 57 |
|   metals | 671.73 |
|     decorative arts | 739.15 |
|     technology | 671.73 |
|   pottery | 666.45 |
|     arts | 738.15 |
|     technology | 666.45 |
|   primary education | 372.52 |
|   technology | 667.6 |
|   textile arts | 746.6 |
|   use in child care | 649.51 |
| Paintings | 750 |
| Pair skating | 796.912 |
| País Vasco (Spain) | T2—466 |
| Paisley (Scotland) | T2—414 37 |
| Paiute Indians | T5—974 576 9 |
| Paiute language | 497.457 69 |
| | T6—974 576 9 |
| Paiwan (Taiwan people) | T5—992 5 |
| Pakistan | 954.91 |
| | T2—549 1 |
|   ancient | 934.91 |
| | T2—349 1 |
| Pakistan (1947–1971) | 954.9 |
| | T2—549 |
|   ancient | 934.9 |
| | T2—349 |
| Pakistanis | T5—914 122 |
| Pakpak | T5—992 246 6 |
| Palaces | |
|   architecture | 728.82 |
|     official residences | 725.17 |
|     private residences | 728.82 |
| Palaeanodonta | 569.31 |
| Palaeognathae | 598.5 |
|   paleozoology | 568.5 |
| Palaic language | 491.998 |
| | T6—919 98 |
| Palate | |
|   human anatomy | 611.315 |
|   human physiology | 612.31 |
|     speech | 612.78 |
|   regional medicine | 617.522 5 |
|   surgery | 617.522 5 |
| Palatinate (Germany) | T2—434 35 |

Palau 996.6
  T2—966
Palauan language 499.52
  T6—995 2
Palauans T5—995 2
Palawan (Philippines) T2—599 4
Palawan Island (Philippines) T2—599 4
Palencia (Spain : Province) T2—462 2
Paleo-Asiatics T5—946
Paleobiology 560
Paleobotanists 561.092
Paleobotany 561
Paleocene epoch 551.783
  geology 551.783
  paleontology 560.178 3
Paleoclimatology 551.609 01
  specific areas 551.69
Paleoecology 560.45
  botanical 561.1
  zoological 560.45
Paleogene period 551.782
  geology 551.782
  paleontology 560.178 2
Paleogeography 551.7
Paleography 417.7
  T4—7
  handwriting 411.7
    specific languages T4—11
Paleolithic Age 930.12
  fine arts 709.011 2
  painting 759.011 2
  sculpture 732.22
Paleomagnetism 538.727
Paleontologists 560.92
Paleontology 560
  *see Manual at* 551.7 vs. 560;
    *also at* 576.8 vs. 560
Paleopalynology 561.13
Paleosiberian languages 494.6
  T6—946
Paleosiberian literatures 894.6
Paleosiberian peoples T5—946
Paleovolcanism 551.210 901
Paleozoic era 551.72
  geology 551.72
  paleontology 560.172
Paleozoology 560
Palermo (Italy) T2—458 231
Palermo (Italy : Province) T2—458 23
  ancient T2—378 23

Palestine 956.94
  T2—569 4
  ancient 933
  T2—33
  Biblical geography and history 220.9
Palestine Liberation Organization
  history 956.940 5
  political party 324.256 940 83
Palestinian Arab women 305.488 927 4
Palestinian Arabs T5—927 4
Palestinian architecture
  ancient 722.33
Palestinian National Authority 351.569 53
Palestinian sculpture 732.3
Palestinian Talmud 296.124
Palestinians (Ethnic group) T5—927 4
Palestinians (Palestinian
  National Authority) T5—927 569 53
Palestrina (Italy)
  ancient T2—376 3
Pali language 491.37
  T6—913 7
Pali literature 891.37
Palindromes 793.734
Palladium 669.7
  chemical engineering 661.063 6
  chemistry 546.636
  metallography 669.957
  metallurgy 669.7
  physical metallurgy 669.967
  *see also* Chemicals
Pallets
  wooden 674.82
Palliative care
  medicine 616.029
Palm Beach County (Fla.) T2—759 32
Palm oil 641.338 51
  cooking 641.638 51
  food 641.338 51
  food technology 664.36
Palm reading 133.6
Palm Sunday 263.925
  devotional literature 242.35
  music 781.726
  sermons 252.625
Palm Valley National Park
  (N.T.) T2—942 91
Palma (Majorca) T2—467 542
Palma de Mallorca
  (Majorca) T2—467 542
Palmae 584.5
  *see also* Palms
Palmales 584.5
  *see also* Palms

Palmerston North (N.Z.)    T2—935 8
Palmerston North City
   (N.Z.)    T2—935 8
Palmettos    584.5
Palmistry    133.6
Palmists    133.609 2
Palms    584.5
   botany    584.5
   forestry    634.974
   ornamental arboriculture    635.977 45
   ornamental gardening    635.934 5
   paleobotany    561.45
Palmyra (Extinct city)    T2—394 32
Palmyra Atoll (Line Islands)    T2—969 9
Palo Alto County (Iowa)    T2—777 155
Palo Pinto County (Tex.)    T2—764 552
Palomino horse    636.13
Palouse River (Idaho and
   Wash.)    T2—797 39
Palpigradi    595.452
Palynology    571.845 2
   paleobotany    561.13
   physiology    571.845 2
Pama-Maric languages    499.15
     T6—991 5
Pama-Nyungan languages    499.15
     T6—991 5
Pamir    T2—586
Pamir languages    491.59
     T6—915 9
Pamir literatures    891.59
Pamiri    T5—915 9
Pamlico County (N.C.)    T2—756 194
Pamlico Sound (N.C.)    551.461 348
     T2—163 48
Pampa (Argentina :
   Province)    T2—821 3
Pampanga (Philippines)    T2—599 1
Pampas    333.74
     T2—153
   biology    578.744
   ecology    577.44
   *see also* Grasslands
Pampas grass    584.9
Pamphlets
   bibliographies    011.33
   cataloging    025.342
   library treatment    025.172
Pamphylia    T2—392 9
Pamplona (Spain)    T2—465 2
Pan (Chimpanzees)    599.885
Pan-Africanism    320.540 96
Pan-Arabism    320.540 917 492 7
Pan fishing    799.12

Pan-German People's Party
   (Austria)    324.243 602 3
Pan-Germanism    320.540 943
Pan movements    320.54
Pan-nationalism    320.54
Pan pipes    788.37
   *see also* Woodwind instruments
Pan-Slavism    320.540 947
Panama    972.87
     T2—728 7
Panama (Panama :
   Province)    T2—728 731
Panama, Gulf of (Panama)    551.461 41
     T2—164 1
Panama Canal (Panama)    386.44
     T2—728 75
Panama hat palm    584.62
Panamanian literature    860
Panamanians    T5—687 287
Panay Island (Philippines)    T2—599 5
Pancake mixes    664.753
Pancakes    641.815 3
Panchromatic photography    778.62
Pancreas    573.377
   biology    573.377
   human anatomy    611.37
   human physiology    612.34
   medicine    616.37
   surgery    617.557
   *see also* Digestive system
Pancreatic cancer
   incidence    614.599 943 7
   medicine    616.994 37
   *see also* Cancer — humans
Pancreatic diseases
   medicine    616.37
   *see also* Digestive system
     diseases   humans
Pancreatic secretions
   human physiology    612.34
Panda (Giant)    599.789
   conservation technology    639.979 789
   resource economics    333.959 789
Panda (Lesser)    599.763
Pandanales    584.66
Pandemics
   social effects    303.485
Pandionidae    598.93
Pando (Bolivia : Dept.)    T2—844 3
Panel heating
   buildings    697.72
Paneling
   household management    645.2
   interior decoration    747.3

Panentheism 211.2
  philosophy 147
Pangasinan (Philippines) T2—599 1
Pangnirtung (Nunavut) T2—719 52
Pangolins 599.31
Panic
  social psychology 302.17
Panic disorder
  medicine 616.852 23
  *see also* Mental disorders
Panic grasses 584.92
  forage crop 633.257 1
Panicoideae 584.92
  forage crops 633.27
Panics (Economics) 338.542
Panicum 584.92
  food crop 633.171
  *see also* Millets
Panjabi language 491.42
  T6—914 2
Panjabi literature 891.42
Panjabis T5—914 21
Pannirtuuq (Nunavut) T2—719 52
Pannonia 936.39
  T2—363 9
Panoan languages 498.4
  T6—984
Panoan peoples T5—984
Panola County (Miss.) T2—762 84
Panola County (Tex.) T2—764 187
Panoramas 745.8
  decorative arts 745.8
  paintings 751.74
Panoramic cinematography 777.6
Panoramic photography 778.36
Panoramic videography 777.6
Panpipes 788.37
  instrument 788.371 9
  music 788.37
  *see also* Woodwind instruments
Panpsychism 141
Pans
  kitchen utensils 643.3
    manufacturing technology 683.82
Pansies 635.933 625
  botany 583.625
  floriculture 635.933 625
Pantelleria Island (Italy) T2—458 24
Pantheism 211.2
  philosophy 147
Pantheistic religions 201.4
Panther (Puma) 599.752 4
  conservation technology 639.979 752 4
  resource economics 333.959 752 4

Panthera 599.755
Panto 792.38
Pantodonta 569.62
Pantomime 792.3
Pantomime (Christmas
  entertainment) 792.38
Pantomime (Silent entertainment) 792.3
Pantomime (United Kingdom) 792.38
Pants (Trousers) 391.476
  commercial technology 687.116
  customs 391.476
  home economics 646.3
  home sewing 646.436
  *see also* Clothing
Pants (Undergarments) 391.423
  *see also* Undergarments
Papa Doc
  Haitian history 972.940 72
Papacy 262.13
Papago Indians T5—974 552
Papakura District (N.Z.) T2—932 6
Papal administration 262.136
Papal bulls and decrees 262.91
Papal infallibility 262.131
Papal schism, 1378–1417 282.090 23
Papal States 945.6
  T2—456
Papal systems (Ecclesiology) 262.3
Paparoa National Park
  (N.Z.) T2—937 3
Papaverales 583.35
Papaws (Annonaceae) 641.344 1
  botany 583.22
  cooking 641.644 1
  food 641.344 1
  orchard crop 634.41
Papaws (Caricaceae, Papayas) 641.346 51
  *see also* Papayas
Papayas 641.346 51
  agriculture 634.651
  botany 583.626
  commercial processing 664.804 651
  cooking 641.646 51
  food 641.346 51
Paper 676
  handicrafts 745.54
  manufacturing technology 676
  materials science 620.197
  photographic materials 771.532 3
  sculpture material 731.2
Paper airplanes 745.592
Paper bags 676.33
Paper boxes 676.32
  handicrafts 745.54

Paper chromatography          543.84
Paper covers
  bookbinding                 686.344
Paper cups                    676.34
Paper cutting                 736.98
Paper dolls                   769.53
Paper folding                 736.98
Paper industry workers        676.092
Paper money                   332.42
  arts                        769.55
  economics                   332.42
  form of currency            332.404 4
  printing                    686.288
Paper plates                  676.34
Paper production              676.2
Paper recycling               676.142
Paper standard                332.42
Paper work
  child care                  649.51
  primary education           372.55
Paperbacks                    002
  bibliographies              011.32
  publishing                  070.573
  reviews                     028.132
Paperboard                    676.288
  materials science           620.197
  structural engineering      624.189 7
Paperboard boxes              676.32
  handicrafts                 745.54
Paperhangers                  698.609 2
Paperhanging                  698.6
  interior decoration         747.3
Papermaking                   676
  equipment manufacturing
    technology                681.767 6
Paperweights
  glass
    decorative arts           748.84
Paphiopedeliums               635.934 4
  botany                      584.4
  floriculture                635.934 4
Paphlagonia                   T2—393 17
Papiamento dialect            467.972 986
                              T6—68
Papiamento literature         860
Papier-mâché
  handicrafts                 745.542
  sculpture material          731.2
Papilionoidea                 595.789
Papillomavirus                579.244 5

Papillomavirus diseases
  humans
    incidence                 614.581
    medicine                  616.911
    *see also* Communicable
      diseases — humans
Papillon                      636.76
Papineau (Quebec :
  Regional County
  Municipality)               T2—714 227
Papineau-Labelle Wildlife
  Reserve (Quebec)            T2—714 241
Papio                         599.865
Papovaviridae                 579.244 5
Pappophoreae                  584.9
Paprika                       641.338 4
  botany                      583.952
  *see also* Hot spices
Papua                         995.4
                              T2—954
Papua (Indonesia : province : 995.1
  1963–2003)                  T2—951
Papua (Indonesia :
  province : 2003– )          T2—951 6
Papua (Territory)             995.402 2
                              T2—954
Papua and New Guinea          995.304
  (Territory)                 T2—953
Papua New Guinea              995.3
                              T2—953
Papuan languages             499.12
                              T6—991 2
Papuan literatures           899.12
Papuans                       T5—991 2
Papyrus                       584.84
Pará (Brazil : State)         T2—811 5
Para (Suriname)               T2—883 4
Parables in the Gospels       226.8
Parabola                      516.152
Parabolic equations           515.353 4
Parabolic functions           515.9
Paracanthopterygii            597.62
  paleozoology                567.62
Paracel Islands               T2—59
Parachute troops              356.166
Parachutes                    629.134 386
Parachuting
  sports                      797.56
Paraconsistent logic          511.31
Parades                       394.5
  circuses                    791.38
  customs                     394.5
  performing arts             791.6
Paradisaeidae                 598.865

Paradise | 202.3
Christianity | 236.24
Islam | 297.23
Paradoxes
logic | 165
Paraffin (Kerosene) | 665.538 3
Paraffin (Wax) | 547.77
natural | 665.4
petroleum product | 665.538 5
Paraffins (Alkanes) | 547.411
chemical engineering | 661.814
Paragraphs
rhetoric | 808
Paraguarí (Paraguay) | T2—892 123
Paraguay | 989.2
| T2—892
Paraguay River | T2—892
Paraguay tea | 641.337 7
*see also* Maté
Paraguayan literature | 860
Paraguayan War, 1865–1870 | 989.205
Paraguayans | T5—688 92
Parah | 296.123 6
Paraíba (Brazil : State) | T2—813 3
Paraíso (Honduras : Dept.) | T2—728 34
Parakeets | 598.71
animal husbandry | 636.686 5
Parakeets (Lovebirds) | 636.686 4
animal husbandry | 636.686 4
zoology | 598.71
Paralegals | 340.092
malpractice | 347.050 41
practice | 347.050 4
Paralipomena (Biblical books) | 222.6
Parallax
stars | 523.81
Parallax corrections | 522.9
Parallel bars (Gymnastic
equipment) | 796.442
Parallel giant slalom racing | 796.939
Parallel processing | 004.35
*see also* Processing modes —
computer science
Parallel processors | 004.35
engineering | 621.391
*see also* Processing modes —
computer science
Parallel programming | 005.275
Parallelism | 147
Paralympics | 796.045 6
Paralysis
medicine | 616.842
*see also* Nervous system
diseases — humans

Paralytic shellfish poisoning
human toxicology | 615.945
Paramagnetism | 538.43
Paramaribo (Suriname :
District) | T2—883 52
Paramecium | 579.495
Parametric inference | 519.54
Parametric statistical methods | 519.5
Paramillo National Park
(Colombia) | T2—861 26
Paramo
ecology | 577.538
Paramotoring | 797.55
Paramours | 306.736
Paramyxoviridae | 579.256
Paraná (Brazil : State) | T2—816 2
Paraná River (Brazil-
Argentina) | T2—822
Argentina | T2—822
Brazil | T2—816
Paranasal sinus diseases
medicine | 616.212
*see also* Respiratory tract
diseases — humans
Paranasal sinuses
human anatomy | 611.21
human physiology | 612.232
medicine | 616.212
Paranoid disorders
medicine | 616.897
*see also* Mental disorders
Paranoid personality disorder
medicine | 616.858 1
*see also* Mental disorders
Paranormal phenomena | 130
Paranthropus | 569.93
Paraphrase
musical element | 781.377
musical forms | 781.826
instrumental | 784.182 6
Paraplegia
medicine | 617.58
neurology | 616.842
*see also* Nervous system
diseases — humans
Parapsychologists | 130.92
Parapsychology | 130
*see Manual at* 001.9 *and* 130;
*also at* 130 *vs.* 200
Parapsychology and religion | 201.613
Christianity | 261.513
Islam | 297.261
Judaism | 296.371

Pararthropoda 592.7
  paleozoology 562.7
Parasaurolophus 567.914
Parasites 578.65
Parasitic animals 591.65
Parasitic diseases 571.999
  agriculture 632.62
  animals 571.999 1
    veterinary medicine 636.089 696
  humans 362.196 96
    incidence 614.55
    medicine 616.96
    social services 362.196 96
  plants 571.999 2
    agriculture 632.62
  *see also* Communicable
    diseases; Parasitism
Parasitic plants 581.65
  agricultural pests 632.52
Parasitic skin diseases
  humans
    incidence 614.595 7
    medicine 616.57
    *see also* Skin diseases —
      humans
Parasitiformes 595.429
Parasitism 571.999
  animals 591.785 7
  ecology 577.857
  pathology 571.999
  plants 581.785 7
  *see also* Parasitic diseases
Parasitology
  medicine 616.96
Parasols 391.44
  *see also* Accessories (Clothing)
Parasympathetic nervous system
  human physiology 612.89
  medicine 616.856 9
Parasympathetic nervous system
  diseases
  medicine 616.856 9
  *see also* Nervous system
    diseases — humans
Parasympatholytics
  pharmacokinetics 615.784
Parathyroid diseases
  medicine 616.445
  *see also* Endocrine
    diseases — humans
Parathyroid glands 573.478
  biology 573.478
  human anatomy 611.44
  human physiology 612.448

Parathyroid glands (continued)
  medicine 616.445
  surgery 617.539
  *see also* Endocrine system
Paratroops 356.166
Paratyphoid fever
  incidence 614.511 4
  medicine 616.927 4
  *see also* Communicable
    diseases — humans
Parazoa 593.4
  paleozoology 563.4
Parc national de la Vanoise
  (France) T2—445 85
Parc national de Port-Cros
  (France) T2—449 3
Parc national des Cévennes
  (France) T2—448 1
Parc national des Ecrins
  (France) T2—449 7
Parc national des Pyrénées
  occidentales (France) T2—447 8
Parc national du Mercantour
  (France) T2—449 4
Parcels
  postal handling 383.125
  *see also* Postal service
Parchim (Germany :
  Landkreis) T2—431 76
Parchment papers 676.284 5
Parchments (Skins)
  manufacturing technology 685
Pardon 364.65
  law 345.077
  penology 364.65
Pardubický kraj (Czech
  Republic) T2—437 19
Parenchyma 571.585
Parent abuse 362.829 2
  *see also* Family violence
Parent-child relations 306.874
  law 346.017
  psychological influence 155.924
  sociology 306.874
Parent participation in schools 371.192
  primary education 372.119 2
    reading 372.425
Parent-school relations 371.192
Parent-teacher associations 371.192 06
Parent-teacher conferences 371.103
Parent-teacher relations 371.192
Parental behavior (Animals) 591.563

| | |
|---|---|
| Parental kidnapping | 362.829 7 |
| law | 344.032 829 7 |
| social welfare | 362.829 7 |
| *see also* Families — social welfare | |
| Parental leave | 331.257 63 |
| personnel management | 658.312 2 |
| Parental rights | 346.017 |
| Parenteral infusions | |
| administering | 615.6 |
| Parenteral nutrition | |
| medicine | 615.854 84 |
| Parenteral therapy | |
| medicine | 615.855 |
| Parenthood | 306.874 |
| child rearing | 649.1 |
| customs | 392.3 |
| sociology | 306.874 |
| Parenting | 649.1 |
| home economics | 649.1 |
| personal religion | 204.41 |
| Christianity | 248.845 |
| Judaism | 296.74 |
| sociology | 306.874 |
| Parents | 306.874 |
| | T1—085 |
| Christian devotional literature | 242.645 |
| family relationships | 306.874 |
| guides to religious life | 204.41 |
| Christianity | 248.845 |
| Judaism | 296.74 |
| psychology | 155.646 |
| social welfare | 362.82 |
| law | 344.032 82 |
| public administration | 353.533 1 |
| Pareto, Vilfredo | |
| economic school | 330.154 3 |
| Pari-mutuel betting | 798.401 |
| Paria, Gulf of (Venezuela and Trinidad and Tobago) | 551.461 366 |
| | T2—163 66 |
| Parianeae | 584.9 |
| Paridae | 598.824 |
| Paris (France) | T2—443 61 |
| Paris, Treaty of, 1783 | |
| United States history | 973.317 |
| Paris Commune, 1871 | 944.081 2 |
| Paris metropolitan area (France) | T2—443 6 |
| Parish houses | |
| architecture | 726.4 |
| Parish libraries | 027.67 |
| Parish missions | 266.022 |
| Parish welfare work | 361.75 |

| | |
|---|---|
| Parishes | 250 |
| administration | 254 |
| ecclesiology | 262.22 |
| *see Manual at* 260 vs. 251–254, 259 | |
| Park, Chung Hee | |
| South Korean history | 951.950 43 |
| Park buildings | |
| architecture | 725.7 |
| Park County (Colo.) | T2—788 59 |
| Park County (Mont.) | T2—786 661 |
| Park County (Wyo.) | T2—787 42 |
| Park lodges | 910.462 |
| *see also* Resorts | |
| Park police | 363.28 |
| Park Range (Colo. and Wyo.) | T2—788 66 |
| Parke County (Ind.) | T2—772 465 |
| Parker County (Tex.) | T2—764 553 |
| Parking | 388.474 |
| *see also* Parking facilities | |
| Parking aprons | 625.889 |
| Parking facilities | 388.474 |
| architecture | 725.38 |
| area planning | 711.73 |
| construction | 690.538 |
| law | 343.098 2 |
| public administration | 354.765 |
| urban transportation services | 388.474 |
| Parking turnouts | 625.77 |
| Parkinson disease | |
| medicine | 616.833 |
| *see also* Nervous system diseases — humans | |
| Parks | 363.68 |
| area planning | 711.558 |
| community redevelopment | 307.346 |
| land economics | 333.783 |
| landscape architecture | 712.5 |
| reserved lands | 719.32 |
| law | 346.046 783 |
| public administration | 353.78 |
| recreation centers | 790.068 |
| social services | 363.68 |
| *see Manual at* T2—4–9 | |
| Parkways | 388.122 |
| *see also* Roads | |
| Parliamentary constituencies | 328.334 5 |
| Parliamentary elections | 324 |
| Parliamentary libraries | 027.65 |
| Parliamentary papers | 328.4–.9 |
| Parliamentary rules | 060.42 |
| legislatures | 328.1 |
| Parliaments | 328 |

Parlors 643.54
  home economics 643.54
  interior decoration 747.75
Parma (Italy) T2—454 41
  ancient T2—372 641
Parma (Italy : Province) T2—454 4
  ancient T2—372 64
Parmer County (Tex.) T2—764 836
Parmesan cheese 641.373 54
  cooking 641.673 54
  food 641.373 54
  processing 637.354
Parnassiaceae 583.72
Parochial schools 371.071
Parody
  literary criticism 809.7
    theory 808.7
  literary history 809.7
  literature 808.87
    specific literatures T3B—7
  musical element 781.377
  musical form 781.826
    instrumental 784.182 6
  rhetoric 808.7
Parole 364.62
  law 345.077
  penology 364.62
  public administration 353.39
Parole administration 364.620 68
Paronym dictionaries 413.1
  specific languages T4—31
Paros Island (Greece) T2—495 85
Parotid gland
  human anatomy 611.316
  medicine 616.316
  surgery 617.522
Parque Nacional Natural El
  Cocuy (Colombia) T2—861 44
Parque Nacional Natural El
  Tuparro (Colombia) T2—861 92
Parque Nacional Natural
  Farallones de Cali
  (Colombia) T2—861 52
Parque Nacional Natural
  Los Picahos (Colombia) T2—861 94
Parque Nacional Natural
  Nevado del Huila
  (Colombia) T2—861 39
Parque Nacional Natural
  Paramillo (Colombia) T2—861 26
Parque Nacional Natural
  Puracé (Colombia) T2—861 53
Parque Nacional Natural
  Sanquianga (Colombia) T2—861 58

Parque Nacional Natural
  Serrania de La Macarena
  (Colombia) T2—861 94
Parque Nacional Natural
  Sierra Nevada de Santa
  Marta (Colombia) T2—861 16
Parque Nacional Natural
  Sumapaz (Colombia) T2—861 46
Parque Nacional Natural
  Tama (Colombia) T2—861 24
Parramatta (N.S.W.) T2—944 1
Parrotfishes 597.7
Parrots 598.71
  animal husbandry 636.686 5
  conservation technology 639.978 71
  resource economics 333.958 71
Parry Sound (Ont. : District) T2—713 15
Parseeism 295
Parsers (Computer science)
  natural languages 415.028 563 5
    specific languages T4—502 856 35
  programming languages 005.45
Parsi language (Pahlavi) 491.53
   T6—915 3
Parsi literature (Pahlavi) 891.53
Parsing (Computers)
  natural languages 415.028 563 5
    specific languages T4—502 856 35
Parsley 641.357
  botany 583.849
  *see also* Herbs
Parsnip River (B.C.) T2—711 82
Parsnips 641.351 4
  botany 583.849
  commercial processing 664.805 14
  cooking 641.651 4
  food 641.351 4
  garden crop 635.14
Parsonages
  architecture 726.9
Part-of-speech tagging 415.028 563 5
  specific languages T4—502 856 35
Part songs 783.1
Part-time employment 331.257 27
  personnel management 658.312 1
Part-time enterprises
  management 658.041
Part-time work 331.257 27
Part-whole relationships 111.82
Part-word method (Reading)
  primary education 372.465
Partei der Arbeit der Schweiz 324.249 407 4
Partei des Demokratischen
  Sozialismus (Germany) 324.243 074

| | |
|---|---|
| Parthenogenesis | 571.887 |
| Parthenopaean Republic | 945.707 |
| Parthia | T2—396 |
| Parthian Empire | 935.064 |
| Parti communiste français | 324.244 075 |
| Parti québécois | 324.271 409 84 |
| Partial differential equations | 515.353 |
| numerical solutions | 518.64 |
| Partial differential operators | 515.724 2 |
| Partial differentiation | 515.33 |
| Partial hearing loss | |
| medicine | 617.8 |
| *see also* Ear diseases — | |
| humans | |
| Partially ordered sets | 511.332 |
| Participatory democracy | 323.042 |
| Participatory management | 331.011 2 |
| personnel management | 658.315 2 |
| public administration | 352.68 |
| Participles | 415.6 |
| specific languages | T4—56 |
| Particle acceleration | 539.73 |
| Particle beams | 539.73 |
| Particle board | 674.836 |
| Particle colliders | 539.73 |
| Particle mechanics | 530.12 |
| classical physics | 531.16 |
| quantum mechanics | 530.12 |
| *see Manual at* 530.475 vs. | |
| 530.12, 531.16 | |
| Particle physics | 539.72 |
| Particle radiation | 539.72 |
| biophysics | 571.459 |
| humans | 612.014 486 |
| nuclear physics | 539.72 |
| Particles (Grammar) | 415.7 |
| specific languages | T4—57 |
| Particles (Matter) | |
| classical mechanics | 531.16 |
| meteorology | 551.511 3 |
| nuclear physics | 539.72 |
| technology | 620.43 |
| Partido Revolucionario | |
| Institucional (Mexico) | 324.272 05 |
| Parties (Entertainments) | 793.2 |
| *see also* Entertainments | |
| (Partics) | |
| Parties (Politics) | 324.2 |
| *see also* Political parties | |
| Partisan troops | 356.15 |
| Partitas | 784.185 4 |

| | |
|---|---|
| Partitions (Building element) | 721.2 |
| architecture | 721.2 |
| construction | 690.12 |
| interior decoration | 747.3 |
| Partitions (Mathematics) | |
| number theory | 512.73 |
| Partitions, 1772–1795 (Poland) | 943.802 5 |
| Partito comunista italiano | 324.245 075 2 |
| Partito d'azione (Italy : | |
| 1853–1867) | 324.245 026 |
| Partito d'azione (Italy : | |
| 1942–1947) | 324.245 06 |
| Partito dei lavoratori italiani | 324.245 027 |
| Partito della rifondazione | |
| comunista (Italy) | 324.245 075 |
| Partito democratico (Italy) | 324.245 06 |
| Partito democratico della sinistra | |
| (Italy) | 324.245 07 |
| Partito fascista repubblicano | |
| (Italy) | 324.245 023 8 |
| Partito liberale italiano | |
| (1943–1994) | 324.245 04 |
| Partito liberale italiano (2004– ) | 324.245 04 |
| Partito nazionale fascista (Italy) | 324.245 023 8 |
| Partito popolare italiano | |
| (1919–1926) | 324.245 028 2 |
| Partito popolare italiano | |
| (1994–2002) | 324.245 082 |
| Partito radicale (Italy) | 324.245 06 |
| Partito radicale transnazionale | |
| (Italy) | 324.245 06 |
| Partito repubblicano italiano | 324.245 05 |
| Partito socialista dei lavoratori | |
| italiani (1893–1895) | 324.245 027 |
| Partito socialista dei lavoratori | |
| italiani (1925–1927) | 324.245 027 |
| Partito socialista dei lavoratori | |
| italiani (1947–1951) | 324.245 072 2 |
| Partito socialista democratico | |
| italiano (1952–1995) | 324.245 072 2 |
| Partito socialista democratico | |
| italiano (2004– ) | 324.245 072 |
| Partito socialista di unità | |
| proletaria (Italy : 1943–1947) | 324.245 074 2 |
| Partito socialista di unità | |
| proletaria (Italy : 1947–1951) | 324.245 074 |
| Partito socialista italiano | 324.245 074 2 |
| Partito socialista unitario (Italy : | |
| 1922–1930) | 324.245 027 |
| Partito socialista unitario (Italy : | |
| 1969–1971) | 324.245 072 2 |

Partnership associations 338.7
  *see also* Business enterprises;
    Unincorporated business
    enterprises
Partnerships 338.73
  accounting 657.92
  economics 338.73
  income tax 336.242 3
    law 343.052 662
  law 346.068 2
  management 658.042
    initiation 658.114 2
    *see Manual at* 658.04 vs.
      658.114, 658.402
  taxes 336.207
    law 343.066 2
Partridgeberry 583.93
Partridges 598.623
  sports hunting 799.246 23
Parts of Holland (England) T2—425 39
Parts of Kesteven (England) T2—425 35
Parts of Lindsey (England) T2—425 31
Parts of speech (Grammar) 415
  specific languages T4—5
Parturition 573.67
  human physiology 612.63
  mammals 573.67
    reproductive behavior 599.156
  obstetrics 618.4
    disorders 618.5
  *see also* Childbirth
Party costumes
  home sewing 646.478
Party finance (Politics) 324.21
Party leadership (Politics) 324.22
Party membership (Politics) 324.21
Party of Democratic Socialism
  (Germany) 324.243 074
Party of Italian Communists 324.245 075
Party of Italian Workers 324.245 027
Party organization (Politics) 324.21
  legislative bodies 328.369
  political process 324.21
  sociology 306.26
Parulidae 598.872
Parvoviridae 579.247
Parys (South Africa :
  District) T2—685 2
Pas (Man.) T2—712 72
Pas-de-Calais (France) T2—442 72
Pasadena (Calif.) T2—794 93
Pasargadae (Extinct city) T2—357 72
Pasco (Peru : Dept.) T2—852 3
Pasco County (Fla.) T2—759 69

Pashto language 491.593
    T6—915 93
Pashto literature 891.593
Pashtoon T5—915 93
Pashtun T5—915 93
Pasquotank County (N.C.) T2—756 142
Passacaglias 781.827
  instrumental 784.182 7
Passage of legislation 328.375
Passaic County (N.J.) T2—749 23
Passaic River (N.J.) T2—749 3
Passamaquoddy Indians T5—973 4
Passamaquoddy language 497.34
    T6—973 4
Passau (Germany) T2—433 55
Passementerie 677.76
  arts 746.27
Passenger automobiles 388.342
  driving 629.283
  engineering 629.222
  military engineering 623.747 2
  repair 629.287 2
  transportation services 388.342
  *see also* Automobiles
Passenger services 388.042
  air 387.742
    airport services 387.736 4
    law 343.097 8
  automobile 388.321
    urban 388.413 21
  bus 388.322
    law 343.094 82
    terminal services 388.33
    urban 388.413 22
      terminal services 388.473
  canal 386.404 22
  ferries 386.6
  ground 388.042
    law 343.093 3
  inland waterway 386.242
    law 343.096 8
    port services 386.862
  lake 386.542
  law 343.093 3
  marine 387.542
    law 343.096 8
    port services 387.162
  ports 387.162
  public administration 354.763
  railroad 385.22
    law 343.095 8
    public administration 354.767 3
    special purpose 385.5
    terminal services 385.262

Passenger services
  railroad (continued)
    urban — 388.42
      terminal services — 388.472
    river — 386.352
Passenger ships
  power-driven — 387.243
    design — 623.812 43
    engineering — 623.824 3
Passenger terminals
  architecture — 725.3
  area planning — 711.7
  construction — 690.53
  inland waterway — 386.852
  ports — 387.152
  railroad — 385.314
Passenger-train cars — 385.33
  engineering — 625.23
  *see also* Rolling stock
Passenger transportation — 388.042
  *see also* Passenger services
Passer sparrows — 598.887
Passeres — 598.8
  *see Manual at* 598.824–.88
Passeriformes — 598.8
  paleozoology — 568.8
Passerines — 598.8
Passifloraceae — 583.626
  edible fruits — 641.344 2
    cooking — 641.644 2
    food — 641.344 2
    orchard crop — 634.42
Passiflorales — 583.626
Passing
  American football — 796.332 25
Passing off (Offense) — 364.166 8
  law — 345.026 68
Passion fruit — 641.344 25
  cooking — 641.644 25
  food — 641.344 25
  orchard crop — 634.425
Passion of Jesus Christ — 232.96
  music — 782.23
Passion plays
  literature — 808.825 16
    history and criticism — 809.251 6
    specific literatures — T3B—205 16
      individual authors — T3A—2
  religious significance — 246.723
  stage presentation — 792.16
Passionflowers — 583.626
  floriculture — 635.933 626

Passionists — 255.62
  church history — 271.62
Passiontide — 263.92
  devotional literature — 242.34
  music — 781.725 5
  sermons — 252.62
Passive-aggressive personality
  disorder
  medicine — 616.858 1
  *see also* Mental disorders
Passive resistance
  political action — 322.4
  social conflict — 303.61
Passive smoking
  human toxicology — 615.952 395 2
  respiratory diseases — 616.200 471
  *see also* Respiratory tract
    diseases — humans
Passover — 296.437
  customs — 394.267
  liturgy — 296.453 7
Passover Haggadah — 296.453 71
Passports — 323.67
  law — 342.082
  political science — 323.67
  public administration — 353.13
Past lives (Occultism) — 133.901 35
Pasta — 641.822
  commercial processing — 664.755
  home preparation — 641.822
Pastaza (Ecuador :
  Province) — T2—866 42
Pasteboard — 676.288
Pastel drawing — 741.235
Pasteurella — 579.34
Pasteurella infections
  incidence — 614.573
  medicine — 616.923
  *see also* Communicable
    diseases — humans
Pasteurization
  alcoholic beverages — 663.15
  milk processing — 637.141
Pastoral counseling — 206.1
  Christianity — 253.5
  Judaism — 296.61
Pastoral Epistles — 227.83
Pastoral psychology — 206.1
  Christianity — 253.52
Pastoral systems — 636.084 5

astoral themes
  arts — 700.458 209 734
    T3C—358 209 734
  literature — 808.803 582 097 34
    history and criticism — 809.933 582 097 34
    specific literatures — T3B—080 358 209 734
      history and
        criticism — T3B—093 582 097 34
astoral theology — 206.1
  Christianity — 253
  Islam — 297.61
  Judaism — 296.61
astors — 270.092
  ecclesiology — 262.14
  *see also* Clergy — Christian
astries — 641.865
  commercial processing — 664.752 5
  home preparation — 641.865
astry mixes — 664.753
asture lands — 333.74
  *see also* Grasslands
astures — 633.202
asturing animals — 636.084 5
atagonia (Argentina and
  Chile) — T2—827
  Argentina — T2—827
  Chile — T2—836 44
atagonian weasel — 599.766 3
atañjali's philosophy — 181.452
atasse, Ange-Félix
  Central African history — 967.410 53
atavium (Italy) — T2—373 41
atchwork
  arts — 746.46
atellas
  human anatomy — 611.718
atent infringement — 364.166 2
  criminal law — 345.026 62
atent law — 346.048 6
atent leather — 675.25
atent medicines — 615.1
atentees — 609.2
atents — 346.048 6
  collections — 608
    T1—027 2
  law — 346.048 6
  public administration — 352.749
aternity — 346.017 5
aternity leave — 331.257 63
  personnel management — 658.312 2
aternosters (Channel
  Islands) — T2—423 49
âtés — 641.812
ath spaces (Mathematics) — 514.224

Pathogenesis
  medicine — 616.071
Pathogenic microorganisms — 579.165
  medical microbiology — 616.904 1
  *see Manual at* 579.165 vs.
    616.9041
Pathogenicity — 571.9
  *see also* Pathology
Pathological aging — 571.939
Pathological anatomy — 571.933
  humans — 616.07
Pathological biochemistry — 571.94
  human metabolic diseases — 616.39
    *see also* Digestive system
      diseases — humans
Pathological gambling
  medicine — 616.858 41
    *see also* Mental disorders
Pathological physiology — 571.9
Pathological processes
  medicine — 616.047
Pathological psychology — 616.89
Pathology — 571.9
  cytology — 571.936
    humans — 611.018 15
  humans — 616.07
  injuries
    medicine — 617.107
  surgery — 617.07
  *see Manual at* 571–575 vs. 630
Pathophysiology — 571.9
  *see also* Pathology
Patience — 179.9
  moral theology — 205.699
  *see also* Virtues
Patience (Game) — 795.43
Patient compliance
  medicine — 615.5
Patient education
  medicine — 615.507 1
Patient isolation
  disease control — 614.45
Patients' libraries — 027.662
Patinating
  decorative arts — 739.15
Patio furniture — 645.8
  *see also* Outdoor furniture
Patio gardening — 635.967 1
Patio lighting — 621.322 9
Patios — 721.84
  architecture — 721.84
  construction — 690.184

Patios (continued)

| | |
|---|---|
| domestic | 643.55 |
|   architecture | 728.93 |
|   construction | 690.893 |
|   home economics | 643.55 |
| Patmos Island (Greece) | T2—495 87 |
| Patois | 417.2 |
|   specific languages | T4—7 |
| Patriarchal family | 306.858 |
| Patriarchate | 262.13 |
| Patriarchs | 200.92 |
|   Biblical | 222.110 922 |
|   biography | 200.92 |
|   Christian | 270.092 |
|     biography | 270.092 |
|       specific denominations | 280 |
|       *see Manual at* 230–280 | |
|   ecclesiology | 262.13 |
| Patriarchy (System of government) | 321.1 |
| Patricia Portion (Ont.) | T2—713 1 |
| Patrick County (Va.) | T2—755 695 |
| Patrilineal kinship | 306.83 |
| Patriotic holidays | 394.26 |
|   law | 344.091 |
|   *see also* Holidays | |
| Patriotic music | 781.599 |
|   songs | 782.421 599 |
| Patriotic pageants | 394.5 |
|   customs | 394.5 |
|   performing arts | 791.624 |
| Patriotic societies | 369.2 |
|   biography | 369.209 2 |
|   United States | 369.1 |
| Patristic philosophy | 189.2 |
| Patristics (Christianity) | 270 |
| Patrol | |
|   military operation | 355.413 |
|   police services | 363.232 |
| Patrol boats (Military) | 359.835 8 |
|   design | 623.812 58 |
|   engineering | 623.825 8 |
|   naval equipment | 359.835 8 |
|   naval units | 359.325 8 |
| Patrol boats (Police) | 363.286 |
|   design | 623.812 63 |
|   engineering | 623.826 3 |
|   police services | 363.286 |
| Patron and client | 306.2 |
| Patronage | 306.2 |
|   political science | 324.204 |
| Patronage of individuals | T1—079 |
| Pattern lumber | 674.43 |

| | |
|---|---|
| Pattern perception | |
|   visual | |
|     psychology | 152.142 3 |
| Pattern poetry | 808.814 |
|   history and criticism | 809.14 |
|   specific literatures | T3B—104 |
| Pattern recognition | |
|   computer science | 006.4 |
| | T1—028 564 |
|   engineering | 621.399 4 |
| Patternmaking | |
|   clothing | 646.407 2 |
|     commercial technology | 687.042 |
|     home sewing | 646.407 2 |
|   metal casting | 671.23 |
|   metal rolling | 671.821 |
| Patterns (Geometry) | 516.15 |
| Patterns (Sewing) | 646.407 |
|   design | 646.407 2 |
|   home sewing | 646.407 |
| Patuxent River (Md.) | T2—752 4 |
| Paucituberculata | 599.27 |
| Paul I, Emperor of Russia | |
|   Russian history | 947.071 |
| Paulatuk (N.W.T.) | T2—719 3 |
| Paulding County (Ga.) | T2—758 373 |
| Paulding County (Ohio) | T2—771 17 |
| Pauline epistles | 227 |
| Paulpietersburg (South Africa : District) | T2—684 2 |
| Pauropoda | 595.64 |
| Pauses (Linguistics) | 414.6 |
|   specific languages | T4—16 |
| Pavans | 793.3 |
|   music | 784.188 23 |
| Pavements | |
|   airport runways | 629.136 34 |
|   road surfaces | 625.8 |
| Pavia (Italy) | |
|   ancient | T2—372 29 |
| Pavia (Italy : Province) | T2—452 9 |
|   ancient | T2—372 29 |
| Paving roads | 625.8 |
| Pavlovian conditioning | 153.152 6 |
| Pavlovian psychological system | 150.194 4 |
| Pavo | 598.625 8 |
| Pawnbrokers | 332.34 |
| Pawnbroking | 332.34 |
|   law | 346.025 |
| Pawnee County (Kan.) | T2—781 49 |
| Pawnee County (Neb.) | T2—782 284 |
| Pawnee County (Okla.) | T2—766 26 |
| Pawnee Indians | T5—979 33 |

awnee language 497.933
  T6—979 33
awnee literature 897.933
awns (Chess) 794.142
awnshops 332.34
ay-cable television 384.555 4
  *see also* Television
ay differentials 331.22
ay equity 331.215 3
  law 344.012 153
ay telephones
  engineering 621.386 9
ay television 384.555
  *see also* Television
ay television (Canada) 384.555 4
  *see also* Television
ayette County (Idaho) T2—796 24
ayments in lieu of taxes
  public finance 336.185
ayne County (Okla.) T2—766 34
ayroll accounting 657.742
ayroll administration 658.321
  armed forces 355.64
  public administration 352.47
ayroll tax 336.242 2
  law 343.052 42
ays Basque (France) T2—447 16
ays de la Loire (France) T2—441 6
ays-d'en-Haut (Quebec) T2—714 244
aysandú (Uruguay : Dept.) T2—895 31
az (Bolivia : Dept.) T2—841 2
az (El Salvador : Dept.) T2—728 425
az (Honduras : Dept.) T2—728 36
CB (Chemical)
  human toxicology 615.951 2
CP abuse 362.294
  medicine 616.863 4
  personal health 613.83
  social welfare 362.294
  *see also* Substance abuse
DA (Computers) 004.167
  *see also* Handheld computing
    devices; Personal
    computers
dA (Swiss political party) 324.249 407 4
ea beans 641.356 52
  *see also* Kidney beans
eace 303.66
  arts 700.458 1
  T3C—358 1
  Civil War (United States) 973.712

Peace (continued)
  ethics 172.42
    religion 205.624 2
      Christianity 241.624 2
      Islam 297.562 42
  international politics 327.172
  law of nations 341.73
  literature 808.803 581
    history and criticism 809.933 581
    specific literatures T3B—080 358 1
    history and
      criticism T3B—093 581
  social theology 201.727 3
    Buddhism 294.337 273
    Christianity 261.873
    Hinduism 294.517 273
    Islam 297.27
    Judaism 296.382 7
  World War I 940.312
  World War II 940.531 2
  *see also* Social history
Peace conferences 341.73
Peace Corps (U.S.) 361.6
Peace movements 327.172
  sociology 303.66
Peace pipe 399
Peace River (Alta.) T2—712 31
Peace River (B.C. :
  Regional district) T2—711 87
Peace River (B.C. and Alta.) T2—712 31
  Alberta T2—712 31
  British Columbia T2—711 87
Peace River (Fla.) T2—759 57
Peace River-Liard (B.C.) T2—711 87
Peace treaties 341.66
Peaceful occupation
  law of nations 341.722
Peaceful settlement of disputes 303.69
  international relations 327.17
  law of nations 341.52
  sociology 303.69
Peacekeeping forces 355.357
  law of nations 341.584
Peacekeeping operations 355.4
Peach County (Ga.) T2—758 556
Peaches 641.342 5
  botany 583.73
  commercial processing 664.804 25
  cooking 641.642 5
  food 641.342 5
  orchard crop 634.25
Peafowl 598.625 8
  animal husbandry 636.595

| | |
|---|---|
| Pe'ah | 296.123 1 |
|   Mishnah | 296.123 1 |
|   Palestinian Talmud | 296.124 1 |
| Peak District (England) | T2—425 11 |
| Peanut flour | 664.726 |
| Peanut meal | 664.726 |
| Peanut worms | 592.35 |
| Peanuts | 641.356 596 |
|   agricultural economics | 338.173 368 |
|   botany | 583.74 |
|   commercial processing | 664.805 659 6 |
|     economics | 338.476 647 26 |
|     technology | 664.726 |
|   cooking | 641.656 596 |
|   field crop | 633.368 |
|   food | 641.356 596 |
|   garden crop | 635.659 6 |
| Pearl Harbor, Attack on, 1941 | 940.542 669 3 |
| Pearl oysters | |
|   culture | 639.412 |
| Pearl River (Miss. and La.) | T2—762 5 |
| Pearl River County (Miss.) | T2—762 15 |
| Pearlfishes | 597.63 |
| Pears | 641.341 3 |
|   botany | 583.73 |
|   commercial processing | 664.804 13 |
|   cooking | 641.641 3 |
|   food | 641.341 3 |
|   orchard crop | 634.13 |
| Pearson, Lester B. | |
|   Canadian history | 971.064 3 |
| Pearston (South Africa : | |
|   District) | T2—687 54 |
| Peas | 641.356 5 |
|   botany | 583.74 |
|   commercial processing | 664.805 65 |
|   cooking | 641.656 5 |
|   field crop | 633.3 |
|   food | 641.356 5 |
|   garden crop | 635.65 |
| Peas (Pisum sativum) | 641.356 56 |
|   botany | 583.74 |
|   commercial processing | 664.805 656 |
|   cooking | 641.656 56 |
|   field crop | 633.37 |
|   food | 641.356 56 |
|   garden crop | 635.656 |
| Peasants | 305.563 3 |
| | T1—088 63 |
| Peasants' War, 1524–1525 | 943.031 |
| Peat | 553.21 |
|   economic geology | 553.21 |
|   mining | 622.331 |
| Peat (continued) | |
|   properties | 662.622 1 |
|   use as soil conditioner | 631.826 |
| Peat bogs | |
|   biology | 578.768 7 |
|   ecology | 577.687 |
| Peat coal | 553.21 |
|   *see also* Peat | |
| Peat mosses | 588.29 |
| Peatlands | |
|   biology | 578.768 7 |
|   ecology | 577.687 |
| Peba-Yaguan languages | 498.9 |
| | T6—989 |
| Pecans | 641.345 2 |
|   agriculture | 634.52 |
|   botany | 583.49 |
|   cooking | 641.645 2 |
|   food | 641.345 2 |
| Peccaries | 599.634 |
| Pecopteris | 561.597 |
| Pecos County (Tex.) | T2—764 923 |
| Pecos River (N.M. and | |
|   Tex.) | T2—764 9 |
|   New Mexico | T2—789 4 |
|   Texas | T2—764 9 |
| Pectins | 572.566 |
|   biochemistry | 572.566 |
|   food technology | 664.25 |
|   *see also* Carbohydrates | |
| Pedagogy | 370 |
| Pedaliaceae | 583.95 |
| Pedaling | |
|   music | 784.193 8 |
| Peddie (South Africa : | |
|   District) | T2—687 55 |
| Pedernales (Dominican | |
|   Republic : Province) | T2—729 323 |
| Pedestals | 721.3 |
|   architecture | 721.3 |
|   construction | 690.13 |
| Pedestrian facilities | 388.41 |
|   area planning | 711.74 |
|   landscape architecture | 717 |
|   use | 388.41 |
| Pedestrian malls | 388.411 |
|   area planning | 711.74 |
|   landscape architecture | 717 |
| Pedestrian paths | 388.12 |
|   area planning | 711.74 |
|   use | 388.12 |
|     local | 388.411 |
| Pedestrian traffic | 388.41 |
|   law | 343.098 1 |

Pedi (African people)    T5—963 977 1
Pedi language    496.397 71
   T6—963 977 1
Pediatric cardiology    618.921 2
Pediatric dentistry    617.645
Pediatric disorders
   incidence    614.599 292
   medicine    618.92
Pediatric gynecology    618.920 98
Pediatric nursing    618.920 023 1
Pediatric pharmacology    615.108 3
Pediatric preventive measures    613.043 2
Pediatric services    362.198 92
   *see also* Health services
Pediatric surgery    617.98
Pediatric therapeutics    615.542
Pediatric toxicology    615.900 83
Pediatricians    618.920 009 2
   role and function    618.920 023 2
Pediatrics    618.92
   *see Manual at* 616 vs. 618.92;
     *also at* 618.92097 vs. 617
Pediculosis
   medicine    616.572
   *see also* Skin diseases —
     humans
Pedicuring    646.727
Pedigrees
   animal husbandry    636.082 2
Pediments    721.5
   architecture    721.5
   construction    690.15
Pee Dee River (N.C. and
   S.C.)    T2—757 8
Peel (Ont. : Regional
   municipality)    T2—713 535
Peer counseling of students    371.404 7
Peer group
   influence on crime    364.253
   socialization    303.327
Peer pressure    303.327
Peer review
   health services    362.106 8
Peer-to-peer architecture
   computer science    004.652
Peerage
   genealogy    929.7
Pegasiformes    597.64
Pegmatite dikes    553.16
   determinative mineralogy    549.116
Peking (China)    T2—511 56
Peking man    569.97
Pekingese (Dog)    636.76
Pelagian Islands    T2—458 22

Pelagianism    273.5
Pelargoniums    635.933 79
   botany    583.79
   floriculture    635.933 79
Pelecaniformes    598.43
   paleozoology    568.4
Pelecanoididae    598.42
Pelgrimsrus 1 (South
   Africa : District)    T2—682 71
Pelgrimsrus 2 (South
   Africa : District)    T2—682 74
Pelicans    598.43
Pella (Greece : Nome)    T2—495 65
Pellagra
   medicine    616.393
   *see also* Digestive system
     diseases — humans
Pelly Bay (Nunavut)    T2—719 55
Pelobatoidea    597.86
Pelomedusidae    597.929
Peloncillo Mountains (Ariz.
   and N.M.)    T2—789 693
Peloponnesian War, 431–404
   B.C.    938.05
Peloponnēsos (Greece)    T2—495 2
Peloponnēsos (Greece :
   Periphereia)    T2—495 22
Peloponnesus (Greece)    T2—495 2
   ancient    T2—386
Peloponnesus (Greece :
   Periphereia)    T2—495 22
Pelvic bones
   human anatomy    611.71
   medicine    616.71
Pelvic muscles
   human anatomy    611.736
Pelvic region
   human anatomy    611.96
   human physiology    612.96
   regional medicine    617.55
   surgery    617.55
Pelycosauria    567.93
Pemba (Tanzania)    967.81
   T2—678 1
Pemba North (Tanzania)    T2—678 1
Pemba South (Tanzania)    T2—678 1
Pemberton (B.C.)    T2—711 31
Pembina County (N.D.)    T2—784 19
Pembrokeshire (Wales)    T2—429 62
Pemiscot County (Mo.)    T2—778 996
Pemón language    498.42
   T6—984 2
Pen-and-ink drawing    741.26
P'en ching    635.977 2

Penal colonies    365.34
   *see also* Penal institutions
Penal institutions    365
   accounting    657.832
   area planning    711.556
   buildings    365.5
    architecture    725.6
   energy economics    333.796 4
   institutional housekeeping    647.966
   law    344.035
   psychological influence    155.962
   reform    365.7
Penal reform    364.6
Penalties
   personnel management    658.314 4
Penance    203.4
   Christianity    234.166
    public worship    265.6
    theology    234.166
Penarth (Wales)    T2—429 89
Penas    787.6
   *see also* Stringed instruments
Pencil drawing    741.24
Pencil fishes    597.48
Pencils
   mechanical    681.6
   wood-cased    674.88
Pend d'Oreille language    497.943 5
   T6—979 435
Pend d'Oreille literature    897.943 5
Pend Oreille County
   (Wash.)    T2—797 21
Pende (African people)    T5—963 93
Pende languages    496.393
   T6—963 93
Pender County (N.C.)    T2—756 25
Pendle (England)    T2—427 645
Pendleton County (Ky.)    T2—769 33
Pendleton County (W. Va.)    T2—754 91
Pendulum motion    531.324
Pendulums    531.324
   clockworks    681.112
   dowsing    133.323
   fortune-telling    133.3
Penetrating wounds
   medicine    617.14
Penetration
   materials science    620.112 6
Penguins    598.47
Penicillin
   pharmacology    615.329 565 4
Penicillium    579.565 4

Penile diseases
   medicine    616.66
   *see also* Male genital
    diseases — humans
Peninsular Malaysia    T2—595 1
Peninsular War, 1807–1814    940.27
Penis    573.656
   biology    573.656
   human anatomy    611.64
   human physiology    612.616
   medicine    616.66
   *see also* Male genital system
Penitentiaries    365.34
   *see also* Penal institutions
Penjing    635.977 2
Penmanship    652.1
   primary education    372.634
Pennine Alps (Italy and
   Switzerland)    T2—494 79
Pennine Chain (England)    T2—428
Pennines (England)    T2—428
Pennington County (Minn.)    T2—776 965
Pennington County (S.D.)    T2—783 93
Pennsylvania    974.8
   T2—748
Pennsylvania Dutch    T5—310 748
Pennsylvania Dutch dialect    437.974 8
   T6—38
Pennsylvania German dialect    437.974 8
   T6—38
Pennsylvania Germans    T5—310 748
Pennsylvanian period    551.752
   geology    551.752
   paleontology    560.175 2
Penny stocks
   speculation    332.632 28
Penny whistles    788.35
   *see also* Woodwind instruments
Pennyroyal Plateau (Ky.)    T2—769 6
Penobscot County (Me.)    T2—741 3
Penobscot River (Me.)    T2—741 3
Penology    364.6
   public administration    353.39
Penrith (N.S.W.)    T2—944 1
Pens (Writing)
   manufacturing technology    681.6
Pensacola (Fla.)    T2—759 99
Pension funds    331.252 4
   investment by    332.672 54
   tax law    343.064
   *see also* Pensions
Pension reform    331.252 2
   *see also* Pensions

Pension trusts 331.252 4
  investment by 332.672 54
  tax law 343.064
  *see also* Pensions
Pensions 331.252
  accounting 657.75
  annuities
    insurance 368.37
  economics 331.252
  law 344.012 52
  personnel management 658.325 3
    executives 658.407 253
  public administration 353.54
  social security 368.43
Penstemon 635.933 95
  botany 583.95
  floriculture 635.933 95
Penstocks
  dam engineering 627.882
Pentaerythritol tetranitrate 662.27
Pentane 665.773
Pentastomida 592.76
Pentateuch 222.1
Pentatonicism 781.265
Pentecost 263.94
  devotional literature 242.38
  Jewish 296.438
    liturgy 296.453 8
  music 781.729 3
  sermons 252.64
Pentecostal churches 289.94
Pentecostalism 270.82
  independent denominations 289.94
  Protestantism 280.4
Pentecostals
  biography 289.940 92
Penthouse gardens
  landscape architecture 712.6
Penticton (B.C.) T2—711 5
Pentland Hills (Scotland) T2—413 5
Pentyrch (Wales) T2—429 87
Penutian languages 497.41
  T6—974 1
Penutian peoples T5—974 1
Penwith (England) T2—423 7
Penza (Russia : Oblast) T2—474 6
Penzenskaia oblast′ (Russia) T2—474 6
Peonies 635.933 62
  botany 583.62
  floriculture 635.933 62
Peons 305.56
  T1—086 25

People T1—08
  groups T1—08
    government programs 353.53
  individuals T1—092
    collected biography T1—092 2
  literature
    specific literatures T3B—080 351
  *see also* Persons (Individuals)
  *see Manual at* T1—08 and
    306.2–.6
People movers
  engineering 621.868
People of God (Church) 262.7
People with mental retardation 305.908 4
  T1—087 4
  education 371.928
  law 344.079 128
  *see also* Mentally disabled
    people
People's Democratic Republic of 951.93
  Korea T2—519 3
People's Party of America 324.273 27
People's Republic of China T2—51
Peoria County (Ill.) T2—773 52
Peperomias 583.25
Pepin County (Wis.) T2—775 47
Pepos 641.356 1
  *see also* Melons
Pepper-shrikes 598.878
Pepperbushes 583.66
Peppers 641.338 4
  botany 583.952
  *see also* Hot spices; Sweet
    peppers
Peppers (Piperaceae) 641.338 4
  botany 583.25
  *see also* Hot spices
Peppers (Solanaceae) 641.338 4
  botany 583.952
  food 641.338 4
    hot peppers 641.338 4
    sweet peppers 641.356 43
  *see also* Hot spices; Sweet
    peppers
Peptic ulcers
  medicine 616.343
  *see also* Digestive system
    diseases — humans
Peptides 572.65
  humans 612.015 756
  *see also* Proteins
Peptones 572.65
  *see also* Proteins

| | |
|---|---|
| Pequot dialect | 497.344 |
| | T6—973 44 |
| Pequot Indians | T5—973 44 |
| Pequot War, 1636–1638 | 973.22 |
| Peracarida | 595.37 |
| paleozoology | 565.37 |
| Perak | T2—595 1 |
| Peramelidae | 599.26 |
| Peramelina | 599.26 |
| Peravia (Dominican Republic : Province) | T2—729 373 |
| Percentage | 513.245 |
| Percentage renting | |
| land economics | 333.563 |
| Perception | 153.7 |
| educational psychology | 370.155 |
| epistemology | 121.34 |
| psychology | 153.7 |
| sensory | 152.1 |
| *see Manual at* 153.7 vs. 152.1 | |
| Perception theory | 003.52 |
| | T1—011 52 |
| Perceptrons | 006.32 |
| Perch trout | 597.73 |
| Percheron horse | 636.15 |
| Perches | 597.75 |
| sports fishing | 799.177 5 |
| Perching birds | 598.8 |
| Percichthyidae | 597.73 |
| Percidae | 597.75 |
| Perciformes | 597.7 |
| paleozoology | 567.7 |
| Percoidea | 597.72 |
| Percoidei | 597.7 |
| Percolation (Statistical physics) | 530.13 |
| Percolation theory | 530.13 |
| Percopsiformes | 597.62 |
| Percussed idiophones | 786.84 |
| set | 786.84 |
| single | 786.884 |
| *see also* Percussion instruments | |
| Percussion bands | 784.68 |
| Percussion caps | 662.4 |
| military engineering | 623.454 2 |
| Percussion ensembles | 785.68 |
| Percussion instruments | 786.8 |
| bands and orchestras | 784 |
| chamber ensembles | 785 |
| mixed | 785.2–.5 |
| single type | 785.68 |
| construction | 786.819 23 |
| by hand | 786.819 23 |
| by machine | 681.868 |
| solo music | 786.8 |

| | |
|---|---|
| Perdix perdix | 598.623 2 |
| Pereira, Aristides | |
| Cape Verdean history | 966.580 31 |
| Perennials (Plants) | 582.16 |
| floriculture | 635.932 |
| Perfect binding | |
| bookbinding | 686.35 |
| Perfectionism | |
| ethical systems | 171.3 |
| personality trait | 155.232 |
| Perforating tools | 621.95 |
| Performance (Law) | 346.022 |
| Performance art | 700 |
| fine arts | 709.040 755 |
| techniques | 702.81 |
| Performance auditing | 658.401 3 |
| public administration | 352.43 |
| Performance audits | 658.401 3 |
| public administration | 352.439 |
| Performance awards | 331.216 4 |
| labor economics | 331.216 4 |
| personnel management | 658.322 5 |
| Performance contracting | |
| students | 371.393 |
| teachers | 371.15 |
| Performance evaluation | |
| computer science | 004.029 |
| engineering | 621.390 29 |
| for design and improvement | 004.24 |
| engineering | 621.392 |
| *see Manual at* 004.1 vs. 004.24 | |
| executive management | 658.401 3 |
| military services | 355.685 |
| public administration | 352.35 |
| Performance evaluation of employees | 658.312 5 |
| public administration | 352.66 |
| Performance rating | |
| personnel management | 658.312 5 |
| executives | 658.407 125 |
| Performance scores | 780 |
| treatises | 780.264 |
| Performance standards | |
| commerce | 389.63 |
| personnel management | 658.312 5 |
| production management | 658.562 |
| Performance techniques | |
| music | 781.43 |
| Performance tests | |
| automotive vehicles | 629.282 4 |
| Performances | 790.2 |
| ethics | 175 |
| music | 780.78 |

Performers (Entertainers)   791.092
  *see Manual at* 780.92 and
   791.092
Performing arts   790.2
  public administrative support   353.77
  sociology   306.484
  *see Manual at* 780.079 vs.
   790.2
Performing arts centers
  architecture   725.83
  area planning   711.558
Perfume-producing plants
  agriculture   633.81
  economic botany   581.636
Perfumes   668.54
  customs   391.63
Pergamum (Turkey)   T2—562 5
  ancient   T2—392 3
Periapical abscesses
  dentistry   617.632
Pericardium   573.172 5
  biology   573.172 5
  human anatomy   611.11
  human physiology   612.17
  medicine   616.11
  *see also* Cardiovascular system
Pericardium diseases
  medicine   616.11
  *see also* Cardiovascular
   diseases — humans
Peridotite   552.3
Peridural anesthesia
  surgery   617.964
Périgord (France)   T2—447 2
Perimenopause
  disorders
   gynecology   618.175
   *see also* Female genital
    diseases — humans
Perimetrium   573.667 25
  human physiology   612.627
  *see also* Female genital system
Perinatal death
  medicine   618.392
Perinatal medicine   618.32
Perinatology   618.32
Perineum
  human anatomy   611.96
  human physiology   612.96
  surgery   617.555
Period costumes
  home sewing   646.478
Period furniture   749.090 1–090 5

Period novels   808.838 1
  history and criticism   809.381
  specific literatures   T3B—308 1
  individual authors   T3A—3
Periodic law   546.8
Periodic table   546.8
Periodicals   050
       T1—05
  *see also* Serials
Periodicity (Biology)   571.77
Periodicity (Chemistry)   546.8
Periodontal diseases
  dentistry   617.632
Periodontics   617.632
Periodontitis
  dentistry   617.632
Periosteum   573.762 5
  human histology   612.751 045
  *see also* Musculoskeletal
   system
Periostitis
  medicine   616.712
  *see also* Musculoskeletal
   diseases — humans
Peripheral control units   004.64
  engineering   621.398 1
Peripheral nerves   573.85
  human physiology   612.81
  medicine   616.856
  *see also* Nervous system
Peripheral nervous system
  diseases
  medicine   616.856
  *see also* Nervous system
   diseases — humans
Peripheral vascular diseases
  medicine   616.131
  *see also* Cardiovascular
   diseases — humans
Peripherals (Computers)   004.7
       T1—028 547
  engineering   621.398 4
Perischoechinoidea   593.95
Periscopes   623.46
Perissodactyla   599.66
  paleozoology   569.66
Peritoneal dialysis
  medicine   617.461 059
Peritoneal diseases
  medicine   616.38
  *see also* Digestive system
   diseases — humans

| | | | |
|---|---|---|---|
| Peritoneum | 573.325 | Perón, Isabel | |
| human anatomy | 611.38 | Argentine history | 982.064 |
| human physiology | 612.33 | Perón, Juan Domingo | |
| medicine | 616.38 | Argentine history | 982.062 |
| surgery | 617.558 | 1946–1955 | 982.062 |
| *see also* Digestive system | | 1973–1974 | 982.064 |
| Periwinkles (Plants) | | Perón, María Estela | |
| botany | 583.93 | Argentine history | 982.064 |
| Perjury | 364.134 | Peronosporalcs | 579.546 |
| law | 345.023 4 | Perouse Strait | 551.461 453 |
| Perkins County (Neb.) | T2—782 88 | | T2—164 53 |
| Pcrkins County (S.D.) | T2—783 45 | Peroxidation | |
| Perlis | T2—595 1 | chemical engineering | 660.284 43 |
| Permaculture | 631.58 | Peroxisomes | 571.655 |
| Permafrost | 551.384 | Perquimans County (N.C.) | T2—756 144 |
| biology | 578.758 6 | Perry County (Ala.) | T2—761 44 |
| ecology | 577.586 | Perry County (Ark.) | T2—767 39 |
| engineering geology | 624.151 36 | Perry County (Ill.) | T2—773 93 |
| Permanent Court of Arbitration | 341.522 2 | Perry County (Ind.) | T2—772 29 |
| Permanent Court of International | | Perry County (Ky.) | T2—769 173 |
| Justice | 341.552 | Perry County (Miss.) | T2—762 175 |
| Permanent deformation | 531.385 | Perry County (Mo.) | T2—778 694 |
| materials science | 620.112 33 | Perry County (Ohio) | T2—771 59 |
| *see also* Plasticity | | Perry County (Pa.) | T2—748 45 |
| Permanent education | 374 | Perry County (Tenn.) | T2—768 38 |
| | T1—071 5 | Persecutions (Christian church | |
| *see also* Adult education | | history) | 272 |
| Permanent magnetic fields | | Persepolis (Iran) | T2—357 72 |
| (Earth) | 538.72 | Pershing County (Nev.) | T2—793 53 |
| Permanent-mold casting | | Persia | T2—55 |
| metals | 671.253 | ancient | 935.7 |
| Permanent waving | 646.724 | | T2—357 |
| Permanent way (Railroad) | 385.312 | Persian cat | 636.832 |
| engineering | 625.1 | Persian Empire | 935.05 |
| transportation services | 385.312 | | T2—35 |
| Permeability | | Egyptian history | 932.016 |
| foundation soils | 624.151 36 | Mesopotamian history | 935.05 |
| Permiaks | T5—945 3 | Middle Eastern history | 939.403 |
| Permian languages | 494.53 | Palestinian history | 933.03 |
| | T6—945 3 | Persian Gulf | 551.461 535 |
| Permian literatures | 894.53 | | T2—165 35 |
| Permian period | 551.756 | Persian Gulf Crisis, 1990–1991 | 956.704 42 |
| geology | 551.756 | Persian Gulf Region | 953 |
| paleontology | 560.175 6 | | T2—53 |
| Permians | T5—945 3 | ancient | 939.49 |
| Permic languages | 494.53 | | T2—394 9 |
| | T6—945 3 | Persian Gulf States | 953.6 |
| Permic literatures | 894.53 | | T2—536 |
| Permskaĩa oblast' (Russia) | T2—474 3 | ancient | 939.49 |
| Permutation groups | 512.21 | | T2—394 9 |
| Permutations (Mathematics) | 511.64 | Persian Gulf syndrome | |
| Perm' (Russia : Oblast) | T2—474 3 | medicine | 616.98 |
| Pernambuco (Brazil) | T2—813 4 | Persian Gulf War, 1980–1988 | 955.054 2 |
| Peromyscus | 599.355 | Persian Gulf War, 1991 | 956.704 42 |

Persian language 491.55
T6—915 5
Persian literature 891.55
Persian rugs
arts 746.755
Persian Wars, 500–479 B.C. 938.03
Persians T5—915 5
Persimmons 641.344 5
botany 583.674
cooking 641.644 5
food 641.344 5
orchard crop 634.45
Persis T2—357 72
Persistence
insurance 368.016
Person (Grammar) 415.5
specific languages T4—55
Person County (N.C.) T2—756 573
Person of Jesus Christ 232.8
Personal actions (Law) 347.053
Personal analysis
applied psychology 158.1
Personal appearance 646.7
customs 391.6
ethics 177.4
*see also* Ethical problems
Personal-area networks 004.68
Personal beauty
arts 700.453
T3C—353
literature 808.803 53
history and criticism 809.933 53
specific literatures T3B—080 353
history and
criticism T3B—093 53
Personal cleanliness 613.4
customs 391.64
health 613.4
Personal coaching
psychology 158.3
Personal computers 004.16
architecture 004.256
buyers' guides 004.160 29
communications 004.616
programming 005.712 6
programs 005.713 6
engineering 621.391 6
graphics programming 006.676
graphics programs 006.686
interfacing 004.616
programming 005.712 6
programs 005.713 6
multimedia-systems
programming 006.776

Personal computers (continued)
multimedia-systems programs 006.786
operating systems 005.446
performance evaluation 004.160 29
for design and improvement 004.256
programming 005.26
programs 005.36
purchasing manuals 004.160 29
systems analysis 004.256
systems design 004.256
*see Manual at* 004.11–.16
Personal conduct
public administrative control 353.37
Personal construct psychology 150.198 5
Personal construct theory 150.198 5
Personal counseling 361.06
education 371.46
*see also* Counseling
Personal digital assistants 004.167
*see also* Handheld computing
devices; Personal
computers
Personal efficiency
business 650.11
executives 658.409 3
Personal finance 332.024
Personal fulfillment
ethical systems 171.3
Personal grooming 646.7
Personal grooming accessories
manufacturing technology 688.5
Personal health 613
primary education 372.37
sociology 306.461 3
Personal hygiene 613
primary education 372.37
Personal improvement
applied psychology 158.1
Personal income 339.32
macroeconomics
distribution 339.22
Personal income tax 336.242
law 343.052 62
public administration 352.44
public finance 336.242
Personal information
management programs 005.57
Personal injury (Law) 346.032 3
Personal keyboarding 652.32
Personal liability insurance 368.56
Personal liberty 323.44
*see also* Civil rights
Personal life 646.7
Personal loans 332.743

Personal names | 929.4
  law | 346.012
Personal narratives
  American Revolution | 973.309 2
  Chaco War | 989.207 160 92
  Civil War (England) | 942.062 092
  Civil War (Spain) | 946.081 092
  Civil War (United States) | 973.781
    Confederate States of
       America | 973.782
    United States | 973.781
  Crimean War | 947.073 809 2
  Franco-German War | 943.082 092
  Hundred Years' War | 944.025 092
  Indo-Pakistan War, 1971 | 954.920 510 92
  Indochinese War | 959.704 109 2
  Iraqi-Iranian Conflict | 955.054 209 2
  Korean War | 951.904 209 2
  Mexican War | 973.620 92
  South African War | 968.048 092
  Spanish-American War | 973.890 92
  Thirty Years' War | 940.240 92
  Vietnamese War | 959.704 309 2
  War of the Pacific | 983.061 609 2
  World War I | 940.481–.482
  World War II | 940.548 1
Personal property
  law | 346.047
    private ownership | 346.047
    public ownership | 343.023
Personal property tax | 336.23
  law | 343.054
  public administration | 352.44
  public finance | 336.23
Personal religion | 204
  Buddhism | 294.344
  Christianity | 240
  Hinduism | 294.54
  Islam | 297.57
    Sufi | 297.4
  Judaism | 296.7
Personal risks | 368.07
Personal safety | 613.6
      T1—028 9
  primary education | 372.37
Personal security
  civil rights issues | 323.43
Personal selling | 381.1
  management | 658.85
      T1—068 8
Personal shorthand | 653.18
Personal space
  sociology | 304.23

Personal survival
  occultism | 133.901 3
Personal wealth
  taxes | 336.24
Personales | 583.95
Personalism
  philosophy | 141.5
Personality | 155.2
  applied psychology | 158.1
  children | 155.418 2
  educational psychology | 370.153 2
  folklore | 398.273
    history and criticism | 398.353
  philosophy | 126
Personality (Law) | 346.012
Personality assessment | 155.28
Personality development | 155.25
Personality disorders
  medicine | 616.858 1
  *see also* Mental disorders
Personality inventories | 155.283
Personality questionnaires | 155.283
Personality tests | 155.28
Personality types | 155.26
Personalized reading instruction
  primary education | 372.417
Personifications (Religion) | 202.14
Personnel
  libraries | 023
  museums | 069.63
  office services | 651.3
Personnel information
  management | 658.301
Personnel management | 658.3
      T1—068 3
  armed forces | 355.61
  executives | 658.407
  libraries | 023
  museums | 069.63
  public administration | 352.6
  schools | 371.201
    higher education | 378.11
Personnel planning | 658.301
Personnel policy | 658.301
Personnel selection
  management | 658.311 2
Personnel transports
  military engineering | 623.746 5
Personnel utilization
  management | 658.312 8
  public administration | 352.66

| | |
|---|---|
| Persons (Individuals) | T1—092 |
| | T2—2 |
| arts | 700.451 |
| | T3C—351 |
| biography | 920 |
| | T1—092 |
| collected biography | T1—092 2 |
| folklore | 398.22 |
| history and criticism | 398.352 |
| groups | T1—08 |
| *see also* People | |
| literature | 808.803 51 |
| history and criticism | 809.933 51 |
| specific literatures | T3B—080 351 |
| history and | |
| criticism | T3B—093 51 |
| objects of worship | 202.13 |
| *see Manual at* T1—092 | |
| Persons (Legal concept) | |
| law | 346.012 |
| Persoonia | 583.89 |
| Perspective | |
| arts | 701.82 |
| technical drawing | 604.245 |
| Perspiration | |
| human physiology | 612.793 |
| Persuasion | 303.342 |
| logic | 168 |
| political science | 320.014 |
| psychology | 153.852 |
| rhetoric | 808 |
| social process | 303.342 |
| PERT (Network analysis) | 658.403 2 |
| Perth (Ont. : County) | T2—713 23 |
| Perth (W.A.) | T2—941 1 |
| Perth and Kinross | |
| (Scotland) | T2—412 8 |
| Perturbation theory | 515.392 |
| Perturbations | |
| celestial mechanics | 521.4 |
| Pertussis | |
| incidence | 614.543 |
| medicine | 616.204 |
| *see also* Respiratory tract | |
| diseases — humans | |
| pediatrics | 618.922 04 |
| Peru | 985 |
| | T2—85 |
| Peru-Bolivian Confederation | 984.044 |
| Bolivian history | 984.044 |
| Peruvian history | 985.05 |
| Peru Current | 551.462 141 |
| Perugia (Italy) | T2—456 511 |
| ancient | T2—375 731 |
| Perugia (Italy : Province) | T2—456 51 |
| ancient | T2—374 3 |
| Etruria | T2—375 73 |
| Umbria | T2—374 3 |
| Perusia (Italy) | T2—375 731 |
| Peruvian lily | 635.934 34 |
| botany | 584.34 |
| floriculture | 635.934 34 |
| Peruvian literature | 860 |
| Peruvians | T5—688 5 |
| Pervasive development disorders | |
| medicine | 616.858 82 |
| pediatrics | 618.928 588 2 |
| Pesach | 296.437 |
| customs | 394.267 |
| liturgy | 296.453 7 |
| Pesaḥim | 296.123 2 |
| Babylonian Talmud | 296.125 2 |
| Mishnah | 296.123 2 |
| Palestinian Talmud | 296.124 2 |
| Pesaro (Italy) | |
| ancient | T2—374 2 |
| Pesaro e Urbino (Italy : | |
| Province) | T2—456 77 |
| ancient | T2—374 2 |
| Pescara (Italy : Province) | T2—457 17 |
| ancient | T2—377 36 |
| Peshawar District (Pakistan) | T2—549 123 |
| Pessimism | |
| philosophy | 149.6 |
| Pest control | 363.78 |
| agriculture | 632.9 |
| *see Manual at* 632.95 vs. | |
| 632.2–.8 | |
| conservation technology | 639.966 |
| control technology | 628.96 |
| disease carriers | |
| medicine | 614.43 |
| household sanitation | 648.7 |
| law | 344.046 |
| public administration | 354.339 |
| social welfare | 363.78 |
| Pest Megye (Hungary) | T2—439 1 |
| Pest resistance | |
| materials science | 620.112 2 |
| Pest-resistant construction | 693.84 |
| Pesticide pollution | 363.738 498 |
| *see also* Pesticides — pollution | |
| Pesticide resistance | |
| agriculture | 632.950 42 |

Pesticides   632.95
  adverse effects
    agriculture   632.950 42
    bee keeping   638.159
    wildlife conservation   639.969
  agricultural use   632.95
    *see Manual at* 632.95 vs.
      632.2–.8
  chemical engineering   668.65
  human toxicology   615.902
  pest control technology   628.96
  pollution   363.738 498
    ecology   577.279
    environmental engineering   628.529
    law   344.046 334
    *see also* Pollution
  public safety   363.179 2
    *see also* Hazardous materials
  toxicology   571.959
  water pollution engineering   628.168 42
Pests   591.65
  agriculture   632.6
  *see also* Pest control
PET (Tomography)
  medicine   616.075 75
Pet food   636.088 7
  animal husbandry   636.088 7
  manufacturing technology   664.66
Pet names   929.97
Petals   575.69
Pétanque   796.31
Petauridae   599.23
Petén (Guatemala : Dept.)   T2—728 12
Peter (Biblical books)   227.92
Peter I, Emperor of Russia
  Russian history   947.05
Peter II, Emperor of Russia
  Russian history   947.061
Peter III, Emperor of Russia
  Russian history   947.062
Peter Lougheed Provincial
  Park (Alta.)   T2—712 332
Peterborough (England :
  City)   T2—426 51
Peterborough (Ont. :
  County)   T2—713 67
Petersburg (Va.)   T2—755 581
Petit basset griffon vendén   636.753 6
Petition
  civil right   323.48
PETN (Explosives)   662.27
Petorca (Chile : Province)   T2  832 48
Petra (Extinct city)   T2—394 8
Petrels   598.42

Petri nets   511.35
Petrified Forest National
  Park (Ariz.)   T2—791 37
Petrified wood   561.16
Petrochemicals   665.538
  chemical engineering   661.804
  human toxicology   615.951
  petroleum product   665.538
Petrogenesis   552.03
Petroglyphs   709.011 3
Petrography   552
Petrol   665.538 27
Petrolatum   665.538 5
Petroleum   553.28
  chemistry   547.83
  dowsing   133.323 7
  economic geology   553.28
  extraction   622.338
    equipment manufacturing
      technology   681.766 5
  extractive economics   338.272 8
    law   343.077 2
  pipeline transportation   388.55
    law   343.093 95
  processing   665.5
    economics   338.476 655
    enterprises   338.766 55
  prospecting   622.182 8
  public administration   354.45
  resource economics   333.823
    law   346.046 823
Petroleum chemicals   665.538
  chemical engineering   661.804
  petroleum product   665.538
Petroleum coke   665.538 8
Petroleum County (Mont.)   T2—786 28
Petroleum engineers   665.509 2
Petroleum gas   665.773
Petroleum geology   553.28
Petroleum industry   338.272 8
  law   343.077 2
Petrologists   552.009 2
Petrology   552
Petrusburg (South Africa :
  District)   T2—685 7
Pets   636.088 7
  art representation   704.943 2
  arts   T3C—362
  therapeutic use   615.851 58
  *see Manual at* 800, T3C—362
    vs. 398.245, 590, 636
Pettis County (Mo.)   T2—778 48
Petty officers   359.009 2
  role and function   359.338

Petunias 635.933 952
  botany 583.952
  floriculture 635.933 952
Pews 247.1
  architecture 726.529 3
Pewter
  decorative arts 739.533
Pezizales 579.578
Pfäffikon (Switzerland :
  Bezirk) T2—494 574 5
Pfiesteriaceae 579.87
pH 541.372 8
  chemical engineering 660.297 28
Phacidiales 579.57
Phaeophyceae 579.88
Phaeophyta 579.88
Phaethontidae 598.43
Phages 579.26
Phagocytes 571.968
  human immunology 616.079 9
Phalaborwa (South Africa :
  District) T2—682 59
Phalacrocoracidae 598.43
Phalaenopsis 584.4
  floriculture 635.934 4
Phalanger 599.232
Phalangeridae 599.232
Phalangeroidea 599.23
Phalanges
  human anatomy 611.718
  hands 611.717
Phalangida 595.43
Phalansterianism (Socialist
  school)
  economics 335.23
Phalanxes (Military units) 355.31
Phalarideae 584.9
Phalaropes 598.33
Phalaropodidae 598.33
Phallales 579.599
Phanarists
  Romanian history 949.801 5
Phanerite 552.3
Phanerozoic eon 551.7
Phanerozonia 593.93
  paleozoology 563.93
Phantasms 133.14
Pharaoh hound 636.753 6
Phareae 584.9
Pharisees 296.812
Pharmaceutical arithmetic 615.140 151 3
Pharmaceutical chemistry 615.19

Pharmaceutical drugs 615.1
  *see also* Drugs
    (Pharmaceuticals)
Pharmaceutical industry 338.476 151
Pharmaceutical services
  insurance 368.382 4
  social welfare 362.178 2
Pharmaceutical technology 615.19
Pharmacists 615.109 2
  law 344.041 6
Pharmacodynamics 615.7
  *see Manual at* 615.1 vs. 615.7;
    *also at* 615.7 vs. 615.9
Pharmacognosy 615.321
Pharmacokinetics 615.7
  *see Manual at* 615.1 vs. 615.7;
    *also at* 615.2–.3 vs. 615.7;
    *also at* 615.7 vs. 615.9
Pharmacologists 615.109 2
Pharmacology 615.1
  adolescent medicine 615.108 35
  pediatrics 615.108 3
  veterinary medicine 636.089 51
  *see Manual at* 615.1 vs. 615.7
Pharmacopoeias 615.11
Pharmacy 615.1
  law 344.041 6
Pharyngeal diseases
  medicine 616.32
    *see also* Digestive system
      diseases — humans
  surgery 617.532
Pharynx
  human anatomy 611.32
  human physiology 612.31
  medicine 616.32
  surgery 617.532
Phascolarctidae 599.25
Phase changes 530.474
  *see also* Phase transformations
Phase diagrams 530.474
  metallurgy 669.94
  *see also* Phase transformations
Phase equilibria 530.474
  *see also* Phase transformations
Phase-locked loops
  electronic circuits 621.381 536 4
Phase modulators
  electronic circuits 621.381 536 4
Phase stability 530.474
  *see also* Phase transformations
Phase transformations 530.474
  chemical engineering 660.296 3
  fluid-state physics 530.424

Phase transformations (continued)
   physics 530.474
   solid-state physics 530.414
   thermochemistry 541.363
Phase transitions 530.474
   *see also* Phase transformations
Phasemeters 621.374 9
Phases
   moon 523.32
Phasianidae 598.62
Phasianus colchicus 598.625 2
Phasmatodea 595.729
Phasmida 595.729
Pheasants 598.625
   animal husbandry 636.594
   conservation technology 639.978 625
   resource economics 333.958 625
   sports hunting 799.246 25
Phelps County (Mo.) T2—778 594
Phelps County (Neb.) T2—782 392
Phencyclidine abuse 362.294
   medicine 616.863 4
   personal health 613.83
   social welfare 362.294
   *see also* Substance abuse
Phenolics 668.422 2
Phenology 578.42
Phenols 547.632
   chemical engineering 661.82
Phenomenalism 142.7
Phenomenological psychology 150.192
Phenomenology 142.7
Phenotypes 576.53
Phenylketonuria
   medicine 616.399
   *see also* Digestive system
     diseases — humans
Phigalia (Extinct city) T2—388
Philadelphia (Pa.) T2—748 11
Philadelphia County (Pa.) T2—748 11
Philanthropists 361.740 92
Philanthropy
   ethics 177.7
   *see also* Ethical problems
   social welfare 361.74
Philately 769.56
Philemon (Biblical book) 227.86
Philesiaceae 584.35
Philibert II, Duke of Savoy
   Piedmontese history 945.105
Philinoglossacea 594.34
Philip I, King of France
   French history 944.022

Philip II, King of France
   French history 944.023
Philip II, King of Spain
   Spanish history 946.043
Philip III, King of France
   French history 944.024
Philip III, King of Spain
   Spanish history 946.051
Philip IV, King of France
   French history 944.024
Philip IV, King of Spain
   Spanish history 946.052
Philip V, King of France
   French history 944.024
Philip V, King of Spain
   Spanish history 946.055
Philip VI, King of France
   French history 944.025
Philippians (Biblical book) 227.6
Philippine-American War,
   1898–1901 959.903 1
Philippine campaign, 1898 973.893 7
Philippine Independent Church 284.8
   *see also* Old Catholic churches
Philippine languages 499.21
   T6—992 1
Philippine literatures 899.21
Philippine people T5—992 1
Philippine Sea 551.461 458
   T2—164 58
Philippines 959.9
   T2—599
Philippolis (South Africa :
   District) T2—685 7
Philipstown (South Africa :
   District) T2—687 13
Philistia 939.48
   T2—394 8
Phillip Island (Vic.) T2—945 2
Phillips County (Ark.) T2—767 88
Phillips County (Colo.) T2—788 77
Phillips County (Kan.) T2—781 17
Phillips County (Mont.) T2—786 16
Philodendrons 635.934 64
   botany 584.64
   floriculture 635.934 64
Philologists 409.2
   linguistics specialists 410.92
Philology 400
   linguistics 410
Philosophers 180–190
   ancient 180
   eastern 181
   medieval western 189

Philosophers (continued)
  modern — 190
  *see Manual at* 180–190
Philosopher's stone — 540.112
  folklore — 398.26
    history and criticism — 398.465
Philosophical anthropology — 128
Philosophical counseling — 128.4
Philosophical logic — 160
Philosophy — 100
                T1—01
  arts — T3C—384
  literature — 808.803 84
    history and criticism — 809.933 84
    specific literatures — T3B—080 384
      history and
        criticism — T3B—093 84
  *see Manual at* T1—01; *also at*
    200 vs. 100
Philosophy and religion — 201.61
  Christianity — 261.51
  Islam — 297.261
  Judaism — 296.371
Philosophy of language — 121.68
  linguistics — 401
Philosophy of nature — 113
Philosophy of religion — 210
Philosophy of science — 501
Philydraceae — 584.35
Phiomorpha — 599.359
Phishing — 364.163 2
  law — 345.026 32
Phlebitis
  medicine — 616.142
  *see also* Cardiovascular
      diseases — humans
Phlebotomy
  diagnosis
    general disease — 616.075 61
Phloem — 575.452
Phlorina (Greece : Nome) — T2—495 62
Phloxes — 635.933 94
  botany — 583.94
  floriculture — 635.933 94
Phobias
  medicine — 616.852 25
  *see also* Mental disorders
Phobic disorders
  medicine — 616.852 25
  *see also* Mental disorders
Phoca — 599.792
Phocidae — 599.79
Phocis (Greece) — T2—495 15
  ancient — T2—383

Phocoena — 599.539
Phocoenidae — 599.539
Phoenicia — 939.44
                T2—394 4
Phoenician architecture — 722.31
Phoenician language — 492.6
                T6—926
Phoenician literature — 892.6
Phoenician sculpture — 732.944
Phoenicians — T5—926
Phoenicopteriformes — 598.35
  paleozoology — 568.3
Phoenix — 398.245 4
  *see also* Legendary animals
Phoenix (Ariz.) — T2—791 73
Phoka (African people) — T5—963 91
Phōkis (Greece) — T2—495 15
Pholidota — 599.31
  paleozoology — 569.31
Phonemics — 414
  specific languages — T4—15
Phonetic method (Reading)
  primary education — 372.465
Phonetic shorthand systems
  English language — 653.42
Phonetics — 414.8
  primary education — 372.465
  specific languages — T4—158
Phonics
  primary education — 372.465
Phonocardiography
  medicine — 616.120 754 4
Phonodiscs — 384
  *see also* Sound recordings
Phonograph records — 384
  *see also* Sound recordings
Phonographs — 621.389 33
Phonology — 414
  specific languages — T4—15
Phonons
  solid-state physics — 530.416
Phonorecords — 384
  *see also* Sound recordings
Phoridae — 595.774
Phoronida — 592.3
  paleozoology — 562.3
Phosphatases — 572.755 3
  *see also* Enzymes
Phosphates — 553.64
  chemical engineering — 661.43
  economic geology — 553.64
  mineralogy — 549.72
  mining — 622.364
Phosphatocopida — 565.3

Phosphenes
  chemical engineering — 661.87
Phosphinic acids
  chemical engineering — 661.87
Phosphoacids
  chemical engineering — 661.87
Phosphoalcohols
  chemical engineering — 661.87
Phosphoaldehydes
  chemical engineering — 661.87
Phosphoketones
  chemical engineering — 661.87
Phospholipids — 572.57
  *see also* Lipids
Phosphonic acids
  chemical engineering — 661.87
Phosphonium compounds
  chemical engineering — 661.87
Phosphoproteins — 572.68
  *see also* Proteins
Phosphorescence — 535.353
Phosphoric acid
  chemical engineering — 661.25
Phosphorus
  applied nutrition — 613.285
  biochemistry — 572.553
    humans — 612.015 24
  chemical engineering — 661.071 2
  chemistry — 546.712
  metabolism
    human physiology — 612.392 4
  organic chemistry — 547.07
    aliphatic — 547.47
    applied — 661.87
Phosphorus fertilizers — 631.85
  chemical engineering — 668.625
Phosphorus salts
  chemical engineering — 661.43
Photo-offset printing — 686.232 5
Photo-optics — 621.367
Photobacterium — 579.34
Photobiochemistry — 572.435
Photoceramic processes — 773.6
Photochemistry — 541.35
  atmosphere — 551.511
  chemical engineering — 660.295
Photocomposition — 686.225 44
Photoconductive cells — 621.381 542
Photoconductivity — 537.54
Photocopying — 686.4
  equipment — 686.402 84
    manufacturing technology — 681.65
  library services — 025.12

Photocopying (continued)
  office use — 652.4
  technology — 686.4
Photoduplication — 686.4
Photoelasticity
  materials science — 620.112 95
Photoelectric components — 621.381 542
Photoelectric photometry
  astronomy — 522.623
Photoelectricity — 537.54
Photoelectronic components — 621.381 542
Photoemission — 537.54
Photoemissive cells — 621.381 542
Photoenamel processes — 773.6
Photoengraving — 686.232 7
Photogrammetry — 526.982
  military engineering — 623.72
Photograph files
  police records — 363.24
Photographers — 770.92
  *see Manual at* 779 vs. 770.92
Photographic chemicals — 771.5
  chemical engineering — 661.808
Photographic digital images — 779
  processing — 771.4
Photographic equipment — 771
  manufacturing technology — 681.418
Photographic images — 779
  arts — 779
  distribution — 771.48
  manipulation — 771.44
  organization — 771.48
  preparation — 771.44
  preservation — 771.45
  processing — 771.4
  storage — 771.45
  *see Manual at* 779 vs. 770.92
Photographic photometry
  astronomy — 522.622
Photographic prints
  processing — 771.4
Photographic projection — 771.48
  motion pictures — 777.57
  transparencies (photographs) — 771.48
Photographic surveying — 526.982
Photographs — 779
    T1—022 2
  arts — 779
  criminal investigation — 363.258
  processing — 771.4
  *see Manual at* 779 vs. 770.92
Photography — 770
  arts — 770
  astronomy — 522.63

Photography (continued)
  engineering 621.367
  green technology 771.402 86
  military engineering 623.72
  nuclear physics 539.778
  technique 771
  waste technology 771.402 86
Photogravure 686.232 7
Photointaglio 686.232 7
Photoionization of gases 530.444
Photojournalism 070.49
  education 371.897
Photolithography 686.232 5
Photoluminescence 535.355
Photomacrography 778.324
  cinematography 777.6
  videography 777.6
Photomechanical printing 686.232
Photometers
  manufacturing technology 681.415
Photometry 535.220 287
  astronomy 522.62
  engineering 621.321 1
Photomicrography 778.31
  biology 570.282
  cinematography 777.6
  science 502.82
  videography 777.6
Photomontage 778.8
Photomultipliers 621.381 542
Photon propulsion 629.475 4
Photonics 621.365
Photonovels 741.5
  *see also* Fotonovelas
Photons 539.721 7
Photonuclear reactions 539.756
Photopsychography 778.3
Photosensitive surfaces
  chemical engineering 661.808
  photography 771.53
Photosensitivity
  animals 573.88
  *see also* Eyes
Photosensitivity disorders
  medicine 616.515
  *see also* Skin diseases —
    humans
Photosphere
  sun 523.74
Photostating
  technology 686.45
Photostats
  technical drawing 604.25
Photosynthesis 572.46

Photosynthetic bacteria 579.38
Phototherapy
  medicine 615.831
Phototransistors 621.381 528
Phototubes 621.381 542
Photovoltaic cells 621.381 542
Photovoltaic effect 537.54
Photovoltaic generation 621.312 44
Phrase books 418
  specific languages T4—83
Phrases (Grammar) 415
  specific languages T4—5
Phrenology 139
Phrygia T2—392 6
Phrygia Pacatiana T2—392 6
Phrygia Salutaris T2—392 6
Phrygian language 491.993
   T6—919 93
Phrynophiurida 593.94
Phthiōtis (Greece) T2—495 15
  ancient T2—383
Phthiraptera 595.756
Phú Thọ (Vietnam :
  Province) T2—597 2
Phú Yên (Vietnam :
  Province) T2—597 5
Phutthayọ̄tfā Čhulālōk, King of
  Siam
  Thai history 959.303 1
Phycid hakes 597.632
Phycologists 579.809 2
Phycology 579.8
Phycomycetes 579.53
Phylacteries 296.461 2
Phyllocarida 595.379 2
Phyllodocida 592.62
Phyllosilicates
  mineralogy 549 67
Phyllostomatidae 599.45
Phyllostomidac 599.45
Phylogeny 576.88
  animals 591.38
  microorganisms 579.138
  plants 581.38
Physarales 579.52
Physeter 599.547
Physeteridae 599.547
Physical anthropologists 599.909 2
Physical anthropology 599.9
Physical biochemistry 572.43
  humans 612.015 83
Physical chemistry 541
  applied 660.29
  *see Manual at* 541 vs. 546

| | | | |
|---|---|---|---|
| Physical conditions of work | 331.256 | Physically disabled people | 305.908 |
| *see also* Work environment | | | T1—087 |
| Physical constants | 530.81 | education | 371.91 |
| Physical crystallography | 548.8 | social group | 305.908 |
| Physical diagnosis | | social welfare | 362.4 |
| medicine | 616.075 4 | Physically handicapped people | 305.908 |
| Physical distribution of goods | | | T1—087 |
| management | 658.788 | *see also* Physically disabled | |
| | T1—068 8 | people | |
| Physical education | 613.7 | Physician and patient | 610.696 |
| health | 613.7 | Physician assistants | 610.737 209 2 |
| primary education | 372.86 | role and function | 610.737 206 9 |
| sports | 796.07 | services | 610.737 2 |
| Physical environment | | Physicians | 610.92 |
| influence on crime | 364.22 | health services | 362.172 |
| psychological influence | 155.91 | *see also* Health services | |
| Physical ethnologists | 599.970 92 | law | 344.041 2 |
| Physical ethnology | 599.97 | malpractice | 344.041 21 |
| Physical evidence | | role and function | 610.695 |
| criminal investigation | 363.256 2 | Physicians' liability insurance | 368.564 2 |
| criminal law | 345.064 | Physicists | 530.092 |
| law | 347.064 | Physics | 530 |
| Physical fitness | 613.7 | ecology | 577.13 |
| health | 613.7 | engineering | 621 |
| public administration | 353.627 4 | law | 344.095 3 |
| sociology | 306.461 3 | Physics and religion | 201.653 |
| Physical geography | 910.02 | Christianity | 261.55 |
| *see Manual at* 550 vs. 910; *also* | | philosophy of religion | 215.3 |
| *at* 909, 930–990 vs. 910 | | Physiocracy (Economic school) | 330.152 |
| Physical geology | 551 | Physiognomy | |
| Physical gerontology | 612.67 | divination | 138 |
| Physical illness | 362.1 | Physiographic features | T2—1 |
| medicine | 616 | *see Manual at* T2—4–9 | |
| *see also* Diseases — humans | | Physiographic regions | T2—1 |
| Physical instruments | | folklore | 398.23 |
| manufacturing technology | 681.753 | history and criticism | 398.322 |
| Physical metallurgy | 669.9 | *see Manual at* T2—4–9 | |
| Physical mineralogy | 549.12 | Physiological balance | 571.75 |
| Physical oceanography | 551.46 | *see also* Endocrine system | |
| Physical operations | | Physiological drives | 152.5 |
| chemical engineering | 660.284 2 | Physiological genetics | 572.8 |
| Physical optics | 535.2 | humans | 611.018 16 |
| Physical organic chemistry | 547.13 | Physiological optics | |
| Physical sciences | 500.2 | humans | 612.84 |
| Physical therapy | | Physiological pathology | 571.9 |
| medicine | 615.82 | *see also* Pathology | |
| psychiatry | 616.891 3 | Physiology | 571 |
| Physical training | | animals | 571.1 |
| health | 613.7 | domestic animals | 636.089 2 |
| Physical typology | | humans | 612 |
| influence on crime | 364.24 | *see Manual at* 612 vs. 611; | |
| Physical units | 530.81 | *also at* 612.1–.8; *also at* | |
| Physical yoga | | 613 vs. 612, 615.8; *also* | |
| health | 613.704 6 | *at* 616 vs. 612 | |

Physiology (continued)
  plants    571.2
  *see Manual at* 571–575 vs.
    630; *also at* 579–590 vs.
    571–575
Physiotherapy
  medicine    615.82
Phytochemicals    572.2
Phytoflagellates    579.82
Phytogeography    581.9
Phytolaccaceae    583.53
Phytomastigophorea    579.82
Phytophthora    579.546
Phytoplankton    579.817 76
  freshwater    579.817 6
PI (Macroeconomics)    339.32
  distribution    339.22
Pi-mesons    539.721 62
Pi pas    787.82
  *see also* Stringed instruments
Piacenza (Italy : Province)    T2—454 6
  ancient    T2—372 66
Pianists    786.209 2
Piano accordions    788.865
  instrument    788.865 19
  music    788.865
  *see also* Woodwind instruments
Piano concertos    784.262
Piano-vocal scores    780
  treatises    780.264
Pianolas    786.66
  *see also* Mechanical musical
    instruments
Pianos    786.2
  instrument    786.219
  music    786.2
  *see also* Keyboard instruments
Piarists    255.58
  church history    271.58
Piast dynasty    943.802 2
Piatt County (Ill.)    T2—773 673
Piauí (Brazil)    T2—812 2
Piave River (Italy)    T2—453
Picahos National Park
  (Colombia)    T2—861 94
Picardie (France)    T2—442 6
Picardy (France)    T2—442 6
Picaresque fiction    808.838 77
  history and criticism    809.387 7
  specific literatures    T3B—308 77
    individual authors    T3A—3

Piccolos    788.33
  instrument    788.331 9
  music    788.33
  *see also* Woodwind instruments
Picenum    T2—374 5
Pichincha (Ecuador :
  Province)    T2—866 13
Pici    598.72
Piciformes    598.72
  paleozoology    568.7
Pickaback plants    583.72
Pickaway County (Ohio)    T2—771 815
Pickens County (Ala.)    T2—761 85
Pickens County (Ga.)    T2—758 255
Pickens County (S.C.)    T2—757 23
Pickerels    597.59
Picketing    331.892 7
Pickett County (Tenn.)    T2—768 687
Pickled foods    641.462
  commercial preservation    664.028 6
  cooking with    641.616 2
  home preservation    641.462
Pickles
  commercial preservation    664.028 6
  cooking with    641.616 2
  home preservation    641.462
Pickling foods    664.028 6
  commercial preservation    664.028 6
  home preservation    641.462
Pickup trucks    388.343 2
  driving    629.284 32
  engineering    629.223 2
  repair    629.287 32
  transportation services    388.343 2
  *see also* Trucks
Picnic areas
  road engineering    625.77
Picnic cooking    641.578
Picnics    642.3
Picornaviridae    579.257 2
Pictorial arts    740
Pictorial journalism    070.49
Pictorial works    T1—022 2
Pictou (N.S. : County)    T2—716 13
Picture dictionaries    413.17
  specific languages    T4—317
  specific subjects    T1—03
Picture frames    684
  furniture arts    749.7
  wooden    674.88
Picture framing    749.7
Pictures    T1—022 2
  bibliographies    011.376
  cataloging    025.347 1

| | |
|---|---|
| Pictures (continued) | |
| fine arts | 740 |
| instructional use | 371.335 2 |
| library treatment | 025.177 1 |
| textile arts | 746.3 |
| Pidgin English | 427.9 |
| | T6—217 |
| Pidgins | 417.22 |
| specific languages | T4—7 |
| *see Manual at* T4—7 | |
| Pidyon haben | 296.442 3 |
| liturgy | 296.454 23 |
| Pie mixes | 664.753 |
| Piecework | 331.216 4 |
| labor economics | 331.216 4 |
| personnel management | 658.322 5 |
| Piedmont (Italy : Region) | 945.1 |
| | T2—451 |
| ancient | T2—372 22 |
| Piedmont (U.S. : Region) | T2—75 |
| Alabama | T2—761 5 |
| Georgia | T2—758 4 |
| Maryland | T2—752 7 |
| North Carolina | T2—756 5 |
| South Carolina | T2—757 3 |
| Virginia | T2—755 6 |
| Piegan Indians | T5—973 52 |
| Piemonte (Italy) | 945.1 |
| | T2—451 |
| ancient | T2—372 22 |
| Pier foundations | 624.158 |
| Pierce, Franklin | |
| United States history | 973.66 |
| Pierce County (Ga.) | T2—758 792 |
| Pierce County (N.D.) | T2—784 591 |
| Pierce County (Neb.) | T2—782 56 |
| Pierce County (Wash.) | T2—797 78 |
| Pierce County (Wis.) | T2—775 42 |
| Pieria (Greece) | T2—495 65 |
| Pierre (S.D.) | T2—783 29 |
| Piers (Columns) | 721.3 |
| architecture | 721.3 |
| construction | 690.13 |
| structural engineering | 624.16 |
| Piers (Port facilities) | 387.15 |
| engineering | 627.31 |
| *see also* Port facilities | |
| Pies | 641.865 2 |
| commercial processing | 664.752 5 |
| home preparation | 641.865 2 |
| Piet Retief (South Africa : | |
| District) | T2—682 79 |
| Pietermaritzburg (South | |
| Africa : District) | T2—684 75 |

| | |
|---|---|
| Pietersburg (South Africa : | |
| District) | T2—682 56 |
| Pietism | 273.7 |
| Piezoelectricity | 537.244 6 |
| Piezomagnetism | 538.3 |
| Pig iron | 669.141 3 |
| Pigeon English | 427.9 |
| | T6—217 |
| Pigeons | 598.65 |
| agricultural pests | 632.686 5 |
| animal husbandry | 636.596 |
| sports hunting | 799.246 5 |
| Piggyback transportation | 385.72 |
| public administration | 354.764 |
| Pigment processes | |
| photographic printing | 773 |
| Pigmentation | |
| human physiology | 612.792 7 |
| *see also* Skin | |
| physical anthropology | 599.95 |
| Pigmented cells | |
| human histology | 611.018 2 |
| Pigments | 667.29 |
| biochemistry | 572.59 |
| humans | 612.015 28 |
| chemistry | 547.869 |
| economic geology | 553.662 |
| paint technology | 667.623 |
| painting material | |
| arts | 751.2 |
| technology | 667.29 |
| Pigmy hippopotamus | 599.635 |
| Pigmy rattlesnake | 597.963 8 |
| Pigmy shrew | 599.336 2 |
| Pigs | 636.4 |
| agricultural pests | 632.696 33 |
| animal husbandry | 636.4 |
| big game hunting | 799.276 332 |
| experimental animals | |
| medicine | 616.027 3 |
| pest control | |
| conservation technology | 639.966 |
| zoology | 599.633 |
| Pikas (Conies) | 599.329 |
| Pike County (Ala.) | T2—761 35 |
| Pike County (Ark.) | T2—767 485 |
| Pike County (Ga.) | T2—758 453 |
| Pike County (Ill.) | T2—773 453 |
| Pike County (Ind.) | T2—772 36 |
| Pike County (Ky.) | T2—769 23 |
| Pike County (Miss.) | T2—762 23 |
| Pike County (Mo.) | T2—778 36 |
| Pike County (Ohio) | T2—771 847 |
| Pike County (Pa.) | T2—748 24 |

Pike perches 597.758
Pikes (Fishes) 597.59
  conservation technology 639.977 59
  resource economics 333.956 59
  sports fishing 799.175 9
Piketberg (South Africa :
  District) T2—687 32
Piła (Poland : Voivodeship) T2—438 49
Pilanesberg National Park
  (South Africa) T2—682 48
Pilasters 721.3
  architecture 721.3
  construction 690.13
Pilates method 613.719 2
Pilchards 641.392
  cooking 641.692
  food 641.392
  zoology 597.45
Pile foundations 624.154
Pile rugs
  arts 746.75
Pile-weave fabrics 677.617
  *see also* Textiles
Pileas 583.45
Pilgrimage to Mecca 297.352
Pilgrimages 203.51
  Christianity 263.041
  Islam 297.35
  Judaism 296.481
Pilgrim's Rest 1 (South
  Africa : District) T2—682 71
Pilgrim's Rest 2 (South
  Africa : District) T2—682 74
Piling (Foundation engineering) 624.154
Pilipino language 499.211
  T6—992 11
Pilipino literature 899.211
Pill beetles 595.763
Pill bugs 595.372
Pillage 364.16
  law 345.026
Pillars of Islam 297.31
Pillow lava 552.26
Pillowcases 645.4
  arts 746.97
  home sewing 646.21
  household equipment 645.4
Pills (Contraceptives)
  health 613.943 22
  medicine 618.182 2
    *see also* Birth control
  pharmacokinetics 615.766
Pills (Pharmaceuticals)
  pharmaceutical chemistry 615.19

Pilot ejection seats 629.134 386
Pilot errors
  air transportation 363.124 14
Pilot guides
  aeronautics 629.132 54
  seamanship 623.892 2
Pilot plants
  chemical engineering 660.280 72
Pilot whales 599.53
Piloting
  aeronautics 629.132 52
  commercial aircraft 629.132 521 6
  manned space flight 629.458 2
  military aeronautics 623.746 048
  private aircraft 629.132 521 7
  seamanship 623.892 2
Piloting services 387.166
  inland ports 386.866
  law 343.096 7
Piloting systems
  spacecraft 629.474 2
  unmanned spacecraft 629.464 2
Pilotless aircraft
  military engineering 623.746 9
Pilots
  aircraft 629.130 92
Pilots (Television programs) 791.45
  *see Manual at* 791.43 vs.
    791.45
Pilot's license
  aircraft 343.097 5
  ships 343.096 5
Piltdown forgery 569.9
PIM (Computer software) 005.57
Pima County (Ariz.) T2—791 77
Pima Indians T5—974 552 9
Pima language 497.455 29
  T6—974 552 9
Pima literature 897.455 29
Pimento (Allspice) 641.338 3
  botany 583.765
  *see also* Spices
Pimientos (Peppers) 641.356 43
  botany 583.952
  *see also* Sweet peppers
Pinaceae 585.2
  paleobotany 561.52
Pinal County (Ariz.) T2—791 75
Pinang T2—595 1
Pinar del Río (Cuba :
  Province) T2—729 11
Pinball games 794.75
Pinching bugs 595.764 9
Pindus Mountains (Greece) T2—495 3

| | |
|---|---|
| Pine Barrens (N.J.) | T2—749 61 |
| Pine beetles | 595.763 |
| forestry pests | 634.975 167 63 |
| Pine County (Minn.) | T2—776 62 |
| Pine Point (N.W.T.) | T2—719 3 |
| Pine River (B.C.) | T2—711 87 |
| Pineal gland | |
| human anatomy | 611.47 |
| human physiology | 612.492 |
| light sensing | 573.88 |
| medicine | 616.48 |
| Pineal gland diseases | |
| medicine | 616.48 |
| *see also* Endocrine diseases — humans | |
| Pineapples | 641.347 74 |
| botany | 584.85 |
| commercial processing | 664.804 774 |
| cooking | 641.647 74 |
| fiber crop | 633.576 |
| food | 641.347 74 |
| horticulture | 634.774 |
| Pinecone fishes | 597.64 |
| Pinellas County (Fla.) | T2—759 63 |
| Pines | 585.2 |
| forestry | 634.975 1 |
| lumber | 674.144 |
| ornamental arboriculture | 635.977 52 |
| Pinetown (South Africa : District) | T2—684 5 |
| Piney Woods (Miss. : Region) | T2—762 5 |
| Pinhole photography | 771 |
| Pinicae | 585 |
| Pinks (Flowers) | 635.933 53 |
| botany | 583.53 |
| floriculture | 635.933 53 |
| Pinnacles | 721.5 |
| architecture | 721.5 |
| construction | 690.15 |
| Pinnipedia | 599.79 |
| paleozoology | 569.79 |
| Pinochle | 795.416 |
| Piñons | 585.2 |
| Pinophyta | 585 |
| paleobotany | 561.5 |
| Pins (Numismatics) | 737.24 |
| Pins (Sewing equipment) | |
| home sewing | 646.19 |
| Pinta | |
| medicine | 616.523 |
| *see also* Skin diseases — humans | |
| Pinto horse | 636.13 |
| Pintupi dialect | 499.15 |
| | T6—991 5 |
| Pioneer (Space probes) | 629.435 4 |
| Pions | 539.721 62 |
| Piophilidae | 595.774 |
| Piotrków Trybunalski (Poland : Voivodeship) | T2—438 47 |
| Pious societies | |
| Christianity | 267 |
| Pipe fitters | 696.209 2 |
| Pipe fitting | |
| buildings | 696.2 |
| Pipe snakes | 597.967 |
| Pipe-threading tools | 621.944 |
| Pipefishes | 597.679 |
| Pipeline processing | 004.3 |
| *see also* Processing modes — computer science | |
| Pipeline processors | 004.3 |
| engineering | 621.391 |
| Pipeline transportation | 388.5 |
| gas technology | 665.744 |
| law | 343.093 9 |
| petroleum technology | 665.544 |
| public administration | 354.764 |
| transportation services | 388.5 |
| Pipelines | |
| engineering | 621.867 2 |
| Piperales | 583.25 |
| Pipes (Conduits) | 621.867 2 |
| chemical engineering | 660.283 |
| machine engineering | 621.867 2 |
| metalworking | 671.832 |
| road engineering | 625.734 |
| ship power plants | 623.873 |
| water supply engineering | 628.15 |
| Pipes (Tobacco) | 688.42 |
| Pipestone County (Minn.) | T2—776 26 |
| Pipeworts | 584.87 |
| Pipidae | 597.865 |
| Pipits | 598.854 |
| Pipoidea | 597.865 |
| Pipridae | 598.822 |
| Piquetberg (South Africa : District) | T2—687 32 |
| Piracy | 364.164 |
| law | 345.026 4 |
| Piranhas | 597.48 |
| Pirated editions | 364.166 2 |
| law | 345.026 62 |
| Pirates' expeditions | 910.45 |
| Pires, Pedro Verona Rodrigues | |
| Cape Verdean history | 966.580 33 |
| Pirin Macedonia | T2—499 8 |

| | |
|---|---|
| Pirke Avot | 296.123 47 |
| Pisa (Italy) | T2—455 51 |
| ancient | T2—375 5 |
| Pisa (Italy : Province) | T2—455 5 |
| ancient | T2—375 5 |
| Pisacha languages | 491.499 |
| | T6—914 99 |
| Pisacha literatures | 891.499 |
| Pisaurum (Italy) | T2—374 2 |
| Piscataquis County (Me.) | T2—741 25 |
| Pisces | 597 |
| Pisces (Zodiac) | 133.527 7 |
| Pisé | |
| building construction | 693.22 |
| Pisidia | T2—392 7 |
| Pistachios | 641.345 74 |
| agriculture | 634.574 |
| botany | 583.77 |
| commercial processing | 664.804 574 |
| cooking | 641.645 74 |
| food | 641.345 74 |
| Pistils | 575.66 |
| Pistoia (Italy : Province) | T2—455 2 |
| ancient | T2—375 2 |
| Pistols | 683.432 |
| art metalwork | 739.744 32 |
| manufacturing technology | 683.432 |
| military engineering | 623.443 2 |
| sports | 799.202 833 |
| *see also* Guns (Small arms) | |
| Piston-driven airplanes | 387.733 43 |
| engineering | 629.133 343 |
| transportation services | 387.733 43 |
| *see also* Aircraft | |
| Piston engines | |
| aircraft | 629.134 352 |
| Piston-turbine engines | |
| aircraft | 629.134 352 |
| Pistons | 621.84 |
| internal-combustion engines | 621.437 |
| Pisum sativum | 641.356 56 |
| *see also* Peas (Pisum sativum) | |
| Pit bull terriers | 636.755 9 |
| Pita | 641.815 |
| Pitakas | 294.382 |
| Pitcairn Island | T2—961 8 |
| Pitch (Aeronautics) | 629.132 364 |
| Pitch (Linguistics) | 414.6 |
| specific languages | T4—16 |
| Pitch (Natural asphalt) | 553.27 |
| *see also* Asphalt | |
| Pitch (Petroleum product) | 665.538 8 |

| | |
|---|---|
| Pitch (Sound) | |
| musical element | 781.232 |
| perception | |
| psychology | 152.152 |
| Pitcher plants | 583.75 |
| Pitcher plants (New World) | 583.36 |
| Pitcher plants (Old World) | 583.75 |
| Pitching (Aeronautics) | 629.132 364 |
| Pitching (Baseball) | 796.357 22 |
| Pitching (Golf) | 796.352 34 |
| Pitching games | 796.24 |
| Pite Saami language | 494.574 |
| | T6—945 74 |
| Pite Sámi language | 494.574 |
| | T6—945 74 |
| Pith | 571.585 |
| Pithecanthropus erectus | 569.97 |
| Pitkin County (Colo.) | T2—788 43 |
| Pitman shorthand systems | 653.424 |
| Pitt County (N.C.) | T2—756 44 |
| Pitt Meadows (B.C.) | T2—711 33 |
| Pitt River (B.C.) | T2—711 37 |
| Pittas | 598.822 |
| Pittidae | 598.822 |
| Pittosporaceae | 583.72 |
| Pittsburg County (Okla.) | T2—766 75 |
| Pittsburgh (Pa.) | T2—748 86 |
| Pittsylvania County (Va.) | T2—755 665 |
| Pituitary diseases | |
| medicine | 616.47 |
| *see also* Endocrine | |
| diseases — humans | |
| Pituitary gland | 573.45 |
| biology | 573.45 |
| human anatomy | 611.47 |
| human physiology | 612.492 |
| medicine | 616.47 |
| *see also* Endocrine system | |
| Pituitary hormones | 573.454 |
| human physiology | 612.492 |
| pharmacology | 615.363 |
| *see also* Endocrine system | |
| Piura (Peru : Dept.) | T2—851 3 |
| Piute County (Utah) | T2—792 53 |
| Piyyutim | 296.452 |
| Pizza | 641.824 8 |
| commercial processing | 664.65 |
| home preparation | 641.824 8 |
| Place names | 910.014 |
| Place settings | |
| table service | 642.6 |
| Placebo effect | |
| medicine | 615.5 |

| | |
|---|---|
| Placement (Education) | 371.264 |
|   colleges and universities | 378.166 4 |
|   *see Manual at* 371.262 vs. | |
|    371.264 | |
| Placement of workers | 331.128 |
|   economics | 331.128 |
|   personnel management | 658.312 8 |
|   public administration | 352.66 |
| Placement tests (Education) | 371.262 |
| Placenta | |
|   human physiology | 612.63 |
|   obstetrical surgery | 618.8 |
|   obstetrics | 618.34 |
| Placental extracts | |
|   pharmacology | 615.39 |
| Placental mammals | 599 |
| Placer County (Calif.) | T2—794 38 |
| Placer deposits | 553.13 |
| Placer mining | 622.292 7 |
| Places | 900 |
| | T1—09 |
|   arts | 700.458 |
| | T3C—358 |
|   folklore | 398.23 |
|    history and criticism | 398.32 |
|   geography | |
|    arts | 700.42 |
| | T3C—32 |
|     literature | 808.803 2 |
|      history and criticism | 809.933 2 |
|      specific literatures | T3B—080 32 |
|     motion pictures | 791.436 2 |
|   legendary | 398.234 |
|   *see also* Legendary places | |
|   literature | 808.803 58 |
|    history and criticism | 809.933 58 |
|    specific literatures | T3B—080 358 |
|     history and | |
|      criticism | T3B—093 58 |
| Placodermi | 567.2 |
| Placodontia | 567.93 |
| Plagiarism | |
|   composition | 808.025 |
| Plague | |
|   incidence | 614.573 2 |
|   medicine | 616.923 2 |
|   *see also* Communicable | |
|    diseases — humans | |
| Plaice | 597.694 |
| Plain-woven rugs | |
|   arts | 746.72 |
| Plains | 551.453 |
| | T2—145 |
|   geography | 910.914 5 |
| Plains (continued) | |
|   geomorphology | 551.453 |
|   physical geography | 910.021 45 |
| Plains Algonquian languages | 497.35 |
| | T6—973 5 |
| Plains Indians | T5—970 78 |
| Plainsong | 782.292 |
| Plaintiffs | 347.052 |
| Planarians | 592.42 |
| Planctosphaeroidea | 593.99 |
|   paleozoology | 563.99 |
| Plane geometry | 516.22 |
|   analytic | 516.32 |
|   Euclidean | 516.22 |
| Plane surveying | 526.9 |
| Plane trees | 583.44 |
|   forestry | 634.973 44 |
|   ornamental arboriculture | 635.977 344 |
| Plane trigonometry | 516.242 |
| Planers | 621.912 |
| Planes (Geometry) | 516.154 |
| Planes (Tools) | 621.912 |
| Planetariums | 520.74 |
| Planetary atmospheres | |
|   astronautic engineering | 629.415 |
| Planetary flights | 919.920 4 |
|   manned | 629.455 |
|   unmanned | 629.435 4 |
| Planetary nebulas | 523.113 5 |
| Planetary rings | 523.98 |
| Planetary systems | 523.2 |
| Planetary transits | 523.99 |
| Planetary wind systems | 551.518 3 |
| Planetoids | 523.44 |
| | T2—992 4 |
| Planets | 523.4 |
| | T2—992 |
|   astrology | 133.53 |
|   astronomy | 523.4 |
|   law of nations | 341.47 |
| Planing mills | 674.42 |
| Plank roads | |
|   engineering | 625.83 |
| Plankton | 578.776 |
|   ecology | 577.76 |
|    freshwater | 577.6 |
|   freshwater | 578.76 |
| Planned economies | 330.124 |
|   economic theory | 335 |
| Planning | 320.6 |
|   executive management | 658.401 2 |
| | T1—068 4 |
|   higher education | 378.107 |

Planning (continued)
military administration     355.684
production management     658.503
public administration     352.34
    community development     354.279 3
public policy     320.6
sales management     658.810 1
social action     361.25
Planographic printing     686.231 5
graphic arts     763
Plans     912
    T1—022 3
architectural design     729.2
geography     912
*see Manual at* T1—0222 vs.
    T1—0223
Plant-animal relationships     577.8
Plant arrangements     745.92
Plant biotechnology     630
Plant breeding     631.52
forestry     634.956
Plant closing     338.604 2
labor economics     331.259 6
    employment security     331.259 6
    unemployment     331.137
labor law     344.012 596
production economics     338.604 2
Plant communities     581.782
Plant containers
manufacturing technology     681.763 1
Plant crops     630
public administration     354.54
*see Manual at* 633–635
Plant culture     630
equipment manufacturing
    technology     681.763 1
Plant diseases     571.92
agricultural economics     338.14
agriculture     632.3
Plant ecology     581.7
Plant genetics     581.35
agriculture     631.523 3
Plant injuries     571.975 2
agriculture     632
Plant introduction     631.523
Plant layout
management     658.23
Plant lice     595.752
agricultural pests     632.752
Plant location
management     658.21
    libraries     022.1
    museums     069.21
    schools     371.61

Plant maintenance
management     658.202
Plant management     658.2
    T1—068 2
libraries     022
museums     069.2
public administration     352.56
schools     371.6
    special education     371.904 5
*see Manual at* 647.068, 658.2,
    T1—0682
Plant pathology     571.92
agriculture     632
Plant pest control
environmental engineering     628.97
Plant physiology     571.2
Plant propagation     631.53
agriculture     631.53
forestry     634.956 5
Plant protection     632.9
Plant quarantine     632.93
Plant regulators
agriculture     631.89
biology     571.72
Plant resources     333.953
public administration     354.349
Plant respiration     572.472
Plant sanitation     363.729 5
engineering     628.51
Plant selection     631.52
Plant shutdowns     338.604 2
Plant spacing (Agriculture)     631.53
Plant supports     631.546
manufacturing technology     681.763 1
Plant training     631.546
Plant varieties
agriculture     631.57
resource economics     333.953 4
Plant viruses     579.28
agriculture     632.8
Plantagenet, House of     942.03
English history     942.03
genealogy     929.72
Irish history     941.503
Plantaginaceae     583.95
Plantagos     583.95
Plantain lilies     635.934 32
botany     584.32
floriculture     635.934 32
Plantains (Fruits)     641.347 73
botany     584.39
commercial processing     664.804 773
cooking     641.647 73

Plantains (Fruits) (continued)
food 641.347 73
horticulture 634.773
Plantains (Plantagos) 583.95
Plantation crops 633
see Manual at 633–635
Plantation houses
architecture 728.8
Plantations
community sociology 307.72
system of production
sociology 306.349
Planting 631.53
equipment manufacturing
technology 681.763 1
Plants 580
agricultural pests 632.5
agriculture 630
anatomy 571.32
art representation 704.943 4
arts 700.464
T3C—364
Bible 220.858
biography T1—092 9
botany 580
coevolution with insects 576.875
comparative psychology 156.9
conservation technology 639.99
drawing 743.7
folklore 398.242
history and criticism 398.368
legendary 398.468
real 398.368
food source 641.303
see Manual at 583–585 vs.
600
influence on precipitation 551.577 5
landscape architecture 715
literature 808.803 64
history and criticism 809.933 64
specific literatures T3B—080 364
history and
criticism T3B—093 64
painting 758.5
paleobotany 561
pathology 571.92
agriculture 632
physiology 571.2
resource economics 333.953
Plants (Buildings and equipment)
architecture 725.4
construction 690.54

Plants (Buildings and equipment) (continued)
location
management 658.21
see also Plant location —
management
management 658.2
T1—068 2
see also Plant management
prisons 365.5
Plaquemines Parish (La.) T2—763 37
Plasma (Blood) 573.156
biology 573.156
human histology 612.116
human physiology 612.116
pharmacology 615.39
see also Cardiovascular system
Plasma (Ionized gas) 530.44
applied physics 621.044
chemical engineering 660.044
physics 530.44
Plasma chemistry 541.042 4
engineering 660.044
Plasma engineering 621.044
Plasma membranes 571.64
Plasma motors 621.46
Plasma physics 530.44
applied physics 621.044
Plasma propulsion 629.475 5
Plasmapheresis
pharmacology 615.39
Plasmid DNA 572.869
Plasmids 572.869
Plasmodiophoromycetes 579.53
Plassey, Battle of, 1757 954.029 4
Plaster casting
sculpture 731.452
Plaster of paris 666.92
Plasterers 693.609 2
Plastering 693.6
architectural construction 721.044 6
Plastic arts 730
see Manual at 731–735 vs.
736–739
Plastic arts (Visual arts) 700
Plastic deformation 531.385
see also Plasticity
Plastic films 668.495
Plastic flow
materials science 620.112 33
Plastic foams 668.493
Plastic furniture 645.4
manufacturing technology 684.106
see also Furniture
Plastic surgery 617.952

Plasticity | 531.385
crystals | 548.842
materials science | 620.112 33
physics | 531.385
Plasticizers (Paints) | 667.622
Plasticizers (Plastics) | 668.411
Plastics | 668.4
architectural construction | 721.044 992 3
building materials | 691.92
construction materials | 693.992 3
handicrafts | 745.572
materials science | 620.192 3
sculpture material | 731.2
ship design | 623.818 923
shipbuilding | 623.820 7
structural engineering | 624.189 23
Plastics casting
sculpture | 731.453
Plastics industry | 338.476 684
equipment manufacturing
technology | 681.766 8
Plastids | 571.659
Plata, Rio de la (Argentina and | 551.461 368
Uruguay) | T2—163 68
Plata, Río de la (Viceroyalty) | 982.024
| T2—82
Platanaceae | 583.44
Platanistidae | 599.538
Plate glass | 666.153
Plate glass insurance | 368.6
Plate tectonics | 551.136
Plateau Penutian languages | 497.412
| T6—974 12
Plateau State (Nigeria) | T2—669 52
Plateaus | 551.434
| T2—143
*see also* Mountains
Platelets | 573.159
histology | 573.159
human histology | 612.117
human physiology | 612.117
medicine | 616.157
physiology | 573.159
*see also* Cardiovascular system
Plates (Musical instruments) | 786.82
*see also* Bars (Musical
instruments)
Plates (Photosensitive surfaces) | 661.808
chemical engineering | 661.808
photography | 771.532 2
Plates (Printing surfaces)
flat surfaces | 686.231 5
raised surfaces | 686.231 4

Plates (Structural elements) | 624.177 65
naval architecture | 623.817 765
Plates (Tableware) | 642.7
paper | 676.34
Platform diving | 797.24
Platform foundations | 624.156
Platform speeches
literature | 808.851
history and criticism | 809.51
specific literatures | T3B—501
individual authors | T3A—5
rhetoric | 808.51
Platforms (Party programs) | 324.23
Platinotype processes | 772.3
Platinum | 669.24
chemical engineering | 661.064 5
chemistry | 546.645
economic geology | 553.422
materials science | 620.189 24
metallography | 669.952 4
metallurgy | 669.24
metalworking | 673.24
mining | 622.342 4
physical metallurgy | 669.962 4
*see also* Chemicals; Metals
Platinum metals | 669.7
chemical engineering | 661.063
chemistry | 546.63
economic geology | 553.495
metallography | 669.957
metallurgy | 669.7
physical metallurgy | 669.967
Platinum printing-out process | 772.3
Platinumwork
decorative arts | 739.24
Platonism | 184
ancient | 184
modern | 141.2
Platoons (Military units) | 355.31
Platt National Park (Okla.) | T2—766 57
Plattdeutsch | 439.4
| T6—394
Plattdeutsch literature | 839.4
Platte County (Mo.) | T2—778 135
Platte County (Neb.) | T2—782 52
Platte County (Wyo.) | T2—787 17
Platte River (Neb.) | T2—782
Platy | 597.667
Platycopa | 595.33
paleozoology | 565.33
Platyhelminthes | 592.4
paleozoology | 562.4
Platypus | 599.29

| | |
|---|---|
| Platyrrhini | 599.85 |
| paleozoology | 569.85 |
| Platysternidae | 597.926 |
| Play | 790 |
| child care | 649.5 |
| psychology | 155 |
| recreation | 790 |
| sociology | 306.481 |
| *see also* Recreation | |
| Play (Animals) | 591.563 |
| Play groups | |
| preschool education | 372.21 |
| Play schools | |
| primary education | 372.21 |
| Play therapy | |
| medicine | 615.851 53 |
| psychiatry | 616.891 653 |
| pediatrics | 618.928 916 53 |
| Player pianos | 786.66 |
| *see also* Mechanical musical | |
| instruments | |
| Playground equipment | |
| manufacturing technology | 688.76 |
| Playgrounds | 796.068 |
| Playing cards | 795.4 |
| manufacturing technology | 688.754 |
| Playing time | |
| musical technique | 781.432 |
| Plays | |
| literature | 808.82 |
| *see also* Drama (Literature) | |
| musical | 782.14 |
| music | 782.14 |
| stage presentation | 792.6 |
| theater | 792 |
| *see also* Theater | |
| Playwrights | 809.2 |
| collected biography | 809.2 |
| specific literatures | T3B—200 9 |
| individual biography | T3A—2 |
| Playwriting | 808.2 |
| Plazas | |
| area planning | 711.55 |
| Plea bargaining | 345.072 |
| Pleading (Law) | 347.072 |
| criminal law | 345.072 |
| Pleasant Island | 996.85 |
| | T2—968 5 |
| Pleasants County (W. Va.) | T2—754 21 |
| Pleasure | 152.42 |
| ethical systems | 171.4 |
| psychology | 152.42 |
| sociology | 306.481 |

| | |
|---|---|
| Pleasure craft | 387.204 23 |
| design | 623.812 042 3 |
| engineering | 623.820 23 |
| handling | 623.881 23 |
| power-driven | 387.231 |
| design | 623.812 31 |
| engineering | 623.823 1 |
| handling | 623.882 31 |
| transportation services | 387.231 |
| transportation services | 387.204 23 |
| wind-driven | 387.223 |
| design | 623.812 23 |
| engineering | 623.822 3 |
| handling | 623.882 23 |
| transportation services | 387.223 |
| Pleasures of food and drink | 641.013 |
| Plecoptera | 595.735 |
| Plectomycetes | 579.565 |
| Plectral instruments | 787.7 |
| *see also* Stringed instruments | |
| Plectral lutes | 787.8 |
| *see also* Stringed instruments | |
| Pledges (Law) | 346.025 |
| Pleinairism | 709.034 4 |
| painting | 759.054 |
| Pleistocene epoch | 551.792 |
| geology | 551.792 |
| paleontology | 560.179 2 |
| Pleosporales | 579.564 |
| Plesianthropus | 569.93 |
| Plesiosauria | 567.937 |
| Plessur (Switzerland) | T2—494 732 2 |
| Plethodon | 597.859 2 |
| Plethodontidae | 597.859 |
| Pleura | 573.252 5 |
| biology | 573.252 5 |
| human anatomy | 611.25 |
| human physiology | 612.25 |
| medicine | 616.25 |
| surgery | 617.543 |
| *see also* Respiratory system | |
| Pleuracanthodii | 567.3 |
| Pleural diseases | |
| medicine | 616.25 |
| *see also* Respiratory tract | |
| diseases — humans | |
| Pleural pneumonia | |
| medicine | 616.241 |
| *see also* Respiratory tract | |
| diseases — humans | |
| Pleurodira | 597.929 |
| Pleuromeiales | 561.79 |
| Pleuronectidae | 597.694 |

| | |
|---|---|
| Pleuronectiformes | 597.69 |
| paleozoology | 567.69 |
| Pliocene epoch | 551.788 |
| geology | 551.788 |
| paleontology | 560.178 8 |
| Ploceidae | 598.887 |
| Płock (Poland : | |
| Voivodeship) | T2—438 41 |
| Ploieşti (Romania) | T2—498 2 |
| Plots | |
| literature | 808.802 4 |
| history and criticism | 809.924 |
| specific literatures | T3B—080 24 |
| history and | |
| criticism | T3B—092 4 |
| music | 780 |
| treatises | 782.002 69 |
| Plotters (Computer devices) | 006.62 |
| engineering | 621.399 6 |
| Plovdiv (Bulgaria : Oblast) | T2—499 7 |
| Plovdivska oblast (Bulgaria) | T2—499 7 |
| Plovers | 598.33 |
| Plowing | 631.51 |
| Plows | 631.51 |
| manufacturing technology | 681.763 1 |
| Plucked board zithers | 787.75 |
| *see also* Stringed instruments | |
| Plucked drums | 786.97 |
| *see also* Percussion instruments | |
| Plucked idiophones | 786.85 |
| set | 786.85 |
| single | 786.887 |
| *see also* Percussion instruments | |
| Plucked instruments | 787.7 |
| *see also* Stringed instruments | |
| Plumas County (Calif.) | T2—794 29 |
| Plumb-yews | 585.3 |
| Plumbaginales | 583.5 |
| Plumbago (Graphite) | 553.26 |
| *see also* Graphite | |
| Plumbers | 696.109 2 |
| Plumbing | 696.1 |
| household management | 644.6 |
| Plumbing fixtures | 644.6 |
| building construction | 696.1 |
| household management | 644.6 |
| Plumeria | 583.93 |
| floriculture | 635.933 93 |
| Plums | 641.342 2 |
| botany | 583.73 |
| cooking | 641.642 2 |
| food | 641.342 2 |
| orchard crop | 634.22 |

| | | |
|---|---|---|
| Plundering | | 364.16 |
| law | | 345.026 |
| Pluralism (Philosophy) | | 147.4 |
| Pluralism (Religion) | | 201.5 |
| Buddhism | | 294.335 |
| Christianity | | 261.2 |
| Hinduism | | 294.515 |
| Islam | | 297.28 |
| Judaism | | 296.39 |
| Pluralism (Social sciences) | | 305.8 |
| education | | 370.117 |
| political science | | 323.1 |
| sociology | | 305.8 |
| Pluriarcs | | 787.93 |
| instrument | | 787.931 9 |
| music | | 787.93 |
| *see also* Stringed instruments | | |
| Plush | | 677.617 |
| Plush-capped finch | | 598.88 |
| Pluto (Planet) | | 523.492 2 |
| | T2—992 9 | |
| astrology | | 133.539 2 |
| Plutocracy | | 321.5 |
| Plutonic rocks | | 552.3 |
| Plutonium | | 669.293 4 |
| chemical engineering | | 661.043 4 |
| chemistry | | 546.434 |
| human toxicology | | 615.925 434 |
| metallography | | 669.952 934 |
| metallurgy | | 669.293 4 |
| physical metallurgy | | 669.962 934 |
| *see also* Chemicals | | |
| Plymouth (England) | T2 | 423 58 |
| Plymouth Brethren | | 289.9 |
| *see also* Christian | | |
| denominations | | |
| Plymouth County (Iowa) | T2—777 16 | |
| Plymouth County (Mass.) | T2—744 82 | |
| Plymouth Rock chicken | | 636.582 |
| Plywood | | 674.834 |
| Plzeňský kraj (Czech | | |
| Republic) | T2—437 14 | |
| PMS (Syndrome) | | |
| gynecology | | 618.172 |
| *see also* Female genital | | |
| diseases — humans | | |
| Pneumatic clocks | | |
| technology | | 681.115 |
| Pneumatic construction | | 693.98 |
| architecture | | 721.044 98 |
| Pneumatic control | | 629.804 5 |
| Pneumatic conveyor systems | | |
| office use | | 651.79 |
| Pneumatic engineering | | 621.51 |

| | |
|---|---|
| Pneumatic engineers | 621.510 92 |
| Pneumatic pumps | 621.69 |
| Pneumatic tools | 621.904 |
| Pneumatics | 533 |
|   engineering | 621.51 |
|   physics | 533 |
| Pneumoconiosis | |
|   medicine | 616.244 |
|   *see also* Respiratory tract | |
|     diseases — humans | |
| Pneumocystis carinii pneumonia | |
|   medicine | 616.241 |
|   *see also* Respiratory tract | |
|     diseases — humans | |
| Pneumonia | |
|   medicine | 616.241 |
|   *see also* Respiratory tract | |
|     diseases — humans | |
| Po River (Italy) | T2—452 |
| Poaching | 364.162 859 1 |
|   birds | 364.162 859 8 |
|     law | 345.026 285 98 |
|   fish | 364.162 859 7 |
|     law | 345.026 285 97 |
|   law | 345.026 285 91 |
|   mammals | 364.162 859 9 |
|     law | 345.026 285 99 |
| Poales | 584.9 |
|   paleobotany | 561.49 |
| Pocahontas County (Iowa) | T2—777 19 |
| Pocahontas County (W. Va.) | T2—754 87 |
| Pocket billiards | 794.73 |
| Pocket calculators | 681.145 |
|   mathematics | 510.284 |
| Pocket gophers | 599.359 9 |
| Pocket mice | 599.359 8 |
| Pocket scores | 780 |
|   treatises | 780.265 |
| Pocono Mountains (Pa.) | T2—748 2 |
| Podargidae | 598.99 |
| Podcasting | 006.787 6 |
| Podiatry | 617.585 |
| Podicipediformes | 598.443 |
|   paleozoology | 568.4 |
| Podkarpackie Voivodeship | |
|   (Poland) | T2—438 66 |
| Podlaskie Voivodeship | |
|   (Poland) | T2—438 36 |
| Podocarpaceae | 585.3 |
|   paleobotany | 561.53 |
| Podocarpuses | 585.3 |
| Podocopa | 595.33 |
|   paleozoology | 565.33 |
| Podophyllaceae | 583.34 |

| | |
|---|---|
| Podostemales | 583.82 |
| Poeciliidae | 597.667 |
| Poems | 808.81 |
|   music | 780 |
|   treatises | 780.268 |
|   *see also* Poetry | |
| Poetic books (Old Testament) | 223 |
|   pseudepigrapha | 229.912 |
| Poetic drama | |
|   literature | 808.82 |
|     history and criticism | 809.2 |
|     specific literatures | T3B—2 |
|      individual authors | T3A—2 |
| Poetics | 808.1 |
| Poetry | 808.81 |
|   criticism | 809.1 |
|   theory | 808.1 |
|   history | 809.1 |
|   rhetoric | 808.1 |
|   specific literatures | T3B—1 |
|     individual authors | T3A—1 |
|   *see Manual at* T3B—1 | |
| Poetry slams | 808.545 |
| Poets | 809.1 |
|   collected biography | 809.1 |
|     specific literatures | T3B—100 9 |
|   individual biography | T3A—1 |
| Pogolo (African people) | T5—963 91 |
| Pogolo languages | 496.391 |
| | T6—963 91 |
| Pogonophora | 592.3 |
|   paleozoology | 562.3 |
| Pogoro (African people) | T5—963 91 |
| Pogoro languages | 496.391 |
| | T6—963 91 |
| Pohamba, Hifikepunye Lucas | |
|   Namibian history | 968.810 42 |
| Pohjois-Karjala (Finland) | T2—489 75 |
| Pohjois-Karjalan lääni | |
|   (Finland) | T2—489 75 |
| Poikilothermy | 571.76 |
| Poinsett County (Ark.) | T2—767 96 |
| Poinsettias | 635.933 69 |
|   botany | 583.69 |
|   floriculture | 635.933 69 |
| Point-of-sale advertising | 659.157 |
| Point processes | 519.23 |
| Point set topology | 514.322 |
| Point sets | 511.33 |
| Point-to-point communications | 004.692 |
| Pointe-Claire (Quebec) | T2—714 28 |
| Pointe Coupee Parish (La.) | T2—763 454 |
| Pointers (Dogs) | 636.752 5 |

| | |
|---|---|
| Pointillism | 709.034 5 |
| painting | 759.055 |
| Poison arrow frogs | 597.877 |
| Poison gas | |
| ethics | 172.42 |
| military engineering | 623.459 2 |
| Poison gas projectiles | 623.451 6 |
| Poison hemlocks | 583.849 |
| Poison ivies | 583.77 |
| Poison oaks | 583.77 |
| Poisoning | |
| human toxicology | 615.9 |
| incidence | 615.904 |
| Poisonous animals | 591.65 |
| human toxicology | 615.94 |
| Poisonous fishes | 597.165 |
| human toxicology | 615.945 |
| Poisonous food animals | |
| human toxicology | 615.945 |
| Poisonous microorganisms | 579.165 |
| Poisonous organisms | 578.65 |
| Poisonous plants | 581.659 |
| human toxicology | 615.952 |
| Poisons | 363.179 1 |
| human toxicology | 615.9 |
| personal safety | 615.905 |
| public safety | 363.179 1 |
| toxicology | 571.95 |
| *see also* Hazardous materials | |
| Poisson distribution | 519.24 |
| Poisson integral | 515.43 |
| Poisson-Stieltjes integral | 515.43 |
| Poisson's ratio | 531.381 |
| Poitiers (France) | T2—446 34 |
| Poitou (France) | T2—446 |
| Poitou-Charentes (France) | T2—446 |
| Poker (Game) | 795.412 |
| Pokeweed | 583.53 |
| Polabian language | 491.89 |
| | T6—918 9 |
| Polabian literature | 891.89 |
| Poland | 943.8 |
| | T2—438 |
| Poland China swine | 636.482 |
| Polar bear | 599.786 |
| conservation technology | 639.979 786 |
| resource economics | 333.959 786 |
| Polar regions | T2—11 |
| *see also* Frigid zones | |
| Polarimeters | |
| manufacturing technology | 681.25 |
| Polarimetry | |
| astronomy | 522.65 |
| Polaris missiles | 359.981 782 |
| engineering | 623.451 97 |
| military equipment | 359.981 782 |
| Polariscopic analysis | 543.59 |
| Polarization of light | 535.52 |
| Polarography | 543.4 |
| Polders | |
| engineering | 627.549 |
| Pole vaulting | 796.434 |
| Polecats (New World) | 599.768 |
| Polecats (Old World) | 599.766 2 |
| Polela (South Africa : District) | T2—684 7 |
| Polemics | |
| Christianity | 239 |
| comparative religion | 202 |
| Islam | 297.29 |
| Judaism | 296.35 |
| Polemoniales | 583.94 |
| Poles (People) | T5—918 5 |
| Polesine (Italy) | T2—453 3 |
| Police | 363.2 |
| law | 344.052 |
| public administration | 353.36 |
| sociology | 306.28 |
| Police boats | 363.286 |
| design | 623.812 63 |
| engineering | 623.826 3 |
| police services | 363.286 |
| Police buildings | |
| architecture | 725.18 |
| Police corruption | 364.132 3 |
| law | 345.023 23 |
| public administration | 353.46 |
| Police dogs | 636.737 6 |
| Police functions | 363.23 |
| Police misconduct | 364.132 |
| Police officers | 363.209 2 |
| role and function | 363.22 |
| Police patrols | 363.232 |
| Police powers (Constitutional law) | 342.041 8 |
| Police questioning | 363.254 |
| Police records | 363.24 |
| Police services | 363.2 |
| *see also* Police | |
| Police surveillance | 363.232 |
| Policy making | 320.6 |
| executive management | 658.401 2 |
| military administration | 355.684 |
| political science | 320.6 |
| public administration | 352.34 |

| | | | |
|---|---|---|---|
| Policy making (continued) | | Political crimes | 364.131 |
| social processes | 303.3 | law | 345.023 1 |
| see Manual at 300, 320.6 vs. | | Political culture | 306.2 |
| 352–354 | | Political divisions | |
| Policy studies | 320.6 | historical geography | 911 |
| Poliomyelitis | | Political elites | 305.524 |
| incidence | 614.549 | | T1—086 21 |
| medicine | 616.835 | Political ethics | 172 |
| see also Nervous system | | religion | 205.62 |
| diseases — humans | | Buddhism | 294.356 2 |
| pediatrics | 618.928 35 | Christianity | 241.62 |
| Poliovirus | 579.257 2 | Hinduism | 294.548 62 |
| Polish language | 491.85 | Islam | 297.562 |
| | T6—918 51 | Judaism | 296.362 |
| Polish literature | 891.85 | Political history | 900 |
| Polish people | T5—918 5 | see Manual at 900; also at 909, | |
| Polishing | 667.72 | 930–990 vs. 320 | |
| gems | 736.202 8 | Political ideologies | 320.5 |
| housecleaning | 648.5 | party programs | 324.23 |
| metals | 671.72 | Political institutions | |
| woodwork | | description and appraisal | 320.9 |
| buildings | 698.33 | social welfare | 361.613 |
| Polishing wheels | 621.922 | sociology | 306.2 |
| Politeness | | Political justice | 320.011 |
| ethics | 177.1 | Political machines | 324.21 |
| Political action committees | 324.4 | sociology | 306.26 |
| law | 342.078 | Political movements | 320.5 |
| Political action groups | 322.4 | see Manual at 324 vs. 320.5, | |
| law | 342.078 | 320.9, 909, 930–990 | |
| political process | 324.4 | Political music | 781.599 |
| relations with government | 322.4 | songs | 782.421 599 |
| Political activity of government | | Political parties | 324.2 |
| employees | | sociology | 306.26 |
| law | 342.068 4 | specific countries | 324.24–.29 |
| Political alliances | T2—171 2 | see Manual at 324.2094–.2099 | |
| Political anthropology | 306.2 | and 324.24–.29; also at | |
| Political buttons | | 909, 930–990 vs. 320 | |
| numismatics | 737.242 | Political patronage | 324.204 |
| Political campaign strategy | 324.72 | sociology | 306.2 |
| Political campaigns | 324.9 | Political persecution | 323.044 |
| see also Campaigns (Politics) | | Political persuasion | 320.014 |
| Political causes of war | 355.027 2 | Political philosophers | 320.092 |
| World War I | 940.311 2 | Political pins | |
| World War II | 940.531 12 | numismatics | 737.242 |
| Political change | 320.011 | Political prisoners | 365.450 92 |
| Political clubs | 324.3 | labor economics | 331.51 |
| Political conditions | 320.9 | Political prisons | 365.45 |
| see Manual at 909, 930–990 vs. | | see also Penal institutions | |
| 320 | | Political process | 324 |
| Political conventions | 324.56 | see Manual at 302–307 vs. 320 | |
| Political corruption | 364.132 3 | Political programs (Party | |
| law | 345.023 23 | platforms) | 324.23 |
| public administration | 353.46 | Political propaganda | 320.014 |

| | |
|---|---|
| Political refugees | 325.21 |
| *see also* Refugees | |
| Political rights | 323.5 |
| Political science | 320 |
| Political scientists | 320.092 |
| Political situation | 320.9 |
| *see Manual at* 909, 930–990 vs. 320 | |
| Political sociology | 306.2 |
| *see Manual at* 320 vs. 306.2 | |
| Political songs | 782.421 599 |
| Political theories | 320.011 |
| Politicians | |
| biography | 324.209 2 |
| characteristics | 324.22 |
| ethics | 172.2 |
| Politics | 320 |
| arts | 700.458 1 |
| | T3C—358 1 |
| folklore | 398.278 1 |
| history and criticism | 398.358 1 |
| journalism | 070.449 32 |
| literature | 808.803 581 |
| history and criticism | 809.933 581 |
| specific literatures | T3B—080 358 1 |
| history and criticism | T3B—093 581 |
| sociology | 306.2 |
| *see Manual at* 324 vs. 320 | |
| Politics and religion | 322.1 |
| political science | 322.1 |
| social theology | 201.72 |
| Buddhism | 294.337 2 |
| Christianity | 261.7 |
| Hinduism | 294.517 2 |
| Islam | 297.272 |
| *see Manual at* 297.26–.27 | |
| Judaism | 296.382 |
| *see Manual at* 322.1 vs. 201.72, 261.7, 292–299 | |
| Politics as a profession | 324.22 |
| Polk, James K. (James Knox) | |
| United States history | 973.61 |
| Polk County (Ark.) | T2—767 45 |
| Polk County (Fla.) | T2—759 67 |
| Polk County (Ga.) | T2—758 375 |
| Polk County (Iowa) | T2—777 58 |
| Polk County (Minn.) | T2—776 95 |
| Polk County (Mo.) | T2—778 77 |
| Polk County (N.C.) | T2—756 915 |
| Polk County (Neb.) | T2—782 352 |
| Polk County (Or.) | T2—795 38 |
| Polk County (Tenn.) | T2—768 875 |
| Polk County (Tex.) | T2—764 165 |
| Polk County (Wis.) | T2—775 17 |
| Polkas | 793.33 |
| music | 784.188 44 |
| Poll tax | 336.25 |
| law | 343.062 |
| public administration | 352.44 |
| public finance | 336.25 |
| qualification for voting | 324.62 |
| Polled Shorthorn cattle | 636.226 |
| Pollen | 571.845 2 |
| paleobotany | 561.13 |
| Pollen control | |
| air conditioning | |
| buildings | 697.932 4 |
| Pollination | 571.864 2 |
| coevolution | 576.875 |
| Polling | 324.65 |
| Pollocks | 641.392 |
| cooking | 641.692 |
| food | 641.392 |
| zoology | 597.632 |
| Pollutants | 363.738 |
| law | 344.046 33 |
| *see also* Pollution | |
| Pollution | 363.73 |
| criminology | 364.145 |
| criminal law | 345.024 5 |
| crop damage | 632.19 |
| ecology | 577.27 |
| human toxicology | 615.902 |
| law | 344.046 32 |
| public administration | 354.335 |
| cleanup | 353.93 |
| social effects | 304.28 |
| social theology | 201.77 |
| Christianity | 261.88 |
| social welfare | 363.73 |
| toxicology | 571.95 |
| *see Manual at* 333.7–.9 vs. 363.1, 363.73, 577; *also at* 363.73 vs. 571.95, 577.27 | |
| Pollution control equipment | |
| manufacturing technology | 681.76 |
| Pollution control technology | 628.5 |
| | T1—028 6 |
| aircraft | 629.134 35 |
| architecture | 720.47 |
| automotive | 629.25 |
| construction | 690.028 6 |
| glassmaking | 666.14 |
| paper manufacturing | 676.042 |
| petroleum | 665.538 9 |
| plastic technology | 668.419 2 |
| rubber manufacturing | 678.29 |

Pollution control technology (continued)
   water      628.168
   wood products      674.84
Pollution liability insurance      368.563
Polo      796.353
Polo players      796.353 092
Polokwane (South Africa :
   District)      T2—682 56
Polonaises      793.3
   music      784.188 4
Polonium
   chemical engineering      661.072 8
   chemistry      546.728
   metallurgy      669.79
Poltava (Ukraine : Oblast)      T2—477 6
Poltavs'ka oblast' (Ukraine)      T2—477 6
Poltergeists      133.142
Polyacrylics      668.423 2
   textiles      677.474 2
   *see also* Textiles
Polyamides      668.423 5
   textiles      677.473
   *see also* Textiles
Polyandry      306.842 3
Polybutadiene rubber      678.72
Polycarbonates      668.423
Polychaeta      592.62
Polychlorinated biphenyl
   human toxicology      615.951 2
Polycythemia
   medicine      616.153
   *see also* Cardiovascular
      diseases — humans
Polyesters      668.422 5
   textiles      677.474 3
   *see also* Textiles
Polyethers      668.423
Polyethylene      668.423 4
   textiles      677.474 5
   *see also* Textiles
Polyfluoro hydrocarbons      668.423 8
   textiles      677.474 8
   *see also* Textiles
Polygalales      583.82
Polygamists      306.842 3
      T1—086 59
Polygamy      306.842 3
   customs      392.5
Polyglandular disorders
   medicine      616.48
   *see also* Endocrine
      diseases — humans
Polyglot Bibles      220.51

Polyglot dictionaries      413
      T1—03
Polygonales      583.57
Polygons      516.154
   Euclidean geometry      516.215 4
Polygraph tests      363.254
   *see also* Lie detectors
Polygyny      306.842 3
Polyhedra      516.156
Polyhydroxy aromatics      547.633
Polyisobutylenes      668.423 4
Polymer clay
   handicrafts      745.572 3
Polymer painting      751.49
Polymer sequence      572.33
Polymerization      547.28
   chemical engineering      668.92
   inorganic chemistry      541.39
   organic chemistry      547.28
Polymerization plastics      668.42
Polymers      547.7
   biochemistry      572.33
   chemical engineering      668.9
   inorganic chemistry      541.225 4
   liquid-state physics      530.429
   materials science      620.192
   organic chemistry      547.7
   shipbuilding      623.820 7
   state of matter      530.413
   structural engineering      624.189 2
Polymixiiformes      597.62
Polymorphism
   crystallography      548.3
Polynesia      996
      T2—96
Polynesian languages      499.4
      T6—994
Polynesian literatures      899.4
Polynesian religion      299.924
Polynesians      T5—994
Polynomial equations      512.942 2
   algebra      512.942 2
   calculus      515.252
Polyolefins      668.423 4
Polyomavirus      579.244 5
Polypeptides      572.65
   humans      612.015 756
   *see also* Proteins
Polyphaga      595.76
Polyphenyl hydrocarbons      547.613
   chemical engineering      661.816
Polyphony      781.286
Polyplacophora      594.27
Polyploidy      572.87

| | | | |
|---|---|---|---|
| Polypodiales | 587.3 | Pomorskie Voivodeship | |
| Polypodiopsida | 587.3 | (Poland) | T2—438 22 |
| paleobotany | 561.73 | Pompeii (Extinct city) | T2—377 256 8 |
| Polyporales | 579.597 | Ponape (Micronesia) | T2—966 |
| Polypropylene | 668.423 4 | Ponape language | 499.52 |
| textiles | 677.474 5 | | T6—995 2 |
| see also Textiles | | Ponca Indians | T5—975 253 9 |
| Polypteriformes | 597.42 | Ponca language | 497.525 39 |
| paleozoology | 567.42 | | T6—975 253 9 |
| Polyradiculoneuritis | | Ponce (P.R. : District) | T2—729 57 |
| medicine | 616.856 | Pond Inlet (Nunavut) | T2—719 52 |
| see also Nervous system | | Pondera County (Mont.) | T2—786 53 |
| diseases — humans | | Pondicherry (India : Union | |
| Polysaccharides | 572.566 | Territory) | T2—548 6 |
| see also Carbohydrates | | Pondoland (South Africa) | T2—687 58 |
| Polystyrenes | 668.423 3 | Ponds | 551.482 |
| Polytheism | 211.32 | | T2—169 2 |
| comparative religion | 202.11 | biology | 578.763 6 |
| philosophy of religion | 211.32 | ecology | 577.636 |
| Polytheistic religions | 201.4 | fish culture | 639.31 |
| Polytopes | 516.158 | hydrology | 551.482 |
| Polyurethane rubber | 678.72 | landscape architecture | 714 |
| Polyurethanes | 668.423 9 | resource economics | 333.916 3 |
| polyesters | 668.422 5 | Pondweeds | 584.742 |
| thermoplastic | 668.423 9 | Pongidae | 599.88 |
| Polyvinyls | 668.423 6 | paleozoology | 569.88 |
| textiles | 677.474 4 | Pongo | 599.883 |
| see also Textiles | | Pongola River | T2—684 2 |
| Polyzoa | 594.67 | Mozambique | T2—679 1 |
| Pomacanthidae | 597.72 | South Africa | T2—684 2 |
| Pomacentridae | 597.72 | Ponies | 636.16 |
| Pomaceous fruits | 641.341 | Pons Variolii | |
| botany | 583.73 | human anatomy | 611.81 |
| cooking | 641.641 | human physiology | 612.826 7 |
| food | 641.341 | medicine | 616.8 |
| orchard crops | 634.1 | Pontarddulais (Wales) | T2—429 82 |
| Pombaline reforms | 946.903 3 | Pontchartrain, Lake (La.) | T2—763 34 |
| Pomegranates | 641.346 4 | Pontederiaceae | 584.35 |
| agriculture | 634.64 | Pontevedra (Spain : | |
| botany | 583.76 | Province) | T2—461 7 |
| cooking | 641.646 4 | Pontiac (Quebec : Regional | |
| food | 641.346 4 | County Municipality) | T2—714 21 |
| Pomerania (Poland and | | Pontiac's Conspiracy, 1763–1764 | 973.27 |
| Germany) | T2—438 16 | Pontificale Romanum | 264.025 |
| Germany | T2—431 78 | Pontine Islands (Italy) | T2—456 23 |
| Poland | T2—438 16 | Pontine Marshes (Italy) | T2—456 23 |
| Pomeranian (Dog) | 636.76 | Pontoporiidae | 599.538 |
| Pomerelia (Poland) | T2—438 22 | Pontotoc County (Miss.) | T2—762 932 |
| Pomeroon-Supenaam | | Pontotoc County (Okla.) | T2—766 69 |
| Region (Guyana) | T2—881 2 | Pontus (Roman diocese) | T2—393 |
| Pommel horse | 796.442 | Pontus (Roman province) | T2—393 3 |
| Pomo Indians | T5—975 74 | Pontus Polemoniacus | T2—393 37 |
| Pomo languages | 497.574 | Pontypridd (Wales) | T2—429 78 |
| | T6—975 74 | Pony express | 383.18 |

Ponza Islands (Italy)    T2—456 23
Poodle    636.728
Poodle (Toy dog)    636.76
Pooideae    584.9
   forage crops    633.2
Pool (Game)    794.733
   equipment technology    688.747 33
Pool halls
   architecture    725.84
Pool players    794.733 092
Poole (Dorset, England)    T2—423 37
Pools (Organizations)    338.87
   *see also* Combinations
     (Enterprises)
Pools (Water)    551.482
   *see also* Ponds
Poor children    305.230 869 42
   social welfare    362.775 69
Poor Clares    255.973
   church history    271.973
Poor laws    362.5
   social aspects    362.5
   welfare law    344.032 5
Poor people    305.569
      T1—086 942
   government programs    353.533 2
   institutional buildings    362.585
   social theology    201.762 5
     Buddhism    294.337 625
     Christianity    261.832 5
     Hinduism    294.517 625
     Judaism    296.38
   social welfare    362.5
     public administration    353.533 2
   welfare law    344.032 5
   *see also* Poverty
Poor women
   social welfare    362.839 85
Poor youth    305.235 086 942
   social welfare    362.775 69
Pop art    709.040 71
   painting    759.067 1
   sculpture    735.230 471
Popcorn    641.356 77
   commercial processing    664.805 677
   cooking    641.656 77
   food    641.356 77
   garden crop    635.677
Pope County (Ark.)    T2—767 32
Pope County (Ill.)    T2—773 991
Pope County (Minn.)    T2—776 46
Popes    282.092
   biography    282.092
   ecclesiology    262.13

Popguns
   music    786.99
   *see also* Percussion
     instruments
Poplars    583.65
   forestry    634.972 3
   lumber    674.142
   ornamental arboriculture    635.977 365
Poppies    635.933 35
   botany    583.35
   floriculture    635.933 35
   narcotic crop    633.75
Popular culture    306
Popular education    370
   social education    370.115
Popular music    781.63
   sociology    306.484 23
   *see Manual at* 781.62 vs.
     781.63–.66
Popular practices (Islam)    297.39
Popular songs    782.421 63
   western    782.421 64
Population    304.6
   social problems    363.9
   sociology    304.6
Population biology    577.88
   animals    591.788
   microorganisms    579.178 8
   plants    581.788
Population control    363.96
   demography    304.66
   social theology    201.7
   *see also* Birth control
Population control (Animals)
   conservation technology    639.93
Population density    304.61
Population dynamics (Ecology)    577.88
Population ecology    577.88
   animals    591.788
   microorganisms    579.178 8
   plants    581.788
Population exchanges    325
Population genetics    576.58
Population geography    304.6
Population movement    304.8
   Civil War (United States)    973.714
   public administration    353.59
   World War II    940.531 45
Population transfers    325
   World War II    940.531 45
Populism
   political ideology    320.566 2
Populist Party (U.S.)    324.273 27
Populus    583.65

| | |
|---|---|
| Poquoson (Va.) | T2—755 422 |
| Porcelain | 666.5 |
|   arts | 738.2 |
|   materials science | 620.146 |
|   technology | 666.5 |
| Porch furniture | 645.8 |
|   *see also* Outdoor furniture | |
| Porches | 721.84 |
|   architecture | 721.84 |
|   construction | 690.184 |
|   home economics | 643.55 |
| Porcupine fishes | 597.64 |
| Porcupines | 599.359 7 |
| Porcupines (New World) | 599.359 74 |
| Porcupines (Old World) | 599.359 7 |
| Pordenone (Italy : Province) | T2—453 94 |
|   ancient | T2—373 94 |
| Pore fungi | 579.597 |
| Porgies | 597.72 |
|   sports fishing | 799.177 2 |
| Porifera | 593.4 |
|   paleozoology | 563.4 |
| Porirua City (N.Z.) | T2—936 2 |
| Pork | 641.364 |
|   commercial processing | 664.92 |
|   cooking | 641.664 |
|   food | 641.364 |
| Pornography | 363.47 |
|   arts | 700.453 8 |
| | T3C—353 8 |
|   criminology | 364.174 |
|     law | 345.027 4 |
|   ethics | 176.7 |
|     religion | 205.667 |
|       Christianity | 241.667 |
|   fine arts | 704.942 8 |
|   law | 344.054 7 |
|   literature | 808.803 538 |
|     history and criticism | 809.933 538 |
|     specific literatures | T3B—080 353 8 |
|       history and | |
|         criticism | T3B—093 538 |
|   painting | 757.8 |
|   social problem | 363.47 |
|     public administrative control | 353.37 |
|   sociology | 306.77 |
| Porous materials | |
|   materials science | 620.116 |
| Porous solids | 530.413 |
| Porphyria | |
|   medicine | 616.399 |
|   *see also* Digestive system | |
|     diseases — humans | |
| Porphyrins | 547.593 |
|   chemical engineering | 661.894 |
| Porphyry | 552.3 |
| Porpoises | 599.539 |
| Porrentruy (Switzerland : District) | T2—494 366 |
| Port Arthur (Tas.) | T2—946 4 |
| Port-au-Prince (Haiti) | T2—729 452 |
| Port Augusta (S. Aust.) | T2—942 38 |
| Port buildings | 387.15 |
|   *see also* Port facilities | |
| Port Coquitlam (B.C.) | T2—711 33 |
| Port Cros National Park (France) | T2—449 3 |
| Port Cygnet (Tas.) | T2—946 2 |
| Port Elizabeth (South Africa : District) | T2—687 52 |
| Port Elizabeth-Uitenhage-Despatch industrial area | T2—687 52 |
| Port facilities | 387.15 |
|   architecture | 725.34 |
|   area planning | 711.76 |
|   engineering | 627.3 |
|   military engineering | 623.64 |
|   transportation services | 387.15 |
|     inland waterway | 386.85 |
|   *see also* Ports | |
| Port Fairy (Vic.) | T2—945 7 |
| Port Harcourt (Nigeria) | T2—669 42 |
| Port Hedland (W.A.) | T2—941 3 |
| Port installations | 387.15 |
|   *see also* Port facilities | |
| Port Kembla (N.S.W.) | T2—944 6 |
| Port Lincoln (S. Aust.) | T2—942 38 |
| Port Louis (Mauritius) | T2—698 2 |
| Port Macquarie (N.S.W.) | T2—944 2 |
| Port maintenance | 387.16 |
| Port Moody (B.C.) | T2—711 33 |
| Port Moresby (Papua New Guinea) | T2—954 5 |
| Port Nelson (Man.) | T2—712 71 |
| Port Pirie (S. Aust.) | T2—942 32 |
| Port Renfrew (B.C.) | T2—711 28 |
| Port Said (Egypt : Province) | T2—621 5 |
| Port Shepstone (South Africa : District) | T2—684 5 |
| Port St. Johns (South Africa : District) | T2—687 58 |
| Port Sudan (Sudan) | T2—625 |
| Port wine | 641.222 609 469 15 |
|   commercial processing | 663.226 094 691 5 |
| Portability | |
|   computer software | 005 |

| | |
|---|---|
| Portable buildings | 720.442 |
|   architecture | 720.442 |
|   construction | 690.342 |
| Portable computers | 004.16 |
|   *see also* Personal computers | |
| Portable document software | 005.726 |
| Portable firearms | 683.4 |
|   military engineering | 623.442 |
|   *see also* Guns (Small arms) | |
| Portable flight vehicles | |
|   engineering | 629.14 |
| Portable heaters | |
|   buildings | 697.24 |
| Portable lights | |
|   mining | 622.473 |
|   nautical equipment | 623.86 |
| Portable radios | 621.384 5 |
| Portable steam engines | 621.15 |
| Portable telephones | 384.53 |
|   communications services | 384.53 |
|   engineering | 621.384 56 |
|   military engineering | 623.734 5 |
| Portage County (Ohio) | T2—771 37 |
| Portage County (Wis.) | T2—775 53 |
| Portage la Prairie (Man.) | T2—712 73 |
| Portal hypertension | |
|   medicine | 616.362 |
|   *see also* Digestive system | |
|     diseases — humans | |
| Portalegre (Portugal : | |
|   District) | T2—469 51 |
| Portals | |
|   sculpture | 731.542 |
| Porter County (Ind.) | T2—772 98 |
| Portes Gil, Emilio | |
|   Mexican history | 972.082 42 |
| Portfolio analysis | 332.6 |
| Portfolio management | 332.6 |
| Porthcawl (Wales) | T2—429 71 |
| Portillo, Alfonso | |
|   Guatemalan history | 972.810 532 |
| Portland (Me.) | T2—741 91 |
| Portland (Or.) | T2—795 49 |
| Portland (Vic.) | T2—945 7 |
| Portland cement | 666.94 |
| Portneuf (Quebec : Regional | |
|   County Municipality) | T2—714 46 |
| Portneuf Wildlife Reserve | |
|   (Quebec) | T2—714 46 |
| Porto (Portugal : District) | T2—469 15 |
| Porto-Novo (Benin) | T2—668 3 |

| | |
|---|---|
| Portraits | |
|   art representation | 704.942 |
|   drawing | 743.42 |
|   painting | 757 |
| Ports | 387.1 |
|   engineering | 627.2 |
|   inland waterway | 386.8 |
|   law | 343.096 7 |
|   public administration | 354.78 |
|   transportation services | 387.1 |
|   *see also* Port facilities | |
| Portsmouth (England) | T2—422 792 |
| Portsmouth (N.H.) | T2—742 6 |
| Portsmouth (Va.) | T2—755 522 |
| Portugal | 946.9 |
| | T2—469 |
|   ancient | 936.69 |
| | T2—366 9 |
| Portuguesa (Venezuela) | T2—874 5 |
| Portuguese (Ethnic group) | T5—69 |
| Portuguese (National group) | T5—691 |
| Portuguese adder | 597.963 6 |
| Portuguese folk music | 781.626 91 |
| Portuguese folk songs | 782.421 626 91 |
| Portuguese Guinea | 966.570 2 |
| | T2—665 7 |
| Portuguese India | T2—547 8 |
| Portuguese language | 469 |
| | T6—69 |
| Portuguese literature | 869 |
| Portuguese man-of-war | 593.55 |
| Portuguese Timor | 959.87 |
| | T2—598 7 |
| Portuguese water dog | 636.73 |
| Portulacaceae | 583.53 |
| Portulacas | 583.53 |
| Posey County (Ind.) | T2—772 34 |
| Posidoniaceae | 584.74 |
| Position classification | 658.306 |
| Position-finding devices | |
|   marine navigation | 623.893 |
|   radio engineering | 621.384 191 |
| Positional astronomy | 522 |
|   mathematical geography | 526.6 |
| Positive psychology | 150.198 8 |
| Positives (Photography) | 771.44 |
|   distribution | 771.48 |
|   manipulation | 771.44 |
|   organization | 771.48 |
|   preparation | 771.44 |
|   preservation | 771.46 |
|   storage | 771.46 |
| Positivism | 146.4 |
|   ethics | 171.2 |

Positron emission tomography
  medicine      616.075 75
Positrons      539.721 4
Posology
  pharmacology      615.14
Possible worlds      511.314
Possums      599.23
Possums (America)      599.276
Possums (Australasia)      599.23
Post cxchanges      355.341
Post-Keynesian economics      330.156
Post-mortem examination
  medicine      616.075 9
Post offices      383.42
  architecture      725.16
  *see also* Postal service
Post-production
  videography      777.55
Post-traumatic stress disorders
  medicine      616.852 1
    *see also* Mental disorders
  pediatrics      618.928 521
Postage-due stamps
  prints      769.57
Postage stamps      383.23
  investment economics      332.63
  philately      769.56
  postal service      383.23
    *see also* Postal service
  printing      686.288
Postal cards      383.122
  *see also* Postal service
Postal clerks      383.492
Postal codes      383.145 5
  *see also* Postal service
Postal communication      383
  *see also* Postal service
Postal inspection      383.46
Postal insurance      368.2
Postal law      343.099 2
Postal offenses      364.136
  law      345.023 6
Postal organization      383.4
  law      343.099 25
Postal rates      383.23
  law      343.099 23
Postal routes      383.143
  law      343.099 25
Postal savings banks      332.22
Postal savings stamps
  prints      769.57

Postal service      383
  armed services      355.693
  law      343.099 2
  public administration      354.759
Postal service workers      383.492
Postal stationery
  philately      769.566
Postal zones      383.145
  *see also* Postal service
Postcard illustration      741.683
Postcards      383.122
  philately      769.566
  *see also* Postal service
Postclassical Greek language      487.3
                 T6—87
Postclassical Latin language      477
                 T6—71
Postcoital contraceptives
  health      613.943 2
  medicine      618.182 5
    *see also* Birth control
Postcoordinate indexing      025.47
Postdoctoral programs      378.155
Postencephalitic Parkinson
  disease
  medicine      616.833
    *see also* Nervous system
      diseases — humans
Posters
  arts      741.674
    illustration      741.674
    prints      769.5
Postglacial epoch      551.793
  geology      551.793
  paleontology      560.179 3
Posthypnotic phenomena      154.774
Postimpressionism      709.034 6
  painting      759.056
Postludes      784.189 3
Postmarks
  philately      769.567
Postmasburg (South Africa :
  District)      T2—687 11
Postmenopause
  disorders
    gynecology      618.175
    *see also* Female genital
      diseases — humans

Postmodernism 149.97
  arts 700.411 3
    T3C—113
  literature 808.801 13
    history and criticism 809.911 3
    specific literatures T3B—080 113
      history and
        criticism T3B—091 13
  philosophy 149.97
Postnatal care
  obstetrics 618.6
Postnatal development
  humans 612.6
Postoperative care
  medicine 617.919 5
Postoperative complications
  medicine 617.919 5
Postpartum depression
  medicine 618.76
Postpartum hemorrhage
  obstetrics 618.7
Postpoliomyelitis syndrome
  incidence 614.549
  medicine 616.835
    *see also* Nervous system
      diseases — humans
Posts (Columns) 721.3
  architecture 721.3
  construction 690.13
Posts (Military installations) 355.7
  law 343.015 7
Poststructuralism
  philosophy 149.97
Posture 613.78
Postwar period (World War II) 909.825
    T1—090 45
Pot abuse 362.295
  medicine 616.863 5
  personal health 613.835
  social welfare 362.295
  *see also* Substance abuse
Pot gardening 635.986
Potable water 363.61
  *see also* Drinking water;
    Municipal water supply
Potaliaceae 583.93
Potamogetonaceae 584.742
Potamogetonales 584.74
Potaro-Siparuni Region
  (Guyana) T2—881 87
Potash 546.383 22
  chemical engineering 661.334

Potash salts 553.636
  economic geology 553.636
  mining 622.363 6
Potassium 669.725
  chemical engineering 661.038 3
  chemistry 546.383
  metallurgy 669.725
  mining 622.363 6
  organic chemistry 547.053 83
    applied 661.895
  physical metallurgy 669.967 25
  *see also* Chemicals
Potassium alkalis 546.383 22
  chemical engineering 661.33
Potassium bicarbonate 546.383 22
  chemical engineering 661.333
Potassium carbonate 546.383 22
  chemical engineering 661.334
Potassium fertilizers 631.83
  chemical engineering 668.623
Potassium hydroxide 546.383 22
  chemical engineering 661.332
Potassium minerals
  economic geology 553.636
Potato printing 761
Potato starch
  food technology 664.22
Potato whiskey 641.25
  commercial processing 663.5
Potatoes 641.352 1
  agriculture 635.21
  botany 583.952
  commercial processing 664.805 21
  cooking 641.652 1
  food 641.352 1
Potawatomi Indians T5—973 16
Potawatomi language 497.316
    T6—973 16
Potchefstroom (South
  Africa : District) T2—682 42
Potential energy 531.6
Potential offenders
  identification 364.41
Potential theory 515.96
Potentiometers 621.374 3
Potenza (Italy : Province) T2—457 71
  ancient T2—377 75
Potgietersrus (South Africa :
  District) T2—682 53
Potichomania
  handicrafts 745.546

| | | | |
|---|---|---|---|
| Potomac River | T2—752 | Poverty (continued) | |
| Maryland | T2—752 | literature | 808.803 556 |
| Virginia | T2—755 2 | history and criticism | 809.933 556 |
| West Virginia | T2—754 9 | specific literatures | T3B—080 355 6 |
| Potoos | 598.99 | history and | |
| Potosí (Bolivia : Dept.) | T2—841 4 | criticism | T3B—093 556 |
| Potpourris (Dried plants) | 668.542 | macroeconomics | 339.46 |
| Pots | | religious practice | 204.47 |
| kitchen utensils | 643.3 | Buddhism | 294.344 47 |
| manufacturing technology | 683.82 | Christianity | 248.47 |
| Potsdam (Germany) | T2—431 546 | Hinduism | 294.544 7 |
| Potsdam (Germany : Bezirk) | T2—431 54 | social theology | 201.762 5 |
| Potsdam-Mittelmark | | Buddhism | 294.337 625 |
| (Germany : Landkreis) | T2—431 54 | Christianity | 261.832 5 |
| Pottawatomie County (Kan.) | T2—781 32 | Hinduism | 294.517 625 |
| Pottawatomie County | | Judaism | 296.38 |
| (Okla.) | T2—766 36 | social welfare | 362.5 |
| Pottawattamie County | | public administration | 353.533 2 |
| (Iowa) | T2—777 71 | social welfare facilities | 362.583 |
| Potted plants | 635.986 | architecture | 725.55 |
| houseplants | 635.965 | Poverty-stricken people | 305.569 |
| Potted trees | 635.977 | | T1—086 942 |
| houseplants | 635.965 | | |
| Potter County (Pa.) | T2—748 55 | *see also* Poor people | |
| Potter County (S.D.) | T2—783 19 | Powder metal products | 671.87 |
| Potter County (Tex.) | T2—764 825 | Powder metallurgy | 671.37 |
| Potters | 738.092 | Powder post beetles | 595.763 |
| Potter's wheels | 666.43 | Powder processes | |
| decorative arts | 738.13 | photographic printing | 773.2 |
| sculpture | 731.3 | Powder River County | |
| technology | 666.43 | (Mont.) | T2—786 37 |
| Pottery | 666.3 | Powder rooms | 643.52 |
| arts | 738 | home economics | 643.52 |
| technology | 666.3 | interior decoration | 747.78 |
| Poultry (Animals) | 636.5 | Powder technology | 620.43 |
| agricultural economics | 338.176 5 | Powdered eggs | 641.375 4 |
| zoology | 598.6 | cooking | 641.675 4 |
| Poultry (Meat) | 641.365 | food | 641.375 4 |
| commercial processing | 664.93 | processing | 637.54 |
| economics | 338.476 649 3 | Powdered soaps | 668.124 |
| cooking | 641.665 | Powders (Pharmaceuticals) | |
| food | 641.365 | pharmaceutical chemistry | 615.19 |
| home preservation | 641.493 | Powell, Lake (Utah and | |
| Poured concrete | 624.183 4 | Ariz.) | T2—792 59 |
| building construction | 693.5 | Powell County (Ky.) | T2—769 585 |
| with reinforcement | 693.541 | Powell County (Mont.) | T2—786 86 |
| without reinforcement | 693.521 | Powell River (B.C.) | T2—711 31 |
| structural engineering | 624.183 4 | Powell River (B.C. : | |
| Poverty | 362.5 | Regional District) | T2—711 31 |
| arts | 700.455 6 | Power (Energy) | 333.79 |
| | T3C—355 6 | Power (Social sciences) | 303.3 |
| influence on crime | 364.2 | international relations | 327.101 |
| law | 344.032 5 | political science | 320.011 |
| | | sociology | 303.3 |
| | | Power control devices | 621.812 |

Power County (Idaho)    T2—796 49
Power-driven ships    387.204 4
   design    623.812 044
   engineering    623.820 4
   handling    623.881 4
   *see also* Ships
Power electronics    621.317
Power equipment
   agricultural use    631.37
   textile technology    677.028 5
Power-factor meters    621.374 9
Power failure
   electrical engineering    621.319
Power hammers    621.974
Power interruption insurance    368.7
Power of attorney    346.029
Power plant insurance    368.7
Power plants (Electric
   generation)    621.312 1
   nuclear engineering    621.483
Power plants (Engines)    621.4
   aircraft    629.134 35
   ships    623.87
   unmanned spacecraft    629.465
Power politics    327.1
Power residues    512.72
Power resources    333.79
Power saws
   use in home woodworking    684.083 34
Power series    515.243 2
Power shovels    621.865
Power supply
   communications engineering    621.382 32
   electronics    621.381 044
Power tools    621.9
   use in home woodworking    684.083
Power transmission
   machine engineering    621.85
Powers (Mathematics)    512.922
Poweshiek County (Iowa)    T2—777 596
Powhatan County (Va.)    T2—755 612
Powhatan Indians    T5—973 47
Powhatan language    497.347
   T6—973 47
POWs    355.113
   *see also* Prisoners of war
Powys (Wales)    T2—429 5
Poxviridae    579.243 2
Poznań (Poland :
   Voivodeship)    T2—438 49
Pozzuoli (Italy)
   ancient    T2—377 25
Practical astronomy    522
Practical ethics    170.44

Practical nurses    610.730 92
   role and function    610.730 693
Practical politics    324.7
Practical printing    686.225
Practice of law    347.050 4
Practice teaching    370.71
   T1—071
Praeneste (Italy)    T2—376 3
Praenestian language    479.4
   T6—794
Pragmatic reductionism
   (Psychology)    150.194 34
Pragmatics    401.45
   discourse analysis    401.41
     specific languages    T4—014 1
   linguistics    401.45
     specific languages    T4—014 5
   psycholinguistics    401.9
     specific languages    T4—019
   sociolinguistics    306.44
   specific languages    T4—014 5
   *see Manual at* 401.43 vs.
     306.44, 401.45, 401.9, 412,
     415
Pragmatism    144.3
   education    370.12
Prague (Czech Republic)    T2—437 12
Praha (Czech Republic)    T2—437 12
Prahova (Romania)    T2—498 2
Praia (Cape Verde)    T2—665 8
Prairie chickens    598.637
Prairie County (Ark.)    T2—767 77
Prairie County (Mont.)    T2—786 25
Prairie dogs    599.367
Prairie Provinces    971.2
   T2—712
Prairies    333.74
   T2—153
   biology    578.744
   ecology    577.44
   geography    910.915 3
   physical geography    910.021 53
   *see also* Grasslands
Prajadhipok, King of Siam
   Thai history    959.304 2
Prakrit languages    491.3
   T6—913
Prakrit literatures    891.3
Praseodymium
   chemistry    546.413
Prasinophyceae    579.83
Prato (Italy : Province)    T2—455 19
   ancient    T2—375 19
Pratt County (Kan.)    T2—781 815

Prättigau-Davos
  (Switzerland)     T2—494 732 5
Prawns     595.388
  *see also* Shrimps
Prayer     204.3
  Buddhism     294.344 3
  Christianity     248.32
  Hinduism     294.543
  Islam     297.382
    Sufi     297.438 2
  Judaism     296.45
  public worship     203.8
    Buddhism     294.343 8
    Christianity     264.1
    Hinduism     294.538
    Judaism     296.45
Prayer books     204.33
  Buddhism     294.344 33
  Christianity     242.8
    public worship     264.13
  Hinduism     294.543 3
  Islam     297.382 4
    Sufi     297.438 24
  Judaism     296.45
Prayer desks
  church architecture     726.529 2
  church furniture     247.1
Prayer in public schools     379.28
  law     344.079 6
Prayer meetings
  Christianity
    public worship     264.7
Prayer of Manasseh (Bible)     229.6
Prayer plant     635.934 39
  botany     584.39
  floriculture     635.934 39
Prayer shawls     296.461
Prayers (Private devotions)     204.33
  Buddhism     294.344 33
  Christianity     242
  Hinduism     294.543 3
  Islam     297.382 4
    Sufi     297.438 24
  Judaism     296.45
Prayers (Public worship)     203.8
  Buddhism     294.343 8
  Christianity     264.13
  Hinduism     294.538
  Islam     297.382 4
    Sufi     297.438 24
  Judaism     296.45
Pre-Aryan period
  Indian history     934.01

Pre-Columbian art     709.7
  Latin America     709.8
Pre-Islamic prophets     297.246
Pre-Socratic philosophy     182
Preaching     206.1
  Christianity     251
  Islam     297.37
  Judaism     296.47
Preaching orders (Christianity)     255.04
  church history     271.04
Preble County (Ohio)     T2—771 71
Precalculus     510
  *see Manual at* 510
Precambrian era     551.71
  geology     551.71
  paleontology     560.171
Precast concrete     624.183 414
  building construction     693.5
    with reinforcement     693.544
    without reinforcement     693.522
  manufacturing technology     666.893
  materials science     620.137
  structural engineering     624.183 414
Precedence (Heraldry)     929.7
Precession
  celestial mechanics     521.9
    corrections     522.9
Precious metals     669.2
  decorative arts     739.2
  economic geology     553.42
  handicrafts     745.56
  materials science     620.189 2
  metallography     669.952
  metallurgy     669.2
  metalworking     673.2
  mining     622.342
  physical metallurgy     669.962
Precious stones     553.8
  *see also* Gems
Precipitates     541.348 5
  chemical engineering     660.294 85
Precipitation (Chemicals)     541.34
  chemical engineering     660.284 24
Precipitation (Meteorology)     551.577
  geologic agent     551.35
  weather forecasting     551.647 7
  weather modification     551.687 7
Precision (Information science)     025.04
Precision casting
  metals     671.255
Precision diving     797.24
Precision engineering     620.004 5
Precision instruments
  technology     681

| | |
|---|---|
| Preclassical Greek language | 487.1 |
| | T6—87 |
| Preclassical Latin language | 477 |
| | T6—71 |
| Preclassicism | |
| music | 780.903 3 |
| Precognition | 133.86 |
| Precoordinate indexing | 025.47 |
| Predation (Biology) | 591.53 |
| plants | 575.99 |
| Predator control | |
| animal husbandry | 636.083 9 |
| conservation technology | 639.966 |
| Predator-prey relations | 591.53 |
| Predatory animals | 591.53 |
| small game hunting | 799.259 7 |
| Predelinquents | 305.230 869 23 |
| | T1—086 923 |
| social group | 305.230 869 23 |
| social welfare | 362.74 |
| Predestination | 202.2 |
| Christianity | 234.9 |
| Islam | 297.227 |
| Predicate and subject (Grammar) | 415 |
| specific languages | T4—5 |
| Predicate calculus | 511.3 |
| mathematical logic | 511.3 |
| philosophical logic | 160 |
| Prediction | 003.2 |
| probabilities | 519.287 |
| statistical mathematics | 519.54 |
| Predictions | 003.2 |
| occultism | 133.3 |
| religion | 203.2 |
| eschatological | 202.3 |
| Prefabricated houses | 643.2 |
| *see also* Dwellings | |
| Prefabricated materials | |
| architectural construction | 721.044 97 |
| building materials | 691.97 |
| construction | 693.97 |
| Preferential hiring | |
| personnel management | 658.311 2 |
| public administration | 352.650 8 |
| union security arrangements | 331.889 6 |
| Preferred provider health | |
| insurance | 368.382 |
| Preferred stocks | 332.632 25 |
| speculation | 332.632 28 |
| Prefixes | 415.92 |
| specific languages | T4—592 |
| Pregnancy | 573.67 |
| biology | 573.67 |
| cooking for | 641.563 19 |

| | |
|---|---|
| Pregnancy (continued) | |
| human physiology | 612.63 |
| obstetrics | 618.2 |
| psychology | 155.646 3 |
| social services | 362.198 2 |
| veterinary medicine | 636.089 82 |
| Pregnancy complications | |
| obstetrics | 618.3 |
| Pregnancy programs in schools | 371.714 |
| Pregnancy toxemias | |
| obstetrics | 618.361 32 |
| Prehistoric animals | 560 |
| Prehistoric archaeology | 930.1 |
| Prehistoric humans | 569.9 |
| Prehistoric periods | 930.1 |
| | T1—090 12 |
| Prehistoric religions | 201.42 |
| Prejudice | 303.385 |
| ethics | 177.5 |
| *see also* Discrimination — | |
| ethics | |
| religion | 200.8 |
| Christianity | 270.08 |
| Judaism | 296.08 |
| sociology | 303.385 |
| Preliminary hearings | 345.072 |
| Preliminary Scholastic | |
| Assessment Test | 378.166 2 |
| Preludes | 784.189 28 |
| Premarital counseling | |
| Christian pastoral counseling | 259.13 |
| social welfare | 362.828 6 |
| *see also* Families — social | |
| welfare | |
| Premarital sexual relations | 306.733 |
| social problem | 363.48 |
| *see also* Sexual relations | |
| Premature birth | |
| obstetrics | 618.397 |
| Premature infants | |
| pediatrics | 618.920 11 |
| Premature labor | |
| obstetrics | 618.397 |
| Premenstrual syndrome | |
| gynecology | 618.172 |
| *see also* Female genital | |
| diseases — humans | |
| Premiers | 352.23 |
| cabinet governments | 321.804 3 |
| public administration | 352.23 |
| Premium television | 384.555 4 |
| *see also* Television | |
| Premonstratensians | 255.19 |
| church history | 271.19 |

Přemyslid dynasty 943.702 23
Prenatal care
  obstetrics 618.24
Prentiss County (Miss.) T2—762 985
Prenuptial contracts 346.016 62
Preoperative care
  surgery 617.919 2
Prep schools 373.222
  *see also* Secondary education
Prepaid dental insurance 368.382 3
Prepaid health insurance 368.382
Preparation of food (Cooking) 641.5
Preparatory schools 373.222
  *see also* Secondary education
Prepared doughs 664.753
Prepared ores 669.042
Prepared pianos 786.28
  instrument 786.281 9
  music 786.28
  *see also* Keyboard instruments
Prepositional phrases 415.7
  specific languages T4—57
Prepositions 415.7
  specific languages T4—57
Prerelease guidance centers 365.34
  *see also* Penal institutions
Prerelease programs 365.663
Presbyopia
  optometry 617.755
  *see also* Eye diseases — humans
Presbyterian Church 285
  church government 262.05
    parishes 254.05
  church law 262.985
  doctrines 230.5
    catechism and creeds 238.5
  general councils 262.55
  guides to Christian life 248.485
  missions 266.5
  moral theology 241.045
  public worship 264.05
  religious associations 267.185
  religious education 268.85
  seminaries 230.073 5
  theology 230.5
Presbyterian Church (U.S.A.) 285.137
  *see also* Presbyterian Church
Presbyterian Church in the United States 285.133
  *see also* Presbyterian Church
Presbyterian Church in the United States of America 285.132
  *see also* Presbyterian Church

Presbyterian Church of Wales 285.235
  *see also* Presbyterian Church
Presbyterian sacred music 781.715
  public worship 782.322 5
  music 782.322 5
  religion 264.050 2
Presbyterians
  biography 285.092
Presbyteries
  Christian ecclesiology 262.4
Preschool children 305.233
  T1—083 3
  development
    physiology 612.654
  home care 649.123
  psychology 155.423
  reading
    library science 028.533
  social aspects 305.233
Preschool education 372.21
  child rearing 649.68
  federal aid 379.121 22
  public support 379.112 2
  *see also* Primary education
Preschool teachers 372.11
Prescott and Russell (Ont.) T2—713 85
Prescribed burning
  forestry 634.955
Prescription drug abuse 362.299
  medicine 616.86
  personal health 613.8
  social welfare 362.299
  *see also* Substance abuse
Prescription drugs 615.1
  insurance 368.382 4
  pharmacology 615.1
  *see also* Drugs (Pharmaceuticals)
Prescription filling 615.4
Prescription writing 615.14
Prescriptive grammar 418
  specific languages T4—82
Prescriptive linguistics 418
  specific languages T4—8
  *see Manual at* 410
Preseli (Wales) T2—429 62
Presentation (Parturition)
  obstetrics 618.42
Presentation of Jesus Christ 232.928
Presentation religious orders 255.977
  church history 271.977
Presentation software 005.58

| | |
|---|---|
| Preservation | T1—028 8 |
| arts | 702.88 |
| bibliographic materials | 025.84 |
| biological specimens | 570.752 |
| botanical specimens | 580.752 |
| cinematography | 777.58 |
| lumber | 674.386 |
| museology | 069.53 |
| negatives | 771.45 |
| positives (photographs) | 771.46 |
| videography | 777.58 |
| zoological specimens | 590.752 |
| *see also* Historic preservation | |
| Preserved Context Indexing System | 025.47 |
| Preserved foods | |
| cooking | 641.61 |
| home economics | 641.4 |
| Preserves (Jams) | 641.852 |
| commercial processing | 664.152 |
| home preparation | 641.852 |
| Preserves (Whole fruits) | 641.34 |
| cooking with | 641.64 |
| food | 641.34 |
| home preparation | 641.4 |
| Preserving biological specimens | 578.075 2 |
| Presidente Hayes (Paraguay : Dept.) | T2—892 23 |
| Presidential government | 321.804 2 |
| Presidents | 352.23 |
| democratic systems | 321.804 2 |
| public administration | 352.23 |
| Presidio County (Tex.) | T2—764 933 |
| Prešovský kraj (Slovakia) | T2—437 36 |
| Presque Isle County (Mich.) | T2—774 82 |
| Press | 070 |
| civil rights issues | 323.445 |
| influence on crime | 364.254 |
| Press control | 363.31 |
| *see also* Censorship | |
| Press law | 343.099 8 |
| Pressing clothes | |
| home economics | 648.1 |
| Pressing equipment | 621.98 |
| Pressing glass | 666.123 |
| Pressing metals | 671.33 |
| Pressing textiles | 677.028 25 |
| Pressure | |
| biophysics | 571.437 |
| humans | 612.014 415 |
| extraterrestrial biophysics | |
| humans | 612.014 535 |
| mechanics | 531.1 |
| Pressure cooking | 641.587 |
| Pressure distribution | |
| aeronautics | 629.132 35 |
| Pressure groups | 322.43 |
| political process | 324.4 |
| relations with government | 322.43 |
| Pressure perception | |
| psychology | 152.182 3 |
| Pressure regulators | |
| steam engineering | 621.185 |
| Pressure surge | |
| engineering | 620.106 4 |
| Pressure vessels | 681.760 41 |
| Pressure welding | 671.529 |
| Pressurization | |
| aircraft | 629.134 42 |
| manned spacecraft | 629.477 5 |
| spacecraft | 629.477 5 |
| Pressurizing oils and gases | 665.028 2 |
| Presswork | |
| printing | 686.23 |
| Prestatyn (Wales) | T2—429 37 |
| Preston (England : Borough) | T2—427 665 |
| Preston County (W. Va.) | T2—754 82 |
| Prestressed concrete | 624.183 412 |
| building construction | 693.542 |
| manufacturing technology | 666.893 |
| materials science | 620.137 |
| structural engineering | 624.183 412 |
| Presumptions (Law) | 347.064 |
| Presupposition | |
| linguistics | 401.454 |
| specific languages | T4—014 54 |
| Preteens | 305.234 |
| *see also* School children | |
| Pretoria (South Africa : District) | T2—682 27 |
| Pretrial procedure | 347.072 |
| criminal law | 345.072 |
| Pretrial release | 345.072 |
| Preventive dentistry | 617.601 |
| Preventive detention | 345.052 7 |
| Preventive medicine | 613 |
| personal | 613 |
| public | 614.44 |
| animal husbandry | 636.089 444 |
| public administration | 353.628 |
| *see Manual at* 362.1–.4 and 614.4–.5 | |
| Preveza (Greece) | T2—495 3 |
| Priapulida | 592.3 |
| paleozoology | 562.3 |

| | | | |
|---|---|---|---|
| Price control (Government) | 338.526 | Prieska (South Africa : | |
| economics | 338.526 | District) | T2—687 12 |
| law | 343.083 | Priesthood | 206.1 |
| public administration | 352.85 | Christianity | 262.1 |
| Price County (Wis.) | T2—775 24 | pastoral theology | 253 |
| Price-demand relationship | 338.521 2 | Jewish | 296.495 |
| Price determination | 338.52 | Priesthood of believers | 234 |
| economics | 338.52 | Priesthood of Jesus Christ | 232.8 |
| marketing management | 658.816 | Priests | 200.92 |
| Price discrimination | | biography | 200.92 |
| criminology | 364.168 | Christian | 270.092 |
| trade law | 343.072 5 | *see also* Clergy — Christian | |
| Price-earnings ratio | 332.632 21 | Jewish | 296.495 |
| Price fixing | 338.523 | role and function | 206.1 |
| criminology | 364.168 | *see Manual at* 200.92 and | |
| criminal law | 345.026 8 | 201–209, 292–299 | |
| economics | 338.523 | Prignitz (Germany : | |
| trade law | 343.072 5 | Landkreis) | T2—431 54 |
| Price indexes | 338.528 | Prignitz-Oberhavel | |
| Price leadership | 338.523 | (Germany : | |
| Price levels | 338.528 | Raumordnungsregion) | T2—431 54 |
| Price lists | T1—029 | Prima facie evidence | 347.064 |
| Price policy | 338.52 | Primaries (Elections) | 324.54 |
| Price statistics | 338.528 | specific countries | 324.24–.29 |
| Price-supply relationship | 338.521 3 | Primary batteries | 621.312 423 |
| Price supports | | Primary education | 372 |
| agricultural economics | 338.18 | federal aid | 379.121 2 |
| law | 343.076 1 | law | 344.074 |
| public administration | 354.528 5 | public administrative support | 353.8 |
| economics | 338.52 | public support | 379.112 |
| law | 343.074 2 | law | 344.076 82 |
| public administration | 352.85 | special education | 371.904 72 |
| Price trends | | *see Manual at* 372.24 and | |
| collectibles | T1—075 | 373.23 | |
| Prices | 338.52 | Primary elections | 324.54 |
| agricultural industries | 338.13 | specific countries | 324.24–.29 |
| economics | 338.52 | Primary epidermis (Plants) | 575.451 |
| land economics | 333.332 3 | Primary groups (Social groups) | 302.34 |
| macroeconomics | 339.42 | Primary industries | 338 |
| mineral industries | 338.23 | economics | 338 |
| regulation | 338.526 | law | 343.076 |
| economics | 338.526 | products | 338.02 |
| law | 343.083 | commerce | 381.4 |
| public administration | 352.85 | foreign | 382.4 |
| secondary industries | 338.43 | public administration | 354.73 |
| stocks | 332.632 22 | public administration | 354.3 |
| theories | 338.521 | Primary metal products | 671.8 |
| Pricing | 338.52 | Primary productivity (Ecology) | 577.15 |
| marketing management | 658.816 | Primary roads | 388.12 |
| Pride | 179.8 | Primary school buildings | 372.16 |
| arts | T3C—353 | architecture | 727.1 |
| folklore | 398.273 | Primary school libraries | 027.822 2 |
| *see also* Vices | | Primary school teachers | 372.11 |
| | | Primary school teaching | 372.110 2 |

| | |
|---|---|
| Primary schools | 372 |
|   *see also* Primary education | |
| Primates | 599.8 |
|   animal husbandry | 636.98 |
|   conservation technology | 639.979 8 |
|   experimental animals | |
|     medicine | 616.027 38 |
|   paleozoology | 569.8 |
|   resource economics | 333.959 8 |
|   zoology | 599.8 |
| Prime (Divine office) | 264.15 |
|   music | 782.324 |
| Prime ministers | 352.23 |
|   cabinet governments | 321.804 3 |
|   public administration | 352.23 |
| Prime movers | |
|   technology | 621.4 |
| Prime numbers | 512.723 |
| Primers (Detonators) | 662.4 |
|   military engineering | 623.454 2 |
| Primers (Readers) | 418 |
|   specific languages | T4—86 |
|     for nonnative speakers | T4—864 |
| Primitive art | 700 |
|   nonliterate peoples | 709.011 |
| Primitive Baptists | 286.4 |
|   *see also* Baptists | |
| Primitive law | 340.52 |
| Primitive Methodist Church | 287.4 |
|   *see also* Methodist Church | |
| Primitive religions | 201.42 |
| Primitive societies | 301.7 |
| Primitive weapons | |
|   art metalwork | 739.744 1 |
| Primitivism | |
|   arts | 700.414 5 |
| | T3C—145 |
|   literature | 808.801 45 |
|     history and criticism | 809.914 5 |
|     specific literatures | T3B—080 145 |
|       history and | |
|         criticism | T3B—091 45 |
| Primorskiĭ kraĭ (Russia) | T2—577 |
| Primor'ye (Russia : Kray) | T2—577 |
| Primroses | 583.675 |
|   floriculture | 635.933 675 |
| Primulales | 583.675 |
| Primulas | 583.675 |
|   floriculture | 635.933 675 |
| Prince (P.E.I.) | T2—717 1 |
| Prince Albert (Sask.) | T2—712 42 |
| Prince Albert (South | |
|   Africa : District) | T2—687 39 |
| Prince Albert's yew | 585.3 |
| Prince Edward (Ont.) | T2—713 587 |
| Prince Edward County (Va.) | T2—755 632 |
| Prince Edward Island | 971.7 |
| | T2—717 |
| Prince Edward Islands | 969.9 |
| | T2—699 |
| Prince George (B.C.) | T2—711 82 |
| Prince George County (Va.) | T2—755 585 |
| Prince George's County | |
|   (Md.) | T2—752 51 |
| Prince of Wales Island | |
|   (Nunavut) | T2—719 55 |
| Prince Rupert (B.C.) | T2—711 1 |
| Prince William County | |
|   (Va.) | T2—755 273 2 |
| Princes | 305.522 |
|   *see also* Royalty | |
| Princesses | 305.522 |
|   *see also* Royalty | |
| Princeton (B.C.) | T2—711 5 |
| Principal components analysis | 519.535 4 |
| Principals (Criminal law) | 345.03 |
| Principals (School) | |
|   biography | 371.200 92 |
|   public control | 379.157 |
|   role and function | 371.201 2 |
| Print making | |
|   graphic arts | 760 |
| Print media | |
|   journalism | 070.17 |
|   sociology | 302.232 |
| Print specimens | 686.224 |
| Printed advertising | 659.132 |
| Printed books | 094 |
| Printed circuits | 621.381 531 |
| Printed music | 780 |
|   treatises | 780.263 |
| Printers | 686.209 2 |
| Printers (Equipment) | |
|   computer science | 004.77 |
|     engineering | 621.398 7 |
|   manufacturing technology | 681.62 |
| Printing | 686.2 |
|   photography | 771.44 |
|   textile arts | 746.62 |
|   textiles | 667.38 |
| Printing apparatus | |
|   photography | 771.44 |
| Printing ink | 667.5 |
| Printing presses | |
|   manufacturing technology | 681.62 |
| Printing solutions | |
|   photography | 771.54 |

Printing telegraphy 384.14
  wireless 384.524
  *see also* Telegraphy
Printmakers 769.92
  *see Manual at* 769.9
Prints
  arts 769
  cataloging 025.347 1
  library treatment 025.177 1
Prion diseases
  medicine 616.83
    *see also* Nervous system
      diseases — humans
Prions (Subviral organisms) 579.29
Priories
  architecture 726.7
  church history 271
  religious significance of
    buildings 246.97
Pripet Marshes (Belarus and
  Ukraine) T2—478
Prisms 535.420 284
  geometry 516.156
  manufacturing technology 681.42
Prison administration 365.068
  public administration 353.39
Prison administrators 365.92
Prison camps 365.34
  military 365.48
  *see also* Penal institutions
Prison chaplaincy 206.1
  Christianity 259.5
Prison discipline 365.643
  law 344.035 643
Prison farms 365.34
  *see also* Penal institutions
Prison libraries 027.665
  administration 025.197 665
  collection development 025.218 766 5
Prison life 365.6
Prison psychology 155.962
Prison reform 365.7
Prison security 365.641
Prisoner discharge 365.647
Prisoner-of-war camps 355.71
  Algerian Revolution 965.046 7
  American Revolution 973.371
    American 973.372
    British 973.371
  Chaco War 989.207 167
  Civil War (England) 942.062 7
  Civil War (Spain) 946.081 7

Prisoner-of-war camps (continued)
  Civil War (United States) 973.771
    Confederate States of
      America 973.771
    United States 973.772
  Crimean War 947.073 87
  Falkland Islands War 997.110 247
  Franco-German War 943.082 7
  Hundred Years' War 944.025 7
  Indo-Pakistan War, 1971 954.920 517
  Indochinese War 959.704 17
  Iraq War, 2003– 956.704 437
  Iraqi-Iranian Conflict 955.054 27
  Korean War 951.904 27
  living conditions 355.129 6
  Napoleonic Wars 940.277
  Persian Gulf War, 1991 956.704 427
  South African War 968.048 7
  Thirty Years' War 940.247
  Vietnamese War 959.704 37
  War of the Pacific 983.061 67
  World War I 940.472
  World War II 940.547 2
Prisoner release 365.647
Prisoners (Convicts) 365.6
  T1—086 927
  labor economics 331.51
  legal status 344.035 6
Prisoner's base 796.14
Prisoners exchange
  World War I 940.473
  World War II 940.547 3
Prisoners of war 355.113
  Algerian Revolution 965.046 7
  American Revolution 973.371
  Chaco War 989.207 167
  Civil War (England) 942.062 7
  Civil War (Spain) 946.081 7
  Civil War (United States) 973.771
  Crimean War 947.073 87
  Falkland Islands War 997.110 247
  Franco-German War 943.082 7
  Hundred Years' War 944.025 7
  Indo-Pakistan War, 1971 954.920 517
  Indochinese War 959.704 17
  Iraq War, 2003– 956.704 437
  Iraqi-Iranian Conflict 955.054 27
  Korean War 951.904 27
  labor economics 331.51
  law 341.65
  military operations 355.41
  Napoleonic Wars 940.277
  Persian Gulf War, 1991 956.704 427

Prisoners of war (continued)
  prisons and camps 355.71
    living conditions 355.129 6
  service status 355.113
  South African War 968.048 7
  Thirty Years' War 940.247
  Vietnamese War 959.704 37
  war customs 399
  War of the Pacific 983.061 67
  World War I 940.472
  World War II 940.547 2
Prisons 365
  *see also* Penal institutions
Privacy 323.448
  civil right 323.448
  law 342.085 8
Private accounting 657.63
Private airplanes
  engineering 629.133 340 422
  piloting 629.132 521 7
Private banks 332.123
Private bills
  enactment 328.378
Private carriers 388.041
  truck 388.324 3
  *see also* Freight services;
    Passenger services
Private colleges 378.04
  *see also* Higher education
Private companies 338.7
  law 346.066 8
  *see also* Business enterprises
Private detective services 363.289
Private duty nursing 610.732
Private education 371.02
  law 344.072
  *see also* Private schools
Private enterprise 338.61
Private international law 340.9
  *see Manual at* 340.9
Private investment 332.6
  economics 332.6
  international 332.673
Private investors 332.6
  economics 332.6
  international 332.673
Private land 333.3
  landscape architecture 712.6
  *see also* Land
Private law 346
Private libraries 027.1
  catalogs 017.2
Private parks
  landscape architecture 712.6

Private police services 363.289
Private presses
  bibliographies of publications 011.55
Private property
  land economics 333.3
  *see also* Land tenure
Private publishers 070.593
Private schools 371.02
  adult education 374
    public support 379.326
  finance 371.206
    law 344.076
  higher education 378.04
    public support 379.324
  law 344.072
  preschool education
    public support 379.322 2
  primary education 372.104 22
    public support 379.322
  public policy 379.3
  public support 379.32
  secondary education 373.222
    public support 379.323
  special education 371.9
    public support 379.328
  *see Manual at* 371 vs. 353.8,
    371.2, 379
Private television 384.550 65
Private universities 378.04
  *see also* Higher education
Private welfare services 361.7
  *see also* Welfare services
Privateering
  naval operations 359.4
  *see also* Naval operations
Privatization 338.925
Privets 635.933 87
  botany 583.87
  floriculture 635.933 87
Privileges (Military awards) 355.134
Privileges of chief executives
  public administration 352.235
Privileges of diplomats 327.2
Privileges of legislators 328.347
Prize contests
  advertising 659.197 901 34
  sales promotion 658.82
  use in advertising 659.17
Prize law 343.096
  law of nations 341.63
Prizes T1—079
  research 001.44

| | |
|---|---|
| Pro-choice movement | 363.46 |
|   law | 342.087 8 |
|   *see also* Abortion | |
| Pro-life movement | 363.46 |
|   law | 342.085 |
|   *see also* Abortion | |
| Probabilistic logic | 511.318 |
|   mathematical logic | 511.318 |
|   philosophical logic | 160.119 88 |
| Probabilistic methods | 518.28 |
| Probabilistic number theory | 512.76 |
| Probabilities | 519.2 |
|   epistemology | 121.63 |
|   gambling | 795.015 192 |
|   insurance | 368.01 |
|   management decision making | 658.403 4 |
|   primary education | 372.79 |
|   *see Manual at* 795.015192 vs. | |
|     519.27 | |
| Probability calculus | 519.2 |
| Probability distribution | 519.24 |
| Probability theory | 519.2 |
| Probate law | 346.052 |
| Probation | 364.63 |
|   law | 345.077 |
|   penology | 364.63 |
|   public administration | 353.39 |
| Probation after death | 236.4 |
| Probation of teachers | 371.144 |
| Problem employees | |
|   personnel management | 658.304 5 |
| Problem of few bodies | 530.14 |
| Problem of *n* bodies | 530.144 |
|   astronomy | 521 |
| Problem of three bodies | 530.14 |
|   astronomy | 521 |
| Problem soils | |
|   floriculture | 635.955 |
| Problem solving | 153.43 |
|   artificial intelligence | 006.333 |
|   educational psychology | 370.152 4 |
|   executive management | 658.403 |
|   psychology | 153.43 |
| Problem students | 371.93 |
| Problems | |
|   study and teaching | T1—076 |
| Proboscidea | 599.67 |
|   paleozoology | 569.67 |
| Proboscis worms | 592.32 |
| Procaryotes | 579.3 |
| Procedural rights | 347.05 |
|   military | 343.014 3 |
|   public administration | 352.88 |
| Procedure (Law) | 347.05 |

| | |
|---|---|
| Procellariiformes | 598.42 |
|   paleozoology | 568.4 |
| Process | |
|   philosophy of nature | 116 |
| Process analysis | |
|   production management | 658.5 |
| Process control | 003.5 |
| | T1—011 5 |
|   chemical engineering | 660.281 5 |
|   production management | 658.5 |
| Process design | |
|   chemical engineering | 660.281 2 |
| Process management | |
|   systems programs | 005.434 |
| Process metallurgy | 669 |
| Process philosophy | 146.7 |
| Process research | |
|   production management | 658.577 |
| Process serving | 347.072 |
| Process theology | 230.046 |
| Processed cheese | 641.373 58 |
|   cooking | 641.673 58 |
|   food | 641.373 58 |
|   manufacturing | 637.358 |
| Processing (Archives) | 025.341 4 |
| Processing (Libraries) | 025.02 |
| Processing centers | |
|   library operations | 025.02 |
| Processing modes | |
|   computer science | 004.3 |
| | T1—028 543 |
|     communications | 004.618 |
|       programming | 005.712 7 |
|       programs | 005.713 7 |
|     graphics programming | 006.677 |
|     graphics programs | 006.687 |
|     interfacing | |
|       programming | 005.712 7 |
|       programs | 005.713 7 |
|     multimedia-systems | |
|       programming | 006.777 |
|     multimedia-systems | |
|       programs | 006.787 |
|     operating systems | 005.447 |
|       programming | 005.27 |
|       programs | 005.37 |
|   *see Manual at* 004.1 vs. | |
|     004.3 | |
| Processions | 394.5 |
|   customs | 394.5 |
|   performing arts | 791.6 |
|   religious rites | 203.8 |
|     Christianity | 265.9 |

Processors
  computer hardware — 004
    engineering — 621.39
    *see Manual at* 004.1
  programming-language
    translators — 005.45
Prochlorales — 579.39
Proconsular Africa — T2—397 3
Procrastination — 179.8
  religion — 205.698
Proctology — 616.35
Procurators fiscal — 345.411 01
Procurement — 658.72
  — T1—068 7
  air forces — 358.416 212
  armed forces — 355.621 2
  naval forces — 359.621 2
  public administration — 352.53
    specific forms of property — 352.55–.57
Procurement of capital — 658.152 2
  — T1—068 1
Procyon — 599.763 2
Procyonidae — 599.763
Produce (Agricultural products) — 338.17
  *see also* Agricultural products
Produce trade — 381.41
Producer brands
  sales promotion — 658.827
Producer gas — 665.772
Producers' cooperatives — 334.6
  management — 658.87
Product accounts
  (Macroeconomics) — 339.31
Product catalogs — 338.020 29
  — T1—029
  manufacturing industries — 338.402 9
  *see Manual at* T1—025 vs.
    T1—029
Product comparisons — T1—029
Product control — 363.19
  production management — 658.56
  *see also* Product safety
Product counterfeiting — 364.166 8
  law — 345.026 68
Product design
  management — 658.575 2
Product development
  management — 658.575
Product directories — 338.020 29
  — T1—029
  manufacturing industries — 338.402 9
  *see Manual at* T1—025 vs.
    T1—029
Product evaluation — 381.33

Product evaluations — T1—029
Product liability — 346.038
  production management — 658.56
Product liability insurance — 368.562
Product life cycle
  management — 658.5
Product listings — T1—029
Product management — 658.5
  marketing — 658.8
  production — 658.5
Product planning — 658.503 8
Product recall — 363.19
  law — 344.042
  product safety — 363.19
  production management — 658.56
Product returns
  marketing management — 658.812
Product safety — 363.19
  criminology — 364.142
    criminal law — 345.024 2
  law — 344.042
  production management — 658.56
  social services — 363.19
    public administration — 353.99
Product servicing
  marketing management — 658.812
Product specifications
  production management — 658.562
Product standards
  production management — 658.562
Production (Performing arts) — 792.023 2
  ballet — 792.84
  motion pictures — 791.430 232
  musical plays — 792.64
  opera — 792.54
  radio — 791.440 232
  stage — 792.023 2
  television — 791.450 232
Production capacity
  secondary industries — 338.45
Production control
  management — 658.5
Production controls (Economic
  programs) — 338.9
  law — 343.075
  public administration — 354.28
Production cooperatives — 334.6
Production economics — 338
Production efficiency — 338.06
  agricultural industries — 338.16
  economics — 338.06
  mineral industries — 338.26

Production efficiency (continued)
  promotion of
    management    658.515
    secondary industries    338.45
Production engineering    670
Production forecasting    338.544
Production forecasts    338.544 3
Production illustration    604.242
Production management    658.5
             T1—068 5
Production planning
  management    658.503
Production resources    338.09
Production systems
  sociology    306.34
Productivity
  agricultural industries    338.16
  labor economics    331.118
  mineral industries    338.26
  production economics    338.06
  production management
    public administration    352.375
  promotion of
    personnel management    658.314
      executives    658.407 14
      public administration    352.66
    production management    658.515
  secondary industries    338.45
Products    338.02
  agricultural industries    338.17
  *see also* Agricultural products
  commerce    381
    public administration    354.73
  economics    338.02
  liability    346.038
  mineral industries    338.27
    commerce    381.42
    production economics    338.27
  secondary industries    338.4
    commerce    381.45
    production economics    338.4
Products research
  technology    607.2
Profanity    179.5
  customs    394
  ethics    179.5
  religion    205.695
    *see also* Blasphemy
  *see also* Ethical problems
Profession of faith
  Islam    297.34
Professional cinematography    777

Professional corporations    338.761
  accounting    657.834
  law    346.066 8
  mergers    338.836 1
  restrictive practices    338.826 1
Professional education    378.013
           T1—071 1
  *see also* Higher education
Professional employees    331.71
  *see also* Professional workers
Professional ethics    174
  religion    205.64
  *see also* Ethical problems
Professional fees
  labor economics    331.216 6
Professional liability    346.033
Professional liability insurance    368.564
Professional licensing    354.93
  law    344.017
Professional nurses    610.730 92
  role and function    610.730 692
Professional relationships    T1—023
  economics    331.7
  ethics    174
    *see also* Ethical problems
Professional schools    378.155
  architecture    727.4
  area planning    711.57
Professional services    338.46
Professional sports    796.044
  law    344.099
  *see Manual at* 796.08 vs.
    796.04
Professional videography    777
Professional workers    331.71
           T1—086 22
  labor economics    331.71
  personnel management    658.304 4
  public administration    354.93
  social class    305.553
  training
    personnel management    658.312 45
Professional writing    808.066
Professionals    T1—086 22
  *see also* Professional workers
Professions    331.71
           T1—023
Professors    378.12
Profit and loss statements
  financial management    658.151 2
Profit sharing    331.216 47
  labor economics    331.216 47
  personnel management    658.322 5

Profits                                   338.516
  accounting                    657.7
  agricultural industries       338.13
  financial management          658.155
  income distribution           339.21
  increasing
    financial management   658.155 4
  mineral industries            338.23
  production economics          338.516
  secondary industries          338.43
  taxes                         336.243
    law                 343.052 44
    public administration   352.44
Progeny                                   306.874
                T1—085 4

Prognosis
  medicine                      616.075
Progoneata                                595.6
  paleozoology                  565.6
Program auditing                          658.401 3
  public administration         352.43
Program audits                            658.401 3
  public administration         352.439
Program design                            005.12
Program documentation
  preparation                   005.15
  text                          005.3
Program evaluation techniques
  (Network analysis)            658.403 2
Program maintenance                       005.16
Program music                             781.56
Program notes (Music)                     780.15
Program reliability                       005
Program verification                      005.14
Programmable calculators                  510.285 41
  *see Manual at* 004.1
Programmable controllers
  control engineering           629.895
Programmed instruction                    371.394 4
                T1—07
  electronic                    371.334
  adult education               374.26
Programming
  dramatic performances         792.023 6
    motion pictures     791.430 236
    radio               791.440 236
    stage               792.023 6
    television          791.450 236
Programming (Mathematics)                 519.7
Programming computers                     005.1
                T1—028 551
  *see also* Computer
    programming

Programming language
  translators                   005.45
Programming languages                     005.13
  computer graphics             006.663
Programs (Broadcasting)                   384.544 3
  communications                384.544 3
  radiobroadcasting             384.544 3
    communications      384.544 3
    performing arts     791.44
  television broadcasting       384.553 2
    communications      384.553 2
    performing arts     791.45
Programs (Computers)                      005.3
                T1—028 553
  *see also* Computer programs
Programs (Party platforms)                324.23
Programs (Social action)                  361.25
  public administration         351
Progreso (Guatemala :
  Dept.)                        T2—728 153
Progress                                  303.44
Progressions                              515.24
Progressive Conservative Party of
  Canada                        324.271 04
Progressive jazz                          781.655
Progressive National Baptist
  Convention                    286.135
  *see also* Baptists
Progressive Party (U.S. : 1912)           324.273 27
Progressive Party (U.S. : 1924)           324.273 27
Progressive Party (U.S. : 1948)           324.273 7
Progressive rock                          781.66
Progressive taxation                      336.293
Prohibited books                          098.1
Prohibition Party (U.S.)                   324.273 8
Prohibitive tariffs                       382.73
  *see also* Customs (Tariff)
Project Apollo                            629.454
Project Gemini                            629.454
Project management                        658.404
  public administration         352.365
Project Mariner                           629.435 4
Project Mercury                           629.454
Project method of teaching                371.36
Project Ranger                            629.435 3
Projectiles                               531.55
  military engineering          623.451
  physics                       531.55
Projection welding                        671.521 3
Projections
  technical drawing             604.245
Projective geometry                       516.5
Projective techniques
  psychological testing         155.284

Projectors
  manufacturing technology    681.418
Prokaryotes    579.3
  paleontology    561.91
Prolapse of uterus
  gynecology    618.144
    *see also* Female genital
      diseases — humans
Proletarian dictatorship    321.92
Proletariat    305.562
     T1—086 23
  *see also* Working class
Promethium
  chemistry    546.414
Promiscuity
  ethics    176.4
    *see also* Sexual relations —
      ethics
Promissory notes    332.77
  law    346.096
Promotion (Personnel)
  armed forces    355.112
  personal success    650.14
  personnel management    658.314 24
  public administration    352.66
Promotion (Students)    371.283
Pronghorn    599.639
  conservation technology    639.979 639
  resource economics    333.959 639
Pronouncing dictionaries    413.1
  specific languages    T4—31
Pronouns    415.55
  specific languages    T4—555
Pronunciation    414
  applied linguistics    418
    specific languages    T4—813
    specific subjects    T1—014
  linguistics    414
    specific languages    T4—152
  primary education    372.622
  singing    783.043
  specialized dictionaries    413.1
    specific languages    T4—31
Proof theory
  mathematical logic    511.36
Proofreading    808.027
  printing    686.225 5
Proofs of God's existence    212.1
Propaganda    303.375
  American Revolution    973.388
  armed services    355.34
    *see also* Unconventional
      warfare
  Civil War (United States)    973.788

Propaganda (continued)
  international politics    327.14
  political parties    324.23
  political science    320.014
  social control    303.375
  World War I    940.488
  World War II    940.548 8
Propagation of sound    534.2
Propane    665.773
Propellants    662.26
  aircraft    629.134 351
  military explosives    623.452 6
Propeller-driven airplanes    387.733 43
  engineering    629.133 343
  military engineering    623.746 042
  transportation services    387.733 43
    *see also* Aircraft
Propellers
  aircraft    629.134 36
  ships    623.873
Proper integrals    515.43
Proper of the mass    264.36
  music    782.323 5
    choral and mixed voices    782.532 35
    single voices    783.093 235
Property
  economic theory    330.17
  Holocaust, 1933–1945    940.531 813 2
  law    346.04
  sociology    306.32
Property damage insurance    368.1
Property insurance    368.1
  commercial    368.12
Property law    346.04
Property loss insurance    368.1
Property management
  public administration    352.5
Property offenses    364.16
  law    345.026
Property rights    323.46
  law    346.042
Property risks    368.06
Property tax    336.22
  law    343.054
  public administration    352.44
Prophecies    133.3
  occultism    133.3
  religion    203.2
    Biblical    220.15
    eschatological    202.3
      Christianity    236
      Judaism    296.33

Prophecies
  religion (continued)
    messianic
      Christianity    232.12
      Judaism    296.336
Prophecy (Concept)    202.117
  Christianity    231.745
    spiritual gift    234.13
  in Bible    220.15
  Islam    297.211 5
  Judaism    296.311 55
Prophetic books (Old Testament)    224
Prophetic books
  (Pseudepigrapha)    229.913
Prophetic message
  Bible    220.15
Prophetic office of Jesus Christ    232.8
Prophets    200.92
  biography    200.92
  Islam    297.246
  role and function    206.1
  *see Manual at* 200.92 and
    201–209, 292–299
Prophets (Biblical books)    224
Prophylaxis
  public health    614.44
Propjet engines
  aircraft    629.134 353 2
Proportion (Architecture)
  horizontal plane    729.23
  vertical plane    729.13
Proportion (Mathematics)    512.924
  algebra    512.924
  arithmetic    513.24
Proportional counters
  nuclear physics    539.773
Proportional representation    328.334 7
  law    342.053
Proportional taxation    336.293
Propositional calculus    511.3
  mathematical logic    511.3
  philosophical logic    160
Propositions
  philosophical logic    160
Proprietary libraries    027.2
Proprietor's income
  macroeconomics    339.21
Proprietorships    338.72
  accounting    657.91
  economics    338.72
  income tax    336.242 3
    law    343.052 68
  law    346.065

Proprietorships (continued)
  management    658.041
    initiation    658.114 1
  *see Manual at* 658.04 vs.
    658.114, 658.402
  taxes    336.207
  law    343.068
Proprioceptive organs
  human anatomy    611.8
  human physiology    612.88
Proprioceptive perception
  psychology    152.188 2
Propulsion systems    621.4
  air-cushion vehicles    629.314
  spacecraft    629.475
  unmanned spacecraft    629.465
Prose literature    808.888
  history and criticism    809.988
  specific literatures    T3B—808
    individual authors    T3A—8
Prose poems    808.81
  history and criticism    809.1
  specific literatures    T3B—1
    individual authors    T3A—1
Prosecution    345.050 42
Proselytizing
  Judaism    296.69
Prosencephalon
  human physiology    612.825
  medicine    616.8
Prosimii    599.83
  paleozoology    569.83
Prosobranchia    594.32
  paleozoology    564.32
Prosodic analysis (Linguistics)    414.6
  specific languages    T4—16
Prosody    808.1
  linguistics    414.6
    specific languages    T4—16
Prospecting    622.1
Prospectors    622.109 2
Prosperity
  economics    338.542
Prostate    573.658
  biology    573.658
  human anatomy    611.63
  human physiology    612.616
  medicine    616.65
  *see also* Male genital system
Prostate cancer
  incidence    614.599 946 3
  medicine    616.994 63
  *see also* Cancer — humans

Prostatic diseases
  medicine — 616.65
   *see also* Male genital
    diseases — humans
Prostheses — 617.9
Prosthetic dentistry — 617.69
Prosthetic devices
  manufacturing technology — 681.761
Prosthetic ophthalmology — 617.79
Prosthodontics — 617.69
Prostitutes — 306.74
Prostitution — 306.74
  criminology — 364.153 4
   criminal law — 345.025 34
  ethics — 176.5
   *see also* Sexual relations —
    ethics
  public control — 363.44
   law — 344.054 4
    public administration — 353.37
  sociology — 306.74
Protacanthopterygii — 597.5
Protactinium
  chemistry — 546.424
  metallurgy — 669.292 4
Proteales — 583.89
Proteas — 635.933 89
  botany — 583.89
  floriculture — 635.933 89
Proteases — 572.76
  *see also* Enzymes
Protection of natural resources — 333.72
Protectionism — 382.73
Protective adaptation — 578.47
  animals — 591.47
  plants — 581.47
Protective barriers
  road engineering — 625.795
Protective behavior (Animals) — 591.566
Protective clothing — 391.48
  commercial technology — 687.162
  customs — 391.48
  *see also* Clothing
Protective coatings — 667.9
Protective coloration (Biology) — 578.47
  animals — 591.472
  plants — 581.47
Protective construction
  military engineering — 623.38
Protective gloves
  manufacturing technology — 685.43
Protective headwear — 391.43
  *see also* Headwear

Protective tariffs — 382.73
  *see also* Customs (Tariff)
Protectorates — 321.08
  *see also* Semisovereign states
Protein cooking — 641.563 8
Protein deficiency — 571.946
Protein plastics — 668.43
Proteins — 572.6
  applied nutrition — 613.282
   animal husbandry — 636.085 22
  biochemistry — 572.6
   humans — 612.015 75
  chemistry — 547.7
  metabolic disorders — 571.946
   medicine — 616.399 5
    *see also* Digestive system
     diseases — humans
  metabolism
   human physiology — 612.398
Proteinuria
  medicine — 616.63
   *see also* Urologic diseases —
    humans
Proteolytic enzymes — 572.76
  *see also* Enzymes
Proterozoic era — 551.715
  geology — 551.715
  paleontology — 560.171 5
Protest — 303.6
  social action — 361.23
Protest groups — 322.4
Protest music — 781.592
Protest stoppages — 331.892
  *see also* Strikes (Work
   stoppages)
Protestant art
  religious significance — 246.4
Protestant churches — 280.4
  *see also* Protestantism
Protestant men
  religious associations — 267.240 4
Protestant Methodists — 287.53
  *see also* Methodist Church
Protestant People's Party of
  Switzerland — 324.249 408 2
Protestant regions — T2—176 14
Protestant women
  religious associations — 267.440 4
Protestant young adults
  religious associations — 267.620 4
Protestantism — 280.4
  church law — 262.980 4
  conversion to — 248.244
  doctrines — 230.044

Protestantism (continued)

| | |
|---|---|
| guides to Christian life | 248.480 4 |
| missions | 266 |
| moral theology | 241.040 4 |
| public worship | 264 |
| religious associations | 267.180 4 |
| religious education | 268.804 |
| seminaries | 230.071 1 |
| theology | 230.044 |

Protestants

| | |
|---|---|
| biography | 280.409 2 |
| Protista | 579 |

*see also* Microorganisms

| | |
|---|---|
| Proto-Malay languages | 499.28 |
| | T6—992 8 |
| Proto-Nordic language | 439.5 |
| | T6—395 |
| Protobranchia | 594.4 |
| Protoceratops | 567.915 |
| Protocol (Diplomacy) | 327.2 |

Protocols (Standards)

| | |
|---|---|
| communications engineering | 621.382 12 |
| computer communications | 004.62 |
| interfacing | 004.62 |

Protocols (Treaties)

| | |
|---|---|
| law of nations | 341.37 |
| texts | 341.026 |
| Protolepidodendrales | 561.79 |
| Protomycetales | 579.562 |
| Proton spin tomography | 616.075 48 |
| Protons | 539.721 23 |
| Protophytes | 579 |
| Protoplasm | 571.6 |
| Prototheria | 599.29 |
| paleozoology | 569.29 |
| Protozoa | 579.4 |
| medical microbiology | 616.936 01 |
| paleontology | 561.99 |
| Protozoan diseases | 571.994 |

*see also* Protozoan infections

| | |
|---|---|
| Protozoan infections | 571.994 |
| agriculture | 632.3 |
| animals | 571.994 11 |
| veterinary medicine | 636.089 693 6 |
| biology | 571.994 |
| humans | 362.196 936 |
| incidence | 614.53 |
| medicine | 616.936 |
| social services | 362.196 936 |
| plants | 571.994 12 |
| agriculture | 632.3 |

*see also* Communicable
   diseases

| | |
|---|---|
| Protozoologists | 579.409 2 |

| | |
|---|---|
| Protozoology | 579.4 |
| medicine | 616.936 01 |
| paleontology | 561.99 |
| Protura | 595.722 |
| Provability logic | 511.314 |

Provençal dialect (Occitan

| | |
|---|---|
| language) | 449.709 449 |
| | T6—491 |
| Provençal language | 449 |
| | T6—491 |
| Provençal literature | 849 |
| Provence (France) | T2—449 |

Provence-Alpes-Côte

| | |
|---|---|
| d'Azur (France) | T2—449 |

Provence-Côte d'Azur

| | |
|---|---|
| (France) | T2—449 |
| Proverbs | 398.9 |
| Proverbs (Biblical book) | 223.7 |
| Providence (R.I.) | T2—745 2 |
| Providence County (R.I.) | T2—745 1 |
| Providence of God | 214.8 |
| Christianity | 231.5 |
| comparative religion | 202.117 |
| Judaism | 296.311 4 |
| philosophy of religion | 214.8 |
| Provident societies | 334.7 |
| economics | 334.7 |
| insurance | 368.3 |
| Province of Canada | 971.04 |
| | T2—71 |
| Provinces | 320.83 |
| local government units | 320.83 |

*see also* Counties

| | |
|---|---|
| public administration | 352.14 |
| support and control | 353.33 |

*see Manual at* 351.3–.9
   vs. 352.13–.19; *also at*
   352.13 vs. 352.15

| | |
|---|---|
| state-level units | 321.023 |

*see also* States (Members of
   federations)

| | |
|---|---|
| Provincial administration | 352.14 |

*see also* Provinces — public
   administration

| | |
|---|---|
| Provincial banks | 332.122 4 |
| Provincial-local relations | 320.404 9 |
| law | 342.042 |
| public administration | 353.334 |

Provincial planning

| | |
|---|---|
| civic art | 711.3 |
| economics | 338.9 |

| | |
|---|---|
| Provincial taxation | 336.201 3 |
| law | 343.043 |
| public administration | 352.442 13 |
| public finance | 336.201 3 |
| Provincialisms | |
| linguistics | 417.2 |
| specific languages | T4—7 |
| Provisional courts | 342.066 4 |
| Prowers County (Colo.) | T2—788 98 |
| Proximity spaces | 514.323 |
| Proxy | |
| law | 346.066 6 |
| Prudence | 179.9 |
| *see also* Virtues | |
| Pruning | 631.542 |
| equipment manufacturing | |
| technology | 681.763 1 |
| fruit crops | 634.044 2 |
| horticulture | 635.044 2 |
| ornamental arboriculture | 635.977 |
| ornamental plants | 635.915 42 |
| Pruntrut (Switzerland : | |
| Bezirk) | T2—494 366 |
| Prussia (Kingdom) | 943.07 |
| | T2—43 |
| Prussia, East (Poland and | |
| Russia) | T2—438 32 |
| Poland | T2—438 32 |
| Russia | T2—472 4 |
| Prussia, West (Poland) | T2—438 2 |
| Prussian language, Old | 491.91 |
| | T6—919 1 |
| Prussian literature, Old | 891.91 |
| Prussian Saxony | T2—431 8 |
| Przemyśl (Poland : | |
| Voivodeship) | T2—438 66 |
| Przewalski's horse | 599.665 5 |
| Psalms | 223.2 |
| music | 782.294 |
| choral and mixed voices | 782.529 4 |
| single voices | 783.092 94 |
| Psalteries | 787.75 |
| *see also* Stringed instruments | |
| Psalters | 264.15 |
| Anglican | 264.030 15 |
| texts | 264.038 |
| Roman Catholic | 264.020 15 |
| texts | 264.028 |
| PSAT (Assessment test) | 378.166 2 |
| Pselaphidae | 595.764 2 |
| Pseudemys | 597.925 94 |
| Pseudepigrapha | 229.9 |
| Pseudo-Demetrius I | |
| Russian history | 947.045 |
| Pseudo-Demetrius II | |
| Russian history | 947.045 |
| Pseudo gospels | 229.8 |
| Pseudoanalytic functions | 515.98 |
| Pseudoborniales | 561.72 |
| Pseudomonas | 579.332 |
| Pseudomonas infections | |
| incidence | 614.57 |
| medicine | 616.92 |
| *see also* Communicable | |
| diseases — humans | |
| Pseudomorphism | |
| crystallography | 548.3 |
| Pseudonymous works | |
| bibliographies | 014 |
| Pseudopoda | 571.67 |
| Pseudoscorpiones | 595.47 |
| Psi phenomena | 133.8 |
| Psilophytales | 561.74 |
| Psilopsida | 587.4 |
| paleobotany | 561.74 |
| Psilotales | 587.4 |
| paleobotany | 561.74 |
| Psittaciformes | 598.71 |
| paleozoology | 568.7 |
| Psittacosis | |
| animals | |
| veterinary medicine | 636.686 539 |
| humans | |
| incidence | 614.566 |
| medicine | 616.958 |
| *see also* Communicable | |
| diseases — humans | |
| Pskov (Russia : Oblast) | T2—472 3 |
| Pskovskaia oblast' (Russia) | T2—472 3 |
| Psocoptera | 595.732 |
| Psophiidae | 598.32 |
| Psoriasis | |
| medicine | 616.526 |
| Psychedelic drugs | |
| pharmacokinetics | 615.788 3 |
| Psychedelics abuse | 362.294 |
| medicine | 616.863 4 |
| personal health | 613.83 |
| social welfare | 362.294 |
| *see also* Substance abuse | |
| Psychiatric clinics | 362.22 |
| *see also* Mental health services | |
| Psychiatric disorders | |
| medicine | 616.89 |
| *see also* Mental disorders | |
| Psychiatric hospitals | 362.21 |
| architecture | 725.52 |
| *see also* Mental health services | |

| | |
|---|---|
| Psychiatric insurance | 368.382 5 |
| Psychiatric nursing | 616.890 231 |
| Psychiatric social work | 362.204 25 |
| Psychiatrists | |
|   law | 344.041 2 |
|   malpractice | 344.041 21 |
| Psychiatry | 616.89 |
|   geriatrics | 618.976 89 |
|   pediatrics | 618.928 9 |
|   *see Manual at* 616.89 vs. | |
|     150.195 | |
| Psychic communication | 133.8 |
| Psychic gifts | 133.8 |
| Psychic healing | |
|   medicine | 615.852 8 |
| Psychic messages | 133.93 |
| Psychic phenomena | 133.8 |
| Psychic surgery | |
|   medicine | 615.852 8 |
| Psychic talents | 133.8 |
| Psychic therapy | |
|   medicine | 615.852 8 |
| Psychoanalysis | 150.195 |
|   psychiatry | 616.891 7 |
|   psychology | 150.195 |
|   *see Manual at* 616.89 vs. | |
|     150.195 | |
| Psychobiology | 573.8 |
|   humans | 612.8 |
| Psychodidae | 595.772 |
| Psychodrama | |
|   psychiatry | 616.891 523 |
| Psychokinesis | 133.88 |
| Psycholinguistics | 401.9 |
|   specific languages | T4—019 |
| Psychological causes of war | 355.027 5 |
|   World War I | 940.311 4 |
|   World War II | 940.531 14 |
| Psychological characteristics | |
|   influence on crime | 364.24 |
| Psychological fiction | 808.838 3 |
|   history and criticism | 809.383 |
|   specific literatures | T3B—308 3 |
|     individual authors | T3A—3 |
| Psychological principles | T1—019 |
| Psychological systems | 150.19 |
|   *see Manual at* 152–158 vs. | |
|     150.19 | |

| | | |
|---|---|---|
| Psychological themes | | |
|   arts | T3C—353 | |
|   literature | | 808.803 53 |
|     history and criticism | | 809.933 53 |
|     specific literatures | T3B—080 353 | |
|     history and | | |
|      criticism | T3B—093 53 | |
| Psychological therapies | | |
|   medicine | | 615.851 |
| Psychological warfare | | 355.343 4 |
|   *see also* Unconventional | | |
|     warfare | | |
| Psychologists | | 150.92 |
| Psychology | | 150 |
| | T1—019 | |
|   information systems | | 025.061 5 |
|   *see Manual at* 302–307 vs. 150, | | |
|     T1—019 | | |
| Psychology (Animals) | | 591.5 |
| Psychology and religion | | 201.615 |
|   Christianity | | 261.515 |
|   Islam | | 297.261 |
|   Judaism | | 296.371 |
| Psychology of religion | | 200.19 |
| Psychometrics | | 150.151 95 |
|   tests | | 150.287 |
| Psychopathic personality | | |
|   medicine | | 616.858 2 |
|   *see also* Mental disorders | | |
| Psychopathology | | 616.89 |
| Psychopharmacology | | 615.78 |
| Psychophysiology | | |
|   humans | | 612.8 |
| Psychoses | | 362.26 |
|   medicine | | 616.89 |
|   *see also* Mental disorders | | |
|   puerperal diseases | | |
|     medicine | | 618.76 |
|   social welfare | | 362.26 |
| Psychosexual disorders | | |
|   medicine | | 616.858 3 |
| Psychosomatic medicine | | 616.08 |
| Psychosurgery | | 617.481 |
| Psychotherapy | | |
|   psychiatry | | 616.891 4 |
| Psychotic disorders | | |
|   medicine | | 616.89 |
|   *see also* Mental disorders | | |
| Psychotropic drugs | | |
|   pharmacokinetics | | 615.788 |
| Psychrometrics | | |
|   air conditioning | | |
|     buildings | | 697.931 5 |

PT boats — 359.835 8
  design — 623.812 58
  engineering — 623.825 8
  naval equipment — 359.835 8
  naval units — 359.325 8
Ptarmigans — 598.633
Pteranodon — 567.918
Pteridophyta — 587
  paleobotany — 561.7
Pteridospermales — 561.595
Pterobranchia — 593.99
  paleozoology — 563.99
Pteroclididae — 598.65
Pterodactylus — 567.918
Pteromedusae — 593.55
Pterophyllum — 597.74
Pteropoda — 594.37
Pteropodidae — 599.49
Pterosauria — 567.918
Pterygota — 595.7
  paleozoology — 565.7
Ptilogonatidae — 598.853
Ptolemaic dynasty — 932.021
Puberty — 612.661
  customs — 392.14
  etiquette — 395.24
  human physiology — 612.661
  music — 781.583
Public accounting — 657.61
  law — 346.063
Public address systems
  engineering — 621.389 2
  office use — 651.79
Public administration — 351
  armed forces — 355.6
  ethics — 172.2
    *see also* Political ethics
  subordinate jurisdictions — 352.14
  support and control — 353.33
    *see Manual at* 351.3–.9
      vs. 352.13–.19; *also at*
      352.13 vs. 352.15
    *see Manual at* T1—068 vs.
      353–354; *also at* 320.9,
      320.4 vs. 351; *also at* 363
      vs. 344.02–.05, 353–354
Public administrators — 352.3
  biography — 351.092
  executive management — 352.3
  investigation
    public administration — 353.46
  law — 342.068
  role and function — 352.3

Public behavior
  customs — 390
  etiquette — 395.53
Public borrowing — 336.34
  *see also* Public debt
Public broadcasting — 384.54
  radio — 384.54
  television — 384.554
Public buildings
  architecture — 725
  interior decoration — 747.85
  law — 344.067 2
    public property — 343.025 6
  plant management — 352.56
  public works — 363
    public administration — 352.77
Public carriers — 388.041
  *see also* Common carriers
Public colleges — 378.05
  *see also* Higher education
Public contracts — 352.53
  law — 346.023
Public credit
  public finance — 336.34
Public debt — 336.34
  administration — 352.45
  law — 343.037
  macroeconomic policy — 339.523
  public finance — 336.34
Public defenders — 345.012 63
Public discussion
  literature — 808.853
    specific literatures — T3B— 503
    individual authors — T3A—5
  rhetoric — 808.53
Public education — 370
  financial management — 371.206
  government control — 379.15
  law — 344.071
  policy issues — 379
  public support — 379.11
    law — 344.076
  revenue sources — 379.13
  *see also* Education
Public employees — 352.63
  *see also* Government workers
Public enterprise (Organization of
  production) — 338.62
Public enterprises — 338.749
Public entertainment — 791
  ethics — 175
  music — 781.55

| | |
|---|---|
| Public expenditures | 336.39 |
| administration | 352.46 |
| law | 343.034 |
| macroeconomic policy | 339.522 |
| public finance | 336.39 |
| Public expenditures limitation | 336.39 |
| law | 343.034 |
| public finance | 336.39 |
| Public facilities | |
| safety | 363.1 |
| public administration | 353.97 |
| sanitation services | 363.729 |
| public administration | 353.94 |
| Public finance | 336 |
| accounting | 657.835 |
| administration | 352.4 |
| economics | 336 |
| law | 343.03 |
| *see Manual at* 332, 336 vs. 339 | |
| Public forests | 333.75 |
| economics | 333.75 |
| acquisition and disposal | 333.11 |
| *see also* Forest lands | |
| Public health | 362.1 |
| law | 344.04 |
| medicine | 614 |
| public administration | 353.6 |
| social welfare | 362.1 |
| Public health law | 344.04 |
| Public health nursing | 610.734 |
| Public health offenses | 364.142 |
| law | 345.024 2 |
| Public hearings | |
| legislative | 328.345 |
| law | 348.01 |
| *see Manual at* 300–330, 355–390 vs. 342–347, 352–354 | |
| nomination of officials | 351 |
| *see Manual at* 300, 320.6 vs. 352–354 | |
| public administration | 351 |
| Public housekeeping | 647 |
| Public housing | 363.585 |
| household management | 647.92 |
| law | 344.063 635 |
| *see also* Housing | |
| Public insolvency | 336.368 |
| Public international law | 341 |
| Public investigations | |
| official misconduct | 353.463 |
| Public investment | 332.672 52 |
| international | 332.673 12 |
| Public issues (Securities) | 332.632 |
| Public land sales | 333.16 |
| economics | 333.16 |
| law | 343.025 3 |
| Public lands | 333.1 |
| administration | 352.57 |
| economics | 333.1 |
| landscape architecture | 712.5 |
| law | 343.025 |
| revenue source | 336.12 |
| Public law | 342 |
| Public lending rights (Intellectual property) | 346.048 |
| Public liability insurance | 368.56 |
| Public libraries | 027.4 |
| administration | 025.197 4 |
| collection development | 025.218 74 |
| public administrative support | 353.73 |
| publications for | |
| bibliographies | 011.67 |
| use studies | 025.587 4 |
| Public library buildings | |
| architecture | 727.824 |
| Public life of Jesus Christ | 232.95 |
| Public lighting | 628.95 |
| Public limited companies | 338.749 |
| law | 346.066 8 |
| *see also* Corporations | |
| Public offerings (Securities) | 332.632 |
| corporate law | 346.066 2 |
| financial economics | 332.632 |
| financial management | 658.152 24 |
| public finance | 336.36 |
| Public opinion | 303.38 |
| Public order | |
| public administration | 353.3 |
| Public order offenses | 364.143 |
| law | 345.024 3 |
| Public ownership | |
| land economics | 333.1 |
| Public parks | 363.68 |
| *see also* Parks | |
| Public performances | 791 |
| ethics | 175 |
| Public policy | 320.6 |
| law | 342.041 |
| *see Manual at* 300, 320.6 vs. 352–354 | |
| Public preventive medicine | 613 |
| *see also* Preventive medicine | |
| Public property | |
| land economics | 333.1 |
| law | 343.02 |
| management | 352.5 |
| Public prosecutors | 345.012 62 |

Public radio   384.54
Public records   352.387
  archival treatment   025.171 4
  civil rights issues   323.448 3
  law   342.066 2
  public administration   352.387
Public relations   659.2
  armed forces   355.342
  arts   700.455 3
                 T3C—355 3
  libraries   021.7
  literature   808.803 553
    history and criticism   809.933 553
  local churches   254.4
  public administration   352.748
  religion   200
Public safety   363.1
Public safety offenses   364.142
  law   345.024 2
Public sanitation   363.72
  technology   628
  *see also* Sanitation
Public schools   371.01
  finance   379.11
   law   344.076
  law   344.071
  primary education   372.104 21
  secondary education   373.224
  *see Manual at* 371 vs. 353.8,
    371.2, 379
Public schools (Private schools)   371.02
  secondary education   373.222
Public service (Civil service)   352.63
Public service (Voluntarism)   361.37
  public administrative support   352.78
Public service workers   352.63
  *see also* Government workers
Public services
  libraries   025.5
  museums   069.1
           T1—075
Public speaking   808.51
  primary education   372.622
Public speeches
  literature   808.851
    history and criticism   809.51
    specific literatures   T3B—501
      individual authors   T3A—5
  rhetoric   808.51
Public spending   336.39
  *see also* Public expenditures
Public structures
  architecture   725

Public television   384.554
  *see also* Television
Public toilets   363.729 4
  technology   628.45
  *see also* Sanitation
Public transportation   388
  *see also* Transportation
Public transportation vehicles   388.34
  driving   629.283 3
  engineering   629.222 3
  transportation services   388.34
Public universities   378.05
  *see also* Higher education
Public utilities   363.6
  accounting   657.838
  area planning   711.7
  law   343.09
  public administration   354.728
    energy   354.428
  social services   363.6
  *see Manual at* 333.7–.9 vs.
    363.6; *also at* 363.5, 363.6,
    363.8 vs. 338
Public utility workers   363.609 2
Public welfare   361.6
  law   344.031 6
  *see also* Welfare services
Public works   363
  law   344.06
    public property   343.025 6
  public administration   352.77
  *see Manual at* 363 vs. 302–307,
    333.7, 570–590, 600
Public worship   203.8
  Buddhism   294.343 8
  Christianity   264
  flower arrangements   745.926
  Hinduism   294.538
  Islam   297.38
  Judaism   296.45
  music   782.3
    choral and mixed voices   782.53
    single voices   783.093
  *see also* Worship
Publicity   659
  public administration   352.748
Publishers   070.5
  biography   070.509 2
  business organizations   338.761 070 5
  journalism   070.5
  occupational ethics   174.907
  relations with authors   070.52
Publishers' catalogs   015

| | |
|---|---|
| Publishing | 070.5 |
|   accounting | 657.84 |
|   journalism | 070.5 |
|   law | 343.099 8 |
| Pubs | 647.95 |
|   *see also* Drinking places | |
| Puddings | 641.864 4 |
| Puddling (Furnace practice) | 669.141 4 |
| Puducherry (India) | T2—548 6 |
| Puebla (Mexico : State) | T2—724 8 |
| Pueblo County (Colo.) | T2—788 55 |
| Pueblo Indians | 978.900 497 4 |
| | T5—974 |
| Puerperal diseases | |
|   obstetrics | 618.7 |
| Puerperal infections | |
|   obstetrics | 618.74 |
| Puerperal perticemia | |
|   obstetrics | 618.74 |
| Puerperal pyemia | |
|   incidence | 614.545 |
|   obstetrics | 618.74 |
| Puerperal septicemia | |
|   incidence | 614.545 |
|   obstetrics | 618.74 |
| Puerperium | |
|   obstetrics | 618.6 |
| Puerto Plata (Dominican | |
|   Republic) | T2—729 358 |
| Puerto Rican campaign, 1898 | 973.893 5 |
| Puerto Rican literature | 860 |
| Puerto Ricans | 305.868 729 5 |
| | T5—687 295 |
| Puerto Rico | 972.95 |
| | T2—729 5 |
| Puffballs | 579.599 |
| Puffbirds | 598.72 |
| Puffer fishes | 597.64 |
| Puffins | 598.33 |
| Pug (Dog) | 636.76 |
| Puget Sound (Wash.) | 551.461 432 |
| | T2—164 32 |
| Puglia (Italy) | T2—457 5 |
|   ancient | T2—377 5 |
| Pukaki, Lake (N.Z.) | T2—938 8 |
| Pulaski County (Ark.) | T2—767 73 |
| Pulaski County (Ga.) | T2—758 523 |
| Pulaski County (Ill.) | T2—773 998 |
| Pulaski County (Ind.) | T2—772 925 |
| Pulaski County (Ky.) | T2—769 63 |
| Pulaski County (Mo.) | T2—778 57 |
| Pulaski County (Va.) | T2—755 775 |
| Pulau Pinang (State) | T2—595 1 |
| Puli | 636.737 |

| | |
|---|---|
| Pullovers | 391.46 |
|   commercial technology | 687.14 |
|   home sewing | 646.45 |
|   *see also* Outerwear | |
| Pulmonary abscesses | |
|   medicine | 616.244 |
|   *see also* Respiratory tract | |
|     diseases — humans | |
| Pulmonary diseases | |
|   medicine | 616.24 |
|   *see also* Respiratory tract | |
|     diseases — humans | |
| Pulmonary embolisms | |
|   medicine | 616.249 |
|   *see also* Respiratory tract | |
|     diseases — humans | |
| Pulmonary heart disease | |
|   medicine | 616.12 |
|   *see also* Cardiovascular | |
|     diseases — humans | |
| Pulmonary hypertension | |
|   medicine | 616.24 |
|   *see also* Respiratory tract | |
|     diseases — humans | |
| Pulmonary sarcoidosis | |
|   medicine | 616.429 |
| Pulmonary thromboses | |
|   medicine | 616.249 |
|   *see also* Respiratory tract | |
|     diseases — humans | |
| Pulmonary tuberculosis | |
|   incidence | 614.542 |
|   medicine | 616.995 |
|   *see also* Respiratory tract | |
|     diseases — humans | |
| Pulmonary valve | |
|   human anatomy | 611.12 |
|   human physiology | 612.17 |
|   medicine | 616.125 |
| Pulmonary valve diseases | |
|   medicine | 616.125 |
|   *see also* Cardiovascular | |
|     diseases — humans | |
| Pulmonata | 594.38 |
| Pulp | 676.1 |
| Pulp industry workers | 676.109 2 |
| Pulpboards | 676.183 |
| Pulpit platforms | |
|   church architecture | 726.593 |
| Pulpits | |
|   church architecture | 726.529 2 |
| Pulpwood | |
|   forest product | 634.983 |

| | |
|---|---|
| Pulque | 641.23 |
| commercial processing | 663.49 |
| Pulsars | 523.887 4 |
| Pulsating stars | 523.844 25 |
| Pulsating variables | 523.844 25 |
| Pulse | |
| human physiology | 612.14 |
| musical element | 781.222 |
| Pulse circuits | |
| electronic circuits | 621.381 534 |
| Pulse detectors | |
| electronic circuits | 621.381 536 5 |
| Pulse generators | |
| electronic circuits | 621.381 534 |
| Pulse-jet engines | |
| aircraft | 629.134 353 6 |
| Pulse-modulated radar systems | |
| engineering | 621.384 85 |
| Pulse modulators | |
| electronic circuits | 621.381 536 5 |
| Pulse processes | |
| electronics | 621.381 534 |
| Puma | 599.752 4 |
| conservation technology | 639.979 752 4 |
| resource economics | 333.959 752 4 |
| Pumice | 553.65 |
| petrology | 552.23 |
| Pumping stations | |
| sewer engineering | 628.29 |
| water supply engineering | 628.144 |
| Pumpkins | 641.356 2 |
| botany | 583.63 |
| commercial processing | 664.805 62 |
| cooking | 641.656 2 |
| food | 641.356 2 |
| garden crop | 635.62 |
| Pumps | 621.69 |
| hydraulic | 621.252 |
| ships | 623.873 |
| Punched card readers | 004.76 |
| computer engineering | 621.398 6 |
| Punched cards | 004.56 |
| electronic data processing | 004.56 |
| nonelectronic data processing | 004.9 |
| Punching tools | 621.96 |
| Punctuated equilibrium | 576.82 |
| Punctuation | 411 |
| specific languages | T4—11 |
| Puncture wounds | |
| medicine | 617.143 |
| Punic language | 492.6 |
| | T6—926 |
| Punic Wars, 264–146 B.C. | 937.04 |

| | |
|---|---|
| Punishment | |
| armed forces | 355.133 25 |
| law | 345.077 |
| penology | 364.6 |
| prisons | 365.644 |
| social control | 303.36 |
| social theology | 201.764 |
| Christianity | 261.833 6 |
| student discipline | 371.54 |
| Punjab (India) | T2—545 52 |
| Punjab (India : Province) | T2—545 |
| Punjab (India : State) | T2—545 5 |
| Punjab (Pakistan) | T2—549 14 |
| Punjabi language | 491.42 |
| | T6—914 2 |
| Punjabi literature | 891.42 |
| Punjabis | T5—914 21 |
| Punk rock | 781.66 |
| Puno (Peru : Dept.) | T2—853 6 |
| Puntarenas (Costa Rica : Province) | T2—728 67 |
| Punting (Boating) | 797.123 |
| Punting (Kicking) | |
| American football | 796.332 27 |
| Punu language | 496.396 |
| | T6—963 96 |
| Puppet films | 791.433 4 |
| Puppet masters | 791.530 92 |
| Puppeteers | 791.530 92 |
| Puppetry | 791.53 |
| Christian religious use | 246.725 |
| religious education | 268.67 |
| primary education | 372.674 |
| production scripts | 791.538 |
| Puppets | 791.53 |
| making | 688.722 4 |
| handicrafts | 745.592 24 |
| technology | 688.722 4 |
| performing arts | 791.53 |
| see also Toys | |
| Puracé National Park (Colombia) | T2—861 53 |
| Puranas | 294.592 5 |
| Purari River (Gulf Province, Papua New Guinea) | T2—954 7 |
| Purbeck (England) | T2—423 36 |
| Purcell Mountains (B.C. and Mont.) | T2—711 65 |
| Purchase contracts | |
| accounting | 657.75 |
| materials management | 658.723 |

| | |
|---|---|
| Purchase of real property | 333.33 |
| economics | 333.33 |
| private ownership | 333.33 |
| public ownership | 333.13 |
| law | 346.043 62 |
| private ownership | 346.043 62 |
| public ownership | 343.025 2 |
| Purchasing | 658.72 |
| | T1—068 7 |
| *see also* Procurement | |
| Purchasing manuals | 381.33 |
| Purchasing power | 339.42 |
| cost of living | 339.42 |
| value of money | 332.41 |
| Purchasing power parity | 332.456 |
| Pure food control | 363.192 |
| *see also* Food — product safety | |
| Pure Land Buddhism | 294.392 6 |
| Pure mathematics | 510 |
| Pure sciences | 500 |
| *see also* Science | |
| Purépecha language | 497.96 |
| | T6—979 6 |
| Purgatives | |
| pharmacokinetics | 615.732 |
| Purgatory | |
| Christianity | 236.5 |
| Purification | |
| oils and gases | 665.028 3 |
| petroleum distillates | 665.534 |
| Purified pulp | 676.4 |
| Purim | 296.436 |
| liturgy | 296.453 6 |
| Purines | 547.596 |
| chemical engineering | 661.894 |
| Puritanism | 285.9 |
| doctrines | 230.59 |
| moral theology | 241.045 9 |
| persecution of others | 272.8 |
| Puritans | |
| biography | 285.909 2 |
| Purple bacteria | 579.38 |
| Purple nonsulfur bacteria | 579.385 |
| Purpose | |
| philosophy | 124 |
| Purposive psychology | 150.193 |
| Purses (Handbags) | 391.44 |
| customs | 391.44 |
| manufacturing technology | 685.51 |
| *see also* Accessories (Clothing) | |
| Purslanes | 583.53 |
| Pursuit (Law enforcement) | 363.232 |
| Pursuit forces (Air warfare) | 358.43 |

| | |
|---|---|
| Pursuit planes | 358.438 3 |
| engineering | 623.746 4 |
| military equipment | 358.438 3 |
| Pus | 571.937 9 |
| Pushball | 796.33 |
| Pushmataha County (Okla.)  T2—766 65 | |
| Pushto language | 491.593 |
| | T6—915 93 |
| Pushto literature | 891.593 |
| Puss in corner | 796.14 |
| Puteoli (Italy) | T2—377 25 |
| Putin, Vladimir Vladimirovich | |
| Russian history | 947.086 2 |
| Putnam County (Fla.) | T2—759 17 |
| Putnam County (Ga.) | T2—758 576 |
| Putnam County (Ill.) | T2—773 375 |
| Putnam County (Ind.) | T2—772 49 |
| Putnam County (Mo.) | T2—778 232 |
| Putnam County (N.Y.) | T2—747 32 |
| Putnam County (Ohio) | T2—771 18 |
| Putnam County (Tenn.) | T2—768 67 |
| Putnam County (W. Va.) | T2—754 35 |
| Putonghua (Standard Chinese | 495.1 |
| language) | T6—951 1 |
| Puts (Finance) | 332.645 3 |
| multiple forms of investment | 332.645 3 |
| stocks | 332.632 283 |
| Puts and calls | 332.645 3 |
| multiple forms of investment | 332.645 3 |
| stocks | 332.632 283 |
| Putters (Golf equipment) | 796.352 35 |
| Putting | 796.352 35 |
| Putumayo (Colombia : | |
| Dept.) | T2—861 63 |
| Puy-de-Dôme (France) | T2—445 91 |
| Puzzles | 793.73 |
| Pwani (Tanzania) | T2—678 23 |
| Pycnogonida | 595.496 |
| paleozoology | 565.49 |
| Pyelitis | |
| medicine | 616.613 |
| *see also* Urologic diseases — humans | |
| Pyelocystitis | |
| medicine | 616.613 |
| *see also* Urologic diseases — humans | |
| Pyelonephritis | |
| medicine | 616.613 |
| *see also* Urologic diseases — humans | |

Pyemia
  incidence                                          614.577
  medicine                                           616.944
    *see also* Communicable
      diseases — humans
  puerperal diseases
    incidence                                        614.545
    obstetrics                                       618.74
Pygmies (African peoples)    T5—960 67
Pygmy right whale                                    599.52
Pygmy sperm whales                                   599.547
Pygopodidae                                          597.952
Pylorus                                              573.36
  biology                                            573.36
  human anatomy                                      611.33
  medicine                                           616.33
  surgery                                            617.553
    *see also* Digestive system
Pylorus diseases
  medicine                                           616.33
    *see also* Digestive system
      diseases — humans
Pyorrhea
  dentistry                                          617.632
Pyracanthas                                          635.933 73
  botany                                             583.73
  floriculture                                       635.933 73
Pyralidoidea                                         595.78
Pyramid power                                        001.94
Pyramidellacea                                       594.34
Pyramids (Buildings)                                 909
  Aztec                                              972.018
  Egyptian                                           932
  Incan                                              985.019
  Mayan                                              972.810 16
    Guatemala                                        972.810 16
    Mexico                                           972.650 16
  Mexican                                            972.01
  Toltec                                             972.017
Pyramids (Geometry)                                  516.156
Pyramids (Marketing)                                 381.1
  management                                         658.872
Pyrans                                               547.592
  chemical engineering                               661.8
Pyrazoles                                            547.593
  chemical engineering                               661.894
Pyrenees (France and Spain)  T2—465
  France                     T2—447 3
  Spain                      T2—465
Pyrénées-Atlantiques
  (France)                   T2—447 16
Pyrenees National Park       T2—447 8
Pyrénées-Orientales
  (France)                   T2—448 9

Pyrenomycetes                                        579.567
Pyridines                                            547.593
  chemical engineering                               661.894
Pyrite
  mineralogy                                         549.32
Pyroclastic rocks                                    552.23
Pyrography                                           745.514
Pyrolaceae                                           583.66
Pyromagnetism                                        538.3
Pyromania
  medicine                                           616.858 43
    *see also* Mental disorders
Pyrometallurgy                                       669.028 2
Pyrometers
  manufacturing technology                           681.2
Pyrometry                                            536.52
Pyrophyllite
  mineralogy                                         549.67
Pyrotechnical devices
  military communications
    engineering                                     623.731 3
Pyrotechnics                                         662.1
Pyrotheria                                           569.62
Pyroxenes
  mineralogy                                         549.66
Pyrrhonic philosophy                                 186.1
Pyrroles                                             547.593
  chemical engineering                               661.894
Pyrrophyta                                           579.87
Pythagorean philosophy                               182.2
Pythagorean theorem                                  516.22
Pythoninae                                           597.967 8
Pythons                                              597.967 8

# Q

Q fever
  incidence                                          614.526 5
  medicine                                           616.922 5
    *see also* Communicable
      diseases — humans
Q hypothesis (Gospels)                               226.066
Qacentina (Algeria :
  Province)                  T2—655
Qaḍarif (Sudan : State)      T2—625
Qādarīyah (Islamic sect)                             297.835
Qaddafi, Muammar
  Libyan history                                     961.204 2
Qādirīyah (Sufi order)                               297.48
Qādisīyah (Iraq)             T2—567 5
Qāhirah (Egypt : Province)   T2—621 6
Qalyūbīyah (Egypt)           T2—621
Qamani'tuaq (Nunavut)        T2—719 58

| | | | |
|---|---|---|---|
| Qatar | 953.63 | Qualitative analysis | 543.1 |
| | T2—536 3 | Qualitative research | 001.42 |
| ancient | 939.49 | | T1—072 1 |
| | T2—394 9 | Quality control | |
| Qataris | T5—927 536 3 | management | 658.401 3 |
| Qattara Depression (Egypt) | T2—622 | military administration | 355.685 7 |
| Qausuittuq (Nunavut) | T2—719 52 | production management | 658.562 |
| Qazvīn (Iran: Province) | T2—551 8 | public administration | 352.357 |
| Qi gong | 613.714 89 | statistical mathematics | 519.86 |
| Qiblah | 297.382 | Quality engineering | 620.004 5 |
| Qigong | 613.714 89 | Quality of life | 306 |
| Qikiqtaaluk (Nunavut) | T2—719 52 | Quality of work life | 306.361 |
| Qin dynasty | 931.04 | labor economics | 331.256 |
| Qinā (Egypt : Province) | T2—623 | Quality standards | |
| Qing dynasty | 951.03 | commerce | 389.63 |
| Qinghai Sheng (China) | T2—514 7 | Quảng Bình (Vietnam) | T2—597 4 |
| Qirā'āt | 297.122 404 5 | Quảng Nam (Vietnam : | |
| Qohelet | 223.8 | Province) | T2—597 5 |
| Qoran | 297.122 | Quảng Ngãi (Vietnam : | |
| Quackery | | Province) | T2—597 5 |
| medicine | 615.856 | Quảng Ninh (Vietnam : | |
| Quad roller hockey | 796.356 64 | Province) | T2—597 2 |
| Quadra Island (B.C.) | T2—711 2 | Quảng Trị (Vietnam : | |
| Quadraphonic sound systems | | Province) | T2—597 4 |
| engineering | 621.389 334 | Quangos | 352.8 |
| Quadratic equations | 512.942 22 | law | 346.067 |
| algebra | 512.942 22 | Quantitative analysis | 543.1 |
| calculus | 515.252 | Quantitative research | 001.42 |
| Quadratic forms | 512.74 | | T1—072 1 |
| Quadratic programming | 519.76 | Quantity | |
| Quadratic residues | 512.72 | philosophy | 119 |
| Quadrature | 515.43 | Quantity standards | |
| Quadrilaterals | 516.154 | commerce | 389.62 |
| Quadrilles | 793.34 | Quantity surveying | 692.5 |
| Quadros, Jânio | | | T1—029 |
| Brazilian history | 981.062 | Quantity theory | |
| Quadruplets | 306.875 | monetary economics | 332.401 |
| *see also* Siblings | | Quantock Hills (England) | T2—423 85 |
| Quagga | 599.665 716 8 | Quantum chemistry | 541.28 |
| Quails | 598.627 | Quantum chromodynamics | 539.754 8 |
| conservation technology | 639.978 627 | Quantum electrodynamics | 530.143 3 |
| resource economics | 333.958 627 | Quantum electronics | 537.5 |
| sports hunting | 799.246 27 | Quantum field theory | 530.143 |
| Quakers | 289.6 | Quantum flavor | 539.721 67 |
| biography | 289.609 2 | Quantum mechanics | 530.12 |
| *see also* Society of Friends | | Quantum physics | 539 |
| Qualifications of employees | 331.114 | Quantum statistical mechanics | 530.133 |
| economics | 331.114 | Quantum statistics | 530.133 |
| personnel management | 658.306 | Quantum theory | 530.12 |
| job analysis | 658.306 | Quantum theory of light | 535.15 |
| public administration | 352.64 | Quapaw Indians | T5—975 25 |
| public administration | 352.64 | Quarantine | |
| selection | 658.311 2 | disease control | 614.46 |
| public administration | 352.65 | law | 344.043 |

Quarks 539.721 67
Quarrying 622.35
Quarter (Law of war) 341.65
Quarter horse 636.133
Quarters (Time interval) 529.2
Quarters for military personnel 355.71
Quartets
  chamber music 785.14
  vocal music 783.14
Quartic equations 512.942 2
  algebra 512.942 2
  calculus 515.252
Quartz
  materials science 620.198
  mineralogy 549.68
Quartzite 552.4
Quasars 523.115
Quasi contract 346.029
Quasi-judicial agencies 352.8
Quaternary period 551.79
  geology 551.79
  paleontology 560.179
Quaternions 512.5
Quay County (N.M.) T2—789 26
Quays 387.15
  engineering 627.31
  *see also* Port facilities
Queanbeyan (N.S.W.) T2—944 7
Quebec (Province) 971.4
  T2—714
  *see Manual at* T2—713 *and*
    T2—714
Québec (Quebec) T2—714 471
Québec (Quebec : Urban
  agglomeration) T2—714 471
Quebec Act, 1774 971.022
Quebec Conference, 1864 971.049
Québec Metropolitan
  Community (Quebec) T2 714 47
Quebec Sign Language 419.714
  T6—999 871 4
Quechan language 497.572
  T6—975 72
Quechua Indians T5—983 23
Quechua language 498.323
  T6—983 23
Quechua literature 898.323
Quechuan Indians T5—983 23
Quechuan languages 498.323
  T6—983 23
Queen Anne's County (Md.) T2—752 34
Queen Anne's lace 583.849
Queen Anne's War, 1701–1714 940.252 6
  North American history 973.25

Queen bees
  apiculture 638.145
Queen Charlotte Islands
  (B.C.) T2—711 12
Queen Charlotte Sound (B.C.) 551.461 433
  T2—164 33
Queen Charlotte Strait (B.C.) 551.461 433
  T2—164 33
Queen Maud Land T2—989
Queens (Chessmen) 794.146
Queens (N.B.) T2—715 42
Queens (N.S. : Regional
  municipality) T2—716 24
Queens (New York, N.Y.) T2—747 243
Queens (P.E.I.) T2—717 4
Queens (Rulers) 352.23
  *see also* Monarchs; Royalty
Queenscliff (Vic.) T2—945 2
Queensland T2—943
Queenstown (South Africa :
  District) T2—687 55
Queenstown (Tas.) T2—946 6
Queenstown-Lakes District
  (N.Z.) T2—939 5
Queleas 598.887
  agricultural pests 632.688 87
Quenas 788.35
  *see also* Woodwind instruments
Quenching metals 671.36
Quercoideae 583.46
Querétaro (Mexico : State) T2—724 5
Quesnay, François
  economic school 330.152
Quesnel (B.C.) T2—711 75
Quesnel Lake (B.C.) T2—711 75
Quesnel River (B.C.) T2—711 75
Question
  philosophical logic 160.119
Question-answering systems 006.3
Questione meridionale 945.709
Questionnaires
  descriptive research 001.433
  T1—072 3
Questions and answers
  study and teaching T1—076
Quetta District (Pakistan) T2—549 152
Quetzals 598.73
Queuing processes 519.82
Queuing theory 519.82
  management decision making 658.403 4
Quezaltenango (Guatemala :
  Dept.) T2—728 182
Quezon (Philippines :
  Province) T2—599 1

| | |
|---|---|
| Quicas | 786.98 |
| *see also* Percussion instruments | |
| Quiché (Guatemala) | T2—728 172 |
| Quiché Indians | T5—974 23 |
| Quiché language | 497.423 |
| | T6—974 23 |
| Quiché literature | 897.423 |
| Quichean languages | 497.42 |
| | T6—974 2 |
| Quichean-Mamean languages | 497.42 |
| | T6—974 2 |
| Quiches | 641.82 |
| Quick breads | 641.815 7 |
| commercial baking | 664.752 3 |
| Quiddity | 111.1 |
| Quietism | 273.7 |
| persecution of | 272.5 |
| Quileute Indians | T5—979 |
| Quilling | |
| handicrafts | 745.54 |
| Quillota (Chile : Province) | T2—832 52 |
| Quillworts | 587.9 |
| Quilting | |
| arts | 746.46 |
| home sewing | 646.21 |
| Quilts | 645.4 |
| arts | 746.46 |
| household equipment | 645.4 |
| Quinary system (Numeration) | 513.5 |
| Quinces | 641.341 4 |
| botany | 583.73 |
| cooking | 641.641 4 |
| food | 641.341 4 |
| orchard crop | 634.14 |
| Quindío (Colombia) | T2—861 34 |
| Quinine | |
| medicinal crop | 633.883 93 |
| Quinoidals | 667.256 |
| Quinolines | 547.596 |
| chemical engineering | 661.894 |
| Quinonization | |
| chemical engineering | 660.284 43 |
| Quintana Roo (Mexico : State) | T2—726 7 |
| Quintets | |
| chamber music | 785.15 |
| vocal music | 783.15 |
| Quintuplets | 306.875 |
| *see also* Siblings | |
| Quirino, Elpidio | |
| Philippine history | 959.904 2 |
| Quitman County (Ga.) | T2—758 924 |
| Quitman County (Miss.) | T2—762 453 |
| Quito (Ecuador) | T2—866 13 |

| | |
|---|---|
| Quito Presidency | 986.604 |
| | T2—866 |
| Quizzes | |
| recreation | 793.73 |
| Qum (Iran : Province) | T2—552 6 |
| Qumbu (South Africa : District) | T2—687 58 |
| Qumran community | 296.815 |
| Dead Sea Scrolls | 296.155 |
| Qunaytirah (Syria : Province) | T2—569 14 |
| Quoits | 796.24 |
| Quorn (S. Aust.) | T2 942 36 |
| Quotas | |
| import trade | 382.52 |
| *see also* Import trade | |
| Quotations | 080 |
| literature | 808.882 |
| specific literatures | T3B—802 |
| individual authors | T3A—8 |
| *see Manual at* 080 vs. 800; *also at* 081–089 | |
| Quran | 297.122 |
| Qwabe (Kingdom) | 968.403 8 |
| | T2—684 |
| Qwaqwa (South Africa) | T2—685 1 |

## R

| | |
|---|---|
| R and D (Research) | |
| production management | 658.57 |
| R&B | 781.644 |
| Rabat (Morocco) | T2—643 6 |
| Rabat (Morocco : Prefecture) | T2—643 6 |
| Rabat-Salé-Zemmour-Zaër (Morocco) | T2—643 6 |
| Rabaul (Papua New Guinea) | T2—958 5 |
| Rabbinical literature | 296.1 |
| Rabbinical seminaries | 296.071 1 |
| Rabbis | 296.092 |
| biography | 296.092 |
| specific denominations | 296.8 |
| professional ethics | 296.364 1 |
| role and function | 296.61 |
| training | 296.071 1 |
| Rabbit hair textiles | 677.35 |
| *see also* Textiles | |
| Rabbits | 599.32 |
| agricultural pests | 632.693 2 |
| animal husbandry | 636.932 2 |
| conservation technology | 639.979 32 |
| experimental animals medicine | 616.027 3 |

Rabbits (continued)
  resource economics          333.959 32
  small game hunting          799.259 32
  zoology                     599.32
Rabies
  animals
    incidence                 636.089 456 3
    veterinary medicine       636.089 695 3
  humans
    incidence                 614.563
    medicine                  616.953
      *see also* Communicable
        diseases — humans
Rabies virus                  579.256 6
Rabun County (Ga.)            T2—758 123
Raccoons                      599.763 2
  trapping                    639.117 632
Race discrimination           305.8
  law                         342.087 3
Race discrimination in
    employment                331.6
  law                         344.016
Race relations                305.8
  religion                    200.89
    Christianity              270.089
  sociology                   305.8
Race walking                  796.429
Racehorses                    636.12
  sports                      798.4
Racerunners (Lizards)         597.958 25
Races (Ethnology)             305.8
  physical ethnology          599.97
Races (Sports)                796
  *see also* Racing
Racetracks
  architecture                725.89
  automobiles                 796.720 68
  horses                      798.400 68
  humans                      796.420 68
Rachidia (Morocco :
    Province)                 T2—645
Racial characteristics
  physical ethnology          599.972
Racial conflict               305.8
  influence on crime          364.256
Racial discrimination         305.8
Racial groups                 305.8
                              T1—089
  *see also* Ethnic groups
Racial minorities             305.8
  *see also* Ethnic groups
Racially mixed people         T5—05
Racine County (Wis.)          T2—775 96

Racing                        796
  aircraft                    797.52
  animals                     798
    dogs                      798.8
    horses                    798.4
  automobiles                 796.72
  bicycles                    796.62
  BMX bicycles                796.622
  boats                       797.14
  cyclo-cross bicycles        796.624
  humans                      796.42
  midget cars                 796.76
  motor scooters              796.75
  motor vehicles              796.7
  motorcycles                 796.75
  mountain bicycles           796.63
  road bicycles               796.626
  soapboxes                   796.6
  track bicycles              796.628
Racing animals
  animal husbandry            636.088 8
Racing cars                   796.72
  driving                     629.284 8
  engineering                 629.228
  repair                      629.287 8
  sports                      796.72
Racism                        305.8
                        T1—089
  ethics                      177.5
    *see also* Discrimination —
      ethics
  political ideology          320.569
  religion                    200.89
    Christianity              270.089
Racism in textbooks
  public control              379.156
Rack railroads                385.6
  engineering                 625.33
  transportation services     385.6
Racket games                  796.34
  equipment technology        688.763 4
Racketeering                  364.106 7
  law                         345.02
Rackets (Game)                796.343
Rackets players               796.343 092
Racketts                      788.5
  *see also* Woodwind instruments
Racon                         621.384 8
  marine navigation           623.893 3
Racquetball                   796.343
Radar                         621.384 8
  airport engineering         629.136 6
  electronic engineering      621.384 8
  marine navigation           623.893 3

Radar (continued)
| | |
|---|---|
| military engineering | 623.734 8 |
| military gunnery | 623.557 |
| nautical engineering | 623.856 48 |
| weather reporting | 551.635 3 |

| | |
|---|---|
| Rade language | 499.22 |
| | T6—992 2 |
| Radford (Va.) | T2—755 786 |
| Radha Soami Satsang | 294 |

Radial street patterns
| | |
|---|---|
| area planning | 711.41 |
| Radiant energy | 539.2 |

Radiant panel heating
| | |
|---|---|
| buildings | 697.72 |

Radiant points
| | |
|---|---|
| astronomy | 523.53 |
| Radiation | 539.2 |
| biophysics | 571.45 |
| humans | 612.014 48 |
| effect on materials | 620.112 28 |
| effect on space flight | 629.416 |
| meteorology | 551.527 |
| physics | 539.2 |
| solid-state physics | 530.416 |
| Radiation (Biological evolution) | 576.84 |
| Radiation biology | 571.45 |
| humans | 612.014 48 |
| Radiation chemistry | 541.382 |
| applied | 660.298 2 |

Radiation dosimetry
| | |
|---|---|
| human biophysics | 612.014 480 287 |
| radiotherapy | 615.842 |
| Radiation injuries | 571.934 5 |
| agriculture | 632.3 |
| animals | 571.934 51 |
| veterinary medicine | 636.089 698 97 |
| humans | 362.196 989 7 |
| medicine | 616.989 7 |
| social services | 362.196 989 7 |

*see also* Environmental
diseases — humans
| | |
|---|---|
| plants | 571.934 52 |
| Radiation measurement | 539.77 |
| Radiation safety | 363.179 9 |
| public administration | 353.999 |

*see also* Hazardous materials
| | |
|---|---|
| Radiation sickness | 571.934 5 |

*see also* Radiation injuries
Radiation therapy
| | |
|---|---|
| medicine | 615.842 |
| Radiation warfare | 358.39 |
| Radiation weapons | 358.398 2 |
| engineering | 623.446 |
| military equipment | 358.398 2 |

Radiative heating
| | |
|---|---|
| buildings | 697.1 |

Radiators
| | |
|---|---|
| heating buildings | 697.07 |
| steam | 697.507 |

Radical Democratic Party (Swiss
| | |
|---|---|
| political party) | 324.249 406 |
| Radical Party (Italy) | 324.245 06 |
| Radical theory | 512.4 |

Radicalism
| | |
|---|---|
| agent of social change | 303.484 |
| political ideology | 320.53 |
| Radicals (Chemicals) | 541.224 |
| Radiesthesia | 133.323 |

Radii (Bones)
| | |
|---|---|
| human anatomy | 611.717 |
| Radio | 384.5 |
| accounting | 657.84 |
| communications services | 384.5 |
| engineering | 621.384 |
| influence on crime | 364.254 |
| instructional use | 371.333 1 |
| adult level | 374.26 |
| | T1—071 5 |
| journalism | 070.194 |
| law | 343.099 45 |
| marine navigation | 623.893 2 |
| military engineering | 623.734 |
| nautical engineering | 623.856 4 |
| performing arts | 791.44 |
| public administration | 354.75 |
| religion | 201.7 |
| Christianity | 261.52 |
| evangelism | 269.26 |
| preaching | 251.07 |
| use by local Christian | |
| church | 253.78 |
| administration | 254.3 |
| sociology | 302.234 4 |

*see Manual at* 384.54, 384.55,
384.8 vs. 791.4
| | |
|---|---|
| Radio adaptations | 791.446 |
| Radio advertising | 659.142 |
| Radio astronomy | 522.682 |

Radio beacons
| | |
|---|---|
| engineering | 621.384 191 |

Radio comment
| | |
|---|---|
| journalism | 070.442 |
| Radio communication | 384.5 |

Radio compasses
| | |
|---|---|
| aircraft engineering | 629.135 1 |
| engineering | 621.384 191 |
| marine navigation | 623.893 2 |

Radio control
  airport engineering    629.136 6
  engineering    621.384 196
Radio direction finders
  aircraft engineering    629.135 1
Radio drama    791.447
  *see also* Radio plays
Radio engineers    621.384 092
Radio evangelism    269.26
Radio frequency allocation    384.545 24
Radio frequency identification    006.245
  computer science    006.245
  engineering    621.384 192
Radio-frequency spectroscopes
  manufacturing technology    681.414 8
Radio genres    791.446
Radio music    781.544
Radio networks    384.540 65
  enterprises    384.540 65
  facilities    384.545 5
  performing arts    791.44
Radio news    070.43
Radio plays    791.447
  literature    808.822 2
    history and criticism    809.222
    specific literatures    T3B—202 2
      individual authors    T3A—2
  radio programs    791.447
  rhetoric    808.222
  *see Manual at* 791.437 and
    791.447, 791.457, 792.9;
    *also at* 808.82 vs. 791.437,
    791.447, 791.457, 792.9
Radio programs    384.544 3
  broadcasting    384.544 3
  performing arts    791.44
Radio public speaking    808.51
Radio relay
  telephone engineering    621.387 82
Radio scripts    791.447
  rhetoric    808.066 791
  *see also* Radio plays
Radio stations    384.545 3
  architecture    725.23
  engineering    621.384
  enterprises    384.540 65
  facilities    384.545 3
  performing arts    791.44
Radio telescopes    522.682
Radio towers
  architecture    725.23
Radio waves    537.534
  biophysics    571.453
    humans    612.014 481

Radio waves (continued)
  physics    537.534
  propagation and transmission    621.384 11
Radioactivation analysis    543.63
Radioactive fallout    363.738
  physics    539.753
  social problem    363.738
  *see also* Pollution
Radioactive materials
  public administration    353.999
  public safety    363.179 9
Radioactive pollution    363.738
  effect on natural ecology    577.277
  *see also* Pollution
Radioactive substances    539.752
Radioactive tracers
  analytical chemistry    543.63
Radioactive wastes    363.728 9
  environmental engineering    628.5
    air pollution    628.535
    water pollution    628.168 5
  law    344.046 22
  public administration    353.999
  social services    363.728 9
  technology    621.483 8
Radioactivity    539.752
Radioactivity prospecting    622.159
Radiobiology    571.45
  humans    612.014 48
Radiobroadcasting    384.54
  *see Manual at* 384.54, 384.55,
    384.8 vs. 791.4
Radiochemical analysis    543.63
Radiochemistry    541.38
  chemical engineering    660.298
Radiocommunication    384.5
  *see also* Radio
Radioecology    577.277
Radioelements    539.752
Radiofrequency spectroscopy
  engineering    621.361
  physics    537.534
Radiogenetics    572.838
Radiographic testing
  materials science    620.112 72
Radiography
  engineering    621.367 3
  medicine    616.075 72
Radioimmunoassay
  medicine    616.075 7
Radioimmunoimaging
  medicine    616.075 75
Radioisotope scanning
  medicine    616.075 75

| | |
|---|---|
| Radioisotope therapy | |
| medicine | 615.842 4 |
| Radioisotopes | 539.752 |
| chemical engineering | 660.298 84 |
| chemistry | 541.388 4 |
| physics | 539.752 |
| technology | 621.483 7 |
| therapeutics | 615.842 4 |
| Radiolaria | 579.45 |
| paleontology | 561.995 |
| Radiology | |
| medicine | 616.075 7 |
| Radiology services | 362.177 |
| *see also* Health services | |
| Radiolysis | 541.382 |
| chemical engineering | 660.298 2 |
| Radiometry | |
| human biophysics | 612.014 480 287 |
| radiotherapy | 615.842 |
| Radionuclide imaging | |
| medicine | 616.075 75 |
| Radionuclides | 539.752 |
| Radios | 621.384 18 |
| automobile | 629.277 |
| Radioscopic diagnosis | |
| medicine | 616.075 7 |
| Radioscopic urinalysis | |
| medicine | 616.075 7 |
| Radiosondes | |
| weather reporting | 551.635 2 |
| Radiotelegraphy | 384.52 |
| communications services | 384.52 |
| engineering | 621.384 2 |
| military engineering | 623.734 2 |
| *see also* Radio | |
| Radiotelephony | 384.53 |
| communications services | 384.53 |
| engineering | 621.384 5 |
| military engineering | 623.734 5 |
| *see also* Radio | |
| Radiotherapy | |
| medicine | 615.842 |
| Radishes | 641.351 5 |
| botany | 583.64 |
| commercial processing | 664.805 15 |
| cooking | 641.651 5 |
| food | 641.351 5 |
| garden crop | 635.15 |
| Radium | 669.725 |
| chemical engineering | 661.039 6 |
| chemistry | 546.396 |
| economic geology | 553.493 |
| human toxicology | 615.925 396 |

| | |
|---|---|
| Radium (continued) | |
| metallurgy | 669.725 |
| *see also* Chemicals | |
| Radium therapy | |
| medicine | 615.842 3 |
| Radnor (Wales : District) | T2—429 51 |
| Radom (Poland : | |
| Voivodeship) | T2—438 41 |
| Radon | |
| air pollution | 363.738 |
| *see also* Pollution | |
| air pollution technology | 628.535 |
| chemistry | 546.756 |
| economic geology | 553.97 |
| gas technology | 665.822 |
| Radon transforms | 515.723 |
| Rae Lakes (N.W.T.) | T2—719 3 |
| Raetia | T2—369 47 |
| Austria | T2—363 64 |
| Switerland | T2—369 47 |
| Raeto-Romance languages | 459.9 |
| | T6—599 |
| Raeto-Romance literatures | 859.9 |
| Raffia | |
| textile arts | 746.41 |
| textiles | 677.54 |
| *see also* Textiles | |
| Raffia palm | 584.5 |
| Rafflesiales | 583.2 |
| Raft zithers | 787.73 |
| *see also* Stringed instruments | |
| Rafting (Sports) | 797.121 |
| Rafts | 386.229 |
| design | 623.812 9 |
| engineering | 623.829 |
| transportation services | 386.229 |
| Rag pulp | 676.13 |
| Rāgas | 781.264 |
| Ragtime | 781.645 |
| Ragusa (Italy : Province) | T2—458 15 |
| ancient | T2—378 15 |
| Ragweeds | 583.99 |
| Ragworts | 583.99 |
| Rail fastenings | |
| railroad engineering | 625.15 |
| Rail transit services | 388.42 |
| *see also* Local rail transit | |
| systems | |
| Railings | |
| church architecture | 726.529 6 |
| Railroad accidents | 363.122 |
| *see also* Railroad safety | |
| Railroad atlases | 385.022 3 |
| specific areas | 385.09 |

Railroad bridges 385.312
  *see also* Bridges
Railroad buildings 385.314
  architecture 725.33
  *see also* Railroad terminals
Railroad cars 385.32–.34
  *see also* Rolling stock
Railroad construction workers 625.100 92
Railroad crossings 385.312
  engineering 625.163
  transportation services 385.312
Railroad engineers 625.100 92
Railroad freight stations 385.314
  architecture 725.32
  *see also* Railroad terminals
Railroad insurance
  inland marine 368.233
Railroad mail 383.143
  *see also* Postal service
Railroad passenger stations 385.314
  architecture 725.31
  *see also* Railroad terminals
Railroad police 363.287 4
Railroad post offices 383.42
  *see also* Postal service
Railroad safety 363.122
  engineering 625.100 289
  law 343.095
  public administration 353.98
  social services 363.122
Railroad stations 385.314
Railroad terminals 385.314
  architecture 725.31
  area planning 711.75
  engineering 625.18
    special purpose 625.3–.6
  institutional housekeeping 647.963 1
  law 343.095 2
  transportation services 385.314
    special purpose 385.5
  urban 388.472
Railroad ties 625.143
Railroad tracks 385.312
  engineering 625.14
    interurban railroads 625.65
    local railroads 625.65
  law 343.095 2
  military engineering 623.631
  transportation services 385.312
Railroad transportation 385
  engineering 625.1
  law 343.095

Railroad transportation (continued)
  local transit 388.42
    *see also* Local rail transit
      systems
  public administration 354.767
  transportation services 385
  *see also* Railroads
Railroad transportation workers 385.092
Railroad workers 385.092
  construction 625.100 92
Railroad yards 385.314
  engineering 625.18
  law 343.095 2
  transportation services 385.314
Railroads 385
  electrification
    technology 621.33
  engineering 625.1
  investment in 332.672 2
  landscape architecture 713
  military engineering 623.63
  mining 622.66
  transportation services 385
  *see also* Railroad transportation
Rails (Birds) 598.32
Rails (Railroads) 625.15
Railway carriages 385.32–.34
  *see also* Rolling stock
Railways 385
  *see also* Railroads
Rain 551.577
  crop damage 632.16
  meteorology 551.577
  weather forecasting 551.647 7
  weather modification 551.687 7
Rain forests 333.75
   T2—152
  biology 578.734
  ecology 577.34
  *see also* Forest lands
Rainbows 551.567
Raincoats 391.46
  customs 391.46
  home sewing 646.45
  *see also* Clothing
Rainfall 551.577
Rains County (Tex.) T2—764 275
Rainy Lake (Minn. and
  Ont.) T2—776 79
Rainy River (Minn. and
  Ont.) T2—776 79
Rainy River (Ont. : District) T2—713 117
Raised-character publications
  publishing 070.579 2

Raja yoga | 181.45
  Hinduism | 294.543 6
  philosophy | 181.45
Rajasthan (India) | T2—544
Rajasthani language | 491.479
 | T6—914 79
Rajasthani literature | 891.479
Rajasthani-speaking people | T5—914 79
Rajiformes | 597.35
  paleozoology | 567.35
Rājshāhi (Bangladesh :
  Division) | T2—549 24
Raleigh (N.C.) | T2—756 55
Raleigh County (W. Va.) | T2—754 73
Rallidae | 598.32
Rallies (Automobile sport) | 796.73
Ralls County (Mo.) | T2—778 355
RAM (Computer memory) | 004.53
  engineering | 621.397 3
Rama I, King of Siam
  Thai history | 959.303 1
Rama II, King of Siam
  Thai history | 959.303 2
Rama III, King of Siam
  Thai history | 959.303 3
Rama IV, King of Siam
  Thai history | 959.303 4
Rama V, King of Siam
  Thai history | 959.303 5
Rama VI, King of Siam
  Thai history | 959.304 1
Rama VII, King of Siam
  Thai history | 959.304 2
Rama VIII, King of Thailand
  Thai history | 959.304 3
Rama IX, King of Thailand
  Thai history | 959.304 4
Ramadan | 297.362
Ramakrishna movement | 294.555
Raman effect | 535.846
Raman spectroscopes
  manufacturing technology | 681.414 6
Raman spectroscopy | 543.57
  analytical chemistry | 543.57
  engineering | 621.361
  physics | 535.846
Rāmānujāchārya (Philosophy) | 181.483
Ramayana | 294.592 2
Rameses II, King of Egypt
  Egyptian history | 932.014
Ramie
  botany | 583.45
  fiber crop | 633.55

Ramie (continued)
  textiles | 677.15
  *see also* Textiles
Ramjet engines
  aircraft | 629.134 353 5
Ramos, Fidel V.
  Philippine history | 959.904 8
Ramos, Nereu
  Brazilian history | 981.062
Ramphastidae | 598.72
Ramps | 721.83
  architecture | 721.83
  canal engineering | 627.135 3
  construction | 690.183
Ramses II, King of Egypt
  Egyptian history | 932.014
Ramsey County (Minn.) | T2—776 58
Ramsey County (N.D.) | T2—784 36
Ramu languages | 499.12
 | T6—991 2
Rana | 597.892
Ranales | 583.34
Ranch-style houses
  architecture | 728.373
Ranchers | 636.010 92
Ranches | 636.01
Ranchowner insurance | 368.096
Randall County (Tex.) | T2—764 834
Randburg (South Africa :
  District) | T2—682 26
Randfontein (South Africa :
  District) | T2—682 22
Randolph County (Ala.) | T2—761 57
Randolph County (Ark.) | T2—767 24
Randolph County (Ga.) | T2—758 932
Randolph County (Ill.) | T2—773 92
Randolph County (Ind.) | T2—772 66
Randolph County (Mo.) | T2—778 283
Randolph County (N.C.) | T2—756 61
Randolph County (W. Va.) | T2—754 85
Random-access memory | 004.53
  engineering | 621.397 3
Random fields | 519.23
Random processes | 519.23
Random walks | 519.282
Ranganathan's Colon
  Classification | 025.435
Range finders
  military engineering | 623.46
  photography | 771.37
Range management | 636.084 5
  animal husbandry | 636.084 5
  forage agriculture | 633.202

Rangelands 333.74
  ecology 577.4
  *see also* Grasslands
Rangeley Lakes (Me. and
    N.H.) T2—741 7
Ranger project 629.435 3
Rangers (Armed forces) 356.167
Ranges (Stoves)
  manufacturing technology 683.88
Rangifer 599.658
  animal husbandry 636.294 8
Rangitikei District (N.Z.) T2—935 5
  Hawke's Bay Region T2—934 64
  Manawatu-Wanganui
    Region T2—935 5
Ranidae 597.89
Rank (Heraldry) 929.7
Rankin County (Miss.) T2—762 59
Rankin Inlet (Nunavut) T2—719 58
Ranks (Military grades) 355.33
Ranoidea 597.89
Ransom County (N.D.) T2—784 315
Ransom insurance 368.82
Ranunculales 583.34
Ranunculidae 583.3
Rao, P. V. Narasimha
  Indian history 954.052
Rap (Music) 781.649
  songs 782.421 649
Rapanui language 499.4
  T6—994
Rapateaceae 584.86
Rape (Crime) 364.153 2
  law 345.025 32
Rape prevention 362.883
  self-defense 613.663
Rape victims 362.883
  *see also* Victims of crime
Rapes (Plants) 583.64
  oil crop 633.853
Rapeseed
  oil crop 633.853
Raphidiodea 595.747
Rapid calculations 513.9
Rapid reading 418.4
  specific languages T4—843 2
Rapid transit 388.4
  *see also* Urban transportation
Rapid transit facilities
  architecture 725.33
  area planning 711.75

Rapid transit railroads 388.42
  engineering 625.4
  *see also* Local rail transit
    systems
Rapides Parish (La.) T2—763 69
Rappahannock County (Va.) T2—755 395
Rappahannock River (Va.) T2—755 2
Rapping (Spiritualism) 133.92
Raptors (Birds) 598.9
  conservation technology 639.978 9
  resource economics 333.958 9
Rapture (Christian doctrine) 236.9
Raqqah (Syria : Province) T2—569 12
Rare animals 333.954 2
  biology 591.68
  resource economics 333.954 2
Rare birds 333.958 22
  biology 598.168
  resource economics 333.958 22
Rare book libraries 026.09
Rare books 090
  bibliographies 011.44
  cataloging 025.341 6
  library treatment 025.171 6
Rare earths 669.291
  chemical engineering 661.041
  chemistry 546.41
  economic geology 553.494
  materials science 620.189 291
  metallography 669.952 91
  metallurgy 669.291
  physical metallurgy 669.962 91
  *see also* Chemicals
Rare fishes 333.956 8
  biology 597.168
  resource economics 333.956 8
Rare gases
  chemistry 546.75
  economic geology 553.97
  technology 665.822
Rare mammals 333.954 2
  biology 599.168
  resource economics 333.954 2
Rare plants 333.953 2
  biology 581.68
  resource economics 333.953 2
Rare reptiles 333.957 2
  biology 597.916 8
  resource economics 333.957 2
Rare species 333.952 2
  biology 578.68
  law 346.046 95
  resource economics 333.952 2
Rarefied-gas electronics 537.53

| | |
|---|---|
| Raritan River (N.J.) | T2—749 44 |
| Rarotongan language | 499.44 |
| | T6—994 4 |
| Ras al Khaimah (United Arab Emirates : Emirate) | T2—535 7 |
| Ra's al Khaymah (United Arab Emirates : Emirate) | T2—535 7 |
| Ras Tafari | |
| Ethiopian history | 963.055 |
| as emperor | 963.055 |
| as regent and king | 963.054 |
| Ras Tafari movement | 299.676 |
| Rashidun Caliphate | 297.090 212 |
| Raspberries | 641.347 11 |
| botany | 583.73 |
| commercial processing | 664.804 711 |
| cooking | 641.647 11 |
| food | 641.347 11 |
| horticulture | 634.711 |
| Rasps | 621.924 |
| Rastafari, Jah | |
| Ethiopian history | 963.055 |
| as emperor | 963.055 |
| as regent and king | 963.054 |
| Rastafarians | |
| biography | 299.676 092 |
| Rastatt (Germany : Landkreis) | T2—434 643 |
| Rat control | 363.78 |
| social welfare | 363.78 |
| technology | 628.969 3 |
| agriculture | 632.693 52 |
| *see also* Pest control | |
| Rat kangaroos | 599.22 |
| Ratchets | 621.83 |
| music | 786.886 |
| *see also* Percussion instruments | |
| Rates (Prices) | |
| communications industry | 384.041 |
| insurance | 368.011 |
| transportation services | 388.049 |
| Rates (Real property taxes) | 336.22 |
| law | 343.054 |
| public finance | 336.22 |
| Rätikon Mountains | T2—494 732 5 |
| Ratio | 512.924 |
| algebra | 512.924 |
| arithmetic | 513.24 |
| Ration coupons | |
| prints | 769.57 |
| Rational functions | 512.96 |
| Rational numbers | 512.782 |
| Rational psychology | 150.192 |
| Rationalism | 149.7 |
| Christian polemics | 239.7 |
| philosophy | 149.7 |
| philosophy of religion | 211.4 |
| political ideology | 320.512 |
| Rationality | 128.33 |
| Rationing | 333.717 |
| law | 343.07 |
| public administration | 352.86 |
| social welfare | 361.6 |
| *see Manual at* 333.7–.9 vs. 363.6 | |
| Ratites | 598.5 |
| animal husbandry | 636.69 |
| paleozoology | 568.5 |
| Rats (Muridae) | 599.35 |
| *see also* Rodents | |
| Rats (Rattus) | 599.352 |
| agricultural pests | 632.693 52 |
| animal husbandry | 636.935 2 |
| experimental animals | |
| medicine | 616.027 33 |
| household sanitation | 648.7 |
| pest control | 363.78 |
| social welfare | 363.78 |
| technology | 628.969 3 |
| agriculture | 632.693 52 |
| *see also* Pest control | |
| small game hunting | 799.259 352 |
| zoology | 599.352 |
| Ratsiraka, Didier | |
| Malagasy history | 969.105 2 |
| 1975–1993 | 969.105 2 |
| 1997–2002 | 969.105 4 |
| Rattan | |
| basketwork crop | 633.58 |
| Rattan furniture | 645.4 |
| manufacturing technology | 684.106 |
| *see also* Furniture | |
| Rattan palms | 584.5 |
| Rattan textiles | 677.54 |
| *see also* Textiles | |
| Ratting | |
| sports hunting | 799.259 352 |
| Rattle drums | 786.96 |
| *see also* Percussion instruments | |
| Rattled idiophones | 786.885 |
| *see also* Percussion instruments | |
| Rattles | |
| musical instruments | 786.885 |
| *see also* Percussion instruments | |
| Rattlesnake ferns | 587.33 |
| Rattlesnakes | 597.963 8 |

Rattus — 599.352
Rauwolfias — 583.93
Ravalli County (Mont.) — T2—786 89
Ravalomanana, Marc
  Malagasy history — 969.105 5
Ravenna (Italy) — T2—454 71
  ancient — T2—372 671
Ravenna (Italy : Province) — T2—454 7
  ancient — T2—372 67
Ravens — 598.864
Ravines — 551.442
  — T2—144
  geography — 910.914 4
  geomorphology — 551.442
  physical geography — 910.021 44
Raw food diet
  health — 613.265
Raw materials — 333.7
  economics — 333.7
  military resources — 355.24
Rāwalpindi (Pakistan :
  District) — T2—549 142
Rawlings, Jerry J.
  Ghanaian history — 966.705 2
Rawlins County (Kan.) — T2—781 125
Ray County (Mo.) — T2—778 19
Ray-finned fishes — 597
  *see also* Fishes
Ray tracing
  computer graphics — 006.693
Rayon
  textiles — 677.46
  arts — 746.044 6
   *see also* Textiles
Rays (Fishes) — 597.35
  cooking — 641.692
  food — 641.392
Rays (Nuclear physics) — 539.722
Razavi Khorāsān (Iran) — T2—559 2
Razing buildings — 690.26
Razors
  manufacturing technology — 688.5
Reaction kinetics — 541.394
  biochemistry — 572.44
  chemical engineering — 660.299 4
  enzymes — 572.744
  organic chemistry — 547.214
Reaction-time studies — 152.83
Reactions (Chemical reactions)
  biochemistry — 572.43
  chemical engineering — 660.299
  chemistry — 541.39
Reactions (Classical mechanics) — 531.113
Reactions (Chemical reactions) — 541.39

Reactor physics
  nuclear engineering — 621.483 1
Reactors
  nuclear engineering — 621.483
Read Island (B.C. : Island) — T2—711 1
Read-only memory — 004.53
  engineering — 621.397 3
Readability
  rhetoric — 808
Reader advisory services
  library operations — 025.54
Readers (Textbooks) — 418
  applied linguistics — 418
   specific languages — T4—86
    for new literates — T4—862
   for nonnative
    speakers — T4—864
  rhetoric — 808
   specific languages — 808.04
  *see Manual at* 420–490
Readers' theater
  primary education — 372.676
Reading — 418.4
  child care — 649.58
  home preschool teaching — 649.68
  library science — 028
  primary education — 372.4
   home schools — 372.4
  recreation — 790.138
  sociology — 306.488
  specific languages — T4—84
Reading (England) — T2—422 93
Reading, Rufus Daniel Isaacs,
  Marquess of
  Indian history — 954.035 7
Reading aids
  library science — 028
Reading aloud
  child care — 649.58
  rhetoric — 808.54
Reading comprehension
  primary education — 372.47
Reading disorders
  special education — 371.914 4
Reading failure
  primary education — 372.43
Reading for content — 371.302 81
Reading groups
  adult education — 374.22
Reading habits — 028.9
Reading interests — 028.9
Reading materials — 418
  — T4—8
  *see also* Readers (Textbooks)

| | |
|---|---|
| Reading programs | |
| primary education | 372.42 |
| Reading readiness | 372.414 |
| Reading-skill strategies | |
| primary education | 372.45 |
| Ready-mix concrete | 666.893 |
| Ready reckoners (Arithmetic) | 513.9 |
| Ready-to-eat cereals | |
| commercial processing | 664.756 |
| Reagan, Ronald | |
| United States history | 973.927 |
| Reagan County (Tex.) | T2—764 873 |
| Reagents | |
| analytical chemistry | 543.028 4 |
| Real analysis | 515.8 |
| Real County (Tex.) | T2—764 883 |
| Real estate | 333.3 |
| accounting | 657.833 5 |
| investment economics | 332.632 4 |
| law | 346.092 2 |
| land economics | 333.3 |
| law | 346.043 |
| private ownership | 346.043 |
| public administration | 354.34 |
| *see Manual at* 333.73–.78 vs. | |
| 333, 333.1–.5 | |
| Real estate business | 333.33 |
| law | 346.043 7 |
| malpractice | 346.043 71 |
| Real estate development | 333.731 5 |
| Real estate finance | 332.72 |
| Real estate investment trusts | 332.632 47 |
| Real estate market | 333.332 2 |
| Real estate sales tax | |
| law | 343.054 6 |
| Real estate syndication | 332.632 47 |
| Real functions | 515.8 |
| Real numbers | 512.786 |
| Real property | 333.3 |
| Real property insurance | 368.096 |
| Real property market | 333.332 2 |
| Real property tax | 336.22 |
| law | 343.054 |
| public administration | 352.44 |
| Real-time locating systems | |
| engineering | 621.384 192 |
| Real-time processing | 004.33 |
| communications | 004.618 3 |
| programming | 005.273 |
| programs | 005.373 |
| *see also* Processing modes — | |
| computer science | |
| Real-time programming | 005.273 |
| Real-valued functions | 515.7 |

| | |
|---|---|
| Real variable functions | 515.8 |
| Realia | |
| cataloging | 025.349 |
| library treatment | 025.179 |
| Realism | |
| education | 370.12 |
| fine arts | 709.034 3 |
| literature | 808.801 2 |
| history and criticism | 809.912 |
| specific literatures | T3B—080 12 |
| history and | |
| criticism | T3B—091 2 |
| painting | 759.053 |
| philosophy | 149.2 |
| sculpture | 735.22 |
| Realistic fiction | 808.838 3 |
| history and criticism | 809.383 |
| specific literatures | T3B—308 3 |
| individual authors | T3A—3 |
| Reality | |
| philosophy | 111 |
| Reamers | 621.954 |
| Reaping | 631.55 |
| Reapportionment (Legislatures) | 328.334 5 |
| Rear axles | |
| automotive engineering | 629.245 |
| Reason | 128.33 |
| epistemology | 121.3 |
| ethical systems | 171.2 |
| philosophical anthropology | 128.33 |
| theology | |
| Christianity | 231.042 |
| Reasoning | 153.43 |
| artificial intelligence | 006.333 |
| educational psychology | 370.152 4 |
| philosophical logic | 160 |
| psychology | 153.43 |
| Rebates | |
| law | 343.072 |
| Rebekah (Biblical matriarch) | 222.110 92 |
| Rebellion (Political offense) | 364.131 |
| law | 345.023 1 |
| Rebuses | 793.73 |
| Recall (Elections) | 324.68 |
| Recall (Information science) | 025.04 |
| Recall (Memory) | 153.123 |
| Recataloging | |
| library operations | 025.39 |
| Receivership | 332.75 |
| *see also* Bankruptcy | |
| Receiving operations | |
| materials management | 658.728 |
| Receiving sets | |
| radio | 621.384 18 |

Recent epoch 551.793
  geology 551.793
  paleontology 560.179 3
Recently extinct species 333.952 2
  *see also* entries beginning Rare
Receptionists
  office services 651.374 3
Receptions
  meal service 642.4
Receptive processes
  (Psychology) 152.1
Recession (Economics) 338.542
Recidivists 364.3
  T1—086 927
Recipes T1—021 2
  cooking 641.5
Reciprocal equations 515.253
Reciprocal trade 382.9
  law 343.087
Reciprocating engines
  aircraft 629.134 352
Reciprocating pumps 621.65
  hydraulic 621.252
Reciprocating steam engines 621.164
Reciprocity (Mathematics)
  number theory 512.74
Recitals
  music 780.78
Recitation (Education) 371.37
Recitation (Reading aloud)
  Koran 297.122 404 5
  rhetoric 808.54
Recitations
  literature 808.854
    history and criticism 809.54
    specific literatures T3B—504
      individual authors T3A—5
Recklinghausen's disease
  incidence 614.599 9
  medicine 616.993 83
Reclaimed rubber 678.29
Reclamation
  natural resources 333.715 3
Reclamation of land 333.731 53
Reclassification
  library operations 025.39
Recognition (Law of nations) 341.26
Recognition (Psychology) 153.124
Recognition of unions 331.891 2
Recoil
  military gunnery 623.57
Recollection (Psychology) 153.123
Recombinant DNA 660.65
Recombination (Genetics) 572.877

Reconciliation (Christian
  doctrine) 234.5
Reconnaissance (Military
  operations) 355.413
Reconnaissance aircraft 358.458 3
  military engineering 623.746 7
  military equipment 358.458 3
Reconnaissance forces (Air
  warfare) 358.45
Reconnaissance surveys
  (Geodesy) 526.31
Reconnaissance topography
  military engineering 623.71
Reconstruction (Aftermath of
  war) 355.028
  Iraq War, 2003– 956.704 43
  United States history 973.8
  World War I 940.314 4
  World War II 940.531 44
Reconstruction (Linguistics) 417.7
  specific languages T4—7
Reconstructionist Judaism 296.834 4
  liturgy 296.450 48
Reconstructive surgical
  procedures 617.952
Record buildings
  architecture 725.15
Recorders (Musical instruments) 788.36
  instrument 788.361 9
  music 788.36
  *see also* Woodwind instruments
Recording
  music 781.49
Recording devices
  communications engineering 621.382 34
  physical quantities 530.7
  manufacturing technology 681.2
Recordings (Sound) 384
  bibliographies 011.38
  *see also* Sound recordings
Recordkeeping
  accounting 657.2
Records management 651.5
  office services 651.5
  public administration 352.387
Recovering substance
  abusers T1—087 4
Recovery (Business cycle)
  economics 338.542
Recovery (Law) 346.043 2
Recovery from addiction
  devotional literature 204.32
    Christianity 242.4

Recovery from addiction (continued)
  pastoral theology    206.1
    Christianity    259.429
  rehabilitation    616.860 3
  religious guidance    204.42
    Christianity    248.862 9
  social services    362.291 86
  social theology    201.762 29
    Christianity    261.832 29
  therapy    616.860 6
Recreation    790
  armed forces    355.346
  arts    700.457 9
                T3C—357 9
  child care    649.5
  church work    253.7
  crime prevention    364.44
  ethics    175
    religion    205.65
      Christianity    241.65
      Islam    297.565
      Judaism    296.365
  folklore    398.277 9
    history and criticism    398.357 9
  human physiology    612.044
  influence on crime    364.25
  land economics    333.78
  law    344.099
  literature    808.803 579
  museum services    069.16
  prisoner services    365.668
  public administrative support    353.78
  social welfare    361.05
  sociology    306.48
Recreation centers    790.068
  architecture    725.804 2
Recreation facilities    790.068
  architecture    725.8
  community redevelopment    307.346
  recreation    790.068
  sanitation services    363.729 2
  social services    363.68
Recreation leaders    790.092
Recreation policy (Government
  policy)    790
Recreation rooms    643.55
  home economics    643.55
  interior decoration    747.791
Recreation safety    363.14
  law    344.047 6
*see also* Safety

Recreation vehicle camps    910.468
  household management    647.942
  *see also* Lodging (Temporary
    housing)
Recreational activities    790.1
Recreational areas (House and
  yard)    643.55
  home economics    643.55
  interior decoration    747.791
Recreational areas (Public areas)
  area planning    711.558
Recreational arts    790
  *see also* Arts; Recreation
Recreational equipment
  manufacturing technology    688.7
Recreational equipment makers    688.709 2
Recreational lands    333.78
  community sociology    307.334
  economics    333.78
    government acquisition and
      disposal    333.11
Recreational music    781.594
Recreational reading    790.138
  library science    028.8
Recreational therapy
  medicine    615.851 53
Recreational vehicles    388.346
  engineering    629.226
  transportation services    388.346
  travel    910
  *see also* Motor homes
Recreational water resources    333.784
Recreational waters
  hydraulic engineering    627.046
Recruiting
  armed forces    355.223
    law    343.012
  personnel management    658.311 1
    executives    658.407 111
    libraries    023.9
    public administration    352.65
Rectal anesthesia
  surgery    617.962
Rectal diseases
  medicine    616.35
  *see also* Digestive system
    diseases — humans
Rectifiers
  electrical engineering    621.313 7
  electronic circuits    621.381 532 2
  radio engineering    621.384 12
Rectum    573.379
  biology    573.379
  human anatomy    611.35

Rectum (continued)
  human physiology — 612.36
  medicine — 616.35
  surgery — 617.555
  *see also* Digestive system
Recurrent education — 374
                T1—071 5
  *see also* Adult education
Recursion theory — 511.35
Recursive functions — 511.352
Recycling paper — 676.142
Recycling technology — 628.445 8
Recycling waste — 363.728 2
  *see also* Waste control
Red algae — 579.89
Red-bellied turtles — 597.925 94
Red cedars — 585.4
Red corpuscles — 573.153 6
  human histology — 612.111
  human physiology — 612.111
  *see also* Cardiovascular system
Red Crescent — 361.763 4
  *see also* Welfare services
Red Cross — 361.772
  international — 361.772
  national — 361.763 4
  World War I — 940.477 1
  World War II — 940.547 71
  *see also* Welfare services
Red Cross nursing — 610.734
Red Crystal — 361.763 4
Red deer — 599.654 2
  animal husbandry — 636.294 42
  big game hunting — 799.276 542
  conservation technology — 639.979 654 2
Red Deer (Alta.) — T2—712 33
Red Deer River (Alta. and
  Sask.) — T2—712 33
Red drum — 597.725
Red dwarfs — 523.88
Red fox — 599.775
Red kangaroo — 599.222 3
Red Lake County (Minn.) — T2—776 963
Red meat — 641.36
  commercial processing — 664.92
  home preservation — 641.492
  *see also* Meat
Red panda — 599.763
Red peppers — 641.356 43
  botany — 583.952
  *see also* Sweet peppers
Red River (China and
  Vietnam) — T2—597 3
Red River (Minn.-Man.) — T2—784 1

Red River (Tex.-La.) — T2—766 6
  Louisiana — T2—763 6
  Oklahoma — T2—766 6
Red River County (Tex.) — T2—764 212
Red River Delta (Vietnam) — T2—597 3
Red River of the North — T2—784 1
  Manitoba — T2—712 74
  Minnesota — T2—776 9
  North Dakota — T2—784 1
Red River Parish (La.) — T2—763 64
Red River Rebellion, 1869–1870 — 971.051
Red River Valley (Minn.-
  Man.) — T2—784 1
Red Sea — 551.461 533
          T2—165 33
Red Sea (Sudan) — T2—625
Red seaweeds — 579.89
Red squirrels (Eurasia) — 599.362
Red squirrels (North America) — 599.363
Red tide — 579.87
Red Willow County (Neb.) — T2—782 843
Red wine — 641.222 3
  commercial processing — 663.223
  fortified — 641.222 6
  sparkling — 641.222 4
    commercial processing — 663.224
Red wolf — 599.773
Redaction criticism
  sacred books — 208.2
    Bible — 220.66
    Talmud — 296.120 66
Redbridge (London,
  England) — T2—421 73
Redbuds — 635.977 374 9
  botany — 583.749
  ornamental arboriculture — 635.977 374 9
Redcar and Cleveland
  (England) — T2—428 54
Reddersburg (South Africa :
  District) — T2—685 6
Redditch (England) — T2—424 43
Redemption — 202.2
  Christian doctrine — 234.3
    Christology — 232.3
  Judaism — 296.32
Redemption (Public debt)
  public finance — 336.363
Redemptorists — 255.64
  church history — 271.64
Redevelopment
  community sociology — 307.34
Rediscount — 332.84
Redistribution (Election districts) — 328.334 5
Redistricting (Legislatures) — 328.334 5

Redox reaction
  chemical engineering 660.284 43
  organic chemistry 547.23
Redpolls (Birds) 598.885
Reduced cultivation methods 631.581
Reduced instruction set
  computing 004.3
  *see also* Processing modes —
    computer science
Reduced work week 331.257
Reducing 613.712
  dietetics 613.25
  exercise 613.712
Reducing diet
  health 613.25
Reducing enzymes 572.791
  *see also* Enzymes
Reducing exercises
  physical fitness 613.712
Reducing solutions
  photography 771.54
Reduction (Chemical reaction) 541.393
  organic chemistry 547.23
Reduction in force
  economics 331.259 6
    employment security 331.259 6
    unemployment 331.137
  law 344.012 596
  personnel management 658.313 4
  public administration 352.69
Reductionism (Psychology) 150.194
Reductive algebras 512.55
Redwood (Sequoia) 585.5
  forestry 634.975 8
  lumber 674.144
Redwood County (Minn.) T2—776 35
Redwood National Park
  (Calif.) T2—794 12
Reed instruments 788.4
  *see also* Woodwind instruments
Reed organs 786.55
  instrument 786.551 9
  music 786.55
  *see also* Keyboard instruments
Reedbucks 599.645
Reedfishes 597.42
Reeds 584.9
Reefs 551.424
  T2—142
  biology 578.778 9
  ecology 577.789
  geography 910.914 2
  geomorphology 551.424
  physical geography 910.021 42

Reel-to-reel tapes (Computers) 004.563
  engineering 621.397 63
Reelfoot Lake (Tenn.) T2—768 12
Reeling textiles 677.028 22
  arts 746.12
  manufacturing technology 677.028 22
Reels (Dances) 793.34
Reengineering
  executive management 658.406 3
Reentry problems
  space flight 629.415
Reeves County (Tex.) T2—764 924
Refectories
  architecture 726.79
Refereeing (Recreation) 790.1
  American football 796.332 3
  basketball 796.323 3
  Canadian football 796.335 3
  golf 796.352 4
  ice hockey 796.962 3
  rugby 796.333 3
  soccer 796.334 3
  tennis 796.342 3
  volleyball 796.325 3
Reference 401.456
  linguistics 401.456
    specific languages T4—014 56
  philosophy of language 121.68
Reference books 028.7
  bibliographies 011.02
  reviews 028.12
  use 028.7
Reference groups
  social psychology 302.5
Reference services 025.52
Reference works 028.7
  bibliographies 011.02
  reviews 028.12
  use 028.7
Referendum (Legislation) 328.23
Referral services
  physicians 362.172
Refined grain
  commercial processing 664.720 7
Reflection of light
  physics 535.323
Reflection of sound
  engineering 620.21
  physics 534.204
Reflexes
  psychology 152.322
Reflexology
  psychology 150.194 4
Reflexology (Therapy) 615.822 4

| | | | |
|---|---|---|---|
| Reforestation | 333.751 53 | Reformed Church (American Reformed) | |
| law | 346.046 751 53 | (continued) | |
| resource economics | 333.751 53 | seminaries | 230.073 57 |
| silviculture | 634.956 | theology | 230.57 |
| Reform Judaism | 296.834 1 | Reformed Church in America | 285.732 |
| liturgy | 296.450 46 | *see also* Reformed Church | |
| Reform movements | 303.484 | (American Reformed) | |
| agent of social change | 303.484 | Reformed Church in the United | |
| relations with government | 322.44 | States | 285.733 |
| religion | 209 | *see also* Reformed Church | |
| social action | 361.24 | (American Reformed) | |
| Reform Party of Canada | 324.271 04 | Reformed Episcopal Church | 283.3 |
| Reform schools | 365.42 | *see also* Anglican Communion | |
| *see also* Penal institutions | | Reformed Hinduism | 294.556 |
| Reformation | 270.6 | Reformed natural gas | 665.773 |
| European history | 940.23 | Reformed Presbyterian churches | 285.136 |
| German history | 943.03 | *see also* Presbyterian Church | |
| Reformation of offenders | 364.601 | Reformed refinery gas | 665.773 |
| Reformatories | 365.34 | Refraction errors | |
| juvenile offenders | 365.42 | incidence | 614.599 7 |
| *see also* Penal institutions | | optometry | 617.755 |
| Reformed Christians | 284.2 | *see also* Eye diseases — | |
| American | 285.7 | humans | |
| biography | 285.709 2 | Refraction of light | 535.324 |
| biography | 284.209 2 | astronomical corrections | 522.9 |
| European | 284.2 | Refraction of sound | |
| biography | 284.209 2 | acoustical engineering | 620.21 |
| Reformed Church | 284.2 | Refractivity | |
| church government | 262.042 | materials science | 620.112 95 |
| parishes | 254.042 | Refractometry | 543.59 |
| church law | 262.984 2 | Refractory materials | 553.67 |
| doctrines | 230.42 | economic geology | 553.67 |
| catechisms and creeds | 238.42 | materials science | 620.143 |
| guides to Christian life | 248.484 2 | metallurgical furnaces | 669.82 |
| missions | 266.42 | technology | 666.72 |
| moral theology | 241.044 2 | Refrigerants | |
| public worship | 264.042 | refrigeration engineering | 621.564 |
| religious associations | 267.184 2 | Refrigerating foods | 664.028 52 |
| religious education | 268.842 | commercial preservation | 664.028 52 |
| seminaries | 230.073 42 | home preservation | 641.452 |
| theology | 230.42 | Refrigeration | 621.56 |
| Reformed Church (American | | alcoholic beverages | 663.15 |
| Reformed) | 285.7 | nautical engineering | 623.853 5 |
| church government | 262.057 | Refrigeration engineers | 621.560 92 |
| parishes | 254.057 | Refrigerator cars | 385.34 |
| church law | 262.985 7 | engineering | 625.24 |
| doctrines | 230.57 | *see also* Rolling stock | |
| catechisms and creeds | 238.57 | Refrigerators | 621.57 |
| guides to Christian life | 248.485 7 | kitchen appliances | 641.452 028 4 |
| missions | 266.57 | low-temperature engineering | 621.57 |
| moral theology | 241.045 7 | Refugees | 305.906 914 |
| public worship | 264.057 | | T1—086 914 |
| religious associations | 267.185 7 | asylum | 323.631 |
| religious education | 268.857 | citizenship law | 342.083 |

Refugees (continued)
immigration law 342.082
law of nations 341.486
political science 325.21
political status 323.631
social group 305.906 914
social theology 201.762 87
Christianity 261.832 8
social welfare 362.87
public administration 353.533 8
women
social welfare 362.839 814
young people
social welfare 362.779 14
Refugio County (Tex.) T2—764 119
Refuse 363.728
military sanitation 623.754
waste technology 628.44
rural 628.744
*see also* Waste control
Regalia 391
Regals (Music) 786.55
instrument 786.551 9
music 786.55
*see also* Keyboard instruments
Regattas 797.14
Regeneration (Christian doctrine) 234.4
Regeneration (Developmental
biology) 571.889
Regensburg (Germany) T2—433 47
Reggae 781.646
songs 782.421 646
Regge poles 539.721
Reggio di Calabria (Italy) T2—457 831
ancient T2—377 831
Reggio di Calabria (Italy :
Province) T2—457 83
ancient T2—377 83
Reggio Emilia (Italy :
Province) T2—454 3
ancient T2—372 63
Reggio nell'Emilia (Italy :
Province) T2—454 3
ancient T2—372 63
Regiments (Military units) 355.31
Regina (Sask.) T2—712 445
Región Autónoma del
Atlántico Norte
(Nicaragua) T2—728 537
Región Autónoma
del Atlántico Sur
(Nicaragua) T2—728 532

Région de Bruxelles-
Capitale (Belgium) T2—493 32
Région parisienne (France) T2—443 6
Région-Sherbrookoise
(Quebec) T2—714 66
Regional anatomy
animals 573.993 3
humans 611.9
Regional anesthesia
surgery 617.964
Regional associations 341.24
Regional bibliographies 015
Regional cytology
humans 612.9
Regional development 338.9
law 343.074 6
Regional field offices
public administration 352.288
Regional histology 571.59
animals 573.99
humans 612.9
plants 575.435 9
Regional medicine 617.5
anesthesiology 617.967 5
geriatrics 618.977 5
pediatrics 618.920 975
surgery 617.5
*see Manual at* 617.5
Regional nationalism 320.54
Regional organizations 341.24
Regional physiology 571.59
animals 573.99
humans 612.9
plants 575.4
Regional planning 307.12
civic art 711.3
community sociology 307.12
economics 338.9
law 346.045
Regional surgery 617.5
anesthesiology 617.967 5
*see Manual at* 617.5
Regional treatment T1—09
Regionalist parties 324.218 4
Regions T2—1
Regions (Local government
units) 320.83
*see also* Counties
Regions (State-level units) 321.023
*see also* States (Members of
federations)
Registered mail 383.182
*see also* Postal service

Registered nursing assistants 610.730 92
  role and function 610.730 693
Registered partners 306.841
                T1—086 56
Registered partnerships 306.841
                T1—086 56
  law 346.016
Registration 352.84
  *see also* Licensing
Registration for military service 355.223 6
Registration of voters 324.64
Registration plates 929.9
Regression analysis 519.536
Regressive taxation 336.293
Regular Baptists 286.1
  *see also* Baptists
Regulation (Public
  administration) 352.8
Regulation of conduct
  armed forces 355.133
Regulations (Laws) 348.025
  United States 348.732 5
Regulatory agencies 352.8
  decisions 348.045
    United States 348.734 5
  law 342.066 4
  rulings 348.045
    United States 348.734 5
Rehabilitation
  geriatrics 618.977 03
  health services 362.178 6
    medicine 617.03
  housing services 363.583
  injuries
    medicine 617.103
  natural resources 333.715 3
  prisoner services 365.661
  social services 362.042 5
Rehabilitation (Restoration of
  rights) 345.077
Rehabilitation training 362.042 5
  labor economics 331.259 2
  personnel management 658.312 44
  public administration 352.669
Rehabilitative therapy 617.06
  injuries
    medicine 617.106
Rehearsal
  musical technique 781.44
Reid, G. H. (George Houstoun)
  Australian history 994.041
Reigate and Banstead
  (England) T2—422 17
Reign of Terror, 1793–1794 944.044

Reiki (Therapy)
  medicine 615.852
Reimbursement health insurance 368.382
Reims (France) T2—443 22
Reina, Carlos Roberto
  Honduran history 972.830 535
Reincarnation
  occultism 133.901 35
  philosophy 129
  religion 202.37
    Buddhism 294.342 37
    Hinduism 294.523 7
Reindeer 599.658
  animal husbandry 636.294 8
  conservation technology 639.979 658
  resource economics 333.959 658
Reindexing
  library operations 025.39
Reinforced concrete 624.183 41
  architectural construction 721.044 54
  building construction 693.54
  foundation materials 624.153 37
  materials science 620.137
  ship design 623.818 341
  ship hulls 623.845 41
  shipbuilding 623.820 7
  structural engineering 624.183 41
Reinforced plastics 668.494
Reinforcement (Psychology) 153.85
Reinforcing plastics 668.416
Reinstatement (Military
  personnel) 355.114
Reinsurance 368.012 2
  law 346.086 012 2
Reinventing government 352.3
REIT 332.632 47
Reitz (South Africa :
  District) T2—685 1
Relapsing fevers
  incidence 614.574 4
  medicine 616.924 4
  *see also* Communicable
    diseases — humans
Relation (Philosophy) 111
Relational databases
  computer science 005.756
Relational grammar 415.018
  specific languages T4—501 8
Relations (Mathematics) 511.326
Relative indexing 025.47
Relatives (People) 306.87
                T1—085

| | |
|---|---|
| Relativism | 149 |
| epistemology | 121 |
| ethics | 171.7 |
| Relativistic particles | 539.72 |
| Relativity theory | 530.11 |
| philosophy | 115 |
| Relaxation (Humans) | |
| physical fitness | 613.792 |
| Relaxation (Physics) | |
| solid-state physics | 530.416 |
| Relaxation methods (Numerical | |
| methods) | 518.63 |
| Relaxing (Hairdressing) | 646.724 |
| Relay communication | |
| engineering | 621.382 5 |
| Relay races | 796.427 |
| Relay systems | |
| radio engineering | 621.384 156 |
| Relays (Electrical) | 621.317 |
| electronic circuits | 621.381 537 |
| Relevance (Information science) | 025.04 |
| Relevance logic | 511.31 |
| Reliability | |
| computer software | 005 |
| Reliability engineering | 620.004 52 |
| Reliability theory | 519.287 |
| Reliance (N.W.T.) | T2—719 3 |
| Relics | |
| Christianity | 235.2 |
| theft of | 364.162 823 52 |
| law | 345.026 282 352 |
| Passion of Jesus Christ | 232.966 |
| Relief (Sculpture) | 731.54 |
| architectural decoration | 729.5 |
| Relief (Welfare) | 361.05 |
| *see also* Welfare services | |
| Relief printing | 761 |
| Relief valves | |
| steam engineering | 621.185 |
| Relief work | 361.3 |
| *see also* Welfare services | |
| Religion | 200 |
| art representation | 704.948 |
| arts | 700.482 |
| | T3C—382 |
| law | 344.096 |
| literature | 808.803 82 |
| history and criticism | 809.933 82 |
| specific literatures | T3B—080 382 |
| history and | |
| criticism | T3B—093 82 |
| painting | 755 |
| primary education | 372.84 |
| public administrative support | 353.7 |

| | |
|---|---|
| Religion (continued) | |
| sociology | 306.6 |
| *see Manual at* 130 vs. 200; | |
| *also at* 200 vs. 100; *also at* | |
| 201–209 and 292–299 | |
| Religion and culture | 201.7 |
| Christianity | 261 |
| Islam | 297.27 |
| Judaism | 296.38 |
| sociology | 306.6 |
| Religion and politics | 322.1 |
| social theology | 201.72 |
| *see also* Politics and religion | |
| Religion and science | 201.65 |
| *see also* Science and religion | |
| Religion and secular disciplines | 201.6 |
| Buddhism | 294.336 |
| Christianity | 261.5 |
| *see Manual at* 261.5 | |
| Hinduism | 294.516 |
| Islam | 297.26 |
| *see Manual at* 297.26–.27 | |
| Judaism | 296.37 |
| philosophy of religion | 215 |
| Religion and state | 322.1 |
| social theology | 201.72 |
| *see also* Politics and religion | |
| Religion historians | 200.92 |
| Religion in public schools | 379.28 |
| law | 344.079 6 |
| Religions | 200 |
| *see also* Religion | |
| *see Manual at* 201–209 and | |
| 292–299 | |
| Religious (Members of Christian | |
| orders) | 255 |
| biography | 271.009 2 |
| *see Manual at* 230–280 | |
| church history | 271 |
| ecclesiology | 262.24 |
| guides to Christian life | 248.894 |
| Religious arts | 700.482 |
| | T3C—382 |
| fine arts | 704.948 |
| religious significance | 203.7 |
| *see also* Arts — religious | |
| significance | |
| Religious authority | 206.5 |
| Christianity | 262.8 |
| Judaism | 296.67 |
| Religious broadcasting | |
| Christianity | 269.26 |

| | |
|---|---|
| Religious buildings | |
| architecture | 726 |
| area planning | 711.56 |
| institutional housekeeping | 647.98 |
| interior decoration | 747.86 |
| religious significance | 203.5 |
| Christianity | 246.9 |
| Judaism | 296.46 |
| Religious conflict | 306.6 |
| influence on crime | 364.256 |
| Religious dance | |
| religious significance | 203.7 |
| Christianity | 246.7 |
| *see also* Arts — religious significance | |
| Religious dietary limitations | 204.46 |
| cooking for | 641.567 |
| Hinduism | 294.544 6 |
| Islam | 297.576 |
| Judaism | 296.73 |
| Religious education | 207.5 |
| Buddhism | 294.375 |
| Christianity | 268 |
| Hinduism | 294.575 |
| Islam | 297.77 |
| Judaism | 296.68 |
| *see Manual at* 207.5, 268 vs. 200.71, 230.071, 292–299 | |
| Religious ethics | 205 |
| Buddhism | 294.35 |
| Christianity | 241 |
| Hinduism | 294.548 |
| Islam | 297.5 |
| Sufi | 297.45 |
| Judaism | 296.36 |
| Religious experience | 204.2 |
| Buddhism | 294.344 2 |
| Christianity | 248.2 |
| Hinduism | 294.542 |
| Islam | 297.57 |
| Sufi | 297.4 |
| Judaism | 296.71 |
| Religious freedom | 323.442 |
| civil right | 323.442 |
| law | 342.085 2 |
| law of nations | 341.483 2 |
| social theology | 201.723 |
| Christianity | 261.72 |
| *see also* Politics and religion — social theology | |
| Religious groups | T1—088 2 |
| collected biography | T1—092 8 |
| journalism for | 070.482 |
| Religious groups (continued) | |
| labor economics | 331.58 |
| legal status | 346.013 |
| constitutional law | 342.087 |
| private law | 346.013 |
| libraries for | 027.67 |
| relations with state | 322.1 |
| sociology | 305.6 |
| *see Manual at* 305.6 vs. 305.92, 306.6 | |
| Religious healing | |
| religion | 203.1 |
| *see also* Spiritual healing — religion | |
| Religious holidays | 203.6 |
| customs | 394.265 |
| *see Manual at* 203.6, 263.9, 292–299 vs. 394.265–.267 | |
| *see also* Holidays; Holy days | |
| Religious ideologies | |
| political science | 320.55 |
| Religious institutions | |
| accounting | 657.832 |
| Religious language | 210.14 |
| Christianity | 230.014 |
| Religious law | 208.4 |
| Buddhism | 294.384 |
| Christianity | 262.9 |
| Hinduism | 294.594 |
| Islam | 297.14 |
| Judaism | 296.18 |
| Religious leaders | 200.92 |
| biography | 200.92 |
| Buddhist | 294.309 2 |
| biography | 294.309 2 |
| specific sects | 294.39 |
| role and function | 294.361 |
| Christian | 270.092 |
| biography | 270.092 |
| specific denominations | 280 |
| *see Manual at* 230–280 | |
| ecclesiology | 262.1 |
| occupational ethics | 241.641 |
| pastoral theology | 253 |
| personal religion | 248.892 |
| training | 230.071 1 |
| Hindu | 294.509 2 |
| biography | 294.509 2 |
| specific sects | 294.55 |
| role and function | 294.561 |
| Islamic | 297.092 |
| biography | 297.092 |
| specific sects | 297.8 |

Religious leaders
  Islamic (continued)
    role and function     297.61
    *see Manual at* 297.092
    Jewish     296.092
      biography     296.092
        specific denominations     296.8
      professional ethics     296.364 1
      role and function     296.61
      training     296.071 1
    occupational ethics     174.1
      religion     205.641
    role and function     206.1
    social group     305.92
    *see Manual at* 200.92 and
      201–209, 292–299
Religious life     204.4
  Buddhism     294.344 4
  Christianity     248.4
  Hinduism     294.544
  Islam     297.57
    Sufi     297.44
  Judaism     296.7
  *see also* Monasticism
Religious medals
  numismatics     737.224
  religious significance     203.7
  *see also* Symbolism —
    religious significance
Religious mythology     201.3
  art representation     704.948
  arts     700.482 013
        T3C—382 013
  literature     808.803 820 13
    history and criticism     809.933 820 13
    specific literatures   T3B—080 382 013
      history and
        criticism   T3B—093 820 13
Religious observances     203
  Christianity     263
  Judaism     296.4
  private     204.46
    Christianity     248.46
    Judaism     296.7
Religious orders     206.57
  Buddhism     294.365 7
  Christianity     255
    church history     271
    ecclesiology     262.24
    organization     255

Religious organizations     206.5
  Christianity     260
    associations for religious
      work     267
    denominations     280
    local church     250
      specific local churches     280
    religious orders     255
    *see Manual at* 260 vs.
      251–254, 259
  congregations     206.5
  Islam     297.65
  Judaism     296.67
  publishing     070.594
  relations with state     322.1
  sociology     306.6
  welfare services     361.75
  *see Manual at* 322.1 vs. 201.72,
    261.7, 292–299
Religious pageants
  performing arts     791.622
  religious significance     203.7
    Christianity     246.72
Religious plays
  literature     808.825 16
    history and criticism     809.251 6
    specific literatures   T3B—205 16
      individual authors   T3A—2
  religious significance     203.7
    Christianity     246.72
      religious education     268.67
  stage presentation     792.16
Religious pluralism     201.5
  *see also* Pluralism (Religion)
Religious policy (Government
  policy)     322.1
Religious political parties     324.218 2
  international organizations     324.182
Religious publishers     070.594
Religious rites     203.8
  *see also* Rites — religion
Religious schools (General
  education)     371.07
  libraries     027.83
Religious services     203.8
  armed forces     355.347
  penal institutions     365.665
  *see also* Rites — religion
Religious socialization     303.325
Religious studies     200.71
  *see Manual at* 207.5, 268 vs.
    200.71, 230.071, 292–299

Religious symbolism 203.7
  art representation 704.948
  painting 755
  *see also* Symbolism —
    religious significance
Religious therapy
  medicine 615.852
Reliquaries
  Christianity 247
Relishes 641.812
Relizane (Algeria :
  Province) T2—651
Remarriage 306.84
  ethics 173
  Judaism 296.444
  social theology 201.7
    Christianity 261.835 84
Remedial education
  adult level 374.012
Remedial reading 418.4
  primary education 372.43
  specific languages T4—842
Remedies (Legal actions) 347.077
Remembrance days
  Holocaust, 1933–1945 940.531 862
Reminiscences 920
    T1—092
  biography 920
  literature 808.883
    history and criticism 809.983
    specific literatures T3B—803
      individual authors T3A—8
Remodeling of buildings 690.24
  architecture 720.286
  home economics 643.7
  *see Manual at* 690 vs. 643.7
Remodeling of clothes 646.4
Remonstrant churches 284.9
Remonstrants
  biography 284.9
Remote control 620.46
  radio engineering 621.384 196
Remote-control models 796.15
  *see Manual at* 796.15 vs.
    629.0460228
Remote-control vehicles
  engineering 629.046
  recreation 796.15
Remote procedure calls 005.71
Remote sensing technology 621.367 8
Remount services 357.2
Removal from office
  recall elections 324.68
Renaissance architecture 724.12

Renaissance art 709.024
  religious significance 246.4
Renaissance decoration 745.409 024
Renaissance music 780.903 1
Renaissance painting 759.03
Renaissance period
  European history 940.21
  Italian history 945.05
Renaissance revival architecture 724.52
Renaissance sculpture 735.21
Renal dialysis
  medicine 617.461 059
Renal disease
  medicine 616.61
  *see also* Urologic diseases —
    humans
Renal failure
  medicine 616.614
  *see also* Urologic diseases —
    humans
Renal hypertension
  medicine 616.132
  *see also* Cardiovascular
    diseases — humans
Rendering oils and gases 665.028 2
Rendezvous
  manned space flight 629.458 3
Renegotiation of government
  contracts 352.53
Renewable energy resources 333.794
  economics 333.794
  engineering 621.042
Renewal theory 519.287
Renfrew (Ont. : County) T2—713 81
Renfrew (Scotland) T2—414 37
Renfrew (Scotland :
  District) T2—414 37
Renfrewshire (Scotland) T2—414 37
Renmark (S. Aust.) T2—942 33
Rennellese language 499.46
    T6—994 6
Rennes (France) T2—441 54
Reno (Nev.) T2—793 55
Reno County (Kan.) T2—781 83
Renovation 690.24
  home economics 643.7
  *see Manual at* 690 vs. 643.7
Rensselaer County (N.Y.) T2—747 41
Rent
  income distribution 339.21
  land economics 333.5
  law 346.043 44
  public revenue 336.12
Rent (Economic theory) 333.012

| | | | |
|---|---|---|---|
| Rent control | 363.583 | Reports | |
| law | 346.043 44 | audits | 657.452 |
| Rent subsidies | 363.582 | financial management | 658.151 2 |
| Rental collections | | office records | 651.78 |
| museology | 069.56 | Repossession | 347.077 |
| Rental housing | 363.5 | installment sales | 346.074 |
| household management | | Repoussé | |
| apartments | 647.92 | decorative arts | 739.14 |
| Rental libraries | 027.3 | sculpture | 731.41 |
| Rental services | | Representation | 324.63 |
| museology | 069.13 | electoral politics | 324.63 |
| Renting | | legislative districts | 328.334 5 |
| land economics | 333.5 | political right | 323.5 |
| Renville County (Minn.) | T2—776 34 | Representation theory | |
| Renville County (N.D) | T2—784 64 | operational calculus | 515.722 3 |
| Reorganization | | Representations | |
| management | 658.16 | fine arts | 704.9 |
| internal organization | 658.402 | museology | 069.134 |
| public administration | 352.28 | Representations of groups | 512.22 |
| public administration | 352.2 | Repression | 323.044 |
| Reorganized Church of Jesus | | Reprieve | 364.63 |
| Christ of Latter Day Saints | 289.333 | Reprimands | |
| *see also* Mormon Church | | personnel management | 658.314 4 |
| Reoviridae | 579.254 | Reprints | |
| Repairs | 620.004 6 | bibliographies | 011.47 |
| | T1—028 8 | Reprisals | |
| buildings | 690.24 | international relations | 327.117 |
| *see Manual at* 690 vs. 643.7 | | law | 341.582 |
| home economics | 643.7 | Reproducers | |
| library materials | 025.84 | sound engineering | 621.389 33 |
| Reparations | | Reproduction | 571.8 |
| law of war | 341.66 | animals | 573.6 |
| revenue source | 336.182 | biology | 571.8 |
| World War I | 940.314 22 | ethics | 176 |
| World War II | 940.531 422 | religion | 205.66 |
| Reparative surgery | 617.952 | Buddhism | 294.356 6 |
| Repatriation | 323.64 | Christianity | 241.66 |
| Repayment (Public debt) | | Hinduism | 294.548 66 |
| public finance | 336.363 | Islam | 297.566 |
| Repeal of legislation | 328.37 | Judaism | 296.366 |
| Repentance | 202.2 | human physiology | |
| Christianity | 234.5 | primary education | 372.372 |
| Islam | 297.22 | microorganisms | 571.842 9 |
| Judaism | 296.32 | plants | 575.6 |
| Repetition learning | | *see Manual at* 571.8 vs. 573.6, | |
| psychology | 153.152 2 | 575.6 | |
| Report writing (Study technique) | 371.302 81 | Reproduction (Memory) | 153.123 |
| Reporters | 070.430 92 | Reproductions | |
| Reporting | | arts | 702.872 |
| executive management | 658.45 | paintings | 751.5 |
| military administration | 355.688 | Reproductive adaptation | 578.46 |
| public administration | 352.38 | animals | 591.46 |
| financial management | 658.151 2 | plants | 581.46 |
| journalism | 070.43 | Reproductive behavior (Animals) | 591.56 |

Reproductive hormones    571.837 4
   *see also* Sex hormones
Reproductive organs    573.6
   *see also* Genital system
Reproductive system    573.6
   animals    573.6
    descriptive zoology    591.46
    physiology    573.6
    *see also* Genital system
   biology    573.6
   plants    575.6
    descriptive botany    581.46
    physiology    575.6
Reproductive technology
   humans
    ethics    176.2
     *see also* Reproduction —
     ethics
    health    613.94
    infertility
     gynecology    618.178 06
    medicine    616.692 06
Reproductive toxicology
   medicine    616.650 71
Reprography    686
   equipment manufacturing
    technology    681.6
   library services    025.12
   office use    652.4
Reptantia    595.38
Reptiles    597.9
   agriculture    639.39
   art representation    704.943 279
   arts    T3C—362 79
   big game hunting    799.279
   commercial hunting    639.14
   conservation technology    639.977 9
   drawing    743.679
   food    641.396
    cooking    641.696
   paleozoology    567.9
   resource economics    333.957
   zoology    597.9
Reptiles as pets    639.39
Republic County (Kan.)    T2—781 24
Republic of Korea    951.95
     T2—519 5
Republic of South Africa    968
     T2—68
Republic of Texas    976.404
Republic of the Congo    967.24
   (Brazzaville)    T2—672 4
Republican Party (U.S. :
   1792–1828)    324.273 26

Republican Party (U.S. : 1854– )    324.273 4
Republican Party of Germany    324.243 03
Republican River (Neb. and
   Kan.)    T2—781 2
   Kansas    T2—781 2
   Nebraska    T2—782 37
Republics    321.86
Republikaner (German political
   party)    324.243 03
Repudiation of debt
   public finance    336.368
Repulse Bay (Nunavut)    T2—719 58
Requiem mass    264.36
   music    782.323 8
    choral and mixed voices    782.532 38
    single voices    783.093 238
Required courses    375.002
   higher education    378.24
Requisition
   military resources    355.28
Reredoses    247.1
   architecture    726.529 6
Res judicata    347.077
Resampling methods    519.54
Rescission (Law)    346.022
Rescue aircraft
   military engineering    623.746 6
Rescue dogs    636.708 86
Rescue operations    363.348 1
   disaster relief    363.348 1
   engineering    628.92
   fire safety    363.378 1
    technology    628.922
   Holocaust, 1933–1945    940.531 835
   mining technology    622.89
   seamanship    623.888 7
Research    001.4
     T1—072
   public administrative support    352. /4
   *see Manual at* T1—072 vs.
    T1—0601–0609
Research and development
   air force supplies    358.407
   military science    355.07
   naval forces    359.07
   production management    658.57
   public administration    354.27
    noneconomic fields    352.7
   public contract law    346.023
Research buildings    001.4
   *see also* Laboratories
Research ethics    174

Research methods      001.42
     T1—072 1
  *see Manual at*
     T1—07201–07209 vs.
     T1—0721
Research reports
  biology      570
  *see Manual at* 571–573 vs.
     610
  medicine      610
  rhetoric      808.02
Researchers      001.409 2
Resedaceae      583.64
Reservation systems
  transportation      388.042
  air service      387.742 2
  *see also* Passenger services
Reservations (Military
  installations)      355.7
Reserve collections in libraries      025.6
Reserve Officer Training Corps      355.223 207 1173
Reserve requirements
  central banking      332.113
Reserve status (Armed forces)      355.113
Reserve training (Armed forces)      355.223 2
Reserves (Armed forces)      355.37
Reserves (Capital management)      658.152 26
Reserves (Natural resources)      333.711
Reservoir engineering
  oil extraction      622.338 2
Reservoirs      627.86
  biology      578.763
  ecology      577.63
  flood control      627.44
  landscape architecture      719.33
  recreational resources      333.784 6
  recreational use      797
  water supply engineering      628.132
Resettlement
  community sociology      307.2
  housing services      363.583
  *see also* Housing
  public administration      353.59
Residency (Training)      T1—071 55
Residential buildings      643.1
  *see also* Dwellings
Residential cities
  area planning      711.45
Residential finance      332.722
Residential homes      362.61
Residential land      333.77
  area planning      711.58
  community sociology      307.336

Residential land (continued)
  resource economics      333.77
  taxation      336.225
Residential water supply      363.61
  economics      333.912 2
Residents (Students)
  training      T1—071 55
Residues
  petroleum      665.538 8
  wood      674.84
Residues (Mathematics)      512.72
Resignation of employees
  armed forces      355.114
  personnel management      658.313
    public administration      352.69
Resin-derived plastics      668.45
Resin-producing plants
  agriculture      633.895
  economic botany      581.636
Resins
  chemistry      547.843 4
  commercial processing      668.37
  fossil      553.29
  materials science      620.192 4
  recovery from pulp      676.5
Resist-dyeing
  textile arts      746.66
Resistance
  materials science      620.112
Resistance boxes      621.374 2
Resistance movements
  Holocaust, 1933–1945      940.531 832
  World War II      940.533 6
Resistance thermometry      536.502 87
Resistance to government      323.044
Resistance warfare      355.021 8
Resistance welding      671.521 3
Resistant construction
  buildings      693.8
  ship hulls      623.848
Resistivity
  skin
    human physiology      612.791
Resistivity in semiconductors      537.622 6
Resistors
  radio engineering      621.384 133
Resolute (Nunavut)      T2—719 52
Resolutions (Legislation)
  enactment      328.377
Resonance
  musical technique      781.48
    instrumental      784.193 2
Resonance accelerators      539.733
Resorcinols      547.633

Resorts 910.462
  accounting 657.837 4
  architecture 728.5
  area planning 711.557
  community sociology 307.334
  household management 647.94
  land economics 333.78
  landscape architecture 712.7
  management 647.940 68
  personal health 613.122
  recreational sociology 306.481 9
  sanitation services 363.729 8
    law 344.046 4
  travel 910.462
Resource Description Framework 025.042 7
Resource development
  banking 332.153
    domestic 332.28
    international 332.153
  natural resources 333.715
Resource recovery 363.728 2
  *see also* Waste control
Resources
  education and research T1—07
    *see Manual at* 016 vs. 026,
    T1—07
  military science 355.2
    law 343.013
  natural 333.7
Respect 179.9
Respiration 572.47
  animals 573.2
  biochemistry 572.47
  human biochemistry 612.22
  human biophysics 612.21
  human physiology 612.2
  microorganisms 572.472 9
  plants 572.472
  *see also* Respiratory system
Respiration disorders
  medicine 616.2
  *see also* Respiratory tract
    diseases — humans
Respiratory agents
  pharmacokinetics 615.72
Respiratory allergies
  medicine 616.202
  *see also* Respiratory tract
    diseases — humans
Respiratory diseases 573.239
  *see also* Respiratory tract
    diseases
Respiratory mechanics
  humans 612.21

Respiratory organs 573.2
  *see also* Respiratory system
Respiratory sounds
  human physiology 612.21
Respiratory system 573.2
  biology 573.2
  diseases 573.239
    *see also* Respiratory tract
    diseases
  human anatomy 611.2
  human histology 612.204 5
  human physiology 612.2
  medicine 616.2
  surgery 617.54
Respiratory therapy
  medicine 615.836
Respiratory tract diseases 573.239
  animals 573.239
    veterinary medicine 636.089 62
  humans 362.196 2
    cancer 362.196 994 2
      incidence 614.599 942
      medicine 616.994 2
      social services 362.196 994 2
      *see also* Cancer — humans
    geriatrics 618.976 2
    incidence 614.592
    medicine 616.2
    nursing 616.200 423 1
    pediatrics 618.922
    pharmacokinetics 615.72
    social services 362.196 2
    surgery 617.54
Respiratory tract infections
  medicine 616.2
  *see also* Respiratory tract
    diseases — humans
Responsa (Jewish law) 296.185
Responses
  music 782.292
Responsibility
  executive management 658.402
  law 346.022
  military administration 355.685
  public administration 352.35
Responsive readings
  public worship 203.8
    Christianity 264.4
    Judaism 296.45
Rest
  animal physiology 573.79
  human physiology 612.76
  physical fitness 613.79

Rest areas
  road engineering     625.77
Rest homes     362.61
  *see also* Health care facilities
Rest periods
  labor economics     331.257 6
  personnel management     658.312 2
Restaurant cooking     641.572
Restaurant meal service     642.5
Restaurants     647.95
  arts     T3C—356 4
  literature     808.803 564
    history and criticism     809.933 564
  *see also* Eating places
Restaurateurs     647.950 92
Restigouche (N.B.)     T2—715 11
Restigouche River (N.B.
  and Quebec)     T2—715 11
Restionales     584.8
Restitution (Law of war)     341.66
  Holocaust, 1933–1945     940.531 814 4
Restitution coefficient     531.382
Restoration     T1—028 8
  arts     702.88
  cinematography     777.58
  engineering     620.004 6
  library materials     025.84
  museology     069.53
  videography     777.58
  wooden furniture     684.104 42
Restoration (France), 1815–1848     944.06
Restoration (Great Britain),
  1660–1688     941.066
  English history     942.066
  Scottish history     941.106 6
Restoration (Spain), 1814–1833     946.072
Restoration (Spain), 1871–1873     946.073
Restoration movement (Christian
  movement)     286.6
  biography     286.609 2
  church government     262.066
    parishes     254.066
  church law     262.986 6
  doctrines     230.66
    catechisms and creeds     238.66
  guides to Christian life     248.486 6
  missions     266.66
  moral theology     241.046 6
  public worship     264.066
  religious associations     267.186 6
  religious education     268.866
  seminaries     230.073 66
  theology     230.66
Restoration of natural resources     333.715 3

Restorative surgery     617.952
Restoring torques
  aeronautics     629.132 364
Restormel (England)     T2—423 7
Restraint
  social control     303.36
Restraint of trade (Competition)     338.604 8
  criminology     364.168
    criminal law     345.026 8
  economics     338.604 8
  law     343.072 3
Restrictive environments
  psychology     155.96
Restrictive practices     338.82
  economics     338.82
  international economics     338.884
Rests (Music)     781.236
Résumé writing     650.142
Résumés (Employment)     650.142
Resurfacing
  road maintenance     625.761
Resurrection     202.3
  Christianity     236.8
  Islam     297.23
  Judaism     296.33
Resurrection of Jesus Christ     232.5
  life     232.97
Resurrection plants     587.9
Resuscitation
  medicine     616.025
Retail advertising     659.131 4
Retail chains     381.12
  management     658.870 2
  *see also* Commerce
Retail credit
  marketing management     658.883
Retail marketing     381.1
  management     658.87
  *see also* Commerce
Retail salesmanship     381.1
  etiquette     395.53
  management     658.85
Retail stores     381.1
  management     658.87
Retail trade     381.1
  accounting     657.839
  marketing management     658.87
  *see also* Commerce
Retail trade buildings
  architecture     725.21
Retained profits
  capital formation     332.041 52

| | |
|---|---|
| Retaining walls | 721.2 |
|   architecture | 721.2 |
|   construction | 690.12 |
|   railroad engineering | 625.13 |
|   structural engineering | 624.164 |
| Retalhuleu (Guatemala : | |
|   Dept.) | T2—728 183 |
| Retarding (Plants) | 631.583 |
|   floriculture | 635.982 |
|   gardening | 635.048 3 |
| Retention | |
|   archives | 025.281 4 |
| Retention (Memory) | 153.122 |
| Retention of records | 651.51 |
| Rethymnē (Greece) | T2—495 9 |
| Reticular tissues | |
|   human histology | 611.018 2 |
| Reticulated beetles | 595.762 |
| Reticuloendothelial system | |
|   human immunology | 616.079 9 |
| Reticulosis | |
|   incidence | 614.599 944 2 |
|   medicine | 616.994 42 |
|     *see also* Cancer — humans | |
| Retinal diseases | |
|   incidence | 614.599 7 |
|   ophthalmology | 617.735 |
|     *see also* Eye diseases — | |
|       humans | |
| Retinas | |
|   human anatomy | 611.84 |
|   human physiology | 612.843 |
|   ophthalmology | 617.735 |
| Retinitis pigmentosa | |
|   ophthalmology | 617.735 |
|     *see also* Eye diseases — | |
|       humans | |
| Retired people | 306.38 |
| | T1—086 96 |
|   labor economics | 331.5 |
|   psychology | 155.672 |
|   religion | 200.869 6 |
|     Christianity | 270.086 96 |
|   social welfare | 362.899 6 |
|   women | 306.380 82 |
|     social welfare | 362.839 84 |
| Retirees | 306.38 |
| | T1—086 96 |
|   *see also* Retired people | |
| Retirement | 306.38 |
|   armed forces | 355.114 |
|   financial planning | 332.024 014 |
|   personnel management | 658.313 2 |
|     public administration | 352.69 |
| Retirement (continued) | |
|   psychology | 155.672 |
|   sociology | 306.38 |
| Retirement age | |
|   economics | 331.252 |
|   personnel management | 658.313 2 |
| Retirement benefits | 331.252 |
|   law | 344.012 52 |
|     public employees | 342.068 6 |
| Retirement counseling | |
|   personnel management | 658.385 |
| Retirement guides | |
|   life skills | 646.79 |
| Retirement income | 332.024 014 |
|   pensions | 331.252 |
|     *see also* Pensions | |
|   personal finance | 332.024 014 |
|   tax economics | 336.242 8 |
|   tax law | 343.052 4 |
| Retirement investment plans | 332.024 014 5 |
| Retirement planning | 332.024 014 |
| Retracts | 514.24 |
| Retraining | |
|   labor economics | 331.259 24 |
|   law | 344.012 592 4 |
|     public employees | 342.068 6 |
|   personnel management | 658.312 43 |
|   social welfare | 362.042 5 |
|   vocational education | 370.113 |
| Retreats (Military tactics) | 355.422 |
| Retreats (Religion) | |
|   Christianity | 269.6 |
| Retribution | |
|   penology | 364.601 |
| Retrieval of information | |
|   information science | 025.524 |
| Retrievers | 636.752 7 |
| Retrospective conversion | |
|   library operations | 025.317 3 |
| Retroviridae | 579.256 9 |
|   medical microbiology | 616.918 801 |
| Retroviridae infections | |
|   incidence | 614.588 |
|   medicine | 616.918 8 |
|     *see also* Communicable | |
|       diseases — humans | |
| Retroviruses | 579.256 9 |
| Rett syndrome | |
|   medicine | 616.858 84 |
|   pediatrics | 618.928 588 4 |
| Return to Orthodox Judaism | 296.715 |
| Returned merchandise | |
|   marketing management | 658.812 |
| Reunification of Germany | 943.087 8 |

| | |
|---|---|
| Réunion | 969.81 |
| | T2—698 1 |
| Reusability | |
| computer software | 005 |
| Reuss River (Switzerland) | T2—494 566 |
| Revegetation | 631.64 |
| Revelation (Biblical book) | 228 |
| Revelation of God | 212.6 |
| Bible | 220.13 |
| Christianity | 231.74 |
| comparative religion | 202.117 |
| Islam | 297.211 5 |
| Judaism | 296.311 5 |
| philosophy of religion | 212.6 |
| Revelstoke (B.C.) | T2—711 68 |
| Revenue | 336.02 |
| financial management | 658.155 4 |
| law | 343.036 |
| public administration | 352.44 |
| public finance | 336.02 |
| Revenue budgets (Public) | 352.48 |
| *see also* Budgets (Public) | |
| Revenue cutters | 363.286 |
| design | 623.812 63 |
| engineering | 623.826 3 |
| police services | 363.286 |
| Revenue offenses | 364.133 |
| law | 345.023 3 |
| Revenue sharing | 336.185 |
| law | 343.034 |
| public administration | 352.73 |
| public finance | 336.185 |
| Revenue stamps | 336.272 |
| prints | 769.572 |
| public finance | 336.272 |
| Revenue tariffs | 382.72 |
| *see also* Customs (Tariff) | |
| Reveries | 154.3 |
| Reverse dictionaries | 413.1 |
| specific languages | T4—31 |
| Reverse osmosis | |
| desalinization | 628.167 44 |
| Review | |
| study and teaching | T1—076 |
| Reviews | |
| ballet | 792.845 |
| books | 028.1 |
| films | 791.437 5 |
| musical plays | 792.645 |
| opera | 792.545 |
| radio programs | 791.447 5 |
| television programs | 791.457 5 |
| Revised English Bible | 220.520 6 |
| Revised Standard version Bible | 220.520 42 |

| | |
|---|---|
| Revised versions of Bible | 220.520 4 |
| Revival meetings | 269.24 |
| Revolution | 303.64 |
| ethics | 172.1 |
| political science | 321.094 |
| social change | 303.4 |
| social conflict | 303.64 |
| social theology | 201.72 |
| Buddhism | 294.337 2 |
| Christianity | 261.7 |
| Hinduism | 294.517 2 |
| Judaism | 296.382 |
| *see Manual at* 909, 930–990 vs. 320.4, 321, 321.09 | |
| Revolution of 1891 (Chilean history) | 983.062 |
| Revolution of 1911–1912 (Chinese history) | 951.036 |
| Revolution of 1918 (German history) | 943.085 1 |
| Revolution of 1958 (Venezuelan history) | 987.063 3 |
| Revolution of April 1870 (Venezuelan history) | 987.062 |
| Revolution of October 1945 (Venezuelan history) | 987.063 2 |
| Revolutionäre Marxistische Liga (Swiss political party) | 324.249 407 5 |
| Revolutionary activities | 322.42 |
| Revolutionary groups | 322.42 |
| Revolutionary Marxist League (Swiss political party) | 324.249 407 5 |
| Revolutionary unions | |
| labor economics | 331.886 |
| Revolutionary warfare | 355.021 8 |
| Revolutions of 1848 | 940.284 |
| German history | 943.074 |
| Revolvers | 683.436 |
| art metalwork | 739.744 36 |
| manufacturing technology | 683.436 |
| military engineering | 623.443 6 |
| *see also* Guns (Small arms) | |
| Revues | 782.14 |
| music | 782.14 |
| stage presentation | 792.6 |
| Rewards | |
| armed forces | 355.134 |
| social control | 303.35 |
| student discipline | 371.53 |
| Reweaving | 646.25 |
| clothing care | 646.6 |
| home sewing | 646.25 |
| Rex cat | 636.822 |

Reye syndrome
  medicine        616.83
    *see also* Nervous system
      diseases — humans
  pediatrics      618.928 3
Reynolds County (Mo.)    T2—778 885
Reza Shah Pahlavi, Shah of Iran
  Iranian history      955.052
RFD (Mail delivery)      383.145
  *see also* Postal service
RFID (Radio frequency
  identification)      006.245
  computer science      006.245
  engineering      621.384 192
Rh factor
  human physiology      612.118 25
  incompatibility
    pediatrics      618.921 5
    perinatal medicine      618.326 1
    *see also* Cardiovascular
      diseases — humans
Rhabdocoela      592.42
Rhabdofario      597.57
Rhabdoviridae      579.256 6
Rhade (Vietnamese people)    T5—992 2
Rhaetia    T2—369 47
  Austria    T2—363 64
  Switzerland    T2—369 47
Rhaetian Alps    T2—494 732
Rhaetian languages      459.9
    T6—599
Rhaetian literatures      859.9
Rhaetians    T5—599
Rhaeto-Romanic languages      459.9
    T6—599
Rhaeto-Romanic literatures      859.9
Rhagionidae      595.773
Rhamnales      583.86
Rhapsodies (Music)      784.189 45
Rhea County (Tenn.)    T2—768 834
Rheas      598.522
Rhegium (Italy)    T2—377 831
Rheiformes      598.522
  paleozoology      568.5
Rheims-Douay Bible      220.520 2
Rhein-Neckar (Germany :
  Metropolregion)    T2—434 645
Rhein-Neckar-Kreis
  (Germany : Landkreis)    T2—434 645
Rhein-Pfalz-Kreis
  (Germany : Landkreis)    T2—434 353
Rheinfelden (Switzerland :
  Bezirk)    T2—494 564 3

Rheinhessen-Pfalz
  (Germany :
  Regierungsbezirk)    T2—434 35
Rheinland-Pfalz (Germany)    T2—434 3
Rheintal (Switzerland)    T2—494 721
Rhenish Prussia (Germany)    T2—434 3
Rhenium      669.7
  chemical engineering      661.054 5
  chemistry      546.545
  metallurgy      669.7
  physical metallurgy      669.967
  *see also* Chemicals
Rheology      531.113 4
Rheostats      621.317
Rhesus monkey      599.864 3
Rheto-Romance languages      459.9
    T6—599
Rheto-Romance literatures      859.9
Rhetoric      808
Rheumatic diseases
  medicine      616.723
    *see also* Musculoskeletal
      diseases — humans
Rheumatic fever
  incidence      614.597 23
  medicine      616.991
    *see also* Communicable
      diseases — humans
  pediatrics      618.929 91
Rheumatic heart disease
  medicine      616.127
    *see also* Cardiovascular
      diseases — humans
Rheumatism
  medicine      616.723
    *see also* Musculoskeletal
      diseases — humans
Rheumatoid arthritis
  medicine      616.722 7
    *see also* Musculoskeletal
      diseases — humans
Rheumatology      616.723
Rhinbund      943.06
Rhine, Confederation of the      943.06
Rhine Province (Germany)    T2—434 3
Rhine River    T2—434
  Germany    T2—434
  Switzerland    T2—494
Rhineland-Palatinate
  (Germany)    T2—434 3
Rhinencephalon
  human physiology      612.825
  medicine      616.8

| | |
|---|---|
| Rhinoceroses | 599.668 |
|   conservation technology | 639.979 668 |
|   resource economics | 333.959 668 |
| Rhinocerotidae | 599.668 |
| Rhinology | 616.21 |
| Rhipiceroidea | 595.763 |
| Rhiptoglossidea | 597.956 |
| Rhizobium | 579.334 |
| Rhizocephala | 595.35 |
| Rhizomes | 581.46 |
|   descriptive botany | 581.46 |
|   physiology | 575.497 |
| Rhizomyidae | 599.35 |
| Rhizophoraceae | 583.763 |
| Rhizopodea | 579.43 |
| Rhizopus | 579.53 |
| Rhizosphere | 577.57 |
| Rhizostomeae | 593.53 |
| Rhode Island | 974.5 |
| | T2—745 |
| Rhode Island Red chicken | 636.584 |
| Rhode Island Sound (Mass. and | 551.461 346 |
|   R.I.) | T2—163 46 |
| Rhodes (Greece : Island) | T2—495 87 |
|   ancient | T2—391 6 |
| Rhodesia (1964–1980) | 968.910 4 |
| | T2—689 1 |
| Rhodesia and Nyasaland | 968.903 |
| | T2—689 |
| Rhodesian man | 569.98 |
| Rhodesian ridgeback | 636.753 6 |
| Rhodesians | T5—968 91 |
| Rhodium | 669.7 |
|   chemical engineering | 661.063 4 |
|   chemistry | 546.634 |
|   metallography | 669.957 |
|   metallurgy | 669.7 |
|   physical metallurgy | 669.967 |
|   *see also* Chemicals | |
| Rhodobacter | 579.385 |
| Rhododendrons | 583.66 |
|   floriculture | 635.933 66 |
| Rhodope (Greece) | T2—495 7 |
| Rhodope Mountains | T2—499 7 |
| Rhodophyceae | 579.89 |
| Rhodophyta | 579.89 |
| Rhodopseudomonas | 579.385 |
| Rhoeadales | 583.35 |
| Rhön (Germany) | T2—433 3 |
| Rhondda (Wales) | T2—429 78 |
| Rhondda Cynon Taff | |
|   (Wales) | T2—429 78 |
| Rhône (France) | T2—445 82 |
| Rhône-Alpes (France) | T2—445 8 |
| Rhône River (Switzerland | |
|   and France) | T2—445 8 |
|   France | T2—445 8 |
|   Switzerland | T2—494 79 |
| Rhubarb | 641.354 8 |
|   botany | 583.57 |
|   commercial processing | 664.805 48 |
|   cooking | 641.654 8 |
|   food | 641.354 8 |
|   garden crop | 635.48 |
| Rhuddlan (Wales : | |
|   Borough) | T2—429 37 |
| Rhum, Isle of (Scotland) | T2—411 54 |
| Rhyl (Wales) | T2—429 37 |
| Rhyme | 808.1 |
| Rhymes | |
|   folk literature | 398.8 |
| Rhyming | 808.1 |
| Rhyming dictionaries | 413.1 |
|   specific languages | T4—31 |
| Rhyming games | 398.8 |
| Rhymney Valley (Wales) | T2—429 76 |
| Rhynchobdellida | 592.66 |
| Rhynchocephalia | 597.945 |
|   paleozoology | 567.945 |
| Rhynchocoela | 592.32 |
| Rhyolite | 552.22 |
| Rhythm (Linguistics) | 414.6 |
|   specific languages | T4—16 |
| Rhythm (Musical element) | 781.224 |
| Rhythm and blues | 781.643 |
| Rhythm bands | 784.68 |
| Rhythm method (Birth control) | |
|   health | 613.943 4 |
|   medicine | 618.184 |
|   *see also* Birth control | |
| Rhythm perception | 153.753 |
| Rhythmic arts | |
|   religious significance | 203.7 |
|     Christianity | 246.7 |
|   *see also* Arts — religious | |
|     significance | |
| Rhythmic gymnastics | 796.443 |
| Riau (Indonesia) | T2—598 14 |
| Riau Islands (Indonesia) | T2—598 192 |
| Riazanskaia oblast' (Russia) | T2—473 3 |
| Rib vaults | 721.45 |
|   architecture | 721.45 |
|   construction | 690.145 |
| Ribatejo (Portugal) | T2—469 45 |
| Ribble, River (England) | T2—427 685 |
| Ribble Valley (England) | T2—427 685 |
| Ribbon seal | 599.792 |
| Ribbon worms | 592.32 |

| | | | |
|---|---|---|---|
| Ribbons | 677.76 | Richland Parish (La.) | T2—763 86 |
| Ribbons (Gymnastic equipment) | 796.443 | Richmond (B.C.) | T2—711 33 |
| Ribe amt (Denmark) | T2—489 5 | Richmond (N.S. : County) | T2—716 98 |
| Ribes | 583.72 | Richmond (Natal, South | |
| edible fruits | 641.347 2 | Africa : District) | T2—684 7 |
| cooking | 641.647 2 | Richmond (Northern Cape, | |
| food | 641.347 2 | South Africa : District) | T2—687 13 |
| horticulture | 634.72 | Richmond (Va.) | T2—755 451 |
| Ribonucleic acid | 572.88 | Richmond County (Ga.) | T2—758 64 |
| Ribose | 572.565 | Richmond County (N.C.) | T2—756 34 |
| *see also* Carbohydrates | | Richmond County (N.Y.) | T2—747 26 |
| Ribosomes | 571.658 | Richmond County (Va.) | T2—755 23 |
| Ribs | | Richmond River (N.S.W.) | T2—944 3 |
| human anatomy | 611.712 | Richmond upon Thames | |
| medicine | 616.71 | (London, England) | T2—421 95 |
| surgery | 617.471 | Richmondshire (England) | T2—428 48 |
| Ricardo, David | | Richtersveld National Park | |
| economic rent theory | 333.012 | (South Africa) | T2—687 19 |
| economic school | 330.153 | Ricinulei | 595.455 |
| Ricciaceae | 588.3 | Rickets | |
| Rice | 641.331 8 | medicine | 616.395 |
| agricultural economics | 338.173 18 | *see also* Digestive system | |
| botany | 584.9 | diseases — humans | |
| commercial processing | | Rickettsiae | |
| economics | 338.476 647 25 | medical microbiology | 616.922 01 |
| technology | 664.725 | Rickettsial diseases | 571.993 27 |
| cooking | 641.631 8 | agriculture | 632.32 |
| food | 641.331 8 | animals | 571.993 271 1 |
| food crop | 633.18 | veterinary medicine | 636.089 692 2 |
| Rice County (Kan.) | T2—781 543 | biology | 571.993 27 |
| Rice County (Minn.) | T2—776 555 | humans | 362.196 922 |
| Rice Lake (Ont.) | T2—713 57 | incidence | 614.526 |
| Rice wine | 641.23 | medicine | 616.922 |
| commercial processing | 663.49 | *see also* Communicable | |
| Ricercares | 784.187 6 | diseases — humans | |
| Rich County (Utah) | T2—792 13 | social services | 362.196 922 |
| Rich Internet applications | 006.78 | plants | 571.993 271 2 |
| Rich people | 305.523 4 | agriculture | 632.32 |
| | T1—086 21 | Rickettsias | 579.327 |
| Richard I, King of England | | Rickshaws | 388.341 |
| English history | 942.032 | manufacturing technology | 688.6 |
| Richard II, King of England | | Riddles | 808.882 |
| English history | 942.038 | folk literature | 398.6 |
| Richard III, King of England | | jokes | |
| English history | 942.046 | literature | 808.882 |
| Richards Bay (South Africa) | T2—684 3 | history and criticism | 809.982 |
| Richardson County (Neb.) | T2—782 282 | specific literatures | T3B—802 |
| Richelieu River (Quebec) | T2—714 3 | individual | |
| Richland County (Ill.) | T2—773 77 | authors | T3A—8 |
| Richland County (Mont.) | T2—786 23 | literature | 808.882 |
| Richland County (N.D.) | T2—784 12 | history and criticism | 809.982 |
| Richland County (Ohio) | T2—771 28 | specific literatures | T3B—802 |
| Richland County (S.C.) | T2—757 71 | individual authors | T3A—8 |
| Richland County (Wis.) | T2—775 75 | recreation | 793.735 |

| | |
|---|---|
| Ridesharing | 388.413 212 |
| Riding-club buildings | |
| architecture | 725.88 |
| Riding horses (Breeds) | 636.13 |
| Riding horses (Recreation) | 798.23 |
| Ridley turtles | 597.928 |
| Riel's Rebellion, 1869–1870 | 971.051 |
| Riel's Rebellion, 1885 | 971.054 |
| Riemann hypothesis | 512.73 |
| Riemann integral | 515.43 |
| Riemann surfaces | 515.93 |
| Riemannian geometry | 516.373 |
| Riemannian manifolds | 516.362 |
| Riesz spaces | 515.73 |
| Rieti (Italy : Province) | T2—456 24 |
| ancient | T2—377 35 |
| RIF (Layoff) | |
| economics | 331.259 6 |
| employment security | 331.259 6 |
| unemployment | 331.137 |
| law | 344.012 596 |
| personnel management | 658.313 4 |
| public administration | 352.69 |
| Rif language | 493.3 |
| | T6—933 |
| Rif Mountains (Morocco) | T2—643 2 |
| Riffle beetles | 595.764 5 |
| Rifle grenades | 623.451 14 |
| Rifles | 683.422 |
| art metalwork | 739.744 25 |
| manufacturing technology | 683.422 |
| military engineering | 623.442 5 |
| military equipment | 355.824 25 |
| sports | 799.202 832 |
| *see also* Guns (Small arms) | |
| Rift Valley fever | |
| incidence | 614.588 |
| medicine | 616.918 |
| Rift Valley Province | |
| (Kenya) | T2—676 27 |
| Rift valleys | 551.872 |
| Riga, Gulf of (Latvia and | 551.461 334 |
| Estonia) | T2—163 34 |
| Rigging equipment | |
| aircraft | 629.134 37 |
| Right and wrong | 170 |
| religion | 205 |
| Right-eyed flounders | 597.694 |
| Right-hand techniques | |
| music | 784.193 67 |
| Right of assembly | 323.47 |
| law | 342.085 4 |
| Right of asylum | 323.631 |
| law | 342.083 |

| | |
|---|---|
| Right of petition | 323.48 |
| law | 342.085 4 |
| Right of privacy | 323.448 |
| Right of property | 323.46 |
| Right of way | 346.043 5 |
| economics | |
| sale and rental | 333.336 |
| Right to bear arms | 323.43 |
| Right to counsel | 345.056 |
| Right to die | |
| ethics | 179.7 |
| religion | 205.697 |
| Christianity | 241.697 |
| Judaism | 296.369 7 |
| law | 344.041 97 |
| medical ethics | 179.7 |
| Right to education | 379.26 |
| law | 344.079 |
| Right to hold office | 323.5 |
| Right to information | 323.445 |
| law | 342.066 2 |
| Right to labor | 331.889 2 |
| Right to learn | 379.26 |
| law | 344.079 |
| Right to life | 323.43 |
| ethics | 179.7 |
| religion | 205.697 |
| Christianity | 241.697 |
| Judaism | 296.369 7 |
| law | 342.085 |
| Right to life (Prenatal) | |
| ethics | 179.76 |
| religion | 205.697 6 |
| *see also* Abortion — ethics | |
| law | 342.085 |
| social theology | 201.763 46 |
| Christianity | 261.836 |
| Judaism | 296.38 |
| Right-to-life movement | |
| social theology | 201.763 46 |
| Christianity | 261.836 |
| Judaism | 296.38 |
| Right to read | 379.24 |
| Right to representation | 323.5 |
| Right to strike | 331.892 01 |
| Right to vote | 324.62 |
| law | 342.072 |
| Right to work | 331.889 2 |
| Right whale | 599.527 3 |
| Righteous Gentiles | |
| Holocaust, 1933–1945 | 940.531 835 |
| Righteousness (Christian | |
| doctrine) | 234 |

Rightist parties 324.213
  international organizations 324.13
Rights of humanity 323
  *see also* Civil rights
Rigid airships 387.732 5
  engineering 629.133 25
  military engineering 623.743 5
  transportation services 387.732 5
Rigid bodies
  mechanics 531
Rigidity
  materials science 620.112 5
Rigveda 294.592 12
Riksdag Act, 1866
  Swedish history 948.504 1
Riksmål language 439.82
                  T6—398 2
Riksmål literature 839.82
Riley County (Kan.) T2—781 28
Rimini (Italy)
  ancient T2—372 686
Rimini (Italy : Province) T2—454 86
  ancient T2—372 686
Rimouski-Neigette
  (Quebec) T2—714 771
Ring-necked pheasant 598.625 2
  sports hunting 799.246 252
Ringed seal 599.792
Ringette 796.966
Ringgold County (Iowa) T2—777 873
Ringkøbing amt (Denmark) T2—489 5
Rings (Jewelry) 391.72
  customs 391.72
  making 739.278 2
    costume jewelry 688.2
      handicrafts 745.594 2
    fine jewelry 739.278 2
Rings (Mathematics) 512.4
  number theory 512.74
Rings (Planets) 523.98
Ringworm
  medicine 616.579
  *see also* Skin diseases —
      humans
Rink bandy 796.963
Rink hockey 796.356 64
Rinks
  architecture 725.86
Rinzai 294.392 7
Rio Arriba County (N.M.) T2—789 52
Rio Blanco County (Colo.) T2—788 15
Rio Branco (Brazil :
  Territory) T2—811 4

Rio de Janciro (Brazil :
  State) T2—815 3
Rio de la Plata (Argentina and 551.461 368
  Uruguay) T2—163 68
Río de la Plata (Viceroyalty) 982.024
                  T2—82
Rio de Oro T2—648
Rio Grande T2—764 4
  Colorado T2—788 3
  Mexico T2—721
  New Mexico T2—789 6
  Texas T2—764 4
Rio Grande County (Colo.) T2—788 37
Rio Grande do Norte
  (Brazil) T2—813 2
Rio Grande do Sul (Brazil) T2—816 5
Rio Grande Valley T2—764 4
Rio Maputo T2—684 2
  Mozambique T2—679 1
  South Africa T2—684 2
Río Muni T2—671 83
Río Negro (Argentina) T2—827 3
Río Negro (Uruguay) T2—895 28
Río San Juan (Nicaragua) T2—728 531
Rioja (Argentina : Province) T2—824 6
Rioja (Spain) T2—463 54
Ríos (Ecuador) T2—866 33
Riot and civil commotion
  insurance 368.125
Riot control 363.323
Riot insurance 368.125
Rioting 364.143
  law 345.024 3
Riots 303.623
  political action 322.4
  prisons 365.641
  public safety 363.323
  social conflict 303.623
  social services 363.323
  *see also* Disasters
Riparian biology 578.768
Riparian ecology 577.68
Riparian rights
  law 346.043 2
Ripened cheeses 641.373 53
  cooking 641.673 53
  food 641.373 53
  processing 637.353
Ripley County (Ind.) T2—772 14
Ripley County (Mo.) T2—778 894
Ripon, George Frederick Samuel
  Robinson, Marquess of
  Indian history 954.035 3

Risaralda (Colombia :
   Dept.)           T2—861 32
RISC (Computer science)    004.3
   *see also* Processing modes —
     computer science
Rishonim            296.180 92
Risk
   economics          338.5
   insurance           368
Risk assessment
   natural resources     333.714
    *see Manual at* 333.7–.9 vs.
      363.1, 363.73, 577
   public safety        363.102
   social services      361.1
Risk capital          332.041 54
Risk factors
   medicine           616.071
Risk management       368
   financial management   658.155
   insurance           368
Risk of consequential loss   368.08
Risk perception
   social psychology     302.12
Risorgimento         945.083
   Lombardian history    945.208 3
   Piedmontese history   945.108 3
   Venetian history     945.308 3
Ritavi (South Africa :
   District)         T2—682 59
Ritchie County (W. Va.)   T2—754 24
Rites              390
   customs           390
   magic            133.43
   religion           203.8
    African religions     299.613 8
    Buddhism         294.343 8
    Christianity        264
    comparative religion   203.8
    Hinduism         294.538
    Islam           297.38
    Judaism          296.45
    music           782.3
   witchcraft         133.43
Ritual bath
   Judaism           296.75
Ritual purity
   Islam            297.38
   Judaism
    family purity       296.742
Ritual slaughter (Dietary laws)  204.46
   Islam            297.576
   Judaism          296.73
Rituale Romanum      264.025

Rituals             203.8
   *see also* Rites — religion
Rivas (Nicaragua : Dept.)   T2—728 517
River basins
   land economics      333.73
River beds          551.442
                  T2—144
   geography         910.914 4
   geomorphology      551.442
   physical geography    910.021 44
River boats          386.224 36
   design           623.812 436
   engineering        623.824 36
   freight services      386.244
   passenger services    386.242
   transportation services   386.224 36
   *see also* Ships
River dogfishes       597.41
River dolphins       599.538
River ice           551.345
River mouths
   engineering        627.124
River Nile (Sudan)     T2—625
River otters         599.769 2
   *see also* Otters (River otters)
River police         363.287 2
River steamers       386.224 36
   *see also* River boats
River transportation     386.3
   *see also* Inland water
    transportation
Rivera (Uruguay : Dept.)   T2—895 34
Rivers             551.483
                  T2—169 3
   biology           578.764
   ecology           577.64
   geography         910.916 93
   hydraulic engineering   627.12
   hydrology         551.483
   interactions with atmosphere  551.524 8
   landscape architecture   714
   law             346.046 916 2
   law of nations       341.442
   recreational resources   333.784 5
   recreational use      797
   resource economics    333.916 2
   travel           910.916 93
   water supply engineering  628.112
Rivers State (Nigeria)    T2—669 42
Riversdale (South Africa :
   District)         T2—687 37
Riverside County (Calif.)   T2—794 97
Riverweeds         583.82

| | | | |
|---|---|---|---|
| Riveting | 671.59 | Road transportation | 388.31 |
| decorative arts | 739.14 | law | 343.094 |
| sculpture | 731.41 | public administration | 354.77 |
| ship hulls | 623.843 2 | urban | 388.413 1 |
| Riveting equipment | 621.978 | Roadability tests | |
| Rivets | 621.884 | automotive vehicles | 629.282 5 |
| Riviera | T2—449 4 | Roadbeds | |
| France | T2—449 4 | railroad engineering | 625.123 |
| Italy | T2—451 8 | interurban railroads | 625.65 |
| Riviera (Switzerland) | T2—494 783 | local railroads | 625.65 |
| Riviera-Pays-d'Enhaut | | road engineering | 625.733 |
| (Switzerland) | T2—494 524 7 | Roadrunners | 598.74 |
| Rivière-du-Loup (Quebec : | | Roads | 388.1 |
| Regional County | | agricultural use | 631.28 |
| Municipality) | T2—714 764 | area planning | 711.7 |
| Rivière-du-Nord (Quebec) | T2—714 246 | effect on natural ecology | 577.272 |
| Rivne (Ukraine : Oblast) | T2—477 9 | engineering | 625.7 |
| Rivnens´ka oblast´ | | forestry | 634.93 |
| (Ukraine) | T2—477 9 | land economics | 333.77 |
| Riwayah | 297.125 16 | acquisition and disposal | 333.11 |
| Rizal (Philippines : | | urban land use | 333.77 |
| Province) | T2—599 1 | landscape architecture | 713 |
| Rize İli (Turkey) | T2—566 22 | law | 343.094 2 |
| ancient | T2—393 37 | military engineering | 623.62 |
| RML (Swiss political party) | 324.249 407 5 | public administration | 354.77 |
| RNA (Genetics) | 572.88 | transportation services | 388.1 |
| RNA virus infections | | urban | 388.411 |
| animals | | use | 388.314 |
| veterinary medicine | 636.089 691 8 | urban | 388.413 14 |
| humans | | Roadside areas | 625.77 |
| incidence | 614.588 | road transportation | 388.312 |
| medicine | 616.918 | Roadside barriers | 625.795 |
| RNA viruses | 579.25 | Roadside biology | 578.755 |
| Roach (Fish) | 597.482 | Roadside ecology | 577.55 |
| sports fishing | 799.174 82 | Roadside shrines | |
| Roaches | 595.728 | architecture | 726.9 |
| Road accidents | 363.125 | Roadside signs | |
| *see also* Highway safety | | outdoor advertising | 659.134 2 |
| Road camps (Correctional | | Roadsteads | 387.1 |
| programs) | 365.34 | hydraulic engineering | 627.22 |
| *see also* Penal institutions | | *see also* Ports | |
| Road cycling | 796.626 | Roan antelope | 599.645 |
| Road engineers | 625.709 2 | Roane County (Tenn.) | T2—768 84 |
| Road maintenance | 625.761 | Roane County (W. Va.) | T2—754 36 |
| Road maps | 912 | Roanoke (Va.) | T2—755 791 |
| Road oils | 665.538 8 | Roanoke County (Va.) | T2—755 792 |
| Road rage | 363.125 1 | Roanoke Island (N.C.) | T2—756 175 |
| Road repair | 625.761 | Roanoke River (Va. and | |
| Road running | 796.425 | N.C.) | T2—756 16 |
| Road safety | 363.125 | North Carolina | T2—756 16 |
| *see also* Highway safety | | Virginia | T2—755 6 |
| Road tests | | Roarers (Musical instruments) | 783.99 |
| automotive vehicles | 629.282 4 | Roasting | |
| | | home cooking | 641.71 |

| | |
|---|---|
| Robalos | 597.72 |
| Robben Island (South Africa) | T2—687 35 |
| Robber flies | 595.773 |
| Robbery | 364.155 2 |
| law | 345.025 52 |
| Robbery insurance | 368.82 |
| Robert II, King of France | |
| French history | 944.021 |
| Robert-Cliche (Quebec) | T2—714 716 |
| Roberts County (S.D.) | T2—783 12 |
| Roberts County (Tex.) | T2—764 818 |
| Robertson (South Africa : District) | T2—687 33 |
| Robertson County (Ky.) | T2—769 415 |
| Robertson County (Tenn.) | T2—768 464 |
| Robertson County (Tex.) | T2—764 239 |
| Robeson County (N.C.) | T2—756 332 |
| Robins | 598.842 |
| Robinson Gorge National Park (Qld.) | T2—943 5 |
| Robot hands | 629.893 3 |
| Robotics | 629.892 |
| Robots | 629.892 |
| engineering | 629.892 |
| factory operations engineering | 670.427 2 |
| primary education | 372.358 |
| recreation | 796.16 |
| social effects | 303.483 4 |
| Rocha (Uruguay : Dept.) | T2—895 16 |
| Rochdale (England : Metropolitan Borough) | T2—427 392 |
| Rochelle (France) | T2—446 42 |
| Rocher-Percé (Quebec) | T2—714 795 |
| Roches Douvres (France) | T2—423 49 |
| Roches moutonnées | 551.315 |
| Rochester (N.Y.) | T2—747 89 |
| Rochester upon Medway (England) | T2—422 32 |
| Rochford (England : District) | T2—426 775 |
| Rock (Music) | |
| attitude of Christianity toward | 261.578 |
| sociology | 306.484 26 |
| Rock art | 709.011 3 |
| painting | 759.011 3 |
| sculpture | 732.23 |
| Rock bass | 597.738 |
| Rock climbing | 796.522 3 |
| Rock County (Minn.) | T2—776 25 |
| Rock County (Neb.) | T2—782 743 |
| Rock County (Wis.) | T2—775 87 |
| Rock cutting | |
| road engineering | 625.733 |

| | |
|---|---|
| Rock failure | |
| mining | 622.28 |
| Rock-fill dams | 627.83 |
| Rock fragmentation | |
| frost action | 551.382 |
| Rock gardens | 635.967 2 |
| Rock Island County (Ill.) | T2—773 393 |
| Rock mechanics | |
| engineering geology | 624.151 32 |
| railroad engineering | 625.122 |
| road engineering | 625.732 |
| Rock mosses | 588.2 |
| Rock music | 781.66 |
| songs | 782.421 66 |
| Rock musicians | 781.660 92 |
| Rock'n' roll | 781.66 |
| Rock pools | |
| biology | 578.769 9 |
| ecology | 577.699 |
| Rock rats | 599.359 |
| Rock River (Wis. and Ill.) | T2—773 3 |
| Rock salt | 553.632 |
| mineralogy | 549.4 |
| *see also* Salt (Sodium chloride) | |
| Rock singers | 782.421 660 92 |
| Rock songs | 782.421 66 |
| Rock whiting | 597.72 |
| Rock wool | |
| materials science | 620.195 |
| Rockbridge County (Va.) | T2—755 852 |
| Rockcastle County (Ky.) | T2—769 623 |
| Rockdale County (Ga.) | T2—758 215 |
| Rocket engines | 621.435 6 |
| aircraft | 629.134 354 |
| spacecraft | 629.475 2 |
| Rocket fuels | 662.666 |
| Rocket launchers (Crew-served weapons) | 355.822 |
| engineering | 623.42 |
| military equipment | 355.822 |
| field artillery | 358.128 2 |
| Rocket launchers (Portable weapons) | 356.162 |
| engineering | 623.442 6 |
| military equipment | 356.162 |
| Rocket planes | |
| engineering | 629.133 38 |
| military engineering | 623.746 045 |
| Rocket propellants | 662.666 |
| Rocket-propelled guided missiles | 358.171 82 |
| engineering | 623.451 9 |
| military equipment | 358.171 82 |

| | |
|---|---|
| Rocket weapons | 358.171 82 |
| engineering | 623.451 9 |
| military equipment | 358.171 82 |
| Rocketry | 621.435 6 |
| Rockets (Ordnance) | 355.825 43 |
| engineering | 623.454 3 |
| military equipment | 355.825 43 |
| Rockfalls | 551.307 |
| Rockfishes | 597.68 |
| cooking | 641.692 |
| food | 641.392 |
| Rockhampton (Qld.) | T2—943 5 |
| Rockingham County (N.C.) | T2—756 63 |
| Rockingham County (N.H.) | T2—742 6 |
| Rockingham County (Va.) | T2—755 922 |
| Rockland County (N.Y.) | T2—747 28 |
| Rockroses | 583.625 |
| Rocks | 552 |
| determinative mineralogy | 549.114 |
| petrology | 552 |
| structural engineering | 624.183 2 |
| Rockwall County (Tex.) | T2—764 278 |
| Rockweeds | 579.888 |
| Rocky Mountain National Park (Colo.) | T2—788 69 |
| Rocky Mountain spotted fever | |
| incidence | 614.526 3 |
| medicine | 616.922 3 |
| *see also* Communicable diseases — humans | |
| Rocky Mountain Trench (B.C. and Mont.) | T2—711 |
| Rocky Mountains | T2—78 |
| Alberta | T2—712 33 |
| British Columbia | T2—711 |
| Canada | T2—711 |
| Colorado | T2—788 |
| Montana | T2—786 5 |
| New Mexico | T2—789 5 |
| United States | T2—78 |
| Utah | T2—792 2 |
| Wyoming | T2—787 2 |
| Rococo architecture | 724.19 |
| Rococo art | 709.033 2 |
| Rococo decoration | 745.409 033 |
| Rococo music | 780.903 3 |
| Rococo painting | 759.047 |
| Rodent control | 363.78 |
| *see also* Rodents — pest control | |
| Rodent-resistant construction | 693.844 |
| Rodentia | 599.35 |
| *see also* Rodents | |
| Rodenticides | 632.951 |
| agricultural use | 632.951 |
| chemical engineering | 668.651 |
| Rodents | 599.35 |
| animal husbandry | 636.935 |
| disease carriers | 571.986 |
| medicine | 614.438 |
| experimental animals | |
| medicine | 616.027 33 |
| paleozoology | 569.35 |
| pest control | 363.78 |
| social welfare | 363.78 |
| technology | 628.969 3 |
| agriculture | 632.693 5 |
| home economics | 648.7 |
| zoology | 599.35 |
| Rodeos | 791.84 |
| Rodney District (N.Z.) | T2—932 1 |
| Rodopē (Greece) | T2—495 7 |
| Rodopi Mountains | T2—499 7 |
| Rodrigues Island (Mauritius) | T2—698 2 |
| Rodríguez, Abelardo L. (Abelardo Luján) | |
| Mexican history | 972.082 44 |
| Rodríguez, Andrés | |
| Paraguayan history | 989.207 41 |
| Rodríguez, Miguel Angel | |
| Costa Rican history | 972.860 524 |
| Rods (Musical instruments) | 786.82 |
| concussed | 786.872 |
| friction | 786.862 |
| set | 786.862 |
| single | 786.888 |
| percussed | 786.842 |
| set | 786.842 |
| single | 786.884 2 |
| plucked | 786.85 |
| set | 786.85 |
| single | 786.887 |
| *see also* Percussion instruments | |
| Rods (Structural elements) | 624.177 4 |
| Roe deer | 599.659 |
| Roentgenium | |
| chemistry | 546.65 |
| Roentgenology | |
| medicine | 616.075 72 |
| Rogaland fylke (Norway) | T2—483 4 |
| Roger Mills County (Okla.) | T2—766 16 |
| Rogers County (Okla.) | T2—766 94 |
| Roggeveld Range (South Africa) | T2—687 17 |
| Rogue River (Or.) | T2—795 21 |
| Role conflict | 302.15 |

| | | | |
|---|---|---|---|
| Role playing | | ROM (Computer memory) | 004.53 |
| psychiatry | 616.891 523 | engineering | 621.397 3 |
| Role-playing games | 793.93 | Roma (Italy) | T2—456 32 |
| *see Manual at* 793.932 vs. | | ancient | T2—376 3 |
| 794.822 | | Roma (Italy : Province) | T2—456 3 |
| Role theory | 302.15 | ancient | T2—376 3 |
| Rolette County (N.D.) | T2—784 592 | Etruria | T2—375 9 |
| Rolfing | | Latium | T2—376 3 |
| therapeutics | 615.822 | Roma (People) | T5—914 97 |
| Roll (Aeronautics) | 629.132 364 | social aspects | 305.891 497 |
| Roll on/roll off shipping | 387.544 2 | Roman architecture | 722.7 |
| Roller bearings | 621.822 | Roman calligraphy | 745.619 78 |
| Roller hockey | 796.356 6 | Roman Catholic cathedrals | |
| Roller painting | 751.49 | architecture | 726.64 |
| Roller skates | | Roman Catholic Church | 282 |
| manufacturing technology | 688.762 1 | canon law | 262.9 |
| Roller skating | 796.21 | church government | 262.02 |
| Rollerblading | 796.21 | parishes | 254.02 |
| Rollers (Agricultural tools) | | conversion to | 248.242 |
| manufacturing technology | 681.763 1 | doctrines | 230.2 |
| Rollers (Birds) | 598.78 | catechisms and creeds | 238.2 |
| Rolling metals | 671.32 | general councils | 262.52 |
| decorative arts | 739.14 | guides to Christian life | 248.482 |
| sculpture | 731.41 | Inquisition | 272.2 |
| Rolling stock | 385.37 | liturgy | 264.02 |
| engineering | 625.2 | missions | 266.2 |
| law | 343.095 5 | moral theology | 241.042 |
| military | 358.25 | papacy | 262.13 |
| engineering | 623.633 | persecution under Queen | |
| mining | 622.66 | Elizabeth | 272.7 |
| monorail | 388.42 | public worship | 264.02 |
| engineering | 625.44 | religious associations | 267.182 |
| operation | 385.204 4 | religious education | 268.82 |
| production economics | 338.476 252 | religious orders | 255 |
| public administration | 354.767 | church history | 271 |
| rapid transit | 388.42 | women | 255.9 |
| engineering | 625.4 | church history | 271.9 |
| special purpose | 385.5 | seminaries | 230.073 2 |
| engineering | 625.3–.6 | social teaching | 261.808 828 2 |
| transportation services | 385.37 | theology | 230.2 |
| *see Manual at* 629.046 vs. 388 | | *see Manual at* 270, 230.11–.14 | |
| Rolls | 641.815 | vs. 230.15–.2, 281.5–.9, 282 | |
| commercial processing | 664.752 3 | Roman Catholic sacred music | 781.712 |
| home preparation | 641.815 | public worship | 782.322 2 |
| Rolls of honor | | music | 782.322 2 |
| armed forces | 355.134 | religion | 264.020 2 |
| World War I | 940.467 | Roman Catholic schisms | 284.8 |
| World War II | 940.546 7 | *see also* Old Catholic churches | |
| *see also* Military | | Roman Catholic schools | 371.071 2 |
| commemorations | | Roman Catholics | 282.092 |
| Rolong (African people) | T5—963 977 5 | Roman-Dutch law | 340.56 |
| Rolong dialect | 496.397 757 | Roman Empire | 937.06 |
| | T6—963 977 5 | | T2—37 |
| | | Austrian history | 936.360 3 |

Roman Empire (continued)
Belgian history 936.930 2
Dutch history 936.920 2
Egyptian history 932.022
English history 936.204
European history 936.03
French history 936.402
Greek history 938.09
Libyan history 939.740 3
Liechtenstein history 936.364 803
Luxembourgian history 936.935 02
Middle Eastern history 939.405
Moroccan history 939.712 04
North African history 939.703
Palestinian history 933.05
Portuguese history 936.690 3
Spanish history 936.603
Swiss history 936.940 2
Tunisian history 939.730 3
Roman Kingdom 937.01
T2—37
Roman law 340.54
Roman philosophy 180.937
Roman question 945.084
Roman religion 292.07
Roman Republic 937.02
T2—37
Roman revival architecture 724.22
Roman sculpture 733.5
Roman type 686.224 7
Romana (Dominican
Republic : Province) T2—729 383
Romance language literatures 840
Romance languages 440
T6—4
Romances (Music) 784.189 68
Romances (Prose) 808.83
history and criticism 809.3
medieval 808.83
history and criticism 809.3
specific literatures T3B—3
individual authors T3A—3
modern 808.838 5
history and criticism 809.385
specific literatures T3B—308 5
individual authors T3A—3
Romances (Verse) 808.813 3
history and criticism 809.133
specific literatures T3B—103 3
individual authors T3A—1
Romanesque architecture 723.4
Romanesque art 709.021 6
religious significance 246.2

Romanesque decoration 745.409 021
Romanesque painting 759.021 6
Romanesque revival architecture 724.52
Romanesque sculpture 734.24
Romani language 491.497
T6—914 97
Romani literature 891.497
Romania 949.8
T2—498
ancient 939.88
T2—398 8
Romanian language 459
T6—591
Romanian literature 859
Romanians T5—591
Romanies T5—914 97
Holocaust, 1933–1945 940.531 808 991 497
social aspects 305.891 497
Romanov, House of 947.046
genealogy 929.77
Romans (Ancient people) T5—71
Romans (Biblical book) 227.1
Romansch T5—599 6
Romansch language 459.96
T6—599 6
Romansch literature 859.96
Romansh T5—599 6
Romansh language 459.96
T6—599 6
Romansh literature 859.96
Romantic fiction 808.838 5
history and criticism 809.385
specific literatures T3B—308 5
individual authors T3A—3
Romanticism
arts 700.414 5
T3C—145
decoration 745.409 034
fine arts 709.034 2
literature 808.801 45
history and criticism 809.914 5
specific literatures T3B—080 145
history and
criticism T3B—091 45
music 780.903 4
painting 759.052
philosophy 141.6
sculpture 735.22
Romany language 491.497
T6—914 97
Romany literature 891.497
Romany people T5—914 97
Romblon (Philippines :
Province) T2—599 5

| | | | |
|---|---|---|---|
| Rome (Italy) | T2—456 32 | Roots (Plants) | 581.498 |
| ancient | T2—376 3 | descriptive botany | 581.498 |
| Rome (Italy : Province) | T2—456 3 | physiology | 575.54 |
| ancient | T2—376 3 | Rope climbing | 796.46 |
| Etruria | T2—375 9 | Roper River (N.T.) | T2—942 95 |
| Latium | T2—376 3 | Ropes | 677.71 |
| Rommelpots | 786.98 | knotting and splicing | 623.888 2 |
| *see also* Percussion instruments | | materials science | 620.197 |
| Ronde bosse | | power transmission | 621.853 |
| ceramic arts | 738.4 | sculpture material | 731.2 |
| Rondônia (Brazil : State) | T2—811 1 | ship gear | 623.862 |
| Rondos | 781.824 | structural engineering | 624.189 7 |
| instrumental | 784.182 4 | Ropes (Gymnastic equipment) | 796.443 |
| Ronga language | 496.397 8 | Roraima (Brazil) | T2—811 4 |
| | T6—963 978 | Rorquals | 599.524 |
| Rood screens | 247.1 | Rorschach (Switzerland : | |
| architecture | 726.529 6 | Wahlkreis) | T2—494 722 |
| Roodepoort (South Africa : | | Rorschach personality theory | 155.264 |
| District) | T2—682 22 | Rorschach tests | 155.284 2 |
| Roof failure (Mining) | 622.28 | Rosa (Roses) | 583.734 |
| Roof furniture | 645.8 | Rosales | 583.73 |
| *see also* Outdoor furniture | | Rosary | 242.74 |
| Roof gardening | 635.967 1 | Roscher, Wilhelm | |
| Roofers | 695.092 | economic school | 330.154 2 |
| Roofing | 695 | Roscommon (Ireland : | |
| Roofing paper | 676.289 | County) | T2—417 5 |
| Roofing tiles | 666.732 | Roscommon County (Mich.) | T2—774 76 |
| Roofs | 721.5 | Rose apples | 583.765 |
| architecture | 721.5 | Rose of Sharon | 635.933 685 |
| construction | 690.15 | botany | 583.685 |
| Rooks (Birds) | 598.864 | floriculture | 635.933 685 |
| Rooks (Chessmen) | 794.143 | Rosé wine | 641.222 32 |
| Rooks County (Kan.) | T2—781 18 | commercial processing | 663.223 2 |
| Rooming houses | 910.464 | Roseau County (Minn.) | T2—776 98 |
| *see also* Lodging (Temporary | | Rosebud County (Mont.) | T2—786 32 |
| housing) | | Rosefinches | 598.885 |
| Roosevelt, Franklin D. (Franklin | | Rosellas (Birds) | 598.71 |
| Delano) | | Rosemaling | 745.723 |
| United States history | 973.917 | Rosemary | 641.357 |
| Roosevelt, Theodore | | botany | 583.96 |
| United States history | 973.911 | *see also* Herbs | |
| Roosevelt County (Mont.) | T2—786 22 | Roses | 635.933 734 |
| Roosevelt County (N.M.) | T2—789 32 | botany | 583.734 |
| Root canal surgery | 617.634 205 9 | floriculture | 635.933 734 |
| Root celery | 641.351 28 | Roses, Wars of the, 1455–1485 | 942.04 |
| *see also* Celeriac | | Rosetta stone | 493.1 |
| Root crops | 635.1 | Rosh Hashanah (Holy day) | 296.431 5 |
| agriculture | 635.1 | customs | 394.267 |
| cooking | 641.651 | liturgy | 296.453 15 |
| food | 641.351 | Rosh Hashanah (Tractate) | 296.123 2 |
| Root extraction (Mathematics) | 512.923 | Babylonian Talmud | 296.125 2 |
| arithmetic | 513.23 | Mishnah | 296.123 2 |
| Roots (Mathematics) | | Palestinian Talmud | 296.124 2 |
| number theory | 512.72 | Rosicrucianism | 135.43 |

Rosicrucians · 135.430 92
Rosidae · 583.7
Roskilde amt (Denmark) · T2—489 1
Ross and Cromarty
  (Scotland) · T2—411 56
Ross County (Ohio) · T2—771 82
Ross-on-Wye (England) · T2—424 2
Ross Sea (Antarctic regions) · 551.461 74
  · T2—167 4
Ross seal · 599.796
Rossendale (England) · T2—427 63
Rossland (B.C.) · T2—711 62
Rostock (Germany) · T2—431 745
Rostock (Germany : Bezirk) · T2—431 74
Rostov (Russia : Oblast) · T2—474 9
Rostovskaia oblast′ (Russia) · T2—474 9
Rostral furniture
  church architecture · 726.529 2
Rot
  agriculture · 632.4
  materials science · 620.112 23
Rotary blowers · 621.62
Rotary fans · 621.62
Rotary files (Records
  management) · 651.54
Rotary International · 369.52
  biography · 369.520 92
Rotary pumps · 621.66
  hydraulic · 621.252
Rotation
  celestial bodies · 521
  earth · 525.35
  sun · 523.73
Rotation groups · 512.2
Rotation of crops
  cultivation technique · 631.582
  economics · 338.162
  soil conservation · 631.452
Rotational motion · 531 113
  classical mechanics · 531.113
  fluid mechanics · 532.059 5
  gas mechanics · 533.295
  liquid mechanics · 532.595
  solid bodies · 531.34
ROTC (Reserve training) · 355.223 207 1173
Rote learning
  education · 371.39
  psychology · 153.152 2
Rother (England) · T2—422 52
Rotherham (England :
  Metropolitan Borough) · T2—428 23
Rotifera · 592.52
Rotifers · 592.52
Rotis · 641.84

Rotor ships · 387.22
  engineering · 623.822
  transportation services · 387.22
  *see also* Ships
Rotors
  aircraft · 629.134 36
  machine engineering · 621.82
Rotorua District (N.Z.) · T2—934 23
  Bay of Plenty Region · T2—934 23
  Waikato Region · T2—933 67
Rotterdam (Netherlands) · T2—492 385
Rottweiler · 636.73
Rouen (France) · T2—442 52
Rouergue (France) · T2—447 4
Rough carpentry · 694.2
Rough lumber · 674.28
Roughness
  materials science · 620.112 92
Roughy (Trachichthyidae) · 597.64
Roulette · 795.23
Roumania · 949.8
  · T2—498
  ancient · 939.88
  · T2—398 8
Round-backed lutes · 787.82
  *see also* Stringed instruments
Round dances · 793.33
Roundabouts (Traffic circles) · 388.13
  area planning · 711.7
  engineering · 625.7
  transportation services · 388.13
  urban · 388.411
Roundhouses · 385.314
  architecture · 725.33
Roundworm-caused diseases
  humans
    incidence · 614.555
    medicine · 616.965
    *see also* Communicable
      diseases — humans
Roundworms · 592.57
Roussillon (France :
  Province) · T2—448 9
Roussillon (Quebec) · T2—714 34
Routers (Woodworking tools)
  use in home woodworking · 684.083 21
Routes
  air · 387.72
  bus · 388.322 1
    urban · 388.413 22
  maritime · 387.52
  truck · 388.324 2
    urban · 388.413 24

| | | | |
|---|---|---|---|
| Routing | | RU486 (Drug) | |
| production management | 658.53 | medicine | 618.29 |
| transportation | 388.041 | pharmacokinetics | 615.766 |
| *see also* Scheduling — | | Rúa, Fernando de la | |
| transportation | | Argentine history | 982.071 |
| Routt County (Colo.) | T2—788 14 | Ruanda language | 496.394 61 |
| Rouville (Quebec) | T2—714 53 | | T6—963 946 1 |
| Rouville (Quebec : Regional | | Ruanda literature | 896.394 61 |
| County Municipality) | T2—714 53 | Ruanda-Rundi languages | 496.394 6 |
| Rouxville (South Africa : | | | T6—963 946 |
| District) | T2—685 6 | Ruanda-Urundi | 967.570 3 |
| Rouyn-Noranda (Quebec) | T2—714 136 | | T2—675 7 |
| Rove beetles | 595.764 2 | Ruapehu District (N.Z.) | T2—935 2 |
| Rovigo (Italy : Province) | T2—453 3 | Rub'al-Khali | T2—538 |
| ancient | T2—373 3 | Rubato | 781.46 |
| Row houses | | Rubber | 678.2 |
| architecture | 728.312 | chemistry | 547.842 6 |
| Rowan County (Ky.) | T2—769 57 | handicrafts | 745.57 |
| Rowan County (N.C.) | T2—756 71 | materials science | 620.194 |
| Rowan trees | 583.73 | shipbuilding | 623.820 7 |
| Rowboat racing | 797.14 | structural engineering | 624.189 4 |
| Rowboats | 386.229 | Rubber bands | 678.35 |
| design | 623.812 9 | Rubber hydrochloride | 678.68 |
| engineering | 623.829 | Rubber industry workers | 678.209 2 |
| transportation services | 386.229 | Rubber plant (Ficus) | 635.933 45 |
| Rowing | | botany | 583.45 |
| sports | 797.123 | floriculture | 635.933 45 |
| Roxas, Manuel | | rubber crop | 633.895 |
| Philippine history | 959.904 1 | Rubber products | 678.3 |
| Roxburgh (Scotland : | | Rubber-stamp printing | 761 |
| District) | T2—413 7 | Rubber stamps | |
| Royal commissions | 352.743 | manufacturing technology | 681.6 |
| Royal fern | 587.3 | Rubber tree (Hevea) | 633.895 2 |
| Royal houses | | botany | 583.69 |
| genealogy | 929.7 | rubber crop | 633.895 2 |
| Royal Natal National Park | | Rubbings | |
| (South Africa) | T2—684 7 | graphic arts | 740 |
| Royal National Park | | research technique | 739.522 |
| (N.S.W.) | T2—944 6 | Rubella | |
| Royal office of Jesus Christ | 232.8 | incidence | 614.524 |
| Royal tennis | 796.34 | medicine | 616.916 |
| Royalty | 305.522 | *see also* Communicable | |
| | T1—086 21 | diseases — humans | |
| customs | 390.22 | pediatrics | 618.929 16 |
| dress | 391.022 | Rubeola | |
| folklore | 398.22 | incidence | 614.523 |
| history and criticism | 398.352 | medicine | 616.915 |
| genealogy | 929.7 | *see also* Communicable | |
| social group | 305.522 | diseases — humans | |
| RSFSR (Russia) | 947 | pediatrics | 618.929 15 |
| | T2—47 | Rubiaceae | 583.93 |
| RSS feeds | 006.787 6 | Rubidium | 669.725 |
| | | chemical engineering | 661.038 4 |
| | | chemistry | 546.384 |

Rubidium (continued)
metallurgy 669.725
*see also* Chemicals
Rubies 553.84
economic geology 553.84
jewelry 739.27
mining 622.384
synthetic 666.88
Rubus berries 641.347 1
*see also* Cane fruits
Rudd, Kevin
Australian history 994.072
Rudders 623.862
aircraft 629.134 33
Rudolf, Lake (Kenya and
Ethiopia) T2—676 27
Rudolf II, Holy Roman Emperor
German history 943.034
Rues (Plants) 583.77
Ruffed grouse 598.635
sports hunting 799.246 35
Rugby 796.333
Rugby (England : Borough) T2—424 85
Rugby League 796.333 8
Rugby players 796.333 092
Rugby Union 796.333
Rügen (Germany :
Landkreis) T2—431 78
Rugs 645.12
arts 746.7
building construction 698.9
household management 645.12
interior decoration 747.5
manufacturing technology 677.643
nonwoven felts 677.632
Ruhr River (Germany) T2—435 5
Ruiz Cortines, Adolfo
Mexican history 972.082 8
Rukwa Region (Tanzania) T2— 678 28
Rule-based programming 005.115
Rule of law 340.11
Rule of the road at sea
law 343.096 6
seamanship 623.888 4
Ruled surfaces 516.362
Rules committees (Legislatures) 328.365 8
Rules of order 060.42
legislatures 328.1
committees 328.365 3
Rum 641.259
commercial processing 663.59
Rum, Isle of (Scotland) T2—411 54

Rumania 949.8
T2—498
ancient 939.88
T2—398 8
Rumanians T5—591
Rumbas 793.33
music 784.188 8
Ruminants 599.63
animal husbandry 636.2
paleozoology 569.63
Rummage sales 381.195
Rummy 795.418
Rumor
social psychology 302.24
Runaway children 305.230 869 23
T1—086 923
social group 305.230 869 23
social welfare 362.74
Rundi (African people) T5—963 946 5
Rundi language 496.394 65
T6—963 946 5
Rundi literature 896.394 65
Runes 430
divination 133.33
Runge-Kutta method 518.63
Runnels County (Tex.) T2—764 724
Runners (Athletes) 796.420 92
Runners (Stolons) 581.46
agricultural propagation 631.533
descriptive botany 581.46
physiology 575.499
Running
animal behavior 591.57
animal physiology 573.79
human physiology 612.044
humans
physical fitness 613.717 2
sports 796.42
Running boards 629.26
Running gear
railroad engineering 625.21
Runnymede (England) T2—422 11
Runoff (Hydrology) 551.488
Runways (Airports)
engineering 629.136 3
military airports 623.663
transportation services 387.736 2
Rupert's Land 971.201
T2—712
Ruppiaceae 584.74
Rupture strength
materials science 620.112 6
Rural administration 352.17

| | | | |
|---|---|---|---|
| Rural areas | T2—173 4 | Rusk County (Tex.) | T2—764 185 |
| government | 320.84 | Rusk County (Wis.) | T2—775 19 |
| *see also* Rural government | | Russell County (Ala.) | T2—761 485 |
| social services to residents | 361.917 34 | Russell County (Kan.) | T2—781 51 |
| public administration | 353.533 4 | Russell County (Ky.) | T2—769 655 |
| Rural churches | 250.917 34 | Russell County (Va.) | T2—755 755 |
| administration | 254.24 | Russia | 947 |
| pastoral theology | 253.091 734 | | T2—47 |
| Rural collection | 383.145 | Asia | 957 |
| *see also* Postal service | | | T2—57 |
| Rural communities | 307.72 | Russian blue cat | 636.82 |
| psychological influence | 155.944 | Russian calligraphy | 745.619 917 1 |
| Rural delivery | 383.145 | Russian folk music | 781.629 171 |
| *see also* Postal service | | Russian folk songs | 782.421 629 171 |
| Rural development | 307.141 2 | Russian language | 491.7 |
| law | 343.074 5 | | T6—917 1 |
| public administration | 354.279 4 | Russian literature | 891.7 |
| Rural education | 370.917 34 | Russian Orthodox Church | 281.947 |
| Rural electrification | 333.793 2 | Russian Orthodox Church | |
| Rural exodus | 307.24 | Outside Russia | 281.947 |
| Rural families | 306.852 | Russian Revolution, 1905 | 947.083 |
| Rural Federation (Austrian | | Russian Revolution, 1917 | 947.084 1 |
| political party) | 324.243 602 3 | Russian Soviet Federated | 947 |
| Rural free delivery | 383.145 | Socialist Republic | T2—47 |
| *see also* Postal service | | Russian turnip | 641.351 26 |
| Rural government | 320.84 | *see also* Rutabagas | |
| public administration | 352.17 | Russians | T5—917 1 |
| control by higher | | Russo-Finnish War, 1939–1940 | 948.970 32 |
| jurisdictions | 353.337 | Russo-Japanese War, 1904–1905 | 952.031 |
| public administrative support | 352.794 | Russo-Turkish War, 1877–1878 | 949.603 87 |
| Rural health services | 362.104 257 | Rust | |
| Rural lands | 333.76 | materials science | 620.112 23 |
| sale and rental | 333.335 | Rust diseases | |
| Rural municipalities | 320.84 | agriculture | 632.492 |
| Rural sanitation | 363.720 917 34 | Rust flies | 595.774 |
| technology | 628.7 | Rust fungi | 579.592 |
| Rural schools | 371.009 173 4 | Rust-resistant paints | 667.69 |
| Rural sociology | 307.72 | Rustenburg (South Africa : | |
| Rural-urban migration | 307.24 | District) | T2—682 41 |
| Rural villages | 307.72 | Rustling | 364.162 863 62 |
| Ruscaceae | 584.355 | law | 345.026 286 362 |
| Ruse (Bulgaria : Oblast) | T2—499 3 | Rusts (Fungi) | 579.592 |
| Rusenska oblast (Bulgaria) | T2—499 3 | agricultural diseases | 632.492 |
| Rush County (Ind.) | T2—772 61 | Rutabagas | 641.351 26 |
| Rush County (Kan.) | T2—781 48 | botany | 583.64 |
| Rushcliffe (England) | T2—425 29 | commercial processing | 664.805 126 |
| Rushes | 584.82 | cooking | 641.651 26 |
| textile arts | 746.41 | food | 641.351 26 |
| textiles | 677.54 | garden crop | 635.126 |
| *see also* Textiles | | Rutales | 583.77 |
| Rushmoor (England) | T2—422 725 | Ruth (Biblical book) | 222.35 |
| Rushwork | 746.41 | Ruthenians (Ethnic group) | T5—917 91 |
| Rushworth (Vic.) | T2—945 4 | | |

Ruthenium 669.7
  chemical engineering 661.063 2
  chemistry 546.632
  metallography 669.957
  metallurgy 669.7
  physical metallurgy 669.967
  *see also* Chemicals
Rutherford County (N.C.) T2—756 913
Rutherford County (Tenn.) T2—768 57
Rutherfordium
  chemistry 546.51
Rutherglen (Scotland) T2—414 57
Rutherglen (Vic.) T2—945 5
Rutile
  mineralogy 549.524
Rutland (England) T2—425 45
Rutland County (Vt.) T2—743 7
Ruvuma Region (Tanzania) T2—678 25
RV (Vehicle) 388.346
  engineering 629.226
  *see also* Motor homes
RV camps 910.468
  household management 647.942
  *see also* Lodging (Temporary
    housing)
Rwanda 967.571
 T2—675 71
Rwanda language 496.394 61
 T6—963 946 1
Rwanda literature 896.394 61
Rwanda-Rundi languages 496.394 6
 T6—963 946
Rwandans T5—967 571
Ryazan (Russia : Oblast) T2—473 3
Rye 641.331 4
  botany 584.9
  commercial processing 664.72
  cooking 641.631 4
  food 641.331 4
  food crop 633.14
  forage crop 633.254
Ryedale (England) T2—428 46
Rynchopidae 598.338
Ryukyu Islands T2—522 9
Ryukyuans T5—956
Rzeszów (Poland :
  Voivodeship) T2—438 66

**S**

's-Gravenhage
  (Netherlands) T2—492 382
Saale-Holzlandkreis
  (Germany : Landkreis) T2—432 22

Saale-Orla-Kreis
  (Germany : Landkreis) T2—432 22
Saale River (Germany) T2—431 84
Saalfeld-Rudolstadt
  (Germany : Landkreis) T2—432 22
Saam languages 494.57
 T6—945 7
Saami (European people) T5—945 7
Saami languages 494.57
 T6—945 7
Saami literatures 894.57
Saane (Switzerland) T2—494 535
Saanich (B.C.) T2—711 28
Saanich Peninsula (B.C.) T2—711 28
Saar River (France and
  Germany) T2—434 2
Saarbrücken (Germany) T2—434 21
Saarbrücken (Germany :
  Regionalverband) T2—434 21
Saarbrücken (Germany :
  Stadtverband) T2—434 21
Saarland (Germany) T2—434 2
Saba (Netherlands Antilles) T2—729 77
Sabah T2—595 3
Sabbath 296.41
  Christianity 263.1
  Judaism 296.41
Sabbatianism 296.82
Sabbatical leave 331.257 63
  economics 331.257 63
  education 371.104
    higher education 378.121
  personnel management 658.312 2
Sabbatical Year (Judaism) 296.439 1
Sabellian languages 479.7
 T6—797
Sabellian literatures 879.7
Sabellianism 273.3
Sabers 623.441
  art metalwork 739.722
Sabiaceae 583.78
Sabie River (South Africa) T2—682 71
Sabina (Italy : Region) T2—456 24
  ancient T2—377 35
Sabine County (Tex.) T2—764 177
Sabine Lake (La. and Tex.) T2—763 52
Sabine language 479.7
 T6—797
Sabine Parish (La.) T2—763 62
Sabine River (Tex. and La.) T2—764 14
Sable (Carnivorous mammal) 599.766 5
Sable antelope 599.645
Sable Island (N.S.) T2—716 99

| | |
|---|---|
| Sabotage | 364.164 |
| armed forces | 355.343 7 |
| *see also* Unconventional warfare | |
| labor economics | 331.893 |
| law | 345.026 4 |
| Sabrata (Extinct city) | T2—397 4 |
| Sac County (Iowa) | T2—777 424 |
| Sac language | 497.314 9 |
| | T6—973 149 |
| Saca, Elías Antonio | |
| Salvadoran history | 972.840 543 |
| Sacatepéquez (Guatemala) | T2—728 162 |
| Saccharides | 572.56 |
| *see also* Carbohydrates | |
| Saccharolytic enzymes | 572.756 |
| *see also* Enzymes | |
| Saccharomyces | 579.563 |
| Saccharomycetaceae | 579.562 |
| Saccopharyngidae | 597.43 |
| Saccorhiza | 579.887 |
| Sachs Harbour (N.W.T.) | T2—719 3 |
| Sachsen (Germany) | T2—432 1 |
| Sachsen-Anhalt (Germany) | T2—431 8 |
| Sackville (N.B.) | T2—715 23 |
| Sacoglossa | 594.35 |
| Sacramental furniture | 247.1 |
| architecture | 726.529 1 |
| Sacramentals | 264.9 |
| Sacramentaries | |
| Roman Catholic | 264.020 36 |
| texts | 264.023 |
| Sacramento (Calif.) | T2—794 54 |
| Sacramento County (Calif.) | T2—794 53 |
| Sacramento Mountains (N.M.) | T2—789 65 |
| Sacramento River (Calif.) | T2—794 5 |
| Sacraments | 234.16 |
| public worship | 265 |
| Anglican | 264.030 8 |
| texts | 264.035 |
| Roman Catholic | 264.020 8 |
| texts | 264.025 |
| theology | 234.16 |
| Sacred books | 208.2 |
| Buddhism | 294.382 |
| Christianity | 220 |
| Latter-Day Saints | 289.32 |
| Hinduism | 294.592 |
| Islam | 297.122 |
| Judaism | 296.1 |
| Bible | 221 |
| *see Manual at* 221 | |
| *see Manual at* 130 vs. 200 | |
| Sacred Heart religious orders | 255.93 |
| church history | 271.93 |
| Sacred music | 781.7 |
| public worship | 203.8 |
| *see also* Public worship | |
| religious significance | 203.7 |
| *see also* Music — religion | |
| vocal forms | 782.22 |
| choral and mixed voices | 782.522 |
| instrumental forms | 784.189 92 |
| single voices | 783.092 2 |
| Sacred places | 203.5 |
| Buddhist | 294.343 5 |
| Christianity | 263.042 |
| Hindu | 294.535 |
| Islam | 297.35 |
| Jain | 294.435 |
| Judaism | 296.48 |
| public worship | 203.8 |
| Sikh | 294.635 |
| Sacred songs | 782.25 |
| choral and mixed voices | 782.525 |
| single voices | 783.092 5 |
| Sacred vocal music | 782.22 |
| Sacrifice of Jesus Christ | 232.4 |
| Sacrifices (Religion) | 203.4 |
| Judaism | 296.492 |
| Sacrilege | |
| criminology | 364.188 |
| law | 345.028 8 |
| Sacristies | |
| architecture | 726.596 |
| Ṣadaqah | 297.54 |
| Sadat, Anwar | |
| Egyptian history | 962.054 |
| Saddle block anesthesia | |
| surgery | 617.964 |
| Saddle fungi | 579.578 |
| Saddle horses | 636.13 |
| Saddlers | 685.109 2 |
| Saddlery | 636.108 37 |
| animal husbandry | 636.083 7 |
| horse rearing | 636.108 37 |
| manufacturing technology | 685.1 |
| Sadducees | 296.813 |
| Sadism | |
| medicine | 616.858 35 |
| *see also* Mental disorders | |
| sociology | 306.775 |
| Sadness | 152.4 |
| Sadomasochism | |
| medicine | 616.858 35 |
| *see also* Mental disorders | |
| sociology | 306.775 |

Safari lodges                            910.462
   *see also* Resorts
Safe-deposit services                    332.178
Safes                                    683.34
Safety                                   363.1
  law                          344.047
  management                    658.408
                    T1—068 4
  personal safety              T1—028 9
  personnel management         658.382
    public administration   352.67
  public administration        353.9
  social services              363.1
  *see Manual at* 363 vs. 302–307,
    333.7, 570–590, 600; *also*
    *at* 363.1
Safety engineering                       620.86
                    T1—028 9
  automotive                   629.204 2
   design                    629.231
  construction                 690.22
  military                     623.75
  roads                        625.702 89
  transportation               629.040 289
Safety equipment
  aircraft                     629.134 43
  automobile                   629.276
  plant management             658.28
  ships                        623.865
  tool engineering             621.992
Safety management                        658.408
                    T1—068 4
Safety regulations                       363.1
  public administration        353.9
  *see Manual at* 363.1; *also at*
    363.1 vs. 600
Safety training
  personnel management         658.312 44
  public administration        352.669
Safety valves
  steam engineering            621.185
Safflower                                583.99
Saffron (Crocus)                         584.38
Safi (Morocco : Province)   T2—646 2
Safwa language                           496.391
                    T6—963 91
Saga-ken (Japan)            T2—522 3
Sagadahoc County (Me.)      T2—741 85
Sagas
  Old Norse literature         839.63
Sage                                     641.357
  botany                       583.96
  *see also* Herbs
Sage grouse                              598.636

Sagebrushes                              583.99
Saginaw Bay (Mich.)         T2—774 47
Saginaw County (Mich.)      T2—774 46
Saginaw River (Mich.)       T2—774 47
Sagitta                                  592.38
Sagittariidae                            598.9
Sagittarius (Zodiac)                     133.527 4
Sago                                     641.336 8
  cooking                      641.636 8
  food                         641.336 8
  starch crop                  633.68
Saguache County (Colo.)     T2—788 49
Saguenay (Quebec)           T2—714 162
Saguenay-Lac-Saint-Jean
  (Quebec : Administrative
  region)                   T2—714 14
Saguenay River (Quebec)     T2—714 16
Saguia el Hamra             T2—648
Sahara                       T2—66
Saharan languages                        496.5
                    T6—965
Sahel                        T2—66
Ṣaḥīḥ (Hadith)                           297.125 21
Saïda (Algeria : Province)   T2—651
Saiga                                    599.647
Sail yachting                            797.124 6
Sailboarding                             797.33
Sailboat racing                          797.14
Sailfishes                               597.78
  sports fishing               799.177 8
Sailing
  sports                       797.124
Sailing ships                            387.204 3
  design                       623.812 043
  engineering                  623.820 3
  handling                     623.881 3
  naval equipment              359.832
  naval units                  359.322
  transportation services      387.204 3
  *see also* Ships
Sailors                                  387.509 2
  merchant mariners            387.509 2
  navy personnel               359.009 2
  sports                       797.109 2
  technologists                623.880 92
Sails                                    623.862
Saimiri                                  599.852
Saint-Augustin-de-
  Desmaures (Quebec)        T2—714 471
Saint Barthélemy            T2—729 76
Saint Bernard (Dog)                      636.73
Saint Bernard Parish (La.)   T2—763 36
Saint-Bruno-de-Montarville
  (Quebec)                  T2—714 37

| | |
|---|---|
| Saint Charles County (Mo.) | T2—778 39 |
| Saint Charles Parish (La.) | T2—763 33 |
| Saint Christopher | T2—729 73 |
| Saint Christopher-Nevis | 972.973 |
| | T2—729 73 |
| Saint Christopher-Nevis-Anguilla | T2—729 73 |
| Saint Clair, Lake (Mich. and Ont.) | T2—774 39 |
| Michigan | T2—774 39 |
| Ontario | T2—713 31 |
| Saint Clair, Lake (Tas.) | T2—946 3 |
| Saint Clair County (Ala.) | T2—761 69 |
| Saint Clair County (Ill.) | T2—773 89 |
| Saint Clair County (Mich.) | T2—774 41 |
| Saint Clair County (Mo.) | T2—778 466 |
| Saint Clair River (Mich. and Ont.) | T2—774 41 |
| Michigan | T2—774 41 |
| Ontario | T2—713 27 |
| Saint Croix (V.I.) | T2—729 722 |
| Saint Croix County (Wis.) | T2—775 41 |
| Saint Croix River (Me. and N.B.) | T2—741 42 |
| Maine | T2—741 42 |
| New Brunswick | T2—715 33 |
| Saint Croix River (Wis. and Minn.) | T2—775 1 |
| Saint-Denis (Réunion) | T2—698 1 |
| Saint Edmundsbury (England) | T2—426 44 |
| Saint-Etienne (Loire, France) | T2—445 817 |
| Saint Eustatius (Netherlands Antilles) | T2—729 77 |
| Saint Francis County (Ark.) | T2—767 91 |
| Saint Francois County (Mo.) | T2—778 68 |
| Saint-François River (Quebec) | T2—714 6 |
| Saint Gall (Switzerland) | T2—494 723 4 |
| Saint Gall (Switzerland : Canton) | T2—494 72 |
| Saint Gall (Switzerland : Wahlkreis) | T2—494 723 |
| Saint George's Channel (Ireland and Wales) | 551.461 337 T2—163 37 |
| Saint Helena | 997.3 T2—973 |
| Saint Helena Parish (La.) | T2—763 15 |
| Saint James Parish (La.) | T2—763 31 |
| Saint-Jean (Quebec : County) | T2—714 38 |
| Saint John (N.B. : County) | T2—715 32 |
| Saint John (V.I.) | T2—729 722 |
| Saint John River (Me. and N.B.) | T2—715 5 |
| Saint John the Baptist Parish (La.) | T2—763 32 |
| Saint Johns County (Fla.) | T2—759 18 |
| Saint Johns River (Fla.) | T2—759 1 |
| Saint Joseph County (Ind.) | T2—772 89 |
| Saint Joseph County (Mich.) | T2—774 19 |
| Saint Joseph religious orders | 255.976 |
| church history | 271.976 |
| Saint Kitts | T2—729 73 |
| Saint Kitts-Nevis | 972.973 T2—729 73 |
| Saint Kitts-Nevis-Anguilla | T2—729 73 |
| Saint-Lambert (Quebec) | T2—714 37 |
| Saint Landry Parish (La.) | T2—763 46 |
| Saint-Laurent, Louis Stephen Canadian history | 971.063 3 |
| Saint-Laurent du Maroni (French Guiana) | T2—882 |
| Saint Lawrence, Gulf of | 551.461 344 T2—163 44 |
| Saint Lawrence County (N.Y.) | T2—747 56 |
| Saint Lawrence River | T2—714 |
| New York | T2—747 56 |
| Ontario | T2—713 7 |
| Quebec | T2—714 |
| Saint Lawrence Seaway | 386.509 714 T2—714 |
| Ontario | T2—713 7 |
| Quebec | T2—714 |
| Saint Louis (Mo.) | T2—778 66 |
| Saint-Louis (Senegal : Region) | T2—663 |
| Saint Louis County (Minn.) | T2—776 77 |
| Saint Louis County (Mo.) | T2—778 65 |
| Saint Lucia | 972.984 3 T2—729 843 |
| Saint Lucie County (Fla.) | T2—759 29 |
| Saint Martin | T2—729 76 |
| Guadeloupe | T2—729 76 |
| Netherlands Antilles | T2—729 77 |
| Saint Martin Parish (La.) | T2—763 48 |
| Saint Mary Parish (La.) | T2—763 42 |
| Saint Marys, Lake (Ohio) | T2—771 415 |
| Saint Marys County (Md.) | T2—752 41 |
| Saint Marys River (Ga. and Fla.) | T2—759 11 |
| Saint Marys River (Mich. and Ont.) | T2—774 91 |
| Saint-Maurice (Switzerland : District) | T2—494 796 8 |

Saint-Maurice River
  (Quebec)         T2—714 45
Saint Paul (Minn.)       T2—776 581
Saint Paul Island        969.9
                     T2—699
Saint Petersburg (Russia)  T2—472 1
Saint Pierre and Miquelon   971.88
                     T2—718 8
Saint-Simonism (Socialist
  school)              335.22
Saint Tammany Parish (La.)  T2—763 12
Saint Thomas (V.I.)      T2—729 722
Saint Thomas Christian churches  281.54
  *see also* Eastern churches
Saint Thomas Evangelical
  Church of India       281.54
  *see also* Eastern churches
Saint Vincent         T2—729 844
Saint Vincent and the Grenadines  972.984 4
                     T2—729 844
Sainte-Anne-de-Bellevue
  (Quebec)         T2—714 28
Sainte Genevieve County
  (Mo.)           T2—778 692
Saintes Islands
  (Guadeloupe)     T2—729 76
Saintonge (France)     T2—446 4
Saints                200.92
  art representation     704.948 63
  arts           T3C—382
  biography         200.92
  Christian         270.092
    biography        270.092
      specific denominations   280
      *see Manual at* 230–280
    doctrines         235.2
  Islam
    Sufis           297.409 2
  objects of worship     202.13
  role and function      206.1
  *see Manual at* 200.92 and
    201–209, 292–299
Saints' days          263.98
  devotional literature    242.37
  sermons          252.67
Saipan            T2—967
Saitama-ken (Japan)    T2—521 34
Saite period         932.015
Saivism           294.551 3
Saka language        491.53
                     T6—915 3
Saka literature       891.53
Sakakawea, Lake (N.D.)   T2—784 75

Sakarya İli (Turkey)    T2—563 4
  ancient           T2—393 15
Sake (Japanese rice wine)   641.23
  commercial processing   663.490 952
Sakha (Russia)        T2—575
Sakhalin (Russia : Oblast)  T2—577
Sakhalin Ula (China and
  Russia)           T2—577
Sakhalinskaiͣa oblast′
  (Russia)          T2—577
Salad dressings      641.814
  food technology     664.37
  home preparation    641.814
Salad greens        641.355
  commercial processing   664.805 5
  cooking          641.655
  food            641.355
  garden crop        635.5
Salad oils
  food technology     664.36
Salads             641.83
Ṣalāḥ ad-Dīn (Iraq :
  Province)         T2—567 4
Sălaj (Romania)      T2—498 4
Salamanca (Spain :
  Province)         T2—462 5
Salamanders       597.85
Salamandroidea     597.85
Salampasu (African people)  T5—963 93
Salampasu-Ndembo languages  496.393
                     T6—963 93
Salar language        494.36
                     T6—943 6
Salaries            331.21
  *see also* Wages
Salary scales        331.216
  personnel management   658.322 2
Ṣalāt              297.382 2
Salazar, Antonio de Oliveira
  Portuguese history    946.904 2
Salcedo (Dominican
  Republic : Province)  T2—729 363
Salé (Morocco : Prefecture)  T2—643 6
Sale of businesses
  law             346.065
  management       658.164
Sale of real property    333.333
  economics         333.333
    private ownership    333.333
    public ownership     333.16
  law             346.043 63
    private ownership    346.043 63
    public ownership     343.025 3
Salem (Or.)          T2—795 37

| | |
|---|---|
| Salem (Va.) | T2—755 793 |
| Salem County (N.J.) | T2—749 91 |
| Salerno (Italy) | T2—457 41 |
| ancient | T2—377 271 |
| Salerno (Italy : Province) | T2—457 4 |
| ancient | T2—377 27 |
| Campania | T2—377 27 |
| Lucania | T2—377 77 |
| Salernum (Italy) | T2—377 271 |
| Sales | 381 |
| law | 346.072 |
| management | 658.81 |
| Sales clerks | 381.092 |
| personnel management | 658.304 4 |
| training | 658.312 45 |
| Sales finance institutions | 332.35 |
| Sales forecasting | |
| marketing management | 658.818 |
| Sales management | 658.81 |
| | T1—068 8 |
| Sales meetings | 658.810 6 |
| Sales personnel | 381.092 |
| organization | 658.810 2 |
| personnel management | 658.304 4 |
| training | 658.312 45 |
| Sales planning | 658.810 1 |
| Sales promotion | 658.82 |
| Sales tax | 336.271 3 |
| law | 343.055 2 |
| public administration | 352.44 |
| Salesmanship | 381 |
| etiquette | 395.53 |
| management | 658.85 |
| Salesmen | 381.092 |
| personnel management | 658.304 4 |
| training | 658.312 45 |
| Salford (England : City) | T2—427 32 |
| Salian emperors | |
| German history | 943.023 |
| Salicales | 583.65 |
| Salientia | 597.8 |
| Salinas de Gortari, Carlos | |
| Mexican history | 972.083 5 |
| Salinas River (Calif.) | T2—794 76 |
| Saline County (Ark.) | T2—767 72 |
| Saline County (Ill.) | T2—773 992 |
| Saline County (Kan.) | T2—781 545 |
| Saline County (Mo.) | T2—778 47 |
| Saline County (Neb.) | T2—782 327 |
| Saline water | 553.72 |
| Saline water conversion | |
| water supply engineering | 628.167 |

| | |
|---|---|
| Salinity | |
| sea water | 551.466 4 |
| soil science | 631.416 |
| Salisbury (England : | |
| District) | T2—423 19 |
| Salisbury (S. Aust.) | T2—942 32 |
| Salisbury Island (Nunavut) | T2—719 52 |
| Salisbury Plain (England) | T2—423 19 |
| Salish Indians | T5—979 435 |
| Salish language | 497.943 5 |
| | T6—979 435 |
| Salishan Indians | T5—979 4 |
| Salishan languages | 497.94 |
| | T6—979 4 |
| Saliva | 573.353 79 |
| human physiology | 612.313 |
| *see also* Digestive system | |
| Salivan languages | 498.9 |
| | T6—989 |
| Salivary gland diseases | |
| medicine | 616.316 |
| *see also* Digestive system | |
| diseases — humans | |
| Salivary glands | 573.353 79 |
| biology | 573.353 79 |
| human anatomy | 611.316 |
| human physiology | 612.313 |
| medicine | 616.316 |
| *see also* Digestive system | |
| Salix | 583.65 |
| Salliq (Nunavut) | T2—719 58 |
| Salmo | 597.57 |
| Salmo salar | 597.56 |
| Salmon | 641.392 |
| commercial fishing | 639.275 6 |
| conservation technology | 639.977 56 |
| cooking | 641.692 |
| culture | 639.375 6 |
| economics | 338.371 375 6 |
| food | 641.392 |
| resource economics | 333.956 56 |
| sports fishing | 799.175 6 |
| zoology | 597.56 |
| Salmon Arm (B.C.) | T2—711 68 |
| Salmon River (Idaho) | T2—796 82 |
| Salmon River Mountains | |
| (Idaho) | T2—796 7 |
| Salmonella | 579.344 |
| Salmonella diseases | 571.993 44 |
| *see also* Salmonella infections | |
| Salmonella infections | 571.993 44 |
| animals | 571.993 44 |
| veterinary medicine | 636.089 692 7 |

Salmonella infections (continued)
  humans                          362.196 927
    incidence                     614.511
    medicine                      616.927
    social services               362.196 927
  *see also* Communicable
    diseases
Salmonidae                        597.55
  conservation technology         639.977 55
  culture                         639.375 5
  resource economics              333.956 55
  sports fishing                  799.175 5
Salmoniformes                     597.5
  paleozoology                    567.5
Salon orchestras                  784.4
Salop (England)          T2—424 5
Salpingitis
  gynecology                      618.12
  *see also* Female genital
    diseases — humans
Salsify                           641.351 6
  botany                          583.99
  cooking                         641.651 6
  food                            641.351 6
  garden crop                     635.16
Salt (Sodium chloride)            553.632
  applied nutrition               613.285 22
  biochemistry                    572.523 822 4
    humans                        612.015 24
  chemistry                       546.382 24
  cooking with                    641.6
  economic geology                553.632
  food technology                 664.4
  metabolism                      572.523 822 4
    human physiology              612.392 6
  mineralogy                      549.4
  mining                          622.363 2
Salt-free cooking                 641.563 23
Salt-free diet
  health                          613.285 223
Salt Lake City (Utah)    T2—792 258
Salt Lake County (Utah)  T2—792 25
Salt lakes                        551.482 9
  biology                         578.763 9
  ecology                         577.639
  resource economics              333.916 4
Salt marshes
  biology                         578.769
  ecology                         577.69
Salta (Argentina : Province)  T2—824 2
Saltarellos                       793.319 45
  music                           784.188 2
Salto (Uruguay : Dept.)  T2—895 35
Salton Sea (Calif.)      T2—794 99

Saltpeter                         553.64
  economic geology                553.64
  mineralogy                      549.732
Salts                             546.34
  biochemistry                    572.51
  chemical engineering            661.4
  chemistry                       546.34
  economic geology                553.63
  metabolism                      572.51
    human physiology              612.392 6
  *see also* Chemicals; Salt
    (Sodium chloride)
Saltwater biology                 578.77
Saltwater desalinization          628.167
Saltwater ecology                 577.7
Saltwater fishes                  597.177
  culture                         639.32
Saltwater fishing                 639.22
  commercial                      639.22
  sports                          799.16
Saltwater intrusion               363.738
  engineering                     628.114
  social problem                  363.738
  *see also* Pollution
Saltwater lagoons                 551.461 8
                         T2—168
  biology                         578.778
  ecology                         577.78
Saltwater wetlands
  biology                         578.769
  ecology                         577.69
Saluda County (S.C.)     T2—757 38
Saluki                            636.753 2
Salvador, El                      972.84
                         T2—728 4
Salvadoran literature             860
Salvadorans              T5—687 284
Salvage operations
  disaster relief                 363.348 1
  maritime law                    343.096 8
  maritime transportation         387.55
  underwater engineering          627.703
Salvation                         202.2
  Christianity                    234
  Islam                           297.22
  Judaism                         296.32
  *see also* Humans — religion
Salvation Army                    287.96
  *see also* Christian
    denominations
Salvator Rosa National Park
  (Qld.)                 T2—943 5
Salvelinus                        597.554
Salviniales                       587.3

| | | | |
|---|---|---|---|
| Salzburg (Austria) | T2—436 32 | Samoyedic languages | 494.4 |
| Salzburg (Austria : Land) | T2—436 3 | | T6—944 |
| Samaná (Dominican | | Samoyedic literatures | 894.4 |
| Republic : Province) | T2—729 365 | Sample preparation | |
| Samar (Philippines) | T2—599 5 | analytical chemistry | 543.19 |
| Samara (Russia : Oblast) | T2—474 4 | Samples | |
| Samaria | T2—335 3 | sales promotion | 658.82 |
| Samaritan Aramaic language | 492.29 | Sampling techniques | 001.433 |
| | T6—922 9 | | T1—072 3 |
| Samaritan language | 492.29 | Sampling theory | 519.52 |
| | T6—922 9 | Sampson County (N.C.) | T2—756 375 |
| Biblical texts | 220.45 | Samsun İli (Turkey) | T2—563 8 |
| Samaritan literature | 892.29 | ancient | T2—393 32 |
| Samaritans (Judaism) | 296.817 | Samuel (Biblical books) | 222.4 |
| Samarium | | San (African people) | T5—961 |
| chemistry | 546.415 | San Andres Mountains | |
| Samarskaīa oblast′ (Russia) | T2—474 4 | (N.M.) | T2—789 67 |
| Samaveda | 294.592 13 | San Andrés y Providencia | |
| Samba (Game) | 795.418 | (Colombia) | T2—861 11 |
| Sambalic languages | 499.21 | San Antonio (Chile : | |
| | T6—992 1 | Province) | T2—832 58 |
| Sambar | 599.654 | San Antonio (Tex.) | T2—764 351 |
| Sambas | 793.33 | San Antonio River (Tex.) | T2—764 12 |
| music | 784.188 8 | San Augustine County | |
| Same languages | 494.57 | (Tex.) | T2—764 175 |
| | T6—945 7 | San Benito County (Calif.) | T2—794 75 |
| Same literatures | 894.57 | San Bernardino County | |
| Same-sex marriage | 306.848 | (Calif.) | T2—794 95 |
| law | 346.016 8 | San Bernardino Mountains | |
| Samhitas | 294.592 1 | (Calif.) | T2—794 95 |
| Sámi (European people) | T5—945 7 | San Blas Cuna Indians | T5—978 3 |
| Sami languages | 494.57 | San Blas Cuna language | 497.83 |
| Sámi languages | 494.57 | | T6—978 3 |
| Sami languages | T6—945 7 | San Blas Cuna literature | 897.83 |
| Sámi languages | T6—945 7 | San Blas Kuna Indians | T5—978 3 |
| Sámi literatures | 894.57 | San Blas Kuna language | 497.83 |
| Samnium | T2—377 3 | | T6—978 3 |
| Samoa | 996.14 | San Blas Kuna literature | 897.83 |
| | T2—961 4 | San Cristóbal (Dominican | |
| Samoan Islands | T2—961 3 | Republic : Province) | T2—729 374 |
| Samoan language | 499.462 | San Diego (Calif.) | T2—794 985 |
| | T6—994 62 | San Diego County (Calif.) | T2—794 98 |
| Samoan literature | 899.462 | San Felipe (Chile : | |
| Samoans | T5—994 62 | Province) | T2—832 45 |
| Samoic Outlier languages | 499.46 | San Francisco (Calif.) | T2—794 61 |
| | T6—994 6 | San Francisco Bay (Calif.) | 551.461 432 |
| Samos (Greece : Nome) | T2—495 82 | | T2—164 32 |
| Samos Island (Greece) | T2—495 82 | San Francisco Bay Area | |
| ancient | T2—391 4 | (Calif.) | T2—794 6 |
| Samothrace Island (Greece) | T2—495 7 | San Francisco County | |
| ancient | T2—391 1 | (Calif.) | T2—794 61 |
| Samoycd | T5—944 | San Francisco earthquake, 1906 | 979.461 051 |
| Samoyed (Dog) | 636.73 | San Gabriel Mountains | |
| | | (Calif.) | T2—794 93 |

San hsiens     787.85
  *see also* Stringed instruments
San Jacinto County (Tex.)    T2—764 167
San Joaquin County (Calif.)    T2—794 55
San Joaquin River (Calif.)    T2—794 8
San Jorge River (Colombia)    T2—861 12
San Jose (Calif.)    T2—794 74
San José (Costa Rica :
   Province)    T2—728 63
San José (Uruguay : Dept.)    T2—895 12
San Juan (Argentina :
   Province)    T2—826 3
San Juan (Dominican
   Republic : Province)    T2—729 342
San Juan (P.R. : District)    T2—729 51
San Juan County (Colo.)    T2—788 25
San Juan County (N.M.)    T2—789 82
San Juan County (Utah)    T2—792 59
San Juan County (Wash.)    T2—797 74
San Juan Mountains (Colo.
   and N.M.)    T2—788 3
San Juan River (B.C.)    T2—711 28
San Juan River (Colo.-Utah)    T2—792 59
San languages    496.1
   T6—961
San Luis (Argentina :
   Province)    T2—826 2
San Luis Obispo County
   (Calif.)    T2—794 78
San Luis Potosí (Mexico :
   State)    T2—724 4
San Luis Valley (Colo. and
   N.M.)    T2—788 3
San Marcos (Guatemala :
   Dept.)    T2—728 184
San Marino    945.49
   T2—454 9
   ancient    937.269
   T2—372 69
San Martín (Peru : Dept.)    T2—854 5
San Martín (Peru : Region)    T2—854 5
San Mateo County (Calif.)    T2—794 69
San Miguel (El Salvador :
   Dept.)    T2—728 432
San Miguel County (Colo.)    T2—788 23
San Miguel County (N.M.)    T2—789 55
San Patricio County (Tex.)    T2—764 115
San Pedro (Paraguay :
   Dept.)    T2—892 136
San Pedro de Macorís
   (Dominican Republic :
   Province)    T2—729 382
San Saba County (Tex.)    T2—764 68

San Salvador (El Salvador :
   Dept.)    T2—728 423
San Salvador Island
   (Bahamas)    T2—729 6
San Sebastián (Spain)    T2—466 1
San Vicente (El Salvador :
   Dept.)    T2—728 427
Sanaga languages    496.396
   T6—963 96
Sanatoriums    362.16
   mental illness    362.23
   physical illness    362.16
   *see also* Health care facilities;
     Mental health services
Sanborn County (S.D.)    T2—783 33
Sánchez Ramírez
   (Dominican Republic :
   Province)    T2—729 368
Sancti Spíritus (Cuba :
   Province)    T2—729 145
Sanctification (Christian
   doctrine)    234.8
Sanctifying grace    234.1
Sanctions (International politics)    327.117
   law of nations    341.582
Sanctuaries
   architecture    726.593
Sanctus    264.36
   music    782.323 2
Sand    553.622
   economic geology    553.622
   materials science    620.191
   mining    622.362 2
   petrology    552.5
Sand adder    597.963 6
Sand casting
   metals    671.252
   sculpture    731.45
Sand dollars    593.95
Sand dunes    551.375
   biology    578.758 3
   ecology    577.583
   geomorphology    551.375
   land economics    333.73
Sand fleas    595.378
Sand grouse    598.65
Sand painting    751.49
Sand sculpture    736.96
Sand yachting    796.68
Sandalwood
   botany    583.88
   forestry    634.973 88
Sandaun Province (Papua
   New Guinea)    T2—957 7

| | |
|---|---|
| Sandblasting | 621.54 |
| glass arts | 748.6 |
| pneumatic engineering | 621.54 |
| Sandcastles | 736.96 |
| Sanders County (Mont.) | T2—786 833 |
| Sandlot baseball | 796.357 62 |
| Sandoval County (N.M.) | T2—789 57 |
| Sandpaper blocks | |
| music | 786.863 |
| *see also* Percussion | |
| instruments | |
| Sandpipers | 598.33 |
| Sandstone | 553.53 |
| building material | 691.2 |
| economic geology | 553.53 |
| petrology | 552.5 |
| quarrying | 622.353 |
| Sandusky Bay (Ohio) | T2—771 214 |
| Sandusky County (Ohio) | T2—771 214 |
| Sandwell (England) | T2—424 94 |
| Sandwich construction | 624.177 9 |
| naval architecture | 623.817 79 |
| Sandwich panels | |
| architectural construction | 721.044 92 |
| construction materials | 693.92 |
| wood | 674.835 |
| *see also* Wood | |
| Sandwiches | 641.84 |
| Sandy soils | |
| floriculture | 635.955 |
| Sangamon County (Ill.) | T2—773 56 |
| Sangamon River (Ill.) | T2—773 55 |
| Sango language | 496.361 6 |
| | T6—963 616 |
| Sango literature | 896.361 6 |
| Sangre de Cristo Mountains | |
| (Colo. and N.M.) | T2—788 49 |
| Sanguinetti, Julio María | |
| Uruguayan history | 989.506 71 |
| 1985–1990 | 989.506 71 |
| 1995–2000 | 989.506 73 |
| Sanhedrin | 296.67 |
| Sanhedrin (Tractate) | 296.123 4 |
| Babylonian Talmud | 296.125 4 |
| Mishnah | 296.123 4 |
| Palestinian Talmud | 296.124 4 |
| Sanikiluaq (Nunavut) | T2—719 52 |
| Sanilac County (Mich.) | T2—774 43 |
| Sanirajak (Nunavut) | T2—719 52 |
| Sanitariums | 362.16 |
| mental illness | 362.23 |
| physical illness | 362.16 |
| *see also* Health care facilities; | |
| Mental health services | |
| Sanitary engineering | 628 |
| military engineering | 623.75 |
| Sanitary engineers | 628.092 |
| Sanitary landfills | 363.728 |
| technology | 628.445 64 |
| sewage sludge | 628.364 |
| water pollution engineering | 628.168 25 |
| *see also* Waste control | |
| Sanitary napkins | 677.8 |
| Sanitation | 363.72 |
| armed forces | 355.345 |
| customs | 392.36 |
| home economics | 648 |
| law | 344.046 4 |
| enforcement | 363.233 |
| mining | 622.49 |
| public administration | 353.93 |
| public facilities | 353.94 |
| ships | 623.854 6 |
| social services | 363.72 |
| spacecraft | 629.477 4 |
| World War I | 940.475 2 |
| World War II | 940.547 52 |
| *see also* Waste control | |
| Sanitation equipment | |
| plant management | 658.28 |
| Sanitation facilities | |
| area planning | 711.8 |
| Sanitation services | 363.72 |
| *see also* Sanitation | |
| Sanitoriums | 362.16 |
| mental illness | 362.23 |
| physical illness | 362.16 |
| *see also* Health care facilities; | |
| Mental health services | |
| Sankara, Thomas | |
| Burkinan history | 966.250 52 |
| Śaṅkarācārya (Philosophy) | 181.482 |
| Sankhya (Philosophy) | 181.41 |
| Sankt Gallen (Switzerland) | T2—494 723 4 |
| Sankt Gallen (Switzerland : Canton) | T2—494 72 |
| Sankt Gallen (Switzerland : Wahlkreis) | T2—494 723 |
| Şanlıurfa İli (Turkey) | T2—565 1 |
| Sanpete County (Utah) | T2—792 563 |
| Sanquianga National Park (Colombia) | T2—861 58 |
| Sansevierias | 584.352 |
| Sanskrit language | 491.2 |
| | T6—912 |
| Vedas | 294.592 104 1 |
| Sanskrit literature | 891.2 |

Santa Ana (El Salvador : Dept.) T2—728 412
Santa Ana Mountains (Calif.) T2—794 96
Santa Bárbara (Honduras) T2—728 385
Santa Barbara County (Calif.) T2—794 91
Santa Barbara Islands (Calif.) T2—794 91
Santa Catarina (Brazil : State) T2—816 4
Santa Clara County (Calif.) T2—794 73
Santa Cruz (Argentina : Province) T2—827 5
Santa Cruz (Bolivia : Dept.) T2—843
Santa Cruz, Andrés
  Bolivian history 984.044
Santa Cruz County (Ariz.) T2—791 79
Santa Cruz County (Calif.) T2—794 71
Santa Cruz de Tenerife (Canary Islands : Province) T2—649
Santa Fe (Argentina : Province) T2—822 4
Santa Fe County (N.M.) T2—789 56
Santa Lucia Range (Calif.) T2—794 78
Santa Rosa (Guatemala) T2—728 144
Santa Rosa County (Fla.) T2—759 985
Santal (South Asian people) T5—959 5
Santalales 583.88
Santali language 495.95
T6—959 5
Santander (Colombia : Dept.) T2—861 25
Santander (Spain) T2—463 51
Santarém (Portugal : District) T2—469 45
Santee River (S.C.) T2—757 8
Santeria 299.674
Santiago (Chile) T2—833 15
Santiago (Chile : Province) T2—833 1
Santiago (Dominican Republic) T2—729 356
Santiago de Compostela (Spain) T2—461 1
Santiago de Cuba (Cuba : Province) T2—729 165
Santiago del Estero (Argentina : Province) T2—825 2
Santiago Rodríguez (Dominican Republic : Province) T2—729 353
Santirs 787.74
  *see also* Stringed instruments

Santo Domingo (Dominican Republic) T2—729 375
Santoríni Island (Greece) T2—495 85
Santos
  fine arts 704.948 2
  religious significance 246.53
Santos, José Eduardo dos
  Angolan history 967.304 2
Sanzas 786.85
  *see also* Percussion instruments
São Francisco River (Brazil) T2—814 2
São Paulo (Brazil : State) T2—816 1
São Tomé (Sao Tome and Principe) T2—671 5
Sao Tome and Principe 967.15
T2—671 5
Sao Tomeans T5—967 15
Saône-et-Loire (France) T2—444 3
Saône River (France) T2—444
Sap 575.75
  forest product 634.986
SAP (Swiss political party) 324.249 407 5
Sap beetles 595.769
Sapindales 583.78
Sápmi T2—48
Sapodilla 583.674
  *see also* Sapotaceae
Saponification 547.27
  chemical engineering 660.284 4
Saponins 572.567
  *see also* Carbohydrates
Sapotaceae 583.674
  edible fruits 641.344 3
    cooking 641.644 3
    food 641.344 3
  orchard crop 634.43
Sapphires 553.84
  economic geology 553.84
  glyptics 736.25
  jewelry 739.27
  mining 622.384
  synthetic 666.88
Saprolegniales 579.542
Sara Gambai dialect 496.5
T6—965
Saracenic architecture
  medieval 723.3
Saragossa (Spain : Province) T2—465 53
Sarah (Biblical matriarch) 222.110 92
Sarajevo (Bosnia and Hercegovina) T2—497 42
Saramacca (Suriname : District) T2—883 3

| | |
|---|---|
| Sarangis | 787.6 |
| *see also* Stringed instruments | |
| Sarans | |
| textiles | 677.474 4 |
| *see also* Textiles | |
| Sarasota County (Fla.) | T2—759 61 |
| Saratoga County (N.Y.) | T2—747 48 |
| Saratov (Russia : Oblast) | T2—474 6 |
| Saratovskaia oblast′ (Russia) | T2—474 6 |
| Saravastivada Buddhism | 294.391 |
| Sarawak | T2—595 4 |
| Sarcodina | 579.43 |
| Sarcoidosis | 362.196 429 |
| medicine | 616.429 |
| social services | 362.196 429 |
| Sarcoma | |
| incidence | 614.599 9 |
| medicine | 616.994 |
| *see also* Cancer — humans | |
| Sarcomastigophora | 579.4 |
| Sarcophagidae | 595.774 |
| Sarcopterygii | 597.39 |
| paleozoology | 567.39 |
| Sardegna (Italy) | 945.9 |
| | T2—459 |
| ancient | 937.9 |
| | T2—379 |
| Sardines | 641.392 |
| conservation technology | 639.977 45 |
| cooking | 641.692 |
| food | 641.392 |
| resource economics | 333.956 45 |
| zoology | 597.45 |
| Sardines (Young herring) | 641.392 |
| fishing | 639.274 52 |
| zoology | 597.452 |
| *see also* Sardines | |
| Sardinia (Italy) | 945.9 |
| | T2—459 |
| ancient | 937.9 |
| | T2—379 |
| Sardinia (Kingdom) | 945.107 |
| Piedmontese history | 945.107 |
| Sardinian history | 945.907 |
| Sardinian language | 459.982 |
| | T6—599 82 |
| Sardinian literature | 859.982 |
| Sardinians | T5—599 82 |
| Sardis (Extinct city) | T2—392 2 |
| Saren (Switzerland) | T2—494 764 4 |
| Sarganserland (Switzerland) | T2—494 729 |

| | |
|---|---|
| Sargasso Sea | 551.461 362 |
| | T2—163 62 |
| biology | 578.776 362 |
| ecology | 577.763 62 |
| Sargassum | 579.888 |
| Sargent County (N.D.) | T2—784 314 |
| Sargodha District (Pakistan) | T2—549 14 |
| Sarine (Switzerland) | T2—494 535 |
| Sark (Channel Islands) | T2—423 45 |
| Sarmatia | 939.52 |
| | T2—395 2 |
| Sarney, José | |
| Brazilian history | 981.064 |
| Sarpy County (Neb.) | T2—782 256 |
| Sarraceniales | 583.36 |
| Sarsaparillas | 584.356 |
| Sarthe (France) | T2—441 7 |
| Sasakian geometry | 516.373 |
| Sashes (Clothing) | 391.44 |
| *see also* Accessories (Clothing) | |
| Saskatchewan | 971.24 |
| | T2—712 4 |
| Saskatchewan River (Sask. and Man.) | T2—712 42 |
| Saskatoon (Sask.) | T2—712 425 |
| Sasolburg (South Africa : District) | T2—685 25 |
| Sasquatch | 001.944 |
| Sassafras | |
| botany | 583.23 |
| food | 641.338 2 |
| Sassafras tea | 641.338 2 |
| commercial processing | 663.96 |
| cooking with | 641.638 2 |
| home preparation | 641.877 |
| Sassanian Empire | 935.07 |
| | T2—35 |
| Sassari (Italy : Province) | T2—459 3 |
| ancient | T2—379 3 |
| Sassou Nguesso, Denis | |
| Congolese history | 967.240 52 |
| 1979–1992 | 967.240 52 |
| 1997– | 967.240 54 |
| SAT (Assessment test) | 378.166 2 |
| Satan | |
| Christianity | 235.47 |
| Islam | 297.216 |
| Judaism | 296.316 |
| occultism | 133.422 |
| Satanism | 133.422 |
| religion | 299 |
| Satellite cells | |
| human cytology | 612.810 46 |

Satellite communication | 384.51
  communications services | 384.51
  engineering | 621.382 5
  law | 343.099 4
  radio | 384.545 6
   engineering | 621.384 156
  television | 384.552
   engineering | 621.388 53
Satellite dishes (Television) | 384.552
  engineering | 621.388 35
Satellite insurance | 368.2
Satellites (Moons) | 523.98
  | T2—992
Sati | 393.930 954
Satire | 808.87
  literary criticism | 809.7
   theory | 808.7
  literary history | 809.7
  literature | 808.87
   specific literatures | T3B—7
  rhetoric | 808.7
  *see Manual at* T1—0207 vs.
   T3B—7, T3A—8 + 02,
   T3B—802, T3B—8 + 02,
   T3A—8 + 07, T3B—807,
   T3B—8 + 07
Satirical poetry | 808.817
  history and criticism | 809.17
  specific literatures | T3B—107
   individual authors | T3A—1
Satirists | 809.7
  collected biography | 809.7
  specific literatures | T3B—700 9
Satisfaction (Christian rite) | 265.63
Satu Mare (Romania :
  Judeţ) | T2—498 4
Saturating paper | 676.284 4
Saturday
  music | 781.522 8
Saturn (Planet) | 523.46
  | T2—992 6
  astrology | 133.537
Satyromania
  medicine | 616.858 33
Sauces | 641.814
  commercial processing | 664.58
  home preparation | 641.814
Saudi Arabia | 953.8
  | T2—538
  ancient | 939.49
  | T2—394 9
Saudi Arabians | T5—927 538
Saudis | T5—927 538
Sauger | 597.758

Sauk County (Wis.) | T2—775 76
Sauk Indians | T5—973 149
Sauk language | 497.314 9
  | T6—973 149
Saul, King of Israel
  Biblical leader | 222.430 92
  Palestinian history | 933.02
Saunas | 613.41
  architecture | 725.73
   domestic | 728.96
   public | 725.73
  construction | 690.573
   domestic | 690.896
   public | 690.573
  health | 613.41
Saunders County (Neb.) | T2—782 296
Sauraism | 294.551 7
Saurauiaceae | 583.66
Sauria | 597.95
  paleozoology | 567.95
Sauria Paharia language | 494.83
  | T6—948 3
Saurischia | 567.912
Sauropodomorpha | 567.913
Sauropterygia | 567.937
Saururaceae | 583.25
Sausage | 641.36
  cooking | 641.66
  food | 641.36
Sautéing | 641.77
Sautrantika Buddhism | 294.391
Savannah (Ga.) | T2—758 724
Savannah River (Ga. and
  S.C.) | T2—758 1
  Georgia | T2—758 1
  South Carolina | T2—757 9
Savannas | 333.74
  | T2—153
  biology | 578.748
  ecology | 577.48
  *see also* Grasslands
Savings | 332.041 5
  capital management | 658.152 26
  financial economics | 332.041 5
  macroeconomics | 339.43
Savings accounts | 332.175 2
Savings and loan associations | 332.32
  law | 346.082 32
  public administration | 354.86
Savings and Loan Bailout, 1989– | 332.320 973
Savings banks | 332.21
Savings-consumption relationship | 339.43
Savings departments | 332.175 2

| | |
|---|---|
| Savings stamps | |
| prints | 769.57 |
| Savoie (France) | T2—445 85 |
| Savona (Italy : Province) | T2—451 84 |
| ancient | T2—371 3 |
| Savories | 641.812 |
| Savoy (Duchy) | T2—445 85 |
| Savoy (France and Italy) | T2—445 85 |
| Savoy, House of | |
| Italian history | 945.084 |
| Piedmontese history | 945.105 |
| Savu Sea | 551.461 474 |
| | T2—164 74 |
| Sawdust | 674.84 |
| fuel | 662.65 |
| Sawfishes | 597.35 |
| Sawflies | 595.79 |
| agricultural pests | 632.79 |
| Ṣawm | 297.53 |
| Ṣawm Ramaḍān | 297.362 |
| Sawmill operations | 674.2 |
| Saws | 621.934 |
| music | 786.888 |
| *see also* Percussion | |
| instruments | |
| Sawtooth Mountains (Idaho) | T2—796 72 |
| Sawtooth Range (Idaho) | T2—796 29 |
| Sawyer County (Wis.) | T2—775 16 |
| Saxhorns | 788.97 |
| instrument | 788.971 9 |
| music | 788.97 |
| *see also* Brass instruments | |
| Saxifragales | 583.72 |
| Saxifrages | 583.72 |
| floriculture | 635.933 72 |
| Saxons | |
| English history | 942.017 |
| Saxony (Germany) | T2—432 1 |
| Saxony (Prussia) | T2—431 8 |
| Saxony, House of | 943.022 |
| Saxony-Anhalt (Germany) | T2—431 8 |
| Saxophones | 788.7 |
| instrument | 788.719 |
| music | 788.7 |
| *see also* Woodwind instruments | |
| Saxophonists | 788.709 2 |
| Say, Jean Baptiste | |
| economic school | 330.153 |
| Sayan Mountains (Russia) | T2—575 |
| Sayyid dynasty | 954.024 2 |

| | |
|---|---|
| Scabies | |
| humans | |
| medicine | 616.573 |
| *see also* Skin diseases — | |
| humans | |
| Scalar field theory | 515.63 |
| Scalds | |
| medicine | 617.11 |
| Scale insects | 595.752 |
| agricultural pests | 632.752 |
| Scale mosses | 588.3 |
| Scales (Integument) | 591.477 |
| descriptive zoology | 591.477 |
| physiology | 573.595 |
| Scales (Maps) | 912.014 8 |
| Scales (Music) | 781.246 |
| Scalic formations (Music) | 781.246 |
| Scaliger, House of | |
| Venetian history | 945.304 |
| Scallops | 641.394 |
| conservation technology | 639.974 4 |
| cooking | 641.694 |
| fishing and culture | 639.46 |
| food | 641.394 |
| commercial processing | 664.94 |
| resource economics | 333.955 46 |
| zoology | 594.4 |
| Scalp diseases | |
| medicine | 616.546 |
| *see also* Skin diseases — | |
| humans | |
| Scaly anteaters | 599.31 |
| Scaly reptiles | 597.94 |
| Scaly-tailed possums | 599.232 |
| Scandentia | 599.338 |
| paleozoology | 569.338 |
| Scandinavia | 948 |
| | T2—48 |
| ancient | 936.8 |
| | T2—368 |
| Scandinavian languages | 439.5 |
| | T6—395 |
| Scandinavian literatures | 839.5 |
| Scandinavian religion | 293 |
| Scandinavians | T5—395 |
| Scandium | 669.290 1 |
| chemical engineering | 661.040 1 |
| chemistry | 546.401 |
| economic geology | 553.494 2 |
| metallurgy | 669.290 1 |
| *see also* Chemicals; Metals | |
| Scanners | |
| computer graphics | 006.62 |

| | |
|---|---|
| Scaphopoda | 594.29 |
| paleozoology | 564.29 |
| Scapolite | |
| mineralogy | 549.68 |
| Scapulas | |
| human anatomy | 611.717 |
| Scarabaeidae | 595.764 9 |
| Scarabaeoidea | 595.764 9 |
| Scarabs | |
| glyptics | 736.209 32 |
| Scarborough (England : | |
| Borough) | T2—428 47 |
| Scarborough (Toronto, Ont.) | T2—713 541 |
| Scarification | |
| customs | 391.65 |
| Scarlatina | |
| incidence | 614.522 |
| medicine | 616.929 87 |
| *see also* Communicable | |
| diseases — humans | |
| Scarlet fever | |
| incidence | 614.522 |
| medicine | 616.929 87 |
| *see also* Communicable | |
| diseases — humans | |
| Scarves | 391.41 |
| home sewing | 646.48 |
| *see also* Accessories (Clothing) | |
| Scarves (Table linens) | |
| arts | 746.96 |
| Scatophagidae | 595.774 |
| Scattered disk objects | 523.494 |
| Scattering (Physics) | 539.758 |
| solid-state physics | 530.416 |
| Scattering of light | 535.43 |
| meteorology | 551.566 |
| Scavenger cells | 571.968 |
| human immunology | 616.079 9 |
| Scenarios | |
| music | 780 |
| treatises | 782.002 69 |
| Scene paintings | 751.75 |
| Scene understanding | |
| artificial intelligence | 006.37 |
| Scenery | |
| dramatic performances | 792.025 |
| motion pictures | 791.430 25 |
| stage | 792.025 |
| television | 791.450 25 |
| Scenic rivers | 333.784 5 |
| law | 346.046 784 5 |
| natural resources | 333.784 5 |
| Scent hounds | 636.753 6 |
| Schaffhausen (Switzerland) | T2—494 586 |
| Schaffhausen (Switzerland : | |
| Canton) | T2—494 58 |
| Scheduled castes | 305.568 8 |
| *see also* Dalits | |
| Scheduling | |
| broadcasting services | 384.544 2 |
| radio | 384.544 2 |
| television | 384.553 1 |
| education | 371.242 |
| production management | 658.53 |
| transportation | 388.041 |
| air | 387.740 42 |
| automobile | 388.321 |
| bus | 388.322 042 |
| urban | 388.413 22 |
| canal | 386.404 204 2 |
| ferries | 386.6 |
| inland waterway | 386.240 42 |
| lake | 386.540 42 |
| marine | 387.540 42 |
| railroad | 385.204 2 |
| urban | 388.42 |
| river | 386.350 42 |
| truck | 388.324 042 |
| urban | 388.413 24 |
| Scheelite | |
| mineralogy | 549.74 |
| Schefferville (Quebec) | T2—714 117 |
| Schenectady County (N.Y.) | T2—747 44 |
| Scheuchzeriaceae | 584.74 |
| Schiffli embroidery | 677.77 |
| Schipperke | 636.72 |
| Schism between Eastern and | |
| Western Church | 270.38 |
| Schisms | |
| Christianity | 262.8 |
| church history | 273 |
| Judaism | 296.67 |
| Schist | 552.4 |
| Schistosomiasis | |
| incidence | 614.553 |
| medicine | 616.963 |
| *see also* Communicable | |
| diseases — humans | |
| Schizanthuses | 635.933 952 |
| botany | 583.952 |
| floriculture | 635.933 952 |
| Schizoid personality disorder | |
| medicine | 616.858 1 |
| *see also* Mental disorders | |
| Schizomida | 595.45 |
| Schizomycetes | 579.3 |

| | | | |
|---|---|---|---|
| Schizophrenia | 362.26 | School children | 305.234 |
| medicine | 616.898 | | T1—083 4 |
| social welfare | 362.26 | development | |
| *see also* Mental disorders | | human physiology | 612.654 |
| Schizophyta | 579.3 | home care | 649.124 |
| Schleicher County (Tex.) | T2—764 876 | psychology | 155.424 |
| Schleswig-Holstein | | reading | |
| (Germany) | T2—435 12 | library science | 028.534 |
| Schleswig-Holstein War, 1864 | 943.076 | social aspects | 305.234 |
| Schley County (Ga.) | T2—758 495 | transportation | 371.872 |
| Schmalkalden-Meiningen | | School choice | 379.111 |
| (Germany : Landkreis) | T2—432 26 | School closings | 379.153 5 |
| Schmalkaldic War, 1546–1547 | 943.031 | School cooking | 641.571 |
| Schmidt, Helmut | | School credits | 371.218 |
| German history | 943.087 7 | School custodians | 371.68 |
| Schmitt, Pál | | School day | 371.244 |
| Hungarian history | 943.905 44 | law | 344.079 2 |
| Schmoller, Gustav von | | School desegregation | 379.263 |
| economic school | 330.154 2 | law | 344.079 8 |
| Schnauzers | 636.73 | School discipline | 371.5 |
| Schoharie County (N.Y.) | T2—747 45 | School districts | 379.153 5 |
| Scholarship | 001.2 | liability | 344.075 |
| Scholarships | 371.223 | School dropouts | 371.291 3 |
| | T1—079 | School enrollment | 371.219 |
| higher education | 378.34 | secondary education | 373.121 9 |
| law | 344.079 5 | School environment | |
| research | 001.44 | psychological influence | 370.158 |
| Scholastic Assessment Test | 378.166 2 | School equipment | 371.67 |
| Scholastic philosophy | 189.4 | higher education | 378.196 7 |
| modern | 149.91 | special education | 371.904 5 |
| School adjustment | 370.158 | School etiquette | 395.5 |
| School administration | 371.2 | School excursions | 371.384 |
| *see Manual at* 371 vs. 353.8, | | School facilities | 371.6 |
| 371.2, 379 | | *see also* Educational buildings | |
| School administrators | | School failure | 371.285 |
| biography | 371.200 92 | School furniture | 371.63 |
| public control | 379.157 | School girls | T1—083 42 |
| role and function | 371.201 1 | School grounds | 371.61 |
| School and society | 306.432 | landscape architecture | 712.7 |
| School assemblies | 371.895 | School hygiene | 371.71 |
| School attendance | 371.294 | School improvement programs | 371.207 |
| compulsory education | 379.23 | School integration | 379.263 |
| law | 344.079 2 | School journalism | 371.897 |
| School attendance districts | 379.153 5 | School leavers | 371.291 3 |
| School boards | 353.822 5 | secondary level | 373.129 13 |
| local public education | 379.153 1 | School-leaving age | 379.23 |
| public education | 353.822 5 | School libraries | 027.8 |
| School bonds | 379.13 | administration | 025.197 8 |
| School boys | T1—083 41 | collection development | 025.218 78 |
| School buildings | 371.6 | use studies | 025.587 8 |
| *see also* Educational buildings | | School library reading programs | |
| School cafeterias | 371.716 | primary education | 372.427 |
| School calendar | 371.23 | School location | 371.61 |
| School camps | 796.542 2 | | |

School lunch programs 371.716
  law 344.079 42
  meal service 642.57
School management 371.2
School meal service 642.57
School media centers 027.8
School milk programs 371.716
School newspapers
  journalism 371.897 4
School nursing 371.712
School orchestras 784.44
School plays
  primary education 372.66
School policy 371
  *see Manual at* 371 vs. 353.8,
    371.2, 379
School principals
  biography 371.200 92
  public control 379.157
  role and function 371.201 2
School psychologists 371.713
School readiness
  child rearing 649.68
School resource centers 027.8
School safety programs 363.119 371
School schedules 371.242
School sites 371.61
School social services 371.7
School social workers 371.46
School socialization 303.324
School staff 371.201
School superintendents
  biography 371.200 92
  public control 379.157
  role and function 371.201 1
School supervision 371.203
School supervisors 371.203 092
School supplies 371.67
School systems 371
  *see Manual at* 371 vs. 353 8,
    371.2, 379
School tablet paper 676.286
School taxes 379.13
School vandalism 371.782
School violence 371.782
School week 371.242
School year 371.23
  law 344.079 2
School yearbooks
  journalism 371.897 6
Schoolcraft County (Mich.) T2—774 935
Schooling 370
  *see also* Education

Schools 371
  T1—071
  accounting 657.832 7
  area planning 711.57
  centralization 379.153 5
  energy economics 333.796 4
  fire hazards 363.379
    *see also* Fire safety
  law 344.07
  liability 344.075
  meal service 642.57
  public finance 379.11
    law 344.076
  standards
    public policy 379.158
  *see also* entries beginning with
    Student
  *see Manual at* 371 vs. 353.8,
    371.2, 379; *also at*
    371.01–.8 vs. 372–374, 378
Schools (Styles)
  fine arts 709
    *see Manual at* 709.012–.015,
      709.02–.05 vs. 709.3–.9
Schools of thought T1—01
  philosophy 140
  *see Manual at* T1—01
Schröder, Gerhard
  German history 943.088 2
Schrödinger wave mechanics 530.124
Schuster, Rudolf
  Slovak history 943.730 512
Schuyler County (Ill.) T2—773 475
Schuyler County (Mo.) T2—778 262
Schuyler County (N.Y.) T2—747 81
Schuylkill County (Pa.) T2—748 17
Schuylkill River (Pa.) T2—748 1
Schwaben (Germany :
  Regierungsbezirk) T2—433 7
Schweinfurt (Germany) T2—433 36
Schweizer Demokraten (Political
  party) 324.249 403
Schweizer-Reneke (South
  Africa : District) T2—682 45
Schweizerische Volkspartei 324.249 403
Schweizerischer
  Nationalpark
  (Switzerland) T2—494 732 7
Schwerin (Germany) T2—431 76
Schwerin (Germany :
  Bezirk) T2—431 76
Schwyz (Switzerland) T2—494 752 64
Schwyz (Switzerland :
  Bezirk) T2—494 752 6

Schwyz (Switzerland :
  Canton)    T2—494 752
Sciaenidae    597.725
Sciaenops    597.725
Sciaridae    595.772
Sciatica
  medicine    616.856
  *see also* Nervous system
    diseases — humans
Science    500
     T1—015
  arts    700.46
     T3C—36
  folklore    398.26
    history and criticism    398.36
  information systems    025.065
  law    344.095
  libraries    026.5
  literature    808.803 6
    history and criticism    809.933 6
    specific literatures    T3B—080 36
      history and
      criticism    T3B—093 6
  painting    758.95
  primary education    372.35
  public administrative support    352.745
  social effects    303.483
    *see Manual at* 303.483 vs.
      306.45, 306.46
  sociology    306.45
    *see Manual at* 303.483 vs.
      306.45, 306.46
  use in agricultural industries    338.16
  *see Manual at* 500 vs. 001
Science and religion    201.65
  Buddhism    294.336 5
  Christianity    261.55
  Hinduism    294.516 5
  Islam    297.265
  Judaism    296.375
  philosophy of religion    215
Science fair projects    507.8
Science fiction    808.838 762
  arts    700.415
     T3C—15
  history and criticism    809.387 62
  motion pictures    791.436 15
  radio programs    791.446 15
  specific literatures    T3B—308 762
    individual authors    T3A—3
  television programs    791.456 15
Science laboratories    507.2
  architecture    727.55

Science museums    507.4
  architecture    727.65
Science policy    338.926
  *see Manual at* 338.926 vs.
    352.745, 500
Science projects in schools    507.8
Sciences (Knowledge)    001
  *see also* Knowledge
Sciences (Natural sciences)    500
  *see also* Science
Scientific exemptions
  customs duties    382.78
Scientific instruments
  manufacturing technology    681.75
Scientific method    001.42
     T1—072 1
Scientific principles    500
     T1—015
  *see Manual at* T1—015 vs.
    T1—0245–0246
Scientific recreations    793.8
Scientific socialism    335.423
Scientific surveys    508
Scientific techniques    T1—072 1
Scientific toys    790.133
  manufacturing technology    688.725
  recreation    790.133
Scientific travels    508
Scientific writing    808.066 5
Scientists    509.2
  Islamic polemics    297.298
  works for    T1—024 5
  *see Manual at* T1—015 vs.
    T1—0245–0246
Scientology    299.936
  biography    299.936 092
Scilly, Isles of (England)    T2—423 79
Scilly Isles (England)    T2—423 79
Scincidae    597.957
Scincomorphoidea    597.957
Scintillation
  atmospheric optics    551.565
Scintillation counters
  nuclear physics    539.775
Sciomyzidae    595.774
Scioto County (Ohio)    T2—771 87
Scioto River (Ohio)    T2—771 5
Scissors    621.93
  home sewing    646.19
Sciuridae    599.36
  paleozoology    569.36
Sciurus    599.362

Scleral diseases
  ophthalmology    617.719
    *see also* Eye diseases —
      humans
Scleras
  human anatomy    611.84
  human physiology    612.841
  ophthalmology    617.719
Sclerenchyma    571.585
Scleroderma
  medicine    616.544
    *see also* Skin diseases —
      humans
Scleroproteins    572.67
  *see also* Proteins
Scolecophidia    597.969
Scolioidea    595.79
Scoliosis
  medicine    616.73
    *see also* Musculoskeletal
      diseases — humans
Scolopacidae    598.33
Scolytidae    595.768
Scombridae    597.782
Scombroidei    597.78
Sconces
  furniture arts    749.63
Scones    641.815 7
Scooters    388.347 5
  engineering    629.227 5
  *see also* Motorcycles
Scopelomorpha    597.61
  paleozoology    567.61
Score reading    781.423
  primary education    372.873
Scores (Music)    780
  cataloging    025.348 8
  library treatment    025.178 8
  treatises    780.26
  *see Manual at* 780.26; *also at*
    782
Scoring systems
  contract bridge    795.415 4
Scorpaeniformes    597.68
  paleozoology    567.68
Scorpio (Zodiac)    133.527 3
Scorpion fishes    597.68
Scorpion flies    595.744
Scorpion venom
  human toxicology    615.942
Scorpions    595.46
Scotch broom    583.74
Scotia Sea    551.461 73
      T2—167 3

Scotland    941.1
      T2—411
  ancient    936.11
      T2—361 1
  *see Manual at* T2—41 *and*
    T2—42; *also at* 941
Scotland. Children's Hearings    345.411 08
Scotland. Court of Appeal    345.411 016 3
Scotland. Court of First Instance    345.411 016 2
Scotland. Court of Session    347.411 023
Scotland. Court of Session. Inner
  House    347.411 035
Scotland. Court of Session. Outer
  House    347.411 024
Scotland. Court of the Lord Lyon    347.411 04
Scotland. Crown Counsel    345.411 01
Scotland. District Court    345.411 012
Scotland. High Court of
  Justiciary    345.411 016
Scotland. House of Lords (Court
  of last resort)    347.411 039
Scotland. Licensing Appeals
  Court    347.411 04
Scotland. Licensing Courts    347.411 04
Scotland. Lord Advocate    345.411 01
Scotland. Sheriff Court    347.411 021
  criminal law    345.411 014
Scotland. Sheriff-Principal    347.411 032
Scotland. Solicitor-General    345.411 01
Scotland County (Mo.)    T2—778 312
Scotland County (N.C.)    T2—756 335
Scots    T5—916 3
Scots language (English dialect)    427.941 1
      T6—21
Scott County (Ark.)    T2—767 44
Scott County (Ill.)    T2—773 455
Scott County (Ind.)    T2—772 183
Scott County (Iowa)    T2—777 69
Scott County (Kan.)    T2—781 43
Scott County (Ky.)    T2—769 425
Scott County (Minn.)    T2—776 54
Scott County (Miss.)    T2—762 655
Scott County (Mo.)    T2—778 97
Scott County (Tenn.)    T2—768 71
Scott County (Va.)    T2—755 732
Scottburgh (South Africa)    T2—684 5
Scottish Borders (Scotland)    T2—413 7
Scottish deerhound    636.753 2
Scottish English dialect    427.941 1
      T6—21
Scottish Gaelic language    491.63
      T6—916 3
Scottish Gaelic literature    891.63
Scottish Gaels    T5—916 3

Scottish Highlands
  (Scotland)      T2—411 5
Scottish literature
  English      820
  Gaelic      891.63
Scotts Bluff County (Neb.)    T2—782 98
Scottsdale (Tas.)      T2—946 4
Scouring compounds      668.127
Scouts (Boy and girl)      369.409 2
Scows      387.29
  design      623.812 9
  engineering      623.829
  transportation services      387.29
  *see also* Ships
Scranton (Pa.)      T2—748 37
Scrap metal      363.728 8
  metallurgy      669.042
  social services      363.728 8
  *see also* Waste control
Scrapbooking      745.593 8
Scrapbooks
  handicrafts      745.593 8
Scraped idiophones      786.886
  *see also* Percussion instruments
Scratch pad paper      676.286
Scratchboard drawing      741.29
Screamers (Birds)      598.41
Screen process printing      686.231 6
Screening
  chemical engineering      660.284 22
  ores      622.74
  sewage treatment      628.34
  water supply treatment      628.162 2
Screenplays      791.437
  literature      808.823
    history and criticism      809.23
    specific literatures    T3B—203
    individual authors    T3A—2
  motion pictures      791.437
  music      780
    treatises      780.268
  rhetoric      808.23
  *see Manual at* 791.437 and
    791.447, 791.457, 792.9;
    *also at* 808.82 vs. 791.437,
    791.447, 791.457, 792.9
Screens      645.4
  church architecture      726.529 6
  church furniture      247.1
  decorative arts      749.3
  *see also* Furniture
Screenwriting      808.23
Screven County (Ga.)      T2—758 695
Screw-cutting tools      621.944

Screw pines      584.66
Screwdrivers      621.972
Screws      621.882
Scribes
  Judaism      296.461 509 2
Scrimshaws      736.69
Script shorthand systems      653.428
Scripts
  motion pictures      791.437
    *see also* Screenplays
  puppetry      791.538
  radio      791.447
  stage productions      792.9
  television      791.457
Scripture readings
  public worship
    Christianity      264.34
Scriptures (Religion)      208.2
  *see also* Sacred books
Scroll saws      621.934
  wood handicrafts      745.513
Scrollwork
  furniture arts      749.5
  wood handicrafts      745.513
Scrophulariales      583.95
Scrotum      573.655 25
  biology      573.655 25
  human anatomy      611.63
  human physiology      612.614
  medicine      616.67
  *see also* Male genital system
Scrotum diseases
  medicine      616.67
  *see also* Male genital
    diseases — humans
Scrub typhus
  incidence      614.526 4
  medicine      616.922 4
  *see also* Communicable
    diseases — humans
Scrublands
  biology      578.738
  ecology      577.38
Scrummaging      796.333 23
Scuba diving
  sports      797.234
Scuds (Amphipoda)      595.378
Scullin, J. H. (James Henry)
  Australian history      994.042
Sculptors      730.92
Sculptural stone      553.5
  *see also* Stone

| | |
|---|---|
| Sculpture | 730 |
|   architectural decoration | 729.5 |
|   primary education | 372.53 |
|   *see Manual at* 731–735 vs. 736–739 | |
| Scunthorpe (England) | T2—428 32 |
| Scups | 597.72 |
| Scurry County (Tex.) | T2—764 731 |
| Scurvy | |
|   medicine | 616.394 |
|   *see also* Digestive system diseases — humans | |
| Scyphozoa | 593.53 |
|   paleozoology | 563.5 |
| Scyros Island (Greece) | T2—495 15 |
|   ancient | T2—391 1 |
| Scythia | 939.51 |
| | T2—395 1 |
| Scythian languages | 491.53 |
| | T6—915 3 |
| Scythian literatures | 891.53 |
| Scythians | T5—915 |
| SD (Swiss political party) | 324.249 403 |
| SDAP (Austrian political party) | 324.243 602 7 |
| SDI (Information service) | 025.525 |
| SDI (Strategic Defense Initiative) | 358.174 |
| Sea-air-land teams (Military units) | 359.984 |
| Sea anemones | 593.6 |
| Sea basins | T2—182 |
| Sea basses | 597.736 |
| Sea birds | 598.177 |
|   conservation technology | 639.978 177 |
|   resource economics | 333.958 287 |
| Sea breams | 597.72 |
| Sea breezes | 551.518 5 |
| Sea caves | |
|   biology | 578.769 9 |
|   ecology | 577.699 |
| Sea cows | 599.55 |
| Sea cucumbers | 593.96 |
| Sea fans | 593.6 |
| Sea figs | 583.53 |
| Sea floor | 551.468 |
|   *see also* Ocean floor | |
| Sea-floor spreading | 551.136 |
| Sea forces | 359 |
| Sea grass wetlands | |
|   biology | 578.769 4 |
|   ecology | 577.694 |
| Sea hares | 594.37 |
| Sea horses | 597.679 8 |
| Sea ice | 551.343 |
| Sea Islands | T2—757 99 |
|   Georgia | T2—758 7 |
|   South Carolina | T2—757 99 |
| Sea Islands Creole | 427.975 799 |
| | T6—217 |
| Sea lavenders | 583.5 |
| Sea-level changes | 551.458 |
| Sea lilies | 593.92 |
| Sea lions | 599.797 5 |
| Sea mail | 383.142 |
|   *see also* Postal service | |
| Sea mats (Bryozoa) | 594.67 |
| Sea of Azov (Ukraine and Russia) | 551.461 389 |
| | T2—163 89 |
| Sea of Crete (Greece) | 551.461 388 |
| | T2—163 88 |
| Sea of Japan | 551.461 454 |
| | T2—164 54 |
| Sea of Marmara (Turkey) | 551.461 389 |
| | T2—163 89 |
| Sea of Okhotsk | 551.461 453 |
| | T2—164 53 |
| Sea otter | 599.769 5 |
|   conservation technology | 639.979 769 5 |
|   resource economics | 333.959 769 5 |
| Sea pens | 593.6 |
| Sea slugs (Nudibranchia) | 594.36 |
| Sea slugs (Opisthobranchia) | 594.34 |
| Sea snakes | 597.965 |
| Sea songs | 782.421 595 |
| Sea spiders | 595.496 |
| Sea squirts | 596.2 |
| Sea turtles | 597.928 |
|   conservation technology | 639.977 928 |
|   resource economics | 333.957 928 |
| Sea urchins | 593.95 |
|   harvest and culture | 639.7 |
| Sea walnuts | 593.8 |
| Sea warfare | 359 |
| Seabed | 551.468 |
|   law of nations | 341.455 |
|   *see also* Ocean floor | |
| Seabed mining | 622.295 |
| Seabees (Naval forces) | 359.982 |
| Seaborgium | 546.53 |
| Seadromes | |
|   engineering | 629.136 1 |
| Seafaring life | 910.45 |
|   music about | 781.595 |
| Seafood | 641.392 |
|   commercial processing | 664.94 |
|   cooking | 641.692 |
|   home preservation | 641.494 |
| Seahorses | 597.679 8 |

| | | | |
|---|---|---|---|
| Sealants | 668.38 | Seashores | 551.457 |
| building materials | 691.99 | | T2—146 |
| materials science | 620.199 | biology | 578.769 9 |
| structural engineering | 624.189 9 | ecology | 577.699 |
| Sealers (Hunters) | 639.290 92 | health | 613.12 |
| Sealing (Hunting) | 639.29 | *see also* Coasts | |
| economics | 338.372 979 | Seasickness | |
| law | 343.076 929 | medicine | 616.989 2 |
| Sealing devices | 621.885 | *see also* Environmental | |
| Seals (Animals) | 599.79 | diseases — humans | |
| conservation technology | 639.979 79 | Seasonal adaptation | 578.43 |
| hunting | 639.29 | animals | 591.43 |
| resource economics | 333.959 79 | plants | 581.43 |
| Seals (Devices) | 929.9 | Seasonal affective disorder | |
| insignia | 929.9 | medicine | 616.852 7 |
| numismatics | 737.6 | *see also* Mental disorders | |
| SEALs (Military units) | 359.984 | Seasonal changes | |
| Seam welding | 671.521 3 | health | 613.11 |
| Seamanship | 623.88 | Seasonal cooking | 641.564 |
| Seamen | 387.509 2 | Seasonal holidays | 394.26 |
| navy enlisted personnel | 359.009 2 | *see also* Holidays | |
| role and function | 359.338 | Seasonal houses | |
| *see also* Sailors | | architecture | 728.7 |
| Seamoths | 597.64 | Seasonal music | 781.524 |
| Seamstresses | 646.209 2 | Seasonal parties | 793.22 |
| Seaplanes | 387.733 47 | Seasonal unemployment | 331.137 044 |
| engineering | 629.133 347 | Seasoning lumber | 674.38 |
| transportation services | 387.733 47 | Seasonings | 641.338 2 |
| *see also* Aircraft | | cooking with | 641.638 2 |
| Seaports | 387.1 | Seasons | 508.2 |
| *see also* Ports | | arts | T3C—33 |
| Search algorithms | 005.741 | astronomy | 525.5 |
| Search and seizure | | biological adaptation | 578.43 |
| criminal investigation | 363.252 | effect on natural ecology | 577.23 |
| law | 345.052 2 | folklore | 398.236 |
| Search dogs | 636.708 86 | history and criticism | 398.33 |
| Search engines | 025.042 52 | influence on crime | 364.22 |
| Search for moving target | 531.112 | literature | 808.803 3 |
| Search strategy | | history and criticism | 809.933 3 |
| information science | 025.524 | specific literatures | T3B—080 33 |
| Search trees (Computer science) | 005.741 | history and | |
| Searching data | 005.741 | criticism | T3B—093 3 |
| Searcy County (Ark.) | T2—767 195 | music | 781.524 |
| Seas | 551.46 | natural history | 508.2 |
| | T2—162 | Seat belts | |
| *see also* Oceans | | aircraft | 629.134 43 |
| Seascapes | | automobiles | 363.125 7 |
| art representation | 704.943 7 | engineering | 629.276 |
| drawing | 743.837 | highway safety | 363.125 7 |
| painting | 758.2 | law | 343.094 4 |
| Seashells | 594.147 7 | Seat ejectors | |
| Seashore animals | 591.769 9 | aircraft | 629.134 386 |
| | | Seats | |
| | | automobile | 629.26 |

Seattle (Wash.)    T2—797 772
Seatwork    371.3
Seawalls    627.58
   flood control    627.42
   port engineering    627.24
   shore protection    627.58
Seawater    551.46
   desalinization    628.167
   oceanography    551.46
   water supply evaluation    628.116
   *see also* Oceanography
Seawater intrusion    363.738
   engineering    628.114
   social problem    363.738
   *see also* Pollution
Seawater supply
   ship sanitation    623.854 3
Seaweeds    579.88
   culture    639.89
   resource economics    333.953 8
Sebaceous gland diseases
   medicine    616.53
     *see also* Skin diseases —
     humans
Sebaceous glands    573.537 9
   biology    573.537 9
   human anatomy    611.77
   human physiology    612.793
   medicine    616.53
   *see also* Skin
Sebastian County (Ark.)    T2—767 36
Seborrhea
   medicine    616.53
     *see also* Skin diseases —
     humans
Secernentea    592.57
Secession
   United States history    973.713
Second-class mail    383.123
   *see also* Postal service
Second Coming of Christ    236.9
Second Crusade, 1147–1149    956.014
Second Empire (France)    944.07
Second International    324.174
Second language acquisition    401.93
   applied linguistics    418
     education    418.007 1
     specific languages    T4—8
       audio-lingual
         approach    T4—834
       education    T4—800 71
       formal approach    T4—824
     specific languages    T4—019
   *see Manual at* T1—407.1

Second languages
   primary education    372.65
Second Republic (Austria)    943.605 3
Second Republic (France)    944.07
Second Republic (Spain)    946.081
Secondary batteries    621.312 424
Secondary education    373
               T1—071 2
   federal aid    379.121 3
   law    344.074
   public administrative support    353.8
   public support    379.113
     law    344.076 83
   special education    371.904 73
   *see Manual at* 372.24 and
     373.23
Secondary industries    338.4
   enterprises    338.7
   law    343.078
     *see Manual at* 343.078 vs.
     343.08
   mergers    338.83
   multinational enterprises    338.88
     *see also* International
     enterprises
   products    338.4
     commerce    381.45
       foreign    382.45
         public administration    354.73
     public administration    354.6
   restrictive practices    338.82
Secondary recovery
   oil extraction    622.338 2
Secondary roads    388.12
Secondary school buildings
   architecture    727.2
Secondary school graduates
   choice of vocation    331.702 33
   labor force    331.114 43
   unemployment    331.137 804
Secondary school libraries    027.822 3
Secondary school teaching    373.110 2
Secondary schools    373
               T1—071 2
   *see also* Secondary education
Secondary sexual characteristics    591.46
   physical anthropology    599.936
Secondary storage (Computers)    004.56
   engineering    621.397 6
Secondhand stores    381.19
   management    658.87
   *see also* Commerce
Secret agents
   criminal investigation    363.252

Secret codes
  computer science — 005.82
Secret police — 363.283
Secret societies — 366
Secretarial accounting — 657.2
Secretarial bookkeeping — 657.2
Secretariat (United Nations) — 352.113
Secretaries — 651.374 109 2
  office services — 651.374 1
Secretaries of state — 352.293
  *see Manual at* 352–354
Secretary bird — 598.9
Secretion — 571.79
  biology — 571.79
  human physiology — 612.4
  medicine — 616.4
  *see also* Endocrine system
Secretory organs — 571.79
  biology — 571.79
  human anatomy — 611.4
  human physiology — 612.4
  *see also* Endocrine system
Sects (Religion) — 209
  Buddhism — 294.39
    sources — 294.385
  Christianity — 280
  Hinduism — 294.55
    sources — 294.595
  Islam — 297.8
  Jainism — 294.49
  Judaism — 296.8
    sources — 296.15
  sources — 208.5
  *see Manual at* 201–209 and
    292–299
Secular cantatas — 782.48
  choral and mixed voices — 782.548
  single voices — 783.094 8
Secular holidays — 394.26
  *see also* Holidays
Secular humanism — 211.6
  Christian polemics — 239.7
Secular institutes
  Christianity — 255.095
    church history — 271.095
    women — 255.909 5
      church history — 271.909 5
Secular trends (Economics) — 338.54
Secular vocal music — 782.4
  choral and mixed voices — 782.54
  single voices — 783.094
Secularism — 211.6
Secured transactions
  law — 346.074

Securities — 332.632
  income tax — 336.242 6
    law — 343.052 46
  investment economics — 332.632
  law — 346.092 2
    corporate law — 346.066 6
  printing — 686.288
  public administration — 354.88
  theft of — 364.162 833 263 2
    law — 345.026 283 326 32
Securities brokers — 332.62
  law — 346.092 6
  public administration — 354.88
Securities exchange — 332.642
  international — 332.65
Securities fraud — 364.163
  law — 345.026 8
Securities violations — 364.168
  law — 345.026 8
Security classification
  (Government documents) — 352.379
  armed forces — 355.343 3
  law — 342.068 4
  public administration — 352.379
Security electronics — 621.389 28
Security measures
  computers — 005.8
  household security — 643.16
  library operations — 025.82
  management — 658.47
    armed forces — 355.343 3
    public administration — 352.379
  museology — 069.54
  office services — 651
  penology — 365.641
SED (German political party) — 324.243 075
Sedang language — 495.93
             T6—959 3
Sedative abuse — 362.299
  medicine — 616.86
  personal health — 613.8
  social welfare — 362.299
  *see also* Substance abuse
Sedatives
  pharmacokinetics — 615.782
Seder service — 296.453 71
Sedgefield (England) — T2—428 62
Sedgemoor (England) — T2—423 81
Sedges — 584.84
  forage crop — 633.26
Sedgwick County (Colo.) — T2—788 76
Sedgwick County (Kan.) — T2—781 86

| | | | |
|---|---|---|---|
| Sediment transport | 551.303 | Seeds (continued) | |
| by water | 551.353 | food | |
| by wind | 551.373 | commercial processing | 664.7 |
| Sedimentary basins | 551.44 | forest products | 634.987 |
| Sedimentary rocks | 552.5 | nursery production | 631.521 |
| Sedimentation | 551.303 | forestry | 634.956 2 |
| in water | 551.353 | ornamental plants | 635.915 21 |
| sewage treatment | 628.353 | paleobotany | 561.14 |
| primary | 628.34 | physiology | 575.68 |
| secondary | 628.353 | sowing | 631.531 |
| water supply treatment | 628.162 2 | forestry | 634.956 5 |
| Sedimentology | 552.5 | ornamental plants | 635.915 31 |
| surface processes | 551.3 | Seeland (Switzerland) | T2—494 545 3 |
| Sediments | 551.304 | Seeland (Switzerland : | |
| glacier borne | 551.314 | Verwaltungsregion) | T2—494 545 |
| ocean floor | 551.468 6 | Sees | |
| river engineering | 627.122 | Christian ecclesiology | 262.3 |
| water borne | 551.354 | Sefrou (Morocco : Province) | T2—643 4 |
| wind borne | 551.374 | Sefton (England) | T2—427 59 |
| Seditious libel | 364.131 | Segesta (Extinct city) | T2—378 24 |
| law | 345.023 1 | Segmented worms | 592.6 |
| Seduction | | Segovia (Spain : Province) | T2—463 57 |
| criminology | 364.153 | Segregation in education | 379.263 |
| criminal law | 345.025 3 | law | 344.079 8 |
| Sedums | 583.72 | Sei whale | 599.524 |
| floriculture | 635.933 72 | Seibo (Dominican | |
| See (Switzerland) | T2—494 538 | Republic : Province) | T2—729 384 |
| See-Gaster (Switzerland) | T2—494 727 | Seiches | 551.463 |
| Seed arrangements | | lakes | 551.482 |
| decorative arts | 745.928 | oceanography | 551.463 |
| Seed-bearing plants | 580 | Seine-et-Marne (France) | T2—443 7 |
| Seed capital | 332.041 54 | Seine-Maritime (France) | T2—442 5 |
| Seed catalogs | 631.521 029 | Seine River (France) | T2—443 6 |
| Seed ferns | 561.595 | Seine-Saint-Denis (France) | T2—443 62 |
| Seed-hair fibers | | Seining | |
| textiles | 677.2 | sports | 799.13 |
| *see also* Textiles | | Seismic prospecting | 622.159 2 |
| Seed industry | 338.17 | Seismic sea waves | 551.463 7 |
| Seed oil | 665.35 | Seismic waves | 551.22 |
| food technology | 664.3 | Seismography | 551.220 287 |
| industrial oils | 665.35 | Seismology | 551.22 |
| Seed plants | 580 | Seismosaurus | 567.913 |
| Seed shrimps | 595.33 | Sekgosese (South Africa : | |
| Seeding clouds | 551.687 6 | District) | T2—682 57 |
| Seedless plants | 586 | Sekhukhuneberg Range | |
| Seedlings | | (South Africa) | T2—682 55 |
| nursery production | 631.52 | Sekhukhuneland (South | |
| forestry | 634.956 2 | Africa : District) | T2—682 55 |
| planting | 631.536 | Selachii | 597.3 |
| forestry | 634.956 5 | paleozoology | 567.3 |
| Seeds | 581.467 | Selaginellales | 587.9 |
| animal feeds | | Selangor | T2—595 1 |
| commercial processing | 664.76 | Selby (England : District) | T2—428 45 |
| descriptive botany | 581.467 | | |

| | |
|---|---|
| Select committees | |
| legislative bodies | 328.365 7 |
| Selected laws | 348.024 |
| United States federal laws | 348.732 4 |
| Selection of animals | 636.081 |
| Selection procedures | |
| personnel management | 658.311 2 |
| public administration | 352.65 |
| Selective dissemination of | |
| information | 025.525 |
| Selective service | 355.223 63 |
| law | 343.012 2 |
| Selenides | |
| mineralogy | 549.32 |
| Selenium | |
| biochemistry | 572.555 |
| chemical engineering | 661.072 4 |
| chemistry | 546.724 |
| metallurgy | 669.79 |
| organic chemistry | 547.057 24 |
| applied | 661.895 |
| Selenography | 919.91 |
| Seletar (Malaysian people) | T5—992 8 |
| Seleucid Empire | 935.062 |
| | T2—35 |
| Self | |
| literature | 808.803 84 |
| history and criticism | 809.933 84 |
| specific literatures | T3B—080 384 |
| history and | |
| criticism | T3B—093 84 |
| philosophy | 126 |
| arts | T3C—384 |
| psychology | 155.2 |
| arts | T3C—353 |
| Self-acceptance | 155.2 |
| applied psychology | 158.1 |
| Self-actualization | 155.2 |
| applied psychology | 158.1 |
| Self-adjoint operator algebras | 512.556 |
| Self-confidence | 155.2 |
| applied psychology | 158.1 |
| Self-contained communities | 307.77 |
| Self-control | 179.9 |
| moral theology | 205.699 |
| psychology | 153.8 |
| development | 155.25 |
| *see also* Virtues | |
| Self-defense | 613.66 |
| children | 613.660 83 |
| military training | 355.548 |
| personal safety | 613.66 |
| women | 613.660 82 |
| Self-defense (Law) | 345.04 |

| | |
|---|---|
| Self-destructive behavior | |
| medicine | 616.858 2 |
| Self-determination of states | 320.15 |
| law of nations | 341.26 |
| Self-development reading | |
| library science | 028.8 |
| Self-employed people | |
| income tax | |
| law | 343.052 6 |
| Self-employment enterprises | |
| management | 658.041 |
| initiation | 658.114 1 |
| Self-esteem | 155.2 |
| applied psychology | 158.1 |
| Self-financing | 332.041 52 |
| Self-help devices | |
| injured people | 617.103 |
| Self-help groups | 361.43 |
| Self-hypnosis | |
| therapeutic use | 615.851 22 |
| Self-improvement | |
| applied psychology | 158.1 |
| Self-incrimination | 345.056 |
| Self-instruction | 371.394 3 |
| Self-organizing systems | 003.7 |
| Self-publishing | 070.593 |
| Self-realization | 155.2 |
| applied psychology | 158.1 |
| ethical systems | 171.3 |
| Self-reliance | 179.9 |
| child training | 649.63 |
| *see also* Virtues | |
| Self-respect | 155.2 |
| applied psychology | 158.1 |
| Selinus (Extinct city) | T2—378 24 |
| Seljuk dynasty | 956.014 |
| Middle Eastern history | 956.014 |
| Turkish history | 956.101 4 |
| Selkirk (Man.) | T2—712 74 |
| Selkirk Mountains | T2—711 68 |
| Selkup language | 494.4 |
| | T6—944 |
| Selling | 381 |
| commerce | 381 |
| management | 658.81 |
| | T1—068 8 |
| techniques for individuals | 658.85 |
| Selosesha (South Africa : | |
| District) | T2—682 48 |
| Selwyn District (N.Z.) | T2—938 5 |
| Semaeostomeae | 593.53 |
| Semang | T5—959 3 |
| Semang languages | 495.93 |
| | T6—959 3 |

Semantic web | 025.042 7
Semantics
  linguistics | 401.43
    specific languages | T4—014 3
    *see Manual at* 401.43 vs.
      306.44, 401.45, 401.9,
      412, 415
  philosophical system | 149.94
  philosophy of language | 121.68
Semaphores
  military engineering | 623.731 2
  nautical engineering | 623.856 12
Semara (Morocco :
  Province) | T2—648
Semi-detached houses
  architecture | 728.312
Semi-enclosed spaces
  architecture | 721.84
Semi-industrial unions | 331.883 3
  *see also* Labor unions
Semiarid lands | 551.415
  | T2—154
  *see also* Arid lands
Semibituminous coal | 553.24
  properties | 662.622 4
  *see also* Coal
Semicircular canal diseases
  medicine | 617.882
    *see also* Ear diseases —
    humans
Semicircular canals
  human physiology | 612.858
  medicine | 617.882
Semiconductivity | 537.622
  materials science | 620.112 972
Semiconductor circuits | 621.381 5
Semiconductor memory | 004.53
  engineering | 621.397 32
Semiconductor storage | 004.568
  engineering | 621.397 68
Semiconductors | 621.381 52
  chemical engineering | 660.297 7
  electrochemistry | 541.377
  physics | 537.622
  radio engineering | 621.384 134
  television engineering | 621.388 32
Semidetached houses
  architecture | 728.312
Semidiesel engines | 621.436
  ships | 623.872 36
Semidiesel locomotives | 385.366
  engineering | 625.266
  transportation services | 385.366
  *see also* Rolling stock

Semigroups | 512.27
Semimetals
  chemistry | 546.71
  economic geology | 553.499
  mineralogy | 549.25
Seminaries | 200.711
  Christianity | 230.071 1
  Judaism | 296.071 1
Seminars | 371.37
  higher education | 378.177
Seminole County (Fla.) | T2—759 23
Seminole County (Ga.) | T2—758 996
Seminole County (Okla.) | T2—766 71
Seminole Indians | T5—973 859
Seminole language | 497.385 9
  | T6—973 859
Seminole War, 1818 | 973.54
Seminole War, 1835–1842 | 973.57
Semionotiformes | 597.41
Semiotics | 302.2
  linguistics | 401.4
    specific languages | T4—014
    specific subjects | T1—014
  philosophy | 121.68
  social aspects | 302.2
Semiprecious stones | 553.87
  carving | 736.2
  economic geology | 553.87
  jewelry | 739.27
  materials science | 620.198
  mining | 622.387
  occultism | 133.255 387
    divination | 133.322
  prospecting | 622.188 7
  synthetic | 666.88
Semiregular variable stars | 523.844 26
Semirigid airships | 387.732 6
  engineering | 629.133 26
  military engineering | 623.743 6
  transportation services | 387.732 6
Semisecret societies | 366
Semiskilled workers | 331.794
  labor economics | 331.794
  labor force | 331.114 2
  personnel management | 658.304 4
  unemployment | 331.137 804
Semisovereign states | 321.08
  law of nations | 341.27
  public administration | 353.15
    specific states | 351.3–.9
Semites | T5—92
  religion | 299.2

| | |
|---|---|
| Semitic languages | 492 |
| | T6—92 |
|   Biblical texts | 220.4 |
| Semitic literatures | 892 |
| Semitic peoples | T5—92 |
|   religion | 299.2 |
| Semitrailers (Freight) | 388.344 |
|   engineering | 629.224 |
|   *see also* Trucks | |
| Semnān (Iran) | T2—552 4 |
| Sena language | 496.391 |
| | T6—963 91 |
| Senari language | 496.35 |
| | T6—963 5 |
| Seneca County (N.Y.) | T2—747 69 |
| Seneca County (Ohio) | T2—771 24 |
| Seneca Indians | T5—975 546 |
| Seneca language | 497.554 6 |
| | T6—975 546 |
| Senegal | 966.3 |
| | T2—663 |
| Senegal languages | 496.321 |
| | T6—963 21 |
| Senegalese | T5—966 3 |
| Senegambia | 966.305 1 |
| | T2—663 |
| Senegambian languages | 496.321 |
| | T6—963 21 |
| Senekal (South Africa : | |
|   District) | T2—685 1 |
| Senescence | 571.878 |
|   *see also* Aging | |
| Senga-Sena languages | 496.391 |
| | T6—963 91 |
| Senile dementia | |
|   geriatrics | 618.976 83 |
|   medicine | 616.83 |
|     *see also* Nervous system | |
|       diseases — humans | |
| Senior citizens | 305.26 |
| | T1—084 6 |
|   *see also* Older people | |
| Senior high schools | 373.238 |
|   *see also* Secondary education | |
| Seniority | |
|   labor economics | 331.259 6 |
|   personnel management | 658.312 |
| Sennas | 583.749 |
| Senneville (Quebec) | T2—714 28 |
| Senoic languages | 495.93 |
| | T6—959 3 |

| | |
|---|---|
| Sensation | 152.1 |
|   biology | 573.87 |
|   epistemology | 121.35 |
|   *see also* Sense organs | |
| Sensationalism (Philosophical | |
|   school) | 145 |
| Sensations (Art styles) | 709.040 7 |
| Sense knowledge | 121.35 |
| Sense organs | 573.87 |
|   animal physiology | 573.87 |
|   descriptive zoology | 591.4 |
|   human anatomy | 611.8 |
|   human histology | 612.8 |
|   human physiology | 612.8 |
|   *see also* Nervous system | |
| Senses | 573.87 |
|   psychology | 152.1 |
|   *see also* Sense organs | |
| Sensitive plants | 583.748 |
| Sensitivity in plants | 575.98 |
| Sensitivity training | |
|   applied psychology | 158.2 |
|   social psychology | 302.14 |
| Sensitometry | 661.808 |
| Sensorineural hearing loss | |
|   medicine | 617.886 |
|     *see also* Ear diseases — | |
|       humans | |
| Sensors | |
|   manufacturing technology | 681.2 |
| Sensory evaluation | |
|   food | 664.072 |
| Sensory functions | 573.87 |
|   human physiology | 612.8 |
|   localization in brain | |
|     human physiology | 612.825 5 |
|   *see also* Nervous system | |
|   *see Manual at* 612.8 vs. 152 | |
| Sensory influences | |
|   psychology | 155.911 |
| Sensory nerves | 573.872 8 |
|   human physiology | 612.811 |
|   *see also* Nervous system | |
| Sensory perception | 152.1 |
|   comparative psychology | 156.21 |
|   educational psychology | 370.155 |
|   epistemology | 121.35 |
|   psychological influence | 155.911 |
|   *see Manual at* 153.7 vs. 152.1; | |
|     *also at* 612.8 vs. 152 | |
| Sentences (Grammar) | 415 |
|   specific languages | T4—5 |
| Sentences (Legal decisions) | 345.077 |
|   penology | 364.6 |

| | |
|---|---|
| Sentencing | 345.077 2 |
| Sentential calculus | 511.3 |
| mathematical logic | 511.3 |
| philosophical logic | 160 |
| Sentiments | 152.4 |
| Senufo (African people) | T5—963 5 |
| Senufo language | 496.35 |
| | T6—963 5 |
| Sepals | 575.69 |
| Separate maintenance | 346.016 68 |
| Separate property | 346.042 |
| divorce law | 346.016 64 |
| Separated men | 306.892 |
| Separated people | 306.89 |
| | T1—086 53 |
| family relationships | 306.89 |
| guides to religious life | |
| Christianity | 248.846 |
| social group | 306.89 |
| social welfare | 362.829 4 |
| Separated women | 306.893 |
| social welfare | 362.839 59 |
| Separation (Domestic relations) | 306.89 |
| ethics | 173 |
| Judaism | 296.444 4 |
| law | 346.016 68 |
| social theology | 201.7 |
| Christianity | 261.835 89 |
| Separation from parents | |
| child psychology | 155.44 |
| Separation from service | |
| personnel management | 658.313 |
| public administration | 352.69 |
| Separation of powers | 320.404 |
| law | 342.044 |
| Separation processes | |
| chemical engineering | 660.284 2 |
| Separatist parties | 324.218 4 |
| Sephardic liturgy | 296.450 42 |
| Sepik-Ramu languages | 499.12 |
| | T6—991 2 |
| Sepik River (New Guinea) | T2—957 5 |
| Sepioidea | 594.58 |
| Sepoy Mutiny, 1857–1858 | 954.031 7 |
| Sept-Rivières (Quebec) | T2—714 176 |
| Septets | |
| chamber music | 785.17 |
| vocal music | 783.17 |
| Septic tanks | |
| technology | 628.742 |
| Septicemia | |
| incidence | 614.577 |
| medicine | 616.944 |
| *see also* Communicable | |
| diseases — humans | |
| puerperal diseases | |
| incidence | 614.545 |
| obstetrics | 618.74 |
| Septoria | 579.55 |
| Septuagint | 221.48 |
| Sepulchral slabs | 736.5 |
| Sequatchie County (Tenn.) | T2—768 77 |
| Sequatchie River (Tenn.) | T2—768 77 |
| Sequence | 264.36 |
| music | 782.323 5 |
| Sequences (Mathematics) | 515.24 |
| Sequences of integers | 512.72 |
| Sequencing | |
| production management | 658.53 |
| Sequential analysis | 519.54 |
| Sequential machines | 511.35 |
| Sequoia National Park | |
| (Calif.) | T2—794 86 |
| Sequoias | 585.5 |
| forestry | 634.975 8 |
| Sequoyah County (Okla.) | T2—766 81 |
| Serbia | 949.71 |
| | T2—497 1 |
| ancient | 939.871 |
| | T2—398 71 |
| Serbia and Montenegro | 949.710 31 |
| | T2—497 1 |
| Serbian language | 491.82 |
| | T6—918 2 |
| Serbian literature | 891.82 |
| Serbian Orthodox Church | 281.949 71 |
| Serbians | T5—918 2 |
| Serbo-Croatian language | 491.82 |
| | T6—918 2 |
| Serbo-Croatian literature | 891.82 |
| Serbs | T5—918 2 |
| Serenades | 784.185 6 |
| Serengeti National Park | |
| (Tanzania) | T2— 678 27 |
| Serer (African people) | T5—963 21 |
| Serer language | 496.321 |
| | T6—963 21 |
| Serer-Sine language | 496.321 |
| | T6—963 21 |
| Serfdom | 306.365 |
| Serfs | 306.365 |
| | T1—086 25 |
| customs | 390.25 |
| dress | 391.025 |

| | |
|---|---|
| Serging | 646.204 4 |
| Sergipe (Brazil) | T2—814 1 |
| Seri Indians | T5—975 7 |
| Serial murderers | 364.152 32 |
| biography | 364.152 320 92 |
| Serial murders | 364.152 32 |
| law | 345.025 232 |
| Serial publications | 050 |
| | T1—05 |
| *see also* Serials | |
| Serialism | |
| music | 781.33 |
| Serials | 050 |
| | T1—05 |
| bibliographies | 011.34 |
| cataloging | 025.343 2 |
| indexes | 050 |
| journalism | 070.175 |
| library treatment | 025.173 2 |
| postal handling | 383.123 |
| *see also* Postal service | |
| publishing | 070.572 |
| sociology | 302.232 4 |
| Sericulture | 638.2 |
| Series (Mathematics) | 515.243 |
| Series (Publications) | |
| bibliographies | 011.48 |
| Serigraphy | 764.8 |
| Sermon on the Mount | 226.9 |
| Christian moral theology | 241.53 |
| Sermon outlines | 251.02 |
| Sermon preparation | 206.1 |
| Christianity | 251.01 |
| Sermons | 204.3 |
| Christianity | 252 |
| Islam | 297.37 |
| Jewish | 296.47 |
| Serology | |
| medicine | 616.079 5 |
| diagnosis | 616.075 6 |
| Serous membranes | |
| human histology | 611.018 7 |
| Serows | 599.647 |
| Serpentine | 553.55 |
| building material | 691.2 |
| economic geology | 553.55 |
| mineralogy | 549.67 |
| petrology | 552.4 |
| quarrying | 622.355 |
| Serpents | 597.96 |
| paleozoology | 567.96 |
| Serpents (Musical instruments) | 788.99 |
| *see also* Brass instruments | |
| Serrai (Greece : Nome) | T2—495 65 |

| | |
|---|---|
| Serrania de La Macarena | |
| National Park | |
| (Colombia) | T2—861 94 |
| Serranidae | 597.736 |
| Serums | |
| pharmacology | 615.37 |
| Serval | 599.752 |
| Servants | |
| home economics | 640.46 |
| public households | 647.2 |
| hours and duties | 647.6 |
| legal status | 346.024 |
| Server class computers | 004.14 |
| engineering | 621.391 4 |
| *see also* Midrange computers | |
| Servers (Computers) | 004.36 |
| Servian language | 491.82 |
| | T6—918 2 |
| Servian literature | 891.82 |
| Servians | T5—918 2 |
| Service (Tennis) | 796.342 21 |
| Service academies (Armed | |
| forces) | 355.007 11 |
| Service clubs | 369.5 |
| biography | 369.509 2 |
| Service comparisons | T1—029 |
| Service contracts | 346.024 |
| armed forces | 355.621 2 |
| public administration | 352.538 |
| Service directories | 338.470 002 9 |
| | T1—029 |
| *see Manual at* T1—025 vs. | |
| T1—029 | |
| Service districts | |
| local public administration | 352.19 |
| Service evaluations | T1—029 |
| Service industries | 338.47 |
| accounting | 657.83 |
| commerce | 381.45 |
| foreign | 382.45 |
| cooperatives | 334.681 |
| enterprises | 338.761 |
| labor economics | 331.793 |
| law | 343.078 |
| mergers | 338.836 1 |
| multinational enterprises | 338.887 1 |
| production efficiency | 338.456 1 |
| public administration | 354.68 |
| restrictive practices | 338.826 1 |
| Service listings | T1—029 |
| Service marks | 929.95 |
| | T1—027 5 |
| Service-oriented architecture | |
| computer science | 004.654 |

Service periods (Armed forces)   355.11
Service stations
   automotive engineering   629.286
Service workers   331.793
   labor economics   331.793
    labor force   331.119 042
    labor market   331.129 042
Serviceberries   583.73
Services (Economic goods)   338.47
   marketing management   658.8
Serviettes   642.7
   arts   746.96
   home sewing   646.21
   table setting   642.7
Serving at table   642.6
Servites   255.47
   church history   271.47
Servitudes   346.043 5
   law of nations   341.4
Servomechanisms
   automation engineering   629.832 3
Sesames   583.95
   botany   583.95
   food   641.338 5
    cooking   641.638 5
   oil crop   633.85
Sesamoids
   human anatomy   611.718
   hands   611.717
Seshego (South Africa :
   District)   T2—682 56
Sesotho language   496.397 72
   T6—963 977 2
Sesquilinear forms
   algebraic geometry   516.35
Session laws   348.022
Sessions (Legislative bodies)   328.35
Set algebra   511.324
Set idiophones   786.84
   see also Percussion instruments
Set theory   511.322
SETI (Search for extraterrestrial
   intelligence)   999
Sétif (Algeria : Province)   T2—655
Seto-naikai (Japan)   551.461 455
   T2—164 55
Sets   511.32
Settat (Morocco : Province)   T2—643 9
Setters (Dogs)   636.752 6
Setting (Literature)   808.802 2
   history and criticism   809.922
   specific literatures   T3B—080 22
    history and criticism   T3B—092 2

Setting (Performances)   792.025
   motion pictures   791.430 25
   stage   792.025
   television   791.450 25
Settlement (Insurance)   368.014
Settlement (Population)   307.14
   land reform   333.31
   public administration   353.59
Settlement (Real estate)   346.043 73
Settling
   water supply treatment   628.162 2
Setúbal (Portugal : District)   T2—469 44
Seven last words on cross   232.963 5
Seven Weeks' War, 1866   943.076
Seven Years' War, 1756–1763   940.253 4
   North American history   973.26
Seveners (Islamic sect)   297.822
   Hadith   297.125 922
Sevenoaks (England :
   District)   T2—422 36
Seventeenth century   909.6
   T1—090 32
Seventh century   909.1
   T1—090 21
Seventh-Day Adventist Church   286.732
   see also Adventists
Seventh-Day Baptists   286.3
   see also Baptists
Severance pay   331.216 6
   personnel management   658.322 2
Severance tax   336.271 6
   law   343.055
Severn, River (Wales and
   England)   T2—424
   England   T2—424
   Wales   T2—429 51
Severnaia Osetiia (Russia)   T2—475 2
Severnaia Zemlia (Russia)   T2—987
Severnaya Zemlya (Russia)   T2—987
Severočeský kraj (Czech
   Republic)   T2—437 16
Severomoravský kraj
   (Czech Republic)   T2—437 28
Sevier County (Ark.)   T2—767 47
Sevier County (Tenn.)   T2—768 893
Sevier County (Utah)   T2—792 55
Seville (Spain : Province)   T2—468 6
Sewage disposal   363.728 493
   social services   363.728 493
   technology   628.36
   see also Sewage treatment
Sewage effluent   363.728 493
   disposal technology   628.362
   social services   363.728 493

| | |
|---|---|
| Sewage effluent (continued) | |
|   water pollution engineering | 628.168 2 |
|   *see also* Sewage treatment | |
| Sewage irrigation | 628.362 3 |
| Sewage lagoons | |
|   sanitary engineering | 628.351 |
| Sewage sludge | 363.728 493 |
|   sanitary engineering | 628.364 |
|   social services | 363.728 493 |
|   use as fertilizer | 631.869 |
|   *see also* Sewage treatment | |
| Sewage treatment | 363.728 493 |
|   law | 344.046 22 |
|   military engineering | 623.753 |
|   rural | 628.742 |
|   social services | 363.728 493 |
|   technology | 628.3 |
|   *see also* Waste control | |
| Seward County (Kan.) | T2—781 735 |
| Seward County (Neb.) | T2—782 324 |
| Seward Peninsula (Alaska) | T2—798 6 |
| Sewerage | 628.2 |
| Sewers | 628.2 |
| Sewing | 646.2 |
|   home economics | 646.2 |
|   primary education | 372.54 |
| Sewing equipment | 646.19 |
|   home sewing | 646.19 |
|   manufacturing technology | 681.767 7 |
| Sewing machines | |
|   home economics | 646.204 4 |
|   manufacturing technology | 681.767 7 |
| Sewing materials | 646.1 |
|   commercial technology | 687.8 |
|   home economics | 646.1 |
| Sex | 306.7 |
|   arts | 700.453 8 |
| | T3C—353 8 |
|   customs | 392.6 |
|   evolution | 576.855 |
|   folklore | 398.273 8 |
|     history and criticism | 398.353 8 |
|   human physiology | 612.6 |
|   literature | 808.803 538 |
|     history and criticism | 809.933 538 |
|     specific literatures | T3B—080 353 8 |
|      history and | |
|       criticism | T3B—093 538 |
|   psychology | 155.3 |
|     adolescents | 155.53 |
|     children | 155.43 |
|   religious worship | 202.12 |
|   sociology | 306.7 |
| Sex (continued) | |
|   theological anthropology | 202.2 |
|     Christianity | 233.5 |
|     *see also* Humans — religion | |
| Sex addiction | |
|   medicine | 616.858 33 |
| Sex cells | 571.845 |
| Sex characteristics | |
|   animals | 591.46 |
|   physical anthropology | 599.936 |
| Sex crimes | 364.153 |
|   law | 345.025 3 |
|   school problem | 371.786 |
| Sex differences | 578.46 |
|   animals | 591.46 |
|   physical anthropology | 599.936 |
|   psychology | 155.33 |
|     adolescents | 155.53 |
|     children | 155.43 |
|   sociology | 305.3 |
| Sex differentiation | 571.882 |
| Sex differentiation disorders | |
|   medicine | 616.694 |
| Sex discrimination against men | 305.32 |
| Sex discrimination against | |
|   women | 305.42 |
|   labor economics | 331.413 3 |
|     law | 344.014 133 |
|   law | 342.087 8 |
| Sex discrimination in education | 370.81 |
|   law | 344.079 8 |
| Sex disorders | |
|   gynecology | 618.17 |
|     *see also* Female genital | |
|      diseases — humans | |
|   medicine | 616.69 |
|     *see also* Genital diseases — | |
|      humans | |
| Sex education | 613.907 1 |
|   home child care | 649.65 |
|   primary level | 372.372 |
| Sex hormones | 571.837 4 |
|   biology | 571.837 4 |
|     animal reproduction | 573.637 4 |
|   human physiology | 612.6 |
|   pharmacology | 615.366 |
|   *see also* Genital system | |
| Sex hygiene | 613.95 |
|   school programs | 371.714 |
| Sex instruction | 613.907 1 |
|   home child care | 649.65 |
|   primary education | 372.372 |
| Sex manuals | 613.96 |

| | | | |
|---|---|---|---|
| Sex offenses | 364.153 | Sexual ethics | 176.4 |
| law | 345.025 3 | religion | 205.66 |
| Sex role | 305.3 | *see also* Sexual relations — | |
| | T1—081 | ethics | |
| arts | 700.452 1 | Sexual excitement | |
| | T3C—352 1 | psychology | 155.31 |
| literature | | Sexual factors in evolution | 576.855 |
| specific literatures | T3B—080 352 1 | Sexual harassment | |
| history and | | prevention | |
| criticism | T3B—093 521 | personnel management | 658.314 5 |
| psychology | 155.33 | Sexual harassment of women | |
| Sexadecimal system | 513.5 | labor economics | 331.413 3 |
| Sexes | | sociology | 305.42 |
| evolution | 576.855 | Sexual intercourse | |
| psychology | 155.33 | psychology | 155.35 |
| social aspects | 305.3 | sociology | 306.77 |
| Sexism | 305.3 | Sexual love | 306.7 |
| Sexism in textbooks | | psychology | 155.3 |
| public control | 379.156 | Sexual orientation | 306.76 |
| Sext | 264.15 | arts | 700.453 |
| music | 782.324 | | T3C—353 |
| Sextants | | literature | 808.803 53 |
| astronomy | 527.028 4 | history and criticism | 809.933 53 |
| Sextets | | specific literatures | T3B—080 353 |
| chamber music | 785.16 | history and | |
| vocal music | 783.16 | literature | T3B—093 53 |
| Sexual abstinence | | psychology | 155.34 |
| health | 613.9 | social groups | T1—086 6 |
| birth control | 613.94 | sociology | 306.76 |
| Sexual abuse of adolescents | | Sexual practices | 306.77 |
| medicine | 616.858 36 | psychology | 155.35 |
| Sexual abuse of children | 362.76 | public control | 363.4 |
| medicine | 616.858 36 | public administration | 353.37 |
| school problem | 371.786 | sociology | 306.77 |
| *see also* Child abuse | | Sexual relations | 306.7 |
| Sexual behavior (Animals) | 591.562 | customs | 392.6 |
| Sexual desire disorders | | ethics | 176.4 |
| psychiatry | 616.858 3 | religion | 205.66 |
| Sexual deviation | | Buddhism | 294.356 6 |
| criminology | 364.153 6 | Christianity | 241.66 |
| criminal law | 345.025 36 | Hinduism | 294.548 66 |
| medicine | 616.858 3 | Islam | 297.566 |
| Sexual disorders | | Judaism | 296.366 |
| gynecology | 618.17 | laws of family purity | 296.742 |
| *see also* Female genital | | social theology | 201.7 |
| diseases — humans | | Christianity | 261.835 7 |
| medicine | 616.69 | sociology | 306.7 |
| *see also* Genital diseases — | | technique | 613.96 |
| humans | | Sexual reproduction | 571.8 |
| psychiatry | 616.858 3 | animals | 573.6 |
| Sexual division of labor | 306.361 5 | microorganisms | 571.845 29 |
| | | plants | 575.6 |
| | | *see also* Genital system | |
| | | Sexual selection (Animals) | 591.562 |

Sexuality
  arts                                          700.453 8
                                  T3C—353 8
  literature                                    808.803 538
    history and criticism                       809.933 538
    specific literatures         T3B—080 353 8
    history and
      criticism                  T3B—093 538
  psychology                                    155.3
Sexually abused children
  pediatrics                                    618.928 583 6
  social theology                               201.762 76
    Christianity                                261.832 72
  social welfare                                362.76
Sexually transmitted diseases
  incidence                                     614.547
  law                                           344.043 695 1
  medicine                                      616.951
  *see also* Communicable
    diseases — humans
Seychelles                                      969.6
                                  T2—696
Seychellois                       T5—969 696
Seymour River (Columbia-
  Shuswap, B.C.)                  T2—711 68
Sforza, House of
  Lombardian history                            945.206
Sgrafitto decoration                            666.45
  arts                                          738.15
  technology                                    666.45
Shaanxi Sheng (China)            T2—514 3
Shabbat                                         296.41
Shabbat (Tractate)                              296.123 2
  Babylonian Talmud                             296.125 2
  Mishnah                                       296.123 2
  Palestinian Talmud                            296.124 2
Shabuoth                                        296.438
  liturgy                                       296.453 8
Shackelford County (Tex.)        T2—764 734
Shade plants
  floriculture                                  635.954 3
Shade-tolerant plants
  floriculture                                  635.954 3
Shade trees                                     635.977
Shades (Furnishings)                            645.3
  household management                          645.3
  manufacturing technology                      684
Shadh (Hadith)                                  297.125 22
Shadow boxes
  furniture arts                                749.7
Shadow puppets                                  791.53
  *see also* Puppets
Shadow theaters                                 791.53

Shadows                                         535.4
  art                                           701.82
  drawing                                       742
  technical drawing                             604.243
Shads                                           641.392
  cooking                                       641.692
  food                                          641.392
  zoology                                       597.45
Shafiites (Islamic sect)                        297.812
Shaft currents (Electricity)                    621.310 42
Shaft sinking                                   624.19
  mining                                        622.25
  underground construction                      624.19
Shafts (Mechanisms)                             621.823
  ship power plants                             623.873
Shah Jahan, Emperor of India
  Indian history                                954.025 7
Shahāda                                         297.34
Shahjahan, Emperor of India
  Indian history                                954.025 7
Shaivism                                        294.551 3
Shaka, Zulu Chief
  KwaZulu-Natal history                         968.403 9
Shaka language                                  496.395
                                  T6—963 95
Shakers                                         289.8
  biography                                     289.809 2
  *see also* Christian
    denominations
Shakes (Roofing)                                695
Shakespeare, William                            822.33
Shaktaism                                       294.551 4
Shakuhachis                                     788.35
Shale
  petrology                                     552.5
Shale oil                                       553.283
  *see also* Oil shale
Shallots                                        641.352 6
  botany                                        584.33
  cooking                                       641.652 6
  food                                          641.352 6
  garden crop                                   635.26
Shamāl Baḥr al Ghazāl
  (Sudan)                        T2—629 4
Shamāl Dārfūr (Sudan :
  State)                         T2—627
Shamāl Kurdufān (Sudan)          T2—628
Shamāl Sīnā' (Egypt)             T2—531
Shamālīyah (Sudan)               T2—625
Shamanism                                       201.44

| | |
|---|---|
| Shamans | 200.92 |
| biography | 200.92 |
| role and function | 206.1 |
| *see Manual at* 200.92 and | |
| 201–209, 292–299 | |
| Shambala languages | 496.391 |
| | T6—963 91 |
| Shame | 152.44 |
| Shamisens | 787.85 |
| *see also* Stringed instruments | |
| Shamrocks (Clovers) | 583.74 |
| Shamrocks (Wood sorrel) | 583.79 |
| Shan | T5—959 19 |
| Shan language | 495.919 |
| | T6—959 19 |
| Shan literature | 895.919 |
| Shandong Sheng (China) | T2—511 4 |
| Shang dynasty | 931.02 |
| Shanghai (China) | T2—511 32 |
| Shankara (Philosophy) | 181.482 |
| Shanmukaism | 294.551 6 |
| Shannon County (Mo.) | T2—778 873 |
| Shannon County (S.D.) | T2—783 66 |
| Shannon River (Ireland) | T2—417 |
| Shansi Province (China) | T2—511 7 |
| Shantung Province (China) | T2—511 4 |
| Shanxi Sheng (China) | T2—511 7 |
| Shape | |
| animals | 591.41 |
| biological organisms | 578.41 |
| plants | 581.41 |
| Shape theory (Topology) | 514.24 |
| Shaped charges | |
| military engineering | 623.454 5 |
| Shapers (Tools) | 621.912 |
| Shaping metals | |
| decorative arts | 739.14 |
| sculpture | 731.41 |
| Shar-Pei | 636.72 |
| Share renting | |
| agricultural land economics | 333.335 563 |
| land economics | 333.563 |
| Sharecroppers | 306.365 |
| | T1—088 63 |
| Sharecropping | 306.365 |
| economics | 333.335 563 |
| Shared custody | 306.89 |
| Shared memory | 005.71 |
| Shareholders' meetings | |
| law | 346.066 6 |
| Shares (Corporate equity securities) | 332.632 2 |
| Sharia | 340.59 |
| religious law | 297.14 |
| secular law | 340.59 |
| Shāriqah (United Arab Emirates : Emirate) | T2—535 7 |
| Shārjah (United Arab Emirates : Emirate) | T2—535 7 |
| Sharkey County (Miss.) | T2—762 414 |
| Sharks | 597.3 |
| commercial fishing | 639.273 |
| cooking | 641.692 |
| food | 641.392 |
| paleozoology | 567.3 |
| sports fishing | 799.173 |
| zoology | 597.3 |
| Sharkskin fabrics | 677.615 |
| *see also* Textiles | |
| Sharp County (Ark.) | T2—767 23 |
| Sharp-tailed grouse | 598.637 8 |
| Sharpeville Massacre, 1960 | 968.058 |
| Sharpshooters | 356.162 |
| Sharq al-Istiwā'īyah (Sudan) | T2—629 5 |
| Sharqīyah (Egypt) | T2—621 |
| Shasta County (Calif.) | T2—794 24 |
| Shastri, Lal Bahadur | |
| Indian history | 954.043 |
| Shavers | |
| manufacturing technology | 688.5 |
| Shaving | 646.724 |
| customs | 391.5 |
| personal care | 646.724 |
| Shavings | |
| wood | 674.84 |
| Shavuot | 296.438 |
| liturgy | 296.453 8 |
| Shawano County (Wis.) | T2—775 36 |
| Shawinigan (Quebec) | T2—714 453 |
| Shawls | 391.44 |
| *see also* Accessories (Clothing) | |
| Shawnee County (Kan.) | T2—781 63 |
| Shawnee Indians | T5—973 17 |
| Shawnee language | 497.317 |
| | T6—973 17 |
| Shawnigan Lake (B.C.) | T2—711 2 |
| Shawns | 788.52 |
| *see also* Woodwind instruments | |
| Shearing animals | 636.083 3 |
| Shearing sheds | |
| architecture | 725.37 |
| Shearing stress | |
| effect on materials | 620.112 45 |
| Shearing textiles | 677.028 25 |
| Shears | 621.93 |
| home sewing | 646.19 |

| | |
|---|---|
| Shearwaters | 598.42 |
| Sheaths (Nerve tissue) | 573.852 5 |
| human histology | 612.810 45 |
| *see also* Nervous system | |
| Sheaths (Tendon) | 573.753 56 |
| *see also* Tendon sheaths | |
| Sheaves (Mathematics) | 514.224 |
| Sheboygan County (Wis.) | T2—775 69 |
| Sheds | |
| architecture | 725.372 |
| construction | 690.537 2 |
| domestic | |
| architecture | 728.922 |
| construction | 690.892 2 |
| Sheehan's syndrome | |
| obstetrics | 618.7 |
| Sheep | 636.3 |
| animal husbandry | 636.3 |
| big game hunting | 799.276 49 |
| zoology | 599.649 |
| Sheep dogs | 636.737 |
| Sheep's milk | 641.371 7 |
| cooking | 641.671 7 |
| food | 641.371 7 |
| processing | 637.17 |
| Sheep's wool textiles | 677.31 |
| arts | 746.043 1 |
| *see also* Textiles | |
| Sheet metal | 671.823 |
| Sheet music illustration | 741.66 |
| Sheeting | |
| rubber | 678.36 |
| Sheets | 645.4 |
| arts | 746.97 |
| home sewing | 646.21 |
| household equipment | 645.4 |
| Sheffield (England : City) | T2—428 21 |
| Shehitah | 296.73 |
| Shekalim | 296.123 2 |
| Mishnah | 296.123 2 |
| Palestinian Talmud | 296.124 2 |
| Shekhar, Chandra | |
| Indian history | 954.052 |
| Shelburne (N.S. : County) | T2—716 25 |
| Shelby County (Ala.) | T2—761 79 |
| Shelby County (Ill.) | T2—773 798 |
| Shelby County (Ind.) | T2—772 59 |
| Shelby County (Iowa) | T2—777 484 |
| Shelby County (Ky.) | T2—769 435 |
| Shelby County (Mo.) | T2—778 323 |
| Shelby County (Ohio) | T2—771 45 |
| Shelby County (Tenn.) | T2—768 19 |
| Shelby County (Tex.) | T2—764 179 |

| | |
|---|---|
| Sheldon, William Herbert | |
| personality theory | 155.264 |
| Shelf fungi | 579.597 |
| Shelf ice | 551.342 |
| Shelflisting | |
| library science | 025.428 |
| Shelikof Strait (Alaska) | 551.461 434 |
| | T2—164 34 |
| Shell carving | 736.6 |
| Shell model (Nuclear physics) | 539.743 |
| Shell parakeets | 636.686 4 |
| Shellac | 667.79 |
| Shellfish | 594 |
| conservation technology | 639.974 |
| cooking | 641.694 |
| culture | 639.4 |
| economics | 338.371 4 |
| fishing | 639.4 |
| fishing industry | 338.372 4 |
| food | 641.394 |
| commercial processing | 664.94 |
| resource economics | 333.955 |
| sports fishing | 799.254 |
| zoology | 594 |
| Shellfishing | |
| economics | 338.372 4 |
| sports | 799.254 |
| Shelling crops | 631.56 |
| Shells (Ammunition) | |
| artillery | 623.451 3 |
| small arms | |
| military engineering | 623.455 |
| Shells (Animals) | 591.477 |
| carving | 736.6 |
| descriptive zoology | 591.477 |
| mollusks | 594.147 7 |
| handicrafts | 745.55 |
| physiology | 573.77 |
| Shells (Structural elements) | 624.177 62 |
| naval architecture | 623.817 762 |
| structural engineering | 624.177 62 |
| concrete | 624.183 462 |
| Shelter | |
| social welfare | 361.05 |
| Sheltered employment | 362.404 848 |
| *see also* Employment | |
| services — social services | |
| Sheltered housing | 362.61 |
| Shelving | |
| household management | 645.4 |
| library collections maintenance | 025.81 |
| library plant management | 022.4 |
| manufacturing technology | 684.16 |
| Shemittah | 296.439 1 |

Shenandoah County (Va.)   T2—755 95
Shenandoah National Park
  (Va.)   T2—755 9
Shenandoah River Valley
  (Va. and W. Va.)   T2—755 9
Shengs   788.82
  *see also* Woodwind instruments
Shensi Province (China)   T2—514 3
Shepherd's purse   583.64
Shepparton (Vic.)   T2—945 4
Shepway (England)   T2—422 395
Sherbet   641.863
  commercial processing   637.4
  home preparation   641.863
Sherbrooke (Quebec)   T2—714 66
Sherbrooke (Quebec :
  Regional County
  Municipality)   T2—714 66
Sherburne County (Minn.)   T2—776 66
Sheridan County (Kan.)   T2—781 145
Sheridan County (Mont.)   T2—786 218
Sheridan County (N.D.)   T2—784 76
Sheridan County (Neb.)   T2—782 92
Sheridan County (Wyo.)   T2—787 32
Sheriffs
  law   347.016
  police services   363.282
Sherman County (Kan.)   T2—781 115
Sherman County (Neb.)   T2—782 44
Sherman County (Or.)   T2—795 64
Sherman County (Tex.)   T2—764 813
Sherman's March to the Sea,
  1864   973.737 8
Sherry   641.222 609 468 8
  commercial processing   663.226 094 688
Sherwood Forest (England)   T2—425 24
Shetland (Scotland)   T2—411 35
Shetland Islands (Scotland)   T2—411 35
Shetland pony   636.16
Shevi'it   296.123 1
  Mishnah   296.123 1
  Palestinian Talmud   296.124 1
Shevu'ot   296.123 4
  Babylonian Talmud   296.125 4
  Mishnah   296.123 4
  Palestinian Talmud   296.124 4
Shewa (Ethiopia)   T2—633
Sheyenne River (N.D.)   T2—784 3
Shi language   496.394
                T6—963 94
Shia Islam   297.82
  doctrines   297.204 2
  Hadith   297.125 92

Shia Islam (continued)
  relations with Sunni Islam   297.804 2
  worship   297.302
Shiatsu
  therapeutics   615.822 2
Shiawassee County (Mich.)   T2—774 25
Shielding
  nuclear reactors   621.483 23
Shields (Armor)   623.441
  art metalwork   739.752
Shieldtail snakes   597.967
Shift systems   331.257 25
Shift work   331.257 25
  personnel management   658.312 1
Shifting cultivation
  agricultural technology   631.581 8
Shiga-ken (Japan)   T2—521 85
Shigella   579.34
Shigellosis
  incidence   614.516
  medicine   616.935 5
    *see also* Communicable
      diseases — humans
Shih Tzu (Dog)   636.76
Shiites   297.82
Shikoku Island (Japan)   T2—523
Shikoku Region (Japan)   T2—523
Shilha language   493.3
               T6—933
Shilluk language   496.5
               T6—965
Shimane-ken (Japan)   T2—521 96
Shin (Sect)   294.392 6
Shina language   491.499
               T6—914 99
Shina literature   891.499
Shinano River (Japan)   T2—521 52
Shiners   597.482
Shingles (Disease)
  medicine   616.522
    *see also* Skin diseases —
      humans
Shingles (Roofing)   695
Shinto   299.561
Shinto philosophy   181.095 61
Shinto temples and shrines   299.561 35
  architecture   726.195 61
Shintoism   299.561
  art representation   704.948 995 61
Shintoists
  biography   299.561 092
Shinyanga Region
  (Tanzania)   T2—678 28

Ship accidents    363.123
   *see also* Water transportation —
     safety
Ship canals    386.4
   engineering    627.137
   transportation services    386.4
     interoceanic    386.42
     noninteroceanic canals    386.47
   *see also* Canals
Ship canneries
   engineering    623.824 8
Ship fitting    623.843 3
Ship flags    929.92
Ship gear    623.862
Ship handling    623.881
Ship railroads    385.77
   engineering    625.39
   transportation services    385.77
Ship timber beetles    595.763
Ship-to-shore communication    384.53
   communications services    384.53
   port services    387.166
Shipboard cooking    641.575 3
Shipboard health    613.68
Shipbuilding    623.82
Shipbuilding industry    338.476 238 2
   law    343.078 623 82
Shiplap    674.43
Shipment
   materials management    658.788
Shipping    387.5
   law    343.096
   materials management    658.788
   *see also* Inland water
     transportation; Ocean
     transportation
Shipping conferences (Business
   enterprises)    387.506 5
Ships    387.2
   arts    T3C—356
   design    623.81
   engineering    623.82
   folklore    398.276
     history and criticism    398.356
   gear and rigging    623.862
   inland water    386.22
     transportation services    386.22
   law    343.096 5
   literature    808.803 56
     history and criticism    809.933 56
     specific literatures    T3B—080 356
       history and
         criticism    T3B—093 56
   naval equipment    359.83

Ships (continued)
   naval units    359.32
     *see Manual at* 359.32 vs.
      359.83
   operation    387.540 44
     nautical engineering    623.881
     transportation services    387.540 44
      canal    386.404 204 4
      inland waterway    386.240 44
      lake    386.540 44
      river    386.350 44
   ordnance    623.825 1
   sanitation services    363.729 3
   transportation services    387.2
   *see Manual at* 629.046 vs. 388
Ships in bottles    745.592 8
Shipworms    594.4
Shipwrecks    363.123
   adventure    910.452
   transportation safety    363.123
   *see also* Water
     transportation — safety
Shipwrights' work    623.844
Shipyards
   architecture    725.4
   production economics    338.476 238 3
   technology    623.83
Shira-Punu languages    496.396
                T6—963 96
Shire horse    636.15
Shires    320.83
   *see also* Counties
Shirts    391.475
   commercial technology    687.115
   customs    391.475
   home economics    646.3
   home sewing    646.435
   *see also* Clothing
Shish kebabs
   home preparation    641.82
Shivaism    294.551 3
Shizuoka-ken (Japan)    T2—521 65
Shoa (Ethiopia)    T2—633
Shoah    940.531 8
   *see also* Holocaust, 1933–1945
Shoalhaven National Park
   (N.S.W.)    T2—944 7
Shoalhaven River (N.S.W.)    T2—944 7
Shock (Pathological)
   medicine    616.047 5
   result of injury    617.21
Shock absorbers
   automotive engineering    629.243

Shock resistance
   materials science   620.112 5
Shock-resistant construction   624.176
   buildings   693.85
Shock therapy
   psychiatry   616.891 2
Shock tunnels
   aircraft   629.134 52
Shock waves   531.113 3
   fluid mechanics   532.059 3
   gas mechanics   533.293
   liquid mechanics   532.593
   solid mechanics   531.33
Shoe buckles   391.7
   customs   391.7
   making   739.278
     costume jewelry   688.2
      handicrafts   745.594 2
     fine jewelry   739.278
Shoe repairers   685.310 092
Shoemakers   685.310 092
Shoes   391.413
   commercial technology   685.31
   customs   391.413
   *see also* Clothing
Shoghi, Effendi
   works by   297.938 6
Shogi   794.18
Shona (African people)   T5—963 975
Shona language   496.397 5
   T6—963 975
Shona literature   896.397 5
Shooting game
   sports   799.21
Shooting stars (Plants)   583.675
Shoots (Plants)   581.495
   descriptive botany   581.495
   physiology   575.4
Shop stewards   331.873 3
Shop technology   670.42
Shoplifting   364.162 32
   law   345.026 232
Shoppers' clubs   381.149
   management   658.879
Shopping   381.1
   etiquette   395.53
   *see also* Commerce
Shopping centers   381.11
   architecture   725.21
   area planning   711.552 2
   management   658.87
   *see also* Commerce

Shopping malls   381.11
   *see also* Commerce; Shopping
     centers
Shops (Retail trade)   381.1
   architecture   725.21
   management   658.87
   *see also* Commerce
Shoran   621.384 8
   marine navigation   623.893 3
Shore, John, Baron Teignmouth
   Indian history   954.031 1
Shore biology   578.769 9
Shore birds   598.33
   sports hunting   799.248 33
Shore ecology   577.699
Shore flies   595.774
Shore protection   333.917 16
   engineering   627.58
   land economics   333.917 16
Shore reclamation   333.917 153
   engineering   627.58
   land economics   333.917 153
Shorebirds   598.33
   sports hunting   799.248 33
Shorelands   551.457
                   T2—146
   *see also* Coasts
Shorelines   551.458
                   T2—146
   geography   910.914 6
   geomorphology   551.458
   physical geography   910.021 46
Shoring
   structural engineering   624.152
Short-haired cats   636.82
Short-necked lutes   787.8
   *see also* Stringed instruments
Short-order cooking   641.57
Short-range ballistic missiles   358.175 282
   engineering   623.451 952
   military equipment   358.175 282
Short-range weather forecasting   551.636 2
Short stories   808.831
   history and criticism   809.31
   specific literatures   T3B—301
     individual authors   T3A—3
Short takeoff and landing
   airplanes
   engineering   629.133 340 426
Short-term capital
   financial management   658.152 44
Short-term government securities   336.31
Short-term loans receivable
   financial management   658.152 44

| | | | |
|---|---|---|---|
| Short track speed skating | 796.914 | Shrew opossums | 599.27 |
| Shortages | | Shrews | 599.336 |
| agricultural industries | 338.17 | Shrewsbury and Atcham | |
| natural resources | 333.711 | (England) | T2—424 54 |
| production | 338.02 | Shrike-vireos | 598.878 |
| secondary industries | 338.47 | Shrikes | 598.862 |
| Shorthair cats | 636.82 | Shrimp culture | 639.68 |
| Shorthand | 653 | Shrimping | 639.58 |
| Shorthorn cattle | 636.222 | economics | 338.372 538 8 |
| Shorts (Clothing) | 391.476 | Shrimps | 595.388 |
| *see also* Pants (Trousers) | | conservation technology | 639.975 388 |
| Shortwave electronics | 621.381 | cooking | 641.695 |
| physics | 537.534 3 | culture | 639.68 |
| Shortwave radio systems | | fishing | 639.58 |
| engineering | 621.384 151 | fishing industry | 338.372 538 8 |
| military engineering | 623.734 1 | food | 641.395 |
| Shoshone County (Idaho) | T2—796 91 | commercial processing | 664.94 |
| Shoshoni Indians | T5—974 574 | resource economics | 333.955 58 |
| Shoshoni language | 497.457 4 | zoology | 595.388 |
| | T6—974 574 | Shriners | 366.16 |
| Shoshoni literature | 897.457 4 | biography | 366.160 92 |
| Shot peening | 671.36 | Shrines | 203.5 |
| Shot-putting | 796.435 | architecture | 726.1 |
| Shotguns | 683.426 | Buddhist | 294.343 5 |
| manufacturing technology | 683.426 | Christianity | 263.042 |
| sports | 799.202 834 | Hindu | 294.535 |
| *see also* Guns (Small arms) | | Islamic | 297.35 |
| Shoulder muscles | | Jain | 294.435 |
| human anatomy | 611.737 | Shinto | 299.561 35 |
| Shoulders (Body parts) | 612.97 | Sikh | 294.635 |
| physiology | 612.97 | Shrinkage-controlled fabrics | 677.688 |
| regional medicine | 617.572 | *see also* Textiles | |
| surgery | 617.572 059 | Shropshire (England) | T2—424 5 |
| *see also* Upper extremities | | Shroud of Turin | 232.966 |
| Shoulders (Highways) | | Shrublands | |
| maintenance | | biology | 578.738 |
| engineering | 625.761 | ecology | 577.38 |
| Show animals | 791.8 | Shrubs | 582.17 |
| animal husbandry | 636.081 1 | floriculture | 635.976 |
| performing arts | 791.8 | landscape architecture | 715.3 |
| Show jumping | 798.250 79 | *see Manual at* 635.9 vs. 582.1 | |
| Show windows | | Shuar Indians | T5—983 72 |
| advertising | 659.157 | Shuar language | 498.372 |
| Shōwa period | 952.033 | | T6—983 72 |
| Showboats | 792.022 | Shuar literature | 898.372 |
| Showcase displays | | Shuara literature | 898.372 |
| advertising | 659.157 | Shuffleboard | 796.2 |
| Showering | 613.41 | Shulḥan 'arukh | 296.182 |
| Showing livestock | 636.081 1 | Shunts (Electrical instrument) | 621.374 2 |
| Shows | 791 | Shuswap Indians | T5—979 43 |
| advertising | 659.152 | Shuswap Lake (B.C.) | T2—711 68 |
| performances | 791 | Shuswap language | 497.943 |
| Shrapnel devices | 623.451 4 | | T6—979 43 |
| Shreveport (La.) | T2—763 99 | Shuswap River (B.C.) | T2—711 5 |

| | |
|---|---|
| Shut-in people | 305.908 7 |
| | T1—087 7 |
| health services | 362.14 |
| home care | 649.8 |
| recreation | 790.196 |
| indoor | 793.019 6 |
| outdoor | 796.087 7 |
| Shutters (Cameras) | 771.36 |
| Shuttle cars | |
| mining | 622.66 |
| Shyness | 155.232 |
| SI (Metric system) | 530.812 |
| social aspects | 389.15 |
| Sialidae | 595.747 |
| Siam | T2—593 |
| Siam, Gulf of | 551.461 472 |
| | T2—164 72 |
| Siamang | 599.882 |
| Siamese | T5—959 11 |
| Siamese cat | 636.825 |
| Siamese fighting fish | 597.7 |
| Siamese language | 495.91 |
| | T6—959 11 |
| Siamese literature | 895.91 |
| Siassi Islands (Papua New Guinea) | T2—957 1 |
| Sibasa (South Africa : District) | T2—682 57 |
| Siberia (Russia) | 957 |
| | T2—57 |
| Siberia, Eastern (Russia) | T2—575 |
| Siberia, Western (Russia) | T2—573 |
| Siberian husky | 636.73 |
| Siberian Yupik | T5—971 4 |
| Siberian Yupik languages | T6—971 4 |
| Sibiu (Romania : Judeţ) | T2—498 4 |
| Sibley County (Minn.) | T2—776 33 |
| Siblings | 306.875 |
| | T1—085 5 |
| child care handbooks | 649.102 45 |
| family relationships | 306.875 |
| home care | 649.143 |
| psychological influence | 155.924 |
| psychology | 155.443 |
| adulthood | 155.646 |
| Sibyls | |
| parapsychology | 133.324 8 |
| religion | 206.1 |
| Sichuan Sheng (China) | T2—513 8 |
| Sicilian dialect | T6—51 |
| Sicilianas | 793.3 |
| music | 784.188 3 |
| Sicily (Italy) | 945.8 |
| | T2—458 |
| ancient | 937.8 |
| | T2—378 |
| Sicily (Kingdom) | 945.8 |
| Sicily, Strait of | 551.461 381 |
| | T2—163 81 |
| Sick leave | 331.257 62 |
| economics | 331.257 62 |
| personnel management | 658.312 2 |
| Sick people | 305.908 7 |
| | T1—087 7 |
| architecture for | 720.877 |
| clothing | |
| home sewing | 646.401 |
| collected biography | T1—092 7 |
| cooking for | 641.563 1 |
| devotional literature | |
| Christianity | 242.4 |
| government programs (nonhealth) | 353.539 |
| guides to religious life | 204.42 |
| Christianity | 248.861 |
| health services | 362.1 |
| public administration | 353.6 |
| home care | 649.8 |
| pastoral care | 206.1 |
| Christianity | 259.41 |
| recreation | 790.196 |
| indoor | 793.019 6 |
| outdoor | 796.087 7 |
| religious rites | 203.8 |
| Christianity | 265.82 |
| social group | 305.908 7 |
| social theology | 201.762 1 |
| Christianity | 261.832 1 |
| social welfare | 362.1 |
| *see Manual at* 362.1 .4 vs. 610 | |
| Sickle cell anemia | |
| medicine | 616.152 7 |
| *see also* Cardiovascular diseases — humans | |
| Sickness | 362.1 |
| medicine | 616 |
| *see also* Diseases — humans | |
| Sickness insurance | 368.382 |
| Sidama (African people) | T5—935 |
| Sidamo (African people) | T5—935 |
| Sidamo languages | 493.5 |
| | T6—935 |
| Siddurim | 296.45 |

Side arms
  art metalwork 739.72
  military engineering 623.44
Side-blown flutes 788.32
  *see also* Woodwind instruments
Side chapels
  architecture 726.595
Side dishes 641.81
Side drums 786.94
  *see also* Percussion instruments
Side effects of drugs
  pharmacokinetics 615.704 2
Side-necked turtles 597.929
Side-sewing
  bookbinding 686.35
Sideline markets 381.1
  *see also* Commerce
Sideline stores 381.1
  *see also* Commerce
Sidereal clocks
  astronomy 522.5
Sidereal day 529.1
Sidereal month 523.33
Siderite
  mineralogy 549.782
Siders (Switzerland :
  Bezirk) T2—494 796 1
Sideshows 791.35
Sidewalks 388.411
  road engineering 625.88
  transportation services 388.411
Sidi Bel Abbès (Algeria :
  Province) T2—651
Sidi Bernoussi-Zenata
  (Morocco) T2—643 8
Sidi Kacem (Morocco :
  Province) T2—643 5
Sidi-Youssef-Ben-Ali
  (Morocco) T2—646 4
Sidings (Railroads) 625.163
Sidings (Walls)
  buildings 698
  wood 674.43
Sidney (B.C.) T2—711 28
Sidon (Lebanon) T2—569 2
  ancient T2—394 4
Sidonian architecture 722.31
SIDS (Syndrome)
  pediatrics 618.920 26
Siedlce (Poland :
  Voivodeship) T2—438 41
Siege of Vicksburg, 1863 973.734 4
Siege warfare 355.44
Siemens process 669.142 2

Siena (Italy) T2—455 81
  ancient T2—375 66
Siena (Italy : Province) T2—455 8
  ancient T2—375 66
Sieradz (Poland :
  Voivodeship) T2—438 47
Sierra (Ecuador) T2—866 1
Sierra County (Calif.) T2—794 36
Sierra County (N.M.) T2—789 67
Sierra Leone 966.4
  T2—664
Sierra Leoneans T5—966 4
Sierra Madre del Sul
  (Mexico) T2—727 3
Sierra Madre Occidental
  (Mexico) T2—723
Sierra Madre Oriental
  (Mexico) T2—724
Sierra Nevada de Santa
  Marta National Park
  (Colombia) T2—861 16
Sierra Nevada Mountains
  (Calif. and Nev.) T2—794 4
Sierra Region (Ecuador) T2—866 1
Sierre (Switzerland :
  District) T2—494 796 1
Sieves (Mathematics) 512.73
Sifakas 599.83
Siftings
  cereal grains
    commercial processing 664.720 8
    wheat 664.722 8
Sight 573.88
  *see also* Vision
Sight method (Reading)
  primary education 372.462
Sight-reading (Music) 781.423
  primary education 372.873
Sighthounds 636.753 2
Sighting apparatus
  military engineering 623.46
Sigillography 929.9
  insignia 929.9
  numismatics 737.6
Sigismund III, King of Poland
  and Sweden
  Swedish history 948.503 24
Sigmodon 599.357 2
Sigmoid colon
  human anatomy 611.347
  human physiology 612.36
  medicine 616.34
  surgery 617.554 7

Sigmoid flexure
  human anatomy    611.347
  human physiology    612.36
  medicine    616.34
  surgery    617.554 7
Sign language literatures    899.98
Sign languages    419
           T6—999 8
  primary education    372.6
  special education    371.912 46
Sign painting    667.6
Signal corps    358.24
Signal generators
  electronics    621.381 548
Signal processing    621.382 2
Signal propagation
  communications engineering    621.382 4
  satellite communication    621.382 54
Signal theory    003.54
  communications engineering    621.382 23
  systems    003.54
Signals    302.23
  communications engineering    621.382 2
  railroad transportation    385.316
    engineering    625.165
    law    343.095 2
    transportation services    385.316
  road transportation    388.312 2
    engineering    625.794
    law    343.094 6
    transportation services    388.312 2
  social psychology    302.23
  street transportation    388.413 122
    engineering    625.794
    law    343.098 2
    transportation services    388.413 122
  transportation    388.041
    engineering    629.040 289
    law    343.093
    transportation services    388.041
Signboards
  social psychology    302.23
Signed English
  American    428.917
  British    428.914 1
Signets
  numismatics    737.6
Signs    302.23
  advertising    659.134
  law    346.045
  social psychology    302.23
  transportation    388.041
    engineering    629.040 289
    transportation services    388.041

Signs (continued)
  wooden    674.88
  *see also* Signals
Ṣiḥāḥ
  Hadith    297.125 4
Siirt İli (Turkey)    T2—566 78
  ancient    T2—394 2
Sikh gurus    294.609 2
  biography    294.609 2
  role and function    294.663
Sikh philosophy    181.046
Sikh temples and shrines    294.635
  architecture    726.146
Sikhism    294.6
  art representation    704.948 946
  Islamic polemics    297.294
Sikhism and Islam    294.615
  Islamic view    297.284 6
  Sikh view    294.615
Sikhs
  biography    294.609 2
Sikkim (India)    T2—541 67
Sikkimese    T5—914 17
  1975–    T5—914 11
Sikoku Island (Japan)    T2—523
Sikoku Region (Japan)    T2—523
Siksika Indians    T5—973 52
Siksika language    497.352
           T6—973 52
Silage    636.086 2
  forage crop    633.2
Silence
  musical element    781.236
Silencers (Automobile part)    629.252
Silesia    T2—438 5
  Czech Republic    T2—437 28
  Poland    T2—438 5
Silesian War, 1740–1742    943.054
Silesian War, 1744–1745    943.054
Silesian War, 1756–1763    940.253 4
Silhouettes    741.7
  animals    591.41
  cutting    736.984
  drawing    741.7
  plants    581.41
Silicates
  mineralogy    549.6
Silicon    553.6
  chemical engineering    661.068 3
  chemistry    546.683
  economic geology    553.6
  materials science    620.193

Silicon (continued)
  organic chemistry    547.08
    aliphatic    547.48
    applied    661.88
  *see also* Chemicals
Silicon salts
  chemical engineering    661.43
Silicones    668.422 7
Silicosis
  medicine    616.244
    *see also* Respiratory tract
      diseases — humans
Silk books    096.2
Silk cotton tree    583.68
Silk ribbon embroidery    746.447
Silk-screen printing    686.231 6
  graphic arts    764.8
  textile arts    746.62
Silk textiles    677.39
  arts    746.043 9
  *see also* Textiles
Silk tree    583.748
Silkworms    638.2
  culture    638.2
  zoology    595.78
Silky flycatchers    598.853
Silky terrier    636.76
Sillimanite
  mineralogy    549.62
Sills (Geology)    551.88
Silo machinery
  manufacturing technology    681.763 1
Silos    633.208 68
Silphidae    595.764 2
Silt
  petrology    552.5
  reservoir engineering    627.86
  river engineering    627.122
Silurian period    551.732
  geology    551.732
  paleontology    560.173 2
Siluriformes    597.49
  paleozoology    567.49
Silva, Luiz Inácio da
  Brazilian history    981.065
Silver    669.23
  chemical engineering    661.065 4
  chemistry    546.654
  economic geology    553.421
  materials science    620.189 23
  metallography    669.952 3
  metallurgy    669.23
  metalworking    673.23
  mining    622.342 3

Silver (continued)
  physical metallurgy    669.962 3
  production economics    338.274 21
  *see also* Chemicals; Metals
Silver Bow County (Mont.)    T2—786 68
Silver coins    332.404 2
  investment economics    332.63
  monetary economics    332.404 2
  numismatics    737.4
Silver processes
  photography    772.4
Silver question    332.423 097 3
Silver standard    332.422 3
Silverfish (Insects)    595.723
Silverpoint drawing    741.25
Silversides    597.66
Silversmithing    739.23
Silversmiths    739.230 92
Silverware
  arts    739.238 3
  table setting    642.7
Silviculture    634.95
Simaroubaceae    583.77
Simbu Province (Papua
  New Guinea)    T2—956 7
Simcoe (Ont. : County)    T2—713 17
Simdlangentsha (South
  Africa : District)    T2—684 2
Simḥat Torah    296.433 9
  liturgy    296.453 39
Similarity (Mathematics)    516.2
Simile    808.032
Simmering
  home cooking    641.73
Simmonds' disease
  medicine    616.47
    *see also* Endocrine
      diseases — humans
Simonstown (South Africa :
  District)    T2—687 35
Simple microscopes
  biology    570.282 3
Simple proteins    572.66
  *see also* Proteins
Simples
  pharmacognosy    615.321
Simplexes    514.223
Simpson County (Ky.)    T2—769 735
Simpson County (Miss.)    T2—762 585
Simpson Desert National
  Park (Qld.)    T2—943 7
Simpson Peninsula
  (Nunavut)    T2—719 55

| | |
|---|---|
| Simulation | 003 |
| | T1—011 |
| engineering | 620.004 4 |
| instructional use | 371.397 |
| management decision making | 658.403 52 |
| mathematics | 511.8 |
| Simuliidae | 595.772 |
| Simultaneous play (Chess) | 794.17 |
| Sin | 202.2 |
| Buddhism | 294.342 2 |
| Christianity | 241.3 |
| original sin | 233.14 |
| Hinduism | 294.522 |
| Islam | 297.22 |
| Judaism | 296.32 |
| moral theology | 205 |
| Buddhism | 294.35 |
| Christianity | 241.3 |
| Hinduism | 294.548 |
| Islam | 297.5 |
| Judaism | 296.36 |
| Sinai (Egypt) | 953.1 |
| | T2—531 |
| Sinai Campaign, 1956 | 956.044 |
| Sinai Peninsula (Egypt) | T2—531 |
| ancient | 939.48 |
| | T2—394 8 |
| Sinaloa (Mexico : State) | T2—723 2 |
| Sindh (Pakistan) | T2—549 18 |
| Sindhi | T5—914 25 |
| Sindhi language | 491.41 |
| | T6—914 11 |
| Sindhi literature | 891.41 |
| Sine-Saloum (Senegal) | T2—663 |
| Sinfonia concertantes | 784.184 5 |
| Sinfoniettas | 784.184 |
| musical form | 784.184 |
| orchestral music | 784.218 4 |
| Singapore | 959.57 |
| | T2—595 7 |
| Singapore Strait | 551.461 472 |
| | T2—164 72 |
| Singeing textiles | 677.028 25 |
| Singers | 782.009 2 |
| Singh, Charan | |
| Indian history | 954.052 |
| Singh, Manmohan | |
| Indian history | 954.053 2 |
| Singh, Vishwanath Pratap | |
| Indian history | 954.052 |
| Singida Region (Tanzania) | T2—678 26 |
| Singine (Switzerland) | T2—494 539 |
| Singing games | 796.13 |

| | |
|---|---|
| Single column tariffs | 382.752 |
| *see also* Customs (Tariff) | |
| Single fatherhood | 306.874 22 |
| Single idiophones | 786.88 |
| *see also* Percussion instruments | |
| Single-lens reflex cameras | 771.32 |
| Single-line outlets (Marketing) | 381.14 |
| *see also* Commerce | |
| Single men | 306.815 2 |
| | T1—086 52 |
| psychology | 155.642 2 |
| social group | 306.815 2 |
| Single motherhood | 306.874 32 |
| social welfare | 362.839 532 |
| Single mothers | 306.874 32 |
| social welfare | 362.839 532 |
| Single-parent family | 306.856 |
| social theology | 201.7 |
| Christianity | 261.835 856 |
| social welfare | 362.829 4 |
| *see also* Families — social welfare | |
| Single parents | 306.856 |
| child care handbooks | 649.102 43 |
| religion | 204.41 |
| Single people | 306.815 |
| | T1—086 52 |
| psychology | 155.642 |
| social group | 306.815 |
| Single-photon emission-computed tomography | 616.075 75 |
| Single-piece processes | |
| production management | 658.533 |
| Single-reed bagpipes | 788.49 |
| *see also* Woodwind instruments | |
| Single-reed instruments | 788.6 |
| *see also* Woodwind instruments | |
| Single-shot pistols | 683.432 |
| *see also* Pistols | |
| Single-sideband radio systems | 621.384 153 |
| Single-stage programming | 519.702 |
| Single-story buildings | 720.48 |
| architecture | 720.48 |
| construction | 690.38 |
| Single-story houses | |
| architecture | 728.373 |
| Single-tax school of economics | 330.155 |
| Single teenage fatherhood | 306.874 22 |
| Single teenage motherhood | 306.874 32 |
| social welfare | 362.787 432 |
| Single-wicket cricket | 796.358 8 |
| Single wingback formation | 796.332 22 |

| | | | |
|---|---|---|---|
| Single women | 306.815 3 | Siouan Indians | T5—975 2 |
| | T1—086 52 | Siouan languages | 497.52 |
| psychology | 155.642 3 | | T6—975 2 |
| social group | 306.815 3 | Sioux City (Iowa) | T2—777 41 |
| Singles (Tennis) | 796.342 27 | Sioux County (Iowa) | T2—777 13 |
| Singleton (N.S.W.) | T2—944 2 | Sioux County (N.D.) | T2—784 88 |
| Singspiels | 782.13 | Sioux County (Neb.) | T2—782 99 |
| music | 782.13 | Sioux Falls (S.D.) | T2—783 371 |
| stage presentation | 792.5 | Sipaliwini (Suriname : | |
| Singularities (Mathematics) | | District) | T2—883 95 |
| algebraic geometry | 516.35 | Siphonales | 579.835 |
| functions of several complex | | Siphonaptera | 595.775 |
| variables | 515.94 | Siphonocladales | 579.83 |
| Singularity theory | 514.746 | Siphonophora | 593.55 |
| Sinhala language | 491.48 | Siphunculata | 595.756 |
| | T6—914 8 | Sipuncula | 592.35 |
| Sinhala literature | 891.48 | paleozoology | 562.35 |
| Sinhalese | T5—914 8 | Sira languages | 496.396 |
| Sinhalese language | 491.48 | | T6—963 96 |
| | T6—914 8 | Sirach (Bible) | 229.4 |
| Sinhalese literature | 891.48 | Siracusa (Italy) | T2—458 141 |
| Sinhalese-Maldivian languages | 491.48 | ancient | T2—378 141 |
| | T6—914 8 | Siracusa (Italy : Province) | T2—458 14 |
| Sinhalese-Maldivian literatures | 891.48 | ancient | T2—378 14 |
| Sink holes | 551.447 | Sirenia | 599.55 |
| | T2—144 | paleozoology | 569.5 |
| *see also* Caves | | Sirenidae | 597.85 |
| Sinkiang Uighur | | Sirens (Amphibians) | 597.85 |
| Autonomous Region | | Sirens (Noisemakers) | 621.389 2 |
| (China) | T2—516 | music | 786.99 |
| Sinking | 532.25 | *see also* Percussion | |
| Sinking funds | | instruments | |
| public finance | 336.363 | warning device | 621.389 2 |
| Sinn Fein Rebellion, 1916 | 941.508 21 | Şırnak İli (Turkey) | T2—566 78 |
| Sinnār (Sudan) | T2—626 4 | ancient | T2—394 2 |
| Sino-Indian Border Dispute, 1957 | 954.042 | Sisal | |
| Sino-Japanese Conflict, | | botany | 584.352 |
| 1937–1945 | 940.53 | fiber crop | 633.577 |
| 1937–1941 | 951.042 | Siskins | 598.885 |
| 1941–1945 | 940.53 | Siskiyou County (Calif.) | T2—794 21 |
| Sino-Japanese War, 1894–1895 | 951.035 | Sissach (Switzerland : | |
| Sino-Tibetan languages | 495 | Bezirk) | T2—494 339 |
| | T6—95 | Sīstān va Balūchestān (Iran) | T2—558 3 |
| Sino-Tibetan literatures | 895 | Sister-brother relationship | 306.875 3 |
| Sinop İli (Turkey) | T2—563 8 | Sister-sister relationship | 306.875 4 |
| ancient | T2—393 32 | Sisters | 306.875 |
| Sintering metals | 671.373 | | T1—085 5 |
| Sinuses | | *see also* Siblings | |
| paranasal | | Sisters (Nurses) | 610.730 92 |
| human anatomy | 611.21 | role and function | 610.730 69 |
| human physiology | 612.232 | Sisters (Women religious) | 255.9 |
| medicine | 616.212 | biography | 271.900 2 |
| Sion (Switzerland) | T2—494 796 44 | *see Manual at* 230–280 | |
| Sion (Switzerland : District) | T2—494 796 4 | | |

Sisters (Women religious) (continued)
  ecclesiology 262.24
  guides to Christian life 248.894 3
Sisters and brothers 306.875 3
  psychology 155.443
Sisters of Bon Secours 255.94
  church history 271.94
Sisters of Charity 255.91
  church history 271.91
Sisters of Mercy 255.92
  church history 271.92
Sistrums 786.885
  *see also* Percussion instruments
Sistrurus 597.963 8
SiSwati language 496.398 7
  T6—963 987
SiSwati literature 896.398 7
Sit-ins
  social conflict 303.61
Sitars 787.82
  *see also* Stringed instruments
Site planning
  architecture 720.28
Site selection
  home economics 643.12
  nuclear engineering 621.483 2
Sitka (Alaska) T2—798 2
Sitten (Switzerland) T2—494 796 44
Sitten (Switzerland :
  District) T2—494 796 4
Sittidae 598.82
Situation ethics 171.7
Situational influences
  psychology 155.93
Sivas İli (Turkey) T2—565 5
  ancient T2—395 5
Siwa language 493.3
  T6 933
Siwi language 493.3
  T6—933
Six Days' War, 1967 956.046
Six-man football 796.332 8
Sixteenth century 909.5
  T1—090 31
Sixth century 909.1
  T1—090 21
Sixth-form colleges 373.238
Size 530.81
  animals 591.41
  biological organisms 578.41
  plants 581.41
Size of enterprise 338.64
  economics 338.64
  microeconomics 338.514 4

Size of farm
  economics 338.16
Size perception
  psychology 153.752
Size standards
  commerce 389.62
  production management 658.562
Sizing coal 662.623
Sizing ores 622.74
Sizing paper 676.234
Sizuoka-ken (Japan) T2—521 65
Sjælland (Denmark) T2—489 1
Sjogren's syndrome
  medicine 616.775
  *see also* Musculoskeletal
    diseases — humans
Ska (Music) 781.646
Skagerrak (Denmark and 551.461 336
  Norway) T2 163 36
Skagit County (Wash.) T2—797 72
Skamania County (Wash.) T2—797 84
Skåne län (Sweden) T2—486 1
Skåne landskap (Sweden) T2—486 1
Skaraborgs län (Sweden) T2—486 7
Skateboarding 796.22
Skateboards 796.22
  manufacturing technology 688.762 2
Skater hockey 796.356 6
Skates (Fishes) 597.35
Skating (Ice) 796.91
  hockey 796.962 2
Skating (Roller) 796.21
Skeena Mountains (B.C.) T2—711 85
Skeena-Queen Charlotte
  (B.C.) T2—711 1
Skeena River (B.C.) T2—711 85
Skeet shooters 799.313 209 2
Skeet shooting 799.313 2
Skeletal muscle tissues
  human histology 612.740 45
Skeletal system 573.76
Skeleton 573.76
  human physiology 612.751
Skeleton (Sports) 796.956
Skepticism
  philosophy 149.73
    ancient 186
    epistemology 121.2
    philosophy of religion 211.7
Sketch books
  music 780
    treatises 780.262

Sketches (Drama)
  literature 808.824 1
    history and criticism 809.241
      specific literatures T3B—204 1
        individual authors T3A—2
Sketches (Drawings) T1—022 2
Skew bevel gears 621.833 2
Skewer cooking 641.76
Skhirate-Témara (Morocco :
  Prefecture) T2—643 6
Ski cross 796.937
Ski lifts 621.868
Ski troops 356.164
Skierniewice (Poland :
  Voivodeship) T2—438 47
Skiers 796.930 92
Skiff beetles 595.762
Skiffle 781.64
Skiing 796.93
  equipment technology 688.769 3
Skikda (Algeria : Province) T2—655
Skilled workers 331.794
  labor economics 331.794
  labor force 331.114 22
  personnel management 658.304 4
  unemployment 331.137 804
Skillet cooking 641.77
Skills shortages 331.136
Skim milk 641.371 47
  cooking 641.671 47
  food 641.371 47
  processing 637.147
Skimmers (Birds) 598.338
Skin 573.5
  anesthesiology 617.967 477
  animal physiology 573.5
  anthropometry 599.945
  descriptive zoology 591.47
  diseases 573.539
  *see also* Skin diseases
  human anatomy 611.77
  human biochemistry 612.792
  human biophysics 612.791
  human histology 612.790 45
  human physiology 612.79
  medicine 616.5
  personal care 646.726
  surgery 617.477
Skin allergies
  incidence 614.599 33
  medicine 616.973
Skin beetles 595.763

Skin diseases 573.539
  animals 573.539
    veterinary medicine 636.089 65
  humans 362.196 5
    anesthesiology 617.967 477
    cancer 362.196 994 77
      incidence 614.599 947 7
      medicine 616.994 77
      social services 362.196 994 77
      *see also* Cancer — humans
    geriatrics 618.976 5
    incidence 614.595
    medicine 616.5
    pediatrics 618.925
    pharmacokinetics 615.778
    social services 362.196 5
    surgery 617.477
Skin diving 797.232
Skin glands
  human physiology 612.793
Skinks 597.957
Skinner, B. F. (Burrhus Frederic)
  psychological system 150.194 34
Skipjack (Tuna) 597.783
Skipper flies 595.774
Skippers 595.788
Skips (Containers) 622.68
Skirmishing (Tactics) 355.422
Skirts 391.477
  commercial technology 687.117
  customs 391.477
  home economics 646.34
  home sewing 646.437
  *see also* Clothing
Skis 796.93
  manufacturing technology 688.769 3
Skitswish Indians T5—979 43
Skitswish language 497.943
  T6—979 43
Skittles 794.6
Skolt Saami language 494.576
  T6—945 76
Skolt Sámi language 494.576
  T6—945 76
Skuas 598.338
Skull
  anthropometry 599.948
  fractures
    medicine 617.155
  human anatomy 611.715
  human physiology 612.751
  medicine 616.71
  surgery 617.514

Skull base
  surgery    617.514
Skunk cabbages    584.64
Skunks    599.768
Sky
  atmospheric optics    551.565
  meteorology    551.5
  religious worship    202.12
Sky color    551.566
Sky marshals    363.287 6
Skydivers    797.560 92
Skydiving    797.56
Skye, Island of (Scotland)    T2—411 54
Skye and Lochalsh
  (Scotland)    T2—411 54
Skylights    721.5
  architecture    721.5
  construction    690.15
Skyros Island (Greece)    T2—495 15
  ancient    T2—391 1
Skyscrapers    720.483
  *see also* Tall buildings
Skysurfing    797.56
Slabs
  structural engineering    624.177 2
    concrete    624.183 42
Slacks    391.476
  *see also* Pants (Trousers)
Slag (Metallurgy)    669.84
Slalom skiing    796.935
Slander    364.156
  ethics    177.3
  law    345.025 6
    criminal law    345.025 6
    torts    346.034
Slang    417.2
  specific languages    T4—7
    *see Manual at* T4—7
Slang dictionaries    T1—03
Slash-and-burn agriculture
  technology    631.581 8
Śląskie Voivodeship
  (Poland)    T2—438 58
Slate    553.54
  building material    691.2
  economic geology    553.54
  petrology    552.4
  quarrying    622.354
Slaughterhouse residues
  use as fertilizer    631.843
Slaughterhouses
  meat processing    664.902 9
Slave kings
  Indian history    954.023 2

Slave labor    331.117 34
Slave River (Alta. and
  N.W.T.)    T2—719 3
Slave trade    306.362
  commerce    381.44
    international commerce    382.44
  criminology    364.15
  law    345.025
  ethics    177.5
  sociology    306.362
Slavery    306.362
  Civil War (United States) cause    973.711 2
  ethics    177.5
    *see also* Discrimination —
      ethics
  labor economics    331.117 34
  law    342.087
  political science    326
Slaves    306.362
      T1—086 25
  customs    390.25
    dress    391.025
  legal status    346.013
    constitutional law    342.087
    private law    346.013
Slavic languages    491.8
      T6—918
Slavic literatures    891.8
Slavic people    T5—918
Slavonia (Croatia)    T2—497 2
Slavonic languages    491.8
      T6—918
Slavonic literatures    891.8
Slavs    T5—918
Sled dog racing    798.83
Sled dogs    636.73
Sledding    796.95
Sleep    154.6
  animal behavior    591.519
  animal physiology    573.868
  comparative psychology    156.4
  human physiology    612.821
  physical fitness    613.794
  psychology    154.6
  *see also* Nervous system
Sleep apnea syndromes
  medicine    616.209
    *see also* Respiratory tract
      diseases — humans
Sleep disorders
  medicine    616.849 8
    *see also* Nervous system
      diseases — humans

Sleep initiation and maintenance disorders
medicine — 616.849 82
*see also* Nervous system diseases — humans
Sleeper services — 388.042
*see also* Passenger services
Sleepers (Ties) — 625.143
Sleeping bags
manufacturing technology — 685.53
Sleeping cars — 385.33
engineering — 625.23
*see also* Rolling stock
Sleeping pills
pharmacokinetics — 615.782
Sleeping services — 388.042
*see also* Passenger services
Sleepwalking
medicine — 616.849 8
*see also* Nervous system diseases — humans
psychology — 154.64
Sleepwear — 391.426
commercial technology — 687.165
customs — 391.426
home sewing — 646.475
*see also* Clothing
Slender blind snakes — 597.969
Slicers — 621.93
Slide preparation — 502.82
biology — 570.282 7
botany — 580.282 7
zoology — 590.282 7
Slide rules
manufacturing technology — 681.14
mathematics — 510.284
Sliders (Turtles) — 597.925 9
Slides (Photographs) — 779
bibliographies — 011.37
cataloging — 025.347 3
instructional use — 371.335 22
library treatment — 025.177 3
processing — 771.4
*see Manual at* 779 vs. 770.92
Sliding bearings — 621.822
Sligo (Ireland) — T2—417 25
Sligo (Ireland : County) — T2—417 2
Slime molds — 579.52
Slings
sports — 799.202 82
Slip laws — 348.01
United States — 348.731

Slip tracing — 666.45
arts — 738.15
technology — 666.45
Slipcovers — 645.4
arts — 746.95
commercial technology — 684.3
home sewing — 646.21
household management — 645.4
Slips (Plant propagation) — 631.535
Slocan Lake (B.C.) — T2—711 62
Slope County (N.D.) — T2—784 93
Slope failure — 551.307
Slopes — 551.43
T2—143
*see also* Mountains
Slopestyle snowboarding — 796.939
Slot machines — 795.27
equipment technology — 688.752
Sloth — 179.8
*see also* Vices
Sloths — 599.313
Slotters — 621.912
Slough (England) — T2—422 97
Slovak language — 491.87
T6—918 7
Slovak literature — 891.87
Slovakia — 943.73
T2—437 3
Slovaks — T5—918 7
Slovene language — 491.84
T6—918 4
Slovenes — T5—918 4
Slovenia — 949.73
T2—497 3
ancient — 939.873
T2—398 73
Slovenian language — 491.84
T6—918 4
Slovenian literature — 891.84
Slovenians — T5—918 4
Slow cooking — 641.588
Slow food movement — 641.013
Slow learners — 371.926
Sludge digestion — 628.354
Slugs (Land) — 594.38
agricultural pests — 632.643 8
control technology — 628.964
culture — 639.483 8
Slugs (Mollusks) — 594.3
Sluices
canal engineering — 627.135 2
dam engineering — 627.882
Slum clearance — 307.344

| | |
|---|---|
| Slums | 307.336 4 |
| area planning | 711.5 |
| social services to residents | |
| public administration | 353.533 3 |
| Słupsk (Poland : | |
| Voivodeship) | T2—438 22 |
| Småland landskap (Sweden) | T2—486 4 |
| Small arms ammunition | 683.406 |
| manufacturing technology | 683.406 |
| military engineering | 623.455 |
| Small business | 338.642 |
| accounting | 657.904 2 |
| economics | 338.642 |
| financial management | 658.159 2 |
| government programs | 354.279 9 |
| income tax | 336.242 3 |
| law | 343.052 68 |
| investment in | 332.672 22 |
| law | 343.07 |
| economic law | 343.07 |
| private law | 346.065 2 |
| management | 658.022 |
| personnel management | 658.303 |
| taxes | 336.207 |
| law | 343.068 |
| Small business loans | 332.742 |
| Small-claims courts | 347.04 |
| Small craft (Boats) | 387.204 2 |
| design | 623.812 042 |
| engineering | 623.820 2 |
| handling | 623.881 2 |
| transportation services | 387.204 2 |
| *see also* Ships | |
| Small craft canals | 386.48 |
| engineering | 627.138 |
| transportation services | 386.48 |
| *see also* Canals | |
| Small firearms | 683.4 |
| military engineering | 623.44 |
| *see also* Guns (Small arms) | |
| Small forge work | 682 |
| Small fruit flies | 595.774 |
| Small fruits | 581.464 |
| horticulture | 634.7 |
| *see also* Berries | |
| Small game hunting | |
| sports | 799.25 |
| Small-group reading | |
| primary education | 372.416 2 |
| Small groups | 302.34 |
| pastoral work | |
| Christianity | 253.7 |
| Small industry | 338.642 |
| Small intestine | 573.378 |
| biology | 573.378 |
| human anatomy | 611.341 |
| human physiology | 612.33 |
| medicine | 616.34 |
| surgery | 617.554 1 |
| *see also* Digestive system | |
| Small-scale systems | 003.7 |
| Small states | 321.06 |
| international role | 327.101 |
| Small towns | 307.762 |
| Smallmouth bass | 597.738 8 |
| Smallpox | |
| incidence | 614.521 |
| medicine | 616.912 |
| *see also* Communicable | |
| diseases — humans | |
| Smara (Morocco : Province) | T2—648 |
| Smart cards | 006.246 |
| banking services | 332.178 |
| computer science | 006.246 |
| credit economics | 332.76 |
| Smartphones | 004.167 |
| Smell | 573.877 |
| animal physiology | 573.877 |
| human physiology | 612.86 |
| Smell disorders | |
| medicine | 616.856 |
| *see also* Nervous system | |
| diseases — humans | |
| Smell perception | |
| psychology | 152.166 |
| Smelting | 669.028 2 |
| Smelts | 641.392 |
| cooking | 641.692 |
| food | 641.392 |
| zoology | 597.5 |
| Smilacaccac | 584.356 |
| Smilaxes (Cat briers) | 584.356 |
| Smilaxes (Ornamentals) | |
| botany | 584.355 |
| Smith, Adam | |
| economic school | 330.153 |
| Smith, Ian Douglas | |
| Zimbabwean history | 968.910 4 |
| Smith County (Kan.) | T2—781 213 |
| Smith County (Miss.) | T2—762 582 |
| Smith County (Tenn.) | T2—768 52 |
| Smith County (Tex.) | T2—764 225 |
| Smithers (B.C.) | T2—711 82 |
| Smithfield (South Africa : | |
| District) | T2—685 6 |
| Smithton (Tas.) | T2—946 5 |

Smocking
  arts     746.44
Smog     363.739 2
  air pollution     363.739 2
  pollution technology     628.532
  *see also* Pollution
Smoke     541.345 15
  colloid chemistry     541.345 15
    applied     660.294 515
  pollution technology     628.532
Smoke bomb launchers     623.445
Smoke bombs     623.451 6
Smoke damage insurance     368.12
Smoke pollution     363.738 7
  *see also* Pollution
Smoke signals
  social psychology     302.222
Smoke trees (Anacardiaceae)     583.77
Smoke trees (Fabaceae)     583.74
Smoked foods
  cooking     641.616
Smokeless powder
  military engineering     623.452 6
Smokers' supplies     688.4
Smoking     394.14
  addiction     362.296
    medicine     616.865
    personal health     613.85
    social welfare     362.296
    *see also* Substance abuse
  customs     394.14
  law     344.054
  social problem     363.4
Smoking cessation
  medicine     616.865 06
Smoking foods     664.028 6
  commercial preservation     664.028 6
  home preservation     641.46
Smolensk (Russia : Oblast)     T2—472 7
Smolenskaïa oblast'
  (Russia)     T2—472 7
Smooth muscle tissues
  human histology     612.740 45
SMP (Insurance)     368.094
Smuggling     364.133 6
  law     345.023 36
Smut fungi     579.593
  agricultural diseases     632.493
Smuts     579.593
  agricultural diseases     632.493
Smuts, Jan Christiaan
  South African history     968.053
    1919–1924     968.053
    1939–1948     968.055

Smyrna (Turkey)     T2—562 5
  ancient     T2—392 3
Smyth County (Va.)     T2—755 723
Snacks     642
  commercial processing     664.6
  cooking     641.53
  customs     394.125 3
Snail farming     639.483 8
Snails     594.3
Snails (Land)     594.38
  agricultural pests     632.643 8
  control technology     628.964
  culture     639.483 8
  food     641.394
    commercial processing     664.95
    cooking     641.694
  zoology     594.38
Snake eels     597.43
Snake flies     595.747
Snake-necked turtles     597.929
Snake plants     584.352
Snake River (Wyo.-Wash.)     T2—796 1
  Idaho     T2—796 1
  Oregon     T2—795 7
  Washington     T2—797 4
  Wyoming     T2—787 55
Snake venom
  human toxicology     615.942
Snakeflies     595.747
Snakeheads (Fishes)     597.64
Snakes     597.96
  resource economics     333.957 96
  small game hunting     799.257 96
Snakes as pets     639.396
Snap beans     641.356 52
  botany     583.74
  cooking     641.656 52
  food     641.356 52
Snapdragons     635.933 95
  botany     583.95
  floriculture     635.933 95
Snappers (Fishes)     597.72
  cooking     641.692
  food     641.392
  sports fishing     799.177 2
Snapping beetles     595.765
Snapping turtles     597.922
Snare drums     786.94
  *see also* Percussion instruments
Snares Islands (N.Z.)     T2—939 9
Snipe flies     595.773
Snipers     356.162
Snipes (Birds)     598.33

| | |
|---|---|
| Snobbishness | |
| arts | T3C—353 |
| literature | 808.803 53 |
| history and criticism | 809.933 53 |
| specific literatures | T3B—080 353 |
| history and criticism | T3B—093 53 |
| Snohomish County (Wash.) | T2—797 71 |
| Snooker | 794.735 |
| Snooks | 597.72 |
| sports fishing | 799.177 2 |
| Snoring | |
| medicine | 616.209 |
| Snorkeling | 797.232 |
| Snout beetles | 595.768 |
| Snow | 551.578 4 |
| building construction | 693.91 |
| meteorology | 551.578 4 |
| weather forecasting | 551.647 84 |
| weather modification | 551.687 84 |
| Snow camping | 796.54 |
| Snow carving | 736.94 |
| Snow-compacted roads | 388.12 |
| engineering | 625.792 |
| Snow control | |
| airport engineering | 629.136 37 |
| road engineering | 625.763 |
| Snow cover | 551.578 46 |
| biology | 578.758 6 |
| ecology | 577.586 |
| *see also* Snow | |
| Snow drifts | 551.578 47 |
| Snow fences | |
| railroad engineering | 625.13 |
| road engineering | 625.763 |
| Snow goose | 598.417 5 |
| Snow leopard | 599.755 5 |
| conservation technology | 639.979 755 5 |
| resource economics | 333.959 755 5 |
| Snow monkey | 599.864 4 |
| Snow-on-the-mountain (Plant) | 583.69 |
| Snow removal | |
| airport engineering | 629.136 37 |
| road engineering | 625.763 |
| road transportation | 388.312 |
| Snow sports | 796.9 |
| equipment technology | 688.769 |
| Snow surveys | 551.579 |
| Snowballs (Plants) | 635.933 92 |
| botany | 583.92 |
| floriculture | 635.933 92 |
| Snowboard cross | 796.939 |
| Snowboarding | 796.939 |
| Snowdonia (Wales) | T2—429 25 |
| Snowfall | 551.578 4 |
| *see also* Snow | |
| Snowmobiles | 388.34 |
| driving | 629.283 042 |
| engineering | 629.220 42 |
| repair | 629.287 042 |
| sports | 796.94 |
| transportation services | 388.34 |
| *see also* Automotive vehicles | |
| Snowplowing | |
| railroad engineering | 625.100 288 |
| road engineering | 625.763 |
| Snowplows | |
| railroad engineering | 625.22 |
| Snowsheds | 625.13 |
| Snowshoeing | 796.92 |
| Snowshoes | |
| manufacturing technology | 688.769 2 |
| Snowstorms | 551.555 |
| social services | 363.349 25 |
| *see also* Disasters | |
| Snowy Mountains (N.S.W.) | T2—944 7 |
| Snuffboxes | |
| handicrafts | 745.593 4 |
| Snyder County (Pa.) | T2—748 49 |
| Soap carving | 736.95 |
| Soap operas | 791.446 |
| radio programs | 791.446 |
| television programs | 791.456 |
| Soapberries | 583.78 |
| Soapbox racing | 796.6 |
| Soaps | 668.12 |
| Soapstone | 553.55 |
| building material | 691.2 |
| economic geology | 553.55 |
| quarrying | 622.355 |
| Soaring | |
| aeronautics | 629.132 31 |
| sports | 797.55 |
| Sobhuza II, King of Swaziland | |
| Swazi history | 968.870 3 |
| Sobolev spaces | 515.782 |
| Sóc Trăng (Vietnam : Province) | T2—597 9 |
| Soccer | 796.334 |
| electronic games | 794.863 34 |
| Soccer players | 796.334 092 |
| Social acceptance | 302.14 |
| Social action | 361.2 |
| Social adjustment | 302.14 |
| Social anthropologists | 306.092 |
| Social anthropology | 306 |
| Social attitudes | 303.38 |

Social behavior — 302
*see Manual at* 302–307 vs. 156
Social behavior (Animals) — 591.56
Social breakdown — 361.1
Social casework — 361.32
Social causes of war — 355.027 4
  World War I — 940.311 4
  World War II — 940.531 14
Social change — 303.4
Social choice — 302.13
Social classes — 305.5
            T1—086 2
  civil rights — 323.322
  customs — 390.2
  dress — 391.02
  dwellings — 392.360 86
  relations with government — 323.322
  religion — 200.862
    Christianity — 270.086 2
  social welfare — 362.892
  *see Manual at* 305.9 vs. 305.5
Social classification — 025.487
Social classification systems — 025.487
Social clubs — 367
Social conflict — 303.6
  influence on crime — 364.256
  public safety — 363.32
Social contract — 320.11
Social control — 303.33
Social credit money — 332.56
Social Credit Party of Canada — 324.271 05
Social customs — 390
  armed forces — 355.1
Social dancing — 793.3
Social decay — 303.45
Social democracy — 335.5
  economic system — 335.5
  political ideology — 320.531 5
Social democratic parties — 324.217 2
  international organizations — 324.172
Social Democratic Party of
  Austria — 324.243 607 2
Social Democratic Party of
  Germany — 324.243 072
Social Democratic Party of
  Switzerland — 324.249 407 2
Social Democratic Worker Party
  (Austria) — 324.243 602 7
Social deterioration — 303.45
Social determinants
  individual psychology — 155.234

Social dysfunction
  collective behavior — 302.17
  individual interactions — 302.542
  individual reactions — 302.54
Social education — 370.115
Social environment
  psychological influence — 155.92
Social equality — 305
  religion — 200.8
    Christianity — 270.08
    Judaism — 296.08
Social ethics — 170
  sociology — 303.372
  *see also* Ethical problems
Social evolution — 303.4
Social forecasts — 303.49
Social gerontology — 362.6
Social groups — 305
            T1—08
  influence on crime — 364.253
  religion — 200.8
    Christianity — 270.08
    Judaism — 296.08
  *see also* People
  *see Manual at* 306 vs. 305, 909,
    930–990
Social history — 306.09
  Algerian Revolution — 965.046 1
  American Revolution — 973.31
  Chaco War — 989.207 161
  Civil War (England) — 942.062 1
  Civil War (Spain) — 946.081 1
  Civil War (United States) — 973.71
  Crimean War — 947.073 81
  Falkland Islands War — 997.110 241
  Franco-German War — 943.082 1
  Hundred Years' War — 944.025 1
  Indo-Pakistan War, 1971 — 954.920 511
  Indochinese War — 959.704 11
  Iraq War, 2003– — 956.704 431
  Iraqi-Iranian Conflict — 955.054 21
  Korean War — 951.904 21
  Mexican War — 973.621
  Napoleonic Wars — 940.271
  Persian Gulf War, 1991 — 956.704 421
  South African War — 968.048 1
  Spanish-American War — 973.891
  Thirty Years' War — 940.241
  Vietnamese War — 959.704 31
  War of 1812 — 973.521
  War of the Pacific — 983.061 61
  World War I — 940.31
  World War II — 940.531
Social identity — 305

Social indexing                               025.487
Social inequality                             305
Social influence                              302.13
    psychology                                155.92
Social innovation                             303.484
Social insects                                595.79
    physiology of caste                       571.882 157 9
Social institutions                           306
    *see Manual at* 302–307 vs. 320
Social insurance                              368.4
    law                                       344.02
    public administration                     353.54
Social interaction                            302
Social justice                                303.372
    law                                       340.115
Social law                                    344.01
Social learning                               303.32
Social legislation                            344.01
Social market economy                         330.126
Social mobility                               305.513
Social movements                              303.484
Social networks                               302.3
Social norms                                  306
    social control                            303.37
Social ownership of means of
    production
    Marxian theory                            335.41
Social participation                          302.14
Social pathology                              361.1
    collective behavior                       302.17
    individual interactions                   302.542
    influence on crime                        364.256
    *see Manual at* 301–307 vs.
        361–365
Social perception                             302.12
Social planning                               361.25
Social policy                                 361.25
    governmental                              361.61
Social prediction                             303.49
Social pressure                               303.3
    executive management                      658.409 5
Social problems                               361.1
    arts                                      700.455 6
                                    T3C—355 6
    influence on crime                        364.256
    literature                                808.803 556
        history and criticism                 809.933 556
        specific literatures      T3B—080 355 6
            history and
                criticism         T3B—093 556
    social theology                           201.76
        Buddhism                              294.337 6
        Christianity                          261.83
        Hinduism                              294.517 6

Social problems
    social theology (continued)
        Islam                                 297.27
        Judaism                               296.38
        welfare                               362.042
    *see Manual at* 301–307 vs.
        361–365; *also at* 361 vs.
        362–363; *also at* 361–365;
        *also at* 361–365 vs. 353.5;
        *also at* 362–363 vs. 364.1;
        *also at* 363 vs. 344.02–.05,
        353–354
Social processes                              303
    *see Manual at* 302–307 vs. 320
Social progress                               303.44
Social protest                                303.6
Social psychology                             302
    *see Manual at* 302–307 vs. 150,
        T1—019
Social reform                                 303.484
    *see also* Reform movements
Social reformers                              303.484 092
    welfare                                   361.240 92
Social relations                              302
    ethics                                    177
        *see also* Ethical problems
Social responsibility
    educational objective                     370.115
    executive management                      658.408
Social role                                   302.15
Social sciences                               300
    descriptive research                      300.723
    information systems                       025.063
    public administrative support             352.745
    *see Manual at* 300 vs. 600
Social scientists                             300.92
Social security                               362
    government-sponsored
        insurance                             368.4
        law                                   344.02
        old-age and survivors                 368.43
            law                               344.023
        public administration                 353.54
    public administration                     353.5
    social welfare                            362
        law                                   344.032
    United States                             368.430 097 3
        law                                   344.730 23
    *see also* Insurance
Social security tax                           336.249
    accounting                                657.46
    law                                       343.052 42
    public finance                            336.249

| | |
|---|---|
| Social services | 361 |
|   *see also* Welfare services | |
| Social skills | 302.14 |
|   life skills | 646.76 |
|   primary education | 372.374 |
|   social psychology | 302.14 |
| Social stratification | 305 |
|   social classes | 305.512 |
| Social studies | 300 |
|   primary education | 372.89 |
| Social survey methodology | 300.723 |
| Social tagging | 025.487 |
| Social teaching of the Church | 261 |
| Social themes | |
|   arts | 700.455 |
|               T3C—355 | |
|   folklore | 398.275 |
|     history and criticism | 398.355 |
|   literature | 808.803 55 |
|     history and criticism | 809.933 55 |
|     specific literatures | T3B—080 355 |
|       history and | |
|         criticism | T3B—093 55 |
| Social theology | 201.7 |
|   Buddhism | 294.337 |
|   Christianity | 261 |
|     *see Manual at* 241 vs. 261.8 | |
|   Hinduism | 294.517 |
|   Islam | 297.27 |
|   Judaism | 296.38 |
| Social understanding | 302.12 |
| Social values | 303.372 |
| Social welfare | 361 |
|   *see also* Welfare services | |
| Social welfare reformers | 361.240 92 |
| Social work | 361.3 |
| Social workers | 361.309 2 |
| Socialism | 335 |
|   economics | 335 |
|   political ideology | 320.531 |
|   sociology | 306.345 |
|   *see Manual at* 335 vs. 306.345, | |
|     320.53 | |
| Socialist communities | 307.77 |
| Socialist ethics | 171.7 |
| Socialist International | 324.174 |
| Socialist Labor Party (U.S.) | 324.273 7 |
| Socialist parties | 324.217 4 |
|   international organizations | 324.174 |
| Socialist Party (U.S.) | 324.273 7 |
| Socialist Party of Italian Workers | |
|   (1893–1895) | 324.245 027 |
| Socialist Party of Italian Workers | |
|   (1925–1927) | 324.245 027 |
| Socialist Party of Italian Workers | |
|   (1947–1951) | 324.245 072 2 |
| Socialist Party of Proletarian | |
|   Unity (Italy : 1943–1947) | 324.245 074 2 |
| Socialist Party of Proletarian | |
|   Unity (Italy : 1947–1951) | 324.245 074 |
| Socialist Unity Party of Germany | 324.243 075 |
| Socialist Worker Party | |
|   (Switzerland) | 324.249 407 5 |
| Socialist Workers Party (U.S.) | 324.273 7 |
| Socialists | 335.009 2 |
| Socialization | 303.32 |
| Socially disadvantaged children | 305.230 869 4 |
|   home care | 649.156 7 |
|   psychology | 155.456 7 |
|   social group | 305.230 869 4 |
| Socially disadvantaged people | 305.56 |
|               T1—086 94 | |
|   government programs | 353.53 |
|   libraries for | 027.6 |
|   religion | 200.869 4 |
|   social group | 305.56 |
|   social welfare | 362 |
|     public administration | 353.53 |
| Socially responsible investments | 332.604 2 |
| Societies | 060 |
|   fraternal organizations | 369 |
|   *see also* Nonprofit | |
|     organizations | |
| Society | 301 |
| Society Islands | T2—962 1 |
| Society of Friends | 289.6 |
|   biography | 289.609 2 |
|   church government | 262.096 |
|     parishes | 254.096 |
|   church law | 262.989 6 |
|   doctrines | 230.96 |
|     catechisms and creeds | 238.96 |
|   general councils | 262.596 |
|   guides to Christian life | 248.489 6 |
|   missions | 266.96 |
|   moral theology | 241.049 6 |
|   persecution of | 272.8 |
|   public worship | 264.096 |
|   religious associations | 267.189 6 |
|   religious education | 268.896 |
|   seminaries | 230.073 96 |
|   theology | 230.96 |
| Society of Jesus | 255.53 |
|   church history | 271.53 |
| Society of the Cincinnati | 369.13 |
| Socinianism | 289.1 |

| | |
|---|---|
| Sociobiology | 304.5 |
| animal behavior | 591.56 |
| biological ecology | 577.8 |
| ethical systems | 171.7 |
| human behavior | 304.5 |
| *see Manual at* 302–307 vs. 156 | |
| Socioeconomic classes | 305.5 |
| | T1—086 2 |
| *see also* Social classes | |
| Socioeconomic problems | 361.1 |
| influence on crime | 364.256 |
| social theology | 201.76 |
| Christianity | 261.8 |
| Islam | 297.27 |
| *see Manual at* 297.26–.27 | |
| Judaism | 296.38 |
| Sociolinguistics | 306.44 |
| Sociological fiction | 808.838 3 |
| history and criticism | 809.383 |
| specific literatures | T3B—308 3 |
| individual authors | T3A—3 |
| Sociological jurisprudence | 340.115 |
| Sociologists | 301.092 |
| Sociology | 301 |
| arts | 700.455 2 |
| | T3C—355 2 |
| literature | 808.803 552 |
| history and criticism | 809.933 552 |
| specific literatures | T3B—080 355 2 |
| history and | |
| criticism | T3B—093 552 |
| *see Manual at* 301–307 vs. | |
| 361–365 | |
| Sociology and religion | |
| Christianity | 261.5 |
| Islam | 297.27 |
| Judaism | 296.38 |
| Sociology of knowledge | 306.42 |
| Sociology of religion | 306.6 |
| *see Manual at* 305.6 vs. 305.92, | |
| 306.6 | |
| Sociometry | 302.015 195 |
| Sociopathic personality | |
| medicine | 616.858 2 |
| *see also* Mental disorders | |
| Sockets | |
| electrical engineering | 621.319 24 |
| Socks | |
| commercial technology | 687.3 |
| home sewing | 646.42 |
| Socorro County (N.M.) | T2—789 62 |
| Socotrans | T5—929 |
| Socratic philosophy | 183.2 |
| Soda niter | |
| mineralogy | 549.732 |
| Soda process | |
| wood pulp | 676.124 |
| Sodalities | 267 |
| Sodas (Chemicals) | 546.382 2 |
| chemical engineering | 661.32 |
| Södermanland landskap | |
| (Sweden) | T2—487 2 |
| Södermanlands län | |
| (Sweden) | T2—487 2 |
| Sodium | |
| applied nutrition | 613.285 22 |
| biochemistry | 572.523 82 |
| humans | 612.015 24 |
| chemical engineering | 661.038 2 |
| chemistry | 546.382 |
| economic geology | 553.499 |
| metabolism | |
| human physiology | 612.392 4 |
| metallurgy | 669.725 |
| organic chemistry | |
| applied | 661.895 |
| Sodium bicarbonate | 546.382 22 |
| chemical engineering | 661.323 |
| Sodium carbonate | 546.382 24 |
| chemical engineering | 661.324 |
| Sodium chloride | 553.632 |
| chemistry | 546.382 24 |
| *see also* Salt (Sodium chloride) | |
| Sodium-free salt | |
| food technology | 664.4 |
| Sodium hydroxide | 546.382 22 |
| chemical engineering | 661.322 |
| Sodium nitrate | 553.64 |
| Sodium-restricted diet | |
| health | 613.285 223 |
| Sodium-vapor lighting | 621.327 6 |
| Sodomy | 306.77 |
| criminology | 364.153 6 |
| criminal law | 345.025 36 |
| sociology | 306.77 |
| Soeharto | |
| Indonesian history | 959.803 7 |
| Soekarno | |
| Indonesian history | 959.803 5 |
| Soekarnoputri, Megawati | |
| Indonesian history | 959.804 1 |
| Sofala (Mozambique : | |
| Province) | T2—679 4 |
| Sofas | 645.4 |
| manufacturing technology | 684.12 |
| *see also* Furniture | |
| Soferim | 296.461 509 2 |

Soferim (Talmudic)    296.120 092
Sofia (Bulgaria)    T2—499 9
Sofia (Bulgaria : Oblast)    T2—499 8
Sofiĭska (Bulgaria : Oblast)    T2—499 8
Soft drinks    641.26
   *see also* Nonalcoholic
     beverages
Soft-fiber crops    633.5
Soft rock    781.66
Soft-shelled turtles    597.926
Soft toys
   making    688.724
     handicrafts    745.592 4
     technology    688.724
Soft-winged flower beetles    595.763
Softball    796.357 8
Softening (Water treatment)    628.166 6
Software    005.3
   *see also* Computer programs
   *see Manual at* 004 vs. 005
Software compatibility    005
Software documentation
   preparation    005.15
   text    005.3
Software engineering    005.1
Software maintenance    005.16
Software measurement    005.14
Software metrics    005.14
Software packages    005.3
Software piracy    364.166 2
   law    345.026 62
Software portability    005
Software reliability    005
Software testing    005.14
Software verification    005.14
Softwoods
   forestry    634.975
   lumber    674.144
Sofʹia Alekseevna, Regent of
   Russia
   Russian history    947.049
Sogdian language    491.53
      T6—915 3
Sogdian literature    891.53
Sogdiana    T2—396
Soglo, Nicéphore Dieudonné
   Beninese history    966.830 52
Sogn og Fjordane fylke
   (Norway)    T2—483 8
Soil    631.4
   *see also* Soils
Soil acidity    631.42
Soil alkalinity    631.42

Soil biochemistry
   soil science    631.417
Soil biology    578.757
   agriculture    631.46
Soil chemistry    631.41
Soil classification    631.44
Soil compaction    624.151 363
Soil conditioners    631.82
   chemical engineering    668.64
Soil conservation    333.731 6
   agriculture    631.45
   land economics    333.731 6
   law    346.046 731 6
   public administration    354.343 4
Soil consolidation    624.151 362
Soil ecology    577.57
Soil erosion    551.302
   agriculture    631.45
   engineering    627.5
   geology    551.302
   *see also* Erosion
Soil factors
   floriculture    635.955
Soil fertility    631.422
Soil formation    551.305
   frost action    551.38
Soil mechanics    624.151 36
   agriculture    631.433
   engineering geology    624.151 36
   railroad engineering    625.122
   road engineering    625.732
Soil moisture    631.432
Soil physics
   soil science    631.43
Soil pollution    363.739 6
   law    344.046 34
   public administration    354.343 5
   social welfare    363.739 6
   technology    628.55
   *see also* Pollution
Soil science    631.4
Soil stabilization    624.151 363
Soil surveys    631.47
   agriculture    631.47
   engineering    624.151 7
Soil temperature    631.436
Soil texture
   agriculture    631.433
   conditioners    631.826
Soil working    631.51
   equipment manufacturing
     technology    681.763 1
Soilless culture    631.585

| | |
|---|---|
| Soils | 631.4 |
| | T2—148 |
| agriculture | 631.4 |
| biology | 578.757 |
| ecology | 577.57 |
| engineering geology | 624.151 |
| materials science | 620.191 |
| petrology | 552.5 |
| railroad engineering | 625.122 |
| road engineering | 625.732 |
| Sojas | 583.74 |
| *see also* Soybeans | |
| Sōka Gakkai | 294.392 8 |
| Sokoto State (Nigeria) | T2—669 62 |
| Sokotrans | T5—929 |
| Sokotri language | 492.9 |
| | T6—929 |
| Sokotri literature | 892.9 |
| Sokotri people | T5—929 |
| Solanaceae | 583.952 |
| Solano County (Calif.) | T2—794 52 |
| Solar batteries | 621.312 44 |
| Solar cells | 621.312 44 |
| Solar collectors | 621.472 |
| Solar day | 529.1 |
| Solar desalinization | 628.167 25 |
| Solar energy | 333.792 3 |
| architectural consideration | 720.472 4 |
| astronomy | 523.72 |
| economics | 333.792 3 |
| engineering | 621.47 |
| law | 343.092 8 |
| public administration | 354.48 |
| Solar energy-powered automobiles | |
| engineering | 629.229 5 |
| Solar engineers | 621.470 92 |
| Solar engines | 621.473 |
| automotive | 629.250 8 |
| ships | 623.872 7 |
| Solar flares | 523.75 |
| Solar furnaces | 621.477 |
| Solar granulation | 523.74 |
| Solar heating | 621.47 |
| buildings | 697.78 |
| Solar houses | 643.2 |
| architecture | 728.370 472 |
| home economics | 643.2 |
| *see also* Dwellings | |
| Solar interior | 523.76 |
| Solar prominences | 523.75 |
| Solar radiation | 523.72 |
| meteorology | 551.527 1 |
| Solar system | 523.2 |
| | T2—99 |
| Solar wind | 523.58 |
| Soldering | 671.56 |
| decorative arts | 739.14 |
| sculpture | 731.41 |
| Soldering equipment | 621.977 |
| Soldier beetles | 595.764 4 |
| Soldier flies | 595.773 |
| Soldierfishes | 597.64 |
| Soldierly qualities | 355.13 |
| Soldiers | 355.009 2 |
| law | 343.01 |
| civil rights | 342.085 |
| law of war | 341.67 |
| Soldiers of fortune | 355.354 |
| Sole bargaining rights | 331.889 6 |
| Sole proprietorships | 338.72 |
| *see also* Proprietorships | |
| Sole traders | |
| law | 346.068 |
| Solenodons | 599.33 |
| Solenogastres | 594.2 |
| Soles (Fishes) | 597.69 |
| cooking | 641.692 |
| food | 641.392 |
| Soleure (Switzerland : Canton) | T2—494 35 |
| Solicitors (Lawyers) | 340.092 |
| Solid dynamics | 531.3 |
| Solid foams | 541.345 13 |
| chemical engineering | 660.294 513 |
| Solid-gas interfaces | 530.417 |
| Solid geometry | 516.23 |
| analytic | 516.33 |
| Euclidean | 516.23 |
| Solid-liquid interfaces | 530.417 |
| Solid mechanics | 531 |
| engineering | 620.105 |
| Solid particles | 530.413 |
| classical mechanics | 531.16 |
| solid-state physics | 530.413 |
| Solid propellants | 662.26 |
| aircraft | 629.134 351 |
| military engineering | 623.452 6 |
| spacecraft | 629.475 24 |
| Solid solutions | |
| metallurgy | 669.94 |
| Solid-state chemistry | 541.042 1 |
| Solid-state lasers | 621.366 1 |
| Solid-state physics | 530.41 |
| *see Manual at* 548 vs. 530.41 | |
| Solid-state storage | 004.568 |
| engineering | 621.397 68 |

| | | | |
|---|---|---|---|
| Solid wastes | 363.728 5 | Solution chemistry | 541.34 |
| law | 344.046 22 | applied | 660.294 |
| social services | 363.728 5 | Solution mining | 622.22 |
| technology | 628.44 | Solutions (Pharmaceuticals) | |
| rural | 628.744 | pharmaceutical chemistry | 615.19 |
| *see also* Waste control | | Solutrean culture | 930.128 |
| Solidification | 536.42 | Solvent abuse | 362.299 3 |
| metallurgy | 669.94 | Solvent extraction | |
| Solids | | chemical engineering | 660.284 248 |
| chemical engineering | 660.041 | Solvents | 541.348 2 |
| expansion and contraction | 536.414 | chemical engineering | 660.294 82 |
| geometry | 516.156 | organic | 661.807 |
| heat transfer | 536.23 | Solway Firth (England and | 551.461 337 |
| mechanics | 531 | Scotland) | T2—163 37 |
| sound transmission | 534.22 | Sólyom, László | |
| specific heat | 536.63 | Hungarian history | 943.905 43 |
| state of matter | 530.41 | Somali | T5—935 4 |
| Solifugae | 595.48 | Somali Democratic Republic | 967.73 |
| Solihull (England : | | | T2—677 3 |
| Metropolitan Borough) | T2—424 97 | people | T5—935 4 |
| Solipsism | | Somali-Ethiopian Conflict, | |
| epistemology | 121.2 | 1978–1991 | 963.071 |
| Solitaire | 795.43 | Somali kelel (Ethiopia) | T2—632 |
| Solitary confinement | 365.644 | Somali language | 493.54 |
| Solitude | | | T6—935 4 |
| psychology | 155.92 | Somali literature | 893.54 |
| religious practice | 204.47 | Somalia | 967.73 |
| Christianity | 248.47 | | T2—677 3 |
| Solo instruments | 786–788 | Somaliland | 967.7 |
| bands and orchestras | 784 | | T2—677 |
| chamber ensembles | 785 | Somalis | T5—935 4 |
| Solo voices | 783.2 | Somaschi | 255.54 |
| Sologne (France) | T2—445 3 | church history | 271.54 |
| Sololá (Guatemala : Dept.) | T2—728 164 | Somatization disorder | |
| Solomon, King of Israel | | medicine | 616.852 4 |
| Biblical leader | 222.530 92 | *see also* Mental disorders | |
| Palestinian history | 933.02 | Somatoform disorders | |
| Solomon Islands | 995.93 | medicine | 616.852 4 |
| | T2—959 3 | *see also* Mental disorders | |
| Solomon River (Kan.) | T2—781 2 | Somatotypes | 599.949 |
| Solomon Sea | 551.461 476 | Somerset (England) | T2—423 8 |
| | T2—164 76 | Somerset County (Md.) | T2—752 23 |
| Solothurn (Switzerland) | T2—494 357 7 | Somerset County (Me.) | T2—741 22 |
| Solothurn (Switzerland : | | Somerset County (N.J.) | T2—749 44 |
| Canton) | T2—494 35 | Somerset County (Pa.) | T2—748 79 |
| Solothurn-Lebern | | Somerset East (South | |
| (Switzerland) | T2—494 357 | Africa : District) | T2—687 53 |
| Solpugida | 595.48 | Somerset Island (Nunavut) | T2—719 52 |
| Solubility | 541.342 | Somerset West (South | |
| chemical engineering | 660.294 2 | Africa : District) | T2—687 34 |
| Soluble soaps | 668.124 | Somervell County (Tex.) | T2—764 521 |
| Solutes | 541.348 3 | Somme (France) | T2—442 62 |
| chemical engineering | 660.294 83 | Somme, 1st Battle of the, 1916 | 940.427 2 |

Sömmerda (Germany :
  Landkreis)     T2—432 24
Somnambulism
  medicine     616.849 8
  *see also* Nervous system
    diseases — humans
  psychology     154.64
Somogy Megye (Hungary)   T2—439 7
Sơn La (Vietnam :
  Province)     T2—597 1
Son of God (Christian doctrines)   231.2
Sonar     621.389 5
  marine navigation     623.893 8
Sonata form     784.183
Sonata-rondos     781.824
  instrumental     784.182 4
Sonatas     784.183
Sonatinas     784.183 2
Sønderjyllands amt
  (Denmark)     T2—489 5
Sondrio (Italy : Province)   T2—452 5
  ancient     T2—372 266
Song cycles     782.47
  choral and mixed voices     782.547
  single voices     783.094 7
Song dynasty     951.024
Song of Solomon     223.9
Song of Songs     223.9
Song of the Three Children
  (Bible)     229.6
Songbirds     598.8
  animal husbandry     636.68
  *see Manual at* 598.824–.88
Songe languages     496.393
    T6—963 93
Songhai (African people)   T5—965
Songhai Empire     966.201 8
    T2—662
Songhai language     496.5
    T6—965
Songhai literature     896.5
Songs     782.42
  choral and mixed voices     782.542
  folk literature     398.87
  single voices     783.094 2
Songs without words     784.189 6
Songwriting     782.421 3
Songye languages     496.393
    T6—963 93
Sonic booms
  aeronautics     629.132 304
Sonics
  engineering     620.2

Sonneberg (Germany :
  Landkreis)     T2—432 26
Sonneratiaceae     583.763
Sonnets     808.814 2
  history and criticism     809.142
  specific literatures     T3B—104 2
  individual authors     T3A—1
Sonography
  medicine     616.075 43
Sonoma County (Calif.)   T2—794 18
Sonora (Mexico : State)   T2—721 7
Sonora Island (B.C.)   T2—711 1
Sonoran Desert     T2—721 7
  Arizona     T2—791 7
  Mexico     T2—721 7
Sonoran languages     497.454
    T6—974 54
Sons     306.874
    T1—085 4
Sons of the American Revolution   369.13
Sonsonate (El Salvador :
  Dept.)     T2—728 413
Sooke (B.C.)     T2—711 28
Sooke Lake (B.C.)     T2—711 28
Sophia, Regent of Russia
  Russian history     947.049
Sophistic philosophy     183.1
Sophonias (Biblical book)   224.96
Sopranino recorders     788.363
  *see also* Woodwind instruments
Soprano recorders     788.364
  *see also* Woodwind instruments
Soprano saxophones     788.72
  *see also* Woodwind instruments
Soprano voices     782.66
  children's     782.76
    choral and mixed voices     782.76
    single voices     783.76
  general works     782.66
    choral and mixed voices     782.66
    single voices     783.66
  women's     782.66
    choral and mixed voices     782.66
    single voices     783.66
Sør-Trøndelag fylke
  (Norway)     T2—484 1
Sorbet     641.863
  commercial processing     637.4
  home preparation     641.863
Sorbian language     491.88
    T6—918 8
Sorbian literature     891.88
Sorbs     T5—918 8

| | | | |
|---|---|---|---|
| Sorcerers (Religious leaders) | 200.92 | Soteriology (continued) | |
| biography | 200.92 | Judaism | 296.32 |
| role and function | 206.1 | *see also* Humans — religion | |
| *see Manual at* 200.92 and | | Sotho (African people) | T5—963 977 |
| 201–209, 292–299 | | Sotho languages | 496.397 7 |
| Sordariales | 579.567 | | T6—963 977 |
| Sorex | 599.336 2 | Sotho-Tswana languages | 496.397 7 |
| Sorghum sugars | 641.336 2 | | T6—963 977 |
| commercial processing | 664.133 | Soto | 294.392 7 |
| food | 641.336 2 | Soufflés | 641.82 |
| *see also* Sugar | | Souk Ahras (Algeria : | |
| Sorghum syrup | 641.336 2 | Province) | T2—655 |
| commercial processing | 664.133 | Soul | 128.1 |
| food | 641.336 2 | philosophy | 128.1 |
| *see also* Sugar | | religion | 202.2 |
| Sorghums | 584.92 | Christianity | 233.5 |
| botany | 584.92 | Islam | 297.225 |
| forage crop | 633.257 4 | Judaism | 296.32 |
| grain crop | 633.174 | *see also* Humans — religion | |
| syrup crop | 633.62 | Soul food cooking | 641.592 960 73 |
| Sorgo | 633.62 | Soul music | 781.644 |
| forage crop | 633.257 4 | songs | 782.421 644 |
| syrup crop | 633.62 | Sound | 534 |
| Soria (Spain : Province) | T2—463 55 | biophysics | 571.444 |
| Soriano (Uruguay : Dept.) | T2—895 27 | humans | 612.014 453 |
| Soricidae | 599.336 | cinematography | 777.53 |
| Sørlandet (Norway) | T2—483 | diagnosis | 616.075 44 |
| Sororities | 369.082 | engineering | 620.2 |
| education | 371.856 | musical element | 781.23 |
| Sorosilicates | | physics | 534 |
| mineralogy | 549.63 | therapeutic use | 615.83 |
| Sorrel (Polygonaceae) | 641.355 6 | videography | 777.53 |
| botany | 583.57 | Sound, The (Denmark and | 551.461 334 |
| cooking | 641.655 6 | Sweden) | T2—163 34 |
| food | 641.355 6 | Sound effects | 792.024 |
| garden crop | 635.56 | *see also* Special effects — | |
| Sorrento (Vic.) | T2—945 2 | dramatic performances | |
| Sorrow | 152.4 | Sound engineering | 620.2 |
| Sorsogon (Philippines : | | Sound engineers | 620.209 2 |
| Province) | T2—599 1 | Sound-induced illness | |
| Sort algorithms | 005.741 | medicine | 616.989 6 |
| Sorting data | 005.741 | *see also* Environmental | |
| Sorting machines | | diseases — humans | |
| manufacturing technology | 681.14 | Sound processing | |
| Soshanguve (South Africa : | | computer science | 006.45 |
| District) | T2—682 28 | Sound-ranging devices | 621.389 5 |
| Sotah | 296.123 3 | communications engineering | 621.389 5 |
| Babylonian Talmud | 296.125 3 | marine navigation | 623.893 8 |
| Mishnah | 296.123 3 | Sound recording systems | 621.389 3 |
| Palestinian Talmud | 296.124 3 | Sound recordings | 384 |
| Sotalia | 599.538 | bibliographies | 011.38 |
| Soteriology | 202.2 | cataloging | 025.348 2 |
| Christianity | 234 | communications services | 384 |
| Islam | 297.22 | engineering | 621.389 32 |

Sound recordings (continued)
  instructional use | 371.333 2
  library treatment | 025.178 2
  music | 780
    cover illustration | 741.66
    treatises | 780.266
    *see Manual at* 780.26
  reviews | 028.138
Sound reproducing systems | 621.389 3
Sound synchronization
  motion pictures | 777.53
Sound synthesis
  computer science | 006.5
    T1—028 565
    engineering | 621.399
Sounding devices | 621.389 5
  communications engineering | 621.389 5
  marine navigation | 623.893 8
Soundproofing | 620.23
  aircraft | 629.134 42
  buildings | 693.834
Soupfin sharks | 597.34
Soups | 641.813
Sour gums (Plants) | 583.84
Sour milk cheeses | 641.373 56
  cooking | 641.673 56
  food | 641.373 56
  processing | 637.356
Sources (Quebec) | T2—714 573
Souris River | T2—784 6
Sourwood | 583.66
Sousaphones | 788.98
  *see also* Brass instruments
Souss Massa-Draâ
  (Morocco) | T2—646 6
South Africa | 968
    T2—68
South African Blacks | T5—968
South African literature
  Afrikaans | 839.36
  Bantu languages | 896.39
  English | 820
South African Republic | 968.204 5
    T2—682
South African War, 1899–1902 | 968.048
  Great Britain | 968.048 31
  Orange Free State | 968.048 32
  South African Republic | 968.048 32
South Africans (Afrikaners) | T5—393 6
South Africans (British
  origin) | T5—28
South Africans (National
  group) | T5—968

South America | 980
    T2—8
  travel | 918.04
South American native languages | 498
    T6—98
South American native literatures | 898
South American native
  peoples | T5—98
South Arabian languages | 492.9
    T6—929
South Arabian literatures | 892.9
South Arabic peoples | T5—929
South Asia | 954
    T2—54
  ancient | 934
    T2—34
South Asian ancestry | T5—914
South Asian languages | T6—911
South Asian theater (World War
  II) | 940.542 5
South Asians | T5—914
South Atlantic Ocean | 551.461 35
    T2—163 5
South Atlantic States | 975
    T2—75
South Australia | T2—942 3
South Ayrshire (Scotland) | T2—414 64
South Bedfordshire
  (England) | T2—425 65
South Bend (Ind.) | T2—772 89
South Bucks (England) | T2—425 98
South Cambridgeshire
  (England) | T2—426 57
South Carolina | 975.7
    T2—757
South Caucasian languages | 499.968
    T6—999 68
South Central States | 976
    T2—76
South China Sea | 551.461 472
    T2—164 72
South Coast (South Africa) | T2—684 5
South Cotabato
  (Philippines) | T2—599 7
South Dakota | 978.3
    T2—783
South Derbyshire (England) | T2—425 19
South Dobruja | T2—499 4
South Downs (England) | T2—422 6
South Dravidian languages | 494.81
    T6—948 1
South Dravidian literatures | 894.81
South Dravidians | T5—948 1

South-East Sulawesi
(Indonesia)    T2—598 48
South frigid zone    T2—116
South Georgia and South
Sandwich Islands    T2—971 2
South Georgia Island    T2—971 2
South Glamorgan (Wales)    T2—429 87
South Gloucestershire
(England)    T2—423 91
South Halmahera-West New
Guinea languages    499.5
   T6—995
South Hams (England)    T2—423 592
South Herefordshire
(England)    T2—424 2
South Holland (England)    T2—425 39
South Holland
(Netherlands)    T2—492 38
South Island (N.Z.)    T2—937
South Kalimantan
(Indonesia)    T2—598 36
South Kesteven (England)    T2—425 38
South Khorāsān (Iran)    T2—559 2
South Korea    951.95
   T2—519 5
South Lakeland (England)    T2—427 83
South Lanarkshire
(Scotland)    T2—414 57
South Mbundu languages    496.399
   T6—963 99
South Ndebele (South
Africa)    T2—682 75
South Norfolk (England)    T2—426 19
South Northamptonshire
(England)    T2—425 59
South Orange (N.J.)    T2—749 33
South Orkney Islands    T2—989
South Osset (Georgia)    T2—475 8
South Oxfordshire
(England)    T2—425 79
South Pacific Ocean    551.461 48
   T2—164 8
South Pembrokeshire
(Wales)    T2—429 62
South Platte River (Colo.
and Neb.)    T2—788 7
South Pole    T2—989
South Ribble (England)    T2—427 67
South Saami language    494.572 2
   T6—945 722
South Saami literature    894.572 2
South Sámi language    494.572 2
   T6—945 722
South Sámi literature    894.572 2

South Sandwich Islands    T2—971 2
South Saskatchewan River
(Alta. and Sask.)    T2—712 42
South Semitic languages    492.8
   T6—928
South Semitic literatures    892.8
South Shetland Islands    T2—989
South Shropshire (England)    T2—424 57
South Slavic languages    491.81
   T6—918 1
South Slavic literatures    891.81
South Slavic peoples    T5—918 1
South Slavs    T5—918 1
South Somerset (England)    T2—423 89
South Staffordshire
(England)    T2—424 66
South Sulawesi (Indonesia)    T2—598 47
South Sumatra (Indonesia)    T2—598 16
South Taranaki District
(N.Z.)    T2—934 88
South temperate zone    T2—126
South Thompson River
(B.C.)    T2—711 72
South Tyneside (England)    T2—428 75
South Tyrol (Italy)    T2—453 83
South Tyrolean People's Party
(Italy)    324.245 084
South Vietnam (1954–1975)    959.770 43
   T2—597 7
South Waikato District
(N.Z.)    T2—933 63
South Wairarapa District
(N.Z.)    T2—936 6
South Wales    T2—429 4
South-West Africa    T2—688 1
South-Western Region
(China)    T2—513
South Wight (England :
Borough)    T2—422 8
South Yorkshire (England)    T2—428 2
Southampton (England)    T2—422 76
Southampton County (Va.)    T2—755 552
Southampton Island
(Nunavut)    T2—719 58
Southeast Asia    959
   T2—59
Southeast Asian languages    495
   T6—95
Southeast Asian literatures    895
Southeast Asian theater (World
War II)    940.542 59
Southeast Asians    T5—95
Southeast Atlantic Ocean    551.461 37
   T2—163 7

Southeast Pacific Ocean 551.461 41
  T2—164 1
Southeastern Asia 959
  T2—59
Southeastern Europe 949.6
  T2—496
  ancient 939.8
  T2—398
Southeastern States 975
  T2—75
Southend-on-Sea (England) T2—426 795
Southern Aegean (Greece) T2—495 85
Southern Africa 968
  T2—68
Southern Alps (N.Z.) T2—937 1
Southern Bantu languages 496.397
  T6—963 97
Southern Baptist Convention 286.132
  *see also* Baptists
Southern Britain 942
  T2—42
  ancient 936.2
  T2—362
Southern California T2—794 9
Southern Cameroons T2—671 1
Southern Darfur (Sudan :
  State) T2—627
Southern dynasties
  Chinese history 951.015
Southern England T2—422
Southern Europe 940
  T2—4
  ancient 938
  T2—38
Southern Finland (Finland) T2—489 71
Southern France T2—448
Southern fur seals 599.797 38
Southern Hemisphere T2—181 4
Southern Highlands
  Province (Papua New
  Guinea) T2—956 1
Southern India T2—548
Southern Italy 945.7
  T2—457
  ancient T2—377
Southern Kordofan (Sudan) T2—628
Southern Leyte
  (Philippines) T2—599 5
Southern Low Countries 949.3
  T2—493
Southern Min dialects 495.172 4
  T6—951 7

Southern Nations,
  Nationalities, and
  Peoples Federal State
  (Ethiopia) T2—633
Southern Paiute Indians T5—974 576 9
Southern Paiute language 497.457 69
  T6—974 576 9
Southern Province (Zambia) T2—689 4
Southern question (Italy) 945.709
Southern Rhodesia 968.910 2
  T2—689 1
Southern Sotho language 496.397 72
  T6—963 977 2
Southern Sotho literature 896.397 72
Southern Sporades (Greece) T2—495 87
  ancient T2—391 6
Southern States 975
  T2—75
  War of 1812 973.523 8
Southern Tiwa Indians T5—974 97
Southern Tiwa language 497.497
  T6—974 97
Southern Turkic languages 494.36
  T6—943 6
Southern Uplands
  (Scotland) T2—413 7
Southern Vietnam T2—597 7
Southern Yemen 953.35
  T2—533 5
Southern Yemenis T5—927 533 5
Southland District (N.Z.) T2—939 6
Southland Region (N.Z.) T2—939 6
Southport (Qld.) T2—943 2
Southwark (London,
  England) T2—421 64
Southwest, New 979
  T2—79
Southwest, Old 976
  T2—76
Southwest jazz 781.653
Southwest Pacific Ocean 551.461 47
  T2—164 7
Southwest Turkic languages 494.36
  T6—943 6
Southwestern Ontario T2—713 2
Soutpansberg (South
  Africa : District) T2—682 57
Soutpansberg (South
  Africa : Mountains) T2—682 57
Sovereigntist parties 324.218 4
Sovereignty 320.15
  law of nations 341.26

Sovereignty of God 212.7
  Christianity 231.7
  comparative religion 202.112
  Judaism 296.311 2
  philosophy of religion 212.7
Soviet Central Asia 958.4
  T2—584
Soviet communism 335.43
  economics 335.43
  political ideology 320.532 2
Soviet people T5—917
Soviet Union 947.084
  T2—47
  Asia 957
  T2—57
Soviets (People) T5—917
Sow bugs 595.372
Soweto (South Africa) T2—682 21
Soweto Uprising, 1976 968.062 7
Sowing 631.531
Soy oil 641.356 55
  cooking 641.656 55
  food 641.356 55
  food technology 664.368
Soyas 583.74
  *see also* Soybeans
Soybean flour 664.726
Soybean glue 668.33
Soybean meal 664.726
Soybean milk
  commercial processing 663.64
Soybeans 583.74
  agricultural economics 338.173 34
  botany 583.74
  commercial processing 664.805 655
    economics 338.476 647 26
    technology 664.726
  cooking 641.656 55
  field crop 633.34
  food 641.356 55
  garden crop 635.655
Soyfoods
  commercial processing
    technology 664.726
Sozialdemokratische
  Arbeiterpartei (Austria) 324.243 602 7
Sozialdemokratische Partei der
  Schweiz 324.249 407 2
Sozialdemokratische Partei
  Deutschlands 324.243 072
Sozialdemokratische Partei
  Österreichs 324.243 607 2
Sozialistische Arbeiterpartei
  (Switzerland) 324.249 407 5

Sozialistische Einheitspartei
  Deutschlands 324.243 075
Space T2—19
  astronomy 520
  law of nations 341.47
  philosophy 114
  physics 530.1
  resource economics 333.94
  *see Manual at* T2—99 vs.
    T2—19; *also at* 520 vs.
    500.5, 523.1, 530.1, 919.9
Space (Area)
  arts 701.8
    drawing 741.018
Space and time 530.11
  philosophy 115
  physics 530.11
Space art 709.040 7
  sculpture 735.230 479
Space artillery
  engineering 623.419
Space biology 571.091 9
Space cinematography 777.6
Space colonies
  engineering 629.442
Space communications
  engineering 621.382 38
  radio engineering 621.384 197
Space engineering 620.419
Space exploration
  unmanned 629.435
Space facilities
  military engineering 623.69
Space flight 387.8
  engineering 629.41
  transportation services 387.8
  *see Manual at* 629.43, 629.45
    vs. 559.9, 919.904
Space forces (Military science) 358.8
Space forces personnel 358.809 2
Space hazards
  engineering 629.416
Space heaters 697.2
Space industrialization
  in extraterrestrial worlds 338.099 9
Space laboratories
  engineering 629.442
Space law 341.47
Space mail 383.144
  *see also* Postal service
Space medicine 616.980 214
Space perception
  psychology 153.752
  visual perception 152.142

Space photography 778.35
  military engineering 623.72
Space physiology 571.091 9
  humans 612.014 5
Space ports
  spacecraft 629.478
Space probes 629.435
Space psychology 155.966
Space rights
  sale and rental 333.339
  zoning 333.771 7
    law 346.045
Space sciences 500.5
  law 344.095 2
  public administrative support 352.745
Space shuttle 387.8
  engineering 629.441
  transportation services 387.8
  *see also* Space transportation
Space stations 629.442
Space suits 629.477 2
Space surveying 526.982
Space telescopes 522.291 9
Space-time 530.11
  philosophy 115
  physics 530.11
Space transportation 387.8
  engineering 629.4
  law 343.097 9
  public administration 354.79
  transportation services 387.8
Space transportation safety 363.124
  *see also* Transportation safety
Space transportation workers 387.809 2
Space videography 777.6
Space walks 629.458 4
Space warfare 358.8
Spacecraft
  engineering 629.47
  military engineering 623.749
  psychological influence 155.966
Spacecraft accidents 363.124
  *see also* Transportation safety
Spacecraft gunnery 623.556
Spacecraft rendezvous
  manned space flight 629.458 3
Spaces (Mathematics) 516
  combinatorial topology 514.224
  geometry 516
Spadefoots 597.86
Spaghetti 641.822
  commercial processing 664.755
  home preparation 641.822

Spain 946
    T2—46
  ancient 936.6
    T2—366
Spalacidae 599.35
Spalding County (Ga.) T2—758 443
Spaniards T5—61
Spaniels 636.752 4
Spanish T5—61
Spanish America 980
    T2—8
Spanish-American literature 860
Spanish-American War, 1898 973.89
  societies 369.181
Spanish Americans T5—68
Spanish Armada, 1588 942.055
Spanish folk music 781.626 1
Spanish folk songs 782.421 626 1
Spanish Guinea T2—671 8
Spanish language 460
    T6—61
  foreign language instruction
    primary education 372.656 1
Spanish literature 860
Spanish Merino sheep 636.366
Spanish-Moroccan War,
  1859–1860 964.03
Spanish Morocco T2—642
Spanish moss 584.85
Spanish plums 641.344 4
  botany 583.77
  cooking 641.644 4
  food 641.344 4
Spanish Sahara T2—648
Spanish Succession, War of the,
  1701–1714 940.252 6
  North American history 973.25
Spanish West Africa T2—648
Spanners 621.972
Spar varnishes 667.79
Sparganiaceae 584.68
Sparganium 584.68
Sparidae 597.72
Spark control devices
  automotive 629.258
Spark-ignition engines 621.434
  automotive 629.250 4
  ships 623.872 34
Sparkling wine 641.222 4
  commercial processing 663.224
Sparrows 598.883
Sparrows (Fringillidae) 598.883
Sparrows (Passer) 598.887
Spars 623.862

| | |
|---|---|
| Sparta (Greece) | T2—495 22 |
| ancient | T2—389 |
| Spartan supremacy | 938.06 |
| Spartanburg County (S.C.) | T2—757 29 |
| Spas | |
| health | 613.122 |
| therapeutics | 615.853 |
| Spatial behavior | |
| human ecology | 304.23 |
| Spatial databases | |
| computer science | 005.753 |
| Spatial perception | |
| psychology | 153.752 |
| Spatial planning | |
| arts | 711 |
| Spatsizi River (B.C.) | T2—711 85 |
| SPD (German political party) | 324.243 072 |
| Speaker recognition | |
| computer science | 006.454 |
| engineering | 621.399 4 |
| Speakers (Communications devices) | 621.382 84 |
| Speaking | |
| applied linguistics | 418 |
| specific languages | T4—83 |
| rhetoric | 808.5 |
| Speaking in tongues | 234.132 |
| Speaking voices | 782.96 |
| choral and mixed voices | 782.96 |
| single voices | 783.96 |
| Spearfishes | 597.78 |
| Spearfishing | 799.14 |
| Spears | 623.441 |
| art metalwork | 739.72 |
| sports | 799.202 82 |
| Special assessments | 336.2 |
| law | 343.042 |
| public administration | 352.44 |
| Special delivery | 383.183 |
| *see also* Postal service | |
| Special districts | 352.19 |
| Special drawing rights | 332.45 |
| Special education | 371.9 |
| federal aid | 379.121 6 |
| law | 344.079 1 |
| public administrative support | 353.89 |
| public support | 379.119 |
| Special effects | 792.024 |
| cinematography | 777.9 |
| dramatic performances | 792.024 |
| motion pictures | 791.430 24 |
| radio | 791.440 24 |
| stage | 792.024 |
| television | 791.450 24 |

| | |
|---|---|
| Special effects (continued) | |
| photography | 778.8 |
| videography | 777.9 |
| Special functions (Mathematics) | 515.5 |
| Special handling | 383.183 |
| *see also* Postal service | |
| Special-interest groups | |
| adult education | 374.22 |
| Special libraries | 026 |
| architecture | 727.83 |
| Special materials | |
| cataloging | 025.34 |
| library acquisitions | 025.28 |
| library treatment | 025.17 |
| Special multi-peril insurance | 368.094 |
| Special Olympics | 796.087 4 |
| Special-purpose paints | 667.69 |
| Special-purpose railroads | 385.5 |
| Special-purpose systems | |
| computer science | 006.2 |
| Special services (Armed forces) | 355.346 |
| Specialist schools | 373.241 |
| Specialization | |
| economics | 338.604 6 |
| international commerce | 382.104 2 |
| social process | 303.44 |
| Specialty advertising | 659.131 |
| Specialty papers | 676.284 |
| Specialty plywoods | 674.835 |
| *see also* Wood | |
| Specialty shops | 381.14 |
| *see also* Commerce | |
| Speciation (Biology) | 576.86 |
| Species | 578.012 |
| evolution | 576.86 |
| Species diversity | 577 |
| Species pools | 577 |
| Specific gravity | 531.14 |
| gas mechanics | 533.15 |
| liquid mechanics | 532.4 |
| solid mechanics | 531.54 |
| Specific heat | 536.6 |
| Specifications | T1—021 2 |
| production management | 658.562 |
| Specimen preservation | |
| biology | 570.752 |
| Speckled trout | 597.554 |
| SPECT (Tomography) | |
| medicine | 616.075 75 |
| Spectral regions | |
| engineering | 621.361 |
| light physics | 535.01 |
| Spectral theory | |
| operational calculus | 515.722 2 |

Spectral types (Stars) 523.87
Spectrochemical analysis 543.5
Spectrography 621.367
Spectrophotometry 543.55
Spectroscopes
  manufacturing technology 681.414
Spectroscopic binaries 523.842
Spectroscopy 543.5
  analytical chemistry 543.5
  astronomy 522.67
  engineering 621.361
  interpretation of nuclear
    structure 539.744
  nonoptical methods 543.6
  physics 535.84
  stars 523.87
Spectrum analysis 543.5
  physics 535.84
Speculation (Finance) 332.645
  guides 332.678
  stocks 332.632 28
Speculative psychology 150.19
Speech 302.224 2
  civil rights issues 323.443
  human physiology 612.78
  primary education 372.622
  psychology 153.6
  social interaction 302.224 2
Speech acts 401.452
  linguistics 401.452
    specific languages T4—014 52
  specific languages T4—014 52
Speech disorders
  medicine 616.855
  *see also* Communication
    disorders
  special education 371.914 2
Speech errors 401.9
  specific languages T4—019
Speech-impaired people T1—087
  special education 371.914 2
Speech output devices 006.54
  engineering 621.399
Speech perception 401.95
  specific languages T4—019
Speech processing
  computer science 006.454
Speech recognition
  computer science 006.454
  engineering 621.399 4
Speech synthesis
  computer science 006.54
  engineering 621.399

Speech therapy
  medicine 616.855 06
  special education 371.914 2
Speeches 080
  literary criticism 809.5
    theory 808.5
  literary history 809.5
  literature 808.85
    specific literatures T3B—5
      individual authors T3A—5
  rhetoric 808.5
Speechreading
  applied linguistics
    specific languages T4—895 4
Speechwriting 808.5
Speed control devices 621.812
Speed drills and tests
  keyboarding 652.307
  shorthand 653.15
Speed letters
  office use 651.75
Speed limits 388.314 4
  law 343.094 6
  urban 388.413 144
Speed reading 418.4
  specific languages T4—843 2
Speed skating 796.914
Speedboats 387.231
  design 623.812 31
  engineering 623.823 1
  handling 623.882 31
  transportation services 387.231
  *see also* Ships
Speedways
  automobile racing 796.720 68
Speller-dividers 413.1
  specific languages T4—31
Spellers 418
  specific languages T4—813
Spelling 411
  applied linguistics 418
    specific languages T4—813
    specific subjects T1—014
  linguistics 411
    specific languages T4—152
  primary education 372.632
  standard language 410
Spelling checkers (Computer
  programs) 005.52
Spelling reform 418
  specific languages T4—813
Spells (Occultism) 133.44
Spelthorne (England) T2—422 12
Spelunkers 796.525 092

| | |
|---|---|
| Spelunking | 796.525 |
| Spence Bay (Nunavut) | T2—719 55 |
| Spencer County (Ind.) | T2—772 31 |
| Spencer County (Ky.) | T2—769 455 |
| Spending | 339.47 |
| Sperm | 571.845 1 |
| Sperm banks | 362.178 3 |
| Sperm whale | 599.547 |
| Spermaceti | |
|   chemical engineering | 665.13 |
| Spermatocidal agents | |
|   health | 613.943 2 |
|   medicine | 618.182 |
|   pharmacokinetics | 615.766 |
| Spermatophyta | 580 |
|   *see also* Plants | |
| Spermophilus | 599.365 |
| Sperrin Mountains | |
|   (Northern Ireland) | T2—416 2 |
| Spey, River (Scotland) | T2—411 58 |
| Spezia (Province) | T2—451 83 |
| Sphaeropsidales | 579.55 |
| Sphagnales | 588.29 |
| Sphalerite | |
|   mineralogy | 549.32 |
| Sphecoidea | 595.798 |
| Sphenisciformes | 598.47 |
|   paleozoology | 568.4 |
| Sphenodontidae | 597.945 |
| Sphenophyllales | 561.72 |
| Sphenopsida | 587.2 |
|   paleobotany | 561.72 |
| Sphenopteris | 561.597 |
| Spheres | 516.154 |
| Spheres of influence | 327.114 |
| Spherical astronomy | 522.7 |
| Spherical harmonics | 515.53 |
| Spherical projection | |
|   technical drawing | 604.245 |
| Spherical trigonometry | 516.244 |
|   analytic | 516.34 |
| Sphygmomanometry | |
|   human physiology | 612.140 287 |
| Spices | 641.338 3 |
|   agriculture | 633.83 |
|   commercial processing | 664.53 |
|   cooking with | 641.638 3 |
|   economic botany | 581.632 |
|   food | 641.338 3 |
| Spider beetles | 595.763 |
| Spider fishes | 597.61 |
| Spider lilies | 635.934 34 |
|   botany | 584.34 |
|   floriculture | 635.934 34 |

| | |
|---|---|
| Spider monkeys | 599.858 |
| Spider venom | |
|   human toxicology | 615.942 |
| Spiderfishes | 597.61 |
| Spiderflowers (Capparaceae) | 583.64 |
| Spiders | 595.44 |
| Spiderworts | 584.86 |
| Spies | |
|   armed forces | 355.343 209 2 |
|   biography | 327.120 92 |
| Spike mosses | 587.9 |
| Spike rushes | 584.84 |
| Spillimacheen River (B.C.) | T2—711 68 |
| Spillways | 627.883 |
| Spin | |
|   nuclear physics | 539.725 |
|   solid dynamics | 531.34 |
| Spin-fishing | 799.126 |
| Spina bifida | |
|   medicine | 616.83 |
|     orthopedic aspects | 616.73 |
|     *see also* Musculoskeletal | |
|       diseases — humans | |
|     *see also* Nervous system | |
|       diseases — humans | |
|   surgery | 617.482 |
| Spinach | 641.354 1 |
|   botany | 583.53 |
|   commercial processing | 664.805 41 |
|   cooking | 641.654 1 |
|   food | 641.354 1 |
|   garden crop | 635.41 |
| Spinal anesthesia | |
|   surgery | 617.964 |
| Spinal column | |
|   fractures | |
|     medicine | 617.151 |
|   human anatomy | 611.711 |
|   human physiology | 612.751 |
|   medicine | 616.73 |
|   surgery | 617.471 |
| Spinal cord | 573.869 |
|   biology | 573.869 |
|   human anatomy | 611.82 |
|   human physiology | 612.83 |
|   medicine | 616.83 |
|   surgery | 617.482 |
|   *see also* Nervous system | |
| Spinal cord diseases | |
|   medicine | 616.83 |
|     *see also* Nervous system | |
|       diseases — humans | |

Spinal deformities
  medicine — 616.73
  *see also* Musculoskeletal
    diseases — humans
Spinal diseases
  medicine — 616.73
  *see also* Musculoskeletal
    diseases — humans
Spinal dysraphism
  medicine — 616.83
    orthopedic aspects — 616.73
    *see also* Musculoskeletal
      diseases — humans
    *see also* Nervous system
      diseases — humans
  surgery — 617.482
Spinal nerve diseases
  medicine — 616.856
    *see also* Nervous system
      diseases — humans
Spinal nerves
  human physiology — 612.819
  medicine — 616.856
Spine
  human anatomy — 611.711
  human physiology — 612.751
  medicine — 616.73
Spine fungi — 579.6
Spinel
  mineralogy — 549.526
Spinets — 786.4
  instrument — 786.419
  music — 786.4
  *see also* Keyboard instruments
Spink County (S.D.) — T2—783 217
Spinner dolphins — 599.534
Spinning (Fishing) — 799.126
Spinning machines
  textile technology — 677.028 52
Spinning textiles — 677.028 22
  arts — 746.12
  manufacturing technology — 677.028 22
Spinor algebras — 512.57
Spinor analysis — 515.63
Spinulosa — 593.93
Spiny anteaters — 599.29
Spiny eels — 597.7
Spiny-headed worms — 592.33
Spiny rats — 599.359
Spiny-rayed fishes — 597.64
Spiral gears — 621.833 3
Spirals — 516.152

Spireas — 635.933 73
  botany — 583.73
  floriculture — 635.933 73
Spires — 721.5
  architecture — 721.5
  construction — 690.15
Spirit leveling — 526.36
Spirit photography — 133.92
Spirit varnishes — 667.79
Spirit writings — 133.93
Spirits (Discarnate beings) — 133.9
  apparitions — 133.1
Spiritual beings — 202.1
  Christianity — 235
Spiritual direction — 206.1
  Christianity — 253.53
Spiritual exercises — 204.3
  Christianity — 248.3
Spiritual gifts
  Christian doctrines — 234.13
Spiritual healing
  medicine — 615.852
  religion — 203.1
    African religions — 299.613 1
    Christianity — 234.131
      miracles — 231.73
      miracles — 202.117
    Native American religions — 299.713 1
Spiritual life — 204.4
  Buddhism — 294.344 4
  Christianity — 248.4
  Hinduism — 294.544
  Islam — 297.57
  Judaism — 296.7
Spiritual renewal — 203
  Christianity — 269
  Islam — 297.3
Spiritual therapies
  medicine — 615.852
Spiritual warfare — 235.4
Spiritual world
  occultism — 133.901 3
Spiritualism — 133.9
  comparative religion — 202.1
  literature — 808.803 7
    history and criticism — 809.933 7
    specific literatures — T3B—080 37
      history and
        criticism — T3B—093 7
  philosophy — 141
  therapy
    medicine — 615.852 8
Spiritualists — 133.909 2

| | |
|---|---|
| Spirituality | 204 |
| Buddhism | 294.344 |
| Christianity | 248 |
| Hinduism | 294.54 |
| Islam | 297.57 |
| Judaism | 296.7 |
| Spirituals | 782.253 |
| choral and mixed voices | 782.525 3 |
| single voices | 783.092 53 |
| Spirochetes | 579.32 |
| Spitsbergen Island | |
| (Norway) | T2—981 |
| Spleen | 573.155 5 |
| biology | 573.155 5 |
| human anatomy | 611.41 |
| human physiology | 612.415 |
| medicine | 616.41 |
| surgery | 617.551 |
| *see also* Hematopoietic system | |
| Spleenworts | 587.3 |
| Splenic diseases | |
| medicine | 616.41 |
| *see also* Hematopoietic | |
| system diseases — | |
| humans | |
| Splicing | |
| ropes and cables | 623.888 2 |
| Splines | 511.422 3 |
| Split-level houses | |
| architecture | 728.373 |
| Split T formation | 796.332 22 |
| SPÖ (Austrian political party) | 324.243 607 2 |
| Spodumene | |
| mineralogy | 549.66 |
| Spokane (Wash.) | T2—797 37 |
| Spokane County (Wash.) | T2—797 37 |
| Spokane Indians | T5—979 43 |
| Spokane language | 497.943 |
| | T6—979 43 |
| Spondylitis | |
| medicine | 616.73 |
| *see also* Musculoskeletal | |
| diseases — humans | |
| Sponges | 593.4 |
| paleozoology | 563.4 |
| Spongillidae | 593.46 |
| Spontaneous abortion | |
| obstetrics | 618.392 |
| Spontaneous generation | 576.83 |
| Spools | |
| wooden | 674.88 |
| Spoonbills (Birds) | 598.34 |
| Spoonworms | 592.3 |

| | |
|---|---|
| Sporades (Greece) | T2—495 8 |
| ancient | T2—391 |
| Sporangia | 575.6 |
| Spores | 571.847 |
| paleobotany | 561.13 |
| Sporoboleae | 584.9 |
| Sporozoa | 579.47 |
| Sport animals | |
| animal husbandry | 636.088 8 |
| Sport climbing | 796.522 4 |
| Sport coats | 391.473 |
| home sewing | 646.433 |
| *see also* Clothing | |
| Sport policy (Government policy) | 796 |
| Sporting dogs (Dogs as sport | |
| animals) | 636.708 88 |
| *see Manual at* 636.70886, | |
| 636.70888 vs. 636.73, | |
| 636.752 | |
| Sporting dogs (United Kingdom) | 636.75 |
| Sporting dogs (United States) | 636.752 |
| *see Manual at* 636.70886, | |
| 636.70888 vs. 636.73, | |
| 636.752 | |
| Sporting goods | |
| manufacturing technology | 688.76 |
| Sports | 796 |
| arts | 700.457 9 |
| | T3C—357 9 |
| child care | 649.57 |
| ethics | 175 |
| *see also* Recreation — ethics | |
| human physiology | 612.044 |
| journalism | 070.449 796 |
| law | 344.099 |
| literature | |
| history and criticism | 809.933 579 |
| specific literatures | T3B—080 357 9 |
| history and | |
| criticism | T3B—093 579 |
| physical fitness | 613.711 |
| public administrative support | 353.78 |
| safety | 363.14 |
| public administration | 353.97 |
| techniques | 796.028 9 |
| sociology | 306.483 |
| Sports acrobatics | 796.476 |
| Sports aerobics | 796.44 |
| Sports buttons | |
| numismatics | 737.243 |
| Sports cards | 796.075 |
| Sports cars | 388.342 1 |
| driving | 629.283 |
| recreation | 796.72 |

| | | | |
|---|---|---|---|
| Sports cars (continued) | | Spouses | 306.872 |
| engineering | 629.222 1 | | T1—086 55 |
| repair | 629.287 21 | law | 346.016 3 |
| transportation services | 388.342 1 | *see also* Married people | |
| *see also* Automobiles | | Spouses of alcoholics | |
| Sports centers | 796.068 | medicine | 616.861 9 |
| architecture | 725.804 3 | social welfare | 362.292 3 |
| construction | 690.580 43 | Spouses of clergy | |
| Sports clothes (Activewear) | 391.48 | Christianity | 253.22 |
| *see also* Activewear | | biography | |
| Sports clothes (Casual wear) | 391 | specific denominations | 280 |
| *see also* Casual wear | | pastoral theology | 253.22 |
| Sports complexes | 796.068 | Spouses of substance abusers | |
| architecture | 725.804 3 | medicine | 616.869 |
| construction | 690.580 43 | social welfare | 362.291 3 |
| Sports equipment | | Sprains | |
| manufacturing technology | 688.76 | medicine | 617.17 |
| Sports etiquette | 395.5 | Sprang | |
| Sports for disabled people | 796.087 | arts | 746.422 4 |
| Sports journalism | 070.449 796 | Sprat | 641.392 |
| Sports medicine | 617.102 7 | cooking | 641.692 |
| Sports music | 781.594 | food | 641.392 |
| Sports pavilions | 796.068 | zoology | 597.452 |
| architecture | 725.804 3 | Spratly Islands | T2—59 |
| construction | 690.580 43 | Spray painting | 667.6 |
| Sports pins | | Sprayed latex | 678.538 |
| numismatics | 737.243 | Spraying | |
| Sports policy (Government | | agricultural pest control | 632.94 |
| policy) | 796 | painting | 667.6 |
| Sportsmanship | | Spraying plants | |
| ethics | 175 | manufacturing technology | 681.763 1 |
| Sportsmen | 796.092 | Spread formation | |
| *see Manual at* 796.092 | | American football | 796.332 22 |
| Sportswear (Activewear) | 391.48 | Spread latex | 678.538 |
| *see also* Activewear | | Spread rubber | 678.36 |
| Sportswear (Casual wear) | 391 | Spreading latex | 678.527 |
| *see also* Casual wear | | Spreadsheets (Computer | |
| Sporulation | 571.847 | programs) | 005.54 |
| Spot removal | | Sprechgesang | 782.97 |
| household sanitation | 648.1 | choral and mixed voices | 782.97 |
| Spot tests (Chemicals) | 543.22 | single voices | 783.97 |
| Spot welding | 671.521 3 | Spree-Neisse (Germany : | |
| Spotsylvania County (Va.) | T2—755 365 | Landkreis) | T2—431 51 |
| Spotted dolphins | 599.534 | Spring | 508.2 |
| Spotted seal | 599.792 | music | 781.524 2 |
| Spotted turtle | 597.925 7 | *see also* Seasons | |
| Spouse abuse | 362.829 2 | Spring-flowering plants | 581.43 |
| criminology | 364.155 53 | floriculture | 635.953 |
| criminal law | 345.025 553 | Spring guns | |
| family relationships | 306.872 | art metalwork | 739.73 |
| medicine | 616.858 22 | Springboard diving | 797.24 |
| social welfare | 362.829 2 | Springbok | 599.646 |
| *see also* Family violence | | Springfield (Ill.) | T2—773 56 |
| | | Springfield (Mass.) | T2—744 26 |

| | | | |
|---|---|---|---|
| Springhaas | 599.359 | Squash players | 796.343 092 |
| Springs (Mechanisms) | 621.824 | Squashes | 641.356 2 |
| automotive engineering | 629.243 | botany | 583.63 |
| railroad engineering | 625.21 | commercial processing | 664.805 62 |
| Springs (South Africa : | | cooking | 641.656 2 |
| District) | T2—682 24 | food | 641.356 2 |
| Springs (Water) | 551.498 | garden crop | 635.62 |
| water supply engineering | 628.112 | Squatter's right | 346.043 2 |
| Springtails | 595.725 | Squawfishes | 597.482 |
| Sprinkler systems | | Squid | 594.58 |
| fire technology | 628.925 2 | cooking | 641.694 |
| Sprinters | 796.422 092 | fishing | 639.485 8 |
| Sprints | 796.422 | food | 641.394 |
| Spruce budworm | | commercial processing | 664.94 |
| forest pest | 634.975 267 8 | zoology | 594.58 |
| Spruces | 585.2 | Squirrel monkeys | 599.852 |
| forestry | 634.975 2 | Squirrelfishes | 597.64 |
| lumber | 674.144 | Squirrels | 599.36 |
| SPS (Swiss political party) | 324.249 407 2 | agricultural pests | 632.693 6 |
| Spur gears | 621.833 1 | small game hunting | 799.259 36 |
| Spurge laurel | 583.67 | Sranan language | 427.988 3 |
| Spurges (Euphorbiaceae) | 583.69 | | T6—217 |
| Spurious knowledge | 001.9 | Sranan Tongo | 427.988 3 |
| Sputtering (Physics) | | | T6—217 |
| solid-state physics | 530.416 | Sranantonga | 427.988 3 |
| Spy stories | 808.838 72 | | T6—217 |
| history and criticism | 809.387 2 | Srê language | 495.93 |
| specific literatures | T3B—308 72 | | T6—959 3 |
| individual authors | T3A—3 | Sri Lanka | 954.93 |
| Spying | 327.12 | | T2—549 3 |
| *see also* Espionage | | Sri Lankans | T5—914 13 |
| Spyware | 005.84 | Śrīharṣa | |
| Squadrons (Air force units) | 358.413 1 | Indian history | 934.07 |
| Squadrons (Naval air units) | 359.943 4 | St. Albans (England : City | |
| Squadrons (Naval units) | 359.31 | and District) | T2—425 85 |
| Squads (Military units) | 355.31 | St. Bride's Major (Wales) | T2—429 89 |
| Squalidae | 597.36 | St. Helens (England : | |
| Squaliformes | 597.36 | Metropolitan Borough) | T2—427 57 |
| Squamata | 597.94 | St. John's (N.L.) | T2—718 1 |
| paleozoology | 567.94 | St. Thomas Christian churches | 281.54 |
| Squamish (B.C.) | T2—711 31 | *see also* Eastern churches | |
| Squamish-Lillooet (B.C.) | T2—711 31 | St. Thomas Christians | 281.54 |
| Squamous epithelia | | *see also* Eastern churches | |
| human histology | 611.018 7 | St. Thomas Evangelical Church | |
| Square books | 099 | of India | 281.54 |
| Square dances | 793.34 | *see also* Eastern churches | |
| music | 784.188 7 | Stab wounds | |
| Square root | 513.23 | medicine | 617.143 |
| Square-wave generators | | Stabiae (Extinct city) | T2—377 258 |
| electronics | 621.381 548 | Stabiles | 731.55 |
| Squares (City planning) | 711.55 | Stability | |
| Squares (Geometry) | 516.154 | aeronautics | 629.132 36 |
| Squaring the circle | 516.204 | foundation soils | 624.151 36 |
| Squash (Game) | 796.343 | Stability theory | 515.392 |

Stabilization ponds
  sewage treatment    628.351
Stabilizers
  aircraft    629.134 33
Stable flies    595.774
Stable management    636.083
Stable waste
  animal husbandry    636.083 8
Stables    636.083 1
Stacks (Library)
  collections maintenance    025.81
  plant management    022.4
Stadiums    796.068
  architecture    725.827
Staff and line organization    658.402
  armed forces    355.330 4
  public administration    352.283
Staff development    370.113
  *see also* Vocational education
Staff notation    780.148
Staff trees    583.85
Staffing patterns    658.312 8
Stafford (England :
  Borough)    T2—424 64
Stafford County (Kan.)    T2—781 813
Stafford County (Va.)    T2—755 26
Staffordshire (England)    T2—424 6
Staffordshire Moorlands
  (England)    T2—424 61
Stag beetles    595.764 9
Stage fright    792.028 019
  motion pictures    791.430 280 19
  radio    791.440 280 19
  stage    792.028 019
  television    791.450 280 19
Stage presentations    792
  *see also* Theater
Stagecoach transportation    388.322 8
Stagecoaches    388.341
  manufacturing technology    688.6
  transportation services    388.341
Stagflation    332.41
Staghorn ferns    587.3
Stags    599.65
  big game hunting    799.276 5
Stained glass
  arts    748.5
Staining (Microscopy)    502.82
  biology    570.282 7
Staining (Woodwork)
  buildings    698.32
Stainless steel    669.142
  decorative arts    739.4
  *see also* Steel

Stains
  manufacturing technology    667.2
Stairs    721.832
  architecture    721.832
  construction    690.183 2
Stalin, Joseph
  Russian history    947.084 2
Stalingrad, Battle of, 1942–1943    940.542 174 7
Stalk-eyed flies    595.774
Stalkers
  biography    364.158 092
Stalking    364.158
  law    345.025 8
Stamens    575.65
Stamford (Conn.)    T2—746 9
Stammering
  medicine    616.855 4
  *see also* Communication
    disorders
  pediatrics    618.928 554
Stamp Act, 1765–1766
  United States history    973.311 1
Stamp tax    336.272
  law    343.057
  public administration    352.44
  public finance    336.272
Stamping metals    671.334
  decorative arts    739.14
  sculpture    731.41
Stamping tools    621.984
Stamps (Postage)    383.23
  *see also* Postage stamps
Stamps (Seals)
  numismatics    737.6
Stand-up comedians    792.760 280 92
Stand-up comedy    792.76
Standard deviation    519.534
Standard gage railroads    385
Standard industrial classifications    338.020 12
Standard language
  applied linguistics    418
    education    418.007 1
      specific languages    T4—800 71
  description and analysis    411–415
  specific languages
    applied linguistics    T4—8
    description and analysis    T4—1–5
Standard Malay language    499.28
      T6—992 8
Standard Malay literature    899.28
Standard of living
  macroeconomics    339.47
Standard time    389.17
Standardbred horse    636.175

| | |
|---|---|
| Standardization | 389.6 |
| | T1—021 8 |
| commerce | 389.6 |
| law | 343.075 |
| production management | 658.562 |
| public administration | 352.83 |
| Standardized tests | 371.262 |
| primary education | 372.126 2 |
| reading | 372.482 |
| *see Manual at* 371.262 vs. 371.264 | |
| Standards | 389.6 |
| | T1—021 8 |
| collections | 389.6 |
| executive management | 658.401 3 |
| public administration | 352.35 |
| law | 343.075 |
| production management | 658.562 |
| public administration | 352.83 |
| technology | 602.18 |
| Standards (Flags) | 929.92 |
| armed forces | 355.15 |
| Standerton (South Africa : District) | T2—682 79 |
| Standing orders | |
| library acquisitions | 025.233 |
| Stanger (South Africa) | T2—684 4 |
| Stanislaus County (Calif.) | T2—794 57 |
| Stanley (Tas.) | T2—946 5 |
| Stanley County (S.D.) | T2—783 55 |
| Stanley Cup | 796.962 648 |
| Stanly County (N.C.) | T2—756 73 |
| Stann Creek District (Belize) | T2—728 23 |
| Stans (Switzerland) | T2—494 762 4 |
| Stanthorpe (Qld.) | T2—943 3 |
| Stanton County (Kan.) | T2—781 712 |
| Stanton County (Neb.) | T2—782 535 |
| Staphyleaceae | 583.78 |
| Staphylinidae | 595.764 2 |
| Staphylinoidea | 595.764 2 |
| Staphylococcal infections | |
| incidence | 614.579 7 |
| medicine | 616.929 7 |
| *see also* Communicable diseases — humans | |
| Staphylococcus | 579.353 |
| Star anise | 641.338 2 |
| botany | 583.3 |
| *see also* Flavorings | |
| Star apples | 583.674 |
| floriculture | 635.933 674 |
| *see also* Sapotaceae | |
| Star catalogs | 523.802 16 |

| | |
|---|---|
| Star clusters | 523.85 |
| Star formation | 523.88 |
| Star routes | 383.143 |
| *see also* Postal service | |
| Star wars (Military science) | 358.174 |
| Starch crops | 633.68 |
| Starch paste | 668.33 |
| Starches | 572.566 |
| applied nutrition | 613.283 |
| biochemistry | 572.566 |
| chemistry | 547.78 |
| cooking | 641.636 8 |
| food | 641.336 8 |
| food technology | 664.2 |
| metabolism | |
| human physiology | 612.396 |
| *see also* Carbohydrates | |
| Starfish | 593.93 |
| paleozoology | 563.93 |
| Stargazers (Fishes) | 597.7 |
| Stark County (Ill.) | T2—773 513 |
| Stark County (N.D.) | T2—784 844 |
| Stark County (Ohio) | T2—771 62 |
| Starke County (Ind.) | T2—772 923 |
| Starlings | 598.863 |
| Starr County (Tex.) | T2—764 485 |
| Stars | 523.8 |
| *see Manual at* 520 vs. 523.1, 523.112, 523.8 | |
| Starters (Appetizers) | 641.812 |
| Starting devices | |
| automotive | 629.257 |
| State (Political body) | 320.1 |
| State administration | 352.13 |
| specific states | 351.3–.9 |
| *see also* States (Members of federations) — public administration | |
| State aid | |
| education | 379.122 |
| private schools | 379.32 |
| State bankruptcy | 336.368 |
| State banks | 332.122 4 |
| State colleges | 378.053 |
| *see also* Higher education | |
| State courts (United States) | 347.733 |
| State flags | 929.92 |
| State governments | 321.023 |
| *see also* States (Members of federations) | |
| State labor (Drafted workers) | 331.117 32 |
| State-local relations | 320.404 9 |
| law | 342.042 |
| public administration | 353.334 |

State of the Union messages — 352.238 409 73
State planning
  civic art — 711.3
  economics — 338.9
State socialism — 335
  economics — 335
  political ideology — 320.53
State succession
  law of nations — 341.26
State taxation — 336.201 3
  law — 343.043
  public administration — 352.442 13
  public finance — 336.201 3
State universities — 378.053
  *see also* Higher education
State visits
  customs — 394.4
Stateless persons — 305.906 914
  T1—086 914
  law — 342.083
  law of nations — 341.486
  social welfare — 362.87
  women
    social welfare — 362.839 814
  young people
    social welfare — 362.779 14
Staten Island (New York, N.Y.) — T2—747 26
States (Independent governments) — 320.1
  governing systems — 321
  law of nations — 341.26
  public administration — 351
    specific states — 351.3–.9
States (Members of federations) — 321.023
  law — 342.042
  public administration — 352.13
    grants-in-aid — 352.734 3
    specific states — 351.3–.9
    support and control — 353.333
  *see Manual at* 351.3–.9
    vs. 352.13–.19; *also at*
    352.13 vs. 352.15
States of matter — 530.4
  chemical engineering — 660.04
States of the Church — 945.6
  T2—456
States' Rights Party (U.S.) — 324.273 3
Static determinacy — 624.171 3
Static indeterminacy — 624.171 3
Statically indeterminate structures — 624.171 3

Statics — 531.12
  air — 533.61
    engineering — 620.107 3
  engineering — 620.103
  fluids — 532.02
    engineering — 620.106 3
  gases — 533.12
    engineering — 620.107 3
  liquids — 532.2
    engineering — 620.106 3
  solids — 531.2
    engineering — 620.105 3
Station posters
  transportation advertising — 659.134 4
Station wagons
  driving — 629.283
  engineering — 629.222
  repair — 629.287 2
Stationary processes — 519.232
Stationary steam engines — 621.16
Stationary targets
  gun sports — 799.312
Stationery — 676.282 3
Stations of the cross — 232.96
Stations of the Cross
  Roman Catholic liturgy — 264.027 4
Statistical graphs — T1—021
  presentation of statistical data — 001.422 6
    T1—072 8
    computer graphics — 001.422 602 856 6
Statistical hypothesis testing — 519.56
Statistical inference — 519.54
Statistical mathematics — 519.5
  primary education — 372.79
  *see Manual at* 519.5,
    T1—015195 vs. 001.422,
    T1—0727
Statistical mechanics — 530.13
Statistical methods — 001.422
    T1—072 7
  numerical methods — 518.28
  systems analysis — T1—011
  *see Manual at* 519.5,
    T1—015195 vs. 001.422,
    T1—0727
Statistical programs — 005.55
Statistical software — 005.55
Statisticians — 310.92
Statistics (Collections) — 310
  T1—021
  presentation of statistical data — 001.422 6
    T1—072 8
    computer graphics — 001.422 602 856 6
Statuary — 731.7

| | |
|---|---|
| Status (Law) | 346.013 |
| Status offenders | 364.36 |
| Statutes | 348.02 |
| Statutory actions | 347.053 |
| Statutory liability risks | 368.08 |
| Statutory rape | 364.153 |
|   law | 345.025 3 |
| Staunton (Va.) | T2—755 911 |
| Staurolite | |
|   mineralogy | 549.62 |
| Stauromedusae | 593.53 |
| Stavropol' (Russia : Kray) | T2—475 2 |
| Stavropol'skiĭ kraĭ (Russia) | T2—475 2 |
| Stawell (Vic.) | T2—945 8 |
| STD (Diseases) | |
|   incidence | 614.547 |
|   medicine | 616.951 |
|   *see also* Communicable | |
|     diseases — humans | |
| Stealing | 364.162 |
|   *see also* Theft | |
| Steam cooking | 641.587 |
| Steam distilling oils and gases | 665.028 2 |
| Steam engineering | 621.1 |
| Steam engineers | 621.109 2 |
| Steam engines | 621.1 |
|   automotive | 629.250 1 |
|   ships | 623.872 2 |
| Steam fitting | |
|   buildings | 696.3 |
| Steam heating | 621.1 |
|   buildings | 697.5 |
| Steam locomotives | 385.361 |
|   engineering | 625.261 |
|   transportation services | 385.361 |
|   *see also* Rolling stock | |
| Steam pipes | 621.185 |
|   buildings | |
|     installation | 696.3 |
| Steam-powered automobiles | |
|   engineering | 629.229 2 |
| Steam-powered electric | |
|   generation | 621.312 132 |
| Steam tractors | |
|   driving | 629.284 92 |
|   engineering | 629.229 2 |
|   repair | 629.287 92 |
| Steam turbines | 621.165 |
| Steaming | |
|   home cooking | 641.73 |
| Steamrollers | |
|   driving | 629.284 92 |
|   engineering | 629.229 2 |
|   repair | 629.287 92 |

| | |
|---|---|
| Steamships | 387.204 4 |
|   engineering | 623.820 4 |
|   transportation services | 387.204 4 |
|   *see also* Ships | |
| Stearns County (Minn.) | T2—776 47 |
| Steatite | 553.55 |
| Steel | 669.142 |
|   architectural construction | 721.044 71 |
|   building construction | 693.71 |
|   building material | 691.7 |
|   materials science | 620.17 |
|   metallography | 669.951 42 |
|   metallurgy | 669.142 |
|   metalworking | 672 |
|   physical metallurgy | 669.961 42 |
|   production economics | 338.476 691 42 |
|   ship design | 623.818 21 |
|   shipbuilding | 623.820 7 |
|   structural engineering | 624.182 1 |
|   *see also* Metals | |
| Steel drums | 786.843 |
|   *see also* Percussion instruments | |
| Steel truss bridges | |
|   construction | 624.217 |
| Steel workers | 669.109 2 |
|   metallurgy | 669.109 2 |
|   metalworking | 672.092 |
| Steele County (Minn.) | T2—776 193 |
| Steele County (N.D.) | T2—784 33 |
| Steenrod algebras | 512.55 |
| Steeplechase races | |
|   horses | 798.45 |
|   humans | 796.426 |
| Steeplechasing | |
|   equipment technology | 688.78 |
| Steeples | |
|   Christian church architecture | 726.597 |
| Steering gear | |
|   automotive engineering | 629.247 |
|   ships | 623.862 |
| Stegosauria | 567.915 |
| Stegosaurus | 567.915 3 |
| Steiermark (Austria) | T2—436 5 |
| Stein algebras | 512.55 |
| Stellar evolution | 523.88 |
| Stellar magnitudes | 523.822 |
| Stellar radiation | 523.82 |
| Stellenbosch (South Africa : | |
|   District) | T2—687 34 |
| Stelleroidea | 593.93 |
|   paleozoology | 563.93 |
| Steller's sea cow | 599.559 168 |

Stem cells
  experimental research
    medicine      616.027 74
Stem vegetables
  garden crops      635.3
Stemonitales      579.52
Stems (Plants)      581.495
  descriptive botany      581.495
  physiology      575.4
  reproductive adaptation      581.46
Stenciling
  decorative arts      745.73
Stencils
  mechanical printing technique      686.231 6
  office use      652.4
Stenella      599.534
Stenographers      651.374 109 2
  office services      651.374 1
Stenographic machines
  manufacturing technology      681.61
Stenography      653.14
Stenolaemata      594.67
Stepbrothers      306.875
     T1—085 5
  *see also* Siblings
Stepchildren      306.874 7
     T1—085 4
Stepfamilies      306.874 7
Stephanotises      583.93
Stephen, King of England
  English history      942.024
Stephens County (Ga.)      T2—758 132
Stephens County (Okla.)      T2—766 53
Stephens County (Tex.)      T2—764 546
Stephenson County (Ill.)      T2—773 33
Stepmothers
  social welfare      362.839 57
Stepparents      306.874 7
     T1—085
Steppes      333.74
     T2—153
  biology      578.744
  ecology      577.44
  *see also* Grasslands
Stepps (Scotland)      T2—414 52
Steps
  landscape architecture      717
Stepsisters      306.875
     T1—085 5
  *see also* Siblings
Stercorariidae      598.338
Sterculiaceae      583.68
Sterea Hellada (Greece)      T2—495 15

Stereo systems
  automobile      629.277
Stereochemistry      547.122 3
  inorganic chemistry      541.223
  organic chemistry      547.122 3
Stereology      502.82
  biology      570.282
Stereophonic sound systems
  engineering      621.389 334
Stereoscopic cinematography      777.65
Stereoscopic photography      778.4
Stereoscopic projection      778.4
Stereoscopic videography      777.65
Stereotypes
  sociology      303.385
Sterility
  gynecology      618.178
    *see also* Female genital
      diseases — humans
  medicine      616.692
    *see also* Genital diseases —
      humans
Sterilization (Birth control)      363.97
  health      613.942
  social services      363.97
  surgery
    tubal ligation      618.120 59
    vasectomy      617.463
  *see also* Birth control
Sterilization (Microorganism
  elimination)
  public health      614.48
  spacecraft      629.477 4
  surgery      617.910 1
Sterkspruit (South Africa :
  District)      T2—687 56
Sterkstroom (South Africa :
  District)      T2  687 55
Sterling County (Tex.)      T2—764 871
Sternoptychidae      597.5
Sternum
  human anatomy      611.713
  human physiology      612.751
  medicine      616.71
  surgery      617.471
Steroids      572.579
  biochemistry      572.579
    humans      612.015 77
  chemistry      547.7
Sterols      572.579 5
Stethoscopes
  manufacturing technology      681.761
  use      616.075 440 28
Steuben County (Ind.)      T2—772 78

| | | | |
|---|---|---|---|
| Steuben County (N.Y.) | T2—747 83 | Stimulant abuse (continued) | |
| Stevenage (England) | T2—425 82 | social welfare | 362.299 5 |
| Stevens, Siaka Probyn | | *see also* Substance abuse | |
| Sierra Leonean history | 966.404 2 | Stimulants | |
| Stevens County (Kan.) | T2—781 725 | pharmacokinetics | 615.785 |
| Stevens County (Minn.) | T2—776 42 | Stinkhorns | 579.599 |
| Stevens County (Wash.) | T2—797 23 | Stipeae | 584.9 |
| Stewardship (Christian practice) | 248.6 | Stipple engraving | 765.5 |
| Stewart (B.C.) | T2—711 85 | Stir frying | 641.774 |
| Stewart County (Ga.) | T2—758 922 | Stirling (Scotland) | T2—413 12 |
| Stewart County (Tenn.) | T2—768 35 | Stirling engines | 621.42 |
| Stewart Island (N.Z.) | T2—939 6 | Stirling Range (W.A.) | T2—941 2 |
| Stewartia | 583.624 | Stirling Range National | |
| Stewartry (Scotland) | T2—414 7 | Park (W.A.) | T2—941 2 |
| Stewing | | Stizostedion | 597.758 |
| home cooking | 641.73 | Stoat | 599.766 2 |
| Stews | | Stochastic analysis | 519.22 |
| commercial processing | 664.65 | Stochastic approximation | 519.623 |
| home preparation | 641.823 | Stochastic games | 519.27 |
| Steynsburg (South Africa : | | Stochastic integrals | 519.22 |
| District) | T2—687 56 | Stochastic methods | 518.28 |
| Steytlerville (South Africa : | | Stochastic optimization | 519.62 |
| District) | T2—687 51 | Stochastic processes | 519.23 |
| Stick fighting | 796.8 | Stochastic systems | 003.76 |
| Stick insects | 595.729 | | T1—011 76 |
| culture | 638.572 9 | Stock breeding | 636.082 |
| Stick zithers | 787.72 | Stock control | |
| *see also* Stringed instruments | | materials management | 658.787 |
| Stickhandling | | Stock exchange buildings | |
| ice hockey | 796.962 2 | architecture | 725.25 |
| Sticklebacks | 597.672 | Stock exchanges | 332.642 |
| Sticks | | law | 346.092 6 |
| music | 786.82 | Stock index futures | 332.632 28 |
| *see also* Rods (Musical | | Stock issues | |
| instruments) | | capital management | 658.152 24 |
| Stigmata | 248.29 | Stock market | 332.642 |
| Stikine (B.C. : Region) | T2—711 85 | Stock options | 332.632 283 |
| Stikine River (B.C. and | | Stock ownership plans | 331.216 49 |
| Alaska) | T2—711 85 | labor economics | 331.216 49 |
| Stiletto flies | 595.773 | personnel management | 658.322 59 |
| Still fishing | 799.122 | Stock prices | 332.632 22 |
| Still life | | Stock purchase plans | 331.216 49 |
| art representation | 704.943 5 | Stock rights | 332.632 2 |
| painting | 758.4 | Stock speculation | 332.632 28 |
| Still rings (Gymnastic equipment) | 796.442 | Stock tickers | 384.14 |
| Stillbirth | | wireless | 384.524 |
| medicine | 618.392 | *see also* Telegraphy | |
| Stillwater County (Mont.) | T2—786 651 | Stock warrants | 332.632 2 |
| Stilts (Footwear) | | Stockbridge Indians | T5—973 449 |
| commercial technology | 688.7 | Stockholders' meetings | |
| Stimulant abuse | 362.299 5 | law | 346.066 6 |
| medicine | 616.864 | Stockholm (Sweden) | T2—487 3 |
| personal health | 613.84 | Stockholms län (Sweden) | T2—487 3 |

Stockings   391.423
  *see also* Hosiery
Stockmen   636.009 2
Stockpiles
  secondary industries   338.47
Stockport (England :
  Metropolitan Borough)   T2—427 34
Stocks   332.632 2
  accounting   657.76
  income tax   336.242 6
   law   343.052 46
  law   346.092 2
   corporate law   346.066 6
  *see Manual at* 332.6322 vs.
   332.6323
Stocks (Matthiola)   583.64
Stockton-on-Tees
  (England : Borough)   T2—428 51
Stockton Plateau (Tex.)   T2—764 92
Stockyards
  animal husbandry   636.083 1
Stoddard County (Mo.)   T2—778 95
Stoic ethics   171.2
Stoic philosophy   188
Stoichiometry   541.26
  applied chemistry   660.7
Stoke-on-Trent (England)   T2—424 63
Stokes County (N.C.)   T2—756 64
Stokes' integral   515.43
STOL airplanes
  engineering   629.133 340 426
Stoles   391.46
  commercial technology   687.14
  fur   685.24
  *see also* Outerwear
Stolons   581.46
  agricultural propagation   631.533
  descriptive botany   581.46
  physiology   575.499
Stomach   573.36
  biology   573.36
  human anatomy   611.33
  human physiology   612.32
  medicine   616.33
  surgery   617.553
  *see also* Digestive system
Stomach cancer
  incidence   614.599 943 3
  medicine   616.994 33
   *see also* Cancer — humans
Stomach diseases
  medicine   616.33
   *see also* Digestive system
    diseases — humans

Stomach ulcers
  medicine   616.334
   *see also* Digestive system
    diseases — humans
Stomatopoda   595.379 6
Stomiatiformes   597.5
Stomiatoidei   597.5
Stomiiformes   597.5
Stone   553.5
  architectural construction   721.044 1
  architectural decoration   729.6
  building construction   693.1
  building materials   691.2
  economic geology   553.5
  materials science   620.132
  sculpture material   731.2
  structural engineering   624.183 2
Stone Age   930.12
   T1—090 12
Stone carving   736.5
Stone County (Ark.)   T2—767 283
Stone County (Miss.)   T2—762 162
Stone County (Mo.)   T2—778 794
Stone flies   595.735
Stone fruits
  botany   583.73
  orchard crops   634.2
Stone lithography   763.22
Stone pavements   625.82
Stone plants   583.53
Stone sculpturing   731.463
Stonecrops   583.72
Stonewall County (Tex.)   T2—764 737
Stoneware   666.6
  arts   738.3
  technology   666.6
Stoneworts   579.839
Stop motion (Animation)   777 7
Stopwatches
  technology   681.118
Storage
  cinematography   777.58
  coal technology   662.624
  gas technology   665.742
  home economics   648.8
  museology   069.53
   T1—075
  negatives   771.45
  petroleum technology   665.542
  positives (photographs)   771.46
  videography   777.58
  warehouse management   658.785
  water supply engineering   628.13

| | |
|---|---|
| Storage (Computers) | 004.5 |
| | T1—028 545 |
| engineering | 621.397 |
| Storage (Mathematics) | 519.83 |
| Storage areas | |
| home economics | 643.5 |
| Storage batteries | 621.312 424 |
| Storage buildings | |
| architecture | 725.35 |
| Storage centers | |
| library role | 021 |
| Storage containers | |
| warehouse management | 658.785 |
| Storage elevators | |
| architecture | 725.36 |
| Storage of office records | 651.53 |
| Storage services | 388.044 |
| *see also* Freight services | |
| Storaxes | 583.674 |
| Store Bælt (Denmark) | 551.461 334 |
| | T2—163 34 |
| Store detectives | 363.289 |
| Stores (Retail trade) | 381.1 |
| architecture | 725.21 |
| institutional housekeeping | 647.962 1 |
| management | 658.87 |
| *see also* Commerce | |
| Storey County (Nev.) | T2—793 56 |
| Storing clothes | |
| home economics | 646.6 |
| Storing crops | 631.568 |
| Storing electric power | 621.312 6 |
| Storing food | |
| home economics | 641.48 |
| Storing food (Animal behavior) | 591.53 |
| Storing household goods | 648.8 |
| Storks | 598.34 |
| Storm insurance | 368.122 |
| Storm petrels | 598.42 |
| Storm sewers | 628.212 |
| Storm surges | |
| oceanography | 551.463 |
| Stormberg Range (South Africa) | T2—687 55 |
| Stormont, Dundas and Glengarry (Ont.) | T2—713 75 |
| Storms | 551.55 |
| meteorology | 551.55 |
| social services | 363.349 2 |
| weather forecasting | 551.645 |
| weather modification | 551.685 |
| *see also* Disasters | |
| Storstrøms amt (Denmark) | T2—489 1 |
| Story County (Iowa) | T2—777 546 |

| | |
|---|---|
| Storytelling | 808.543 |
| child care | 649.58 |
| library services | 027.625 1 |
| primary education | 372.677 |
| rhetoric | 808.543 |
| Stour, River (Wiltshire-Dorset, England) | T2—423 3 |
| Stoves | |
| ceramic arts | 738.8 |
| heating buildings | 697.22 |
| household appliances | 644.1 |
| kitchen appliances | 643.3 |
| manufacturing technology | 683.88 |
| Strabane (Northern Ireland : District) | T2—416 41 |
| Strabismus | |
| ophthalmology | 617.762 |
| *see also* Eye diseases — humans | |
| Strafford County (N.H.) | T2—742 5 |
| Straightening tools | 621.98 |
| Strain gauges | |
| materials science | 620.112 302 87 |
| Strains | 531.381 |
| bridge engineering | 624.252 |
| materials science | 620.112 3 |
| naval architecture | 623.817 6 |
| physics | 531.381 |
| structural analysis | 624.176 |
| Strains (Injuries) | |
| medicine | 617.17 |
| Strait of Dover | 551.461 336 |
| | T2—163 36 |
| Strait of Georgia (B.C.) | 551.461 433 |
| | T2—164 33 |
| Strait of Gibraltar | 551.461 381 |
| | T2—163 81 |
| Strait of Hormuz | 551.461 535 |
| | T2—165 35 |
| Strait of Juan de Fuca (B.C. and Washington) | 551.461 432 |
| | T2—164 32 |
| Strait of Magellan (Chile and Argentina) | 551.461 74 |
| | T2—167 4 |
| Strait of Malacca | 551.461 565 |
| | T2—165 65 |
| Strait of Mandab | 551.461 532 |
| | T2—165 32 |
| Strait of Messina (Italy) | 551.461 386 |
| | T2—163 86 |
| Strait of Sicily | 551.461 381 |
| | T2—163 81 |
| Straits | |
| law of nations | 341.446 |

| | | | |
|---|---|---|---|
| Straits of Florida | 551.461 363 | Stratford-on-Avon | |
| | T2—163 63 | (England : District) | T2—424 89 |
| Straits of Mackinac (Mich.) | T2—774 923 | Strathclyde (Scotland) | T2—414 |
| Stralsund (Germany) | T2—431 78 | Strathkelvin (Scotland) | T2—414 36 |
| Strand (South Africa : | | Strathmore (Scotland) | T2—412 6 |
| District) | T2—687 34 | Stratifications (Rock formations) | 551.81 |
| Strange particles | 539.721 6 | economic geology | 553.14 |
| Strangeness (Nuclear physics) | 539.721 6 | specific areas | 554–559 |
| Strangers | | Stratigraphic paleobotany | 561.11 |
| applied psychology | 158.27 | Stratigraphic paleontology | 560.17 |
| psychological influence | 155.927 | Stratigraphic paleozoology | 560.17 |
| Strangford Lough (Northern | | Stratigraphy | 551.7 |
| Ireland) | T2—416 54 | Stratiomyidae | 595.773 |
| Strasbourg (France) | T2—443 954 | Stratosphere | 551.514 2 |
| Strasser, Valentine E. M. | | | T2—161 3 |
| Sierra Leonean history | 966.404 4 | Straw pulp | 676.14 |
| Strategic arms limitation | 327.174 7 | Strawberries | 641.347 5 |
| Strategic Defense Initiative | 358.174 | botany | 583.73 |
| Strategic geography | 355.47 | commercial processing | 664.804 75 |
| Strategic management | 658.401 2 | cooking | 641.647 5 |
| military administration | 355.684 | food | 641.347 5 |
| public administration | 352.34 | horticulture | 634.75 |
| Strategic materials | 355.24 | Stream of consciousness | |
| land economics | 333.8 | literature | 808.802 5 |
| law | 343.01 | history and criticism | 809.925 |
| military science | 355.24 | specific literatures | T3B—080 25 |
| Strategic missile forces | 358.17 | history and | |
| land | 358.175 4 | criticism | T3B—092 5 |
| navy | 359.981 7 | Streaming (Education) | 371.254 |
| Strategic missiles | 358.171 82 | Streams | 551.483 |
| engineering | 623.451 9 | *see also* Rivers | |
| law of nations | 341.738 | Středočeský kraj (Czech | |
| military equipment | 358.171 82 | Republic) | T2—437 11 |
| Strategic planning (Management) | 658.401 2 | Středoslovenský kraj | |
| military administration | 355.684 | (Slovakia) | T2—437 34 |
| public administration | 352.34 | Street art (Murals) | 751.73 |
| Strategic weapons | 358.171 82 | Street cleaning | 363.729 1 |
| engineering | 623.451 9 | public administration | 353.94 |
| law of nations | 341.738 | technology | 628.46 |
| military equipment | 358.171 82 | *see also* Sanitation | |
| Strategy | 355.02 | Street cries | 398.87 |
| Civil War (United States) | 973.730 1 | Street fighting (Military science) | 355.426 |
| military operations | 355.4 | Street furniture | |
| overall military objectives | 355.02 | landscape architecture | 717 |
| World War I | 940.401 | Street hockey | 796.356 4 |
| World War II | 940.540 1 | Street luge racing | 796.67 |
| *see also* Military history | | Street markets | 381.18 |
| Stratford Avon River | | management | 658.87 |
| (England) | T2—424 4 | *see also* Commerce | |
| Stratford District (N.Z.) | T2—934 85 | Street music | 781.532 |
| Manawatu-Wanganui | | Street noise | 363.741 |
| Region | T2—935 3 | *see also* Noise | |
| Taranaki Region | T2—934 85 | Street patterns | |
| | | area planning | 711.41 |

| | |
|---|---|
| Street signals | 388.413 122 |
|   engineering | 625.794 |
|   law | 343.098 2 |
|   transportation services | 388.413 122 |
| Street signs | 388.413 122 |
|   *see also* Street signals | |
| Street songs | 398.87 |
| Street theater | 792.022 |
| Street trees | 635.977 |
| Street vending | 381.18 |
| Streetcars | 388.46 |
|   engineering | 625.66 |
|   transportation services | 388.46 |
| Streets | 388.411 |
|   engineering | 625.7 |
|   law | 343.098 2 |
|   transportation services | 388.411 |
|   *see also* Roads | |
| Strength | |
|   crystals | 548.842 |
|   materials science | 620.112 |
| Strepsiptera | 595.76 |
| Streptochaeteae | 584.9 |
| Streptococcal infections | |
|   incidence | 614.579 8 |
|   medicine | 616.929 8 |
|   *see also* Communicable | |
|     diseases — humans | |
| Streptococcus | 579.355 |
| Streptomyces | 579.378 |
| Streptomycetes | 579.378 |
| Streptoneura | 594.32 |
| Stress | |
|   medicine | 616.98 |
|   psychiatry | 616.89 |
|   psychology | 155.904 2 |
|     children | 155.418 904 2 |
|     late adulthood | 155.671 890 42 |
| Stress (Linguistics) | 414.6 |
|   specific languages | T4—16 |
| Stress-induced diseases | |
|   medicine | 616.98 |
|   *see also* Environmental | |
|     diseases — humans | |
|   psychiatry | 616.89 |
| Stress management | |
|   psychology | 155.904 2 |
| Stresses (Physical forces) | 531.381 |
|   bridge engineering | 624.252 |
|   crystals | 548.842 |
|   naval architecture | 623.817 6 |
|   physics | 531.381 |
|   structural analysis | 624.176 |
| Stretching exercises | 613.718 2 |

| | |
|---|---|
| Striated muscle tissues | |
|   human histology | 612.740 45 |
| Strict liability | 346.038 |
| Stridulation | 595.715 94 |
|   insect communication | 595.715 94 |
|   physiology | 573.927 |
| Strigiformes | 598.97 |
|   paleozoology | 568.9 |
| Strijdom, Johannes Gerhardus | |
|   South African history | 968.057 |
| Strike insurance | 368.815 |
| Strikebreaking | 331.894 |
| Strikes (Geology) | 551.85 |
| Strikes (Work stoppages) | 331.892 |
|   economics | 331.892 |
|     government measures | 331.898 |
|     management measures | 331.894 |
|     public administration | 354.97 |
|   labor law | 344.018 92 |
|   personnel management | 658.315 4 |
|   public administration | 352.68 |
| String art | 746.047 1 |
| String beans | 641.356 52 |
|   *see also* Snap beans | |
| String ensembles | 785.7 |
| String games | 793.96 |
| String orchestras | 784.7 |
| String quartets | 785.719 4 |
| String theory | 539.725 8 |
| String trios | 785.719 3 |
| Stringed instruments | 787 |
|   bands and orchestras | 784 |
|   chamber ensembles | 785 |
|     mixed | 785.2–.5 |
|     single type | 785.7 |
|   construction | 787.192 3 |
|     by hand | 787.192 3 |
|     by machine | 681.87 |
|   solo music | 787 |
| Strings | 677.71 |
| Strip cartoons | 741.56 |
|   *see also* Comic strips | |
| Strip cropping (Soil conservation) | 631.456 |
| Strip-mined lands | 333.765 |
|   economics | 333.765 |
|   reclamation technology | 631.64 |
| Strip mining | 622.292 |
|   law | 346.046 765 |
| Striped bass | 641.392 |
|   cooking | 641.692 |
|   culture | 639.377 32 |
|   food | 641.392 |
|   sports fishing | 799.177 32 |
|   zoology | 597.732 |

| | | | |
|---|---|---|---|
| Striped dolphins | 599.534 | Structural engineering | 624.1 |
| Striped polecat | 599.766 | *see Manual at* 624.1 | |
| Striped weasels | 599.766 3 | Structural engineers | 624.109 2 |
| Striper (Striped bass) | 641.392 | Structural failure | 624.171 |
| *see also* Striped bass | | Structural foam products | 668.493 |
| Stroboscopic photography | 621.367 | Structural geology | 551.8 |
| Stroessner, Alfredo | | Structural linguistics | 410.18 |
| Paraguayan history | 989.207 3 | specific languages | T4—018 |
| Stroke (Disorder) | | Structural materials | |
| medicine | 616.81 | construction | 691 |
| *see also* Nervous system | | nuclear reactors | 621.483 32 |
| diseases — humans | | Structural optimization | 624.177 13 |
| Stromatoporoidea | 563.58 | Structural polysaccharides | 572.566 8 |
| Stromboli (Italy) | T2—458 11 | Structural proteins | 572.67 |
| Stromiatiformes | 597.5 | Structural stability | 624.171 |
| Stromiiformes | 597.5 | Structural stone | 553.5 |
| Strong interaction (Nuclear | | *see also* Stone | |
| particles) | 539.754 8 | Structural theory | 624.17 |
| Strongboxes | 683.34 | Structural unemployment | 331.137 041 |
| Strontium | 669.725 | Structuralism | |
| chemical engineering | 661.039 4 | fine arts | 709.040 7 |
| chemistry | 546.394 | sculpture | 735.230 477 |
| metallurgy | 669.725 | philosophy | 149.97 |
| physical metallurgy | 669.967 25 | Structure (Philosophy) | 117 |
| *see also* Chemicals | | Structure-activity relationships | 572.4 |
| Strophic form | 781.823 | biochemistry | 572.4 |
| instrumental | 784.182 3 | pharmacology | 615.19 |
| Stroud (England : District) | T2—424 19 | Structured programming | 005.113 |
| Struck board zithers | 787.74 | Structures (Buildings) | |
| *see also* Stringed instruments | | architecture | 720 |
| Struck drums | 786.92 | construction | 690 |
| *see also* Percussion instruments | | engineering | 624.1 |
| Struck stringed instruments | 787.7 | interior decoration | 747.8 |
| *see also* Stringed instruments | | landscape architecture | 717 |
| Structural analysis | 624.17 | Structures (Mathematics) | 511.33 |
| bridges | 624.25 | combinatorial topology | 514.224 |
| construction | 690.21 | geometry | 516 |
| naval architecture | 623.817 1 | topology | 514 |
| Structural chemistry | 541.2 | Struthioniformes | 598.524 |
| Structural clay products | 666.73 | paleozoology | 568.5 |
| materials science | 620.142 | Stuart, House of | 941.06 |
| Structural control (Engineering) | 624.171 | British history | 941.06 |
| Structural crystallography | 548.81 | English history | 942.06 |
| Structural decoration | 729 | genealogy | 929.72 |
| *see Manual at* 729 | | Irish history | 941.506 |
| Structural design | 624.177 1 | Stuccowork | 693.6 |
| naval architecture | 623.817 71 | architectural construction | 721.044 6 |
| Structural dynamics | 624.171 | Studbooks | 636.082 2 |
| Structural elements | 721 | Student academic activities | 371.2 |
| architecture | 721 | Student activism | 371.81 |
| area planning | 711.6 | Student activities | 371.8 |
| construction | 690.1 | | |
| engineering | 624.17 | | |

Student adjustment — 370.158
Student aid — 371.22
 — T1—079
  higher education — 378.3
  law — 344.079 5
Student assessment — 371.26
Student clubs — 371.83
Student competitions — 371.89
Student councils — 371.59
Student counseling — 371.4
Student crime — 371.782
Student discipline — 371.5
  law — 344.079 3
Student employment — 371.225
 — T1—079
  higher education — 378.365
  *see also* Scholarships
Student exchanges — 370.116 2
  higher education — 378.016 2
  law — 344.08
  secondary education — 373.011 62
Student expenditures
  higher education — 378.38
Student experiments — T1—078
Student expulsion — 371.543
Student failure — 371.285
Student government — 371.59
Student guidance — 371.4
Student health programs — 371.71
Student housing — 371.871
Student journalism — 371.897
Student life — 371.8
Student loans — 371.224
 — T1—079
  higher education — 378.362
  law — 344.079 5
Student magazines
  journalism — 371.897 5
Student mobility — 371.291
  higher education — 378.169 1
Student movements — 371.81
Student newspapers
  journalism — 371.897 4
Student organizations — 371.83
 — T1—06
Student participation in
  administration — 371.59
Student periodicals
  journalism — 371.897
Student personnel services — 371.4
Student probation — 371.543
Student projects — T1—078
Student protest — 371.81

Student rights
  law — 344.079 3
Student service (Community
  service)
  higher education — 378.103
  secondary education — 373.119
Student services (Welfare) — 371.7
  law — 344.079 4
Student strikes — 371.81
Student suspension — 371.543
Student-teacher relations — 371.102 3
Student teaching — 370.71
Student transportation — 371.872
Student unions
  architecture — 727.38
Student unrest — 371.81
Student welfare — 371.7
  law — 344.079 4
Students — 371.8
  legal status — 344.079
  role in counseling — 371.404 7
Studies (Rooms) — 643.58
  home economics — 643.58
  residential interior decoration — 747.73
Studies (Subject-oriented
  programs) — T1—07
Studios
  broadcast engineering — 621.384
  communications engineering — 621.382 3
  photography — 771.1
Study abroad — 370.116
Study and teaching — T1—07
Study clubs — 367
Study collections
  museology — 069.55
Study facilities — 371.621
Study groups
  adult education — 374.22
Study methods — 371.302 81
Study scores — 780
  treatises — 780.265
Study skills — 371.302 81
Stuffed toys
  making — 688.724
   handicrafts — 745.592 4
   technology — 688.724
Stunt animals
  animal husbandry — 636.088 8
Stunt flyers — 797.540 92
Stunt flying — 797.54
Stuntmen — 791.430 280 92
Stunts
  motion pictures — 791.430 28
  television — 791.450 28

| | |
|---|---|
| Sturgeons | 597.42 |
| Sturnidae | 598.863 |
| Stutsman County (N.D.) | T2—784 52 |
| Stutterers | T1—087 |
| Stutterheim (South Africa : District) | T2—687 55 |
| Stuttering | |
| medicine | 616.855 4 |
| *see also* Communication disorders | |
| pediatrics | 618.928 554 |
| special education | 371.914 2 |
| Stuttgart (Germany) | T2—434 715 |
| Stuttgart (Germany : Regierungsbezirk) | T2—434 71 |
| Stuttgart (Germany : Region) | T2—434 71 |
| Stylasterina | 593.55 |
| Style | |
| fine arts | 701.8 |
| drawing | 741.018 |
| literary criticism | 809 |
| specific literatures | T3B—09 |
| rhetoric | 808 |
| Style checkers (Computer programs) | 005.52 |
| Style manuals | 808.027 |
| typing | 652.3 |
| Style sheet languages | 006.74 |
| Styles (Fine arts) | 709 |
| *see Manual at* 704.9 and 753–758; *also at* 709.012–.015, 709.02–.05 vs. 709.3–.9 | |
| Stylidiaceae | 583.98 |
| Stylommatophora | 594.38 |
| Styracaceae | 583.674 |
| Styrenes | 668.423 3 |
| Styria (Austria) | T2—436 5 |
| Suazo Córdova, Roberto | |
| Honduran history | 972.830 532 |
| Sub-Saharan Africa | 967 |
| | T2—67 |
| Subantarctic Islands (N.Z.) | T2—939 9 |
| Subatomic particles | 539.72 |
| Subconscious | 154.2 |
| comparative psychology | 156.4 |
| educational psychology | 370.15 |
| philosophy | 127 |
| Subcontracting | 346.022 |
| armed forces | 355.621 2 |
| management | 658.405 8 |
| Subcontracting fees | |
| labor economics | 331.216 6 |
| Subcultures | 306.1 |
| Subdivision of land | 333.3 |
| law | 346.043 77 |
| public administration | 354.34 |
| Subgroups | 512.2 |
| Subia languages | 496.399 |
| | T6—963 99 |
| Subject analysis | |
| information science | 025.4 |
| Subject and predicate (Grammar) | 415 |
| specific languages | T4—5 |
| Subject authority files | 025.47 |
| Subject bibliographies | 016 |
| *see Manual at* 016 vs. 026, T1—07 | |
| Subject cataloging | 025.47 |
| Subject catalogs | |
| specific subjects | 016 |
| Subject control | |
| information science | 025.4 |
| Subject headings | 025.47 |
| specific languages | 025.472–.479 |
| Subject indexing | 025.47 |
| Subject vocabularies | 025.47 |
| specific languages | 025.472–.479 |
| Subjective knowledge | 121.4 |
| Subjectivism | 141 |
| Subjectivity | 126 |
| epistemology | 121.4 |
| Subjectless constructions | 415 |
| specific languages | T4—5 |
| Sublanguage | 401.47 |
| applied linguistics | 401.47 |
| specific languages | T4—014 7 |
| Sublette County (Wyo.) | T2—787 65 |
| Sublimation | 530.414 |
| Subliminal perception | |
| psychology | 153.736 |
| Sublittoral biology | 578.778 |
| Sublittoral ecology | 577.78 |
| Submachine guns | 355.824 24 |
| military engineering | 623.442 4 |
| military equipment | 355.824 24 |
| Submanifolds | 516.362 |
| Submarine cable telegraphy | 384.1 |
| *see also* Telegraphy | |
| Submarine geology | 551.468 |
| Submarine geomorphology | 551.468 3 |
| Submarine medicine | 616.980 22 |
| Submarine mining | 622.295 |
| Submarine physiology | |
| humans | 612.014 415 |
| Submarine sandwiches | 641.84 |

| | | | |
|---|---|---|---|
| Submarine swimming | 627.72 | Subsonic vibrations | 534.52 |
|   hydraulic engineering | 627.72 |   biophysics | 571.443 |
|   sports | 797.23 |     humans | 612.014 45 |
| Submarine warfare | 359.93 |   engineering | 620.28 |
|   World War I | 940.451 |   physics | 534.52 |
|   World War II | 940.545 1 | Substance (Philosophy) | 111.1 |
| Submarines | 359.938 3 | Substance abuse | 362.29 |
|   design | 623.812 57 |   arts | T3C—356 1 |
|   engineering | 623.825 7 |   child rearing | 649.48 |
|   environmental psychology | 155.963 |   criminology | 364.177 |
|   naval equipment | 359.938 3 |   devotional literature | 204.32 |
|   naval units | 359.933 |     Christianity | 242.4 |
| Submerged lands | 551.41 |   ethics | 178 |
|   *see also* Wetlands | |   health insurance | 368.382 5 |
| Submersible craft | 387.204 5 |   law | 344.044 6 |
|   design | 623.812 045 |     criminal law | 345.027 7 |
|   engineering | 623.820 5 |     social welfare law | 344.044 6 |
|   transportation services | 387.204 5 |   literature | 808.803 561 |
|   *see also* Ships | |     history and criticism | 809.933 561 |
| Submissiveness | |     specific literatures | T3B—080 356 1 |
|   personality trait | 155.232 |       history and | |
| Subordinate constructions | |         criticism | T3B—093 561 |
|   (Grammar) | 415 |   medicine | 616.86 |
|   specific languages | T4—5 |   pastoral theology | 206.1 |
| Subordinate levels of | |     Christianity | 259.429 |
|   administration | 352.14 |   personal health | 613.8 |
| Subornation of perjury | 364.134 |   personnel management | 658.382 2 |
|   law | 345.023 4 |     public administration | 352.67 |
| Subrings | 512.4 |   pregnancy complications | |
| Subscription books | |     obstetrics | 618.368 6 |
|   publishing | 070.573 |   primary education | 372.378 |
| Subscription libraries | 027.2 |   prisoner services | 365.667 29 |
| Subscription television | 384.555 4 |   religious guidance | 204.42 |
|   *see also* Television | |     Christianity | 248.862 9 |
| Subsidence | 551.307 |   school problem | 371.784 |
| Subsidiary corporations | 338.8 |   social theology | 201.762 29 |
|   *see also* Combinations | |     Christianity | 261.832 29 |
|     (Enterprises) | |   social welfare | 362.29 |
| Subsidies | |     public administration | 353.64 |
|   agricultural industries | 338.18 |   transportation safety | 363.120 1 |
|   export trade | 382.63 |     traffic accidents | 363.125 14 |
|     *see also* Export trade | |   *see Manual at* 616.86 vs. 158.1, | |
|   law | 343.074 2 |     204.42, 248.8629, 292–299, | |
|   natural resources | 333.715 8 |     362.29 | |
|   production economics | 338.922 | Substance abusers | T1—087 4 |
| Subsidized housing | 363.582 | Substance-related disorders | |
|   *see also* Housing | |   medicine | 616.86 |
| Subsistence hunting | 639.1 |   perinatal medicine | 618.326 86 |
| Subsistence theory of wages | 331.210 1 |   pregnancy complications | |
| Subsonic flow | 533.273 |     obstetrics | 618.368 6 |
|   air mechanics | 533.62 | Substitute teaching | 371.141 22 |
|     aeronautics | 629.132 303 | Substitution (Chemical reaction) | 541.39 |
| | |   organic chemistry | 547.2 |
| | | Substructural logic | 511.31 |

| | | | |
|---|---|---|---|
| Subsurface mining | 622.2 | Subway stations | 388.472 |
| Subsurface resources | | architecture | 725.31 |
| land economics | 333.8 | construction | 690.531 |
| public administration | 354.39 | transportation services | 388.472 |
| Subsurface water | 553.79 | Subway transportation | 388.42 |
| *see also* Groundwater | | *see also* Subways (Rail) | |
| Subterranean land vehicles | | Subways (Pedestrian) | 388.411 |
| engineering | 629.292 | Subways (Rail) | 388.42 |
| Subtiaba-Tlapanec languages | 497.9 | engineering | 625.42 |
| | T6—979 | law | 343.098 3 |
| Subtraction | 512.92 | public administration | 354.769 |
| algebra | 512.92 | transportation services | 388.42 |
| arithmetic | 513.212 | Success | 650.1 |
| Subtractive processes | | applied psychology | 158 |
| color photography | 778.66 | children | 155.419 |
| Subtropical fruits | | arts | T3C—353 |
| cooking | 641.646 | business | 650.1 |
| food | 641.346 | folklore | 398.273 |
| orchard crops | 634.6 | home economics | 646.7 |
| Subud | 299.933 | literature | 808.803 53 |
| Suburban administration | 352.169 | history and criticism | 809.933 53 |
| Suburban areas | 307.74 | specific literatures | T3B—080 353 |
| | T2—173 3 | history and | |
| *see also* Suburbs | | criticism | T3B—093 53 |
| Suburban biology | 578.756 | parapsychology | 131 |
| Suburban ecology | 577.56 | public situations | 650.1 |
| Suburban sociology | 307.74 | social psychology | 302.14 |
| Suburban transportation | 388.4 | Success in business | 650.1 |
| railroad | | Success runs (Mathematics) | 519.84 |
| engineering | 625.4 | Successful living | 646.7 |
| Suburbs | 307.74 | Succession (Law) | 346.052 |
| | T2—173 3 | Succubi | 133.423 |
| psychological influence | 155.943 | *see also* Legendary beings | |
| public administration | 352.169 | Succulent plants | 581.754 |
| control by higher | | floriculture | 635.952 5 |
| jurisdictions | 353.336 9 | Suceava (Romania : Judeţ) | T2—498 1 |
| Subversion (Political) | 327.12 | Suchitepéquez (Guatemala) | T2—728 165 |
| *see also* Subversive activities | | Suckers (Fishes) | 597.48 |
| Subversive activities | 327.12 | Suckers (Plants) | |
| armed forces | 355.343 7 | agricultural propagation | 631.533 |
| *see also* Unconventional | | Sucking lice | 595.756 |
| warfare | | Sucre (Bolivia) | T2—842 4 |
| criminology | 364.131 | Sucre (Colombia : Dept.) | T2—861 13 |
| criminal law | 345.023 1 | Sucre (Venezuela : State) | T2—875 3 |
| international politics | 327.12 | Sucrose | 572.565 |
| political groups | 322.42 | *see also* Carbohydrates | |
| public administration | 353.17 | Sucumbíos (Ecuador : | |
| Subversive groups | 322.42 | Province) | T2—866 412 |
| Subversive material | | Sud (Haiti) | T2—729 462 |
| postal handling | 383.120 5 | Sud-Est (Haiti : Dept.) | T2—729 456 |
| Subviral organisms | 579.29 | Sud-Kivu (Congo) | T2—675 17 |
| | | Sudan | 962.4 |
| | | | T2—624 |
| | | Sudan grass | 584.92 |

| | |
|---|---|
| Sudanese | T5—927 624 |
| Sudanic languages (Chari-Nile) | 496.5 |
| | T6—965 |
| Sudbury (Ont. : District) | T2—713 133 |
| Sudbury (Ont. : Regional municipality) | T2—713 133 |
| Sudden infant death | |
| pediatrics | 618.920 26 |
| Śuddhādvaita (Philosophy) | 181.484 4 |
| Sudetenland (Czech Republic) | T2—437 1 |
| Südlicher Oberrhein (Germany : Region) | T2—434 626 |
| Südtirol (Italy) | T2—453 83 |
| Südtiroler Volkspartei (Italy) | 324.245 084 |
| Suede leather | 675.25 |
| Suez (Egypt : Province) | T2—621 5 |
| Suez, Gulf of | 551.461 533 |
| | T2—165 33 |
| Suez, Isthmus of | T2—621 5 |
| Suez Canal (Egypt) | 386.43 |
| | T2—621 5 |
| Suffering | |
| consolatory devotions | 204.32 |
| Christianity | 242.4 |
| philosophy | 128.4 |
| religious guidance | 204.42 |
| Christianity | 248.86 |
| theodicy | 202.118 |
| *see also* Theodicy | |
| theological anthropology | 202.2 |
| *see also* Humans — religion | |
| Suffixes | 415.92 |
| specific languages | T4—592 |
| Suffolk (England) | T2—426 4 |
| Suffolk (Va.) | T2—755 53 |
| Suffolk Coastal (England) | T2—426 46 |
| Suffolk County (Mass.) | T2—744 6 |
| Suffolk County (N.Y.) | T2—747 25 |
| Suffolk horse | 636.15 |
| Suffrage | 324.62 |
| law | 342.072 |
| Suffrages (Liturgy) | 264.13 |
| music | 782.292 |
| Sufi orders | 297.48 |
| Sufis | 297.409 2 |
| Sufism | 297.4 |
| Sugar | 641.336 |
| agriculture | 633.6 |
| biochemistry | 572.565 |
| commercial processing | 664.1 |
| cooking with | 641.636 |
| food | 641.336 |
| *see also* Carbohydrates | |
| Sugar beets | 633.63 |
| agriculture | 633.63 |
| botany | 583.53 |
| Sugar crops | 633.6 |
| Sugar-free cooking | 641.563 837 |
| Sugar-free diet | |
| health | 613.283 32 |
| Sugar maple | 633.64 |
| botany | 583.78 |
| syrup crop | 633.64 |
| Sugar substitutes | |
| food technology | 664.5 |
| Sugarcane | 633.61 |
| agricultural economics | 338.173 61 |
| agriculture | 633.61 |
| botany | 584.92 |
| Sugars | 572.565 |
| *see also* Carbohydrates | |
| Sūhāj (Egypt : Province) | T2—623 |
| Suharto | |
| Indonesian history | 959.803 7 |
| Suhl (Germany) | T2—432 26 |
| Suhl (Germany : Bezirk) | T2—432 26 |
| Sui dynasty | 951.016 |
| Suicidal behavior | 362.28 |
| medicine | 616.858 445 |
| *see also* Suicide | |
| Suicide | 362.28 |
| criminology | 364.152 2 |
| criminal law | 345.025 22 |
| customs | 394.88 |
| ethics | 179.7 |
| religion | 205.697 |
| Buddhism | 294.356 97 |
| Christianity | 241.697 |
| Hinduism | 294.548 697 |
| Judaism | 296.369 7 |
| medicine | 616.858 445 |
| pastoral care | 206.1 |
| Christianity | 259.428 |
| social theology | 201.762 28 |
| Christianity | 261.832 28 |
| social welfare | 362.28 |
| *see also* Mental illness | |
| Suidae | 599.633 |
| Suiformes | 599.633 |
| Suir River (Ireland) | T2—419 1 |
| Suitcases | |
| manufacturing technology | 685.51 |
| Suites | 784.185 8 |
| Suits (Clothing) | 391.473 |
| commercial technology | 687.113 |
| customs | 391.473 |
| home economics | 646.3 |

Suits (Clothing) (continued)
  home sewing    646.433
  *see also* Clothing
Suits (Law)    347.053
  procedure    347.050 4
Sukarno
  Indonesian history    959.803 5
Sukhothai (Kingdom)    959.302 2
Sukkah    296.123 2
  Babylonian Talmud    296.125 2
  Mishnah    296.123 2
  Palestinian Talmud    296.124 2
Sukkot    296.433
  liturgy    296.453 3
Suku (African people)    T5—963 93
Suku language    496.393
   T6—963 93
Sukuma (African people)    T5—963 94
Sukuma-Nyamwezi languages    496.394
   T6—963 94
Sukunka River (B.C.)    T2—711 87
Sulawesi (Indonesia)    T2—598 4
Sulawesi Barat (Indonesia)    T2—598 46
Sulawesi languages    499.226
   T6—992 26
Sulawesi Selatan
  (Indonesia)    T2—598 47
Sulawesi Tengah
  (Indonesia)    T2—598 44
Sulawesi Tenggara
  (Indonesia)    T2—598 48
Sulawesi Utara (Indonesia)    T2—598 42
Sulaymānīyah (Iraq :
  Province)    T2—567 2
Sulfate process
  wood pulp    676.126
Sulfated hydrocarbons    668.14
Sulfated oils    668.14
Sulfates    546.723 24
  chemical engineering    661.63
  mineralogy    549.75
Sulfides    546.723 2
  chemical engineering    661.63
  mineralogy    549.32
  organic chemistry    547.061
Sulfinic acids    547.066
  chemical engineering    661.896
Sulfite process
  wood pulp    676.125
Sulfites    546.723 24
  chemical engineering    661.63
Sulfonation    547.27
  chemical engineering    660.284 4

Sulfones    547.065
  chemical engineering    661.896
Sulfonic acids    547.067
  chemical engineering    661.896
Sulfosalts
  mineralogy    549.35
Sulfoxides    547.065
  chemical engineering    661.896
Sulfur    553.668
  applied nutrition    613.285
  biochemistry    572.554
    humans    612.015 24
  chemical engineering    661.072 3
  chemistry    546.723
  economic geology    553.668
  metabolism
    human physiology    612.392 4
  mining    622.366 8
  organic chemistry    547.06
    aliphatic    547.46
    applied    661.896
    aromatic    547.66
  *see also* Chemicals
Sulfur bacteria    579.38
Sulfur dioxide
  gas technology    665.84
Sulfur salts
  chemical engineering    661.63
Sulfuric acid
  chemical engineering    661.22
Sulidae    598.43
Sullivan, Harry Stack
  psychological system    150.195 7
Sullivan County (Ind.)    T2—772 41
Sullivan County (Mo.)    T2—778 235
Sullivan County (N.H.)    T2—742 75
Sullivan County (N.Y.)    T2—747 35
Sullivan County (Pa.)    T2—748 59
Sullivan County (Tenn.)    T2—768 96
Sully County (S.D.)    T2—783 284
Sulphur    553.668
  *see also* Sulfur
Sulpicians    255.75
  church history    271.75
Sultan Kudarat (Philippines)    T2—599 7
Sulu (Philippines)    T2—599 9
Sulu Archipelago
  (Philippines)    T2—599 9
Sulu Sea    551.461 473
   T2—164 73
Sumacs    583.77
Sumapaz National Park
  (Colombia)    T2—861 46
Sumatera (Indonesia)    T2—598 1

| | |
|---|---|
| Sumatera Barat (Indonesia) | T2—598 13 |
| Sumatera Selatan (Indonesia) | T2—598 16 |
| Sumatera Utara (Indonesia) | T2—598 12 |
| Sumatra (Indonesia) | T2—598 1 |
| Sumba Island (Indonesia) | T2—598 68 |
| Sumbawa (Indonesia) | T2—598 65 |
| Sumer | 935.501 |
| | T2—355 |
| Sumerian language | 499.95 |
| | T6—999 5 |
| Sumerian literature | 899.95 |
| Sumerians | T5—999 5 |
| Sumie | 751.425 2 |
| Summability | 515.243 |
| Summaries | |
|   rhetoric | 808.062 |
| Summation (Calculus) | 515.43 |
| Summation (Law) | 347.075 |
| Summer | 508.2 |
|   music | 781.524 4 |
|   *see also* Seasons | |
| Summer air conditioning | |
|   building systems | 697.933 3 |
| Summer-flowering plants | 581.43 |
|   floriculture | 635.953 |
| Summer school | 371.232 |
| Summer theater | 792.022 4 |
| Summers County (W. Va.) | T2—754 76 |
| Summit County (Colo.) | T2—788 45 |
| Summit County (Ohio) | T2—771 36 |
| Summit County (Utah) | T2—792 14 |
| Summons | 347.072 |
|   criminal law | 345.072 |
| Sumner County (Kan.) | T2—781 87 |
| Sumner County (Tenn.) | T2—768 47 |
| Sumner's method | |
|   celestial navigation | 527.3 |
| Sumo | 796.812 5 |
| Sums´ka oblast´ (Ukraine) | T2—477 6 |
| Sumter County (Ala.) | T2—761 41 |
| Sumter County (Fla.) | T2—759 73 |
| Sumter County (Ga.) | T2—758 913 |
| Sumter County (S.C.) | T2—757 69 |
| Sumy (Ukraine : Oblast) | T2—477 6 |
| Sun | 523.7 |
| | T2—994 |
|   astrology | 133.531 |
|   astronomy | 523.7 |
|   gravity | 523.71 |
|   religious worship | 202.12 |
| Sun bathing | |
|   health | 613.193 |

| | |
|---|---|
| Sun-dried blocks | |
|   architectural construction | 721.044 22 |
|   building construction | 693.22 |
| Sun spiders | 595.48 |
| Sun tables | |
|   earth astronomy | 525.38 |
| Sunan (Hadith) | 297.125 5 |
| Sunbeam snakes | 597.967 |
| Sunburn | |
|   medicine | 616.515 |
|   *see also* Skin diseases — humans | |
| Sunbury (N.B.) | T2—715 43 |
| Sunbury (Vic.) | T2—945 2 |
| Sunda Islands | T2—598 |
| Sunda Islands, Lesser (Indonesia) | T2—598 6 |
| Sunda language | 499.223 2 |
| | T6—992 232 |
| Sunda literature | 899.223 2 |
| Sundanese | T5—992 232 |
| Sundanese language | 499.223 2 |
| | T6—992 232 |
| Sundanese literature | 899.223 2 |
| Sunday | |
|   Christian observance | 263.3 |
|   music | 781.522 2 |
| Sunday school | 268 |
|   Jewish | 296.680 83 |
| Sunday school buildings | |
|   administration | 268.2 |
|   architecture | 726.4 |
| Sunday work | 331.257 4 |
|   economics | 331.257 4 |
|   personnel management | 658.312 1 |
| Sunderland (England : Metropolitan Borough) | T2—428 71 |
| Sundews | 583.75 |
| Sundials | |
|   technology | 681.111 2 |
| Sunfishes | 597.738 |
| Sunflower County (Miss.) | T2—762 47 |
| Sunflowers | 583.99 |
|   floriculture | 635.933 99 |
| Sung dynasty | 951.024 |
| Sunlight-favoring plants | |
|   floriculture | 635.954 |
| Sunni Islam | 297.81 |
|   doctrines | 297.204 1 |
|   relations with Shia Islam | 297.804 2 |
|   worship | 297.301 |
| Sunshine Coast (B.C.) | T2—711 31 |
| Sunshine law | 342.066 2 |
| Sunspiders | 595.48 |

| | | | |
|---|---|---|---|
| Sunspots | 523.74 | Superintendents of schools | |
| geomagnetic effects | 538.746 | biography | 371.200 92 |
| Sunwar language | 495.49 | public control | 379.157 |
| | T6—954 9 | role and function | 371.201 1 |
| Suomi language | 494.541 | Superior (Wis.) | T2—775 11 |
| | T6—945 41 | Superior, Lake | T2—774 9 |
| Suomi literature | 894.541 | Michigan | T2—774 9 |
| Super Bowl (Football) | 796.332 648 | Ontario | T2—713 12 |
| Supcrannuation (Pension) | 331.252 | Superior courts | 347.02 |
| Supercolliders | 539.736 | Superior intelligence | 153.98 |
| Supercomputers | 004.11 | Supermarkets | 381.149 |
| architecture | 004.251 | discount stores | 381.149 |
| communications | 004.611 | management | 658.879 |
| programming | 005.712 1 | food stores | 381.456 413 |
| programs | 005.713 1 | management | 658.879 |
| engineering | 621.391 1 | *see also* Commerce | |
| graphics programming | 006.671 | Supernatural | |
| graphics programs | 006.681 | occultism | 130 |
| interfacing | 004.611 | Supernatural beings | |
| programming | 005.712 1 | religious | 202.11 |
| programs | 005.713 1 | *see also* Gods and goddesses | |
| multimedia-systems | | secular | 398.21 |
| programming | 006.771 | *see also* Legendary beings | |
| multimedia-systems programs | 006.781 | Supernatural in literature | 808.803 7 |
| operating systems | 005.441 | history and criticism | 809.933 7 |
| performance evaluation | 004.110 29 | specific literatures | T3B—080 37 |
| for design and improvement | 004.251 | history and criticism | T3B—093 7 |
| programming | 005.21 | Supernovas | 523.844 65 |
| programs | 005.31 | Supersonic flow | 533.275 |
| systems analysis | 004.251 | air mechanics | 533.62 |
| systems design | 004.251 | aeronautics | 629.132 305 |
| *see Manual at* 004.11–.16 | | Superstitions | 001.96 |
| Superconducting supercolliders | 539.736 | folklore | 398.41 |
| Superconductivity | 537.623 | Superstores | 381.149 |
| engineering | 621.35 | management | 658.879 |
| materials science | 620.112 973 | Superstring theory | 539.725 8 |
| Superconductor circuits | 621.381 5 | Superstrings | 539.725 8 |
| Superconductors | 537.623 | Supersymmetry | 539.725 |
| engineering | 621.35 | Supertanker berthing areas | 387.1 |
| Supercritical fluid | | engineering | 627.22 |
| chromatography | 543.86 | *see also* Ports | |
| Supercritical gas chromatography | 543.86 | Supervised activities | |
| Supercross | 796.756 | child care | 649.5 |
| Superego | | Supervision of dramatic | |
| subconscious | 154.2 | performances | 792.023 |
| Superfluidity | 530.42 | motion pictures | 791.430 23 |
| Supergiant slalom skiing | 796.935 | radio | 791.440 23 |
| Supergravity | 530.142 3 | stage | 792.023 |
| Superheaters | | television | 791.450 23 |
| nuclear reactors | 621.483 4 | Supervision of employees | 658.302 |
| steam engineering | 621.197 | executive personnel | 658.407 |
| | | library personnel | 023.9 |
| | | military personnel | 355.330 41 |
| | | public administration | 352.66 |

Supervisors
  labor economics    331.794
  role and function    658.302
Suppers    642
  cooking    641.53
    light meals    641.53
    main meals    641.54
  customs    394.125 3
    light meals    394.125 3
    main meals    394.125 4
Supplemental budgets (Public)    352.48
  *see also* Budgets (Public)
Supplies
  armed forces    355.8
  management    658.7
    armed forces    355.621
    public administration    352.55
  office services    651.29
Supply (Quantity)
  communications industry    384.041
  forecasts    338.02
    agricultural industries    338.17
    production economics    338.02
    secondary industries    338.47
  microeconomics    338.521 3
  natural resources    333.711
  transportation services    388.049
Supply and demand    338.521
  monetary economics    332.401
  production economics    338.521
Supply depots (Armed forces)    355.75
Supply management    658.7
  armed forces    355.621
  public administration    352.55
Supply services (Armed forces)    355.621
  issuing units    355.341
Supply ships (Military)    359.985 83
  *see also* Military supply ships
Supply-side economics    330.155 4
Support (Domestic relations)    346.016 63
Support groups    361.43
Supporting garments    391.423
  commercial technology    687.2
  customs    391.423
  home sewing    646.42
  *see also* Clothing
Suppressed books    098.1
Suppuration    571.937 9
Supramolecular chemistry    547.122 6
  inorganic chemistry    541.226
Supranational states    321.04
Suprasegmental phonology    414.6
  specific languages    T4—16
Supreme court justices    347.035 092

Supreme courts    347.035
  criminal law    345.014 44
Suras (Koran)    297.122 9
Surety bonds
  insurance    368.84
Suretyship    346.074
Surf riding    797.32
Surface-active agents    668.1
Surface chemistry    541.33
  applied    660.293
Surface engineering    620.44
Surface finishing
  home woodworking    684.084
  wooden furniture    684.104 3
Surface integrals    515.43
Surface-mined lands    333.765
  economics    333.765
  reclamation technology    631.64
Surface mining    622.292
Surface-painted enamels
  ceramic arts    738.46
Surface physics    530.417
  liquids    530.427
  solids    530.417
Surface processes (Geology)    551.3
  *see Manual at* 551.302–.307 vs.
    551.35
Surface prospecting    622.12
Surface rail transit systems    388.42
  engineering    625.6
  public administration    354.769
  transportation services    388.42
Surface refinishing
  wooden furniture    684.104 43
Surface tension    530.427
  chemical engineering    660.293
Surface tillage    631.581
Surface-to-air guided missiles    358.174 82
  engineering    623.451 94
  military equipment    358.174 82
Surface-to-air missile forces    358.174
Surface-to-surface guided
  missiles    358.171 82
  engineering    623.451 95
  military equipment    358.171 82
Surface-to-underwater guided
  missiles    358.176 82
  engineering    623.451 96
  military equipment    358.176 82
Surface transportation    388
  mining    622.69
  *see also* Ground transportation
Surface treatment
  metals    671.7

Surface water | 553.78
| T2—169
  economic geology | 553.78
  hydrology | 551.48
  resource economics | 333.91
Surfaced lumber | 674.42
Surfaces
  geometry
    algebraic | 516.352
    configurations | 516.154
    differential | 516.36
    integral | 516.362
Surfacing roads | 625.8
  dirt roads | 625.75
  paved roads | 625.8
Surfactants | 668.1
Surfers | 797.320 92
Surfers Paradise (Qld.) | T2—943 2
Surfing | 797.32
Surgeons | 617.092
  law | 344.041 2
  malpractice | 344.041 21
  role and function | 617.023 2
Surgery | 617
  gynecology | 618.105 9
  obstetrics | 618.8
  veterinary medicine | 636.089 7
  *see Manual at* 616 vs. 617.4;
    *also at* 617
Surgery (Topology) | 514.72
Surgical abortion | 362.198 88
  medicine | 618.88
  *see also* Abortion
Surgical assistants
  role and function | 617.023 3
Surgical complications
  anesthesiology | 617.960 41
  medicine | 617.919
Surgical dressings
  use | 617.93
Surgical equipment | 617.9
Surgical gauzes | 677.8
  manufacturing technology | 677.8
  use | 617.93
Surgical infections
  medicine | 617.919 5
Surgical insurance | 368.382 2
Surgical nurses
  role and function | 617.023 1
Surgical nursing | 617.023 1
Surgical physician assistants
  role and function | 617.023 32
Surgical shock
  medicine | 617.21

Surgical technicians
  role and function | 617.023 3
Surigao del Norte
  (Philippines) | T2—599 7
Surigao del Sur
  (Philippines) | T2—599 7
Surinam toad | 597.865
Suriname | 988.3
| T2—883
Surinamers | T5—914 1
Surnames | 929.42
Surpluses
  agricultural industries | 338.17
  military supplies | 355.621 37
  natural resources | 333.711
  production | 338.02
  secondary industries | 338.47
Surrealism
  arts | 700.411 63
| T3C—116 3
  fine arts | 709.040 63
  literature | 808.801 163
    history and criticism | 809.911 63
    specific literatures | T3B—080 116 3
    history and
      criticism | T3B—091 163
  painting | 759.066 3
  sculpture | 735.230 463
Surrey (B.C.) | T2—711 33
Surrey (England) | T2—422 1
Surrey Heath (England) | T2—422 13
Surrogate motherhood | 306.874 3
  ethics | 176.2
    *see also* Reproduction —
      ethics
  law | 346.017
Surry County (N.C.) | T2—756 65
Surry County (Va.) | T2—755 562
Sursee (Switzerland : Amt) | T2—494 555
Surselva (Switzerland) | T2—494 735 8
Surveillance
  civil rights issue | 323.448 2
  engineering | 621.389 28
  law | 345.052
  law enforcement | 363.232
Survey methodology | 001.433
| T1—072 3
Surveying | 526.9
  canal engineering | 627.131
  dam engineering | 627.81
  railroad engineering | 625.11
  road engineering | 625.723
Surveying equipment
  manufacturing technology | 681.76

| | | | |
|---|---|---|---|
| Surveyors | 526.909 2 | Sustainable engineering | 628 |
| Surveys | | | T1—028 6 |
| descriptive research | 001.433 | Sustut River (B.C.) | T2—711 85 |
| | T1—072 3 | Susu language | 496.34 |
| marketing management | 658.83 | | T6—963 4 |
| marketing reports | 381 | Sutherland (Scotland) | T2—411 52 |
| public administration | 352.75 | Sutherland (South Africa : | |
| Survival | 613.69 | District) | T2—687 17 |
| Survival analysis | 519.546 | Sūtrapiṭaka | 294.382 3 |
| Survival housekeeping | 613.69 | Suttapiṭaka | 294.382 3 |
| Survival skills | 613.69 | Suttee | 393.930 954 |
| Survival training (Military | | customs | 393.930 954 |
| training) | 355.54 | Hindu practice | 294.538 8 |
| Survivors' insurance | 368.3 | Sutter County (Calif.) | T2—794 34 |
| government-sponsored | 368.43 | Sutton (London, England) | T2—421 92 |
| law | 344.023 | Sutton County (Tex.) | T2—764 879 |
| Sus | 599.633 2 | Sutures | |
| Susa (Extinct city) | T2—357 64 | surgical use | 617.917 8 |
| Susanna (Deuterocanonical book) | 229.6 | Suwałki (Poland : | |
| Sushi | 641.82 | Voivodeship) | T2—438 32 |
| Susliks | 599.365 | Suwannee County (Fla.) | T2—759 82 |
| Suspended ceilings | | Suwannee River (Ga. and | |
| buildings | 698 | Fla.) | T2—759 8 |
| Suspended sentence | 364.63 | Suwaydā' (Syria : Province) | T2—569 14 |
| Suspense drama | 792.27 | Suways (Egypt : Province) | T2—621 5 |
| literature | 808.825 27 | SV40 (Virus) | 579.244 5 |
| history and criticism | 809.252 7 | Svalbard (Norway) | T2—981 |
| specific literatures | T3B—205 27 | Svan language | 499.968 |
| individual authors | T3A—2 | | T6—999 68 |
| stage presentation | 792.27 | Svealand (Sweden) | T2—487 |
| Suspense stories | 808.838 72 | Sverdlovsk (Russia : Oblast) | T2—474 3 |
| history and criticism | 809.387 2 | Sverdlovskaia oblast´ | |
| specific literatures | T3B—308 72 | (Russia) | T2—474 3 |
| individual authors | T3A—3 | Svetambara (Jainism) | 294.492 |
| Suspension bridges | | SVP (Swiss political party) | 324.249 403 |
| construction | 624.23 | Swabia (Germany) | T2—434 6 |
| Suspension of rights | 323.49 | Bavaria | T2—433 7 |
| Suspension systems | | Swabian Alps (Germany) | T2—434 73 |
| automotive engineering | 629.243 | Swabian dialect | 437.943 37 |
| Suspensions (Chemistry) | 541.34 | | T6—33 |
| chemical engineering | 660.294 | Swabian Jura (Germany) | T2—434 73 |
| Susquehanna County (Pa.) | T2—748 34 | Swabians | |
| Susquehanna River | T2—748 | Sicilian history | 945.804 |
| Maryland | T2—752 74 | Southern Italian history | 945.704 |
| Pennsylvania | T2—748 | Swahili language | 496.392 |
| Susquehanna River, West | | | T6—963 92 |
| Branch (Pa.) | T2—748 5 | Swahili literature | 896.392 |
| Sussex (England) | T2—422 5 | Swahili-speaking peoples | T5—963 92 |
| Sussex cattle | 636.222 | Swain County (N.C.) | T2—756 96 |
| Sussex County (Del.) | T2—751 7 | Swale (England) | T2—422 33 |
| Sussex County (N.J.) | T2—749 76 | Swale, River (England) | T2—428 48 |
| Sussex County (Va.) | T2—755 565 | Swallow-tanager | 598.875 |
| Sustainable architecture | 720.47 | Swallowers (Chiasmodontidae) | 597.7 |
| Sustainable development | 338.927 | Swallowers (Saccopharyngidae) | 597.43 |

| | | | |
|---|---|---|---|
| Swallows | 598.826 | Swedes (Plants) | 641.351 26 |
| Swamp eels | 597.64 | *see also* Rutabagas | |
| Swamp rats | 599.35 | Swedish language | 439.7 |
| Swamps | 551.417 | | T6—397 |
| biology | 578.768 | Swedish literature | 839.7 |
| ecology | 577.68 | Swedish people | T5—397 |
| *see also* Wetlands | | Swedish turnip | 641.351 26 |
| Swan Hill (Vic.) | T2—945 9 | *see also* Rutabagas | |
| Swan River (W.A.) | T2—941 2 | Sweep generators | |
| Swans | 598.418 | electronics | 621.381 548 |
| animal husbandry | 636.681 | Sweeping | |
| Swansea (Wales) | T2—429 82 | housecleaning | 648.5 |
| Swanskin fabrics | 677.624 | Sweet bay | 641.357 |
| *see also* Textiles | | botany | 583.23 |
| Swaps (Finance) | 332.645 7 | *see also* Herbs | |
| Swarming of bees | 595.799 156 | Sweet cider | 641.341 1 |
| apiculture | 638.146 | commercial processing | 663.63 |
| Swartruggens (South | | cooking with | 641.641 1 |
| Africa : District) | T2—682 48 | food | 641.341 1 |
| Swat (Pakistan) | T2—549 122 | Sweet clovers | 633.366 |
| Swati language | 496.398 7 | botany | 583.74 |
| | T6—963 987 | forage crop | 633.366 |
| Swazi (Ethnic group) | T5—963 987 | Sweet corn | 641.356 72 |
| Swazi (National group) | T5—968 87 | commercial processing | 664.805 672 |
| Swazi language | 496.398 7 | cooking | 641.656 72 |
| | T6—963 987 | food | 641.356 72 |
| Swazi literature | 896.398 7 | garden crop | 635.672 |
| Swaziland | 968.87 | Sweet gale | 583.43 |
| | T2—688 7 | Sweet Grass County (Mont.) | T2—786 64 |
| Swearing | | Sweet gums | 583.44 |
| customs | 394 | forestry | 634.973 44 |
| ethics | 179.5 | ornamental arboriculture | 635.977 344 |
| Sweat gland diseases | | Sweet herbs | 641.357 |
| medicine | 616.56 | *see also* Herbs | |
| *see also* Skin diseases — | | Sweet peas (Flowers) | 635.933 74 |
| humans | | botany | 583.74 |
| Sweat glands | 573.537 9 | floriculture | 635.933 74 |
| biology | 573.537 9 | Sweet peppers | 641.356 43 |
| human anatomy | 611.77 | botany | 583.952 |
| human physiology | 612.793 | commercial processing | 664.805 643 |
| medicine | 616.56 | cooking | 641.656 43 |
| *see also* Skin | | food | 641.356 43 |
| Sweaters | 391.46 | garden crop | 635.643 |
| commercial technology | 687.14 | Sweet potatoes | 641.352 2 |
| home sewing | 646.45 | agriculture | 635.22 |
| *see also* Outerwear | | botany | 583.94 |
| Sweden | 948.5 | commercial processing | 664.805 22 |
| | T2—485 | cooking | 641.652 2 |
| ancient | 936.85 | food | 641.352 2 |
| | T2—368 5 | Sweet sorghums | 633.62 |
| Swedenborgianism | 289.4 | Sweetened condensed milk | 641.371 424 |
| Swedenborgians | | cooking | 641.671 424 |
| biography | 289.409 2 | food | 641.371 424 |
| Swedes | T5—397 | processing | 637.142 4 |

| | |
|---|---|
| Sweeteners | |
| commercial processing | 664.1 |
| Sweetleaf | 583.674 |
| Sweets (Candy) | 641.853 |
| commercial processing | 664.153 |
| home preparation | 641.853 |
| Sweets (Desserts and | |
| confections) | 641.86 |
| Sweetwater County (Wyo.) | T2—787 85 |
| Swellendam (South Africa : | |
| District) | T2—687 36 |
| Swells (Wind effects) | 551.463 |
| lakes | 551.482 |
| Świętokrzyskie Voivodeship | |
| (Poland) | T2—438 45 |
| Swift County (Minn.) | T2—776 41 |
| Swift Current (Sask.) | T2—712 43 |
| Swifts | 598.762 |
| Swimmers | 797.210 92 |
| Swimming | 797.21 |
| animal behavior | 591.57 |
| physical fitness | 613.716 |
| Swimming pools | 797.2 |
| architecture | 725.74 |
| domestic | 643.556 |
| architecture | 728.962 |
| construction | 690.896 2 |
| home economics | 643.556 |
| public | 797.2 |
| architecture | 725.74 |
| construction | 690.574 |
| sanitation services | 363.729 2 |
| Swindon (England : | |
| Borough) | T2—423 13 |
| Swine | 636.4 |
| Swing (Golf) | 796.352 3 |
| Swing (Music) | 781.654 |
| Swisher County (Tex.) | T2—764 838 |
| Swiss | T5—35 |
| Swiss cheese | 641.373 54 |
| cooking | 641.673 54 |
| food | 641.373 54 |
| processing | 637.354 |
| Swiss Democrats (Political party) | 324.249 403 |
| Swiss-German dialect | 437.949 4 |
| | T6—35 |
| Swiss Germans | T5—35 |
| Swiss Labour Party | 324.249 407 4 |
| Swiss Liberal Party | 324.249 406 |
| Swiss literature | |
| French | 840 |
| German | 830 |
| Italian | 850 |
| Swiss National Park | T2—494 732 7 |
| Swiss People's Party | 324.249 403 |
| Switchboard operators | |
| office services | 651.374 3 |
| Switchboards | |
| communications services | 384.65 |
| telephony | 621.387 |
| Switches | |
| electrical engineering | 621.317 |
| interior wiring | 621.319 24 |
| railroad engineering | 625.163 |
| Switching | |
| communications engineering | 621.382 16 |
| computer communications | 004.66 |
| engineering | 621.398 1 |
| computer engineering | 621.395 |
| telephone engineering | 621.385 7 |
| Switching circuits | |
| electronics | 621.381 537 |
| Switching equipment | |
| electrical engineering | 621.317 |
| Switching theory | |
| electronics | 621.381 537 2 |
| Switzerland | 949.4 |
| | T2—494 |
| ancient | 936.94 |
| | T2—369 4 |
| Switzerland County (Ind.) | T2—772 125 |
| Swivel embroidery | 677.77 |
| Sword dances | 793.35 |
| Sword fighting | 796.86 |
| Sword lilies | 635.934 38 |
| botany | 584.38 |
| floriculture | 635.934 38 |
| Swordfish | 597.78 |
| Swordplay | 796.86 |
| Swords | 623.441 |
| art metalwork | 739.722 |
| Swordtail (Fish) | 597.667 |
| Sycamores | 583.44 |
| forestry | 634.973 44 |
| ornamental arboriculture | 635.977 344 |
| Sydney (N.S.W.) | T2—944 1 |
| Syenite | 553.52 |
| economic geology | 553.52 |
| petrology | 552.3 |
| quarrying | 622.352 |
| Sylhet (Bangladesh : | |
| Division) | T2—549 27 |
| Syllabaries | 411 |
| specific languages | T4—11 |
| Syllabi (Outlines) | T1—020 2 |
| Syllogisms | 166 |
| Syllogistic logic | 160 |
| Sylviidae | 598.843 |

Sylvilagus 599.324
Symbiosis 577.85
  animals 591.785
  factor in evolution 576.85
  plants 581.785
Symbolic divination 133.33
Symbolic logic 511.3
  computer programming
    languages 005.131
Symbolic programming 005.1
Symbolism 302.222 3
  art representation 704.946
  arts 700.415
       T3C—15
  Bible 220.64
  literature 808.801 5
    history and criticism 809.915
    specific literatures T3B—080 15
      history and
        criticism T3B—091 5
  of divinatory arts 133.3
  paintings 753.6
  religious significance 203.7
    Buddhism 294.343 7
    Hinduism 294.537
    Islam 297.3
    Judaism 296.46
  social psychology 302.222 3
  Talmud 296.120 64
Symbolism (Art style) 709.034 7
  painting 759.057
Symbolism of numbers 133.335
Symbols 302.222 3
       T1—014 8
  cultural institutions 306.4
  dictionaries 413.15
    specific languages T4—315
    specific subjects T1—014 8
  linguistics 411
    specific languages T4—11
  social psychology 302.222 3
Symmetric functions 515.22
Symmetric spaces 516.362
Symmetry
  arts 701.8
  geometry 516.1
Symmetry (Nuclear physics) 539.725
Sympathetic nervous system
  human physiology 612.89
  medicine 616.856 9

Sympathetic nervous system
  diseases
    medicine 616.856 9
    *see also* Nervous system
      diseases — humans
Symphonic poems 784.184 3
  musical form 784.184 3
  orchestral music 784.218 43
Symphonies 784.184
  musical form 784.184
  orchestral music 784.218 4
Symphonions 786.65
  *see also* Mechanical musical
    instruments
Symphony orchestras 784.2
Symphyla 595.63
Symphyseotomy
  obstetrical surgery 618.85
Symphysodon 597.74
Symphyta 595.79
Symplectic manifolds 516.36
Symplocaceae 583.674
Symptomatology 616.047
Symptoms
  medicine 616.047
Synagogue dedication 296.446
  liturgy 296.454 6
Synagogues 296.65
  architecture 726.3
  history of specific
    congregations 296.09
  organization 296.65
  religious symbolism of
    buildings 296.46
Synapsida 567.93
Synbranchiformes 597.64
Syncarida 595.379
Synchro-cyclotrons 539.735
Synchronic linguistics 410
  *see Manual at* 410
Synchronized swimming 797.217
Synchronized trampoline 796.474
Synchronous accelerators 539.735
Synchronous converters 621.313 5
Synchronous generators 621.313 4
Synchronous machinery 621.313 3
Synchronous transfer modes
  communications engineering 621.382 16
  computer communications 004.66
    engineering 621.398 1
Synchroscopes 621.374 9
Synchrotrons 539.735
Synclines 551.86

| | |
|---|---|
| Syncretism | |
| philosophy | 148 |
| Syndetic structure | 025.322 2 |
| authority files | 025.322 2 |
| subject authority files | 025.47 |
| Syndicalism | 335.82 |
| economics | 335.82 |
| political ideology | 320.53 |
| sociology | 306.34 |
| Syndicated crime | 364.106 8 |
| Syndicates | |
| banking | 332.16 |
| real estate investment | 332.632 47 |
| unincorporated business | |
| enterprises | 338.7 |
| *see also* Business enterprises; | |
| Unincorporated business | |
| enterprises | |
| Synecology | 577.8 |
| animals | 591.78 |
| microorganisms | 579.178 |
| plants | 581.78 |
| Synesthesia | |
| psychology | 152.189 |
| Syngnathidae | 597.679 |
| Synod of Bishops | 262.136 |
| Synod of Evangelical Lutheran | |
| Churches | 284.132 3 |
| *see also* Lutheran church | |
| Synodontidae | 597.61 |
| Synods | |
| Christian ecclesiology | 262.4 |
| Synonym dictionaries | 413.1 |
| specific languages | T4—312 |
| specific subjects | T1—03 |
| Synopses | T1—020 2 |
| music | 780 |
| treatises | 780.269 |
| vocal music | |
| treatises | 782.002 69 |
| Synoptic Gospels | 226 |
| Synoptic problem (Gospels) | 226.066 |
| Syntax | 415 |
| specific languages | T4—5 |
| Synthesis | |
| chemical engineering | 660.284 4 |
| chemistry | 541.39 |
| organic chemistry | 547.2 |
| Synthesizers | 786.74 |
| instrument | 786.741 9 |
| music | 786.74 |
| *see also* Electrophones | |
| Synthetic building materials | 666.89 |

| | |
|---|---|
| Synthetic chemicals | |
| organic | 661.805 |
| Synthetic drugs | |
| pharmacology | 615.31 |
| Synthetic drugs of abuse | 362.299 |
| personal health | 613.8 |
| social welfare | 362.299 |
| *see also* Substance abuse | |
| Synthetic dyes | 667.25 |
| Synthetic fuels | 662.66 |
| Synthetic gems | 666.88 |
| Synthetic glue | 668.31 |
| Synthetic meat | 664.64 |
| Synthetic minerals | 666.86 |
| Synthetic petroleum | 662.662 |
| Synthetic textile fibers | 677.4 |
| Synthetism | 709.034 7 |
| painting | 759.057 |
| Syphilis | |
| incidence | 614.547 2 |
| medicine | 616.951 3 |
| *see also* Communicable | |
| diseases — humans | |
| Syracusae (Italy) | T2—378 141 |
| Syracuse (Italy) | T2—458 141 |
| ancient | T2—378 141 |
| Syracuse (Italy : Province) | T2—458 14 |
| ancient | T2—378 14 |
| Syracuse (N.Y.) | T2—747 66 |
| Syria | 956.91 |
| | T2—569 1 |
| ancient | 939.43 |
| | T2—394 3 |
| Syriac Church | 281.63 |
| *see also* Eastern churches | |
| Syriac language | 492.3 |
| | T6—923 |
| Biblical texts | 220.43 |
| Syriac literature | 892.3 |
| Syriac Orthodox Church | 281.63 |
| *see also* Eastern churches | |
| Syrian Desert | T2—569 |
| Iraq | T2—567 4 |
| Jordan | T2—569 59 |
| Saudi Arabia | T2—538 |
| Syria | T2—569 12 |
| Syrian Orthodox Church | 281.63 |
| *see also* Eastern churches | |
| Syrians | T5—927 569 1 |
| Syrians (Religious order) | 255.18 |
| church history | 271.18 |
| Syringas | 583.72 |
| Syro-Malabar Christians | 281.52 |
| *see also* Eastern churches | |

| | | | |
|---|---|---|---|
| Syrphidae | 595.774 | Systems programs | 005.43 |
| Syrup crops | 633.6 | *see Manual at* 005.3, 005.5 vs. | |
| Syrups | 641.336 | 005.43–.45 | |
| commercial processing | 664.1 | Systems stability | 003.5 |
| food | 641.336 | Systems theory | 003 |
| *see also* Sugar | | management | 658.403 2 |
| Systellommatophora | 594.38 | Szabolcs-Szatmár-Bereg | |
| System administration (Computer | | Megye (Hungary) | T2—439 9 |
| science) | 005.43 | Szczecin (Poland : | |
| System analysis | 003 | Voivodeship) | T2—438 16 |
| *see also* Systems analysis | | Szechwan Province (China) | T2—513 8 |
| System design | 003 | Szondi tests | 155.284 3 |
| *see also* Systems design | | | |
| System identification | 003.1 | | |
| Systematic bibliography | 010.44 | | |
| Systematics (Biology) | 578.012 | | |
| Système international | 530.812 | | |
| social aspects | 389.15 | | |

# T

| | | | |
|---|---|---|---|
| Systemic lupus erythematosus | | T cells | 571.966 |
| medicine | 616.772 | human immunology | 616.079 7 |
| *see also* Musculoskeletal | | T formation | 796.332 22 |
| diseases — humans | | T lymphocytes | 571.966 |
| Systems | 003 | humans | 616.079 7 |
| | T1—011 | Ta'anit (Tractate) | 296.123 2 |
| *see Manual at* 510, T1—0151 | | Babylonian Talmud | 296.125 2 |
| vs. 003, T1—011 | | Mishnah | 296.123 2 |
| Systems analysis | 003 | Palestinian Talmud | 296.124 2 |
| computer science | 004.21 | Tabanidae | 595.773 |
| | T1—028 542 1 | Tabankulu (South Africa : | |
| engineering | 621.392 | District) | T2—687 59 |
| software | 005.12 | Ṭabaqāt al-Ruwāh | 297.125 261 |
| *see Manual at* 004.21 vs. | | Ṭabarānī, Sulaymān ibn Aḥmad | |
| 004.22, 621.392 | | Hadith | 297.125 63 |
| management | 658.403 2 | Tabasaran language | 499.964 |
| public administration | 352.33 | | T6—999 64 |
| military administration | 355.683 | Tabasco (Mexico : State) | T2—726 3 |
| Systems analysts | 003.092 | Tabby | |
| Systems control | 003.5 | building construction | 693.22 |
| Systems design | 003 | Tabernacles | |
| computer science | 004.21 | Christian church furniture | 247.1 |
| engineering | 621.392 | architecture | 726.529 1 |
| software | 005.12 | Judaism | 296.49 |
| *see Manual at* 004.21 vs. | | Tabes dorsalis | |
| 004.22, 621.392 | | medicine | 616.83 |
| Systems engineering | 620.001 171 | *see also* Nervous system | |
| Systems engineers | 620.009 2 | diseases — humans | |
| Systems of government | 321 | Tablas | 786.93 |
| Systems optimization | 003 | *see also* Percussion instruments | |
| | T1—011 | Tablature | 780.148 |
| Systems programming | 005.42 | Table decorations | 642.8 |
| *see Manual at* 005.1–.2 vs. | | Table furnishings | 642.7 |
| 005.42 | | Table linens | 642.7 |
| | | arts | 746.96 |
| | | home sewing | 646.21 |
| | | table setting | 642.7 |
| | | Table manners | 395.54 |

Table Mountain (Western
  Cape, South Africa)   T2—687 355
Table salt   553.632
  *see also* Salt (Sodium chloride)
Table service   642.6
Table setting   642.6
Table tennis   796.346
Table tennis players   796.346 092
Table tipping (Spiritualism)   133.92
Tableaux   793.24
Tablecloths   642.7
  arts   746.96
  home sewing   646.21
  table setting   642.7
Tables (Furniture)   645.4
  decorative arts   749.3
  outdoor   645.8
    *see also* Outdoor furniture
  *see also* Furniture
Tables (Lists)   T1—021
Tabletop fountains   745.594 6
Tabletop photography   778.8
Tablets (Pharmaceuticals)
  pharmaceutical chemistry   615.19
Tableware   642.7
  earthenware   666.68
    arts   738.38
    technology   666.68
  glass
    arts   748.2
  gold
    arts   739.228 3
  handicrafts   745.593
  ironwork
    arts   739.48
  porcelain   666.58
    arts   738.28
    technology   666.58
  pottery   666.3
    arts   738
    technology   666.3
  silver
    arts   739.238 3
  table setting   642.7
  wood
    arts   736.4
Taboos   390
Tabora Region (Tanzania)   T2—678 28
Tabulated materials   T1—021
Tacanan languages   498.9
    T6—989
Taccaccac   584.35
Tachinid flies   595.774
Tachinidae   595.774

Táchira (Venezuela)   T2—871 2
Tachometers
  technology   681.118
Tachyglossidae   599.29
Tackles (Mechanisms)   621.863
Tackling
  American football   796.332 26
Tacna (Peru : Dept.)   T2—853 5
Tacoma (Wash.)   T2—797 788
Tacos   641.84
Tactical exercises (Military
  training)   355.54
Tactical geography   355.47
Tactical missile forces   358.175 2
Tactical rockets   355.825 43
  engineering   623.454 3
  military equipment   355.825 43
Tactics (Military science)   355.42
Tactile organs
  cancer
    incidence   614.599 948 8
    medicine   616.994 88
  human anatomy   611.88
  human physiology   612.88
Tactile perception
  psychology   152.182
Tacuarembó (Uruguay :
  Dept.)   T2—895 32
Tadla-Azilal (Morocco)   T2—644
Tadpole shrimps   595.32
Tadpoles   597.813 92
Tadzhik   T5—915 7
Tadzhik language   491.57
    T6—915 7
Tadzhik literature   891.57
Tadzhikistan   958.6
    T2—586
Taekwondo   796.815 7
Taeniodontia   569.31
Taff Ely (Wales)   T2—429 78
Ṭafīlah (Jordan : Province)   T2—569 567
Taft, William H. (William
  Howard)
  United States history   973.912
Tag sales   381.195
Tagalog language   499.211
    T6—992 11
Tagalog literature   899.211
Tagmemics   415
  specific languages   T4—5
Taguchi methods (Quality
  control)
  production management   658.562

| | | |
|---|---|---|
| Tagus River (Spain and | | |
| Portugal) | T2—469 45 | |
| Portugal | T2—469 45 | |
| Spain | T2—462 8 | |
| Tahiti | T2—962 11 | |
| Tahitian language | 499.444 | |
| | T6—994 44 | |
| Tahitian literature | 899.444 | |
| Tahitians | T5—994 44 | |
| Tahitic languages | 499.44 | |
| | T6—994 4 | |
| Tahoe, Lake (Calif. and | | |
| Nev.) | T2—794 38 | |
| California | T2—794 38 | |
| Nevada | T2—793 57 | |
| Tai chi | 613.714 8 | |
| T'ai chi ch'üan | 613.714 8 | |
| Tai-Kadai languages | 495.9 | |
| | T6—959 | |
| Tai languages | 495.91 | |
| | T6—959 1 | |
| Tai literatures | 895.91 | |
| Tai peoples | T5—959 1 | |
| Taigas | | |
| biology | 578.737 | |
| ecology | 577.37 | |
| Tailless whip scorpions | 595.453 6 | |
| Tailoring | 646.4 | |
| commercial technology | 687.044 | |
| home sewing | 646.4 | |
| Tailors | 646.400 92 | |
| commercial | 687.044 092 | |
| Taĭmyr (Russia : Okrug) | T2—575 | |
| Taĭmyrskiĭ avtonomnyĭ | | |
| okrug (Russia) | T2—575 | |
| Taino Indians | T5—979 22 | |
| Taino language | 497.922 | |
| | T6—979 22 | |
| Taiping Rebellion, 1850–1864 | 951.034 | |
| Taishō period | 952.032 | |
| Taita language | 496.395 | |
| | T6—963 95 | |
| Taiwan | 951.249 | |
| | T2—512 49 | |
| ancient | 931.249 | |
| | T2—312 49 | |
| Taiwan native peoples | T5—992 5 | |
| Taiwan Strait | 551.461 457 | |
| | T2—164 57 | |
| Tajik | T5—915 7 | |
| Tajik language | 491.57 | |
| | T6—915 7 | |
| Tajik literature | 891.57 | |
| Tajikistan | 958.6 | |
| | T2—586 | |
| ancient | 939.6 | |
| | T2—396 | |
| Tajwīd | 297.122 404 5 | |
| Tāk Sin, King of Siam | | |
| Thai history | 959.302 4 | |
| Takapuna (N.Z.) | T2—932 2 | |
| Take-overs | 338.83 | |
| *see also* Mergers | | |
| Takeoff | | |
| aeronautics | 629.132 521 2 | |
| manned space flight | 629.452 | |
| space flight | 629.41 | |
| unmanned space flight | 629.432 | |
| Takeoff accidents | 363.124 92 | |
| *see also* Air safety | | |
| Takhrījāt | 297.125 7 | |
| Taki-Taki | 427.988 3 | |
| | T6—217 | |
| Takla Lake (B.C.) | T2—711 82 | |
| Talbot County (Ga.) | T2—758 483 | |
| Talbot County (Md.) | T2—752 32 | |
| Talc | 553.676 | |
| economic geology | 553.676 | |
| mineralogy | 549.67 | |
| mining | 622.367 6 | |
| technology | 666.72 | |
| Talca (Chile : Province) | T2—833 5 | |
| Talented people | 305.908 9 | |
| | T1—087 9 | |
| Taliaferro County (Ga.) | T2—758 616 | |
| Talismans | 133.44 | |
| Islamic popular practices | 297.39 | |
| numismatics | 737.23 | |
| religious significance | 203.7 | |
| *see also* Symbolism — | | |
| religious significance | | |
| Talk shows | 791.446 | |
| radio programs | 791.446 | |
| television programs | 791.456 | |
| Talking books | | |
| bibliographies | 011.384 | |
| Tall buildings | 720.483 | |
| architecture | 720.483 | |
| construction | 690.383 | |
| fire hazards | 363.379 | |
| *see also* Fire safety | | |
| Tall oil | | |
| recovery from pulp | 676.5 | |
| Talladega County (Ala.) | T2—761 61 | |
| Tallahassee (Fla.) | T2—759 88 | |
| Tallahatchie County (Miss.) | T2—762 455 | |
| Tallapoosa County (Ala.) | T2—761 53 | |

Tallapoosa River (Ga. and
   Ala.)     T2—761 5
Tallit     296.461
Tallow     665.2
Tallow tree     583.69
Talmud     296.12
Talmud Bavli     296.125
Talmud Yerushalmi     296.124
Talmudic literature     296.12
Talmudic period     956.940 2
Talpidae     599.335
Talurqjuak (Nunavut)     T2—719 55
Tama County (Iowa)     T2—777 56
Tama National Park
   (Colombia)     T2—861 24
Tamahaq language     493.38
    T6—933 8
Tamahaq literature     893.38
Tamang language     495.4
    T6—954
Tamanrasset (Algeria :
   Province)     T2—657
Tamar, River (England)     T2—423 5
Tamar River (Tas.)     T2—946 5
Tamaracks     585.2
   *see also* Larches
Tamaricales     583.628
Tamarind     641.344 6
   botany     583.74
   cooking     641.644 6
   food     641.344 6
   orchard crop     634.46
Tamarins     599.84
   conservation technology     639.979 84
   resource economics     333.959 84
Tamarisk     583.628
Tamashek language     493.38
    T6—933 8
Tamashek literature     893.38
Tamasheq language     493.38
    T6—933 8
Tamasheq literature     893.38
Tamaulipas (Mexico)     T2—721 2
Tamazight language     493.33
    T6—933 3
Tamazight literature     893.33
Tambacounda (Senegal :
   Region)     T2—663
Tambourines     786.95
   *see also* Percussion instruments
Tambov (Russia : Oblast)     T2—473 5
Tambovskaia oblast´
   (Russia)     T2—473 5

Tamburas     787.82
   *see also* Stringed instruments
Tamerlane
   Asian history     950.24
Tameside (England)     T2—427 35
Tamiasciurus     599.363
Tamid     296.123 5
   Mishnah     296.123 5
   Palestinian Talmud     296.124 5
Tamil     T5—948 11
Tamil language     494.811
    T6—948 11
Tamil literature     894.811
Tamil Nadu (India)     T2—548 2
Ta'mim (Iraq : Province)     T2—567 4
Tampa (Fla.)     T2—759 65
Tamworth (England)     T2—424 69
Tamworth (N.S.W.)     T2—944 4
Tan-Tan (Morocco :
   Province)     T2—646 8
Tanagers     598.875
Tanaidacea     595.374
Tanakh     221
   *see Manual at* 221
Tandem bicycles
   engineering     629.227 6
   repair     629.287 76
   riding     629.284 76
Tandja, Mamadou
   Nigerien (Niger) history     966.260 53
Tandridge (England :
   District)     T2—422 18
Taney County (Mo.)     T2—778 797
Tang dynasty     951.017
Tanga Region (Tanzania)     T2—678 22
Tanganyika     967.820 3
    T2—678 2
Tanganyika, Lake     T2—678 28
Tangible property risks     368.062
Tangier-Assilah (Morocco)     T2—642
Tangier-Tétouan (Morocco)     T2—642
Tangipahoa Parish (La.)     T2—763 13
Tangkhul language     495.4
    T6—954
Tangos     793.33
   music     784.188 85
Tank cars     385.34
   engineering     625.24
   *see also* Rolling stock
Tank warfare     358.18
Tankers (Ships)     387.245
   engineering     623.824 5
   petroleum technology     665.543
   *see also* Ships

Tanks (Containers)
    water supply engineering    628.13
Tanks (Vehicles)    358.188 3
    engineering    623.747 52
    military equipment    358.188 3
Tankwa-Karoo National
    Park (South Africa)    T2—687 17
Tannaim    296.120 092
Tanners    675.230 92
Tanning leather    675.23
Tannins    572.567
    agricultural production    633.87
    biochemistry    572.567
    *see also* Carbohydrates
Tano languages    496.338
    T6—963 38
Tanoan Indians    T5—974 9
Tanoan languages    497.49
    T6—974 9
Tantalum    669.735
    chemical engineering    661.052 6
    chemistry    546.526
    economic geology    553.465
    materials science    620.189 35
    metallography    669.957 35
    metallurgy    669.735
    metalworking    673.735
    physical metallurgy    669.967 35
    *see also* Chemicals; Metals
Tantras
    Buddhist    294.385
    Hindu    294.595
Tantric Buddhism    294.392 5
Tantric Hinduism    294.551 4
Tanzania    967.8
    T2—678
Tanzanians    T5—967 8
Taoism
    art representation    704.948 995 14
    arts    T3C—382 995 14
    philosophy    181.114
    religion    299.514
Taoist holidays
    customs    394.265 951 4
Taoist philosophy    181.114
Taoists
    philosophy    181.114
    religion    299.514 092
Taos County (N.M.)    T2—789 53
Taos Indians    T5—974 96
Taos language    497.496
    T6—974 96
Taounate (Morocco :
    Province)    T2—643 2

Taourirt (Morocco :
    Province)    T2—643 3
Tap dancing    792.78
Tapas    641.812
Tape drives (Computers)
    computer science    004.563
    engineering    621.397 63
Tape players
    automobile    629.277
    sound reproduction    621.389 324
Tape recorders
    automobile    629.277
    sound reproduction    621.389 324
Tape recordings
    sound reproduction    621.389 324
Tapes (Adhesives)    668.38
Tapes (Computers)
    computer science    004.563
    engineering    621.397 63
Tapes (Recording devices)    621.382 34
Tapes (Sound)    384
    bibliographies    011.38
    *see also* Sound recordings
Tapes (Textiles)    677.76
Tapestries    677.64
    manufacturing technology    677.64
    textile arts    746.3
Tapestry makers    746.392
Tapestry-woven rugs
    arts    746.72
Tapestry yard goods    677.642
Tapeworm-caused diseases
    incidence    614.554
    medicine    616.964
        *see also* Communicable
            diseases — humans
Tapeworms    592.46
Taphonomy    560.41
Taphrinales    579.562
Tapia
    building construction    693.22
Tapioca    641.336 82
    cooking    641.636 82
    food    641.336 82
Tapiridae    599.66
Tapirs    599.66
Tapping tools    621.955
Taps (Valves)    621.84
Tar
    materials science    620.196
Tar pavements    625.85

Tar sands 553.283
    economic geology 553.283
    mining 622.338 3
        law 343.077 2
    processing 665.4
Taraba State (Nigeria) T2—669 89
Tarahumara Indians T5—974 546
Tarahumara language 497.454 6
    T6—974 546
Tarahumaran languages 497.454 6
    T6—974 546
Taranaki Region (N.Z.) T2—934 8
Taranto (Italy)
    ancient T2—377 67
Taranto (Italy : Province) T2—457 55
    ancient T2—377 67
Taranto, Gulf of (Italy) 551.461 386
    T2—163 86
Tarapacá (Chile : Region) T2—831 2
Tararua District (N.Z.) T2—935 7
    Manawatu-Wanganui
        Region T2—935 7
    Wellington Region T2—936 9
Tarascan languages 497.96
    T6—979 6
Tarasco Indians T5—979 6
Tarasco language 497.96
    T6—979 6
Tardigrada 592.72
Tardive dyskinesia
    medicine 616.83
    *see also* Nervous system
        diseases — humans
Taree (N.S.W.) T2—944 2
Tarentum (Italy) T2—377 67
Tarf (Algeria : Province) T2—655
Target selection
    military gunnery 623.557
Target shooting 799.3
Targets
    shooting sports 799.3
        manufacturing technology 688.793
Targums 221.42
Tariff 382.7
    *see also* Customs (Tariff)
Tarija (Bolivia : Dept.) T2—842 5
Tarka (South Africa :
    District) T2—687 55
Tarlac (Philippines :
    Province) T2—599 1
Tarn (France) T2—447 37
Tarn-et-Garonne (France) T2—447 5
Tarnobrzeg (Poland :
    Voivodeship) T2—438 66

Tarnów (Poland :
    Voivodeship) T2—438 62
Taro 641.336 8
    botany 584.64
    cooking 641.636 8
    food 641.336 8
    starch crop 633.68
Tarot 133.324 24
Taroudant (Morocco :
    Province) T2—646 6
Tarpons 597.43
    sports fishing 799.174 3
Tarquinia (Italy)
    ancient T2—375 8
Tarraconensis T2—366
Tarragon 641.357
    *see also* Herbs
Tarragona (Spain :
    Province) T2—467 3
Tarrant County (Tex.) T2—764 531
Tarsals
    human anatomy 611.718
Tarsiers 599.83
Tarsiidae 599.83
Tarsipedidae 599.23
Tarsus (Turkey) T2—564 6
Tartans
    heraldry 929.6
Tarts 641.865 2
    commercial processing 664.752 5
    home preparation 641.865 2
Ṭarṭūs (Syria : Province) T2—569 13
Taseko River (B.C.) T2—711 75
Task forces (Naval units) 359.31
Tasman District (N.Z.) T2—937 7
    Nelson-Marlborough
        Region T2—937 7
    West Coast Region T2—937 4
Tasman Peninsula (Tas.) T2—946 4
Tasman Sea 551.461 478
    T2—164 78
Tasmania T2—946
Tasmanian cedar 585.5
Tasmanian devil 599.27
Tasmanian languages 499.15
    T6—991 59
Tasmanian tiger 599.27
Tasmanian wolf 599.27
Tasmanians (Aboriginal
    people) T5—991 59
Taste (Aesthetics)
    music 781.17

| | |
|---|---|
| Taste (Sense) | 573.878 |
|   animal physiology | 573.878 |
|   human anatomy | 611.87 |
|   human physiology | 612.87 |
|   psychology | 152.167 |
| Taste buds | 573.878 |
| Taste disorders | |
|   medicine | 616.856 |
|     *see also* Nervous system | |
|       diseases — humans | |
| Taste perception | |
|   psychology | 152.167 |
| Tata (Morocco : Province) | T2—646 8 |
| Tatar language | 494.387 |
| | T6—943 87 |
|   Crimean | 494.388 |
| | T6—943 88 |
| Tatar literature | 894.387 |
|   Crimean | 894.388 |
| Tatar Strait (Russia) | 551.461 454 |
| | T2—164 54 |
| Tatar suzerainty | |
|   Russian history | 947.03 |
| Tatars | T5—943 87 |
|   Crimean | T5—943 88 |
| Tatarstan (Russia) | T2—474 5 |
| Tate County (Miss.) | T2—762 85 |
| Tatted fabrics | 677.663 |
|   *see also* Textiles | |
| Tatting | |
|   arts | 746.436 |
| Tattnall County (Ga.) | T2—758 775 |
| Tattooing | |
|   customs | 391.65 |
| Taung (South Africa : | |
|   District) | T2—682 46 |
| Taunton Deane (England) | T2—423 87 |
| Taunus (Germany) | T2—434 16 |
| Taupo, Lake (N.Z.) | T2—933 9 |
| Taupo District (N.Z.) | T2—933 9 |
|   Bay of Plenty Region | T2—934 24 |
|   Hawke's Bay Region | T2—934 63 |
|   Manawatu-Wanganui | |
|     Region | T2—935 13 |
|   Waikato Region | T2—933 9 |
| Tauranga District (N.Z.) | T2—934 21 |
| Taurus (Zodiac) | 133.526 3 |
| Taurus Mountains (Turkey) | T2—564 |
| Tautomerism | 547.122 52 |
|   inorganic chemistry | 541.225 2 |
|   organic chemistry | 547.122 52 |
| Tawhid | 297.211 3 |
| Tawi-Tawi (Philippines) | T2—599 9 |
| Tawitawi (Philippines) | T2—599 9 |

| | |
|---|---|
| Tax accounting | 657.46 |
|   law | 343.042 |
|     income tax | 343.052 044 |
| Tax administration | 352.44 |
|   law | 343.04 |
|   *see Manual at* 343.04–.06 vs. | |
|     336.2, 352.44 | |
| Tax appeals | |
|   law | 343.042 |
| Tax assessment | 336.2 |
|   income tax | 336.241 |
|     law | 343.052 042 |
|   law | 343.042 |
|   property tax | 336.222 |
|     law | 343.054 2 |
|   public administration | 352.44 |
| Tax auditing | |
|   law | 343.04 |
| Tax avoidance | 336.206 |
|   income tax | 336.241 6 |
|     corporate | 336.243 16 |
|     law | 343.052 3 |
|     personal | 336.242 16 |
|   law | 343.04 |
|   property tax | 336.22 |
|     law | 343.054 3 |
|   public finance | 336.206 |
| Tax collection | 352.44 |
|   law | 343.042 |
| Tax credits | 336.206 |
|   income tax law | 343.052 37 |
|   *see also* Tax avoidance | |
| Tax deductions | 336.206 |
|   *see also* Tax avoidance | |
| Tax evasion | 364.133 8 |
|   law | 345.023 38 |
| Tax-exempt organizations | |
|   law | 343.066 |
| Tax-exempt securities | |
|   law | 346.092 2 |
| Tax exemptions | 336.206 |
|   *see also* Tax avoidance | |
| Tax expenditures | 336.206 |
| Tax incentives | 336.206 |
|   income tax law | 343.052 304 |
|   *see also* Tax avoidance | |
| Tax incidence | 336.294 |
| Tax law | 343.04 |
|   *see Manual at* 343.04–.06 vs. | |
|     336.2, 352.44 | |
| Tax limitations | |
|   law | 343.034 |
| Tax lists | |
|   genealogy | 929.3 |

Tax loopholes 336.206
  *see also* Tax avoidance
Tax planning
  law 343.04
    income tax 343.052
Tax rates 336.2
  import tax 336.265
Tax rebates 336.206
  *see also* Tax avoidance
Tax reduction 336.206
  *see also* Tax avoidance
Tax reform 336.205
  income tax 336.241 5
    corporate 336.243 15
    personal 336.242 15
Tax returns
  income tax law 343.052 044
Tax shelters 336.206
  income tax law 343.052 38
  investment economics 332.604 22
  *see also* Tax avoidance
Taxales 585.6
  paleobotany 561.56
Taxation 336.2
  American Revolution cause 973.311 4
  *see also* Taxes
Taxation power (Legislative
  bodies) 328.341 2
Taxes 336.2
  accounting 657.46
  financial management 658.153
  law 343.04
  macroeconomic policy 339.525
  public administration 352.44
    litigation 353.43
Taxicab drivers 388.413 214 092
Taxicab service 388.413 214
  law 343.098 2
  public administration 354.765 3
  transportation services 388.413 214
Taxicabs 388.342 32
  driving 629.283 32
  engineering 629.222 32
  repair 629.287 232
  transportation services 388.342 32
  *see also* Automobiles
Taxidermy 590.752
Taxodiaceae 585.5
  paleobotany 561.55
Taxonomic biology 578
Taxonomic nomenclature 578.014
  *see Manual at* 579–590
Taxonomy (Biology) 578.012
Tay, River (Scotland) T2—412 8

Tây Ninh (Vietnam :
  Province) T2—597 7
Tay-Sachs disease
  medicine 616.858 845
  pediatrics 618.928 588 45
Taya, Maawiya Ould Sid'Ahmed
  Mauritanian history 966.105 3
Tayassuidae 599.634
Taylor, Charles Ghankay
  Liberian history 966.620 33
Taylor, Zachary
  United States history 973.63
Taylor County (Fla.) T2—759 86
Taylor County (Ga.) T2—758 493
Taylor County (Iowa) T2—777 79
Taylor County (Ky.) T2—769 673
Taylor County (Tex.) T2—764 727
Taylor County (W. Va.) T2—754 55
Taylor County (Wis.) T2—775 26
Tayside (Scotland) T2—412 8
Taza (Morocco : Province) T2—643 2
Taza-Al Hoceïma-Taounate
  (Morocco) T2—643 2
Tazewell County (Ill.) T2—773 54
Tazewell County (Va.) T2—755 763
TCA cycle 572.475
Te Anau, Lake (N.Z.) T2—939 6
Tea 641.337 2
  agricultural economics 338.173 72
  agriculture 633.72
  botany 583.624
  commercial processing
    economics 338.476 639 4
    technology 663.94
  cooking with 641.637 2
  customs 394.15
  food 641.337 2
  home preparation 641.877
Tea Act, 1773
  United States history 973.311 5
Tea leaves
  divination 133.324 4
Teacher-administrator relations 371.106
Teacher aides 371.141 24
Teacher burnout 371.100 19
Teacher certification 371.12
Teacher-community relations 306.432
  education 371.19
  sociology 306.432
Teacher education 370.711
Teacher evaluation 371.144
Teacher exchanges 370.116 3
  law 344.08
Teacher morale 371.100 19

Teacher-parent conferences 371.103
Teacher-parent relations 371.192
Teacher participation in
   administration 371.106
Teacher qualifications 371.12
  higher education 378.124
Teacher-staff relations 371.106
Teacher-student relations 371.102 3
Teacher training 370.711
              T1—071 1
Teacher turnover 371.14
Teacher workload 371.141 2
Teachers 371.1
  biography 371.100 92
  higher education 378.12
  law 344.078
  public control 379.157
  religious educators 207.509 2
    Christian 268.092
      biography 268.092
       *see Manual at* 230–280
      role and function 268.3
    Jewish 296.680 92
      biography 296.680 92
      role and function 296.68
  role in guidance 371.404 6
  workload 371.141 2
    higher education 378.122 12
Teachers' assistants 371.141 24
Teachers' colleges 370.711
Teaching 371.102
              T1—071
  educational psychology 370.15
  higher education 378.125
  law 344.078
  professional education 370.711
  special education 371.904 3
Teaching (Spiritual gift) 234.13
Teaching aids 371.33
              T1—078
Teaching load 371.141 2
  higher education 378.122 12
Teaching machines
  adult education 374.26
Teaching materials 371.33
  *see also* Instructional materials
Teaching methods 371.3
              T1—071
  personnel training 658.312 404
  primary education 372.13
  religious education 207.5
    Christianity 268.6
  special education 371.904 3
Teaching office of the church 262.8

Teaching orders (Christianity) 255.03
  church history 271.03
  women 255.903
    church history 271.903
Teachings of Jesus Christ 232.954
Teak
  botany 583.96
  forestry 634.973 96
  lumber 674.144
Team handball 796.327
Team management 658.402 2
  *see also* Work teams
Team teaching 371.148
Teamsters 388.324 092
Tear ducts
  human physiology 612.847
Tear gas
  military engineering 623.459 2
Tear-gas canister launchers 623.445
Teas (Meals) 642
  cooking 641.53
    light meals 641.53
    main meals 641.54
  customs 394.125 3
    light meals 394.125 3
    main meals 394.125 4
Teasels 583.92
Teasing 302.3
Tébessa (Algeria : Province) T2—655
Technetium
  chemical engineering 661.054 3
  chemistry 546.543
Technical assistance
  economics 338.91
  public finance 336.185
Technical chemistry 660
Technical drawing 604.2
Technical education T1—071
Technical high schools 373.246
  *see also* Secondary education
Technical libraries 026.6
Technical processes (Libraries) 025.02
Technical reports
  cataloging 025.343 6
  library treatment 025.173 6
Technical services (Libraries) 025.02
Technical training 607
  armed forces 355.56
Technical writing 808.066
Techno music 781.648
Technological archaeology 609

Technological innovations
  agricultural industries    338.16
  cause of social change    303.483
    *see Manual at* 303.483 vs.
      306.45, 306.46
  economics    338.064
  executive management    658.406 2
  mineral industries    338.26
  production management    658.514
Technological instruments
  manufacturing technology    681.76
Technological unemployment    331.137 042
Technologists    609.2
  works for    T1—024 6
  *see Manual at* T1—015 vs.
    T1—0245–0246
Technology    600
  art representation    704.949 6
  arts    700.456
        T3C—356
  folklore    398.276
    history and criticism    398.356
  law    344.095
  literature    808.803 56
    history and criticism    809.933 56
    specific literatures    T3B—080 356
    history and
      criticism    T3B—093 56
  painting    758.96
  primary education    372.358
  production management    658.514
  public administrative support    352.745
  social effects    303.483
    *see Manual at* 303.483 vs.
      306.45, 306.46
  sociology    306.46
    *see Manual at* 303.483 vs.
      306.45, 306.46
  *see Manual at* 300 vs. 600
Technology and religion    201.66
  Christianity    261.56
  Islam    297.266
  Judaism    296.376
  philosophy of religion    215
Technology assessment    303.483
  economic development    338.9
    public administration    354.27
  health services potential    362.104 2
  natural resources impact    333.714
  safety risk    363.1
  social change potential    303.483
Technology transfer    338.926
  economics    338.926
  law    343.074

Tecophilaeaceae    584.35
Tectibranchia    594.37
Tectonics    551.8
Tectosilicates
  mineralogy    549.68
Teddy bears
  making    688.724 3
    handicrafts    745.592 43
  technology    688.724 3
Teenage boys    305.235 1
        T1—083 51
  *see also* Young men — under
    twenty one
Teenage fathers    306.874 2
  social welfare    362.787 42
Teenage girls    305.235 2
        T1—083 52
  *see also* Young women —
    under twenty one
Teenage mothers    306.874 3
  social welfare    362.787 43
Teenage pregnancy
  obstetrics    618.200 835
  social welfare    362.787 43
Teenagers    305.235
        T1—083 5
  *see also* Adolescents
Tees, River (England)    T2—428 5
Teesdale (England)    T2—428 61
Teeth    591.44
  animal physiology    573.356
  anthropometry    599.943
  dentistry    617.6
  descriptive zoology    591.44
  diseases    573.356 39
    *see also* Tooth diseases
  human anatomy    611.314
  human physiology    612.311
Teeth diseases    573.356 39
  *see also* Tooth diseases
Tefillin    296.461 2
Tegucigalpa (Honduras)    T2—728 371
Tehama County (Calif.)    T2—794 27
Tehran (Iran)    T2—552 5
Tehran (Iran : Province)    T2—552 5
Tehuantepec, Gulf of (Mexico)    551.461 41
        T2—164 1
Tehuantepec Canal    386.447
Teichmüller spaces    515.94
Teignbridge (England)    T2—423 55
Teignmouth, John Shore, Baron
  Indian history    954.031 1
Teiidae    597.958 2

Tejan Kabbah, Amad
  Sierra Leonean history — 966.404 5
Teke languages — 496.396
  T6—963 96
Tekirdağ İli (Turkey) — T2—496 16
Tekrur (Kingdom) — 966.301
  T2—663
Tel Aviv (Israel : District) — T2—569 48
Telangiectasis
  medicine — 616.148
  *see also* Cardiovascular
    diseases — humans
Telangitis
  medicine — 616.148
  *see also* Cardiovascular
    diseases — humans
Telecommunication — 384
  accounting — 657.84
  communications services — 384
  engineering — 621.382
  law — 343.099 4
  public administration — 354.75
Telecommunication workers — 384.092
Telecommuting — 331.256 8
  labor economics — 331.256 8
  personnel management — 658.312 3
Teleconferencing
  instructional use — 371.358
Telecontrol
  engineering — 620.46
  radio engineering — 621.384 196
Telefacsimile — 384.14
  *see also* Facsimile transmission
Telefax — 384.14
  *see also* Facsimile transmission
Telegraphy — 384.1
  communications services — 384.1
  engineering — 621.383
  law — 343.099 4
  military engineering — 623.732
  nautical engineering — 623.856 2
  public administration — 354.75
  sociology — 302.235
  wireless — 384.52
Telegraphy stations
  communications industry — 384.15
Telemark fylke (Norway) — T2—482 8
Telemarketing — 381.142
  management — 658.872
Teleology — 124
  philosophy — 124
  philosophy of religion — 210
Teleorman (Romania) — T2—498 2

Teleostei — 597
  *see also* Fishes
Telepathists — 133.820 92
Telepathy — 133.82
Telephone — 384.6
  communications services — 384.6
  engineering — 621.385
  law — 343.099 43
  military engineering — 623.733
  public administration — 354.75
  sociology — 302.235
  wireless — 384.53
Telephone answering machines
  engineering — 621.386 7
  office services — 651.73
Telephone books — 910.25
  *see Manual at* T1—025 vs.
    T1—029
Telephone calls — 384.64
  wireless — 384.534
  *see also* Telephone
Telephone counseling — 361.06
Telephone engineers — 621.385 092
Telephone etiquette — 395.59
Telephone lines
  communications services — 384.65
Telephone-order houses — 381.142
  management — 658.872
  *see also* Commerce
Telephone selling — 381.142
  management — 658.872
    techniques for individuals — 658.85
Telephone services — 384.64
  wire — 384.64
  wireless — 384.534
Telephone shopping — 381.142
Telephone stations
  communications services — 384.65
  wireless — 384.535
Telephone switching systems — 621.387
Telephones — 621.386
  automobile — 629.277
  office services — 651.73
Telephony — 384.6
  *see also* Telephone
Telephotography — 778.322
Telescopes — 522.2
  astronomy — 522.2
  manufacturing technology — 681.412 3
Teleshopping — 381.142
  law — 343.081 142 8
  *see also* Commerce

| | |
|---|---|
| Teletext | 004.69 |
| *see also* Computer communications | |
| Teletype | 384.14 |
| wireless | 384.524 |
| *see also* Telegraphy | |
| Television | 384.55 |
| accounting | 657.84 |
| communications services | 384.55 |
| engineering | 621.388 |
| ethics | 175 |
| religion | |
| Christianity | 241.65 |
| *see also* Recreation — ethics | |
| influence on crime | 364.254 |
| instructional use | 371.335 8 |
| adult level | 374.26 |
| | T1—071 5 |
| journalism | 070.195 |
| law | 343.099 46 |
| military engineering | 623.735 |
| performing arts | 791.45 |
| *see Manual at* 791.43, 791.45 vs. 777 | |
| public administration | 354.75 |
| religion | 201.7 |
| Christianity | 261.52 |
| evangelism | 269.26 |
| preaching | 251.07 |
| use by local Christian church | 253.78 |
| administration | 254.3 |
| sociology | 302.234 5 |
| *see Manual at* 384.54, 384.55, 384.8 vs. 791.4 | |
| Television adaptations | 791.456 |
| Television advertising | 659.143 |
| Television broadcasting | 384.55 |
| *see Manual at* 384.54, 384.55, 384.8 vs. 791.4 | |
| Television dinners | |
| commercial processing | 664.65 |
| home serving | 642.1 |
| Television drama | |
| literature | 808.822 5 |
| history and criticism | 809.225 |
| specific literatures | T3B—202 5 |
| individual authors | T3A—2 |
| performing arts | 791.457 |
| rhetoric | 808.225 |
| Television engineers | 621.388 009 2 |
| Television evangelism | 269.26 |
| Television genres | 791.456 |
| Television graphics | 777.55 |

| | |
|---|---|
| Television mini-series | 791.45 |
| *see Manual at* 791.43 vs. 791.45 | |
| Television music | 781.546 |
| Television networks | 384.550 65 |
| enterprises | 384.550 65 |
| facilities | 384.552 3 |
| performing arts | 791.45 |
| Television news | 070.43 |
| Television photography | 777 |
| Television pilot programs | 791.45 |
| *see Manual at* 791.43 vs. 791.45 | |
| Television plays | |
| literature | 808.822 5 |
| history and criticism | 809.225 |
| specific literatures | T3B—202 5 |
| individual authors | T3A—2 |
| performing arts | 791.457 |
| rhetoric | 808.225 |
| Television programs | 384.553 2 |
| broadcasting | 384.553 2 |
| performing arts | 791.45 |
| Television public speaking | 808.51 |
| Television recorders | |
| videography | 777.36 |
| Television scripts | |
| rhetoric | 808.066 791 |
| Television selling | 381.142 |
| management | 658.872 |
| Television selling organizations | |
| management | 658.872 |
| Television sets | 621.388 8 |
| automobile | 629.277 |
| Television shopping | 381.142 |
| Television speeches | |
| literature | 808.851 |
| history and criticism | 809.51 |
| specific literatures | T3B—501 |
| individual authors | T3A—5 |
| Television stations | 384.552 2 |
| architecture | 725.23 |
| engineering | 621.388 6 |
| enterprises | 384.550 65 |
| facilities | 384.552 2 |
| performing arts | 791.45 |
| Television towers | |
| architecture | 725.23 |
| Television transmission | |
| engineering | 621.388 1 |
| Telex | 384.14 |
| wireless | 384.524 |
| *see also* Telegraphy | |
| Telfair County (Ga.) | T2—758 843 |

Telford and Wrekin
  (England)          T2—424 56
Telford pavements        625.86
Teller County (Colo.)      T2—788 58
Tellurides
  mineralogy           549.32
Tellurium
  chemical engineering    661.072 6
  chemistry            546.726
  economic geology      553.499
  metallurgy           669.79
Telopea               583.89
Telpherage            621.868
Teltow-Fläming (Germany :
  Landkreis)           T2—431 54
Telugu                T5—948 27
Telugu language         494.827
                  T6—948 27
Telugu literature        894.827
Tem (African people)    T5—963 5
Tem language          496.35
                  T6—963 5
Témiscamingue (Quebec :
  Regional County
  Municipality)        T2—714 137
Témiscouata (Quebec :
  Regional County
  Municipality)        T2—714 762
Temne (African people)   T5—963 2
Temne language         496.32
                  T6—963 2
Temotu (Solomon Islands)   T2—959 39
Temouchent (Algeria :
  Province)           T2—651
Tempera painting        751.43
Temperament (Musical
  instruments)          784.192 8
Temperament (Psychology)   155.262
Temperance           178
  *see also* Virtues
Temperate basses       597.73
Temperate Zones       T2—12
Temperate zones
  diseases
    medicine           616.988 2
    *see also* Environmental
        diseases — humans
Temperature           536.5
  biophysics          571.46
    humans           612.014 46
  health             613.1
  meteorology         551.525
  physics            536.5

Temperature (continued)
  seawater           551.465 3
    meteorological effect   551.524 6
  weather forecasting     551.642 5
Temperature adaptation    578.42
  animals            591.42
  plants             581.42
Temperature changes
  effect on materials     620.112 15
  geologic work        551.39
  meteorology         551.525 3
Temperature control
  buildings           697.932 2
  mining             622.43
  ships              623.853
  spacecraft          629.477 5
Temperature-salinity
  relationships        551.466 43
Tempering glass        666.129
Tempering metals       671.36
Templars             255.791 3
  church history       271.791 3
Temple of Jerusalem     296.491
Temples              203.5
  architecture         726.1
  Buddhist           294.343 5
  Hindu             294.535
  Jain               294.435
  Jewish             296.65
    *see also* Synagogues
  Jewish temple in Jerusalem   296.491
  Mormon           246.958 93
  Shinto            299.561 35
  Sikh               294.635
Tempo (Music)         781.22
Temporal constructions
  (Grammar)          415
  specific languages     T4—5
Temporal databases
  computer science      005.753
Temporal logic         511.314
Temporal power of pope   262.132
Temporary buildings     720.444
  architecture         720.444
  construction         690.344
Temporary deformation    531.382
  materials science      620.112 32
  *see also* Elasticity
Temporary employees    331.257 29
Temporary employment   331.257 29
Temporary help        331.257 29
Temporary help services   331.128
Temporary housing
  social welfare        361.05

| | |
|---|---|
| Temporomandibular joint dysfunction | |
| regional medicine | 617.522 |
| Temptation | |
| moral theology | 205 |
| Christianity | 241.3 |
| Temptation of Jesus Christ | 232.95 |
| Temuan (Malaysian people) | T5—992 8 |
| Temuan language | T6—992 8 |
| Temurah | 296.123 5 |
| Babylonian Talmud | 296.125 5 |
| Mishnah | 296.123 5 |
| Ten Commandments | 222.16 |
| moral theology | |
| Christianity | 241.52 |
| Judaism | 296.36 |
| Ten kingdoms (China) | 951.018 |
| Ten Sikh gurus | 294.609 2 |
| biography | 294.609 2 |
| role and function | 294.663 |
| Ten Thousand Islands (Fla.) | T2—759 44 |
| Tenancy | |
| land economics | 333.53 |
| law | 346.043 4 |
| Tenant-landlord relations | 333.54 |
| law | 346.043 4 |
| Tenants' liability insurance | 368.56 |
| Tenbury Wells (England) | T2—424 47 |
| Tench | 597.482 |
| sports fishing | 799.174 82 |
| Tenda (African people) | T5—963 2 |
| Tenda language | 496.32 |
| | T6—963 2 |
| Tende-Yanzi languages | 496.396 |
| | T6—963 96 |
| Tender offers (Securities) | 332.632 2 |
| financial economics | 332.632 2 |
| law | 346.066 2 |
| management | 658.16 |
| production economics | 338.83 |
| Tenderizers | |
| food technology | 664.4 |
| Tendinitis | |
| medicine | 616.75 |
| *see also* Musculoskeletal diseases — humans | |
| Tendon diseases | |
| medicine | 616.75 |
| *see also* Musculoskeletal diseases — humans | |
| Tendon sheath diseases | |
| medicine | 616.76 |
| *see also* Musculoskeletal diseases — humans | |
| Tendon sheaths | 573.753 56 |
| human anatomy | 611.75 |
| human physiology | 612.75 |
| medicine | 616.76 |
| *see also* Musculoskeletal system | |
| Tendons | 573.753 56 |
| biology | 573.753 56 |
| human anatomy | 611.74 |
| human physiology | 612.75 |
| medicine | 616.75 |
| surgery | 617.474 |
| *see also* Musculoskeletal system | |
| Tendrils | 581.48 |
| Tendring (England) | T2—426 725 |
| Tenebrionidae | 595.769 |
| Tenedos Island (Turkey) | T2—562 2 |
| ancient | T2—391 1 |
| Tenements | 647.92 |
| architecture | 728.314 |
| construction | 690.831 4 |
| household management | 647.92 |
| *see also* Dwellings | |
| Tenericutes | 579.328 |
| Tennant Creek (N.T.) | T2—942 95 |
| Tennessee | 976.8 |
| | T2—768 |
| Tennessee River | T2—768 |
| Alabama | T2—761 9 |
| Tennessee | T2—768 |
| Tennessee Walking Horse | 636.13 |
| Tennis | 796.342 |
| electronic games | 794.863 42 |
| equipment technology | 688.763 42 |
| Tennis courts | 796.342 068 |
| Tennis players | 796.342 092 |
| Tenor horns | 788.974 |
| *see also* Brass instruments | |
| Tenor recorders | 788.366 |
| *see also* Woodwind instruments | |
| Tenor saxophones | 788.74 |
| *see also* Woodwind instruments | |
| Tenor viols | 787.64 |
| *see also* Stringed instruments | |
| Tenor voices | 782.87 |
| choral and mixed voices | 782.87 |
| single voices | 783.87 |
| Tenos Island (Greece) | T2—495 85 |
| Tenpins | 794.6 |
| Tenrecs | 599.33 |
| Tensas Parish (La.) | T2—763 79 |
| Tension (Mechanical stress) | |
| effect on materials | 620.112 41 |

Tension headache
  medicine                 616.849 14
  *see also* Nervous system
    diseases — humans
Tensor algebra          512.57
Tensor analysis         515.63
Tensor calculus         515.63
Tent shows            792.022
Tentaculata            593.8
Tenterfield (N.S.W.)     T2—944 4
Tentering textiles      677.028 25
Tenth century          909.1
                   T1—090 21
Tenth of Muḥarram     297.36
Tents               796.540 284
  manufacturing technology   685.53
Tenure              331.259 6
  labor economics      331.259 6
  law
    public employees     342.068 6
    personnel management  658.312
    teachers          371.104
      higher education   378.121 4
    public administration  354.98
Tepiman languages     497.455
                 T6—974 55
Tepo language         496.33
                 T6—963 3
Tequila (Distilled liquor)  641.25
  commercial processing  663.5
Tequila (Plant)       584.352
Ter Saami language    494.576
                 T6—945 76
Ter Sámi language     494.576
                 T6—945 76
Teramo (Italy : Province)  T2—457 15
  ancient            T2—374 9
Teratogenic agents
  medicine           616.043
Teratology
  biology             571.976
  medicine           616.043
Terbium
  chemistry          546.416
Terce               264.15
  music             782.324
Terengganu         T2—595 1
Tergeste (Italy)      T2—373 91
Term life insurance    368.323
Term limitation
  chief executives      352.23
  legislators         328.33
Term logic            160

Terminal ballistics
  military engineering   623.516
Terminal care        362.175
  ethics             179.7
  law               344.041 97
  medicine           616.029
  nursing            616.029
  pastoral theology     206.1
    Christianity       259.417 5
  social theology     201.762 175
    Christianity       261.832 175
  social welfare      362.175
  *see also* Health services
Terminals (Computers)   004.75
  engineering        621.398 5
  graphics          006.62
    engineering       621.399 6
Terminals (Transportation)  388.04
  *see also* Transportation
    facilities
Termination
  insurance          368.016
Terminology         401.4
                 T1—014
  dictionaries        413
  specific languages    T4—014
    dictionaries       T4—3
    usage (Applied
     linguistics)       T4—81
    *see Manual at* T4—3 vs.
     T4—81
  usage (Applied linguistics)  418
Termite damage prevention  691.14
Termite-resistant construction  693.842
Termites            595.736
  control technology    628.965 7
Ternary form         781.822 3
  instrumental       784.182 2
Ternary system (Numeration)  513.5
Terni (Italy : Province)   T2—456 52
  ancient            T2—374 4
    Etruria         T2—375 76
    Umbria         T2—374 4
Ternopil' (Ukraine : Oblast)  T2—477 9
Ternopil's'ka oblast'
  (Ukraine)          T2—477 9
Terns               598.338
Ternstrocmiaceae      583.624
Terpenes
  chemistry          547.71
Terra-cotta
  architectural construction  721.044 3
  building construction   693.3

Terra-cotta (continued)
building materials — 691.4
materials science — 620.142
Terrace (B.C.) — T2—711 85
Terrace houses
architecture — 728.312
Terraces
landscape architecture — 717
Terracing (Soil conservation) — 631.455
Terrapins — 597.925
Terrariums — 578.073
animals — 590.73
floriculture — 635.982 4
plants — 580.73
Terrebonne Parish (La.) — T2—763 41
Terrell County (Ga.) — T2—758 935
Terrell County (Tex.) — T2—764 922
Terrestrial ecology — 577
Terrestrial photogrammetry — 526.982 5
Terrestrial radiation
meteorology — 551.527 2
Terrestrial turtles — 597.924
Terriers — 636.755
Terriers (Toy dogs) — 636.76
Territorial property — 320.12
law of nations — 341.42
Territorial waters
law — 342.041 3
law of nations — 341.448
Territoriality
animal behavior — 591.566
human ecology — 304.23
Territories (Local government
units) — 320.83
see also Counties
Territories (State-level units) — 321.023
see also States (Members of
federations)
Territories under international
control — 321
law — 341.29
public administration — 353.159
Territory of states — 320.12
law — 342.041 3
law of nations — 341.42
Terrorism — 363.325
criminology — 364.131 7
law — 345.023 17
ethics — 172.1
international relations — 327.117
prevention
management — 658.473
social conflict — 303.625
Terry cloth — 677.617

Terry County (Tex.) — T2—764 859
Tersinidae — 598.875
Tertiary education — 378
— T1—071 1
see also Higher education
Tertiary period — 551.78
geology — 551.78
paleontology — 560.178
Tertiary recovery
oil extraction — 622.338 2
Teruel (Spain : Province) — T2—465 51
Terumot — 296.123 1
Mishnah — 296.123 1
Palestinian Talmud — 296.124 1
Teso language — 496.5
— T6—965
Tessellations (Mathematics) — 516.132
Euclidean geometry — 516.213 2
Tessin (Switzerland) — T2—494 78
Test, River (England) — T2—422 732
Test anxiety — 371.260 19
Test bias
education — 371.260 13
psychology — 150.287
Test construction
education — 371.261
— T1—076
teacher-prepared tests — 371.271
Test reliability
education — 371.260 13
Test-taking skills
education — 371.26
Test-tube babies
ethics — 176.2
see also Reproduction —
ethics
medicine — 618.178 059 9
Test tubes — 542.2
Test validity
education — 371.260 13
Test Valley (England) — T2—422 732
Testaments
pseudepigrapha — 229.914
Testes — 573.655
biology — 573.655
human anatomy — 611.63
human physiology — 612.614
medicine — 616.68
see also Male genital system
Testicles — 573.655
see also Testes

Testicular cancer  
  incidence      614.599 946 3  
  medicine      616.994 63  
  *see also* Cancer — humans  
Testicular diseases  
  medicine      616.68  
  *see also* Male genital  
    diseases — humans  
Testing      T1—028 7  
  chemistry      542.3  
  education      371.26  
     T1—076  
    teacher-prepared tests      371.271  
  physics      530.8  
Testing devices  
  electronics      621.381 548  
  manufacturing technology      681.2  
  radio engineering      621.384 133  
Tests      T1—028 7  
  education      371.26  
     T1—076  
    teacher-prepared tests      371.271  
    *see Manual at* 371.262 vs.  
    371.264  
  personnel selection      658.311 25  
  public administration      352.65  
Testudines      597.92  
  paleozoology      567.92  
Testudinidae      597.924  
Testudinoidea      597.92  
Tetanus  
  incidence      614.512 8  
  medicine      616.931 8  
  *see also* Communicable  
    diseases — humans  
Tete (Mozambique :  
  Province)      T2—679 5  
Tetela languages      496.396  
     T6—963 96  
Teton County (Idaho)      T2—796 54  
Teton County (Mont.)      T2—786 55  
Teton County (Wyo.)      T2—787 55  
Teton Indians      T5—975 244  
Teton language      497.524 4  
     T6—975 244  
Teton Range (Wyo. and  
  Idaho)      T2—787 55  
Tétouan (Morocco :  
  Province)      T2—642  
Tetrahedrite  
  mineralogy      549.35  
Tetrao      598.634  
Tetraodontiformes      597.64  
Tetraonidae      598.63  

Tetrapoda      596  
Tetras      597.48  
Teuthoidea      594.58  
Teutoburg Forest  
  (Germany)      T2—435 65  
Teutonic Knights      255.791 4  
  church history      271.791 4  
Teutonic languages      430  
     T6—3  
Teutonic literatures      830  
Tevul Yom      296.123 6  
Tewa Indians      T5—974 94  
Tewa language      497.494  
     T6—974 94  
Tewa literature      897.494  
Tewkesbury (England :  
  Borough)      T2—424 12  
Texada Island (B.C.)      T2—711 31  
Texas      976.4  
     T2—764  
Texas, East      T2—764 14  
Texas County (Mo.)      T2—778 84  
Texas County (Okla.)      T2—766 135  
Texas Panhandle (Tex.)      T2—764 8  
Texas Republic      976.404  
Texoma, Lake (Okla. and  
  Tex.)      T2—766 61  
Text editors (Computer  
  programs)      005.52  
  programming aids      005.13  
Text encoding      005.72  
Text processing      005.52  
Textbook bias      371.32  
  public control      379.156  
Textbooks      371.32  
  bibliographies      011.7  
  law      344.077  
  public control      379.156  
  teaching use      371.32  
Textile arts      746  
Textile chemicals      677.028 35  
Textile handicrafters      746.092  
Textile handicrafts      746  
Textile industry      338.476 77  
  law      343.078 677  
Textile plants (Living organisms)      677  
  *see Manual at* 583–585 vs. 600  
Textile printing      667.38  
Textile workers      677.009 2  
Textiles      677  
  equipment manufacturing  
    technology      681.767 7  
  field crops      633.5  
  handicrafts      746

Textiles (continued)

| | |
|---|---|
| home sewing | 646.11 |
| manufacturing technology | 677 |
| materials science | 620.197 |
| product safety | 363.19 |
| sculpture material | 731.2 |
| ship design | 623.818 97 |
| shipbuilding | 623.820 7 |

Texts (Music) 780

treatises 780.268

Textual criticism

| | | |
|---|---|---|
| literature | | 809 |
| specific literatures | T3B—09 | |
| theory | | 801.959 |
| sacred books | | 208.2 |
| Bible | | 220.404 6 |
| Talmud | | 296.120 4 |

Texture

materials science 620.112 92

Texture (Music) 781.28

Thaba Nchu (South Africa :
   District) T2—685 5

Thabamoopo (South Africa :
   District) T2—682 55

Thabazimbi (South Africa :
   District) T2—682 51

Thai T5—959 11

Thái Bình (Vietnam :
   Province) T2—597 3

| | |
|---|---|
| Thai language | 495.91 |
| | T6—959 11 |

Thai literature 895.91

Thái Nguyên (Vietnam :
   Province) T2—597 1

| | |
|---|---|
| Thailand | 959.3 |
| | T2—593 |
| Thailand, Gulf of | 551.461 472 |
| | T2—164 72 |

Thal (Switzerland : Bezirk) T2—494 353 7

Thal-Gäu (Switzerland) T2—494 353

Thalamus

| | |
|---|---|
| human anatomy | 611.81 |
| human physiology | 612.826 2 |
| medicine | 616.8 |

Thalassemia

medicine 616.152

*see also* Cardiovascular
    diseases — humans

Thaliacea 596.2

Thallium 669.79

| | |
|---|---|
| chemical engineering | 661.067 8 |
| chemistry | 546.678 |
| metallurgy | 669.79 |

Thallium (continued)

physical metallurgy 669.967 9

*see also* Chemicals

| | |
|---|---|
| Thallobionta | 579 |
| Thallophyta | 579 |
| Thames, River (England) | T2—422 |

Thames Coromandel
   District (N.Z.) T2—933 23

Thamesdown (England) T2—423 13

Thanet (England) T2—422 357

Thanh Hóa (Vietnam :
   Province) T2—597 4

| | |
|---|---|
| Thanksgiving | 394.264 9 |
| cooking | 641.568 |
| handicrafts | 745.594 164 9 |

Thao (Taiwan people) T5—992 5

Thar Desert (India and
   Pakistan) T2—544

Thasos Island (Greece) T2—495 7

ancient T2—391 1

Thatch grasses 584.92

Thayer County (Neb.) T2—782 335

The Pas (Man.) T2—712 72

The Weald (England) T2—422 5

| | |
|---|---|
| Theales | 583.624 |
| Theater | 792 |
| accounting | 657.84 |
| influence on crime | 364.254 |
| instructional use | 371.399 |
| performing arts | 792 |
| primary education | 372.66 |
| religious significance | 203.7 |
| Christianity | 246.72 |
| religious education | 268.67 |

*see also* Arts — religious
    significance

sociology 306.484 8

| | |
|---|---|
| Theater etiquette | 395.53 |
| Theater-in-the-round | 792.022 8 |
| Theater television | 384.556 |

*see also* Television

Theaters (Buildings)

| | |
|---|---|
| architecture | 725.822 |
| area planning | 711.558 |
| institutional housekeeping | 647.968 22 |
| music | 781.538 |
| Theatines | 255.51 |
| church history | 271.51 |
| Theatrical costumes | 792.026 |
| dramatic performances | 792.026 |
| home sewing | 646.478 |

*see also* Costumes

| | |
|---|---|
| Theatrical dancing | 792.78 |
| Theatrical performers | 792.028 092 |

Theban supremacy 938.06
Thebes (Egypt : Extinct
   city) T2—323
Thebes (Greece) T2—384
Thecodontia 567.91
Thecosomata 594.34
Theft 364.162
  law 345.026 2
  prevention
    household security 643.16
    management 658.473
    museology 069.54
     T1—075
Theft insurance 368.82
Theism 211.3
  Christianity 231
  comparative religion 202.11
  Islam 297.211
  Judaism 296.311
  philosophy of religion 211.3
Theistic religions 201.4
Thelephoraceae 579.6
Theligonales 583.5
Thelon Game Sanctuary
  (N.W.T. and Nunavut) T2—719 3
Thelon River (N.W.T. and
  Nunavut) T2—719 58
Thematic apperception tests 155.284 4
Thematic catalogs 780.216
Theme and variations 781.825
  instrumental 784.182 5
Theme parks 791.068
  *see also* Amusement parks
Themes
  arts 700.42–.49
     T3C—3
  literature 808.803
    history and criticism 809.933
    specific literatures T3B—080 3
      history and
        criticism T3B—093
    *see Manual at*
      T3B—102–107,
      T3B—205, T3B—308 vs.
      T3C—1, T3C—3
  musical element 781.248
Theocracy 321.5
  political ideology 320.55
  political system 321.5
  religion 201.721
    Christianity 261.73
Theodicy 202.118
  Christianity 231.8
  comparative religion 202.118

Theodicy (continued)
  Islam 297.211 8
  Judaism 296.311 8
  philosophy of religion 214
Theodore I, Czar of Russia
  Russian history 947.044
Theodore II, Negus of Ethiopia
  Eritrean history 963.504 1
  Ethiopian history 963.041
Theodore III, Czar of Russia
  Russian history 947.049
Theologians 202.092
  Christian 230.092
    *see Manual at* 230–280
Theological anthropology 202.2
  *see also* Humans — religion
Theological seminaries
  Christianity 230.071 1
Theology 202
  Buddhism 294.342
  Christianity 230
  Hinduism 294.52
  Islam 297.2
    Sufi 297.41
  Judaism 296.3
Theophanies
  Christianity 231.74
Theophrastaceae 583.675
Theoretical biochemistry 572.33
  humans 612.015 82
Theoretical chemistry 541.2
  *see Manual at* 541 vs. 546
Theoretical organic chemistry 547.12
Theory T1—01
  *see Manual at* T1—01
Theosis
  Christian doctrine 234.8
Theosophists
  biography 299.934 092
Theosophy 299.934
Theotokos 232.91
Thera Island (Greece) T2—495 85
  ancient T2—391 5
Therapeutic manipulations
  medicine 615.82
Therapeutic services 362.178
  *see also* Health services
Therapeutic spells and charms 133.446
Therapeutic systems 615.53
  *see Manual at* 615.53
Therapeutic touch
  medicine 615.852

| | |
|---|---|
| Therapeutics | 615.5 |
|   adolescent medicine | 615.508 35 |
|   pediatrics | 615.542 |
|   veterinary medicine | 636.089 55 |
|   *see Manual at* 613 vs. 612, | |
|     615.8; *also at* 615.8 | |
| Therapists | 615.509 2 |
| Therapsida | 567.93 |
| Therapy | 615.5 |
|   *see Manual at* 617 | |
| Theravada Buddhism | 294.391 |
| Theremins | 786.73 |
|   *see also* Electrophones | |
| Thérèse-De Blainville | |
|   (Quebec) | T2—714 248 |
| Therevidae | 595.773 |
| Thermal analysis | 543.26 |
| Thermal capacity | 536.6 |
| Thermal conductivity | 536.201 2 |
| Thermal convective storms | 551.554 |
| Thermal cracking | |
|   petroleum | 665.533 |
| Thermal diffusivity | 536.201 4 |
| Thermal dissociation | 541.364 |
|   chemical engineering | 660.296 4 |
| Thermal effects of electricity | 537.624 |
| Thermal engineering | 621.402 |
| Thermal expansion | 536.41 |
| Thermal forces | |
|   materials science | 620.112 1 |
| Thermal insulation | 693.832 |
| Thermal ocean power conversion | 333.914 |
| Thermal perception | 152.182 2 |
| Thermal pollution | 363.739 4 |
|   effect on natural ecology | 577.627 26 |
|   social welfare | 363.739 4 |
|   water supply engineering | 628.168 31 |
|   *see also* Pollution | |
| Thermal properties | |
|   materials science | 620.112 96 |
| Thermal waters | 333.88 |
|   economics | 333.88 |
|   geophysics | 551.23 |
| Thermal weapons | 623.446 |
| Thermionic converters | 621.312 43 |
| Thermistors | 621.381 548 |
| Thermit welding | 671.529 |
| Thermobiology | 572.436 |
|   biochemistry | 572.436 |
|   body temperature | 571.76 |
|   humans | 612.014 46 |
| Thermobiophysics | 571.46 |
|   humans | 612.014 46 |

| | |
|---|---|
| Thermochemistry | 541.36 |
|   biochemistry | 572.436 |
|   chemical engineering | 660.296 |
| Thermocouples | 536.52 |
| Thermodynamics | 536.7 |
|   biochemistry | 572.436 |
|   chemical engineering | 660.296 9 |
|   chemistry | 541.369 |
|   engineering | 621.402 1 |
|   meteorology | 551.522 |
|   physics | 536.7 |
| Thermoelectric generation | 621.312 43 |
| Thermoelectricity | 537.65 |
| Thermography | |
|   medicine | 616.075 4 |
| Thermogravimetry | 543.26 |
| Thermoluminescence | 535.356 |
| Thermometry | 536.502 87 |
| Thermonuclear reaction | 539.764 |
| Thermonuclear reactors | 621.484 |
| Thermopenetration | |
|   therapeutics | 615.832 3 |
| Thermoplastic elastomers | 678 |
| Thermoplastic plastics | 668.423 |
| Thermosbaenacea | 595.373 |
| Thermosetting plastics | 668.422 |
| Thermostats | |
|   air conditioning buildings | 697.932 2 |
|   heating buildings | 697.07 |
| Thermotherapy | |
|   medicine | 615.832 |
| Theropoda | 567.912 |
| Thesauri (Controlled | |
|   vocabularies) | 025.47 |
| Thesauri (Synonym dictionaries) | 413.1 |
|   specific languages | T4—312 |
|   specific subjects | T1—03 |
| Theses (Academic) | 378.242 |
|   bibliographies | 011.75 |
|   rhetoric | 808.066 378 |
|   specific places | 015 |
| Thesprōtia (Greece) | T2—495 3 |
| Thessalia (Greece) | T2—495 4 |
| Thessalonians (Biblical books) | 227.81 |
| Thessalonikē (Greece : | |
|   Nome) | T2—495 65 |
| Thessaly (Greece) | T2—495 4 |
|   ancient | T2—382 |
| Theta function | 515.984 |
| Theunissen (South Africa : | |
|   District) | T2—685 3 |
| Thiazoles | 547.594 |
| Thierstein (Switzerland) | T2—494 355 3 |
| Thiès (Senegal : Region) | T2—663 |

Thigh muscles
  human anatomy 611.738
Thighs 612.98
  physiology 612.98
  regional medicine 617.582
  surgery 617.582
  *see also* Lower extremities
Thimbles
  home sewing 646.19
Thin-film circuits 621.381 5
Thin-film memory 004.53
  engineering 621.397 32
Thin-film technology 621.381 52
Thin films 530.427 5
  liquid-state physics 530.427 5
  solid-state physics 530.417 5
Thin-layer chromatography 543.84
Things (Law) 346.04
Things (Philosophy) 111
Thinking 153.42
  human physiology 612.823 342
  psychology 153.42
Thinners
  paint technology 667.624
Thio acids 547.064
  chemical engineering 661.896
Thioalcohols
  chemical engineering 661.896
Thioaldehydes 547.065
  chemical engineering 661.896
Thioethers 547.061
  chemical engineering 661.896
Thioketones 547.065
  chemical engineering 661.896
Thiophenes 547.594
Thiqāt (Hadith) 297.125 262
Third-class mail 383.124
  *see also* Postal service
Third Crusade, 1189–1192 956.014
Third International 324.175
Third Order Regular of St.
  Francis 255.38
  church history 271.38
  women 255.973
    church history 271.973
Third orders
  religious orders 255.094
    church history 271.094
    women 255.909 4
      church history 271.909 4
Third parties (Law) 346.022
Third Reich 943.086
Third Republic (France) 944.081
Third stream jazz 781.681 75

Third World (Developing
  regions) T2—172 4
Third World (Unaligned
  blocs) T2—171 6
Thirst
  human physiology 612.391
  psychology 152.188 6
Thirteen Articles of Faith
  (Judaism) 296.3
Thirteenth century 909.2
   T1—090 22
Thirty Years' War, 1618–1648 940.24
Thistles 583.99
Thlaping Tlaro (South
  Africa : District) T2—682 46
Thohoyandou (South
  Africa : District) T2—682 57
Thomas County (Ga.) T2—758 984
Thomas County (Kan.) T2—781 132
Thomas County (Neb.) T2—782 774
Thomist philosophy 189.4
  modern 149.91
Thompson (Man.) T2—712 71
Thompson, John S. D. (John
  Sparrow David), Sir
  Canadian history 971.055
Thompson-Nicola (B.C.) T2—711 72
Thompson River (B.C.) T2—711 72
Thonga (African people) T5—963 97
Thonga language 496.397
   T6—963 97
Thoracic surgery 617.540 59
Thoracica 595.35
Thorax 573.996
  biology 573.996
  human anatomy 611.94
  human physiology 612.94
  regional medicine 617.54
  surgery 617.540 59
Thorium 669.292 2
  chemistry 546.422
  economic geology 553.493
  metallurgy 669.292 2
  *see also* Chemicals; Metals
Thorndike, Edward L. (Edward
  Lee)
  psychological system 150.194 4
Thorns 581.47
  descriptive botany 581.47
  physiology 575.457
Thorough bass 781.47
Thoroughbred horse 636.132
Thothmes III, King of Egypt
  Egyptian history 932.014

Thought 153.42
  philosophy 128.3
  psychology 153.42
Thousand Islands (N.Y. and
  Ont.) T2—747 58
  New York T2—747 58
  Ontario T2—713 7
Thrace T2—495 7
  ancient T2—398 61
  Bulgaria T2—499 5
  Greece T2—495 7
Thrace, Eastern (Turkey) 949.61
   T2—496 1
  ancient 939.861
   T2—398 61
Thracian language 491.993
   T6—919 93
Thraco-Phrygian languages 491.993
   T6—919 93
Thrashers (Birds) 598.844
Thraupidae 598.875
Thread 677.028 62
  home sewing 646.19
  manufacturing technology 677.028 62
Threatened species 333.952 2
  *see also* entries beginning with
    Rare
Threats
  international relations 327.117
  social control 303.36
Three-day event (Horsemanship) 798.242
Three-dimensional chess 794.18
Three-dimensional graphics
  computer graphics 006.693
Three-quarter play
  rugby 796.333 25
Three Rivers (England) T2—425 88
Three-wheel vehicles
  engineering 629.220 4
Three wise men (Christian
  doctrines) 232.923
Thresholds (Psychology) 152.1
  quantitative studies 152.82
Threskiornithidae 598.34
Thrift industry 332.32
  law 346.082 32
  public administration 354.86
Thrift institutions 332.32
  law 346.082 32
  public administration 354.86
Thrift shops 381.19
Thrifts (Plants) 635.933 5
  botany 583.5
  floriculture 635.933 5

Thrips 595.758
Throat
  human anatomy 611.32
  human physiology 612.31
  medicine 616.31
  regional medicine 617.531
  surgery 617.531 059
Throat diseases
  medicine 616.31
  *see also* Digestive system
    diseases — humans
Throckmorton County
  (Tex.) T2—764 735
Thrombin
  human physiology 612.115
Thrombocytes 573.159
  human histology 612.117
  *see also* Cardiovascular system
Thromboembolisms
  arteries
    medicine 616.135
    *see also* Cardiovascular
     diseases — humans
  veins
    medicine 616.145
    *see also* Cardiovascular
     diseases — humans
Thrombophlebitis
  medicine 616.142
  *see also* Cardiovascular
    diseases — humans
Thromboses
  arteries
    medicine 616.135
    *see also* Cardiovascular
     diseases — humans
  lungs
    medicine 616.249
    *see also* Respiratory tract
     diseases — humans
  medicine 616.135
  *see also* Cardiovascular
    diseases — humans
  veins
    medicine 616.145
    *see also* Cardiovascular
     diseases — humans
Throttles
  automotive 629.258
Throughways 388.122
  *see also* Roads
Thrushes 598.842
Thrust (Aeronautics) 629.132 33
Thừa Thiên-Huế (Vietnam) T2—597 4

| | |
|---|---|
| Thulium | |
|   chemistry | 546.418 |
| Thumb pianos | 786.85 |
|   *see also* Percussion instruments | |
| Thun, Lake of (Switzerland) | T2—494 541 5 |
| Thunder Bay (Ont. : | |
|   District) | T2—713 12 |
| Thunderstorms | 551.554 |
|   social services | 363.349 24 |
| Thuner See (Switzerland) | T2—494 541 5 |
| Thunnus | 597.783 |
| Thur River (Switzerland) | T2—494 59 |
| Thurgau (Switzerland) | T2—494 59 |
| Thüringen (Germany) | T2—432 2 |
| Thuringia (Germany) | T2—432 2 |
| Thuringian Forest | T2—432 26 |
| Thurniaceae | 584.82 |
| Thurrock (England) | T2—426 78 |
| Thurston County (Neb.) | T2—782 227 |
| Thurston County (Wash.) | T2—797 79 |
| Thutmose III, King of Egypt | |
|   Egyptian history | 932.014 |
| Thylacine | 599.27 |
| Thymallus | 597.559 |
| Thyme | 641.357 |
|   botany | 583.96 |
|   *see also* Herbs | |
| Thymelaeales | 583.67 |
| Thymus-derived lymphocytes | 571.966 |
|   humans | 616.079 7 |
| Thymus gland | |
|   human anatomy | 611.43 |
|   human physiology | 612.43 |
|   medicine | 616.43 |
|   surgery | 617.546 |
| Thymus gland diseases | |
|   medicine | 616.43 |
|   *see also* Endocrine | |
|     diseases — humans | |
| Thyristors | 621.381 528 7 |
| Thyroid cancer | |
|   incidence | 614.599 944 4 |
|   medicine | 616.994 44 |
|   *see also* Cancer — humans | |
| Thyroid diseases | |
|   medicine | 616.44 |
|   *see also* Endocrine | |
|     diseases — humans | |
| Thyroid gland | 573.47 |
|   biology | 573.47 |
|   human anatomy | 611.44 |
|   human physiology | 612.44 |
|   medicine | 616.44 |
| Thyroid gland (continued) | |
|   surgery | 617.539 |
|   *see also* Endocrine system | |
| Thysanolaeneae | 584.9 |
| Thysanoptera | 595.758 |
| Thysanura | 595.723 |
| Tianjin (China) | T2—511 54 |
| Tiaras | 391.7 |
|   customs | 391.7 |
|   making | 739.278 |
|     costume jewelry | 688.2 |
|     handicrafts | 745.594 2 |
|     fine jewelry | 739.278 |
| Tiaret (Algeria : Province) | T2—651 |
| Tibet (China) | T2—515 |
| Tibet Autonomous Region | |
|   (China) | T2—515 |
| Tibetan Buddhism | 294.392 3 |
| Tibetan language | 495.4 |
| | T6—954 1 |
| Tibetan literature | 895.4 |
| Tibetan spaniel | 636.72 |
| Tibetan terrier | 636.72 |
| Tibetans | T5—954 1 |
| Tibeto-Burman languages | 495.4 |
| | T6—954 |
| Tibeto-Burman literatures | 895.4 |
| Tibeto-Burman peoples | T5—954 |
| Tibias | |
|   human anatomy | 611.718 |
| Ticino (Switzerland) | T2—494 78 |
| Ticino League (Swiss political | |
|   party) | 324.249 408 4 |
| Ticinum (Italy) | T2—372 29 |
| Tick-borne rickettsia infections | |
|   incidence | 614.526 3 |
|   medicine | 616.922 3 |
|   *see also* Communicable | |
|     diseases — humans | |
| Ticker tapes | |
|   investment analysis | 332.632 042 |
| Ticks | 595.429 |
|   disease carriers | 571.986 |
|     medicine | 614.433 |
| Tidal currents | 551.464 |
| Tidal flats | 551.457 |
|   biology | 578.769 9 |
|   ecology | 577.699 |
|   *see also* Coasts | |
| Tidal power plants | 621.312 134 |
| Tidal waves | 551.463 7 |
| Tide marshes | |
|   biology | 578.769 |
|   ecology | 577.69 |

Tide pools
  biology   578.769 9
  ecology   577.699
Tide tables
  navigation aids   623.894 9
Tidelands (Shorelands)   551.457
  *see also* Coasts
Tidelands (Wetlands)   551.41
  *see also* Wetlands
Tides   551.464
Tidewater (Va. : Region)   T2—755 1
Tie-dyeing
  textile arts   746.664
Tie plates   625.143
Tiền Giang (Vietnam)   T2—597 8
Tien Shan   T2—516
  China   T2—516
  Kyrgyzstan   T2—584 3
Tientos   784.187 6
Tientsin (China)   T2—511 54
Tierra del Fuego
  (Argentina)   T2—827 6
Tierra del Fuego (Argentina
  and Chile)   T2—827 6
Tierra del Fuego (Chile)   T2—836 46
Ties (Neckwear)   391.41
  *see also* Accessories (Clothing)
Ties (Railroad)   625.143
Tift County (Ga.)   T2—758 882
Tiger   599.756
  big game hunting   799.277 56
  conservation technology   639.979 756
  resource economics   333.959 756
Tiger beetles   595.762
Tiger fishes (Characidae)   597.48
Tiger shark   597.34
Tigerfishes (Characidae)   597.48
Tigerflowers
  botany   584.38
Tightrope walking
  circuses   791.34
  sports   796.46
Tigray kelel (Ethiopia)   T2—634
Tigre (African people)   T5—928
Tigré language   492.82
    T6—928 2
Tigré literature   892.82
Tigrigna language   T6—928 3
Tigrigna literature   892.83
Tigrinya (African people)   T5—928
Tigrinya language   492.83
    T6— 928 3
Tigrinya literature   892.83
Tigris River   T2—567 4

Tigua Indians   T5—974 96
Tigua language   497.496
    T6—974 96
Tijānīyah   297.48
Tikar (African people)   T5—963 6
Tikar language   496.36
    T6—963 6
Tilapias   641.392
  cooking   641.692
  culture   639.377 4
  food   641.392
  zoology   597.74
Tile drains   666.733
Tile furniture   645.4
  manufacturing technology   684.106
  *see also* Furniture
Tile piping   666.733
Tiles
  architectural construction   721.044 3
  building construction   693.3
  building materials   691.4
  ceramic arts   738.6
  floor coverings
    building construction   698.9
  materials science   620.142
  rubber   678.34
  structural engineering   624.183 6
Tiliaceae   583.68
Tilings (Mathematics)   516.132
  Euclidean geometry   516.213 2
Till (Geologic landforms)   551.315
Till (Geologic material)   551.314
Tillage   631.51
Tillamook County (Or.)   T2—795 44
Tillman County (Okla.)   T2—766 46
Tillodontia   569.31
Timaliidae   598.834
Timaru District (N.Z.)   T2—938 7
Timber   338.174 98
  agricultural economics   338.174 98
  building material   691.1
  resource economics   333.751 1
  *see Manual at* 583–585 vs. 600
Timber resources   333.751 1
  *see also* Forest lands
Timber truss bridges
  construction   624.218
Timber wolf   599.773
Timbre (Sound)
  musical element   781.234
Timbre perception
  psychology   152.157

Time
  arts       701.8
                     T3C—384
    drawing       741.018
  chronology       529
  literature       808.803 84
    history and criticism       809.933 84
    specific literatures    T3B—080 384
      history and
        criticism    T3B—093 84
  philosophy       115
  sociology       304.237
Time (Music)       781.22
Time and date recorders
  technology       681.118
Time clocks
  technology       681.118
Time deposits       332.175 2
Time estimates
  building construction       692.5
  commercial    T1—029
Time-invariant systems       003.8
Time-lapse cinematography       777.6
Time-lapse videography       777.6
Time management       650.11
  business       650.11
    executives       658.409 3
    home economics       640.43
Time of day
  influence on crime       364.22
Time of Troubles, 1605–1613       947.045
Time payments (Wages)       331.216 2
  personnel management       658.322 2
Time perception       153.753
Time series       519.232
Time-series analysis       519.55
Time-sharing (Computers)       005.434
  computer hardware       004.3
  systems programs       005.434
Time-sharing (Real estate)       333.323 4
  economics       333.323 4
  law       346.043 3
Time studies
  production management       658.542 1
Time systems       389.17
Time-varying systems       003.8
Time wage rate       331.216 2
  personnel management       658.322 2
Time zones       389.17
Timepieces
  technology       681.11

Times
  arts    T3C—33
  folklore       398.236
    history and criticism       398.33
  literature       808.803 3
    history and criticism       809.933 3
    specific literatures    T3B—080 33
      history and
        criticism    T3B—093 3
  music       781.52
  religious observance       203.6
    Christianity       263
    Islam       297.36
    Judaism       296.43
Times Roman type       686.224 7
Timesaving cooking       641.555
Timework       331.216 2
  personnel management       658.322 2
Timiş (Romania)    T2—498 4
Timiskaming (Ont.)    T2—713 144
Timor Island (Indonesia)    T2—598 68
Timor Sea       551.461 574
                     T2—165 74
Timor Tengah (Indonesia)    T2—598 68
Timor Timur       959.87
                     T2—598 7
Timothy (Biblical books)       227.83
Timothy (Grass)       633.24
  botany       584.9
  forage crop       633.24
Timpani       786.93
  *see also* Percussion instruments
Timur
  Asian history       950.24
Tin       669.6
  architectural construction       721.044 76
  building construction       693.76
  building material       691.86
  chemical engineering       661.068 6
  chemistry       546.686
  decorative arts       739.532
  economic geology       553.453
  materials science       620.185
  metallography       669.956
  metallurgy       669.6
  metalworking       673.6
  mining       622.345 3
  physical metallurgy       669.966
  *see also* Chemicals; Metals
Tin soldiers
  handicrafts       745.592 82
Tinamiformes       598.55
  paleozoology       568.5
Tinamous       598.55

Tindouf (Algeria : Province) T2—657
Tinea
  medicine      616.579
Tineoidea      595.78
Tinian (Northern Mariana
  Islands)      T2—967
Tinne Indians      T5—972
Tinned foods
  cooking      641.612
  product safety      363.192 9
    *see also* Food — product
      safety
Tinos Island (Greece)      T2—495 85
Tinsel
  textiles      677.76
    *see also* Textiles
Tintype process      772.14
Tioga County (N.Y.)      T2—747 77
Tioga County (Pa.)      T2—748 56
Tipaza (Algeria : Province)      T2—653
Tipiṭaka      294.382
Tippah County (Miss.)      T2—762 923
Tippecanoe County (Ind.)      T2—772 95
Tipperary (Ireland : County)      T2—419 2
Tipping
  economics      331.216 6
  etiquette      395.5
Tipton County (Ind.)      T2—772 555
Tipton County (Tenn.)      T2—768 17
Tipulidae      595.772
Tires      678.32
  automotive engineering      629.248 2
Tirmidhī, Muḥammad ibn ʿĪsá
  Hadith      297.125 43
Tirol (Austria)      T2—436 42
Tiryns (Extinct city)      T2—388
Tishah b'Av      296.439
  liturgy      296.453 9
Tishomingo County (Miss.)      T2—762 995
Tissemsilt (Algeria :
  Province)      T2—651
Tissue anatomy      571.533
  humans      611.018
Tissue banks      362.178 3
    *see also* Health services
Tissue biology      571.5
  humans      611.018
Tissue culture      571.538
  experimental research
    medicine      616.027
    humans      612.028
Tissue degeneration      571.935
Tissue differentiation      571.835

Tissue grafting
  surgery      617.954
Tissue morphology      571.533
  humans      611.018
Tissue paper      676.284 2
  handicrafts      745.54
Tissue regeneration      571.889 35
  humans      611.018
Tissue respiration      572.47
  human physiology      612.26
    *see also* Respiratory system
Tissues      571.5
  humans      611.018
Titanium      669.732 2
  chemical engineering      661.051 2
  chemistry      546.512
  economic geology      553.462 3
  materials science      620.189 322
  metallography      669.957 322
  metallurgy      669.732 2
  metalworking      673.732 2
  physical metallurgy      669.967 322
    *see also* Chemicals; Metals
Titanium group
  chemical engineering      661.051
  chemistry      546.51
Tithes
  Christian practice      248.6
  local church fund raising      254.8
Titicaca Lake (Peru and
  Bolivia)      T2—841 2
  Bolivia      T2—841 2
  Peru      T2—853 6
Title (Property)      346.043 8
  law      346.043 8
  public administration      354.34
Title examinations      346.043 8
Title insurance      368.88
  law      346.086 88
Title manipulation
  subject cataloging      025.486
Title searching      346.043 8
Titles of honor
  genealogy      929.7
Titling
  cinematography      777.55
  technical drawing      604.243
  videography      777.55
Titmice      598.824
Tito, Josip Broz
  Yugoslavian history      949.702 3
Titoism      335.434 4
  economics      335.434 4
  political ideology      320.532 309 497

| | |
|---|---|
| Titration | 543.24 |
| Titus (Biblical book) | 227.85 |
| Titus County (Tex.) | T2—764 215 |
| Tiumenskaĩa oblast´ (Russia) | T2—573 |
| Tiv (African people) | T5—963 6 |
| Tiv language | 496.36 |
| | T6—963 6 |
| Tivi (African people) | T5—963 6 |
| Tivi language | 496.36 |
| | T6—963 6 |
| Tiwa Indians | T5—974 96 |
| Tiwa language | 497.496 |
| | T6—974 96 |
| Tiwi language (Melville Island) | 499.15 |
| | T6—991 5 |
| Tizi Ouzou (Algeria : Province) | T2—653 |
| Tiznit (Morocco : Province) | T2—646 6 |
| Tlaxcala (Mexico : State) | T2—724 7 |
| Tlemcen (Algeria : Province) | T2—651 |
| Tlingit Indians | T5—972 7 |
| Tlingit language | 497.27 |
| | T6—972 7 |
| TMJ dysfunction | |
| regional medicine | 617.522 |
| TNT (Explosive) | 662.27 |
| military engineering | 623.452 7 |
| Toadfishes | 597.62 |
| Toads | 597.87 |
| Toadstools | 579.6 |
| Toamasina (Madagascar : Province) | T2—691 |
| Toasting | 394.12 |
| Toasts | 394.12 |
| customs | 394.12 |
| literature | 808.851 |
| history and criticism | 809.51 |
| specific literatures | T3B—501 |
| individual authors | T3A—5 |
| rhetoric | 808.512 |
| Toba Batak | T5—992 246 2 |
| Toba Batak language | 499.224 62 |
| | T6—992 246 2 |
| Toba Batak literature | 899.224 62 |
| Tobacco | |
| agriculture | 633.71 |
| botany | 583.952 |
| customs | 394.14 |
| ethics | 178.7 |
| *see also* Ethical problems | |
| human toxicology | 615.952 395 2 |
| manufacturing technology | 679.7 |
| Tobacco (continued) | |
| smuggling | 364.133 6 |
| law | 345.023 36 |
| Tobacco abuse | 362.296 |
| effect on fetus | |
| perinatal medicine | 618.326 86 |
| medicine | 616.865 |
| personal health | 613.85 |
| pregnancy complications | |
| obstetrics | 618.368 6 |
| social welfare | 362.296 |
| *see also* Substance abuse | |
| Tobacco industry | 338.173 71 |
| agricultural economics | 338.173 71 |
| law | 343.076 371 |
| manufacturing | 338.476 797 |
| Tobacco industry workers | 679.709 2 |
| Tobacco smuggling | 364.133 6 |
| law | 345.023 36 |
| Tobacco substitutes | 688.4 |
| Tobago | 972.983 |
| | T2—729 83 |
| Tobias (Deuterocanonical book) | 229.22 |
| Tobit (Deuterocanonical book) | 229.22 |
| Tobogganing | 796.95 |
| Tobote language | 496.35 |
| | T6—963 5 |
| Tocantins (Brazil) | T2—811 7 |
| Toccatas | 784.189 47 |
| Tocharian language | 491.994 |
| | T6—919 94 |
| Tocharish language | 491.994 |
| | T6—919 94 |
| Tochigi-ken (Japan) | T2—521 32 |
| Tocopilla (Chile : Province) | T2—831 32 |
| Toda (Dravidians) | T5—948 1 |
| Toda language | 494.81 |
| | T6—948 1 |
| Toda literature | 894.81 |
| Today's English Bible | 220.520 82 |
| Todd County (Ky.) | T2—769 77 |
| Todd County (Minn.) | T2—776 88 |
| Todd County (S.D.) | T2—783 62 |
| Tofu | 641.356 55 |
| commercial processing | 664.805 655 |
| cooking | 641.656 55 |
| food | 641.356 55 |
| Togaviridae | 579.256 2 |
| Toggenburg (Switzerland) | T2—494 726 |
| Togo | 966.81 |
| | T2—668 1 |

| | |
|---|---|
| Togoland | 966.810 2 |
| | T2—668 1 |
| Ghana | T2—667 |
| Togo | T2—668 1 |
| Togolese | T5—966 81 |
| Tōhoku Region (Japan) | T2—521 1 |
| Tohono O'Odham Indians | T5—974 552 |
| Tohono O'Odham language | 497.455 2 |
| | T6—974 552 |
| Tohono O'Odham literature | 897.455 2 |
| Tohorot (Order or tractate) | 296.123 6 |
| Babylonian Talmud | 296.125 6 |
| Mishnah | 296.123 6 |
| Palestinian Talmud | 296.124 6 |
| Toilet paper | 676.284 2 |
| Toilet training | 649.62 |
| Toilets | |
| construction | 690.42 |
| Tojiki language | 491.57 |
| | T6—915 7 |
| Tok Pisin | 427.995 3 |
| | T6—217 |
| Toka (African people) | T5—963 91 |
| Toka language | 496.391 |
| | T6—963 91 |
| Tokamaks | 621.484 |
| Tokat İli (Turkey) | T2—565 6 |
| ancient | T2—393 37 |
| Tokelau Islands | 996.15 |
| | T2—961 5 |
| Tokelau language | 499.46 |
| | T6—994 6 |
| Tokelauan dialect | 499.46 |
| | T6—994 6 |
| Tokelauans (New Zealand people) | T5—994 6 |
| Token coins | 332.404 3 |
| Tokens | |
| numismatics | 737.3 |
| Tokharian language | 491.994 |
| | T6—919 94 |
| Tokugawa period | 952.025 |
| Tokushima-ken (Japan) | T2—523 4 |
| Tokyo (Japan) | T2—521 35 |
| Tolecraft | 745.723 |
| Toledo (Ohio) | T2—771 13 |
| Toledo (Spain : Province) | T2—464 3 |
| Toledo Bend Reservoir (La. and Tex.) | T2—763 62 |
| Toledo District (Belize) | T2—728 24 |
| Toledo Manrique, Alejandro | |
| Peruvian history | 985.064 4 |

| | |
|---|---|
| Toleration | 179.9 |
| moral theology | 205.699 |
| social theology | 201.723 |
| Christianity | 261.72 |
| *see also* Politics and religion — social theology | |
| *see also* Virtues | |
| Toliara (Madagascar : Province) | T2—691 |
| Tolima (Colombia : Dept.) | T2—861 36 |
| Tolland County (Conn.) | T2—746 43 |
| Tolls | |
| roads | 388.114 |
| transportation services | 388.049 |
| Tollways | 388.122 |
| *see also* Roads | |
| Tolman, Edward Chace | |
| psychological system | 150.194 34 |
| Tolna Megye (Hungary) | T2—439 7 |
| Toltec empire | 972.017 |
| | T2—72 |
| Tom Green County (Tex.) | T2—764 721 |
| Tomahawks | 623.441 |
| Tomatoes | 641.356 42 |
| botany | 583.952 |
| commercial processing | 664.805 642 |
| cooking | 641.656 42 |
| food | 641.356 42 |
| garden crop | 635.642 |
| Tombigbee River (Miss. and Ala.) | T2—761 2 |
| Tombs | |
| architecture | 726.8 |
| Tomography | |
| medicine | 616.075 7 |
| Tompkins County (N.Y.) | T2—747 71 |
| Tomsk (Russia : Oblast) | T2—573 |
| Tomskaia oblast' (Russia) | T2—573 |
| Tonal systems (Music) | 781.26 |
| Tonality | 781.258 |
| Tonbridge and Malling (England) | T2—422 372 |
| Tønder amt (Denmark) | T2—489 5 |
| Tone color | |
| musical element | 781.234 |
| perception | |
| psychology | 152.157 |
| Tone River (Japan) | T2—521 3 |
| Tonga | 996.12 |
| | T2—961 2 |
| Tonga (Mozambique and South African people) | T5—963 97 |
| Tonga (Zambian people) | T5—963 91 |

Tonga language (Inhambane)        496.397
                                  T6—963 97
Tonga language (Nyasa)            496.391
                                  T6—963 91
Tonga language (Tonga Islands)    499.482
                                  T6—994 82
Tonga language (Zambesi)          496.391
                                  T6—963 91
Tonga literature (Tonga Islands)  899.482
Tongaat (South Africa)      T2—684 4
Tongaland (South Africa)    T2—684 3
Tongan language                   499.482
                                  T6—994 82
Tongan literature                 899.482
Tongans                     T5—994 82
Tongariro National Park
  (N.Z.)                    T2—935 2
Tongic languages                  499.48
                                  T6—994 8
Tongue                            573.357
  biology                         573.357
  human anatomy                   611.313
  human physiology                612.312
    tasting                       612.87
  medicine                        616.31
  surgery                         617.522
  *see also* Digestive system
Tongue-and-groove products        674.43
Tongue diseases
  medicine                        616.31
  *see also* Digestive system
            diseases — humans
Tongue twisters                   808.882
  folk literature                 398.8
  literature                      808.882
    history and criticism         809.982
    specific literatures    T3B—802
      individual authors    T3A—8
Tongueless frogs                  597.865
Tonguing (Music)                  784.193 4
Tongwe languages                  496.394
                                  T6—963 94
Tonic sol-fa                      780.148
Toning solutions
  photography                     771.54
Tonnage                           387.2
  inland water                    386.22
  ocean                           387.2
Tonsil diseases
  medicine                        616.314
  *see also* Digestive system
            diseases — humans

Tonsillitis
  medicine                        616.314
  *see also* Digestive system
            diseases — humans
Tonsils
  human anatomy                   611.32
  human physiology                612.312
  medicine                        616.314
  surgery                         617.532
Tonus
  muscles
    human physiology              612.741
  skin
    human physiology              612.791
Tooele County (Utah)        T2—792 43
Tool engineering                  621.9
Tool engineers                    621.900 92
Toole County (Mont.)        T2—786 12
Tooling
  bookbinding                     686.36
Tools                             621.9
Toombs County (Ga.)         T2—758 782
Tooth diseases                    573.356 39
  animals                         573.356 39
  humans
    cancer                        616.994 314
    dentistry                     617.63
    incidence                     614.599 6
Tooth extraction                  617.66
Tooth shells                      594.29
Tooth sockets
  dentistry                       617.632
Tooth tissues
  dentistry                       617.634
Toothbrushing                     617.601
Toothed whales                    599.5
Toothpicks
  wooden                          674.88
Toowoomba (Qld.)            T2—943 3
Top-down programming              005.11
Top games                         795.2
  equipment technology            688.752
Top management                    658.42
  public administration           352.285
Topaz
  mineralogy                      549.62
Topcoats                          391.46
  customs                         391.46
  home sewing                     646.45
  *see also* Clothing
Tope                              597.34
Topectomy
  surgery                         617.481
Topeka (Kan.)               T2—781 63

Topiary work 715.1
Topic and comment (Grammar) 415
  specific languages T4—5
Topical drug administration 615.6
Topminnows 597.66
Topographic surveying 526.98
Topographical anatomy
  humans 611.9
Topography 910
  city planning 711.42
  geographic description 910
  geomorphology 551.41
  influence on crime 364.22
  influence on precipitation 551.577 5
  mapping 526
  military engineering 623.71
  ocean floor 551.468 3
Topological algebras 512.55
Topological K-theory 514.23
Topological manifolds 514.34
Topological spaces 514.32
Topological transformation
  groups 514
Topological vector spaces 515.73
Topology 514
Toposes 512.62
Tops (Clothing) 391.475
  commercial technology 687.115
  customs 391.475
  home economics 646.3
  home sewing 646.435
  *see also* Clothing
Tops (Coverings)
  automobile 629.26
Toradja languages 499.226
  T6—992 26
Toradjas T5—992 26
Torah (Bible) 222.1
Torah scrolls 296.461 5
Toraja (Indonesian people) T5—992 26
Toraja languages 499.226
  T6—992 26
Toraja Sa'dan language 499.226
  T6—992 26
Torbay (England) T2—423 595
Torches 621.323
  *see also* Lighting
Torfaen (Wales) T2—429 97
Tories
  Canadian history 971.024
  United States history 973.314
Torino (Italy) T2—451 21
  ancient T2—372 221

Torino (Italy : Province) T2—451 2
  ancient T2—372 22
Tornadoes 551.553
  meteorology 551.553
  social services 363.349 23
  weather forecasting 551.645 3
  weather modification 551.685 3
  *see also* Disasters
Tornedalen Finnish 494.54
  T6—945 4
Tornedalen Finnish literature 894.54
Toronto (Ont.) T2—713 541
Toros Dağları (Turkey) T2—564
Torpedo boats 359.835 8
  design 623.812 58
  engineering 623.825 8
  naval equipment 359.835 8
  naval units 359.325 8
Torpedoes (Ammunition) 359.825 17
  engineering 623.451 7
  naval equipment 359.825 17
Torpedoes (Fishes) 597.35
Torquay (Vic.) T2—945 2
Torque 531.34
Torrance County (N.M.) T2—789 63
Torres Strait (Qld. and Papua 551.461 476
  New Guinea) T2—164 76
Torres Strait Islanders T5—991 2
Torres Strait Islands (Qld.) T2—943 8
Torricelli languages T6—991 2
Torrid Zone T2—13
Torrid zone
  biology 578.091 3
  ecology 577.091 3
  geography 910.913
Torridge (England) T2—423 51
Torrijos Espino, Martín
  Panamanian history 972.870 542
Torsion (Mathematics) 516.36
Torsion (Mechanics)
  effect on materials 620.112 43
Tort liability 346.03
Tortillas 641.815
Tortoises 597.924
  conservation technology 639.977 924
  resource economics 333.957 924
Tortola (V.I.) T2—729 725
Tortricoidea 595.78
Torts 346.03
  *see Manual at* 345.02 vs.
    346.03
Tortuga Island (Haiti) T2—729 42
Torture
  war customs 399

Toruń (Poland :
  Voivodeship) — T2—438 26
Tory Party (Great Britain) — 324.241 02
Toscana (Italy) — 945.5
  — T2—455
  ancient — T2—375
Tosefta — 296.126 2
Total derivatives — 515.33
Total differentiation — 515.33
Total productive maintenance — 658.202
Total quality management — 658.401 3
  production management — 658.562
Total war — 355.02
Totalitarian government — 321.9
Totalitarianism — 320.53
Totem poles
  religious significance — 299.713 7
  sculpture — 731.77
Totemic kinship — 306.83
Totemism — 202.11
Totonac Indians — T5—979
Totonacan languages — 497.9
  — T6—979
Totonicapán (Guatemala :
  Dept.) — T2—728 181
Tottori-ken (Japan) — T2—521 93
Touareg — T5—933
Toucans — 598.72
  animal husbandry — 636.68
Touch — 573.875
  animal physiology — 573.875
  human physiology — 612.88
  psychology — 152.182
  *see also* Nervous system
Touch football
  American — 796.332 8
  Canadian — 796.335 8
Touch-me-nots — 583.79
Touch techniques
  music — 784.193 68
Touchtone devices
  computer science — 004.76
  engineering — 621.398 6
Toulouse (France) — T2—447 367
Touracos — 598.74
Touraine (France) — T2—445 4
Touré, Ahmadou
  Malian history — 966.230 53
Touré, Ahmed Sékou
  Guinean history — 966.520 51
Tourette syndrome
  medicine — 616.83
    *see also* Nervous system
      diseases — humans

Tourism — 910
  industry — 338.479 1
  recreation — 790.18
  sociology — 306.481 9
  travel — 910
    *see also* Travel
Tourist exemptions
  customs duties — 382.78
    *see also* Customs (Tariff)
Tourist industry — 338.479 1
  air service — 387.742
  boat service — 387.542
  bus service — 388.322 2
    urban — 388.413 22
  economics — 338.479 1
  law — 343.078 91
    transportation law — 343.093 3
  public administration — 354.73
  railroad service — 385.22
  sociology — 306.481 9
  transportation services — 388.042
Tourmaline — 553.87
  mineralogy — 549.64
  *see also* Semiprecious stones
Tournaments (Contests)
  customs — 394.7
Tournaments (Graphs) — 511.54
Tours (France) — T2—445 45
Towada Lake (Japan) — T2—521 12
Towboats — 387.232
  design — 623.812 32
  engineering — 623.823 2
  *see also* Ships
Towed boats — 387.29
  design — 623.812 9
  engineering — 623.829
  transportation services — 387.29
  *see also* Ships
Toweling
  arts — 746.98
Towels — 643.52
  arts — 746.98
  home economics — 643.52
  home sewing — 646.21
Tower Hamlets (London,
  England) — T2—421 5
Towers (Structural elements) — 721.5
  architecture — 721.5
  Christian church architecture — 726.597
  construction — 690.15
Towers (Structures)
  architecture — 725.97
Towhees — 598.883

Town halls
  architecture 725.13
Town planning 307.121 6
  *see also* City planning
Towner County (N.D.) T2—784 38
Townhouses 643.1
  architecture 728.312
  *see also* Dwellings
Towns 307.76
  *see also* Cities
Towns County (Ga.) T2—758 282
Townshend Acts, 1767
  United States history 973.311 2
Townsville (Qld.) T2—943 6
Toxic chemicals 363.179 1
  hazardous materials technology 604.7
    chemical engineering 660.280 4
  pollution 363.738 4
    *see also* Pollution
  public safety 363.179 1
  *see also* Hazardous materials
Toxic drug reactions
  pharmacokinetics 615.704
Toxic materials 363.179
  *see also* Hazardous materials
Toxic shock syndrome
  incidence 614.579 7
  medicine 616.929 7
    *see also* Communicable
      diseases — humans
Toxic spills 363.728 7
  *see also* Waste control
Toxic torts 346.038
Toxic wastes 363.728 7
  technology 628.42
  *see also* Waste control
Toxicity testing 615.907
Toxicologists 615.900 92
Toxicology 571.95
  adolescent medicine 615.900 835
  medicine 615.9
    *see Manual at* 615.7 vs.
      615.9
  pediatrics 615.900 83
  veterinary medicine 636.089 59
Toxins
  human toxicology 615.95
  toxicology 571.957
Toxoids
  pharmacology 615.372
Toy dogs 636.76
Toy instrument orchestras 784.46
Toy makers 688.720 92
Toy Manchester terrier 636.76

Toy soldiers
  handicrafts 745.592 82
Toy theaters 791.5
Toyama-ken (Japan) T2—521 53
Toys 790.133
  cataloging 025.349 6
  customs 394.3
  library treatment 025.179 6
  making 688.72
    handicrafts 745.592
    technology 688.72
  product safety 363.19
    law 344.042 35
  recreation 790.133
  use in child care 649.55
Toys (Dogs) 636.76
TPM (Maintenance management) 658.202
TQM (Management) 658.401 3
  production management 658.562
Trà Vinh (Vietnam) T2—597 8
Trabzon İli (Turkey) T2—565 8
Trace elements 572.515
  applied nutrition 613.285
    animal husbandry 636.085 27
  biochemistry 572.515
    humans 612.015 24
  metabolism
    human physiology 612.392 4
Trace fossils 560.43
Tracer testing
  materials science 620.112 73
Trachea 573.26
  biology 573.26
  human anatomy 611.23
  human physiology 612.234
  medicine 616.23
  surgery 617.533
  *see also* Respiratory system
Tracheal diseases
  medicine 616.23
    *see also* Respiratory tract
      diseases — humans
Tracheitis
  medicine 616.23
    *see also* Respiratory tract
      diseases — humans
Trachemys 597.925 9
Tracheophytes 580
  *see also* Plants
Trachichthyidae 597.64

Trachoma
  incidence — 614.599 7
  ophthalmology — 617.772
    *see also* Eye diseases —
      humans
Trachylina — 593.55
Track (Sports) — 796.42
Track and field — 796.42
  biography — 796.420 92
Track and field athletics — 796.42
Track cycling — 796.628
Track laying — 625.144
Tracking
  space flight — 629.457
  unmanned space flight — 629.437
Tracking hounds — 636.753 6
Tracking systems
  spacecraft — 629.474 3
  unmanned spacecraft — 629.464 3
Tracks (Animals) — 591.479
Tracks (Railroad) — 385.312
Tract (Music) — 782.323 5
Traction systems
  electrical engineering — 621.33
Tractor trailers — 388.344
  engineering — 629.224
  *see also* Trucks
Tractors — 629.225 2
  agricultural use — 631.372
  driving — 629.284 52
  engineering — 629.225 2
  repair — 629.287 52
Trade — 381
  *see also* Commerce
Trade acceptances — 332.77
  exchange medium — 332.55
  law — 346.096
Trade advertising — 659.131 5
Trade agreements — 382.9
  law — 343.087 026 1
Trade associations — 381.06
  law — 346.064
Trade barriers — 382.7
Trade bibliographies — 015
Trade cards
  illustration — 741.685
Trade catalogs — 381.029
    T1—029
  *see Manual at* T1—025 vs.
    T1—029; *also at* T1—074
    vs. T1—029
Trade fairs — 381.1
Trade promotion
  international banking — 332.154

Trade secrets
  law — 346.048
  management — 658.472
Trade shows — 381.1
  advertising — 659.152
Trade unions — 331.88
  *see also* Labor unions
Trade winds — 551.518 3
Trademark infringement — 364.166 3
  criminal law — 345.026 63
Trademarks — 929.95
    T1—027 5
  law — 346.048 8
  products — 602.75
  public administration — 352.749
  sales promotion — 658.827
Traders — 381.092
Trading cards
  illustration — 741.6
Trading stamps
  sales promotion — 658.82
Tradition (Theology)
  Christianity — 231.042
Traditional medicine — 610
Traditional remedies
  therapeutics — 615.88
Traditionalism
  philosophy — 148
  political ideology — 320.52
Trafalgar, Battle of, 1805 — 940.274 5
Traffic accidents — 363.125
  *see also* Highway safety;
    Transportation safety
Traffic circles — 388.13
  area planning — 711.7
  engineering — 625.7
  transportation services — 388.13
  urban — 388.411
Traffic control — 388.041
  air transportation — 387.740 426
  *see also* Air traffic control
  canal transportation — 386.404 204 2
  inland waterway — 386.240 42
  lake transportation — 386.540 42
  railroad transportation — 385.204 2
    engineering — 625.165
  river transportation — 386.350 42
  road transportation — 388.312
    engineering — 625.794
    law — 343.094 6
    police services — 363.233 2
    public administration — 354.772 8
    urban — 388.413 12
      law — 343.098 2

| | |
|---|---|
| Traffic control failures | 363.120 1 |
|   air transportation | 363.124 18 |
|   railroad transportation | 363.122 1 |
|   *see also* Transportation safety | |
| Traffic engineering (Urban) | 388.413 12 |
|   law | 343.098 |
|   public administration | 354.772 8 |
| Traffic flow (Road) | 388.31 |
|   urban | 388.413 1 |
| Traffic noise | 363.741 |
|   *see also* Noise | |
| Traffic patterns | |
|   highways | 388.314 3 |
|   streets | 388.413 143 |
| Traffic regulations | 343.094 6 |
|   urban transportation | 343.098 |
| Traffic safety | 363.125 |
|   *see also* Highway safety; | |
|     Transportation safety | |
| Traffic signals | 388.312 2 |
|   *see also* Traffic signs | |
| Traffic signs | 388.312 2 |
|   engineering | 625.794 |
|   law | 343.094 6 |
|   transportation services | 388.312 2 |
|   urban | 388.413 122 |
|   law | 343.098 2 |
| Traffic surveys | |
|   roads | 388.314 |
|   urban | 388.413 14 |
| Traffic violations | 364.147 |
|   law | 345.024 7 |
| Traffic volume | |
|   highways | 388.314 2 |
|   streets | 388.413 142 |
| Trafficways | |
|   engineering | 629.047 |
|   landscape architecture | 713 |
| Trafford (England) | T2—427 31 |
| Tragedies (Drama) | 792.12 |
|   literature | 808.825 12 |
|     history and criticism | 809.251 2 |
|     specific literatures | T3B—205 12 |
|       individual authors | T3A—2 |
|   stage presentation | 792.12 |
| Tragedy | |
|   arts | T3C—162 |
|   literature | 808.801 62 |
|     history and criticism | 809.916 2 |
|     specific literatures | T3B—080 162 |
|       history and | |
|         criticism | T3B—091 62 |
| Tragelaphus | 599.642 3 |
| Tragicomedies (Drama) | |
|   literature | 808.825 23 |
|     history and criticism | 809.252 3 |
|     specific literatures | T3B—205 23 |
|       individual authors | T3A—2 |
| Tragulidae | 599.63 |
| Trail (B.C.) | T2—711 62 |
| Trailer camps | 910.468 |
|   household management | 647.942 |
|   *see also* Lodging (Temporary | |
|     housing) | |
| Trailer parks | 647.92 |
|   area planning | 711.58 |
|   household management | 647.92 |
| Trailers (Freight) | 388.344 |
|   engineering | 629.224 |
|   *see also* Trucks | |
| Trailers (Passenger) | 388.346 |
|   architecture | 728.79 |
|   engineering | 629.226 |
|   pulling | 629.284 6 |
|   repair | 629.287 6 |
|   travel | 910 |
|   *see also* Motor homes | |
| Traill County (N.D.) | T2—784 14 |
| Train accidents | 363.122 |
|   *see also* Railroad safety | |
| Trainers (Aircraft) | |
|   military engineering | 623.746 2 |
| Training | |
|   armed forces | 355.5 |
|   child care | 649.6 |
|   employee education | 370.113 |
|   *see also* Vocational education | |
| Training plants | 631.546 |
| Training programs | |
|   personnel management | 658.312 404 |
|     public administration | 352.669 |
|   public administration | 354.968 |
| Training schools (Correctional | |
|   institutions) | 365.42 |
|   *see also* Penal institutions | |
| Training teachers | T1—071 1 |
| Trains | 385.37 |
|   engineering | 625.2 |
|   sanitation services | 363.729 3 |
|   transportation services | 385.37 |
|   *see also* Rolling stock | |
| Traits | |
|   individual psychology | 155.232 |
| Trajectories | |
|   military engineering | 623.514 |
| Tramp routes | 387.523 |
| Trampoline | 796.474 |

| | |
|---|---|
| Trampolining | 796.474 |
| Tramps | 305.569 |
| | T1—086 942 |
| Trams | |
|   engineering | 625.66 |
| Tramways | 388.46 |
|   engineering | 625.6 |
|   public transportation | 354.769 |
|   transportation services | 388.46 |
| Trance music | 781.648 |
| Trance phenomena (Hypnotism) | 154.772 |
| Tranquilizer abuse | 362.299 |
|   medicine | 616.86 |
|   personal health | 613.8 |
|   social welfare | 362.299 |
|   *see also* Substance abuse | |
| Tranquilizers | |
|   pharmacokinetics | 615.788 2 |
| Trans-Neptunian objects | 523.49 |
| | T2—992 9 |
| Trans-New Guinea languages | 499.12 |
| | T6—991 2 |
| Trans-Uranian planets | 523.48 |
| Transaction processing systems | 005.745 |
| Transaction tax | 336.27 |
|   law | 343.055 |
|   public administration | 352.44 |
|   public finance | 336.27 |
| Transactional analysis | |
|   applied psychology | 158.2 |
|     system | 158.9 |
|   psychiatry | 616.891 45 |
| Transborder data flow | 384.3 |
|   computer communications | |
|     services | 384.3 |
|   law | 344.09 |
| Transcarpathia (Ukraine : | |
|   Oblast) | T2—477 9 |
| Transcaucasus | 947.5 |
| | T2—475 |
| Transcendence of God | 212.7 |
|   *see also* Attributes of God | |
| Transcendental functions | 515.22 |
| Transcendental meditation | 158.125 |
|   system | 158.9 |
| Transcendental numbers | 512.73 |
| Transcendentalism | |
|   arts | T3C—384 |
|   literature | 808.803 84 |
|     history and criticism | 809.933 84 |
|     specific literatures | T3B—080 384 |
|       history and | |
|         criticism | T3B—093 84 |
|   philosophy | 141.3 |

| | |
|---|---|
| Transcription (Genetics) | 572.884 5 |
| Transcription (Language) | |
|   linguistics | 411 |
|     specific languages | T4—11 |
|   shorthand notes | 653.14 |
| Transcription (Music) | 781.37 |
| Transduction (Genetics) | 571.964 8 |
| Transepts | |
|   Christian church architecture | 726.592 |
| Transfection | 571.964 8 |
| Transfer (Law) | 346.043 6 |
| Transfer of employees | |
|   personnel management | 658.312 8 |
|   public administration | 352.66 |
| Transfer of learning | |
|   psychology | 153.154 |
| Transfer painting | |
|   pottery | 666.45 |
|   arts | 738.15 |
|   technology | 666.45 |
| Transfer payments | |
|   macroeconomic policy | 339.522 |
| Transfer RNA | 572.886 |
| Transfer students | 371.291 4 |
|   higher education | 378.169 14 |
| Transfer tax (Inheritance) | 336.276 |
|   law | 343.053 |
| Transfer tax (Transactions) | 336.27 |
|   law | 343.055 |
|   public finance | 336.27 |
| Transferases | 572.792 |
|   *see also* Enzymes | |
| Transfiguration of Jesus Christ | 232.956 |
| Transfinite numbers | 511.322 |
| Transformation (Genetics) | 571.964 8 |
| Transformation of energy | 531.68 |
| Transformational grammar | 415.018 2 |
|   specific languages | T4 501 82 |
| Transformations (Mathematics) | 511.326 |
|   geometry | 516.1 |
|   mathematical logic | 511.326 |
| Transformer substations | 621.312 6 |
| Transformers (Electrical | |
|   equipment) | 621.314 |
| Transforms | 515.723 |
| Transgender people | 306.768 |
| | T1—086 7 |
|   labor economics | 331.5 |
|   psychology | 155.33 |
|   social welfare | 362.897 |
| Transgender young people | |
|   social services | 362.785 |
| Transgenderism | 306.768 |

| | |
|---|---|
| Transgenderist young people | |
|   social services | 362.785 |
| Transgenderists | 306.768 |
| | T1—086 7 |
|   psychology | 155.33 |
|   social welfare | 362.897 |
| Transgenic mammals | |
|   experimental animals | |
|     medicine | 616.027 3 |
| Transient magnetism | |
|   (Geomagnetism) | 538.74 |
| Transients (Electricity) | 621.319 21 |
| Transistors | 621.381 528 |
|   television engineering | 621.388 32 |
| Transit insurance | 368.2 |
| Transit police | 363.287 |
| Transit tax | 382.7 |
|   public finance | 336.263 |
|   *see also* Customs (Tariff) | |
| Transition metals | |
|   chemical engineering | 661.06 |
|   chemistry | 546.6 |
| Transitional flow | 532.052 6 |
|   gas mechanics | 533.216 |
|   liquid mechanics | 532.516 |
| Transits | 523.99 |
|   Mercury | 523.91 |
|   Venus | 523.92 |
| Transkei (South Africa) | T2—687 58 |
| Translating | |
|   linguistics | 418.02 |
|     specific languages | T4—802 |
|     specific subjects | 418.03 |
|       specific languages | T4—803 |
| Translation (Genetics) | 572.645 |
| Translation (Linguistics) | 418.02 |
|   specific languages | T4—802 |
|   specific subjects | 418.03 |
|     specific languages | T4—803 |
| Translations | |
|   bibliographies | 011.7 |
| Translator stations | 384.554 |
|   *see also* Television | |
| Translators (Computer science) | |
|   microprogramming languages | 005.18 |
|   programming languages | 005.45 |
| Translators (Interpreters) | |
|   specific languages | T4—802 092 |
| Transliteration | 411 |
|   specific languages | T4—11 |
| Translocation (Genetics) | 572.877 |
| Transmigration | |
|   occultism | 133.901 35 |
|   philosophy | 129 |
| Transmission devices | |
|   automotive engineering | 629.244 |
| Transmission facilities | |
|   communications engineering | 621.382 3 |
| Transmission media | |
|   computer communications | 004.64 |
|     engineering | 621.398 1 |
| Transmission modes | |
|   communications engineering | 621.382 16 |
|   computer communications | 004.66 |
|     engineering | 621.398 1 |
| Transmission of light | 535.3 |
| Transmission of sound | 534.2 |
| Transmitters | |
|   radio engineering | 621.384 131 |
|   television engineering | 621.388 31 |
| Transmitting electricity | 621.319 |
| Transmitting heat | |
|   engineering | 621.402 2 |
| Transmitting steam | 621.185 |
| Transnational Radical Party | |
|   (Italy) | 324.245 06 |
| Transoceanic flights | |
|   engineering | 629.130 916 2 |
| Transonic flow | 533.274 |
|   air mechanics | 533.62 |
|   aeronautics | 629.132 304 |
| Transpadane Gaul | T2—372 2 |
| Transparencies (Photographs) | 779 |
|   processing | 771.4 |
|   *see Manual at* 779 vs. 770.92 | |
| Transpersonal psychology | 150.198 7 |
| Transpiration | 575.8 |
|   meteorology | 551.572 |
| Transplanting (Plant propagation) | 631.536 |
| Transplants (Medical) | 362.197 95 |
|   *see also* Organ transplants | |
| Transport aircraft | |
|   military engineering | 623.746 5 |
| Transport phenomena | 530.475 |
|   chemical engineering | 660.284 2 |
|   *see also* Mass transfer | |
| Transport proteins | 572.696 |
| Transport theory (Statistical | |
|   mechanics) | 530.138 |
| Transport workers | 388.092 |
| Transportation | 388 |
|   arts | T3C—355 8 |
|   coal technology | 662.624 |
|   distribution of goods | |
|     management | 658.788 2 |
|   energy economics | 333.796 8 |
|   gas technology | 665.743 |
|   law | 343.093 |

Transportation (continued)
literature — 808.803 558
   history and criticism — 809.933 558
military engineering — 623.6
mining — 622.6
museology — 069.53
           T1—075
petroleum technology — 665.543
public administration — 354.76
safety — 363.12
   *see also* Transportation safety
social effects — 303.483 2
transportation services — 388
  *see Manual at* 380
Transportation (Spiritualism) — 133.92
Transportation accidents — 363.12
  *see also* Transportation safety
Transportation advertising — 659.134 4
Transportation diseases
medicine — 616.980 2
  *see also* Environmental
    diseases — humans
Transportation engineering — 629.04
Transportation equipment
engineering — 629.046
theft of — 364.162 862 904
   law — 345.026 286 290 4
Transportation facilities — 388.04
architecture — 725.3
area planning — 711.7
construction — 690.53
military resources — 355.27
Transportation for employees
personnel management — 658.383
Transportation injuries
medicine — 617.102 8
Transportation insurance — 368.2
Transportation law — 343.093
Transportation liability insurance — 368.57
Transportation police — 363.287
Transportation safety — 363.12
fire hazards — 363.379
  *see also* Fire safety
law — 343.093 8
public administration — 353.98
social services — 363.12
  *see Manual at* 900
Transportation workers — 388.092
Transports (Ships) — 359.985 83
design — 623.812 64
engineering — 623.826 4
naval equipment — 359.985 83
naval units — 359.985 3
Transposition (Music) — 781.436

Transposons — 572.869
Transsexual adolescents
social services — 362.785
Transsexualism — 306.768
psychology — 155.33
Transsexuality — 306.768
psychology — 155.33
Transsexuals — 306.768
           T1—086 7
psychology — 155.33
social welfare — 362.897
Transuranium elements — 546.44
  *see also* Chemicals
Transvaal (Colony) — 968.204 9
           T2—682
Transvaal (South Africa) — 968.205
           T2—682
Transverse flutes — 788.32
  *see also* Woodwind instruments
Transvestism — 306.778
Transvestites — 306.778
Transylvania (Principality) — T2—498 4
Transylvania Colony — 976.902
           T2—769
Transylvania County (N.C.) — T2—756 93
Traoré, Moussa
Malian history — 966.230 51
Trapaceae — 583.76
Trapani (Italy : Province) — T2—458 24
ancient — T2—378 24
Trapeze work
circuses — 791.34
sports — 796.46
Trappers — 639.109 2
Trapping — 639.1
commercial — 639.1
sports — 799.2
Trappists — 255.125
church history — 271.125
Traps
military engineering — 623.31
Traps Islands (N.Z.) — T2—939 9
Trapshooters — 799.313 209 2
Trapshooting — 799.313 2
Traralgon (Vic.) — T2—945 6
Trás-os-Montes (Portugal) — T2 469 2
Trás-os-Montes e Alto
   Douro (Portugal) — T2—469 2
Trash (Art style) — 709.034 8
Trauma centers — 362.18
Traumatic neuroses
medicine — 616.852 1
  *see also* Mental disorders

| | |
|---|---|
| Traumatic shock | |
| medicine | 617.21 |
| Traumatology | |
| medicine | 617.1 |
| Travel | 910 |
| arts | 700.42 |
| | T3C—32 |
| industry | 338.479 1 |
| literature | 808.803 2 |
| history and criticism | 809.933 2 |
| specific literatures | T3B—080 32 |
| history and | |
| criticism | T3B—093 2 |
| meal service | 642.3 |
| natural history | 508 |
| recreation | 790.18 |
| sociology | 306.481 9 |
| *see Manual at* 550 vs. 910; | |
| *also at* 900; *also at* 909, | |
| 930–990 vs. 910; *also at* | |
| 913–919 | |
| Travel by bicycle | 796.64 |
| Travel cooking | 641.575 |
| Travel diseases | |
| medicine | 616.980 2 |
| *see also* Environmental | |
| diseases — humans | |
| Travel facilities | 910.46 |
| *see also* Lodging (Temporary | |
| housing) | |
| Travel guides | 910.202 |
| Travel health | 613.68 |
| Travelers | 910.92 |
| Traveling displays | |
| transportation advertising | 659.134 4 |
| Traveling shows | 791.1 |
| Traveling-wave tubes | 621.381 335 |
| Traverse County (Minn.) | T2—776 435 |
| Traversing (Surveying) | 526.33 |
| Travertine | 553.516 |
| Travis County (Tex.) | T2—764 31 |
| Trawlers | 387.28 |
| design | 623.812 8 |
| engineering | 623.828 2 |
| *see also* Ships | |
| Treason | 364.131 |
| American Revolution | 973.381 |
| law | 345.023 1 |
| Treasure County (Mont.) | T2—786 313 |
| Treasure hunting | 622.19 |
| Treasury bills | 332.632 32 |
| *see also* Government securities | |
| Treasury certificates | 332.632 32 |
| *see also* Government securities | |

| | |
|---|---|
| Treasury departments (Public | |
| administration) | 352.4 |
| Treasury notes | 332.632 32 |
| *see also* Government securities | |
| Treaties | 341.37 |
| sources of law of nations | 341.1 |
| texts | 341.026 |
| Treaty Establishing a | |
| Constitution for Europe, 2004 | 341.242 202 65 |
| Treaty Establishing the European | |
| Community, 1957 | 341.242 202 65 |
| Treaty of Campo Formio, 1797 | 945.307 |
| Treaty of Nice, 2001 | 341.242 202 65 |
| Treaty of Noyon, 1516 | 945.306 |
| Treaty of Paris, 1783 | |
| United States history | 973.317 |
| Treaty of Verdun, 843 | 943.021 |
| Treaty of Versailles, 1783 | |
| United States history | 973.317 |
| Treaty of Versailles, 1919 | |
| European history | 940.314 1 |
| Treaty on European Union, 1992 | 341.242 202 65 |
| Treaty powers (Legislative | |
| bodies) | 328.346 |
| Trebizond İli (Turkey) | T2—565 8 |
| Treble recorders | 788.365 |
| *see also* Woodwind instruments | |
| Treble viols | 787.63 |
| *see also* Stringed instruments | |
| Treble voices | |
| men's | 782.86 |
| choral and mixed voices | 782.86 |
| single voices | 783.86 |
| women's | 782.66 |
| *see also* Soprano voices | |
| Tredegar (Wales) | T2—429 95 |
| Tree crops | 634 |
| Tree frogs | 597.878 |
| Tree kangaroos | 599.22 |
| Tree lily | 584.354 |
| Tree of heaven | 635.977 377 |
| botany | 583.77 |
| ornamental arboriculture | 635.977 377 |
| Tree planting | 634.956 5 |
| ornamental arboriculture | 635.977 |
| Tree shrews | 599.338 |
| Tree squirrels | 599.362 |
| Tree swifts | 598.762 |
| Treenware | 674.88 |
| Trees | 582.16 |
| art representation | 704.943 4 |
| arts | T3C 364 216 |
| drawing | 743.76 |
| forestry | 634.9 |

Trees (continued)
  landscape architecture — 715.2
  literature — 808.803 642 16
    history and criticism — 809.933 642 16
    specific literatures — T3B—080 364
      history and
        criticism — T3B—093 64
  ornamental agriculture — 635.977
  paleobotany — 561.16
  religious worship — 202.12
  *see Manual at* 633–635; *also at*
    635.9 vs. 582.1
Trees (Mathematics) — 511.52
Trefoils — 633.32
  botany — 583.74
  forage crop — 633.32
Trego County (Kan.) — T2—781 165
Treinta y Tres (Uruguay :
  Dept.) — T2—895 22
Trellises
  plant training — 631.546
Trematoda — 592.48
Trematode infections
  incidence — 614.553
  medicine — 616.963
    *see also* Communicable
      diseases — humans
Tremellales — 579.59
Trempealeau County (Wis.) — T2—775 49
Trench mouth
  medicine — 616.312
    *see also* Digestive system
      diseases — humans
Trench warfare — 355.44
Trenčiansky kraj (Slovakia) — T2—437 38
Trent, River (England) — T2—425
Trentino-Alto Adige (Italy) — 945.38
  — T2—453 8
  ancient — T2—373 7
Trento (Italy : Province) — T2—453 85
  ancient — T2—373 75
Trenton (N.J.) — T2—749 66
Trespass (Law) — 346.036
Treutlen County (Ga.) — T2—758 682
Treviño (Spain) — T2—466 7
Treviso (Italy) — T2—453 61
  ancient — T2—373 65
Treviso (Italy : Province) — T2—453 6
  ancient — T2—373 65
Triakidae — 597.36
Trial-and-error learning
  psychology — 153.152 4
Trial courts — 347.02
  criminal law — 345.014 2

Trial of Jesus Christ — 232.962
Trial practice — 347.075
  criminal law — 345.075
Trial procedure — 347.075
Trials (Law) — 347.07
  criminal law — 345.07
Triangles (Geometry) — 516.154
Triangles (Music) — 786.884 2
  *see also* Percussion instruments
Triangulation — 526.33
Triassic period — 551.762
  geology — 551.762
  paleontology — 560.176 2
Triathlon — 796.425 7
Tribal communities — 307.772
  government — 321.1
Tribal fighting (Military tactics) — 355.425
Tribal groups — 305.8
Tribal land
  economics — 333.2
Triboelectricity — 537.21
Tribology — 621.89
Tribulation (Christian doctrine) — 236.9
Tribunals
  papal administration — 262.136
Tricarboxylic acid cycle — 572.475
Triceratops — 567.915 8
Trichechidae — 599.55
Trichechus — 599.55
Trichiales — 579.52
Trichinosis
  incidence — 614.562
  medicine — 616.965 4
    *see also* Communicable
      diseases — humans
Trichiuridae — 597.78
Trichoderma — 579.567 7
Trichomycetes — 579.53
Trichoptera — 595.745
Trick cinematography — 777.9
Trick games — 793.5
Trick photography — 778.8
Trick videography — 777.9
Tricks — 793.8
  manufacturing technology — 688.726
Tricuspid valve
  human anatomy — 611.12
  human physiology — 612.17
  medicine — 616.125
Tricuspid valve diseases
  medicine — 616.125
    *see also* Cardiovascular
      diseases — humans

| | |
|---|---|
| Tricycles | |
| engineering | 629.227 3 |
| repair | 629.287 73 |
| riding | 629.284 73 |
| Trier (Germany) | T2—434 313 |
| Trier (Germany : | |
| Regierungsbezirk) | T2—434 31 |
| Trieste (Italy) | T2—453 931 |
| ancient | T2—373 91 |
| Trieste (Italy : Province) | T2—453 93 |
| ancient | T2—373 9 |
| Trifolium | 633.32 |
| botany | 583.74 |
| forage crop | 633.32 |
| Trigg County (Ky.) | T2—769 79 |
| Trigger circuits | |
| electronics | 621.381 537 |
| Triggerfishes | 597.64 |
| Trigonometric leveling | 526.38 |
| Trigonometry | 516.24 |
| Trihydroxy aromatics | 547.633 |
| Trikala (Greece : Nome) | T2—495 4 |
| Trilateration | 526.33 |
| Trilliums | 584.32 |
| floriculture | 635.934 32 |
| Trills | 781.247 |
| Trilobita | 565.39 |
| Trimble County (Ky.) | T2—769 375 |
| Trimmers | 621.93 |
| Trimmings | |
| textiles | 677.7 |
| Trinidad | 972.983 |
| | T2—729 83 |
| Trinidad and Tobago | 972.983 |
| | T2—729 83 |
| Trinidadians | T5—969 729 83 |
| Trinitarians (Religious order) | 255.42 |
| church history | 271.42 |
| Trinity | 231.044 |
| art representation | 704.948 52 |
| arts | T3C—382 310 44 |
| Trinity County (Calif.) | T2—794 14 |
| Trinity County (Tex.) | T2—764 172 |
| Trinity River (Tex.) | T2—764 14 |
| Trinity Sunday | 263.94 |
| devotional literature | 242.38 |
| music | 781.729 4 |
| sermons | 252.64 |
| Trionychidae | 597.926 |
| Trios | |
| chamber music | 785.13 |
| vocal music | 783.13 |
| Triphenylmethane dyes | 667.254 |
| Tripiṭaka | 294.382 |

| | |
|---|---|
| Triple Alliance, War of the, | |
| 1865–1870 | 989.205 |
| Triple jump | 796.432 |
| Triple points | 530.474 |
| *see also* Phase transformations | |
| Triplets | 306.875 |
| psychology | 155.444 |
| *see also* Siblings | |
| Tripods (Cameras) | 771.38 |
| Tripoli (Libya) | T2—612 |
| Tripolis (Libya) | 961.2 |
| | T2—612 |
| ancient | 939.74 |
| | T2—397 4 |
| Tripolitan War, 1801–1805 | 973.47 |
| Tripp County (S.D.) | T2—783 61 |
| Tripura (India) | T2—541 5 |
| Triremes | 387.21 |
| design | 623.812 1 |
| engineering | 623.821 |
| handling | 623.882 1 |
| transportation services | 387.21 |
| *see also* Ships | |
| Trisecting an angle | 516.204 |
| Tristan da Cunha Islands | T2—973 |
| Tritium | 546.213 |
| *see also* Chemicals | |
| Trituberculata | 569.2 |
| Triumphs | |
| customs | 394.4 |
| Triuridales | 584.37 |
| tRNA | 572.886 |
| Trnavský kraj (Slovakia) | T2—437 32 |
| Troas | T2—392 1 |
| Trobriand Islands (Papua | |
| New Guinea) | T2—954 1 |
| Troches | |
| pharmaceutical chemistry | 615.19 |
| Trochili | 598.764 |
| Trochilidae | 598.764 |
| Trochodendrales | 583.43 |
| Troglodytidae | 598.833 |
| Trogoniformes | 598.73 |
| paleozoology | 568.7 |
| Trogons | 598.73 |
| Trois-Rivières (Quebec) | T2—714 451 |
| Trojan horses (Computer | |
| security) | 005.84 |
| Trojan War | 939.21 |
| Trolley cars | 388.46 |
| Trolleybus transportation | 388.413 223 |
| engineering | 625.6 |
| transportation services | 388.413 223 |

Trolleybuses 388.34
  engineering 625.66
  transportation services 388.34
Trolling (Fishing) 799.128
Trolls 398.21
  *see also* Legendary beings
Trombones 788.93
  instrument 788.931 9
  music 788.93
  *see also* Brass instruments
Trombonists 788.930 92
Trompsburg (South Africa :
  District) T2—685 7
Troms fylke (Norway) T2—484 5
Trøndelag (Norway) T2—484
Troop movements 355.411
Troop support 355.415
Troopships 359.985 83
  *see also* Transports (Ships)
Tropaeolaceae 583.79
Tropes (Music) 782.297
  choral and mixed voices 782.529 7
  single voices 783.092 97
Tropic birds 598.43
Tropical animals 591.709 13
Tropical biology 578.091 3
Tropical climate 551.691 3
  health 613.113
Tropical cooking 641.591 3
Tropical cyclones 551.552
  *see also* Hurricanes
Tropical diseases
  medicine 616.988 3
    *see also* Environmental
      diseases — humans
Tropical ecology 577.091 3
Tropical forests
  biology 578.730 913
  ecology 577.309 13
Tropical fruits
  cooking 641.646
  food 641.346
  orchard crops 634.6
Tropical grasslands
  biology 578.748
  ecology 577.48
Tropical medicine 616.988 3
Tropical plants 581.709 13
  floriculture 635.952 3
Tropical rain forests
  biology 578.734
  ecology 577.34

Tropics T2—13
  biology 578.091 3
  ecology 577.091 3
Troposphere 551.513
   T2—161 2
Trotskyism 335.433
  economics 335.433
  political ideology 320.532 3
Trotskyist International 324.175
Trotters (Horses) 636.175
Troubadour poetry 808.814
  history and criticism 809.14
  specific literatures T3B—104
    individual authors T3A—1
Troubled young people
  social welfare 362.74
Trough zithers 787.72
  *see also* Stringed instruments
Troughs
  music 786.82
    concussed 786.874
    friction 786.864
      set 786.864
      single 786.888
    percussed 786.844
      set 786.844
      single 786.884 4
    *see also* Percussion
      instruments
Troup County (Ga.) T2—758 463
Trousdale County (Tenn.) T2—768 482
Trousers 391.476
  *see also* Pants (Trousers)
Trout 641.392
  commercial fishing 639.275 7
  conservation technology 639.977 57
  cooking 641.692
  culture 639.375 7
    economics 338.371 375 7
  food 641.392
  resource economics 333.956 57
  sports fishing 799.175 7
  zoology 597.57
Trout-perches 597.62
Trover and conversion 346.036
Trovoada, Miguel
  Sao Tomean history 967.150 22
Troy (Extinct city) 939.21
   T2—392 1
Truancy 371.295
  law 344.079 2
Truant officers 371.295
Trucial States T2—535 7

| | |
|---|---|
| Truck accidents | 363.125 9 |
| *see also* Highway safety | |
| Truck cavalry | 357.54 |
| Truck farming | 635 |
| Truck terminals | 388.33 |
| transportation services | 388.33 |
| urban | 388.473 |
| Truck transportation | 388.324 |
| law | 343.094 83 |
| public administration | 354.765 4 |
| transportation services | 388.324 |
| urban | 388.413 24 |
| law | 343.098 2 |
| Truckers | 388.324 092 |
| Trucks | 388.344 |
| agricultural use | 631.373 |
| driving | 629.284 4 |
| engineering | 629.224 |
| military engineering | 623.747 4 |
| operation | 388.324 044 |
| urban | 388.413 24 |
| repair | 629.287 4 |
| transportation services | 388.344 |
| *see also* Automotive vehicles | |
| Trudeau, Pierre Elliott | |
| Canadian history | 971.064 4 |
| 1968–1979 | 971.064 4 |
| 1980–1984 | 971.064 6 |
| True bugs | 595.754 |
| True cedars | 585.2 |
| True fungi | 579.5 |
| True lice | 595.756 |
| True seals | 599.79 |
| True swifts | 598.762 |
| True wasps | 595.798 |
| True water beetles | 595.762 |
| Truffles | 641.358 |
| agriculture | 635.8 |
| biology | 579.57 |
| commercial processing | 664.805 8 |
| cooking | 641.658 |
| food | 641.358 |
| Trujillo (Venezuela : State) T2—871 4 | |
| Trujillo Molina, Rafael Léonidas | |
| Dominican history | 972.930 53 |
| Truk (Micronesia) T2—966 | |
| Truman, Harry S. | |
| United States history | 973.918 |
| Trumbull County (Ohio) T2—771 38 | |
| Trumpet creepers | 635.933 95 |
| botany | 583.95 |
| floriculture | 635.933 95 |
| Trumpet fishes | 597.67 |
| Trumpeter swan | 598.418 4 |

| | |
|---|---|
| Trumpeters (Birds) | 598.32 |
| Trumpeters (Musicians) | 788.920 92 |
| Trumpets | 788.92 |
| instrument | 788.921 9 |
| music | 788.92 |
| *see also* Brass instruments | |
| Trunks (Luggage) | |
| manufacturing technology | 685.51 |
| Trường Sơn Mountain | |
| Range (Vietnam) T2—597 4 | |
| Truro (N.S.) T2—716 12 | |
| Truss bridges | |
| construction | 624.217 |
| Trusses (Structural elements) | 624.177 3 |
| naval architecture | 623.817 73 |
| Trust companies | 332.26 |
| Trust services | 332.178 |
| Trust territories | 321.08 |
| *see also* Semisovereign states | |
| Trust Territory of the Pacific | 996.5 |
| Islands T2—965 | |
| Trustees | |
| executive management | 658.422 |
| libraries | 021.82 |
| Trusteeships (Territories) | 321.08 |
| *see also* Semisovereign states | |
| Trusts (Fiduciary) | 346.059 |
| accounting | 657.47 |
| income tax law | 343.052 64 |
| tax law | 343.064 |
| Trusts (Organizations) | 338.85 |
| *see also* Combinations | |
| (Enterprises) | |
| Truth | 121 |
| Truth in lending | 346.073 |
| Truth tables | 511.3 |
| mathematical logic | 511.3 |
| philosophical logic | 160 |
| Truthfulness | |
| ethics | 177.3 |
| *see also* Ethical problems | |
| Trypanosomiasis | |
| incidence | 614.533 |
| medicine | 616.936 3 |
| *see also* Communicable | |
| diseases — humans | |
| Trypetidae | 595.774 |
| Tsafon (Israel : District) T2—569 45 | |
| Tsetse flies | 595.774 |
| Tshivenda language | 496.397 6 |
| T6—963 976 | |
| Tshivenda literature | 896.397 6 |

Tshwane (South Africa :
  Metropolitan
  Municipality)      T2—682 27
Tsimshian Indians      T5—974 128
Tsimshian language      497.412 8
     T6—974 128
Tsimshian languages      497.412
     T6—974 12
Tsin dynasty      931.04
Tsinghai Province (China)      T2—514 7
Tsiranana, Philibert
  Malagasy history      969.105 1
Tsitsikamma Forest and
  Coastal National Park
  (South Africa)      T2—687 51
Tsitsikamma National Park
  (South Africa)      T2—687 51
Tsogo languages      496.396
     T6—963 96
Tsolo (South Africa :
  District)      T2—687 58
Tsomo (South Africa :
  District)      T2—687 58
Tsonga (African people)      T5—963 978
Tsonga language      496.397 8
     T6—963 978
Tsonga literature      896.397 8
Tsugaru Strait (Japan)      551.461 454
     T2—164 54
Tsunamis      551.463 7
  social services      363.349 4
Tsutsugamushi disease
  incidence      614.526 4
  medicine      616.922 4
  *see also* Communicable
    diseases — humans
Tswa-Ronga languages      496.397 8
     T6—963 978
Tswana (African people)      T5—963 977 5
Tswana language      496.397 75
     T6—963 977 5
Tswana literature      896.397 75
Tu language      T6—942
Tuamotu Islands      T2—963 2
Tuareg      T5—933
Tuareg language      493.38
     T6—933 8
Tuareg literature      893.38
Tuatara      597.945
Tubal pregnancy
  obstetrics      618.31

Tubal sterilization
  health      613.942
  *see also* Birth control
  surgery      618.120 59
Tubas      788.98
  instrument      788.981 9
  music      788.98
  *see also* Brass instruments
Tube feeding
  medicine      615.854 82
Tube zithers      787.72
  *see also* Stringed instruments
Tuberales      579.57
Tuberculosis      362.196 995
  incidence      614.542
  law      344.043 699 5
  medicine      616.995
  social services      362.196 995
  *see also* Communicable
    diseases — humans
Tubers      581.46
  cooking      641.652
  descriptive botany      581.46
  food      641.352
  food crops      635.2
  nursery production      631.526
    ornamental plants      635.915 26
  physiology      575.498
  planting      631.532
    ornamental plants      635.915 32
Tubes
  music      786.82
    concussed      786.875
    friction      786.865
      set      786.865
      single      786.888
    percussed      786.845
      set      786.845
      single      786.884 5
  *see also* Percussion
    instruments
Tübingen (Germany :
  Regierungsbezirk)      T2—434 73
Tubuai Islands      T2—962 2
Tubular bridges
  construction      624.21
Tubular drums      786.94
  *see also* Percussion instruments
Tubulidentata      599.31
  paleozoology      569.31
Tucano Indians      T5—983 5
Tucano language      498.35
     T6—983 5

| | | | |
|---|---|---|---|
| Tucanoan languages | 498.35 | Tumble bugs | 595.764 9 |
| | T6—983 5 | Tumbler Ridge (B.C.) | T2—711 87 |
| Tucker County (W. Va.) | T2—754 83 | Tumbling | 796.472 |
| Tucson (Ariz.) | T2—791 776 | Tumbling flower beetles | 595.769 |
| Tucumán (Argentina) | T2—824 3 | Tumboa plant | 585.8 |
| Tudor, House of | 942.05 | Tumbuka (African people) | T5—963 91 |
| English history | 942.05 | Tumbuka language | 496.391 |
| genealogy | 929.72 | | T6—963 91 |
| Irish history | 941.505 | Tumors | 571.978 |
| Tufa | 552.5 | humans | |
| Tuff | 552.23 | incidence | 614.599 9 |
| Tug Fork | T2—754 4 | medicine | 616.994 |
| Kentucky | T2—769 2 | *see also* Cancer | |
| West Virginia | T2—754 4 | Tunas | 641.392 |
| Tug services | 387.166 | commercial fishing | 639.277 83 |
| inland ports | 386.866 | conservation technology | 639.977 783 |
| law | 343.096 7 | cooking | 641.692 |
| Tugboats | 387.232 | food | 641.392 |
| design | 623.812 32 | resource economics | 333.956 783 |
| engineering | 623.823 2 | zoology | 597.783 |
| *see also* Ships | | Tunas (Cuba : Province) | T2—729 162 |
| Tugela (South Africa) | T2—684 4 | Tunbridge Wells (England : | |
| Tugela River (South Africa) | T2—684 | Borough) | T2—422 38 |
| Tughluk dynasty | 954.023 6 | Tunceli İli (Turkey) | T2—566 75 |
| Tuition | 371.206 | ancient | T2—394 2 |
| higher education | 378.106 | Tundras | 551.453 |
| Tuktoyaktuk (N.W.T.) | T2—719 3 | | T2—153 |
| Tuktut Nogait National Park | | biology | 578.758 6 |
| (N.W.T.) | T2—719 3 | ecology | 577.586 |
| Tula (Russia : Oblast) | T2—473 4 | geography | 910.915 3 |
| Tulameen River (B.C.) | T2—711 5 | geomorphology | 551.453 |
| Tulare County (Calif.) | T2—794 86 | physical geography | 910.021 53 |
| Tularemia | | Tung oil | 665.333 |
| incidence | 614.573 9 | Tung tree | 583.69 |
| medicine | 616.923 9 | Tungstates | |
| *see also* Communicable | | mineralogy | 549.74 |
| diseases — humans | | Tungsten | 669.734 |
| Tularosa Valley (N.M.) | T2—789 65 | chemical engineering | 661.053 6 |
| Tulbagh (South Africa : | | chemistry | 546.536 |
| District) | T2—687 33 | economic geology | 553.464 9 |
| Tulcea (Romania : Judeţ) | T2—498 3 | materials science | 620.189 34 |
| Tulip tree | 583.22 | metallography | 669.957 34 |
| forestry | 634.973 22 | metallurgy | 669.734 |
| Tulips | 635.934 32 | metalworking | 673.734 |
| botany | 584.32 | mining | 622.346 49 |
| floriculture | 635.934 32 | physical metallurgy | 669.967 34 |
| Tulita (N.W.T.) | T2—719 3 | *see also* Chemicals; Metals | |
| Tulles | 677.654 | Tungurahua (Ecuador) | T2—866 15 |
| *see also* Textiles | | Tungus | T5—941 |
| Tulsa County (Okla.) | T2—766 86 | Tungus languages | 494.1 |
| Tulums | 788.49 | | T6—941 |
| *see also* Woodwind instruments | | Tungus-Manchu languages | 494.1 |
| Tul′skaĩa oblast′ (Russia) | T2—473 4 | | T6—941 |
| Tumbes (Peru : Dept.) | T2—851 2 | | |

| | | | |
|---|---|---|---|
| Tungusic languages | 494.1 | Turbines | 621.406 |
| | T6—941 | hydraulic power | 621.24 |
| Tungusic literatures | 894.1 | steam engineering | 621.165 |
| Tungusic peoples | T5—941 | Turbojet engines | 621.435 2 |
| Tunica County (Miss.) | T2—762 86 | aircraft | 629.134 353 3 |
| Tunicata | 596.2 | Turbojet fuel | 665.538 25 |
| paleozoology | 566 | Turbomachines | 621.406 |
| Tuning | 784.192 8 | Turboprop airplanes | 387.733 43 |
| Tunis (Tunisia) | T2—611 | engineering | 629.133 343 |
| Tunisia | 961.1 | transportation services | 387.733 43 |
| | T2—611 | *see also* Aircraft | |
| ancient | 939.73 | Turboprop engines | |
| | T2—397 3 | aircraft | 629.134 353 2 |
| Tunisians | T5—927 611 | Turboramjet engines | |
| Tunnel diodes | 621.381 522 | aircraft | 629.134 353 4 |
| Tunnel engineers | 624.193 092 | Turbots | 597.69 |
| Tunnel vaults | 721.45 | Turbulence | |
| architecture | 721.45 | oceanography | 551.462 |
| construction | 690.145 | Turbulent flow | 532.052 7 |
| Tunneling (Construction) | 624.193 | aeronautics | 629.132 32 |
| mining | 622.26 | air mechanics | 533.62 |
| Tunneling (Physics) | 530.416 | gas mechanics | 533.217 |
| semiconductors | 537.622 6 | liquid mechanics | 532.517 |
| Tunnels | 388.13 | Turco-Tataric languages | 494.3 |
| architecture | 725.98 | | T6—943 |
| construction | 624.193 | Turcomans | T5—943 64 |
| military engineering | 623.68 | Turdidae | 598.842 |
| mining | 622.26 | Turf | |
| psychological influence | 155.964 | floriculture | 635.964 2 |
| public administration | 354.76 | Turfanish language | 491.994 |
| transportation services | 388.13 | | T6—919 94 |
| railroads | 385.312 | Turin (Italy) | T2—451 21 |
| roads | 388.13 | ancient | T2—372 221 |
| Tununirusiq (Nunavut) | T2—719 52 | Turin (Italy : Province) | T2—451 2 |
| Tuolumne County (Calif.) | T2—794 45 | ancient | T2—372 22 |
| Tupaiidae | 599.338 | Turing machines | 511.35 |
| paleozoology | 569.338 | Turkana (African people) | T5—965 |
| Tuparro National Park | | Turkana, Lake (Kenya and | |
| (Colombia) | T2—861 92 | Ethiopia) | T2—676 27 |
| Tupelos | 583.84 | Turkana language | 496.5 |
| Tupí Indians | T5—983 832 | | T6—965 |
| Tupí language | 498.383 2 | Turkestan | 958.4 |
| | T6—983 832 | | T2—584 |
| Tupí languages | 498.38 | Turkey | 956.1 |
| | T6—983 8 | | T2—561 |
| Tupí literature | 898.383 2 | ancient | 939.2 |
| Tupinambá Indians | T5—983 83 | | T2—392 |
| Tupinambá language | 498.383 | Turkey (Meat) | 641.365 92 |
| | T6—983 83 | commercial processing | 664.93 |
| Tupper, Charles, Sir | | cooking | 641.665 92 |
| Canadian history | 971.055 | food | 641.365 92 |
| Tuque (Quebec) | T2—714 459 | | |
| Turacos | 598.74 | | |
| Turbellaria | 592.42 | | |

| | | | |
|---|---|---|---|
| Turkey in Europe | 949.61 | Turner, John | |
| | T2—496 1 | Canadian history | 971.064 6 |
| ancient | 939.861 | Turner County (Ga.) | T2—758 885 |
| | T2—398 61 | Turner County (S.D.) | T2—783 385 |
| Turkey vulture | 598.92 | Turneraceae | 583.626 |
| Turkeys | 636.592 | Turnicidae | 598.32 |
| animal husbandry | 636.592 | Turning | |
| conservation technology | 639.978 645 | home woodworking | 684.083 |
| resource economics | 333.958 645 | Turning tools | 621.94 |
| sports hunting | 799.246 45 | Turnip celery | 641.351 28 |
| zoology | 598.645 | *see also* Celeriac | |
| Turkic languages | 494.3 | Turnips | 641.351 25 |
| | T6—943 | botany | 583.64 |
| Turkic literatures | 894.3 | commercial processing | 664.805 125 |
| Turkic peoples | T5—943 | cooking | 641.651 25 |
| Turkish baths | 613.41 | food | 641.351 25 |
| Turkish language | 494.35 | garden crop | 635.125 |
| | T6—943 5 | Turnouts | |
| Turkish literature | 894.35 | railroad engineering | 625.163 |
| Turkish rugs | | Turnover of employees | |
| arts | 746.756 1 | personnel management | 658.314 |
| Turkish Thrace | 949.61 | public administration | 352.66 |
| | T2—496 1 | Turnover tax | 336.27 |
| ancient | 939.861 | law | 343.055 |
| | T2—398 61 | public administration | 352.44 |
| Turkish Van cat | 636.83 | public finance | 336.27 |
| Turkmen | T5—943 64 | Turnovers (Stuffed foods) | 641.84 |
| Turkmen language | 494.364 | Turnpikes | 388.122 |
| | T6—943 64 | *see also* Roads | |
| Turkmen literature | 894.364 | Turnstones | 598.33 |
| Turkmen rugs | | Turpentine | 665.332 |
| arts | 746.758 4 | agriculture | 633.895 9 |
| Turkmenbashy, Saparmyrat | | chemical technology | 665.332 |
| Turkmenistan history | 958.508 61 | recovery from pulp | 676.5 |
| Turkmenistan | 958.5 | Turquoise | 553.87 |
| | T2—585 | mineralogy | 549.72 |
| ancient | 939.6 | *see also* Semiprecious stones | |
| | T2—396 | Turs | 599.648 |
| Turko-Tatar languages | 494.3 | Tursiops | 599.533 |
| | T6—943 | Turtle farming | 639.392 |
| Turkoman language | 494.364 | Turtle grass | 584.73 |
| | T6—943 64 | Turtles | 597.92 |
| Turkoman literature | 894.364 | agriculture | 639.392 |
| Turkomans | T5—943 64 | conservation technology | 639.977 92 |
| Turks | T5—943 5 | food | |
| *see Manual at* T5—9435 | | commercial processing | 664.95 |
| Turks and Caicos Islands | T2—729 61 | resource economics | 333.957 92 |
| Turku ja Pori (Finland : | | zoology | 597.92 |
| Lääni) | T2—489 73 | Turun ja Porin lääni | |
| Turku-Pori (Finland : Lääni) | T2—489 73 | (Finland) | T2—489 73 |
| Turmeric | 641.338 3 | Tuscaloosa County (Ala.) | T2—761 84 |
| botany | 584.39 | Tuscan Apennines (Italy) | T2—454 |
| *see also* Spices | | | |
| Turn and bank indicators | 629.135 2 | | |

| | |
|---|---|
| Tuscany (Grand Duchy) | 945.507 |
| 1569–1801 | 945.507 |
| 1814–1860 | 945.508 3 |
| Tuscany (Italy) | 945.5 |
| | T2—455 |
| ancient | T2—375 |
| Tuscarawas County (Ohio) | T2—771 66 |
| Tuscarora language | 497.55 |
| | T6—975 5 |
| Tuscola County (Mich.) | T2—774 45 |
| Ṭūsī, Muḥammad ibn al-Ḥasan | |
| Hadith | 297.125 921 3 |
| Tusk shells | 594.29 |
| Tusks | 591.47 |
| descriptive zoology | 591.47 |
| physiology | 573.356 |
| Tussah silk textiles | 677.392 |
| *see also* Textiles | |
| Tutankhamen, King of Egypt | |
| Egyptian history | 932.014 |
| Tutoring | 371.394 |
| Tutsi (African people) | T5—963 946 1 |
| Tuva (Russia) | T2—575 |
| Tuva-Altai languages | 494.33 |
| | T6—943 3 |
| Tuvalu | 996.82 |
| | T2—968 2 |
| Tuvalu language | 499.46 |
| | T6—994 6 |
| Tuvaluans | T5—994 6 |
| Tuvinian language | 494.33 |
| | T6—943 3 |
| Tuyên Quang (Vietnam : | |
| Province) | T2—597 1 |
| TV | 384.55 |
| *see also* Television | |
| TV dinners | |
| commercial processing | 664.65 |
| home serving | 642.1 |
| Tverskaĩa oblast′ (Russia) | T2—472 8 |
| Tver′ (Russia : Oblast) | T2—472 8 |
| Tweed, River (Scotland and | |
| England) | T2—413 7 |
| Tweeddale (Scotland) | T2—413 7 |
| Tweedsmuir Provincial Park | |
| (B.C.) | T2—711 82 |
| Tweezers | |
| manufacturing technology | 688.5 |
| Twelfth century | 909.1 |
| | T1—090 21 |
| Twelve patriarchs | |
| pseudepigrapha | 229.914 |
| Twelve prophets (Bible) | 224.9 |
| Twelve step programs | |
| devotional literature | 204.32 |
| Christianity | 242.4 |
| pastoral theology | 206.1 |
| Christianity | 259.429 |
| religious guidance | 204.42 |
| Christianity | 248.862 9 |
| social theology | 201.762 29 |
| Christianity | 261.832 29 |
| substance abuse | |
| rehabilitation | 616.860 3 |
| therapy | 616.860 6 |
| Twelve-tone system | 781.268 |
| Twelve Tribes | 933.02 |
| Twelvers (Islamic sect) | 297.821 |
| Hadith | 297.125 921 |
| Twentieth century | 909.82 |
| | T1—090 4 |
| Twenty-first century | 909.83 |
| | T1—090 5 |
| Twenty-one (Game) | 795.423 |
| Twi (Ghanaian people) | T5—963 385 |
| Twi language (Ghana) | 496.338 5 |
| | T6—963 385 |
| Twi literature (Ghana) | 896.338 5 |
| Twiggs County (Ga.) | T2—758 545 |
| Twilight | 525.7 |
| meteorology | 551.566 |
| Twill-woven rugs | |
| arts | 746.72 |
| Twin Cities Metropolitan | |
| Area (Minn.) | T2—776 579 |
| Twin Falls County (Idaho) | T2—796 37 |
| Twines | 677.71 |
| Twining | |
| arts | 746.42 |
| Twins | 306.875 |
| obstetrics | 618.25 |
| psychology | 155.444 |
| *see also* Siblings | |
| Twisters (Tornadoes) | 551.553 |
| Twisting textiles | 677.028 22 |
| arts | 746.12 |
| manufacturing technology | 677.028 22 |
| Two-way radios | |
| automobile | 629.277 |
| Tyler, John | |
| United States history | 973.58 |
| Tyler County (Tex.) | T2—764 163 |
| Tyler County (W. Va.) | T2—754 19 |
| Tympanic membrane diseases | |
| medicine | 617.85 |
| *see also* Ear diseases — | |
| humans | |

Tympanic membranes
  human anatomy — 611.85
  human physiology — 612.854
  medicine — 617.85
Tympanuchus — 598.637
Tyndale Bible — 220.520 1
Tyne, River (England) — T2—428 7
Tyne and Wear (England) — T2—428 7
Tynedalc (England) — T2—428 81
Type 1 diabetes — 362.196 462 2
  medicine — 616.462 2
  pregnancy complications
    obstetrics — 618.364 6
  social services — 362.196 462 2
  *see also* Endocrine diseases —
    humans
Type 2 diabetes — 362.196 462 4
  medicine — 616.462 4
  pregnancy complications
    obstetrics — 618.364 6
  social services — 362.196 462 4
  *see also* Endocrine diseases —
    humans
Type ornaments — 686.224
Type theory — 511.3
Typecasting — 686.221
Typefaces — 686.224
Typefounding — 686.221
Typesetters — 686.225 092
Typesetting — 686.225
Typewriter art — 740
Typewriters — 652.3
  manufacturing technology — 681.61
  office practice — 652.3
Typewriting — 652.3
Typewriting analysis
  criminal investigation — 363.256 5
Typha — 584.68
Typhales — 584.68
Typhlopidae — 597.969
Typhlopoidea — 597.969
Typhoid fever
  incidence — 614.511 2
  medicine — 616.927 2
  *see also* Communicable
    diseases — humans
Typhoons — 551.552
  *see also* Hurricanes
Typhus
  incidence — 614.526 2
  medicine — 616.922 2
  *see also* Communicable
    diseases — humans
Typing — 652.3

Typists — 651.374 109 2
  office services — 651.374 1
Typographic masterpieces
  books — 094.4
Typographical designs
  graphic arts — 740
Typography — 686.22
Typology (Linguistics) — 410.1
  grammar — 415.01
    specific languages — T4—501
Typology (Psychology) — 155.26
Typology (Theology)
  Biblical interpretation — 220.64
  Christian doctrines — 232.1
  Talmudic interpretation — 296.120 64
Tyrannidae — 598.823
Tyrannosaurus — 567.912 9
Tyranny — 321.9
Tyrant flycatchers — 598.823
Tyre (Lebanon) — T2—569 2
  ancient — T2—394 4
Tyrian architecture — 722.31
Tyrol (Austria) — T2—436 42
Tyrolean zithers — 787.75
  *see also* Stringed instruments
Tyrone (Northern Ireland) — T2—416 4
Tyrrell County (N.C.) — T2—756 172
Tyrrhenian Sea — 551.461 383
  — T2—163 83
Tytonidae — 598.97
Tyumen (Russia : Oblast) — T2—573
Tzeltal Indians — T5—974 28
Tzeltal language — 497.428
  — T6—974 28
Tzotzil Indians — T5—974 287
Tzotzil language — 497.428 7
  — T6—974 287
Tzotzil literature — 897.428 7
Tzutujil Indians — T5—974 2
Tzutujil language — 497.42
  — T6—974 2

# U

Ubangi-Shari — 967.410 3
  — T2—674 1
Ubangian languages — 496.361
  — T6—963 61
Ubombo (South Africa :
  District) — T2—684 3
Ubykh language — 499.962
  — T6—999 62
Ucayali (Peru) — T2—854 3
Ucayali (Peru : Region) — T2—854 3

Uckermark (Germany :
  Landkreis)    T2—431 53
Uckermark-Barnim
  (Germany :
  Raumordnungsregion)    T2—431 53
Udine (Italy : Province)    T2—453 91
  ancient    T2—373 81
Udmurt language    494.53
    T6— 945 3
Udmurt literature    894.53
Udmurtia (Russia)    T2—474 6
Udmurtiia (Russia)    T2—474 6
Udmurts    T5—945 3
Uecker-Randow (Germany :
  Landkreis)    T2—431 78
UFOs (Objects)    001.942
Uganda    967.61
    T2—676 1
Ugandans    T5—967 61
Ugarit (Extinct city)    T2—394 33
Ugaritic language    492.67
    T6—926 7
Ugaritic literature    892.67
Ugliness
  personal
    arts    T3C—353
    literature    808.803 53
      history and criticism    809.933 53
      specific literatures    T3B—080 353
        history and
        criticism    T3B—093 53
Ugrians    T5—945 1
Ugric languages    494.51
    T6—945 1
Ugric literatures    894.51
Ugric peoples    T5—945 1
UHF radio systems    621.384 151
Uíge (Angola : Province)    T2—673 2
Uighur    T5—943 23
Uighur language    494.323
    T6—943 23
Uighur literature    894.323
Uillean pipes    788.49
  *see also* Woodwind instruments
Uinta County (Wyo.)    T2—787 84
Uinta Mountains (Utah and
  Wyo.)    T2—792 14
Uintah County (Utah)    T2—792 21
Uitenhage (South Africa :
  District)    T2—687 52
Ukaan language    496.33
    T6—963 3

Ukraine    947.7
    T2—477
  ancient    939.52
    T2—395 2
Ukrainian Autocephalous
  Orthodox Church    281.947 7
Ukrainian language    491.79
    T6—917 91
Ukrainian literature    891.79
Ukrainian Orthodox Church
  (Kyivan Patriarchate)    281.947 7
Ukrainian Orthodox Church
  (Moscow Patriarchate)    281.947 7
Ukrainians    T5—917 91
Ukuleles    787.89
  instrument    787.891 9
  music    787.89
  *see also* Stringed instruments
Ukzin    296.123 6
Ulama
  role and function    297.61
Ulawa (Solomon Islands)    T2—959 38
Ulbricht, Walter
  German history    943.108 75
Ulcerations
  skin
    medicine    616.545
    *see also* Skin diseases —
      humans
Ulcerative colitis
  medicine    616.344 73
Ulcers
  digestive system
    medicine    616.343
    *see also* Digestive system
      diseases — humans
Ulema
  role and function    297.61
Ulladulla (N.S.W.)    T2—944 7
Ullapool (Scotland)    T2—411 52
Ulmaceae    583.45
Ulnas
  human anatomy    611.717
Ulrika Eleonora, Queen of
  Sweden
    Swedish history    948.503 61
Ulster (Northern Ireland and    941.6
  Ireland)    T2—416
Ulster County (N.Y.)    T2—747 34
Ultima Esperanza (Chile)    T2—836 42
Ultimatums
  law of nations    341.58
Ultrahigh-frequency electronics
  physics    537.534 4

Ultrahigh-frequency radio
  systems      621.384 151
Ultrahigh-speed photography    778.37
Ultralight airplanes      387.733 43
  engineering      629.133 343
  transportation services      387.733 43
  *see also* Aircraft
Ultramicrobes
  medical microbiology      616.910 1
Ultrasonic cardiography
  medicine      616.120 754 3
Ultrasonic diagnosis
  medicine      616.075 43
Ultrasonic imaging
  medicine      616.075 43
Ultrasonic testing
  materials science      620.112 74
Ultrasonic therapy
  medicine      615.832 3
Ultrasonic vibrations      534.55
  biophysics      571.445
    humans      612.014 455
  engineering      620.28
  physics      534.55
Ultrasonic weapons      623.447
Ultrasonic welding      671.529
Ultrasonography
  medicine      616.075 43
Ultrastructure (Biology)      571.633
Ultraviolet photography
  engineering      621.367 2
Ultraviolet radiation      535.014
  biophysics      571.456
    humans      612.014 484
  chemical effect      541.353 4
  chemical engineering      660.295 34
  engineering      621.364
  military engineering      623.042
  physics      535.014
  therapeutics      615.831 5
  water supply treatment      628.166 2
Ultraviolet spectroscopes
  manufacturing technology      681.414 4
Ultraviolet spectroscopy      543.5
  analytical chemistry      543.5
  engineering      621.361
  physics      535.844
Ultraviolet therapy      615.831 5
Uluru (Ayers Rock)-Mt.
  Olga National Park
  (N.T.)      T2—942 91
Ul'ianovskaia oblast'
  (Russia)      T2—474 6

Ul'yanovsk (Russia :
  Oblast)      T2—474 6
Umatilla County (Or.)      T2—795 69
Umatilla Indians      T5—974 12
Umatilla language      497.412
     T6—974 12
Umbanda      299.672
Umbelliferae      583.849
Umberto I, King of Italy
  Italian history      945.084
  Lombardian history      945.208 4
  Piedmontese history      945.108 4
  Sardinian history      945.908 4
  Sicilian history      945.808 4
  Southern Italian history      945.708 4
  Tuscan history      945.508 4
  Venetian history      945.308 4
Umbrella liability insurance      368.5
Umbrella plant (Cyperales)      584.84
Umbrellas      391.44
Umbria (Italy)      T2—456 5
  ancient      T2—374 2
  Etruria      T2—375 7
Umbrian language      479.9
     T6—799
Umbrians      T5—79
Umbumbulu (South Africa :
  District)      T2—684 5
Umbundu languages      496.399
     T6—963 99
Ume Saami language      494.572
     T6—945 72
Ume Sámi language      494.572
     T6—945 72
Umhlanga (South Africa)      T2—684 4
Umhlanga Rocks (South
  Africa)      T2—684 4
Umingmaktok (Nunavut)      T2—719 55
Umlazi (South Africa :
  District)      T2—684 5
Umm al-Qaiwain (United
  Arab Emirates : Emirate)    T2—535 7
Umm al-Qaywayn (United
  Arab Emirates : Emirate)    T2—535 7
Umpiring (Recreation)      790.1
  American football      796.332 3
  baseball      796.357 3
  Canadian football      796.335 3
  cricket      796.358 3
  rugby      796.333 3
  soccer      796.334 3
  volleyball      796.325 3
Umpqua River (Or.)      T2—795 29
UMT (Military training)      355.225

Umtata (South Africa :
  District)           T2—687 58
Umvoti (South Africa :
  District)           T2—684 7
Umzimkulu (South Africa :
  District)           T2—687 59
Umzinto (South Africa :
  District)           T2—684 5
UN (United Nations)      341.23
Unaligned blocs         T2—171 6
Unami language         497.345
                     T6—973 45
Unarmed combat        796.81
  military training      355.548
  sports             796.81
Unborn children
  law               346.017 1
Unclaimed estates      346.057
Uncles              306.87
                     T1—085
Unconscious
  philosophy         127
  psychology         154.2
Unconventional warfare  355.343
  Algerian Revolution    965.046 8
  American Revolution    973.385
  Chaco War        989.207 168
  Civil War (England)    942.062 8
  Civil War (Spain)      946.081 8
  Civil War (United States)  973.785
  Crimean War       947.073 88
  Falkland Islands War   997.110 248
  Franco-German War    943.082 8
  Hundred Years' War    944.025 8
  Indo-Pakistan War, 1971  954.920 518
  Indochinese War     959.704 18
  Iraq War, 2003–      956.704 438
  Iraqi-Iranian Conflict   955.054 28
  Korean War        951.904 28
  Mexican War        973.628
  Napoleonic Wars     940.278
  Persian Gulf War, 1991  956.704 428
  South African War    968.048 8
  Spanish-American War   973.898
  Thirty Years' War     940.248
  Vietnamese War      959.704 38
  War of the Pacific     983.061 68
  World War I        940.485
  World War II       940.548 5
Uncovered spaces
  architecture        721.84
Undaria              579.887
Underachievers (Students)  371.28
  special education     371.9

Underberg District (South
  Africa)            T2—684 7
Undercover police work  363.232
Underdeveloped areas   T2—172 4
Underemployed people   331.13
Underemployment      331.13
Undergarments       391.423
  commercial technology  687.2
  customs         391.423
  home sewing       646.42
  *see also* Clothing
Underglaze painting    666.45
  arts             738.15
  technology        666.45
Underground architecture 720.473
Underground areas
  environmental psychology 155.964
Underground construction  624.19
Underground disposal    363.728
  sewage sludge disposal  628.366
  solid waste technology  628.445 66
  *see also* Waste control
Underground electrical lines 621.319 23
Underground mining    622.2
Underground movements
  World War II      940.533 6
Underground publications
  bibliographies      011.56
Underground railroad (Rescue
  operation)
  Civil War (United States) cause 973.711 5
Underground railroads   388.42
  *see also* Subways (Rail)
Underground shelters
  military engineering   623.38
Underground stems     581.46
  descriptive botany    581.46
  physiology        575.49
Underground transportation 388.42
  *see also* Subways (Rail)
Underground water     553.79
  *see also* Groundwater
Underpopulation      363.91
Undertaking (Mortuary)  363.75
  customs         393
  economics        338.473 637 5
  funerals         393.93
    *see also* Funerals
  law              344.045
  music          781.588
  social services      363.75
    public administration  353.6
  technology        614.6
  *see also* Death

| | |
|---|---|
| Underwater acoustics | |
| engineering | 620.25 |
| Underwater archaeology | 930.102 804 |
| Underwater cinematography | 777.6 |
| Underwater construction | 627.702 |
| Underwater demolition | |
| military engineering | 623.27 |
| Underwater demolition units | |
| (Navy) | 359.984 |
| Underwater engineering | 627.7 |
| Underwater foundations | 624.157 |
| Underwater guided missiles | 359.981 782 |
| engineering | 623.451 97 |
| military equipment | 359.981 782 |
| Underwater hockey | 797.25 |
| Underwater mining | 622.295 |
| Underwater photography | 778.73 |
| Underwater prospecting | 622.17 |
| Underwater reconnaissance | |
| military engineering | 623.71 |
| naval operations | 359.984 |
| Underwater swimming | |
| sports | 797.23 |
| Underwater tunnels | |
| construction | 624.194 |
| Underwater videography | 777.6 |
| Underwater welding | 671.52 |
| Underwear | 391.423 |
| *see also* Undergarments | |
| Underweight people | |
| weight-gaining diet | 613.24 |
| Underwriters | 368.012 092 |
| Underwriting | 368.012 |
| Undistributed profits tax | 336.243 2 |
| Unemployed people | 305.906 94 |
| | T1—086 941 |
| labor economics | 331.137 |
| social group | 305.906 94 |
| social welfare | 362.899 4 |
| Unemployed poor people | |
| social welfare | 362.594 |
| Unemployed youth | |
| social welfare | 362.779 4 |
| Unemployment | 331.137 |
| economics | 331.137 |
| *see Manual at* 331.120424 | |
| vs. 331.1377 | |
| influence on crime | 364.2 |
| sociology | 306.361 |
| Unemployment compensation | 368.44 |
| *see also* Unemployment | |
| insurance | |

| | |
|---|---|
| Unemployment insurance | 368.44 |
| labor economics | 331.255 2 |
| law | 344.024 |
| public administration | 353.54 |
| Unesco | 001.060 1 |
| law | 344.09 |
| public administration | 353.721 1 |
| Uneven bars (Gymnastic | |
| equipment) | 796.442 |
| Unfair economic practices | 338.604 8 |
| criminology | 364.168 |
| criminal law | 345.026 8 |
| economics | 338.604 8 |
| law | 343.072 |
| Ungava Bay Region | |
| (Quebec and Nunavut) | T2—714 111 |
| Ungraded schools | 371.255 |
| Ungulates | 599.6 |
| conservation technology | 639.979 6 |
| paleozoology | 569.6 |
| resource economics | 333.959 6 |
| Unicameral legislatures | 328.39 |
| UNICEF (Children's Fund) | 362.7 |
| public administration | 353.536 211 |
| Unicoi County (Tenn.) | T2—768 982 |
| Unicorn fishes | 597.64 |
| Unicorn plants | 635.933 95 |
| botany | 583.95 |
| floriculture | 635.933 95 |
| Unicorns | 398.245 4 |
| *see also* Legendary animals | |
| Unidentified flying objects | 001.942 |
| Unification Church | 289.96 |
| biography | 289.960 92 |
| *see also* Christian | |
| denominations | |
| Unified field theory | 530.142 |
| Unified operations (Armed | |
| forces) | 355.46 |
| Uniflagellate molds | 579.53 |
| Uniform algebras | 512.55 |
| Uniform functions | 515.22 |
| Uniform spaces | 516 |
| geometry | 516 |
| topology | 514.32 |
| Uniform titles | |
| cataloging | 025.322 |
| Uniforms | 391.48 |
| armed forces | 355.14 |
| issue and use | 355.81 |
| *see Manual at* 355.1409 | |
| commercial technology | 687.15 |
| customs | 391.48 |
| *see also* Clothing | |

Unincorporated business
  enterprises  338.7
  law  346.068
  management  658.044
    initiation  658.114 4
    *see Manual at* 658.04 vs.
      658.114, 658.402
  production economics  338.7
  *see also* Business enterprises
Unincorporated societies  060
  *see also* Nonprofit
    organizations
Unión (El Salvador : Dept.)  T2—728 434
Union (Philippines)  T2—599 1
Union catalogs  025.31
  bibliography  017
  library cooperation  021.642
  library science  025.31
Union County (Ark.)  T2—767 61
Union County (Fla.)  T2—759 14
Union County (Ga.)  T2—758 285
Union County (Ill.)  T2—773 995
Union County (Ind.)  T2—772 625
Union County (Iowa)  T2—777 853
Union County (Ky.)  T2—769 885
Union County (Miss.)  T2—762 925
Union County (N.C.)  T2—756 755
Union County (N.J.)  T2—749 36
Union County (N.M.)  T2—789 23
Union County (Ohio)  T2—771 532
Union County (Or.)  T2—795 71
Union County (Pa.)  T2—748 48
Union County (S.C.)  T2—757 41
Union County (S.D.)  T2—783 392
Union County (Tenn.)  T2—768 935
Union dues checkoff  331.889 6
Union federations  331.872
  *see also* Labor unions
Union Islands  996.15
    T2—961 5
Union leaders  331.880 92
  biography  331.880 92
  role and function  331.873 3
Union of Christian and Center
  Democrats (Italian political
  party)  324.245 082
Union of Kalmar  948.03
  *see also* Kalmar Union
Union of Soviet Socialist  947.084
  Republics  T2—47
Union organizing  331.891 2
Union Parish (La.)  T2—763 89
Union pipes  788.49
  *see also* Woodwind instruments

Union racketeering  364.106 7
Union recognition  331.891 2
Union republics (Soviet Union)  321.023
  *see also* States (Members of
    federations)
Union security  331.889
Union shop  331.889 2
Union sympathizers
  Civil War (United States)  973.717
Union Valdôtaine (Italian
  political party)  324.245 084
Uniondale (South Africa :
  District)  T2—687 38
Unione dei democratici cristiani e
  democratici di centro (Italian
  political party)  324.245 082
Unionidae  594.4
Unions  331.88
  *see also* Labor unions
Uniramia  595.7
  paleozoology  565.7
Unison voices  782.5
Unit method of teaching  371.36
Unit operations
  chemical engineering  660.284 2
Unit processes
  chemical engineering  660.284 4
Unit theory (Mathematics)  512.74
Unit trusts  332.632 7
Unitarian and Universalist
  churches  289.1
  church government  262.091
    parishes  254.091
  doctrines  230.91
  guides to Christian life  248.489 1
  missions  266.91
  moral theology  241.049 1
  public worship  264.091
  religious associations  267.189 1
  religious education  268.891
  seminaries  230.073 91
  theology  230.91
Unitarian churches  289.133
  *see also* Unitarian and
    Universalist churches
Unitarian Universalist
  Association  289.132
  *see also* Unitarian and
    Universalist churches
Unitarianism  289.1
Unitarians
  biography  289.109 2
Unitary spaces  515.73

| | |
|---|---|
| Unitary state (System of government) | 321.01 |
| United Arab Emirates | 953.57 |
| | T2—535 7 |
| ancient | 939.49 |
| | T2—394 9 |
| United Arab Republic | 962.053 |
| | T2—62 |
| Egyptian history | 962.053 |
| Syrian history | 956.910 42 |
| United Brethren in Christ | 289.9 |
| *see also* Christian denominations | |
| United charities | 361.8 |
| United Christian Democrats (Italian political party) | 324.245 082 |
| United Church of Canada | 287.92 |
| *see also* Christian denominations | |
| United Church of Christ | 285.834 |
| *see also* Congregationalism | |
| United Church of Religious Science | 299.93 |
| United Confederate Veterans | 369.17 |
| United Conference of Methodist Churches | 287.532 |
| *see also* Methodist Church | |
| United Daughters of the Confederacy | 369.17 |
| United Evangelical Lutheran Church | 284.131 3 |
| *see also* Lutheran church | |
| United Kingdom | 941 |
| | T2—41 |
| *see Manual at* 941 | |
| United Lutheran Church in America | 284.133 5 |
| *see also* Lutheran church | |
| United Methodist Church (Great Britain) | 287.53 |
| *see also* Methodist Church | |
| United Methodist Church (U.S.) | 287.6 |
| *see also* Methodist Church | |
| United Methodist Free Churches | 287.53 |
| *see also* Methodist Church | |
| United Nations | 341.23 |
| armed forces | 355.357 |
| finance | 336.091 63 |
| law of nations | 341.23 |
| public administration | 352.113 |
| law | 341.233 |
| United Nations. Charter | 341.232 |
| United Nations. Economic and Social Council | 341.232 5 |

| | |
|---|---|
| United Nations. General Assembly | 341.232 2 |
| United Nations. Security Council | 341.232 3 |
| United Nations (Military alliance) World War II | 940.533 2 |
| United Nations Children's Fund | 362.7 |
| public administration | 353.536 211 |
| United Nations Educational, Scientific, and Cultural Organization | 001.060 1 |
| law | 344.09 |
| public administration | 353.721 1 |
| United Nations International Children's Emergency Fund public administration | 353.536 211 |
| United Nations philatelic issues | 769.561 |
| United Nations treaties series | 341.026 2 |
| United Pentecostal Church | 289.94 |
| United Presbyterian Church in the U.S.A. | 285.131 |
| *see also* Presbyterian Church | |
| United Presbyterian Church of North America | 285.134 |
| *see also* Presbyterian Church | |
| United Provinces of Central America | 972.804 |
| | T2—728 |
| Costa Rican history | 972.860 42 |
| Guatemalan history | 972.810 42 |
| Honduran history | 972.830 4 |
| Nicaraguan history | 972.850 42 |
| Salvadoran history | 972.840 42 |
| United Provinces of the Netherlands | 949.204 |
| | T2—492 |
| United Reformed Church in the United Kingdom | 285.232 |
| *see also* Presbyterian Church | |
| United Socialist Party (Italy : 1922–1930) | 324.245 027 |
| United Socialist Party (Italy : 1969–1971) | 324.245 072 2 |
| United Society of Believers in Christ's Second Appearing | 289.8 |
| *see also* Christian denominations | |
| United States | 973 |
| | T2—73 |
| Dutch explorations | 973.19 |
| English explorations | 973.17 |
| French explorations | 973.18 |
| geography | 917.3 |
| Norse explorations | 973.13 |
| Spanish and Portuguese explorations | 973.16 |

United States (continued)
travel | 917.304
*see Manual at* T2—73 vs.
T2—71
United States. Central
Intelligence Agency | 327.127 3
United States. Continental
Congress
United States history | 973.312
United States. Court of Customs
and Patent Appeals | 347.732 8
United States. Navy. SEALs | 359.984
United States. Supreme Court | 347.732 6
reports | 348.734 13
United States Code | 348.732 3
United States customary
measurements | 530.813
United States federal law reporter
system for the Atlantic region | 348.734 22
United States federal reporter
system for the Northeast
region | 348.734 23
United States federal reporter
system for the Northwest
region | 348.734 24
United States federal reporter
system for the Pacific region | 348.734 28
United States federal reporter
system for the South region | 348.734 27
United States federal reporter
system for the Southeast
region | 348.734 25
United States federal reporter
system for the Southwest
region | 348.734 26
United States national reporter
system | 348.734 2
United States of Colombia | 986.106 1
T2—861
Colombian history | 986.106 1
Panamanian history | 972.870 3
United States Pacific seawaters | 551.461 432
T2—164 32
United States people
(National group) | T5—13
United States Sanitary
Commission
Civil War (United States) | 973.777
Uniting Church in Australia | 287.93
*see also* Christian
denominations
Unitized cargo services | 385.72
public administration | 354.764

Units | 530.81
Unity | 111.82
Christian church | 262.72
Unity School of Christianity | 289.97
*see also* Christian
denominations
Universal algebra | 512
Universal bibliographies | 011.1
Universal Decimal Classification | 025.432
Universal history | 909
Universal House of Justice
works by | 297.938 7
Universal joints | 621.825
Universal languages | 401.3
Universal life insurance | 368.324
Universal military training | 355.225
law | 343.012 2
Universal priesthood | 234
Universal time | 389.17
Universalist churches | 289.134
*see also* Unitarian and
Universalist churches
Universalists
biography | 289.109 2
Universals (Philosophy) | 111.2
Universe
astronomy | 523.1
philosophy | 113
Universities | 378
T1—071 1
area planning | 711.57
liability | 344.075
*see also* Higher education
Universities without walls | 378.03
*see also* Higher education
University autonomy | 378.1
University buildings | 378.196
*see also* College buildings
University extension | 378.175
University graduates
choice of vocation | 331.702 35
labor force | 331.114 45
social group | 305.55
unemployment | 331.137 804
University libraries | 027.7
*see also* Academic libraries
University presses
bibliographies of publications | 011.54
publishing | 070.594
Unjust enrichment | 346.029
Unlawful assembly | 364.143
law | 345.024 3
Unleavened breads | 641.815

Unloading operations
    materials management     658.788 5
    ships     623.888 1
Unmanned space flight
    engineering     629.43
Unmanned spacecraft
    engineering     629.46
    military engineering     623.749
Unmarried couples     306.841
         T1—086 56
    law     346.016
Unmarried fathers     306.874 22
Unmarried mothers     306.874 32
         T1—086 947
    government programs     353.533 1
    psychology     155.642 3
    social group     306.874 32
    social welfare     362.839 532
        public administration     353.533 1
Unmarried parenthood     306.856
    *see also* Unwed parenthood
Unmarried parents     306.856
Unmarried teenage mothers
    social welfare     362.787 432
Unsized papers     676.286
Unskilled workers     331.798
         T1—086 24
    labor economics     331.798
    labor force     331.114 2
    personnel management     658.304 4
    unemployment     331.137 804
Unspecified keyboard
    instruments     786
    *see also* Keyboard instruments
Unspecified melody instrument     787
    *see also* Stringed instruments
Unstrut-Hainich-Kreis
    (Germany : Landkreis)     T2—432 24
Unterer Neckar (Germany :
    Region)     T2—434 645
Unterfranken (Germany)     T2—433 3
Untouchables     305.568 8
         T1—086 94
    religion     200.869 4
        Hinduism     294.508 694
Unwed fatherhood     306.874 22
Unwed motherhood     306.874 32
Unwed parenthood     306.856
    ethics     173
        *see also* Family ethics
    social theology     201.7
        Christianity     261.835 856
Upanishads     294.592 18

Upholstered furniture     645.4
    manufacturing technology     684.12
    *see also* Furniture
Upholstery     645.4
    arts     746.95
    home sewing     646.21
    household management     645.4
    interior decoration     747.5
Upholstery fabrics     677.616
    *see also* Textiles
Upholstery trimmings     677.76
Upland ecology     577.5
Upland game birds     598.6
    conservation technology     639.978 6
    resource economics     333.958 6
    sports hunting     799.246
Upland rice
    food crop     633.179
Upper Arrow Lake (B.C.)     T2—711 62
Upper atmosphere     551.514
    winds     551.518 7
Upper Austria (Austria)     T2—436 2
Upper Avon River
    (England)     T2—424 4
Upper Bavaria (Germany)     T2—433 6
Upper Canada     971.03
         T2—71
    Ontario     971.302
         T2—713
Upper chambers (Legislative
    bodies)     328.31
Upper class     305.52
         T1—086 21
Upper Demerara-Berbice
    Region (Guyana)     T2—881 4
Upper Egypt     T2—623
Upper extremities     612.97
    anatomy     611.97
    bones     612.751
        anatomy     611.717
        medicine     616.71
        physiology     612.751
        surgery     617.471
    fractures
        medicine     617.157
    joints
        medicine     616.72
        surgery     617.57
    muscles
        anatomy     611.737
    physiology     612.97
    regional medicine     617.57
    surgery     617.570 59
Upper Franconia (Germany)     T2—433 1

| | | | |
|---|---|---|---|
| Upper Guinea | T2—665 | Uranium (continued) | |
| Upper houses (Legislative | | prospecting | 622.184 932 |
| bodies) | 328.31 | *see also* Chemicals; Metals | |
| Upper Hutt City (N.Z.) | T2—936 5 | Urantia | 299 |
| Upper Karoo (South Africa) | T2—687 13 | Uranus (Planet) | 523.47 |
| Upper Mesopotamia | T2—567 4 | | T2—992 7 |
| ancient | 935.4 | astrology | 133.538 |
| | T2—354 | Urban administration | 352.16 |
| Upper Nile (Sudan : | | Urban areas | 307.76 |
| Province) | T2—629 3 | | T2—173 2 |
| Upper Nile (Sudan : | | *see also* Cities | |
| Region) | T2—629 3 | Urban biology | 578.756 |
| Upper Palatinate (Germany) | T2—433 4 | Urban communities | 307.76 |
| Upper Paleolithic Age | 930.128 | *see also* Cities | |
| Upper Peninsula (Mich.) | T2—774 9 | Urban development | 307.141 6 |
| Upper Takutu-Upper | | law | 344.06 |
| Essequibo Region | | public administration | 354.279 3 |
| (Guyana) | T2—881 84 | Urban dialects | 417.209 173 2 |
| Upper Volta | 966.250 3 | linguistics | 417.209 173 2 |
| | T2—662 5 | specific languages | T4—7 |
| Upper Volta people | T5—966 25 | sociolinguistics | 306.440 917 32 |
| Uppland landskap (Sweden) | T2—487 4 | Urban ecology (Biology) | 577.56 |
| Uppsala län (Sweden) | T2—487 4 | Urban economics | 330.917 32 |
| Upshur County (Tex.) | T2—764 222 | Urban education | 370.917 32 |
| Upshur County (W. Va.) | T2—754 62 | Urban exodus | 307.26 |
| Upson County (Ga.) | T2—758 486 | Urban families | 306.854 |
| Upton County (Tex.) | T2—764 863 | Urban forestry | 635.977 |
| Upton upon Severn | | Urban government | 320.85 |
| (England) | T2—424 47 | Urban heat islands | 551.525 091 732 |
| Upwelling | | Urban homesteading | 363.583 |
| oceanography | 551.462 | *see also* Housing | |
| Ur (Extinct city) | T2—355 | Urban lands | 333.77 |
| Urabá, Gulf of (Colombia) | 551.461 365 | economics | 333.77 |
| | T2—163 65 | sale and rental | 333.337 |
| Ural-Altaic languages | 494 | public administration | 354.35 |
| | T6—94 | Urban mass transportation | 388.4 |
| Ural-Altaic literatures | 894 | *see also* Urban transportation | |
| Ural Mountains (Russia) | T2—474 3 | Urban ministry | 253.091 732 |
| Uralic languages | 494.5 | church administration | 254.22 |
| | T6—945 | Urban municipalities | 320.85 |
| Uralic literatures | 894.5 | Urban renewal | 307.341 6 |
| Uraninite | | civic art | 711.4 |
| mineralogy | 549.528 | Urban runoff | 363.728 4 |
| Uranium | 669.293 1 | sewer systems | 628.21 |
| chemical engineering | 661.043 1 | social services | 363.728 4 |
| chemistry | 546.431 | *see also* Waste control | |
| economic geology | 553.493 2 | Urban-rural migration | 307.26 |
| human toxicology | 615.925 431 | Urban schools | 371.009 173 2 |
| materials science | 620.189 293 1 | Urban sociology | 307.76 |
| metallography | 669.952 931 | Urban transportation | 388.4 |
| metallurgy | 669.293 1 | law | 343.098 |
| mining | 622.349 32 | public administration | 354.769 |
| physical metallurgy | 669.962 931 | railroad | |
| production economics | 338.274 932 | engineering | 625.4 |

Urban transportation (continued)
safety    363.125
   public administration    353.98
   *see also* Transportation safety
transportation services    388.4
Urban warfare    355.426
Urdu language    491.439
     T6—914 39
Urdu literature    891.439
Ure, River (England)    T2—428 48
Urea fertilizers    631.841
   chemical engineering    668.624 1
Ureas    668.422 3
Uredinales    579.592
Uremia
   medicine    616.635
   *see also* Urologic diseases —
     humans
Ureteral diseases
   medicine    616.61
   *see also* Urologic diseases —
     humans
Ureters    573.49
   biology    573.49
   human anatomy    611.61
   human physiology    612.467
   medicine    616.61
   surgery    617.461
   *see also* Urinary system
Urethra    573.49
   biology    573.49
   human anatomy    611.62
   human physiology    612.467
   medicine    616.62
     men    616.64
   surgery    617.462
   *see also* Urinary system
Urethral diseases
   medicine    616.62
     men    616.64
   *see also* Urologic diseases —
     humans
Urethritis
   medicine    616.624
   *see also* Urologic diseases —
     humans
Urewera National Park
   (N.Z.)    T2—934 25
Urfa İli (Turkey)    T2—565 1
Urhobo (African people)    T5—963 3
Urhobo language    496.33
     T6— 963 3
Uri (Switzerland)    T2—494 77

Urinalysis
   diagnosis
     general disease    616.075 66
Urinary calculi
   medicine    616.622
   *see also* Urologic diseases —
     humans
Urinary diseases    573.493 9
   *see also* Urologic diseases
Urinary incontinence
   medicine    616.62
   *see also* Urologic diseases —
     humans
Urinary system    573.49
   anesthesiology    617.967 461
   biology    573.49
   diseases    573.493 9
   *see also* Urologic diseases
   human anatomy    611.61
   human histology    612.460 45
   human physiology    612.46
   medicine    616.6
   surgery    617.461
Urination disorders
   medicine    616.62
   *see also* Urologic diseases —
     humans
Urine
   human physiology    612.461
Urochordata    596.2
   paleozoology    566
Urodela    597.85
   paleozoology    567.8
Urogenital diseases    573.639
   animals    573.639
     veterinary medicine    636.089 66
   humans
     cancer
       incidence    614.599 946
       medicine    616.994 6
     medicine    616.6
     pharmacokinetics    615.76
     surgery    617.46
Urogenital organs    573.6
   *see also* Urogenital system
Urogenital system    573.6
   diseases    573.639
   *see also* Urogenital diseases
   human anatomy    611.6
   human physiology    612.46
   medicine    616.6
   surgery    617.46
   *see also* Genital system;
     Urinary system

Urologic diseases 573.493 9
  animals 573.493 9
    veterinary medicine 636.089 66
  humans 362.196 6
    anesthesiology 617.967 461
    cancer 362.196 994 61
      incidence 614.599 946 1
      medicine 616.994 61
      social services 362.196 994 61
    *see also* Cancer — humans
    geriatrics 618.976 6
    incidence 614.596
    medicine 616.6
    pediatrics 618.926
    pharmacokinetics 615.761
    social services 362.196 6
    surgery 617.461
  *see also* Urogenital diseases
Urology 616.6
Uropeltidae 597.967
Uropygi 595.453 2
Ursidae 599.78
  paleozoology 569.78
Ursulines 255.974
  church history 271.974
Ursus 599.78
Ursus americanus 599.785
Ursus arctos 599.784
Ursus maritimus 599.786
Urticales 583.45
Urticaria
  medicine 616.517
  *see also* Skin diseases — humans
Uru-Chipaya languages 498.9
  T6—989
Uruguay 989.5
  T2—895
Uruguay River T2—822
  Argentina T2—822
  Uruguay T2—895
Uruguayan literature 860
Uruguayans T5—688 95
Usability
  computer software 005.019
  computers 004.019
Usage (Applied linguistics) 418
  specific languages T4—8
Uşak İli (Turkey) T2—562 8
  ancient T2—392 6
Use tax 336.271
  law 343.055
  public administration 352.44
  public finance 336.271

Useful animals 591.63
Useful organisms 578.63
  *see Manual at* 630 vs. 579–590, 641.3
Useful plants 581.63
  *see Manual at* 583–585 vs. 600
Usenet newsgroups 004.693
User charges 336.16
  *see also* User fees
User education
  libraries 025.56
User fees 336.16
  law 343.055
  library services 025.11
  public administration 352.44
  public finance 336.16
User interfaces 005.437
  graphics programming 006.678 4
  graphics programs 006.688 4
  multimedia-systems programming 006.778 4
  multimedia-systems programs 006.788 4
  systems programming 005.428
  systems programs 005.437
  *see Manual at* 005.269 and 005.284, 005.3684, 005.384
Usk (Wales) T2—429 98
USSR 947.084
  T2—47
Ust-Orda Buriat (Russia : Okrug) T2—575
Ust-Orda Buriatskiĭ avtonomnyĭ okrug (Russia) T2—575
Ústecký kraj (Czech Republic) T2—437 16
Uster (Switzerland : Bezirk) T2—494 574 1
Ustilaginales 579.593
Usulután (El Salvador : Dept.) T2—728 431
Usury 332.83
  law 346.073
Utah 979.2
  T2—792
Utah County (Utah) T2—792 24
Utari T5—946
Ute Indians T5—974 576
Ute language 497.457 6
  T6—974 576
Uteem, Cassam
  Mauritian history 969.820 41
Utensils
  manufacturing technology 683.8

Uterine cervix
  gynecology            618.14
  human anatomy        611.66
  human physiology     612.627
  surgery              618.145
Uterine diseases
  gynecology            618.14
  *see also* Female genital
    diseases — humans
Uterine hemorrhage
  obstetrics             618.54
Uterine infections
  gynecology            618.142
  *see also* Female genital
    diseases — humans
Uterine malformations
  gynecology            618.144
  *see also* Female genital
    diseases — humans
Uterus                  573.667
  biology               573.667
  gynecology            618.14
  human anatomy        611.66
  human physiology     612.627
  surgery               618.145
Utican architecture      722.32
Utilitarianism           144.6
  ethics                171.5
Utilities (Buildings facilities)   644
  construction          696
  household management   644
  museums            069.29
  plant management     658.26
                     T1—068 2
    public administration   352.56
Utilities (Public services)   363.6
  *see also* Public utilities
Utility dogs (United Kingdom)   636.72
Utility programs       005.43
Utility theory         330.157
Uto-Aztecan Indians    T5—974 5
Uto-Aztecan languages   497.45
                     T6—974 5
Utopian socialism      335.02
  English system       335.12
Utopias               321.07
  arts                T3C—372
  literature           808.803 72
    history and criticism   809.933 72
    specific literatures   T3B—080 372
      history and
        criticism     T3B—093 72
  political system      321.07
  socialism            335.02

Utrecht (Netherlands :
  Province)           T2—492 32
Utrecht (South Africa :
  District)            T2—684 1
Uttar Pradesh (India)     T2—542
Uttarakhand (India)      T2—545 1
Uttaranchal (India)       T2—545 1
Uttlesford (England)     T2—426 712
Uudenmaan lääni (Finland)  T2—489 71
Uusimaa (Finland)        T2—489 71
Uvalde County (Tex.)     T2—764 432
Uveal diseases
  incidence           614.599 7
  ophthalmology       617.72
    *see also* Eye diseases —
      humans
Uveas
  human anatomy        611.84
  human physiology     612.842
  ophthalmology       617.72
Uyghur              T5—943 23
Uyghur language       494.323
                     T6—943 23
Uyghur literature        894.323
Uzbek               T5—943 25
Uzbek language         494.325
                     T6—943 25
Uzbek literature         894.325
Uzbekistan            958.7
                     T2—587
  ancient             939.6
                     T2—396

# V

Vaal River (South Africa)  T2—682
Vaal Triangle (South
  Africa)             T2—682 23
Vaalbos National Park
  (South Africa)       T2—687 11
Vaasa (Finland : Lääni)   T2—489 73
Vaasan Lääni (Finland)   T2—489 73
Vacation homes        643.25
  architecture         728.72
  construction         690.872
  home economics      643.25
  *see also* Dwellings
Vacation schools
  adult education       374.8
Vacations
  labor economics     331.257 6
  personnel management   658.312 2
  recreation           790.1
  sociology           306.481 25

Vaccination
  disease control                  614.47
  law                             344.043
Vaccines
  pharmacology                    615.372
Vacuoles                          571.655
Vacuum deposition
  metal finishing                 671.735
Vacuum electronics                537.53
Vacuum metallizing                671.735
Vacuum metallurgy                 669.028 4
Vacuum pumps                      621.55
Vacuum technology                 621.55
Vacuum tubes
  electronics                     621.381 512
  radio engineering               621.384 132
Vacuum ultraviolet spectroscopes
  manufacturing technology        681.414 5
Vacuum ultraviolet spectroscopy
  physics                         535.845
Vacuums                           533.5
  engineering                     621.55
Vagala language                   496.35
                                  T6—963 5
Vagina
  gynecology                      618.15
  human anatomy                   611.67
  human physiology                612.628
Vaginal diaphragms
  health                          613.943 5
  medicine                        618.185
  *see also* Birth control
Vaginal diseases
  gynecology                      618.15
  *see also* Female genital
      diseases — humans
Vaginiperineotomy
  obstetrical surgery             618.85
Vagrancy                          364.148
  law                             345.024 8
Vagrants                          305.569
                                  T1—086 942
Vai (African people)             T5—963 4
Vai language                      496.34
                                  T6—963 4
Vaiśeṣika (Philosophy)            181.44
Vaisheshika (Philosophy)          181.44
Vaishnavism                       294.551 2
Vaisnavism                        294.551 2
Vajiravudh, King of Siam
  Thai history                    959.304 1
Val-de-Marne (France)            T2—443 63
Val-de-Ruz (Switzerland :
    District)                    T2—494 383

Val-de-Travers
  (Switzerland)                  T2—494 389
Val-d'Oise (France)              T2—443 67
Val-Saint-François
  (Quebec)                       T2—714 65
Val Verde County (Tex.)          T2—764 881
Valais (Switzerland)             T2—494 79
Valdivia (Chile : Province)      T2—835 2
Valdotanian Union (Italian
    political party)                        324.245 084
Vale of Glamorgan (Wales)        T2—429 89
Vale of White Horse
  (England)                      T2—425 76
Vale Royal (England)             T2—427 15
Valemount (B.C.)                 T2—711 82
Valence (Chemistry)              541.224
Valencia (Spain : Province)      T2—467 63
Valencia (Spain : Region)        T2—467 6
Valencia County (N.M.)           T2—789 92
Valentine's Day                  394.261 8
  handicrafts                    745.594 161 8
Valerianaceae                    583.92
Valerians                        583.92
Validation
  data                           005.72
    file processing              005.74
  programming                    005.14
Valises
  manufacturing technology       685.51
Vallabhācārya (Philosophy)       181.484 4
Valladolid (Spain :
  Province)                      T2—462 3
Valle (Honduras : Dept.)         T2—728 352
Valle d'Aosta (Italy)            945.11
                                 T2—451 1
  ancient                        T2—372 21
Valle del Cauca (Colombia)       T2—861 52
Vallée-de-la-Gatineau
  (Quebec)                       T2—714 224
Vallée de l'Or (Quebec)          T2—714 139
Vallée-du-Richelieu
  (Quebec)                       T2—714 365
Vallemaggia (Switzerland)        T2—494 789
Valley County (Idaho)            T2—796 76
Valley County (Mont.)            T2—786 17
Valley County (Neb.)             T2—782 48
Valley Forge
  United States history          973.334 1
Valley of Mexico (Mexico)        T2—725
Valley winds                     551.518 5
Valleys                          551.442
                                 T2—144
  geography                      910.914 4

Valleys (continued)
  geomorphology — 551.442
  physical geography — 910.021 44
Valois, House of — 944.025
  genealogy — 929.74
Valparaíso (Chile :
  Province) — T2—832 55
Valparaíso (Chile : Region) — T2—832 4
Valréas (France) — T2—445 88
Valuation
  businesses
    financial management — 658.15
    law — 346.065
  investment economics — 332.632 21
  real property — 333.332
    law — 346.043 7
Valuation of assets
  accounting — 657.73
Valuation theory — 515.78
Value — T1—01
  labor theory
    Marxian economics — 335.412
  microeconomics — 338.521
Value-added networks — 004.69
  computer communications
    services — 384.33
  *see also* Computer
    communications
Value-added tax — 336.271 4
  law — 343.055
  public administration — 352.44
  public finance — 336.271 4
Value analysis (Cost control) — 658.155 2
Value cognition
  psychology — 153.45
Values
  epistemology — 121.8
  social control — 303.372
Valvatida — 593.93
Valverde (Dominican
  Republic : Province) — T2—729 357
Valves — 621.84
  internal-combustion engines — 621.437
Valvular activity
  heart
    human physiology — 612.171
Valvular heart diseases
  medicine — 616.125
  *see also* Cardiovascular
    diseases — humans
Vampire bats — 599.45
Vampires — 398.21
  *see also* Legendary beings

Vampyromorpha — 594.55
Van Allen radiation belts — 538.766
Van Buren, Martin
  United States history — 973.57
Van Buren County (Ark.) — T2—767 29
Van Buren County (Iowa) — T2—777 98
Van Buren County (Mich.) — T2—774 13
Van Buren County (Tenn.) — T2—768 657
Van İli (Turkey) — T2—566 28
  ancient — T2—395 5
Van pools — 388.413 212
Van Wert County (Ohio) — T2—771 413
Van Zandt County (Tex.) — T2—764 276
Vanadates
  mineralogy — 549.72
Vanadium — 669.732
  chemical engineering — 661.052 2
  chemistry — 546.522
  economic geology — 553.462 6
  materials science — 620.189 32
  metallography — 669.957 32
  metallurgy — 669.732
  metalworking — 673.732
  organic chemistry
    applied — 661.895
  physical metallurgy — 669.967 32
  *see also* Chemicals; Metals
Vanadium group
  chemical engineering — 661.052
  chemistry — 546.52
Vance County (N.C.) — T2—756 532
Vancouver (B.C.) — T2—711 33
Vancouver Island (B.C.) — T2—711 2
Vandal language — 439.9
                — T6—399
Vandal period
  Libyan history — 939.740 4
  Moroccan history — 939.712 05
  North Africa — 939.704
  Tunisian history — 939.730 4
Vandalic language — 439.9
                — T6—399
Vandalism — 364.164 4
  law — 345.026 44
  schools — 371.782
Vandalism insurance — 368.12
Vandals (Germanic people) — T5—39
  Sardinian history — 945.901
Vanderbijlpark (South
  Africa : District) — T2—682 23
Vanderburgh County (Ind.) — T2—772 33
Vanderhoof (B.C.) — T2—711 82
Vanderkloof Dam (South
  Africa) — T2—687 13

Vänern (Sweden)     T2—486 7
Vanga shrikes     598.8
Vanillas     641.338 2
  botany     584.4
  *see also* Flavorings
Vanishing species     333.952 2
  *see also* entries beginning with
    Rare
Vanoise, Parc national de la
  (France)     T2—445 85
Vanrhynsdorp (South
  Africa : District)     T2—687 31
Vans     388.343 4
  driving     629.284 34
  engineering     629.223 4
  repair     629.287 34
  transportation services     388.343 4
  *see also* Trucks
Vanuatu     995.95
     T2—959 5
Vapor lighting     621.327
Vapor-phase deposition
  metal finishing     671.735
Vapor plating
  metal finishing     671.735
Vaporization     536.44
Var (France)     T2—449 3
Varactors     621.381 522
Varanidae     597.959 6
Varanus     597.959 6
Varanus komodoensis     597.959 68
Vardar Macedonia     T2—497 6
Vardar River     T2—497 6
Varese (Italy : Province)     T2—452 2
  ancient     T2—372 25
Vargas, Getúlio
  Brazilian history     981.061
Variable annuities
  insurance     368.375
Variable costs     338.514 2
  financial management     658.155 3
Variable life insurance     368.325
Variable rate securities     332.632 044
Variable stars     523.844
Variables     511.326
Variation (Biology)     576.54
  humans     599.94
Variations (Mathematics)     515.64
Variations (Musical forms)     781.825
  instrumental     784.182 5

Varicella
  incidence     614.525
  medicine     616.914
  *see also* Communicable
    diseases — humans
Varicose veins
  medicine     616.143
  *see also* Cardiovascular
    diseases — humans
Varietal wines     641.22
  commercial processing     663.2
Varieties
  agriculture     631.57
Variety drama
  literature     808.825 7
    history and criticism     809.257
    specific literatures     T3B—205 7
     individual authors     T3A—2
Variety shows     792.7
Variety stores     381.14
  *see also* Commerce
Variola major
  incidence     614.521
  medicine     616.912
  *see also* Communicable
    diseases — humans
Variola minor
  incidence     614.521
  medicine     616.913
  *see also* Communicable
    diseases — humans
Variola vaccinia
  incidence     614.521
  medicine     616.913
  *see also* Communicable
    diseases — humans
Varix
  medicine     616.143
  *see also* Cardiovascular
    diseases — humans
Varmints
  small game hunting     799.25
Värmland landskap
  (Sweden)     T2—487 7
Värmlands län (Sweden)     T2—487 7
Varna (Bulgaria : Oblast)     T2—499 4
Varnenska oblast (Bulgaria)     T2—499 4
Varnish trees     583.77
Varnishes     667.79
Varnishing     667.79
  technology     667.79
  woodwork
    buildings     698.34
Vas Megye (Hungary)     T2—439 7

| | |
|---|---|
| Vasa, House of | 948.503 2 |
| Vascongadas (Spain) | T2—466 |
| Vascular circulation | 573.18 |
|   human physiology | 612.13 |
|   *see also* Cardiovascular system | |
| Vascular cryptogams | 587 |
| Vascular dementia | |
|   medicine | 616.81 |
|   *see also* Nervous system | |
|     diseases — humans | |
| Vascular diseases | |
|   medicine | 616.13 |
|   *see also* Cardiovascular | |
|     diseases — humans | |
|   pregnancy complications | |
|     obstetrics | 618.361 3 |
| Vascular headaches | |
|   medicine | 616.849 1 |
|   *see also* Nervous system | |
|     diseases — humans | |
| Vascular plants | 580 |
| Vascular seedless plants | 587 |
| Vascular surgery | 617.413 |
| Vasectomy (Birth control) | |
|   health | 613.942 |
|   *see also* Birth control | |
|   surgery | 617.463 |
| Vases | |
|   sculpture | 731.72 |
| Vaslui (Romania : Judeţ) | T2—498 1 |
| Vasoconstrictors (Drugs) | |
|   pharmacokinetics | 615.71 |
| Vasoconstrictors (Nerves) | |
|   human physiology | 612.18 |
| Vasodilators (Drugs) | |
|   pharmacokinetics | 615.71 |
| Vasodilators (Nerves) | |
|   human physiology | 612.18 |
| Vasomotors | |
|   human physiology | 612.18 |
| Vasopressin | |
|   human physiology | 612.492 |
|   pharmacology | 615.363 |
| Västerbotten landskap | |
|   (Sweden) | T2—488 7 |
| Västerbottens län (Sweden) | T2—488 7 |
| Västergötland landskap | |
|   (Sweden) | T2—486 7 |
| Västernorrlands län | |
|   (Sweden) | T2—488 5 |
| Västmanland landskap | |
|   (Sweden) | T2—487 5 |
| Västmanlands län (Sweden) | T2—487 5 |

| | |
|---|---|
| Västra Götalands län | |
|   (Sweden) | T2—486 7 |
| VAT (Tax) | 336.271 4 |
|   law | 343.055 |
|   public administration | 352.44 |
|   public finance | 336.271 4 |
| Vaterländische Front (Austrian | |
|   political party) | 324.243 602 43 |
| Vatican City | 945.634 |
| | T2—456 34 |
|   ancient | T2—376 3 |
| Vättern (Sweden) | T2—486 4 |
| Vaucluse (France : Dept.) | T2—449 2 |
| Vaud (Switzerland) | T2—494 52 |
| Vaudeville | 792.7 |
| Vaudreuil-Soulanges | |
|   (Quebec) | T2—714 26 |
| Vault (Gymnastic equipment) | 796.442 |
| Vaults | 721.43 |
|   architecture | 721.43 |
|   construction | 690.143 |
| Vaupés (Colombia) | T2—861 65 |
| Vázquez, Tabaré | |
|   Uruguayan history | 989.506 75 |
| VdU (Austrian political party) | 324.243 603 |
| Veal | 641.362 |
|   commercial processing | 664.92 |
|   cooking | 641.662 |
|   food | 641.362 |
| Vector algebra | 512.5 |
| Vector analysis | 515.63 |
| Vector bundles | 514.224 |
| Vector calculus | 515.63 |
| Vector geometry | 516.182 |
| Vector processing | 004.35 |
|   *see also* Processing modes — | |
|     computer science | |
| Vector processors | 004.35 |
|   engineering | 621.391 |
|   *see also* Processing modes — | |
|     computer science | |
| Vector quantities | |
|   mechanics | 531.112 |
| Vector spaces | 512.52 |
| Vector-valued functions | 515.7 |
| Vectorcardiography | |
|   medicine | 616.120 754 7 |
| Vectors (Disease carriers) | 571.986 |
|   biology | 571.986 |
|   medicine | 614.43 |
| Vedanta (Philosophy) | 181.48 |
| Vedas | 294.592 1 |
| Vedda | T5—914 8 |

Vedic language 491.29
   T6—912 9
Vedic literature 891.29
Vedic period 934.02
Vedic religion 294.509 013
Vega (Dominican Republic :
  Province) T2—729 369 7
Vegan diet
  health 613.262 2
Vegetable arrangements 745.924
Vegetable drugs
  pharmacology 615.321
Vegetable fats 665.3
  food technology 664.3
  industrial technology 665.3
Vegetable fibers
  textiles 677.54
   *see also* Textiles
Vegetable gardening 635
Vegetable glue 668.33
Vegetable juices 641.35
  commercial processing 663.63
  cooking with 641.65
  food 641.35
  home preparation 641.875
Vegetable manures
  agricultural use 631.87
Vegetable oils 665.3
  cooking 641.638 5
  food 641.338 5
  food technology 664.3
  industrial technology 665.3
Vegetable poisons
  human toxicology 615.952
Vegetable waxes 665.12
Vegetables 641.35
  commercial preservation 664.8
  commercial processing 664.8
  cooking 641.65
  food 641.35
  garden crop 635
  home preservation 641.4
Vegetarian cooking 641.563 6
Vegetarian diet
  health 613.262
Vegetarian foods 641.303
Vegetarianism
  dietary regimen 613.262
  ethics 179.3
   religion 205.693
    Buddhism 294.356 93
    Christianity 241.693
    Hinduism 294.548 693

Vegetation and climate
  influence on precipitation 551.577 5
Vegetation regions T2—15
Vegetative reproduction 571.89
  agriculture 631.53
  plants 575.49
  *see Manual at* 571.8 vs. 573.6,
   575.6
Vegliote dialect T6—57
Vegliote literature 850
Vehicle failures 363.120 1
  air transportation 363.124 16
  *see also* Transportation safety
Vehicles 388.04
  engineering 629.046
  law 343.093
  military engineering 623.74
  military equipment 355.83
  transportation services 388.04
  *see Manual at* 629.046 vs. 388
Vehicular accidents 363.125
  *see also* Transportation safety
Vehicular safety 363.125
  *see also* Transportation safety
Vehicular transportation
  (Automotive) 388.3
  law 343.094
  public administration 354.765
  transportation services 388.3
  urban 388.41
   law 343.098 2
Vei (African people) T5—963 4
Vei language 496.34
  T6—963 4
Veii (Extinct city) T2—375 95
Veinakh languages 499.964 1
  T6—999 641
Veins 573.186
  biology 573.186
  human anatomy 611.14
  human physiology 612.134
  medicine 616.14
  surgery 617.414
  *see also* Cardiovascular system
Veins (Geology) 553.19
  economic geology 553.19
  structural geology 551.88
Vejle amt (Denmark) T2—489 5
Velathri (Italy) T2—375 5
Velloziaceae 584.354
Vellum books 096.2
Velocity (Mechanics) 531.112

Velocity of flow
 air mechanics    533.62
 fluid mechanics    532.053 2
 gas mechanics    533.27
 liquid mechanics    532.57
Velocity of light    535.24
Velocity of sound    534.202
Velocity of stars    523.83
Velocity theory
 monetary economics    332.401
Velour    677.617
 *see also* Textiles
Velvet    677.617
 *see also* Textiles
Velveteen    677.617
 *see also* Textiles
Venango County (Pa.)    T2—748 96
Venda (African people)    T5—963 976
Venda (South Africa)    T2—682 57
Venda language    496.397 6
    T6—963 976
Venda literature    896.397 6
Vendean War, 1793–1800    944.042
Vendée (France)    T2—441 69
Vendettas
 influence on crime    364.256
Vending machines    629.82
Vendor selection
 library acquisitions    025.233
 materials management    658.722
Vendors and purchasers    346.043 63
Veneers    674.833
 architectural decoration    729.6
Venereal diseases
 incidence    614.547
 law    344.043 695 1
 medicine    616.951
 *see also* Communicable
  diseases — humans
Venetia    T2—373
Venetia (Italy : Region)    945.3
    T2—453
Venetiaan, Runaldo Ronald
 Surinamese history    988.303 22
 1991–1996    988.303 22
 2000–    988.303 24
Venetian League (Italian political
 party)    324.245 308 4
Venetian Republic    945.308 3
Venetic language    479.4
    T6—794
Veneto (Italy)    945.3
    T2—453
 ancient    T2—373

Venezia (Italy)    T2—453 11
Venezia (Italy : Province)    T2—453 1
 ancient    T2—373 5
Venezuela    987
    T2—87
Venezuela, Gulf of (Colombia    551.461 365
 and Venezuela)    T2—163 65
Venezuelan literature    860
Venezuelans    T5—688 7
Venial sin    241.31
Venice (Italy)    T2—453 11
 ancient    T2—373 5
Venice (Italy : Province)    T2—453 1
 ancient    T2—373 5
Venice (Republic)    945.3
Venice, Gulf of (Italy)    551.461 385
    T2—163 85
Venison    641.391
 commercial processing    664.92
 cooking    641.691
 food    641.391
Venoms
 human toxicology    615.942
Venous diseases
 medicine    616.14
 *see also* Cardiovascular
  diseases — humans
Venous embolisms
 medicine    616.145
 *see also* Cardiovascular
  diseases — humans
Venous thromboses
 medicine    616.145
 *see also* Cardiovascular
  diseases — humans
Ventersburg (South Africa :
 District)    T2—685 3
Ventersdorp (South Africa :
 District)    T2—682 42
Venterstad (South Africa :
 District)    T2—687 56
Ventilation
 aircraft    629.134 42
 automobile    629.277 2
 buildings    697.92
 household management    644.5
 library buildings    697.978
  plant management    022.8
 mining    622.42
 museums    069.29
 plant management    658.25
 sewers    628.23
 underground construction    624.19
 vehicles    629.040 289

Ventilation engineers | 697.920 92
Ventricle diseases (Heart)
  medicine | 616.12
  *see also* Cardiovascular
    diseases — humans
Ventricles (Heart)
  human anatomy | 611.12
  human physiology | 612.17
  medicine | 616.12
Ventricular fibrillation
  medicine | 616.128
  *see also* Cardiovascular
    diseases — humans
Ventriloquism | 793.89
Ventura County (Calif.) | T2—794 92
Venture capital | 332.041 54
Venus (Planet) | 523.42
  | T2—992 2
  astrology | 133.534
  unmanned flights to | 629.435 42
Venus's flytrap | 583.75
Veps | T5—945 4
Veps language | 494.54
  | T6—945 4
Veps literature | 894.54
Veracruz (Mexico : State) | T2—726 2
Veraguas (Panama :
  Province) | T2—728 722
Verandas | 721.84
Verb phrases | 415.6
  specific languages | T4—56
Verb tables
  applied linguistics | 418
  specific languages | T4—82
Verbal communication | 302.224
  psychology | 153.6
Verband der Unabhängigen
  (Austrian political party) | 324.243 603
Verbania (Italy . Province) | T2—451 65
  ancient | T2—372 245
Verbano-Cusio-Ossola
  (Italy) | T2—451 65
  ancient | T2—372 245
Verbenaceae | 583.96
Verbenas | 635.933 96
  botany | 583.96
  floriculture | 635.933 96
Verbs | 415.6
  specific languages | T4—56
Vercelli (Italy : Province) | T2—451 7
  ancient | T2—372 23

Verd antique marble | 553.55
  economic geology | 553.55
  quarrying | 622.355
Verdicts | 347.075
  criminal law | 345.075
Verdun, Treaty of, 843 | 943.021
Vereeniging (South Africa :
  District) | T2—682 23
Vérendrye Wildlife Reserve
  (Quebec) | T2—714 224
Verification
  musical instruments | 784.192 7
  programming | 005.14
Vermicides | 632.951
  agricultural use | 632.951
  chemical engineering | 668.651
Vermiculite | 553.678
  economic geology | 553.678
  mining | 622.367 8
Vermiform appendix
  human anatomy | 611.345
  human physiology | 612.33
  medicine | 616.34
  surgery | 617.554 5
Vermiform appendix diseases
  medicine | 616.34
  *see also* Digestive system
    diseases — humans
Vermilion County (Ill.) | T2—773 65
Vermilion Parish (La.) | T2—763 51
Vermillion County (Ind.) | T2—772 462
Vermont | 974.3
  | T2—743
Vernon (B.C.) | T2—711 5
Vernon County (Mo.) | T2—778 44
Vernon County (Wis.) | T2—775 73
Vernon Parish (La.) | T2—763 61
Verona (Italy) | T2—453 41
  ancient | T2—373 21
Verona (Italy : Province) | T2—453 4
  ancient | T2—373 2
Verrucae
  medicine | 616.544
  *see also* Skin diseases —
    humans
Versailles (France) | T2— 443 663
Versailles, Treaty of, 1783
  United States history | 973.317
Versailles, Treaty of, 1919
  European history | 940.314 1

| | |
|---|---|
| Verse drama | |
| literature | 808.82 |
| history and criticism | 809.2 |
| specific literatures | T3B—2 |
| individual authors | T3A—2 |
| Versification | 808.1 |
| Version | |
| obstetrical surgery | 618.82 |
| Verte, Île (Quebec) | T2—714 764 |
| Vertebrate viruses | 579.2 |
| Vertebrates | 596 |
| agricultural pests | 632.66 |
| conservation technology | 639.9 |
| paleozoology | 566 |
| resource economics | 333.954 |
| zoology | 596 |
| Vertical combinations | |
| (Enterprises) | 338.804 2 |
| *see also* Combinations | |
| (Enterprises) | |
| Vertical lift rotors | |
| aircraft | 629.134 36 |
| Vertical-speed indicators | 629.135 2 |
| Vertical takeoff and landing | |
| aircraft | 387.733 5 |
| engineering | 629.133 35 |
| military engineering | 623.746 047 |
| transportation services | 387.733 5 |
| Vertigo | |
| medicine | 616.841 |
| *see also* Nervous system | |
| diseases — humans | |
| Vervains | 635.933 96 |
| botany | 583.96 |
| floriculture | 635.933 96 |
| Verwoerd, Hendrik Frensch | |
| South African history | 968.058 |
| Very-high-frequency radio | |
| systems | 621.384 151 |
| Very large scale integration | 621.395 |
| Very-low-frequency radio | |
| systems | 621.384 153 |
| Vesicles | 571.655 |
| Vespers | 264.15 |
| Anglican | 264.030 15 |
| texts | 264.034 |
| music | 782.324 |
| Vespertilionidae | 599.47 |
| Vespoidea | 595.798 |
| Vessel flutes | 788.38 |
| *see also* Woodwind instruments | |

| | |
|---|---|
| Vessels | |
| music | 786.82 |
| concussed | 786.876 |
| friction | 786.866 |
| set | 786.866 |
| single | 786.888 |
| percussed | 786.846 |
| set | 786.846 |
| single | 786.884 6 |
| *see also* Percussion | |
| instruments | |
| Vessels (Nautical) | 387.2 |
| *see also* Ships | |
| Vest-Agder fylke (Norway) | T2—483 2 |
| Vested rights (Pensions) | 331.252 2 |
| *see also* Pensions | |
| Vesterålen (Norway) | T2—484 4 |
| Vestfold fylke (Norway) | T2—482 7 |
| Vestibular diseases | |
| medicine | 617.882 |
| *see also* Ear diseases — | |
| humans | |
| Vestibular perception | 152.188 2 |
| Vestibules (Ears) | |
| human anatomy | 611.85 |
| human physiology | 612.858 |
| medicine | 617.882 |
| Vestibulocochlear nerve diseases | |
| medicine | 617.886 |
| *see also* Ear diseases — | |
| humans | |
| Vestinian language | 479.7 |
| | T6—797 |
| Vestlandet (Norway) | T2—483 3 |
| Vestments | 391.48 |
| commercial technology | 687.15 |
| customs | 391.48 |
| *see also* Clothing | |
| Vests (Undergarments) | 391.423 |
| *see also* Undergarments | |
| Vests (Waistcoats) | 391.473 |
| commercial technology | 687.113 |
| customs | 391.473 |
| home sewing | 646.433 |
| *see also* Clothing | |
| Vestsjælland (Denmark) | T2—489 1 |
| Veszprém Megye (Hungary) | T2—439 7 |
| Vetches | 633.35 |
| botany | 583.74 |
| forage crop | 633.35 |

| | |
|---|---|
| Veterans | 305.906 97 |
| | T1—086 97 |
| education benefits | 371.223 |
| college and university | 378.32 |
| law | 343.011 3 |
| financial assistance | |
| social welfare | 362.868 2 |
| government programs | 353.538 |
| health services | |
| law | 343.011 5 |
| labor economics | 331.52 |
| law | 343.011 4 |
| law | 343.011 |
| rehabilitation | |
| law | 343.011 5 |
| social group | 305.906 97 |
| social welfare | 362.86 |
| law | 343.011 |
| public administration | 353.538 |
| Veterans' benefits | 362.86 |
| Veterans' homes | 362.160 869 7 |
| architecture | 725.594 |
| Veterans' life insurance | 368.364 |
| Veterans of Foreign Wars of the | |
| United States | 369.11 |
| Veterans' pensions | 331.252 913 55 |
| law | 343.011 2 |
| Veterans' preference | 352.650 869 7 |
| Veterans' rights | 362.86 |
| Veterinarians | 636.089 092 |
| law | 344.049 |
| Veterinary epidemiology | 636.089 44 |
| Veterinary hospitals | 636.083 21 |
| architecture | 725.592 |
| Veterinary hygiene | 636.089 3 |
| Veterinary law | 344.049 |
| Veterinary medicine | 636.089 |
| Veterinary public health | 636.083 2 |
| law | 344.049 |
| Veterinary sciences | 636.089 |
| Veterinary services | |
| armed forces | 355.345 |
| Veveyse (Switzerland) | T2—494 531 |
| VFW (Veterans' organization) | 369.11 |
| VHF radio systems | 621.384 151 |
| Viana do Castelo (Portugal : | |
| District) | T2—469 11 |
| Viaticum | 265.7 |
| Viborg amt (Denmark) | T2—489 5 |
| Vibraphones | 786.843 |
| *see also* Percussion instruments | |
| Vibration perception | |
| psychology | 152.182 3 |
| Vibration prospecting | 622.159 2 |
| Vibration weapons | 623.447 |
| Vibrational spectra (Molecules) | 539.6 |
| Vibrations | 620.3 |
| aeronautics | 629.132 362 |
| biophysics | 571.443 |
| humans | 612.014 45 |
| effect on materials | 620.112 48 |
| engineering | 620.3 |
| fluid mechanics | 532.05 |
| machinery | 621.811 |
| solid-state physics | 530.416 |
| solids | 531.32 |
| Vibrato | 781.43 |
| instrumental technique | 784.193 68 |
| Viburnums | 635.933 92 |
| botany | 583.92 |
| floriculture | 635.933 92 |
| Vice-presidents | 352.239 |
| democratic systems | 321.804 2 |
| public administration | 352.239 |
| Vicenary system (Numeration) | 513.5 |
| Vicenza (Italy) | T2—453 51 |
| ancient | T2—373 62 |
| Vicenza (Italy : Province) | T2—453 5 |
| ancient | T2—373 62 |
| Viceroys | 352.23 |
| Vices | 179.8 |
| arts | T3C—353 |
| literature | 808.803 53 |
| history and criticism | 809.933 53 |
| specific literatures | T3B—080 353 |
| history and | |
| criticism | T3B—093 53 |
| religion | 205.698 |
| Buddhism | 294.356 98 |
| Christianity | 241.3 |
| Hinduism | 294.548 |
| Islam | 297.5 |
| Judaism | 296.369 8 |
| Vichada (Colombia) | T2—861 92 |
| Vicksburg, Siege of, 1863 | 973.734 4 |
| Victimology | 362.88 |
| Victims of abuse | |
| social welfare | 362.885 |
| Victims of crime | 362.88 |
| | T1—086 949 |
| insurance | 368.82 |
| law | 344.028 |
| school programs | 371.782 |
| social welfare | 362.88 |
| law | 344.032 88 |
| public administration | 353.533 7 |

Victims of oppression
  social welfare — 362.87
    public administration — 353.533 8
Victims of war — 305.906 95
  *see also* War victims
Victor Amadeus II, King of
  Sardinia
  Piedmontese history — 945.107
  Sardinian history — 945.907
Victor Amadeus III, Duke of
  Savoy
  Piedmontese history — 945.107
  Sardinian history — 945.907
Victor Emmanuel I, King of
  Sardinia
  Piedmontese history — 945.108 2
    1796–1815 — 945.108 2
    1815–1861 — 945.108 3
Victor Emmanuel II, King of
  Italy
  Italian history — 945.084
  Lombardian history — 945.208 4
  Piedmontese history — 945.108 4
  Sardinian history — 945.908 4
  Sicilian history — 945.808 4
  Southern Italian history — 945.708 4
  Tuscan history — 945.508 4
  Venetian history — 945.308 4
Victor Emmanuel III, King of
  Italy
  Italian history — 945.091
  Lombardian history — 945.209 1
  Piedmontese history — 945.109 1
  Sardinian history — 945.909 1
  Sicilian history — 945.809 1
  Southern Italian history — 945.709 1
  Tuscan history — 945.509 1
  Venetian history — 945.309 1
Victor Harbour (S. Aust.) — T2—942 32
Victoria — T2—945
Victoria (B.C.) — T2—711 28
Victoria (N.B. : County) — T2—715 53
Victoria (N.S. : County) — T2—716 93
Victoria (Ont. : County) — T2—713 64
Victoria (Seychelles) — T2—696
Victoria, Lake — T2—678 27
Victoria, Queen of Great Britain
  British history — 941.081
  English history — 942.081
  Scottish history — 941.108 1
Victoria County (Tex.) — T2—764 125
Victoria East (South Africa :
  District) — T2—687 55
Victoria Falls — T2—689 1

Victoria Island (Nunavut
  and N.W.T.) — T2—719 55
Victoria swine — 636.484
Victoria West (South
  Africa : District) — T2—687 17
Victorian architecture — 724.5
Victualing
  aircraft — 387.736 4
  boats — 387.168
  buses — 388.33
  ships — 387.168
  trains — 385.26
  transportation services — 388.041
Vicuña — 599.636 7
  animal husbandry — 636.296
Vicuña wool textiles — 677.32
  *see also* Textiles
Video animation — 777.7
Video art — 777
  computer art — 776.6
Video cassettes — 384.558
  *see also* Video recordings
Video discs
  computer storage — 004.565
    engineering — 621.397 67
  recordings — 384.558
    *see also* Video recordings
Video display components — 621.381 542 2
Video display screens
  computer science — 004.77
  engineering — 621.398 7
Video games — 794.8
Video mini-series — 791.45
  *see Manual at* 791.43 vs.
    791.45
Video photography — 777
Video production — 384.558
  communications services — 384.558
  videography — 777
Video recorders — 384.558
  communications services — 384.558
  engineering — 621.388 33
  videography — 777.36
  *see also* Television
Video recording — 777
Video recordings — 384.558
  bibliographies — 011.373
  cataloging — 025.347 3
  communications services — 384.558
  engineering — 621.388 332
  instructional use — 371.335 23
    adult level — 374.26
  library treatment — 025.177 3

Video recordings (continued)
 music   780
  treatises   780.267
  *see Manual at* 780.26
 performing arts   791.43
 videography   777.38
 *see also* Television
Video records   384.558
 *see also* Video recordings
Video tapes   384.558
 *see also* Video recordings
Videocassettes   384.558
 *see also* Video recordings
Videoconferencing
 instructional use   371.335 8
Videodiscs
 computer storage   004.565
  engineering   621.397 67
 recordings   384.558
 *see also* Video recordings
Videography   777
 *see Manual at* 791.43, 791.45
  vs. 777
Videorecordings   384.558
 *see also* Video recordings
Videorecords   384.558
 *see also* Video recordings
Videotapes   384.558
 *see also* Video recordings
Videotex   004.69
 communications services   384.35
 *see also* Computer
  communications
Vieira, João Bernardo
 Guinean (Guinea-Bissau)
  history   966.570 32
   1980–1999   966.570 32
   2005–2009   966.570 34
Vielles   787.69
 instrument   787.691 9
 music   787.69
 *see also* Stringed instruments
Vienna (Austria)   T2—436 13
Vienne (France : Dept.)   T2—446 3
Vieques Island (P.R.)   T2—729 59
Vierwaldstätter See
 (Switzerland)   T2—494 557
Việt-Cộng (Vietnamese history)   959.704 332 2
Viet-Muong languages   495.92
   T6—959 2
Viet-Muong literatures   895.92
Viet-Muong peoples   T5—959 2
Vietcong (Vietnamese history)   959.704 332 2

Vietnam   959.7
   T2—597
Vietnamese   T5—959 22
Vietnamese communism   335.434 6
Vietnamese language   495.922
   T6—959 22
Vietnamese literature   895.922
Vietnamese War, 1961–1975   959.704 3
 North Vietnam   959.704 331
 societies   369.2
  United States   369.186
 South Vietnam   959.704 332
Viewdata   004.69
 *see also* Computer
  communications
Viewer access
 communications services   384.555 3
Viewfinders   771.37
Vige language   496.35
   T6—963 5
Vigesimal system (Numeration)   513.5
Vigo County (Ind.)   T2—772 45
Vihuelas   787.86
 instrument   787.861 9
 music   787.86
 *see also* Stringed instruments
Vijnana Buddhism   294.392
Viking Mars Program   629.435 43
Viking period   948.022
 Danish history   948.901 4
 Norwegian history   948.101 4
 Swedish history   948.501 4
Vikings   T5—395
Vila Real (Portugal :
 District)   T2—469 23
Vilas County (Wis.)   T2—775 23
Vîlcea (Romania)   T2—498 2
Viljoenskroon (South
 Africa : District)   T2—685 2
Villa Clara (Cuba :
 Province)   T2—729 142
Villages   307.762
   T2—173 2
 area planning   711.43
 government   320.8
  cities   320.85
 *see Manual at* T2—4–9
Villancicos   782.43
 carols   782.281 723
Villas
 architecture   728.8
Vinayapiṭaka   294.382 2
Vincentians   255.77
 church history   271.77

| | | | |
|---|---|---|---|
| Vindelicia | T2—363 3 | Violence (continued) | |
| Vinegar | | public safety | 363.32 |
| commercial processing | 664.55 | social conflict | 303.6 |
| cooking with | 641.62 | Violence in schools | 371.782 |
| Vinegar flies | 595.774 | Violence in the workplace | |
| Vines | 582.18 | prevention | |
| floriculture | 635.974 | management | 658.473 |
| landscape architecture | 715.4 | Violent behavior | |
| *see Manual at* 635.9 vs. 582.1 | | medicine | 616.858 2 |
| Vĩnh Long (Vietnam : | | Violent crimes | 364.15 |
| Province) | T2—597 8 | prevention | 364.4 |
| Vĩnh Phúc (Vietnam : | | self-defense | 613.66 |
| Province) | T2—597 2 | *see also* Crime | |
| Vinnytsa (Ukraine : Oblast) | T2—477 8 | Violets | 583.625 |
| Vinnyts´ka oblast´ | | floriculture | 635.933 625 |
| (Ukraine) | T2—477 8 | Violin concertos | 784.272 |
| Vinton County (Ohio) | T2—771 837 | Violin family | 787.2 |
| Vinylidene chlorides | 668.423 7 | *see also* Stringed instruments | |
| Vinyls | 668.423 6 | Violin makers | 787.219 092 |
| textiles | 677.474 4 | Violinists | 787.209 2 |
| *see also* Textiles | | Violins | 787.2 |
| Vinyons | | instrument | 787.219 |
| textiles | 677.474 4 | music | 787.2 |
| *see also* Textiles | | *see also* Stringed instruments | |
| Viola concertos | 784.273 | Violoncellists | 787.409 2 |
| Viola da gambas | 787.65 | Violoncellos | 787.4 |
| instrument | 787.651 9 | instrument | 787.419 |
| music | 787.65 | music | 787.4 |
| *see also* Stringed instruments | | *see also* Stringed instruments | |
| Viola d'amores | 787.66 | Viols | 787.6 |
| instrument | 787.661 9 | instrument | 787.619 |
| music | 787.66 | music | 787.6 |
| *see also* Stringed instruments | | *see also* Stringed instruments | |
| Violales | 583.625 | Vipera | 597.963 6 |
| Violas | 787.3 | Viperfishes | 597.5 |
| instrument | 787.319 | Viperidae | 597.963 |
| music | 787.3 | Vipers | 597.963 |
| *see also* Stringed instruments | | Viral diseases | 571.992 |
| Violence | 303.6 | *see also* Virus diseases | |
| arts | 700.455 2 | Viral hepatitis | |
| | T3C—355 2 | medicine | 616.362 3 |
| ethics | 179.7 | *see also* Digestive system | |
| religion | 205.697 | diseases — humans | |
| Buddhism | 294.356 97 | Viral skin diseases | |
| Christianity | 241.697 | medicine | 616.522 |
| Hinduism | 294.548 697 | *see also* Skin diseases — | |
| Islam | 297.569 7 | humans | |
| Judaism | 296.369 7 | Vireolaniidae | 598.878 |
| literature | 808.803 552 | Vireonidae | 598.878 |
| history and criticism | 809.933 552 | Vireos | 598.878 |
| specific literatures | T3B—080 355 2 | conservation technology | 639.978 878 |
| history and | | resource economics | 333.958 878 |
| criticism | T3B—093 552 | Virgin birth of Jesus Christ | 232.921 |
| | | Virgin Gorda (V.I.) | T2—729 725 |

Virgin Islanders    T5—969 729 72
Virgin Islands    972.972
   T2—729 72
Virgin Islands, British    T2—729 725
Virgin Islands National Park
   (Saint John, V.I.)    T2—729 722
Virgin Islands of the United
   States    T2—729 722
Virginals    786.4
   instrument    786.419
   music    786.4
   *see also* Keyboard instruments
Virginia    975.5
   T2—755
Virginia (South Africa :
   District)    T2—685 3
Virginia Beach (Va.)    T2—755 51
Virginia City (Nev.)    T2—793 56
Virginia cowslip    635.933 94
   botany    583.94
   floriculture    635.933 94
Virginia creeper    583.86
Virginia deer    599.652
   conservation technology    639.979 652
   resource economics    333.959 652
Virginia reels    793.34
Virginia willow    583.72
Virginity of Mary    232.913
Virgo (Zodiac)    133.526 7
Viroids    579.29
Virologists    579.209 2
Virology    579.2
   medicine    616.910 1
Virtual memory    005.435
   computer hardware    004.5
   programs    005.435
Virtual private networks    004.678
Virtual reality    006.8
   computer art    776
Virtual reference services
   (Libraries)    025.52
Virtue    179.9
Virtues    179.9
   arts    700.453
   T3C—353
   literature    808.803 53
    history and criticism    809.933 53
    specific literatures    T3B—080 353
     history and
      criticism    T3B—093 53
   religion    205.699
    Buddhism    294.356 99
    Christianity    241.4
    Hinduism    294.548

Virtues
   religion (continued)
    Islam    297.5
    Judaism    296.369 9
Virus diseases    571.992
   agriculture    632.8
   animals    571.992 11
    veterinary medicine    636.089 691
   biology    571.992
   humans    362.196 91
    incidence    614.58
    medicine    616.91
    social services    362.196 91
   plants    571.992 12
    agriculture    632.8
   *see also* Communicable
    diseases
Viruses (Computer security)    005.84
Viruses (Microorganisms)    579.2
   medical microbiology    616.910 1
   *see Manual at* 579.24–.25
Visas    323.67
   law    342.082
   political science    323.67
   public administration    353.13
Visayan Islands
   (Philippines)    T2—599 5
Viscaceae    583.88
Visceral leishmaniasis
   incidence    614.534
   medicine    616.936 4
   *see also* Communicable
    diseases — humans
Visceral perception
   psychology    152.188 6
Visconti, House of
   Lombardian history    945.205
Viscose rayon    677 463
   *see also* Textiles
Viscosity    531.113 4
   fluid mechanics    532.053 3
   gas mechanics    533.28
   liquid mechanics    532.58
   solid mechanics    531.4
Viscous flow    532.053 3
   gas mechanics    533.28
   liquid mechanics    532.58
Vises    621.992
Viseu (Portugal : District)    T2—469 31
Vishnuism    294.551 2
Visibility
   aeronautics    629.132 4
   meteorology    551.568

| | |
|---|---|
| Visible light | 535 |
| *see also* Light | |
| Visible light spectroscopes | |
| manufacturing technology | 681.414 3 |
| Visigothic domination | |
| Spanish history | 946.01 |
| Vision | 573.88 |
| artificial intelligence | 006.37 |
| arts | 701.8 |
| epistemology | 121.35 |
| human physiology | 612.84 |
| psychology | 152.14 |
| *see also* Eyes | |
| Visions | |
| religious experience | 204.2 |
| Christianity | 248.29 |
| Viśiṣṭādvaita (Philosophy) | 181.483 |
| Visitation rights (Domestic law) | 346.017 3 |
| Visitation Sisters | 255.975 |
| church history | 271.975 |
| Visiting housekeepers | |
| social welfare | 362.828 3 |
| Visiting nurses | 610.734 3 |
| medicine | 610.734 3 |
| social welfare | 362.14 |
| *see also* Health services | |
| Visp (Switzerland : Bezirk) | T2—494 794 6 |
| Visual arts | 700 |
| Visual-auditory memory | 153.134 |
| Visual binaries | 523.841 |
| Visual display units | |
| computer science | 004.77 |
| engineering | 621.398 7 |
| Visual effects | |
| dramatic performances | 792.024 |
| *see also* Special effects — | |
| dramatic performances | |
| Visual memory | 153.132 |
| Visual novels | 741.5 |
| Visual perception | |
| psychology | 152.14 |
| Visual programming | 005.118 |
| Visual signaling | |
| communications services | 384 |
| military engineering | 623.731 |
| nautical engineering | 623.856 1 |
| Visualization (Psychology) | 153.32 |
| Visually-impaired people | 305.908 1 |
| | T1—087 1 |
| education | 371.911 |
| library services | 027.663 |
| social welfare | 362.41 |
| Vitaceae | 583.86 |
| Vitalism | 147 |

| | |
|---|---|
| Vitamin D treatment | |
| milk processing | 637.141 |
| Vitamin therapy | 615.328 |
| Vitamins | 572.58 |
| applied nutrition | 613.286 |
| animal husbandry | 636.085 28 |
| biochemistry | 572.58 |
| humans | 612.399 |
| chemistry | 547.7 |
| metabolism | |
| human physiology | 612.399 |
| pharmacology | 615.328 |
| Vitebsk (Belarus : Voblasts) | T2—478 4 |
| Vitebskaĩa voblasts' | |
| (Belarus) | T2—478 4 |
| Viterbo (Italy) | T2—456 251 |
| ancient | T2—375 8 |
| Viterbo (Italy : Province) | T2—456 25 |
| ancient | T2—375 8 |
| Viticulture | 634.8 |
| Vitiligo | |
| medicine | 616.55 |
| *see also* Skin diseases — | |
| humans | |
| Vitoria (Spain) | T2—466 5 |
| Vitreous bodies | |
| human anatomy | 611.84 |
| human physiology | 612.844 |
| ophthalmology | 617.746 |
| Vitreous body diseases | |
| ophthalmology | 617.746 |
| *see also* Eye diseases — | |
| humans | |
| Viverridae | 599.742 |
| Vivisection | |
| ethics | 179.4 |
| *see also* Animals — | |
| treatment of — ethics | |
| Vizcaya (Spain) | T2—466 3 |
| Vizsla | 636.752 |
| Vlaams-Brabant (Belgium) | T2—493 31 |
| Vladimir (Russia : Oblast) | T2—473 3 |
| Vladimirskaĩa oblast' | |
| (Russia) | T2—473 3 |
| VLF radio systems | 621.384 153 |
| VLSI (Computer circuits) | 621.395 |
| VMM insurance | 368.12 |

| | |
|---|---|
| Vocabulary | 401.4 |
| dictionaries | 413 |
| specific languages | T4—014 |
| dictionaries | T4—3 |
| usage (Applied | |
| linguistics) | T4—81 |
| *see Manual at* T4—3 vs. | |
| T4—81 | |
| usage (Applied linguistics) | 418 |
| Vocabulary development | |
| primary education | 372.44 |
| Vocal communication | |
| animals | 596.159 4 |
| physiology | 573.92 |
| Vocal cord diseases | |
| medicine | 616.22 |
| *see also* Respiratory tract | |
| diseases — humans | |
| Vocal cords | 573.925 |
| biology | 573.925 |
| medicine | 616.22 |
| surgery | 617.533 |
| *see also* Respiratory system | |
| Vocal duets | 783.12 |
| Vocal expression | |
| psychology | 152.384 2 |
| Vocal forms | 782 |
| Vocal music | 782 |
| diction | 783.043 |
| *see Manual at* 782 | |
| Vocal quartets | 783.14 |
| Vocal trios | 783.13 |
| Vocalises | 782.4 |
| Vocalists | 782.009 2 |
| Vocalization | |
| animals | 596.159 4 |
| physiology | 573.92 |
| Vocation (Career) | 331.7 |
| *see also* Occupations, | |
| Vocational guidance | |
| Vocation (Religious calling) | 253.2 |
| ecclesiology | 262.1 |
| guides to life | 248.892 |
| monastic and religious orders | 255 |
| men | 255 |
| guides to life | 248.894 22 |
| women | 255.9 |
| guides to life | 248.894 32 |
| Vocational counseling | 331.702 |
| *see also* Vocational guidance | |
| Vocational education | 370.113 |
| | T1—071 |
| adult level | 374.013 |

| | |
|---|---|
| Vocational education (continued) | |
| on the job | 331.259 2 |
| personnel management | 658.312 4 |
| | T1—068 3 |
| executives | 658.407 124 |
| public administration | 352.669 |
| secondary level | 373.246 |
| Vocational guidance | 331.702 |
| | T1—023 |
| economics | 331.702 |
| education | 371.425 |
| personnel management | 658.385 |
| psychology | 158.6 |
| Vocational interest tests | 153.94 |
| Vocational interests | |
| applied psychology | 158.6 |
| Vocational qualifications | 331.114 |
| *see also* Qualifications of | |
| employees | |
| Vocational rehabilitation | 362.042 5 |
| *see also* Employment | |
| services — social services | |
| Vocational schools | 370.113 |
| *see also* Vocational education | |
| Vocational training | 370.113 |
| | T1—071 5 |
| *see also* Vocational education | |
| Vochysiaceae | 583.82 |
| Vodka | 641.25 |
| commercial processing | 663.5 |
| Vogul | T5—945 1 |
| Vogul language | 494.51 |
| | T6—945 1 |
| Vogul literature | 894.51 |
| Voice | |
| human physiology | 612.78 |
| music | 783 |
| *see Manual at* 782 | |
| preaching | 251.03 |
| rhetoric of speech | 808.5 |
| Voice (Grammar) | 415.6 |
| specific languages | T4—56 |
| Voice disguisers (Musical | |
| instruments) | 783.99 |
| Voice disorders | |
| medicine | 616.855 6 |
| *see also* Communication | |
| disorders | |
| Voice input devices | 006.454 |
| computer engineering | 621.399 4 |
| Voice instruments | 783.99 |
| Voice mail systems | |
| office services | 651.73 |

| | |
|---|---|
| Voice output devices | 006.54 |
| computer engineering | 621.399 |
| Voice prints | |
| criminal investigation | 363.258 |
| Voice synthesis | 006.54 |
| computer engineering | 621.399 |
| Voiōtia (Greece) | T2—495 15 |
| Voivodina (Serbia) | T2—497 1 |
| Volatiles (Volcanic gases) | 551.23 |
| Volcanic ash | 552.23 |
| Volcanic gases | 551.23 |
| Volcanic rocks | 552.2 |
| Volcanoes | 551.21 |
| disaster services | 363.349 5 |
| *see also* Disasters | |
| Voles | 599.354 |
| Volga languages, Middle | 494.56 |
| | T6—945 6 |
| Volga literatures, Middle | 894.56 |
| Volga River (Russia) | T2—474 |
| Volgograd (Russia : Oblast) | T2—474 7 |
| Volgogradskaīa oblast′ | |
| (Russia) | T2—474 7 |
| Volition | 153.8 |
| Volksrust (South Africa : | |
| District) | T2—682 79 |
| Volleyball | 796.325 |
| Volleyball cards | 796.325 075 |
| Volleyball courts | 796.325 068 |
| Volleyball players | 796.325 092 |
| Vologda (Russia : Oblast) | T2—471 9 |
| Vologodskaīa oblast′ | |
| (Russia) | T2—471 9 |
| Volscian language | 479.7 |
| | T6—797 |
| Volsinii (Terni, Italy) | T2—375 76 |
| Volsinii (Viterbo, Italy : | |
| Extinct city) | T2—375 83 |
| Volsinii Novi (Extinct city) | T2—375 83 |
| Volsinii Veteres (Italy) | T2—375 76 |
| Volt-ammeters | 621.374 6 |
| Volta-Comoe languages | 496.338 |
| | T6—963 38 |
| Volta River (Ghana) | T2—667 |
| Voltage detectors | 621.374 3 |
| Voltaic languages | 496.35 |
| | T6—963 5 |
| Voltaic literatures | 896.35 |
| Voltameters | 621.374 4 |
| Voltans | T5—966 25 |
| Volterra (Italy) | |
| ancıent | T2—375 5 |
| Volterra equations | 515.45 |
| Voltmeters | 621.374 3 |

| | |
|---|---|
| Volume (Sound) | |
| musical element | 781.233 |
| perception | |
| psychology | 152.154 |
| Volumetric analysis | 543.24 |
| Voluntaries (Music) | 784.189 3 |
| Voluntarism | 361.37 |
| philosophy | 141 |
| public administrative support | 352.78 |
| social psychology | 302.14 |
| Voluntary association | 302.3 |
| Voluntary enlistment (Military) | 355.223 62 |
| Voluntary movement | 573.7 |
| psychology | 152.35 |
| Voluntary muscle tissues | 573.753 5 |
| human histology | 612.740 45 |
| *see also* Musculoskeletal | |
| system | |
| Voluntary retail chains | 381.12 |
| management | 658.870 2 |
| *see also* Commerce | |
| Voluntary service groups | |
| international assistance | 361.26 |
| public administrative support | 352.78 |
| Voluntary sterilization | 363.97 |
| *see also* Sterilization (Birth | |
| control) | |
| Volunteer social work | 361.37 |
| Volunteer teacher aides | 371.141 24 |
| Volusia County (Fla.) | T2—759 21 |
| Volvocales | 579.832 |
| Volyn (Ukraine : Oblast) | T2—477 9 |
| Volyns′ka oblast′ (Ukraine) | T2—477 9 |
| Vombatidae | 599.24 |
| Von Mises, Ludwig | |
| economic school | 330.157 |
| Von Neumann algebras | 512.556 |
| Von Willebrand disease | |
| medicine | 616.157 |
| *see also* Cardiovascular | |
| diseases — humans | |
| Voodoo | 299.675 |
| Voodooism | 299.675 |
| Vorarlberg (Austria) | T2—436 45 |
| Voreio Aigaio (Greece) | T2—495 82 |
| Voronezh (Russia : Oblast) | T2—473 5 |
| Voronezhskaīa oblast′ | |
| (Russia) | T2—473 5 |
| Vorpommern (Germany) | T2—431 78 |
| Vorster, B. J. (Balthazar | |
| Johannes) | |
| South African history | 968.062 |

Vortex motion                        532.059 5
  fluid mechanics                    532.059 5
  gas mechanics                      533.295
  liquid mechanics                   532.595
Vosges (France)                      T2—443 89
Vostok (Manned satellite)            629.454
Vote counting                        324.65
Voter registration                   324.64
  law                                342.075
Votic language                       494.54
                                     T6—945 4
Voting behavior                      324.9
Voting machines                      324.65
  manufacturing technology           681.14
Voting offenses                      364.132 4
  law                                345.023 24
Voting procedures                    324.65
  law                                342.075
Voting qualifications                324.62
  law                                342.072
Voting rights                        324.62
  law                                342.072
Votive offerings                     203.7
  Christianity                       246.55
  fine arts                          704.948
    Christianity                     704.948 2
  *see also* Symbolism —
    religious significance
Votyak                               T5—945 3
Votyak language                      494.53
                                     T6—945 3
Votyak literature                    894.53
Voucher system (Education)           379.111
Vowels                               414
  applied linguistics
    specific languages               T4—813
  specific languages                 T4—15
Voyageurs National Park
  (Minn.)                            T2—776 77
VPNs                                 004.678
Vrancea (Romania)                    T2—498 1
Vrede (South Africa :
  District)                          T2—685 1
Vredefort (South Africa :
  District)                          T2—685 2
Vredenburg (South Africa :
  District)                          T2—687 32
Vredendal (South Africa :
  District)                          T2—687 31
Vryburg (South Africa :
  District)                          T2—682 46
Vryheid (South Africa :
  District)                          T2—684 2

VTOL aircraft                        387.733 5
  engineering                        629.133 35
  military engineering               623.746 047
  transportation services            387.733 5
Vulcanization                        678.24
  latex                              678.524
  rubber                             678.24
Vulcanized papers                    676.284 5
Vulcanized rubber                    678.34
Vulci (Extinct city)                 T2—375 82
Vulgar Latin language                477
                                     T6—71
Vulgate Bible                        220.47
Vulpes                               599.775
Vultures                             598.92
Vultures (New World)                 598.92
Vultures (Old World)                 598.94
Vulva
  gynecology                         618.16
  human anatomy                      611.67
  human physiology                   612.628
Vulvar diseases
  gynecology                         618.16
  *see also* Female genital
    diseases — humans
Vuwani (South Africa :
  District)                          T2—682 57
Východočeský kraj (Czech
  Republic)                          T2—437 18
Východoslovenský kraj
  (Slovakia)                         T2—437 35
Vysočina kraj (Czech
  Republic)                          T2—437 22

# W

W*-algebras                          512.556
Waadt (Switzerland)                  T2—494 52
Waadtländer Nordjura
  (Switzerland)                      T2—494 522 5
Wabash County (Ill.)                 T2—773 78
Wabash County (Ind.)                 T2—772 83
Wabash River (Ind.)                  T2—772 4
Wabasha County (Minn.)               T2—776 13
Wabaunsee County (Kan.)              T2—781 61
Wade, Abdoulaye
  Senegalese history                 966.305 2
Wadena County (Minn.)                T2—776 87
Wādī al-Jadīd (Egypt)                T2—622
Wading birds                         598.3
Wafers (Electronics)                 621.381 52
Waffle mixes                         664.753
Waffles                              641.815 3
Wage differentials                   331.22

| | |
|---|---|
| Wage discrimination | 331.215 3 |
| Wage payment systems | 331.216 |
| Wage policy | 331.21 |
| Wage-price policy | 339.5 |
| inflation control | 332.415 |
| Wage scales | 331.216 |
| personnel management | 658.322 2 |
| Wages | 331.21 |
| accounting | 657.742 |
| economics | 331.21 |
| law | 344.012 1 |
| public employees | 342.068 6 |
| personnel management | 658.32 |
| | T1—068 3 |
| armed forces | 355.64 |
| executives | 658.407 2 |
| public administration | 352.67 |
| public administration | 354.98 |
| taxation | 336.242 2 |
| law | 343.052 42 |
| public administration | 352.44 |
| public finance | 336.242 2 |
| Wages fund theory | 331.210 1 |
| Wagga Wagga (N.S.W.) | T2—944 8 |
| Wagner tubas | 788.98 |
| *see also* Brass instruments | |
| Wagoner County (Okla.) | T2—766 87 |
| Wagons | 388.341 |
| agricultural use | 631.373 |
| manufacturing technology | 688.6 |
| Wagtails | 598.854 |
| Waḥdah (Sudan) | T2—629 3 |
| Wahhābīyah (Islamic sect) | 297.814 |
| Wahid, Abdurrahman | |
| Indonesian history | 959.804 1 |
| Wahkiakum County (Wash.) | T2—797 91 |
| Waiheke Island (N.Z.) | T2—932 4 |
| Waikato District (N.Z.) | T2—933 3 |
| Waikato Region (N.Z.) | T2—933 |
| Waimakariri District (N.Z.) | T2—938 2 |
| Waimate District (N.Z.) | T2—938 93 |
| Waipa District (N.Z.) | T2—933 57 |
| Wairarapa (N.Z.) | T2—936 6 |
| Wairoa District (N.Z.) | T2—934 62 |
| Waistcoats | 391.473 |
| *see also* Vests (Waistcoats) | |
| Waitakere City (N.Z.) | T2—932 3 |
| Waitaki District (N.Z.) | T2—939 1 |
| Canterbury Region | T2—938 97 |
| Otago Region | T2—939 1 |
| Waiters and waitresses | 642.6 |
| Waiting on tables | 642.6 |
| Waitomo District (N.Z.) | T2—933 8 |
| Manawatu-Wanganui | |
| Region | T2—935 17 |
| Waikato Region | T2—933 8 |
| Wakashan Indians | T5—979 5 |
| Wakashan languages | 497.95 |
| | T6—979 5 |
| Wakatipu, Lake (N.Z.) | T2—939 5 |
| Wakayama-ken (Japan) | T2—521 82 |
| Wake County (N.C.) | T2—756 55 |
| Wake Island | T2—965 |
| Wakeboarding | 797.3 |
| Wakefield (England : City) | T2—428 15 |
| Wakes | 393.9 |
| Christian rites | 265.85 |
| music | 781.588 |
| Wakkerstroom (South | |
| Africa : District) | T2—682 79 |
| Wakool River (N.S.W.) | T2—944 8 |
| Wakulla County (Fla.) | T2—759 89 |
| Walachia | T2—498 2 |
| Walaga (Ethiopia) | T2—633 |
| Walapai language | 497.572 4 |
| | T6—975 724 |
| Walbiri | T5—991 5 |
| Walbiri language | 499.15 |
| | T6—991 5 |
| Wałbrzych (Poland : | |
| Voivodeship) | T2—438 52 |
| Waldenburg (Switzerland : | |
| Bezirk) | T2—494 337 |
| Waldenses | |
| biography | 284.4 |
| Waldensian churches | 284.4 |
| Waldensianism | 273.6 |
| denomination | 284.4 |
| persecution of | 272.3 |
| Waldo County (Me.) | T2—741 52 |
| Waldorf method | 371.391 |
| Walensee (Switzerland) | T2—494 727 |
| Wales | 942.9 |
| | T2—429 |
| ancient | 936.29 |
| | T2—362 9 |
| *see Manual at* 941 | |
| Wales, North | T2—429 1 |
| Wales, South | T2—429 4 |
| Wales Island (Nunavut) | T2—719 52 |
| Wałęsa, Lech | |
| Polish history | 943.805 71 |
| Walgett (N.S.W.) | T2—944 9 |
| Walker County (Ala.) | T2—761 76 |
| Walker County (Ga.) | T2—758 33 |
| Walker County (Tex.) | T2—764 169 |

Walkie-talkies 621.384 5
Walking
  animal physiology 573.79
  human physiology 612.044
  physical fitness 613.717 6
  sports 796.51
    equipment technology 688.765 1
    *see Manual at* 913–919 vs.
      796.51
Walkingsticks (Insects) 595.729
Wall coverings
  household management 645.2
Walla Walla County
  (Wash.) T2—797 48
Wallabies 599.22
Wallace County (Kan.) T2—781 123
Wallachia T2—498 2
Wallachia (Principality) 949.801 4
  T2—498 2
Wallaroos 599.222
Wallboards
  pulp 676.183
Wallenpaupack, Lake (Pa.) T2—748 23
Waller County (Tex.) T2—764 249
Walleye 597.758
  conservation technology 639.977 758
  resource economics 333.956 758
  sports fishing 799.177 58
Walleyed pike 597.758
Wallflowers (Plants) 583.64
Wallis (Switzerland) T2—494 79
Wallis and Futuna Islands 996.16
  T2—961 6
Wallo (Ethiopia) T2—634
Wallonia (Belgium) T2—493 4
Walloon Brabant (Belgium) T2—493 37
Walloons T5—42
Wallowa County (Or.) T2—795 73
Wallowa Mountains (Or.) T2—795 73
Wallpaper 676.284 8
  handicrafts 745.54
  household management 645.2
  interior decoration 747.3
Walls (Building element) 721.2
  architecture 721.2
  construction 690.12
  interior decoration 747.3
Walls (Structures)
  agricultural use 631.27
  architecture 725.96
Walnuts 641.345 1
  botany 583.49
  cooking 641.645 1
  food 641.345 1

Walnuts (continued)
  forestry 634.973 49
  nut crops 634.51
Walpiri T5—991 5
Walpiri language 499.15
  T6—991 5
Walras, Léon
  economic school 330.157
Walrus 599.799
Walsall (England :
  Metropolitan Borough) T2—424 92
Walsh County (N.D.) T2—784 18
Walthall County (Miss.) T2—762 22
Waltham Forest (London,
  England) T2—421 72
Walton County (Fla.) T2—759 97
Walton County (Ga.) T2—758 212
Waltzes 793.33
  music 784.188 46
Walvis Bay (Namibia) T2—688 1
Walworth County (S.D.) T2—783 18
Walworth County (Wis.) T2—775 89
Wampanoag Indians T5—973 48
Wampanoag language 497.348
  T6—973 48
Wanaka, Lake (N.Z.) T2—939 5
Wandering Jews 584.86
Wandsworth (London,
  England) T2—421 66
Wanganui District (N.Z.) T2—935 4
Wangaratta (Vic.) T2—945 5
Wanica (Suriname :
  District) T2—883 57
Wannsee-Konferenz (1942 :
  Berlin, Germany) 940.531 844
Wansbeck (England) T2—428 86
Wansdyke (England) T2—423 98
Wapello County (Iowa) T2—777 93
Wapiti 599.654 2
  animal husbandry 636.294 42
  big game hunting 799.276 542
  conservation technology 639.979 654 2
War 355.02
  arts 700.458 1
    T3C—358 1
  effect on natural ecology 577.274
  ethics 172.42
    religion 205.624 2
      Buddhism 294.356 242
      Christianity 241.624 2
      Hinduism 294.548 624 2
      Islam 297.562 42
      Judaism 296.362 42

| | |
|---|---|
| War (continued) | |
| folklore | 398.278 2 |
| history and criticism | 398.358 1 |
| law | 341.6 |
| literature | 808.803 581 |
| history and criticism | 809.933 581 |
| specific literatures | T3B—080 358 1 |
| history and | |
| criticism | T3B—093 581 |
| military science | 355.02 |
| social effects | 303.485 |
| social theology | 201.727 3 |
| Buddhism | 294.337 273 |
| Christianity | 261.873 |
| Hinduism | 294.517 273 |
| Islam | 297.27 |
| Judaism | 296.382 7 |
| sociology | 303.66 |
| *see also* Wars | |
| War and emergency legislation | 343.01 |
| War and emergency powers | |
| administrative law | 342.062 |
| constitutional law | 342.041 2 |
| War crime trials | 341.690 268 |
| War crimes | 364.138 |
| criminal law | 345.023 8 |
| law of nations | 341.69 |
| War customs | 399 |
| War dances | 399 |
| War games | |
| military science | 355.48 |
| recreation | 793.92 |
| War loan interest | 336.182 |
| War memorials | 725.94 |
| War neuroses | |
| medicine | 616.852 12 |
| *see also* Mental disorders | |
| War news | |
| journalism | 070.433 3 |
| War of 1812 | 973.52 |
| War of nerves | 327.14 |
| War powers (Legislative bodies) | 328.346 |
| War relief | 363.349 88 |
| War risk insurance | 368.14 |
| War risk life insurance | 368.364 |
| War victims | 305.906 95 |
| | T1—086 949 |
| law of war | 341.67 |
| social group | 305.906 95 |
| social services | 363.349 8 |
| War with Algiers, 1815 | 973.53 |
| Warab (Sudan) | T2—629 4 |
| Warao Indians | T5—989 |
| Warao language | 498.9 |
| | T6—989 |
| Warao literature | 898.9 |
| Waratahs | 583.89 |
| Warble flies | 595.774 |
| Warblers (Old World) | 598.843 |
| Ward (Law) | 346.018 |
| Ward County (N.D.) | T2—784 63 |
| Ward County (Tex.) | T2—764 914 |
| Ward management | 362.173 068 |
| medicine | 610.733 |
| Wards (Election districts) | 328.334 5 |
| Ware County (Ga.) | T2—758 794 |
| Warehouse clubs | 381.149 |
| management | 658.879 |
| Warehouse management | 658.785 |
| military supplies | 355.621 3 |
| Warehouse receipts | |
| law | 346.096 |
| Warehouses | |
| architecture | 725.35 |
| Warehousing | 388.044 |
| commerce | 381 |
| transportation services | 388.044 |
| *see also* Freight services | |
| Warfare | 355.02 |
| *see also* War | |
| Warlocks (Occultists) | 133.430 92 |
| *see also* Legendary beings | |
| Warm-blooded animals | 599 |
| paleozoology | 569 |
| Warmbad (South Africa : District) | T2—682 51 |
| Warmbaths (South Africa : District) | T2—682 51 |
| Warmińsko-Mazurskie Voivodeship (Poland) | T2—438 32 |
| Warning systems | 363.35 |
| civil defense | 363.35 |
| law | 344.053 5 |
| military engineering | 623.737 |
| public administration | 353.95 |
| Warragul (Vic.) | T2—945 6 |
| Warrant officers | 355.009 2 |
| role and function | 355.332 |
| Warrants (Law) | 345.052 |
| Warranty | 343.08 |
| Warren (N.S.W.) | T2—944 9 |
| Warren County (Ga.) | T2—758 625 |
| Warren County (Ill.) | T2—773 415 |
| Warren County (Ind.) | T2—772 96 |
| Warren County (Iowa) | T2—777 82 |
| Warren County (Ky.) | T2—769 74 |
| Warren County (Miss.) | T2—762 29 |

| | |
|---|---|
| Warren County (Mo.) | T2—778 386 |
| Warren County (N.C.) | T2—756 52 |
| Warren County (N.J.) | T2—749 78 |
| Warren County (N.Y.) | T2—747 51 |
| Warren County (Ohio) | T2—771 763 |
| Warren County (Pa.) | T2—748 67 |
| Warren County (Tenn.) | T2—768 653 |
| Warren County (Va.) | T2—755 97 |
| Warrenton (South Africa : | |
| District) | T2—687 11 |
| Warrick County (Ind.) | T2—772 32 |
| Warrington (England : | |
| Borough) | T2—427 19 |
| Warrnambool (Vic.) | T2—945 7 |
| Wars | 355.02 |
| history | 900 |
| military analysis | 355.48 |
| military science | 355.02 |
| social services | 363.349 8 |
| *see also* Disasters; War | |
| *see Manual at* 900; *also at* | |
| 930–990 | |
| Wars between France and Holy | |
| Roman Empire, 1521–1599 | |
| French history | 944.028 |
| Italian history | 945.06 |
| Wars of the Roses, 1455–1485 | 942.04 |
| Warsaw (Poland : | |
| Voivodeship) | T2—438 41 |
| Warsaw Ghetto | 940.531 853 841 |
| Warsaw Pact | 355.031 094 7 |
| Warsaw Treaty Organization | 355.031 094 7 |
| Warships | 359.83 |
| ancient and medieval | 359.832 |
| design | 623.812 1 |
| engineering | 623.821 |
| handling | 623.882 1 |
| naval equipment | 359.83 |
| naval units | 359.32 |
| power-driven | 359.83 |
| design | 623.812 5 |
| engineering | 623.825 |
| naval equipment | 359.83 |
| wind-driven | 359.832 |
| design | 623.812 25 |
| engineering | 623.822 5 |
| Wart snakes | 597.967 |
| Wartburgkreis (Germany : | |
| Landkreis) | T2—432 26 |
| Warthog | 599.633 |
| Warts | |
| medicine | 616.544 |
| *see also* Skin diseases — | |
| humans | |

| | |
|---|---|
| Warwick (England : | |
| District) | T2—424 87 |
| Warwickshire (England) | T2—424 8 |
| Warwickshire Avon River | |
| (England) | T2—424 4 |
| Wasatch County (Utah) | T2—792 23 |
| Wasatch Range (Utah and | |
| Idaho) | T2—792 2 |
| Idaho | T2—796 44 |
| Utah | T2—792 2 |
| Wasco County (Or.) | T2—795 62 |
| Waseca County (Minn.) | T2—776 195 |
| Wash, The (England) | T2—425 3 |
| Washabaugh County (S.D.) | T2—783 64 |
| Washakie County (Wyo.) | T2—787 34 |
| Washboards | |
| music | 786.886 |
| *see also* Percussion | |
| instruments | |
| Washburn County (Wis.) | T2—775 15 |
| Washing clothes | |
| home economics | 648.1 |
| Washing coal | 662.623 |
| Washing fabrics | |
| home economics | 648.1 |
| Washing machines | |
| manufacturing technology | 683.88 |
| Washington | 979.7 |
| | T2—797 |
| Washington (D.C.) | 975.3 |
| | T2—753 |
| Washington (District) | 976.803 |
| | T2—768 |
| Washington, George | |
| United States history | 973.41 |
| 1789–1793 | 973.41 |
| 1793–1797 | 973.43 |
| Washington County (Ala.) | T2—761 243 |
| Washington County (Ark.) | T2—767 14 |
| Washington County (Colo.) | T2—788 79 |
| Washington County (Fla.) | T2—759 963 |
| Washington County (Ga.) | T2—758 672 |
| Washington County (Idaho) | T2—796 25 |
| Washington County (Ill.) | T2—773 88 |
| Washington County (Ind.) | T2—772 22 |
| Washington County (Iowa) | T2—777 923 |
| Washington County (Kan.) | T2—781 273 |
| Washington County (Ky.) | T2—769 493 |
| Washington County (Md.) | T2—752 91 |
| Washington County (Me.) | T2—741 42 |
| Washington County (Minn.) | T2—776 59 |
| Washington County (Miss.) | T2—762 42 |
| Washington County (Mo.) | T2—778 64 |
| Washington County (N.C.) | T2—756 165 |

| | |
|---|---|
| Washington County (N.Y.) | T2—747 49 |
| Washington County (Neb.) | T2—782 245 |
| Washington County (Ohio) | T2—771 98 |
| Washington County (Okla.) | T2—766 96 |
| Washington County (Or.) | T2—795 43 |
| Washington County (Pa.) | T2—748 82 |
| Washington County (R.I.) | T2—745 9 |
| Washington County (Tenn.) | T2—768 97 |
| Washington County (Tex.) | T2—764 245 |
| Washington County (Utah) | T2—792 48 |
| Washington County (Va.) | T2—755 725 |
| Washington County (Vt.) | T2—743 4 |
| Washington County (Wis.) | T2—775 91 |
| Washington Parish (La.) | T2—763 11 |
| Washita County (Okla.) | T2—766 42 |
| Washita River (Tex. and Okla.) | T2—766 5 |
| Washo Indians | T5—975 76 |
| Washo language | 497.576 |
| | T6—975 76 |
| Washoe County (Nev.) | T2—793 55 |
| Washtenaw County (Mich.) | T2—774 35 |
| Wāsiṭ (Iraq) | T2—567 5 |
| Wasmosy, Juan Carlos | |
| Paraguayan history | 989.207 42 |
| Wasps | 595.79 |
| agricultural pests | 632.79 |
| Wasseramt (Switzerland) | T2—494 359 3 |
| Wasseramt-Bucheggberg (Switzerland) | T2—494 359 |
| Waste control | 363.728 |
| law | 344.046 2 |
| production management | 658.567 |
| public administration | 353.93 |
| social services | 363.728 |
| spacecraft | 629.477 4 |
| technology | 628.4 |
| *see also* Waste technology; Wastes | |
| Waste disposal | 363.728 |
| *see also* Waste control; Waste technology | |
| Waste heat | 333.793 |
| Waste lands | 333.731 37 |
| Waste management | 363.728 |
| *see also* Waste control | |
| Waste technology | 628.4 |
| | T1—028 6 |
| architecture | 720.475 |
| construction | 690.028 6 |
| glassmaking | 666.14 |
| nuclear engineering | 621.483 8 |
| paper manufacturing | 676.042 |
| petroleum | 665.538 9 |

| | |
|---|---|
| Waste technology (continued) | |
| plastics | 668.419 2 |
| rubber manufacturing | 678.29 |
| rural | 628.74 |
| wood products | 674.84 |
| *see also* Waste control | |
| Waste utilization | |
| production management | 658.567 |
| Wastelands | |
| public administration | 354.34 |
| Wastepaper pulp | 676.142 |
| Wastes | 363.728 |
| energy production | |
| economics | 333.793 8 |
| fuel technology | 662.87 |
| law | 344.046 2 |
| pollution technology | 628.5 |
| social services | 363.728 |
| utilization | |
| animal feed | 636.085 56 |
| production management | 658.567 |
| water pollution engineering | 628.168 |
| *see also* Waste control; Waste technology | |
| Wastewater | 363.728 4 |
| *see also* Waste control | |
| Watauga County (N.C.) | T2—756 843 |
| Watchdog agencies | 352.88 |
| Watchdogs | 636.73 |
| Watches | 681.114 |
| art metalwork | 739.3 |
| technology | 681.114 |
| Watchmakers | 681.114 092 |
| Watchworks | |
| technology | 681.112 |
| Water | 553.7 |
| biochemistry | 572.539 |
| humans | 612.015 22 |
| chemical engineering | 661.08 |
| chemistry | 546.22 |
| disease transmission | 614.43 |
| dowsing | 133.323 2 |
| economic geology | 553.7 |
| folklore | 398.26 |
| history and criticism | 398.364 |
| geologic agent | 551.35 |
| *see Manual at* 551.302–.307 vs. 551.35 | |
| health | 613.287 |
| hydraulic engineering | 627 |
| hydraulic-power technology | 621.204 22 |
| law | 346.046 91 |
| materials science | 620.198 |

Water (continued)
  metabolism
    human physiology — 612.392 3
  meteorology — 551.57
  plant management — 658.26
  prospecting — 628.114
  public administration — 354.36
  religious worship — 202.12
  resource economics — 333.91
  sanitary engineering — 628.1
  supply services — 363.61
  treatment engineering — 628.162
Water absorption
  plants — 575.76
Water-atmosphere interactions — 551.524
  microclimatology — 551.66
Water balance — 551.48
Water bears — 592.72
Water beetles — 595.762
Water birds — 598.176
  conservation technology — 639.978 176
  paleozoology — 568.4
  resource economics — 333.958 28
Water bodies — 551.46
  — T2—16
  influence on precipitation — 551.577 5
  physical geology — 551.46
  public administration — 354.36
Water buffalo — 636.293
  animal husbandry — 636.293
  zoology — 599.642
Water chestnuts — 583.765
Water clocks
  technology — 681.111
Water clovers — 587.3
Water collection systems
  engineering — 628.142
Water conservation — 333.911 6
  agriculture — 631.7
  engineering — 628.13
  law — 346.046 911 6
  public administration — 354.363 4
  resource economics — 333.911 6
Water detention ponds — 627.44
Water distribution systems — 363.61
  engineering — 628.144
Water diversion
  engineering — 627.123
  flood control — 627.45
Water drainage
  buildings — 696.13
Water-electrolyte balance
  biochemistry — 571.75
    humans — 612.015 22

Water-electrolyte imbalances — 571.937 5
  medicine — 616.399 2
    *see also* Digestive system
      diseases — humans
Water features
  landscape architecture — 714
Water fixtures
  buildings — 696.1
Water fleas — 595.32
Water games — 797.25
Water gardens — 635.967 4
Water gas — 665.772
Water hammer
  engineering — 620.106 4
Water heaters
  buildings — 696.6
  manufacturing technology — 683.88
Water hyacynths — 584.72
Water ices (Desserts) — 641.863
  commercial processing — 637.4
  home preparation — 641.863
Water impoundment
  flood control — 627.44
  water-lifting devices — 621.69
Water lilies — 635.933 29
  botany — 583.29
  floriculture — 635.933 29
Water mains — 628.15
Water mills — 621.21
Water ouzels — 598.832
Water pageantry — 797.203
Water plantains — 584.72
Water pollution — 363.739 4
  effect on natural ecology — 577.627
  law — 344.046 343
  public administration — 354.363 5
  sanitary engineering — 628.168
  social welfare — 363.739 4
  toxicology — 571.95
  *see also* Pollution
Water polo — 797.252
Water poppy — 584.72
Water power — 333.914
  economics — 333.914
  electrical engineering — 621.312 134
  law — 343.092 4
  public administration — 354.362 7
Water purification — 628.162
Water-repellent fabrics — 677.682
  *see also* Textiles
Water resources — 333.91
  engineering — 627
  law — 346.046 91
  public administration — 354.36

| | | | |
|---|---|---|---|
| Water reuse | 363.728 4 | Water voles | 599.354 |
| *see also* Waste control | | Water witching | 133.323 2 |
| Water rights | | Waterberg (South Africa : | |
| law | 346.043 2 | District) | T2—682 53 |
| public control | 346.046 91 | Waterbuck | 599.645 |
| sale and rental | 333.339 | Waterclovers | 587.3 |
| Water safety | 363.123 | Watercolor painting | 751.422 |
| public administration | 353.987 | Watercresses | 641.355 6 |
| sports | 797.200 289 | botany | 583.64 |
| *see also* Safety | | cooking | 641.655 6 |
| Water scavenger beetles | 595.763 | food | 641.355 6 |
| Water skiers | 797.350 92 | garden crop | 635.56 |
| Water skiing | 797.35 | Waterfalls | T2—169 4 |
| Water softeners | | hydrology | 551.484 |
| buildings | 696.12 | Waterford (Ireland) | T2—419 15 |
| hot-water supply | 696.6 | Waterford (Ireland : | |
| Water-soluble mediums | | County) | T2—419 1 |
| painting | 751.42 | Waterfowl | 598.41 |
| Water-soluble paints | 667.63 | conservation technology | 639.978 41 |
| Water solutions | 541.342 2 | food | 641.391 |
| chemical engineering | 660.294 22 | cooking | 641.691 |
| Water spangles | 587.3 | resource economics | 333.958 41 |
| Water sports | 797 | sports hunting | 799.244 |
| Water storage (Plant physiology) | 575.78 | zoology | 598.41 |
| Water striders | 595.754 | Waterfowling | 799.244 |
| Water supply | 363.61 | Waterleafs | 583.94 |
| economic geology | 553.7 | Waterloo (Ont.) | T2—713 45 |
| engineering | 628.1 | Waterloo (Ont. : Regional | |
| rural | 628.72 | municipality) | T2—713 44 |
| household management | 644.6 | Waterloo, Battle of, 1815 | 940.274 2 |
| law | 343.092 4 | Watermarks | 676.280 27 |
| military engineering | 623.751 | Watermeals | 584.64 |
| plumbing | 696.12 | Watermelons | 641.356 15 |
| public administration | 354.366 | botany | 583.63 |
| ships | 623.854 | commercial processing | 664.805 615 |
| social services | 363.61 | cooking | 641.656 15 |
| spacecraft | 629.477 3 | food | 641.356 15 |
| *see Manual at* 363.61 | | garden crop | 635.615 |
| Water table | 551.492 | Waterpower | 333.914 |
| Water temperatures | | Waterproof construction | |
| meteorology | 551.524 | buildings | 693.892 |
| oceanography | 551.465 3 | Waterproof fabrics | 677.682 |
| Water towers | 628.13 | *see also* Textiles | |
| Water transportation | 387 | Watersheds | |
| engineering | 629.048 | land economics | 333.73 |
| law | 343.096 | Waterspouts (Tornadoes) | 551.553 |
| military engineering | 623.8 | Waterton-Glacier | |
| public administration | 354.78 | International Peace Park | |
| safety | 363.123 | (Mont. and Alta.) | T2—786 52 |
| law | 343.096 | Alberta | T2—712 34 |
| public administration | 353.987 | Montana | T2—786 52 |
| transportation services | 387 | Waterton Lakes National | |
| Water treatment | 628.162 | Park (Alta.) | T2—712 34 |
| Water turbines | 621.24 | | |

| | |
|---|---|
| Waterval-Boven (South Africa : District) | T2—682 74 |
| Waterways (Inland transportation) | 386 |
| *see also* Inland waterways | |
| Waterwheels | 621.21 |
| Waterworks | 363.61 |
| *see also* Water supply | |
| Watford (England) | T2—425 892 |
| Watling Island (Bahamas) | T2—729 6 |
| Watonwan County (Minn.) | T2—776 29 |
| Watson, John Christian | |
| Australian history | 994.041 |
| Watsonian behaviorism | 150.194 32 |
| Watt-hour meters | 621.374 5 |
| Wattled crows | 598.8 |
| Wattles (Trees) | 583.748 |
| forestry | 634.973 748 |
| ornamental arboriculture | 635.977 374 8 |
| Wattmeters | 621.374 6 |
| Waukesha County (Wis.) | T2—775 93 |
| Waupaca County (Wis.) | T2—775 38 |
| Waushara County (Wis.) | T2—775 57 |
| Wave action | 551.36 |
| Wave guides | |
| microwave electronics | 621.381 331 |
| Wave mechanics | 530.124 |
| Wave propagation | |
| microwave electronics | 621.381 31 |
| radio engineering | 621.384 11 |
| Wave theories | 530.14 |
| electricity | 537.12 |
| light | 535.13 |
| modern physics | 530.14 |
| Wave transmission | |
| microwave electronics | 621.381 31 |
| radio engineering | 621.384 11 |
| Wavelets (Mathematics) | 515.243 3 |
| Wavell, Archibald Percival Wavell, Earl of | |
| Indian history | 954.035 9 |
| Waveney (England) | T2—426 41 |
| Waveney, River (England) | T2—426 19 |
| Waverley (England) | T2—422 19 |
| Waves | |
| air mechanics | 533.62 |
| fluid mechanics | 532.059 3 |
| gas mechanics | 533.293 |
| liquid mechanics | 532.593 |
| mechanics | 531.113 3 |
| oceanography | 551.463 |
| quantum theory | 530.124 |
| solid mechanics | 531.33 |
| Wax beans | 641.356 52 |
| *see also* Snap beans | |
| Wax carving | 736.93 |
| Wax myrtles | 583.43 |
| Wax painting | 751.46 |
| Waxbills | 598.886 |
| Waxes | 665.1 |
| biochemistry | 572.57 |
| chemistry | 547.77 |
| sculpture material | 731.2 |
| Waxing | |
| woodwork | |
| buildings | 698.33 |
| Waxwings | 598.852 |
| Way of the Cross | 232.96 |
| Roman Catholic liturgy | 264.027 4 |
| Wayne County (Ga.) | T2—758 756 |
| Wayne County (Ill.) | T2—773 792 |
| Wayne County (Ind.) | T2—772 63 |
| Wayne County (Iowa) | T2—777 88 |
| Wayne County (Ky.) | T2—769 64 |
| Wayne County (Mich.) | T2—774 33 |
| Wayne County (Miss.) | T2—762 573 |
| Wayne County (Mo.) | T2—778 92 |
| Wayne County (N.C.) | T2—756 395 |
| Wayne County (N.Y.) | T2—747 87 |
| Wayne County (Neb.) | T2—782 57 |
| Wayne County (Ohio) | T2—771 61 |
| Wayne County (Pa.) | T2—748 23 |
| Wayne County (Tenn.) | T2—768 39 |
| Wayne County (Utah) | T2—792 54 |
| Wayne County (W. Va.) | T2—754 47 |
| Waynesboro (Va.) | T2—755 912 |
| Weak interaction (Nuclear particles) | 539.754 4 |
| Weakfish | 597.725 |
| Weakley County (Tenn.) | T2—768 24 |
| Weald, The (England) | T2 422 5 |
| Wealden (England) | T2—422 51 |
| Wealth | 330.16 |
| distribution | 339.2 |
| economic theory | 330.16 |
| ethics | 178 |
| religion | 205.68 |
| Buddhism | 294.356 8 |
| Christianity | 241.68 |
| Hinduism | 294.548 68 |
| macroeconomics | 339.3 |
| Wealth tax | 336.22 |
| law | 343.054 |
| Wealthy people | 305.523 4 |
| | T1—086 21 |
| customs | 390.1 |
| dress | 391.01 |

| | |
|---|---|
| Weapons | |
| engineering | 623.4 |
| military | 355.8 |
| *see also* Arms (Military) | |
| small firearms | 683.4 |
| *see also* Guns (Small arms) | |
| Weapons industry | 338.476 234 |
| Weapons of mass destruction | 358.3 |
| disarmament | 327.174 5 |
| engineering | 623.451 6 |
| law | 341.735 |
| warfare | 358.3 |
| Weapons testing | |
| law of nations | 341.733 |
| Wear | |
| machine engineering | 621.89 |
| Wear, River (England) | T2—428 6 |
| Wear resistance | |
| materials science | 620.112 92 |
| Wear River Valley | |
| (England) | T2—428 6 |
| Wear Valley (England) | T2—428 64 |
| Wearable computers | 004.16 |
| *see also* Personal computers | |
| Weasel spiders | 595.48 |
| Weasels | 599.766 2 |
| Weather | 551.6 |
| aeronautics | 629.132 4 |
| crop damage | 632.1 |
| earth sciences | 551.6 |
| folklore | 398.26 |
| history and criticism | 398.363 |
| health | 613.11 |
| influence on crime | 364.22 |
| literature | 808.803 6 |
| history and criticism | 809.933 6 |
| specific literatures | T3B—080 36 |
| history and | |
| criticism | T3B—093 6 |
| public administration | 354.37 |
| social effects | 304.25 |
| transportation hazard | 363.120 1 |
| air transportation | 363.124 12 |
| *see also* Transportation safety | |
| *see Manual at* 551.5 vs. 551.6 | |
| Weather bureaus | 354.37 |
| Weather control | 551.68 |
| law | 344.095 5 |
| *see also* Weather | |
| Weather forecasting | 551.63 |
| armed forces | 355.343 2 |
| *see also* Weather | |

| | |
|---|---|
| Weather-induced illnesses | |
| medicine | 616.988 |
| *see also* Environmental | |
| diseases — humans | |
| Weather lore | 551.631 |
| Weather modification | 551.68 |
| law | 344.095 5 |
| *see also* Weather | |
| Weather satellites | |
| use | 551.635 4 |
| Weather stripping | 678.35 |
| Weathering | 551.302 |
| by water | 551.352 |
| by wind | 551.372 |
| materials science | 620.112 23 |
| soil formation | 551.305 |
| Weatherization (Housing | |
| program) | 363.583 |
| Weaver finches | 598.887 |
| Weaver finches (Estrildidae) | 598.886 |
| Weaver finches (Ploceidae) | 598.887 |
| Weaverbirds | 598.887 |
| Weavers (Birds) | 598.887 |
| Weaving | 677.028 242 |
| arts | 746.14 |
| threads and yarns | 746.14 |
| vegetable fibers | 746.41 |
| manufacturing technology | 677.028 242 |
| primary education | 372.54 |
| Web application frameworks | 006.76 |
| Web databases | 005.740 285 467 8 |
| computer science | 005.740 285 467 8 |
| information systems | 025.042 2 |
| Web page design | 006.7 |
| Web programming | 006.76 |
| Web publishing | 070.579 73 |
| computer science | 006.7 |
| Web server programs | 005.376 |
| Web servers | 004.36 |
| Web services | 006.78 |
| Web sites | |
| bibliographies | 025.042 2 |
| specific subjects | 025.06 |
| *see Manual at* 011.39 vs. | |
| 005.3029, 016.0053, | |
| 025.04; *also at* 011.39 | |
| vs. 005.3029, 016.0053, | |
| 025.0422 | |
| cataloging | 025.344 |
| computer science | 006.7 |
| development | 006.7 |
| information systems | 025.042 2 |
| Webb County (Tex.) | T2—764 462 |
| Weber County (Utah) | T2—792 28 |

Webster County (Ga.)    T2—758 916
Webster County (Iowa)    T2—777 51
Webster County (Ky.)    T2—769 883
Webster County (Miss.)    T2—762 697
Webster County (Mo.)    T2—778 823
Webster County (Neb.)    T2—782 374
Webster County (W. Va.)    T2—754 65
Webster Parish (La.)    T2—763 96
Weddell Sea (Antarctic regions)    551.461 73
     T2—167 3
Weddell seal    599.796
Wedding clothes    392.54
   commercial technology    687.16
   customs    392.54
   home sewing    646.476
   *see also* Clothing
Wedding music    781.587
Weddings
   customs    392.5
     dress    392.54
      *see also* Clothing
   etiquette    395.22
   flower arrangements    745.926
   handicrafts    745.594 1
   interior decoration    747.93
   rites    203.85
Weed killers    632.5
   agriculture    632.5
   chemical engineering    668.654
   environmental engineering    628.97
Weeding (Library collections)    025.216
Weeds    632.5
   control    363.78
     agriculture    632.5
     environmental engineering    628.97
     social services    363.78
   economic botany    581.652
Weeks    529.2
Weenen (South Africa :
   District)    T2—684 7
Weevils    595.768
   agricultural pests    632.768
Weight
   biological organisms    578.41
   plants    581.41
Weight-gaining diet
   health    613.24
Weight lifters    796.410 92
Weight lifting    613.713
   physical fitness    613.713
   sports    796.41
Weight-losing diet
   health    613.25

Weight-losing programs
   dietetics    613.25
   exercises    613.712
   health    613.712
Weighting (Compensation)
   labor economics    331.216 6
   personnel management    658.322 2
Weightlessness
   space flight    629.418
Weights and measures    530.81
   law    343.075
   physics    530.81
   public administration    352.83
   social use    389.1
   standardization    389.62
Weimar (Germany)    T2—432 241
Weimar Republic    943.085
Weimaraner (Dog)    636.752
Weimarer Land (Germany :
   Landkreis)    T2—432 24
Weinfelden (Switzerland :
   Bezirk)    T2—494 595
Weirs    627.883
Weld County (Colo.)    T2—788 72
Welded joints    671.520 42
Welders    671.520 92
Welding    671.52
   decorative arts    739.14
   sculpture    731.41
   ship hulls    623.843 2
Welding equipment    621.977
Welding plastics    668.415
Welds    671.520 42
Welensky, Roy
   Rhodesia and Nyasaland
     history    968.903
Welfare    361
   *see also* Welfare services
Welfare economics school    330.155 6
Welfare fraud    364.163
   law    345.026 3
Welfare law    344.03
Welfare liberalism
   political ideology    320.513
Welfare power (Legislative
   bodies)    328.341 3
Welfare reform    361.68
Welfare rights    361.614
Welfare services    361
   accounting    657.832
   Algerian Revolution    965.046 7
   American Revolution    973.37
   arts    700.455 6
     T3C—355 6

Welfare services (continued)
| | |
|---|---|
| Chaco War | 989.207 167 |
| Civil War (England) | 942.062 7 |
| Civil War (Spain) | 946.081 7 |
| Civil War (United States) | 973.777 |
| crime prevention | 364.44 |
| Crimean War | 947.073 87 |
| Falkland Islands War | 997.110 247 |
| Franco-German War | 943.082 7 |
| Holocaust, 1933–1945 | 940.531 87 |
| Hundred Years' War | 944.025 7 |
| Indo-Pakistan War, 1971 | 954.920 517 |
| Indochinese War | 959.704 17 |
| Iraq War, 2003– | 956.704 437 |
| Iraqi-Iranian Conflict | 955.054 27 |
| Korean War | 951.904 27 |
| law | 344.03 |
| literature | 808.803 556 |
| history and criticism | 809.933 556 |
| specific literatures | T3B—080 355 6 |
| history and criticism | T3B—093 556 |
| Napoleonic Wars | 940.277 |
| Persian Gulf War, 1991 | 956.704 427 |
| personnel management | 658.38 |
| prisoner services | 365.66 |
| public administration | 353.5 |
| South African War | 968.048 7 |
| specific groups | 362 |
| law | 344.032 |
| students | 371.7 |
| Thirty Years' War | 940.247 |
| Vietnamese War | 959.704 37 |
| War of the Pacific | 983.061 67 |
| World War I | 940.477 |
| World War II | 940.547 7 |

*see Manual at* 301–307 vs. 361–365; *also at* 361 vs. 362–363; *also at* 361–365; *also at* 361–365 vs. 353.5

Welfare state
| | |
|---|---|
| economics | 330.126 |
| social welfare | 361.65 |
| Welfare workers | 361.92 |
| Welkom (South Africa : District) | T2—685 35 |

Well-being
| | |
|---|---|
| applied psychology | 158 |
| children | 155.419 |
| parapsychology | 131 |

Well blowouts
| | |
|---|---|
| oil extraction | 622.338 2 |
| Well shrimps | 595.378 |
| Welland (Ont. : County) | T2—713 38 |

| | |
|---|---|
| Welland, River (England) | T2—425 39 |
| Welland Canal (Ont.) | T2—713 38 |
| Wellesley, Richard Wellesley, Marquess | |
| Indian history | 954.031 2 |
| Wellingborough (England : Borough) | T2—425 58 |
| Wellington (N.S.W.) | T2—944 5 |
| Wellington (N.Z.) | T2—936 3 |
| Wellington (Ont. : County) | T2—713 42 |
| Wellington (South Africa : District) | T2—687 34 |
| Wellington City (N.Z.) | T2—936 3 |
| Wellington Region (N.Z.) | T2—936 |
| Wells (B.C.) | T2—711 75 |

Wells (Water source)
| | |
|---|---|
| engineering | 628.114 |
| hydrology | 551.498 |
| Wells County (Ind.) | T2—772 72 |
| Wells County (N.D.) | T2—784 58 |
| Wells Gray Provincial Park (B.C.) | T2—711 72 |

Welsers period
| | |
|---|---|
| Venezuelan history | 987.03 |
| Welsh | T5—916 6 |
| Welsh Borders (England and Wales) | T2—424 |
| Welsh Calvinistic Methodist Church | 285.235 |

*see also* Presbyterian Church
| | |
|---|---|
| Welsh corgis | 636.737 |
| Welsh language | 491.66 |
| | T6—916 6 |

Welsh literature
| | |
|---|---|
| English | 820 |
| Welsh | 891.66 |
| Welsh Marches (England and Wales) | T2—424 |
| Welsh pony | 636.16 |
| Welshpool (Wales) | T2—429 51 |
| Welwitschiales | 585.8 |
| Welwyn Hatfield (England) | T2—425 86 |
| Wendish language | 491.88 |
| | T6—918 8 |
| Wendish literature | 891.88 |
| Wendish people | T5—918 8 |
| Wends | T5—918 8 |

Wens (Disorder)
| | |
|---|---|
| medicine | 616.53 |

*see also* Skin diseases — humans
| | |
|---|---|
| Wentworth (Ont.) | T2—713 52 |
| Wepener (South Africa : District) | T2—685 6 |

Werdenberg (Switzerland :
  Wahlkreis)     T2—494 728
Werewolves     398.245 4
  *see also* Legendary animals
Werribee (Vic.)     T2—945 2
Weser-Ems (Germany :
  Regierungsbezirk)     T2—435 91
Weser River (Germany)     T2—435 9
Wesleyan Conference     287.53
  *see also* Methodist Church
Wesleyan Methodist Church     287.1
  *see also* Methodist Church
Wesleyan Reform Union     287.534
  *see also* Methodist Church
Wesleyan Reformers     287.53
  *see also* Methodist Church
Wesselsbron (South Africa :
  District)     T2—685 3
Wessex supremacy     942.016
West (U.S.)     978
     T2—78
  art representation     704.949 978
  arts     700.458 78
     T3C—358 78
  literature     808.803 587 8
    history and criticism     809.933 587 8
    specific literatures     T3B—080 358 78
     history and
      criticism     T3B—093 587 8
  *see also* Westerns — fiction
West (Western world)     909.098 21
     T2—182 1
West Africa     966
     T2—66
West Africans     T5—966
West Atlantic languages (Africa)     496.32
     T6—963 2
West Azerbaijan (Iran)     T2—554
West Bank     956.953
     T2—569 53
  ancient     933.53
     T2—335 3
West Baton Rouge Parish
  (La.)     T2—763 452
West Bengal (India)     T2—541 4
West Berkshire (England :
  District)     T2—422 91
West Berlin (Germany)     T2—431 554
West Branch Susquehanna
  River (Pa.)     T2—748 5
West Carroll Parish (La.)     T2—763 83
West Coast National Park
  (South Africa)     T2—687 32
West Coast Region (N.Z.)     T2—937 1

West Devon (England)     T2—423 53
West Dorset (England)     T2—423 31
West Dunbartonshire
  (Scotland)     T2—414 32
West Equatoria (Sudan)     T2—629 5
West Feliciana Parish (La.)     T2—763 17
West Flanders (Belgium)     T2—493 12
West Frisian Islands
  (Netherlands)     T2—492 13
West Germanic languages     439
     T6—39
West Germanic literatures     839
West Germany (1949–1990)     943.087
     T2—43
West Glamorgan (Wales)     T2—429 82
West Indian boxwood     583.45
West Indian steel drums     786.843
  *see also* Percussion instruments
West Indies     972.9
     T2—729
West Indies, Dutch     T2—729 86
West Indies, French     T2—729 76
West Indies Associated
  States     T2—729 73
West Iranian languages (Ancient)     491.51
     T6—915 1
West Iranian literatures (Ancient)     891.51
West Irian     995.1
     T2—951
West Irian Jaya (Indonesia)     T2—951 2
West Java (Indonesia)     T2—598 24
West Kalimantan
  (Indonesia)     T2—598 32
West Kettle River (B.C.)     T2—711 62
West Lake Region
  (Tanzania)     T2—678 27
West Lancashire (England)     T2—427 612
West Lindsey (England)     T2—425 31
West Lothian (Scotland)     T2—413 3
West Malaysia     T2—595 1
West Midlands (England)     T2—424 9
West Midlands (England :
  Region)     T2—424
West New Britain Province
  (Papua New Guinea)     T2—958 7
West New Guinea     995.1
     T2—951
West New Guinea languages     499.5
     T6—995
West Nile fever
  incidence     614.588 56
  medicine     616.918 56
West Nusa Tenggara
  (Indonesia)     T2—598 65

| | |
|---|---|
| West Orange (N.J.) | T2—749 33 |
| West Oxfordshire (England) | T2—425 71 |
| West Pakistan (Pakistan) | T2—549 1 |
| West Prussia (Germany) | T2—438 2 |
| West Rand (South Africa) | T2—682 22 |
| West Redonda Island (B.C.) | T2—711 1 |
| West Road River (B.C.) | T2—711 75 |
| West Scandinavian languages | 439.5 |
| | T6—395 |
| West Scandinavian literatures | 839.5 |
| West Semitic languages | 492 |
| | T6—92 |
| West Semitic literatures | 892 |
| West Semitic peoples | T5—92 |
| West Sepik Province (Papua New Guinea) | T2—957 7 |
| West Slavic languages | 491.85 |
| | T6—918 5 |
| West Slavic literatures | 891.85 |
| West Slavs | T5—918 5 |
| West Somerset (England) | T2—423 85 |
| West Sulawesi (Indonesia) | T2—598 46 |
| West Sumatra (Indonesia) | T2—598 13 |
| West Sussex (England) | T2—422 6 |
| West Thurlow Island (B.C.) | T2—711 1 |
| West Timor (Indonesia) | T2—598 68 |
| West Vancouver (B.C.) | T2—711 33 |
| West Virginia | 975.4 |
| | T2—754 |
| West-Vlaanderen (Belgium) | T2—493 12 |
| West Wiltshire (England) | T2—423 15 |
| West Yorkshire (England) | T2—428 1 |
| Westchester County (N.Y.) | T2—747 277 |
| Westerlies | 551.518 3 |
| Western Aramaic languages | 492.29 |
| | T6—922 9 |
| Western Aramaic literatures | 892.29 |
| Western architecture | 722–724 |
| ancient | 722.6 |
| Western art music | 781.68 |
| Western Asian intergovernmental organizations | 341.247 7 |
| Western Australia | T2—941 |
| Western Bahr al Ghazal (Sudan) | T2—629 4 |
| Western Bay of Plenty District (N.Z.) | T2—934 22 |
| Western bloc | T2—171 3 |
| Western calendars | 529.4 |
| Western calligraphy | 745.619 7 |
| Western Canada | T2—712 |
| Western Cape (South Africa) | 968.73 |
| | T2—687 3 |
| Western civilization | 909.098 21 |
| Western Darfur (Sudan : State) | T2—627 |
| Western Desert (Egypt) | T2—622 |
| Western desert language | 499.15 |
| | T6—991 5 |
| Western Europe | 940 |
| | T2—4 |
| ancient | 936 |
| | T2—36 |
| Western Finland (Finland) | T2—489 73 |
| Western flower arrangements | 745.922 4 |
| Western folk music modes | 781.263 |
| Western France | T2—446 |
| Western front World War I | 940.414 4 |
| Western Greece (Greece) | T2—495 27 |
| Western Hemisphere | T2—181 2 |
| Western Hemisphere intergovernmental organizations | 341.245 |
| Western Highlands (Papua New Guinea) | T2—956 5 |
| Western Hindi languages | 491.43 |
| | T6—914 3 |
| Western Hindi literatures | 891.43 |
| Western Isles (Scotland) | T2—411 4 |
| Western Kordofan (Sudan) | T2—628 |
| Western Macedonia (Greece) | T2—495 62 |
| Western Mediterranean region | T2—182 21 |
| ancient | 936 |
| | T2—36 |
| Western Mediterranean Sea | 551.461 381 |
| | T2—163 81 |
| Western New Guinea (Indonesia) | 995.1 |
| | T2—951 |
| Western Oregon | T2—795 1 |
| Western Panjabi language | 491.419 |
| | T6—914 19 |
| Western philosophy | 190 |
| Western popular music | 781.64 |
| country music songs | 782.421 642 |
| songs | 782.421 64 |
| Western Province (Kenya) | T2—676 28 |
| Western Province (Papua New Guinea) | T2—954 9 |
| Western Province (Solomon Islands) | T2—959 31 |
| Western Province (Zambia) | T2—689 4 |
| Western Saami languages | 494.572 |
| | T6—945 72 |

Western Sahara 964.8
  T2—648
Western Samar
  (Philippines) T2—599 5
Western Sámi languages 494.572
  T6—945 72
Western Samoa 996.14
Western Samoans T5—994 62
Western Siberia (Russia) T2—573
Western States (U.S.) 978
  T2—78
  *see also* West (U.S.)
Western stories 808.838 74
  history and criticism 809.387 4
  specific literatures T3B—308 74
    individual authors T3A—3
Western Turkic languages 494.38
  T6—943 8
Western Washington T2—797 6
Western world 909.098 21
  T2—182 1
Westerns
  fiction 808.838 74
    history and criticism 809.387 4
    specific literatures T3B—308 74
      individual authors T3A—3
  motion pictures 791.436 587 8
  radio programs 791.446 587 8
  television programs 791.456 587 8
Westland District (N.Z.) T2—937 1
Westland National Park
  (N.Z.) T2—937 1
Westlich Raron
  (Switzerland) T2—494 794 5
Westmeath (Ireland) T2—418 15
Westminster (London,
  England) T2—421 32
Westmoreland County (Pa.) T2—748 81
Westmoreland County (Va.) T2—755 24
Westmorland (N.B. :
  County) T2—715 23
Westmount (Quebec) T2—714 28
Weston County (Wyo.) T2—787 14
Westonaria (South Africa :
  District) T2—682 22
Westösterreich (Austria) T2—436 4
Westphalia (Germany) T2—435 6
Wet-collodion process 772.14
Wet-weather photography 778.75
Wetar Island (Indonesia) T2—598 52
Wetland animals 591.768

Wetlands 551.417
  biology 578.768
    resource economics 333.952 88
      animals 333.954 88
  ecology 577.68
  geomorphology 551.417
  law 346.046 918
  public administration 354.34
  resource economics 333.918
Wetting agents 668.14
Wetzel County (W. Va.) T2—754 18
Wexford (Ireland) T2—418 856
Wexford (Ireland : County) T2—418 85
Wexford County (Mich.) T2—774 67
Weymouth and Portland
  (England) T2—423 35
Whakatane District (N.Z.) T2—934 25
Whale fishes 597.64
Whale lice 595.378
Whale oil 665.2
Whalers 639.280 92
Whales 599.5
  conservation technology 639.979 5
  hunting 639.28
  paleozoology 569.5
  resource economics 333.959 5
    law 346.046 959 5
  zoology 599.5
Whaling
  law 343.076 928
  production economics 338.372 95
  products 338.372 95
    commerce 381.439 5
  technology 639.28
Whaling industry 338.372 95
Whaling ships
  engineering 623.824 8
Whanganui National Park
  (N.Z.) T2—935 2
Whangarei District (N.Z.) T2—931 6
Wharton County (Tex.) T2—764 133
Wharves
  engineering 627.31
Whatcom County (Wash.) T2—797 73
Wheat 641.331 1
  botany 584.9
  commercial processing 664.722
  cooking 641.631 1
  food 641.331 1
  food crop 633.11
  forage crop 633.251
Wheatland County (Mont.) T2—786 63
Wheel games 795.2
  equipment technology 688.752

| | |
|---|---|
| Wheelbarrows | |
|    manufacturing technology | 688.6 |
| Wheelchair basketball | 796.323 8 |
| Wheelchair sports | 796.045 6 |
| Wheelchairs | 617.033 |
| Wheeler County (Ga.) | T2—758 835 |
| Wheeler County (Neb.) | T2—782 762 |
| Wheeler County (Or.) | T2—795 81 |
| Wheeler County (Tex.) | T2 764 828 |
| Wheeler Lake (Ala.) | T2—761 98 |
| Wheeling (W. Va.) | T2—754 14 |
| Wheels | |
|    automotive engineering | 629.248 |
|    railroad engineering | 625.21 |
| Whelks | 594.32 |
| Whey | 641.373 |
|    cooking | 641.673 |
|    food | 641.373 |
|    processing | 637.3 |
| Whig Party (Great Britain) | 324.241 02 |
| Whig Party (U.S.) | 324.273 23 |
| Whip scorpions | 595.453 2 |
| Whippet (Dog) | 636.753 2 |
| Whippoorwill | 598.99 |
| Whips | |
|    music | 786.99 |
|      *see also* Percussion | |
|       instruments | |
| Whiptails (Lizards) | 597.958 25 |
| Whirligig beetles | 595.762 |
| Whisk ferns | 587.4 |
| Whiskey | 641.252 |
|    commercial processing | 663.52 |
| Whisky | 641.252 |
|    commercial processing | 663.52 |
| Whist | 795.413 |
| Whistle (Voices) | 782.98 |
|    choral and mixed voices | 782.98 |
|    single voices | 783.98 |
| Whistle blowing | |
|    law | 342.068 |
|    public administration | 353.46 |
| Whistler (B.C.) | T2—711 31 |
| White bass | 597.732 |
| White blood cells | 571.96 |
|    human immunology | 616.079 |
| White collar crime | 364.168 |
|    law | 345.026 8 |
| White collar workers | 331.792 |
| | T1—086 22 |
|    labor economics | 331.792 |
|      labor force | 331.119 042 |
|      labor market | 331.129 042 |
|      labor unions | 331.883 6 |

| | |
|---|---|
| White collar workers (continued) | |
|    personnel management | 658.304 4 |
|    social class | 305.55 |
| White corpuscles | 571.96 |
|    human histology | 612.112 |
|    human immunology | 616.079 |
|    human physiology | 612.112 |
|    *see also* Cardiovascular system | |
| White County (Ark.) | T2—767 76 |
| White County (Ga.) | T2—758 277 |
| White County (Ill.) | T2—773 96 |
| White County (Ind.) | T2—772 93 |
| White County (Tenn.) | T2—768 66 |
| White dwarfs | 523.887 |
| White elephant sales | 381.195 |
| White-footed mice | 599.355 |
| White-fronted goose | 598.417 3 |
| White mangrove | 583.763 |
| White Mountains (N.H. and | |
|    Me.) | T2—742 2 |
| White Nile (Sudan : State) | T2—626 4 |
| White Nile River | T2—629 3 |
| White perch | 597.732 |
| White Pine County (Nev.) | T2—793 15 |
| White race | 305.809 |
| | T5—09 |
| White River (Ark. and Mo.) | T2—767 2 |
| White River (Ind.) | T2—772 3 |
| White River (South Africa : | |
|    District) | T2—682 71 |
| White Rock (B.C.) | T2—711 33 |
| White Sands National | |
|    Monument (N.M.) | T2—789 65 |
| White Sea (Russia) | 551.461 324 |
| | T2—163 24 |
| White shark | 597.33 |
| White slave traffic | 364.153 4 |
|    law | 345.025 34 |
| White supremacy | |
|    political ideology | 320.569 09 |
| White-tailed deer | 599.652 |
|    big game hunting | 799.276 52 |
|    conservation technology | 639.979 652 |
|    resource economics | 333.959 652 |
| White whale | 599.542 |
| White wine | 641.222 2 |
|    commercial processing | 663.222 |
|    fortified | 641.222 6 |
|    sparkling | 641.222 4 |
|      commercial processing | 663.224 |
| Whitefish Bay (Mich. and | |
|    Ont.) | T2—774 91 |
| Whitefishes | 597.55 |

| | |
|---|---|
| Whiteflies | 595.752 |
| Whitehorse (Yukon) | T2—719 1 |
| Whites | T5—09 |
|   race identity | 305.809 |
| Whiteshell Provincial Park | |
|   (Man.) | T2—712 74 |
| Whiteside County (Ill.) | T2—773 35 |
| Whitetip shark | 597.34 |
| Whitewash | 667.63 |
| Whitewashing | |
|   buildings | 698.2 |
| Whitfield County (Ga.) | T2—758 324 |
| Whiting (Kingfish) | 597.725 |
| Whitings (Cods) | 597.633 |
| Whitings (Whitefishes) | 597.55 |
| Whitlam, Gough | |
|   Australian history | 994.062 |
| Whitley County (Ind.) | T2—772 75 |
| Whitley County (Ky.) | T2—769 132 |
| Whitman County (Wash.) | T2—797 39 |
| Whitney, Mount (Calif.) | T2—794 86 |
| Whitsunday | 263.94 |
|   devotional literature | 242.38 |
|   music | 781.729 3 |
|   sermons | 252.64 |
| Whitsunday Group (Qld.) | T2—943 6 |
| Whitsunday Island National | |
|   Park (Qld.) | T2—943 6 |
| Whittling | 736.4 |
| Whole-class reading | |
|   primary education | 372.416 4 |
| Whole-language approach | |
|   primary education | 372.62 |
|     language arts | 372.62 |
|     reading | 372.475 |
| Whole life insurance | 368.326 |
| Whole tonality | 781.266 |
| Whole-word method (Reading) | |
|   primary education | 372.462 |
| Wholesale clubs | 381.149 |
|   management | 658.879 |
| Wholesale marketing | 381.2 |
|   management | 658.86 |
|   *see also* Commerce | |
| Wholesale outlet stores | 381.15 |
|   management | 658.870 5 |
| Wholesale trade | 381.2 |
|   accounting | 657.839 |
|   law | 343.081 2 |
|   marketing management | 658.86 |
|   *see also* Commerce | |
| Whooping cough | |
|   incidence | 614.543 |
|   medicine | 616.204 |
|   *see also* Respiratory tract | |
|     diseases — humans | |
|   pediatrics | 618.922 04 |
| Whyalla (S. Aust.) | T2—942 38 |
| Wibaux County (Mont.) | T2—786 34 |
| Wicca | |
|   religious practice | 299.94 |
| Wichita (Kan.) | T2—781 86 |
| Wichita County (Kan.) | T2—781 423 |
| Wichita County (Tex.) | T2—764 745 |
| Wichita Indians | T5—979 3 |
| Wichita language | 497.93 |
| | T6—979 3 |
| Wick (Scotland) | T2—411 52 |
| Wickerwork plants | |
|   agriculture | 633.58 |
| Wicketkeeping | 796.358 24 |
| Wicklow (Ireland : County) | T2—418 4 |
| Wicomico County (Md.) | T2—752 25 |
| Wide-area networks | 004.67 |
|   *see also* Computer | |
|     communications | |
| Widgeon grass | 584.74 |
| Widowed people | 306.88 |
| | T1—086 54 |
|   family relationships | 306.88 |
|   psychology | 155.644 |
|   social group | 306.88 |
|   social welfare | 362.829 3 |
| Widowers | 306.882 |
| | T1—086 54 |
|   family relationships | 306.882 |
|   psychology | 155.644 2 |
|   social group | 306.882 |
|   social welfare | 362.829 3 |
| Widows | 306.883 |
| | T1—086 54 |
|   family relationships | 306.883 |
|   psychology | 155.644 3 |
|   social group | 306.883 |
|   social welfare | 362.839 58 |
| Wielkopolskie Voivodeship | |
|   (Poland) | T2—438 49 |
| Wien (Austria) | T2—436 13 |
| Wieringermeer | |
|   (Netherlands) | T2—492 35 |
| Wiesbaden (Germany) | T2—434 165 |
| Wieser, Friedrich, Freiherr von | |
|   economic school | 330.157 |

| | | | |
|---|---|---|---|
| Wife abuse | 362.829 2 | Wild turkeys | 598.645 |
| criminology | 364.155 53 | conservation technology | 639.978 645 |
| criminal law | 345.025 553 | resource economics | 333.958 645 |
| social welfare | 362.829 2 | sports hunting | 799.246 45 |
| *see also* Family violence | | Wild West shows | 791.84 |
| Wife and husband | 306.872 | Wildcat (Felis silvestris) | 599.752 6 |
| law | 346.016 3 | Wildcat (Lynx rufus) | 599.753 6 |
| Wigan (England : | | Wildebeests | 599.645 9 |
| Metropolitan Borough) | T2—427 36 | Wilderness areas | |
| Wight, Isle of (England) | T2—422 8 | conservation | 333.782 16 |
| Wigs | 646.724 8 | law | 346.046 782 |
| customs | 391.5 | natural resources | 333.782 |
| dramatic performances | 792.027 | Wilderness National Park | |
| motion pictures | 791.430 27 | (South Africa) | T2—687 37 |
| stage | 792.027 | Wildfowl | 598.163 |
| television | 791.450 27 | conservation technology | 639.978 163 |
| manufacturing technology | 679 | economic zoology | 598.163 |
| personal care | 646.724 8 | food | 641.391 |
| Wigtown (Scotland) | T2—414 7 | cooking | 641.691 |
| Wijdenbosch, Jules A. | | resource economics | 333.958 29 |
| Surinamese history | 988.303 23 | sports hunting | 799.24 |
| Wikis (Computer science) | 006.75 | waterfowl | 598.41 |
| Wil (Switzerland : | | *see also* Waterfowl | |
| Wahlkreis) | T2—494 725 | Wildfowling | 799.24 |
| Wilbarger County (Tex.) | T2—764 746 | Wildfowling (Waterfowling) | 799.244 |
| Wilcox County (Ala.) | T2—761 38 | Wildlife | 590 |
| Wilcox County (Ga.) | T2—758 845 | resource economics | 333.954 |
| Wild and scenic rivers | 333.784 5 | smuggling | 364.133 67 |
| law | 346.046 784 5 | law | 345.023 367 |
| natural resources | 333.784 5 | *see also* Animals | |
| Wild boars | 599.633 2 | Wildlife conservation | 333.954 16 |
| agricultural pests | 632.696 33 | law | 346.046 951 6 |
| big game hunting | 799.276 332 | technology | 639.9 |
| conservation technology | 639.979 633 2 | Wildlife crimes | 364.162 859 1 |
| resource economics | 333.959 633 2 | law | 345.026 285 91 |
| Wild children | 155.456 7 | Wildlife management | 333.954 |
| Wild edible plants | 641.303 | technology | 639.9 |
| economic botany | 581.632 | Wildlife refuges | 333.954 16 |
| food | 641.303 | Wildlife reserves | 333.954 16 |
| Wild flowers | 582.13 | conservation technology | 639.95 |
| floriculture | 635.967 6 | economics | 333.954 16 |
| Wild horse | 599.665 5 | landscape architecture | 719.36 |
| conservation technology | 639.979 665 5 | law | 346.046 951 6 |
| resource economics | 333.959 665 5 | Wildlife viewing sites | 590.723 4 |
| Wild mango (Dika) | 583.79 | Wildlife watching | 590.723 4 |
| Wild rice | 584.9 | Wilhelmina, Queen of the | |
| cooking | 641.631 78 | Netherlands | |
| food | 641.331 78 | Dutch history | 949.207 1 |
| food crop | 633.178 | Wilhelmshaven (Germany) | T2—435 917 |
| Wild sarsaparilla | 583.84 | Wilkes County (Ga.) | T2—758 172 |
| Wild silk textiles | 677.392 | Wilkes County (N.C.) | T2—756 82 |
| *see also* Textiles | | Wilkin County (Minn.) | T2—776 91 |
| | | Wilkinson County (Ga.) | T2—758 543 |
| | | Wilkinson County (Miss.) | T2—762 25 |

Will 153.8
  philosophy 128.3
    freedom of will 123.5
Will County (Ill.) T2—773 25
Willacy County (Tex.) T2—764 493
Willamette River (Or.) T2—795 3
Willem Pretorius Game
  Reserve (South Africa) T2—685 3
William I, German Emperor
  German history 943.083
William I, King of England
  English history 942.021
William II, German Emperor
  German history 943.084
William II, King of England
  English history 942.022
William III, King of England
  British history 941.068
  English history 942.068
  Scottish history 941.106 8
William IV, King of Great
  Britain
  British history 941.075
  English history 942.075
  Scottish history 941.107 5
Williams County (N.D.) T2—784 73
Williams County (Ohio) T2—771 113
Williams Lake (B.C.) T2—711 75
Williamsburg (Va.) T2—755 425 2
Williamsburg County (S.C.) T2—757 83
Williamson County (Ill.) T2—773 993
Williamson County (Tenn.) T2—768 56
Williamson County (Tex.) T2—764 289
Williamsoniaceae 561.592
Willingdon, Freedman Freedman-
  Thomas, Marquess of
  Indian history 954.035 8
Willisau (Switzerland :
  Amt) T2—494 553
Williston (South Africa :
  District) T2—687 17
Williston Lake (B.C.) T2—711 87
Willmore Wilderness
  Provincial Park (Alta.) T2—712 332
Willowmore (South Africa :
  District) T2—687 51
Willows 583.65
  ornamental arboriculture 635.977 365
Willowvale (South Africa :
  District) T2—687 58
Wills 346.054
  genealogy 929.3
Willy-willies (Hurricanes) 551.552
Wilmington (Del.) T2—751 2

Wilmington (N.C.) T2—756 27
Wilmot Proviso, 1847 973.61
  Civil War (United States) cause 973.711 3
Wilson, Woodrow
  United States history 973.913
Wilson cloud chambers
  nuclear physics 539.777
Wilson County (Kan.) T2—781 925
Wilson County (N.C.) T2—756 43
Wilson County (Tenn.) T2—768 54
Wilson County (Tex.) T2—764 445
Wilsons Promontory
  National Park (Vic.) T2—945 6
Wiltshire (England) T2—423 1
Wimmera (Vic. : District) T2—945 8
Wimmera River (Vic.) T2—945 9
Winburg (South Africa :
  District) T2—685 3
Winches 621.864
Winchester (England : City) T2—422 735
Winchester (Va.) T2—755 991
Wind 551.518
  crop damage 632.16
  geologic agent 551.37
Wind bands 784.8
Wind Cave National Park
  (S.D.) T2—783 95
Wind chimes 786.872
  *see also* Percussion instruments
Wind-driven ships 387.204 3
  design 623.812 043
  engineering 623.820 3
  modern 387.22
    design 623.812 2
    engineering 623.822
    handling 623.882 2
    transportation services 387.22
  transportation services 387.204 3
  *see also* Ships
Wind energy 333.92
Wind engines 621.45
Wind ensembles 785.43
Wind erosion 551.372
Wind instruments 788
  bands and orchestras 784
  chamber ensembles 785
  construction 788.192 3
    by hand 788.192 3
    by machine 681.88
  solo music 788
Wind loads 624.175
Wind-powered electric
  generation 621.312 136
Wind propulsion 621.45

| | |
|---|---|
| Wind River Range (Wyo.) | T2—787 6 |
| Wind scorpions | 595.48 |
| Wind tunnels | |
|   aircraft | 629.134 52 |
| Wind waves | |
|   oceanography | 551.463 |
| Windham County (Conn.) | T2—746 45 |
| Windham County (Vt.) | T2—743 9 |
| Windhoek (Namibia) | T2—688 1 |
| Windlasses | 621.864 |
| Windmills | 621.453 |
| Window-box gardens | 635.967 8 |
| Window displays | |
|   advertising | 659.157 |
| Window furnishings | 645.3 |
|   home sewing | 646.21 |
|   household management | 645.3 |
|   manufacturing technology | 684 |
| Window gardening | 635.967 8 |
| Window glass | 666.152 |
| Window insurance | 368.6 |
| Window managers (Systems | |
|   programs) | 005.437 |
| Windowing programs | 005.437 |
| Windows | |
|   automobile | 629.266 |
|   buildings | 721.823 |
|     architecture | 721.823 |
|     construction | 690.182 3 |
|     interior decoration | 747.3 |
| Windscreen wipers | 678.35 |
|   automobile | 629.276 |
| Windscreens | |
|   automobile | 629.266 |
| Windshield wipers | 678.35 |
|   automobile | 629.276 |
| Windshields | |
|   automobile | 629.266 |
| Windsor (N.S.) | T2—716 35 |
| Windsor (Ont.) | T2—713 32 |
| Windsor, Edward, Duke of | |
|   British history | 941.084 |
|   English history | 942.084 |
|   Scottish history | 941.108 4 |
| Windsor, House of | 941.08 |
|   British history | 941.08 |
|   English history | 942.08 |
|   genealogy | 929.72 |
|   Scottish history | 941.108 |
| Windsor and Maidenhead | |
|   (England) | T2—422 96 |
| Windsor County (Vt.) | T2—743 65 |
| Windsor Tableland National | |
|   Park (Qld.) | T2—943 6 |
| Windstorm insurance | 368.122 |
| Windsurfing | 797.33 |
| Windward Islands | 972.984 |
| | T2—729 84 |
| Wine | 641.22 |
|   commercial processing | 663.2 |
|   cooking with | 641.622 |
|   home economics | 641.22 |
|   home preparation | 641.872 |
| Wings (Air force units) | 358.413 1 |
| Wings (Airplanes) | |
|   engineering | 629.134 32 |
| Wings (Animals) | 591.479 |
|   descriptive zoology | 591.479 |
|     birds | 598.147 9 |
|     insects | 595.714 79 |
|   physiology | 573.798 |
| Wings (Naval air units) | 359.943 4 |
| Winkler County (Tex.) | T2—764 913 |
| Winn Parish (La.) | T2—763 66 |
| Winnebago, Lake | T2—775 64 |
| Winnebago County (Ill.) | T2—773 31 |
| Winnebago County (Iowa) | T2—777 22 |
| Winnebago County (Wis.) | T2—775 64 |
| Winnebago Indians | T5—975 26 |
| Winnebago language | 497.526 |
| | T6—975 26 |
| Winneshiek County (Iowa) | T2—777 32 |
| Winnipeg (Man.) | T2—712 743 |
| Winnipeg, Lake (Man.) | T2—712 72 |
| Winnipegosis, Lake (Man.) | T2—712 72 |
| Winnipesaukee, Lake (N.H.) | T2—742 4 |
| Winona County (Minn.) | T2—776 12 |
| Winooski River (Vt.) | T2—743 17 |
| Winston County (Ala.) | T2—761 74 |
| Winston County (Miss.) | T2—762 692 |
| Winter | 508.2 |
|   music | 781.524 8 |
|   *see also* Seasons | |
| Winter air conditioning | |
|   building systems | 697.933 2 |
| Winter flounder | 597.694 |
| Winter-flowering plants | 581.43 |
|   floriculture | 635.953 |
| Winter Olympic Games | 796.98 |
| Winter sports | 796.9 |
| Winteraceae | 583.22 |
| Wintergreens | 583.66 |
|   flavorings | 641.338 2 |
|   *see also* Flavorings | |
| Winter's bark | 583.22 |
| Winterthur (Switzerland : | |
|   Bezirk) | T2—494 574 7 |

Wire communication systems 384.6
  *see also* Telephone
Wire services
  journalism 070.435
Wire-stitching
  bookbinding 686.35
Wire walking
  sports 796.46
Wired communications 004.6
Wirehaired pointing griffon 636.752
Wireless communication 384.5
  communications services 384.5
  engineering 621.384
  law 343.099 45
  public administration 354.75
Wireless communications 004.6
Wires
  electrical circuits 621.319 33
  metal 671.842
  power transmission 621.854
  sculpture material 731.2
  structural engineering 624.177 4
Wiretapping
  criminal investigation 363.252
  electronic engineering 621.389 28
  law 345.052
Wireworms 595.765
  agricultural pests 632.765
Wirral (England) T2—427 51
Wirt County (W. Va.) T2—754 26
Wisconsin 977.5
  T2—775
Wisconsin Evangelical Lutheran
  Synod 284.134
  *see also* Lutheran church
Wisconsin River (Wis.) T2—775
Wisdom literature (Bible) 223
  Apocrypha 229.3
  Old Testament 223
  pseudepigrapha 229.912
Wisdom of God 212.7
  Christianity 231.6
  comparative religion 202.112
  Judaism 296.311 2
  philosophy of religion 212.7
Wisdom of Solomon (Bible) 229.3
Wise County (Tex.) T2—764 532
Wise County (Va.) T2—755 743
Wise men (Christian doctrines) 232.923
Wisent 599.643
Wismar (Germany) T2—431 76
Wisterias 635.933 74
  botany 583.74
  floriculture 635.933 74

Wit and humor 152.43
Witbank (South Africa :
  District) T2—682 76
Witch hazels (Plants) 583.44
Witchcraft 133.43
  arts T3C—377
  literature 808.803 77
   history and criticism 809.933 77
   specific literatures T3B—080 377
   history and
    criticism T3B—093 77
  religious practice 203.3
   African religions 299.613 3
   modern revivals 299.94
   Native American religions 299.713 3
  sociology 306.4
Witches (Occultists) 133.430 92
  persecution by Church 272.8
  *see also* Legendary beings
Witches (Religious leaders) 200.92
  biography 200.92
  modern revivals of old
   religions 299.94
  role and function 206.1
  *see Manual at* 200.92 and
   201–209, 292–299
Witham, River (England) T2—425 3
Withholding tax 336.242 2
  law 343.052 424
Withlacoochee River (Fla.) T2—759 7
Witness bearing 248.5
Witnesses 347.066
  police interrogation 363.254
  trial procedure 347.075
Witotoan languages 498.9
  T6—989
Witrivier (South Africa :
  District) T2—682 71
Witsieshoek (South Africa :
  District) T2—685 1
Wittmund (Germany :
  Landkreis) T2—435 917
Witwatersrand (South
  Africa) T2—682 2
Wives 306.872 3
  T1—086 55
  social welfare 362.839 52
  *see also* Married women
Wives of alcoholics
  social welfare 362.292 3
Wives of clergymen
  Christianity 253.22
  *see also* Spouses of clergy —
   Christianity

Wives of substance abusers
  social welfare      362.291 3
Wizardry      133.43
  religious practice      203.3
    modern revivals      299.94
Wizards (Occultists)      133.430 92
  *see also* Legendary beings
Wizards (Religious leaders)      200.92
  biography      200.92
  role and function      206.1
  *see Manual at* 200.92 and
    201–209, 292–299
Włocławek (Poland :
  Voivodeship)      T2—438 26
Wobblies      331.886 097 3
Wodehouse (South Africa :
  District)      T2—687 57
Wodonga (Vic.)      T2—945 5
Województwo Dolnośląskie
  (Poland)      T2—438 52
Województwo Kujawsko-
  Pomorskie (Poland)      T2—438 26
Województwo Łódzkie
  (Poland)      T2—438 47
Województwo Lubelskie
  (Poland)      T2—438 43
Województwo Lubuskie
  (Poland)      T2—438 12
Województwo Małopolskie
  (Poland)      T2—438 62
Województwo Mazowieckie
  (Poland)      T2—438 41
Województwo Opolskie
  (Poland)      T2—438 55
Województwo Podkarpackie
  (Poland)      T2—438 66
Województwo Podlaskie
  (Poland)      T2—438 36
Województwo Pomorskie
  (Poland)      T2—438 22
Województwo Śląskie
  (Poland)      T2—438 58
Województwo
  Świętokrzyskie (Poland)      T2—438 45
Województwo Warmińsko-
  Mazurskie (Poland)      T2—438 32
Województwo
  Wielkopolskie (Poland)      T2—438 49
Województwo
  Zachodniopomorskie
  (Poland)      T2—438 16
Wok cooking      641.774
Woking (England)      T2—422 142

Wokingham (England :
  District)      T2—422 94
Wolds, The (England)      T2—428 3
Wolf children      155.456 7
Wolf-Rayet stars      523.88
Wolfe County (Ky.)      T2—769 213
Wolfhounds      636.753 5
Wolfram      669.734
  *see also* Tungsten
Wolframite
  mineralogy      549.74
Wolfsbanes      583.34
Wolfville (N.S.)      T2—716 34
Wollastonite
  mineralogy      549.66
Wollongong (N.S.W.)      T2—944 6
Wolmaransstad (South
  Africa : District)      T2—682 45
Wolof (African people)      T5—963 214
Wolof language      496.321 4
     T6—963 214
Wolof literature      896.321 4
Wolverhampton (England)      T2—424 91
Wolverine      599.766
Wolves      599.773
  animal husbandry      636.977 3
  conservation technology      639.979 773
  predator control technology      636.083 9
    conservation technology      639.966
  resource economics      333.959 773
  zoology      599.773
Wombats      599.24
Women      305.4
     T1—082
  advertising images and themes      659.104 552 2
  art representation      704.942 4
  arts      700.452 2
     T3C—352 2
  Bible      220.830 54
  biography      920.72
  civil and human rights      323.34
    *see also* Women's rights
  criminal offenders      364.374
  drawing      743.44
  education      371.822
  etiquette      395.144
  fine arts      704.042
  government programs      353.535
  grooming      646.704 2
  health      613.042 44
  journalism for      070.483 47
  labor economics      331.4

Women (continued)
  legal status      346.013 4
    constitutional law      342.087 8
    private law      346.013 4
  literature      808.803 522
    history and criticism      809.933 522
    specific literatures      T3B—080 352 2
      history and
        criticism      T3B—093 522
  painting      757.4
  physical fitness      613.704 5
  political organizations      324.3
  psychology      155.333
  recreation      790.194
    indoor      793.019 4
    outdoor      796.082
  relations with government      323.34
  religion      200.82
    Christianity      270.082
      devotional literature      242.643
      guides to Christian life      248.843
    guides to life      204.408 2
    Islam      297.082
      guides to life      297.570 82
    Judaism      296.082
      guides to life      296.708 2
  sex hygiene      613.954
  social aspects      305.4
  social welfare      362.83
    public administration      353.535
  suffrage      324.623
  *see Manual at* T1—081 and
    T1—08351, T1—08352,
    T1—08421, T1—08422
Women and religion      200.82
  *see also* Women — religion
Women authors (Literature)      809.892 87
  specific literatures      T3B—099 287
Women clergy      200.92
  biography      200.92
  Christian      270.092
    biography      270.092
      specific denominations      280
      *see Manual at* 230–280
    ecclesiology      262.1
    ordination      262.14
    pastoral theology      253.082
    *see also* Clergy — Christian
  Judaism      296.092
  ordination      206.108 2
  role and function      206.108 2
  *see Manual at* 200.92 and
    201–209, 292–299

Women in combat      355.408 2
Women in education      370.82
  secondary level      373.082
Women of the Bible      220.920 82
Women rabbis      296.092
  biography      296.092
    specific denominations      296.8
  ordination      296.610 82
  role and function      296.610 82
Women workers      331.4
  economics      331.4
  public administration      354.908 2
Women's baseball      796.357 8
Women's basketball      796.323 8
Women's clothing      391.2
  commercial technology      687.082
  customs      391.2
  home economics      646.34
  home sewing      646.404
  *see also* Clothing
Women's football      796.332 8
Women's movements      305.42
Women's political organizations      324.3
Women's prisons      365.43
  *see also* Penal institutions
Women's rights      323.34
  law      342.087 8
  law of nations      341.485 8
  political science      323.34
  sociology      305.42
Women's shelters      362.838 3
Women's suffrage      324.623
Women's units (Armed forces)      355.348
Women's voices      782.6
  choral and mixed voices      782.6
  single voices      783.6
Wonderboom (South
  Africa : District)      T2—682 28
Wood      575.46
  architectural construction      721.044 8
  architectural decoration      729.6
  biology      575.46
  building material      691.1
  fuel      333.953 97
    chemical technology      662.65
    resource economics      333.953 97
  handicrafts      745.51
  lumber technology      674
  materials science      620.12
  sculpture material      731.2
  ship design      623.818 4
  shipbuilding      623.820 7
  structural engineering      624.184
Wood boring beetles      595.764 8

| | |
|---|---|
| Wood briquettes | 662.65 |
| Wood Buffalo National Park (Alta.) | T2—712 32 |
| Wood carving | 736.4 |
| Wood construction | 694 |
| Wood County (Ohio) | T2—771 16 |
| Wood County (Tex.) | T2—764 223 |
| Wood County (W. Va.) | T2—754 22 |
| Wood County (Wis.) | T2—775 52 |
| Wood duck | 598.412 3 |
|   conservation technology | 639.978 412 3 |
|   resource economics | 333.958 412 3 |
| Wood engraving | 761.2 |
| Wood flour | 674.84 |
| Wood laminates | 674.835 |
|   *see also* Wood | |
| Wood lice | 595.372 |
| Wood mice (Apodemus) | 599.358 5 |
| Wood mice (Peromyscus) | 599.355 |
| Wood oil | 665.33 |
| Wood pavements | 625.83 |
| Wood products | 674.8 |
| Wood products workers | 674.809 2 |
| Wood pulp | 676.12 |
| Wood rats | 599.357 3 |
| Wood sculpturing | 731.462 |
| Wood shavings | 674.84 |
| Wood shrews | 599.332 |
| Wood shrikes | 598.8 |
| Wood snakes | 597.967 |
| Wood sorrels | 583.79 |
| Wood-stove cooking | 641.58 |
| Wood swallows | 598.8 |
| Wood technology | |
|   equipment manufacturing technology | 681.767 6 |
| Wood turtle | 597.925 7 |
| Wood-using technologies | 674.8 |
| Wood warblers | 598.872 |
| Woodburning | 745.514 |
| Woodbury County (Iowa) | T2—777 41 |
| Woodchuck | 599.366 |
|   small game hunting | 799.259 366 |
| Woodcocks | 598.33 |
|   sports hunting | 799.248 33 |
| Woodcraft | |
|   camp activity | 796.545 |
| Woodcreepers | 598.822 |
| Wooden furniture | 645.4 |
|   manufacturing technology | 684.104 |
|   *see also* Furniture | |
| Wooden ships | |
|   construction | 623.820 7 |
| Wooden shoes | 391.413 |
|   commercial technology | 685.32 |
|   customs | 391.413 |
|   *see also* Clothing | |
| Woodend (Vic.) | T2—945 3 |
| Woodenware | 674.88 |
| Woodford County (Ill.) | T2—773 53 |
| Woodford County (Ky.) | T2—769 465 |
| Woodland Indians | T5—97 |
| Woodlands | 333.75 |
| | T2—152 |
|   *see also* Forest lands | |
| Woodlark Island (Papua New Guinea) | T2—954 1 |
| Woodlots | |
|   agroforestry | 634.99 |
| Woodpeckers | 598.72 |
| Woodruff County (Ark.) | T2—767 92 |
| Woods (Golf equipment) | 796.352 32 |
| Woods, Lake of the | T2—776 81 |
|   Canada | T2—713 11 |
|   Minnesota | T2—776 81 |
| Woods County (Okla.) | T2—766 21 |
| Woodson County (Kan.) | T2—781 923 |
| Woodspring (England) | T2—423 96 |
| Woodward County (Okla.) | T2—766 19 |
| Woodwind bands | 784.89 |
| Woodwind instruments | 788.2 |
|   bands and orchestras | 784 |
|   chamber ensembles | 785 |
|     mixed | 785.2–.5 |
|     single type | 785.8 |
|   construction | 788.219 23 |
|     by hand | 788.219 23 |
|     by machine | 681.882 |
|   solo music | 788.2 |
| Woodwork | |
|   interior decoration | 747.3 |
| Woodworking | 684.08 |
|   carpentry | 694 |
|   home workshops | 684.08 |
|   lumber technology | 674 |
| Woody plants | 582.16 |
|   landscape architecture | 715 |
| Woody vines | 582.18 |
| Wool growing | 636.314 5 |
| Wool textiles | 677.31 |
|   *see also* Textiles | |
| Wool wax | 665.13 |
| Woolly monkeys | 599.858 |
| Worcester (England) | T2—424 48 |
| Worcester (South Africa : District) | T2—687 33 |
| Worcester County (Mass.) | T2—744 3 |

Worcester County (Md.)          T2—752 21
Worcestershire (England)        T2—424 4
Word-attack skills (Reading)
    primary education           372.46
Word classes                    415
    specific languages          T4—5
Word dividers (Dictionaries)    413.1
    specific languages          T4—31
Word formation                  415.92
    specific languages          T4—592
Word games                      793.734
Word of God
    Bible                       220.13
    Jesus Christ                232.2
Word order                      415
    specific languages          T4—5
Word origins                    412
    specific languages          T4—2
Word processing                 005.52
Word-recognition method
    primary education           372.462
Word sense disambiguation
    natural language processing 401.430 285 635
        specific languages      T4—014 302 856 35
Word study
    primary education           372.61
Word usage
    rhetoric                    808
Words                           401.4
                                T1—014
    dictionaries                413
    music                       780
        treatises               780.268
    specific languages          T4—014
        dictionaries            T4—3
        usage (Applied
            linguistics)        T4—81
        *see Manual at* T4—3 vs.
            T4—81
    usage (Applied linguistics) 418
Work                            331
    *see also* Labor
Work (Mechanics)                531.6
Work (Physiological exertion)   573.79
    human physiology            612.042
Work animals                    636.088 6
Work areas
    home economics              643.58
Work associates
    applied psychology          158.26
    psychological influence     155.926
Work at home
    labor economics             331.256 7

Work camps (Correctional
    programs)                   365.34
    *see also* Penal institutions
Work cars                       385.32
    engineering                 625.22
    transportation services     385.32
    *see also* Rolling stock
Work environment                331.256
    economics                   331.256
    engineering                 620.8
    personnel management        658.38
        public administration   352.67
    public administration       354.98
    safety                      363.11
        public administration   353.96
        *see also* Industrial safety
    sanitation                  363.729 5
        public administration   353.94
Work ethic                      306.361 3
Work force                      331.11
Work-force diversity            331.133
    personnel management        658.300 8
Work furloughs
    penology                    365.65
Work groups                     658.402 2
    *see also* Work teams
Work load
    production management       658.54
Work music                      781.593
Work periods                    331.257
    economics                   331.257
    personnel management        658.312 1
        public administration   352.67
    public administration       354.98
Work places                     331.256
    *see also* Work environment
Work pressures
    executive management        658.409 5
Work productivity
    personnel management
        public administration   352.66
    promotion of
        personnel management    658.314
Work release
    penology                    365.65
Work satisfaction               331.012
    *see also* Job satisfaction
Work sharing                    331.257 2
Work shifts                     331.257 25
Work songs                      782.421 593
Work stress
    labor economics             331.256
Work studies
    production management       658.54

Work-study plan 371.227
  higher education 378.37
  secondary education 373.28
Work-study programs 371.225
  higher education 378.365
Work teams 658.402 2
  group decision making 658.403 6
  internal organization 658.402 2
  personnel utilization
    public administration 352.66
  production management 658.533
    quality control 658.562
Work training 370.113
  *see also* Vocational education
Work vehicles
  automotive engineering 629.225
  driving 629.284 5
  repair 629.287 5
Workaholism
  personality trait 155.232
Workbooks T1—076
Workday 331.257 23
  economics 331.257 23
  personnel management 658.312 1
Worker control of industry 338.69
  production economics 338.69
  theory of union role 331.880 1
Worker parties 324.217
  international organizations 324.17
Worker rights 331.011
  law 344.010 1
Worker security 331.259 6
  law 344.012 596
    public employees 342.068 6
  public administration 354.98
Worker self-management 338.69
  personnel management 658.315 2
  theory of union role 331.880 1
Workers 331.11
  economics 331.11
  public administration 354.9
  social class 305.562
Workers' compensation
  insurance 368.41
  employers' liability 368.56
  government-sponsored 368.41
  law 344.021
  personnel management 658.325 4
  public administration 353.69
Workflow
  production management 658.53
Workhouses (Correctional
  institutions) 365.34
  *see also* Penal institutions

Working capital 332.041 2
  financial management 658.152 44
Working class 305.562
               T1—086 23
  civil rights 323.322 3
  customs 390.1
    dress 391.01
  lower class T1—086 24
  middle class T1—086 23
  relations with government 323.322 3
  social welfare 362.85
    public administration 354.9
Working-class parties 324.217
  international organizations 324.17
Working conditions (Physical) 331.256
  *see also* Work environment
Working dogs (Breeds of dogs) 636.73
  *see Manual at* 636.70886,
    636.70888 vs. 636.73,
    636.752
Working dogs (Dogs as working
  animals) 636.708 86
  *see Manual at* 636.70886,
    636.70888 vs. 636.73,
    636.752
Working environment 331.256
  *see also* Work environment
Working mothers
  economics 331.44
Working ships 387.2
  engineering 623.82
  power-driven 387.248
    engineering 623.824
    transportation services 387.248
  small craft 387.204 26
    engineering 623.820 26
    transportation services 387.204 26
  transportation services 387.2
  wind-driven 387.226
    engineering 623.822 6
    transportation services 387.226
  *see also* Ships
Workmen's compensation
  insurance 368.41
  *see also* Workers'
    compensation insurance
Workplace diversity 331.133
  personnel management 658.300 8
Workplace environment 331.256
  *see also* Work environment
Workplace violence
  prevention
    management 658.473

Workplaces    331.256
*see also* Work environment
Workshops (Seminars)    T1—071 5
Workshops (Workrooms)
   agriculture    631.304
Workstations (Microcomputers)    004.16
*see also* Personal computers
Workweek    331.257
   economics    331.257
   personnel management    658.312 1
World Bank    332.153 2
   law    346.082 153 2
World-circling travel    910.41
World community
   law of nations    341.2
World Community of al-Islam in
   the West    297.87
World Court    341.552
World Cup competition
   soccer    796.334 668
World fairs    907.4
*see also* Exhibitions
World government    321.04
   law    341.21
World history    909
   arts    T3C—358 2
   literature    808.803 582
     history and criticism    809.933 582
     specific literatures    T3B—080 358 2
     history and
       criticism    T3B—093 582
World Party of Socialist
   Revolution    324.175
World politics and religion
   social theology    201.727
     Christianity    261.7
     Judaism    296.382 7
   *see also* Politics and
      religion — social
      theology
World series (Baseball)    796.357 646
World Trade Organization    382.92
World views    140
World War I, 1914–1918    940.3
      T1—090 41
   societies    369.2
     United States    369.186
World War II, 1939–1945    940.53
      T1—090 44
   societies    369.2
     United States    369.186
World Wide Web    004.678
   computer science    004.678
   hypertext    006.7

World Wide Web (continued)
   information systems    025.042
   publishing    070.579 73
   sociology    302.231
   *see Manual at* 004.678 vs.
     006.7, 025.042, 384.33
Worm-caused diseases    571.999
   agriculture    632.623
   animals    571.999 1
     veterinary medicine    636.089 696 2
   humans
     incidence    614.552
     medicine    616.962
     *see also* Communicable
       diseases — humans
   plants    571.999 2
     agriculture    632.623
Worm culture    639.75
WORM discs    004.565
   engineering    621.397 67
Worm farming    639.75
Worm gears    621.833 3
Worm lizards    597.948
Worm snakes    597.969
Worms    592.3
   agricultural pests    632.623
   culture    639.75
   paleozoology    562.3
   plant crop pests    632.623
Worms (Computer security)    005.84
Worms (Germany)    T2—434 352
Wormwood    641.338 2
   botany    583.99
   *see also* Flavorings; Herbs
Wororan languages    499.15
      T6—991 5
Worry    152.46
Worship    204.3
   Buddhism    294.344 3
   Christianity    248.3
   Hinduism    294.543
   Islam    297.3
     Sufi    297.43
   Judaism    296.45
   *see also* Public worship
Worth
   epistemology    121.8
Worth County (Ga.)    T2—758 945
Worth County (Iowa)    T2—777 232
Worth County (Mo.)    T2—778 143
Worthing (England)    T2—422 68

| | | | |
|---|---|---|---|
| Wounds | | Writing instruments | |
| biology | 571.975 | manufacturing technology | 681.6 |
| incidence | 614.3 | Writing skills | |
| medicine | 617.1 | primary education | 372.623 |
| Woven felt | 677.62 | Writing systems (Linguistics) | 411 |
| *see also* Textiles | | specific languages | T4—11 |
| Wrangel Island (Russia) | T2—577 | Writings (Bible) | 223 |
| Wrangell-Saint Elias | | Written communication | 302.224 4 |
| National Park and | | management use | 658.453 |
| Preserve (Alaska) | T2—798 3 | office services | 651.74 |
| Wrapping paper | 676.287 | primary education | 372.623 |
| Wraps (Clothing) | 391.46 | rhetoric | 808 |
| commercial technology | 687.19 | sociology | 302.224 4 |
| home sewing | 646.45 | Written language disorders | |
| *see also* Outerwear | | medicine | 616.855 3 |
| Wraps (Stuffed foods) | 641.84 | *see also* Communication | |
| Wrasses | 597.7 | disorders | |
| Wreaths | 745.926 | Wrocław (Poland : | |
| Wreckage studies | | Voivodeship) | T2—438 52 |
| aeronautics | 629.132 55 | Wrongful death | 346.032 3 |
| automotive | 629.282 6 | Wrongful entry | 346.036 |
| naval architecture | 623.817 6 | Wrought iron | 669.141 4 |
| seamanship | 623.888 5 | decorative arts | 739.4 |
| structural analysis | 624.176 | WTO (World Trade | |
| Wrecking bars | 621.93 | Organization) | 382.92 |
| Wrecking buildings | 690.26 | Wu dialects | 495.172 |
| Wrekin, The (England : | | | T6—951 7 |
| District) | T2—424 56 | Wujs | 787.94 |
| Wren-tit | 598.834 | *see also* Stringed instruments | |
| Wrenches | 621.972 | Wuppertal (Germany) | T2—435 532 |
| Wrens | 598.833 | Württemberg (Germany) | T2—434 7 |
| Wrestlers | 796.812 092 | Würtz-Fittig reaction | |
| Wrestling | 796.812 | chemical engineering | 660.284 4 |
| Wrexham (Wales: County | | Würzburg (Germany) | T2—433 39 |
| Borough) | T2—429 39 | WWW (World Wide Web) | 004.678 |
| Wrexham Maelor (Wales) | T2—429 39 | *see also* World Wide Web | |
| Wright County (Iowa) | T2—777 274 | Wyandot County (Ohio) | T2—771 26 |
| Wright County (Minn.) | T2—776 51 | Wyandot Indians | T5—975 55 |
| Wright County (Mo.) | T2—778 825 | Wyandot language | 497.555 |
| Wrigley (N.W.T.) | T2—719 3 | | T6—975 55 |
| Wrinkle-resistant fabrics | 677.681 | Wyandotte chicken | 636.583 |
| *see also* Textiles | | Wyandotte County (Kan.) | T2—781 39 |
| Wrist techniques | | Wychavon (England) | T2—424 49 |
| music | 784.193 64 | Wycliffe Bible | 220.520 1 |
| Wrists | 612.97 | Wycliffites | 284.3 |
| physiology | 612.97 | Wycombe (England : | |
| regional medicine | 617.574 | District) | T2—425 95 |
| surgery | 617.574 | Wye, River (Wales and | |
| *see also* Upper extremities | | England) | T2—429 5 |
| Write once read many discs | 004.565 | Wynberg (South Africa : | |
| engineering | 621.397 67 | District) | T2—687 35 |
| Write once read many drives | 004.565 | Wyndham (W.A.) | T2—941 4 |
| engineering | 621.397 67 | Wynyard (Tas.) | T2—946 5 |
| Writing (Manual skill) | 652.1 | | |

Wyoming 978.7
 T2—787
Wyoming County (N.Y.) T2—747 93
Wyoming County (Pa.) T2—748 35
Wyoming County (W. Va.) T2—754 45
Wyperfeld National Park
 (Vic.) T2—945 9
Wyre (England) T2—427 682
Wyre Forest (England) T2—424 41
Wythe County (Va.) T2—755 773

# X

X, Malcolm 320.558 092
X-ray astronomy 522.686 3
X-ray computed tomography
 medicine 616.075 722
X-ray electronics 537.535
X-ray equipment
 manufacturing technology 681.753
 public safety 363.189
X-ray examination
 medicine 616.075 72
X-ray metallography 669.950 283
X-ray photography
 engineering 621.367 3
X-ray spectroscopes
 manufacturing technology 681.414 8
X-ray spectroscopy 543.62
 analytical chemistry 543.62
 engineering 621.361
 physics 537.535 2
X-ray testing
 materials science 620.112 72
X-ray therapy
 medicine 615.842 2
X rays 539.722 2
 biophysics 571.457
 humans 612.014 485
Xanthē (Greece : Nome) T2—495 7
Xanthophyta 579.82
Xanthorrhoeaceae 584.35
Xantusiidae 597.959 8
Xavante language 498.4
 T6—984
Xenarthra 599.31
Xenon
 chemistry 546.755
 gas technology 665.822
Xenopeltidae 597.967
Xenopus 597.865 4
Xenosauridae 597.959
Xenungulata 569.62

Xeroderma
 medicine 616.544
 *see also* Skin diseases —
  humans
Xerography 686.442
 equipment manufacturing
  technology 681.65
 office use 652.4
 technology 686.442
Xhosa (African people) T5—963 985
Xhosa language 496.398 5
 T6—963 985
Xhosa literature 896.398 5
Xiang dialects 495.172 15
 T6—951 7
Xinca language 497.9
 T6—979
Xinjiang Uygur Zizhiqu
 (China) T2—516
Xinjiang Weiwuer Zizhiqu
 (China) T2—516
Xiphiidae 597.78
Xiphosura 595.492
 paleozoology 565.492
Xizang Zizhiqu (China) T2—515
Xoloitzcuintli 636.76
Xosa language 496.398 5
 T6—963 985
Xosa literature 896.398 5
Xylariales 579.567
Xylem 575.46
Xylophones 786.843
 *see also* Percussion instruments
Xyridaceae 584.86

# Y

Yacht basins
 engineering 627.38
Yacht racing 797.14
Yachting 797.124 6
Yachts 387.204 23
 engineering 623.820 23
 handling 623.881 23
 power-driven 387.231 4
  engineering 623.823 14
  transportation services 387.231 4
 transportation services 387.204 23
 wind-driven 387.223
  design 623.812 23
  engineering 623.822 3
  transportation services 387.223
 *see also* Ships
Yad ha-ḥazaḳah 296.181 2

YaDabub behér
  béhérasbočenā hezbač
  kelel (Ethiopia)   T2—633
Yadayim   296.123 6
Yadkin County (N.C.)   T2—756 66
Yadkin River (N.C.)   T2—756 68
Yagua language   498.9
  T6—989
Yahya Khan, Aga Muhammad
  Pakistani history   954.904 6
Yajurveda   294.592 14
Yak   599.642 2
Yaka (African people)   T5—963 93
Yakama Indians   979.700 497 412 7
  T5—974 127
Yakama language   497.412 7
  T6—974 127
Yakima County (Wash.)   T2—797 55
Yakima River (Wash.)   T2—797 55
Yakut   T5—943 32
Yakut language   494.332
  T6—943 32
Yakut literature   894.332
Yakutat (Alaska)   T2—798 2
Yakutia (Russia)   T2—575
Yalobusha County (Miss.)   T2—762 82
Yalova İli (Turkey)   T2—563 3
  ancient   T2—393 13
Yamagata-ken (Japan)   T2—521 16
Yamaguchi-ken (Japan)   T2—521 97
Yamal-Nenets (Russia)   T2—573
Yamal-Nenetskiĭ
  avtonomnyĭ okrug
  (Russia)   T2—573
Yamanashi-ken (Japan)   T2—521 64
Yambasa languages   496.396
  T6—963 96
Yamhill County (Or.)   T2—795 39
Yami (Taiwan people)   T5—992 5
Yamoussoukro (Ivory
  Coast)   T2—666 8
Yams (Dioscorea)   641.352 3
  agriculture   635.23
  botany   584.357
  commercial processing   664.805 23
  cooking   641.652 3
  food   641.352 3
Yams (Sweet potatoes)   641.352 2
  botany   583.94
  *so* Sweet potatoes
  ᵒunty (N.C.)   T2—756 873
  787.74
  ᵈd instruments
  ᵗna)   T2—512

Yankton County (S.D.)   T2—783 394
Yanomam languages   498.92
  T6—989 2
Yanomamo Indians   T5—989 2
Yanomamo language   498.92
  T6—989 2
Yanzi language   496.396
  T6—963 96
Yao (African people)   T5—963 97
Yao (Southeast Asian
  people)   T5—959 78
Yao language (Southeastern
  Asia)   495.978
  T6—959 78
Yao languages (Africa)   496.397
  T6—963 97
Yao literature (Southeastern
  Asia)   895.978
Yaoundé (Cameroon)   T2—671 1
Yap (Micronesia)   T2—966
Yapese language   499.52
  T6—995 2
Yaqui Indians   T5—974 542
Yaqui language   497.454 2
  T6—974 542
Yaqui literature   897.454 2
Yaracuy (Venezuela)   T2—872 6
Yar'adua, Umaru Musa
  Nigerian history   966.905 5
Yard goods   677.632
Yard sales   381.195
  management   658.87
  *see also* Commerce
Yards
  landscape architecture   712.6
Yare, River (England)   T2—426 1
Yarmouth (N.S. : County)   T2—716 31
Yarn   677.028 62
  home sewing   646.19
  manufacturing technology   677.028 62
Yaroslavl' (Russia : Oblast)   T2—473 2
Yarra River (Vic.)   T2—945 2
Yaruro language   498.9
  T6—989
Yass (N.S.W.)   T2—944 7
Yates County (N.Y.)   T2—747 82
Yaunde-Fang languages   496.396
  T6—963 96
Yavapai County (Ariz.)   T2—791 57
Yavapai Indians   T5—975 724
Yavapai language   497.572 4
  T6—975 724
Yaw (Aeronautics)   629.132 364

Yawning
  human physiology     612.21
Yaws
  medicine     616.523
  *see also* Skin diseases —
    humans
Yayi, Boni
  Beninese history     966.830 54
Yazd (Iran : Province)     T2—559 4
Yazoo County (Miss.)     T2—762 49
Yazoo Mississippi Delta
  (Miss. : Region)     T2—762 4
Yazoo River (Miss.)     T2—762 4
Year-round school     371.236
Year-round systems
  air conditioning     697.933 4
Yearbooks     050
     T1—05
  encyclopedia     030
  publishing     070.572
Yearly Conference of People
  Called Methodists     287.53
  *see also* Methodist Church
Years     529.2
Yeast breads     641.815
Yeasts     579.562
Yeasts (Basidiomycetes)     579.59
Yeasts (Common yeasts)     579.563
  leaven     664.68
Yeasts (Saccharomycetaceae)     579.562
Yell County (Ark.)     T2—767 38
Yellow-dog contracts     331.894
Yellow-eyed grass     584.86
Yellow fever
  incidence     614.541
  medicine     616.918 54
  *see also* Communicable
    diseases — humans
Yellow-green algae     579.82
Yellow Medicine County
  (Minn.)     T2—776 37
Yellow pages (Directories)     T1—029
  *see Manual at* T1—025 vs.
    T1—029
Yellow poplar     583.22
  forestry     634.973 22
Yellow River (China)     T2—511
Yellow Sea     551.461 456
     T2—164 56
Yellowknife (N.W.T.)     T2—719 3
Yellowstone County
  (Mont.)     T2—786 39
Yellowstone National Park     T2—787 52
  Montana     T2—786 661

Yellowstone River     T2—786 3
Yellowwoods     585.3
Yeltsin, Boris Nikolayevich
  Russian history     947.086 1
Yemen     953.3
     T2—533
  ancient     939.49
     T2—394 9
Yemen (People's Democratic     953.350 52
  Republic)     953.350 52
     T2—533 5
     T2—533 5
Yemen (Republic of Yemen)     953.305 3
     T2—533
Yemen (Yemen Arab Republic)     953.320 52
     T2—533 2
Yemen Arab Republic     953.320 52
     T2—533 2
Yemenis     T5—927 533
  Northern Yemen     T5—927 533 2
  Southern Yemen     T5—927 533 5
Yên Bái (Vietnam :
  Province)     T2—597 1
Yenisei Ostyak     T5—946
Yenisei-Ostyak language     494.6
     T6—946
Yenisei Samoyed language     494.4
     T6—944
Yeppoon (Qld.)     T2—943 5
Yersinia     579.34
Yersinia infections
  incidence     614.573
  medicine     616.923
  *see also* Communicable
    diseases — humans
Yeshivot     296.071 1
Yevamot     296.123 3
  Babylonian Talmud     296.125 3
  Mishnah     296.123 3
  Palestinian Talmud     296.124 3
Yevrey Autonomous Region
  (Russia)     T2—577
Yews     585.6
Yeye language     496.399
     T6—963 99
Yezidis
  religion     299.159
Yi dynasty     951.902
Yiddish language     439.1
     T6—391
Yiddish literature     839.1
Yield point (Mechanics)     531.381
Yields
  crop production     631.558

| | |
|---|---|
| Yin dynasty | 931.02 |
| Yindjibarndi language | 499.15 |
| | T6—991 5 |
| YMCA (Association) | 267.3 |
| Ynys Môn (Wales) | T2—429 21 |
| Yo-Yos | 796.2 |
| Yoakum County (Tex.) | T2—764 849 |
| Yobe State (Nigeria) | T2—669 87 |
| Yodo River (Japan) | T2 521 83 |
| Yoga | 181.45 |
| Buddhism | 294.344 36 |
| comparative religion | 204.36 |
| health | 613.704 6 |
| Hinduism | 294.543 6 |
| philosophy | 181.45 |
| Yogacara Buddhism | 294.392 |
| Yogurt | 641.371 476 |
| cooking | 641.671 476 |
| food | 641.371 476 |
| processing | 637.147 6 |
| Yogyakarta (Indonesia : | |
| Daerah Istimewa) | T2—598 27 |
| Yoho National Park (B.C.) | T2—711 68 |
| Yok-Utian languages | 497.413 |
| | T6—974 13 |
| Yokohama-shi (Japan) | T2—521 364 |
| Yokuts Indians | T5—974 13 |
| Yokuts language | 497.413 |
| | T6—974 13 |
| Yolo County (Calif.) | T2—794 51 |
| Yom Kippur | 296.432 |
| liturgy | 296.453 2 |
| Yom Kippur War, 1973 | 956.048 |
| Yoma | 296.123 2 |
| Babylonian Talmud | 296.125 2 |
| Mishnah | 296.123 2 |
| Palestinian Talmud | 296.124 2 |
| Yonne (France) | T2—444 12 |
| York (England) | T2—428 43 |
| York (N.B.) | T2—715 51 |
| York (Ont. : County) | T2—713 54 |
| York (Ont. : Regional | |
| municipality) | T2—713 547 |
| York (Toronto, Ont.) | T2—713 541 |
| York, House of | 942.04 |
| English history | 942.04 |
| Irish history | 941.504 |
| York County (Me.) | T2—741 95 |
| York County (Neb.) | T2—782 345 |
| York County (Pa.) | T2—748 41 |
| York County (S.C.) | T2—757 43 |
| York County (Va.) | T2—755 423 |
| Yorke Peninsula (S. Aust.) | T2—942 35 |
| Yorkshire (England) | T2—428 1 |

| | |
|---|---|
| Yorkshire Dales (England) | T2—428 4 |
| Yorkshire terrier | 636.76 |
| Yorkshire Wolds (England) | T2—428 3 |
| Yorkton (Sask.) | T2—712 42 |
| Yoro (Honduras : Dept.) | T2—728 314 |
| Yoruba (African people) | T5—963 33 |
| Yoruba language | 496.333 |
| | T6—963 33 |
| Yoruba literature | 896.333 |
| Yoruboid languages | 496.333 |
| | T6—963 33 |
| Yosemite National Park | |
| (Calif.) | T2—794 47 |
| Young adult literature | 808.899 283 |
| history and criticism | 809.892 83 |
| specific literatures | T3B—080 928 3 |
| history and criticism | T3B—099 283 |
| Young adults | 305.242 |
| | T1—084 2 |
| civil rights | 323.353 |
| etiquette | 395.124 |
| health | 613.043 4 |
| journalism for | 070.483 4 |
| labor economics | 331.34 |
| legal status | |
| constitutional law | 342.087 7 |
| life skills | 646.700 842 |
| physiology | 612.661 |
| political organizations | 324.3 |
| psychology | 155.65 |
| recreation | 790.192 |
| indoor | 793.019 2 |
| outdoor | 796.083 5 |
| relations with government | 323.353 |
| religion | 200.842 |
| Christianity | 270.084 2 |
| devotional literature | 242.64 |
| guides to Christian life | 248.84 |
| pastoral care | 259.25 |
| religious associations | 267.6 |
| religious education | 268.434 |
| social aspects | 305.242 |
| social welfare | 362 |
| under eighteen | |
| social welfare | |
| law | 344.032 708 3 |
| under twenty-one | 305.235 |
| | T1—083 5 |
| legal status | 346.013 5 |
| private law | 346.013 5 |
| social welfare | 362.708 3 |
| *see also* Adolescents | |

| | |
|---|---|
| Young animals | 591.392 |
|   domestic animals | 636.07 |
|   mammals | 599.139 2 |
| Young County (Tex.) | T2—764 545 |
| Young men | 305.242 1 |
| | T1—084 21 |
|   etiquette | 395.124 1 |
|   journalism for | 070.483 46 |
|   psychology | 155.65 |
|   social aspects | 305.242 1 |
|   social welfare | 362 |
|   under twenty-one | 305.235 1 |
| | T1—083 51 |
|    etiquette | 395.123 2 |
|    health | 613.042 33 |
|    journalism for | 070.483 36 |
|    psychology | 155.532 |
|    publications for | |
|     bibliographies | 011.624 1 |
|    sex hygiene | 613.953 |
|    social aspects | 305.235 1 |
|    social welfare | 362.708 3 |
|   *see also* Adolescent boys | |
|   *see Manual at* T1—081 *and* | |
|    T1—08351, T1—08352, | |
|    T1—08421, T1—08422 | |
| Young Men's Christian | |
|   Association camps | 796.542 2 |
| Young Men's Christian | |
|   Associations | 267.3 |
| Young parents | |
|   social welfare | 362.787 4 |
| Young people | 305.23 |
| | T1—083 |
|   civil and human rights | 323.352 |
|    law | 342.087 72 |
|   education | 371.82 |
|   government programs | 353.536 |
|   grooming | 646.704 6 |
|   guides to religious life | 204.408 3 |
|    Christianity | 248.82 |
|    Judaism | 296.708 3 |
|   journalism for | 070.483 2 |
|   legal aid | 362.716 |
|   legal status | 346.013 5 |
|    constitutional law | 342.087 72 |
|    private law | 346.013 5 |
|   libraries for | 027.625 |
|   material assistance | 362.71 |
|   publications for | |
|    bibliographies | 011.62 |
|    reviews | 028.162 |
|   reading | |
|    library science | 028.5 |
| Young people (continued) | |
|   reading interests | 028.55 |
|   relations with government | 323.352 |
|   religion | 200.83 |
|    Christianity | 270.083 |
|     devotional literature | 242.62 |
|     pastoral care | 259.2 |
|     religious education | 268.432 |
|    Judaism | 296.083 |
|     religious education | 296.680 83 |
|   sex hygiene | 613.951 |
|   social aspects | 305.23 |
|   social welfare | 362.7 |
|    public administration | 353.536 |
| Young people's books | |
|   bibliographies | 011.62 |
| Young people's societies | 369.4 |
|   biography | 369.409 2 |
| Young women | 305.242 2 |
| | T1—084 22 |
|   etiquette | 395.124 2 |
|   journalism for | 070.483 47 |
|   psychology | 155.65 |
|   social aspects | 305.242 2 |
|   social welfare | 362 |
|   under twenty-one | 305.235 2 |
| | T1—083 52 |
|    etiquette | 395.123 3 |
|    health | 613.042 43 |
|    journalism for | 070.483 37 |
|    psychology | 155.533 |
|    publications for | |
|     bibliographies | 011.624 2 |
|    sex hygiene | 613.955 |
|    social welfare | 362.708 3 |
|   *see Manual at* T1—081 *and* | |
|    T1—08351, T1—08352, | |
|    T1—08421, T1—08422 | |
| Young Women's Christian | |
|   Associations | 267.5 |
| Young workers | 331.34 |
| Youngstown (Ohio) | T2—771 39 |
| Youth | 305.235 |
| | T1—083 5 |
|   over twenty | 305.242 |
| | T1—084 2 |
|   *see also* Young adults | |
|   *see also* Adolescents | |
| Youth hostels | 910.466 |
|   *see also* Lodging (Temporary | |
|    housing) | |
| Yozgat İli (Turkey) | T2—563 8 |
|   ancient | T2—393 32 |

| | |
|---|---|
| Ytterbium | |
|   chemistry | 546.419 |
| Yttrium | 669.290 3 |
|   chemical engineering | 661.040 3 |
|   chemistry | 546.403 |
|   metallurgy | 669.290 3 |
|   physical metallurgy | 669.962 903 |
|   *see also* Chemicals | |
| Yttrium-group metals | |
|   economic geology | 553.494 7 |
| Yuan dynasty | 951.025 |
| Yuat River (Papua New | |
|   Guinea) | T2—957 5 |
| Yuba County (Calif.) | T2—794 35 |
| Yucatán (Mexico : State) | T2—726 5 |
| Yucatán Channel | 551.461 364 |
| | T2—163 64 |
| Yucatec Maya language | 497.427 |
| | T6—974 27 |
| Yucatecan language | 497.427 |
| | T6—974 27 |
| Yucatecan literature | 897.427 |
| Yuccas | 584.352 |
| Yuchi language | 497.9 |
| | T6—979 |
| Yudhoyono, Susilo Bambang | |
|   Indonesian history | 959.804 2 |
| Yue dialects | 495.172 7 |
| | T6—951 7 |
| Yüeh dialects | 495.172 7 |
| | T6—951 7 |
| Yugoslav Banat | T2—497 1 |
| Yugoslav communism | 335.434 4 |
|   economics | 335.434 4 |
|   political ideology | 320.532 309 497 |
| Yugoslavia | 949.702 |
| | T2—497 |
|   ancient | 939.87 |
| | T2—398 7 |
| Yugoslavia (1918–1991) | 949.702 |
| | T2—497 |
| Yugoslavia (1991–2003) | 949.710 31 |
| | T2—497 1 |
| Yugoslavs | T5—918 2 |
| Yui language | 499.12 |
| | T6—991 2 |
| Yuit | T5—971 4 |
| Yuit language | 497.14 |
| | T6—971 4 |
| Yukaghir language | 494.6 |
| | T6—946 |
| Yukaghir literature | 894.6 |
| Yuki Indians | T5—975 |

| | |
|---|---|
| Yuki language | 497.5 |
| | T6—975 |
| Yukon | 971.91 |
| | T2—719 1 |
| Yukon River (Yukon and | |
|   Alaska) | T2—798 6 |
|   Alaska | T2—798 6 |
|   Yukon | T2—719 1 |
| Yuma County (Ariz.) | T2—791 71 |
| Yuma County (Colo.) | T2—788 78 |
| Yuma Indians | T5—975 72 |
| Yuma language | 497.572 |
| | T6—975 72 |
| Yuman Indians | T5—975 72 |
| Yuman languages | 497.572 |
| | T6—975 72 |
| Yunnan Sheng (China) | T2—513 5 |
| Yupik | T5—971 4 |
| Yupik languages | 497.14 |
| | T6—971 4 |
| Yupik literatures | 897.14 |
| Yurak Samoyed language | 494.4 |
| | T6—944 |
| Yurok Indians | T5—973 |
| Yurok language | 497.3 |
| | T6—973 |
| Yvelines (France) | T2—443 66 |
| YWCA (Association) | 267.5 |

# Z

| | |
|---|---|
| Z transform | 515.723 |
| Zacapa (Guatemala : Dept.) | T2—728 132 |
| Zacatecas (Mexico : State) | T2—724 3 |
| Zachodniopomorskie | |
|   Voivodeship (Poland) | T2—438 16 |
| Zagora (Morocco : | |
|   Province) | T2—646 6 |
| Zaire | 967.510 33 |
| | T2—675 1 |
| Zaire (Angola) | T2—673 2 |
| Zaire River | T2—675 1 |
| Zairians | T5—967 51 |
| Zakarpats´ka oblast´ | |
|   (Ukraine) | T2—477 9 |
| Zakat | 297.54 |
| Zakynthos (Greece) | T2—495 5 |
| Zala Megye (Hungary) | T2—439 7 |
| Zambales (Philippines) | T2—599 1 |
| Zambezi River | T2—679 |
| Zambézia (Mozambique) | T2—679 6 |
| Zambia | 968.94 |
| | T2—689 4 |
| Zambians | T5—968 94 |

Zamboanga del Norte
  (Philippines : Province)    T2—599 7
Zamboanga del Sur
  (Philippines)    T2—599 7
Zamfara State (Nigeria)    T2—669 61
Zamora (Spain : Province)    T2—462 4
Zamora-Chinchipe
  (Ecuador)    T2—866 44
Zamość (Poland :
  Voivodeship)    T2—438 43
Zamucoan languages    498.9
    T6—989
Zande (African people)    T5—963 61
Zande language    496.361
    T6—963 61
Zander    597.758
Zanichelliaceae    584.74
Zanjān (Iran : Province)    T2—551 6
Zante (Greece)    T2—495 5
Zanzibar    967.81
    T2—678 1
Zanzibar Central/South
  (Tanzania)    T2—678 1
Zanzibar North (Tanzania)    T2—678 1
Zanzibar Urban/West
  (Tanzania)    T2—678 1
Západočeský kraj (Czech
  Republic)    T2—437 14
Západoslovenský kraj
  (Slovakia)    T2—437 33
Zaparoan languages    498.9
    T6—989
Zapata County (Tex.)    T2—764 483
Zaporizhzhya (Ukraine :
  Oblast)    T2—477 3
Zaporiz′ka oblast′ (Ukraine)    T2—477 3
Zapotec Indians    T5—976 8
Zapotec language    497.68
    T6—976 8
Zapotec literature    897.68
Zapotecan languages    497.68
    T6—976 8
Zaragoza (Spain : Province)    T2—465 53
Zaramo language    496.391
    T6—963 91
Zarma (African people)    T5—965
Zarma language    496.5
    T6—965
Zarqā' (Jordan : Province)    T2—569 593
  ancient    T2—335 93
Zarzuelas    782.12
  music    782.12
  stage presentation    792.5

Zastron (South Africa :
  District)    T2—685 6
Zavala County (Tex.)    T2—764 437
Zavim    296.123 6
Zawā'id    297.125 64
Zaydites (Islamic sect)    297.824
  Hadith    297.125 924
Zealand (Denmark)    T2—489 1
Zealots (Judaism)    296.81
Zebra fishes (Freshwater)    597.482
  culture    639.374 82
Zebra fishes (Marine)    597.68
Zebra plant    635.934 39
  botany    584.39
  floriculture    635.934 39
Zebras    599.665 7
  animal husbandry    636.18
Zebus    636.291
Zechariah (Biblical book)    224.98
Zedillo Ponce de León, Ernesto
  Mexican history    972.083 6
Zeeland (Netherlands :
  Province)    T2—492 42
Zeewolde (Netherlands)    T2—492 2
Zeiformes    597.64
Zen Buddhism    294.392 7
  biography    294.392 709 2
Zener diodes    621.381 522
Zeolite
  mineralogy    549.68
Zephaniah (Biblical book)    224.96
Zera'im    296.123 1
  Babylonian Talmud    296.125 1
  Mishnah    296.123 1
  Palestinian Talmud    296.124 1
Zero-base budgeting    658.154
  public administration    352.48
  *see also* Budgets (Public)
Zero-memory systems    003.8
Zeta function    515.56
  number theory    512.73
Zevahim    296.123 5
  Babylonian Talmud    296.125 5
  Mishnah    296.123 5
Zhejiang Sheng (China)    T2—512 42
Zhong guo gong chan dang
  (Chinese political party)    324.251 075
Zhou dynasty    931.03
Zhytomyr (Ukraine : Oblast)    T2—477 8
Zhytomyrs′ka oblast′
  (Ukraine)    T2—477 8
Ziebach County (S.D.)    T2—783 53
Zielona Góra (Poland :
  Voivodeship)    T2—438 12

| | |
|---|---|
| Ziguinchor (Senegal : | |
| Region) | T2—663 |
| Zigula-Zaramo languages | 496.391 |
| | T6—963 91 |
| Žilinský kraj (Slovakia) | T2—437 37 |
| Zimbabwe | 968.91 |
| | T2—689 1 |
| Zimbabwe Rhodesia | T2—689 1 |
| Zimbabweans | T5—968 91 |
| Zimbabweans (British | |
| origin) | T5—210 689 1 |
| Zinc | 669.52 |
| building construction | 693.752 |
| building material | 691.852 |
| chemical engineering | 661.066 1 |
| chemistry | 546.661 |
| decorative arts | 739.55 |
| economic geology | 553.452 |
| materials science | 620.184 2 |
| metallography | 669.955 2 |
| metallurgy | 669.52 |
| metalworking | 673.52 |
| mining | 622.345 2 |
| organic chemistry | 547.056 61 |
| applied | 661.895 |
| physical metallurgy | 669.965 2 |
| *see also* Chemicals; Metals | |
| Zinc lithography | 763.24 |
| Zincite | |
| mineralogy | 549.522 |
| Zingiberales | 584.39 |
| Zinnias | 635.933 99 |
| botany | 583.99 |
| floriculture | 635.933 99 |
| Zion National Park (Utah) | T2—792 48 |
| Zionism | 320.540 956 94 |
| Zip code | 383.145 5 |
| *see also* Postal service | |
| Ziphiidae | 599.545 |
| Zircon | |
| mineralogy | 549.62 |
| Zirconia | |
| technology | 666.72 |
| Zirconium | 669.735 |
| chemical engineering | 661.051 3 |
| chemistry | 546.513 |
| economic geology | 553.465 |
| materials science | 620.189 352 |
| metallography | 669.957 35 |
| metallurgy | 669.735 |
| metalworking | 673.735 |
| physical metallurgy | 669.967 35 |
| *see also* Chemicals; Metals | |

| | |
|---|---|
| Zithers | 787.7 |
| instrument | 787.719 |
| music | 787.7 |
| *see also* Stringed instruments | |
| Ziwa Magharibi Region | |
| (Tanzania) | T2—678 27 |
| Zlínský kraj (Czech | |
| Republic) | T2—437 25 |
| Zoantharia | 593.6 |
| Zoarcidae | 597.63 |
| Zodiac | |
| astrology | 133.52 |
| astronomy | 523 |
| folklore | 398.26 |
| history and criticism | 398.362 |
| Zodiacal light | 523.59 |
| Zofingen (Switzerland : | |
| Bezirk) | T2—494 562 2 |
| Zohar | 296.162 |
| Zombiism | |
| African religions | 299.675 |
| Zonal regions | T2—1 |
| Zone time | 389.17 |
| Zones of latitude | |
| astronomical geography | 525.5 |
| Zonguldak İli (Turkey) | T2—563 7 |
| ancient | T2—393 17 |
| Zoning | 333.731 7 |
| area planning | 711 |
| urban | 711.4 |
| land use | 333.731 7 |
| urban | 333.771 7 |
| law | 346.045 |
| public administration | 354.333 |
| urban | 354.353 |
| Zoo animals | 590.73 |
| animal husbandry | 636.088 9 |
| Zooflagellates | 579.42 |
| Zoological gardens | 590.73 |
| *see also* Zoos | |
| Zoological paleoecology | 560.45 |
| Zoological specimens | |
| preservation | 590.752 |
| Zoologists | 590.92 |
| Zoology | 590 |
| Zoomastigophorea | 579.42 |
| paleontology | 561.992 |
| Zoonoses | 571.98 |
| animals | |
| veterinary medicine | 636.089 695 9 |

Zoonoses (continued)
humans — 362.196 959
  incidence — 614.56
  medicine — 616.959
  social services — 362.196 959
  *see also* Communicable
  diseases
Zooplankton — 592.177 6
  freshwater — 592.176
Zoos — 590.73
  animal care — 636.088 9
  architecture — 727.659
  landscape architecture — 712.5
Zoque Indians — T5—974 3
Zoque language — 497.43
  — T6—974 3
Zoraptera — 595.738
Zorilla — 599.766
Zoroastrianism — 295
  philosophy — 181.05
Zoroastrians
  biography — 295.092
Zosteraceae — 584.74
Zouagha-Moulay Yacoub
  (Morocco) — T2—643 4
Zoug (Switzerland : Canton) — T2—494 756
Zoysieae — 584.9
Zucchini — 641.356 2
  *see also* Squashes
Zug (Switzerland) — T2—494 756 4
Zug (Switzerland : Canton) — T2—494 756
Zug, Lake (Switzerland) — T2—494 756
Zuger See (Switzerland) — T2—494 756
Zuid-Holland (Netherlands) — T2—492 38
Zuidelijke IJsselmeerpolders
  (Netherlands) — T2—492 2
Zuider Zee (Netherlands) — T2—492 2
Zulia (Venezuela) — T2 872 3
Zulu (African people) — T5—963 986
Zulu language — 496.398 6
  — T6—963 986
Zulu literature — 896.398 6
Zulu War, 1879 — 968.404 5
Zululand (South Africa) — 968.404
  — T2—684
Zuma, Jacob
  South African history — 968.068
Zuni Indians — T5—979 94
Zuni language — 497.994
  — T6—979 94
Zuni literature — 897.994
Zurich (Switzerland) — T2—494 572 6
Zurich (Switzerland :
  Canton) — T2—494 57

Zurich, Lake of
  (Switzerland) — T2—494 572
Zurzach (Switzerland :
  Bezirk) — T2—494 564 7
Zuurberg National Park
  (South Africa) — T2—687 53
Zuzus — 787.92
  *see also* Stringed instruments
Zwelitsha (South Africa :
  District) — T2—687 55
Zygnematales — 579.837
Zygomycetes — 579.53
Zygophyllaceae — 583.79
Zygote intrafallopian transfer
  surgery — 618.178 059 9
Zygotes — 571.864
Zymases — 572.791
  *see also* Enzymes
Zyrian — T5—945 3
Zyrian language — 494.53
  — T6—945 3
Zyrian literature — 894.53

**The 23rd edition of the Dewey Decimal Classification** was produced using the fourth generation of the Editorial Support System (ESS), developed by OCLC Online Computer Library Center, Inc. ESS includes a print module developed by Pansoft GmbH, Karlsruhe, Germany, under an agreement with OCLC. Composition was done in Times Roman and Arial under the supervision of Michael Panzer. The book was printed and bound by Edwards Brothers, Inc., Ann Arbor, Michigan.